FOURTH
EDITION

STRUCTURED
COBOL

FUNDAMENTALS AND STYLE

**FOURTH
EDITION**

STRUCTURED
COBOL

FUNDAMENTALS AND STYLE

TYLER WELBURN
WILSON PRICE

McGRAW-HILL

New York St. Louis San Francisco Auckland Bogotá Caracas
Lisbon London Madrid Mexico Milan Montreal New Delhi Paris
San Juan Singapore Sydney Tokyo Toronto

McGraw-Hill
San Francisco, California

Structured COBOL, 4th Edition
Fundamentals and Style

1 2 3 4 5 6 7 8 9 0 VNH VNH 9 0 9 8 7 6 5 4

P/N 069196-7

Order Information
ISBN 0-07-912044-X (text and *Start-up! with Micro Focus Personal COBOL 2.0*)
ISBN 0-07-912045-8 (Micro Focus Compiler and *Start-up! with Micro Focus Personal COBOL 20*)
ISBN 0-07-912046-6 (text, RM Compiler, and *Start-Up! with RM 5.2*)

Sponsoring Editor: Frank Ruggirello
Editorial Assistant: Debra Colon
Technical Reviewer: Charles Nelson
Production Supervisor: Richard DeVitto
Project Manager: Jane Granoff
Copyeditor: Karen Richardson
Interior designer: John Edeen
Cover designer: John Edeen
Cover art: "Structure" by William Edeen
Compositor: Proctor-Willenbacher
Printer and binder: Von Hoffmann Press, Inc.

Library of Congress Card Catalog No. 94-79026

International Edition

Copyright © 1995
Exclusive rights by McGraw-Hill Inc. for manufacture and export.
This book cannot be re-exported from the country to which it is consigned by McGraw-Hill. The International Edition is not available in North America.

When ordering this title, use ISBN 0-07-113544-8

To my children: Brent, Veronica, and Keith   (TW)

To my mother, Dorothy Price Sawyer, a very special person
who taught me to always be positive.   (WP)

Brief Contents

CONTENTS

CONCEPTS MODULE C   **PRINCIPLES OF REPORT DESIGN**   191

CHAPTER 7   **Report Program Design and Coding**   198

DIRECTORY TO EXAMPLE PROGRAMS

Example Programs and Required Data Files

Note: The extension C74 means the program is coded using COBOL-74 standards. All others (except SORTPP74.CBL) use COBOL-85.

Program	Input File	Comments
Chapter 1		
PATLIST.CBL	PATRON.DAT	Simple file listing
PATLIST.C74	PATRON.DAT	Simple file listing
Chapter 2		
PATDFCT.CBL	PATRON.DAT	Simple file listing with condition
Chapter 3		
No new programs		
Chapter 4		
PATCRE8.CBL		Creates PATRON.DT
PATADD.CBL	PATRON.DT	Add records to PATRON.DT
PATDISP.CBL	PATRON.DAT	Display records on screen
Chapter 5		
PATDFCT2.CBL	PATRON.DAT	Basic report headings
PATADD2.CBL	PATRON.DAT	Screen positioning for DISPLAY
Chapter 6		
PATDFCT3.CBL	PATRON.DAT	Percentage calculation
LOAN-PAY.CBL		Loan payment calculation
Chapter 7		
PATLIST2.CBL	PATRON.DAT	Basic page control & report totals
PATLIST2.C74	PATRON.DAT	Basic page control & report totals
PATLIST3.CBL	PATRON.DAT	Page totals
Chapter 8		
No complete programs		

Program	Input File	Comments
Chapter 9		
SCTLBRK.CBL	SALES_S.DAT	Single-level control break
SCTLBRK.C74	SALES_S.DAT	Single-level control break
MCTLBRK.CBL	SALES_M.DAT	Multiple-level control break
MCTLBRK.C74	SALES_M.DAT	Multiple-level control break
Chapter 10		
DATAVAL.CBL	SALES_TR.ERR	Data validation
DATAENT.CBL	SALES_T.DAT	Data entry/validation
Chapter 11		
AVERAGE.CBL	SALES_S2.DAT	Using an array
HIGHREP1.CBL	SALES_S2.DAT	Loading/processing data in an array
HIGHREP2.CBL	SALES_S2.DAT	Processing with parallel arrays
HIGHREP3.CBL	SALES_S3.DAT	Using an index
BEVERAGE.CBL	none	Searching a table
Chapter 12		
PAYTBLE1.CBL	none	Two-level table—direct lookup
PAYTBLE2.CBL	none	Two-level table lookup—positional/indexed
PAYTBLE3.CBL	none	Two-level table lookup—indexed
PAYTBLE4.CBL	PAY-RATE.TBL	Three-level table processing—input loaded
PAYTBLE5.CBL	none	Printing a three-level table
PAYTBLE6.CBL	none	Three-level table processing
PAYTBLE7.CBL	none	Printing a three-level table
ROOMS.CBL	ROOMS.DAT	Table processing—room chart
Chapter 13		
SORTONLY.CBL	INVEN-U.DAT	Basic sort
SORTPP85.CBL	INVEN-U.DAT	Sort with pre- and post-processing
SORTPP74.CBL	INVEN-U.DAT	Sort with pre- and post-processing—COBOL-74
SORTALPH.CBL	PROS-A.DAT, PROS-B.DAT	Case-insensitive sort
Chapter 14		
SEQ-MNT.CBL	BUDGET1.DAT, BUD-TRA.DAT	Sequential file maintenance
SEQ-MNT.C74	BUDGET1.DAT, BUD-TRA.DAT	Sequential file maintenance
Chapter 15		
EMPCRE8I.CBL	none	Create EMPLOYEE.DAI
EMPCRE8R.CBL	none	Create EMPLOYEE.DAR
EMPADDI.CBL	EMPLOYEE.DAT	Add records to EMPLOYEE.DAI
EMPADDR.CBL	EMPLOYEE.DAT	Add records to EMPLOYEE.DAR
EMPLIST.CBL	EMPLOYEE.DAI	Sequential list of an indexed file
EMPCRE8A.CBL	none	Create EMPLOYEE.DAA
EMPADDA.CBL	EMPLOYEE.DAT	Add records to EMPLOYEE.DAA
EMPLISTA.CBL	EMPLOYEE.DAA	List an indexed file using alternate key
EMPMNT.CBL	EMPLOYEE.DAI	Indexed file maintenance
EMPMNT.C74	EMPLOYEE.DAI	Indexed file maintenance

Program	Input File	Comments
SLSCRE8.CBL	none	Create SALES_MA.DAI
SLSADD.CBL	SALES_MA.DAT	Add records to SALES_MA.DAI
SLSUPD.CBL	SALES_S.DAT	Master-transaction update (indexed files)
SLSUPD.C74	SALES_S.DAT	Master-transaction update (indexed files)
EMPGETA.CBL	EMPLOYEE.DAA	Access indexed records using alternate key
EMPGETA.C74	EMPLOYEE.DAA	Access indexed records using alternate key

Chapter 16

Program	Input File	Comments
PAYTBLE8.CBL	PAY-RATE.TBL	Using the COPY statement
PAYTBLE8.DTA		Source code for the COPY statement
PAYTBLE8.PRO		Source code for the COPY statement
PAY-T-SE.CBL	PAY-RATE.TBL	Subprogram to search a table
PAY-T-LD.CBL	PAY-RATE.TBL	Subprogram to load a table
PAY-T-GL.CBL	PAY-RATE.TBL	Program with nested programs

For Chapter 16 assignment

Program	Input File	Comments
INV-CRE8.CBL LINEITEM.DAI	none	Create INVOICE.DAI and
ORD-CRE8.CBL	CUSTOMER.DAT, SOFTWARE.DAT	Generate customer and software files(16-1)

Appendix A

Program	Input File	Comments
RPATLIST.CBL	PATRON.DAT	Report with headings and report total using Report Writer.
RSLCTBRK.CBL	SALES_S.DAT	Single-level control break using Report Writer.
RMLCTBRK.CBL	SALES_M.DAT	Multiple-level control break using Report Writer.

Appendix C

Program	Input File	Comments
PRNCTL-I.CBL	PATRON.DAT	Switch to compressed font—IBM/Epson
PRNCTL-L.CBL	PATRON.DAT	Switch to compressed font—HP Laserjet

Alphabetic List of Example Programs

Program	Chapter	Description
AVERAGE.CBL	11	Using an array
BEVERAGE.CBL	11	Searching a table
DATAENT.CBL	10	Data entry/validation
DATAVAL.CBL	10	Data validation
EMPADDA.CBL	15	Add records to employee file for EMPMNT
EMPADDI.CBL	15	Add records to an indexed file
EMPADDR.CBL	15	Add records to a relative file

Program	Chapter	Description
EMPCRE8A.CBL	15	Create indexed employee file for EMPMNT
EMPCRE8I.CBL	15	Create an indexed file
EMPCRE8R.CBL	15	Create a relative file
EMPGETA.CBL	15	Access indexed records using alternate key
EMPGETA.C74	15	Access indexed records using alternate key—COBOL-74
EMPLIST.CBL	15	Sequential list of an indexed file
EMPLISTA.CBL	15	Listing an indexed file using alternate key
EMPMNT.C74	15	Indexed file maintenance—COBOL-74
EMPMNT.CBL	15	Indexed file maintenance
HIGHREP1.CBL	11	Loading and processing data in an array
HIGHREP2.CBL	11	Processing with parallel arrays
HIGHREP3.CBL	11	Using an index
LOAN-PAY.CBL	6	Loan payment calculation
MCTLBRK.C74	9	Multiple-level control break—COBOL-74
MCTLBRK.CBL	9	Multiple-level control break
PATADD.CBL	4	Add records to a file
PATADD2.CBL	5	Screen positioning for DISPLAY
PATCRE8.CBL	4	Create an empty file
PATDFCT.CBL	2	Simple file listing with condition
PATDFCT2.CBL	5	Basic report headings
PATDFCT3.CBL	6	Percentage calculation
PATDISP.CBL	4	Display records on screen
PATLIST.C74	1	Simple file listing—COBOL-74
PATLIST.CBL	1	Simple file listing
PATLIST2.C74	7	Basic page control & report totals—COBOL-74
PATLIST2.CBL	7	Basic page control & report totals
PATLIST3.CBL	7	Page totals
PAY-T-GL.CBL	16	Program with nested programs
PAY-T-LD.CBL	16	Subprogram to load a table
PAY-T-SE.CBL	16	Subprogram to search a table
PAYTBLE1.CBL	12	Two-level table—direct lookup
PAYTBLE2.CBL	12	Two-level table lookup—positional/indexed
PAYTBLE3.CBL	12	Two-level table lookup—indexed
PAYTBLE4.CBL	12	Three-level table processing
PAYTBLE5.CBL	12	Printing a three-level table
PAYTBLE6.CBL	12	Three-level table processing
PAYTBLE7.CBL	12	Printing a three-level table
PAYTBLE8.CBL	16	Using the COPY statement
PAYTBLE8.DTA	16	Source code for the COPY statement
PAYTBLE8.PRO	16	Source code for the COPY statement
PRNCTL-I.CBL	App. C	Switch to compressed font—IBM/Epson
PRNCTL-L.CBL	App. C	Switch to compressed font—HP Laserjet

Program	Chapter	Description
RMCTLBRK.CBL	App. A	Multiple-level control break—Report Writer
ROOMS.CBL	9	Table processing—room chart
RPATLIST.CBL	App. A	Report headings and totals—Report Writer
RSCTLBRK.CBL	App. A	Single-level control break—Report Writer
SCTLBRK.C74	9	Single-level control break—COBOL-74
SCTLBRK.CBL	9	Single-level control break
SEQ-MNT.C74	14	Sequential file maintenance—COBOL-74
SEQ-MNT.CBL	14	Sequential file maintenance
SLSADD.CBL	15	Add records to indexed files for SLSUPD
SLSCRE8.CBL	15	Create indexed files for SLSUPD
SLSUPD.CBL	15	Master-transaction update (indexed files)
SLSUPD.C74	15	Master-transaction update (indexed files)—COBOL-74
SORTALPH.CBL	13	Case-insensitive sort
SORTONLY.CBL	13	Basic sort
SORTPP74.CBL	13	Sort with pre- and post-processing—COBOL-74
SORTPP85.CBL	13	Sort with pre- and post-processing

PREFACE

The prefaces to previous editions of this book included the following: "This text utilizes the most current COBOL program design and coding techniques together with contemporary business computer system concepts. It offers a solid foundation for beginning COBOL students to build upon as their knowledge and skills develop and grow along with the exciting field of computer technology."

Since the third edition, two significant changes in the COBOL field have occurred. First, the focus has finally shifted from COBOL-74 to COBOL-85 in our instructional programs (although COBOL-74 and COBOL 9-X are mentioned where appropriate). Second, powerful microcomputer hardware and COBOL software are readily available. These two changes were primary considerations for adjustments to the fourth edition in order to maintain the quality of the first three editions.

Goals for the Fourth Edition

First, this fourth edition has benefited immensely from the observations and criticisms of many users of the third edition. Their input provided us with a solid foundation on which to incorporate needed improvements and updating. In addition to maintaining the quality of the third edition, our broad goals were as follows:

- Incorporate file handling and other advanced topics (covered in the companion volume, *Advanced Structured COBOL: Batch, On-Line, and Data-Base Concepts*) to make this a comprehensive, full year textbook.

- Shift the emphasis from COBOL-74 to COBOL-85, while including suitable references to both COBOL-74 and COBOL-9X.

- Introduce interactive programs early and expand upon interaction in subsequent chapters as appropriate and meaningful.

- Further diversify and expand the complete program examples for illustrating new programming principles.

- Intensify the focus on solid structured methodology, emphasizing programming practices that produce intuitively apparent and easily maintained programs.

Each of these is described in more detail later in this preface.

Key Strengths Retained

In preparing the fourth edition, we made a special effort to maintain—and improve—the qualities and features that instructors and students found useful in the third edition.

Text Organization

The COBOL syntax is presented within the framework of commonly encountered business-system program models. Concepts are developed step by step—proceeding from the simple to the more complex. Each program category builds upon and adds to the knowledge, techniques, and skills developed in the previous one.

The programs presented here also serve as a ready reference for each application type, and they introduce students to the fact that several traditional application-program categories exist. This permits students to analyze programming tasks in relation to program type and to use common approaches rather than to "reinvent the wheel" for each program. Further, with this method of presentation, coding is never divorced from practical application.

Concepts Modules

The third edition included nine *concepts modules* describing general principles related to the programming chapters that followed. Student response to separating general theory from COBOL principles was very positive. Those already familiar with the general theory simply skipped the corresponding module; those requiring the background appreciated the delineation between theory and COBOL. The major criticism was their number. To that end, we took two tacks. First, we cut down the material; second, we incorporated appropriate elements directly into corresponding COBOL chapters. Consequently, this edition includes only five concepts modules.

Programming Style Conventions

Over the years, through trial and error, COBOL installations and programmers have developed programming style conventions. The establishment and use of such conventions significantly aid program readability and maintainability. In this text, therefore, applicable style considerations are presented—along with the syntactical coding rules—to provide an introduction to proper coding form. Through presentation of these style conventions, students can quickly learn sound coding practices that might otherwise take years to acquire. Basic programming conventions are introduced with the first program and are expanded upon as appropriate in later examples.

Comprehensive Program Design Documentation

New concepts are introduced through program examples. Most new sample programming applications include programming specifications, a structure chart, a pseudocode solution, and the COBOL program. Programming specifications include complete input/output descriptions and a detailed list of program operations. Structure charts are provided to show overall program organization and module definition. English-like pseudocode is used to make comprehension of the detailed logic easier for the beginning programming student. The resulting COBOL solution, complete with in-program comments, is evolved logically from the preceding program design documentation.

Combination Tutorial/Reference Approach

Students often react to COBOL textbooks in one of two ways. Typically, either they feel that the text is a good reference manual but doesn't really explain how to write certain types of programs, or they claim that the book explains concepts well but is difficult to use as a reference. This text blends tutorial and reference features. Whenever a subject is presented, it is fully covered in one place. However, to guard against information overload, topics are covered on a step-by-step basis and are integrated with programming examples. Furthermore, subjects are organized to give a quick description, and then go into detail. This enables students to skip much of the detail if desired, progress to the next topic (or chapter), and then return at a later date for the fine points.

Extensive End-of-Chapter Material

At the end of each chapter, a chapter summary is presented. Appropriate chapters also contain COBOL language element summaries and style summaries.

Exercises appear after the summaries. Each chapter includes terms for definition and review questions. Most chapters also contain syntax/debug exercises.

Range of Programming Assignments

Each chapter includes several programming assignments that relate directly to the material covered within the chapter. Most of the assignments are independent of other assignments. Some are cumulative; for instance, Programming Assignment 5-2 requires that the program of 3-2 be expanded.

A complete set of test data is included on the data disk accompanying the book. The program specifications for each programming assignment identify the appropriate data set.

Numerous Illustrations and Examples

Over 350 figures are in the text. The figures include illustrations, diagrams, programming specifications, design documentation and coding examples.

A Complete Teaching Package

This fourth edition is not merely a textbook; it is a *teaching package*, designed to provide you—the instructor—with the broadest possible support. The package consists of the following components:

- A comprehensive **Instructor's Manual,** containing chapter objectives, teaching tips, answers to exercises, test questions, transparency masters, and data files for programming assignments.

- A **data disk** containing a complete set of sample programs from the textbook and data files for each programming assignment.

- A **solutions disk** containing solutions for each programming assignment.

Chapter/Topic Organization

Each chapter contains a preliminary overview discussion. Chapters that cover two or more distinct topics identify these topics as individual entities. Such topic organization clearly indicates the subject of each text segment. This permits easy identification of the material that the instructor might choose to skip or cover in a different sequence.

COBOL-85 Software Available

Because all programs conform to COBOL-85, they can be compiled and run on a mainframe, mini, or personal computer. Students desiring their own personal computer software have two options: Micro Focus or Ryan-McFarland.

Micro Focus COBOL-85

The most comprehensive approach is the purchase of Micro Focus Personal COBOL. It is important to avoid considering this as "microcomputer COBOL," which implies that it is something less than full COBOL-85, or a limited-use educational version. *This is COBOL-85;* it even includes the 1989 Intrinsic Functions package. Although not documented in the *Micro Focus Personal COBOL 2.0 Programmer's Guide*, Personal COBOL also includes the COBOL Report Writer feature. The Report Writer examples programs in Appendix A were tested with Personal COBOL.

The cost of the system, available through Micro Focus to users of this book, was less than $50 at the time of this book's publication.

Ryan-McFarland COBOL-85

For the more economically inclined, this book can be ordered complete with the special education version of the Ryan-McFarland COBOL-85 compiler. It is important to recognize that this version is *not* a watered-down system, useless for all except the simplest problems. In fact, the opposite is true; the compiler includes the following powerful features:

1. COBOL programs of up to 1,000 lines of source code can be compiled.
2. Supported file types include sequential, line sequential, relative, and indexed.
3. File size limitation for indexed files is 100 records; for all others, it is 1,000 records.
4. Records in the File Section can be up to 132 bytes in length.
5. Up to four file definitions may be used in any program (that is, four files may be open at one time).
6. Indexed files may include one or two keys.
7. The CALL statement can be implemented to one level. That is, a program can call another, but the called program cannot call a third program.

This compiler is adequate for all but this book's most advanced applications. For major projects, the restriction on the program size and the number of simultaneous files open can create problems.

Separate "Getting Started" Manuals

For users of Micro Focus or Ryan-McFarland, separate "getting started" student manuals are available through McGraw-Hill.

Start-Up! with Micro Focus Personal COBOL 2.0 provides step-by-step instructions for using the Editor, Checker, and Animator. The wide variety of Micro Focus features are illustrated through a series of example dialogues with the corresponding software. This volume also includes a description of the Micro Focus implementations of: (1) extensions of the ACCEPT and DISPLAY statements, (2) a SCREEN SECTION for interactive input/output, and (3) a screen painter facility to produce the detail code necessary for keyboard/screen activities.

Start-up! with RM 5.2 provides step-by-step instructions for compiling and running programs. A complete chapter is devoted to using RM/COSTAR for managing programs, entering and editing, syntax checking and compiling, and using the debugger. This volume also includes a description of the Ryan-McFarland implementations of: (1) extensions of the ACCEPT and DISPLAY statements, and (2) a SCREEN SECTION for interactive input/output.

Expanded and Updated Material

When preparing this revision, we considered every topic and figure of the third edition in order to present the material as clearly and understandably as possible. Similarly, each topic was reassessed for relevance, and additional topic area candidates were considered. Areas in which significant new material appears are as follows.

Expansion to Include File Processing

The third edition was written to be used in conjunction with *Advanced Structured COBOL: Batch, On-Line, and Data-Base Concepts* to provide a full year's coverage of COBOL. This edition was trimmed where appropriate, then expanded to include advanced file-processing concepts and program management. The following topics are included: sequential file maintenance and updating, random file processing (with a strong focus on interactive file updating), and subprograms (separately called programs and nested programs).

Interactive Programs

Next to expanding the third edition to cover file processing, the most commonly encountered request was to include interactive processing capabilities. When doing this, we gave special consideration to avoid token interaction and incorporate it in a useful, meaningful context. Chapter 4, a short chapter, shows the reader how to (1) create a new field, (2) add records to an existing field, and (3) display records, one at a time, from a file. COBOL-85 versions of the ACCEPT and DISPLAY are used in all examples. These basic concepts are expanded in subsequent chapters with assignments as appropriate.

Chapter 5 deals with improving the appearance of computer output, both printed and displayed on a screen. At this point, nonstandard forms of the ACCEPT and DISPLAY are included, allowing for line/column screen addressing, clearing the screen, and displaying in reverse video. Forms for several compilers are described.

For instructors who don't want to include interactive programs, these sections can be omitted with no loss of continuity.

Tools Chapters

In each chapter, we have sought to maintain a balance between COBOL language features and COBOL programming principles—new features are generously illustrated with complete program applications. However, there are two language-feature exceptions: editing (the first topic of Chapter 5), and conditional operations (Chapter 8). These provide extensive coverage of the corresponding language features. To a degree, they can be considered almost as reference materials. The student does not need to exhibit mastery of all these features after completing each chapters. But he or she should have a basic insight to them and know where to look when they are used in example programs or required for programming assignments. In this sense, these can be considered "tools" chapters.

Complete Programs

Students learn best by working from solid examples of new concepts—we learned this from previous editions. To that end, we illustrate each new principle with one or more examples. In most cases, these examples are not merely abbreviated program segments, but complete programs that both demonstrate the new principles and show them in a typical context. The number of complete programs included in this edition has almost doubled (to approximately 50) over the third edition.

The complete set of example programs is included on the data disk accompanying this book. For each program, the filename is identical to the PROGRAM-ID designated in the program. The name extension is CBL for COBOL-85 programs and C74 for the limited number of COBOL-74 programs. For example, PATLIST is stored as PATLIST.CBL and PATLIST.C74. Test data for the sample programs is also included on the disk; those filenames are as designated in the programming specifications for the program.

Controlling Printer Pitch for Personal Computers

Limited print-line width on personal computers was an expressed concern by several institutions—the recommendation was that all report-generating assignments be limited to a report line maximum of 80 characters. Instead, we included, as Appendix C, COBOL code that can be inserted in any program to change from 10 characters per inch to compressed printing (approximately 17 characters per inch) and back again. Example code is included for the IBM Graphics/Epson printers and the Hewlett-Packard LaserJet. The technique employed is easily converted to any other printer type.

COBOL-85

In the third edition, equal treatment was given to COBOL-74 and COBOL-85. Most current books that place their primary emphasis on COBOL-85 (but include COBOL-74) are written with the constraints of COBOL-74. It is approximately one decade since the 1985 Standard was introduced. We believe the time has arrived to teach COBOL by taking advantage of COBOL-85's many powerful features—without living within the COBOL-74 limitations. To achieve this, the fourth edition maximizes the capabilities of COBOL-85 to produce good, easy-to-follow COBOL programs. However, COBOL-74 is not ignored. Equivalent COBOL-74 forms are described; in a few cases, a complete COBOL-74 program is shown when the differences are substantial.

Significant additions and changes to COBOL scheduled with the next standard (COBOL-9X) are noted where appropriate.

Acknowledgments

Anyone who has written a book knows of the many efforts by people behind the scenes. This book is no exception. At the top of the list, Frank Ruggirello of McGraw-Hill provided the resources to make everything work—and work well. Deborah Colon, also at McGraw-Hill, provided hands-on coordination to ensure that the many facets of the project moved smoothly at all levels.

Overall project coordination from Jane Granoff was the norm for her—outstanding, as usual. Karen Richardson did far more than her normal copyediting task. Not only did she improve significantly on our English, but she did a terrific job of proofreading. We did become weary of her harassing comments and notes, but it was difficult to be critical when she was usually right and added to the book's quality. Rad Proctor, of Proctor-Willenbacher, and her staff did an excellent job of turning a complex manuscript into a well-crafted book.

Chuck Nelson (Programming Assignment solutions) and Jorene Kirkland (Instructor's Manual) deserve special thanks for their efforts in preparing critical and ancillary materials. Numerous others at the nuts-and-bolts level put forth special efforts to ensure that this project was done properly and completed on time. To them and to the following people who provide special assistance in preparation of this book's four editions, we offer our sincere thanks and appreciation.

William Barth
Cayuga Community College

Robert H. Doursen
California Polytechnic State University

Paul Duchow
Pasadena Community College

Janie Epstein
Johnson County Community College

Mary Ann Grams
San Antonio College

Carol C. Grimm
Palm Beach Junior College

R. Wayne Hedrick
Texas A&M University

Susan Hinrichs
Missouri Western State College

Jorene Kirkland
Amarillo College

Dr. Ron Kizior
Loyola University, Chicago

Sue Krimm
Los Angeles Pierce College

David M. Kroenke
Wall Data, Inc.

Marjorie Leeson
Delta College

Anthony Mann
Central State University

Anne M. McBride
California State University, Chico

Joe Murray
North Adams State College

Charles Nelson
Rock Valley College

Jack Olson
Merritt College

Edward Rategan
College of San Mateo

Cyndi Reese
Santa Rosa Junior College

Dan Rota
Robert Morris College

Joseph Southern
LaGuardia Community College

George Vlahakis
Evergreen Valley College

THE PROGRAM DEVELOPMENT PROCESS

MODULE OBJECTIVES

The purpose of this module is to give you an insight to the process of designing and writing a computer program (the program development process). From this module, you will learn the following:

- The four phases of program development: specification, design, coding, and testing.

- The importance of clearly defining exactly what to do before proceeding with the programming task (specification phase).

- The use of two standard tools for designing a program (solving the problem): pseudocode and flowcharts.

- The converting of a design into a COBOL computer program (the coding phase).

- The process of compiling, whereby the computer converts a COBOL program to machine language.

- The testing phase, during which all aspects of the program are tested to ensure that the program functions as intended.

MODULE OUTLINE

Four Phases of Program Development

The Specification Phase
    Determine the Needs of the Users
    Input Data Format
    Illustrative Layouts of the Output Record
    Programming Specifications

The Design Phase
    Program Design Tools
    Structured Walkthrough

The Coding Phase
    Writing the COBOL Program
    Compiling the Program

The Testing Phase
    Execution Errors
    Debugging

Four Phases of Program Development

Assume that you work for Fleetwood Charities (a nonprofit organization) and that one of your tasks is to track individual patrons (contributors). With hundreds of patrons, it is essential that the data pertaining to them be recorded in an organized way. To accomplish this, Fleetwood just created a computerized patron file containing data on each patron. Your supervisor assigned you the task of working with the solicitation department to create a report generation program from data in the file. Because this assignment is fairly complicated, you would not simply sit down and begin programming. The overall program development process consists of four phases: specification, design, coding, and testing, as illustrated in Figure A-1.

The Specification Phase

The ultimate objective of the specification phase is to determine exactly what the end users need from the proposed system or program. Since you are not familiar with the needs of the end users, the specification phase of the program development process consists of:

1. Working with people in the solicitation department, you must determine what they need. From this, you will determine the input data that is required to furnish the desired output.
2. Obtain the input record format and check to ensure that the data you need to generate the desired output is available. (The term *report* means "printed output from the computer.")
3. Prepare a layout of the printed report.
4. Define program specifications that describe the overall purpose of the program, identify the input items and the desired output, and list the major processing operations that must occur.
5. Obtain approval to proceed to the next step of the program development process.

The following expands upon these phase elements.

Determine the Needs of the Users

A program that does not satisfy the needs of the users has little value. So, one of your first actions is to find out what they need. Sometimes users themselves are not clear on this and the programmer/analyst provides "brainstorming" assistance. After this information is obtained, you can design a report form that readily conveys what is needed.

Suppose that from your discussions with Fleetwood Charity users, you found that their most pressing need is a report listing the patrons and their contribution information. Also, it must identify those whose contributions are below their target amounts.

Input Data Format

You might encounter two scenarios when designing a program to fulfill your users' needs. In the first case, the files from which your program is to extract the data already exist. In this case, you are usually restricted to working with the data at hand. You must check that each output item is available in the input data record.

In the second case, you will sometimes encounter situations in which you must design the entire application and create the data files yourself. In this case, you must carefully assess both current and anticipated future needs of the users.

After the input files are identified, the exact position of each data-item must be identified, since these are used in the program. For instance, the patron data format can be given to you as the table in Figure A-2(a) or on the **record layout form** of Figure A-2(b). (Note: Here you can see that the city, state, and zip fields

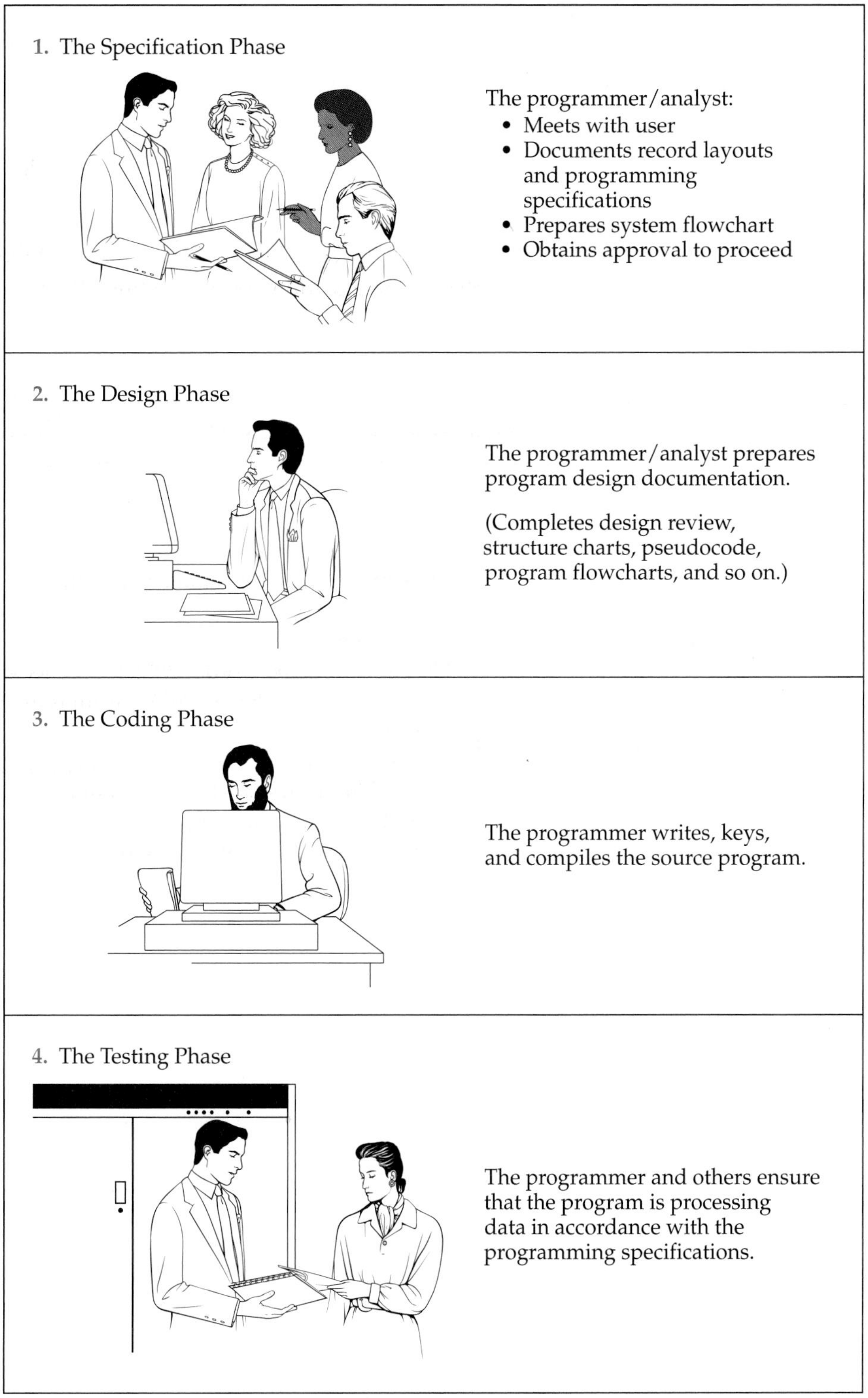

Figure A-1
The program development
process.

1. The Specification Phase

The programmer/analyst:
- Meets with user
- Documents record layouts and programming specifications
- Prepares system flowchart
- Obtains approval to proceed

2. The Design Phase

The programmer/analyst prepares program design documentation.

(Completes design review, structure charts, pseudocode, program flowcharts, and so on.)

3. The Coding Phase

The programmer writes, keys, and compiles the source program.

4. The Testing Phase

The programmer and others ensure that the program is processing data in accordance with the programming specifications.

are combined into a single field. Normally, each of these would be defined as a separate field; however, they are combined for simplicity in this example.)

Illustrative Layouts of the Output Record

After you precisely define the user's needs, you must lay out the report page format by indicating where each field must be printed. For this, you use a **print chart**—a gridlike form to define an output report produced on a computer printer.

Figure A-2 Input data format.

Field	Length	Class	Comments
Name	18	Alphanumeric	
Street address	18	Alphanumeric	
City/state/zip	24	Alphanumeric	
Target contribution	4	Numeric	Whole dollars
Actual contribution	4	Numeric	Whole dollars

(a) In the form of a table.

Input file: Patron record

Name	Address	City/ state/zip	Annual contribution	Target contribution

0 1 2 3 4 5 6 7 8 9 10 11 12 13 14 15 16 17 18 19 20 21 22 23 24 25 26 27 28 29 30 31 32 33 34 35 36 37 38 39 40 41 42 43 44 45 46 47 48 49 50 51 52 53 54 55 56 57 58 59 60 61 62 63 64 65 66 67 68

(b) As a record layout form.

Later in the program development process, it is used as a reference when writing the program code.

Figure A-3 shows a print chart that you might prepare. The preprinted numbers running horizontally across the top of the print chart denote the print positions for each report line. The numbers running vertically down the left side of the chart represent the print lines for each page of the report. The series of Xs are programmer entries that depict positions on the line where data will be printed. Hence, this print chart depicts that output will be printed as follows:

Print Position	Field (Data-Item)
2–19	Name
21–38	Address
40–63	City/state/zip
65–66	**Flag for under target (else blank)

Notice that the printed line is shown twice; that is, one line of Xs is shown at line 7 and the second at line 9. The blank line between the two indicates that the report lines must be double-spaced. This is a common method for indicating line spacing.

Your program will prepare **hard-copy** output that is printed on a page, producing a permanent copy. However, many applications require interaction between the user and the computer via the keyboard and a video display terminal. Output displayed only on a screen is called **soft copy** because no permanent copy is produced; the screen display disappears the instant other information replaces it.

Programming Specifications

Before beginning a detailed design of the program, you should prepare a general description of the program functions, an identification of its input and output records, and a list of its processing operations. Together, these items constitute the

Figure A-3   The patron-address list print chart.

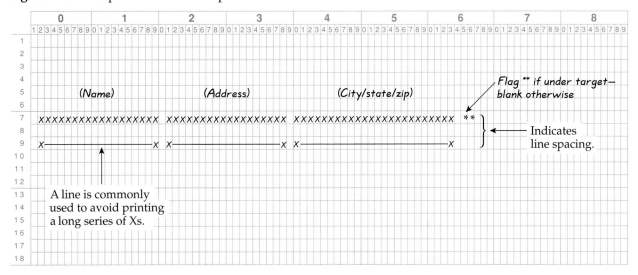

programming specifications. A systems analyst or programmer typically writes such specifications after consultations with the user.

Figure A-4 is a typical set of programming specifications for your application. You also need to draw an overall representation of the data flow in your system. This is called a **system flowchart** and is shown in Figure A-5.

Figure A-4
The patron-address
list programming
specifications.

PROGRAMMING SPECIFICATIONS

Program Name: PATRON LIST   **Program ID:** PATLIST
              (with under-target patrons identified)

Program Description:

     This program is to print a patron address list from input
     patron records. Patrons contributing less than their
     target amount are identified.

Input File:

     Patron File

Output File:

     Patron Address List

List of Program Operations:

A. Read each input patron record.

B. For each record, print the following fields on the employee
    address list in accordance with the format shown on the
    print chart:
         Patron name
         Patron address
         Patron city/state/zip
         Two consecutive asterisk characters (**) if the
         contributed amount is less than the target amount.

C. Double-space each printed line.

Figure A-5
Patron-address list system
flowchart.

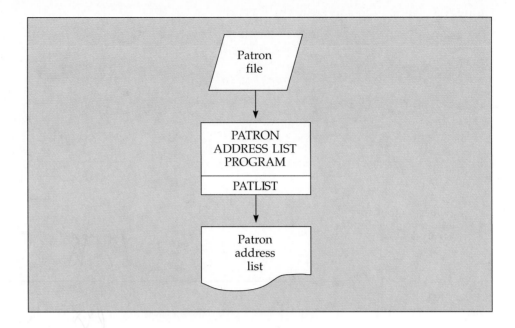

The Design Phase

The first few programs that you write will be relatively basic and you will probably find them fairly easy to visualize. However, most actual business programs are large, complex, and require many conditional operations—making them difficult to visualize. In some respects, designing a program is much like building a house. Long before the carpenter begins sawing wood and pounding nails, an architect must draw detailed plans. Designing and writing a program is no different: the solution must be worked out before detailed coding can begin.

Program Design Tools

Many program design techniques and tools are available to the program designer. For the programs in this text, two primary design tools are used: structure charts and pseudocode. You will learn about structure charts in Module B.

A **pseudocode** solution to a programming problem is an English-like description of how to solve the problem. It describes the necessary sequence of steps, points at which either of two actions is taken depending upon a condition, and repetition of an activity. You can see the program logic, the way in which the program "flows," in Figure A-6(a).

A **program flowchart** is a graphical representation of the problem solution. As you can see in Figure A-6(b), it also depicts the program logic. You will learn about flowchart standards in Module B.

Structured Walkthrough

After completing and checking your program design documentation, it is wise to have someone else check your work. Many organizations use design reviews called **structured walkthroughs**. Typically, a walkthrough is a formally scheduled and conducted meeting with about six participants. During the walkthrough, both design weaknesses and design errors are identified; both must be corrected. After this is completed to the satisfaction of your reviewing colleagues, you will enter the coding phase. While using this book, you will find it valuable to meet with one or more students and review each other's work.

The Coding Phase

During the coding phase, you will work from the input and output documentation and the pseudocode or flowchart to prepare a working computer program. If the program design was comprehensively and properly done, the coding phase is not difficult. These actions typically involve the following three steps:

Figure A-6
Common programming tools.

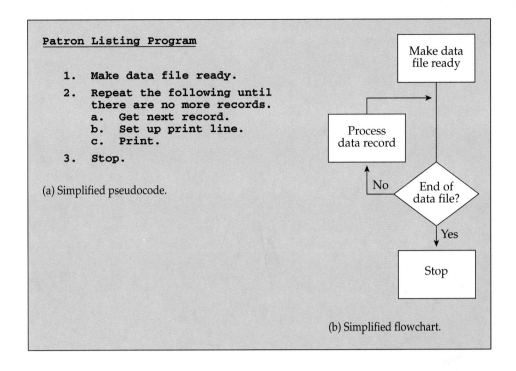

Patron Listing Program

1. **Make data file ready.**
2. **Repeat the following until there are no more records.**
    a. **Get next record.**
    b. **Set up print line.**
    c. **Print.**
3. **Stop.**

(a) Simplified pseudocode.

(b) Simplified flowchart.

1. Prepare a COBOL program equivalent of the pseudocode or flowchart solution.
2. Key the program into the computer so that it is in a computer-readable form.
3. Convert the COBOL program to the language of the computer on which it will run; that is, compile the program.

Writing the COBOL Program

A common error of the beginning programmer is to skip much of the design phase and start writing the program. This might work with the small, simple programs in this book's first few chapters, but it will not work with larger programs. You must work from your pseudocode or flowchart solution.

If you have ready access to a computer or terminal with good editing capabilities, you can compose your program directly into the computer. (That is, you can combine steps 1 and 2, just described.) If you have limited computer access, write out your program with pencil and paper before using the computer. In either case, as you code, you will sometimes encounter operations that can be implemented better with a change in design. When this occurs, you should make appropriate adjustments to your design.

Compiling the Program

COBOL was designed specifically for business data-processing, using an English-like command syntax. Since the COBOL language is standardized, a COBOL program prepared for use on one make of computer can be run—with little or no modification—on another entirely different computer. Hence, COBOL is said to be *machine-independent*. This independence is despite the fact that the internal codes (called the machine-language) of the two computers may be entirely different. The key to program independence is a special type of program called a *language translator*, or **compiler**, that converts your program to the language of the computer you will use. (Compilers are available from independent software companies and computer manufacturers.) After entering your program into a machine-readable form, you must compile it. The computer, under control of the compiler, reads your COBOL program (called the **source program**) and converts the COBOL statements to equivalent machine language instructions for that particular computer. The result of this action, illustrated in Figure A-7, is an **object program** that is ready to run. You should realize that none of the instructions in your program is carried out

Figure A-7
The compiling process.

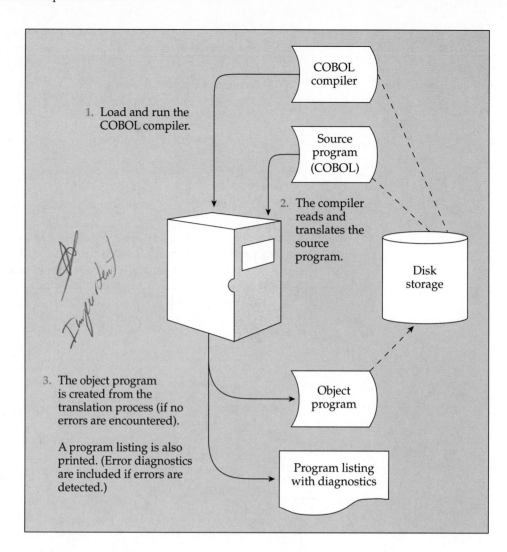

1. Load and run the COBOL compiler.

COBOL compiler

Source program (COBOL)

2. The compiler reads and translates the source program.

Disk storage

3. The object program is created from the translation process (if no errors are encountered).

A program listing is also printed. (Error diagnostics are included if errors are detected.)

Object program

Program listing with diagnostics

during compiling; the compiler simply performs the translation operation and creates the object program.

One of the results the compiler gives you is a **post-compile listing**, a complete printout of the program. If you violated any of the COBOL language rules (for instance, if you typed PREFORM instead of PERFORM), the listing includes an appropriate error message. All such errors must be corrected and the program recompiled. An error-free compile produces an object program that then can be run. Summarizing, the sequence you will follow when preparing and running a program is

1. Write the program.
2. Key it into the computer.
3. Compile the program. If errors are identified by the compiler, correct them and recompile. The end result will be a machine-language equivalent of your COBOL program (the object program).
4. Run the object program, which causes the computer to execute the actions you wrote in your COBOL program.

The exact procedures vary from one type of computer system to another. You must get appropriate instructions from your instructor, computer center supervisor, or other computer authority.

Generally, the type of errors that the compiler can detect are called syntactical or **syntax errors**. Whenever syntax errors are identified by the compiler on the program listing, you must correct the erroneous code of the source program by rekeying the affected entries. Then you must recompile the source program. A compilation in which the compiler does not find any syntax errors is called a *clean compile*. After achieving a clean compile, you can begin testing the resulting object program.

The Testing Phase

Execution Errors

A distinction exists between editing a novel for correct English grammar and reviewing it for story quality. That is, a novel can be grammatically correct, but still have a bad plot. Similarly, just because you obtain a clean compile does not mean that the program will operate correctly. Your program can include errors that will cause it to execute incorrectly. Two general types of such errors are logic errors and runtime errors.

Logic errors occur when you tell the computer to perform the wrong operation. For instance, in a patron listing program to identify those patrons who are below their target amounts, you might accidentally identify those who are above their targets instead.

Runtime errors occur when you tell the computer to do something it cannot do. For instance, if your program divides a total by a count and the count is 0, you have an operation that the computer cannot perform. When something like this occurs, the computer usually terminates your program. Programmers refer to this as a program *crash*.

Debugging

The task of finding program errors, or bugs, is called **debugging** the program. If you are thorough during the design phase, the number of logic and runtime errors should be relatively few. *However, you must never assume that the output you obtain from a computer is correct simply because it is printed by the computer.* The computer does only as you direct it. It is critical that your test data checks all aspects of your program and exercises every possible option.

Finding an error is sometimes very difficult; erroneous results that you see in one part of a program can be the result of an action performed in a completely different part of the program. On the other hand, one of the beauties of program modularization is that modules can often be tested individually, thereby localizing errors and vastly simplifying the debugging process.

Once the program testing is complete, the program can be placed into the production environment to perform the task for which it was written.

Exercises

Terms for Definition

compiler	pseudocode
debugging	record layout form
hard copy	runtime error
logic error	soft copy
object program	source program
post-compile listing	structured walkthrough
print chart	syntax errors
program flowchart	system flowchart
programming specifications	

Review Questions

1. Name the four phases of the program development process.

2. A print layout chart is used for what purpose?

3. _____ is the generic name for an English-like program documentation language.

4. What is a flowchart?

5. A group review of program design or coding is referred to as a(n) _____.

6. Distinguish between a source program and an object program.

7. Name the three types of errors that can appear in a program.

8. Printed output from running a computer program is often called a(n) _____.

A First Look at COBOL

Special Note on 1974, 1985, and 199X Standards

This book focuses on the 1985 Standard (COBOL-85) with appropriate references back to the 1974 Standard (COBOL-74). Examples incorporating COBOL-85 features not compatible with COBOL-74 are pointed out and alternative COBOL-74 forms are described. However, if you want to focus only on COBOL-85, you can easily skip the discussions of COBOL-74 with no loss of continuity. When applicable, notes referring to COBOL-9X, the next standard, are also included.

Chapter Outline

CHAPTER OBJECTIVES

This chapter provides you with a broad overview of a complete COBOL program. If you are a beginning programming student, do not expect to fully understand the details of this program after you've read this chapter. Also, you may not comprehend all of the COBOL language interrelationships yet. The purpose of this chapter is to introduce you to basic concepts of COBOL. The material presented in this overview chapter is further developed in following chapters, so you'll have other chances to master it. From this chapter, you will learn the following:

- The four broad elements of a COBOL program:

IDENTIFICATION DIVISION	Documents the program.
ENVIRONMENT DIVISION	Specifies computer hardware and the data files.
DATA DIVISION	Defines files, records, and fields.
PROCEDURE DIVISION	Expresses the program logic.

- The structure of a COBOL program—consisting of divisions, sections, paragraphs, and sentences.

- The designation and use of memory areas for input and output operations.

- The definition of the format of a record—done in the DATA DIVISION.

- The instructions to the computer to carry out the data-processing activities—done in the PROCEDURE DIVISION. Action statements include:

OPEN	Make data files ready for use.
CLOSE	End use of data files.
READ	Copy a record from a data file into memory.
MOVE	Copy data from one field in memory to another.
WRITE	Copy a record from memory to an output device.
STOP RUN	Terminate execution of a program.
PERFORM	Repeat a sequence of operations.

- The entering of a COBOL program into the computer.

Introducing COBOL

The Patron File

You were introduced to Fleetwood Charities and their patron file in Module A. Recall from Figure A-2 that the record format is as follows:

Field	Length	Class
Name	18	Alphanumeric
Street address	18	Alphanumeric
City/state/zip	24	Alphanumeric
Target contribution	4	Numeric (whole dollars)
Actual contribution	4	Numeric (whole dollars)
Total record size	68	

Your sample data file is stored in the computer as shown in Figure 1-1. Generally, you must have the record format before processing a file. For instance, it is impossible to identify individual numeric fields without the record format description.

A Simple Report from the Patron File

For your first look at COBOL, you will learn how to write the patron listing program described in Module A. However, for simplicity, this program only lists patrons; it will not identify anyone below their targeted amount. The printed output from the file of Figure 1-1 is shown in Figure 1-2. Notice that there is one line of output for each record of the file; single output lines that correspond to an input record are called **detail lines**. (In later chapters, you will learn about heading lines, summary lines, and others.) You can see that data "jammed" together in the input file is separated out so that it is easier to read in the output report. Also, note that not all of the data from the data record is used in printing a detail line.

Generating Output from Input Data

Whenever a data record is read into the computer's memory, it is placed in an input area of memory exactly as it is stored in the record. So, the 68-byte patron record is read into 68 consecutive bytes of memory. One of the programmer's tasks is to define this input area and to break it down into its component fields.

Figure 1-1
Sample patron data file.

```
Acton, Jocelyn      223 Connecticut StSan Francisco, CA 94107 03500350
Anderson, Hazel     1247 Main Street   Woodside, CA 94062      02500100
Baker, Donald       1532 Bancroft RoadBerkeley, CA 94703       03750300
Broadhurst, Ryan    Route 3            Big Trees, CA 95066     05000500
Campbell, J. H.     4892 Powell StreetEmeryville, CA 94608     02000175
Davidson, Harley    349 Airport Way    Concord, CA 94519       02500100
Drumright, Devon    2817 Laguna StreetOakland, CA 94602        01000105
Englehoff, F.       137 Rengstorff Bl.Santa Clara, CA 95051    02500150
Erlicht, Beverly    3814 Marina Blvd. San Francisco, CA 94123  02250225
Fox, Wylie          35 Crescent CircleOrinda, CA 94563         01000100
Grant, Rosalyn P.   4530 17th Street   San Francisco, CA 94114 00750080
Hildebrand, John    211 Central AvenueSanta Cruz, CA 95060     02500200
Jones, Jeanette     453 Bayview Drive Belvedere, CA 94920      03750000
Lacrosse, Larry     1347 Sacramento    Berkeley, CA 94702      04800520
Mattingly, Roscoe   1523 Old Bayshore Mountain View, CA 94043  01800180
Miller, Irwin B.    4237 Doppler Blvd.Daly City, CA 94014      02000185
Molitar, Arnold T.  125 Wharf Circle  Capitola, CA 95010       02000150
Nelson, J. J.       24389 Ballena RoadAlameda, CA 94501        02500000
Pratt, Diane        2201 Pacific Ave.  San Francisco, CA 94115 03750229
Stevenson, Howard   385 C Street       San Rafael, CA 94901    02000000
Unger, William P.   15062 E. 14th St. San Leandro, CA 94578    03000300
Walton, John Jr.    531 Gray Peak RoadBelmont, CA 94002        01500150
Winger, Mandy       1987 Dallas Drive Hayward, CA 94545        02250225
Zener, Eva          515 Bridgeport AveSausalito, CA 94965      02000190
```

Figure 1-2
List of contributors and
their addresses.

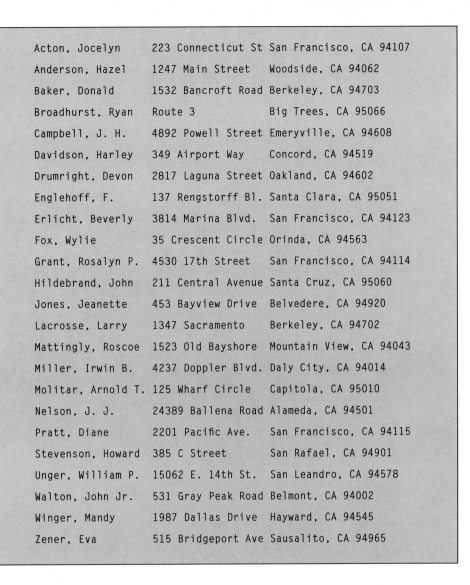

```
Acton, Jocelyn       223 Connecticut St San Francisco, CA 94107
Anderson, Hazel      1247 Main Street    Woodside, CA 94062
Baker, Donald        1532 Bancroft Road Berkeley, CA 94703
Broadhurst, Ryan     Route 3            Big Trees, CA 95066
Campbell, J. H.      4892 Powell Street Emeryville, CA 94608
Davidson, Harley     349 Airport Way    Concord, CA 94519
Drumright, Devon     2817 Laguna Street Oakland, CA 94602
Englehoff, F.        137 Rengstorff Bl. Santa Clara, CA 95051
Erlicht, Beverly     3814 Marina Blvd.  San Francisco, CA 94123
Fox, Wylie           35 Crescent Circle Orinda, CA 94563
Grant, Rosalyn P.    4530 17th Street   San Francisco, CA 94114
Hildebrand, John     211 Central Avenue Santa Cruz, CA 95060
Jones, Jeanette      453 Bayview Drive  Belvedere, CA 94920
Lacrosse, Larry      1347 Sacramento    Berkeley, CA 94702
Mattingly, Roscoe    1523 Old Bayshore  Mountain View, CA 94043
Miller, Irwin B.     4237 Doppler Blvd. Daly City, CA 94014
Molitar, Arnold T.   125 Wharf Circle   Capitola, CA 95010
Nelson, J. J.        24389 Ballena Road Alameda, CA 94501
Pratt, Diane         2201 Pacific Ave.  San Francisco, CA 94115
Stevenson, Howard    385 C Street       San Rafael, CA 94901
Unger, William P.    15062 E. 14th St.  San Leandro, CA 94578
Walton, John Jr.     531 Gray Peak Road Belmont, CA 94002
Winger, Mandy        1987 Dallas Drive  Hayward, CA 94545
Zener, Eva           515 Bridgeport Ave Sausalito, CA 94965
```

Similarly, the programmer must define an output area corresponding to the desired printed line.

With both the input and output areas defined, the action of the program—as illustrated in Figure 1-3—is to:

1. Read a record into the input area.
2. Move the individual fields to their appropriate positions in the output area.
3. Print the data stored in the output area.

Broad Elements of a Program

From these descriptions, it is evident that a program processing data from a file must include the following elements:

1. Designation of the file from which the data will be obtained. Almost all computers have more than one disk drive and each drive probably contains many files.
2. A description of the record format for the data file.
3. A description of the specific sequence of steps (the procedure) to be implemented when processing the data.

Figure 1-3   The read-move-print sequence.

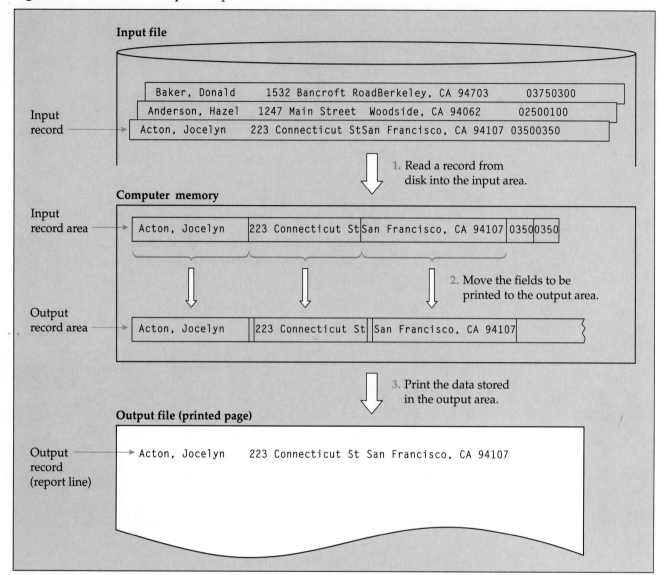

This is not unique to COBOL; the same is necessary in a program written in Pascal, FORTRAN, or BASIC (although the description may be subtle for some types of BASIC files). In addition to these three items, virtually all languages have the capability for the programmer to include an identification of the program and its actions. From one language to another, there are significant differences in the way these elements are implemented, but they exist anyway.

In COBOL, these four elements (including identification information) are explicitly identified as separate components or **divisions** of the COBOL program. Depicted in Figure 1-4, these components are as follows:

- IDENTIFICATION DIVISION   Documents the program.

- ENVIRONMENT DIVISION   Specifies computer hardware and the data files.

- DATA DIVISION   Defines files, records, and fields.

- PROCEDURE DIVISION   Expresses the program logic.

Figure 1-4   COBOL division structure.

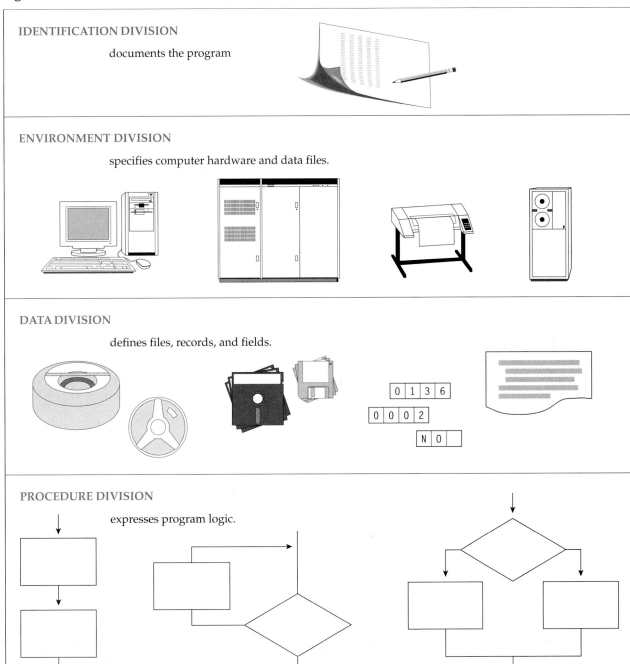

You can see these four elements in the patron list program of Figure 1-5. (Note: The line numbers to the left are not part of the program; they are included for your reference when analyzing the program.) Studying this program gives you a first look at COBOL and furnishes you with sufficient background to write your own simple program. As you will see, some details of this program are postponed to Chapters 2 and 3.

Reserved Words and User-Defined Words

If you glance at this program, you will see that much of it reads like simple English; for instance, line 60 reads:

```
MOVE SPACES TO PATRON-LINE
```

Figure 1-5   Annotated patron list (PATLIST) COBOL program.

```
1        IDENTIFICATION DIVISION.                          33      FD  PATRON-LIST.
2        PROGRAM-ID.    PATLIST.                           34
3                                                          35      01  PATRON-LINE.
4     *      PRICE/WELBURN  6/20/89  revised 1/5/95        36          05  FILLER                PIC X(1).
5                                                          37          05  PL-NAME               PIC X(18).
6     *      This program prints a patron address list.    38          05  FILLER                PIC X(1).
7                                                          39          05  PL-ADDRESS            PIC X(18).
8                                                          40          05  FILLER                PIC X(1).
9        ENVIRONMENT DIVISION.                             41          05  PL-CITY-STATE-ZIP     PIC X(24).
10                                                         42
11       INPUT-OUTPUT SECTION.                             43      WORKING-STORAGE SECTION.
12                                                         44
13       FILE-CONTROL.                                     45      01  SW-SWITCHES.
14           SELECT PATRON-FILE                            46          05  SW-EOF-SWITCH         PIC X(3).
15               ASSIGN TO (system dependent).             47
16           SELECT PATRON-LIST                            48
17               ASSIGN TO (system dependent).             49      PROCEDURE DIVISION.
18                                                         50
19                                                         51      000-PRINT-PATRON-LIST.
20       DATA DIVISION.                                    52          OPEN INPUT PATRON-FILE
21                                                         53               OUTPUT PATRON-LIST
22       FILE SECTION.                                     54          MOVE "NO " TO SW-EOF-SWITCH
23                                                         55          PERFORM UNTIL SW-EOF-SWITCH IS EQUAL TO "YES"
24       FD  PATRON-FILE.                                  56              READ PATRON-FILE
25                                                         57                  AT END
26       01  PATRON-RECORD.                                58                      MOVE "YES" TO SW-EOF-SWITCH
27           05  PR-NAME              PIC X(18).           59                  NOT AT END
28           05  PR-ADDRESS           PIC X(18).           60                      MOVE SPACES TO PATRON-LINE
29           05  PR-CITY-STATE-ZIP    PIC X(24).           61                      MOVE PR-NAME TO PL-NAME
30           05  PR-TARGET-CONTR      PIC 9(4).            62                      MOVE PR-ADDRESS TO PL-ADDRESS
31           05  PR-ACTUAL-CONTR      PIC 9(4).            63                      MOVE PR-CITY-STATE-ZIP TO PL-CITY-STATE-ZIP
32                                                         64                      WRITE PATRON-LINE
                                                           65                          AFTER ADVANCING 2 LINES
                                                           66              END-READ
                                                           67          END-PERFORM
                                                           68          CLOSE PATRON-FILE
                                                           69                PATRON-LIST
                                                           70          STOP RUN
                                                           71          .
```

The words of this statement fall into two distinct categories: user defined and reserved. **Reserved words** have special predefined meanings in COBOL and each can be used only as explicitly allowed by COBOL. In the previous example, MOVE is a reserved word. On the other hand, **user-defined words** are those selected by the programmer to identify data fields and other needed program elements: PATRON-LINE is an example. User-defined words can be up to 30 characters in length and must contain at least one letter. You will learn more about selecting them in Chapter 2.

The IDENTIFICATION DIVISION: Identifying the Program

The **IDENTIFICATION DIVISION**, repeated in Figure 1-6, is the first division of a COBOL program. This division includes two required entries. The first is the **division header** and contains the reserved words IDENTIFICATION DIVISION, exactly as shown. The second entry is PROGRAM-ID (a reserved word). This line includes the name selected by the programmer for this program—PATLIST in this case.

Notice the use of periods in these two entries—they are required. The COBOL language processor looks for periods to terminate various elements of the program. As you will learn when you begin running programs, omitting or misplacing periods usually causes problems.

The asterisk character (*) in each of lines 4 and 6 indicates a descriptive comment that conveys only documentation information to the programmer. Since it is ignored by the COBOL system, you can type whatever descriptive comments you like. Note that blank lines (3 and 5) are used to separate parts of the program and make it easier to read.

Figure 1-6
The IDENTIFICATION
DIVISION for the PATLIST
program.

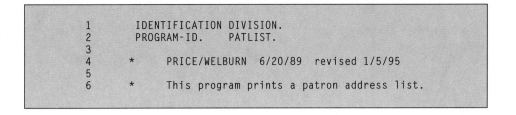

```
1        IDENTIFICATION DIVISION.
2        PROGRAM-ID.    PATLIST.
3
4    *      PRICE/WELBURN  6/20/89  revised 1/5/95
5
6    *      This program prints a patron address list.
```

Some COBOL language processors produce a program printout with blank lines deleted. If yours does that, simply include an * in column 7 to retain the blank line spacing.

The ENVIRONMENT DIVISION: Defining Input-Output

The **ENVIRONMENT DIVISION** is the link between the predominantly hardware-independent COBOL program and the actual computer and input-output device hardware that the program uses. You can see in Figure 1-7(a) the **section header** INPUT-OUTPUT SECTION, which is required of any program that uses one or more data files. (It is one of two allowable sections of this division.)

INPUT-OUTPUT SECTION

The **INPUT-OUTPUT SECTION** designates the data files that the program uses. Each file is identified and associated with a hardware input-output device.

The PATLIST program uses two files—the input file (that is, the patron file) containing name-and-address records, and an output report file containing lines of patron data. Even though the program will send output to the printer, COBOL considers it as file output. Thus, the word *file* is not limited to a collection of data

Figure 1-7
Assigning COBOL
file-names.

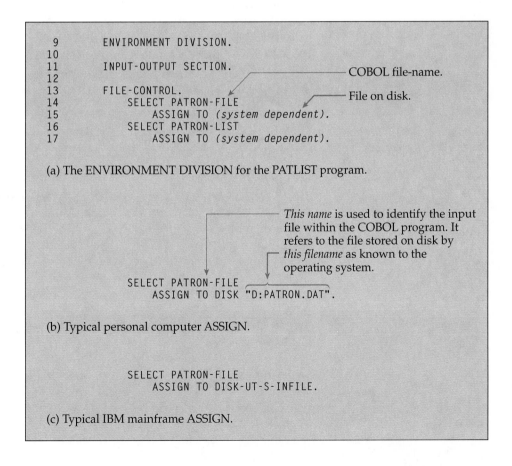

```
 9        ENVIRONMENT DIVISION.
10
11        INPUT-OUTPUT SECTION.
12                                              ── COBOL file-name.
13        FILE-CONTROL.
14            SELECT PATRON-FILE
15                ASSIGN TO (system dependent).     ── File on disk.
16            SELECT PATRON-LIST
17                ASSIGN TO (system dependent).
```

(a) The ENVIRONMENT DIVISION for the PATLIST program.

This name is used to identify the input file within the COBOL program. It refers to the file stored on disk by *this filename* as known to the operating system.

```
SELECT PATRON-FILE
    ASSIGN TO DISK "D:PATRON.DAT".
```

(b) Typical personal computer ASSIGN.

```
SELECT PATRON-FILE
    ASSIGN TO DISK-UT-S-INFILE.
```

(c) Typical IBM mainframe ASSIGN.

stored on disk or tape. Under FILE-CONTROL, you can see two SELECT/ASSIGN TO entries: one for each file used in the program. Each of these identifies the COBOL file-name that will be used to refer to the data file in the COBOL program. For instance, the programmer gave the patron file the name PATRON-FILE; all references within the program to the file are through this name.

The corresponding ASSIGN TO specifies a hardware device and/or operating system filename that the operating system uses to refer to the file. In lines 15 and 17, you see the words *system dependent*. These are not the words you would type into the program; they are simply a message indicating that you must include an entry corresponding to your computer. Figure 1-7(b) is a typical personal computer entry you might encounter; Figure 1-7(c) is a common IBM mainframe form. Before attempting to run any program, you must obtain the exact form to be used at your installation from an instructor, lab director, or other computer authority.

The DATA DIVISION: Defining Files, Records, and Fields

FILE SECTION

As its name implies, the **DATA DIVISION** describes the data processed by the program. The DATA DIVISION for the PATLIST program (shown in Figure 1-8) consists of two sections: the FILE SECTION and the WORKING-STORAGE SECTION. Most programs in this book include these two sections.

Data-items (files, records, and fields) of the input and output files are defined in the **FILE SECTION**. Each file selected in the ENVIRONMENT DIVISION must be described in this section. So, the FILE SECTION is made up of file descriptions for all files that the program uses. A **file-description entry** starts with the reserved word FD (standing for File Description) followed by the COBOL **file-name** defined in the ENVIRONMENT DIVISION (as in Figure 1-8).

COBOL-74

COBOL-74 requires an additional clause with the FD; you will see it in the COBOL-74 equivalent of this program later in the chapter.

Figure 1-8
The DATA DIVISION for the PATLIST program.

```
20      DATA DIVISION.
21
22      FILE SECTION.
23
24      FD  PATRON-FILE. ←——— Data filename, as defined in the SELECT clause.
25
26      01  PATRON-RECORD. ←——— Record name.
27          05  PR-NAME                     PIC X(18).
28          05  PR-ADDRESS ←                PIC X(18).
29          05  PR-CITY-STATE-ZIP           PIC X(24).
30          05  PR-TARGET-CONTR             PIC 9(4).
31          05  PR-ACTUAL-CONTR             PIC 9(4).
32                                          ↑
33      FD  PATRON-LIST.
34                                          └——Field length and class.
35      01  PATRON-LINE.                    ——Field name.
36          05  FILLER                      PIC X(1).
37          05  PL-NAME                     PIC X(18).
38          05  FILLER                      PIC X(1).
39          05  PL-ADDRESS                  PIC X(18).
40          05  FILLER                      PIC X(1).
41          05  PL-CITY-STATE-ZIP           PIC X(24).
42
43      WORKING-STORAGE SECTION.
44
45      01  SW-SWITCHES.
46          05  SW-EOF-SWITCH               PIC X(3).
```

After the FD entry for a file, the record format for that file is described. Each element of the record description in this program has three parts:

1. A two-digit level-number (such as 01 or 05, as in these examples), which determines the hierarchy of the element.
2. A user-defined data-name to identify the record or field—or else the reserved word FILLER. You use the data-name in statements of the PROCEDURE DIVISION when referring to the field.
3. A PICTURE clause (commonly abbreviated with the reserved word **PIC**, as in the PATLIST program), which defines the data class and the length of the field.

As in line 26 of the PATLIST program, the level-number 01 always signifies a record-description entry. Following the level-number 01 is the user-defined record name: PATRON-RECORD. Lines following the record-description entry consist of a sequence of entries (termed **data-item description entries**) describing the fields composing the record. Each must begin with a level-number in the range 02 through 49. Using the level-number 05 in lines 27–31 (a number that is larger than the 01 of PATRON-RECORD) tells the compiler that these data-items are fields that make up the PATRON-RECORD.

In line 27, you can see that the entry following the reserved word PIC (the PICTURE entry) is X(18). The letter X is a code meaning that the data class is alphanumeric; the 18 (enclosed within parentheses) says that the length of this field is 18 positions. In lines 30 and 31, the PIC code is 9—indicating numeric data class.

Beginning with line 33 in Figure 1-8 are the file and record descriptions for the output file PATRON-LIST. Descriptions of the input FD are equally applicable to this output FD. However, since the output line requires that space be inserted between output fields, this record description includes a one-position FILLER entry between each field (lines 36, 38, and 40). The word FILLER is a COBOL reserved word designated specifically for indicating a portion of a record that will not be referenced. In contrast to COBOL-74, COBOL-85 does not require that the word FILLER be included to designate an unreferenced entry. Therefore, in all future programs of this book, filler entries will consist only of the level-number and the PIC designation.

WORKING-STORAGE SECTION

Most programs require other fields in addition to those present in the input and output data records. Some examples are fields used to accumulate totals or to keep track of program status conditions. Such fields are described in the **WORKING-STORAGE SECTION** because they are not part of the input or output records described in the FILE SECTION. Because the PATLIST program is a straightforward read-and-print type of program, only one WORKING-STORAGE field (SW-EOF-SWITCH) is required.

All such fields are defined under a WORKING-STORAGE "record," as in this example. In line 45, you see the record SW-SWITCHES, which includes the single entry SW-EOF-SWITCH.

The PROCEDURE DIVISION: Coding the Program Logic

As the name suggests, the **PROCEDURE DIVISION** contains "procedures" (actions to be implemented) by the program. Generally, the PROCEDURE DIVISION is composed of separate modules called **paragraphs**. To simplify your first look at COBOL, the PROCEDURE DIVISION of PATLIST consists of only one paragraph. You can see in Figure 1-9 the paragraph name 000-PRINT-PATRON-LIST at line 51. This paragraph name is a user-defined word—a name selected by the programmer. In Chapter 2, you will learn the significance of individual paragraphs—but for now, simply consider it a required item.

Figure 1-9
The PROCEDURE
DIVISION for the PATLIST
program.

```
49        PROCEDURE DIVISION.
50
51        000-PRINT-PATRON-LIST.
52            OPEN INPUT PATRON-FILE
53                 OUTPUT PATRON-LIST
54            MOVE "NO " TO SW-EOF-SWITCH
55            PERFORM UNTIL SW-EOF-SWITCH IS EQUAL TO "YES"
56                READ PATRON-FILE
57                    AT END
58                        MOVE "YES" TO SW-EOF-SWITCH
59                    NOT AT END
60                        MOVE SPACES TO PATRON-LINE
61                        MOVE PR-NAME TO PL-NAME
62                        MOVE PR-ADDRESS TO PL-ADDRESS
63                        MOVE PR-CITY-STATE-ZIP TO PL-CITY-STATE-ZIP
64                        WRITE PATRON-LINE
65                            AFTER ADVANCING 2 LINES
66                END-READ
67            END-PERFORM
68            CLOSE PATRON-FILE
69                  PATRON-LIST
70            STOP RUN
71            .
```

Following the paragraph name are statements (lines 52–70). COBOL statements in the PROCEDURE DIVISION designate an operation to take place and therefore begin with a verb: an action word telling the computer to do something. The verbs used in the program are as follows:

```
OPEN and CLOSE
READ
MOVE
WRITE
STOP RUN
PERFORM
```

The OPEN and CLOSE Statements

Each file used in a program must be "made ready" before data can be read from or written to it, which is done with the OPEN statement. In Figure 1-9, you see the following OPEN statement (lines 52 and 53):

```
OPEN INPUT PATRON-FILE
     OUTPUT PATRON-LIST
```

After processing is complete and before the program is terminated, all files that were opened must be closed. This is done in lines 68 and 69 with the statement:

```
CLOSE PATRON-FILE
      PATRON-LIST
```

Do not worry about the slightly different format of these two statements (the OPEN uses the reserved words INPUT and OUTPUT, but the CLOSE does not). This is described more fully in Chapter 3.

The READ Statement

After an input file is open, data can be read from it with the READ statement. This is done at line 56 with the statement:

```
READ PATRON-FILE
```

The verb READ is followed by the name of the file from which the record will be read. Each time the READ is executed, the next data record is read from the input device and placed in the input area defined in the DATA DIVISION.

Figure 1-10
The end-of-file record.

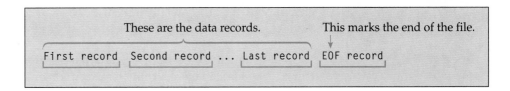

These are the data records.   This marks the end of the file.

```
First record   Second record ... Last record   EOF record
```

Figure 1-11
Features of the AT
END/NOT AT END
portion of the READ.

```
READ PATRON-FILE
    AT END
        (One or more COBOL statements) ← These are executed if the record just
    NOT AT END                            read is the EOF record.
        (One or more COBOL statements) ← These are executed if the record just
END-READ                                  read is a data record.
    │
    └─ Signifies the last of the statements
       involved with the READ operation.
```

Actually, the READ statement is capable of a lot more than simply reading a record. To fully appreciate how it works, you must know how data is stored in a file. In Figure 1-10, you can see that records are stored one after the other. Following the last data record of the file is a special record called the **end-of-file (EOF) record**.

As each record is read, COBOL checks if it is a data record or the EOF record. If it is the EOF, you can direct COBOL to take one set of actions. In COBOL-85 only, if it is a data record, you can direct COBOL to take another set of actions. Figure 1-11 illustrates this feature of the READ statement. The reserved words composing the READ are AT END, NOT AT END, and END-READ. Be aware that END-READ is a single reserved word that includes a hyphen.

In the READ of Figure 1-9, the AT END action causes YES to be moved to the field SW-EOF-SWITCH. As you will see, this controls the repeated reading and processing of data records. On the other hand, the NOT AT END condition means that a data record was read and must be processed. This is accomplished by the sequence of statements at lines 60–65. The purpose of the END-READ is to identify the group of statements whose execution is controlled by the READ.

The MOVE Statement

The operation of moving data from one place in memory to another is done with the MOVE statement, such as that in line 61 of Figure 1-9:

```
MOVE PR-NAME TO PL-NAME
```

This statement copies data from the input field (PR-NAME) to corresponding positions of the output area (PL-NAME). The PATLIST program also includes two minor variations of the MOVE. The MOVE at line 60 moves spaces to the output record (SPACES is a reserved word that represents blank spaces). Also, the MOVE statements at lines 54 and 58 move the words NO and YES into the WORKING-STORAGE field SW-EOF-SWITCH. Items enclosed in quotes this way are called literals and are processed exactly as quoted.

The WRITE Statement

The WRITE statement at lines 64 and 65

```
WRITE PATRON-LINE
    AFTER ADVANCING 2 LINES
```

identifies the output *record* to be written (PATRON-LINE) and sends it to the printer. (Notice that the READ and WRITE differ in this respect. You READ a file and WRITE a record.) This printed record is the output record into which input data was moved. The AFTER ADVANCING controls line spacing and results in a double-spaced report, as you can see back in Figure 1-2 (page 15).

The STOP RUN Statement

The last statement executed in a program must be the STOP RUN; it is at line 70 in Figure 1-9. This statement terminates execution of the program and returns control to the operating system.

The PERFORM Statement

When you run the program, statements are executed one after the other in the order in which they are encountered. The PERFORM is an exception to this because it allows a sequence of statements to be executed repeatedly. This form of the PERFORM consists of the following components:

1. The verb PERFORM and a condition to be tested, which controls repeated execution of statements that follow.
2. One or more statements to be executed under control of the PERFORM. These statements make up a **program loop**.
3. The entry END-PERFORM, which identifies the end of the loop.

Figure 1-12 illustrates the way in which the PERFORM statement works. That is, the sequence of statements composing the loop are executed repeatedly until the WORKING-STORAGE variable SW-EOF-SWITCH contains YES. (Remember, the AT END clause of the READ statement moves YES into this data-item when the EOF record is read.)

Overall Execution of the Program

Throughout this book, you will encounter statements such as, "execution of the MOVE statement causes...." and "...this paragraph will be executed repeatedly..." As you learned in Module A, the COBOL program statements are not executed directly. They are first converted to the computer's machine language; then, the resulting machine language program is executed. So, you should always interpret

Figure 1-12   Repeated execution using a PERFORM statement.

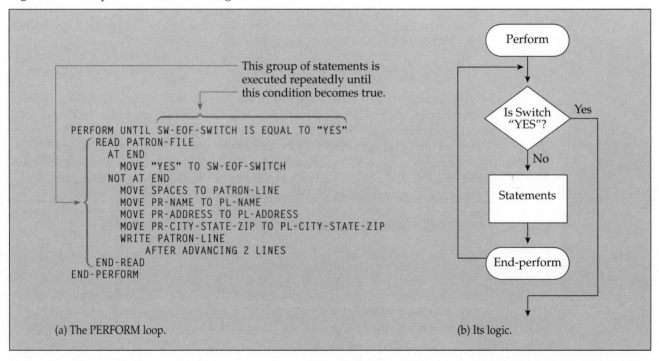

(a) The PERFORM loop.   (b) Its logic.

a description such as "this paragraph is executed repeatedly" as meaning "the machine language program elements resulting from this paragraph are executed repeatedly."

Execution of a program begins with the first statement following the PROCEDURE DIVISION entry and continues statement by statement until the end of the program is encountered. To illustrate, let's walk through this program (Figure 1-9) to trace the logic flow. For this example, assume that the patron file contains two data records plus the EOF record; the action sequence is as follows:

Statement(s)	Action
52, 53	Open the input and output files.
54	Initialize by moving NO to the control field SW-EOF-SWITCH.
55	Because SW-EOF-SWITCH does not contain YES, proceed to the next statement (the first statement of the loop).
56	Read the first record from the data file. This is a data record, so place its contents in the input record area. Since this is not the EOF, proceed to line 60.
60–63	Move data of the first record from the input area to the output area.
64, 65	Print the output record after advancing the paper two lines. The END-READ at line 66 signifies that this completes statement execution under this execution of the READ.
67	Upon encountering the END-PERFORM, return control to the PERFORM statement at line 55.
55	Check to determine if SW-EOF-SWITCH contains YES. It does not, so proceed to the next statement.
56	Read the next (second) record from the data file. This is a data record, so place its contents in the input record area and proceed to line 60.
60–63	Move data of the second record from the input area to the output area.
64, 65	Print the output record after advancing the paper two lines.
67	Upon encountering the END-PERFORM, return control to the PERFORM statement at line 55.
55	Check to determine if SW-EOF-SWITCH contains YES. It does not, so proceed to the next statement.
56	Read the next (third) record from the data file. This is the EOF, so the AT END option is selected; proceed to line 58.
58	Move YES to SW-EOF-SWITCH. This completes the AT END action, so skip to the END-READ (line 66) and then to the END-PERFORM (line 67). Then return control to the PERFORM at line 55.
55	Check to determine if SW-EOF-SWITCH contains YES. It does, so transfer control to the statement following the END-PERFORM (line 68).
68–69	Close the files.
70	Terminate execution of the program.

Preparing the Program for the Computer

The Coding Form

When COBOL was first devised, most programs were punched into 80-column cards and read into the computer by special card readers. As a result, the capacity of the card was a determining factor in defining how a COBOL program was prepared. Although cards were widely replaced by video terminals, the effects of card capacity still remain. For example, a statement in the PROCEDURE DIVISION

Figure 1-13   The COBOL coding form.

System				Keying Instructions						
Program *PATRON LISTING*			Graphic	Ø	O	1	I	2	Z	
Programmer *PRICE / WELBURN* Date *1/5*			Punch	ZERO	ALPHA	ONE	ALPHA	TWO	ALPHA	

```
IDENTIFICATION DIVISION.
PROGRAM-ID.        PATLIST.

*          PRICE/WELBURN     6/20/89     revised  1/5/95

*          This  program  prints  a  patron  address  list.


DATA  DIVISION.

FILE  SECTION.

FD    PATRON-FILE.

01    PATRON-RECORD.
      05    PR-NAME                              PIC  X(18).
      05    PR-ADDRESS                           PIC  X(18).
```

cannot begin on the line before position (column) 12. Generally, it is important that you space over carefully and ensure that your entries start in the correct columns. For convenience, program statements are commonly written on special COBOL coding forms that are vertically ruled with the exact format required by a COBOL program. To give you an idea of how to use a coding form, part of the PATLIST program is written on one in Figure 1-13. This form is divided into four major fields:

Usage	Columns
Sequence number	1–6
Continuation (or * for comment)	7
COBOL statements	8–72
Program identification	73–80 (not shown in Figure 1-13)

With keyboard entry directly into the computer, the Sequence and Identification columns are often not used; examples in this book ignore them. However, some installations do require, as shop standards, entries in one or both of these areas. Referring back to the program listing of Figure 1-5 (page 18), do not confuse the numbers to the left of each statement with any portion of the coding sheet. These numbers were not entered by the programmer; they are generated by the compiler to identify lines of the program in specifying incorrect statements. Virtually all compilers create such line numbers.

Figure 1-13 (continued)

System				Keying Instructions						
Program *PATRON LISTING*			Graphic	Ø	O	I	I	2	Z	
Programmer *PRICE / WELBURN* Date *1/5*			Punch	ZERO	ALPHA ONE	ALPHA TWO	ALPHA			

```
        PROCEDURE  DIVISION.

    000-PRINT-PATRON-LIST.
        OPEN   INPUT   PATRON-FILE
               OUTPUT  PATRON-LIST
        MOVE   "NO"  TO  SW-EOF-SWITCH
        PERFORM UNTIL  SW-EOF-SWITCH  IS  EQUAL  TO  "YES"
            READ  PATRON-FILE
                AT  END
                    MOVE  "YES"  TO  SW-EOF-SWITCH
                .
                .
        CLOSE  PATRON-FILE
               PATRON-LIST
        STOP  RUN
                .
```

Area A and Area B Entries

All COBOL statements of the Figure 1-5 program are entered into the coding form's columns 8–72 (however, the * signifying a comment is entered into column 7). Notice in the coding form that column 8 is marked A and column 12 is marked B. The A marks the first position of **Area A**, which consists of columns 8–11. Similarly, the B marks the first position of **Area B**, which includes columns 12–72. These positions are significant because certain COBOL entries must begin in Area A, and others must begin in Area B. Most entries that must begin in Area A will extend into Area B; this is completely acceptable. In Figure 1-5, the following entries must start in Area A:

Division headers (IDENTIFICATION, ENVIRONMENT, DATA, and PROCEDURE).

Section headers (FILE SECTION and WORKING-STORAGE SECTION).

Paragraph headers (FILE-CONTROL, FD, and 01).

PROCEDURE DIVISION paragraph names (000-PRINT-PATRON-LIST).

All other entries must begin in Area B. When entering a program, you must be careful to use the proper number of spaces so that your entry starts in the proper area. *Do not use the tab key to space across* unless you are using an editor especially designed for COBOL that replaces the tab character with an appropriate number of spaces.

In COBOL-74, no program entry can go beyond column 72. However, the 1985 Standard does not specify an end to Area B. In your career, you might encounter a compiler that allows a COBOL statement to go beyond column 72.

> **COBOL-9X**
>
> Strict margin rules will probably be eliminated in COBOL-9X, allowing the programmer more flexibility for positioning entries on the line.

Spacing and the Use of Periods

At least one blank space must appear between words. Whenever one blank space is used, any number of blank spaces may be used.

In COBOL, a period indicates the end of an entry (described further in Chapter 2). For this chapter's programming assignments, you must use periods in the first three divisions exactly as in the PATLIST program of Figure 1-5. In the PROCEDURE DIVISION, you must use a period after the paragraph name and after the last statement of the paragraph. Notice in Figure 1-9 (page 22) that the paragraph-ending period is included on a separate line following the last statement of the paragraph. It could also be written as

```
STOP RUN.
```

with the period immediately following the last statement. As a style standard to help you avoid pitfalls, the paragraph-ending period is always included on a separate line in this book.

However, you should know that COBOL permits you to terminate *each statement* of the PROCEDURE DIVISION with a period. If you look at other programs, especially those written using COBOL-74, you will see periods following nearly every statement.

Compiling and Running PATLIST—COBOL-85

If you want to compile and run the PATLIST program, you can either key it in from Figure 1-5 (do not type the line numbers to the left) or you can use the copy stored on the disk included with this book. (The COBOL-85 program is stored as PATLIST.CBL.) If entering the program from the keyboard, you must change the entries identified in Figure 1-5 by *(system dependent)* to conform to your computer. The copy on disk includes entries compatible with the Micro Focus and Ryan-McFarland compilers. You must change them if your computer uses different entries.

The PATLIST Program Coded in COBOL-74

If you want to enter and/or compile and run the PATLIST program and cannot access a COBOL-85 compiler, you can use the COBOL-74 version in Figure 1-14. If you do not want to run the program now, you can skip this section. These equivalent COBOL-74 forms are described in Chapter 3's expanded descriptions.

This program includes several additional entries not needed in COBOL-85 (lines 12–15, 31, and 41). They are described in Chapters 2 and 3. To compile and run the program, you can either type it through the keyboard from Figure 1-14 (omit the line numbers to the left) or you can use the copy stored on the disk included with this book. (The program is stored as PATLIST.C74.) If you enter the program from the keyboard, you must change the entries identified in Figure 1-14 by *(system dependent)* to conform to your computer. The copy on disk includes entries oriented to IBM personal computer compilers. Using a COBOL-74 compiler, you will probably need to change them for your computer.

Regarding the PROCEDURE DIVISION code, COBOL-74 lacks two vital elements used in the PATLIST program of Figure 1-5: the NOT AT END phrase of the READ and this particular version of the PERFORM. The PERFORM in Figure 1-14

Figure 1-14   COBOL-74 version of PATLIST.

```
1     IDENTIFICATION DIVISION.                          40    FD  PATRON-LIST
2     PROGRAM-ID.   PATLIST.                            41        LABEL RECORDS ARE OMITTED.
3                                                       42
4     *      PRICE/WELBURN  6/20/89  revised 1/5/95     43    01  PATRON-LINE.
5                                                       44        05  FILLER              PIC X(1).
6     *     This program prints a patron address list   45        05  PL-NAME             PIC X(18).
7     *     using COBOL-74.                             46        05  FILLER              PIC X(1).
8                                                       47        05  PL-ADDRESS          PIC X(18).
9                                                       48        05  FILLER              PIC X(1).
10    ENVIRONMENT DIVISION.                             49        05  PL-CITY-STATE-ZIP   PIC X(24).
11                                                      50
12    CONFIGURATION SECTION.                            51    WORKING-STORAGE SECTION.
13                                                      52
14        SOURCE-COMPUTER. (system dependent).         53    01  SW-SWITCHES.
15        OBJECT-COMPUTER. (system dependent).         54        05  SW-EOF-SWITCH       PIC X(3).
16                                                      55
17    INPUT-OUTPUT SECTION.                             56
18                                                      57    PROCEDURE DIVISION.
19    FILE-CONTROL.                                     58
20        SELECT PATRON-FILE                            59    000-PRINT-PATRON-LIST.
21            ASSIGN TO (system dependent).            60        OPEN INPUT PATRON-FILE
22        SELECT PATRON-LIST                            61             OUTPUT PATRON-LIST
23            ASSIGN TO (system dependent).            62        MOVE "NO " TO SW-EOF-SWITCH
24                                                      63        PERFORM 200-PROCESS-RECORD
25                                                      64            UNTIL SW-EOF-SWITCH IS EQUAL TO "YES"
26    DATA DIVISION.                                    65        CLOSE PATRON-FILE
27                                                      66              PATRON-LIST.
28    FILE SECTION.                                     67        STOP RUN
29                                                      68
30    FD  PATRON-FILE                                   69    200-PROCESS-RECORD.
31        LABEL RECORDS ARE STANDARD.                  70        READ PATRON-FILE
32                                                      71            AT END
33    01  PATRON-RECORD.                                72                MOVE "YES" TO SW-EOF-SWITCH.
34        05  PR-NAME            PIC X(18).             73        IF SW-EOF-SWITCH IS EQUAL TO "NO "
35        05  PR-ADDRESS         PIC X(18).             74            MOVE SPACES TO PATRON-LINE
36        05  PR-CITY-STATE-ZIP  PIC X(24).             75            MOVE PR-NAME TO PL-NAME
37        05  PR-TARGET-CONTR    PIC 9(4).              76            MOVE PR-ADDRESS TO PL-ADDRESS
38        05  PR-ACTUAL-CONTR    PIC 9(4).              77            MOVE PR-CITY-STATE-ZIP TO PL-CITY-STATE-ZIP
39                                                      78            WRITE PATRON-LINE
                                                        79                AFTER ADVANCING 2 LINES.
```

(lines 63 and 64) causes the repeated processing of the paragraph numbered 200 until the end of the data file is detected. The IF statement at line 73 allows the statements that follow to be executed only if the preceding record just read is not the end-of-file. In other words, the IF achieves the same effect as the NOT AT END of Figure 1-5. If you enter the program through the keyboard, be careful to include periods exactly as listed. A more detailed description—plus a commonly used COBOL-74 technique for processing a data file—are included in Chapter 3.

Chapter Summary

This completes your "first look" at COBOL. With this overall view of a simple—but complete—COBOL program, you can now make the basic modification described in the upcoming programming assignment. In Chapters 2 and 3, you will learn enough COBOL language syntax to write a variety of COBOL programs.

A COBOL program is composed of reserved words (words with special meaning to the COBOL system) and user-defined words (words defined by the programmer to identify data elements: files, records, and fields).

The four broad elements (divisions) of a COBOL program are

- IDENTIFICATION DIVISION   Documents the program.
- ENVIRONMENT DIVISION   Specifies computer hardware and the data files.
- DATA DIVISION   Defines files, records, and fields.
- PROCEDURE DIVISION   Expresses the program logic.

The IDENTIFICATION DIVISION is the first entry in the program; this division contains the program identification.

The ENVIRONMENT DIVISION is the link between the hardware-independent COBOL program and the actual computer input/output devices, including auxiliary storage units on which data files to be processed are saved.

The DATA DIVISION contains descriptions of all data items—files, records, and fields—used by the COBOL program. The DATA DIVISION for a typical program contains two sections: the FILE SECTION and the WORKING-STORAGE SECTION.

Each record description entry of the DATA DIVISION is designated by the level-number 01. It consists of one or more fields, each with a PIC clause defining the data class and size.

The WORKING-STORAGE SECTION defines fields that are required in the program, but are not part of an input or output record.

The PROCEDURE DIVISION contains procedural statements describing the actions to be taken in processing the data. Statements used in this chapter include: OPEN, CLOSE, READ, MOVE, WRITE, STOP RUN, and PERFORM. Looping (repetition) capabilities are provided by the PERFORM/UNTIL.

When entering a COBOL program, you must be aware of Area A (columns 8–11) and Area B (columns 12–72). Division headers, section headers, paragraph headers, and PROCEDURE DIVISION paragraph headers must begin in Area A. All other entries begin in Area B.

Exercises

Terms for Definition

Area A
Area B
DATA DIVISION
data-item description entries
detail lines
division
division header
end-of-file (EOF) record
ENVIRONMENT DIVISION
file-description entry
file-name

FILE SECTION
IDENTIFICATION DIVISION
INPUT-OUTPUT SECTION
paragraphs
PIC
PROCEDURE DIVISION
program loop
reserved word
section header
user-defined words
WORKING-STORAGE SECTION

Review Questions

1. List, in correct sequence, the four COBOL divisions and briefly describe the general purpose of each.

2. Name the DIVISION to which each of the following sections belongs:
   a. `WORKING-STORAGE SECTION`
   b. `INPUT-OUTPUT SECTION`
   c. `FILE SECTION`

3. Identify the DIVISION to which each of the following paragraphs belongs:
   a. `PROGRAM-ID`
   b. `SELECT`
   c. `000-PRINT-PATRON-LIST`
   d. `FILE-CONTROL`

4. The reserved word FD is an abbreviation for what?

5. What type of entry does the level-number 01 signify? *Record items*

6. What type of entry do the level-numbers 02 through 49 signify?

Data item

7. Describe briefly what each of the following COBOL reserved words does:
   a. ASSIGN
   b. AT END
   c. CLOSE
   d. MOVE
   e. OPEN
   f. PERFORM UNTIL
   g. READ
   h. SELECT
   i. STOP RUN
   j. WRITE

8. For each of the following line numbers, describe the effect on Figure 1-5's program if that line were removed.
   a. 38
   b. 46
   c. 58
   d. 64, 65

Programming Assignments

Programming Assignment 1-1: Patron Address

Enter, compile, and run the PATLIST program of Figure 1-5.

Programming Assignment 1-2: Patron Address/ Contribution List

Input file: Patron file (PATRON.DAT)

Input-record format:

Note: The following record definition corresponds to the record description in Figure 1-5's PATLIST program.

Positions	Field name	Data class
1–18	Patron name	Alphanumeric
19–36	Patron street address	Alphanumeric
37–60	Patron city/state/zip	Alphanumeric
61–64	Target contribution	Numeric
65–68	Actual contribution	Numeric

Required output:

The program should print a list of all contributors in the patron file. The printed report must include the following input fields with two spaces between fields.

Output report data-items:

Name
City-state-zip
Target contribution
Actual contribution

More on the IDENTIFICATION, ENVIRONMENT, and DATA Divisions

Chapter Outline

CHAPTER

2

CHAPTER OBJECTIVES

At this point, you should now have (1) a knowledge of data files and processing them, (2) an insight to the basic structure of a COBOL program, and (3) a general understanding of the program development process. In this chapter, you will concentrate on the detailed COBOL language specifications necessary to write a COBOL program. From this chapter, you will learn the following:

- The structure of a COBOL program—consisting of divisions, sections, paragraphs, sentences, and statements.

- More about the computer-dependent ENVIRON-MENT DIVISION, which consists of two sections: the CONFIGURATION SECTION and the INPUT-OUTPUT SECTION.

- More about the DATA DIVISION, which describes the input and output processed by the program.

- The use of level-numbers in defining the record, fields within the record, and subfields.

COBOL Format and Terminology

COBOL Format Notation

In this and the following chapters, you will look closely at the precise syntactical format of COBOL language entries. COBOL has a standard **format notation** that presents syntactical rules and requirements. A complete summary of formats is given in Appendix E for COBOL-85. The following is a summary of the meanings for the various symbols used in the format notation.

1. Reserved words required in the statement are printed in capital letters and underscored:

    OPEN

2. Reserved words not required in the statement are printed in capital letters but *not* underscored; for instance, IS and THAN can be omitted in the following:

    IS GREATER THAN

3. Names to be supplied by the programmer are indicated in lowercase by forms such as *data-name*, *record-name*, and *paragraph-name*. The word **identifier** is commonly used in place of data-name; for example:

    ACCEPT identifier   or   ACCEPT data-name

4. When two or more data-names or identifiers are required in a statement, they are called *identifier-1*, *identifier-2*, and so on:

    DIVIDE identifier-1 BY identifier-2

5. The words *comment-entry* indicate that the entry made by the programmer is ignored by the compiler and—as a programmer comment—serves solely for documentation:

    INSTALLATION. [comment-entry]...

6. When one of two or more choices is required, the choices are enclosed within braces, one above the other. For instance, the following means that either identifier or literal may be used:

    DISPLAY $\left\{ \begin{array}{l} \text{identifier} \\ \text{literal} \end{array} \right\}$

7. Brackets enclose an optional part of a statement. For instance,

    WRITE record-name [FROM data-name]

    can also be used in the following form:

    WRITE record-name

8. If the optional component may be one of two or more choices, they are included in brackets in the same way braces represent a choice. For instance, either HIGH or LOW may be selected or they both may be omitted:

    DISPLAY $\left\{ \begin{array}{l} \text{identifier} \\ \text{literal} \end{array} \right\}$ $\left[\begin{array}{l} \underline{\text{HIGH}} \\ \underline{\text{LOW}} \end{array} \right]$

9. Whenever an element may be used more than one time, an ellipsis (three consecutive dots) is used and the optional portion is enclosed within braces, as the following example illustrates:

$$\underline{\text{DISPLAY}} \begin{Bmatrix} \text{identifier} \\ \text{literal} \end{Bmatrix} \dots$$

10. If a period is shown in the general form, then it is required in the COBOL entry.
11. All commas and semicolons shown in the general form are optional.

Reserved Words

You learned in Chapter 1 that certain words, called reserved words, have predefined meanings in COBOL. Consequently, they can be used only in their COBOL-specified contexts. For example, assume that you used the reserved word RANDOM to define a field of a record as follows:

```
05  RANDOM     PIC X(4).
```

Upon encountering this entry, the compiler issues an error message. Record- and field-naming conventions that you will study later in this chapter almost eliminate the likelihood of your accidentally using a reserved word out of context.

User-Defined Words

A user-defined word is created by the programmer in accordance with certain rules. Although 17 categories of user-defined words exist, the patron deficit program uses only three types: program-name, data-name, and procedure-name. A **program-name**—such as PATDFCT—identifies the program as a whole. **Data-names** identify data files, records, and data-items (fields and subfields). **Procedure-names** identify sections or paragraphs within the PROCEDURE DIVISION.

Although COBOL gives you a lot of latitude in selecting user-defined words, each must conform to the following rules:

- Be composed only of alphabetic characters (A through Z and a through z), digits (0 through 9), and hyphens (-).

- Contain at least one letter. (Actually, according to the COBOL standard, procedure-names—though not data-names—may be composed entirely of digits. Such a procedure-name is a poor choice, however, since it is less meaningful than a name containing descriptive words.)

- Not exceed 30 characters.

- Not begin or end with a hyphen.

- Not contain any spaces within the word (that is, embedded blank spaces are not permitted).

- Not be the same as a reserved word.

Figure 2-1 shows examples of valid and invalid user-defined words. When creating a user-defined word, some programmers are tempted to use highly abbreviated forms to avoid excessive writing and keying. Resist this temptation; use meaningful names in order to create a self-documenting program. For instance, if a report total field is called REPORT-TOTAL, this name is easy to remember while coding and later reviewing the program. On the other hand, RT or even R-TOTAL could easily be confused with names you selected for other fields.

The hyphen is included as a legal name character so that you can create names that are easier to read and that better document the program. Note that a name such as INPUT-SUMMARY is valid although part of the name (INPUT) is a reserved word.

COBOL-9X

The allowable length of programmer-selected names will probably be increased in COBOL-9X.

Figure 2-1   Valid and invalid user-defined words.

Valid user-defined words	Invalid user-defined words	Reason invalid
NUMBER-1-GRADE	#1-GRADE	# not allowed.
GROSS-PAY	GROSS.PAY	. not allowed.
GROSSPAY	GROSS PAY	Cannot contain embedded blank.
GROSS-PAYROLL	-GROSS-PAYROLL	Cannot begin with hyphen.
2ND-QUARTER-EARNINGS	2ND-QUARTER-EARNINGS-	Cannot end with hyphen.
YTD-SOCIAL-SECURITY-TAX	YEAR-TO-DATE-SOCIAL-SECURITY-TAX	Cannot contain over 30 characters.
X100	100 (as a data-name)	Must contain at least one alphabetic character.

The PATLIST Program— First Three Divisions

The first three divisions of the program PATLIST are repeated in Figure 2-2. As you can see, the organization is somewhat like that of this book, where each chapter is broken down into major topics, minor headings, paragraphs, and finally, sentences. In all divisions but the PROCEDURE DIVISION, all headers (division, section, and paragraph) are reserved words. In the PROCEDURE DIVISION, paragraph headers are user selected (as you learned in Chapter 1).

Many of this program's features were mentioned in Chapter 1; let's consider them in greater detail.

The IDENTIFICATION DIVISION

The PROGRAM-ID Paragraph

The only paragraph in this IDENTIFICATION DIVISION is the **PROGRAM-ID paragraph**. Following the paragraph header, you must enter the program-name. You may have noticed that the name used for this program is PATLIST rather than something more descriptive, such as PATRON-LIST. This choice appears to contradict the earlier advice of avoiding abbreviations to maintain good readability.

The reason the shorter name was selected is that program-names are a special type of user-defined word. A program-name is used by some computer operating systems to identify the program. The file-name length restrictions on most operating systems are much less than the generous 30 characters allowed for COBOL words (for example, MS-DOS systems allow only 8 characters); some operating systems do not even allow the hyphen. If you choose a name longer than that allowed; the operating system truncates to the maximum length when storing the program. This can result in two or more programs with the same name and the potential loss of one or more of them. Since most operating systems accommodate eight-character names, that standard is used in this book. You should find out what your system permits.

Other Paragraphs

Both COBOL-85 and COBOL-74 include five other optional paragraph entries for this division: AUTHOR, INSTALLATION, DATE-WRITTEN, DATE-COMPILED, and SECURITY. User entries in these paragraphs are solely for documentation and are ignored by the compiler. Exactly the same documenting function can be done with comments (asterisk in column 7). These entries are classed as obsolete and will be deleted from COBOL-9X.

Figure 2-2   Annotated first three divisions of patron list (PATLIST) program.

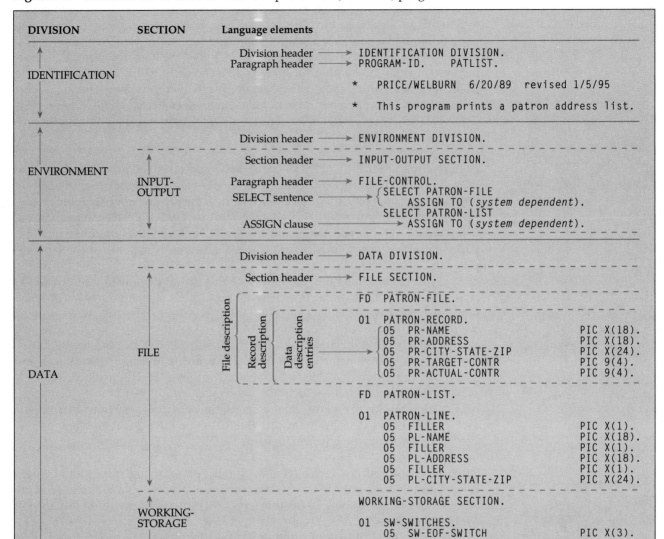

DIVISION	SECTION	Language elements	
IDENTIFICATION		Division header ⟶	`IDENTIFICATION DIVISION.`
		Paragraph header ⟶	`PROGRAM-ID.    PATLIST.`
			`*    PRICE/WELBURN  6/20/89  revised 1/5/95`
			`*    This program prints a patron address list.`
ENVIRONMENT		Division header ⟶	`ENVIRONMENT DIVISION.`
	INPUT-OUTPUT	Section header ⟶	`INPUT-OUTPUT SECTION.`
		Paragraph header ⟶	`FILE-CONTROL.`
		SELECT sentence ⟶	`SELECT PATRON-FILE`
			`    ASSIGN TO (system dependent).`
			`SELECT PATRON-LIST`
		ASSIGN clause ⟶	`ASSIGN TO (system dependent).`

```
DATA DIVISION.

FILE SECTION.

FD  PATRON-FILE.

01  PATRON-RECORD.
    05  PR-NAME                 PIC X(18).
    05  PR-ADDRESS              PIC X(18).
    05  PR-CITY-STATE-ZIP       PIC X(24).
    05  PR-TARGET-CONTR         PIC 9(4).
    05  PR-ACTUAL-CONTR         PIC 9(4).

FD  PATRON-LIST.

01  PATRON-LINE.
    05  FILLER                  PIC X(1).
    05  PL-NAME                 PIC X(18).
    05  FILLER                  PIC X(1).
    05  PL-ADDRESS              PIC X(18).
    05  FILLER                  PIC X(1).
    05  PL-CITY-STATE-ZIP       PIC X(24).

WORKING-STORAGE SECTION.

01  SW-SWITCHES.
    05  SW-EOF-SWITCH           PIC X(3).
```

DATA division rows: Division header ⟶ `DATA DIVISION.`; Section header ⟶ `FILE SECTION.`; FILE section with File description / Record description / Data description entries brackets; WORKING-STORAGE section.

The ENVIRONMENT DIVISION

Although almost the entire COBOL program can be prepared independent of the specific equipment for which it is written, the coding of the ENVIRONMENT DIVISION depends on the computer, compiler, and/or operating system used. Each vendor that supplies a COBOL compiler assigns words, called **system-names**, to input/output devices and other operating features of the environment. The system-names chosen by one vendor usually differ from those selected by another.

Most COBOL applications operate on files stored on disk. One of the computer's operating system's functions is to keep track of these files. For this purpose, each stored file is assigned a name—called a **physical filename**—which the operating system places in its disk directory, together with the location on disk of the file. The name is *external* to the program. Any program processing a file must have access to the file via its physical name. At first glance, it might seem logical to use the physical filename as the reference in the program; for instance, to use the physical filename in the OPEN and READ statements of your program.

There are two reasons COBOL designers did not allow this when they designed the language. First, this method would cause PROCEDURE DIVISION statements to depend on the physical filename. If, for a given run, you wanted to use a different data file (one with the same data format but a different name), you would need to change each statement that included the filename. Second, operating system rules for naming files have no relationship to the rules for selecting COBOL names. For instance, many operating systems allow using a period as part of a filename, whereas a period is not legal in a user-selected COBOL name. It is the INPUT-OUTPUT SECTION that relates COBOL names to external files for processing by the program.

The INPUT-OUTPUT SECTION—FILE-CONTROL

Specifically, the FILE-CONTROL paragraph associates each COBOL file-name with the actual file on an I/O device, which makes the rest of the program entirely independent of the physical filename. To do this, the **file-control entry** contains, as a minimum, two clauses: SELECT and ASSIGN. The SELECT clause introduces the user-defined COBOL file-name, and the ASSIGN clause links the file-name to a particular input/output device and file in a way that is dependent on the computer and compiler.

Figure 2-3(a) illustrates the nature of this link for the IBM mainframe OS environment. Here the connection between the COBOL file-name and the physical filename is as follows:

1. In the SELECT clause, the COBOL file-name PATRON-FILE is assigned to the system name UT-S-INFILE. UT-S are identifying codes; INFILE is an arbitrary name selected by the programmer (or assigned by installation standards).
2. Special OS job control statements tell the operating system what actions to take with this program: link INFILE (from UT-S-INFILE of the ASSIGN) to the physical filename PATRON.DATA.

Since the connection between a name within the program and the external physical filename is done outside the COBOL program, processing a different data file requires no change to the COBOL program. It is only necessary to modify the job control statements.

Figure 2-3(b) illustrates another method for achieving this linkage. This method is used by both the Micro Focus and Ryan-McFarland compilers for the MS-DOS operating system. The same method—plus minor variations of it—are found in several other systems. With this technique, the assignment to disk is explicitly indicated, followed by the physical name of the file. (The physical filename used here is PATRON.DAT, which is consistent with the limitation on the filenames imposed by MS-DOS.) It is also possible to use a variable name in the ASSIGN, which allows the user to type in the physical name of the file when the program is run. For instance, you could use

```
SELECT PATRON FILE
    ASSIGN TO DISK WA-INPUT-FILE-NAME.
```

WA-INPUT-FILE-NAME, a data item defined in the WORKING-STORAGE SECTION, would contain the filename.

Figure 2-3(c) shows the method used by Microsoft and several minicomputer COBOL compilers. Here the clause VALUE OF FILE-ID identifies the physical file (a variable name can also be used in place of the literal). Note that this method causes the DATA DIVISION to be nonstandard.

For each file used by the program, a separate file-control entry must exist. Although they may be listed in any order in the FILE-CONTROL paragraph, programmers commonly list the input file (or files) and then the output file (or files).

Figure 2-3 Linkage between the COBOL program and the physical file.

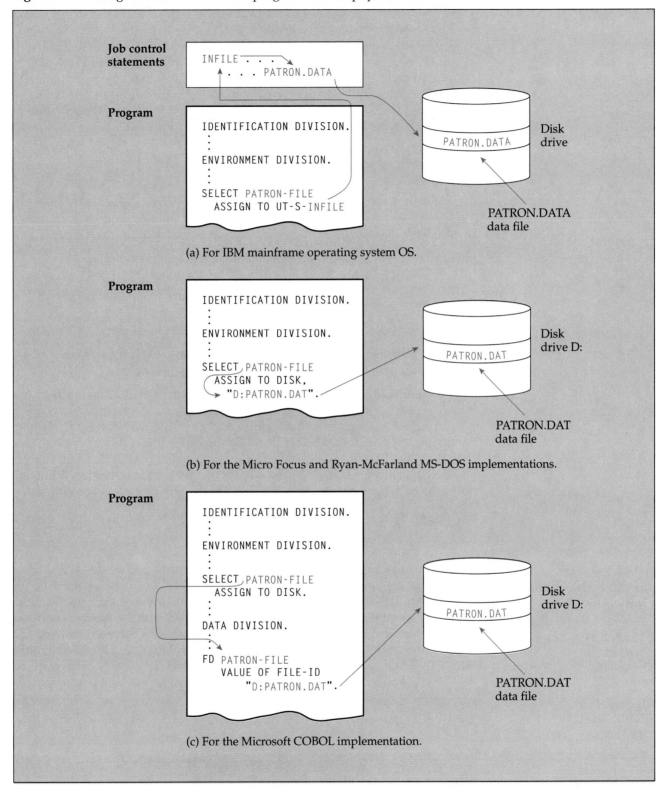

(a) For IBM mainframe operating system OS.

(b) For the Micro Focus and Ryan-McFarland MS-DOS implementations.

(c) For the Microsoft COBOL implementation.

COBOL-74

COBOL-74 requires that the ENVIRONMENT DIVISION also include another section—the CONFIGURATION SECTION. (It is optional in COBOL-85.) The model of the computer used to compile the source COBOL program is designated in the SOURCE-COMPUTER paragraph. The model of the computer used to run the compiled program is designated in the OBJECT-COMPUTER paragraph. For instance, if you use an IBM 3081 to compile and run your program, you would include the following entries:

```
CONFIGURATION SECTION.
SOURCE-COMPUTER. IBM 3081.
OBJECT-COMPUTER. IBM 3081.
```

Format of the ENVIRONMENT DIVISION

Figure 2-4 shows an abbreviated version of the COBOL-85 ENVIRONMENT DIVISION format. As you study this, remember the following standards:

- Entries enclosed in square brackets are optional—they may be included or omitted.

- Reserved words of a statement are printed in capital letters.

- Underscored reserved words are required in the statement. Non-underscored words are optional—they may be omitted.

- Names to be supplied by the programmer are printed in lowercase.

In Figure 2-4, you can see that within the CONFIGURATION SECTION, both paragraphs (SOURCE-COMPUTER and OBJECT-COMPUTER) are optional, plus the entire CONFIGURATION SECTION itself. The INPUT-OUTPUT SECTION is also optional; in a program that does not process files, it is not needed. Although not enclosed in brackets, the entire ENVIRONMENT DIVISION is also optional.

The DATA DIVISION—Basic Components

FILE SECTION— The FD

You learned in Chapter 1 that data-items—files, records, and fields—of the input and output files are defined in the FILE SECTION. Each file selected in the ENVIRONMENT DIVISION must be described in this section. So, the FILE SECTION is composed of file descriptions for all files that the program uses. As mentioned in Chapter 1, a file-description entry starts with the reserved word FD. An FD entry must be specified in the FILE SECTION for each file selected in the FILE-CONTROL paragraph of the ENVIRONMENT DIVISION. The reserved

Figure 2-4
ENVIRONMENT DIVISION format.

```
Format:

        ENVIRONMENT DIVISION.
        [CONFIGURATION SECTION.
        [SOURCE-COMPUTER. computer-name.]
        [OBJECT-COMPUTER. computer-name.]]
        [INPUT-OUTPUT SECTION.
        FILE-CONTROL.
            SELECT file-name
                ASSIGN TO implementor-name.]
```

word FD is a **level indicator.** COBOL level indicators are two-character alphabetic reserved words used to identify a specific type of file. Be aware that the reserved word FD is written in positions 8 and 9—Area A.

Following the FD is the user-selected name for the file, which corresponds to the name defined in the SELECT clause of the ENVIRONMENT DIVISION. The file-name is an Area B item and is written beginning in position 12. The file-name must be spelled exactly the same as it appears in the SELECT clause. The FD entry must be terminated by a period. The FD for a file must be followed by its corresponding record description, as shown in Figure 2-2 (page 37).

In addition to the file description (FD) used in the patron programs, the FILE SECTION can contain three other similar components: SD (for sorting), RD (for report generation), and CD (for communications). This chapter focuses on the FD.

Although not used in this book, the FD can include any of several optional clauses, described in the following section. At this stage, you may want to simply scan the descriptions—you only need to be aware of them. They are included here for completeness.

FD Clauses

In all of this book's programs, the FD entries include only the reserved word FD and the user-selected file-name. However, several other clauses can be included; three are shown in Figure 2-5.

The RECORD CONTAINS clause specifies the length of the logical records in the file. Some programmers like to include it because it documents the program and provides some protection against errors. For instance, assume that you designated the width of PR-ADDRESS (Figure 2-2) to be 20 instead of 18. Then the length of PATRON-RECORD would be 70 instead of 68. With the RECORDS CONTAINS clause (Figure 2-5) designating 68, the compiler issues an error message.

Frequently, you will encounter language elements—such as the LABEL RECORDS clause—that are carry-overs from hardware and/or software limitations that no longer exist. When a data file is stored on magnetic tape, it includes—as a first record—a special label record containing data about the file. When the file was created, the programmer could use standard or nonstandard (installation-written) labels. The LABEL RECORDS clause was a required COBOL element so that the user could identify the label type. As disk storage became predominant, the clause remained an entry, even though disk files do not use labels.

Referring to Figure 2-5, notice that the FD for PATRON-LIST, the printer file, includes LABEL RECORDS ARE OMITTED. Label records do not apply to printers. The LABEL RECORDS clause is required in COBOL-74, optional in COBOL-85, and will not be included in COBOL-9X.

The DATA RECORD clause specifies the name of the record within the file. However, it is not necessary because the record description containing the record-name immediately follows the FD entry. The DATA RECORD clause will not be included in COBOL-9X.

Figure 2-5
Additional FD entries.

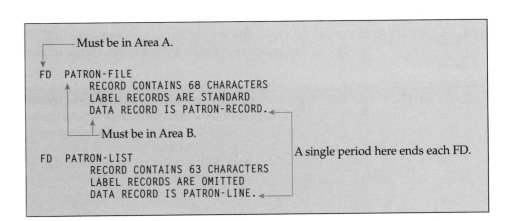

You may encounter one other FD clause in a COBOL production environment: the BLOCK CONTAINS clause. When stored on magnetic media, individual records are commonly blocked into longer physical records to improve efficiency. The BLOCK CONTAINS clause designates the number of data records in a physical record or block. For instance, if a file you are to use was stored on disk with 20 records per block (a blocking factor of 20), you must include the clause:

```
BLOCK CONTAINS 20 RECORDS
```

The system designer provides you with this information. None of the files you use in this book contains blocked records.

Notice the use of the period in the FD examples of Figure 2-5; only one is positioned after the last clause. These additional clauses are all part of the FD entry; the period signifies the end of the entire entry. Also, the FD clauses are all Area B entries. For readability, the clauses were indented four spaces so that each begins in position 16.

The WORKING-STORAGE SECTION

The FILE SECTION of the DATA DIVISION defines the files, records, and fields to be read or written by the program. In addition to this input and output data, most programs process other data-items. The WORKING-STORAGE SECTION is used for the definition and storage of these other records and fields. If you inspect the WORKING-STORAGE SECTION of a typical COBOL program, you will see that it looks much like the FILE SECTION (excluding the FD) because it consists of one or more record descriptions. As in the FILE SECTION, a record can be broken into fields and subfields to meet the needs of your program. Basically, the level-numbers 01 through 49 are used not only for true record/field/subfield relationships, but also to organize independent fields. This organizational technique is used in example programs throughout this book.

When coding the section header, remember that a hyphen is required between the words WORKING and STORAGE.

DATA DIVISION Format

The partial DATA DIVISION format is shown in Figure 2-6. The DATA DIVISION header must appear exactly as shown in Figure 2-6 and must be terminated by a period. Although only two sections—FILE and WORKING-STORAGE—are shown here, this division may include three other sections, not described in this book. This division is optional in COBOL-85, which permits the use of advanced programming techniques. However, all programs in this book require a DATA DIVISION. If the file contains variable-length records (a topic not discussed in this book), the TO clause shown in brackets within the format can be used to provide minimum and maximum record lengths.

Data Descriptions

As you learned in Chapter 1, records and fields are defined by **record-** and **field-description entries,** which can have three parts:

1. A two-digit level-number (01 for records and 02 through 49 for fields), which determines the hierarchy of the element.
2. A user-defined data-name to identify and permit reference to the record or field. Filler items can use the reserved word FILLER or omit it.
3. A PICTURE clause, usually abbreviated with the reserved word PIC, which defines the data class and the length of the field.

Figure 2-6
DATA DIVISION format.

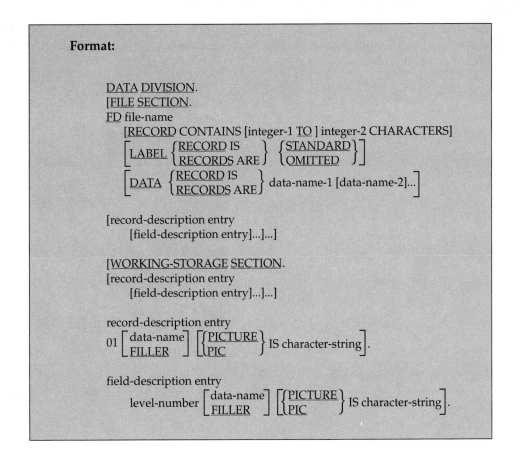

Format:

DATA DIVISION.
[FILE SECTION.
FD file-name
      [RECORD CONTAINS [integer-1 TO] integer-2 CHARACTERS]
      [LABEL {RECORD IS / RECORDS ARE} {STANDARD / OMITTED}]
      [DATA {RECORD IS / RECORDS ARE} data-name-1 [data-name-2]...]

[record-description entry
      [field-description entry]...]...]

[WORKING-STORAGE SECTION.
[record-description entry
      [field-description entry]...]...]

record-description entry
01 [data-name / FILLER] [{PICTURE / PIC} IS character-string].

field-description entry
      level-number [data-name / FILLER] [{PICTURE / PIC} IS character-string].

Level-Numbers in Defining Records, Fields, and Subfields

Records and fields are designated in the DATA DIVISION by **level-numbers**, the two digits that precede each data-item entry. Level-number 01—written in Area A—always defines a record. Fields composing the records are defined with a two-digit level-number in the range 02 through 49, which determines the hierarchy of the element. These are coded in Area B.

In PATLIST, the records (01) are broken down into individual fields—each designated with 05—containing PICTURES to define their sizes. In many cases, it is necessary to break an individual field into subfields. For instance, if the patron file included a contribution date field, the input record description might be as shown in Figure 2-7. Any field that is broken down into subfields *must not* include a PIC clause. For instance, PR-CONTR-DATE is composed of three subfields, each with its own PIC, thereby defining the size of this date field.

In some applications, you may need to break down a field even further than that of Figure 2-7. For instance, consider an inventory system and a corresponding partial record description for the product record shown in Figure 2-8. As the next chapter shows, you can operate on the entire inventory code field or on any component of it within the program.

Any item in a record description that is broken down further is called a **group item**. For instance, PRODUCT-RECORD (the record definition), PR-INVENTORY-CODE, PR-PART-NUMBER, and PR-PRODUCT-CODE are all group items. On the other hand, an item with a PIC, which is not broken down further into subfields, is called an **elementary item**.

As illustrated in both Figures 2-7 and 2-8, level-numbers are assigned on a hierarchical basis. Each subfield has a level-number that is higher in numerical

Figure 2-7
A date field in the input record description for PATRON-RECORD.

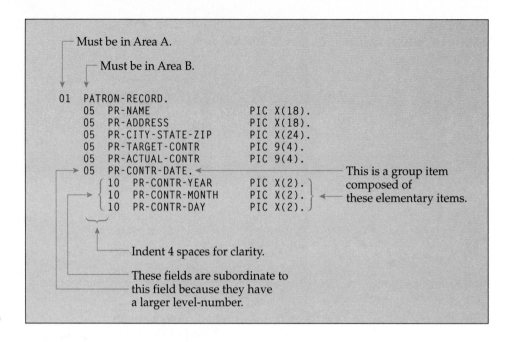

```
                     ┌─ Must be in Area A.

                        ┌─ Must be in Area B.

    01   PATRON-RECORD.
         05   PR-NAME                PIC X(18).
         05   PR-ADDRESS             PIC X(18).
         05   PR-CITY-STATE-ZIP      PIC X(24).
         05   PR-TARGET-CONTR        PIC 9(4).
         05   PR-ACTUAL-CONTR        PIC 9(4).
         05   PR-CONTR-DATE.  ←──────────────────  This is a group item
              10   PR-CONTR-YEAR     PIC X(2).                 composed of
              10   PR-CONTR-MONTH    PIC X(2).  ←──  these elementary items.
              10   PR-CONTR-DAY      PIC X(2).
```

Indent 4 spaces for clarity.

These fields are subordinate to this field because they have a larger level-number.

Figure 2-8   A field definition and the corresponding COBOL record description.

Field	Length
Inventory control part identification code	14
Manufacturing plant location	1
Part number	
Product line identification	3
Product code	
Item code	4
Premium level	1
Surface plating	2
Federal standards code	3
Product description	30

```
01   PRODUCT-RECORD.
     05   PR-INVENTORY-CODE.
          10   PR-PLANT-LOCATION       PIC X(1).
          10   PR-PART-NUMBER.
               15   PR-PRODUCT-LINE-ID  PIC X(3).
               15   PR-PRODUCT-CODE.
                    20   PR-ITEM-CODE       PIC X(4).
                    20   PR-PREMIUM-LEVEL   PIC X(1).
               15   PR-SURFACE-PLATING     PIC X(2).
          10   PR-FEDERAL-CODE            PIC X(3).
     05   PR-PRODUCT-DESCRIPTION        PIC X(30).
     ⋮
```

value (which is lower in hierarchical order) than the field to which it is subordinate.

Obviously, a group item does not require a PICTURE clause designating a length because its length is the sum of its subordinate elementary item lengths.

Suggested Standards for Indention and Level-Numbers

Since level-number 01 is an Area A entry, it is placed in positions 8 and 9. The corresponding name of the record is written in Area B. Level-numbers 02 through 49 may begin in any Area B positions: 12 through 72. It is customary to indent each data-item level four spaces to the right of the higher level that precedes it. For example, level 01 begins in position 8, level 05 indents to position 12, level 10 indents to position 16, and so on. If you have a record with many levels, you may find two-space indentions more practical.

In Figures 2-7 and 2-8, notice that after the 05 number, level-numbers are assigned in increments of 5: 05, 10, 15, and so on. However, increments of 10 would work just as well. This leaves numerical gaps so that fields or subfields can be further subdivided at a later time, if necessary.

Data-Names

Data-names within the record description are the names you define to identify data-items. Data-names must conform to the rules for user-defined words. In addition, they should be meaningful and descriptive. The following convention was used in the selection of PATLIST data-names:

1. The record-name is derived from the file-name. For instance, in PATLIST, the record-name PATRON-RECORD corresponds to the file-name PATRON-FILE. The sole purpose is for its documentation value; this technique is used throughout the book.

2. The file-name and record-name are descriptive, indicating what they represent. For instance:

```
PATRON-FILE        PATRON-LIST
PATRON-RECORD      PATRON-LINE
```

3. Each field within a record includes a two-letter prefix that relates the field to the record. For example, the prefix PR is an abbreviation for PATRON-RECORD and PL for PATRON-LINE. So, you know at a glance when checking a PROCEDURE DIVISION that PR-ADDRESS is a field from the input record PATRON-RECORD and that PL-ADDRESS is a field from the output record PATRON-LINE.

4. Each data-name is unique; that is, no two fields are given the same data-name. For instance, if you use PR-ADDRESS for both the street address and city-state-zip, it is impossible to distinguish one from the other. (Although the current standards allow duplication between records with a means to distinguish between them, that feature will be deleted from COBOL-9X.)

Regarding the choice of prefixes, you should use any abbreviation that is meaningful and reminds you of the record to which the field belongs. Later in this book, you will find some suggestions for various situations. Although two-character prefixes are used throughout this book, you may wish to use three- or four-character prefixes. The key is to make them meaningful without being clumsy.

PICTURE Clauses

Each elementary data-item description must contain a PICTURE clause. This clause specifies the data class and length of the field. A basic PICTURE clause contains the reserved word PICTURE—or the commonly used abbreviation PIC—followed by a blank space and an entry described in the general form as **character-string** (see Figure 2-6). The two **PICTURE symbols** you know so far are X, which defines the field as alphanumeric, and 9, which describes a numeric field. Immediately following the symbol is a number, enclosed in parentheses, indicating the field's length. Two of the fields from PATRON-RECORD are annotated in Figure 2-9.

Figure 2-9
The PICTURE clause.

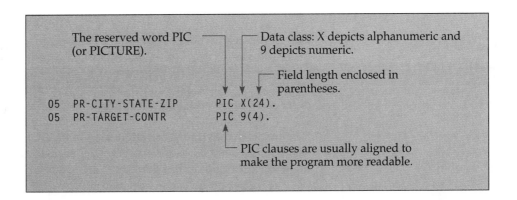

Instead of coding the field length as a value within parentheses, the PICTURE symbol can be repeated so that it appears the number of times equal to the length value. The following alternative to coding some of Figure 2-7's fields illustrates this:

```
05  PR-TARGET-CONTR       PIC 9999.  equivalent to PIC 9(4)
05  PR-ACTUAL-CONTR       PIC 9999.
05  PR-CONTR-DATE.
    10  PR-CONTR-MONTH     PIC XX.    equivalent to PIC X(2)
    10  PR-CONTR-DAY       PIC XX.
    10  PR-CONTR-YEAR      PIC XX.
```

For PICTURE character-strings that contain only one type of symbol, the use of parentheses is superior to such symbol repetition. It is easier to interpret the field length when expressed as a number, especially for longer fields. Also, it is a good idea to sum the values in a column of PICTURE clauses in order to check the length of a record. It is easier to do this with the field width enclosed in parentheses than by interpreting the repeated symbols.

About the 9 PICTURE Symbol

Beginning COBOL students sometimes erroneously think that using a 9 PICTURE symbol when defining a data-item enables the data-item to contain only numeric data. This is wrong. For instance, the definition

```
05  PR-ACTUAL-CONTR   PIC 9(4).
```

does not restrict the program from reading alphanumeric data into the field PR-ACTUAL-CONTR during program execution. For instance, if one of the input records contained the name JOHN in the positions for this field, JOHN is read and stored exactly as if it were defined X(4). However, the 9 symbol does influence actions of the compiler; you will learn about them in Chapters 3 and 4.

In Figure 2-7, you see the date field defined with the X descriptor even though the data-items will only contain digits. For instance, the date March 28, 1931, is stored (using Figure 2-7's format) as 310328. Thus, you could use the 9 descriptor. In practice, you will see it defined both ways. If the date must be verified to ensure that it does not contain nonnumeric data, the X is used. If it is involved in any type of calculation, the 9 is used.

Common Errors of Beginning COBOL Programmers

Certain errors seem to discover beginning COBOL programmers very quickly. So that you can guard against them, they are depicted in Figure 2-10 and discussed here.

Omitted Period

Whenever a period is shown in the COBOL format notation, it must be there. A period is always required to terminate a division header, section header, paragraph header, FD entry (at the end of the complete entry), and a data-item description.

Extra Period

A period placed where it should not be also causes problems. Beginning COBOL programmers sometimes mistakenly place a period between multiclause, multiphrase, or multiline sentences such as the SELECT/ASSIGN file-control entry and the FD entry. Also, a period is sometimes erroneously inserted in a data-item description entry after a data-name and before the PICTURE clause.

Omitted Hyphen

Remember that hyphens are often used in COBOL to join multiple English words into a single COBOL reserved or user-defined word. When a hyphen is specified, it must be used. Required hyphens are often inadvertently omitted from the

Figure 2-10   Checklist of common IDENTIFICATION, ENVIRONMENT, and DATA DIVISION syntactical errors.

Syntactical errors	Division		
	IDENTIFICATION	**ENVIRONMENT**	**DATA**
Omitted period	`IDENTIFICATION DIVISION.`◄ `PROGRAM-ID.`◄ `AUTHOR.`◄ `INSTALLATION.`◄ `DATE-WRITTEN.`◄ `DATE-COMPILED.`◄ `SECURITY.`◄	`ENVIRONMENT DIVISION.`◄ `INPUT-OUTPUT SECTION.`◄ `FILE-CONTROL.`◄	`DATA DIVISION.`◄ `FILE SECTION.`◄ `WORKING-STORAGE SECTION.`◄ To terminate FD sentence To terminate each data-item description sentence
Extra period		`SELECT ` `file-name`◄ `ASSIGN TO ` `implementor-name`	`02  data-name` ◄ ` PIC X(5).`
Omitted hyphen	`PROGRAM-ID` `DATE-WRITTEN` `DATE-COMPILED`	`INPUT-OUTPUT` `FILE-CONTROL`	`WORKING-STORAGE` In data-names
Extra hyphen	`IDENTIFICATION DIVISION`	`ENVIRONMENT DIVISION` `CONFIGURATION SECTION` `INPUT-OUTPUT SECTION` `ASSIGN TO`	`RECORD CONTAINS` `LABEL RECORDS` `DATA RECORDS` `FILE SECTION`
Omitted space			`PIC X(5)`
Inadvertent space			`PIC X(5)`
Incorrect Area A placement			`FD file-name`
Misspelling	All reserved words	All reserved words	All reserved words

reserved words PROGRAM-ID, INPUT-OUTPUT, FILE-CONTROL, WORKING-STORAGE, and so on. Similarly, each user-defined word must be a continuous string of characters. Hyphens must be used rather than spaces when forming a user-defined word from multiple English words or abbreviations.

Extra Hyphen   When coding division and section headers, notice that the division or section name is separated from the reserved word DIVISION or SECTION by a space—not a hyphen. Because hyphens are used so frequently, sometimes new programmers include them where they are not allowed.

Omitted Space   A space must be provided between COBOL words, although a period can follow a COBOL word without an intervening space.

Inadvertent Space   An error never results from using extra spaces when one is required. That is, whenever one space is required, any number of spaces is permissible. However, sometimes one or more spaces are coded where they should not be used. Often a space is erroneously coded into a PICTURE character-string, such as X (2). The space between the X and the open parenthesis is an error because no spaces should be within the character-string. It should read X(2) without the space.

On the other hand, a space is required between the reserved word PIC and the beginning of the PICTURE character-string. So, PICX(2) is invalid; PIC X(2) is the correct coding.

Area A/Area B Mistakes   The names of all divisions, sections, and paragraphs must start in Area A. Also, the indicator FD and the level-number 01 must begin in Area A. All other COBOL statements used in this book start in Area B.

Misspelling   When using a reserved word, it must be spelled exactly as specified in the COBOL list of reserved words. Common misspellings include ENVIORNMENT instead of ENVIRONMENT, LABLE rather than LABEL, PROCEEDURE instead of PROCEDURE, and PREFORM in place of PERFORM.

Chapter Summary

The IDENTIFICATION DIVISION includes one required paragraph: the PROGRAM-ID.

The ENVIRONMENT DIVISION is relatively easy to code, but somewhat difficult to discuss because the specific system-names depend on the particular COBOL compiler used. The division contains two sections: the CONFIGURATION SECTION and the INPUT-OUTPUT SECTION.

The CONFIGURATION SECTION specifies the computer; its use is optional in COBOL-85.

The INPUT-OUTPUT SECTION identifies the input/output files. In the FILE-CONTROL paragraph of the INPUT-OUTPUT SECTION, a file-control entry is specified for each file used by the program. The file-name is defined in the SELECT clause by a file-control entry and is associated with an input/output device by an ASSIGN clause.

The DATA DIVISION commonly contains two sections: the FILE SECTION and the WORKING-STORAGE SECTION.

In the FILE SECTION, an FD entry must be specified for each file selected in the ENVIRONMENT DIVISION. Following each FD entry, a record-description entry must be coded for each record format contained with the file.

Each record contains data-item description entries for fields within the record. A data-item description entry contains a level-number and a user-defined data-name for the field. If an elementary item is described, it also contains a PICTURE clause.

The WORKING-STORAGE SECTION contains data-item descriptions for those fields required by the program that are not defined within the FILE SECTION.

COBOL Language Element Summary

Reserved words have predefined meanings in COBOL. Appendix E contains a complete list of reserved words.

The programmer creates user-defined words according to certain syntactical rules. A user-defined word must:

- Be composed only of alphabetic characters (A through Z and a through z), digits (0 through 9), and hyphens (-).

- Contain at least one letter.

- Not exceed 30 characters.

- Not begin or end with a hyphen.

- Not contain any blank spaces (embedded blanks).

- Not be the same as a reserved word.

Comment lines contain an asterisk (*) in position 7 and include comments within the COBOL program listing. Words and symbols on comment lines are not treated as COBOL language elements.

A system-name is a COBOL word that communicates with the operating environment. Two commonly used types of system-names are computer-names and implementor-names. A computer-name identifies the computer system used; an implementor-name refers to a feature or device available on the computer system. The compiler vendor chooses system-names.

Level indicators identify a specific type of file-description entry.

Level-numbers indicate either (1) the position of a data-item in the hierarchical structure of a logical record, or (2) special properties of a data-description entry.

PICTURE clauses describe certain characteristics of elementary data-items. This chapter discussed data-class and field-length aspects. It introduced alphanumeric (PICTURE symbol X) and numeric (PICTURE symbol 9) specifications. Field length can be expressed either by (1) repeating the symbol so that as many symbols are specified as are characters or digits in the field, or (2) following the X or 9 symbol by the character or digit length enclosed within parentheses.

Style Summary

General Coding Conventions

- Make user-defined words meaningful and descriptive.

- Use hyphens in user-defined words to separate multiple English words and abbreviations.

- Provide vertical spacing among divisions, sections, and certain paragraphs by inserting blank lines or blank comment lines (lines with only an asterisk in column 7).

- Write only one COBOL sentence, statement, clause, or phrase per coding line.

- When a sentence, statement, or clause extends over multiple coding lines, indent each line after the first.

- When indention is necessary, indent in four-space units. Exceptions are cases in which vertical alignment of entries is desired or when four-space indentions consume too much space on the coding line; then, use two spaces.

IDENTIFICATION DIVISION

- Limit the program-name to the maximum number of characters allowed by the operating system used.

ENVIRONMENT DIVISION

- Write the SELECT entry so that the ASSIGN clause begins on a separate line. Indent the ASSIGN clause four spaces (to position 16).

- Sequence the SELECT entries so that the input files are listed first, then the output files.

- Do not choose file-names that refer to specific input/output devices, such as TAPE-FILE or DISK-FILE.

DATA DIVISION

- If you use additional clauses for the FD entry, write each clause on a separate line. Following the filename, indent each clause to position 16.

- Use gap level-number assignment: 01, 05, 10, 15, and so on.

■ Indent each data-item subdivision four spaces (level-number 05 at position 12, level-number 10 at position 16, and so on). If four-space indentions consume too much space on the coding line, use two-space indentions.

■ Prefix each record's data-name with a two-, three-, or four-character abbreviation for that record. The prefix for each record within the program should be unique.

■ Use the abbreviation PIC, rather than the word PICTURE.

■ Vertically align PICTURE clauses within each record description of the DATA DIVISION.

■ Express the field length in the PICTURE character-string by a number enclosed in parentheses, rather than by repetition.

Exercises

Terms for Definition

character-string
data-name
elementary item
field-description entry
file-control entry
format notation
group item
identifier
level indicator

level-number
physical filename
PICTURE symbol
procedure-name
PROGRAM-ID paragraph
program-name
record-description entry
system-name

Review Questions

1. Identify the COBOL format notation conventions that are used to specify the following language entry types.
   a. Required reserved word
   b. Optional reserved word
   c. Programmer-supplied entry
   d. Optional feature or entry
   e. Alternative entries
   f. Entry-repetition permitted

2. For each of the following that is invalid as a user-defined word, explain why it is not valid.
   a. VALIDUSERDEFINEDWORD
   b. INVALID-USER-DEFINED-WORD
   c. A
   d. AR-ACCOUNTS-RECEIVABLE-AMOUNT-OUT *Too long*
   e. AR-PURCHASES *need hyphen*
   f. AR-CREDITLIMIT
   g. AR-E20-20CODE
   h. AR-E
   i. ARE *Reserve word ?*
   j. MTD-SYS-TAX
   k. 25 *need Alpha*
   l. 25-DOLLARS
   m. $25 *no $ nr Alpha*
   n. -25-DOLLARS *cannot star*
   o. 25DOLLARS50CENTS
   p. 25.50-DOLLARS *no .*
   q. 5-POUNDS
   r. 5-LBS
   s. 5# *no #*

3. What is the purpose of the FILE-CONTROL paragraph of the INPUT-OUTPUT SECTION of the ENVIRONMENT DIVISION?

4. If a program has one input file and two output files, a total of ___*3*___ SELECT entries are required in the __*File-Control*__ paragraph of the __*Input-Output*__ SECTION of the __*Environment*__ DIVISION.

5. Each file-name specified in the __*File-Control*__ *Select* entry in the __*Environment*__ DIVISION must have a counterpart entry with that exact file-name in the __*File-Section*__ entry in the __*Data-Division*__ DIVISION.

6. Identify the level-numbers for the following types of data-description entries:
   a. Record-description entry *01*
   b. Data-item (field) description entry *02 - 49*

7. How is a group data-item distinguished from an elementary data-item? *By pic Clause*

8. What PICTURE symbol is used for the following classes of data?
   a. Numeric digits *pic 9( ).*
   b. Alphanumeric characters *pic X( )*

9. Identify which of the following must start in Area A:
   a. Division header *yes*
   b. Section header *yes*
   c. Paragraph header *yes*
   d. Entries within a paragraph *No*
   e. SELECT clause *No*
   f. FD level indicator *yes*
   g. Level 01 entries *yes*
   h. Level 02 through level 49 entries *No*

Syntax/Debug Exercises

1. Some or all of the following ENVIRONMENT DIVISION entries are erroneous. Identify each error and indicate how to correct it. Assume that the system-dependent entries are correct.

```
      ┌── Column 7
      │   1         2         3         4
      ▼ 78901234567890123456789012345678 90

        ENVIORNMENT DIVISION.
        INPUT-OUTPUT SECTION.
        FILE-CONTROL.
        SELECT INPUT-FILE
          → ASSIGN TO UT-S-INFILE.
      → SELECT PRINT-FILE
             ASSIGN TO UT-S-PRTFILE.
```

2. Some or all of the record-description and data-item description entries on the following page are erroneous according to COBOL syntax rules. Identify each error and indicate how to correct it.

```
        ┌─ Column 7
        ▼   1         2         3         4
       78901234567890123456789012345678901234567890123

        01   RECORD.   Reserved
             05  RE-SS-NUM         PIC 9(9).
             05  RE-NAME           PIC X(20).
             05  RE-ADDRESS  PIC   X(24).
             05  RE-CITY-STATE     PIC X (24).
             05  RE-ZIP            PIC X(10).
             05  RE-TELEPHONE      PIC X(13).
             05  RE-BIRTHDATE      PIC X(6).
             10  RE-BIRTHMONTH     PIC XX.
             10  RE-BIRTHDAY       PIC XX.
             10  RE-BIRTHYEAR      PIC XX.
             05  RE-EMPLOYER       PIC X(30).
                 10  RE-NAME       PIC X(20).
                 10  RE-TELEPHONE  PIC X(13).
```

Programming Assignments

The following programming assignments are used for this chapter and for Chapter 3. You can postpone starting them until you finish Chapter 3. Or, you can code the first three divisions now and delay the PROCEDURE DIVISION until you complete Chapter 3. If proceeding now, you should:

1. Prepare a print chart to define the printed output.

2. Code the first three divisions of the COBOL program.

3. To check your code for errors, go ahead and compile. In COBOL-85, the PROCEDURE DIVISION is optional, so you should have no problem. If your compiler requires a PROCEDURE DIVISION, you can include the following "dummy" to avoid extra diagnostics:

```
PROCEDURE DIVISION.
000-DUMMY.
    STOP RUN.
```

About the Data Files

The data disk included with this book contains a data file for each programming assignment. Most of the assignments do not use all of the fields included in the record format. For example, Assignment 2-1 uses the data file STUDENT.DAT. The complete record description consists of 10 fields and the record length is 70 positions. Assignment 2-1 uses only three of the fields, with the third ending in position 50 of the record. Therefore, in your record description, you need to designate fillers to account for all unused positions. *For all programs, your input record description must account for all positions of the input record—even those not used in your program.*

Programming Assignment 2-1: Student List

Background information:

The Bayview Institute of Computer Technology maintains comprehensive student data in computer files. One of the counselors wants to make a brief study of student progress and requires a list of students and the number of units they completed.

Input file: Student file (STUDENT.DAT)

Student record

	Student last name	Student first name		Units completed	
1 2 3 4 5 6 7 8 9 10 11	12 13 14 15 16 17 18 19 20 21 22 23 24 25	26 27 28 29 30 31 32 33 34 35 36 37 38 39 40 41 42 43 44 45 46 47	48 49 50	51 52 53 54 55 56 57 58 59 60 61 62 63 64 65 66 67 68 69 70	

Required output:

Printed report, single-spaced, one line for each input record.

Output report-line format:

Positions	Field
4–13	Student first name
15–28	Student last name
32–34	Units completed

Programming
Assignment 2-2:
Salesperson List

Background information:

Follow-the-Sun Sales maintains a file of their sales representatives. The sales manager wants to perform a study of salesperson performance. For this, she needs a list of all salespeople that indicates their territories and their sales. Most of the records have a value of A for the Status-code field; those that do not must be identified.

Input file: Salesperson file (SALESPER.DAT)

Salesperson record

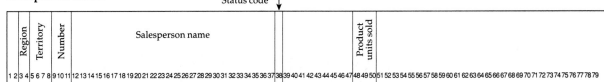

Status code

	Region	Territory	Number	Salesperson name			Product units sold	
1 2	3 4	5 6 7	8 9 10 11	12 13 14 15 16 17 18 19 20 21 22 23 24 25 26 27 28 29 30 31 32 33 34 35 36 37	38 39 40 41 42 43 44 45 46 47	48 49 50	51 52 53 54 55 56 57 58 59 60 61 62 63 64 65 66 67 68 69 70 71 72 73 74 75 76 77 78 79	

Required output:

Printed report, double-spaced, one line for each input record.

Output report-line format:

Positions	Field
7–8	Salesperson region
12–15	Salesperson territory
19–21	Salesperson number
25–50	Salesperson name
54–56	Product-units sold
65	Status code (only if code not A)

Programming
Assignment 2-3:
Company Telephone
Directory List

Background information:

The Century-21 Marketing Agency is a fast-moving, automated company. Virtually all of their activities utilize the computer somehow. However, much to the personnel director's dismay, no one has ever printed a list of employees and their telephone extensions, even though this data is stored in the computer. A company telephone directory must be prepared from the employee file.

Employee record

Input file: Century-21 Employee file (EMPLOYEE.DAT)

	Last name	First name		Telephone ext.
1 2 3 4 5 6 7	8 9 10 11 12 13 14 15 16 17 18	19 20 21 22 23 24 25 26 27	28 29 30 31 32 33 34 35 36 37 38 39 40 41 42 43 44 45 46 47 48 49 50 51 52 53 54 55 56 57 58 59 60 61 62 63 64 65 66 67 68 69 70 71 72 73 74	75 76 77 78

Required output:

Print each employee record two-up (two records on each line) on the output company telephone directory line. Use single-spacing.

Output report-line format:

Positions	Field	
1–11	Employee last name	(first record of two)
13–21	Employee first name	(first record of two)
25–28	Telephone extension	(first record of two)
41–51	Employee last name	(second record of two)
53–61	Employee first name	(second record of two)
65–68	Telephone extension	(second record of two)

Programming
Assignment 2-4:
Employee-Address
Roster

Background information:

The Temp-Surv Company provides temporary office employees for a wide variety of service companies. Because of their high turnover rate, they frequently need to print an employee-address roster from data in their employee file.

Employee record

Input file: Temp-Surv Employee file (EMPLOYEE.DAT)

Employee number	Employee name	Employee address	Employee city/state/zip	
1 2 3 4 5 6 7	8 9 10 11 12 13 14 15 16 17 18 19 20 21 22 23 24 25 26 27 28	29 30 31 32 33 34 35 36 37 38 39 40 41 42 43 44 45 46 47 48 49 50 51	52 53 54 55 56 57 58 59 60 61 62 63 64 65 66 67 68 69 70 71 72 73 74	75 76 77 78

Required output:

For each input employee record, print three output employee lines.

Example: 50873 WESTERBROOK ALEXANDER R
                     21065 NORTHWEST 3RD ST
                     OKLAHOMA CITY OK   73118

Single-space each line that applies to the same employee record; double-space between employees.

Output report-line format:

Employee-Name Line

Positions	Field
6–10	Employee number
14–36	Employee name

Note: The output Employee-name field is two positions longer than the input Employee-name field. Don't worry about this; it is a valid action.

Employee-Address Line

Positions	Field
14–36	Employee address

Employee City/State/Zip/Telephone Line

Positions	Field
14–36	Employee city/state/zip code

Programming Assignment 2-5: Nurses' Duty Roster

Background information:

Brooklawn Hospital maintains a file that contains one record for each nurse employed by the hospital. Like many hospitals, Brooklawn has high turnover rates and has difficulty obtaining nurses for special assignments that meet Brooklawn's standards. The head nurse intends to do a study of the existing nurses' staff and requires a printed report from the computer file.

Input file: Nurses file (NURSES.DAT)

Nurses record

Required output:

A nurses' assignment roster, double-spaced, one line for each input record.

Output report-line format:

Positions	Field	Comments
1–14	Professional specialty	
20	Shift code	Leave blank if Shift Code is 1; otherwise, print the value.
25–47	Name	
53–55	Ward/duty station	

Programming Assignment 2-6: Vehicle Rental Application

Background information:

Rent-Ur-Wheels rents various modes of transportation: cars, bicycles, motorcycles, and trucks. Their business success depends on having a lot of rolling stock and knowing whether or not it is available for rental. To provide this information, the firm maintains a data file that contains one record for each vehicle.

Input file: Vehicle file (VEHICLE.DAT)

Vehicle record

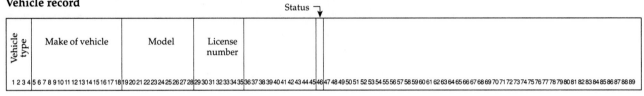

Required output:

Printed report, double-spaced, one line for each vehicle record.

Output report-line format:

Positions	Field
5	Status
10–23	Make of vehicle
26–35	Model
38–41	Vehicle type
45–51	License number

Programming Assignment 2-7: Bookstore Inventory Application

Background information:

Granger and Heatherford, Purveyors of Fine Publications, finally computerized after years of maintaining manual records of their books. Already designed and installed is an inventory file that contains one record for each book title that they carry. They now need programs to print various reports.

Input file: Granger/Heatherford inventory file (GHINVEN.DAT)

GH Inventory record

Title	Author	Subject area		Quanity on hand	

1 2 3 4 5 6 7 8 9 10 11 12 13 14 15 16 17 18 19 20 21 22 23 24 25 26 27 28 29 30 31 32 33 34 35 36 37 38 39 40 41 42 43 44 45 46 47 48 49 50 51 52 53 54 55 56 57 58 59 60 61 62 63 64 65 66 67 68 69

Required output:

Printed report, double-spaced, one line for each input record.

Output report-line format:

Positions	Field
1–8	Subject area
11–25	Author
28–45	Title
47–49	Quantity on hand

**Programming
Assignment 2-8:
Computer Store
Product File**

Background information:

Bob and Helen Smith operate their own business, Complete Computers Corporation, or "3C." Their specialty is configuring complete personal computer systems for individuals, but they also advise users on individual components such as CPUs, hard disks, and monitors.

To keep their operating expenses to a minimum, the Smiths do not maintain a large inventory of computer hardware. Instead, they maintain a comprehensive data file that contains information on the physical characteristics, price, and availability of as many computer components as possible. With this information, they can tailor a computer system to each user's requirements and budget. One of the reports they require is a product/vendor summary.

Input file: CCC Inventory file (CCCINVEN.DAT)

CCC Inventory record

Product category code	Product name		Vendors from whom product is available		
			Vendor #1 Code	Vendor #2 Code	Vendor #3 Code
1 2 3 4 5	6 7 8 9 10 11 12 13 14 15 16 17 18 19 20	21 22 23 24 25 26 27 28 29 30 31 32 33	34 35 36 37 38 39 40 41 42	43 44 45 46 47 48 49 50 51	52 53 54 55 56 57 58 59 60

Required output:

Printed report, single-spaced, one line for each product record.

Output report-line format:

Positions	Field
1–15	Product name
20–24	Product category code
30–32	Vendor code for vendor #1
39–41	Vendor code for vendor #2
48–50	Vendor code for vendor #3

INTRODUCTION TO STRUCTURED PROGRAMMING

MODULE OBJECTIVES

In Module A, you learned about the program development process and you had a brief introduction to techniques used during the design phase. This module expands these concepts and builds a basis that you can use for an organized, structured approach to program design and coding. From this module, you will learn about the following:

- Using flowcharts to graphically illustrate the logic of a program.

- Modularization, whereby a program is broken down into semi-independent segments, each with a defined purpose.

- The basic nature of the structure chart, a device for graphically illustrating the structure of a program and the interrelationships between program modules.

- A module-numbering/naming convention that allows for a consistent physical placement of modules within a program.

MODULE OUTLINE

About Structured Programming

Flowcharting Program Logic
Flowcharting Standards
Structured Programming Constructs

Program Modularization
The Modular Concept
The Notion of a Controlling Module
Structure Charts
Functional Nature of Modules
Module-Naming and Numbering Conventions

Expanding the Patron Program
Definition of the Problem
Ensure That the Input Is Available to Produce the Desired Output
Prepare a Print Chart
Write Programming Specifications
Structure Chart
Pseudocode for PATDFCT

About Structured Programming

Structured programming is a collection of techniques for program design, documentation, coding, and testing to create proper, reliable, and maintainable software products cost-effectively. Two of structured programming's cornerstones are (1) the modularization of a program into independent components and (2) the utilization of basic logical forms in solving programming problems.

Flowcharting Program Logic

Flowcharting Standards

In Module A, you were introduced to pseudocode (an abbreviated English description of the program actions) and to flowcharts (a graphical representation of program actions). Although pseudocode is the common choice for program design, many programmers find flowcharts valuable. Flowcharts are used sparingly in this book, but you should understand some basic flowchart standards.

A program flowchart is a graphic method of illustrating the program logic. It shows *how* things should be done; the *logic* of the program. It pictures the sequence of steps taken, points at which either of two actions is taken depending upon a condition, and repetition of an activity. You can see the way in which the program "flows" in the flowchart for PATLIST in Figure B-1. Flowcharts use the specific symbols—illustrated in this example—connected by flowlines to represent the various program operations.

Structured Programming Constructs

Modern programming theory revolves around the use of three basic structures—**sequence**, **selection**, and **looping**—shown in Figure B-2. If you inspect Figure B-1's flowchart, you will see that it contains combinations of some of these structures.

Program Modularization

The Modular Concept

The single program you studied in Chapter 1 is relatively simple and fairly easy to visualize. However, most actual programs are large, complex, and require many conditional operations, making them much more difficult to visualize. The programmer who begins writing code without first carefully analyzing all aspects of the problem will become hopelessly bogged down. Good programmers recognize the value of breaking a program into a series of semi-independent components or **modules**. This approach is an essential element of modern programming methods.

Let's take another look at the PROCEDURE DIVISION of the PATLIST program (Figure B-3) to see how it could be "modularized." Notice that the overall task can be broken down into three distinct parts, each with a different *function*. The function of the first module is to perform operations that must be completed before record processing begins. These are *initializing actions*.

Corresponding to the first module, the function of the third module is to "finish up" after the last record is processed: The files are closed and execution is terminated.

The function of the second module, which is executed repeatedly, is to perform the job in which you are interested—reading and printing records. As this example shows, the second module forms most of the program. However, the important issue is not the relative sizes of the modules, but that the program is broken down into components based on the functions performed.

The Notion of a Controlling Module

Program modularization is based on two principles. One is breaking a program into independent modules, as just described. The other is the use of a "superior" module that controls execution of the subordinate modules. Although you won't look at actual COBOL code until Chapter 3, you can get an idea of how such a system might work by inspecting the pseudocode solution shown in Figure B-4.

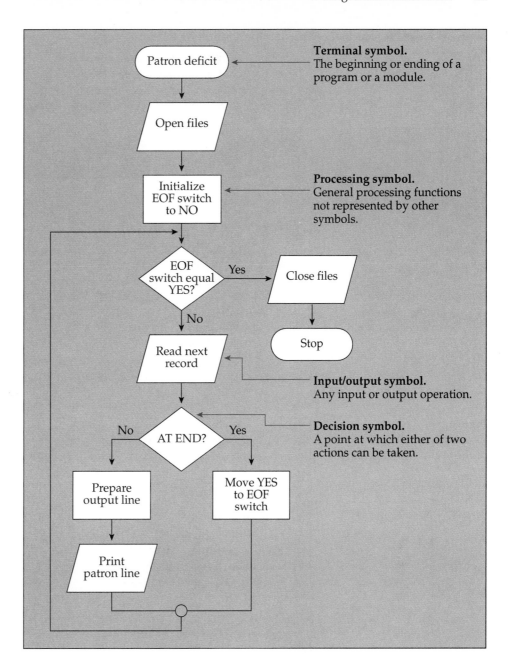

Figure B-1
Flowchart for the
PATLIST program.

Note that the modular organization here is slightly different than that of Figure B-3 in that the opening and closing of files is incorporated in the controlling module. Execution of the modular form in Figure B-4 is via the controlling module and proceeds exactly as the English-like pseudocode suggests:

1. The files are opened.
2. Control is transferred to the Initialize-variable-fields module and EOF switch is set to NO. Then control is returned to the controlling module.
3. The following is repeated until the EOF switch contains YES.
    A record is read.
        If it is the end-of-file record, the EOF switch is set to YES.
        If it is a data record, control is transferred to the Process-patron-record module.
            In the Process-patron-record module, the output line is prepared and the record written.

Figure B-2   Three structures of modern programming theory.

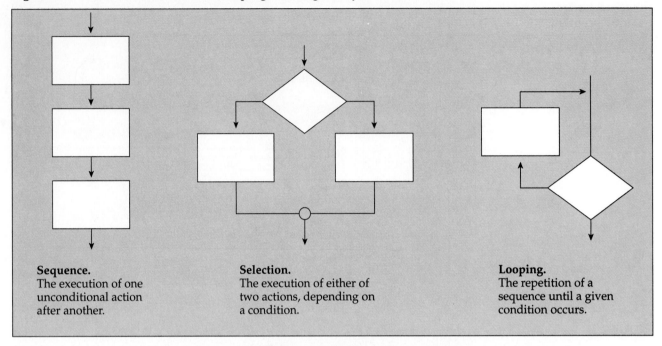

Sequence.
The execution of one
unconditional action
after another.

Selection.
The execution of either of
two actions, depending on
a condition.

Looping.
The repetition of a
sequence until a given
condition occurs.

Figure B-3
Functional components
of the PATLIST program.

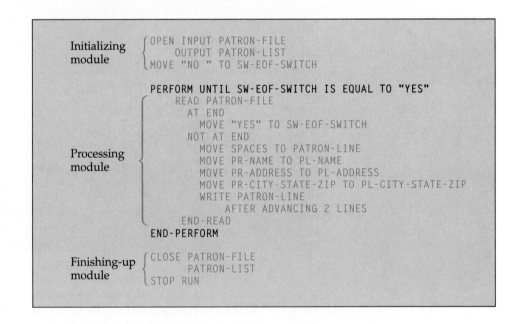

```
Initializing    ┌ OPEN INPUT PATRON-FILE
module          │       OUTPUT PATRON-LIST
                └ MOVE "NO " TO SW-EOF-SWITCH

                PERFORM UNTIL SW-EOF-SWITCH IS EQUAL TO "YES"
                ┌     READ PATRON-FILE
                │       AT END
                │         MOVE "YES" TO SW-EOF-SWITCH
                │       NOT AT END
                │         MOVE SPACES TO PATRON-LINE
Processing      │         MOVE PR-NAME TO PL-NAME
module          ┤         MOVE PR-ADDRESS TO PL-ADDRESS
                │         MOVE PR-CITY-STATE-ZIP TO PL-CITY-STATE-ZIP
                │         WRITE PATRON-LINE
                │             AFTER ADVANCING 2 LINES
                └     END-READ
                END-PERFORM

Finishing-up    ┌ CLOSE PATRON-FILE
module          │       PATRON-LIST
                └ STOP RUN
```

4. The files are closed.
5. Execution is halted at the Stop.

Structure Charts

While pseudocode and program flowcharts show *how* things should be done, Figure B-5's block representation shows *what* should be done. It also shows the relationship among the three elements of the program and displays their *hierarchy*. That is, two modules are subordinate to a controlling module. The form shown here is called a **structure chart** or a **hierarchy chart**. When implemented in a program, modules are commonly known as **procedures**. In COBOL, each module (or box in the structure chart) represents a paragraph in the PROCEDURE DIVISION.

In this example, you see two module *levels*. The **mainline module** or program controlling module is known as the *zero-level module*. Modules subordinate to

Figure B-4
Pseudocode for the modularized PATLIST program.

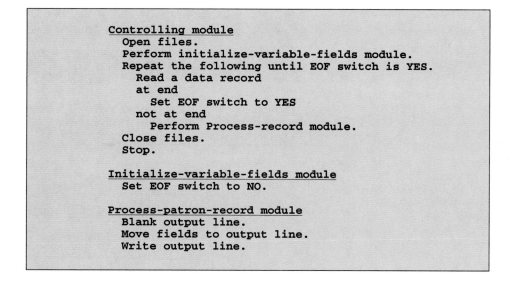

```
Controlling module
   Open files.
   Perform initialize-variable-fields module.
   Repeat the following until EOF switch is YES.
     Read a data record
     at end
        Set EOF switch to YES
     not at end
        Perform Process-record module.
   Close files.
   Stop.

Initialize-variable-fields module
   Set EOF switch to NO.

Process-patron-record module
   Blank output line.
   Move fields to output line.
   Write output line.
```

Figure B-5
Structure chart: a block representation of a program's modules.

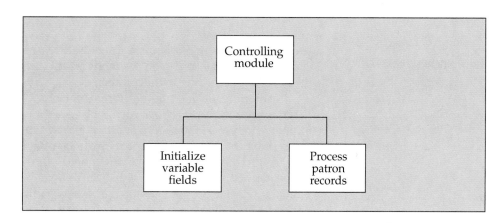

it are called *first-level modules;* Figure B-5 has two. Modules below the first level are termed second-level modules, and so on. At the second level, you begin to see numerous modules in a program structure.

Functional Nature of Modules

As you will learn in later chapters, a critical element in designing a program is repeatedly breaking down large modules into smaller ones. The final result is a set of modules, with each performing a basic task and being relatively independent of the others. Defining a "basic task," however, is rather subjective.

You could argue that the Process-records module includes two different actions—preparing the output line and writing the output line—and they should be represented as two different modules. This book's examples do not draw such a fine line: A balance is maintained between computer science theory and what is practical in a COBOL programming environment.

Module-Naming and Numbering Conventions

Since each program module should handle a specific function, the name chosen for the module should describe that function. As Figure B-6 shows, module names that contain a single verb followed by an optional adjective and an object tend to describe functional modules. By naming modules in this way, you are forced to consider the true function of the module—which also aids in functional module design.

Module numbers are helpful in the reading, writing, and debugging of COBOL programs. Trying to locate a particular unnumbered module of a long program poses difficulties much like those encountered when trying to find a certain topic in a book without an index. Module numbers can be used as references to aid

Figure B-6
Module-naming
convention examples.

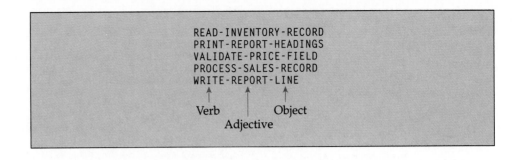

Figure B-7
Module-numbering
conventions.

Module number	Module function
000	Mainline
100–199	Initialization of variable fields
200–699	General processing

speedy location. For example, a three-digit sequence number can be assigned to each module name, and then the modules can be arranged in ascending order in the program, according to the number.

Although specific number ranges for modules—based upon the module's function—can also limit flexibility, they usually provide for organizational commonalty from one program to another. Perhaps more important, consistent module numbering permits one program to be used as a model, or skeleton, for another program with a similar function. Because of this, a module-numbering convention is used for all programs in this book. A portion of that convention, which is relevant to your first programs, is shown in Figure B-7. Chapter 6 expands on this convention.

Expanding the Patron Program

In Chapter 3, you will expand upon Chapter 1's basic principles. To prepare for that, let's slightly expand the patron listing program. The rest of this module applies the problem-solving principles you just learned.

Definition of the Problem

The membership supervisor of Fleetwood Charities wants a report listing all patrons; those with a contribution below their target must be identified. After speaking with the supervisor, you learn that the report must consist of the following:

Patron name

City/state/zip

Target contribution

Actual contribution

Contribution deficit (difference between target and actual)
for those below their target amount

Ensure That the Input Is Available to Produce the Desired Output

The membership supervisor gave you a precise indication of what she desires from the report. Your first step is to ensure that the needed data is available from the patron file. As you know from Chapter 1, this file's record format is as follows.

Positions	Field
1–18	Patron name
19–36	Street address
37–60	City/state/zip
61–64	Target contribution
65–68	Actual contribution

Inspecting this, you see that the required output can come from the input record as follows.

Output field	Source
Patron name	Input record
City/state/zip	Input record
Target contribution	Input record
Actual contribution	Input record
Deficit	Calculate from input (Actual and Target)

Prepare a Print Chart

The next step is to lay out your report's general format and then prepare a print chart showing all details. When doing this, remember to arrange output fields in an easy-to-read format—think of the end user. Sometimes, poorly formatted and difficult-to-read reports go unused, even though they contain valuable information. A finished print chart is shown in Figure B-8.

Write Programming Specifications

The final step in the specification phase is to prepare the programming specifications: a general description of the program function, input and output identification, and a list of processing operations. Figure B-9 shows the programming specifications.

This completes the specification phase. After gaining the approval of the membership supervisor that this satisfies her needs, you proceed to the design phase.

Structure Chart

Often, you will find that one program's structure is very similar to another. From a structure viewpoint, this program is identical to PATLIST and therefore has the same structure chart, which was shown in Figure B-5.

Pseudocode for PATDFCT

The structure chart tells you what must be done; pseudocode tells you how to do it. From an overall logic point-of-view, this application differs from Figure B-4's PATLIST pseudocode only in the conditional printing of the contribution deficit. The logic for this application is shown in Figure B-10. You will see how the PROCEDURE DIVISION coding reflects this in Chapter 3.

Figure B-8   Print chart for patron deficit report (PATDFCT).

Figure B-9
Programming specifications
for patron deficit report.

PROGRAMMING SPECIFICATIONS

Program Name: PATRON LIST   Program ID: PATDFCT
             (with under-target patrons identified)

Program Description:

    This program is to print a list of patrons from input
    patron records. Patrons contributing less than their
    target amount are identified.

Input File:

    Patron File

Output File:

    Patron Contribution Report

List of Program Operations:

A. Read each input patron record.

B. For each record, print the following fields on the employee
    address list in accordance with the format shown on the
    print chart:
        1. Patron name
           Patron city/state/zip
           Target contribution
           Actual contribution
        2. If Actual less than Target, print Difference
           between Actual and Target

C. Single-space each printed line.

Figure B-10
Pseudocode solution for
patron deficit report.

```
000-Print-Contribution-List module
  Open files.
  Perform 100-Initialize-variable-fields module.
  Repeat the following until EOF switch is YES.
    Read a data record
    at end
      Set EOF switch to YES
    not at end
      Perform 200-Process-Patron-Record module.
  Close files.
  Stop.

100-Initialize-Variable-Fields module
  Initialize EOF switch.

200-Process-Patron-Record module
  Blank output line.
  Move input fields to output line.
  If Actual Contribution less than Target Contribution
    Calculate:
      Contribution Deficit = Target Contribution
                                  - Actual Contribution
    Move Contribution Deficit to output line.
  Write output line.
```

Module Summary

Structured programming is a collection of techniques for program design, documentation, coding, and testing to create proper, reliable, and maintainable software products cost-effectively. The structured programming techniques you learned in this chapter include:

- The idea of breaking a program into independent modules and arranging them into the form of a structure chart.

- Program logic, which is comprised entirely of the three basic programming structures: sequence, selection, and looping.

Style Summary

Each module of a program should be given a number and a name that describes what it does. The name should consist of a verb and an object, to show what is being done.

The following is the module-numbering recommendation:

000	Mainline
100–199	Initialization of variable fields
200–699	General processing
800–849	Input operations

Exercises

Terms for Definition

hierarchy chart
looping structure
mainline module
module
procedures

selection structure
sequence structure
structure chart
structured programming

Review Questions

1. What is the main purpose of modularizing a program?

2. What is the difference between a structure chart and a program flowchart?

3. Diagram and describe the function of each of the three basic logic structures.

MORE ON THE
PROCEDURE DIVISION

CHAPTER OUTLINE

CHAPTER

3

CHAPTER OBJECTIVES

This chapter expands upon Chapter 1's PROCEDURE DIVISION elements. After completing this chapter, you will program the PROCEDURE DIVISION for programming assignments started in Chapter 2. From this chapter, you will learn the following:

- More about the structure of the PROCEDURE DIVISION.

- More about the following COBOL verbs: CLOSE, MOVE, OPEN, READ, and WRITE.

- The out-of-line PERFORM and PERFORM/ UNTIL, which make program modularization possible.

- Simple conditional operations using the IF statement—Chapter 8 describes this in more detail.

- Performing simple arithmetic operations— Chapter 6 describes this in more detail.

PROCEDURE DIVISION Elements

You know from Chapter 1 that a COBOL program's PROCEDURE DIVISION expresses the logic that the computer will perform to obtain the specified results. Each procedural step—such as input, arithmetic, data movement, decision, and output—is written as an English-like statement. PROCEDURE DIVISION elements of the PATDFCT program (of Module B) are annotated in Figure 3-1's program listing.

Like other division headers, the PROCEDURE DIVISION header is a required entry and must begin in Area A. It must be spelled exactly as shown in Figure 3-1, it must be followed by a period, and it must appear on a line by itself.

You can see that the PROCEDURE DIVISION is composed of paragraphs. A paragraph within the PROCEDURE DIVISION is also termed a procedure. Each

Figure 3-1   The PATDFCT program.

```
 1        IDENTIFICATION DIVISION.
 2        PROGRAM-ID.    PATDFCT.
 3
 4     *    PRICE/WELBURN  6/20/89  revised 1/5/95
 5
 6     *    This program prints a patron contribution
 7     *    report. Under-target patrons are identified.
 8
 9
10        ENVIRONMENT DIVISION.
11
12        INPUT-OUTPUT SECTION.
13
14        FILE-CONTROL.
15            SELECT PATRON-FILE
16                ASSIGN TO (system dependent).
17            SELECT PATRON-LIST
18                ASSIGN TO (system dependent).
19
20
21        DATA DIVISION.
22
23        FILE SECTION.
24
25        FD  PATRON-FILE.
26        01  PATRON-RECORD.
27            05  PR-NAME                 PIC X(18).
28            05  PR-ADDRESS              PIC X(18).
29            05  PR-CITY-STATE-ZIP       PIC X(24).
30            05  PR-TARGET-CONTR         PIC 9(4).
31            05  PR-ACTUAL-CONTR         PIC 9(4).
32
33        FD  PATRON-LIST.
34        01  PATRON-LINE.
35            05                          PIC X(1).
36            05  PL-NAME                 PIC X(18).
37            05                          PIC X(1).
38            05  PL-CITY-STATE-ZIP       PIC X(24).
39            05                          PIC X(4).
40            05  PL-TARGET-CONTR         PIC 9(4).
41            05                          PIC X(3).
42            05  PL-ACTUAL-CONTR         PIC 9(4).
43            05                          PIC X(3).
44            05  PL-CONTR-DIFFERENCE     PIC 9(4).
45
46        WORKING-STORAGE SECTION.
47
48        01  PROGRAM-SWITCHES.
49            05  PS-END-OF-PATRON-FILE   PIC X(3).
50        01  AR-ARITHMETIC-WORK-AREAS.
51            05  AR-DIFFERENCE           PIC 9(4).
```

paragraph begins with a paragraph- or procedure-name, which is coded starting in position 8 of Area A. Procedure-names are user-defined words and must be terminated by a period. Referring to Module B's program modularization principles, each paragraph is a separate program module. Using this book's style standard, the last statement of a paragraph is followed by a period, which is on the next line. Technically, the end of a paragraph is signaled by the start of another paragraph (a paragraph header in Area A) or by the end of the program (no additional statements).

From PATLIST, you know that the PROCEDURE DIVISION paragraphs contain one or more statements designating the actions to be implemented during execution of the program. A **statement** is a syntactically valid combination of COBOL words that begins with a verb. The PROCEDURE DIVISION's beginning verb must be coded in Area B. Examples of valid statements are

```
MOVE PR-NAME TO PL-NAME
READ PATRON-FILE
```

In general formats for the PROCEDURE DIVISION, you will see commands referred to as **imperative statements**; they cause the program to do something

Figure 3-1   (continued)

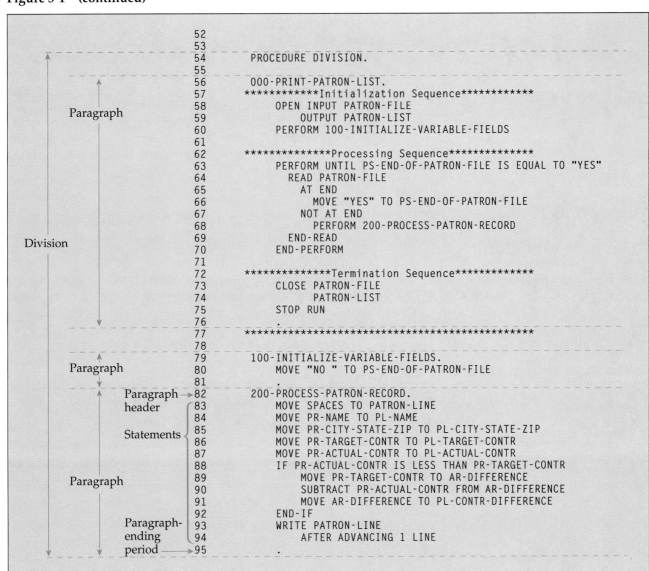

during execution. This is opposed to statements in the DATA DIVISION that are *declarative* in nature; they "declare" areas of memory (data-items) for use by the program.

If you desire, you can use the period to form a **sentence** from one *or more* statements, as illustrated by the following examples of the MOVE:

```
MOVE PR-NAME TO PL-NAME.          One statement, one sentence
MOVE PR-ADDRESS TO PL-ADDRESS.    One statement, one sentence

MOVE PR-NAME TO PL-NAME
MOVE PR-ADDRESS TO PL-ADDRESS.    Two statements, one sentence
```

With today's COBOL capabilities, using periods within paragraphs to form individual sentences has little value. This book's example programs only use the period after the last statement of the paragraph, as required by COBOL syntax.

However, COBOL-74 PROCEDURE DIVISION period usage is different, as is illustrated by an example later in this chapter.

The Out-of-Line PERFORM

In Chapter 1, you learned about one of the PERFORM statement's two forms—the inline PERFORM—which allows you to repeat a sequence of statements. The other form—the *out-of-line* PERFORM—is more general and provides the necessary tool for program modularization. This version of the PERFORM causes the computer to transfer control to another paragraph (module) in the program. When execution of that paragraph is completed, control is returned to the statement following the PERFORM, as Figure 3-2 illustrates. Although not shown in this program, a performed procedure can perform still another procedure. For instance, the mainline procedure could perform procedure A; from within procedure A, a PERFORM statement could refer to procedure B. You can have a limitless number of levels in a program: one procedure can call another, which can call a third, and so on.

As you will learn later in this chapter, the out-of-line PERFORM has a conditional form.

OPEN, CLOSE, and STOP

The OPEN Statement

The first PROCEDURE DIVISION statement of the PATDFCT program is the OPEN. Each file used by a COBOL program must be "opened" before any other input/output operations involving the file can be executed. The OPEN statement initiates processing for a file. It does *not* cause data records to be read from an input file or written to an output file. It does make available to the program a memory

Figure 3-2
Executing a PERFORM.

```
                                            Transfer
              :                             control.
              :
    PERFORM 300-CALCULATE-TOTALS. ─────────────→ 300-CALCULATE-TOTALS.
    MOVE ... ←──────────────────────────┐          :   ┌ Execute procedure.
              :          Return control.  │          :  │
              :                           │          ▼
                                          └───────ADD SUBTOTAL TO LI-TOTAL
                                                        .

                                                  310-SAVE-BASE-VALUES.
              The next paragraph signals the ─┐        :
              end of the preceding procedure,   │        :
              thereby causing return of control.
```

Figure 3-3
The OPEN statement.

Format:

$$\text{OPEN} \begin{Bmatrix} \underline{\text{INPUT}} \text{ file-name-1 [file-name-2]} \dots \\ \underline{\text{OUTPUT}} \text{ file-name-3 [file-name-4]} \dots \end{Bmatrix} \dots$$

Example from PATDFCT:

```
OPEN INPUT PATRON-FILE
     OUTPUT PATRON-LIST
```

buffer area into which a physical input record can be read or from which a physical output record can be written (this is not the record area defined in the FD).

In the OPEN statement format of Figure 3-3, you see that the two lines following the word OPEN are enclosed in braces { }. Recall the formatting standards described in Chapter 2; this means that one of the two must be used in the statement.

The reserved word INPUT must precede the name of the input file. Similarly, the reserved word OUTPUT must precede the name of the output file. If multiple files are within one of these categories, additional files may be listed following the appropriate reserved word—INPUT or OUTPUT—but the reserved word cannot be repeated. Two other open modes exist; they are described in later chapters.

Notice that the OPEN statements of the patron programs were written on two lines in conformance with our general style conventions of one phrase per line and indention of statement lines after the first.

The CLOSE Statement

Each file that is opened in a program must be closed before program execution ends. For most example programs in this book, this takes place immediately before terminating program execution. However, as with opening a file, a file can be closed at any point in the program. For instance, if in the middle of a program, you require one-time access to data in a file, you could write a module to open the file, access the data, and close the file. Then you would execute that procedure when needed.

The action of closing a file causes the following to take place with respect to that file:

1. Terminates processing for that file; the file is no longer accessible to the program.

2. Makes the memory buffer area reserved for the input or output activity available to the operating system.
3. If the output is to an auxiliary device, causes the EOF record to be positioned after the last record and causes the last block of data in the memory buffer (this may consist of one or more logical records) to be written to the storage device.

The CLOSE statement is coded with the reserved word CLOSE, followed by the file-name of each file to be closed—as illustrated in Figure 3-4. Unlike the OPEN statement, the reserved words INPUT and OUTPUT are not specified; the compiler remembers the designation.

The STOP Statement

To end program execution, the STOP RUN statement is used. It terminates execution of the program and returns control of computer resources to the operating system.

Figure 3-4
The CLOSE statement.

Format:

```
CLOSE file-name-1 [file-name-2] . . .
```

Example from PATDFCT:

```
CLOSE PATRON-FILE
      PATRON-LIST
```

The READ Statement

Reading a Record

The READ statement makes a logical record from an input file available to the program. Figure 3-5 shows the partial statement format. As you can see, the reserved word READ is followed by the name of the file from which the record is read. Although the AT END phrase is shown in brackets and so is optional, it is required for any program that reads records from the file serially (one after another) until the end of the file is reached. Such sequential access is always used for magnetic tape and is commonly used for disk files.

In the patron programs, executing a READ statement immediately after opening the files causes the first record of the input PATRON-FILE to be read into the PATRON-RECORD record-description area of the FILE SECTION within the computer's main memory. Whatever was in that area of memory before execution of the READ statement will be overlaid—or replaced—by the data transferred from the input file. Figure 3-6 illustrates this processing. The data read into the input area remains there until the next READ statement is executed, which then overlays the area with the next record's data.

Figure 3-5
The READ statement.

Format:

```
READ file-name
  [[AT END
     imperative-statement-1]
   [NOT AT END
     imperative-statement-2]
  END-READ]
```

Note: Imperative-statement means one or more PROCEDURE DIVISION statements.

Example:

```
READ PATRON-FILE
  AT END
     MOVE "YES" TO PS-END-OF-PATRON-FILE
  NOT AT END
     PERFORM 200-PROCESS-PATRON-RECORD
END-READ
```

The AT END and NOT AT END Phrases

One characteristic of sequential processing of a data file is that processing begins with the first record and proceeds through to the last. You learned from Chapter 1 that the last data record in a file is followed by a special EOF record. This is convenient because the program can be written to process until the EOF is encountered; no attention need be paid to the number of records in the file. The technique works as well with 50,000 records as with 5 records. The COBOL feature you used to control this is the AT END phrase of the READ statement.

Figure 3-6   The effect of the READ statement.

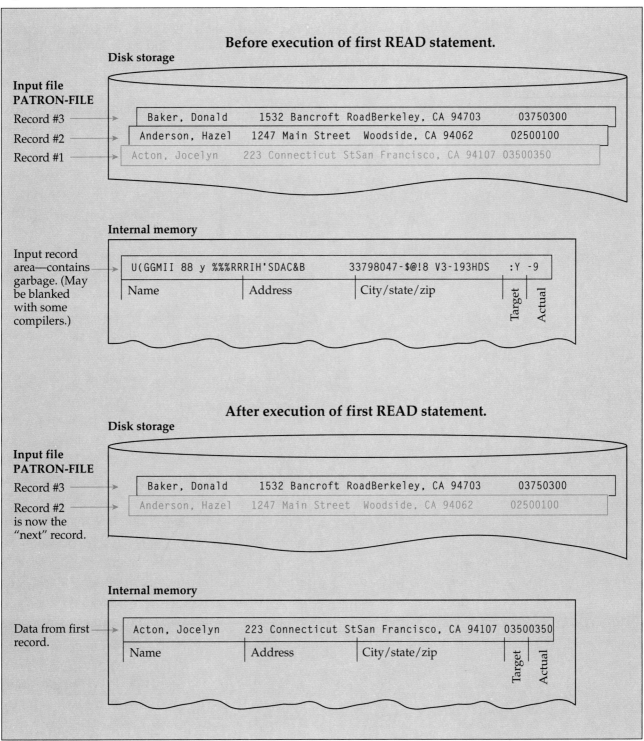

From the format description in Figure 3-5, you can see that one *or more* statements must be written after the reserved words AT END. The purpose of the END-READ is to identify for the compiler where this group of statements ends. The range of statements is called the **scope** of the READ, and the END-READ is called a **scope terminator**.

As illustrated in Figure 3-7, the READ works as follows:

1. If the next available record in the input file is the end-of-file record, the program executes the statement(s) following the reserved words AT END. When finished, processing continues with the statement following the END-READ.
2. If the next available record in the input file is a data record, it is read and the program ignores the AT END sequence and proceeds to the NOT AT END. After completing that sequence, processing continues with the statement following the END-READ.

Recognize that the end-of-file condition is *not* detected when the last data record is read. Instead, end-of-file is identified only when a READ is attempted *after* the last data record was already read.

COBOL-74

COBOL-74 does not include the NOT AT END phrase. Basic processing techniques for COBOL-74 are described at the end of this chapter.

Figure 3-7
AT END phrase logic.

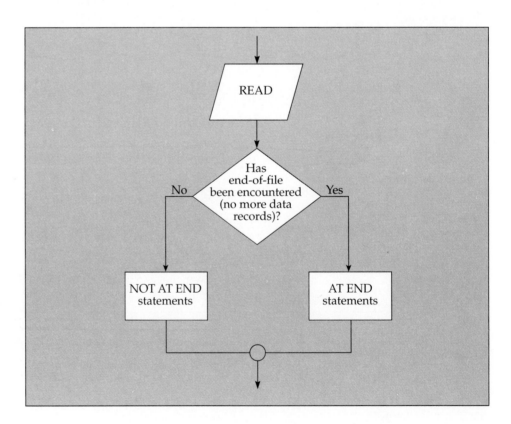

Literals and Figurative Constants

In mathematics, we work with two types of quantities: *variables*, those that change, and *constants*, those that remain fixed. For example, the formula to compute the circumference of a circle is 3.14 times the diameter, or

$$C = 3.14 \times D$$

Here C and D are variables and 3.14 is a constant. Programming languages have equivalent forms. The variables of the patron programs are the DATA DIVISION–defined data-names. Actual values are placed in them by the program operations of reading, moving, and calculating. Corresponding to constants of mathematics are two types of COBOL **literals**: numeric and nonnumeric.

Numeric Literals

A **numeric literal** is simply a number. For example, the 2 in the following statement is a numeric literal:

```
WRITE PATRON-LINE
   AFTER ADVANCING 2 LINES
```

You most commonly use numeric literals in arithmetic statements and in VALUE clauses (described in Chapter 5). For instance, in the statement

```
MULTIPLY .065 BY AR-SALES-AMOUNT
```

the entry .065 is a numeric literal.

Generally, you can form a numeric literal with only the following restrictions:

- It can consist only of digits (0 through 9), a sign character (plus or minus), and a decimal point. For instance, the following are *not* valid:

```
10%     1,275
```

- It can contain from 1 to 18 digits; for example:

```
0     3     162     5170058770
```

- It can contain at most one decimal point; for example:

```
.065    2.6     387.62     11280.00
```

However, a decimal point must not be used after the last digit of a whole number amount—the compiler interprets that as indicating the end of a sentence.

- It can optionally contain either a single plus or a single minus sign; for example:

```
+25     +25.00     -392     -392.79
```

When the sign character is used, it must be the leftmost character of the literal. When the sign character is not used, the literal is considered to be a positive value.

- It must *not* be enclosed in quotes; quotes specify a nonnumeric literal.

Nonnumeric Literals

A **nonnumeric literal** is a sequence of characters enclosed in quotation marks. For instance, the following MOVE statement includes the nonnumeric literal YES:

```
MOVE "YES" TO PS-END-OF-PATRON-FILE
```

Nonnumeric literals are formed according to the following rules:

- The literal must be enclosed in quotation marks, which act as *delimiters* to indicate the start and end of the literal value.

- The literal can range in length from 1 to 120 characters. The delimiting quotes are not counted as part of the literal when determining its length.

- Like an alphanumeric field, a literal can consist of any character of the character set—letters, digits, blank spaces, and special characters. The term *nonnumeric* can be misleading since the literal may consist entirely of digits. Such a literal is nonnumeric in that it cannot be used in arithmetic calculations.

Because the quotation marks act as delimiters, a quotation mark cannot appear singly as part of the literal itself; it would be incorrectly interpreted by the compiler as marking the end of the literal. If quotation marks are supposed to be part of the literal, some compilers permit the coding of two delimiters in a row to be interpreted as that single character within the literal.

Although the current COBOL standards call for conventional quotation marks ("), many compilers allow you to use single quotation marks ('). In fact, due to printer limitations, early IBM compilers used single quotation marks as literal delimiters.

Figurative Constants

The word SPACES is a particular type of reserved word called a **figurative constant**. A figurative constant is similar to a literal in that it provides a way of introducing an actual value into a COBOL program. It differs from a literal because the actual value is specified not with the value itself, but instead by a reserved word, such as SPACES. COBOL includes a few figurative constants other than SPACES; one of them is ZERO, which represents the numeric value zero. (It can also be written ZEROS and ZEROES.) Two others are HIGH-VALUE and LOW-VALUE, which represent the highest and lowest possible values. You will learn how to use these in later chapters.

Although the word SPACES is used in the patron programs, the singular form SPACE is equivalent. Both singular and plural forms are provided to permit COBOL coding in accordance with grammatically correct English.

Changing Field Contents by Moving Data

The MOVE Statement

The MOVE verb transfers data from one area of memory to another. Its format, together with three sample statements from PATDFCT, are shown in Figure 3-8. After the reserved word MOVE, either an identifier or a literal is coded. The term *identifier* means that a field-name from the DATA DIVISION must be coded. The literal can be either a literal or a figurative constant.

Actually, the word MOVE is a misnomer because the action is one of copying. For instance, in Figure 3-8's first example, the value stored in the field PR-NAME (the sending field) is copied into the field PL-NAME (the receiving field), as illustrated in Figure 3-9. Notice that the entire field from PR-NAME—including the spaces—is copied into PL-NAME.

The format notation shows a third identifier enclosed in brackets and followed by an ellipsis (three periods). The ellipsis indicates that additional data-names may be written. Thus, one MOVE statement can be used to transfer data from one sending field to one *or more* receiving fields.

The following MOVE from the patron programs—to initialize the program switch—illustrates two concepts:

```
MOVE "NO " TO PS-END-OF-PATRON-FILE
```

Figure 3-8
The MOVE statement.

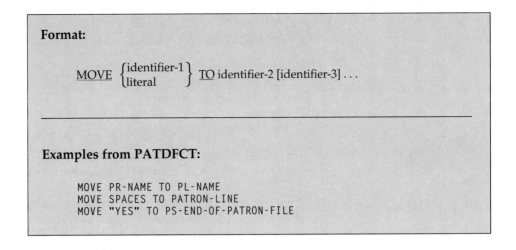

Format:

$$\text{MOVE} \begin{Bmatrix} \text{identifier-1} \\ \text{literal} \end{Bmatrix} \text{TO identifier-2 [identifier-3]} \ldots$$

Examples from PATDFCT:

```
MOVE PR-NAME TO PL-NAME
MOVE SPACES TO PATRON-LINE
MOVE "YES" TO PS-END-OF-PATRON-FILE
```

Figure 3-9
Action of the MOVE statement.

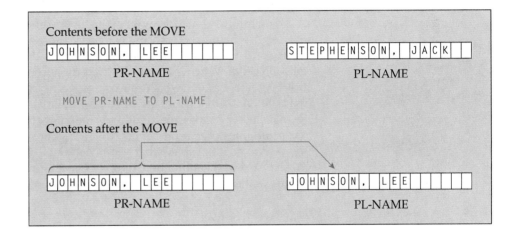

Contents before the MOVE

`JOHNSON, LEE` PR-NAME   `STEPHENSON, JACK` PL-NAME

```
MOVE PR-NAME TO PL-NAME
```

Contents after the MOVE

`JOHNSON, LEE` PR-NAME   `JOHNSON, LEE` PL-NAME

First, the sending field is a nonnumeric literal: The actual data to be used is enclosed in quotation marks. In this case, the literal data is three positions in length—the letters N and O, plus a space.

The second feature of this example MOVE relates to the length of the fields involved in the MOVE. That is, in all MOVE statements of the patron programs, the sending field and the receiving field have both been the same length. Here, the field PS-END-OF-PATRON-FILE is defined in WORKING-STORAGE as PIC X(3), a three-position field—so the literal moved to it includes three characters.

Actually, the following statement in which the sending field is only two characters does exactly the same thing:

```
MOVE "NO" TO PS-END-OF-PATRON-FILE
```

In this case, the space is not required because of the way in which the MOVE treats alphanumeric fields when the lengths are different. When alphanumeric data is moved with fields of different lengths, the following occurs:

- If the sending field is shorter than the receiving field, the sending field data is positioned to the left in the receiving field and remaining positions of the receiving field are filled with spaces.

- If the sending field is longer than the receiving field, data is copied from the leftmost portion of the sending field until the receiving field is full. In other words, data from the sending field is truncated.

If the MOVE is operating on numeric data (defined with the 9 PIC), sending field data is always positioned to the right—or corresponding to the decimal point if one exists—and excess positions in the receiving field are filled with zeros. You will learn more about this in Chapter 5.

One final variation of the MOVE is used in the patron programs. To blank the print line before moving data to it:

```
MOVE SPACES TO PATRON-LINE
```

This statement uses the figurative constant SPACES as the sending field, filling the entire record PATRON-LINE with spaces.

Initializing Fields

When program execution begins, fields defined in the DATA DIVISION contain either (1) unpredictable data left from the previous program that used that area of memory—commonly called **garbage**, or (2) an initialization value used by the compiler to clear memory—typically spaces or binary zeros. The exception to this are fields in the WORKING-STORAGE SECTION defined with a VALUE clause, which Chapter 5 describes.

This means that you must code statements to explicitly initialize all fields that require a specific starting value. In the PATDFCT program, you see two instances of the need for initialization. One is the program switch PS-END-OF-PATRON-FILE. When execution of the program begins, it contains garbage. (This could possibly be YES, which causes processing of the data file to be skipped if PS-END-OF-PATRON-FILE is not initialized to NO.)

The other case of initialization is that of the output line area PATRON-LINE. When program execution begins, this entire area contains garbage. Because the print chart calls for spaces between each data column on the report line, those unused areas—the unnamed filler items—must be blanked out or garbage is printed in these positions of the report.

The simplest way to blank these spaces is to blank the entire output record with the statement:

```
MOVE SPACES TO PATRON-LINE
```

In this instance, since the data for each output field from one record is replaced by data from the next record, you might wonder about placing this initialization statement in the initializing module (100), thereby executing it only once. After all, once the filler areas are set to spaces, nothing in the program changes them. The answer to this relates to means used by many operating systems to speed up input/output operations: Alternate output areas are used with automatic switching between them. The simplest solution to the resulting problem is to clear the line each time before moving data into it.

Simple Editing with the MOVE

Some of the programming assignments at the end of this chapter include a date field stored in the form year-month-day. For instance, December 18, 1995, might be stored as 951218; this format is commonly indicated as *yymmdd*. As you can see, the year is listed first, followed by the month, then the day. You also can see that punctuation required in a report (for example, 12/18/95) is not included.

To illustrate how you would do this, assume that the patron record contains a date-of-contribution field. Then the code of Figure 3-10 would be required to print this date. Notice that each of the three subfields of the date-of-contribution fields—month, day, and year—were moved individually so that the separating slashes could be inserted where they belong on the output line. The last MOVE, which inserts the slashes, is an example of a literal being copied into multiple—in this case, two—receiving fields.

Figure 3-10
A simple editing operation
with multiple MOVE
statements.

```
05  PR-CONTR-DATE.
    10  PR-CONTR-MONTH        PIC X(2). ⎫ Part of input record
    10  PR-CONTR-DAY          PIC X(2). ⎬ definition.
    10  PR-CONTR-YEAR         PIC X(2). ⎭
    ⋮
05  PL-CONTR-DATE.
    10  PL-CONTR-MONTH        PIC X(2). ⎫
    10  PL-DATE-SEPARATOR-1   PIC X(1). ⎪ Part of printer line
    10  PL-CONTR-DAY          PIC X(2). ⎬ record definition.
    10  PL-DATE-SEPARATOR-2   PIC X(1). ⎪
    10  PL-CONTR-YEAR         PIC X(2). ⎭
    ⋮
MOVE PR-CONTR-MONTH TO PL-CONTR-MONTH ⎫ MOVE statements in
MOVE PR-CONTR-DAY TO PL-CONTR-DAY     ⎬ 200-PROCESS-PATRON-RECORDS
MOVE PR-CONTR-YEAR TO PL-CONTR-YEAR   ⎪ paragraph.
MOVE "/" TO PL-DATE-SEPARATOR-1       ⎪
             PL-DATE-SEPARATOR-2      ⎭
```

The WRITE Statement

Writing a Record

After all data to be printed is moved into the output area (PATRON-LINE in the patron programs), that line can be written to the output device. Although the patron programs print the output, the WRITE statement is not limited to printing; it can be used for writing output to any output device. This determination depends upon entries in the ENVIRONMENT DIVISION. The WRITE statement, shown in Figure 3-11, causes a record to be transferred from main storage to an output device. After the reserved word WRITE, you must specify the *record*-name of the record to be written as output. This contrasts with the READ statement, in which you specify the *file*-name.

The ADVANCING Phrase

Because the PATRON-RECORD is directed to a printer file, the ADVANCING phrase is used. Either BEFORE ADVANCING or AFTER ADVANCING could be specified. The former option means that first the line is written and then the paper form is advanced; the line is written BEFORE ADVANCING the form. The latter option is used for the reverse situation: The form is advanced and then the line is written (the line is written AFTER ADVANCING the form). The AFTER

Figure 3-11
The WRITE statement.

Partial format:

WRITE record-name [{ BEFORE / AFTER } ADVANCING { identifier / integer } [LINE / LINES]]

Examples:

```
1. WRITE PATRON-LINE
       AFTER ADVANCING 2 LINES

2. WRITE PATRON-LINE
       AFTER 2
```

ADVANCING option is most commonly used. Note that you should avoid using both the BEFORE and AFTER in the same program. Such a combination can lead to program bugs in which lines are printed on top of each other.

Referring to the format in Figure 3-11, you can see that the BEFORE/AFTER clause is optional. If it is omitted, the AFTER ADVANCING 1 LINE is used as the default. Also, you can see that the words ADVANCING and LINE (or LINES) are optional.

Initial-Character Printer Forms Control

Before a report line is printed, the printer must be informed of the line-spacing or line-skipping requirements for the line. That is, the printer must be told whether the line is to be single-spaced, double-spaced, triple-spaced, or printed at the top of the next page. IBM and certain other early COBOL compilers required the programmer to explicitly allocate the first position of the printer output record for this purpose. If you work on programs written for such systems, you will probably encounter programs in which this "extra" position is included at the beginning of the record.

Conditional Operations

Examples in the Patron Programs

One way of categorizing statement forms is to separate those that cause an action to be taken unconditionally from those that cause an action to be taken depending on some type of condition. For example, consider the READ statement:

```
READ PATRON-FILE
    AT END
        MOVE "YES" TO PS-END-OF-PATRON-FILE
    NOT AT END
        PERFORM 200-PROCESS-PATRON-RECORD
END-READ
```

As you know, after the record is read, execution continues *either* following the AT END *or* following the NOT AT END.

Repeated execution of this READ is controlled by a similar type of conditional action using the following PERFORM:

```
PERFORM UNTIL PS-END-OF-PATRON-FILE IS EQUAL TO "YES"
```

In this case, an action is repeated until a particular test condition becomes true (until the value in PS-END-OF-PATRON-FILE is YES).

The PATDFCT program also includes the IF statement, still another form that causes something to happen on a conditional basis.

The IF Statement

PATDFCT uses the IF statement shown in Figure 3-12 to determine whether or not to calculate and print the patron's deficit amount. This form functions exactly as its English suggests. That is, if Actual-contribution is less than Target-contribution, the sequence of three statements preceding the scope terminator END-IF is executed; otherwise, it is skipped.

The test element that determines whether or not an action is taken is called the **condition**. In this program, both the IF and the PERFORM/UNTIL have condition forms; Figure 3-13 illustrates both of them. Here, two data quantities are linked by *relational operators* that define the type of comparison to be made. The result of evaluating such relational conditions is either a true or a false. For instance, if PS-END-OF-PATRON-FILE contains YES, the relationship is true; otherwise, it is false.

Figure 3-12 The IF statement from PATDFCT.

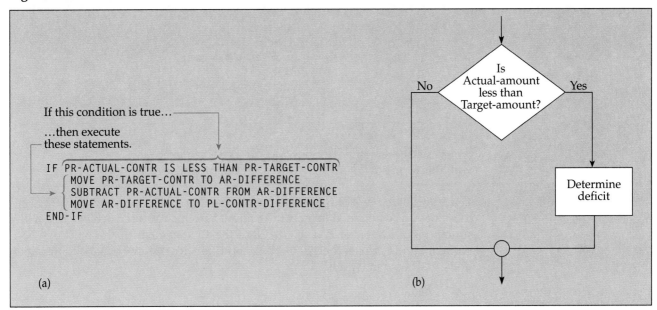

The following are relational operator forms you may want to use. Chapter 8 contains more detailed descriptions.

    IS LESS THAN
    IS GREATER THAN
    IS EQUAL TO
    IS NOT LESS THAN
    IS NOT GREATER THAN
    IS NOT EQUAL TO

In all cases, they execute exactly as the English suggests.

You can also compare a numeric field to a constant value. For instance, if a list of patrons should include everyone contributing $200 or less, the IF takes the following form:

```
IF PR-ACTUAL-CONTR IS NOT GREATER THAN 200
```

Figure 3-14 contains the format of the IF. As shown, you can include an ELSE option. If the condition is true, the statements preceding the ELSE are executed; if

Figure 3-13
Conditional forms.

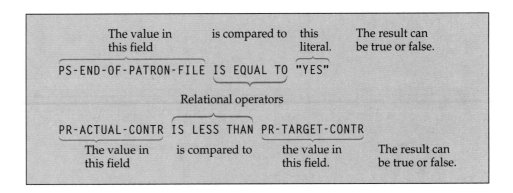

Figure 3-14
Format of the IF statement.

Format:

    IF condition
        imperative-statement-1
    [ELSE
        imperative-statement-2]
    END-IF

it is false, the statements following the ELSE are executed. You can experiment with this form now or you can wait until Chapter 8.

Printing Only the Records with a Deficit

To further illustrate the IF statement, assume that you want a report listing only those patrons who failed to meet their target amounts. You can achieve this with a simple modification of PATDFCT: Place the IF statement in the NOT AT END sequence and perform the 200 module conditionally. Appropriate code modifications are shown in Figure 3-15.

Simple Arithmetic

Another topic you will study in depth later is arithmetic operations. Since the basic forms are relatively intuitive, let's consider them now so that you can use them before the detailed coverage of Chapter 6.

The four basic arithmetic operations—add, subtract, multiply, and divide—each involve three elements: the two numbers being combined and the result. To see how this is implemented in COBOL, consider the following two statements taken from PATDFCT (lines 89 and 90):

```
MOVE PR-TARGET-CONTR TO AR-DIFFERENCE
SUBTRACT PR-ACTUAL-CONTR FROM AR-DIFFERENCE
```

Figure 3-15
Executing module 200 conditionally.

```
**************Processing Sequence**************
        PERFORM UNTIL PS-END-OF-PATRON-FILE IS EQUAL TO "YES"
            READ PATRON-FILE
              AT END
                MOVE "YES" TO PS-END-OF-PATRON-FILE
              NOT AT END
                IF PR-ACTUAL-CONTR IS LESS THAN PR-TARGET-CONTR
                    PERFORM 200-PROCESS-PATRON-RECORD
                END-IF
            END-READ
        END-PERFORM
              .
              .
              .
    200-PROCESS-PATRON-RECORD.
        MOVE SPACES TO PATRON-LINE
        MOVE PR-NAME TO PL-NAME
        MOVE PR-CITY-STATE-ZIP TO PL-CITY-STATE-ZIP
        MOVE PR-TARGET-CONTR TO PL-TARGET-CONTR
        MOVE PR-ACTUAL-CONTR TO PL-ACTUAL-CONTR
        MOVE PR-TARGET-CONTR TO AR-DIFFERENCE
        SUBTRACT PR-ACTUAL-CONTR FROM AR-DIFFERENCE
        MOVE AR-DIFFERENCE TO PL-CONTR-DIFFERENCE
        WRITE PATRON-LINE
            AFTER ADVANCING 1 LINE
          .
```

Here, the actual contribution is subtracted from the target contribution by:

1. Moving the target contribution to a work area (AR-DIFFERENCE) defined in the WORKING-STORAGE section (see Figure 3-1, page 70).
2. Subtracting the actual contribution from the value in the work area. The resulting value in the work area is the desired deficit.

The final action in this conditional sequence is moving the newly calculated deficit to the output line.

The following examples illustrate the four arithmetic forms (in each case, assume that the data-items are appropriately defined in the DATA DIVISION):

```
ADD DR-OVERTIME TO DR-TOTAL-TIME
SUBTRACT 10 FROM CR-ACCOUNT-TOTAL
MULTIPLY PA-FACTOR BY ER-LIMIT
DIVIDE TS-QUANTITY INTO IR-TOTAL-VALUE
```

These execute exactly as the English suggests; the result replaces the original value in the field following the reserved word TO, FROM, BY, or INTO.

If you use arithmetic operations before studying Chapter 6, remember that it is best to avoid performing arithmetic where the result will be in a field defined in an input or output record. Use a work data-item defined in the WORKING-STORAGE section as in the PATDFCT example; then move the result to the output area.

Some COBOL-74 Techniques

When structured programming principles were first widely implemented, most business programmers used COBOL-74. Although COBOL was not tailored to structured programming then, structured methodology techniques were developed.

Although this book's emphasis is on COBOL-85, certain COBOL-74 programming techniques are so widely used that you should know about them.

The Priming READ

Let's leave the details of COBOL momentarily and consider in general terms the processing of data from a file. In its simplest form, we want to carry out the following instruction sequence:

Do the following while the next record is not the EOF
    Read a record
    Process the record
    Write the results.

The problem with using this logic in a COBOL program is that the program cannot "look ahead" to the next record to determine if it is a data record or an EOF record. As you know, the patron programs get around this problem with the NOT AT END phrase of the READ, as follows:

Do the following until end-of-file is YES
    Read a record
        AT END
            Set end-of-file is YES
        NOT AT END
            Process the record
            Write the results

Figure 3-16   Using the priming READ—COBOL-74.

```
1        IDENTIFICATION DIVISION.
2        PROGRAM-ID.   PATDFCT.C74.
3
4     *    PRICE/WELBURN 6/20/89  revised 1/5/95
5
6     *    This program prints a patron contribution
7     *    report. Under-target patrons are identified.
8     *    Coded for COBOL-74.
9
10
11       ENVIRONMENT DIVISION.
12
13       CONFIGURATION SECTION.
14
15           SOURCE-COMPUTER. (system dependent).
16           OBJECT-COMPUTER. (system dependent).
17
18       INPUT-OUTPUT SECTION.
19
20       FILE-CONTROL.
21           SELECT PATRON-FILE
22               ASSIGN TO (system dependent).
23           SELECT PATRON-LIST
24               ASSIGN TO (system dependent).
25
26
27       DATA DIVISION.
28
29       FILE SECTION.
30
31       FD  PATRON-FILE
32           LABEL RECORDS ARE STANDARD.
33       01  PATRON-RECORD.
34           05  PR-NAME               PIC X(18).
35           05  PR-ADDRESS            PIC X(18).
36           05  PR-CITY-STATE-ZIP     PIC X(24).
37           05  PR-TARGET-CONTR       PIC 9(4).
38           05  PR-ACTUAL-CONTR       PIC 9(4).
39
40       FD  PATRON-LIST
41           LABEL RECORDS ARE OMITTED.
42       01  PATRON-LINE.
43           05  FILLER                PIC X(1).
44           05  PL-NAME               PIC X(18).
45           05  FILLER                PIC X(1).
46           05  PL-CITY-STATE-ZIP     PIC X(24).
47           05  FILLER                PIC X(4).
48           05  PL-TARGET-CONTR       PIC 9(4).
49           05  FILLER                PIC X(3).
50           05  PL-ACTUAL-CONTR       PIC 9(4).
51           05  FILLER                PIC X(3).
52           05  PL-CONTR-DIFFERENCE   PIC 9(4).
53
54       WORKING-STORAGE SECTION.
55
56       01  PROGRAM-SWITCHES.
57           05  PS-END-OF-PATRON-FILE      PIC X(3).
58
59       01  AR-ARITHMETIC-WORK-AREAS.
60           05  AR-DIFFERENCE              PIC 9(4).
61
62
63       PROCEDURE DIVISION.
64
65       000-PRINT-PATRON-LIST.
66       ************Initialization Sequence************
67           OPEN INPUT PATRON-FILE
68                OUTPUT PATRON-LIST
69           PERFORM 100-INITIALIZE-VARIABLE-FIELDS
70           READ PATRON-FILE
71               AT END MOVE "YES" TO PS-END-OF-PATRON-FILE.
72
73       **************Processing Sequence**************
74           PERFORM 200-PROCESS-PATRON-RECORD
75               UNTIL PS-END-OF-PATRON-FILE IS EQUAL TO "YES"
76
77       **************Termination Sequence*************
78           CLOSE PATRON-FILE
79                 PATRON-LIST
80           STOP RUN.
81
82       ***********************************************
83
84       100-INITIALIZE-VARIABLE-FIELDS.
85           MOVE "NO " TO PS-END-OF-PATRON-FILE.
86
87       200-PROCESS-PATRON-RECORD.
88           MOVE SPACES TO PATRON-LINE
89           MOVE PR-NAME TO PL-NAME
90           MOVE PR-CITY-STATE-ZIP TO PL-CITY-STATE-ZIP
91           MOVE PR-TARGET-CONTR TO PL-TARGET-CONTR
92           MOVE PR-ACTUAL-CONTR TO PL-ACTUAL-CONTR
93           IF PR-ACTUAL-CONTR IS LESS THAN PR-TARGET-CONTR
94               MOVE PR-TARGET-CONTR TO AR-DIFFERENCE
95               SUBTRACT PR-ACTUAL-CONTR FROM AR-DIFFERENCE
96               MOVE AR-DIFFERENCE TO PL-CONTR-DIFFERENCE.
97           WRITE PATRON-LINE
98               AFTER ADVANCING 1 LINE
99           READ PATRON-FILE
100              AT END MOVE "YES" TO PS-END-OF-PATRON-FILE.
```

Without the NOT AT END, a different technique is used in COBOL-74; it employs the following logic:

Read the first record.
Do the following while the current record is not the EOF
    Process the record
    Write the results
    Read a record.

Notice that the first record is read outside the loop; it is an initializing action. This is commonly called **priming** the input area; the initial read statement is called the **priming READ**. Subsequent records are read at the end of the loop. So, when the EOF record is read, the repeated execution is terminated without processing the EOF record. This is implemented in Figure 3-16's COBOL-74 version of PATDFCT where you see the priming READ at lines 70 and 71, and the end-of-module read at lines 99 and 100.

The Out-of-Line PERFORM/UNTIL

The out-of-line PERFORM allows control to be transferred to another module and returned upon completion. The inline PERFORM allows you to repeat a sequence of statements until a specified condition occurs. The out-of-line PERFORM/UNTIL combines these features in providing for repeated execution of another module. The action of the PERFORM at lines 74 and 75 of Figure 3-16 is as follows:

1. If the condition PS-END-OF-PATRON-FILE IS EQUAL TO "YES" is *true*, the 200 procedure is not performed. Instead, program control continues to the next consecutive statement.
2. If the condition is false, the 200 procedure is performed.
3. Upon return from the performed procedure, the condition is retested. The 200 procedure continues to be performed until the condition becomes true.

Implementing COBOL-85 Techniques with COBOL-74

Although the precise sequential-processing techniques employed in this book cannot be used with COBOL-74, they can be closely simulated (as an alternate to the priming READ). This is done in Figure 3-17, in which the out-of-line PERFORM repeatedly executes the 150 module. This module contains the READ and an IF for conditional execution of the 200 module.

Because COBOL-74 does not include the END scope terminators, every statement that includes one or more conditionally executed statements must terminate with a period. You saw two statements in this category: the READ and the IF. Referring to the code of Figures 3-16 and 3-17, you can see that both terminate with periods. Notice in Figure 3-16 that the scope-defining period of the IF is placed only after the last of the conditionally executed statements (at line 96).

Figure 3-17
An alternate to the priming read—COBOL-74.

```
63          PROCEDURE DIVISION.
64
65          000-PRINT-PATRON-LIST.
66              OPEN INPUT PATRON-FILE
67                   OUTPUT PATRON-LIST
68              PERFORM 100-INITIALIZE-VARIABLE-FIELDS
69
70          **************Processing Sequence**************
71              PERFORM 150-PROCESS-PATRON-RECORD
72                  UNTIL PS-END-OF-PATRON-FILE IS EQUAL TO "YES"
73
74          **************Termination Sequence*************
75              CLOSE PATRON-FILE
76                    PATRON-LIST
77              STOP RUN.
78
79          ************************************************
80
81          100-INITIALIZE-VARIABLE-FIELDS.
82              MOVE "NO " TO PS-END-OF-PATRON-FILE.
83
84          150-READ-INPUT-RECORD.
85              READ PATRON-FILE
86                  AT END MOVE "YES" TO PS-END-OF-PATRON-FILE.
87              IF PS-END-OF-PATRON-FILE IS EQUAL TO "NO "
88                  PERFORM 200-PROCESS-PATRON-RECORD.
89
90          200-PROCESS-PATRON-RECORD.
91              MOVE SPACES TO PATRON-LINE
92              MOVE PR-NAME TO PL-NAME
93              MOVE PR-CITY-STATE-ZIP TO PL-CITY-STATE-ZIP
94              MOVE PR-TARGET-CONTR TO PL-TARGET-CONTR
95              MOVE PR-ACTUAL-CONTR TO PL-ACTUAL-CONTR
96              IF PR-ACTUAL-CONTR IS LESS THAN PR-TARGET-CONTR
97                  MOVE PR-TARGET-CONTR TO AR-DIFFERENCE
98                  SUBTRACT PR-ACTUAL-CONTR FROM AR-DIFFERENCE
99                  MOVE AR-DIFFERENCE TO PL-CONTR-DIFFERENCE.
100             WRITE PATRON-LINE
101                 AFTER ADVANCING 1 LINE.
```

COBOL-74

Figure 3-16's sample COBOL-74 program includes modifications that are common to most COBOL-85 example programs in this book. These include:

1. Insert the CONFIGURATION SECTION and insert the LABEL RECORDS clause in each FD clause.
2. Include the reserved word FILLER in filler entries.
3. Modify the READ sequence to eliminate the NOT AT END. Do this by using the priming READ form (Figure 3-16) or by replacing the NOT AT END with an appropriate IF statement (Figure 3-17).
4. Move the inline code of the processing sequence (repetition) to a separate module and change the PERFORM to execute that module.
5. Replace the END-IF scope terminators with a period on the preceding line.
6. If necessary, move separate-line paragraph-ending periods to the end of the preceding line.
7. Change the ASSIGN clause entry as necessary.

Periods in the PROCEDURE DIVISION

To end each statement of the PROCEDURE DIVISION with a period is common practice with COBOL-74—almost. The difficulty—especially for COBOL beginners—lies with conditionally executed code. Within a paragraph, the period serves two functions: to end each statement (not required) and to define the scope of a conditional sequence (required). Figure 3-18 illustrates problems that can arise from misplaced periods. The version to the left in Figure 3-18(a) is similar to this book's COBOL-85 forms in that it contains only two periods: one to end the IF scope and the other to end the paragraph. The version to the right is a form you will see in most existing COBOL-74 programs. Each sentence ends with a period, except those within the IF scope. These two forms are equivalent.

Figure 3-18(b) illustrates a common error—periods where they do not belong. The first statement under the IF—the MOVE—is followed by a period. This period terminates the IF statement. Consequently, the two statements following the conditionally executed MOVE (SUBTRACT and MOVE) will be executed unconditionally. Actually, the indention is misleading because it implies that all three statements will be executed conditionally. The code to the right, which is identical, includes indention that gives you a visual indication of how the compiler treats the code to the left.

Forgetting the IF scope-ending period causes another problem, as Figure 3-18(c) illustrates. Even though the WRITE and READ are not indented, they become part of the conditionally executed code because the conditional sequence is not terminated until the period. The code on the right gives you a visual

Figure 3-18   Period usage in COBOL-74.

```
200-PROCESS-PATRON-RECORD.                                                    200-PROCESS-PATRON-RECORD.
    MOVE SPACES TO PATRON-LINE                                                    MOVE SPACES TO PATRON-LINE.
    MOVE PR-NAME TO PL-NAME                            EQUIVALENT                 MOVE PR-NAME TO PL-NAME.
    MOVE PR-CITY-STATE-ZIP TO PL-CITY-STATE-ZIP           ←——→                    MOVE PR-CITY-STATE-ZIP TO PL-CITY-STATE-ZIP.
    MOVE PR-TARGET-CONTR TO PL-TARGET-CONTR                                       MOVE PR-TARGET-CONTR TO PL-TARGET-CONTR.
    MOVE PR-ACTUAL-CONTR TO PL-ACTUAL-CONTR                                       MOVE PR-ACTUAL-CONTR TO PL-ACTUAL-CONTR.
    IF PR-ACTUAL-CONTR IS LESS THAN PR-TARGET-CONTR                              IF PR-ACTUAL-CONTR IS LESS THAN PR-TARGET-CONTR
        MOVE PR-TARGET-CONTR TO AR-DIFFERENCE                                         MOVE PR-TARGET-CONTR TO AR-DIFFERENCE ←
        SUBTRACT PR-ACTUAL-CONTR FROM AR-DIFFERENCE                                   SUBTRACT PR-ACTUAL-CONTR FROM AR-DIFFERENCE ←
        MOVE AR-DIFFERENCE TO PL-CONTR-DIFFERENCE.                                    MOVE AR-DIFFERENCE TO PL-CONTR-DIFFERENCE.
    WRITE PATRON-LINE                                                            WRITE PATRON-LINE
        AFTER ADVANCING 1 LINE                                                        AFTER ADVANCING 1 LINE.
    READ PATRON-FILE                                                             READ PATRON-FILE
        AT END MOVE "YES" TO PS-END-OF-PATRON-FILE.                                  AT END MOVE "YES" TO PS-END-OF-PATRON-FILE.
```

(a) VALID—With and without periods after each sentence (except within conditionals).   No periods here.

Figure 3-18   (continued)

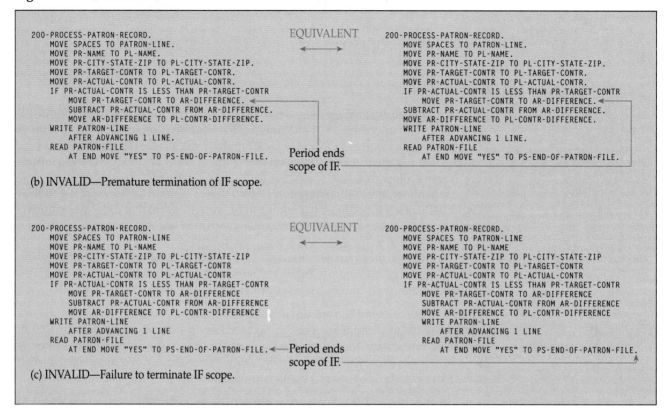

(b) INVALID—Premature termination of IF scope.

(c) INVALID—Failure to terminate IF scope.

representation of how the compiler treats the code to the left. In the versions on the left in both (b) and (c), the indention is misleading to you and me, but not to the compiler.

To avoid problems of this type, periods should be used in the PROCEDURE DIVISION of all COBOL-74 programs only as follows: (1) after the paragraph header, (2) after the last statement of a conditional sequence (AT END and IF), and (3) after the paragraph's last statement.

Formalizing Conventions and Rules

Positioning, Spacing, and Punctuation

Chapter 1 briefly discussed such topics as punctuation and the forms of COBOL program entries. Let's wrap up this chapter by considering these subjects in more detail.

All COBOL entries—except comment lines—can be classified as either Area A (positions 8–11) or Area B (positions 12–72) entries. You may start Area A entries anywhere in Area A (traditionally, programmers start them in position 8). You cannot position Area B entries in Area A, but you can begin them anywhere in Area B.

You know from Chapter 1 that spacing and punctuation conventions for COBOL language entries are similar to those used in English. The following is a summary of these COBOL rules:

- At least one space must appear between words. Whenever one space is used, any number of spaces may be used.

- When a period is shown in the COBOL format notation, the period is required in the coding entry.

- Commas and semicolons improve readability, but are ignored by the compiler. For instance, the OPEN statement of PATDFCT could be written as follows:

```
OPEN INPUT PATRON-FILE,
    OUTPUT PATRON-LIST
```

- Whenever a comma or semicolon is used, it must be followed by a space.

Paragraph-ending periods are always coded on a separate line (column 12) following the paragraph's last statement. This simplifies program modification in which a new statement is inserted as the paragraph's last statement. It also provides a blank-appearing line between paragraphs. Note: Some COBOL-74 compilers may not allow this.

Indentions are typically made in four-space units. However, in a PROCEDURE DIVISION module with complex logic, you may find that four-space indents move everything too far to the right. You may want to use two spaces in such cases.

Vertical Spacing of COBOL Coding Lines

You can enhance program neatness and readability by inserting blank lines—using vertical spacing—to separate different parts of the program. Note that this relates to the appearance of the source program, not to the printed program output.

Caution: Some compilers remove such blank lines, causing your carefully inserted blanks to disappear. Also, the editor furnished with at least one COBOL compiler terminates the program-entry session when the Enter (Return) key is struck twice in succession. If your compiler exhibits similar characteristics, use an asterisk in column 7 to insert a blank comment line.

In this book, line spacing was chosen to provide sufficient white space to make listings easily readable, yet not so generous that the lines consume excessive space. Basic standards are as follows:

- Division headers (except the PROCEDURE DIVISION): preceded by two blank lines and followed by one.

- Section headers: preceded and followed by one blank line.

- 01-level entries: preceded by one blank line.

Chapter Summary

The PROCEDURE DIVISION of a COBOL program expresses the logic that the computer follows to obtain the specified results. The PROCEDURE DIVISION may contain user-defined sections, but typically does not. Paragraph-names within the PROCEDURE DIVISION are user-defined words. Paragraphs and paragraph-names within the PROCEDURE DIVISION are alternatively referred to as procedures and procedure-names, respectively.

A PROCEDURE DIVISION paragraph contains one or more imperative statements (commands). A statement is a syntactically valid combination of COBOL words that begins with a COBOL verb. The following are statements described in this chapter:

CLOSE	Terminates processing for one or more files.
IF	Provides a conditional capability; allows an action to be taken or skipped, or either of two actions to be taken. The scope of the IF is indicated with the END-IF.
MOVE	Copies data from one data-item to another.

OPEN   Makes one or more files ready for processing; must be issued before a file's records can be accessed.

PERFORM   Transfers control to a specified procedure-name and, after the procedure is executed, returns to the next consecutive statement from which control was transferred.

PERFORM/UNTIL (out-of-line)
Operates like a PERFORM statement, except that it transfers control conditionally, depending upon the status of the condition expressed in the UNTIL phrase. Upon return, it retests the condition and so provides iterative processing.

PERFORM/UNTIL (in-line)
Causes a sequence of statements terminated by an END-PERFORM to be executed repeatedly until a designated condition becomes true.

READ   Makes a logical record from an input file available to the program. For sequential input files, it must contain an AT END phrase defining the action to be taken when the file EOF is detected. The scope of the AT END sequence is indicated with an END-READ.

STOP RUN   Terminates program execution and returns computer control to the operating system.

A COBOL verb is a word that expresses an action to be taken by a COBOL program. It must begin in Area B.

Nonnumeric literals are used when it is necessary to introduce actual values into a program. They (1) must be enclosed in quotation marks, (2) may contain any characters acceptable to the computer system used, and (3) must not exceed 120 characters.

Figurative constants are preassigned reserved words that represent actual values.

COBOL Structure Summary

Refer to Figure 3-19.

Style Summary

PROCEDURE DIVISION conventions:

- Code the OPEN statement with each file-name on a separate line. Vertically align each file-name.

- Code the READ statement with the AT END phrase, its conditional action, the NOT AT END, and its conditional action on separate lines. Indent each two spaces.

- When a MOVE statement will not fit on one coding line, write the reserved word TO and the name of the receiving field on a separate line. Indent the second line four spaces.

- Code the WRITE statement with the ADVANCING phrase on a separate line. Indent the ADVANCING phrase four spaces.

- Code the CLOSE statement with each file-name on a separate line; align the file-names.
- In the PROCEDURE DIVISION of COBOL-85 programs, use periods only at the end of a paragraph-name and on the line following the last statement of a paragraph.

Figure 3-19   COBOL structure summary chart.

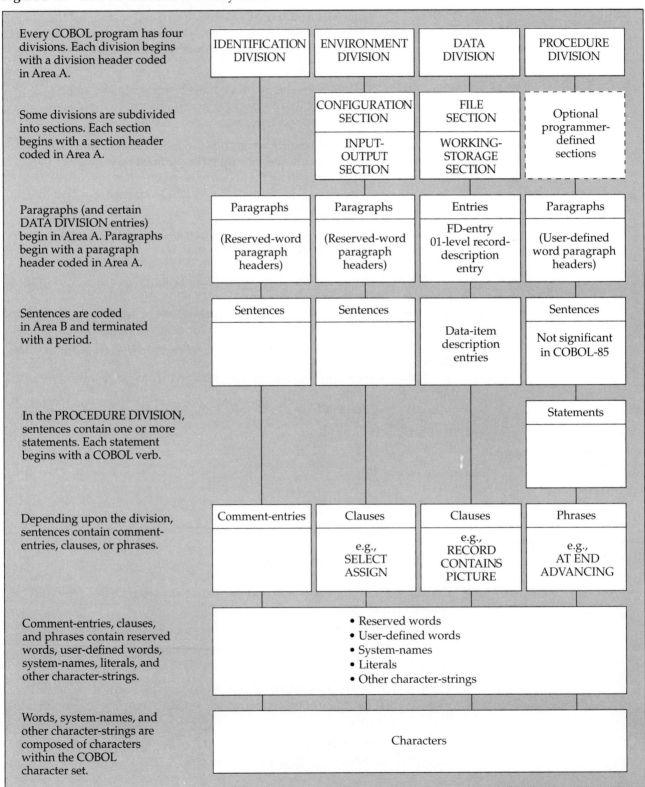

	IDENTIFICATION DIVISION	ENVIRONMENT DIVISION	DATA DIVISION	PROCEDURE DIVISION
Every COBOL program has four divisions. Each division begins with a division header coded in Area A.				
Some divisions are subdivided into sections. Each section begins with a section header coded in Area A.		CONFIGURATION SECTION / INPUT-OUTPUT SECTION	FILE SECTION / WORKING-STORAGE SECTION	Optional programmer-defined sections
Paragraphs (and certain DATA DIVISION entries) begin in Area A. Paragraphs begin with a paragraph header coded in Area A.	Paragraphs (Reserved-word paragraph headers)	Paragraphs (Reserved-word paragraph headers)	Entries: FD-entry 01-level record-description entry	Paragraphs (User-defined word paragraph headers)
Sentences are coded in Area B and terminated with a period.	Sentences	Sentences	Data-item description entries	Sentences: Not significant in COBOL-85
In the PROCEDURE DIVISION, sentences contain one or more statements. Each statement begins with a COBOL verb.				Statements
Depending upon the division, sentences contain comment-entries, clauses, or phrases.	Comment-entries	Clauses e.g., SELECT ASSIGN	Clauses e.g., RECORD CONTAINS PICTURE	Phrases e.g., AT END ADVANCING
Comment-entries, clauses, and phrases contain reserved words, user-defined words, system-names, literals, and other character-strings.	• Reserved words • User-defined words • System-names • Literals • Other character-strings			
Words, system-names, and other character-strings are composed of characters within the COBOL character set.	Characters			

Exercises

Terms for Definition

condition
figurative constant
garbage
imperative statements
literals
nonnumeric literal
numeric literal

priming
priming READ
scope
scope terminator
sentence
statement

Review Questions

1. A paragraph in the PROCEDURE DIVISION can also be termed a(n) _____.

2. A procedure-name is a(n) _____ word.

3. A syntactically valid combination of COBOL words and symbols beginning with a verb is called a(n) _____.

4. Procedure-names begin in Area _____.

5. COBOL verbs begin in Area _____.

6. A(n) _____ statement must be executed before a data file can be processed.

7. The _____ statement transfers data from one data-item to another.

8. The _____ statement makes a data record from an input file available to the program.

9. The _____ statement causes a record to be transferred from an output area to an output device.

10. The _____ statement terminates program execution.

11. The READ statement references the _____-name; the WRITE statement references the _____-name.

12. The COBOL language element used to introduce an actual value into a program is known as a(n) _____.

13. A nonnumeric literal must be enclosed by _____ and is limited to a length of _____ characters.

14. A numeric literal can be composed only of _____, _____, and _____.

15. A numeric literal must contain at least _____ digit(s), but must not contain more than _____ digits.

16. Preassigned words that represent actual values are known as _____.

Questions Pertaining to PATDFCT

1. What would happen during execution of PATDFCT if the data file to be processed contained no data records (it contained only the EOF record)?

2. In the PATDFCT program, the deficit is moved to the output field PL-CONTR-DIFFERENCE if the Actual-contribution is less than the Target-contribution. Why isn't it necessary to blank out this field for records where nothing is to be printed in order to avoid printing the value from a preceding output record?

Programming Assignments

To complete a programming assignment started in Chapter 2, perform the following tasks:

1. Draw a structure chart of the PROCEDURE DIVISION for the problem.

2. Prepare program design documentation (such as pseudocode or a program flowchart) for the PROCEDURE DIVISION.

3. Add the coding for the PROCEDURE DIVISION to the coding of the first three divisions completed for Chapter 2.

4. Obtain a clean compile of the complete program.

5. Execute the program, using the data file specified by your instructor. Check the output carefully to make sure that your program is working properly.

Debugging/Program Testing Supplement

Supplement Objectives

If you coded and compiled any of Chapter 1's programming assignments, you probably learned that the compiler is very fussy about COBOL syntax rules. Perhaps you discovered that an apparently minor error in the DATA DIVISION can have a significant effect on statements in the PROCEDURE DIVISION. The purpose of this debugging/program testing supplement is to give you some pointers on finding errors and preparing programs that work properly. In this supplement, you will learn the following:

- How to recognize the effect in the PROCEDURE DIVISION of errors made in other divisions.

- The types of errors commonly encountered:
  - Syntax errors that are detected by the compiler.
  - Logic errors that direct the computer to perform operations other than those you desire, resulting in incorrect output.
  - Runtime errors that direct the computer to perform an action of which it is not capable, causing termination of the program.

- How to use structured walkthroughs to ensure program soundness.

- The creation and use of test data to ensure that a program performs the functions for which it was intended.

Supplement Outline

Compiler-Detected Errors
Error Diagnostics
About Making Corrections

Logic Errors
Data-Definition Mistakes
Incorrect Logic
Runtime Errors

Error Detection and Correcting
Structured Walkthroughs
Program Testing

Compiler-Detected Errors

Error Diagnostics

At the end of Chapter 2, you learned about syntax errors in the first three divisions and the role of the compiler in detecting them. Most of the common syntactical errors identified in Figure 2-10 (page 47) for the first three divisions also apply to the PROCEDURE DIVISION. In fact, many types of errors made in the DATA DIVISION produce error messages relating to statements of the PROCEDURE DIVISION.

If you make any errors, you will receive appropriate compiler diagnostic messages. Many compilers classify each diagnostic to show how serious it is. At minimum, most have the following two categories:

W   *Warning.*
A warning calls attention to something that may be a problem. Some compilers make assumptions concerning the correct form. A warning does not interrupt the compiling or prevent ultimate execution of the program. However, each warning should be checked and corrected. Ignoring a warning—even though it looks harmless—could lead to execution errors.

E   *Error.*
This indicates a serious error that the compiler could not correct. After detecting an E-level error, the incorrect statement is ignored and compilation of the program continues. All E-level errors must be corrected before attempting to run the program.

Some types of errors result in diagnostic messages that identify the exact location of the error and what you did wrong. Others result in diagnostics that are far removed from the actual error and require some detective work to find the error.

For example, if you misspell ENVIRONMENT DIVISION, the compiler identifies the error immediately. Similarly, the following incorrect form of the MOVE statement is identified clearly:

```
MOVE PR-AMOUNT INTO LC-AMOUNT
```

On the other hand, consider the following segments from PATDFCT (Figure 3-1, pages 70 and 71) in which the work field AR-DIFFERENCE is misspelled as AR-DIFERENCE:

```
50        01  ARITHMETIC-WORK-AREAS.
51            05  AR-DIFERENCE            PIC 9(4).
 :
89                MOVE PR-TARGET-CONTR TO AR-DIFFERENCE
90                SUBTRACT PR-ACTUAL-CONTR FROM AR-DIFFERENCE
91                MOVE AR-DIFFERENCE TO PR-CONTR-DIFFERENCE
```

Each of the three statements in lines 89–91 would be accompanied by a diagnostic indicating that AR-DIFFERENCE is not defined. Obviously, the programmer's mistake was back at line 51—which, to the compiler, was perfectly valid.

You can minimize the chances of misspelling by avoiding the use of names that are confusing abbreviations of the entities they represent. For instance, EM-SVGS-RPRT is a poor abbreviation for an employee savings report because it is too easy to forget your exact abbreviation when coding the PROCEDURE DIVISION. Although EM-SAVINGS-REPORT requires more typing, it is much easier to remember.

About Making Corrections

When you get a post-compile listing with diagnostics, you must inspect each of the messages and write in the corrections adjacent to the statement in error. Then, with an appropriate editor, make the corrections to your program and recompile it.

However, occasionally you will have a relatively minor error in one part of a program that gives you so many diagnostics in the PROCEDURE DIVISION that it is extremely clumsy working through the listing. When a situation like that occurs (sometimes giving you more diagnostic lines than you have program lines), find the problem producing that error, correct it, and run another compile. If you have other errors, you will have a post-compile listing that is far easier to work with than your first one was.

Logic Errors

Logic errors are those in which you tell the computer to do the wrong thing. Some logic errors make the computer do something that is "against the rules," causing your program to terminate or crash. Most others give erroneous results and are found only by testing.

Data-Definition Mistakes

A common error, and one very easy to make, is using an incorrect field length in the record description. It is critical that the definitions of records and fields in the PICTURE clause conform to the actual data as expressed in the programming specifications (which, in turn, should of course define the actual data characteristics stored in the records). Figure 3S-1 provides an example of how the incorrect definition of a field size causes processing of misaligned data. For these two fields, the only detectable error is that the printed output appears strange: an extra character at the end of the name, the first character of the address missing, and so on. However, if the shift resulted in nonnumeric data being part of a numeric field involved in an arithmetic operation, the program could crash.

Incorrect Logic

The PROCEDURE DIVISION statements should be written to correspond to the logic expressed in the pseudocode or flowchart—which should, of course, express the correct logic necessary to achieve the required results. If the logic of your program is incorrect, it will not produce the required results. The only way to detect

Figure 3S-1 Example of a data definition error.

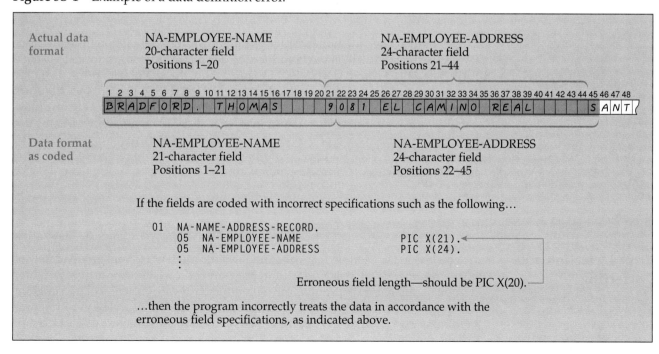

this is through testing: creating a set of test data, determining the exact output that should result from that data, and then comparing the program output to your expected results.

Problems frequently occur in conditionally executed statements. For instance, assume that you must print a list of patrons with contributions below their target amounts. In your program, you use the following:

```
IF PR-ACTUAL-CONTR IS GREATER THAN PR-TARGET-CONTR
    PERFORM 200-PROCESS-PATRON-RECORD
END-IF
```

From this, you obtain a partial listing of the patrons in the file. Unfortunately, this data is the opposite of what you want; it lists patrons who *exceeded* their target amounts. If you did not check the report against the original data, this incorrect report could appear to be reasonable.

Consider another example logic error. Assume that you intend to write the following command that adds the quantity SERVICE-CHARGE to TOTAL-CHARGE:

```
ADD SERVICE-CHARGE TO TOTAL-CHARGE
```

However, while daydreaming, you subtract rather than add, as follows:

```
SUBTRACT SERVICE-CHARGE FROM TOTAL-CHARGE
```

To the compiler during the compile and to the computer during program execution, this is a valid action. The computer does not know what you intend the program to do. The compiler can only check that you wrote the program code in accordance with the syntax requirements of the COBOL language.

Too often, beginning programmers feel that they are finished with a program when it compiles without error messages and produces output when run. Do not fall into this trap; check your work.

Runtime Errors

A runtime error occurs when you direct the computer to do something of which it is not capable. For instance, consider the following statement to divide the total sales by the number of units sold:

```
DIVIDE UNITS-SOLD INTO TOTAL-SALES
```

This is valid syntax and appears to perform the desired calculation (judging from its English form). It will indeed produce the desired result; for instance, if TOTAL-SALES is 1141.44 and UNITS-SOLD is 96, then the calculated result is 11.89. However, what if, for some reason, the value in UNITS-SOLD is 0? Since the computer cannot divide by 0, an error results. When attempting to do this, most computers generate an error and terminate execution of the program, crashing the program. If yours is a production program that the company runs at 2:00 A.M. every morning, you should expect a wake-up call from an irate computer operator who has an important schedule to maintain.

Error Detection and Correcting

Structured Walkthroughs

As you learned in Module A, a structured walkthrough is a formal group review of a programmer or analyst's work for the purpose of detecting errors or faulty design. Recall that walkthroughs can be conducted at various stages of the program development process: (1) in the specification phase after completion of the programming specifications, (2) in the design phase after completion of each design document, (3) in the coding phase after obtaining a clean compile, and (4) during the testing phase. The following is a typical set of guidelines:

1. A walkthrough is not used to review an individual's work performance; it reviews program quality and project progress.
2. Each person attending a walkthrough must function in the role of either reviewee, reviewer, or recording secretary.
3. The reviewee conducts the meeting, since it is his or her work being reviewed.
4. The reviewee is responsible for distributing the material to be reviewed to all the reviewers before the meeting.
5. The walkthrough should not exceed two hours.
6. During the walkthrough, problems may be identified, but not corrected.

While you are taking this course, you may or may not participate in a structured walkthrough. If you do not, you should at least learn to walk through your programs with another student, looking for potential problems. During this course, you will undoubtedly encounter an error in your program that you simply cannot find, no matter how carefully you look. Often the act of explaining your program to another person makes the error obvious to you.

Program Testing

The objective of any program is to process data and produce *correct* output. The only way to be certain the results are correct and that your program does not contain logic errors is by careful **program testing**. To test a program, you must:

1. Prepare a set of test data that exercises every aspect of your program. For instance, the test data for the PATDFCT program must include data with the following characteristics:
   Actual contribution LESS THAN the target contribution
   Actual contribution EQUAL TO the target contribution
   Actual contribution GREATER THAN the target contribution
   In addition, it is often a good idea to include zero data amounts. For instance, you might include a record with a zero target amount, one with a zero actual amount, and one with both. Sometimes zero values give unexpected results. In a program with numerous conditional actions, the test data can be very extensive.
2. Process your test data manually and determine what the computer should print. For instance, you should manually calculate the deficit for one or more of the under-target patrons. If your output differs with the computer's, something is wrong.

For large programs, the testing can become complex and time consuming. However, one of structured programming's strengths using a modular approach is that program testing can be done on a structured basis. Such structured testing is sometimes referred to as **top-down** (or **stub**) **testing**.

Because each structured-code module is relatively independent of the others, modules can be tested either one at a time or within a specific group. This means that testing top-level modules can begin before lower-level modules are completed.

To perform top-down (stub) testing, dummy procedures are inserted in the program for those modules not yet coded. The dummy procedure contains only the procedure-name header and an EXIT statement (a statement that immediately returns control to the module executing the PERFORM). Although this technique is oriented to programs considerably larger than those you will write in this book, you may find the method helpful toward the end of the course.

Supplement Summary

Program errors are best prevented by carefully designing a program, using the good structured techniques described in this book.

An error in the ENVIRONMENT DIVISION or DATA DIVISION can result in diagnostics for many otherwise correct statements in the PROCEDURE DIVISION. If this multiplying effect is great, the best approach is usually to correct the error, then run another compile before proceeding further.

Use extra care in defining input records. If you are off a single position in one field, all fields that follow will be off.

The compiler will not catch logic errors. You must prepare test data that exercises all aspects of your program. Testing is a major element of the programming process.

Exercises

Terms for Definition

program testing
top-down (stub) testing

Review Questions

1. What is meant by, "A clean compile does not mean an error-free program"?

2. What is the difference between a syntax error and a logic error?

Syntax/Debug Exercises

1. The PATDFCT program includes the following IF:

   ```
   IF PR-ACTUAL-CONTR IS LESS THAN PR-TARGET-CONTR
   ```

   What would happen if it were incorrectly entered as follows?

   ```
   IF PR-ACTUAL-CONTR IS LESS THAN PR-ACTUAL-CONTR
   ```

2. Would execution of PATDFCT be any different if the IF statement were as follows? Explain your answer.

   ```
   IF PR-TARGET-CONTR IS NOT GREATER THAN PR-ACTUAL-CONTR
   ```

KEYBOARD INPUT AND SCREEN DISPLAY

Note

This chapter is included at this point so that you can experience writing programs that interact with a user if interactive programs are compatible with your operating environment. If not, you may proceed to Chapter 5 with no loss of continuity.

CHAPTER OUTLINE

CHAPTER 4

CHAPTER OBJECTIVES

So far in this book, the focus has been on sequential file processing—applications in which a record is read, processed, and a line printed. An equally important area is interactive processing, whereby the user—working with a keyboard and a CRT screen—interacts directly with the computer. Although extensive interactive applications come later in this book, this chapter provides you with your first insight into writing interactive programs. From this chapter, you will learn the following:

- The two basic interactive input/output statements: DISPLAY and ACCEPT.

- How to add records to an existing data file.

- How to create a data file from the keyboard.

- How to display the contents of a file on the screen.

Screen I/O with the DISPLAY and ACCEPT

The DISPLAY Statement

In COBOL, the DISPLAY is used for low-volume, terminal output. Its format and several examples are shown in Figure 4-1. From the format, you can see that both literals and data-items can be displayed and that a single DISPLAY can display one or more items. The examples function as follows:

1. The contents of the data-item PR-PATRON-NAME is displayed.
2. The literal value "Sample literal" is displayed.
3. The screen display includes the literal, immediately followed by the contents of the data-item PR-PATRON-NAME. In this example, the two items to be displayed are separated by a comma. The comma is optional and is ignored by the compiler. The following is a typical display:

```
The patron's name is John J. Mudd
```

4. Here, the two entries to be displayed are listed on separate lines. This statement format is consistent with the way in which fields on an output line are listed in the WORKING-STORAGE SECTION. Its output is identical to that of Example 3.
5. When the DISPLAY list consists of two or more entries, they are displayed with no space separation. So, if you want to display the contents of two or more fields, you should separate them with an appropriately sized literal defined with spaces. In this example, the value in WA-AMOUNT is separated from the value in WA-BALANCE by three spaces.
6. This produces the same result as Example 5.

Normally, after a DISPLAY is completed, the cursor advances to the start of the next line (scrolling the screen, if necessary). The WITH NO ADVANCING phrase causes the cursor to remain where it is, following the last position of the displayed elements. This is convenient when you query the user and await a response. You will see it used in this chapter's example programs.

Most compilers include a variety of options for actions such as clearing all or part of the line or screen, positioning the display anywhere on the screen, and highlighting items. Chapter 5 describes some of these capabilities.

Figure 4-1
The DISPLAY format and examples.

Format:

$$\underline{\text{DISPLAY}} \quad \begin{Bmatrix} \text{identifier-1} \\ \text{literal-1} \end{Bmatrix} \dots \quad [\text{WITH } \underline{\text{NO}} \ \underline{\text{ADVANCING}}]$$

Examples:

```
1. DISPLAY PR-PATRON-NAME
2. DISPLAY "Sample literal"
3. DISPLAY "The patron's name is ", PR-PATRON-NAME
4. DISPLAY "The patron's name is "
           PR-PATRON-NAME
5. DISPLAY WA-AMOUNT, "   ", WA-BALANCE
6. DISPLAY WA-AMOUNT
           "   "
           WA-BALANCE
```

The ACCEPT Statement

While the DISPLAY statement allows you to display information on the screen, the ACCEPT allows you to enter data from the keyboard into the program, while simultaneously displaying your entry on the screen. Its format is relatively simple: The reserved word ACCEPT must be followed by a data-name into which the data will be stored. For example, with execution of the statement

```
ACCEPT WA-PAY-RATE
```

the program stops and awaits a keyboard entry. After the user types the input quantity and presses the Enter key, the typed value is stored in WA-PAY-RATE.

Batch and Interactive Processing

The programs you have studied so far have each processed the entire set of data from an input data file. They are simple forms of **batch processing** programs because they process an entire "batch" of data when run. There is no continuous interaction with the user while the program is running.

In contrast, some applications programs require continuous user interaction. For instance, consider your interaction with an ATM (automatic teller machine). You key in your account number, identification number, and amount of withdrawal. The computer accepts it, updates your account, prints a receipt, and initiates delivery of the cash. This is called **interactive processing** because you interact directly with the computer as the transaction occurs.

Adding Records to the Patron File

Program Planning

For your first example of an interactive program, let's consider one that allows you to add records to the patron file. Figure 4-2's sample screen gives you an idea of the dialogue between the user and the computer. Notice the following about this screen:

1. Items typed in from the keyboard (by the user) are in color. All other items on the screen are displayed by the program. The coloring is shown here for clarity; if you ran the program, no items would be colored.
2. An opening announcement is displayed, which describes to the user the purpose of the program and provides the option to continue or to abort the run.
3. The prompt for each field consists of two lines. The first identifies the field to be entered. The second—a row of Xs or 9s—indicates the field length and type, which is analogous to printer spacing chart information.
4. The user must enter the requested data, which must fit within the field size defined by the preceding line.
5. After the last field, the user is queried about entering another record.

As Figure 4-3 illustrates, the program's logic is relatively simple. Actually, it is very similar to the logic of the patron programs.

The EXTEND Mode of the OPEN

Chapter 3's patron program opens the patron file in the INPUT mode; this allows records to be read. The program also opens a printer file in the OUTPUT mode; this provides for the printed report to be written. When an OPEN OUTPUT is executed, an existing file with the same name is erased.

Figure 4-2 Sample screen display for record entry.

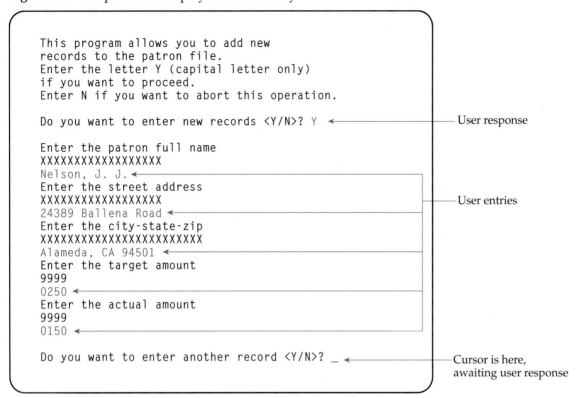

```
This program allows you to add new
records to the patron file.
Enter the letter Y (capital letter only)
if you want to proceed.
Enter N if you want to abort this operation.

Do you want to enter new records <Y/N>? Y  ◄──────────── User response

Enter the patron full name
XXXXXXXXXXXXXXXXXX
Nelson, J. J. ◄
Enter the street address
XXXXXXXXXXXXXXXXXX
24389 Ballena Road ◄                                    User entries
Enter the city-state-zip
XXXXXXXXXXXXXXXXXXXXXXXXXX
Alameda, CA 94501 ◄
Enter the target amount
9999
0250 ◄
Enter the actual amount
9999
0150 ◄

Do you want to enter another record <Y/N>? _  ◄──────── Cursor is here,
                                                        awaiting user response
```

We have a slightly different need (than INPUT or OUTPUT) in this application: We must open the patron file so that we can add records to the current end of the file. In other words, it must be opened for an output function, but without destroying existing data. The EXTEND mode, as the following illustrates, is provided explicitly for this purpose:

```
OPEN EXTEND PATRON-FILE
```

Figure 4-3
Pseudocode to create
a new patron file.

```
000-Create-Patron-File.
   1. Perform 100-Display-Announce-Screen.
   2. Open patron file.
   3. Perform until do-not-continue.
      a. Perform 200-Accept-Patron-Record
      b. Write patron record
      c. Query user about continuing
   4. Close patron file.
   5. Stop run.

100-Display-Announce-Screen.
   1. Display description of program.
   2. Query user about continuing.

200-Accept-Patron-Record.
   1. Accept the following fields
         Patron name
         Street address
         City-state-zip
         Target amount
         Actual amount
```

With this statement's execution, the program (1) opens PATRON-FILE, (2) positions an internal record pointer after the last record, and (3) allows you to WRITE records following the current last record of the file.

A Program to Add Records to the Patron File—PATADD

Figure 4-4's completed program follows directly from the logic of Figure 4-3. At lines 62–64, the user is queried and allowed to respond about continuing or not. The response determines what happens next.

1. The user response is accepted into the program switch SW-ANOTHER-RECORD at line 64. If the response is not Y, the condition at line 43 is true and execution falls through to the CLOSE at line 51. In other words, this loop is not executed.
2. The DISPLAY statement at lines 62 and 63—and the DISPLAY at lines 47 and 48—include the clause WITH NO ADVANCING. This clause is used because it keeps the cursor immediately following the literal display for the ACCEPT. You can see the cursor on the last line of Figure 4-2's screen display. This is easier for the user than having the cursor at the beginning of the next line when a simple yes/no response is required.
3. Repeated execution of the loop sequence at lines 44–49 is controlled by the PERFORM at line 43. The same switch (SW-ANOTHER-RECORD) is used for repetition as was used to determine whether execution was to proceed or be aborted.

Figure 4-4 Interactive program to create a new patron file—PATADD.

```
1      IDENTIFICATION DIVISION.                    38    PROCEDURE DIVISION.
2      PROGRAM-ID.    PATADD.                       39
3                                                   40    000-CREATE-PATRON-FILE.
4      *    W. PRICE 1/9/95                         41        PERFORM 100-DISPLAY-ANNOUNCE-SCREEN
5                                                   42        OPEN EXTEND PATRON-FILE
6      *    This program allows the user to add     43        PERFORM UNTIL SW-ANOTHER-RECORD IS NOT EQUAL TO "Y"
7      *    records to the patron file.             44            PERFORM 200-ACCEPT-PATRON-RECORD
8                                                   45            WRITE PATRON-RECORD
9                                                   46            DISPLAY " "
10     ENVIRONMENT DIVISION.                        47            DISPLAY "Do you want to enter another record <Y/N>? "
11                                                  48                    WITH NO ADVANCING
12     INPUT-OUTPUT SECTION.                        49            ACCEPT SW-ANOTHER-RECORD
13                                                  50        END-PERFORM
14     FILE-CONTROL.                                51        CLOSE PATRON-FILE
15         SELECT PATRON-FILE                       52        STOP RUN
16             ASSIGN TO (system dependent).        53        .
17                                                  54
18                                                  55    100-DISPLAY-ANNOUNCE-SCREEN.
19                                                  56        DISPLAY "This program allows you to add new"
20     DATA DIVISION.                               57        DISPLAY "records to the patron file."
21                                                  58        DISPLAY "Enter the letter Y (capital letter only)"
22     FILE SECTION.                                59        DISPLAY "if you want to proceed."
23                                                  60        DISPLAY "Enter N if you want to abort this operation."
24     FD  PATRON-FILE.                             61        DISPLAY " "
25     01  PATRON-RECORD.                           62        DISPLAY "Do you want to enter new records <Y/N>? "
26         05  PR-NAME              PIC X(18).      63                WITH NO ADVANCING
27         05  PR-ADDRESS           PIC X(18).      64        ACCEPT SW-ANOTHER-RECORD
28         05  PR-CITY-STATE-ZIP    PIC X(24).      65        DISPLAY " "
29         05  PR-TARGET-CONTR      PIC 9(4).       66        .
30         05  PR-ACTUAL-CONTR      PIC 9(4).       67    200-ACCEPT-PATRON-RECORD.
31                                                  68        DISPLAY "Enter the patron full name"
32     WORKING-STORAGE SECTION.                     69        DISPLAY "XXXXXXXXXXXXXXXXXX"
33                                                  70        ACCEPT PR-NAME
34     01  SW-SWITCHES.                             71        DISPLAY "Enter the street address"
35         05  SW-ANOTHER-RECORD    PIC X(1).       72        DISPLAY "XXXXXXXXXXXXXXXXXX"
36                                                  73        ACCEPT PR-ADDRESS
37                                                  74        DISPLAY "Enter the city-state-zip"
                                                    75        DISPLAY "XXXXXXXXXXXXXXXXXXXXXXXX"
                                                    76        ACCEPT PR-CITY-STATE-ZIP
                                                    77        DISPLAY "Enter the target amount"
                                                    78        DISPLAY "9999"
                                                    79        ACCEPT PR-TARGET-CONTR
                                                    80        DISPLAY "Enter the actual amount"
                                                    81        DISPLAY "9999"
                                                    82        ACCEPT PR-ACTUAL-CONTR
                                                    83        .
```

4. After a record is accepted and written, the user is queried about repeating at lines 47–49. A response of Y causes this module to be repeated (from the PERFORM at line 43). Although the prompt tells the user to enter N for no more records, any entry other than Y terminates processing—including the lowercase y.

5. Within the 200 module, each pair of prompt lines is followed by an ACCEPT statement; for instance, see lines 68–70.

6. After all five fields are entered, the new record is written to disk by the WRITE statement at line 45.

The forms of the ACCEPT and DISPLAY used here are relatively primitive, but are all that COBOL-85 provides. Almost all compilers provide far more features for these two statements. For instance, with most compilers you could designate that the ACCEPT statement display a template illustrating the exact form and size of the data-item to be entered. With that capability, field indications (lines 69, 72, and so on) are not needed. You will learn about some typical features in Chapter 5.

COBOL-74

The following changes to PATADD are required to convert it to a COBOL-74 program:

1. Insert the CONFIGURATION SECTION (preceding line 11) and insert the LABEL RECORDS clause in the FD clause of line 24.

2. Make an appropriate entry in the ASSIGN clause at line 16.

3. Move the inline code at lines 44–49 to a separate module; name it 150-PROCESS-LOOP. Change the PERFORM to an out-of-line PERFORM that refers to 150-PROCESS-LOOP. Delete the END-PERFORM at line 50.

4. If necessary, move separate-line paragraph-ending periods to the end of the preceding line.

Creating a New File

If you are preparing a new application and must create new files, it is best to use a two-step process. One program should create a new file (usually, this is a one-time activity). The other program should allow for record entry, as does PATADD of the preceding section. The file-creation program, shown in Figure 4-5, would actually be a short utility. Since the program does not address individual fields, the record is defined as an elementary item of length 68.

COBOL-74

The following changes to PATCRE8 are required to convert it to a COBOL-74 program:

1. Insert the CONFIGURATION SECTION and insert the LABEL RECORDS clause in the FD clause.

2. Make an appropriate entry in the ASSIGN clause.

3. Delete the END-IF at line 43 and insert a period at the end of line 42.

4. If necessary, move the period at line 45 to the end of line 44.

Figure 4-5   Program to create a new file—PATCRE8.

```
 1        IDENTIFICATION DIVISION.              24
 2        PROGRAM-ID.    PATCRE8.               25    WORKING-STORAGE SECTION.
 3                                              26
 4    *      W. PRICE 1/9/95                    27    01  SW-SWITCHES.
 5                                              28        05  SW-CREATE-FILE            PIC X(1).
 6    *      This program creates a new patron file.   29
 7                                              30
 8                                              31    PROCEDURE DIVISION.
 9        ENVIRONMENT DIVISION.                 32
10                                              33    000-CREATE-PATRON-FILE.
11        INPUT-OUTPUT SECTION.                 34        DISPLAY "THIS PROGRAM CREATES A NEW PATRON FILE"
12                                              35        DISPLAY " "
13        FILE-CONTROL.                         36        DISPLAY "Do you want to create a new PATRON file <Y/N>? "
14            SELECT PATRON-FILE                37            WITH NO ADVANCING
15                ASSIGN TO (system dependent). 38        ACCEPT SW-RESPONSE
16                                              39        IF SW-RESPONSE = "Y"
17                                              40            OPEN OUTPUT PATRON-FILE
18        DATA DIVISION.                        41            CLOSE PATRON-FILE
19                                              42            DISPLAY "File created"
20        FILE SECTION.                         43        END-IF
21                                              44        STOP RUN
22        FD  PATRON-FILE.                      45        .
23        01  PATRON-RECORD             PIC X(68).
```

Displaying Records from the Patron File

Program Planning

In Chapter 3, you printed a listing of the patron file records—one line of the output report per record. You could easily send your listing output to the screen by using DISPLAY statements. The problem with this approach is that, for a long file, most of the records scroll off the screen quickly. In Chapter 8, you will learn techniques for avoiding this by counting the number of records displayed and temporarily stopping the output when the screen becomes full. The alternative for now is to display one record at a time, using a full-screen display as illustrated in Figure 4-6. As with the program PATADD, an announcement is displayed and the user is

Figure 4-6   Sample screen for record display.

```
This program allows you to display records,
one at a time, from the patron file.
Enter the letter Y (capital letter only)
if you want to continue.
Enter N if you want to abort this operation.

Do you want to continue <Y/N>? Y          ————— User response


        Patron name: Acton, Jocelyn

            Address: 223 Connecticut St

     City-State-Zip: San Francisco, CA 94107

Target contribution: 0350

Actual contribution: 0350

Do you want to display another record <Y/N>? _   ————— Cursor is here,
                                                        awaiting user response
```

given the option to proceed or to abort the run. In this case, the response is to continue. The next five lines display, appropriately labeled, the five fields from the first record of the file. Then the user is queried about continuing.

With PATADD, the loop is repeated until a keyboard response indicates that no more records will be entered. The display program is different in this respect. That is, records can be displayed until the user indicates that no more are desired or until the end of the file is encountered. Consequently, the overall program logic of this program is slightly different, as illustrated by Figure 4-7's pseudocode. As you can see, conditional execution of the 200-Display module is controlled exclusively by the Perform statement (Number 3) and the Not At End of the Read.

A Program to Display Records from the Patron File—PATDISP

In Figure 4-8's program, you can see that repeated execution of the 200 module is controlled by the switch SW-ANOTHER-RECORD. That switch is used in the two ACCEPT statements of lines 79—the initial request to continue or abort—and 62. If the user elects to abort by entering other than Y at line 79, the loop controlled by the line 49 PERFORM is not executed and execution falls through to line 66.

Execution of the 200 module repeats until: (1) the user enters other than Y at line 62, or (2) the end of file is detected and the switch is changed to N at line 52.

You can see in the DISPLAY statements of the 200 module that the field descriptions are positioned so that the data is printed one field above the other (also, refer to Figure 4-6's sample output). Each of these DISPLAY statements includes a descriptive literal, a space, and the field name. You can separate the literal and field name by a comma and space if it helps make the form more readable. The comma is optional and is ignored by the compiler. As with PATADD, the DISPLAY with quotes enclosing a space causes a blank line to be inserted between other display lines.

One other item is of interest: the ACCEPT statement at line 56. If you want to display a message upon program termination, it is a good idea to include an ACCEPT to halt the computer so that the user can read the message. Otherwise, it may disappear from the screen when your COBOL system takes over. Any

Figure 4-7
Pseudocode to display records of the patron file.

```
000-Display-Patron-Records.
  1. Perform 100-Display-Announce-Screen.
  2. Open patron file.
  3. Perform until not more-display.
        Read patron file
        At End
              a. Set more-display to False
              b. Display EOF message to user
              c. Await user response
        Not At End
              a. Perform 200-Display-Patron-Record
              b. Query user about more-display

100-Display-Announce-Screen.
  1. Display description of program.
  2. Query user about continuing.

200-Display-Patron-Record.
  1. Display the following fields
        Patron name
        Street address
        City-state-zip
        Target amount
        Actual amount
```

Figure 4-8   Interactive program to display records of the patron file—PATDISP.

```
 1        IDENTIFICATION DIVISION.               48    **************Processing Sequence**************
 2        PROGRAM-ID.    PATDISP.                49        PERFORM UNTIL SW-ANOTHER-RECORD IS NOT EQUAL TO "Y"
 3                                               50            READ PATRON-FILE
 4     *      W. PRICE 1/9/95                     51                AT END
 5                                               52                    MOVE "N" TO SW-ANOTHER-RECORD
 6     *    This program allows the user to display 53                DISPLAY " "
 7     *    records from the patron file.        54                    DISPLAY "The above is the last record of the file."
 8                                               55                    DISPLAY " Press Enter to terminate the program."
 9                                               56                    ACCEPT WA-WAIT-FOR-USER
10        ENVIRONMENT DIVISION.                  57                NOT AT END
11                                               58                    PERFORM 200-DISPLAY-PATRON-RECORD
12        INPUT-OUTPUT SECTION.                  59                    DISPLAY " "
13                                               60                    DISPLAY "Do you want to display another record <Y/N>? "
14        FILE-CONTROL.                          61                        WITH NO ADVANCING
15            SELECT PATRON-FILE                 62                    ACCEPT SW-ANOTHER-RECORD
16                ASSIGN TO (system dependent).  63            END-READ
17                                               64        END-PERFORM
18                                               65    **************Termination Sequence*************
19                                               66        CLOSE PATRON-FILE
20        DATA DIVISION.                         67        STOP RUN
21                                               68        .
22        FILE SECTION.                          69    ***************************************************
23                                               70    100-DISPLAY-ANNOUNCE-SCREEN.
24        FD  PATRON-FILE.                       71        DISPLAY "This program allows you to display records,"
25        01  PATRON-RECORD.                     72        DISPLAY "one at a time, from the patron file. "
26            05  PR-NAME           PIC X(18).   73        DISPLAY "Enter the letter Y (capital letter only)"
27            05  PR-ADDRESS        PIC X(18).   74        DISPLAY "if you want to continue."
28            05  PR-CITY-STATE-ZIP PIC X(24).   75        DISPLAY "Enter N if you want to abort this operation."
29            05  PR-TARGET-CONTR   PIC 9(4).    76        DISPLAY " "
30            05  PR-ACTUAL-CONTR   PIC 9(4).    77        DISPLAY "Do you want to continue <Y/N>? "
31                                               78            WITH NO ADVANCING
32        WORKING-STORAGE SECTION.               79        ACCEPT SW-ANOTHER-RECORD
33                                               80        DISPLAY " "
34        01  SW-SWITCHES.                       81        .
35            05  SW-ANOTHER-RECORD PIC X(1).    82    200-DISPLAY-PATRON-RECORD.
36                                               83        DISPLAY " "
37        01  WA-WORK-AREA.                      84        DISPLAY "       Patron name: " PR-NAME
38            05  WA-WAIT-FOR-USER  PIC X(1).    85        DISPLAY " "
39                                               86        DISPLAY "          Address: " PR-ADDRESS
40                                               87        DISPLAY " "
41        PROCEDURE DIVISION.                    88        DISPLAY "   City-State-Zip: " PR-CITY-STATE-ZIP
42                                               89        DISPLAY " "
43        000-DISPLAY-PATRON-RECORDS.            90        DISPLAY "Target contribution: " PR-TARGET-CONTR
44    ************Initialization Sequence*************  91        DISPLAY " "
45            OPEN INPUT PATRON-FILE             92        DISPLAY "Actual contribution: " PR-ACTUAL-CONTR
46            PERFORM 100-DISPLAY-ANNOUNCE-SCREEN 93       DISPLAY " "
47                                               94        .
```

field name could be used with the ACCEPT of line 56, but one *must* be included according to the statement syntax. WA-WAIT-FOR-USER is specifically defined for this purpose. Actually, any data-item could specified here, but it is poor documentation to use, for instance, SW-ANOTHER-RECORD.

COBOL-74

The following changes to PATDISP are required to convert it to a COBOL-74 program:

1. Insert the CONFIGURATION SECTION and insert the LABEL RECORDS clause in the FD clause.

2. Modify the READ sequence to eliminate the NOT AT END. Do this by using the priming READ form (Figure 3-16, page 86) or by replacing the NOT AT END with an appropriate IF statement (Figure 3-17).

3. If necessary, move separate-line paragraph-ending periods to the end of the preceding line.

Chapter Summary

The DISPLAY statement provides for low-volume output to the console. Any combination of literals and data-items can be displayed from a single DISPLAY.

The ACCEPT statement provides for low-volume input from the keyboard. Only one data-item can appear in the list of an ACCEPT statement.

Opening a file for output causes COBOL to erase, without warning, an existing file of the same name.

The OPEN EXTEND opens an existing file for output without destroying its contents. It allows records to be added to the end of the file.

Exercises

Terms for Definition

batch processing
interactive processing

Review Questions

1. Show the exact appearance of the resulting line or lines as displayed on the screen after execution of each of the following. Assume that AF-FIELD contains ABCDEF and AN-FIELD contains 12345.
   a. `DISPLAY "AF-FIELD = ", AF-FIELD`
   b. `DISPLAY "AF-FIELD = " WITH NO ADVANCING`
      `DISPLAY  AF-FIELD`
   c. `DISPLAY AF-FIELD,    AN-FIELD`
   d. `DISPLAY AF-FIELD, " ", AN-FIELD`

2. In response to a prompt, a user types A1578. Show the exact appearance of the resulting line or lines as displayed on the screen after the user entry for each of the following:
   a. `DISPLAY "Please enter your code:"`
      `ACCEPT CA-CODE`
   b. `DISPLAY "Please enter your code:" WITH NO ADVANCING`
      `ACCEPT CA-CODE`
   c. `DISPLAY "Please enter your code:" WITH NO ADVANCING`
      `DISPLAY " "`
      `ACCEPT CA-CODE`
   d. `DISPLAY "Please enter your code:  " WITH NO ADVANCING`
      `ACCEPT CA-CODE`

3. How are the open modes OUTPUT and EXTEND similar? How are they different?

4. How are the open modes INPUT and EXTEND similar? How are they different?

Programming Assignments

1. In Chapter 3, you wrote a program for one or more of the programming assignments. For the data file of each program written in Chapter 3, write a corresponding program that allows you to display the records of the file, one at a time. Provide the user with the ability to terminate the program at any time.

2. Make a copy of the data file for which you wrote a program in Chapter 3 and give it another name. Then write a program that allows you to add additional records to the file. When finished, enter several new records, then print a listing using your Chapter 3 program.

IMPROVING THE APPEARANCE OF COMPUTER OUTPUT

Note

The first topic of this chapter, "PICTURE Clauses," gives you many helpful tools. It covers a wide variety of editing features—much more than you will need to complete the chapter's assignments. Mastering all of these editing features is not essential now. It is more important that you become familiar enough with them so that when your program requires extensive editing, you will recognize the forms and remember where to find them.

CHAPTER OUTLINE

CHAPTER

5

CHAPTER OBJECTIVES

Example programs so far read input data and printed it. However, the form of the output was not designed to help end users interpret the data—just to receive it. This chapter's focus is on making an output report more descriptive and easier to read. From this chapter, you will learn the following:

- The five categories of PICTURE clauses:

    Numeric

    Alphabetic

    Alphanumeric

    Numeric-edited

    Alphanumeric-edited

- Editing that lets you:

    Suppress leading zeros and replace with spaces or asterisks

    Insert punctuation such as the decimal point and the comma

    Insert a minus or a plus sign

    Insert a dollar sign

- Features of the MOVE statement in moving data from one type of field to another—for example, the editing action that occurs when a numeric field is moved to a numeric-edited item.

- The VALUE clause, which allows you to define an initial value in a field of the WORKING-STORAGE SECTION.

- Defining output lines as part of the WORKING-STORAGE SECTION, then moving them to the output area (defined under the FD) before printing.

- The READ/INTO statement.

- Options that can be used with the DISPLAY for screen display.

- Options that can be used with the ACCEPT for keyboard input.

TOPIC

PICTURE Clauses

Basic PICTURE Symbols

From the patron programs, you saw that PICTURE clauses specify the following attributes of an elementary data-item:

1. The data class of the field:

   alphanumeric (indicated with the X symbol)

   numeric (indicated with the 9 symbol)

2. The length of the field

In addition to the symbols X and 9, four other basic symbols exist. One of them, the symbol P, is used for decimal scaling; it is not utilized in this book.

Alphabetic Symbol

The alphabetic symbol denotes a field that can contain only letters of the alphabet and the space (no special characters or digits). The A symbol offers little advantage over the alphanumeric designator and is not used in this book.

Assumed Decimal Point

The patron programs used whole dollar amounts, not dollars and cents, to simplify your first experiences with COBOL. So the input fields were defined with the following PICTURE:

```
PICTURE 9(4)
```

If the data is stored in the file with dollars and cents, it is necessary to designate a decimal point position. For instance, that portion of the input record definition might read as follows:

Field	Columns	Format
Target contribution	61–66	*nnnn͵nn*
Actual contribution	67–72	*nnnn͵nn*

Where *nnnn͵nn* means a six-position field with an assumed decimal point between the fourth and fifth digits.

Notice that the decimal point is not stored in the field, so typical values in these two fields might appear beginning position 61 as:

128075201550

The first six digits, 128075, are the target contribution and represent 1280.75; the next 6 digits, 201550, are the actual contribution and represent 2015.50. Since the decimal point is not stored with the field, the PICTURE clause must indicate its assumed position.

V   Indicates an **assumed decimal point.** When included in a PICTURE, V indicates the position of the assumed decimal point in the number. Since the field will not include an actual decimal point, the V does not cause storage to be reserved. Since a single numeric field value can contain only one decimal point, only one V is allowed in a PICTURE string. If a V is not present, the decimal is assumed to be immediately to the right of the field's rightmost digit. The Target-contribution field just discussed could be defined as either of the following:

```
PR-TARGET-CONTR PICTURE 9999V99
PR-TARGET-CONTR PICTURE 9(4)V9(2)
```

Signed Fields

Any field that may be negative must have an explicit sign designation in its PIC-TURE or the sign is discarded.

S   Indicates that the field might include an arithmetic sign. Generally, a signed field should be specified for:

- Any input-record numeric fields that might be negative.

- All WORKING-STORAGE fields used for computations if any possibility of a negative calculated result exists.

- Any numeric field that might receive data from a signed field.

For example, if the field AR-CURRENT-BALANCE is a calculated field that could contain a negative value, it might be defined as follows:

```
AR-CURRENT-BALANCE PICTURE S9999V99
```

A Simple Editing Example

You probably noticed that although the patron reports print the desired results, the form of the output is not particularly helpful. Compare the report lines of Figure 5-1(a) to those of 5-1(b), in which the fields include dollars and cents. The value of some simple editing on the numeric fields is evident. Eliminating the nonsignificant leading zeros and inserting the comma and decimal point make the report much easier to interpret.

Generally, you can consider **editing** as the operation of changing the form of an output field so that it is more meaningful. This is done by moving the data to an output field defined with an appropriate edit PICTURE. For instance, where the input field for PR-TARGET-CONTR is defined with PIC 9999V99, the output field could be defined with PIC 9,999.99. As you can see, this output PIC includes a comma and a period, which corresponds to the form you desire for the printed

Figure 5-1   Typical report output.

```
Acton, Jocelyn     San Francisco, CA 94107   035050   035050
Anderson, Hazel    Woodside, CA 94062        125000   110000   015000
Baker, Donald      Berkeley, CA 94703        037550   030000   007550
Broadhurst, Ryan   Big Trees, CA 95066       150000   150000


(a) Without editing numeric output.



Acton, Jocelyn     San Francisco, CA 94107     350.50     350.50
Anderson, Hazel    Woodside, CA 94062        1,250.00   1,100.00   150.00
Baker, Donald      Berkeley, CA 94703          375.50     300.50    75.50
Broadhurst, Ryan   Big Trees, CA 95066       1,500.00   1,500.00


(b) With editing numeric output.
```

Figure 5-2
Editing by moving data to
an editing PICTURE.

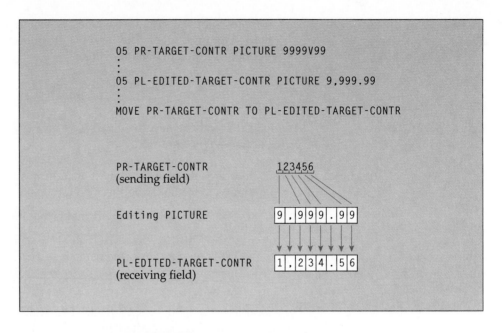

output. This field definition is called a **numeric-edited item.** For your first look at how editing works, let's consider Figure 5-2's example.

The action that takes place during the MOVE operation is as follows:

1. The positions of the decimal point—assumed in the sending field and actual in the receiving field—are aligned. This is critical if the sending field has a different length than the receiving field.
2. Digits from the sending field are moved into corresponding positions of the receiving field containing the 9 PICTURE symbol.
3. Data from the sending field does not disturb "punctuation" defined in the receiving field PICTURE.

As you will learn, editing is done on both numeric and alphanumeric fields. However, numeric editing is by far the most common. In fact, you will use it almost every time you print a numeric field. Like the 9 and V PICTURE symbols that signify a numeric field, 15 different symbols signify a numeric-edited field. The COBOL Standard breaks these down into the following five categories: zero suppression and replacement, simple insertion, special insertion, fixed insertion, and floating insertion. Figure 5-3 summarizes them.

Numeric Editing— Decimal and Comma

Inserting a Decimal Point

Although the computer can utilize assumed decimal points for internal processing, human processing usually demands that the decimal point be displayed on the output. So, the actual decimal point is almost always specified for report and display screen output. The decimal point is called a **special insertion** character (it is the only one) because, in addition to the insertion editing, it specifies how data from the sending field is decimal-point aligned in the editing field.

When the decimal-point editing symbol is specified, as illustrated in Figure 5-4's examples, it is printed, not just assumed. Contrast this actual decimal-point editing PICTURE symbol with the assumed decimal-point V symbol. Recognize that although the assumed decimal-point V symbol does not occupy a storage position, the actual decimal point requires one position.

Obviously, only one decimal-point symbol can be specified in a PICTURE character-string. Also, because a decimal-point symbol as the rightmost character

Figure 5-3
Numeric editing PICTURE
symbols by category.

Data category	Symbol	Meaning
Suppression and replacement	Z	Zero suppression with space replacement
	*	Zero suppression with asterisk replacement
Simple insertion	,	Comma
	/	Slash (stroke, diagonal)
	B	Blank space
	0	Zero
Special insertion	.	Decimal point
Fixed insertion	–	Minus sign (fixed)
	+	Plus sign (fixed)
	CR	Credit symbol
	DB	Debit symbol
	$	Dollar sign (fixed)
Floating insertion	–	Minus sign (floating)
	+	Plus sign (floating)
	$	Dollar sign (floating)

Figure 5-4
Decimal-point insertion
examples.

Special Insertion (Decimal-Point) Editing

Data in storage	Edit field PICTURE	Edited result
103256	PIC 9999.99	1032.56
002500	PIC 9999.99	0025.00
250	PIC 9999.99	0025.00
7	PIC 9999.99	0007.00
000894	PIC 999.99	008.94
00002	PIC 999.99	000.02
000003	PIC 999.99	000.00
103256	PIC 999.999	103.256

Note: ▲ indicates assumed decimal-point location.

of a PICTURE character-string might be interpreted by the compiler as an end-of-sentence period, the decimal-point editing symbol cannot be specified there.

**Inserting One
or More Commas**

When we write integer number values in our everyday lives, we place a comma to the left of each group of three digits so that the number is easier to read. The typical use for the comma PICTURE symbol in COBOL is exactly the same. Figure 5-5 shows some examples of **simple insertion**. Although by tradition we often insert commas three digits from one another, comma symbols can be placed anywhere in the PICTURE character-string—except as the rightmost symbol.

Figure 5-5
Comma insertion examples.

Comma Insertion		
Data in storage	**Edit field PICTURE**	**Edited result**
12345	PIC 99,999	12,345
00020	PIC 99,999	00,020
123456	PIC 9,999.99	1,234.56
012345	PIC 9,999.99	0,123.45
12345	PIC 9,999.99	0,123.45
143002104	PIC 9,999,999.99	1,430,021.04

Note: ▲ indicates assumed decimal-point location.

Numeric Editing— Zero Suppression

Replacement with Spaces

The lengths of most numeric fields are usually greater than most of the data values recorded in them (for instance, the four-digit actual contribution field might contain the two-digit data value 65). When a data value occupies less than the total number of a numeric field's positions, the leftmost positions will contain zeros. These **leading zeros** are alternatively referred to as *leftmost zeros* or *high-order zeros*. Obviously, leading zeros do not affect the value of the data contained in a field. Since they are not needed, they are normally replaced by spaces on printed reports; for instance, 00803 is printed as 803 preceded by two spaces. This action of replacing leading zeros with spaces is called **zero suppression and replacement**. In the value 803, observe that the zero between the eight and the three is not suppressed because it is not a leading zero (it is preceded by a digit other than zero).

COBOL provides for leading-zero suppression with space replacement through the symbol Z, probably the most frequently used editing symbol. Examples of its use are shown in Figure 5-6. In the fourth whole number and second assumed decimal examples, notice that nothing is printed for 0 because all positions are replaced with spaces. In the assumed decimal example where a value 0 is edited into ZZZ.ZZ, you can see that the decimal point is suppressed; it makes no sense to leave it with no digits. Also, if a significant digit does not occur to the

Figure 5-6
Zero suppression and blank-space replacement editing examples.

Zero Suppression and Space Replacement Editing					
With Whole-Number Quantities			**With Assumed Decimal Positioning**		
Data in storage	**Edit field PICTURE**	**Edited result**	**Data in storage**	**Edit field PICTURE**	**Edited result**
10358	PIC ZZ,ZZZ	10,358	00002	PIC ZZZ.ZZ	.02
00803	PIC ZZ,ZZZ	803	00000	PIC ZZZ.ZZ	
00002	PIC ZZ,ZZZ	2	02500	PIC ZZZ.99	25.00
00000	PIC ZZ,ZZZ		00089	PIC ZZ9.99	0.89
00017	PIC ZZ,ZZ9	17	00089	PIC ZZZ.99	.89
00005	PIC ZZ,ZZ9	5	00002	PIC ZZZ.99	.02
00000	PIC ZZ,ZZ9	0	00000	PIC ZZZ.99	.00

Note: ▲ indicates assumed decimal point location.

left of the comma in the whole number examples, the comma is suppressed and replaced by the space character.

Often it is appropriate to zero-suppress all but a certain number of the right-most positions of a field. For instance, in several examples, a 9 symbol specifies unconditional printing of digit positions, even though they may be leading zeros.

For zero suppression, you can specify any combination of Zs and 9s, but the Z symbols must precede the 9 symbols. In other words, a Z symbol cannot appear to the right of a 9 symbol.

Furthermore, you cannot include a combination of Z and 9 symbols to the right of the decimal point. That is, PIC ZZ,ZZZ.Z9 is not valid.

Replacement with Asterisks

In some cases, leading zeros are considered undesirable, but it is not desirable to leave the positions blank. For instance, on a computer-printed check, blank spaces preceding a dollar amount could be replaced with digits to fraudulently increase the check's value. By replacing leading zeros with asterisks (called **asterisk check protection**), tampering with the check amount is more difficult and readability is improved by eliminating leading zeros.

When an asterisk is specified in the PICTURE character-string, leading zeros are replaced by asterisks. In Figure 5-7's examples, you can see that replacement with asterisk is identical to replacement with space, except that the decimal point is not eliminated with a zero amount. Syntax rules are equivalent to those for the Z symbol: Any combination of * symbols and 9 symbols may be specified, but the * symbols must precede the 9 symbols.

Floating Dollar (Currency) Sign

The **floating dollar (currency) sign*** gives you the capability to suppress leading zeros and position a dollar sign to the immediate left of the printed number (with no intervening spaces). As you can see by Figure 5-8's examples, the floating dollar sign symbol is coded in the leftmost position of the PICTURE character-string and is repeated for each position through which it should float. In this sense, its inclusion in the PICTURE clause is the same as that of the Z and * symbols.

Figure 5-7
Zero suppression and asterisk replacement editing examples.

Zero Suppression and Asterisk Replacement Editing

With Whole-Number Quantities			With Assumed Decimal Positioning		
Data in storage	Edit field PICTURE	Edited result	Data in storage	Edit field PICTURE	Edited result
10358	PIC **,***	10,358	00002	PIC ***.**	***.02
00803	PIC **,***	***803	00000	PIC ***.**	***.**
00002	PIC **,***	*****2	02500	PIC ***.99	*25.00
00000	PIC **,***	******	00089	PIC **9.99	**0.89
00017	PIC **,**9	****17	00089	PIC ***.99	***.89
00005	PIC **,**9	*****5	00002	PIC ***.99	***.02
00000	PIC **,**9	*****0	00000	PIC ***.99	***.00

Note: ▲ indicates assumed decimal-point location.

---

*Actually, the currency sign can represent any currency unit: dollars, pounds, francs, marks, and so on. However, in the United States, the floating currency sign is commonly referred to as the floating dollar sign. The currency sign can be changed to other monetary symbols through the SPECIAL-NAMES paragraph of the ENVIRONMENT DIVISION.

Figure 5-8
Floating insertion
editing—dollar sign.

Floating Insertion Editing—Dollar Sign		
Data in storage	Edit field PICTURE	Edited result
104705	PIC $$,$$$.99	$1,047.05
004705	PIC $$,$$$.99	$47.05
000007	PIC $$,$$$.99	$.07
000007	PIC $$,$$9.99	$0.07
000000	PIC $$,$$$.99	$.00
000000	PIC $$,$$$.$$	

Note: ▲ indicates assumed decimal-point location.

Be careful not to make the number of dollar signs exactly equal to the number of zero suppression digits in data value: One extra position is required for the output line. For example,

    PIC ZZ9

is sufficient for the data value 382, but

    PIC $$9

is not because the edited result $382 requires four positions; PIC $$$9 is needed.

Floating Plus and Minus

COBOL includes several means of denoting signs for fields that include a sign (were defined with the S PICTURE symbol). The plus sign (+) symbol is used in exactly the same way as the floating dollar sign symbol. The only difference, as Figure 5-9 illustrates, is that the insertion character is either plus or a minus, depending upon the sign of the sending field. As with the dollar sign, the plus symbol requires an extra position in the receiving field.

The minus sign (–) symbol works the same, except that the sign itself is printed only if the data value is negative. Otherwise, the suppression yields a space. Figure 5-10 illustrates the floating minus sign.

Figure 5-9
Floating insertion
editing—plus sign.

Floating Insertion Editing—Plus Sign			
Data in storage	Sign	Edit field PICTURE	Edited result
218079	–	PIC ++,+++.99	-2,180.79
018079	–	PIC ++,+++.99	-180.79
018079	+	PIC ++,+++.99	+180.79
018079	(no sign)	PIC ++,+++.99	+180.79
000000	(no sign)	PIC ++,+++.99	+.00
000000	(no sign)	PIC ++,+++.++	

Note: ▲ indicates assumed decimal-point location.

Figure 5-10
Floating insertion
editing—minus sign.

Floating Insertion Editing—Minus Sign			
Data in storage	Sign	Edit field PICTURE	Edited result
108659	–	PIC --,---.99	-1,086.59
003000	–	PIC --,---.99	-30.00
003000	+	PIC --,---.99	30.00
003000	(no sign)	PIC --,---.99	30.00
000000	(no sign)	PIC --,---.99	.00
000000	(no sign)	PIC --,---.--	

Note: ▲ indicates assumed decimal-point location.

Numeric Editing— Fixed Position Insertion

With **fixed position insertion**, editing symbols are limited to placement at certain locations within the PICTURE character-string. This contrasts with, for example, the floating dollar sign, where the dollar sign placement depends upon the size of the data value. There are five fixed insertion symbols. Four of them—the – (minus sign), the + (plus sign), CR (credit symbol), and DB (debit symbol)—are conditional PICTURE symbols depending upon the sign of the data field. The fifth fixed insertion symbol is the $ (currency sign).

Fixed Plus and Minus

The fixed plus and minus are similar to their floating counterparts, except (1) the sign is placed in a fixed position independent of the data field size and (2) the sign may be positioned at either the left or the right of the field. The examples of the fixed plus shown in Figure 5-11 illustrate how you use this symbol.

Figure 5-11
Fixed insertion
editing—plus sign.

Fixed Insertion Editing—Plus Sign			
Data in storage	Sign	Edit field PICTURE	Edited result
12345	+	PIC ZZ,ZZ9+	12,345+
02345	–	PIC ZZ,ZZ9+	2,345-
00000	(no sign)	PIC ZZ,ZZ9+	0+
180056	–	PIC Z,ZZZ.99+	1,800.56-
080056	+	PIC Z,ZZZ.99+	800.56+
000000	(no sign)	PIC Z,ZZZ.99+	.00+
12345	+	PIC +ZZ,ZZ9	+12,345
02345	–	PIC +ZZ,ZZ9	- 2,345
00000	(no sign)	PIC +ZZ,ZZ9	+ 0
180056	–	PIC +Z,ZZZ.99	-1,800.56
080056	+	PIC +Z,ZZZ.99	+ 800.56
000000	(no sign)	PIC +Z,ZZZ.99	+ .00

Note: ▲ indicates assumed decimal-point location.

The fixed minus sign allows a minus sign to be printed if the data value is negative. If the value is positive or zero, a blank space appears in the minus-sign location. Figure 5-12 illustrates the fixed minus.

Credit Symbol CR and Debit Symbol DR

The **credit symbol (CR)** operates in a manner similar to that of the fixed minus sign, except (1) it occupies two character-positions and (2) it must occupy the rightmost positions of the PICTURE. You can see from the examples of Figure 5-13 that if the data value placed in the field is negative, the letters CR print; otherwise, the two positions are blank.

In these examples, notice that you can either position the CR adjacent to the digit specification or include a space between the digits and the CR symbol (the B symbol is described later in this section). Assuming there's enough room on the report line, the space makes for easier reading.

A credit symbol typically is preferred to the minus sign for external and formal reports because it provides a more visually definite indication. For internal reports, the minus sign is commonly used because it needs only one print position and so conserves valuable space on a print line or display screen.

The **debit symbol (DB)** works exactly like the credit symbol; it indicates a negative amount. That is, when DB is specified and the data value is negative, DB prints. If the data value is positive or zero, two blank spaces appear.

The CR or the DB are commonly used in accounting. Which of the two is used in a particular instance depends upon the accounting application.

Fixed Dollar (Currency) Sign

The fixed dollar (currency) sign symbol is used to print a dollar sign preceding a number at a fixed location. The fixed dollar sign can only be specified once and it must be the leftmost symbol of the PICTURE character-string, as illustrated in Figure 5-14. Notice that if the data value may be negative, provisions must be made for the sign or it will be lost. If the minus insertion symbol is used, it must be positioned to the right.

The fixed dollar sign is commonly used to indicate columnar dollar amounts on the first line and on total lines of formal accounting reports such as balance sheets and income statements.

Figure 5-12
Fixed insertion editing—minus sign.

Fixed Insertion Editing—Minus Sign			
Data in storage	Sign	Edit field PICTURE	Edited result
02345	−	PIC ZZ,ZZ9-	2,345-
02345	+	PIC ZZ,ZZ9-	2,345
00000	(no sign)	PIC ZZ,ZZ9-	0
080056	−	PIC Z,ZZZ.99-	800.56-
080056	+	PIC Z,ZZZ.99-	800.56
000000	(no sign)	PIC Z,ZZZ.99-	.00
02345	−	PIC -ZZ,ZZ9	- 2,345
02345	+	PIC -ZZ,ZZ9	2,345
00000	(no sign)	PIC -ZZ,ZZ9	0
080056	−	PIC -Z,ZZZ.99	- 800.56
080056	+	PIC -Z,ZZZ.99	800.56
000000	(no sign)	PIC -Z,ZZZ.99	.00

Note: ▲ indicates assumed decimal-point location.

Figure 5-13
Fixed insertion
editing—credit (CR).

Fixed Insertion Editing—Credit

Data in storage	Sign	Edit field PICTURE	Edited result
22500	–	PIC ZZZ.99CR	225.00CR
22500	+	PIC ZZZ.99CR	225.00
00000	(no sign)	PIC ZZZ.99CR	.00
22500	–	PIC ZZZ.99BCR	225.00 CR
22500	+	PIC ZZZ.99BCR	225.00

Note: ▲ indicates assumed decimal-point location.

Figure 5-14
Fixed insertion
editing—dollar sign.

Fixed Insertion Editing—Dollar Sign

Data in storage	Sign	Edit field PICTURE	Edited result
151207	(no sign)	PIC $Z,ZZZ.99	$1,512.07
00008	(no sign)	PIC $ZZZ.99	$ .08
00008	(no sign)	PIC $ZZZ.99	$ 0.08
00700	–	PIC $999.99	$007.00
00700	–	PIC $ZZZ.99-	$ 7.00-
00700	–	PIC $ZZZ.99CR	$ 7.00CR

Note: ▲ indicates assumed decimal-point location.

Simple Insertion Editing—Slash, Blank, and Zero

In addition to the comma, three other simple insertion editing symbols exist: the / (slash), the B (space), and the 0 (zero). Like the period, each of the simple insertion characters, when inserted into a field, requires a separate storage position.

The insertion symbol / (slash) has its most frequent use as a separator between the month, day, and year subfields of numeric-defined dates. Suppose you have an input field defined as numeric that contains a date expressed in six-digit month-day-year format (*mmddyy*—two digits for each month, day, and year). Just as decimal points are not typically stored in numeric amount fields, the month/day/year separating slashes are not normally stored in date fields. Editing of the date can be accomplished with an appropriate edit field PICTURE, as illustrated by Figure 5-15's examples. You should know that dates stored in *yymmdd* format require that each component (month, day, and year) be moved if the desired output format is *mm/dd/yy* (see Chapter 3's example of editing with the MOVE).

Also, notice that slash inserting is not limited to date formats. Any number of / symbols can be specified at any location in a PICTURE character-string.

The space insertion symbol B allows you to separate parts of a field with spaces. For instance, in Figure 5-16's second example, you see the three parts of a Social Security number separated by spaces. As with the slash character, any number of B symbols can be specified at any location in a PICTURE character-string.

Figure 5-15
Simple insertion
editing—slash.

Simple Insertion Editing—Slash		
Data in storage	Edit field PICTURE	Edited result
122595	PIC 99/99/99	12/25/95
030795	PIC 99/99/99	03/07/95
030795	PIC Z9/99/99	3/07/95
516	PIC 99/9	51/6

Figure 5-16
Simple insertion
editing—blank space.

Simple Insertion Editing—Blank Space		
Data in storage	Edit field PICTURE	Edited result
112495	PIC 99B99B99	11 24 95
566509224	PIC 999B99B9999	566 50 9224
2468	PIC 9B9B9B9	2 4 6 8

The insertion symbol 0 (zero) has only a few uses. One example can be drawn from the bean business. Beans and many other dry commodities are sold in bulk by hundred-pound units. If each bean sale is recorded in a field assigned PIC 9(4), the number of pounds of beans sold is always a hundred times greater than the value stored. Suppose a certain output requires the number of pounds sold to be expressed in single-pound units rather than hundredweights. Figure 5-17 shows how to do this with zero insertion.

Other Editing Topics

Alphanumeric-Edited Data-Items

You can see that COBOL includes a wide variety of editing capabilities for numeric fields. On the other hand, there is only one category of alphanumeric editing symbols—those that can be used with the X symbol. The symbols are the simple insertion symbols: / (slash), B (blank space), and 0 (zero). The **alphanumeric editing symbols** are specified and operate exactly like their numeric editing

Figure 5-17
Simple insertion
editing—zero.

Simple Insertion Editing—Zero		
Data in storage	Edit field PICTURE	Edited result
0150	PIC 999900	015000
0150	PIC ZZZ900	15000
015	PIC ZZZ.900	15.000
000	PIC ZZZ.900	000
000	PIC ZZZ.Z00	00

Figure 5-18
Alphanumeric
editing examples.

Alphanumeric Editing Examples			
Symbol	Data in storage	Edit field PICTURE	Edited result
Slash	122595	PIC XX/XX/XX	12/25/95
	030796	PIC XX/XX/XX	03/07/96
	ABC	PIC XX/X	AB/C
Blank space	122595	PIC XXBXXBXX	12 25 95
	XYZ	PIC XBXX	X YZ
	ABC123	PIC XBXX/XXX	A BC/123
Zero	A10	PIC XXX0	A100
	12	PIC 0XX	012

counterparts, except that they are used in conjunction with the alphanumeric PICTURE symbol X, rather than the numeric PICTURE symbols. Figure 5-18 shows examples of alphanumeric editing.

Warning About PICTURE Clauses

When forming a PICTURE clause, be certain to always choose symbols from one data class: numeric, alphabetic, or alphanumeric. Figure 5-19 lists the PICTURE symbols organized by data class. *Symbols cannot be mixed across class lines.* For example, specifying PIC XX,XXX causes the compiler to identify the clause as invalid because it contains both alphanumeric (X) and numeric editing (the comma) symbols.

The BLANK WHEN ZERO Clause

Although BLANK WHEN ZERO is a clause separate from the PICTURE clause, it is closely related because it also controls data output.

Sometimes a numeric editing PICTURE clause is specified for a field, but the editing is not wanted when the value of the edited field is zero. As an example, suppose you have a date represented in an input field by a PICTURE character-string of 9(6). For the output report, the editing PICTURE is 99/99/99. However, not all input records have a date present in the input field; when absent, the date field contains zeros. As a result, those records lacking a date are printed as 00/00/00. Normally, users prefer that a date field be blank rather than printed with zero values. In other words, the desired processing is to edit the date in accordance with the PICTURE clause, but print nothing if the input field value contains zero.

You can use the BLANK WHEN ZERO clause to achieve this result. When the clause is coded for a data-item description entry, it causes the field to be blanked

Figure 5-19
PICTURE symbols by class.

Numeric	Numeric-edited	Alphabetic	Alphanumeric	Alphanumeric-edited
9	Z .	A	X	/
S	* –			0
V	, +			B
P	/ CR			
	0 DB			
	B $			

Figure 5-20
The BLANK WHEN
ZERO clause.

Format:

BLANK WHEN ZERO

Examples:

```
05  WS-PRICE     PIC ZZ,ZZZ.99   BLANK WHEN ZERO.
05  CODE-NUMBER  PIC 99999       BLANK WHEN ZERO.
05  PL-DATE      PIC 99/99/99    BLANK WHEN ZERO.
```

when a value of zeros is moved to it. As Figure 5-20 shows, the reserved words BLANK WHEN ZERO are coded after the PICTURE clause. You should know that this clause can be used only with numeric and numeric-edited data-items.

Some common applications of the blank-when-zero effect can be handled either with the BLANK WHEN ZERO clause or without it. A simple case is when full zero suppression with blank-space replacement is specified. For example, specification of PIC Z,ZZZ together with a BLANK WHEN ZERO clause is redundant. In general, if a 9, *, 0, $, or a fixed + sign appears in the PICTURE character-string and the blank-when-zero effect is desired, the BLANK WHEN ZERO clause must be coded.

TOPIC

The MOVE Statement and Report Headings

Principles of the MOVE

Summary of the MOVE Categories

By now, you've used the MOVE statement under a variety of circumstances. That is, you've used it to move the contents of one numeric field to another and the contents of one alphanumeric to another. You have also learned to move the contents of numeric and alphanumeric fields to numeric and alphanumeric edit fields. Although the MOVE appears at first glance to be a relatively simple statement, it has a wide variety of capabilities.

Figure 5-21 summarizes the many possible MOVE statement combinations. Notice the following about the table:

- The action resulting from each type of sending and receiving field in the MOVE is described in the intersecting box.

- The notation AN/AN means an alphanumeric to alphanumeric move; similarly, N/N means a numeric to numeric move.

- The unshaded boxes indicate the most common moves.

- Some of the moves are noted as ILLEGAL. This means that they are not allowed and the compiler will flag them. The following are illegal moves that beginning COBOL programmers frequently attempt:

Figure 5-21 MOVE statement categories.

Sending Field	Receiving Field				
	Alphanumeric	Alphanumeric edited	Numeric	Numeric edited	Group
Alphanumeric	Left justification Receiving field shorter: truncation Receiving field longer: padded with spaces	Same as AN/AN *also* Editing is performed	ILLEGAL	ILLEGAL	Same as AN/AN
Alphanumeric-edited	De-editing occurs in COBOL-85 Same as AN/AN in COBOL-74	Same as AN/AN *also* Editing is performed	ILLEGAL	ILLEGAL	Same as AN/AN
Numeric Integer	Same as AN/AN	Same as AN/AN *also* Editing is performed	Decimal point alignment Receiving field shorter: truncation		Same as AN/AN
Noninteger	ILLEGAL	ILLEGAL	Receiving field longer: padding with zeros	Same as N/N *also* Editing is performed	
Numeric-edited	Same as AN/AN	Same as AN/AN *also* Editing is performed	De-editing occurs in COBOL-85 ILLEGAL in COBOL-74	ILLEGAL	Same as AN/AN
Group	Same as AN/AN	Same as AN/AN (No editing is performed)	ILLEGAL	ILLEGAL	Same as AN/AN

Note: Unshaded areas indicate most common MOVE categories.   AN/AN = Alphanumeric to alphanumeric. N/N = Numeric to numeric.

MOVE alphanumeric-field TO numeric or numeric-edited field

MOVE numeric-field-with-decimal positions TO alphanumeric field

MOVE group field TO numeric or numeric-edited field

Let's consider details of some frequently encountered variations of the MOVE statement.

Comments About Some Common MOVE Forms

When viewing Figure 5-21, keep in mind the distinction between numeric and alphanumeric movement. As described in Chapter 3, when moving numeric data, the objective is to retain the data's numeric value. In Figure 5-22's examples, you can see that integer data values—numbers without decimal points—are positioned

Figure 5-22
Typical numeric moves.

Sending Field		Receiving Field	
PICTURE	Data	**PICTURE**	Result
PIC 999	341	PIC 9999	0341
PIC 999	341	PIC 9999V99	034100
PIC 999	341	PIC 999V9	3410
PIC 999	341	PIC 999.99	341.00
PIC 999V99	34132	PIC 9999V999	0341320
PIC 999V99	34132	PIC 9999.999	0341.320
PIC 999V99	34132	PIC 99.9	41.3
PIC 999V99	34132	PIC 999	341

to the right in the receiving field and excess positions to the left are filled with zeros. Quantities with decimal points are appropriately positioned around the receiving decimal point and excess positions on both the left and right are filled with zeros. If the receiving field is smaller than the transmitting field, excessive digits are left behind; they are **truncated**.

In contrast, in an alphanumeric move, data is always positioned to the *left* in the receiving field. Excess positions to the right in the receiving field are filled with spaces.

Carefully distinguishing between an alphanumeric and a numeric move is especially significant in some of the MOVE categories. For instance, if a whole number field (numeric) must be moved to an alphanumeric field, the resulting move is an alphanumeric move (see the appropriate table entry in Figure 5-21). This means that the entire number, including leading zeros, moves to the receiving field. If the receiving field is longer than the transmitting field, the value is positioned to the left and unused positions to the right are filled with spaces; the field is said to be **left-justified**.

De-Editing Actions

Because of the widespread use of data entry via video display terminals, COBOL-85 includes the capability to convert data from its edited form to an unedited form. This action, which can be used for both numeric and alphanumeric entries, is called **de-editing** and is exactly the reverse of the corresponding edit action. If the receiving field is properly defined, the resulting action is exactly the opposite of the corresponding edit: All editing insertions are deleted and, for numeric fields, suppressed zeros are reintroduced.

This is done with a MOVE in which the sending field is defined by the appropriate edited item and the receiving field is numeric or alphanumeric. An example of numeric de-editing is shown in Figure 5-23.

Group Field MOVE Operations

The MOVE operations just described and all the earlier examples are elementary field moves. That is, both the sending and receiving fields are elementary data-items. (Remember that an elementary field is the one with the PICTURE clause; a group field does not contain its own PICTURE clause, but is a collection of elementary data-items.)

Group fields can also be specified in a MOVE statement as either the sending field, the receiving field, or both. When a group field is specified as *either* the sending or receiving field, the processing rules for an alphanumeric-to-alphanumeric MOVE operation go into effect, even if the sending field is numeric.

Figure 5-23
De-editing with a numeric-edited sending field and a numeric receiving field.

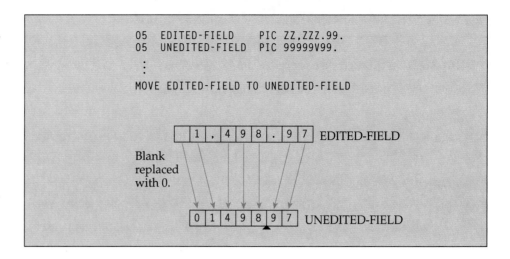

Although a group to alphanumeric-edited MOVE statement is not a common type, it is a tricky one that can puzzle a beginning programmer. Notice in Figure 5-21's table (bottom row, second column) that the move is alphanumeric *without editing*. One case in which you might encounter this is in working with the following date field:

```
05  AR-DATE.
    10  AR-DATE-MONTH   PIC X(2).
    10  AR-DATE-DAY     PIC X(2).
    10  AR-DATE-YEAR    PIC X(2).
05  OU-DATE             PIC XX/XX/XX.
```

If you move AR-DATE to OU-DATE, the six-position date data is left-justified in OU-DATE, with two spaces filling the unused positions to the right.

The REDEFINES Clause

The preceding example illustrates a situation that is occasionally encountered in COBOL: the need to have a field defined in two different ways. That is, a program's particular needs might require that the month, day, and year be defined as individual fields, as shown. However, the editing move requires that the AR-DATE be defined as an elementary item. For needs like this, COBOL allows you to redefine any field to another form. For example, consider:

```
05  EMPLOYEE-NUMBER                PIC 9(4).
05  EMPLOYEE-NUMBER-X
        REDEFINES EMPLOYEE-NUMBER  PIC X(4).
```

Here, EMPLOYEE-NUMBER-X and EMPLOYEE-NUMBER refer to exactly the same four positions of storage. The difference between the two relates to the MOVE statement. That is, if EMPLOYEE-NUMBER is involved in a MOVE, numeric rules apply; if EMPLOYEE-NUMBER-X is involved in a MOVE, alphanumeric rules apply.

Redefining of the required date (from the preceding example) and other REDEFINES samples are shown in Figure 5-24.

Qualification of Data-Names

Although data-name qualification is not used in this book, it is included here for your future information. Later in your studies or career, you may need to know about the qualification of data-names.

When forming data-names for the programs in this text, each one was made unique. Use of data-name prefixes for the fields of a record—as was recommended in Chapter 2—almost ensures that all data-names are different.

Figure 5-24   The REDEFINES clause.

Valid REDEFINES entry examples

The REDEFINES field is shorter than the field being redefined.

```
05   XDATE                        PIC X(6).
05   MONTH REDEFINES XDATE        PIC X(2).
```

The REDEFINES field is longer than the field being redefined (invalid in COBOL-74).

```
05   MONTH                        PIC X(2).
05   XDATE REDEFINES MONTH        PIC X(6).
```

Elementary field REDEFINES group field.

```
05   GROUP-DATE.
     10   MONTH                   PIC X(2).
     10   XDAY                    PIC X(2).
     10   YEAR                    PIC X(2).
05   NUMERIC-DATE
        REDEFINES GROUP-DATE      PIC 9(6).
```

Group field REDEFINES elementary field.

```
05   NUMERIC-DATE                 PIC 9(6).
05   GROUP-DATE REDEFINES NUMERIC-DATE.
     10   MONTH                   PIC X(2).
     10   XDAY                    PIC X(2).
     10   YEAR                    PIC X(2).
```

Multiple REDEFINES entries (note that each entry must refer back to the original entry—not to another REDEFINES item).

```
05   ALPHA-DATE                   PIC X(6).
05   NUMERIC-DATE
        REDEFINES ALPHA-DATE      PIC 9(6).
05   NUMERIC-MONTH
        REDEFINES ALPHA-DATE      PIC 9(2).
```

Invalid REDEFINES entry examples

Invalid: The REDEFINES field is not at the same level as the redefined field.

```
10   ALPHA-DATE                   PIC X(6).
05   NUMERIC-DATE
        REDEFINES ALPHA-DATE      PIC 9(6).
```

Invalid: The REDEFINES entry does not immediately follow the field being redefined.

```
05   ALPHA-DATE                   PIC X(6).
05   QUANTITY                     PIC S9(5).
05   NUMERIC-DATE
        REDEFINES ALPHA-DATE      PIC 9(6).
```

Invalid: Multiple REDEFINES entries, with the second one referencing a REDEFINES item rather than the original redefined item.

```
05   ALPHA-DATE                   PIC X(6).
05   NUMERIC-DATE
        REDEFINES ALPHA-DATE      PIC 9(6).
05   NUMERIC-MONTH
        REDEFINES NUMERIC-DATE    PIC 9(2).
```

However, COBOL does not require that all fields within a program have different names. But, when a data-name is duplicated, there must be a unique data-name at a higher-level field (a data-item with a lower-level number) that can be used to differentiate the fields with duplicate names. (By definition, then, each 01-level record-description data-name is unique, since there can be no level-number hierarchically above 01.)

When a field with a duplicate data-name is referenced in the PROCEDURE DIVISION, it must be qualified by the data-name that differentiates it at a

Figure 5-25
Qualification of data-names.

```
    01  RECORD-IN.
        05  EMPLOYMENT-CODE          PIC X(1).
        05  SS-NUMBER                PIC X(9).
        05  FULL-NAME.
            10  LAST-NAME            PIC X(13).
            10  FIRST-NAME           PIC X(11).
   .
   .
   .
    01  RECORD-OUT.
        05  FULL-NAME.
            10  FIRST-NAME           PIC X(11).
            10  LAST-NAME            PIC X(13).
        05  SS-NUMBER                PIC X(9).
   .
   .
   .
        MOVE SS-NUMBER OF RECORD-IN TO SS-NUMBER OF RECORD-OUT
        MOVE FIRST-NAME OF RECORD-IN TO FIRST-NAME OF RECORD-OUT
        MOVE LAST-NAME OF RECORD-IN TO LAST-NAME OF RECORD-OUT
```

higher level. Figure 5-25 gives an example of duplicate data-names and qualification. Notice that in the first three MOVE statements, each duplicated data-name is followed by the reserved word OF (or IN)—which is, in turn, followed by the differentiating data-name at the higher level.

Reference Modification

You know from Chapter 2 that you can define a record in order to give you access to an entire field or any part of one. For instance, the definition

```
    05  SOCIAL-SECURITY-NUM.
        10  SOCIAL-SECURITY-NUM-1    PIC X(3).
        10  SOCIAL-SECURITY-NUM-2    PIC X(2).
        10  SOCIAL-SECURITY-NUM-3    PIC X(4).
```

allows you to refer to the entire nine-position field by SOCIAL-SECURITY-NUM or to any of the three parts of it by the elementary items. COBOL-85 also includes another technique for gaining access to parts of a field. It is called **reference modification** and gives you access to any part of a field without the group/elementary item definition as above. For example, consider the preceding field, defined as follows:

```
    05  SOCIAL-SECURITY-NUM     PIC X(9).
```

Using reference modification, the three parts are available as:

Field	Columns	Format
Target contribution	61–66	*nnnn.nn*
Actual contribution	67–72	*nnnn.nn*

Where *nnnn.nn* means a six-position field with an assumed decimal point between the fourth and fifth digits.

Thus, the following statements are equivalent:

```
    MOVE SOCIAL-SECURITY-NUM-2 TO SS-HOLD-PART
    MOVE SOCIAL-SECURITY-NUM:2:2 TO SS-HOLD-PART
```

Basic reference modification principles are

- The data-name is followed by the leftmost position within the field and the length of the subfield to be accessed. The colon character separates these entries.

- The leftmost position and length can be numeric data-items (variables).
- If the length is omitted, the subfield is taken from the leftmost position to the end of the field. So, the following two forms are equivalent:

```
SOCIAL-SECURITY-NUM:6:4
SOCIAL-SECURITY-NUM:6
```

Although it is usually best to define a field as a group item consisting of elementary items, in some cases, reference modification is convenient.

Defining Report Headings

The VALUE Clause

Editing helps make an output report easier to read. Another method is to include descriptive headings, as in Figure 5-26's sample output and print chart. The common method of producing such headings is to:

1. Define each heading in a data-item of the WORKING-STORAGE SECTION using a VALUE clause.
2. Move the data-item to the output area, then print.

One way to define the two headings in Figure 5-26 is with the WORKING-STORAGE entries of Figure 5-27. To correlate PL-REPORT-HEADING-LINE with

Figure 5-26 Printed program output.

```
                      PATRON DEFICIT REPORT


PATRON NAME        CITY/STATE/ZIP            TARGET ACTUAL DEFICIT

Acton, Jocelyn     San Francisco, CA 94107     350    350
Anderson, Hazel    Woodside, CA 94062          250    100     150
Baker, Donald      Berkeley, CA 94703          375    300      75
Broadhurst, Ryan   Big Trees, CA 95066         500    500
```

(a) With headings.

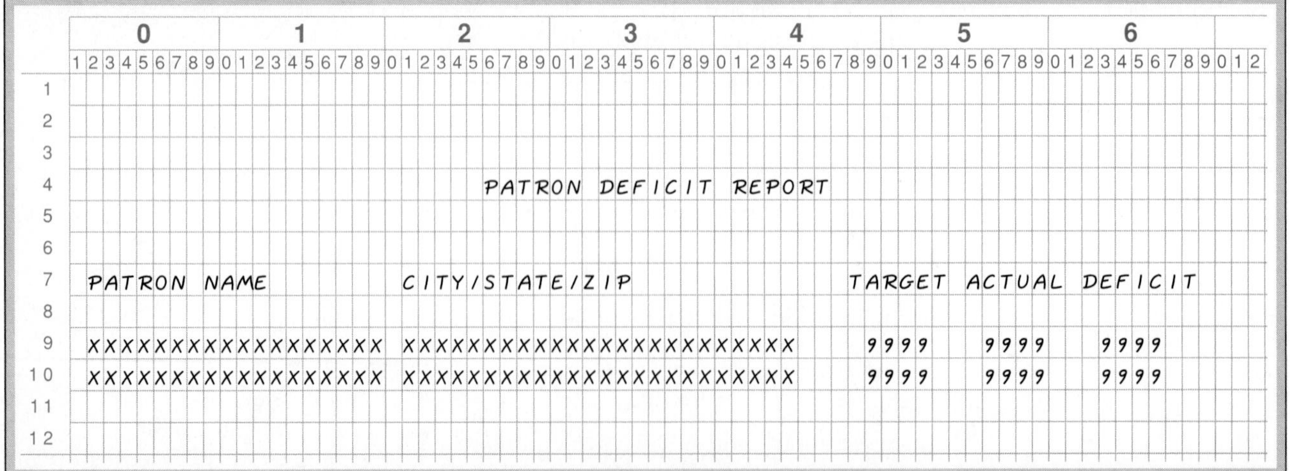

(b) Print chart.

Figure 5-27
VALUE clauses to create heading lines.

```
     01  PL-REPORT-HEADING-LINE.
         05  PIC X(25)    VALUE SPACES.
         05  PIC X(21)    VALUE "PATRON DEFICIT REPORT".

     01  PL-COLUMN-HEADING-LINE.
         05  PIC X(20)    VALUE " PATRON NAME".
         05  PIC X(27)    VALUE "CITY/STATE/ZIP".
         05  PIC X(21)    VALUE "TARGET ACTUAL DEFICIT".
```

the print chart, notice that the report heading is preceded by 25 spaces. This is achieved in the program with the entry

```
     05  PIC X(25)    VALUE SPACES.
```

This entry reserves 25 memory positions *and* fills them with spaces before execution of the program begins. The second entry of that record

```
     05  PIC X(21)    VALUE "PATRON DEFICIT REPORT".
```

reserves 21 memory positions *and* fills them with the quoted literal. So the record-item, PL-REPORT-HEADING-LINE, contains the exact program heading as it is to be printed.

PL-COLUMN-HEADING-LINE is also constructed in multiple parts with field widths defined so that the result corresponds exactly to the layout required for the column heading line. For instance, notice the first definition for the portion of the heading PATRON NAME, in which you can see that the literal can be shorter than the length defined by the PIC clause. The compiler automatically fills the remaining positions with spaces, as Figure 5-28 illustrates. The next column heading *and its included spaces* occupy 27 positions (refer to the print chart), so PIC X(27) is used. With this method, it is relatively easy to properly align your printed report's elements.

COBOL-74

Each of the elementary items in Figure 5-27 requires the word FILLER preceding PIC.

These examples illustrate using the VALUE clause to initialize alphanumeric fields (with alphanumeric data). You can also use the VALUE clause to initialize

Figure 5-28
Information in memory from a literal.

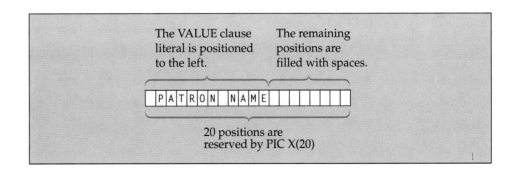

numeric fields, those defined with the 9 PICTURE. However, you must use numeric literals or figurative constants for numeric fields. You will see this in the next chapter when you learn more about COBOL's arithmetic operations.

Characteristics of the VALUE clause can be summarized as follows:

- A VALUE clause can be used with either alphanumeric or numeric fields.

- A VALUE clause can be used with a field that is given a specific name or one defined as filler. If given a name, that field can be referenced in the PROCEDURE DIVISION just like any other field.

- If an alphanumeric literal is shorter than the field length, it is positioned to the left in the field and the extra positions to the right are filled with spaces.

- The literal specified in the VALUE clause must be consistent with the category of data defined by the PICTURE clause. That is, if the field is defined as alphanumeric, a nonnumeric literal must be coded; if defined as numeric, a numeric literal must be specified.

- A figurative constant such as ZERO or SPACE can be used as the literal of a VALUE clause. Recognize, though, that because a space is an alphanumeric character, SPACE and SPACES cannot be coded for a numeric field. On the other hand, since a zero is either a numeric digit or an alphanumeric character, ZERO, ZEROS, and ZEROES can be specified with either numeric or alphanumeric fields.

Sometimes it is tempting to use the VALUE clause when defining an output line in the FILE SECTION. *This is not valid.* The VALUE clause can be used only with WORKING-STORAGE SECTION fields; its use is prohibited in the FILE SECTION. In addition, the VALUE clause cannot be used with the OCCURS clause, a topic covered in a later chapter.

Perhaps it occurred to you that the VALUE clause can be used to initialize the EOF program switch as follows:

```
01  PROGRAM-SWITCHES.
    05  PS-END-OF-PATRON-FILE PIC X(3) VALUE "NO".
```

Then you do not need the initializing statement

```
MOVE "NO" TO PS-END-OF-PATRON-FILE
```

in the 100 module. If so, you are correct. However, many people think this is poor programming practice. A good rule to follow is to use the VALUE clause only for items that will not change in the program: items that are constant. Then you know that those fields to which you assign values with the VALUE clause will remain as defined in the WORKING-STORAGE SECTION. As you will learn in later chapters, some work areas must be initialized more than once in a program, an action that can be done only within the PROCEDURE DIVISION.

COBOL-9X

COBOL-9X will allow VALUE clauses to be used in the FILE SECTION. It is also anticipated that a PICTURE will not be required for definition of an alphanumeric literal; the compiler will determine the length from the literal itself.

Output Lines in the
WORKING-STORAGE
SECTION

PATDFCT includes only one output line format: that needed for the detail lines consisting of data from the input records. The format for this line is defined in the record description under the printer FD. On the other hand, if you look at Figure 5-26(a)'s output, you see that the report includes three different output lines: the report heading line, the column heading line, and the detail lines. In this type of situation, it is best to define all output lines in WORKING-STORAGE, then move the specific output line to the output record before printing. PATDFCT2 in Figure 5-29—a modification of PATDFCT—incorporates these principles.

At line 29, you can see that the output (printer) record is defined as a single 132-position line. The 132-position width is somewhat standard because most mainframe high-speed printers can print 132-position lines. You can use 132 or some smaller value that matches your printer's capability.

In lines 48–58, you see the detail line that was defined in the FILE SECTION of PATDFCT. Because this area is defined in the WORKING-STORAGE SECTION— and will be moved to the output line area—each filler must include a VALUE SPACE clause.

The two other output lines, the headings that you saw earlier, are defined in lines 60–67.

Printing Report Headings

Move/Print Actions

Let's look at the overall structure of Figure 5-29's PROCEDURE DIVISION. Except for the module to print headings (870-Print-Heading), the structure is identical to the PATDFCT program studied in Chapters 2 and 3. You can see that the 870 module is performed from the mainline module at line 77.

In PATDFCT, the individual fields of the output line are defined in the FILE SECTION as part of the printer FD record. Because of this, it was necessary to move spaces to this area before processing to ensure that positions between fields did not contain garbage. This action is not necessary in PATDFCT2 because prior to each WRITE, a record is moved from WORKING-STORAGE (see lines 112, 116, 118, and 121). So, the action of writing each line is a two-step process. For instance, to print the report heading line, PL-REPORT-HEADING-LINE is moved to PATRON-RECORD-LINE (line 116) and then the output record is written (line 117). A similar process produces the column heading line (lines 118–119); notice that desired line spacing is achieved with AFTER ADVANCING 3. The blank line following the heading line is inserted by writing a blank line (lines 121 and 122).

Avoiding Garbage in Printed Output

One other feature of this program illustrates a common problem that plagues students—and even experienced programmers at times. To see this, assume that lines 109 and 110 of Figure 5-29 (the ELSE option) were omitted. Consider the scenario in which the third data record was printed:

```
Baker, Donald       Berkeley, CA 94703          375     300     75
```

In the fourth record, which is about to be processed, the actual and target contributions are equal, so nothing should be printed for the deficit. The following occurs:

1. Individual input fields are moved to corresponding output fields (lines 101–104, Figure 5-29).
2. The actual contribution is compared to the target contribution (line 105). Because they are equal, nothing is moved to PL-CONTR-DIFFERENCE. Remember, this is based on the assumption that the else portion of the program (at lines 109 and 110) was removed.

Figure 5-29 Printing headings—the PATDFCT2 program.

```
1        IDENTIFICATION DIVISION.                              68  /
2        PROGRAM-ID.   PATDFCT2.                               69
3                                                              70      PROCEDURE DIVISION.
4     *  PRICE/WELBURN  6/20/89  revised 1/12/95               71
5                                                              72      000-PRINT-PATRON-LIST.
6     *  This program prints a patron contribution report      73  ***********Initialization Sequence***********
7     *  with headings. Under-target patrons are identified.   74          OPEN INPUT PATRON-FILE
8                                                              75               OUTPUT PATRON-LIST
9                                                              76          PERFORM 100-INITIALIZE-VARIABLE-FIELDS
10       ENVIRONMENT DIVISION.                                 77          PERFORM 700-PRINT-HEADINGS
11                                                             78
12       INPUT-OUTPUT SECTION.                                 79  **************Processing Sequence**************
13                                                             80          PERFORM UNTIL PS-END-OF-PATRON-FILE IS EQUAL TO "YES"
14       FILE-CONTROL.                                         81              READ PATRON-FILE
15           SELECT PATRON-FILE                                82                       INTO PR-PATRON-RECORD
16               ASSIGN TO (system dependent).                 83                  AT END
17           SELECT PATRON-LIST                                84                      MOVE "YES" TO PS-END-OF-PATRON-FILE
18               ASSIGN TO (system dependent).                 85                  NOT AT END
19                                                             86                      PERFORM 200-PROCESS-PATRON-RECORD
20                                                             87              END-READ
21       DATA DIVISION.                                        88          END-PERFORM
22                                                             89
23       FILE SECTION.                                         90  **************Termination Sequence*************
24                                                             91          CLOSE PATRON-FILE
25       FD  PATRON-FILE.                                      92                PATRON-LIST
26       01  PATRON-RECORD          PIC X(68).                 93          STOP RUN
27                                                             94              .
28       FD  PATRON-LIST.                                      95  ******************************************************
29       01  PATRON-LINE-RECORD     PIC X(132).                96
30                                                             97      100-INITIALIZE-VARIABLE-FIELDS.
31       WORKING-STORAGE SECTION.                              98          MOVE "NO" TO PS-END-OF-PATRON-FILE
32                                                             99              .
33       01  PROGRAM-SWITCHES.                                100      200-PROCESS-PATRON-RECORD.
34           05  PS-END-OF-PATRON-FILE PIC X(3).              101          MOVE PR-NAME TO PL-NAME
35                                                            102          MOVE PR-CITY-STATE-ZIP TO PL-CITY-STATE-ZIP
36       01  ARITHMETIC-WORK-AREAS.                           103          MOVE PR-TARGET-CONTR TO PL-TARGET-CONTR
37           05  AR-DIFFERENCE        PIC 9(4).               104          MOVE PR-ACTUAL-CONTR TO PL-ACTUAL-CONTR
38                                                            105          IF PR-ACTUAL-CONTR IS LESS THAN PR-TARGET-CONTR
39    *    Input record definition                            106              MOVE PR-TARGET-CONTR TO AR-DIFFERENCE
40       01  PR-PATRON-RECORD.                                107              SUBTRACT PR-ACTUAL-CONTR FROM AR-DIFFERENCE
41           05  PR-NAME             PIC X(18).               108              MOVE AR-DIFFERENCE TO PL-CONTR-DIFFERENCE
42           05  PR-ADDRESS          PIC X(18).               109          ELSE
43           05  PR-CITY-STATE-ZIP   PIC X(24).               110              MOVE ZERO TO PL-CONTR-DIFFERENCE
44           05  PR-TARGET-CONTR     PIC 9(4).                111          END-IF
45           05  PR-ACTUAL-CONTR     PIC 9(4).                112          MOVE PATRON-LINE TO PATRON-LINE-RECORD
46                                                            113          WRITE PATRON-LINE-RECORD
47    *    PL Print line definitions                          114              .
48       01  PATRON-LINE.                                     115      870-PRINT-HEADINGS.
49           05                      PIC X(1)  VALUE SPACE.   116          MOVE PL-REPORT-HEADING-LINE TO PATRON-LINE-RECORD
50           05  PL-NAME             PIC X(18).               117          WRITE PATRON-LINE-RECORD
51           05                      PIC X(1)  VALUE SPACE.   118          MOVE PL-COLUMN-HEADING-LINE TO PATRON-LINE-RECORD
52           05  PL-CITY-STATE-ZIP   PIC X(24).               119          WRITE PATRON-LINE-RECORD
53           05                      PIC X(4)  VALUE SPACE.   120              AFTER ADVANCING 3
54           05  PL-TARGET-CONTR     PIC Z(4).                121          MOVE SPACES TO PATRON-LINE-RECORD
55           05                      PIC X(3)  VALUE SPACE.   122          WRITE PATRON-LINE-RECORD.
56           05  PL-ACTUAL-CONTR     PIC Z(4).                123              .
57           05                      PIC X(3)  VALUE SPACE.
58           05  PL-CONTR-DIFFERENCE PIC Z(4).
59
60       01  PL-REPORT-HEADING-LINE.
61           05  PIC X(25)   VALUE SPACES.
62           05  PIC X(21)   VALUE "PATRON DEFICIT REPORT".
63
64       01  PL-COLUMN-HEADING-LINE.
65           05  PIC X(20)   VALUE " PATRON NAME".
66           05  PIC X(27)   VALUE "CITY/STATE/ZIP".
67           05  PIC X(21)   VALUE "TARGET ACTUAL DEFICIT".
```

Unfortunately, the output that should be

```
Broadhurst, Ryan   Big Trees, CA 95066        500    500
```

will instead be

```
Broadhurst, Ryan   Big Trees, CA 95066        500    500    75
```

Why was the unwanted deficit amount of 75 printed? It is garbage left from the preceding record. Because nothing was moved into PL-CONTR-DIFFERENCE while processing the fourth record, contents from the third record remained. This was not a problem with PATDFCT because the entire output record—defined in the FILE SECTION—was set to spaces before processing each record.

This problem is avoided in PATDFCT2 by moving zero into PL-CONTR-DIFFERENCE (line 110) under the ELSE option. Because this output field is defined as PIC Z(4)—refer to line 58—it is fully suppressed for the zero amount.

The READ/INTO Statement

With multiple output line requirements, it is best to define all output records in the WORKING-STORAGE SECTION and move each to the FILE SECTION record description immediately before writing. PATDFCT2 takes this one step further and removes the record definition for the input file to the WORKING-STORAGE SECTION as well. Observe in the FD coding (line 26) that the input record PATRON-RECORD is defined as a single field: 68 positions in this case. Upon reading the record, the program can include a MOVE statement that moves the record to the field breakdown record (lines 40–45). However, it is more convenient to use the INTO phrase with the READ (line 82). Figure 5-30 illustrates the way in which the READ/INTO functions.

From a style point-of-view, this technique removes all record definitions from the FILE SECTION and places them in the WORKING-STORAGE SECTION. More importantly, in one situation, it is quite functional. That is, after the end-of-file is read, the COBOL Standard indicates that the contents of the input area are undefined. So, you cannot count on the last record's availability. In some applications, you still need reference to the last data record after EOF detection. By using a WORKING-STORAGE record area, you will have that last data record available. The READ/INTO is used in example programs from now on.

The WRITE/FROM Statement

Although the WRITE/FROM is not used in this book, it's included here for your future information. Later in your studies or career, you may need to know about this statement. Corresponding to the READ/INTO, COBOL includes the WRITE/FROM, which combines a move operation prior to writing. For instance, the following WRITE/FROM statements are equivalent to the corresponding MOVE-WRITE statement sequences of PATDFCT2:

Figure 5-30
The READ/INTO statement.

```
FD  PATRON-FILE.
01  PATRON-RECORD              PIC X(68).
    :
    :
WORKING-STORAGE SECTION.
01  PR-PATRON-RECORD.
    05  PR-NAME                PIC X(18).
    05  PR-ADDRESS             PIC X(18).
    05  PR-CITY-STATE-ZIP      PIC X(24).
        :
        :
    READ PATRON-FILE
              INTO PR-PATRON-RECORD
      AT END
        MOVE "YES" TO PS-END-OF-PATRON-FILE
      NOT AT END
        PERFORM 200-PROCESS-PATRON-RECORD
    END-READ
```

These both accomplish the same thing: move the record just read into the WORKING-STORAGE area.

The above READ is equivalent to the following:

```
    READ PATRON-FILE
      AT END
        MOVE "YES" TO PS-END-OF-PATRON-FILE
      NOT AT END
        MOVE PATRON-RECORD TO PR-PATRON-RECORD
        PERFORM 200-PROCESS-PATRON-RECORD
    END-READ
```

```
        MOVE PATRON-LINE TO PATRON-LINE-RECORD
        WRITE PATRON-LINE-RECORD
                                                        } Equivalent
        WRITE PATRON-LINE-RECORD
            FROM PATRON-LINE
```

```
        MOVE PL-COLUMN-HEADING-LINE TO PATRON-LINE-RECORD
        WRITE PATRON-LINE-RECORD
            AFTER ADVANCING 3
                                                        } Equivalent
        WRITE PATRON-LINE-RECORD
            FROM PL-COLUMN-HEADING-LINE
                AFTER ADVANCING 3
```

Although the WRITE/FROM has its conveniences, generally it will not fit into the techniques for printed output introduced in Chapter 7.

COBOL-74 Modifications to PATDFCT2

The COBOL-74 version of PATDFCT2 differs from the COBOL-85 version only in the features described in Chapters 2 and 3. That is, the following changes are required of Figure 5-29 to be compatible with COBOL-74:

1. Insert the CONFIGURATION SECTION.
2. Insert LABEL RECORDS clauses.
3. Include the reserved word FILLER in the detail line description.
4. Modify the processing sequence (lines 80–88); use the technique of either Figure 3-16 (priming READ; see page 86) or Figure 3-17. Do not forget to follow the READ/AT END with a period to terminate the AT END scope.
5. Remove the scope terminator END-IF at line 111 and terminate the IF scope with a period at the end of line 110.
6. If your compiler does not allow the paragraph-ending period to be on a separate line, remove those periods and place them at the end of the paragraph's last statement.

TOPIC

Interaction with the Computer

Screen Display and Keyboard Input

The ACCEPT and DISPLAY Statements

In Chapter 4, you were introduced to displaying output on the screen (DISPLAY) and accepting input from the keyboard (ACCEPT). Regarding the ACCEPT, the COBOL Standard states that data keyed from the keyboard will replace previous contents of the designated field with left justification and, if necessary, blank fill to the right.

Although the COBOL Standard provides only minimal interactive capabilities, most COBOL implementations include significant enhancements over the basic DISPLAY and ACCEPT. Unfortunately, slight differences exist from implementation to implementation. However, most include basic capabilities to do the following:

1. Position the cursor at any point (line and column) on the screen for the input or output function.
2. Clear the entire screen.
3. Clear a single line of the screen.
4. Change the appearance of a displayed item by highlighting it (reverse video), causing it to blink, and showing it in extra-bright characters.
5. For the ACCEPT, require that an entry be made, or require that the full number of characters be entered into the field.
6. For the ACCEPT, display the current value of the designated data-item as a default entry. Pressing the Enter key without typing data causes the current value in the data-item to remain unchanged.

Partial format of these two statements for several implementations are shown in Figure 5-31. The examples all perform the same functions.

1. In the first DISPLAY example, the screen is cleared, then the literal is displayed beginning screen line 4, column 20.
2. In the second DISPLAY example, the contents of the field PR-NAME are displayed in reverse video beginning screen line 7, column 35.

Figure 5-31
DISPLAY and READ formats and examples.

Format (Micro Focus and IBM AS/400†):

$$\underline{\text{DISPLAY}} \begin{Bmatrix} \text{identifier-1} \\ \text{literal-1} \end{Bmatrix}$$

$$\left[\text{AT} \left[\underline{\text{LINE}} \text{ NUMBER} \begin{Bmatrix} \text{identifier-2} \\ \text{literal-2} \end{Bmatrix} \right] \left[\begin{Bmatrix} \underline{\text{COLUMN}} \\ \underline{\text{COL}} \end{Bmatrix} \text{NUMBER} \begin{Bmatrix} \text{identifier-3} \\ \text{literal-3} \end{Bmatrix} \right] \right]$$

$$\left[\underline{\text{WITH}} \begin{Bmatrix} \underline{\text{REVERSE-VIDEO}} \\ \begin{Bmatrix} \underline{\text{BLANK}} \ \underline{\text{SCREEN}} \\ \underline{\text{BLANK}} \ \underline{\text{LINE}} \end{Bmatrix} \end{Bmatrix} \dots \right]$$

$$\underline{\text{ACCEPT}} \quad \text{identifier-1}$$

$$\left[\text{AT} \left[\underline{\text{LINE}} \text{ NUMBER} \begin{Bmatrix} \text{identifier-2} \\ \text{literal-1} \end{Bmatrix} \right] \left[\begin{Bmatrix} \underline{\text{COLUMN}} \\ \underline{\text{COL}} \end{Bmatrix} \text{NUMBER} \begin{Bmatrix} \text{identifier-3} \\ \text{literal-2} \end{Bmatrix} \right] \right]$$

$$\left[\underline{\text{WITH}} \ \underline{\text{REVERSE-VIDEO}} \right]$$

Examples:

```
DISPLAY "PATRON FILE DATA ENTRY SCREEN"   LINE 4 COL 20
                                          WITH BLANK SCREEN
DISPLAY PR-NAME                           LINE 7 COL 35
                                          WITH REVERSE-VIDEO

ACCEPT PR-ADDRESS                         LINE 9 COL 35
                                          WITH REVERSE-VIDEO
```

†Note: To use these ACCEPT and DISPLAY forms with the AS/400, you must specify the *EXTACCDSP generation option of the CRTCBLPGM command, or use the EXTACCDSP option of the PROCESS stateement.

(continues)

Figure 5-31 (continued)

Format (Ryan-McFarland):

$$\underline{DISPLAY} \left\{ \begin{array}{l} \text{identifier-1} \\ \text{literal-1} \end{array} \right\}$$

$$\left[\underline{LINE} \left\{ \begin{array}{l} \text{identifier-2} \\ \text{literal-2} \end{array} \right\} \right] \left[\underline{POSITION} \left\{ \begin{array}{l} \text{identifier-3} \\ \text{literal-3} \end{array} \right\} \right]$$

$$\left[\begin{array}{l} \underline{REVERSE} \\ \left\{ \begin{array}{l} \underline{ERASE} \\ \underline{ERASE}\ \underline{EOL} \end{array} \right\} \end{array} \right] \dots$$

$$\underline{ACCEPT}\ \ \text{identifier-1}$$

$$\left[\underline{LINE} \left\{ \begin{array}{l} \text{identifier-2} \\ \text{literal-1} \end{array} \right\} \right] \left[\underline{POSITION} \left\{ \begin{array}{l} \text{identifier-3} \\ \text{literal-2} \end{array} \right\} \right]$$

$$\left[\underline{REVERSE} \right]$$

Examples:

```
DISPLAY "PATRON FILE DATA ENTRY SCREEN"   LINE 4 POSITION 20
                                          ERASE
DISPLAY PR-NAME                           LINE 7 POSITION 35
                                          REVERSE

ACCEPT PR-ADDRESS                         LINE 9 POSITION 35
                                          REVERSE
```

3. In the ACCEPT, the cursor is positioned at screen line 9, column 35, awaiting entry from the keyboard for data to be placed in the field PR-ADDRESS. Since PR-ADDRESS is 18 positions in length, 18 positions of the screen beginning with line 9, column 37 is highlighted. This is the area from which the keyboard entry is displayed as it is typed.

A Program Using ACCEPT and DISPLAY—PATADD2

To give you an idea of how to use these features, let's consider Chapter 4's PATADD program to add records to the patron file. This illustrates both the ACCEPT and DISPLAY.

The printer layout form simplifies the task of laying out the exact format of a printed report. From the column numbers, it is easy to determine the exact width of filler fields. The same is true of laying out a screen display. However, with a screen display, you are dealing not only with positioning from one side to the other, but also from the top of the screen to the bottom. Consequently, a word processor is especially useful in designing your screen layout. In fact, Figure 5-32's layout (page 144) was done with a word processor, thereby simplifying the task of moving lines around to obtain a clean, balanced appearance. You can quickly see that, for example, the "Patron full name" literal must begin at line 7, column 17, and that the corresponding ACCEPT must begin at line 7, column 35.

Figure 5-33's PATADD2 program uses the Micro Focus versions of the ACCEPT and DISPLAY. The overall structure and logic are identical to those of PATADD from Chapter 4. The following are significant points about this program:

Figure 5-31 (continued)

Format (Digital Equipment Corporation VAX):

<u>DISPLAY</u> $\begin{Bmatrix} \text{identifier-1} \\ \text{literal-1} \end{Bmatrix}$

$\left[\text{AT } \underline{\text{LINE}} \text{ NUMBER } \begin{Bmatrix} \text{identifier-2} \\ \text{literal-2} \end{Bmatrix} \right]$

$\left[\text{AT } \underline{\text{COLUMN}} \text{ NUMBER } \begin{Bmatrix} \text{identifier-3} \\ \text{literal-3} \end{Bmatrix} \right]$

$\left[\underline{\text{ERASE}} \text{ [TO } \underline{\text{END}} \text{ OF] } \begin{Bmatrix} \underline{\text{SCREEN}} \\ \underline{\text{LINE}} \end{Bmatrix} \right]$

$\left[\underline{\text{REVERSED}} \right]$

<u>ACCEPT</u> $\begin{Bmatrix} \text{identifier-1} \\ \text{literal-1} \end{Bmatrix}$

$\left[\text{FROM } \underline{\text{LINE}} \text{ NUMBER } \begin{Bmatrix} \text{identifier-2} \\ \text{literal-2} \end{Bmatrix} \right]$

$\left[\text{FROM } \underline{\text{COLUMN}} \text{ NUMBER } \begin{Bmatrix} \text{identifier-3} \\ \text{literal-3} \end{Bmatrix} \right]$

$\left[\underline{\text{ERASE}} \text{ [TO } \underline{\text{END}} \text{ OF] } \begin{Bmatrix} \underline{\text{SCREEN}} \\ \underline{\text{LINE}} \end{Bmatrix} \right]$

$\left[\underline{\text{REVERSED}} \right]$

Examples:

```
DISPLAY "PATRON FILE DATA ENTRY SCREEN"    LINE 4 COLUMN 20
                                           ERASE SCREEN
DISPLAY PR-NAME                            LINE 7 COLUMN 35
                                           REVERSED

ACCEPT PR-ADDRESS                          LINE 9 COLUMN 35
                                           REVERSED
```

- An announcement screen is displayed and the user is given the option of proceeding or aborting the run (the same as PATADD).

- In contrast to PATADD, direct screen positioning allows you to display the entire input screen (lines 81–88), then proceed through the data entry (lines 90–99).

Figure 5-32   Screen layout for data entry.

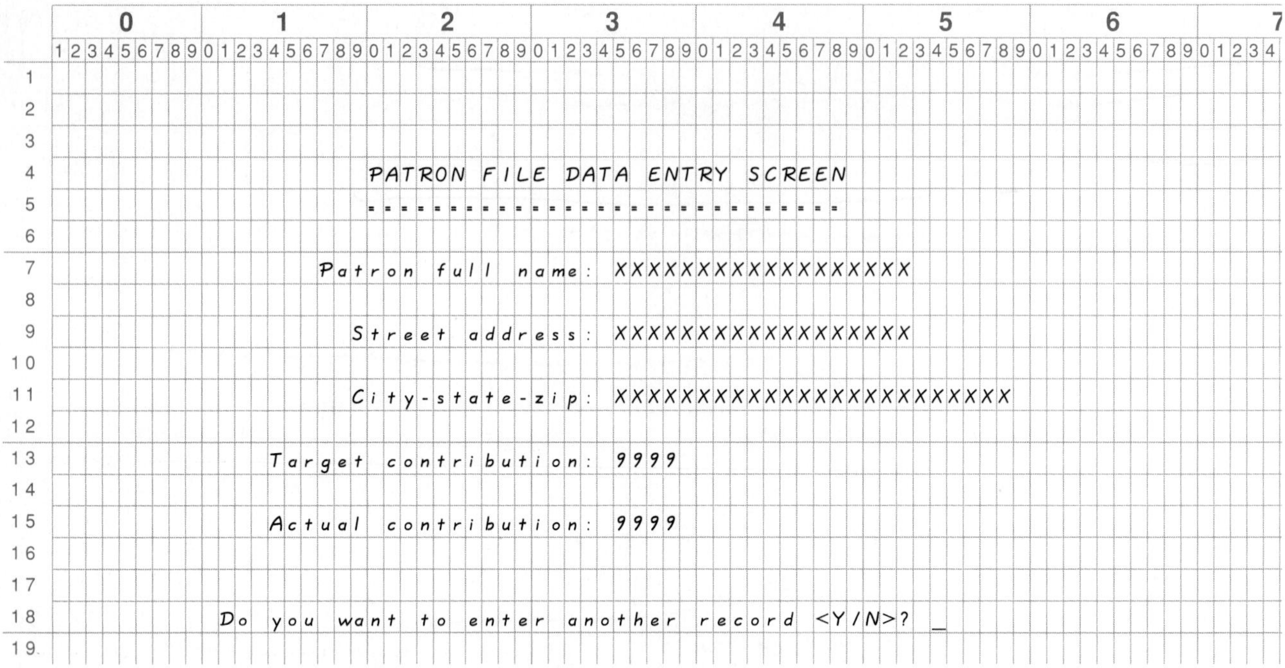

- With Micro Focus COBOL, if the ACCEPT statement includes the LINE and COL options, the current value of the designated data-item is displayed as a default value. For instance, if 1525 was entered into PR-TARGET-CONTR, the next time the ACCEPT was executed, that value would be displayed as a default value if the data-item was not set to 0. Eliminating previous values of each field before repeating the loop is the purpose of lines 78–80.

- Numeric-edited fields are defined for the actual and target contribution fields and are used in the ACCEPT (lines 96 and 98). This produces a form on the screen that is much more intuitive during data entry. De-editing MOVE statements move these edited fields to the output record at lines 100 and 101.

As a rule, if you use cursor positioning within a program for ACCEPT and DISPLAY, use cursor positioning throughout. Avoid mixing cursor positioning forms with the simpler COBOL Standard forms; the results can be confusing.

It is very helpful in understanding interactive programs to experiment with and run them. If you run PATADD2, make some changes and observe what happens. For instance, remove the field initialization statements (lines 78–80) and observe how the previous entries are displayed. Also, use PR-TARGET-CONTR in the ACCEPT of line 96 (and delete the MOVE at line 100) and observe how the input appearance differs from that of PR-ACTUAL-CONTR.

Chapter Summary

PICTURE Clauses

PICTURE clauses describe the following field characteristics:

1. Data class
2. Length (number of digits or characters)
3. Assumed decimal-point location (for numeric fields)

Figure 5-33   Data-entry program—PATADD2.

```
1        IDENTIFICATION DIVISION.                              59
2        PROGRAM-ID.    PATADD2.                               60      100-DISPLAY-ANNOUNCE-SCREEN.
3                                                              61          DISPLAY "This program allows you to add new"
4        *      W. PRICE 1/12/95                               62                                              LINE  8 COL 20
5                                                              63                                              WITH BLANK SCREEN
6        *      This program allows the user to add            64          DISPLAY "records to the Patron file."
7        *      records to the patron file.                    65                                              LINE  9 COL 20
8                                                              66          DISPLAY "Enter the letter Y (capital letter only)"
9                                                              67                                              LINE 10 COL 20
10       ENVIRONMENT DIVISION.                                 68          DISPLAY "if you want to proceed."
11                                                             69                                              LINE 11 COL 20
12       INPUT-OUTPUT SECTION.                                 70          DISPLAY "Enter N if you want to abort this operation."
13                                                             71                                              LINE 12 COL 20
14       FILE-CONTROL.                                         72          DISPLAY "Do you want to enter new records <Y/N>? "
15           SELECT PATRON-FILE                                73                                              LINE 15 COL 20
16               ASSIGN TO (system dependent).                 74          ACCEPT SW-ANOTHER-RECORD
17                                                             75                                              LINE 15 COL 60
18                                                             76
19                                                             77      200-ACCEPT-PATRON-RECORD.
20       DATA DIVISION.                                        78          MOVE SPACES TO PATRON-RECORD
21                                                             79          MOVE ZERO TO SI-TARGET-CONTR
22       FILE SECTION.                                         80                     SI-ACTUAL-CONTR
23                                                             81          DISPLAY "PATRON FILE DATA ENTRY SCREEN" LINE  4 COL 20
24       FD  PATRON-FILE.                                      82                     WITH BLANK SCREEN
25       01  PATRON-RECORD.                                    83          DISPLAY "============================" LINE  5 COL 20
26           05  PR-NAME              PIC X(18).               84          DISPLAY "Patron full name"       LINE  7 COL 17
27           05  PR-ADDRESS           PIC X(18).               85          DISPLAY "Street address"         LINE  9 COL 19
28           05  PR-CITY-STATE-ZIP    PIC X(24).               86          DISPLAY "City-state-zip"         LINE 11 COL 19
29           05  PR-TARGET-CONTR      PIC 9(4).                87          DISPLAY "Target contribution"    LINE 13 COL 14
30           05  PR-ACTUAL-CONTR      PIC 9(4).                88          DISPLAY "Actual contribution"    LINE 15 COL 14
31                                                             89
32       WORKING-STORAGE SECTION.                              90          ACCEPT PR-NAME                    LINE  7 COL 35
33                                                             91                     WITH REVERSE-VIDEO
34       01  SW-SWITCHES.                                      92          ACCEPT PR-ADDRESS                 LINE  9 COL 35
35           05  SW-ANOTHER-RECORD    PIC X(1).                93                     WITH REVERSE-VIDEO
36                                                             94          ACCEPT PR-CITY-STATE-ZIP          LINE 11 COL 35
37       01  SI-SCREEN-INPUT-ITEMS.                            95                     WITH REVERSE-VIDEO
38           05  SI-TARGET-CONTR      PIC ZZZ9.                96          ACCEPT SI-TARGET-CONTR            LINE 13 COL 35
39           05  SI-ACTUAL-CONTR      PIC ZZZ9.                97                     WITH REVERSE-VIDEO
40                                                             98          ACCEPT SI-ACTUAL-CONTR            LINE 15 COL 35
41                                                             99                     WITH REVERSE-VIDEO
42       PROCEDURE DIVISION.                                   100         MOVE SI-TARGET-CONTR TO PR-TARGET-CONTR
43                                                             101         MOVE SI-ACTUAL-CONTR TO PR-ACTUAL-CONTR
44       000-CREATE-PATRON-FILE.                               102         .
45           PERFORM 100-DISPLAY-ANNOUNCE-SCREEN
46           OPEN EXTEND PATRON-FILE
47           PERFORM UNTIL SW-ANOTHER-RECORD IS NOT EQUAL TO "Y"
48               PERFORM 200-ACCEPT-PATRON-RECORD
49               WRITE PATRON-RECORD
50               DISPLAY "Do you want to enter another record <Y/N>?"
51                                       LINE 18 COL 11
52               ACCEPT SW-ANOTHER-RECORD LINE 18 COL 54
53               DISPLAY " "              LINE 18 COL 1
54                                            WITH BLANK LINE
55           END-PERFORM
56           CLOSE PATRON-FILE
57           STOP RUN
58           .
```

4. Arithmetic-sign presence (for numeric fields)
5. Editing to be performed

The five PICTURE clause categories are

1. Numeric
2. Alphabetic
3. Alphanumeric
4. Numeric-edited
5. Alphanumeric-edited

To form PICTURE clauses, the programmer can use the PICTURE symbols summarized in the next section, entitled "COBOL PICTURE Symbol Reference."

Other DATA DIVISION clauses are related to PICTURE clauses. The BLANK WHEN ZERO clause can be specified in the data-item description entry for a numeric or numeric-edited field. When a value of zero is transferred to a field specified with the BLANK WHEN ZERO, spaces—rather than the normal editing specified in the PICTURE clause—appear in the field.

The MOVE Statement and Report Headings

The VALUE clause allows you to define elementary items with initial values. If one follows a PICTURE (WORKING-STORAGE SECTION only), the compiler loads the field with the value indicated in the clause.

If a program is to have more than one print line, it is convenient to define each output line as a separate record in the WORKING-STORAGE SECTION.

Depending upon the MOVE statement sending and receiving field characteristics, one or more of the following actions may occur: right or left justification, truncation, padding, and/or decimal-point alignment. Common categories with the resulting actions are listed in the following four groups:

1. Numeric sending field to numeric receiving field.

    - Decimal-point alignment.

    - If the receiving is shorter (on either side of the decimal point), excess sending field digits are truncated.

    - If the receiving field is longer (on either side of the decimal point), excess receiving field positions are padded with zeros.

2. Numeric sending field to numeric-edited receiving field.

    - Same actions as Group 1.

    - Also, editing is performed for the receiving field in accordance with its PICTURE clause.

3. Alphanumeric sending field to alphanumeric receiving field.
   Numeric integer sending field to alphanumeric receiving field.
   Group sending field.
   Group receiving field.

    - Left justification in receiving field.

    - If the receiving field is shorter, excess rightmost positions from the sending field are truncated.

    - If the receiving field is longer, excess rightmost positions in the receiving field are padded with spaces.

4. Alphanumeric sending field to alphanumeric-edited receiving field.

    - Same actions as Group 3.

    - Also, editing is performed for the receiving field in accordance with its PICTURE clause.

COBOL PICTURE
Symbol Reference

ALPHANUMERIC

Symbol	Description and Syntactical Requirements
X	Alphanumeric character

ALPHABETIC

Symbol	Description and Syntactical Requirements
A	Alphabetic character

NUMERIC

Symbol	Description and Syntactical Requirements	Symbol	Description and Syntactical Requirements
9	**Numeric digit** ■ Each numeric PICTURE character-string must contain at least one 9 symbol. ■ Up to 18 digits may be specified for a numeric field.	**S**	**Arithmetic sign.** The S symbol should generally be specified for: Numeric fields in the FILE SECTION that should or may carry an arithmetic sign. Numeric fields in the WORKING-STORAGE SECTION that will be operated on arithmetically. ■ Only one S may be specified within a numeric PICTURE character-string. ■ When specified, the S must be the leftmost symbol of the PICTURE character-string. ■ If an S is not specified for a numeric field, the field's contents are treated as an absolute value.
V	**Assumed decimal point** ■ Only one V may be specified within a numeric PICTURE character-string. ■ The V is not counted toward the length of the field. ■ The V is not required for integer (whole number) fields.		
		P	**Assumed decimal scaling position.** This is a placeholder to scale to the decimal point. It is not used in this book.

NUMERIC -EDITED

Symbol	Description and Syntactical Requirements	Symbol	Description and Syntactical Requirements
Z	**Zero suppression with blank-space replacement.** Normally used to make fields on output reports and displays more readable. ■ Any number (up to 18) of Z symbols may be specified. ■ The Z symbol cannot be preceded by a 9 symbol. ■ If a Z symbol is specified to the right of a decimal point, then all digit positions of the PICTURE character-string must be represented by the Z symbol.	**.**	**Decimal point.** An actual decimal point is typically used for display on reports and display screens. ■ Only one decimal point symbol may be specified within a numeric editing PICTURE character-string. ■ The decimal point cannot be specified as the rightmost character of a PICTURE character-string.
*	**Zero suppression with asterisk replacement.** Normally used for check protection. ■ Any number of * symbols (up to 18) may be specified. ■ The * symbol cannot be preceded by a 9 symbol. ■ If an * symbol is specified to the right of a decimal point, then all digit positions of the PICTURE character-string must be represented by the * symbol.	**CR**	**Credit symbol.** Normally used to identify credit balances on invoices, customer statements, financial statements, and other formal reports. ■ Only one CR symbol may be specified in a PICTURE character-string. ■ The CR symbol must be specified as the rightmost symbol of the PICTURE character-string. ■ If the field value is negative, the CR symbol is printed; if the field value is positive or zero, the letters CR are replaced with two spaces.
,	**Comma.** Normally used to improve readability when numeric output report or display fields contain more than three integer digit positions. ■ Any number of comma symbols may be specified. ■ The comma symbol may be specified at any location, except as the rightmost symbol of the PICTURE character-string.	**DB**	**Debit symbol.** Not used very often, except for certain accounting reports. ■ Only one DB symbol may be specified in a PICTURE character-string. ■ The DB symbol must be specified as the rightmost symbol of the PICTURE character-string. ■ If the field value is negative, the DB symbol is printed; if the field value is positive or zero, the letters DB are replaced with two spaces.
/	**Slash.** Normally used to separate the month, day, and year of dates expressed in six-digit format. ■ Any number of slash symbols may be specified. ■ The slash symbol can be specified at any location within the PICTURE character-string.	**$**	**Fixed dollar (currency) sign.** Normally specified to identify dollar amounts on invoices, customer statements, financial reports, and other formal reports. ■ Only one fixed dollar symbol may be specified in a PICTURE character-string. ■ The fixed dollar symbol must be specified as the leftmost symbol of the PICTURE character-string.
B	**Blank space.** Normally used to separate groups of digits and/or letters for readability. ■ Any number of B symbols may be specified. ■ The B symbol can be specified at any location within the PICTURE character-string.	**$**	**Floating dollar (currency) sign.** Normally specified to identify dollar amounts on invoices, customer statements, financial reports, and other formal reports. ■ The floating dollar symbol is coded in the leftmost position of the PICTURE character-string and is repeated for each position through which the dollar symbol is to float. ■ If a floating dollar symbol is coded to the right of a decimal point, then all digit positions to the right of the decimal point must be represented by floating dollar symbols.
0	**Zero.** Does not have many applications, but is sometimes convenient for appending zeros to the end or beginning of a value. ■ Any number of zero symbols may be specified. ■ The zero symbol can be specified at any location within the PICTURE character-string.		

NUMERIC-EDITED (continued)

Symbol	Description and Syntactical Requirements	Symbol	Description and Syntactical Requirements
–	**Fixed minus sign.** Normally specified as the rightmost symbol to identify negative values for signed numeric fields. ■ Only one fixed minus sign symbol may be specified in a PICTURE character-string. ■ The fixed minus sign symbol must be specified as either the leftmost or the rightmost symbol of the PICTURE character-string. ■ If the field value is negative, the minus sign is printed; if the field value is positive or zero, the sign is replaced with a space.	+	**Fixed plus sign.** Normally specified as the rightmost symbol to identify positive and negative values for signed numeric fields. ■ Only one fixed plus sign symbol may be specified in a PICTURE character-string. ■ The fixed plus sign symbol must be specified as either the leftmost or the rightmost symbol of the PICTURE character-string. ■ If the field value is positive or zero, the plus sign is printed; if the field value is negative, a minus sign is printed.
–	**Floating minus sign.** Normally specified to identify negative values for signed numeric fields in those situations in which a minus sign is desired on the left-hand side of a zero-suppressed value. ■ The floating minus sign symbol is coded in the leftmost position of the PICTURE character-string and is repeated for each position through which the minus sign is to float. ■ If a floating minus sign symbol is coded to the right of a decimal point, then all digit positions to the right of the decimal point must be represented by floating minus sign symbols. ■ If the field value is negative, the minus sign is printed; if the field value is positive or zero, the sign is replaced with a space.	+	**Floating plus sign.** Normally specified to identify positive and negative values for signed numeric fields in those situations in which the plus or minus sign is desired on the left-hand side of a zero-suppressed value. ■ The floating plus sign symbol is coded in the leftmost position of the PICTURE character-string and is repeated for each position through which the plus or minus sign is to float. ■ If a floating plus sign symbol is coded to the right of a decimal point, then all digit positions to the right of the decimal point must be represented by floating plus sign symbols. ■ If the field value is positive or zero, the plus sign is printed; if the field value is negative, a minus sign is printed. However, if (1) all the digit positions of the PICTURE character-string are represented by the floating plus sign and (2) the value of the field is zero, then the entire field appears as blank spaces.

ALPHANUMERIC-EDITED	Symbol	Description and Syntactical Requirements
Refer to the counterpart symbol in the preceding numeric-edited category; the alphanumeric-edited symbols have the same usage and syntactical requirements.	/ B 0	Slash Blank space Zero

Style Summary

■ Do not use the alphabetic PICTURE symbol A. Instead, use the symbol X for both alphabetic and alphanumeric fields.

■ When an entire field is defined by the same symbol (or the same symbol plus an S), use the parentheses method to express the field length. For example, a seven-character alphanumeric field can be defined as PIC X(7); an eight-integer, signed numeric field can be defined as PIC S9(8).

■ If a PICTURE character-string contains editing symbols, code each symbol with the repetition method so that the desired editing is more easily readable. That is, code PIC $ZZ,ZZZ.99- rather than PIC $Z(2),Z(3).9(2)- to produce clearer results.

■ For report heading modules, use module numbers 870–879.

Features Not in COBOL-74

The de-editing MOVE (move an edited field to a nonedited field) provides for the removal of editing symbols. With appropriately defined pictures, it works exactly the opposite of an editing move.

Exercises

Terms for Definition

alphanumeric
alphanumeric editing symbol
assumed decimal point
asterisk check protection
credit symbol (CR)
debit symbol (DB)
de-edit
edit
fixed position insertion
floating dollar (currency) sign

leading zeros
left-justified
numeric
numeric-edited item
reference modification
simple insertion
special insertion
truncate
zero suppression and replacement

Review Questions

1. A PICTURE clause can identify five characteristics of a field. Name them.

2. List the five data-class categories of PICTURE clauses.

3. Identify the PICTURE symbol and category for each of the following:
   a. Numeric digit
   b. Signed field
   c. Assumed decimal point
   d. Alphabetic character
   e. Alphanumeric character
   f. Zero suppression/blank replacement
   g. Zero suppression/asterisk replacement
   h. Comma insertion
   i. Slash insertion
   j. Zero insertion
   k. Blank-space insertion
   l. Decimal-point insertion
   m. Minus sign
   n. Plus sign
   o. Credit symbol
   p. Debit symbol
   q. Dollar (currency) sign

4. Write PICTURE character-strings for the following field specifications:
   a. Five integer-digit unsigned numeric.
   b. Seven integer-digit signed numeric.
   c. Eight-digit (six integers; two decimal places) unsigned numeric.
   d. Three-digit (no integers; three decimal places) signed numeric.
   e. Two integer-digit representing thousands and hundreds positions (tens and units positions are not stored for the value) unsigned numeric.
   f. One digit representing mils position of a cent amount (tens and hundreds decimal places are not stored for the value) unsigned numeric.
   g. Twenty-two position alphanumeric.
   h. Three integer-digit edited with full leading zero suppression with blank-space replacement.
   i. Four-digit dollars-and-cents (two integer positions; two decimal places) edited with a fixed dollar sign and zero suppression with blank-space replacement of the dollar positions.
   j. Nine-digit (seven integers; two decimal positions) edited with full zero suppression (print nothing for a zero value) and standard comma insertion.
   k. Five-digit dollars-and-cents (three integer positions; two decimal places) edited with a floating dollar sign.

l.   Six-digit dollars-and-cents (four integer positions; two decimal places) edited with a fixed dollar sign and zero suppression with asterisk replacement of the dollar positions.

m.   Five-digit (all integers) edited with zero suppression with blank-space replacement (of all but the units position) and with a fixed minus sign as the rightmost position (provide standard comma insertion).

n.   Six-digit date field edited with slash insertion.

o.   Nine-digit Social Security field edited with blank spaces (where hyphens are typically placed).

5. To cause blank spaces to appear in a numeric or numeric-edited field when the value of the data within the field is zero, the _____ clause can be specified.

6. The literal specified in the VALUE clause must be consistent with the _____ of the PICTURE clause with which it is associated.

7. The VALUE clause cannot be specified in the _____ SECTION.

8. When the same data-name is specified for more than one field in the DATA DIVISION, _____ of that data-name is required in the PROCEDURE DIVISION.

9. When the REDEFINES clause is coded, it must immediately follow the _____ in the data-item description entry.

10. When using the REDEFINES clause, the redefining field (the one with the REDEFINES clause) must be at the same _____ as the redefined field.

Syntax/Debug Exercises

1. Some of the following VALUE clause specifications are not syntactically correct. Identify each erroneous entry.

```
a.  05  AMOUNT   PIC S9(5)      VALUE -5.
b.  05  AMOUNT   PIC S9(5)      VALUE 00000.
c.  05  AMOUNT   PIC S9(5)      VALUE ZEROS.
d.  05  AMOUNT   PIC S9(5)      VALUE SPACES
e.  05  AMOUNT   PIC S9(5)      VALUE +555555.
f.  05  AMOUNT   PIC S9(5)      VALUE "81786".
g.  05  AMOUNT   PIC S9(5)      VALUE +3.1416.
h.  05  DOLLARS  PIC S9(3)V99   VALUE +99998.
i.  05  DOLLARS  PIC S9(3)V99   VALUE 99998.
j.  05  DOLLARS  PIC S9(3)V99   VALUE -998.98.
k.  05  DOLLARS  PIC S9(3)V99   VALUE -998V98.
l.  05  DOLLARS  PIC S9(3)V99   VALUE 99.998.
m.  05  CODE-A   PIC 9(4)       VALUE +1234.
n.  05  CODE-A   PIC 9(4)       VALUE 12V34.
o.  05  FIELD-B  PIC X(3)       VALUE SPACES.
p.  05  FIELD-B  PIC X(3)       VALUE ZEROS.
q.  05  FIELD-B  PIC X(3)       VALUE 123.
r.  05  FIELD-B  PIC X(3)       VALUE "123".
s.  05  FIELD-B  PIC X(3)       VALUE "ABC".
```

2. Some of the following PICTURE character-strings are incorrect. Identify each erroneous entry.

1.	PIC 9(X)	**10.**	PIC ZZ,ZZ,ZZ	**19.**	PIC -ZZZ.99-
2.	PIC 9(5)V	**11.**	PIC ZZ.ZZ.ZZ	**20.**	PIC ZZ,ZZZ.ZZ
3.	PIC S9(5)V99	**12.**	PIC ZZ,ZZZ.Z9	**21.**	PIC Z9/Z9/99
4.	PIC 9(3)S	**13.**	PIC +ZZZ,ZZZ	**22.**	PIC XX/XX/XX
5.	PIC S(9)	**14.**	PIC ZZZ,Z77+	**23.**	PIC 999B99B9999
6.	PIC ZZ,Z99.99	**15.**	PIC 99,999.99	**24.**	PIC XXXBXXBXXXX
7.	PIC ZZ,ZZ9.ZZ	**16.**	PIC $*,***.99CR	**25.**	PIC 99900
8.	PIC 9(19)	**17.**	PIC $Z,ZZZ.99DR	**26.**	PIC XXX00
9.	PIC X(19)	**18.**	PIC ----9.99	**27.**	PIC +++,++9

3. Some of the following MOVE statements are not syntactically correct. Identify each erroneous entry.

```
01  MISCELLANEOUS-FIELDS
    05   NUMERIC-INTEGER-FIELD        PIC 9(7).
    05   NUMERIC-DEC-POSN-FIELD       PIC S9(5)V99.
    05   NUMERIC-EDITED-FIELD         PIC ZZ,ZZZ.99-.
    05   ALPHANUMERIC-FIELD           PIC X(7).
    05   ALPHANUMERIC-EDITED-FIELD    PIC XX/XX/XX.
```

a. MOVE ALPHANUMERIC-FIELD TO NUMERIC-INTEGER-FIELD

b. MOVE NUMERIC-INTEGER-FIELD TO ALPHANUMERIC-FIELD

c. MOVE NUMERIC-DEC-POSN-FIELD TO ALPHANUMERIC-FIELD

d. MOVE ALPHANUMERIC-FIELD TO NUMERIC-DEC-POSN-FIELD

e. MOVE NUMERIC-INTEGER-FIELD TO NUMERIC-EDITED-FIELD

f. MOVE ALPHANUMERIC-FIELD TO NUMERIC-EDITED-FIELD

g. MOVE NUMERIC-EDITED-FIELD TO NUMERIC-EDITED-FIELD

h. MOVE NUMERIC-INTEGER-FIELD TO ALPHANUMERIC-EDITED-FIELD

i. MOVE NUMERIC-DEC-POSN-FIELD TO MISCELLANEOUS-FIELDS

j. MOVE ALPHANUMERIC-FIELD TO MISCELLANEOUS-FIELDS

4. Some of the following REDEFINES clause specifications are not syntactically correct. Identify each erroneous entry.

```
a.  05   FLD-A                        PIC X(5).
    05   FLD-R REDEFINES FLD-A        PIC 9(5).
b.  05   FLD-BPIC 9(5).
    05   FLD-S REDEFINES FLD-B        PIC X(6).
c.  05   FLD-C                        PIC X(6).
    05   FLD-T REDEFINES FLD-C        PIC 9(5).
d.  05   FLD-D                        PIC X(6).
    05   FLD-U REDEFINES FLD-C        PIC 9(6).
e.  05   FLD-E.
         10   FLD-E1                  PIC X(5).
         10   FLD-E2                  PIC S9(5).
    05   FLD-V REDEFINES FLD-E        PIC X(10).
f.  05   FLD-F.
         10    FLD-F1                 PIC X(1).
         10    FLD-F2                 PIC X(2).
         10    FLD-W REDEFINES FLD-F  PIC 9(3).
g.  05   FLD-G                        PIC X(5).
    05   FLD-X REDEFINES FLD-G        PIC 9(5).
    05   FLD-Y REDEFINES FLD-X        PIC 9(3)V99.
```

Programming Assignments

Programming Assignment 5-1: Understocked Inventory Report

Background information:

Tools Unlimited is a wholesale company that stocks and sells tools to retailers. Since the company does none of its own manufacturing, its policy is to maintain a sufficient inventory to satisfy customer needs, taking into account the lag-time between placing an order with its manufacturers and delivery of goods. The inventory file includes one record for each item in the inventory. Included in the record is a field containing the quantity-on-hand and another containing the reorder-point. Whenever the quantity-on-hand drops below the reorder-point, an order must be placed to replenish the stock. Management would like a report of all items for which the quantity-on-hand is less than the reorder-point.

Input file: Inventory file (INVEN.DAT)

Inventory record

	Product identification	Product description		Reorder point	Quanity on hand	

1 2 3|4 5 6 7 8 9 10 11 12 13|14 15 16 17 18 19 20 21 22 23 24 25 26 27 28 29 30 31 32 33 34 35 36 37 38 39|40 41 42 43 44 45 46 47|48 49 50 51|52 53 54 55|56 57 58 59 60 61 62 63 64 65 66 67 68 69 70 71 72 73 74 75 76 77 78 79 80

Required output:

Print a report, doubled-spaced, with one detail line for each input record for which the Quantity-on-hand is less than the Reorder-point (for which a shortfall exists).

Output report-line formats:

Heading lines. Use appropriate report and column headings.

Detail line.

Positions	Field	Comments
4–14	Product identification	Print in form *xxxx/xxxxxx* (insert a slash between subfields).
17–42	Product description	
44–49	Reorder point	Insert comma, zero-suppress.
52–56	Quantity on hand	Same as Reorder point.
60–65	Inventory shortfall	Same as Reorder point.

Program operations:

1. Process only those records for which Quantity-on-hand is less than Reorder-point.

2. Calculate Inventory-shortfall as Reorder-point minus Quantity-on-hand.

Programming Assignment 5-2: Salesperson Performance Report

Background information:

The sales manager of Follow-the-Sun Sales has completed her preliminary study of salesperson performance. She now requires a report giving the sales amounts and commissions for each salesperson from the data in the salesperson file.

Input file: Salesperson file (SALESPER.DAT)

Salesperson record

Required output:

Print a report, single-spaced, with one detail line for each input record (ignore records that do not have a Status-code value of A).

Output report-line formats:

Heading lines. Use appropriate report and column headings.

Detail line.

Positions	Field	Comments
3–4	Salesperson region	
5	Hyphen	Print a hyphen.
6–9	Salesperson territory	
12–14	Salesperson number	
17–42	Salesperson name	
44–48	Product-units sold	Zero-suppress leading zeros, insert floating minus sign, blank if zero.
50–54	Commission percentage	Suppress leading integer digits, print a decimal point. Typical output: 18.75
55	Percent sign	Print a percent sign.
58–67	Sales revenue	Print a fixed dollar sign, zero-suppress with asterisk replacing leading dollar digits, insert a comma, print a decimal point.
72–80	Commission amount	Same as Sales-revenue.

Program operations:

1. Process only those records with a Status-code value of A.

2. Edit output fields as specified.

Programming Assignment 5-3: Gross-Pay Report

Background information:

The payroll department of Silicon Manufacturing maintains an employee payroll file with one record for each employee. Data includes hours worked and pay rate.

Input file: Earnings file (EARNINGS.DAT)

Earnings record

Required output:

Print a report, doubled-spaced, with one detail line for each input record.

Output report-line formats:

Heading lines. Use appropriate report and column headings.

Detail line.

Positions	Field name	Comments
4–14	Employee number	Print in form *xxx-xx-xxxx* (insert hyphens).
17–28	Employee last name	
30–38	Employee first name	
44–49	Hours worked	Zero-suppress leading hour digits, print a decimal point.
54–58	Pay rate	Zero-suppress leading dollar digits, print a decimal point.
66–73	Gross pay	Zero-suppress leading dollar digits, print a decimal point, insert a comma.

Program operations:

1. Process only those records with a value H for the Pay code field.

2. Calculated quantities for detail output are

    Gross-pay is Hours-worked times Pay-rate.

Programming Assignment 5-4: Accounts-Receivable Report

Background information:

One of Silicon Valley Manufacturing's critical functions is keeping an accurate account of the funds owed by customers. Each month, a report is prepared from the customer file that summarizes the purchases and payments for each customer. This is called the accounts-receivable report.

Input file: Customer file (CUSTOMER.DAT)

Customer record

Output report-line formats:

Heading lines. Use appropriate report and column headings.

Detail line.

Positions	Field name	Comments
1–5	Customer number	
7–30	Customer name	
32–44	Balance forward	Zero-suppress leading dollar digits, insert a comma, print a decimal point, print a rightmost fixed space and CR symbol for a negative value.
46–55	New purchases	Zero-suppress leading dollar digits, insert a comma, print a decimal point.
57–66	Payments received	Same as New-purchases.
68–80	New balance	Same as Balance-forward.

Program operations:

1. *Programming option:* As directed by your instructor, either process all records or process only those customer records with a space in the Special-flag field.

2. The New-balance is to be calculated as:

    Balance-forward

    plus New-purchases

    minus Payments-received

Programming Assignment 5-5: Nurses' Salary Increase Projection

Background information:

The management of Brooklawn Hospital (refer to Programming Assignment 2-5) is currently engaged in salary negotiations with the Nurses' Union. The union proposed a salary increase of 9% for employees working the first shift and 14% for employees working the second or third shift. Management wants to find out how much this proposal will impact current salaries. For this assignment, you must modify the program written for Programming Assignments 2-5 and 3-5 as follows.

Input file: Nurses file (NURSES.DAT)

Nurses record

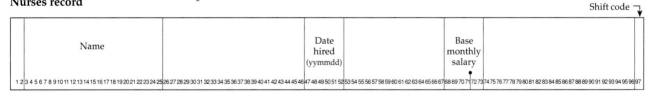

Output report-line formats:

Heading lines. Use appropriate report and column headings.

Detail line.

Positions	Field	Comments
1–23	Name	
26–33	Date-hired	Format *mm/dd/yy* (insert slashes).
35	Shift code	
37–45	Base salary	Insert a floating dollar sign, decimal point, comma; suppress leading zeros.
49–57	New salary	Same as Base-salary.

Program operations:

1. Process each record.

2. Calculate New-salary as follows:

> If Shift-code = 1 New-salary is Base-salary times 1.09
> otherwise New-salary is Base-salary times 1.14

Programming Assignment 5-6: Vehicle Rental Application

Background information:

The management of Rent-Ur-Wheels wants a report that lists all vehicles. However, rental information is to be omitted for those vehicles that are not rented. To accomplish this, modify the program written for Programming Assignment 3-6.

Input file: Vehicle file (VEHICLE.DAT)

Vehicle record

Status ⌐

Vehicle type	Make of vehicle		License number	Daily rental fee		Date due back (yymmdd)		Customer last name	Customer phone number

1 2 3 4 5 6 7 8 9 10 11 12 13 14 15 16 17 18 19 20 21 22 23 24 25 26 27 28 29 30 31 32 33 34 35 36 37 38 39 40 41 42 43 44 45 46 47 48 49 50 51 52 53 54 55 56 57 58 59 60 61 62 63 64 65 66 67 68 69 70 71 72 73 74 75 76 77 78 79 80 81 82 83 84 85 86 87 88 89

Required output:

Heading lines. Use appropriate report and column headings.

Detail line.

Positions	Field	Comments
3–6	Vehicle type	
9–22	Make of vehicle	
24–30	License number	

For only those vehicles that are currently rented:

Positions	Field	Comments
34–38	Date due back	Format *mm/dd*
42–47	Daily rental fee	Insert decimal point, floating dollar sign.
50–63	Customer phone number	Insert punctuation: (415) 554-1234 as an example.
65–80	Customer last name	

Program operations:

1. Process each record.

2. For all vehicles, print the Vehicle type, Make, and License. For only those that are rented (Status field equal to R), print the rental information as described earlier for the detail line.

Programming Assignment 5-7: Bookstore Inventory Application

Background information:

The president of Granger and Heatherford, knowing the value of complete and up-to-date information in business management, requested that a listing be placed on her desk at 8:00 A.M. each day, showing the status of the firm's salable goods. To accomplish this, modify the program written for Programming Assignment 3-7.

Input file: Granger/Heatherford inventory file (GHINVEN.DAT)

GH Inventory record

Title	Author		Unit cost		Quantity on hand	Reorder level	Quantity on order	Date of last order (mmddyy)
1 2 3 4 5 6 7 8 9 10 11 12 13 14 15 16 17 18	19 20 21 22 23 24 25 26 27 28 29 30 31 32 33	34 35 36 37 38 39 40 41 42 43 44 45 46	47 48 49 50	51 52 53 54	55 56 57	58 59 60	61 62 63	64 65 66 67 68 69

Required output:

For this assignment, you must do all format planning. The output report must include appropriate heading lines.

The detail lines must print the following:

> Author
> Title
> Reorder level
> Quantity on order
> Date of last order
> Quantity on hand
> Unit cost
> Inventory value (Quantity-on-hand times Unit-cost)

Use editing that is appropriate to each of the fields.

Programming Assignment 5-8: Interactive Assignment— Record Display

For any one of the preceding assignments, write an interactive program that displays records from the file—one record at a time. Design a clean, balanced screen layout with appropriate descriptions. Give the user the option of viewing the next record in the file or terminating processing.

Programming Assignment 5-9: Interactive Assignment— Data Entry

For any one of the preceding assignments, write an interactive program that allows the user to add records to the file. Design a clean, balanced screen layout with appropriate descriptions. For each record, the program is to:

1. Accept data into all fields.

2. Ask the user if the record should be saved to disk. If the user responds with Y (yes), write the record to disk; otherwise, do not write the record to disk. This is a common procedure; it gives the user a final look at the record before actually writing it.

3. Allow the user to enter another record or terminate processing.

ARITHMETIC OPERATIONS

CHAPTER OUTLINE

CHAPTER

6

CHAPTER OBJECTIVES

In Chapter 3, you learned about the basic forms of the four arithmetic verbs: ADD, SUBTRACT, MULTIPLY, and DIVIDE. This chapter focuses on the many details of COBOL arithmetic operations. From this chapter, you will learn the following:

- Designating a sign on a numeric field.

- Two formats of the ADD statement.

- Two formats of the SUBTRACT statement.

- Two formats of the MULTIPLY statement.

- Rounding of calculated results.

- Five formats of the DIVIDE statement.

- The COMPUTE statement, which can designate calculations by using a form similar to that of algebra.

Negative Numbers in COBOL

You know from earlier descriptions that the compiler reserves one position of storage for each 9 in the PICTURE and none for the V (assumed decimal point).

Interestingly, the S PICTURE symbol (sign) also does not reserve any memory if you do not explicitly tell the compiler to do so. For instance, the field PL-SIGNED-FIELD

```
10  PL-SIGNED-FIELD    PIC S99V99.
```

uses only four bytes. If so, how is it possible to store four digits *and* the sign in only four positions? The answer comes from the early days of punched-card processing, when numerous methods were used to maximize the amount of data stored in an 80-column punched card. One of the methods was to record—or punch—the sign in the same card column as the last digit of the numeric field. This practice carried over to computers and is still used today.

You can use COBOL with almost no knowledge of what is occurring within the computer. However, with signed numbers, you need to know the two ways in which the sign is carried. The default is an **embedded sign** in which the sign is encoded in the last digit of field. The COBOL Standard allows either the first or the last position to be used—the last is most common. Figure 6-1 illustrates the embedded-sign concept. Encoding in this way actually changes the last digit of a number to another character in an implementer-dependent way. For the IBM mainframe, the last digit becomes an uppercase letter according to the following table:

Negative digit	Stored as
–0	}
–1	J
–2	K
–3	L
–4	M

Negative digit	Stored as
–5	N
–6	O
–7	P
–8	Q
–9	R

So, the negative number –128528 is stored internally as 12852Q. Usually, this is unimportant unless you inspect a data file. Fortunately, COBOL handles this automatically.

The second way in which the sign is stored is in a *separate position*. For instance, a six-digit number requires seven positions: six for digits and one for the sign. The **separate sign**, which is designated by the SIGN clause, can be located either at the beginning of the field or at the end. Figure 6-2 illustrates the two cases. Obviously, the SIGN clause is meaningful only with numeric fields that include an

Figure 6-1
Sign embedded in the last digit.

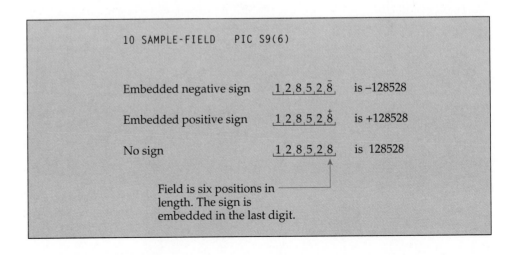

Figure 6-2
Separate sign character.

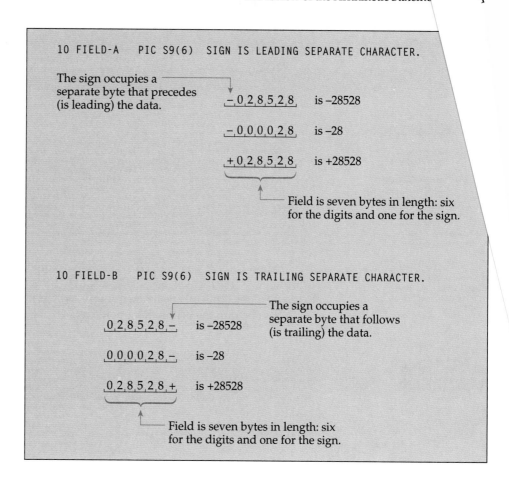

```
10 FIELD-A   PIC S9(6)   SIGN IS LEADING SEPARATE CHARACTER.
```

The sign occupies a separate byte that precedes (is leading) the data.

    - 0 2 8 5 2 8   is -28528

    - 0 0 0 0 2 8   is -28

    + 0 2 8 5 2 8   is +28528

Field is seven bytes in length: six for the digits and one for the sign.

```
10 FIELD-B   PIC S9(6)   SIGN IS TRAILING SEPARATE CHARACTER.
```

    0 2 8 5 2 8 -   is -28528

The sign occupies a separate byte that follows (is trailing) the data.

    0 0 0 0 2 8 -   is -28

    0 2 8 5 2 8 +   is +28528

Field is seven bytes in length: six for the digits and one for the sign.

S in their PICTURE. When used with a group item, this clause applies to all signed numeric fields in that group item.

Although one method might be slightly more efficient than another for various computers, your program will function correctly regardless of the sign convention used in the WORKING-STORAGE SECTION. However, in a record description for an input file, you must be certain that your sign designation corresponds to the way in which the data is stored. In most IBM mainframe environments, you will find that the default of an embedded sign on the rightmost digit is used.

A Preview of the Arithmetic Statements

In Chapter 3, you used simple arithmetic to subtract the Actual-contribution field from the Target-contribution field. Figure 6-3 illustrates the MOVE/SUBTRACT sequence. Notice that data in the first field (the one designated before the FROM) is unchanged, but the value of the second field is replaced with the calculated difference.

Each of the other three basic arithmetic operations has a similar form, as the following examples illustrate:

```
ADD FIELD-A TO FIELD-B
SUBTRACT FIELD-A FROM FIELD-B
MULTIPLY FIELD-A BY FIELD-B
DIVIDE FIELD-A INTO FIELD-B
```

In each case, the value in FIELD-A is "combined" with the value in FIELD-B. FIELD-A is left unchanged; the contents of FIELD-B are replaced with the result of the arithmetic operation.

Figure 6-3
Example of the SUBTRACT
statement.

```
MOVE PR-TARGET-CONTR TO AR-DIFFERENCE
SUBTRACT PR-ACTUAL-CONTR FROM AR-DIFFERENCE
```

Field contents

	PR-TARGET-CONTR	PR-ACTUAL-CONTR	AR-DIFFERENCE
Before MOVE:	0 2 0 0	0 1 8 5	? ? ? ?
After MOVE:	0 2 0 0	0 1 8 5	0 2 0 0
After SUBTRACT:	0 2 0 0	0 1 8 5	0 0 1 5

When coding your DATA DIVISION, remember that all fields upon which arithmetic is performed in the PROCEDURE DIVISION must be defined as numeric items. This means that a numeric-edited item cannot be used as one of the fields involved in the arithmetic operation.

COBOL-9X

COBOL-9X is expected to allow arithmetic operations on numeric-edited data items.

These examples give you an overall idea of the arithmetic tools available. Each statement has various formats and special features that are not shown here, but are discussed in the upcoming sections.

The ADD Statement

The ADD statement has two forms. Although the COBOL Standard calls them Format-1 and Format-2, this text also refers to them by the more meaningful designations of ADD/TO and ADD/GIVING, respectively.

The ADD/TO (Format-1) Statement

As you observed in the PATDFCT program, the ADD/TO statement causes the sum to be developed in the augend (the second of the two quantities)—thereby erasing the augend's original value. The ADD/TO statement is typically used within a series of calculations or when accumulating, as in the PATDFCT program
    The ADD/TO format is shown in Figure 6-4. When interpreting this, remember that:

- Brackets or braces enclosing multiple elements in the format notation means that any one of the alternative elements shown may be specified.

Figure 6-4
The ADD/TO format.

**Partial Format
ADD/TO (Format-1):**

$$\underline{ADD} \left\{ \begin{array}{l} \text{identifier-1} \\ \text{literal-1} \end{array} \right\} \dots \underline{TO} \; \{\text{identifier-2} \; [\underline{ROUNDED}]\} \dots$$

- An element followed by an ellipsis (...) means that element can be repeated one or more times.

Notice in the ADD/TO statement that each addend (the entry before the word TO) can be either an identifier (the data-name of a numeric field) or a numeric literal (an actual numeric value). From this format, you can see that its variations allow you to:

- Add one field to a second

- Add a numeric literal to a field

- Add one or more literals and/or fields to a field

- Add one or more literals and/or fields to two or more fields

The first two cases are relatively straightforward; you probably used them in earlier assignments. The other two variations are shown in Figure 6-5.

In Figure 6-5(a), three addends—SALES-TAX, DELIVERY-CHARGE, and a literal—are added to the augend, SALES-PRICE. Of course, the original value in SALES-PRICE is replaced by the newly calculated sum.

Usually, one or more addends are combined with a single augend, but sometimes more than one augend is needed. Such processing is handled by specifying more than one field after the word TO, as Figure 6-5(b) shows. In this case, two augends exist: TOTAL-PURCHASES and TOTAL-TAXABLE-PURCHASES.

Referring to the ADD format, you should recognize that a numeric literal cannot be written after the TO; the augend(s) receive the sum. The sum must be stored in a field, not in a literal.

Both of the Figure 6-5 examples involve data with two digits to the right of the decimal point—typically dollar and cent amounts. Normally, all fields in an ADD or a SUBTRACT statement have the same number of decimal positions. However, this makes no difference to COBOL because the compiler generates code to align decimal points as appropriate.

Figure 6-5
Examples of the
ADD/TO statement.

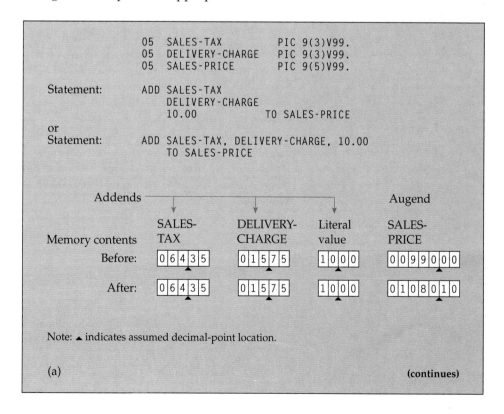

Figure 6-5 (continued)

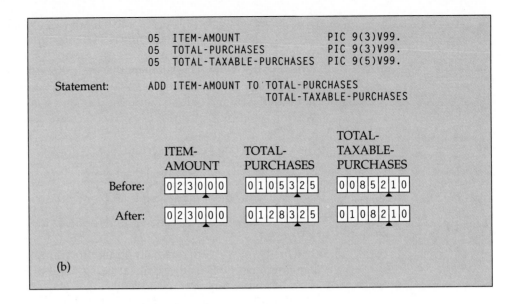

```
                          05    ITEM-AMOUNT              PIC 9(3)V99.
                          05    TOTAL-PURCHASES          PIC 9(3)V99.
                          05    TOTAL-TAXABLE-PURCHASES  PIC 9(5)V99.

        Statement:        ADD ITEM-AMOUNT TO TOTAL-PURCHASES
                                            TOTAL-TAXABLE-PURCHASES
```

	ITEM-AMOUNT	TOTAL-PURCHASES	TOTAL-TAXABLE-PURCHASES
Before:	0 2 3 0 0 0	0 1 0 5 3 2 5	0 0 8 5 2 1 0
After:	0 2 3 0 0 0	0 1 2 8 3 2 5	0 1 0 8 2 1 0

(b)

Referring to Figure 6-4's partial format, note that the optional phrase ROUNDED is included. This relates to the rounding off of the calculated result and is illustrated later with multiplication and division operations.

The ADD/GIVING (Format-2) Statement

The ADD/GIVING statement sums two or more quantities *without* changing any of them and stores the result in one or more separate fields not involved in the calculation. From the general form of the ADD/GIVING in Figure 6-6, notice the following about this statement:

- At least two elements (identifier-1/literal-1 and identifier-2/literal-2) must be specified before the reserved word GIVING. Each can be either a numeric field or a numeric literal.

- The sum of the addition is stored in the field coded after the reserved word GIVING. The field(s) that will receive the sum must have a PICTURE specification that is either numeric or numeric-edited.

- The reserved word TO, which is required by the ADD/TO statement syntax, is optional in the ADD/GIVING statement.

COBOL-74

In COBOL-74, the reserved word TO—which is required by the ADD/TO statement syntax—is prohibited in the ADD/GIVING statement. Beginning COBOL programmers using COBOL-74 compilers often inadvertently specify the word TO in the ADD/GIVING statement and receive a diagnostic error message from the compiler.

Figure 6-6
The ADD/GIVING format.

Partial Format
ADD/GIVING (Format-2):

$$\underline{ADD} \begin{Bmatrix} identifier\text{-}1 \\ literal\text{-}1 \end{Bmatrix} \dots \ TO \ \begin{Bmatrix} identifier\text{-}2 \\ literal\text{-}2 \end{Bmatrix}$$

$$\underline{GIVING} \ \{ \ identifier\text{-}3 \ [\underline{ROUNDED}] \ \} \ \dots$$

A simple example of this statement is shown in Figure 6-7(a). (In this example and most that follow, the PICTURE description is not explicitly shown; it is implied by the memory representation.) Figure 6-7(b) should help you conceptualize how the ADD/GIVING works. The arithmetic operations actually take place using a temporary work area in memory. When the arithmetic is complete, the result is moved to the GIVING field.

Inspecting the general form, you can see that any number of values, either literals or data fields, can be added. Also, the resulting sum can be stored in one or more fields; this action is equivalent to the MOVE, which allows you to move—or copy—a field into multiple receiving fields. The following are two other examples of the ADD/GIVING:

Example
```
ADD FIELD-A
    FIELD-B
    FIELD-C
    25.00
          GIVING FIELD-TOTAL
```

Action Sums the contents of fields FIELD-A, FIELD-B, FIELD-C, and the numeric literal 25, then places the result in FIELD-TOTAL. Here, the fields are stacked one above the other in order to give a visual representation of the action.

Example `ADD FIELD-A TO 25.00 GIVING FIELD-TOTAL, WORK-FIELD`

Action Sums the contents of field FIELD-A and the numeric literal 25, then places a copy of the result in both FIELD-TOTAL and WORK-FIELD. The comma separating the two result fields is optional and is included to give a visual separation of the two fields.

Figure 6-7   ADD/GIVING example and execution sequence.

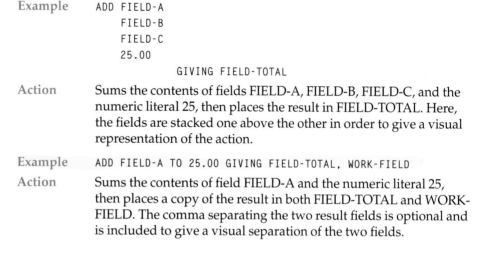

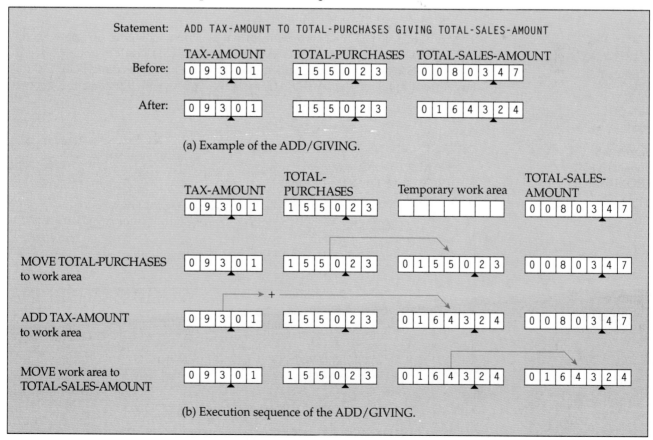

The SUBTRACT Statement

If you understand the ADD statement, you should easily comprehend the SUBTRACT because their general forms are almost the same. Like the ADD, the SUBTRACT has two formats: Format-1 (SUBTRACT/FROM) and Format-2 (SUBTRACT/GIVING).

The SUBTRACT/FROM (Format-1) Statement

Figure 6-8 shows the SUBTRACT/FROM statement format. Its characteristics are illustrated by the following examples:

Example	`SUBTRACT 20.00 FROM FIELD-B`
Action	Subtracts the value 20.00—the *subtrahend*—from the contents of FIELD-B—the *minuend*—with the resulting *difference* stored in FIELD-B.
Example	`SUBTRACT FIELD-A, FIELD-B, 12.25 FROM FIELD-C`
Action	When multiple subtrahends are coded—FIELD-A, FIELD-B, and 12.25, in this case—the COBOL compiler handles the computation by first summing the subtrahends and then subtracting that sum from the minuend(s) written after the reserved word FROM. In this example, the contents of FIELD-A, the contents of FIELD-B, and the numeric literal 12.25 are added (using a temporary work area), then this resulting sum is subtracted from FIELD-C.
Example	`SUBTRACT FIELD-A FROM FIELD-B, FIELD-C`
Action	Subtracts the contents of FIELD-A from the contents of FIELD-B, with the resulting difference stored in FIELD-B. Then subtracts the contents of FIELD-A from the contents of FIELD-C, with that resulting difference stored in FIELD-C. As with the ADD, the element following the FROM (the receiving field) cannot be a literal.

The SUBTRACT/ GIVING (Format-2) Statement

The SUBTRACT/GIVING statement format is shown in Figure 6-9. As with the ADD/GIVING statement, the GIVING field of this SUBTRACT is not included in the calculation and can thus be either a numeric or a numeric-edited field. The following examples of the SUBTRACT/GIVING statement illustrate the general format.

Figure 6-8
The SUBTRACT/ FROM format.

Partial Format
SUBTRACT/FROM (Format-1):

$$\underline{\text{SUBTRACT}} \left\{ \begin{array}{l} \text{identifier-1} \\ \text{literal-1} \end{array} \right\} \dots \underline{\text{FROM}} \; \{ \text{identifier-2} \; [\underline{\text{ROUNDED}}] \} \dots$$

Figure 6-9
The SUBTRACT/ GIVING format.

Partial Format
SUBTRACT/GIVING (Format-2):

$$\underline{\text{SUBTRACT}} \left\{ \begin{array}{l} \text{identifier-1} \\ \text{literal-1} \end{array} \right\} \dots \underline{\text{FROM}} \left\{ \begin{array}{l} \text{identifier-2} \\ \text{literal-2} \end{array} \right\}$$

$$\underline{\text{GIVING}} \; \{ \text{identifier-3} \; [\underline{\text{ROUNDED}}] \} \dots$$

Example   SUBTRACT 10.00, WITH-TAX, FICA, OTHER-DED FROM GROSS-PAY
           GIVING NET-PAY

Action   Calculates the sum of 10.00 and the contents of the fields WITH-
           TAX, FICA, and OTHER-DED. Subtracts this sum from the value in
           GROSS-PAY and stores the result in NET-PAY. The only field
           changed is NET-PAY.

Example   SUBTRACT 1 FROM BONUS-PNTS GIVING CHECK-PNTS, WORK-PNTS

Action   The amount 1 is subtracted from the value in BONUS-PNTS; the
           result is copied into CHECK-PNTS and WORK-PNTS. BONUS-
           PNTS is not changed.

Dealing with Negative Results

As indicated earlier, if a SUBTRACT statement produces a negative result, COBOL
discards the sign unless the receiving field is defined as being signed. For instance,
if you subtract 525 from 300, you will obtain a value of 225 rather than –225. So be
certain to include a sign with your arithmetic work areas.

The MULTIPLY Statement

As with the ADD and SUBTRACT statements, the MULTIPLY statement has
two formats: Format-1 and Format-2. These formats are referred to in the text as
MULTIPLY/BY and MULTIPLY/GIVING, respectively.

The MULTIPLY/BY (Format-1) Statement

Figure 6-10 shows the MULTIPLY/BY format. Notice that the MULTIPLY differs
from the ADD and SUBTRACT in that only a single factor (identifier-1/literal-1)
can precede the keyword BY. Like the equivalent ADD and SUBTRACT forms, the
result is placed in the field following the keyword BY (identifier-2). The following
two examples illustrate the general format:

Example   MULTIPLY 1.1 BY TAX-RATE

Action   The value in TAX-RATE is multiplied by 1.1; the value in TAX-RATE
           is replaced with the calculated product.

Example   MULTIPLY 1.1 BY BASE-TAX-RATE, COUNTY-RATE, SPECIAL-RATE

Action   The values in each of the fields BASE-TAX-RATE, COUNTY-RATE,
           and SPECIAL-RATE are multiplied by 1.1 and replaced by the
           respective products.

The Rounded Clause

A multiplication in which both fields have digits to the right of the decimal point
usually has right digits that are discarded, as Figure 6-11 illustrates. By default,
COBOL truncates. If you want to round the result instead, then you can include
the ROUNDED clause. For example, Figure 6-11's MULTIPLY statement becomes

    MULTIPLY TAX-RATE BY TAX-WORK-AREA ROUNDED.

Figure 6-10
The MULTIPLY/BY format.

> **Partial Format**
> **MULTIPLY/BY (Format-1):**
>
> MULTIPLY $\left\{ \begin{array}{l} \text{identifier-1} \\ \text{literal-1} \end{array} \right\}$ BY { identifier-2 [ROUNDED] } ...

Figure 6-11
Truncating a product.

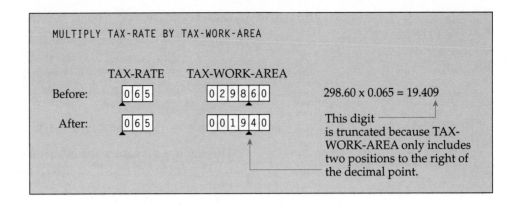

Figure 6-12
The MULTIPLY/
GIVING format.

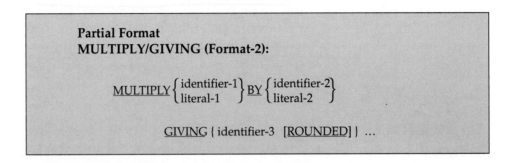

The result stored in TAX-WORK-AREA then becomes 0019.41, instead of 0019.40.

Note that the ROUNDED clause was not required in any of the ADD or SUBTRACT examples because all elements involved in the calculations were shown with the same number of decimal places. However, whenever the result field for any of these arithmetic statements contains fewer places to the right of the decimal point than the expected calculated result, you should consider the ROUNDED clause.

**The MULTIPLY/
GIVING (Format-2)
Statement**

In the MULTIPLY/GIVING partial format of Figure 6-12, both factors to the multiplication operation (identifier-1/literal-1 and identifier-2/literal-2) can be either a numeric field or a numeric literal. The product or products (identifier-3, identifier-4, and so on) may be either numeric or numeric-edited fields. The following example of the MULTIPLY/GIVING is the typical way in which this statement is used:

Example   `MULTIPLY TOTAL-PURCHASES BY TAX-RATE GIVING TAX-AMOUNT`

Action   The values in TOTAL-PURCHASES and TAX-RATE are multiplied. The original value in TAX-AMOUNT is replaced with the calculated product.

**The DIVIDE
Statement**

The DIVIDE statement is somewhat more complicated because it has five formats, Format-1 through Format-5. Three of them are DIVIDE/INTO forms and two are DIVIDE/BY forms. The major difference between the INTO and the BY formats is the relative placement of the divisor and dividend within the DIVIDE statement.

Figure 6-13
The DIVIDE/INTO
and DIVIDE/INTO/
GIVING formats.

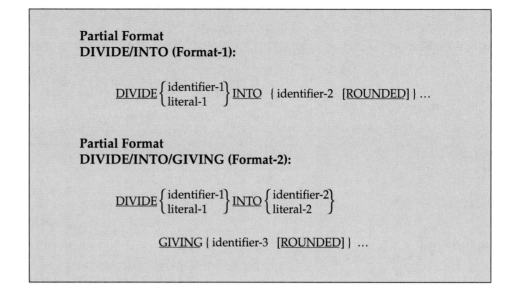

Partial Format
DIVIDE/INTO (Format-1):

$$\underline{DIVIDE} \begin{Bmatrix} \text{identifier-1} \\ \text{literal-1} \end{Bmatrix} \underline{INTO} \ \{ \text{identifier-2} \ [\underline{ROUNDED}] \} \ \dots$$

Partial Format
DIVIDE/INTO/GIVING (Format-2):

$$\underline{DIVIDE} \begin{Bmatrix} \text{identifier-1} \\ \text{literal-1} \end{Bmatrix} \underline{INTO} \begin{Bmatrix} \text{identifier-2} \\ \text{literal-2} \end{Bmatrix}$$

$$\underline{GIVING} \ \{ \text{identifier-3} \ [\underline{ROUNDED}] \} \ \dots$$

The DIVIDE/INTO (Format-1) and the DIVIDE/INTO/GIVING (Format-2) Statements

As you can see by inspecting Figure 6-13, these two DIVIDE statement formats are identical to those of the corresponding MULTIPLY statements. The following two examples illustrate the ways in which you will most commonly use the DIVIDE:

Example   DIVIDE TOTAL-UNITS INTO WORK-POINTS ROUNDED

Action   The value in TOTAL-UNITS, the *divisor,* is divided into the value in WORK-POINTS, the *dividend.* The original value in WORK-POINTS is replaced with the calculated quotient.

Example   DIVIDE TOTAL-UNITS INTO EARNED-POINTS
              GIVING GRADE-POINT-AVERAGE ROUNDED

Action   The value in TOTAL-UNITS is divided into the value in EARNED-POINTS and the quotient is stored in GRADE-POINT-AVERAGE. You will commonly use the ROUNDED clause when dividing, as in this example.

As with all arithmetic statements, fields listed after the word GIVING are not factors to the division operation; they may be either numeric or numeric-edited fields. The original values of the factors listed before the GIVING are not disturbed.

The DIVIDE/INTO/GIVING/REMAINDER (Format-4) Statement

As Figure 6-14 shows, the DIVIDE/INTO/GIVING/REMAINDER format permits specification of a field to hold the remainder from the division operation. Otherwise, the arithmetic is like that provided by the DIVIDE/INTO/GIVING format. After the reserved word REMAINDER is coded, the data-name of an elementary numeric field is coded. This field will receive the remainder value. The REMAINDER phrase is not often specified for DIVIDE operations.

However, remainders are often used in one type of situation—when working with a counting system that does not cycle at 10. A good example is hours and minutes. For instance, 192 minutes is usually represented as 3 hours 12 minutes, rather than 3.2 hours. Notice that if you divide 192 by 60 (do this by hand, not with

Figure 6-14
The DIVIDE/INTO/
GIVING/REMAINDER
format.

Partial Format
DIVIDE/INTO/GIVING/REMAINDER (Format-4):

$$\underline{\text{DIVIDE}} \left\{ \begin{array}{l} \text{identifier-1} \\ \text{literal-1} \end{array} \right\} \underline{\text{INTO}} \left\{ \begin{array}{l} \text{identifier-2} \\ \text{literal-2} \end{array} \right\}$$

$$\underline{\text{GIVING}} \text{ identifier-3 } [\underline{\text{ROUNDED}}] \underline{\text{ REMAINDER}} \text{ identifier-4}$$

a calculator), the quotient is 3 (the number of hours) and the remainder is 12 (the number of minutes). The following is a COBOL statement to perform such an operation:

```
DIVIDE 60 INTO TOTAL-TIME-IN-MINUTES
    GIVING ELAPSED-HOURS REMAINDER ELAPSED-MINUTES
```

The DIVIDE/BY/
GIVING (Format-3)
and the DIVIDE/BY/
GIVING/REMAINDER
(Format-5) Statements

As you can see by comparing the general formats of Figure 6-15 to formats in Figures 6-13 and 6-14, a correspondence occurs between formats of two pairs of the DIVIDE statement:

```
DIVIDE/BY/GIVING            to    DIVIDE/INTO/GIVING
DIVIDE/BY/GIVING/REMAINDER  to    DIVIDE/INTO/GIVING/REMAINDER
```

The differences are (1) the reserved word BY is used instead of the word INTO and (2) the relative location of the divisor and the dividend are switched. For example, the following performs exactly the same function as the earlier example to obtain hours and minutes from minutes:

```
DIVIDE TOTAL-TIME-IN-MINUTES BY 60
    GIVING ELAPSED-HOURS REMAINDER ELAPSED-MINUTES
```

Figure 6-15
The DIVIDE/BY/GIVING
and DIVIDE/BY/
GIVING/REMAINDER
formats.

Partial Format
DIVIDE/BY/GIVING (Format-3):

$$\underline{\text{DIVIDE}} \left\{ \begin{array}{l} \text{identifier-1} \\ \text{literal-1} \end{array} \right\} \underline{\text{BY}} \left\{ \begin{array}{l} \text{identifier-2} \\ \text{literal-2} \end{array} \right\}$$

$$\underline{\text{GIVING}} \{ \text{ identifier-3 } [\underline{\text{ROUNDED}}] \} \dots$$

Partial Format
DIVIDE/BY/GIVING/REMAINDER (Format-5):

$$\underline{\text{DIVIDE}} \left\{ \begin{array}{l} \text{identifier-1} \\ \text{literal-1} \end{array} \right\} \underline{\text{BY}} \left\{ \begin{array}{l} \text{identifier-2} \\ \text{literal-2} \end{array} \right\}$$

$$\underline{\text{GIVING}} \text{ identifier-3 } [\underline{\text{ROUNDED}}] \underline{\text{ REMAINDER}} \text{ identifier-4}$$

The COMPUTE Statement

The COMPUTE statement is an alternative to the four basic arithmetic verbs just described. If you know almost any other computer language (such as BASIC), you will understand the technique employed. It permits the expression of arithmetic calculations in a manner similar to algebraic notation. Figure 6-16 shows the COMPUTE statement, together with examples.

COMPUTE Statement Processing

The five arithmetic operator symbols that may be coded in a COMPUTE statement are as follows:

Operator symbol	Operation
+	Addition
−	Subtraction
*	Multiplication
/	Division
**	Exponentiation

In Figure 6-16's first example, the arithmetic expression consists of three quantities to add and one to subtract:

```
BALANCE-FORWARD + CURRENT-PURCHASES + SERVICE-CHARGE - TOTAL-PAYMENT
```

As you might expect, the arithmetic operations are carried out from left to right; then, the result is stored in the data-item NEW-BALANCE. In contrast, Figure 6-16's third example is more complex and includes a variety of arithmetic operators.

When the arithmetic expression contains more than one arithmetic operator symbol, the operations are executed in a specific order, called the **hierarchy of arithmetic operations** or the **order of precedence**. The order is as follows:

1. **Unary operations** (has only one factor and reverses the sign of a field)
2. **Exponentiation** (raises a value to a power)
3. Multiplication and division
4. Addition and subtraction

Figure 6-16
The COMPUTE statement format and examples.

Partial Format:

COMPUTE { identifier-1 [ROUNDED] } ...

= arithmetic-expression

Examples:

```
COMPUTE NEW-BALANCE = BALANCE-FORWARD
                    + CURRENT-PURCHASES
                    + SERVICE-CHARGE
                    - TOTAL-PAYMENT

COMPUTE INTEREST = PRINCIPAL * RATE * YEARS / 100
COMPUTE AMOUNT = PRINCIPAL * (1.00 + RATE / 100) ** YEARS
```

To illustrate this hierarchy of operations, consider the following statement:

```
COMPUTE X = A + B / C
```

The sequence of operations is

1. The division specified by B / C is performed; division is at hierarchy level 3.
2. The quotient from that division is added to the value of A; addition is at hierarchy level 4 and is therefore performed after division.
3. The result is placed in X; only the value of X changes.

Some expressions contain two or more additions or subtractions (or multiplications or divisions). When this occurs, the operations within each hierarchy level are executed starting from left to right within the expression. To illustrate, consider the statement:

```
COMPUTE X = A - B / C + D * E
```

The sequence in which the calculations occur is as follows:

1. B / C (quotient stored in a temporary work area)
2. D * E (product stored in a temporary work area)
3. A – (quotient from Step 1)
4. (difference from Step 3) + (product from Step 2)

Be careful of this hierarchy or else you could encounter something unanticipated. Suppose you want to add two fields (A and B) and then divide the sum by another field (C). You would not get the correct result using:

```
COMPUTE X = A + B / C   (Does not give the desired result.)
```

The reason is that the division of B by C would occur before A is added to B.

To override this normal sequence of operations, use parentheses—just as in algebra. That is, operations within the innermost set of parentheses are evaluated first and then evaluation proceeds through the outermost set. Equal parentheses levels are evaluated on a left-to-right basis. So, by writing the previous statement with parentheses as follows, you obtain the desired result:

```
COMPUTE X = (A + B) / C
```

It is a good practice to code parentheses within the arithmetic expression—regardless of whether or not they are actually required to override the normal sequence of operations—for two reasons. First, with complex expressions, it is sometimes difficult to determine exactly when the system will perform each operation. It is simpler and less risky to instead code the parentheses where appropriate to ensure the desired sequence. Second, it is easier to read and understand an arithmetic expression written with parentheses.

COMPUTE
Statement Syntax

The identifier coded before the equals sign—that is, the field that will receive the result—can be either numeric or numeric-edited. Each field coded within the arithmetic expression—that is, after the equals sign—must be purely numeric (either a numeric field or a numeric literal).

The equals sign and each arithmetic operator sign must be preceded and followed by a space. For example, the statement

```
COMPUTE X=A+B
```

is syntactically incorrect. It must instead be coded with spaces to separate the elements of the arithmetic expression; that is:

```
COMPUTE X = A + B
```

In most programming languages, spaces are ignored by the compiler, so they can either be omitted or included to improve readability. So if you know some other language, such as BASIC or Pascal, make sure you do not get confused and leave out the spaces.

> **COBOL-9X**
>
> COBOL-9X will relax the requirement of spaces around arithmetic operators, thereby making valid forms such as the following:
>
> ```
> X=A+B
> ```

Although multiply operations are often implied in algebra (the absence of a times sign implies multiplication), all operations must be explicitly coded in the COMPUTE statement arithmetic expression.

When parentheses are coded, they must always appear in pairs and should be coded immediately adjacent to their contents. That is, a left parenthesis should have a space on the left and no space on the right; a right parenthesis should have no space on the left and a space on the right.

A unary operation can be specified to reverse the arithmetic sign of a value within a field. A minus sign coded with no factor to the left is a **unary arithmetic operator.** For example, the statements

```
COMPUTE X = - B + C
COMPUTE X = A + (- B + C)
```

cause the value of B to be multiplied by the numeric literal –1 before it is added to C. Remember that unary operations rank highest in the hierarchy of arithmetic operations.

Note that the general format of COMPUTE allows use of the ROUNDED phrase. It works with the COMPUTE in exactly the same way it works with the four arithmetic statements.

The ON SIZE ERROR Phrase

Perhaps you wonder what happens when an arithmetic calculation generates a value that exceeds the size of the receiving field. The answer is that an **arithmetic overflow** condition occurs and the overflowing digit or digits are lost. In COBOL, it is called a **size error** condition and is illustrated in Figure 6-17. In this case, the overflow of 1 is discarded and the resulting sum in TOTAL-AMOUNT is 0438.86, as shown. COBOL provides no indication of the erroneous result.

However, this size error condition can be detected and an action taken by including the ON SIZE ERROR phrase as follows:

```
ADD NEW-AMOUNTS TO TOTAL-AMOUNT
    ON SIZE ERROR
        PERFORM 999-IDENTIFY-SIZE-ERROR
END-ADD
```

Figure 6-17
A size error condition.

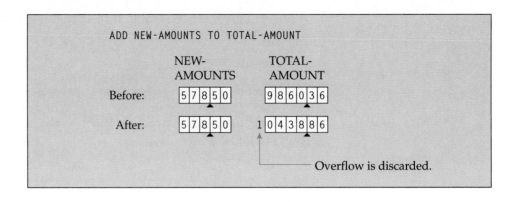

Now when the condition of Figure 6-17 occurs, the 999-IDENTIFY-SIZE-ERROR procedure is performed. When a size error does occur and the phrase is specified, the contents of the receiving field are unpredictable. (Typically, the receiving field is unchanged, rather than filled with a truncated answer.)

In a normal situation when the result can be accommodated within the answer field(s), the ON SIZE ERROR phrase statements are skipped; program processing resumes after the END-ADD scope terminator. Overall, the way in which the ON SIZE ERROR phrase works is virtually identical to the way the AT END phrase of the READ statement functions.

In addition to the ON SIZE ERROR clause, arithmetic statements can include the NOT ON SIZE ERROR, which is roughly equivalent to the NOT AT END of the READ. Figure 6-18 shows the complete format and an example for the ADD/TO. The figure's comments illustrate how this form works. Notice that the format lists imperative statements as the conditional options. Remember, imperative statement means one *or more* PROCEDURE DIVISION statements.

The form of the SIZE ERROR/NOT SIZE ERROR options shown for the ADD in Figure 6-18 applies equally to all arithmetic operations, including the COMPUTE. The only difference is the scope terminator: END-SUBTRACT, END-MULTIPLY, END-DIVIDE, and END-COMPUTE, as appropriate.

Figure 6-18
SIZE ERROR options
with the ADD/TO.

Format
ADD/TO (Format-1):

$$\underline{ADD} \begin{Bmatrix} \text{identifier-1} \\ \text{literal} \end{Bmatrix} \dots \underline{TO} \{ \text{identifier-2} \ [\underline{ROUNDED}] \} \dots$$

[ON <u>SIZE ERROR</u> imperative-statement-1]
[<u>NOT</u> ON <u>SIZE ERROR</u> imperative-statement-2]
[<u>END-ADD</u>]

```
ADD NEW-AMOUNTS TO TOTAL-AMOUNT
    ON SIZE ERROR
        MOVE "NO" TO AR-GOOD-ADD
    NOT ON SIZE ERROR
        MOVE "YES" TO AR-GOOD-ADD
END-ADD
```

If a size error occurs from the ADD, this statement is executed.

If no error occurs, this statement is executed.

The END-ADD scope indicator defines the scope of the SIZE ERROR conditional elements.

COBOL-74

COBOL-74 includes the SIZE ERROR clause, but not the NOT SIZE ERROR clause; the following example illustrates the SIZE ERROR. Notice that a period terminates the scope of the conditionally executed statements.

```
ADD NEW-AMOUNTS TO TOTAL-AMOUNT
    ON SIZE ERROR
        MOVE "NO" TO AR-GOOD-ADD
        PERFORM 999-LOG-SIZE-ERROR.
```

By utilizing proper program design and data checking (a topic of Chapter 10), you can avoid most size errors. A few actions, such as calculating running totals (accumulating), can give unexpected results that cause size errors. In such cases, the ON SIZE ERROR—or alternate program logic—should be used. However, use of the ON SIZE ERROR phrase is discouraged because it is awkward to handle the exception processing. It is best to check data before calculations to ensure that size errors do not occur.

Selecting the Appropriate Arithmetic Form

If you are a little overwhelmed by the vast array of arithmetic forms and wonder what to use when, don't worry; the proper choice is usually obvious by the application needs.

For instance, the GIVING phrase is typically not applicable when running totals are accumulated into a WORKING-STORAGE field or when counting or decrementing (counting backwards); these topics are covered in the next chapter. Statements without the GIVING phrase are more effective.

On the other hand, GIVING should be used when all fields in the calculation are needed for later calculations or other uses. For example, suppose that the sum of fields FIELD-A and FIELD-B is required early in the program processing. Then, later on, the original values of FIELD-A and FIELD-B are needed again. If the ADD statement to produce the sum is written without the GIVING phrase as

```
ADD FIELD-A TO FIELD-B
```

the original value of FIELD-B is lost. Therefore, in this situation, the statement should be written with a GIVING phrase so that a separate field is introduced to hold the sum; for instance:

```
ADD FIELD-A TO FIELD-B GIVING FIELD-C
```

Another situation appropriate for use of the GIVING phrase is when the results of a calculation are to be placed in a numeric-edited field. Remember that a numeric-edited field cannot be used as a field in an arithmetic statement. Assuming that EDITED-FIELD is a numeric-edited item, the form

```
ADD FIELD-A TO EDITED-FIELD
```

is invalid, but the form

```
ADD FIELD-A TO FIELD-B GIVING EDITED-FIELD
```

is valid.

Regarding the COMPUTE, any calculation can be made by either using some combination of the four basic arithmetic verbs or through using the COMPUTE statement. On one hand, most business calculations are relatively simple and the basic arithmetic verbs are adequate. However, if the calculation is complex and requires many operations, the COMPUTE is more concise. Also, if you must do exponentiation (raising a number to a power), the COMPUTE statement is straightforward.

However, a major drawback to the use of the COMPUTE is that the COBOL standards do not define the techniques to be used in handling the size, truncation, and rounding aspects of the intermediate results obtained during the calculation. This means that (1) unexpected result values may occur unless you are aware of the techniques employed by the compiler used, and (2) even if you know the approach followed by a particular vendor's compiler, different results may be obtained when the program is run using another vendor's compiler. Therefore, the COMPUTE statement may introduce unexpected results, which hinders program portability. However, COBOL-9X will remedy this problem.

Packed-Decimal Data Format

Although packed-decimal data format is not used in this book, it's included for your future information. You must understand it if you ever process a file containing data in this format.

In 1964, IBM introduced the System/360 line of computers, which featured the 8-bit storage **byte**. Over the years, the byte has become almost universal as the basic unit of data storage in computers, ranging from the small microcomputers to large mainframes. As used in computers today, the byte can be coded and interpreted in numerous ways, depending upon the types of operations performed and the computer instructions used.

You know from preceding chapters that DATA DIVISION entries such as the following define the number of storage positions (the number of bytes) for data-items:

```
05  ALPHA-FIELD   PIC X(10).
05  NUMBER-FIELD  PIC 9(5).
```

For instance, because of the PIC 9(5), NUMBER-FIELD requires five storage positions. Actually, this represents an inefficient use of computer byte for numeric quantities because the byte has a far greater capacity.

The System/360's designers realized that using an entire byte to store one digit was inefficient because each decimal digit can be represented in binary with four bits, or a half-byte. This is done in IBM mainframes, using a format called **packed-decimal,** in which each byte holds two digits—except the rightmost, which contains one digit plus the sign. For an application in which large quantities of numeric data are stored in a disk file, using a packed format can significantly reduce the file size. Previously, many COBOL applications were written in which data was stored in packed-decimal format to save disk storage. However, using packed-decimal format to save disk storage space is done primarily on mainframes. Modern data compression techniques render packed-decimal unnecessary.

Although COBOL-74 does not support the packed-decimal format, almost all COBOL-74 compilers do support it as a nonstandard extension because of IBM's dominance. COBOL-85 includes support for packed-decimal.

Defining Packed-Decimal in the PICTURE—The USAGE Clause

Whenever you define a data-item in the DATA DIVISION—unless you indicate otherwise—it defaults to a form called **display format,** in which each position of the field width reserves one byte. However, if the file from which you must read data contains fields stored in packed-decimal, you must explicitly define them as such in the record description. To do this, you must utilize the USAGE clause. The following is an example of a field defined this way:

```
05  PR-PACKED-TARGET-CONTR   PIC 9(6)V99  USAGE IS PACKED-DECIMAL.
```

The required key word is USAGE. The word IS is optional; PACKED-DECIMAL is the reserved word specified in the COBOL-85 Standard.

In IBM COBOL, packed-decimal is called COMPUTATIONAL-3—or simply COMP-3—and the preceding definition takes the following form:

```
05  PR-PACKED-TARGET-CONTR   PIC 9(6)V99  USAGE IS COMP-3.
```

The only time you will need to use this clause is if you are processing files in which data is stored in packed-decimal. As stated earlier, packed-decimal is not used in this book's example programs.

A Modification to the Patron Deficit Program

The PATDFCT3 Program

To show how some of this chapter's principles are applied, let's consider a modification to PATDFCT2 that involves the following:

Print only those patrons with the actual contribution less than the target contribution.

Calculate and print the contribution deficiency ratio (as a percentage):

$$\text{Ratio} = \frac{\text{Target-contribution} - \text{Actual-contribution}}{\text{Target-contribution}}$$

Since this is a relatively minor variation of PATDFCT2, the overall program design does not require extensive commentary. To give you an idea of what the printed report looks like, sample output is shown in Figure 6-19. The program, PATDFCT3, is shown in Figure 6-20.

Arithmetic Operations

From Figure 6-19's sample output, you can see that the percentage is calculated to the nearest tenth. For an idea of the ratios that can result from the calculations, consider the following table's examples.

Actual	Target	Deficit	Ratio (Deficit/Target)	Percentage
400	500	100	.2	20.0
322	500	173	.346	34.6
0	500	500	1.0	100.0

Figure 6-19
Sample output for
PATDFCT3.

```
                        PATRON DEFICIT REPORT
   PATRON NAME          CITY/STATE/ZIP          TARGET  ACTUAL     DEFICIT

   Anderson, Hazel      Woodside, CA 94062        250     100      150   60.0%
   Baker, Donald        Berkeley, CA 94703        375     300       75   20.0%
   Campbell, J. H.      Emeryville, CA 94608      200     175       25   12.5%
   Davidson, Harley     Concord, CA 94519         250     100      150   60.0%
   Englehoff, F.        Santa Clara, CA 95051     250     150      100   40.0%
   Hildebrand, John     Santa Cruz, CA 95060      250     200       50   20.0%
   Jones, Jeanette      Belvedere, CA 94920       375       0      375  100.0%
   Miller, Irwin B.     Daly City, CA 94014       200     185       15    7.5%
   Molitar, Arnold T.   Capitola, CA 95010        200     150       50   25.0%
   Nelson, J. J.        Alameda, CA 94501         250       0      250  100.0%
   Pratt, Diane         San Francisco, CA 94115   375     229      146   38.9%
   Stevenson, Howard    San Rafael, CA 94901      200       0      200  100.0%
   Zener, Eva           Sausalito, CA 94965       200     190       10    5.0%
```

Figure 6-20   The PATDFCT3 program.

```
1        IDENTIFICATION DIVISION.                              66     01  PL-REPORT-HEADING-LINE.
2        PROGRAM-ID.    PATDFCT3.                              67         05  PIC X(25)    VALUE SPACES.
3                                                              68         05  PIC X(21)
4    *    PRICE/WELBURN 6/25/89 REVISED 1/12/95                69                 VALUE "PATRON DEFICIT REPORT".
5                                                              70
6    *    This program prints a list of patrons whose         71     01  PL-COLUMN-HEADING-LINE.
7    *    contributions are less than their target amounts.   72         05  PIC X(20)    VALUE " PATRON NAME".
8                                                              73         05  PIC X(27)    VALUE "CITY/STATE/ZIP".
9                                                              74         05  PIC X(24)    VALUE "TARGET ACTUAL    DEFICIT".
10       ENVIRONMENT DIVISION.                                 75
11                                                             76
12       INPUT-OUTPUT SECTION.                                 77     PROCEDURE DIVISION.
13                                                             78
14       FILE-CONTROL.                                         79     000-PRINT-DEFICIENT-LIST.
15           SELECT PATRON-FILE                                80     ************Initialization Sequence************
16               ASSIGN TO (system dependent).                81         OPEN INPUT PATRON-FILE
17           SELECT PATRON-LIST                                82              OUTPUT PATRON-LIST
18               ASSIGN TO (system dependent).                83         PERFORM 100-INITIALIZE-VARIABLE-FIELDS
19                                                             84         PERFORM 870-PRINT-HEADINGS
20                                                             85
21       DATA DIVISION.                                        86     **************Processing Sequence**************
22                                                             87         PERFORM UNTIL PS-END-OF-PATRON-FILE IS EQUAL TO "YES"
23       FILE SECTION.                                         88             READ PATRON-FILE
24                                                             89                     INTO PR-PATRON-RECORD
25       FD  PATRON-FILE.                                      90                 AT END
26       01  PATRON-RECORD                 PIC X(68).          91                     MOVE "YES" TO PS-END-OF-PATRON-FILE
27                                                             92                 NOT AT END
28       FD  PATRON-LIST.                                      93                     IF PR-ACTUAL-CONTR IS LESS THAN PR-TARGET-CONTR
29       01  PATRON-LINE-RECORD            PIC X(132).         94                         PERFORM 200-PROCESS-DEFICIENT-PATRON
30                                                             95                     END-IF
31       WORKING-STORAGE SECTION.                              96             END-READ
32                                                             97         END-PERFORM
33       01  PROGRAM-SWITCHES.                                 98
34           05  PS-END-OF-PATRON-FILE     PIC X(3).           99     **************Termination Sequence*************
35                                                            100         CLOSE PATRON-FILE
36       01  ARITHMETIC-WORK-AREAS.                           101               PATRON-LIST
37           05  AW-DEFICIENCY             PIC 9(4).          102         STOP RUN
38           05  AW-DEFICIENCY-RATIO       PIC 9V999.        103         .
39           05  AW-DEFICIENCY-PERCENT                       104     **************************************************
40               REDEFINES AW-DEFICIENCY-RATIO PIC 999V9.    105
41                                                            106     100-INITIALIZE-VARIABLE-FIELDS.
42   *    Input record definition                            107         MOVE "NO" TO PS-END-OF-PATRON-FILE
43       01  PR-PATRON-RECORD.                                108         .
44           05  PR-NAME                   PIC X(18).         109     200-PROCESS-DEFICIENT-PATRON.
45           05  PR-ADDRESS                PIC X(18).         110         MOVE PR-NAME TO PL-NAME
46           05  PR-CITY-STATE-ZIP         PIC X(24).         111         MOVE PR-CITY-STATE-ZIP TO PL-CITY-STATE-ZIP
47           05  PR-TARGET-CONTR           PIC 9(4).          112         MOVE PR-TARGET-CONTR TO PL-TARGET-CONTR
48           05  PR-ACTUAL-CONTR           PIC 9(4).          113         MOVE PR-ACTUAL-CONTR TO PL-ACTUAL-CONTR
49                                                            114         SUBTRACT PR-ACTUAL-CONTR FROM PR-TARGET-CONTR
50   *    PL-PRINT-LINE-DEFINITIONS                           115             GIVING AW-DEFICIENCY
51       01  PATRON-LINE.                                     116         MOVE AW-DEFICIENCY TO PL-CONTR-DEFICIENCY
52           05                    PIC X(1)  VALUE SPACE.     117         DIVIDE AW-DEFICIENCY BY PR-TARGET-CONTR
53           05  PL-NAME           PIC X(18).                 118             GIVING AW-DEFICIENCY-RATIO ROUNDED
54           05                    PIC X(1)  VALUE SPACE.     119         MOVE AW-DEFICIENCY-PERCENT TO PL-PERCENTAGE
55           05  PL-CITY-STATE-ZIP PIC X(24).                 120         MOVE PATRON-LINE TO PATRON-LINE-RECORD
56           05                    PIC X(3)  VALUE SPACE.     121         WRITE PATRON-LINE-RECORD
57           05  PL-TARGET-CONTR   PIC Z,ZZ9.                 122         .
58           05                    PIC X(2)  VALUE SPACE.     123     870-PRINT-HEADINGS.
59           05  PL-ACTUAL-CONTR   PIC Z,ZZ9.                 124         MOVE PL-REPORT-HEADING-LINE TO PATRON-LINE-RECORD
60           05                    PIC X(2)  VALUE SPACE.     125         WRITE PATRON-LINE-RECORD
61           05  PL-CONTR-DEFICIENCY PIC Z,ZZ9.              126         MOVE PL-COLUMN-HEADING-LINE TO PATRON-LINE-RECORD
62           05                    PIC X(2)  VALUE SPACE.     127         WRITE PATRON-LINE-RECORD
63           05  PL-PERCENTAGE     PIC ZZ9.9.                 128             AFTER ADVANCING 3
64           05                    PIC X(1)  VALUE "%".       129         MOVE SPACES TO PATRON-LINE-RECORD
65                                                            130         WRITE PATRON-LINE-RECORD.
                                                              131         .
```

Two controlling factors determine the field size needed for calculations. First, the ratio field can range up to 1.0 (patron making no contribution). Second, the output report requires the percentage to the nearest tenth of a percent. So, the arithmetic work areas for these two fields need to be 9V999 and 999V9, respectively. At line 38 of Figure 6-20, AW-DEFICIENCY-RATIO includes PIC 9V999. At line 40, AW-DEFICIENCY-PERCENT redefines this field with PIC 999V9. Remember, the data in storage includes no decimal point: its *assumed* position is indicated by the V in the PICTURE. So, for instance, if the number stored is 0346, when referred to by AW-DEFICIENCY-RATIO, it is interpreted as 0.346. But when referred to by AW-DEFICIENCY-PERCENT, it is interpreted as 34.6.

In the PROCEDURE DIVISION, you see the DIVIDE at lines 117 and 118 that performs the division and places the result in AW-DEFICIENCY-RATIO. Notice that the *same quantity* is referred to as AW-DEFICIENCY-PERCENT in being moved to the output area. If it were impossible to redefine a field in COBOL, then it would be necessary to multiply AW-DEFICIENCY-RATIO by 100 to obtain AW-DEFICIENCY-PERCENT.

COBOL-74

The following changes are needed to convert PATDFCT3 to COBOL-74:

1. Insert the CONFIGURATION SECTION and insert the LABEL RECORDS clause in each FD clause.
2. Include the reserved word FILLER in filler entries.
3. Modify the READ sequence to eliminate the NOT AT END. Do this by using the priming READ form (Figure 3-16, page 86) or by replacing the NOT AT END with an appropriate IF statement (Figure 3-17).
4. If necessary, move separate-line paragraph-ending periods to the end of the preceding line.
5. Change the ASSIGN clause entry as necessary.

COBOL-89 Supplement

The COBOL-89 Intrinsic Function Supplement includes several common mathematical functions. Among them are a square root function and a random number generator, both described in Appendix C.

Calculating a Loan Payment—An Interactive Example

Assume that you have a user who needs an interactive program to calculate loan payment amounts. The program should accept the following input items from the keyboard:

Amount of the loan

Loan period in months

Annual interest rate

Then it should calculate and display the monthly payment amount. To make the program more versatile, the user must be able to repeat the activity as many times as desired.

The following formula is used to calculate the monthly payment from the given input entries:

$$\text{Monthly payment} = \frac{i \times (\text{Loan amount})}{1 - (1 + i)^{-n}}$$

where $\quad i =$ Monthly interest rate expressed as a decimal fraction. For instance, an annual rate of 18% gives $i = (18 / 100) / 12 = 0.18 / 12 = 0.015$

$\quad n =$ number of monthly payments

Figure 6-21's program includes a complex calculation using the COMPUTE. The basic logic of program repetition—although a different twist than in previous

Figure 6-21 The LOAN-PAY program.

```
1        IDENTIFICATION DIVISION.              51    ***********************************************
2        PROGRAM-ID. LOAN-PAY.                 52
3                                              53    100-ANNOUNCE-TO-USER.
4    *      W. Price 1/12/95                   54        DISPLAY "        LOAN PAYMENT PROGRAM"
5                                              55        DISPLAY " "
6    *   Loan Payment Calculation Program      56        DISPLAY "This program calculates the required monthly"
7    *   (Refer to 100 paragraph for description) 57     DISPLAY "payment for a loan. The input is:"
8                                              58        DISPLAY " "
9        DATA DIVISION.                        59        DISPLAY "  Amount of loan in whole dollars"
10       WORKING-STORAGE SECTION.              60        DISPLAY "       Maximum input is 9999."
11                                             61        DISPLAY "  Annual interest rate as a percent"
12       01  INPUT-FIELDS.                     62        DISPLAY "       Must include decimal point"
13           05  IP-RATE            PIC V999.  63        DISPLAY "       May have 1 digit to right of decimal"
14           05  IP-ANNUAL-RATE REDEFINES IP-RATE 64     DISPLAY "       Example inputs 14.5   12.0"
15                                 PIC 99V9.   65        DISPLAY "  Number of months for payment"
16           05  IP-AMNT           PIC 9999.   66        DISPLAY "Press the ENTER key to begin"
17           05  IP-PERIODS        PIC 99.     67        ACCEPT CF-DUMMY
18                                             68        .
19       01  DISPLAY-FIELDS.                   69    200-GET-INPUT-VALUES.
20           05  DF-PAYMENT       PIC $$,$$9.99. 70       DISPLAY " "
21           05  DF-RATE          PIC Z9.9.    71        DISPLAY "Enter the amount: " WITH NO ADVANCING
22           05  DF-AMNT          PIC $$,$$9.  72        ACCEPT IP-AMNT
23           05  DF-PERIODS       PIC Z9.      73        DISPLAY "Enter annual rate: "  WITH NO ADVANCING
24                                             74        ACCEPT IP-ANNUAL-RATE
25       01  ARITHMETIC-FIELDS.                75        DISPLAY "Enter the num of periods: " WITH NO ADVANCING
26           05  AF-PAYMENT       PIC 9999V99. 76        ACCEPT IP-PERIODS
27           05  AF-RATE          PIC V9999.   77        .
28                                             78    250-CALCULATE-PAYMENT.
29       01  CONTROL-FIELDS.                   79        COMPUTE AF-RATE = IP-RATE / 12
30           05  CF-DUMMY         PIC X.       80        COMPUTE AF-PAYMENT = (AF-RATE * IP-AMNT)
31           05  CF-CONTIN        PIC 9.       81                    / (1 - (1 + AF-RATE) ** (- IP-PERIODS))
32                                             82        .
33       PROCEDURE DIVISION.                   83    300-DISPLAY-RESULTS.
34                                             84        DISPLAY " "
35       000-COMPUTE-LOAN-PAYMENT.             85        MOVE IP-AMNT TO DF-AMNT
36    ************Initialization Sequence************ 86    DISPLAY "         Loan amount: ", DF-AMNT
37           PERFORM 100-ANNOUNCE-TO-USER      87        MOVE IP-ANNUAL-RATE TO DF-RATE
38           MOVE 1 TO CF-CONTIN               88        DISPLAY "Annual interest rate: ", DF-RATE, "%"
39                                             89        MOVE IP-PERIODS TO DF-PERIODS
40    **************Processing Sequence************** 90    DISPLAY "     Number of months: ", DF-PERIODS
41           PERFORM UNTIL CF-CONTIN = 0       91        MOVE AF-PAYMENT TO DF-PAYMENT
42               PERFORM 200-GET-INPUT-VALUES  92        DISPLAY " "
43               PERFORM 250-CALCULATE-PAYMENT 93        DISPLAY "     The payment is: ", DF-PAYMENT
44               PERFORM 300-DISPLAY-RESULTS   94        DISPLAY " "
45           END-PERFORM                       95        DISPLAY "Enter 1 to repeat, 0 to end"
46    **************Termination Sequence************* 96    ACCEPT CF-CONTIN
47                                             97        .
48           DISPLAY "Processing complete"
49           STOP RUN
50           .
```

programs—is nothing new. Refer to the sample dialogue of Figure 6-22 while studying the following comments about this program. Note that the highlighted portions of this screen represent user input.

1. The WORKING-STORAGE SECTION is broken into records descriptive of the fields of which they are composed. The IP-RATE field is redefined in exactly the same way as the percentage field of the PATDFCT3 program. Edited fields are defined in exactly the way you would define them for a printed report.

COBOL-74

The following changes are needed to convert PATDFCT3 to COBOL-74:

1. Insert the CONFIGURATION SECTION.
2. Convert the inline PERFORM (lines 41–45) to an out-of-line PERFORM and place the three statements (lines 42–44) in an appropriate paragraph.
3. If necessary, move separate-line paragraph-ending periods to the end of the preceding line.

Figure 6-22
Sample screen display
from LOAN-PAY.

```
              LOAN PAYMENT PROGRAM

    This program calculates the required monthly
    payment for a loan. The input is:

       Amount of loan in whole dollars
           Maximum input is 9999.
       Annual interest rate as a percent
           Must include decimal point
           May have 1 digit to right of decimal
           Example inputs 14.5    12.0
       Number of months for payment

    Enter the amount: 2000
    Enter annual rate: 12.5
    Enter the num of periods: 18

            Loan amount: $2,000
    Annual interest rate: 12.5%
        Number of months: 18

          The payment is: $122.41

    Enter 1 to repeat, 0 to end
```

2. Repetition of the sequence occurs via the PERFORM at line 41 and is controlled by the field CF-CONTIN. This field is initialized at line 38 and accepts the user response at line 96.
3. The interest rate is accepted into the variable IP-ANNUAL-RATE (PIC 99V9), which is a redefinition of IP-RATE (PIC V999). IP-RATE is used in the calculation of line 79.
4. The payment is calculated by the COMPUTE at lines 80 and 81. Inspect this statement carefully and ensure that you see how it corresponds to the equation.

Chapter Summary

Each field to be computed arithmetically must be defined as numeric. Also, the field length, decimal-point location, and arithmetic-sign specifications must be considered. To perform arithmetic calculations, either the basic arithmetic statements—ADD, SUBTRACT, MULTIPLY, and DIVIDE—or the COMPUTE statement can be used. Figure 6-23 shows a summary of arithmetic statements.

The optional phrase ROUNDED can be specified for any arithmetic statement answer field to be rounded off. The optional phrase ON SIZE ERROR can be specified to provide exception-condition handling when the result will not fit in the answer field.

Generally, a program's PROCEDURE DIVISION is independent of decimal-point positioning. Once defined in the DATA DIVISION, all PROCEDURE DIVISION statements handle all decimal positioning according to the definitions of fields.

The ACCEPT and DISPLAY are used for low-volume terminal input and output.

Figure 6-23 A summary of arithmetic statements.

Statement (Format)	Operand 1	Keyword	Operand 2	GIVING	Result		REMAINDER	Remainder	ON SIZE ERROR
ADD/TO (Format-1)	Addend(s) — Numeric identifier or Numeric literal	TO	Addend(s)/Sum(s) — Numeric identifier			(ROUNDED)			(ON SIZE ERROR) imperative-statement
ADD/GIVING (Format-2)	Addend — Numeric identifier or Numeric literal		Addend(s) — Numeric identifier / Numeric literal	GIVING	Sum(s) — Numeric identifier or Numeric-edited literal	(ROUNDED)			(ON SIZE ERROR) imperative-statement
SUBTRACT/FROM (Format-1)	Subtrahend(s) — Numeric identifier or Numeric literal	FROM	Minuend(s)/Remainder(s) — Numeric identifier			(ROUNDED)			(ON SIZE ERROR) imperative-statement
SUBTRACT/GIVING (Format-2)	Subtrahend(s) — Numeric identifier or Numeric literal	FROM	Minuend — Numeric identifier / Numeric literal	GIVING	Remainder(s) — Numeric identifier or Numeric-edited literal	(ROUNDED)			(ON SIZE ERROR) imperative-statement
MULTIPLY/BY (Format-1)	Multiplicand — Numeric identifier or Numeric literal	BY	Multiplier(s)/Product(s) — Numeric identifier			(ROUNDED)			(ON SIZE ERROR) imperative-statement
MULTIPLY/GIVING (Format-2)	Multiplicand — Numeric identifier or Numeric literal	BY	Multiplier — Numeric identifier / Numeric literal	GIVING	Product(s) — Numeric identifier or Numeric-edited literal	(ROUNDED)			(ON SIZE ERROR) imperative-statement
DIVIDE/INTO (Format-1)	Divisor — Numeric identifier or Numeric literal	INTO	Dividend(s)/Quotient(s) — Numeric identifier			(ROUNDED)			(ON SIZE ERROR) imperative-statement
DIVIDE/INTO/GIVING (Format-2)	Divisor — Numeric identifier or Numeric literal	INTO	Dividend — Numeric identifier / Numeric literal	GIVING	Quotient(s) — Numeric identifier or Numeric-edited literal	(ROUNDED)			(ON SIZE ERROR) imperative-statement
DIVIDE/BY/GIVING (Format-3)	Dividend — Numeric identifier or Numeric literal	BY	Divisor — Numeric identifier / Numeric literal	GIVING	Quotient(s) — Numeric identifier or Numeric-edited literal	(ROUNDED)			(ON SIZE ERROR) imperative-statement
DIVIDE/INTO/GIVING/REMAINDER (Format-4)	Divisor — Numeric identifier or Numeric literal	INTO	Dividend — Numeric identifier / Numeric literal	GIVING	Quotient — Numeric identifier or Numeric-edited literal	(ROUNDED)	REMAINDER	Numeric identifier	(ON SIZE ERROR) imperative-statement
DIVIDE/BY/GIVING/REMAINDER (Format-5)	Dividend — Numeric identifier or Numeric literal	BY	Divisor — Numeric identifier / Numeric literal	GIVING	Quotient — Numeric identifier or Numeric-edited literal	(ROUNDED)	REMAINDER	Numeric identifier	(ON SIZE ERROR) imperative-statement
COMPUTE	Numeric identifier or Numeric-edited identifier (ROUNDED)	=	Arithmetic expression						(ON SIZE ERROR) imperative-statement

Features Not in COBOL-74

The reserved word TO cannot be used in the ADD/GIVING in COBOL-74.

The scope terminators END-ADD, END-SUBTRACT, END-MULTIPLY, END-DIVIDE, and END-COMPUTE are not available to terminate the scope of the statements of the ON SIZE ERROR clause; a period must be used.

The NOT ON SIZE ERROR is not available.

Exercises

Terms for Definition

arithmetic overflow   order of precedence
byte   packed-decimal
display format   separate sign
embedded sign   size error
exponentiation   unary arithmetic operator
hierarchy of arithmetic operations   unary operation

Review Questions

1. What four properties must be considered when defining a field to be used in arithmetic computations?

2. Numeric literals may be used in arithmetic statements—except for fields that

   _____.

3. An arithmetic statement can contain a numeric-edited item only

   _____.

4. Two phrases that can be specified for any arithmetic statement are

   _____ and _____.

5. An ADD statement may contain how many addends?

   _____.

6. The reserved word FROM _____ (must/must not) be specified for the Format-1 SUBTRACT statement; it _____ (must/must not) be specified for the Format-2 SUBTRACT statement.

7. The reserved word _____ must be specified between the multiplier and the multiplicand of the MULTIPLY statement.

8. When a DIVIDE statement is written with the reserved word operator _____, the first factor is the dividend; the second factor is the divisor.

9. When a DIVIDE statement is written with the reserved word operator _____, the first factor is the divisor; the second factor is the dividend.

10. When the reserved word operator BY is specified in a DIVIDE statement, the _____ phrase must be specified.

11. List the hierarchy of arithmetic operations that apply to the COMPUTE statement.

12. Identify the value of X after execution of the following COMPUTE statements; assume that the values of A, B, and C are as indicated.

     A = 4; B = 10; C = 2

     a. X = A + B / C
     b. X = (A + B) / C
     c. X ROUNDED = A + (B / C)

13. To detect arithmetic overflows, the _____ phrase should be coded

    as part of the arithmetic statement.

14. Why should WORKING-STORAGE SECTION fields used for arithmetic typically be coded with the PICTURE symbol S?

Syntax/Debug Exercises

1. Two fields are defined as follows:

   ```
   AMOUNT     PIC S9999V99
   FACTOR     PIC 9V9.
   ```

   The following statement appears in the PROCEDURE DIVISION:

   ```
   MULTIPLY AMOUNT BY FACTOR GIVING TOTAL
   ```

   Assuming that TOTAL represents a dollar-and-cent amount, what is the smallest clause that should be specified to provide for the correct rounding and sign handling, and to ensure that a SIZE ERROR cannot occur?

2. Some of the following arithmetic statements contain syntax errors. For each statement containing a syntax error, rewrite it correctly. (Consider each data-item to be a numeric field.)

   a. ADD DEPOSIT OLD-BALANCE
   b. ADD DEPOSIT TO OLD-BALANCE
   c. ADD REG-HOURS PREM-HOURS
          GIVING TOTAL-HOURS
   d. ADD AMOUNT TO 10
   e. ADD AMOUNT 10
          GIVING ADJ-AMOUNT
   f. ADD DAY-1 DAY-2 DAY-3
          DAY-4 DAY-5 DAY-6
          DAY-7 GIVING WEEK
   g. SUBTRACT CHECK-AMOUNT
          FROM BALANCE
   h. SUBTRACT CHECK-AMOUNT
          SERVICE-CHARGE
          GIVING BALANCE
   i. SUBTRACT CHECK-AMOUNT
          FROM SERVICE-CHARGE
          GIVING BALANCE
   j. MULTIPLY 60 TIMES HOURS
   k. MULTIPLY HOURS BY 60
   l. MULTIPLY HOURS BY 60
          GIVING MINUTES

   m. DIVIDE MINUTES BY 60
   n. DIVIDE 60 BY MINUTES
   o. DIVIDE MINUTES INTO 60
   p. DIVIDE 60 INTO MINUTES
   q. DIVIDE MINUTES INTO 60
          GIVING HOURS
   r. DIVIDE 60 INTO MINUTES
          GIVING HOURS
   s. DIVIDE MINUTES BY 60
          GIVING HOURS
   t. DIVIDE 60 BY MINUTES
          GIVING HOURS
   u. DIVIDE MINUTES BY 60
          GIVING HOURS
          REMAINDER MINUTES
   v. COMPUTE AVERAGE =
          TOTAL-POINTS / NBR
   w. COMPUTE GROSS-PAY =
          RATE X HOURS
   x. COMPUTE Y = A+B-C
   y. COMPUTE R = (S + T) -
          (V / W)

Questions Pertaining to PATDFCT3

1. Would PATDFCT3 produce any output if the patron file contained no patrons with contributions less than the target amount? Explain your answer.

2. What would happen if one of the input records contained a value of 0 for the Target-contribution field?

Programming Assignments

Note: In the programming assignment descriptions of numeric input and output quantities, formatting notations as illustrated by the following are used:

$nnn_{\blacktriangle}nn$ An input numeric field with an assumed decimal point between the third and fourth digits.

$nnn.nn$ An output numeric field with a printed decimal point between the third and fourth digits.

Programming Assignment 6-1: Expanded Understocked Inventory Report

Background information:

This assignment is an expansion of Assignment 5-1 to take into account the quantity-on-order. It requires that a report be printed for all inventory items of Tools Unlimited for which the quantity-on-hand has dropped below the reorder-point.

Input file: Inventory file (INVEN.DAT)

Inventory record

Product identification	Product description		Unit price	Reorder point	Quantity on hand	Quantity on order		Order quantity	
1 2 3 4 5 6 7 8 9 10 11 12 13 14 15 16 17 18 19 20 21 22 23 24 25 26 27 28 29 30 31 32 33 34 35 36 37 38 39 40		41 42 43 44 45 46 47	48 49 50 51	52 53 54 55	56 57 58 59	60 61 62 63 64 65 66 67 68 69 70	71 72 73 74	75 76 77 78 79 80	

Required output:

Print a report, doubled-spaced, with one detail line for each input record for which the quantity-on-hand plus quantity-on-order is less than the reorder-point (for which a shortfall exists).

Output report-line formats:

Heading lines. Use appropriate report and column headings.

Detail line.

Position	Field	Comments
4–14	Product identification	Print in form *xxxx/xxxxxx* (insert a slash between subfields).
16–41	Product description	
43–48	Quantity on hand	Insert comma, zero-suppress.
50–54	Quantity on order	Same as Quantity on hand.
56–61	Order quantity	Same as Quantity on hand.
63–70	Unit price	Insert comma and decimal point (dollar-and-cent amount), zero-suppress.
72–80	Amount of order	Insert comma and decimal point (dollar-and-cent amount), zero-suppress.

Program operations:

1. Process only those records for which Quantity-on-hand plus Quantity-on-order is less than Reorder-point.

2. Calculate Amount-of-order as Unit-price times Order-quantity. You may assume that data values are such that Amount-of-order will never exceed $99,999.99.

Programming Assignment 6-2: Expanded Salesperson Performance Report

Background information:

In addition to the report of Assignment 5-2, the sales manager of Follow-the-Sun Sales requires a report that displays a comparison of sales revenue and sales quota for each salesperson.

Input file: Salesperson file (SALESPER.DAT)

Salesperson record

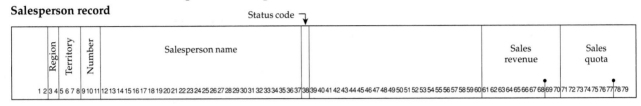

Required output:

Print a report, single-spaced, with one detail line for each input record (ignore records that do not have a Status-code value of A). At the end of the report, print a summary line containing Sales-quota and Sales-revenue (after double-spacing) for these Status-code A records.

Output report-line formats:

Heading lines. Use appropriate report and column headings.

Detail line.

Positions	Field	Comments
1–2	Salesperson region	
3	Hyphen	Print a hyphen.
4–7	Salesperson territory	
9–11	Salesperson number	
15–40	Salesperson name	
42–54	Sales quota	Print a fixed dollar sign, zero-suppress with blank replacement, insert commas, insert a decimal point.
56–69	Sales revenue	Print a fixed dollar sign, zero-suppress with blank replacement, insert commas, insert a decimal point.
71–73	Percent of quota	Whole number: zero-suppress all but last digit.
74	Percent sign	Print a percent sign.
76–78	Indication of quota made	Print "YES" if quota made, else leave blank.

Program operations:

1. Process only those records with the Status-code equal A.

2. Calculate the Percent-of-quota by dividing the Sales-revenue by the Sales-quota. Round the percentage to the nearest whole percentage point.

3. If Sales-revenue equals or exceeds Sales-quota, then print YES for Indication-of-quota-made; otherwise, leave this area blank.

Programming Assignment 6-3: Earnings Report

Background information:

The payroll department of Silicon Manufacturing needs a payroll summary report of current earnings and year-to-date earnings for hourly employees.

Input file: Earnings file (EARNINGS.DAT)

Earnings record

Required output:

Print a report, single-spaced, with one detail line for each hourly employee.

Output report-line formats:

Heading lines. Use appropriate row and column headings.

Detail line.

Positions	Field	Comments
4–14	Employee number	Print in form *xxx-xx-xxxx* (insert hyphens).
17–28	Employee last name	
30–38	Employee first name	
41–48	Gross pay	Zero-suppress leading dollar digits, print a decimal point, insert a comma.
52–61	Year-to-date earnings	Zero-suppress leading dollar digits, print a decimal point, insert comma.
64–73	Updated YTD earnings	Same as Year-to-date (YTD) earnings.

Program operations:

1. Process records only for hourly employees (those with a value of H in the field Pay-code).

2. Gross-pay is calculated as Hours-worked times Pay-rate.

3. Updated YTD earnings is calculated as Year-to-date earnings plus Gross-pay.

Programming Assignment 6-4: Expanded Accounts-Receivable Report

Background information:

The Silicon Valley Manufacturing controller would like the program of Assignment 5-4 modified to indicate the amount past-due by 30 days for each customer.

Input file: Customer file (CUSTOMER.DAT)

Customer name record

Customer number	Customer name		Balance forward	New purchases	Over-30 amount		Special flag	Payments received

1 2 3 4 5 6 7 8 9 10 11 12 13 14 15 16 17 18 19 20 21 22 23 24 25 26 27 28 29 30 31 32 33 34 35 36 37 38 39 40 41 42 43 44 45 46 47 48 49 50 51 52 53 54 55 56 57 58 59 60 61 62 63 64 65 66 67 68 69 70 71 72 73 74 75 76 77 78 79 80

Output report-line formats:

Heading lines. Use appropriate report and column headings.

Detail line.

Positions	Field	Comments
1–5	Customer number	
7–30	Customer name	
32–44	Balance forward	Zero-suppress leading dollar digits, insert a comma, print a decimal point, print a rightmost fixed space and CR symbol for a negative value.
46–55	New purchases	Zero-suppress leading dollar digits, insert a comma, print a decimal point.
57–66	Payments received	Same as New-purchases.
68–80	New balance	Same as Balance-forward.
82–94	New over-30 amount	Same as Balance-forward.

Program operations:

1. *Programming option:* As directed by your instructor, either process all records or process only those customer records with a space in the Special-flag field.

2. The New-balance is to be calculated as:

    Balance-forward

    plus New-purchases

    minus Payments-received

3. If Payments-received field is less than Over-30-amount, then New-over-30-amount is Over-30-amount minus Payments-received; otherwise, it is zero.

Programming Assignment 6-5: Nurses' Annuity Report

Background information:

The investment committee of Brooklawn Hospital needs a report indicating the extent to which employees are saving via the Hospital annuity program.

Nurses record

Input file: Nurses file (NURSES.DAT)

Shift code ⌐

Name		Date hired (yymmdd)		Base monthly salary	Annuity withholding		
1 2 3 4 5 6 7 8 9 10 11 12 13 14 15 16 17 18 19 20 21 22 23 24 25	26 27 28 29 30 31 32 33 34 35 36 37 38 39 40 41 42 43 44 45 46	47 48 49 50 51 52	53 54 55 56 57 58 59 60 61 62 63 64 65 66 67	68 69 70 71 72 73 74 75 76 77 78 79 80 81	82 83 84 85 86 87 88 89 90 91 92 93 94 95 96 97		

Output report-line formats:

Heading lines. Use appropriate report and column headings.

Detail line.

Positions	Field	Comments
1–23	Name	
26–33	Date-hired	Format *mm/dd/yy*
35	Shift code	
37–45	Adjusted salary	Insert a fixed dollar sign, decimal point, comma; suppress leading zeros.
49–55	Annuity withholding	Insert a fixed dollar sign, decimal point; suppress leading zeros.
58–59	Annuity percentage	Whole number: zero-suppress both digits.
60	Percent sign	Print percent sign if Annuity-withholding not zero.

Program operations:

1. Process each record.

2. Calculate adjusted salary as follows:

    If Shift-code = 1 Adjusted-salary is same as Base-monthly-salary.
    Otherwise Adjusted-salary is Base-monthly-salary times 1.25.

3. If Annuity-withholding is greater than 0, calculate Annuity-percentage as Annuity-withholding divided by Adjusted-salary; round to the nearest whole percentage point.

4. Print Annuity-percentage and percent sign only if Annuity-withholding is greater than 0.

Programming Assignment 6-6: Compound Interest Computation

Background information:

Howard Mulch, entrepreneur extraordinaire, wants an interactive program that will aid him in managing his investments.

Keyboard input:

Principal to be invested

Annual interest rate

Maximum number of years

Formula:

to calculate the accumulated amount, use:

$$\text{Amount} = P\,(1+r)^{t}$$

Where P = Principal
r = Annual interest rate
t = time in years

Program screen output:

You have two options for this program; the second involves more complex program logic than the first.

Option 1:   Summary of the input values.
The accumulated Amount using the Maximum-number-of-years input value for the time period.

Option 2:   Summary of the input values.
A table consisting of the number of years and the corresponding accumulated amount for years ranging from 1 to the Maximum-number-of-years input value. For example, 2,500 invested at 7.5% with maximum-years of 5 gives the following output:

1	2687.50
2	2889.63
3	3105.74
4	3338.73
5	3589.07

Program operations:

1. Allow user to repeat.

2. Display an announcement screen.

3. Accept input: Principal to be invested, Annual interest rate, and Maximum number of years.

4. Calculate and display the Amount (or table of amounts for Option 2).

Pseudocode assistance—Option 2:

The following pseudocode illustrates the logic you can use in coding Option 2 of this assignment:

```
Initialize Number-of-years to 0
Perform until Number-of-years = Maximum-number-of-years
   Add 1 to Number-of-years
   Calculate Amount using Time-period in formula
   Display Number-of-years and calculated Amount
```

CONCEPTS
MODULE
C

PRINCIPLES OF REPORT DESIGN

MODULE OBJECTIVES

This book has emphasized designing your printed output so that it clearly illustrates the information you are trying to convey. To do this, each example has utilized a print chart in laying out the printed form. From Chapter 5, you learned about improving the appearance of a report through using appropriate description lines and by editing your output fields. This module describes many of the factors that you must consider in the business environment of report generation. You should note that the principles described here apply to report generation in general, not simply to report generation using the COBOL programming language. From this module, you will learn the following:

- The printed report page is commonly considered to consist of three areas: the heading area, the body area, and the footing area.

- Some of the basic guidelines for good report design are

  - Provide heading-standard information to identify the report.

  - Label all output data and position column headings properly.

  - Plan positioning of fields and provide adequate spacing to make the report easy to read.

  - Use editing that is appropriate to the application.

- Include page totals when appropriate.

Report Areas

Since Chapter 5, you have seen two types of output lines: headings positioned at the beginning of the report and detail lines. Usually, reports consist of three general types of output lines: heading lines, detail lines, and total lines, as Figure C-1 illustrates.

The Heading Area

The **heading lines**, which form the **heading area** of the report, should contain data that identifies the report. Heading lines commonly include the report title, organization name, report date, and page number.

The bottom part of the heading area usually contains column headings for the detail-line fields printed in the body area below it.

In all programs so far, we have not considered the fact that a report might span several pages. Headings are typically repeated on each page of a report. **Page headings** are the most common type of heading and are repeated on each page of a report. Occasionally, an overall **report heading**, containing introductory material, is printed before the first page heading.

The Body Area

The programs you have studied and written so far have included one line for each selected record; as you know, these are called detail lines. (Sometimes, two or more detail lines are printed for each record.) This portion of the report is commonly called the **body area**.

In addition to detail lines, the body can contain **total** or **summary lines** in which multiple input records—but not all the records of the file—are accumulated or otherwise summarized and printed as one report line. This commonly results from control-break processing, Chapter 9's topic.

The Footing Area

Some reports require that for each page of the report, totals of selected columns for that page be printed at the bottom of the page. These so-called **page totals** are especially useful for reports that require manual reconciliation and/or modifications to numeric column amounts.

Total lines display totals of selected fields from detail lines. For instance, in Figure C-1, the sales revenue for all the detail records is totaled and printed. Total lines can appear in the body of the report (control-break processing), at the end of each page, or at the end of the report. Actually, Figure C-1's total line is a **grand-total line** because it consists of the accumulated total of sales revenue for all the detail records. Grand-total lines commonly include record counts, grand totals for columns, and the results of calculations—such as averages, percentages, and so on—that must be made after all applicable input records are processed.

Figure C-1
Report areas.

```
                        COMPARTMENT DEPARTMENT STORES INC.        PAGE   5
                        STORE REVENUE REPORT                      03-13-95
Heading lines →
                        STORE      DEPARTMENT      PRODUCT             SALES
                        NUMBER     NUMBER          DESCRIPTION       REVENUE

                        002        50000          PERFUME             18.95
                        001        60000          WASHER             398.00
Detail lines →          001        50000          COLOGNE              9.98
(Body area              002        70000          VIDEO RECORDER     698.00
of report)              001        60000          REFRIGERATOR       498.00
                        001        50000          PERFUME             29.95
                        002        60000          WASHER             379.00
                        002        70000          TELEVISION         598.00

Total line ─────────────────────────────────→ REPORT TOTAL       3,198.88*
```

The area at the bottom of a page in which page totals and grand totals are printed is called the **footing area**.

Report Design Guidelines

Certain guidelines for report design are helpful when you design a report. Let's consider several basic points; Figure C-2's sample report page illustrates many of them.

Identify the Report and Standardize the Heading-Identification Area

Positioning report-identification items in standard locations from one report to the next makes it easier for users when working with different reports. Every output report should have a title or some other identifier (item 2, Figure C-2). If the output will be read or used by someone outside the company or division, the name of the issuing organization should appear on the report (item 1). A report- and/or program-code identifier that uniquely identifies the report should also be assigned and printed on the output (item 3). For multipage reports, a page number should be provided (item 4).

When dates are printed on reports, it is often appropriate to print two dates: (1) the date to which the report applies, or a **period-ending date**, and (2) the date when the computer actually printed or processed the report, which is the **run date**. For instance, item 5 in Figure C-2 is the period-ending date 07/18/95. Inclusion of run date 08/01/95 (item 6) is very helpful in case the report is modified, corrected, or revised between the period-ending date and the run date.

Label All Output Fields

Even though you and the user may be very familiar with the report while it is being developed, data that is printed on reports without identification soon becomes ambiguous and confusing. Data fields should not be displayed on a report without a descriptive label that explains what each field is. For detail-line fields, such descriptions usually take the form of column headings. For the total line and for other exception fields not covered by the column headings, adjacent descriptive words on the same line may be required. You can see examples of this in Figure C-2's report.

Position Column Headings Properly

If a data field beneath a column heading contains a uniform number of characters to be printed on each line, it is probably most attractive to center the column heading above the data span. Typically, however, numeric fields have blank positions to the left of the value (because of zero suppression) and alphanumeric fields have blank positions to the right of the printed characters (because the length of the field is often longer than most data entries in the field).

Therefore, column headings for numeric fields are usually more visually pleasing when they are offset or justified to the right boundary of the data column; column headings for alphanumeric fields are best positioned at or near the left limit of the data area.

Determine Report Width and Length

Most mainframe computer line printers print 10 characters per inch with a maximum of 132 print positions in a line. Continuous-feed (perforated) forms, with a width of $14\frac{7}{8}$ inches, are commonly used on these printers. Page length, which determines how many lines can be printed on a page, is usually either $8\frac{1}{2}$ or 11 inches.

Serial printers used with microcomputers have a wide variety of capabilities. In addition to 10 characters per inch (cpi), most can print 12 cpi and 17 cpi—thereby giving even the $8\frac{1}{2}$-inch standard page width a considerable line capacity.*

---

*Appendix C describes how to control print character size from your COBOL program.

Figure C-2   Report layout techniques.

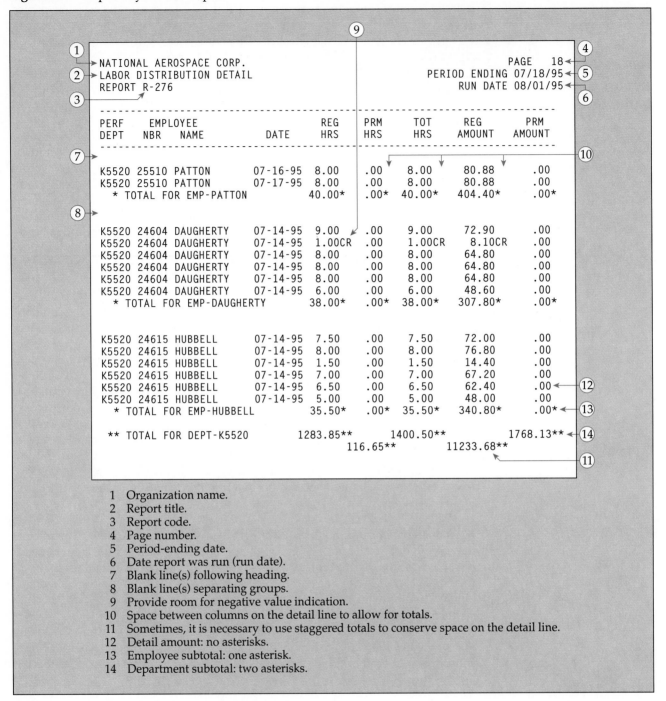

1 Organization name.
2 Report title.
3 Report code.
4 Page number.
5 Period-ending date.
6 Date report was run (run date).
7 Blank line(s) following heading.
8 Blank line(s) separating groups.
9 Provide room for negative value indication.
10 Space between columns on the detail line to allow for totals.
11 Sometimes, it is necessary to use staggered totals to conserve space on the detail line.
12 Detail amount: no asterisks.
13 Employee subtotal: one asterisk.
14 Department subtotal: two asterisks.

Practically all printers print 6 lines to the vertical inch; a standard 11-vertical-inch form therefore accommodates a maximum of 66 print lines. (Usually, though, top and bottom margins occupy some of the print lines.) Many of the 6-lines-per-inch printers can also be operator-set to print 8 lines to the inch. In larger data-processing installations, printers are often set at 8 lines per inch to save paper.

If the report can be accommodated easily in an 8-inch width or less, it is a good idea to keep within that number. This permits the user to copy and file the report with a standard 8½-inch-wide paper dimension. However, if your printer prints only the traditional 10 characters per inch, this severely limits the amount of output you can have on a single line.

**Consider Margin
Requirements**

If the report will be bound on the horizontal edges—as is often done with nylon-post binders—a generous top and bottom margin must be provided. Otherwise, the binding obscures some of the report page.

If a report will be kept in a standard three-ring binder, a left-margin area must be provided for the binder holes. Because of these and other binding considerations, you should investigate binding and filing requirements before specifying margin sizes.

**Make the Report
Visually Attractive**

Do not cram the data together; space the fields across the chosen report width. Provide extra blank lines before and after subtotal and total lines; this **white space** makes the report easier to read. Items 7 and 8 of Figure C-2 illustrate typical placement of blank lines.

For numeric amounts that are the result of an arithmetic operation, provide room for the longest possible value that can occur. When just two values are involved in a calculation, the maximum size can be determined by counting the digits.

In many situations, however, the total amount is the result of successive arithmetic operations. For example, the maximum size of a field that is used to accumulate the grand total of account balances depends upon the number of input records being processed. In this case, you must select the space required based on your knowledge of the data.

**Consider Intercolumn
Space Requirements**

When determining the number of horizontal print positions needed for numeric fields with column totals in the total area, you must provide for the length of the total field, rather than the detail-line field. An alternative method, which conserves horizontal space on the detail line, is to stagger the column totals (item 11 of Figure C-2).

Space for negative-number indication (minus signs, credit symbols, and so on) must also be considered and allocated, when applicable. Items 9 and 10 depict these intercolumn space-requirement considerations.

**Choose Suitable
Negative-Value
Indication**

Most numeric amount fields should provide for negative values so that reversals and negative adjustments can be handled. For internal reports, a minus sign symbol (–) usually indicates a negative value. The minus sign symbol is convenient because it occupies only one character position. However, it is generally preferable to use the CR symbol for formal accounting and other external reports. When displaying a credit balance on a customer's account, it is a good idea to print even further information, such as the following:

```
CREDIT BALANCE--DO NOT PAY
```

This message ensures that the value is understood to be negative. Figure C-3 shows examples of negative-value representations.

Figure C-3
Alternatives for negative-value indication.

```
        SATISFACTORY and appropriate for internal reports:

            1.00-

        BETTER for formal reports and customer statements, invoices, etc.:

            1.00 CR

        BEST for customer statements:

            1.00 CR ** CREDIT BALANCE--DO NOT PAY **
```

Use Appropriate Editing

Leading zeros of numeric amount fields should generally be suppressed, but numeric code numbers—such as Social Security and other account numbers—are easier to manipulate when their leftmost zeros are not suppressed. Insert decimal points when decimal positions must be printed for an amount. If sufficient space is available on the print line, insert commas into amount fields that contain over three or four integers. Place slashes, or hyphens, in six-digit dates. Do not print dollar signs, except on formal financial reports and checks; for internal reports, the column heading (plus the typical dollar-and-cents placement of the decimal point) should indicate that the amount is monetary.

Use check-protection features to avoid fraudulent check alteration. For instance, with asterisk fill, a check amount could print as $**1,234.56. Alternately, use a floating dollar sign, although it is slightly less secure.

Use Asterisks to Identify Total Levels

Asterisks, or another symbol, can distinguish totals and subtotals from detail amounts. They also indicate the composition, or level, of the total amount. Item 12 of Figure C-2 shows a detail line that contains no asterisks. Items 13 and 14 illustrate total-level identification with asterisks. For a grand total of all departments, three asterisks would be used. Accountants often refer to these total levels as "one-star," "two-star," and so on.

Module Summary

There are three general data areas of a report: heading, body, and footing. The heading area generally contains data such as organization name, report title, period-ending date, run date, page number, report number, and column headings. The body area contains detail lines, summary lines, and subtotal lines. The footing area generally contains page and report column totals, the results of calculations, descriptive words, and record counts.

When designing reports, you should use an established set of guidelines to maintain consistency in the appearance of your reports. The following are report design guidelines:

- Identify the report.
- Standardize the heading-identification area.
- Label all output fields.
- Position column headings properly.
- Determine report width and length.
- Consider margin requirements.
- Make the report visually attractive.
- Consider placement of identification information.
- Allow sufficient space for numeric results.
- Consider intercolumn space requirements.
- Choose suitable negative-value indication.
- Use appropriate editing.
- Consider page totals for certain reports.
- Use asterisks to identify total levels.
- Provide check protection for check amounts.

Exercises

Terms for Definition

body area
footing area
grand-total line
heading area
heading lines
page headings

page totals
period-ending date
report heading
run date
total (summary) lines
white space

Review Questions

1. Identify the three general data areas that you must consider when designing a report.

2. List three report identification items that you should consider printing on a report.

3. Name the two types of dates that the programmer/analyst should consider printing on a report.

4. Identify three types of lines that might be found in the body of a report.

5. When page totals or other data are printed at the bottom of each report page, that area is called the _____ area.

6. The end of a report often contains a(n) _____ area.

7. The most common line spacings are either _____ or _____ characters per vertical inch.

8. When a report requires manual reconciliation, it may be appropriate to provide _____ on the report.

Report Program Design and Coding

Chapter Outline

CHAPTER

7

CHAPTER OBJECTIVES

In Module C, you learned about many of the factors you must take into account when designing a report. This chapter's purpose is to apply some of those principles by considering two extensions of the patron listing program. The first example illustrates accumulating a report total and controlling printing from page to page. The second example expands total accumulation to include printing a total for each page of printed output.

Furthermore, these examples illustrate a standard convention for modularizing programs that is used throughout the rest of this book. The second example incorporates the principles described in Module C regarding multipage reports. The program code of these examples can be used as models for practically any straightforward read-and-print program with headings and totals. From this chapter, you will learn the following:

- An expansion of the module-numbering conventions introduced in Module B.

- Accumulating totals on fields of the input record.

- The ADVANCING PAGE option of the WRITE statement, which allows you to position continuous form paper at the top of a new page.

- Using a variable quantity to control line spacing with the WRITE statement.

- Placing the WRITE statement in an independent module so that a single statement writes a given file.

- Using the INITIALIZE statement to give initial values to data-items during program execution.

- The ACCEPT/FROM DATE statement, which allows you to obtain the current date from the computer operating system.

- Recommendations for the organization of entries in the WORKING-STORAGE SECTION.

- Report layout and planning.

- Top-down design—an organized approach to program modularization and construction of a structure chart.

TOPIC

Page Control and Calculating Totals

Some Preliminary Concepts

This chapter's two example programs illustrate some of the elementary report-design principles described in Module C. Before looking at the first example, let's consider some of the principles illustrated by it: module-numbering conventions, the calculation of report totals, and controlling paper positioning within the printer (page control).

Module-Numbering Conventions

In Module B, you were introduced to predetermined numbering ranges for program modules. Although specific number ranges for modules—based upon the module's function—can limit flexibility, they provide for organizational commonalty from one program to another. Perhaps more important, consistent module numbering permits one program to be used as a model, or skeleton, for another program with a similar function. Figure 7-1 summarizes the complete range of module numbers used in this book.

Calculating Totals

The sample report of Figure C-2 (page 194) illustrates various considerations in designing a report that is both functional and easy to read. Let's consider how to program one of its features: calculation of totals.

Assume that you want to enhance the Fleetwood Charities list-of-patrons report by printing the total contributions at the end of the report. To do this, you need to define an arithmetic data-item in WORKING-STORAGE into which you will add the patron contribution for each record as that record is read. In other words, as processing proceeds, the sum of the contributions is accumulated in a data-item serving as an **accumulator**. To incorporate accumulation in your program, you must address the following needs:

Figure 7-1
Module-numbering conventions.

Module number	Module function
000	Mainline
100–199	Initialization of variable fields
200–699	General processing
700–799	End-of-run totals, statistics, etc.
800–849	Input (READ, ACCEPT)
850–869	General nonreport output (WRITE, REWRITE, DELETE, DISPLAY)
870–879	Report headings
880–889	Report top-line output (page skipping)
890–899	Report-line output (line spacing)
900–999	Subprogram communication (CALL) and abnormal program termination

In the DATA DIVISION:

Define the accumulator data-item.

In the PROCEDURE DIVISION:

Initialize the accumulator to zero.

As each record is processed, add the contribution to the accumulator.

After the last record is processed, print the total line, including the accumulator's contents.

Page Control

Until now, your programs have printed with no consideration to individual pages of the computer paper. In fact, perhaps one or more of your assignments has printed a detail line straddling the perforations on the form that separate one page from the next.

Virtually every report-generating program includes some way of controlling the printer. As described in Module C, when a page becomes full, the printer is directed to position the form at the top of the next page before printing continues. This is called **page control** and is implemented by counting each line as it is printed and comparing that count to some predetermined allowable number of lines per page.

To incorporate page control into your program, you must address the following needs:

In the DATA DIVISION:

Define a line-counter data-item.

Define a page-number data-item.

Define the number of lines to be printed on a page.

In the PROCEDURE DIVISION:

Initialize the page-number to zero.

Before printing a detail line, check the line-counter to see if the page is full.

If the page is full, start a new page, initialize the line-counter, and add 1 to the page-number.

As each detail line is printed, add 1 to the line-counter.

Of course, the question arises: "How do I control the printer?" The partial answer is that you already exercised some control over the printer through the AFTER ADVANCING clause of the WRITE statement to produce double-spacing on the printed output. For example, the AFTER ADVANCING 2 LINES phrase causes the printer to move the form forward two lines before printing.

Actually, the WRITE allows for the use of either the ADVANCING phrase or the PAGE phrase where PAGE causes the printer to move the paper to the top of the next page. That is, the AFTER ADVANCING PAGE clause causes the printer to (1) move the form to the next page, then (2) print the output line. Of course, this feature's use depends upon the paper being positioned properly in the printer, as well as the length of the form being coordinated with the printer's form-length settings. The ADVANCING PAGE clause is used in the next example program.

A Program with a Total Field and Page Control

The concepts just described for accumulating and page control are incorporated into Figure 7-2's PATLIST2 program. To minimize bulk within the program and focus on these concepts, the program processes minimal data from the record and prints a single heading line, as you can see by inspecting the sample output shown in Figure 7-3. The elements of this program that implement accumulating and page control are highlighted in Figure 7-2. Without them, the program is identical to simple listing programs you've worked with previously.

Calculating the Total for the Contribution Field

First, let's consider totaling of the contribution field. The contribution-field accumulator (AC-TOTAL-CONTR) is defined at line 37. Because it eventually contains the sum of all patron contributions, its size must be defined accordingly. Here, the field width of 6 is a judgment call. If Fleetwood Charities were a small organization for which total contributions rarely exceeded $200,000, then the six-digit

Figure 7-2   Page control and calculating totals.

```
1        IDENTIFICATION DIVISION.                                60        PROCEDURE DIVISION.
2        PROGRAM-ID.    PATLIST2.                                61
3                                                                62        000-PRINT-PATRON-LIST.
4     *      Price/Welburn   1/15/95                             63
5     *      Calculate grand-total & print w/page control        64        ************Initialization Sequence************
6                                                                65            OPEN INPUT PATRON-FILE
7        ENVIRONMENT DIVISION.                                   66                 OUTPUT PATRON-LIST
8                                                                67            PERFORM 100-INITIALIZE-VARIABLE-FIELDS
9        INPUT-OUTPUT SECTION.                                   68            PERFORM 870-PRINT-HEADINGS
10                                                               69
11       FILE-CONTROL.                                           70        ************Processing Sequence************
12           SELECT PATRON-FILE                                  71            PERFORM UNTIL
13               ASSIGN TO (system dependent).                   72                PS-END-OF-PATRON-FILE IS EQUAL TO "YES"
14           SELECT PATRON-LIST                                  73                READ PATRON-FILE
15               ASSIGN TO (system dependent).                   74                AT END
16                                                               75                    MOVE "YES" TO PS-END-OF-PATRON-FILE
17                                                               76                NOT AT END
18       DATA DIVISION.                                          77                    PERFORM 200-PROCESS-PATRON-RECORD
19                                                               78                END-READ
20       FILE SECTION.                                           79            END-PERFORM
21                                                               80
22       FD  PATRON-FILE.                                        81        ************Termination Sequence************
23       01  PATRON-RECORD.                                      82            PERFORM 700-PRINT-TOTAL-LINE
24           05  PR-NAME            PIC X(18).                   83            CLOSE PATRON-FILE
25           05                     PIC X(46).                   84                  PATRON-LIST
26           05  PR-ACTUAL-CONTR    PIC 9(4).                    85            STOP RUN
27                                                               86            .
28       FD  PATRON-LIST.                                        87        ****************************************************
29       01  PATRON-LINE-RECORD     PIC X(132).                  88        100-INITIALIZE-VARIABLE-FIELDS.
30                                                               89            MOVE "NO" TO PS-END-OF-PATRON-FILE
31       WORKING-STORAGE SECTION.                                90            MOVE ZEROS TO AC-TOTAL-CONTR
32                                                               91                          RC-PAGE-NUMBER
33       01  PROGRAM-SWITCHES.                                   92            .
34           05  PS-END-OF-PATRON-FILE PIC X(3).                 93        200-PROCESS-PATRON-RECORD.
35                                                               94            IF RC-LINES-USED NOT LESS THAN RC-LINES-PER-PAGE
36       01  AC-ACCUMULATORS.                                    95                PERFORM 870-PRINT-HEADINGS
37           05  AC-TOTAL-CONTR      PIC 9(6).                   96            END-IF
38                                                               97            MOVE PR-NAME TO PL-NAME
39       01  REPORT-CONTROLS.                                    98            MOVE PR-ACTUAL-CONTR TO PL-ACTUAL-CONTR
40           05  RC-PAGE-NUMBER      PIC 9(2).                   99            ADD PR-ACTUAL-CONTR TO AC-TOTAL-CONTR
41           05  RC-LINES-USED       PIC 9(2).                   100           MOVE PATRON-LINE TO PATRON-LINE-RECORD
42           05  RC-LINES-PER-PAGE   PIC 9(2) VALUE 20.          101           WRITE PATRON-LINE-RECORD
43                                                               102           ADD 1 TO RC-LINES-USED
44       01  PATRON-LINE.                                        103           .
45           05  PL-NAME             PIC X(18).                  104       700-PRINT-TOTAL-LINE.
46           05                      PIC X(5) VALUE SPACES.      105           MOVE AC-TOTAL-CONTR TO SL-TOTAL-CONTR
47           05  PL-ACTUAL-CONTR     PIC Z,ZZ9.                  106           MOVE SUMMARY-LINE TO PATRON-LINE-RECORD
48                                                               107           WRITE PATRON-LINE-RECORD
49       01  H1-COLUMN-HEADING-LINE.                             108               AFTER ADVANCING 2 LINES
50           05  PIC X(23)   VALUE "PATRON NAME     ".           109           .
51           05  PIC X(10)   VALUE "CONTR".                      110       870-PRINT-HEADINGS.
52           05  PIC X(5)    VALUE "Page ".                      111           ADD 1 TO RC-PAGE-NUMBER
53           05  H1-PAGE-NUMBER      PIC Z(2).                   112           MOVE RC-PAGE-NUMBER TO H1-PAGE-NUMBER
54                                                               113           MOVE H1-COLUMN-HEADING-LINE TO PATRON-LINE-RECORD
55       01  SUMMARY-LINE.                                       114           WRITE PATRON-LINE-RECORD AFTER PAGE
56           05  PIC X(21)  VALUE " TOTAL CONTRIBUTIONS ".       115           MOVE SPACES TO PATRON-LINE-RECORD
57           05  SL-TOTAL-CONTR      PIC ZZZ,ZZ9.                116           WRITE PATRON-LINE-RECORD
58                                                               117           MOVE 2 TO RC-LINES-USED
59                                                               118           .
```

Figure 7-3
Sample output—PATLIST2.

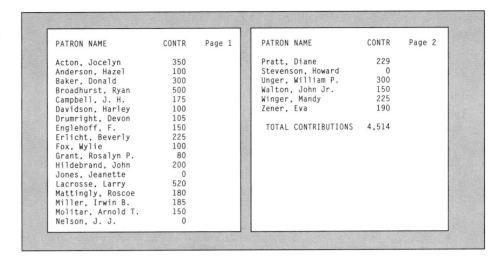

```
PATRON NAME          CONTR    Page 1        PATRON NAME          CONTR    Page 2

Acton, Jocelyn         350                  Pratt, Diane           229
Anderson, Hazel        100                  Stevenson, Howard        0
Baker, Donald          300                  Unger, William P.      300
Broadhurst, Ryan       500                  Walton, John Jr.       150
Campbell, J. H.        175                  Winger, Mandy          225
Davidson, Harley       100                  Zener, Eva             190
Drumright, Devon       105
Englehoff, F.          150                  TOTAL CONTRIBUTIONS  4,514
Erlicht, Beverly       225
Fox, Wylie             100
Grant, Rosalyn P.       80
Hildebrand, John       200
Jones, Jeanette          0
Lacrosse, Larry        520
Mattingly, Roscoe      180
Miller, Irwin B.       185
Molitar, Arnold T.     150
Nelson, J. J.            0
```

choice (at line 37) is adequate. However, a large organization with million-dollar contributions would require seven or eight digits.

In the PROCEDURE DIVISION, you can see that AC-TOTAL-CONTR is set to zero (line 90) as part of the initialization process (executed from line 67 of the main-line module). Then at line 99 in the 200 module, the contribution amount—PR-ACTUAL-CONTR—is added to AC-TOTAL-CONTR as each record is processed.

The 700 module, added to this program to print the total line, includes a statement to move the accumulated contributions to the edited total output field (line 105).

Printing Headings

Implicit with page control is the repeated printing of headings; that is, headings are printed at the top of each page. Actually, headings must be printed under two conditions:

- Before processing the first record (the first page).
- When the current page is full and the form moves to the next page; commonly called a **page break**.

In PATLIST2, page headings are printed by the 870 module—you will look at the details of this module later. It is performed as part of the initialization sequence (line 68) to print the headings on the first page. It is also performed conditionally in the processing module (at line 95) for succeeding pages when page breaks occur.

Page Control

Each data record is processed in the 200 module, which tests to ensure that sufficient room exists on the page before proceeding. The logic of this module is illustrated in the flowchart segment of Figure 7-4. The vehicle for control is the counter RC-LINES-USED, which counts each line as it is printed. Actually, RC-LINES-USED is much like the accumulator AC-TOTAL-CONTR in that a value (in this case, a fixed value of 1) is added to it each time a record is processed; see line 102.

The decision symbol question of Figure 7-4—"Is current page full?"—is implemented in the 200 module by the following IF statement:

```
IF RC-LINES-USED NOT LESS THAN RC-LINES-PER-PAGE
   PERFORM 870-PRINT-HEADINGS
END-IF
```

Here, the counter RC-LINES-USED is compared to the line-maximum item RC-LINES-PER-PAGE, which is set to 20 by a VALUE in the DATA DIVISION (line 42). To see how this works, assume that RC-LINES-USED was incremented to 18, a

Figure 7-4
Page-control logic.

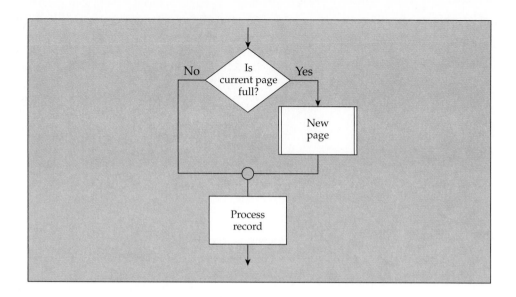

record was read, and control was transferred to the 200 module. The following will take place:

1. In the IF statement, the condition

   18 (in RC-LINES-USED) IS NOT LESS THAN
   20 (in RC-LINES-PER-PAGE)

   is false, so the conditional (line 95) is not executed and processing continues at line 97.
2. At line 102, RC-LINES-USED is incremented to 19.
3. When the next record is read and control is again transferred to the 200 module, the IF statement conditional

   19 (in RC-LINES-USED) IS NOT LESS THAN
   20 (in RC-LINES-PER-PAGE)

   is again false, so line 95 is not executed.
4. At line 102, RC-LINES-USED is incremented to 20.
5. When the next record is read and control is again transferred to the 200 module, the IF statement conditional

   20 (in RC-LINES-USED) IS NOT LESS THAN
   20 (in RC-LINES-PER-PAGE)

   is now true, so control is transferred to the 870 module.

The 870 Module

Now, let's focus on the 870 module. Considering that a new page will start, the page-counter variable is incremented by 1 in the following statement (line 111):

```
ADD 1 TO RC-PAGE-NUMBER
```

That value is then moved to the heading line, which in turn is moved to the printer record from which it is printed at line 114. Since this WRITE statement contains the AFTER ADVANCING PAGE clause, the paper is positioned to a new page before the heading line is printed.

If you look closely at Figure 7-3's report, you will see that the first detail line printed after the headings is double-spaced from the heading line. However, all other detail lines are single-spaced. The easiest way to handle this is to simply print a blank line as part of the heading (in other words, print a two-line heading). The blank line is printed at program lines 115 and 116.

After the two heading lines are printed, the line-counter (RC-LINES-USED) is initialized to a value of 2, reflecting this.

**Other Observations
About PATLIST2**

Assigning a Constant

The maximum number of lines per page is placed in the field RC-LINES-PER-PAGE as the constant value 20. Notice that the only place this field is used in the program is in the condition of the IF; that is:

```
IF RC-LINES-USED NOT LESS THAN RC-LINES-PER-PAGE
```

At first, defining a separate field for the limit appears unnecessary because the IF could be coded as follows:

```
IF RC-LINES-USED NOT LESS THAN 20
```

Generally, program maintainability is improved if such constants are defined as fields in WORKING-STORAGE. Then if at some future date you need to change a value, you can locate it more quickly in WORKING-STORAGE than in the PROCEDURE DIVISION. This becomes even more significant if you use the constant in two or more places in the program.

The IF Statement

The relational operator of the IF statement (line 94) is NOT LESS THAN. So, when the two fields become equal, this condition is true and the heading procedure is performed. Perhaps you wonder why the more obvious IS EQUAL TO operator is not used. The reason is that you want a new page whenever the line count equals *or exceeds* the maximum allowable. To illustrate the potential problem, assume that at a later date you made the following changes to the program:

- Changed the initialization of RC-LINES-USED to 3 (line 117) because you wanted to print three heading lines.

- Changed the detail line WRITE to double-spacing and correspondingly changed the line-counter incrementing to 2 (line 102).

Then during execution, your line-counter progresses from 19 to 21, skipping over the equal condition of 20; page control does not occur. On the other hand, using NOT LESS THAN creates a new page when the counter reaches 21.

**An Alternate Technique
for Printing First-Page
Headings**

In PATLIST2, the page-heading procedure is performed as part of the initialization sequence—before the first record is processed. Another technique that you might encounter involves initializing the line-counter to its full-page value, then allowing program logic to take its course. This method is illustrated in the modified PROCEDURE DIVISION of Figure 7-5, where you can see that the counter is initialized to its full-page value (line 91). Then after the first record is read and control is transferred to the 200 module, the IF condition is true and control is transferred immediately to the 870 module. Of course, the statement to perform module 870 was deleted from the initialization sequence since it is no longer needed (compare line 68 with that of PATLIST2 in Figure 7-2).

Some More COBOL Features

Variable Line Spacing

If you check Figure 7-2, you will find that it includes four WRITE statements. Generally, input and output statements set in action a complex sequence of operations that are subject to numerous types of input/output errors. Consequently, a production program usually includes a variety of input/output error-recovery capabilities. This can add significantly to the COBOL code to accompany a READ or WRITE statement, as well as add complexity to the program. One way to simplify coding and provide a sound structure is to place the WRITE—or READ

Figure 7-5 An alternate solution for printing first-page headings.

```
60      PROCEDURE DIVISION.                                87   100-INITIALIZE-VARIABLE-FIELDS.
61                                                         88       MOVE "NO" TO PS-END-OF-PATRON-FILE
62      000-PRINT-PATRON-LIST.                             89       MOVE ZEROS TO AC-TOTAL-CONTR
63                                                         90                       RC-PAGE-NUMBER
64      ************Initialization Sequence************    91       MOVE RC-LINES-PER-PAGE TO RC-LINES-USED
65          OPEN INPUT PATRON-FILE                         92       .
66               OUTPUT PATRON-LIST                        93   200-PROCESS-PATRON-RECORD.
67          PERFORM 100-INITIALIZE-VARIABLE-FIELDS.        94       IF RC-LINES-USED NOT LESS THAN RC-LINES-PER-PAGE
68                                                         95           PERFORM 870-PRINT-HEADINGS
69      **************Processing Sequence**************    96       END-IF
70          PERFORM UNTIL                                  97       MOVE PR-NAME TO PL-NAME
71              PS-END-OF-PATRON-FILE IS EQUAL TO "YES"    98       MOVE PR-ACTUAL-CONTR TO PL-ACTUAL-CONTR
72              READ PATRON-FILE                           99       ADD PR-ACTUAL-CONTR TO AC-TOTAL-CONTR
73                  AT END                                 100      MOVE PATRON-LINE TO PATRON-LINE-RECORD
74                      MOVE "YES" TO PS-END-OF-PATRON-FILE 101     WRITE PATRON-LINE-RECORD
75                  NOT AT END                             102      ADD 1 TO RC-LINES-USED
76                      PERFORM 200-PROCESS-PATRON-RECORD  103      .
77              END-READ                                   104  700-PRINT-TOTAL-LINE.
78          END-PERFORM                                    105      MOVE AC-TOTAL-CONTR TO SL-TOTAL-CONTR
79                                                         106      MOVE SUMMARY-LINE TO PATRON-LINE-RECORD
80      **************Termination Sequence*************    107      WRITE PATRON-LINE-RECORD
81          PERFORM 700-PRINT-TOTAL-LINE                   108          AFTER ADVANCING 2 LINES
82          CLOSE PATRON-FILE                              109      .
83                PATRON-LIST                              110  870-PRINT-HEADINGS.
84          STOP RUN                                       111      ADD 1 TO RC-PAGE-NUMBER
85          .                                              112      MOVE RC-PAGE-NUMBER TO H1-PAGE-NUMBER
86      *************************************************   113      MOVE H1-COLUMN-HEADING-LINE TO PATRON-LINE-RECORD
                                                           114      WRITE PATRON-LINE-RECORD AFTER PAGE
                                                           115      MOVE SPACES TO PATRON-LINE-RECORD
                                                           116      WRITE PATRON-LINE-RECORD
                                                           117      MOVE 2 TO RC-LINES-USED
                                                           118      .
```

as needed—in a separate module and perform that module whenever an output (or input) operation is needed. However, when implemented with a printer file, special provisions are required to accommodate the report's different line-spacing needs. This is accomplished using a technique called **variable line spacing**, which is implemented in the code segment shown in Figure 7-6. The following are the features of this technique:

1. Because the output lines require different line spacing, the data-item RC-LINE-SPACING is defined in WORKING-STORAGE; it is used for line-spacing control.
2. The WRITE statement is placed in the 890 module.
3. When it is time to print a line, the line-spacing value is moved to RC-LINE-SPACING before performing the 890 module. For instance, see the last two statements of the 700 module:
   a. Move a value of 2 to RC-LINE-SPACING.
   b. Transfer control to the 890 module, which contains the WRITE statement.
4. In the 890 module, the clause

   ```
   AFTER ADVANCING RC-LINE-SPACING
   ```

   includes the data-item RC-LINE-SPACING. In this instance, it contains a value of 2, which causes the desired double-spacing.
5. The line-counting function is included in the 890 module by adding the value in RC-LINE-SPACING to RC-LINES-USED.

However, the AFTER PAGE clause is not amenable to this technique, so it is necessary to include a second module (880) specifically for this situation. You can see that this module is performed by the fourth statement of the 870 module.

Observe the use of the verbs PRINT and WRITE in the module names. The word PRINT is used in this text to describe higher-level modules that either format a report line or handle the printing of more than one line (see modules 700 and 870). The word WRITE is used for the lower-level, independent common modules

Figure 7-6
Using a single-WRITE
module.

```
              05  RC-LINE-SPACING        PIC 9(2).
              .
              .
          200-PROCESS-PATRON-RECORD.
              IF RC-LINES-USED NOT LESS THAN RC-LINES-PER-PAGE
                  PERFORM 870-PRINT-HEADINGS
              END-IF
              MOVE PR-NAME TO PL-NAME
              MOVE PR-ACTUAL-CONTR TO PL-ACTUAL-CONTR
              ADD PR-ACTUAL-CONTR TO AC-TOTAL-CONTR
              MOVE PATRON-LINE TO PATRON-LINE-RECORD
              MOVE 1 TO RC-LINE-SPACING
              PERFORM 890-WRITE-REPORT-LINE
              .
          700-PRINT-TOTAL-LINE.
              MOVE AC-TOTAL-CONTR TO SL-TOTAL-CONTR
              MOVE SUMMARY-LINE TO PATRON-LINE-RECORD
              MOVE 2 TO RC-LINE-SPACING
              PERFORM 890-WRITE-REPORT-LINE
              .
          870-PRINT-HEADINGS.
              ADD 1 TO RC-PAGE-NUMBER
              MOVE RC-PAGE-NUMBER TO H1-PAGE-NUMBER
              MOVE H1-COLUMN-HEADING-LINE TO PATRON-LINE-RECORD
              PERFORM 880-WRITE-REPORT-TOP-LINE
              MOVE SPACES TO PATRON-LINE-RECORD
              PERFORM 890-WRITE-REPORT-LINE
              .
          880-WRITE-REPORT-TOP-LINE.
              WRITE PATRON-LINE-RECORD
                  AFTER ADVANCING PAGE
              MOVE 1 TO RC-LINES-USED
              .
          890-WRITE-REPORT-LINE.
              WRITE PATRON-LINE-RECORD
                  AFTER ADVANCING RC-LINE-SPACING LINES
              ADD RC-LINE-SPACING TO RC-LINES-USED
```

that physically WRITE the line (see modules 880 and 890). This style standard is used throughout this book.

The INITIALIZE Statement

In PATLIST2, you used three data-items as accumulators: the contribution total, the lines-used counter, and the page counter. Before its use, each accumulator in a program must be set to some initial value, usually zero. Actually, a large program can have many accumulators and other work areas—both numeric and nonnumeric—that must be initialized. To simplify this, COBOL-85 includes a special statement called INITIALIZE, as the following example illustrates:

```
        05  RC-LINES-USED        PIC 9(2).
        .
        05  SW-SPECIAL-SWITCH    PIC X(4).
        .
    01  AC-ACCUMULATORS.
        05  AC-PAGE-TOTAL-CONTR  PIC 9(6).
        05  AC-TOTAL-CONTR       PIC 9(6).
        .
        INITIALIZE AC-ACCUMULATORS
                   RC-LINES USED
                   SW-SPECIAL-SWITCH
```

The action of this statement is to set all listed numeric items to zero and nonnumeric items to spaces. In this instance, AC-ACCUMULATORS is a group item, so all elementary items composing this group item are appropriately initialized.

Figure 7-7
Format of the INITIALIZE
statement.

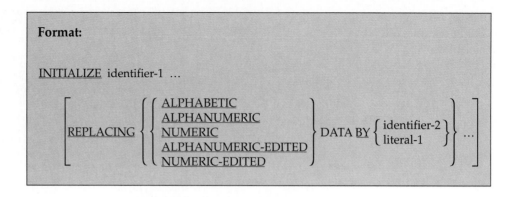

Format:

INITIALIZE identifier-1 ...

Generally, the initialization involves setting numeric and numeric-edited fields to zero; alphanumeric, alphanumeric-edited, and alphabetic fields are set to spaces. As shown in the general format of Figure 7-7, you can include the REPLACING/BY clause to provide selective initialization to different values.

COBOL-74

COBOL-74 does not include the INITIALIZE statement.

The ACCEPT/FROM DATE Statement

The next example report program includes the date that the report was generated. Fortunately, the date maintained by the operating system is available to the program through the ACCEPT/FROM DATE statement. To illustrate, assume that a date field was defined in WORKING-STORAGE as follows:

```
01   WORK-AREAS.
     05   WA-CURRENT-DATE.
          10   CURRENT-YEAR      PIC 9(2).
          10   CURRENT-MONTH     PIC 9(2).
          10   CURRENT-DAY       PIC 9(2).
```

Then, the date is made available to the program by the operating system with execution of the following statement:

ACCEPT WA-CURRENT-DATE FROM DATE

The date from the
operating system is
placed in this field.

This key word tells COBOL
to obtain the current date
from the operating system.

The date is made available to the program as a six-digit, unsigned integer quantity in the *yymmdd* format, where *yy* is the two-digit year number of the century, *mm* is the month number, and *dd* is the day number. The statement moves the date—according to the rules of the MOVE statement—into the field specified in the ACCEPT statement (WA-CURRENT-DATE, in this case). For example, if the current date is March 28, 1995, the contents of WA-CURRENT-DATE are as follows:

WA-CURRENT-DATE

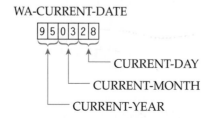

CURRENT-DAY
CURRENT-MONTH
CURRENT-YEAR

Figure 7-8
The ACCEPT/
FROM statement.

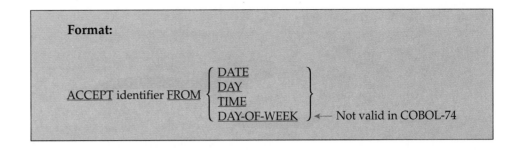

Because the date field is a group item consisting of three subfields, the year, month, and day are available as shown.

Figure 7-8 shows the general format of the ACCEPT/FROM statement. Notice that this statement can also be used to obtain current values for date in year/day form, the time, and the day of the week. The following table includes an example of each:

Option	Field size	Format	Example	Meaning
DAY	5	*yyddd*	95128	Year: 1995, Day: 128
TIME	8	*hhmmsscc*	10223815	Clock time 10 hours 22 minutes 38.15 seconds
DAY-OF-WEEK	1	*d*	2	Tuesday 1–7 corresponds to Monday through Sunday

COBOL-89 Module

The 1989 COBOL Module includes intrinsic functions, one being a date function that returns the current date (much the same as the information returned by the ACCEPT/FROM). It is described in Appendix C.

COBOL-74 Version of PATLIST2

There are two ways to convert PATLIST2 to COBOL-74 code. One is to use the equivalent to COBOL-85 illustrated in Figure 3-17 (page 87). The other is to use a priming READ. With the adoption of only one WRITE or READ statement for a file within a given program as a standard, the priming READ requires some adaptation. Because the technique is so commonly encountered, PATLIST2 is rewritten in Figure 7-9. Here you see all of the standard changes: CONFIGURATION SECTION, LABEL RECORDS clauses, the reserved word FILLER, and removal of END-IF. In addition, the processing sequence was replaced with a PERFORM to another paragraph (200). The READ statement was moved to a separate module (800), which is performed from line 79 (priming READ) and line 105 (read next record).

Figure 7-9   COBOL-74 version of PATLIST2.

```
1        IDENTIFICATION DIVISION.                          63
2        PROGRAM-ID.    PATLIST2.                          64      01  SUMMARY-LINE.
3                                                          65          05  FILLER              PIC X(21)
4     *      Price/Welburn  1/15/95                        66                                  VALUE " TOTAL CONTRIBUTIONS ".
5     *      Calculate grand-total & print w/page control  67          05  SL-TOTAL-CONTR      PIC ZZZ,ZZ9.
6     *      using COBOL-74 and the priming READ.          68
7                                                          69
8        ENVIRONMENT DIVISION.                             70      PROCEDURE DIVISION.
9                                                          71
10       CONFIGURATION SECTION.                            72      000-PRINT-PATRON-LIST.
11                                                         73
12           SOURCE-COMPUTER. IBM-PC.                      74      ************Initialization Sequence************
13           OBJECT-COMPUTER. IBM-PC.                      75          OPEN INPUT PATRON-FILE
14                                                         76               OUTPUT PATRON-LIST
15       INPUT-OUTPUT SECTION.                             77          PERFORM 100-INITIALIZE-VARIABLE-FIELDS
16                                                         78          PERFORM 870-PRINT-HEADINGS
17       FILE-CONTROL.                                     79          PERFORM 800-READ-PATRON-RECORD
18           SELECT PATRON-FILE                            80      *************Processing Sequence**************
19               ASSIGN TO (system dependent).            81          PERFORM 200-PROCESS-PATRON-RECORD
20           SELECT PATRON-LIST                            82               UNTIL PS-END-OF-PATRON-FILE IS EQUAL TO "YES"
21               ASSIGN TO (system dependent).            83
22                                                         84      *************Termination Sequence*************
23                                                         85          PERFORM 700-PRINT-TOTAL-LINE
24       DATA DIVISION.                                    86          CLOSE PATRON-FILE
25                                                         87                PATRON-LIST
26       FILE SECTION.                                     88          STOP RUN.
27                                                         89
28       FD  PATRON-FILE                                   90      ***************************************************
29           LABEL RECORDS ARE STANDARD.                   91      100-INITIALIZE-VARIABLE-FIELDS.
30       01  PATRON-RECORD.                                92          MOVE "NO" TO PS-END-OF-PATRON-FILE
31           05  PR-NAME          PIC X(18).               93          MOVE ZEROS TO AC-TOTAL-CONTR
32           05  FILLER           PIC X(46).               94                        RC-PAGE-NUMBER.
33           05  PR-ACTUAL-CONTR  PIC 9(4).                95
34                                                         96      200-PROCESS-PATRON-RECORD.
35       FD  PATRON-LIST                                   97          IF RC-LINES-USED NOT LESS THAN RC-LINES-PER-PAGE
36           LABEL RECORDS ARE OMITTED.                    98               PERFORM 870-PRINT-HEADINGS.
37       01  PATRON-LINE-RECORD   PIC X(132).              99          MOVE PR-NAME TO PL-NAME
38                                                        100          MOVE PR-ACTUAL-CONTR TO PL-ACTUAL-CONTR
39       WORKING-STORAGE SECTION.                         101          ADD PR-ACTUAL-CONTR TO AC-TOTAL-CONTR
40                                                        102          MOVE PATRON-LINE TO PATRON-LINE-RECORD
41       01  PROGRAM-SWITCHES.                            103          WRITE PATRON-LINE-RECORD
42           05  PS-END-OF-PATRON-FILE PIC X(3).          104          ADD 1 TO RC-LINES-USED
43                                                        105          PERFORM 800-READ-PATRON-RECORD.
44       01  AC-ACCUMULATORS.                             106
45           05  AC-TOTAL-CONTR   PIC 9(6).               107      700-PRINT-TOTAL-LINE.
46                                                        108          MOVE AC-TOTAL-CONTR TO SL-TOTAL-CONTR
47       01  REPORT-CONTROLS.                             109          MOVE SUMMARY-LINE TO PATRON-LINE-RECORD
48           05  RC-PAGE-NUMBER   PIC 9(2).               110          WRITE PATRON-LINE-RECORD
49           05  RC-LINES-USED    PIC 9(2).               111               AFTER ADVANCING 2 LINES.
50           05  RC-LINES-PER-PAGE PIC 9(2) VALUE 20.     112
51                                                        113      800-READ-PATRON-RECORD.
52       01  PATRON-LINE.                                 114          READ PATRON-FILE
53           05  PL-NAME          PIC X(18).              115               AT END MOVE "YES" TO PS-END-OF-PATRON-FILE.
54           05  FILLER           PIC X(5) VALUE SPACES.  116
55           05  PL-ACTUAL-CONTR  PIC Z,ZZ9.              117      870-PRINT-HEADINGS.
56                                                        118          ADD 1 TO RC-PAGE-NUMBER
57       01  H1-COLUMN-HEADING-LINE.                      119          MOVE RC-PAGE-NUMBER TO H1-PAGE-NUMBER
58           05  FILLER           PIC X(23)               120          MOVE H1-COLUMN-HEADING-LINE TO PATRON-LINE-RECORD
59                                VALUE "PATRON NAME     ". 121         WRITE PATRON-LINE-RECORD AFTER PAGE
60           05  FILLER           PIC X(10)  VALUE "CONTR". 122         MOVE SPACES TO PATRON-LINE-RECORD
61           05  FILLER           PIC X(5)   VALUE "Page ". 123         WRITE PATRON-LINE-RECORD
62           05  H1-PAGE-NUMBER   PIC Z(2).               124          MOVE 2 TO RC-LINES-USED
```

Page Totals

Basic Page Total Principles

The focus of PATLIST2 is on the use of an accumulator to obtain a report total on the contribution field of the patron record. It may not be apparent to you that the accumulator AC-TOTAL-CONTR in PATLIST2 is associated with a specific data group; in this case, the data group is the entire file. The accumulator is given an initial value of zero and then increased by the appropriate data-item as each record is processed. After the last record, the value in the accumulator is printed.

In Module C, you learned about another totaling concept: page totals. These are totals on selected fields printed at the bottom of the page for all detail records on that page. You can see the basic features of page totals on the sample output shown in Figure 7-10. An examination of this output reveals that it involves two data groups: the *current page* and the *entire file*. So, it requires two accumulators: a page-total accumulator and a report-total accumulator. Each page total is obtained by adding the current-record contribution to the page-total accumulator, exactly as done with the report total in PATLIST2. Obviously, the page total must be set to zero at the beginning of each new page.

Figure 7-10
Sample output
with page totals.

```
FLEETWOOD CHARITIES      Page  1        FLEETWOOD CHARITIES      Page  2
CONTRIBUTION SUMMARY    12/02/95        CONTRIBUTION SUMMARY    12/02/95

PATRON NAME               CONTR         PATRON NAME               CONTR

Acton, Jocelyn              350         Miller, Irwin B.           185
Anderson, Hazel            100          Molitar, Arnold T.         150
Baker, Donald              300          Nelson, J. J.                0
Broadhurst, Ryan           500          Pratt, Diane               229
Campbell, J. H.            175          Stevenson, Howard            0
Davidson, Harley           100          Unger, William P.          300
Drumright, Devon           105          Walton, John Jr.           150
Englehoff, F.              150          Winger, Mandy              225
Erlicht, Beverly           225          Zener, Eva                 190
Fox, Wylie                 100
Grant, Rosalyn P.           80              PAGE TOTAL           1,429
Hildebrand, John           200
Jones, Jeanette              0          TOTAL CONTRIBUTIONS      4,514
Lacrosse, Larry            520
Mattingly, Roscoe          180

    PAGE TOTAL          3,085
```

The report total can be considered in two ways: as the sum of all individual record contributions or as the sum of the page totals. Using the latter technique, the processing sequence is

1. With each detail record, add the contribution to the page accumulator.
2. At a page break (when a full page occurs):
   a. Print the page-total line.
   b. Progress to a new page and print the headings.
   c. Add the page-accumulator value to the report accumulator.
   d. Set the page accumulator to zero.

So, the report total is a sum of page totals, rather than a sum of detail amounts. This "sum of sums" concept is more efficient for the computer and, overall, is considered a better technique.

In addition to page breaks, two other conditions cause part of these break actions to take place: beginning the first page and detecting the end-of-file (the last page). For the first page, which you can consider a "pseudo-break," both the printing and initializing must occur; page-total printing and accumulation do not occur because no preceding total exists.

On the other hand, following detection of the end-of-file (another pseudo-break), the page-total line must be printed, but neither new page headings nor initialization is required.

These conditions are summarized in Figure 7-11's table, where First refers to the first-record pseudo-break, Other refers to regular page breaks, and Last refers to the end-of-file pseudo-break.

Figure 7-11
Page-break actions.

Action	Pseudo-break		
	First	Other	Last
Print page-total line		X	X
New page and print headings	X	X	
Add page total to report total		X	X
Initialize page-total accumulator	X	X	

PATLIST3—A Basic
Page-Total Program

Actually, once you get the idea of page control and printing page headings, extending to printing page totals is relatively straightforward. The program PATLIST3—from which the report of Figure 7-10 was generated—is shown in Figure 7-12. This program's overall structure is a minor variation of PATLIST2, shown in Figure 7-2 (page 202). PATLIST3 illustrates the following concepts:

1. Page totals
2. Accessing the current date from the system
3. Single WRITE and variable line spacing
4. The INITIALIZE statement
5. The READ/FROM statement

Modifications of PATLIST2 to produce page totals are highlighted in Figure 7-12. Two additions to WORKING-STORAGE are necessary: the page total accumulator (AC-PAGE-TOTAL-CONTR) at line 46 and the page-total print line at lines 78–80.

Correlating the program's actions with Figure 7-11's table, you can see that fields are initialized and the headings printed for the first pseudo-break via the PERFORMs at lines 94 and 95. The accumulators are set to zero by the INITIALIZE statement at line 118.

Within the processing loop, the detail-record contribution amount is added to the page-total accumulator at line 131. When the page becomes full—as indicated by the test at line 127—the four page-break actions occur:

1. The page-total line is printed via the PERFORM at line 128.
2. The page total is added to the report-total accumulator at line 144.
3. The page-total accumulator is set to zero at line 145.
4. The new page headings are printed via the PERFORM at line 129.

When the end-of-file pseudo-break occurs, the page-total line is printed and the final page total added to the report total via the PERFORM at line 109.

Comments About the
WORKING-STORAGE
SECTION

You can see that the WORKING-STORAGE SECTION for each example program is larger than that of the preceding program. Although you can arrange your entries in any order, your program organization is enhanced if you use a common pattern. For the programs in this text, the 01-level record-description entries are arranged in the following order:

1. Switches
2. Report control fields
3. Work areas
4. Accumulator (total) fields
5. Input-record areas
6. Heading-line areas
7. Detail-line areas
8. Total-line areas

For easy identification of the various heading lines, notice that the prefixes H1, H2, and H3 are used (for heading lines 1, 2, and 3, respectively).

Observe that a strict alignment of all PIC clauses within WORKING-STORAGE is no longer maintained. Generally, these are positioned farther to the left to accommodate literals defined with the VALUE clauses. In some cases, VALUE clauses are positioned even farther to the left on a separate line. However, within a given record, you should try to maintain a reasonable degree of alignment simply to make it easier to read and understand your record entries.

Remember, COBOL through the 1985 Standard does not allow you to make program entries beyond column 71. This restriction will not be carried over to

Figure 7-12   PATLIST3—A program to print page totals.

```
1     IDENTIFICATION DIVISION.
2     PROGRAM-ID.    PATLIST3.
3
4     *     Price/Welburn   1/15/95
5     *     Calculate & Print page-totals/report total
6
7     ENVIRONMENT DIVISION.
8
9     INPUT-OUTPUT SECTION.
10
11    FILE-CONTROL.
12        SELECT PATRON-FILE
13            ASSIGN TO (system dependent).
14        SELECT PATRON-LIST
15            ASSIGN TO (system dependent).
16
17
18    DATA DIVISION.
19
20    FILE SECTION.
21
22    FD  PATRON-FILE.
23    01  PATRON-RECORD          PIC X(68).
24
25    FD  PATRON-LIST.
26    01  PATRON-LINE-RECORD     PIC X(132).
27
28    WORKING-STORAGE SECTION.
29
30    01  PROGRAM-SWITCHES.
31        05  PS-END-OF-PATRON-FILE PIC X(3).
32
33    01  RC-REPORT-CONTROLS.
34        05  RC-PAGE-NUMBER      PIC 9(2).
35        05  RC-LINES-USED       PIC 9(2).
36        05  RC-LINES-PER-PAGE   PIC 9(2) VALUE 20.
37        05  RC-LINE-SPACING     PIC 9(2).
38
39    01  WA-WORK-AREAS.
40        05  WA-CURRENT-DATE.
41            10  WA-CURRENT-YEAR  PIC 9(2).
42            10  WA-CURRENT-MONTH PIC 9(2).
43            10  WA-CURRENT-DAY   PIC 9(2).
44
45    01  AC-ACCUMULATORS.
46        05  AC-PAGE-TOTAL-CONTR  PIC 9(6).
47        05  AC-TOTAL-CONTR       PIC 9(6).
48
49    01  PR-PATRON-RECORD.
50        05  PR-NAME             PIC X(18).
51        05                      PIC X(46).
52        05  PR-ACTUAL-CONTR     PIC 9(4).
53
54    01  H1-HEADING-LINE.
55        05                      PIC X(30)
56                VALUE "FLEETWOOD CHARITIES     Page".
57        05  H1-PAGE-NUMBER      PIC Z(2).
58
59    01  H2-HEADING-LINE.
60        05                      PIC X(24)
61                VALUE "CONTRIBUTION SUMMARY".
62        05  H2-CURRENT-DATE.
63            10  H2-CURRENT-MONTH PIC Z9.
64            10                   PIC X(1)  VALUE "/".
65            10  H2-CURRENT-DAY   PIC 9(2).
66            10                   PIC X(1)  VALUE "/".
67            10  H2-CURRENT-YEAR  PIC 9(2).
68
69    01  H3-HEADING-LINE.
70        05              PIC X(27)   VALUE "PATRON NAME".
71        05              PIC X(10)   VALUE "CONTR".
72
73    01  PL-PATRON-LINE.
74        05  PL-NAME             PIC X(18).
75        05                      PIC X(9) VALUE SPACES.
76        05  PL-ACTUAL-CONTR PIC Z,ZZ9.
77
78    01  PT-PAGE-TOTAL-LINE.
79        05      PIC X(25)  VALUE "        PAGE TOTAL".
80        05  PT-TOTAL-CONTR PIC ZZZ,ZZ9.
81
82    01  RT-REPORT-TOTAL-LINE.
83        05      PIC X(25)  VALUE " TOTAL CONTRIBUTIONS".
84        05  RT-TOTAL-CONTR PIC ZZZ,ZZ9.
85
86
87    PROCEDURE DIVISION.
88
89    000-PRINT-PATRON-LIST.
90
91    ************Initialization Sequence************
92        OPEN INPUT PATRON-FILE
93            OUTPUT PATRON-LIST
94        PERFORM 100-INITIALIZE-VARIABLE-FIELDS
95        PERFORM 870-PRINT-HEADINGS
96
97    *************Processing Sequence*************
98        PERFORM UNTIL
99            PS-END-OF-PATRON-FILE IS EQUAL TO "YES"
100           READ PATRON-FILE INTO PR-PATRON-RECORD
101               AT END
102                   MOVE "YES" TO PS-END-OF-PATRON-FILE
103               NOT AT END
104                   PERFORM 200-PROCESS-PATRON-RECORD
105           END-READ
106       END-PERFORM
107
108   **************Termination Sequence*************
109       PERFORM 700-PRINT-PAGE-TOTAL-LINE
110       PERFORM 710-PRINT-REPORT-TOTAL-LINE
111       CLOSE PATRON-FILE
112             PATRON-LIST
113       STOP RUN
114       .
115   *********************************************
116   100-INITIALIZE-VARIABLE-FIELDS.
117       MOVE "NO" TO PS-END-OF-PATRON-FILE
118       INITIALIZE AC-ACCUMULATORS
119             RC-LINES-USED
120             RC-PAGE-NUMBER
121       ACCEPT WA-CURRENT-DATE FROM DATE
122       MOVE WA-CURRENT-MONTH TO H2-CURRENT-MONTH
123       MOVE WA-CURRENT-DAY TO H2-CURRENT-DAY
124       MOVE WA-CURRENT-YEAR TO H2-CURRENT-YEAR
125       .
126   200-PROCESS-PATRON-RECORD.
127       IF RC-LINES-USED NOT LESS THAN RC-LINES-PER-PAGE
128           PERFORM 700-PRINT-PAGE-TOTAL-LINE
129           PERFORM 870-PRINT-HEADINGS
130       END-IF
131       ADD PR-ACTUAL-CONTR TO AC-PAGE-TOTAL-CONTR
132       MOVE PR-NAME TO PL-NAME
133       MOVE PR-ACTUAL-CONTR TO PL-ACTUAL-CONTR
134       MOVE PL-PATRON-LINE TO PATRON-LINE-RECORD
135       MOVE 1 TO RC-LINE-SPACING
136       PERFORM 890-WRITE-REPORT-LINE
137       .
138   700-PRINT-PAGE-TOTAL-LINE.
139       MOVE AC-PAGE-TOTAL-CONTR TO PT-TOTAL-CONTR
140       MOVE 2 TO RC-LINE-SPACING
141       MOVE PT-PAGE-TOTAL-LINE TO PATRON-LINE-RECORD
142       PERFORM 890-WRITE-REPORT-LINE
143   *   Page-break housekeeping
144       ADD AC-PAGE-TOTAL-CONTR TO AC-TOTAL-CONTR
145       MOVE ZERO TO AC-PAGE-TOTAL-CONTR
146       .
147   710-PRINT-REPORT-TOTAL-LINE.
148       MOVE AC-TOTAL-CONTR TO RT-TOTAL-CONTR
149       MOVE 2 TO RC-LINE-SPACING
150       MOVE RT-REPORT-TOTAL-LINE TO PATRON-LINE-RECORD
151       PERFORM 890-WRITE-REPORT-LINE
152       .
153   870-PRINT-HEADINGS.
154       ADD 1 TO RC-PAGE-NUMBER
155       MOVE RC-PAGE-NUMBER TO H1-PAGE-NUMBER
156       MOVE H1-HEADING-LINE TO PATRON-LINE-RECORD
157       PERFORM 880-WRITE-REPORT-TOP-LINE
158       MOVE H2-HEADING-LINE TO PATRON-LINE-RECORD
159       MOVE 1 TO RC-LINE-SPACING
160       PERFORM 890-WRITE-REPORT-LINE
161       MOVE H3-HEADING-LINE TO PATRON-LINE-RECORD
162       MOVE 2 TO RC-LINE-SPACING
163       PERFORM 890-WRITE-REPORT-LINE
164       MOVE 1 TO RC-LINE-SPACING
165       MOVE SPACES TO PATRON-LINE-RECORD
166       PERFORM 890-WRITE-REPORT-LINE
167       .
168   880-WRITE-REPORT-TOP-LINE.
169       WRITE PATRON-LINE-RECORD
170           AFTER ADVANCING PAGE
171       MOVE 1 TO RC-LINES-USED
172       .
173   890-WRITE-REPORT-LINE.
174       WRITE PATRON-LINE-RECORD
175           AFTER ADVANCING RC-LINE-SPACING LINES
176       ADD RC-LINE-SPACING TO RC-LINES-USED
177       .
```

Remember, COBOL through the 1985 Standard does not allow you to make program entries beyond column 71. This restriction will not be carried over to COBOL-9X.

COBOL-74 Modifications to PATLIST3

1. Insert the CONFIGURATION SECTION and LABEL RECORDS clauses.
2. Insert the reserved word FILLER.
3. Modify the processing sequence (lines 98–106); if you use the priming READ, place the READ statement in a separate module.
4. Replace END-IF (line 130) with a period at the end of line 129.
5. Replace INITIALIZE (lines 118–120) with appropriate MOVE statements.

Controlling Printer Line Width—Personal Computers

The output specifications of business reports often require detail line width wider than that available with the standard 8½-inch paper commonly used in personal computer printers. To accommodate this need, most printers provide the capability for printing in a condensed mode, commonly 17 characters per inch. Some printers allow the print mode to be set from printer switches or buttons; others require that the computer send an appropriate binary code or sequence of codes. So, by creating the appropriate code sequence, then writing it to the printer (as part of your initialization sequence), you can set your printer to print condensed type. Appendix D includes a description of how to do this and sample code sequences for two printers.

TOPIC

Designing a Report Program

In the stepwise refinement of the patron list programs, we have not followed the normal program-design process of identifying the application needs, laying out the structure, and writing the pseudocode. Instead, the focus was on the basic principles of using COBOL. Now that you have seen the solution and understand the principles involved, let's backtrack and step through the program-design process.

Programming Specifications for the Contribution Summary Program

The Output Report

Your task is to write a program that generates a patron contribution report with page and report totals. After meeting with the contributions supervisor, you determine the exact output required and formalize it as the print chart depicted in Figure 7-13. On one hand, this chart shows exactly where everything should be on the report page. On the other, it does not indicate how many lines per page should be printed. This determination requires some arithmetic. Referring to Figure 7-13, the headings require five lines and the page total requires two lines—including

Figure 7-13   The print chart for the patron contribution summary report.

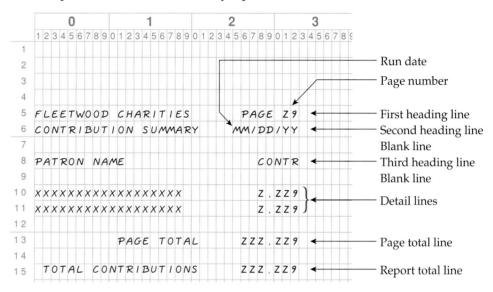

blank lines, in both cases. In addition, the last page requires two additional lines for the report total. Regarding the report-total line, the supervisor indicated that even if the last page of the report is completely full after printing the page-summary line, she does *not* want the report total printed by itself on a separate page. This requirement causes you to divide the page into four sections:

1. The *top margin*—lines at the top of the page on which nothing is printed.
2. The *body*—where detail lines (and some summary lines) are printed.
3. The *footing*—is somewhat of a "printing overflow" area. Its only use is to print summary lines (page total, in this case) that must be kept on the same page as the output preceding it, but might otherwise be printed on the next page. For other remarks on the footing area, refer back to Module C.
4. The *bottom margin*—similar to the top margin, nothing is printed here.

For this application, assume that the form requirements are as follows:

- A standard 11-inch form length (66 lines using 6 lines per inch)
- Top margin of 4 lines
- Bottom margin of 3 lines
- Footing of 5 lines

As you can see in Figure 7-14, this results in a body line span of 54 lines for each page. Referring to PATLIST3 in Figure 7-12, the data-item RC-LINES-PER-PAGE (line 36) would receive a value of 54. (Note: The value of 20 was chosen for Figure 7-12's example report simply to show a two-page report with the small sample data file.)

After determining the user's needs and that required input is available for generating the desired output, you now proceed to the program specifications. In Figure 7-15, requirements are described in detail—reflecting the planning of output format. Notice the explicit description of the output format (items F and G).

Figure 7-14
Computation of
report-line span.

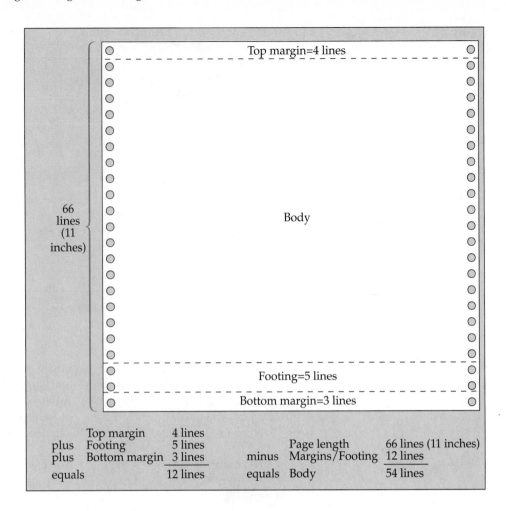

Designing the Structure Chart

Top-Down Design

Each program studied so far was a modest extension of the previous example; this was reflected in the structure. However, the structure of this book's programs now becomes considerably more complex, with greater differences from preceding programs. So, a formalized approach to modularizing an application will become critical. How do you modularize a program? Actually, the process of solving a programming problem is much like building a house. That is, the architect first provides general sketches of the house and its placement on the lot. Next, plans are drawn, beginning with the overall concept and working down to the detail. Only when all of the detailed drawings are complete does actual construction begin.

Similarly, with a programming job, the overall needs and requirements are defined first. Then, the tasks are broken into subtasks until each is a manageable size. The programming begins only after these steps are complete. This process of working from the general to the specific is called **top-down design**. Let's consider the following seven-step approach to designing a structure chart, using the patron contribution application as an example.

The first step is to identify the functional modules that will form your program. You work from a combination of the program specifications and your knowledge of the general operations required for this type of program. Since the program must accumulate, you will need an initialization module. Since detail lines are required, you need a patron-record processing module. Required printed output includes heading lines, page-total lines, and report-total lines. Because of style convention, two modules are also needed for the WRITE statements.

Figure 7-15
Programming specifications
for PATLIST3.

PROGRAMMING SPECIFICATIONS

Program Name: PATRON CONTRIBUTION   **Program ID:** PATLIST3
SUMMARY REPORT

Program Description:

This program prints a detail/summary report from input patron records.

Input File:

Patron File

Output File:

Patron Contribution/Summary Report

List of Program Operations:

A. Read each input patron record.
B. For each record:
    1. Print a detail-line containing the following fields in
        accordance with the format shown on the print-chart:
        - Patron name
        - Contribution

    2. Accumulate both page totals and report totals for the
        contribution field.
C. Each detail-line must be single-spaced from the previous
    detail-line.
D. At the bottom of each page, the program must print the
    total of contributions for that page.
E. After all the input patron records are processed, the
    program must print the total contributions for all
    patrons.
F. Standard 11-inch long continuous forms are used as the
    paper stock. Provide a 4-line margin at the top of the
    form, a 3-line margin at the bottom of the form, and a 5-
    line footing area. Lines are printed at the rate of 6
    lines per vertical inch.
G. Headings are printed on each page of the report. After
    54 lines are used on a report page (including heading
    lines), the program should skip to the next page.
    1. The run date must be obtained from the operating
        system and printed on the second heading-line in
        accordance with the format shown on the print-chart.
    2. The page number must be incremented each time the
        heading is printed and displayed on the heading-line
        in accordance with the format shown on the print-
        chart.
    3. The first detail-line printed after the headings
        should be double-spaced from the last heading-line.

A complete list of the PATLIST3 program functions would therefore appear as shown in step 1 of Figure 7-16. When listing functional program modules, they need not be arranged in any particular sequence. The list is merely for reference while drawing the structure chart to help ensure that all required modules are included.

Notice in the module list that the module-naming conventions introduced earlier are followed. However, no module numbers are assigned yet.

In accordance with top-down program development concepts, the top-level block on the structure chart is drawn to describe the overall program function: print patron list. This is shown in step 2 of Figure 7-16. This top-level module, which is at level 0 on the chart, represents the mainline module of the program.

Figure 7-16 Structure chart design (steps 1–4): patron detail/summary report.

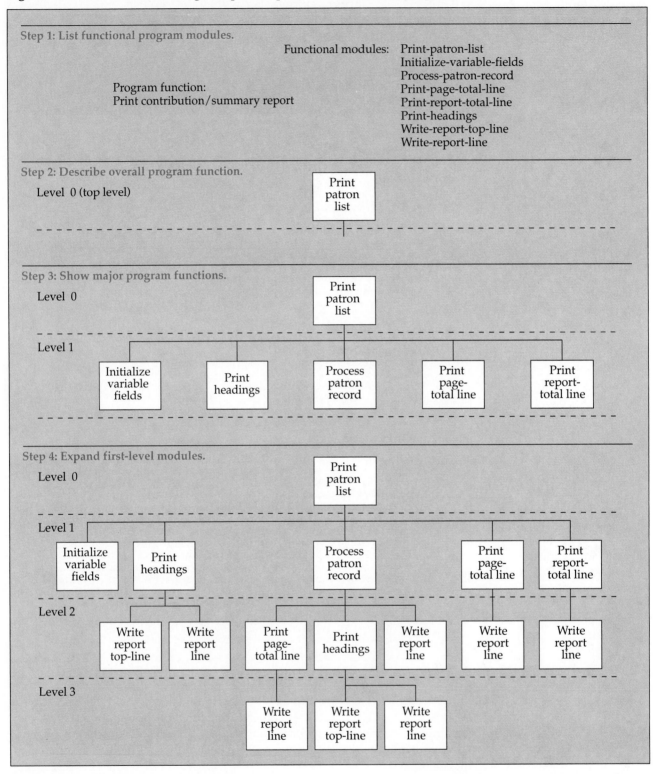

Step 3: Show Major Program Functions

The modules shown at the first structure chart level from the top are those that relate directly to the overall program function. These are the modules that are performed from the mainline module. For PATLIST3, the following five principal modules are shown at level 1:

1. Initialize-variable-fields
2. Print-headings
3. Process-patron-record
4. Print-page-total-line
5. Print-report-total-line

Remember that the purpose of a structure chart is to show how modules relate to one another hierarchically (that is, vertically); sequential (or horizontal) relationships are not necessarily meaningful. However, it is easier to relate the structure chart to the program coding when the modules are arranged on the chart from left to right by the order in which the functions typically occur during program execution. Such a left-to-right arrangement was incorporated into step 3 of Figure 7-16, which shows the levels 0 and 1 of the PATLIST3 structure chart.

Step 4: Expand First-Level Modules

Those first-level modules that will perform other modules are expanded to show the performed modules, as illustrated in step 4 of Figure 7-16. Let's consider each of these first-level modules.

Initialize-Variable-Fields Module

This module is similar in function to that of previous programs in the text. It is executed only once and does not perform any other modules.

Print-Headings Module

Report headings are printed under two conditions: at the start of a run (the first page) and after a page is full and the printer is positioned to a new page. This module as positioned at the first level represents printing the headings for the first page. This module must in turn perform (1) the Write-report-top-line module, which prints the very first heading line on each page and (2) the Write-report-line module, which prints the remaining heading lines. These are shown at level 2.

Process-Patron-Record Module

This module involves the program's read-process cycle. We know that it controls writing of detail lines and page-control operations that, in turn, include printing page totals and headings. It performs the following three modules:

- Print-page-total-line (when page totals are required)
- Print-headings (when headings are required)
- Write-report-line (to print each detail line)

Print-Page-Total-Line Module

This module is performed with each page break. It performs one other module—Write-report-line—to print the page-total line on the report.

Print-Report-Total-Line Module

This module is executed only once after all patron records are processed. It performs one other module—Write-report-line—to print the report-total line on the report.

Step 5: Identify Common Modules

As you observed in the PATLIST3 program, certain modules—especially those that handle input/output operations—will appear on the structure chart more than once. For example, the module Write-report-line appears six times. These common modules are identified by shading the upper right-hand corner of the structure chart block, as you will see later.

Step 6: Review Structure Chart

After finishing the structure chart, you should review it to verify that it is complete and correct. In doing so, refer to your program specifications to ensure that you did not overlook any aspect of the program requirements. Don't expect to get everything the first time. Although the preceding descriptions give the appearance of a 1-2-3 approach where the solution is obvious, that is not the case in practice. Usually, some experimentation (and head-scratching) are involved.

Step 7: Number Each Module

The final step is to number the modules according to the module-numbering conventions of Figure 7-1 (page 200). The completed structure chart is shown in Figure 7-17. Here you see that the common modules are identified by shaded triangles in the upper right-hand corner. Because the common modules need be coded only once, parentheses are affixed to each common module's number after its first occurrence on the chart. This is simply an aid to make it easier to check off completed modules during coding; the duplicated ones with their module numbers in parentheses can be skipped.

A Final Comment About Modular Design

One of this book's programming styles is to use a module-naming convention that identifies the action of the module. So, for instance, the module name 700-Print-Total-Line clearly tells us the single, basic function of the module. If, in your planning phase, you find that you need two verbs to truly describe what the function does, then you should consider two separate modules.

In this respect, it could be argued that the module 710-Print-Page-Totals violates this standard because it includes two actions: setting up for printing *and* updating accumulators. (If you need to refresh your memory, refer to the program in Figure 7-12, page 213.) Therefore, the updating function should be included as a separate module and beneath the 200 module should be the Print-page-total-line

Figure 7-17 Completed structure chart for PATLIST3.

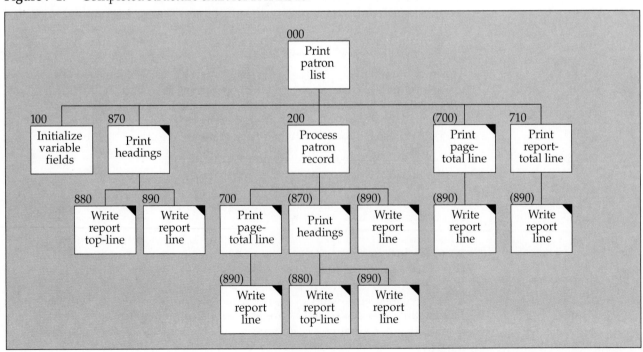

module *and* an Update-accumulators module. Here is an example of when to consider compromise from rigid standards in the interest of practicality. You should consider two factors. First, the function of updating accumulators is directly associated with actions performed when a break is detected—a page break, in this case. In this sense, we could argue that the two actions can reasonably be kept together because they are closely related and they occur simultaneously. (In structured programming theory, grouping actions because they occur simultaneously is called *temporal cohesion*.) Second, in the program, this results in a two-statement module; too many of these could make the program fragmented and difficult to follow. So, it is common practice to include the updating-accumulators action as part of the Print-totals module. The value of this technique is even more significant when working with multiple levels of control breaks, as you will learn in Chapter 9.

Writing the Pseudocode

Since we've already studied the PATLIST3 program, the pseudocode solution should be fairly obvious. However, as done with the structure chart, let's put the program itself out of our minds. Then we can work from the structure chart in determining the pseudocode.

000-Print-Patron-List Module

We know the following general actions of the mainline module:

1. This module will call each of its five subordinate (first-level) modules.
2. From previous programs of this type, we know that the order in which the first-level modules are performed is identical to the left-to-right order in Figure 7-17's structure chart.
3. Execution of the 200-Process-Patron-Record module is repeated within an inline PERFORM statement under control of a READ statement—the standard approach used for processing data files.
4. This module also includes appropriate OPEN and CLOSE statements.

The pseudocode for this module is as follows:

```
000-Print-Patron-List module
   1.  Open the files.
   2.  Perform 100-Initialize-Variable-Fields.
   3.  Perform 870-Print-Headings.
   4.  Perform until end-of-file
          Read a record from the input Patron file;
             if there are no more records
                Move "Yes" to the end-of-file indicator
             if more records
                Perform 200-Process-Patron-Record.
   5.  Perform 700-Print-Page-Total-Line.
   6.  Perform 710-Print-Report-Total-Line.
   7.  Close the files.
   8.  Stop the run.
```

As counterpart initialization modules did in this text's previous programs, this module handles:

1. Setting the end-of-file switch to "no".
2. Setting the accumulator fields to zero. In addition to the report-total field, this program includes the page-total accumulator.
3. Setting fields used for line counting and page numbering to zero.
4. Obtaining the run date from the operating system and placing it in the second heading line.

This module's pseudocode is virtually identical to the previous sequence of steps.

```
100-Initialize-Variable-Fields module
     1.  Set the End-of-file indicator to "No".
     2.  Set the following to zero:
             Page and report accumulator fields
             Lines-used indicator
             Page-count
     3.  Obtain the date from the operating system and move it to the
         second heading-line.
```

200-Process-Patron-Record Module

This is the central-processing module; it carries out essentially the same activities of the corresponding module in PATLIST2. However, referring to the structure chart, we see that it also prints the page-total line, in addition to printing headings and the report detail line. Here the sequencing is important. That is, upon detecting a full page, the page-total line must be printed before progressing to the next page and printing headings. Then the detail line can be set up and printed. Specific actions are described in the following pseudocode solution to this module:

```
200-Process-Patron-Record module
     1.  If the report page is full,
             Perform 710-Report-Total-Line
             Perform 870-Print-Headings.
     2.  Add the Actual-contribution to Page-total.
     3.  Move the following input fields to the detail-line:
             Patron-name
             Actual-contribution
     4.  Move the detail-line to the output-line area.
     5.  Set the line-spacing indicator for single-spacing.
     6.  Perform 890-Write-Report-Line.
```

700 and 710 Total Line Modules

Referring to the structure chart, you can see that the 700-Print-Page-Total-Line module is performed under two different conditions: from the 200 module when a page is found to be full and from the mainline module after the end-of-file condition occurs. It serves two broad functions: (1) set up and print the page-total summary line and (2) do the page-break housekeeping functions. You see details of this activity in the following pseudocode:

```
700-Print-Page-Total-Line module
     1.  Move the Page-total field to the Page-total-line.
     2.  Move the Page-total-line to the output area.
     3.  Set the line-spacing indicator for double-spacing.
     4.  Perform 890-Write-Report-Line.
     5.  Add the Page-total to the Report-total.
     6.  Set the Page-total to 0.
```

On the other hand, the 710-Print-Report-Total-Line module is executed only after all the records are processed; it does not require the housekeeping functions of the page-total module.

```
710-Print-Report-Total-Line module
     1.  Move the Report-total field to the Report-total-line.
     2.  Move the Report-total-line to the output area.
     3.  Set the line-spacing indicator for double-spacing.
     4.  Perform 890-Write-Report-Line.
```

This module handles the printing of all the heading lines and is reasonably straightforward. Note the following four points:

1. The page number must be incremented by 1 and moved to the appropriate heading line.

2. The first heading line must cause the printer to progress to a new page before printing.
3. Care must be taken in setting the line-spacing variable to a value in accordance with the print chart requirements before printing each heading line.
4. The blank line preceding the first detail line is achieved by printing a blank line, as in PATLIST2.

The following is the pseudocode for this module:

```
870-Print-Headings module
     1.  Add 1 to the Page-count.
     2.  Move the Page-count to the Page-number field in the first
         heading-line.
     3.  Move Heading-line-1 to the output print-line area.
     4.  Perform 880-Write-Report-Top-Line.
     5.  Move Heading-line-2 to the output print-line area.
     6.  Set the line-spacing indicator for single-spacing.
     7.  Perform 890-Write-Report-Line.
     8.  Move Heading-line-3 to the output print-line area.
     9.  Set the line-spacing indicator for double-spacing.
    10.  Perform 890-Write-Report-Line.
    11.  Clear the output print-line area.
    12.  Set the line-spacing indicator for single-spacing.
    13.  Perform 890-Write-Report-Line.
```

880 and 890 Write Modules

The 880 module is used only to print the first heading line on each page. After the write operation, the lines-used indicator is set to 1 because one line—the first heading line—has now been used on the current report page.

The 890 module is used to print all lines—heading, detail, and total—of the report, except for the first heading line. It provides for line spacing (single-, double-, or triple-spacing) in accordance with the value present in the line-spacing indicator field at the time the line is printed.

After printing the line, the value of the line-spacing indicator is added to the lines-used field to keep track of how many lines were printed on the current page. (Recall that the lines-used field is tested in the 200-Process-Patron-Record module to determine when a page is full, at which time the continuous form must be positioned to a new page.)

```
880-Write-Report-Top-Line module
     1.  Advance to the top of the next report page and write the
         output print-line area.
     2.  Set the Lines-used indicator to 1.

890-Write-Report-Line module
     1.  Write the print-line area after advancing the forms in
         accordance with the value in the line-spacing indicator
         field.
     2.  Add the line-spacing indicator to the Lines-used field.
```

Chapter Summary

An accumulator is a data-item used to obtain the total of a field for all—or part—of the records in a file. It must be set to zero at the beginning of the processing sequence and incremented with each record.

The INITIALIZE statement (not included in COBOL-74) provides for initializing all elementary items under a group item. The initialization involves setting numeric and numeric-edited fields to zero; alphanumeric, alphanumeric-edited, and alphabetic fields are set to spaces.

The PAGE option of the ADVANCING phrase allows you to cause the printer to position the paper at the top of a new page.

The current date, day, or time may be obtained from the operating system by this statement: ACCEPT identifier FROM DATE, DAY, TIME, or (not included in COBOL-74) DAY-OF-WEEK.

Page control is accomplished by counting lines printed. To determine the total allowable lines, you must work from the print chart—accounting for the form length, top and bottom margins, and the footing area.

With large programs, an orderly approach to program design is essential. Top-down design is a step-by-step approach of proceeding from the general to the modularized detail until a large, complex task is broken down into a collection of interrelated, basic tasks. The following is a seven-step approach to creating a structure chart:

1. List the functional program modules.
2. Describe the overall program function on the top level of the structure chart.
3. Show the major program functions on the first level of the structure chart.
4. Expand the first-level modules to show the modules that are performed at lower levels. Expand lower levels until further breakdown is no longer necessary.
5. Identify common modules.
6. Review the structure chart.
7. Number each module.

Style Summary

A program module that appears in more than one place on the structure chart is called a common module. Identify common modules on the structure chart by shading upper-right corners.

Use a standardized module-numbering convention—such as that in Figure 7-1—to provide consistency among programs.

Initialize constant fields with VALUE clauses in the WORKING-STORAGE SECTION of the DATA DIVISION; initialize variable fields with PROCEDURE DIVISION statements. Doing this aids program documentation and provides more flexibility for repeated execution of modules.

Define input and output records in the WORKING-STORAGE SECTION. For input records, this permits reference to the fields of a record after the last record in the file is read. For output records, it allows VALUE clauses to be used for the initialization of constant fields within the record.

Arrange your WORKING-STORAGE SECTION entries in an organized way. The following is a recommended order:

1. Switches
2. Report control fields
3. Work areas
4. Accumulator (total) fields
5. Input-record areas
6. Heading-line areas
7. Detail-line areas
8. Total-line areas

Use only one READ and one WRITE statement for each file—except that you need two WRITE statements if a top-of-page action is needed. Do this by including each statement in a separate module.

Avoid use of the WRITE/FROM option for report lines because it is not consistent with the use of common, independent I/O modules.

Exercises

Terms for Definition

accumulator   top-down design
page break   variable line spacing
page control

Review Questions

1. List the seven steps of preparing a structure chart.

2. Why is it preferable to define output records in the WORKING-STORAGE SECTION, rather than the FILE SECTION?

3. Why is it preferable to define input records in the WORKING-STORAGE SECTION, rather than the FILE SECTION?

4. With the ACCEPT/FROM DATE statement, the field that receives the date should be _____ positions in length; after execution, the field contains the date in _____ format.

5. With the ACCEPT/FROM DAY statement, the field that receives the day number should be _____ positions in length; after execution, the field contains the day number in _____ format.

6. To provide for skipping to the top of the next report page, the _____ option of the ADVANCING phrase is used.

Questions About the Example Programs

PATLIST2—Refer to Figure 7-2

1. PATRON-LINE-RECORD is defined as a 132-position output line in the FD (line 29). However, each of the three WORKING-STORAGE output lines (which will be moved to PATRON-LINE-RECORD) consists of fewer than 132 positions. Explain why this discrepancy is valid.

2. A beginning programmer forgets the VALUE clause in the definition of PATRON-LINE (line 46). What effect does this have on the printed output?

3. Describe what will occur if the statements initializing the accumulators (lines 90 and 91) are omitted.

4. What will happen if the data file contains no records (only the EOF)?

5. What will happen if the line-counter statement at line 102 is omitted?

PATLIST3—Refer to Figure 7-12

1. Describe the program output if the initial value of RC-LINES-PER-PAGE is accidentally entered as 6 instead of 20.

2. This program includes two counters: RC-PAGE-NUMBER and RC-LINES-USED. There is an important conceptual difference between the way in which these accumulators are used in the program. Identify that difference.

3. Describe the printed output if the IF (line 127) were accidentally coded as:

```
IF RC-LINES-USED IS LESS THAN RC-LINES-PER-PAGE
```

4. Describe the printed output if the MOVE statement at line 171 were omitted.

5. How would it affect the printed output if the ADD statement at line 144 were omitted?

6. How would it affect the printed output if the MOVE statement at line 145 were omitted?

Programming Assignments

Programming Assignment 7-1: Price List

Background information:

The sales manager of Tools Unlimited needs a new report prepared from the inventory file. It must list each item in the product line and its price.

Input file: Inventory file (INVEN.DAT)

Inventory record

	Product identification	Product description		Unit price	

Inventory class

1 2 3 4 5 6 7 8 9 10 11 12 13 14 15 16 17 18 19 20 21 22 23 24 25 26 27 28 29 30 31 32 33 34 35 36 37 38 39 40 41 42 43 44 45 46 47 48 49 50 51 52 53 54 55 56 57 58 59 60 61 62 63 64 65 66 67 68 69 70 71 72 73 74 75 76 77 78 79 80

Output-report format:

```
                              PRICE LIST (7-1)

PROD IDENT          PRODUCT DESCRIPTION                    PRICE

  XXXXXXXXXX        XXXXXXXXXXXXXXXXXXXXXXXXXXXX        Z,ZZZ.99
  XXXXXXXXXX        XXXXXXXXXXXXXXXXXXXXXXXXXXXX        Z,ZZZ.99

NUMBER OF RECORDS PROCESSED ZZZ9
```

Program operations:

1. Process each input part record—except those with a value X for the Inventory-class field.

2. Count each record that is processed.

3. Print the two heading lines on the first page and on each following page of the list.

4. Print an output price list detail line for each part record as specified on the print chart.

5. Single-space each detail line (except double-space between the last heading line and the first detail line on each page, as shown on the print chart). Provide for a span of 54 lines per page.

6. After all input records are processed, print a double-spaced total line with the count of number of records processed.

Programming Assignment 7-2: Earnings Report

Background information:

The personnel manager of Silicon Manufacturing wants a program to print an employee earnings report from data in the earnings file.

Input file: Earnings file (EARNINGS.DAT)

Earnings record

	Employee number	Employee last name	Employee first name		Pay code	Year-to-date earnings	

1 2 3 4 5 6 7 8 9 10 11 12 13 14 15 16 17 18 19 20 21 22 23 24 25 26 27 28 29 30 31 32 33 34 35 36 37 38 39 40 41 42 43 44 45 46 47 48 49 50 51 52 53 54 55 56 57 58 59 60 61 62 63 64 65 66 67 68 69 70 71 72 73 74 75 76 77 78 79

Output file:

Earnings Report

Output-report format:

```
                    0         1         2         3         4         5         6
          1234567890123456789012345678901234567890123456789012345678901234567890123456789
 1
 2
 3
 4  EARNINGS  REPORT  (7-2)                        MM/DD/YY   PAGE  ZZ9
 5
 6      EMPLOYEE           ----EMPLOYEE  NAME-----      YEAR-TO-DATE
 7      NUMBER         LAST            FIRST                EARNINGS
 8
 9  999-99-9999        XXXXXXXXXXX  XXXXXXXXX         ZZZ,ZZZ.99
10
11  999-99-9999        XXXXXXXXXXX  XXXXXXXXX         ZZZ,ZZZ.99
12
13
14                 HOURLY  TOTAL  EARNINGS   Z,ZZZ,ZZZ.99*
15                 SALARIED  TOTAL  EARNINGS  Z,ZZZ,ZZZ.99*
16
17
```

Program operations:

1. Process each input earnings record.

2. Print the three heading lines on the first page and on each following page of the report.
   a. Print the run date on the first heading line as specified on the print chart.
   b. Accumulate and print the page number on the first heading line as specified on the print chart.

3. For each input employee record, do the following:
   a. Print an output earnings detail line as specified on the print chart.
   b. Accumulate the total earnings for hourly employees (Pay-code is H) and for salaried employees (Pay-code is S).

4. Double-space each detail line. Provide for a span of 40 lines per page.

5. After all input earnings records are processed, print two total lines—one for the hourly employees and the other for the salaried employees. For the first total line, triple-space from the last detail line as specified on the print chart.

Programming Assignment 7-3: Sales Quota Report

Background information:

The sales manager of Follow-the-Sun Sales wants to know how each member of the sales staff is performing relative to his or her sales quota. For this, a sales quota report must be printed from the salesperson file.

Input file: Salesperson file (SALEPER.DAT)

Salesperson record

Region	Territory	Number	Salesperson name		Sales revenue	Sales quota
1 2	3 4	5 6 7 8	9 10 11 12 13 14 15 16 17 18 19 20 21 22 23 24 25 26 27 28 29 30 31 32 33 34 35 36 37	38 39 40 41 42 43 44 45 46 47 48 49 50 51 52 53 54 55 56 57 58 59 60	61 62 63 64 65 66 67 68 69 70	71 72 73 74 75 76 77 78 79

Output-report format:

YES or blank

```
        0         1         2         3         4         5         6         7         8
   1234567890123456789012345678901234567890123456789012345678901234567890123456789012345678901
 1
 2
 3
 4 FOLLOW-THE-SUN SALES                                            RUN DATE MM/DD/YY
 5 SALES QUOTA REPORT (7-3)                                                 PAGE ZZ9
 6
 7 REGION    ----------SALESPERSON----------      SALES          SALES     PERCENT QUOTA
 8   TERR.   NBR    NAME                           QUOTA          REVENUE   OF QUOTA MADE
 9
10 XX-9999   999    XXXXXXXXXXXXXXXXXXXXXXXXX    Z,ZZZ,ZZZ.99   ZZ,ZZZ,ZZZ.99     ZZ9%      YES
11
12 XX-9999   999    XXXXXXXXXXXXXXXXXXXXXXXXX    Z,ZZZ,ZZZ.99   ZZ,ZZZ,ZZZ.99     ZZ9%
13
14                          PAGE TOTALS   ZZ,ZZZ,ZZZ.99*  ZZZ,ZZZ,ZZZ.99*
15
16
17            TOTAL SALESPERSONS Z,ZZ9*      ZZ,ZZZ,ZZZ.99*  ZZZ,ZZZ,ZZZ.99*     ZZ9%
18
19
```

Program operations:

1. Process each input salesperson record.

2. Print the four heading lines on the first page and on each following page of the report.
   a. Print the run date on the first heading line as specified on the print chart.
   b. Accumulate and print the page number on the second heading line as specified on the print chart.

3. For each input salesperson record, do the following:
   a. Calculate the percent-of-quota by dividing the sales revenue by the sales quota. Round the percentage to the nearest percentage point.
   b. Print an output detail line as specified on the print chart.

c. If the salesperson makes his or her quota (Sales-revenue not less than Sales-quota), then print the word "YES" as indicated on the print chart. Otherwise, leave this entry blank.

d. Accumulate the total number of salespersons, the total sales quota, and the total sales revenue.

4. Double-space each detail line. Provide for a span of 55 lines per page.

5. *Assignment option to be included as required by your instructor.*
Print a total line at the bottom of each page as shown on the print chart. The page total is to consist of totals for the Sales-quota and Sales-revenue fields.

6. After all input salesperson records are processed:
   a. Calculate the total percent-of-quota.
   b. Print the output report total line (triple-spaced from the last detail line) as specified on the print chart. If you do the page-total option of this assignment (step 5), include two asterisks after the printed totals.

Programming Assignment 7-4: Aged Analysis Report

Background information:

One of Silicon Valley Manufacturing's subsidiaries follows standard accounts-receivable procedures for "aging" amounts due. The amount owed by each customer is broken down into categories identifying whether it is a current amount owed, past due by more than 30 days, or past due by more than 60 days. A report of amounts owed by customers identified by these categories is called an aged analysis report. One is required by the accounting manager.

Input file: Customer file (CUSTOMER.DAT)

Customer name record

Customer number	Customer name		Account balance	Current amount	Over-30 amount	Over-60 amount	

Output-report format:

```
EFFICIENT CHIPS MFG. CO                                              PAGE ZZ9
AGED ANALYSIS REPORT (7-4)                     RUN TIME HH:MM:SS  RUN DATE  MM/DD/YY

CUSTOMER                          ACCOUNT           CURRENT         OVER-30         OVER-60
 NUMBER      CUSTOMER NAME        BALANCE           AMOUNT          AMOUNT          AMOUNT

  99999   XXXXXXXXXXXXXXXXXXXXX  ZZZ,ZZZ.99CR    ZZZ,ZZZ.99CR    ZZZ,ZZZ.99CR    ZZZ,ZZZ.99CR
  99999   XXXXXXXXXXXXXXXXXXXXX  ZZZ,ZZZ.99CR    ZZZ,ZZZ.99CR    ZZZ,ZZZ.99CR    ZZZ,ZZZ.99CR

             PAGE TOTAL     Z,ZZZ,ZZZ.99CR*   Z,ZZZ,ZZZ.99CR*  Z,ZZZ,ZZZ.99CR*  Z,ZZZ,ZZZ.99CR*

             REPORT TOTAL ZZ,ZZZ,ZZZ.99CR**  ZZ,ZZZ,ZZZ.99CR**  ZZ,ZZZ,ZZZ.99CR**  ZZ,ZZZ,ZZZ.99CR**
```

Program operations:

1. Read each input customer record.

2. Print the four heading lines on the first page and on each following page of the report.
   a. Accumulate and print the page number on the first heading line as specified on the print chart.
   b. Print the run time and date on the second heading line as specified on the print chart.

3. For each input customer record, do the following:
    a. Print an output detail line as specified on the print chart.
    b. Accumulate the total account balance, current amount, over-30 amount, and over-60 amount.

4. Single-space each detail line (except double-space between the last heading line and the first detail line on each page, as shown on the print chart). Provide for a span of 53 lines per page—not counting the page-total line.

5. Print a page-total line at the bottom of each report page as shown on the print chart. The page-total line should contain a total of the account balances, current amounts, over-30 amounts, and over-60 amounts printed on that page.

6. After all input salesperson records are processed:
    a. Print the last page-total line.
    b. Print the report total line (double-spaced from the last detail line) as specified on the print chart.

Programming Assignment 7-5: Nurses' Shift Differential Summary

Background information:

The management of Brooklawn Hospital, in their continued union negotiations, require more information on shift differential pay.

Input file: Nurses file (NURSES.DAT)

Nurses record

Output-report format:

Program operations:

1. Process each input record.

2. Print the four heading lines on the first page and on each following page of the report.
    a. Print the run date on the first heading line as specified on the print chart.
    b. Accumulate and print the page number on the second heading line as specified on the print chart.

3. For each input record, do the following:
    a. Calculate the Shift-differential-pay as follows:

        If Shift-code = 1, use 0
        If Shift-code = 2, use .4 times Base-monthly-salary
        If Shift-code = 3, use .6 times Base-monthly-salary

    b. Calculate the Total-pay as Base-monthly-salary plus Shift-differential-pay.
    c. Print an output detail line that includes Base-monthly-salary, Shift-differential-pay, and Total-pay as specified on the print chart.
    d. Accumulate totals for the New-base-monthly-salary and the New-total-monthly-salary.
    e. Maintain a count of the number of records processed and the number of nurses receiving a shift differential.

4. Double-space each detail line as shown on the print chart. Provide for a span of 53 lines per page (not counting the total lines).

5. Print the two page total lines as shown on the print chart.

Programming Assignment 7-6: Vehicle Rental Application

Background information:

The program of Assignment 5-6 must be expanded to include the following:

1. A two-page heading line that includes the date and page number.

2. One or two column heading lines (as appropriate).

3. Detail lines as in Assignment 5-6.

4. Page and report totals giving counts of the number of vehicles rented and the number not rented.

5. Provisions for a span of 36 lines per page.

Programming Assignment 7-7: Computer Store Average Prices

Background information:

Complete Computers Corporation (Programming Assignments 2-8/3-8) configures personal computer systems based on an individual's specific needs. One of their data files includes information on the various computer products they must order to conduct business. This file includes one record for each product item, identifying vendors from which it can be ordered—as well as pertinent pricing information. For each item, the Smiths (owners of the company) have identified two prices to consider when ordering. First is a target price (one they can reasonably expect to get) and the other is a maximum price (the point beyond which they lose money). For further costing studies, they want a report that includes some pricing averages.

Input file: The CCC Inventory file (CCCINVEN.DAT)

CCC Inventory record

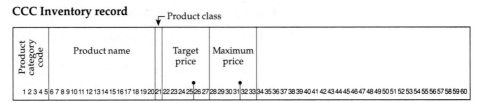

Output report-line format:

```
                    0                   1                   2                   3                   4                   5                   6                 7
        1 2 3 4 5 6 7 8 9 0 1 2 3 4 5 6 7 8 9 0 1 2 3 4 5 6 7 8 9 0 1 2 3 4 5 6 7 8 9 0 1 2 3 4 5 6 7 8 9 0 1 2 3 4 5 6 7 8 9 0 1 2 3 4 5 6 7 8 9 0 1 2 3 4
  1
  2
  3
  4   COMPLETE COMPUTERS CORP.                                    RUN DATE MM/DD/YY
  5   PRODUCT COMPONENT COST SUMMARY (7-7)                        PAGE ZZ9
  6
  7   PRODUCT                          PRODUCT           TARGET        MAXIMUM
  8   CODE            PRODUCT          CLASS             PRICE          PRICE
  9
 10   XXXXX       XXXXXXXXXXXXXXX        X             Z,ZZZ.99      Z,ZZZ.99
 11
 12   XXXXX       XXXXXXXXXXXXXXX        X             Z,ZZZ.99      Z,ZZZ.99
 13
 14
 15               AVERAGES:  CLASS A                   Z,ZZZ.99      Z,ZZZ.99
 16                          CLASS B                   Z,ZZZ.99      Z,ZZZ.99
 17
 18
```

Program operations:

1. Process each input inventory record.

2. Print the four heading lines on each page of the report.

3. For each input record, do the following:
    a. Print an output detail line as specified on the print chart.
    b. Determine whether or not the Product Class is A. If A, accumulate Class A totals for the Target Price and Maximum Price; if not A, accumulate for Class B totals for the Target Price and Maximum Price. (Note: This processing causes any record containing other than A or B for this field to be treated as if it were B, an acceptable action for this assignment.)
    c. Maintain a count of the number of Class A records and Class B records.

4. Double-space each detail line as shown on the print chart. Provide for a span of 44 lines per page (not counting the total lines).

5. After the last record is processed, calculate the averages for the prices (the A prices divided by the A count and the B prices divided by the B count).

6. Print the two report-total lines as shown on the print chart.

CONDITIONAL OPERATIONS

Note

In a sense, you can consider this chapter a "tools" chapter. It covers a wide variety of COBOL's conditional capabilities: far more than you will need to complete the assignments. Mastery of all this chapter's techniques and conditional forms is not essential now. It is more important that you become sufficiently familiar with them so that when tackling programs with complex logic, you will recognize the forms and remember where to find them in this chapter.

CHAPTER OUTLINE

CHAPTER

8

CHAPTER OBJECTIVES

In preceding chapters, you used a simple form of the IF statement to determine actions to take. This provided you with an insight to its basic capabilities. Actually, the IF is a powerful COBOL statement that takes many forms. From this chapter, you will learn about its many details:

- The IF general format.

- Four types of condition tests: relation, class, sign, and condition-name.

    Relation condition—compare one quantity to another.

    Class condition—determine if a field is numeric or alphabetic.

    Sign condition—determine if a quantity is negative, zero, or positive.

    Condition-name—substitute a name (providing better documentation) for an equal condition.

- The AND and OR operators, which allow you to combine two or more conditions into a single test.

- The NOT operator, which allows you to negate a condition (check for the opposite sense).

- Nested IF statements in which the conditionally executed statements under an IF include other IF statements.

- The EVALUATE statement that simplifies a test in which any one of several alternative actions is to be executed depending on the results of one or more tests.

Basics of the IF Statement

CONTINUE and NEXT SENTENCE

COBOL includes two statements that effectively "do nothing," but are used in IF statements under certain circumstances: CONTINUE and NEXT SENTENCE. The COBOL-85 Standard defines CONTINUE as an imperative statement that performs no operation. It can be used anywhere a conditional statement or an imperative statement is used. For instance, upon encountering the CONTINUE in the sequence

```
MOVE DETAIL-LINE TO REPORT-LINE
CONTINUE
WRITE REPORT-LINE
```

execution immediately progresses from the MOVE statement to the WRITE statement as if the CONTINUE were not there. Obviously, it serves no useful purpose in this example, but you will see how it is used in an IF.

> **COBOL-74**
>
> COBOL-74 does not include the CONTINUE statement.

Although NEXT SENTENCE is included in both the 1974 and 1985 Standards, its use is based on the COBOL-74 practice of ending statements of the PROCEDURE DIVISION with periods, thereby creating sentences. When used in a COBOL-74 environment within an IF, it causes execution to progress from the IF to the next sentence in the program. A later example illustrates its use.

Because of this book's style convention of including a period only at the end of the paragraph, the NEXT SENTENCE statement will not function as intended. However, you will study one situation in which it simplifies coding.

The IF General Format

As you know from previous examples, the IF statement provides you with the capability to code the selection (if-then-else) structure of structured programming theory. Figure 8-1 shows the format of the COBOL-85 IF as it is used in this book—plus the format of the COBOL-74 IF. Examples in earlier chapters used the IF both with and without the ELSE clause.

Basically, you can write the simple IF statement three ways: with both true and false actions, with true actions only, and with false actions only. These are illustrated in Figure 8-2. You are familiar with the first two forms: with both true and false actions (using the ELSE), and with true actions only. Figure 8-2(c), with false actions only, uses the CONTINUE.

> **COBOL-74**
>
> For COBOL-74, replace CONTINUE with NEXT SENTENCE, and utilize the period in place of END-IF to indicate the IF scope.

Examples of the IF shown in Figure 8-3 summarize all of the principles you already learned. Remember that one of the IF characteristics is its scope: the range of statements that are conditionally executed under the IF.

Since COBOL-85 includes scope terminators, you can explicitly indicate the scope of an IF by using the END-IF. You will have no problem inadvertently terminating the scope of an IF by following the recommended rules for periods in the

Figure 8-1
The IF statement format.

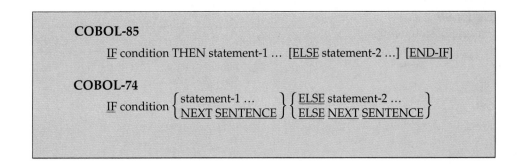

COBOL-85

IF condition THEN statement-1 … [ELSE statement-2 …] [END-IF]

COBOL-74

IF condition { statement-1 … / NEXT SENTENCE } { ELSE statement-2 … / ELSE NEXT SENTENCE }

PROCEDURE DIVISION: use only after the paragraph name and the last statement in the paragraph. If you insert a period following any conditional statement between the IF and END-IF, that period acts as a scope terminator, thereby ending the IF (see the remark to Example 4 of Figure 8-3). You will then have a dangling END-IF—or ELSE and END-IF—that will produce a compiler diagnostic.

In COBOL-74, the period defines the scope. A misplaced period can cause considerable trouble. For instance, in Figure 8-3's Example 2, both the ADD and the MOVE are executed conditionally. However, if you accidentally place a period following the ADD statement, that period terminates the IF. Then, only the ADD is executed conditionally; the MOVE is executed unconditionally. Even though indenting suggests that it is part of the conditional operation, the compiler ignores all such indenting and ends the IF with the first period it finds. Note that because this is *not* a syntax error, it is *not* detected by the compiler.

In Figure 8-1's general format, you can see that the optional word THEN can be used in the IF to be more consistent with the if-then-else terminology. Example 4 of Figure 8-3 also includes the THEN. Its inclusion does not affect the execution of the IF statement in any way. Note that COBOL-74 does not include this option.

Figure 8-2   The three simple IF configurations.

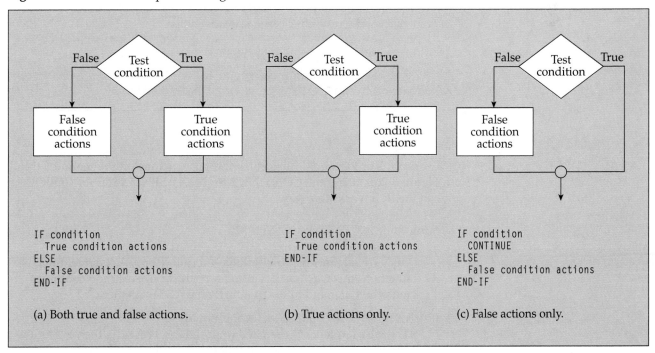

Figure 8-3
Sample IF statements.

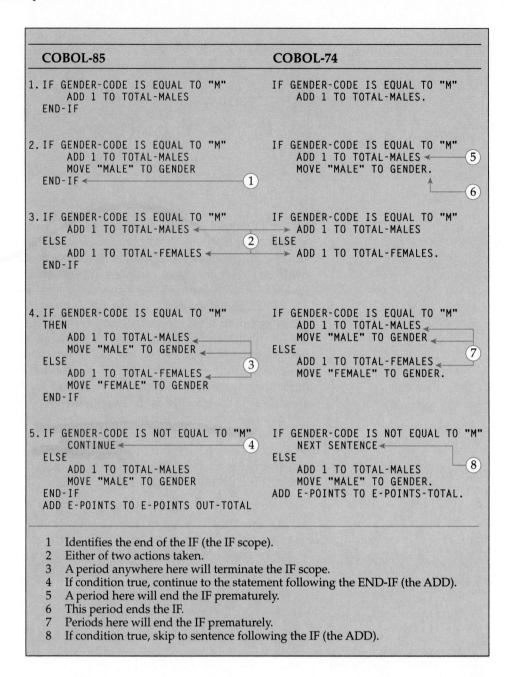

```
COBOL-85                                    COBOL-74

1. IF GENDER-CODE IS EQUAL TO "M"           IF GENDER-CODE IS EQUAL TO "M"
        ADD 1 TO TOTAL-MALES                    ADD 1 TO TOTAL-MALES.
   END-IF


2. IF GENDER-CODE IS EQUAL TO "M"           IF GENDER-CODE IS EQUAL TO "M"
        ADD 1 TO TOTAL-MALES                    ADD 1 TO TOTAL-MALES ←──  (5)
        MOVE "MALE" TO GENDER                   MOVE "MALE" TO GENDER.
   END-IF ←──────────────────  (1)
                                                                     ──  (6)

3. IF GENDER-CODE IS EQUAL TO "M"           IF GENDER-CODE IS EQUAL TO "M"
        ADD 1 TO TOTAL-MALES ←──                → ADD 1 TO TOTAL-MALES
   ELSE                        (2)          ELSE
        ADD 1 TO TOTAL-FEMALES ←──          →  ADD 1 TO TOTAL-FEMALES.
   END-IF


4. IF GENDER-CODE IS EQUAL TO "M"           IF GENDER-CODE IS EQUAL TO "M"
   THEN                                         ADD 1 TO TOTAL-MALES
        ADD 1 TO TOTAL-MALES                    MOVE "MALE" TO GENDER
        MOVE "MALE" TO GENDER               ELSE
   ELSE                          (3)            ADD 1 TO TOTAL-FEMALES      (7)
        ADD 1 TO TOTAL-FEMALES                  MOVE "FEMALE" TO GENDER.
        MOVE "FEMALE" TO GENDER
   END-IF

5. IF GENDER-CODE IS NOT EQUAL TO "M"       IF GENDER-CODE IS NOT EQUAL TO "M"
        CONTINUE ←──              (4)            NEXT SENTENCE ←──
   ELSE                                      ELSE
        ADD 1 TO TOTAL-MALES                     ADD 1 TO TOTAL-MALES         (8)
        MOVE "MALE" TO GENDER                    MOVE "MALE" TO GENDER.
   END-IF                                    ADD E-POINTS TO E-POINTS-TOTAL.
   ADD E-POINTS TO E-POINTS OUT-TOTAL
```

1   Identifies the end of the IF (the IF scope).
2   Either of two actions taken.
3   A period anywhere here will terminate the IF scope.
4   If condition true, continue to the statement following the END-IF (the ADD).
5   A period here will end the IF prematurely.
6   This period ends the IF.
7   Periods here will end the IF prematurely.
8   If condition true, skip to sentence following the IF (the ADD).

Example 5 in Figure 8-3 illustrates the false-actions-only version of the IF from Figure 8-2(c), using the CONTINUE (or NEXT SENTENCE for COBOL-74) option of the IF. It works this way:

If the value in GENDER-CODE is M:
> The statement following the IF is executed. This statement, CONTINUE, means, "do nothing—continue on." A statement that functions this way is called a *null statement*. So, execution continues with the statement following the IF: the ADD statement.

Else (if the value in GENDER-CODE is not M):
> The false sequence is executed (the ADD and MOVE), then execution continues with the statement following the IF: the ADD statement.

If you compare this example to Examples 2 and 5 in Figure 8-3, you will see that their overall actions are identical. Notice that the action to be taken is switched from a true action in Example 2 to a false action in Example 5, simply by changing the sense of the test from IS EQUAL TO to IS NOT EQUAL TO. Generally, any IF requiring a false action can be changed to a true action by changing the sense of the condition. So, you might question the value of the false action form and the use of CONTINUE. However, it has documentation value in some instances.

About Indenting

When coding simple IF statements, you should use the form of the examples: indent the action statement verbs either two or four spaces to the right. Four spaces is often used, but if you have many levels of indention, you may choose only two spaces. Also, place the word ELSE on a line by itself; do not code the word ELSE on the same line as the preceding or following statements. (The exception is when using a nested IF, described later in this chapter.) You will find that program modifications often require action statements to be added or deleted. By coding the word ELSE on a line by itself, such changes are made with minimum IF statement disruption and error.

Recognize that IF statement indention is provided only for program readability and *does not affect execution of the statement*. The IF statement selection control is determined solely by the word ELSE and the scope terminator.

Types of Conditions

All of the conditions used so far involved comparing one entity to another—looking at the *relation* between two entities. For example, in PATDFCT (Figure 3-1, page 70), the relation between actual contribution and target contribution determined whether or not a computation was performed. Actually, this is one of four types of conditions—relation, class, sign, and condition-name—that are expressed within an IF statement. The relation is discussed in the next section; the other three are described later.

IF Statement—The Relation Condition

Basics of the Relation Condition

The **relation condition** is the most frequently used type. All of the IF statements encountered so far use relation conditions. Figure 8-4 shows the relation condition format. As you can see, the element preceding the operator is called the **subject** of the relation and the element following the operator is called the **object**. Usually, the subject is specified as an identifier—that is, a field name—and the object is either an identifier or a literal.

The subject can be tested to determine if it is greater than, less than, equal to, not greater than, not less than, or not equal to the object. COBOL-85 also allows the combination operators: greater than or equal to, and less than or equal to. In all cases, the standard mathematical symbols >, <, and = (reserved words in COBOL) can be used to specify the operator. Because they are concise—and commonly encountered in programming—the mathematical symbols are used in most of this text's programs.

The data class of the relation condition's object should be consistent with the subject. That is, if the subject is numeric, the object should be numeric. If the subject is alphanumeric, the object should be alphanumeric. Although you can use certain other combinations, you must be aware of the specific comparison processing that will occur. Figure 8-5 shows a table of comparison processing.

Numeric Comparisons

When the subject and object are both defined as numeric data-items, comparison of the two values is made according to their algebraic values. The relative length of the fields does not matter. For example, a three-digit integer field containing 687 is equal to a seven-digit integer field with a value of 0000687. Similarly, 0003.25 is

Figure 8-4 Relation condition format.

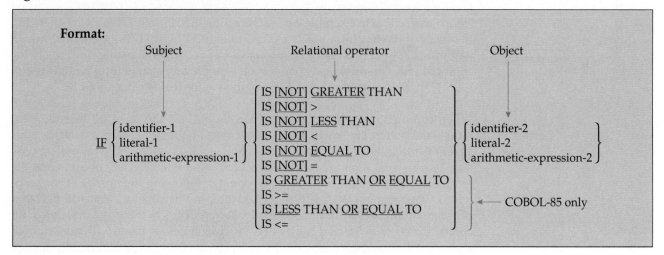

Figure 8-5 Relation condition table.

Subject field	Object Field	
	Numeric data-item or Numeric literal	**Alphanumeric data-item or Nonnumeric literal or Group item**
Numeric data-item or Numeric literal	**Numeric** (algebraic) comparison	**Alphanumeric** (character-by-character) comparison
Alphanumeric data-item or Non-numeric literal or Group item	**Alphanumeric** (character-by-character) comparison	**Alphanumeric** (character-by-character) comparison

equal to 03.2500; the location of the assumed decimal point does not affect the comparison values.

Also, arithmetic signs affect the comparison. Positive values are greater than negative values. For example, +07 is greater than –98.

Alphanumeric Comparisons

The result of alphanumeric comparisons depends upon the collating sequence of the computer used. **Collating sequence** refers to the order of character values and is determined by the binary value used to code each character. As expected, an alphanumeric value of 3 is less than 7. Similarly, the letter B is less than R in accordance with normal alphabetic sequencing. But how does a dollar sign ($) compare to the letter E? Or, which is greater in value—a letter or a digit? Figure 8-6 summarizes the collating sequences of the two commonly used data representation formats: ASCII and EBCDIC. Observe that in EBCDIC, digits are higher than letters; in ASCII, the converse is true.

With alphanumeric fields, comparison begins at the leftmost character position and proceeds to the right. Figure 8-7 provides an example of an alphanumeric comparison; note from the PICs that these fields are equal in length.

When alphanumeric subject and object fields are of different lengths, the shorter field is internally extended on the right with spaces until it is the same length as the longer field. Then the comparison takes place as if the fields were equal in length.

Figure 8-6
ASCII and EBCDIC
collating sequences.

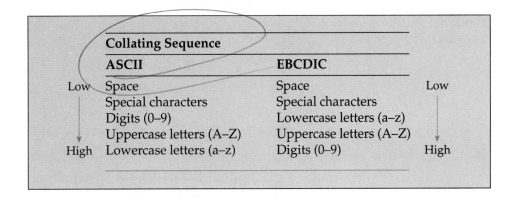

Collating Sequence		
ASCII	**EBCDIC**	
Low Space	Space	Low
Special characters	Special characters	
Digits (0–9)	Lowercase letters (a–z)	
Uppercase letters (A–Z)	Uppercase letters (A–Z)	
High Lowercase letters (a–z)	Digits (0–9)	High

Figure 8-7
Alphanumeric relation
condition tests: equal-length
fields.

```
05   TRANSACTION-NAME             PIC X(10).
05   MASTER-NAME                  PIC X(10).

IF   TRANSACTION-NAME IS LESS THAN MASTER-NAME
     PERFORM 999-PROCESS-LOW-TRANSACTION
END-IF
MOVE ...
```

Value in TRANSACTION-NAME field	Value in MASTER-NAME field	Condition test result	Next statement executed
JONES	JONES	False	MOVE
JONES	SMITH	True	PERFORM
SMITH	SMITHSON	True	PERFORM
THORPE	THORP	False	MOVE

The NOT Operator

The PATLIST2 program (see Figure 7-2, page 202) uses the following IF test to determine when a printed page is full, requiring positioning to a new page:

```
IF RC-LINES-USED NOT LESS THAN RC-LINES-PER-PAGE
```

Referring to Figure 8-4's IF format, you can see that the NOT can be used with any of the single-comparison operators. When used, the NOT and the next keyword are considered to be a single operator. For instance, LESS (the only required word of the operator) is one relational operator; NOT LESS is treated by COBOL as a different operator.

The IF Statement—Other Condition Types

Class Condition

The **class condition** tests whether a field contains only numeric digits or only alphabetic characters. As shown in Figure 8-8's class condition format, a field can be tested to determine if its contents are

Numeric	Not numeric
Alphabetic (regardless of case)	Not alphabetic (regardless of case)
Uppercase alphabetic	Not uppercase alphabetic
Lowercase alphabetic	Not lowercase alphabetic

Figure 8-8
Class condition format.

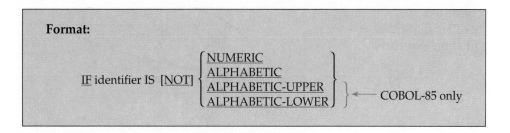

Format:

IF identifier IS [<u>NOT</u>] { NUMERIC / ALPHABETIC / ALPHABETIC-UPPER / ALPHABETIC-LOWER } ← COBOL-85 only

For a value to be considered NUMERIC, the field must contain only digits from 0 (zero) through 9 and an optional sign. For the three alphabetic categories, the field may contain only the following:

ALPHABETIC	A through Z, a through z, and space
ALPHABETIC-UPPER	A through Z and space
ALPHABETIC-LOWER	a through z and space

NUMERIC class tests can be made on alphanumeric (PIC X) and numeric (PIC 9) fields; this test is *not* limited to fields defined with the 9 PICTURE symbol. Figure 8-9 shows NUMERIC test examples. ALPHABETIC class tests can be made on alphanumeric, alphabetic, and group fields. Figure 8-10 provides examples of the ALPHABETIC test.

COBOL-74

COBOL-74 does not include ALPHABETIC-UPPER and ALPHABETIC-LOWER.

Programmer-Defined Class Condition

COBOL-85 permits the specification of a programmer-defined class that can be tested with a class-condition IF statement. The class condition is defined in the SPECIAL-NAMES paragraph of the CONFIGURATION SECTION of the

Figure 8-9
NUMERIC class test examples.

```
05  PRICE                        PIC 9(3)V99.

IF PRICE IS NUMERIC
    PERFORM 999-VALIDATE-PRICE
ELSE
    PERFORM 999-IDENTIFY-PRICE-ERROR.
END-IF
```

Value in PRICE field	Class	Condition test result	Statement executed
02999	Numeric	True	999-VALIDATE-PRICE
02999	Alphanumeric	True	999-VALIDATE-PRICE
2999	Numeric	False	999-IDENTIFY-PRICE-ERROR
2999	Alphanumeric	False	999-IDENTIFY-PRICE-ERROR

Note: ▲ indicates assumed decimal-point location.

Figure 8-10
ALPHABETIC class test examples.

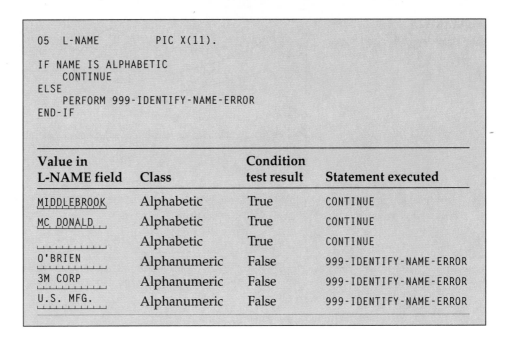

```
05  L-NAME          PIC X(11).

IF NAME IS ALPHABETIC
    CONTINUE
ELSE
    PERFORM 999-IDENTIFY-NAME-ERROR
END-IF
```

Value in L-NAME field	Class	Condition test result	Statement executed
MIDDLEBROOK	Alphabetic	True	CONTINUE
MC DONALD	Alphabetic	True	CONTINUE
	Alphabetic	True	CONTINUE
O'BRIEN	Alphanumeric	False	999-IDENTIFY-NAME-ERROR
3M CORP	Alphanumeric	False	999-IDENTIFY-NAME-ERROR
U.S. MFG.	Alphanumeric	False	999-IDENTIFY-NAME-ERROR

ENVIRONMENT DIVISION and is tested by an IF statement in the PROCEDURE DIVISION. Figure 8-11's examples illustrate the basic feature of the CLASS clause. Its first use in the SPECIAL-NAMES paragraph designates the letters A, E, I, O, and U as belonging to the class identified as VOWEL. Because the word VOWEL signifies the designated five letters, it is analogous to—for example—the COBOL predefined word ALPHABETIC-UPPER, which signifies all the uppercase letters. The second example, SPECIAL-LETTER, illustrates how to designate the members of a class when they are consecutive characters in the collating sequence. Notice that a period does not follow the first CLASS definition. Because the CLASS entry is a clause, a period belongs *only* after the last CLASS clause.

The PROCEDURE DIVISION segment in Figure 8-11 shows that you use the programmer-defined class in exactly the same way you use the standard classes. So, in the second IF—whenever the field LETTER-FIELD contains only the characters A, E, I, O, or U—the condition is true and the 400 module is performed.

Sign Condition

The **sign condition** tests whether the value of a numeric field is POSITIVE, NEGATIVE, or ZERO. Because it has narrower applicability, the sign test is used much less frequently than relation and class tests.

Figure 8-11
The CLASS condition clause.

```
ENVIRONMENT DIVISION.
CONFIGURATION SECTION.
SPECIAL-NAMES.                                        No period here
    CLASS VOWEL IS "AEIOU"
    CLASS SPECIAL-LETTER IS "W" THRU "Z".
    ⋮
PROCEDURE DIVISION.                                   Period after last
    ⋮                                                 CLASS clause
    IF LETTER-FIELD IS ALPHABETIC-UPPER
        PERFORM 400-PROCESS-WORD
    END-IF
    IF LETTER-FIELD IS VOWEL
        PERFORM 400-PROCESS-WORD
    END-IF
```

Figure 8-12
Sign condition format
and examples.

Format:

$$\text{IF} \left\{ \begin{array}{l} \text{identifier} \\ \text{arithmetic-expression} \end{array} \right\} \text{IS [\underline{NOT}]} \left\{ \begin{array}{l} \underline{\text{POSITIVE}} \\ \underline{\text{NEGATIVE}} \\ \underline{\text{ZERO}} \end{array} \right\}$$

Examples:

```
05  BANK-BALANCE          PIC S9(8)V99.

IF BANK-BALANCE IS POSITIVE
    PERFORM 999-PROCESS-CHECK
END-IF

IF BANK-BALANCE IS NEGATIVE
    PERFORM 999-PREPARE-OVERDRAFT-NOTICE
END-IF

IF BANK-BALANCE IS ZERO
    PERFORM 999-TEST-CLOSED-ACCOUNT
END-IF

IF BANK-BALANCE - MINIMUM-BALANCE IS NEGATIVE
    PERFORM 999-ASSESS-SERVICE-CHARGE
END-IF
```

Figure 8-12 shows the sign condition format and examples. When the value tested is zero, it is considered to be ZERO, a unique value that is neither positive nor negative.

Observe in Figure 8-12's last example that it is sometimes appropriate and convenient to use an arithmetic expression as the subject of a sign condition.

Condition-Names

Condition-Name Condition

A **condition-name condition** is a special way of writing a relation condition in order to improve its readability. For instance, suppose you are working on a program in which the field COLOR-CODE can have either of two values: 1 or 2. If code 1 means the color white and code 2 means blue, then you might have a statement such as the following in a program:

```
IF COLOR-CODE = "1"
    PERFORM 400-PROCESS-SPECIAL
ELSE
    PERFORM 450-PROCESS-NORMAL
END-IF
```

If you are like most people, you would have trouble remembering whether 1 is the code for white or for blue—the statement is not very self-documenting. However, if written as follows, it tells you the color:

```
IF WHITE
    PERFORM 400-PROCESS-SPECIAL
ELSE
    PERFORM 450-PROCESS-NORMAL
END-IF
```

Figure 8-13
88-level item example.

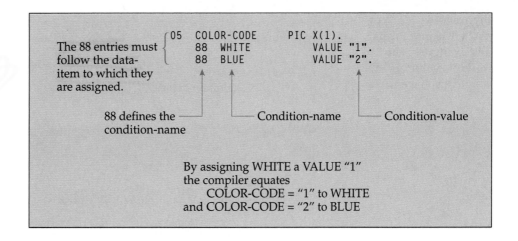

The 88 entries must follow the data-item to which they are assigned.

```
05  COLOR-CODE      PIC X(1).
    88  WHITE           VALUE "1".
    88  BLUE            VALUE "2".
```

88 defines the condition-name

Condition-name

Condition-value

By assigning WHITE a VALUE "1" the compiler equates
COLOR-CODE = "1" to WHITE
and COLOR-CODE = "2" to BLUE

The word WHITE is called a condition-name condition and must be defined as a special entry in the DATA DIVISION: an 88-level entry. Figure 8-13 shows an example of an 88-level item. Each condition-name you use in an IF statement must be defined as an 88-level entry. The 88-level item is coded subordinate to the data-item description entry for the field to which it corresponds.

In the example, COLOR-CODE is a one-character field that will contain a code (1 or 2) indicating whether the color is white or blue. The two 88-level items following this field definition show that the condition-name WHITE is assigned to a value of 1 and the condition-name BLUE is assigned to a value of 2 in the COLOR-CODE field. That is, when the field COLOR-CODE contains 1, the condition WHITE is true; otherwise, it is false. When COLOR-CODE contains 2, the condition BLUE is true; otherwise, it is false.

As Figure 8-14's condition-name condition format and examples show, 88-level entries are not limited to the simple form of the color-code example. That is, the VALUE clause of an 88-level item may contain multiple values or a range of values. The reserved word THRU is used to define a range of values. For instance, if MONTH-ABBREV contains any one of the four values APR, JUN, SEP, or NOV, then the condition 30-DAY-MONTH is true. Similarly, if MONTH-NBR contains 10, 11, or 12, then the condition QUARTER-4 is true.

The condition-name can be preceded by the word NOT, thereby "reversing" the sense of the test. For instance, if you need to take some action if TEST-PERIOD contains one of the months 1, 2, or 3 (Figure 8-14), you would code:

```
IF QUARTER-1
    PERFORM 999-QUARTER-1-ROUTINE
```

If you need to take an action when TEST-PERIOD contains other than one of the months 1, 2, or 3, you would code:

```
IF NOT QUARTER-1
    PERFORM 999-OTHER-QUARTER-ROUTINE
```

About the VALUE Clause

Note that the COBOL language is somewhat ambiguous regarding the meaning of the VALUE clause; it is used in two different ways:

- In 01- through 49-level WORKING-STORAGE fields to establish initial values

- In 88-level items to associate values with a condition-name

Figure 8-14
VALUE clause format and examples with multiple value and range of value entries.

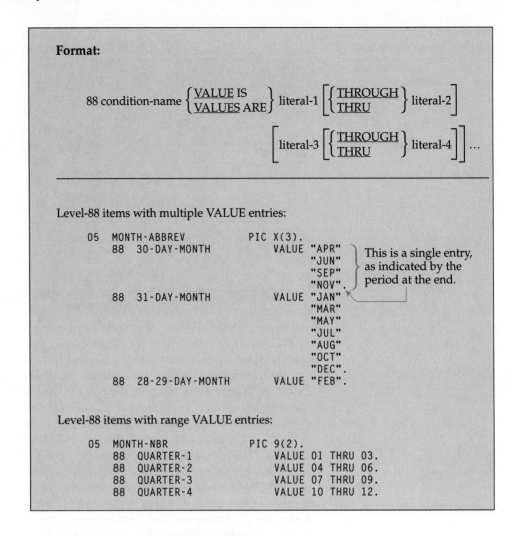

Format:

$$88 \text{ condition-name } \left\{ \begin{array}{l} \underline{\text{VALUE}} \text{ IS} \\ \underline{\text{VALUES}} \text{ ARE} \end{array} \right\} \text{literal-1} \left[\left\{ \begin{array}{l} \underline{\text{THROUGH}} \\ \underline{\text{THRU}} \end{array} \right\} \text{literal-2} \right]$$

$$\left[\text{literal-3} \left[\left\{ \begin{array}{l} \underline{\text{THROUGH}} \\ \underline{\text{THRU}} \end{array} \right\} \text{literal-4} \right] \right] \dots$$

Level-88 items with multiple VALUE entries:

```
05  MONTH-ABBREV          PIC X(3).
    88  30-DAY-MONTH          VALUE "APR"
                                    "JUN"      This is a single entry,
                                    "SEP"      as indicated by the
                                    "NOV".     period at the end.
    88  31-DAY-MONTH          VALUE "JAN"
                                    "MAR"
                                    "MAY"
                                    "JUL"
                                    "AUG"
                                    "OCT"
                                    "DEC".
    88  28-29-DAY-MONTH       VALUE "FEB".
```

Level-88 items with range VALUE entries:

```
05  MONTH-NBR             PIC 9(2).
    88  QUARTER-1             VALUE 01 THRU 03.
    88  QUARTER-2             VALUE 04 THRU 06.
    88  QUARTER-3             VALUE 07 THRU 09.
    88  QUARTER-4             VALUE 10 THRU 12.
```

Recognize that these two uses for VALUE clauses are quite different. For 01- through 49-level items, the VALUE clause causes the field to be initialized with the corresponding value; this could be termed an **initializing VALUE clause**. The **condition-name VALUE clause** used with an 88-level item does *not* initialize, however. It instead associates a condition-name with a value.

Recall that you learned special limitations for using the initializing VALUE clauses; in contrast, a condition-name VALUE clause:

- Can be specified in either the FILE SECTION or the WORKING-STORAGE SECTION (initializing VALUE clauses cannot be specified in the FILE SECTION)

- Can be associated with a data-item description that contains a REDEFINES clause (described in Chapter 11)

- Can be associated with a data-item description that contains an OCCURS clause (the OCCURS clause is introduced in Chapter 11)

- Can contain multiple values or a range of values

Using the SET Command with Condition-Names

The COBOL-85 Standard includes an extension of previous versions that is convenient to use for conditions that can be either true or false. For instance, consider our conventional sequential file-processing operations illustrated in Figure 8-15(a),

Figure 8-15 The SET statement.

```
                                              10  S1-END-OF-FILE-SWITCH  PIC X.
                                                  88  S1-END-OF-FILE       VALUE "Y"
10   PS-END-OF-FILE-SWITCH        PIC X.           88  S1-NOT-END-OF-FILE  VALUE "N"
  :                                             :
  :                                             :
MOVE "N" TO PS-END-OF-FILE-SWITCH            SET S1-NOT-END-OF-FILE TO TRUE
  :                                             :
  :                                             :
PERFORM UNTIL PS-END-OF-FILE = "Y"           PERFORM UNTIL S1-END-OF-FILE
  READ INPUT-FILE                              READ INPUT-FILE
    AT END                                       AT END
      MOVE "Y" TO PS-END-OF-FILE-SWITCH            SET S1-END-OF-FILE TO TRUE
    NOT AT END                                   NOT AT END
```

(a) Conventional EOF processing.   (b) Using condition-names and the SET.

in which the switch PS-END-OF-FILE is initialized to N (for No), tested for a value of Y (for Yes), and given a value of Y upon detection of the end-of-file.

The following commentary describes the condition-name principles introduced in Figure 8-15(b).

1. The switch is defined as one position in length because the actual values to be used are immaterial. All reference is through the condition-names.
2. The switch is assigned condition-names S1-END-OF-FILE and S1-NOT-END-OF-FILE, representing the end-of-file and not-end-of-file conditions.
3. The SET statement

   ```
   SET S1-NOT-END-OF-FILE TO TRUE
   ```

   performs the same operation as the corresponding statement

   ```
   MOVE "N" TO PS-END-OF-FILE-SWITCH
   ```

4. Some programs require the use of numerous switches and corresponding condition-names. In order to clearly relate the condition-name to its corresponding switch, the naming convention illustrated in Figure 8-15(b) is used throughout this book. That is, a prefix consisting of the letter S and one (or two) digits is affixed to each switch entry. That same prefix is used on each condition-name subordinate to the switch.

Combined Conditions

Suppose you are working in a college data-processing department and the program you are preparing requires that students be identified for the dean's list. The requirement is that a student must be currently enrolled in more than 11 units and have a grade-point average greater than 3.5. In pseudocode form, you write this:

```
IF  current-units greater than 11
AND grade-point-average (GPA) greater than 3.5
    place student on the dean's list
```

You might also have the task of sending special notices to students who are currently enrolled in less than 9 units or who have not accumulated more than 30 total units. This pseudocode takes the form:

```
IF current-units less than 9
OR cumulative-units not greater than 30
    send special notice
```

In COBOL, you can build multiple conditions such as these, using the **logical operators** AND or OR. In fact, the COBOL form is almost identical to the pseudocode form. Multiple conditions interrelated by logical operators are called **combined conditions** and have the format shown in Figure 8-16.

The AND Logical Operator

When the AND logical operator is used, both conditions must be true for the combined condition to be considered true. If either one or both of the conditions are false, the combined condition is considered false. A graphical way of representing an AND complex condition is called a **boolean diagram** and is illustrated in Figure 8-17. You can think of this figure as an electric wire with two on-off switches: C (representing current-units) and G (representing GPA). Electricity flows from point 1 to point 2 only if both switches are on (true); if either is off (false), electricity does not flow. This corresponds to the AND operator: The action is carried out only if both conditions are true.

The AND operator is used in the following statement to satisfy the need for identifying those students taking more than 11 units and having a grade-point average greater than 3.5:

```
IF  CURRENT-UNITS IS GREATER THAN 11.0
AND GPA IS GREATER THAN 3.5
    PERFORM 300-PLACE-ON-DEANS-LIST
END-IF
```

Here, if a student is both taking more than 11 units *and* has a GPA greater than 3.5, the statement PERFORM 300-PLACE-ON-DEANS-LIST is executed. If either one or both of the two conditions are false, the statement is skipped.

Use of the AND operator is not limited to simply two conditions, as illustrated by this example. For instance, Figure 8-18 is an example in which five conditions are combined. If all five are true, the true-action statement PERFORM 400-PROCESS-DATE is executed. If any one or more are false, the false-action statement PERFORM 999-IDENTIFY-DATE-ERROR is executed. Observe that

Figure 8-16
The combined IF statement format.

Format:

$$\text{condition-1} \left\{ \left\{ \frac{\text{AND}}{\text{OR}} \right\} \text{condition-2} \right\}$$

Figure 8-17
Boolean diagram for the AND condition.

Electricity flows from point 1 to point 2 only if both C and R are **on**. Similarly, the corresponding COBOL action is taken only if both the cumulative-units and GPA requirements are **true**.

Figure 8-18
A combined IF statement with multiple AND operators.

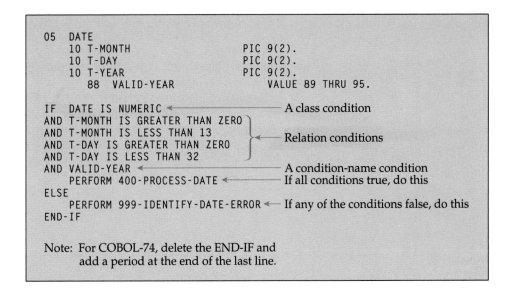

```
05  DATE
    10  T-MONTH               PIC 9(2).
    10  T-DAY                 PIC 9(2).
    10  T-YEAR                PIC 9(2).
        88  VALID-YEAR              VALUE 89 THRU 95.

IF  DATE IS NUMERIC ◄─────────────────── A class condition
AND T-MONTH IS GREATER THAN ZERO ⎫
AND T-MONTH IS LESS THAN 13      ⎪
AND T-DAY IS GREATER THAN ZERO   ⎬◄── Relation conditions
AND T-DAY IS LESS THAN 32        ⎪
AND VALID-YEAR ◄───────────────── A condition-name condition
    PERFORM 400-PROCESS-DATE ◄─────────── If all conditions true, do this
ELSE
    PERFORM 999-IDENTIFY-DATE-ERROR ◄── If any of the conditions false, do this
END-IF
```

Note: For COBOL-74, delete the END-IF and
add a period at the end of the last line.

different condition types can be combined; this example includes class, relation, and condition-name conditions.

The OR Logical Operator

The other combined condition that you encountered at the beginning of this section uses the logical OR and is represented by the following pseudocode:

```
IF current-units less than 9
OR cumulative-units not greater than 30
    send special notice
```

The following is the COBOL equivalent of this pseudocode:

```
IF  CURRENT-UNITS IS LESS THAN 11.0
OR  CUM-UNITS IS NOT GREATER THAN 30.0
    PERFORM 370-SEND-SPECIAL-NOTICE
END-IF
```

Although the AND requires all conditions to be true, the OR is much less restrictive. If any one or more of the conditions are true, the combined condition is considered to be true. Only if all conditions are false, is the combined condition considered to be false. This is illustrated by the boolean diagram in Figure 8-19.

As with the AND operator, two or more conditions can be linked with an OR operator.

Complex Conditions

When the operators AND and OR are both used within the same IF statement, the resulting expression is referred to as a **complex condition**. For example, assume that you are working on an application and you are informed that any record for which the complex condition on the next page is true must be deleted.

Figure 8-19
Boolean diagram for the OR condition.

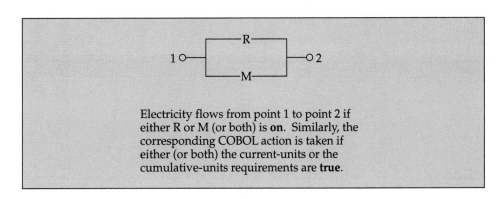

Electricity flows from point 1 to point 2 if
either R or M (or both) is **on**. Similarly, the
corresponding COBOL action is taken if
either (or both) the current-units or the
cumulative-units requirements are **true**.

If record-code is equal to 23, *or* update-code is equal to D, *and* balance is zero

This is confusing. In which order must you apply the conditions? Representing this in boolean diagram form, is it interpreted as illustrated in Figure 8-20(a), or as represented in (b)?

If the rules of logic are applied to ordinary English, logic rules dictate that in a complex form such as this, the *and* association is made first, then the *or* association is made. So, this form is interpreted as in Figure 8-20(a).

Figure 8-21 shows the equivalent COBOL statement. Although interpreting this is confusing to many people, the compiler will perform the conditional evaluation as illustrated in the sample.

Figure 8-20
Dual interpretation of a combined AND and OR.

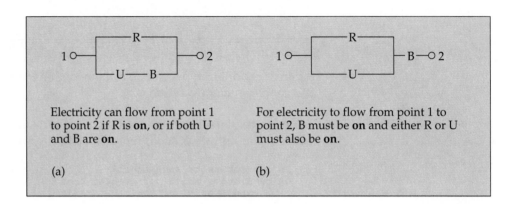

Electricity can flow from point 1 to point 2 if R is **on**, or if both U and B are **on**.

(a)

For electricity to flow from point 1 to point 2, B must be **on** and either R or U must also be **on**.

(b)

Figure 8-21   A complex condition IF statement example and its evaluation sequence.

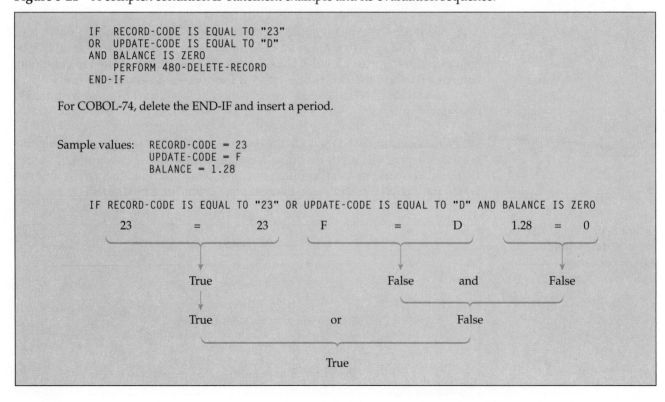

If this is not the way in which you want the condition evaluated, then by using parentheses, you must explicitly tell COBOL the order in which you want the AND and OR operators applied. So, to achieve the form of the representation in Figure 8-20(b), you would use parentheses as shown in Figure 8-22. Evaluation of the condition is illustrated by the same sample values used in Figure 8-21. Notice that the condition evaluates to true in Figure 8-21 but—using the exact same data values—it evaluates to false in Figure 8-22.

Overall, complex conditions are confusing when you write them and also when you later review or modify them. When writing complex conditions, *always* use parentheses to explicitly specify the evaluation sequence and to make the condition more understandable.

Other IF Capabilities

Negated Conditions

A **negated condition** is created merely by inserting the operator NOT immediately before the condition. The operator NOT reverses the truth value of the condition to which it is applied. For instance, suppose that the college application (used previously to illustrate the AND) requires that you perform an action for those students not on the dean's list—those with current-units not greater than 11 and GPA not greater than 3.5. For this, you could use the form shown in Example C in Figure 8-23.

When the operator NOT is coded to form a negated condition, the resulting expression is considered a complex condition. In a condition consisting of all three operators—NOT, AND, and OR—the NOT is evaluated first (from left to right), unless overridden by parentheses. Note: Do not confuse a negated condition

Figure 8-22   Changing the evaluation sequence with parentheses.

```
        IF  (RECORD-CODE IS EQUAL TO "23"
            OR  UPDATE-CODE IS EQUAL TO "D")
        AND BALANCE IS ZERO
            PERFORM 480-DELETE-RECORD
        END-IF
```

For COBOL-74, delete the END-IF and insert a period.

Sample values: RECORD-CODE = 23
                  UPDATE-CODE = F
                  BALANCE = 1.28

IF (RECORD-CODE IS EQUAL TO "23" OR UPDATE-CODE IS EQUAL TO "D") AND BALANCE IS ZERO

| 23 | = | 23 | F | = | D | 1.28 | = | 0 |

True   or   False   False

True   and   False

False

Figure 8-23 Negated condition examples.

```
      A. Negated relation condition

          IF NOT COLOR-CODE = "1"
              MOVE "BLUE" TO LI-COLOR-CODE
          END-IF


      B. Negated condition-name condition

          IF NOT WHITE
              MOVE "BLUE" TO LI-COLOR-CODE
          END-IF


      C. Negated combined IF condition
                                                        This entire expression
                                                        is evaluated, then
          IF NOT (CURRENT-UNITS IS GREATER THAN 11.0)   the result is negated
                  AND GPA IS GREATER THAN 3.5)          (reversed).
              PERFORM 500-PROCESS-AS-STANDARD
          END-IF


      D. An alternative to the negated combined IF condition

          COBOL-85                              COBOL-74


          IF CURRENT-UNITS IS GREATER THAN 11.0   IF CURRENT-UNITS IS GREATER THAN 11.0
          AND GPA IS GREATER THAN 3.5             AND GPA IS GREATER THAN 3.5
              CONTINUE                                NEXT SENTENCE
          ELSE                                    ELSE
              PERFORM 500-PROCESS-AS-STANDARD         PERFORM 500-PROCESS-AS-STANDARD.
          END-IF
```

NOT—which *precedes the condition*—with the word NOT used within the condition, as in NOT EQUAL TO. These are two distinct entities.

As is evident by Example C in Figure 8-23, negated conditions are sometimes difficult to understand. Often, an alternative form produces the same results, yet is easier to understand. Example D in Figure 8-23 is an equivalent alternative to Example C.

Implied Subjects and Relation Operators

It is possible to compare one subject with two or more objects and not repeat the subject. For instance, Figure 8-24's two IF statements produce exactly the same result. In the second, MONTH is the **implied subject** for the second and third comparisons.

Similarly, **implied relation operators** are also permitted, as illustrated in Figure 8-25. Notice that the relation operator IS LESS THAN is not coded preceding CREDIT-LIMIT, but implied. Implied subjects and relation operators apply only to relation conditions.

It is suggested that you do not use implied subjects and relation operators because they can cause confusion. Instead, you should explicitly code both the subjects and the operators. However, if you decide to use them, be careful; they tend to be misleading and difficult to understand.

The Nested IF

Frequently, processing requirements necessitate making a further test within a conditional sequence of a test. For instance, assume that in a voter's survey, one of the tasks is to count the number of persons falling in each of the following categories:

Figure 8-24
Implied subject example.

The combined IF statement relation condition...

```
IF  MONTH IS GREATER THAN ZERO
AND MONTH IS LESS THAN "13"
AND MONTH IS NOT EQUAL TO "02"
    PERFORM 450-STANDARD-DAY-CHECK
END-IF
```

...may be written with implied subjects as follows:

```
IF  MONTH IS GREATER THAN ZERO
AND LESS THAN "13"
AND NOT EQUAL TO "02"
    PERFORM 450-STANDARD-DAY-CHECK
END-IF
```

For COBOL-74, delete the END-IF and insert a period.

Figure 8-25
Implied subject and
relation operator example.

The combined IF statement relation condition...

```
IF  BALANCE IS LESS THAN 10000.00
AND BALANCE IS LESS THAN CREDIT-LIMIT
    PERFORM 300-POST-PAYMENT
END-IF
```

...may be written with implied subject and relation operator as follows:

```
IF BALANCE IS LESS THAN 1000.00
                AND CREDIT-LIMIT
    PERFORM 300-POST-PAYMENT
END-IF
```

For COBOL-74, delete the END-IF and insert a period.

Registered voters who voted

Registered voters who did not vote

Nonregistered persons

Using IF capabilities, the logic to carry out this activity is illustrated by the pseudocode and flowchart in Figure 8-26. You can see that the Yes condition action of the first test (Registered?) involves another test. This example is coded in Figure 8-27. When the reserved word IF is specified more than once within an IF statement, the resulting statement is referred to as a **nested IF statement**.

The structure of this example is relatively basic and its logic should be easy to follow. However, applications are commonly encountered in which two or more levels of nesting are required with complex and confusing logic. Then the challenge begins. The results are commonly combinations that are confusing to follow and prone to hard-to-find coding errors.

Figure 8-26 The logic of the nested IF.

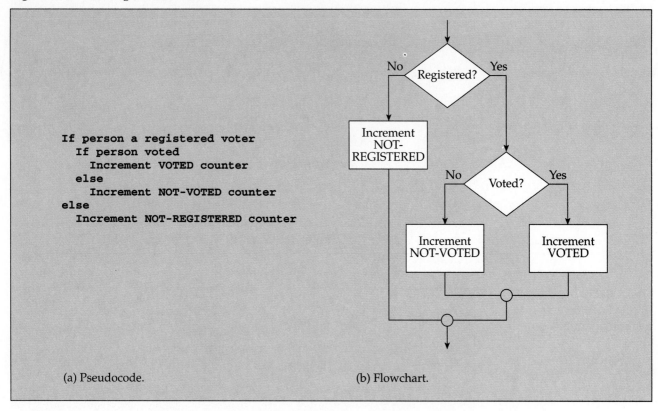

```
If person a registered voter
   If person voted
     Increment VOTED counter
   else
     Increment NOT-VOTED counter
else
   Increment NOT-REGISTERED counter
```

(a) Pseudocode.

(b) Flowchart.

Figure 8-27 Nested IF example.

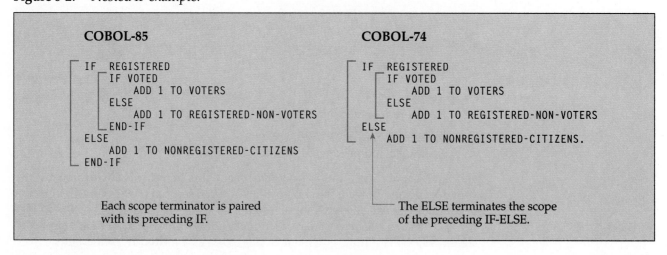

COBOL-85

```
IF  REGISTERED
     IF VOTED
          ADD 1 TO VOTERS
     ELSE
          ADD 1 TO REGISTERED-NON-VOTERS
     END-IF
ELSE
     ADD 1 TO NONREGISTERED-CITIZENS
END-IF
```

Each scope terminator is paired
with its preceding IF.

COBOL-74

```
IF  REGISTERED
     IF VOTED
          ADD 1 TO VOTERS
     ELSE
          ADD 1 TO REGISTERED-NON-VOTERS
ELSE
     ADD 1 TO NONREGISTERED-CITIZENS.
```

The ELSE terminates the scope
of the preceding IF-ELSE.

The EVALUATE Statement

The Case Structure

Assume that you are working on a program that controls access to the patron file of Fleetwood Charities. One element of the program gives the user access to certain functions through the following screen menu:

```
              FLEETWOOD CHARITIES
            PATRON FILE UPDATE MENU


        E - Enter/Delete/Edit records
        D - Display selected records
        F - Form letter processing
        M - Maintenance operations

        X - eXit the System


        Please enter the desired option letter:
```

Your task is to write the COBOL code that will take action depending upon the user selection, as follows:

User-selection	Action
E	Perform Process-records
D	Perform Display-records
F	Perform Create-form-letters
M	Perform Do-maintenance
X	Set exit switch to true
Any other value	Perform Request-another-entry

Figure 8-28 shows the simplest way of illustrating the logic. In structured programming, this is called the **case structure**. As you can see, it involves multiple options based on a condition test. Using IF statements, the case structure requires multiple uses of nested IF statements. However, COBOL-85 includes a statement specifically designed to handle the case structure: the EVALUATE statement. Let's begin your consideration of the EVALUATE with the solution to this menu application, shown in Figure 8-29. Although this example is almost self-explanatory, the following are important points:

1. The entry immediately following the keyword EVALUATE (USER-CHOICE, in this case) is called the **selection subject**. It is the entry against which comparisons that follow are made.
2. The entry immediately following each keyword WHEN is called the **selection object**. This is the entry to which the selection subject is compared.
3. For evaluation purposes, the comparisons are made in exactly the same way as an equal comparison in an IF statement. The first equal condition that occurs causes the corresponding sequence of object statements to be executed. Upon completion of the sequence, control is passed to the END-EVALUATE and execution of the EVALUATE

Figure 8-28 The case structure.

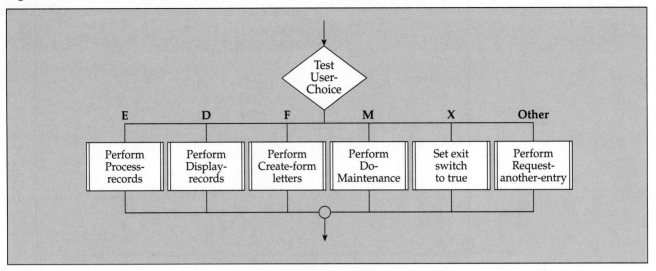

Figure 8-29
The EVALUATE statement.

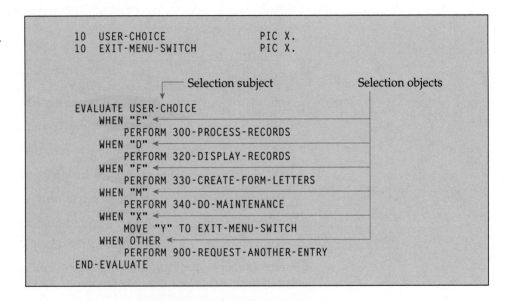

is completed. For instance, if USER-CHOICE contains F, then 330-CREATE-FORM-LETTERS is executed. Upon return, control is passed to the END-EVALUATE.

4. Although only one statement is included for each case in this example (PERFORM), there may be any number of statements, including IF statements or another EVALUATE statement.

5. If none of the preceding WHENs produces an equal condition, then the OTHER option is executed. This option is not required and can be omitted if no action is to be taken when none of the preceding conditions is satisfied.

You will study an alternate solution later in this chapter that uses condition-names and the SET statement.

Although not illustrated by this example, a range of values may be specified as the selection object. For instance, assume that an instructor wants to assign letter grades for an exam in which the grades range from 0 to 100. In Figure 8-30, the selection object is a range of values: for instance, 90 THRU 100. If the value in

Figure 8-30
Using the THRU option in
the EVALUATE.

```
         10   SCORE        PIC 9(3).
         10   GRADE        PIC X.



         EVALUATE SCORE
              WHEN 90 THRU 100
                     MOVE "A" TO GRADE
              WHEN 80 THRU 89
                     MOVE "B" TO GRADE
              WHEN 65 THRU 79
                     MOVE "C" TO GRADE
              WHEN 50 THRU 64
                     MOVE "D" TO GRADE
              WHEN  0 THRU 49
                     MOVE "F" TO GRADE
              WHEN OTHER
                     PERFORM 900-PROCESS-SCORE-ERROR
         END-EVALUATE
```

SCORE is within that range, then the condition is true and A is moved to GRADE. (Note: Either the keyword THRU or THROUGH may be used.)

Multiple Selection Objects/Subjects

The preceding examples of EVALUATE merely scratch the surface of this powerful statement. To illustrate two or more objects/subjects, consider the following example of a payroll program, in which each employee's gross pay is determined as follows:

```
If employee is hourly
  If hours worked is 40 or less
    Gross pay equals pay rate times hours worked
  If hours worked is more than 40 but not more than 48
    Gross pay equals pay rate times 40
                    plus overtime rate times excess hours over 40
  If hours worked is more than 48
    Gross pay equals pay rate times 40
                    plus overtime rate times 8
                    plus premium-time rate times excess over 48
else
  Gross pay equals salary
```

Notice that for hourly employees, the hours worked must be compared to both 40 and 48 to determine the gross pay calculation method. In the EVALUATE solution of Figure 8-31, assume that all variables are appropriately defined and that HOURLY is a properly defined condition-name (88-level item). The following commentary describes this example:

1. The EVALUATE includes three selection objects:

   HOURLY
   HOURS > 40
   HOURS > 48

   These coincide with the needs described in the preceding pseudocode.
2. Each WHEN includes three selection subjects, coinciding exactly with the selection objects.
3. Consecutive selection objects and selection subjects are separated by the reserved word *also*. Uppercase (ALSO) could be used as well, but lowercase focuses attention on the objects (and subjects) themselves.
4. During execution, each object is compared to its corresponding subject. If the comparison is satisfied for every comparison object, that WHEN

Figure 8-31
The EVALUATE with multiple selection objects/subjects.

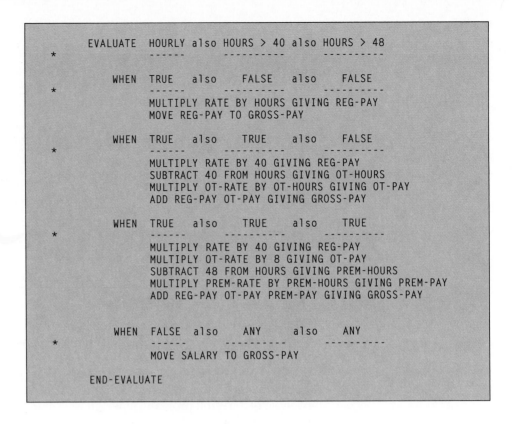

```
              EVALUATE   HOURLY also HOURS > 40 also HOURS > 48
     *                   ------      ----------      ----------

         WHEN   TRUE   also    FALSE   also    FALSE
     *          ------         ----------      ----------
                MULTIPLY RATE BY HOURS GIVING REG-PAY
                MOVE REG-PAY TO GROSS-PAY

         WHEN   TRUE   also    TRUE   also    FALSE
     *          ------         ----------      ----------
                MULTIPLY RATE BY 40 GIVING REG-PAY
                SUBTRACT 40 FROM HOURS GIVING OT-HOURS
                MULTIPLY OT-RATE BY OT-HOURS GIVING OT-PAY
                ADD REG-PAY OT-PAY GIVING GROSS-PAY

         WHEN   TRUE   also    TRUE   also    TRUE
     *          ------         ----------      ----------
                MULTIPLY RATE BY 40 GIVING REG-PAY
                MULTIPLY OT-RATE BY 8 GIVING OT-PAY
                SUBTRACT 48 FROM HOURS GIVING PREM-HOURS
                MULTIPLY PREM-RATE BY PREM-HOURS GIVING PREM-PAY
                ADD REG-PAY OT-PAY PREM-PAY GIVING GROSS-PAY


         WHEN   FALSE also    ANY    also    ANY
     *          ------         ----------      ----------
                MOVE SALARY TO GROSS-PAY

           END-EVALUATE
```

phrase is selected and its statements are executed. For instance, for an hourly employee working 45 hours, the following truth values result:

HOURLY	true
HOURS > 40	true
HOURS > 48	false

The second WHEN is satisfied and the pay calculated accordingly.

5. In this example, three reserved words—TRUE, FALSE, and ANY— are used as selection subjects. Each of them functions exactly as the English suggests. For TRUE and FALSE, the object must be true or false. ANY means that the particular test must not be made because any value is acceptable.

6. For style, spacing is used so that each subject aligns with its corresponding object. Underscoring is used via comment lines to clearly show relationships, resulting in a tabular form that is clear and understandable.*

7. The mathematical symbol > is used in place of the bulkier IS GREATER THAN. These symbols are used frequently in programs that follow because they are more compact.

Simulating the EVALUATE Statement with COBOL-74

Coding the preceding pay calculation with COBOL-74's nested IFs can be very confusing and can result in a form that does not work the way you expect. The best solution is to simulate the EVALUATE format; Figure 8-32 is an example of how to do this.

Another Form of the EVALUATE Statement

In some instances, the table form of the EVALUATE (illustrated in Figure 8-31) does not best fit the conditional need of the application. To illustrate, assume that you are at a point in a program where the action to be taken is as follows:

---

*If you have ever studied the subject of decision tables, you will recognize that this form of the EVALUATE closely resembles a decision table.

Figure 8-32
Simulating an EVALUATE with COBOL-74.

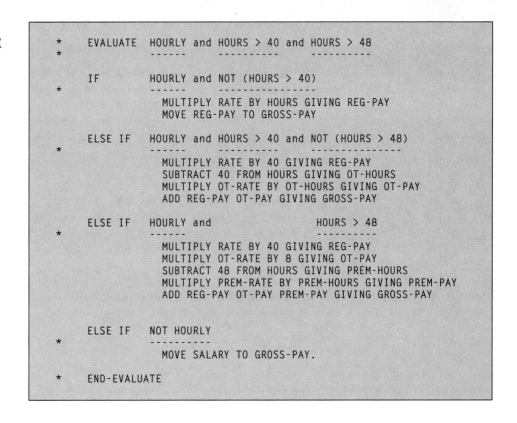

```
*      EVALUATE   HOURLY and HOURS > 40 and HOURS > 48
*                 ------     ----------     ----------

       IF         HOURLY and NOT (HOURS > 40)
*                 ------     ----------------
                     MULTIPLY RATE BY HOURS GIVING REG-PAY
                     MOVE REG-PAY TO GROSS-PAY

       ELSE IF    HOURLY and HOURS > 40 and NOT (HOURS > 48)
*                 ------     ----------     ----------------
                     MULTIPLY RATE BY 40 GIVING REG-PAY
                     SUBTRACT 40 FROM HOURS GIVING OT-HOURS
                     MULTIPLY OT-RATE BY OT-HOURS GIVING OT-PAY
                     ADD REG-PAY OT-PAY GIVING GROSS-PAY

       ELSE IF    HOURLY and                 HOURS > 48
*                 ------                      ----------
                     MULTIPLY RATE BY 40 GIVING REG-PAY
                     MULTIPLY OT-RATE BY 8 GIVING OT-PAY
                     SUBTRACT 48 FROM HOURS GIVING PREM-HOURS
                     MULTIPLY PREM-RATE BY PREM-HOURS GIVING PREM-PAY
                     ADD REG-PAY OT-PAY PREM-PAY GIVING GROSS-PAY


       ELSE IF    NOT HOURLY
*                 ----------
                     MOVE SALARY TO GROSS-PAY.

*      END-EVALUATE
```

```
If TOTAL-AMOUNT is greater than CREDIT-LIMIT
  then perform the 400-CHECK-OVER-LIMIT module
else if CREDIT-AMOUNT is greater than 0
       then save CREDIT-AMOUNT and perform 410-CHECK-CR-AMOUNT
else if NO-INPUT is true
       then perform 920-PROCESS-NO-INPUT
otherwise
  Initialize accumulators and perform 260-GET-NEXT-AMOUNT
```

This can be coded with the form of the EVALUATE shown in Figure 8-33. When studying this example, the following are important points to note.

Figure 8-33
Using TRUE as the EVALUATE selection object.

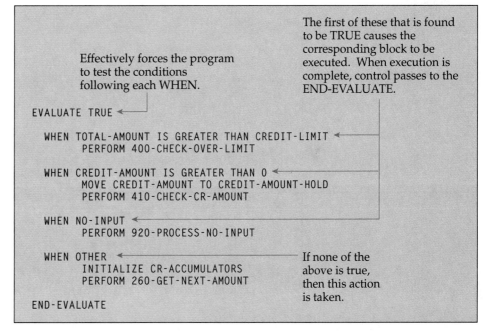

Effectively forces the program to test the conditions following each WHEN.

The first of these that is found to be TRUE causes the corresponding block to be executed. When execution is complete, control passes to the END-EVALUATE.

```
EVALUATE TRUE

    WHEN TOTAL-AMOUNT IS GREATER THAN CREDIT-LIMIT
         PERFORM 400-CHECK-OVER-LIMIT

    WHEN CREDIT-AMOUNT IS GREATER THAN 0
         MOVE CREDIT-AMOUNT TO CREDIT-AMOUNT-HOLD
         PERFORM 410-CHECK-CR-AMOUNT

    WHEN NO-INPUT
         PERFORM 920-PROCESS-NO-INPUT

    WHEN OTHER
         INITIALIZE CR-ACCUMULATORS
         PERFORM 260-GET-NEXT-AMOUNT

END-EVALUATE
```

If none of the above is true, then this action is taken.

1. The selection subject is simply the reserved word TRUE, a logical value. So, the selection objects must provide the logical values of either true or false.
2. Execution of this statement involves evaluating the selection objects (following the WHENs) until one is found with a truth value matching the selection subject (TRUE, in this case). When that occurs, the corresponding object statements are executed and control passes to the END-EVALUATE.
3. If none of the WHEN subjects is true, then the OTHER option is executed.

The EVALUATE TRUE form of the EVALUATE and condition-names can be combined to produce a form of the menu selection example (Figure 8-29, page 256) that is both functional and understandable. In Figure 8-34, you see that the selection subject is the reserved word TRUE and the selection objects are appropriate condition-names.

General Format of the EVALUATE

The preceding EVALUATE examples illustrate the variety of forms this statement can assume. The general format of Figure 8-35 displays its complexity.

About the PERFORM

The PERFORM WITH TEST AFTER

With the following PERFORM example, you know that the 500 module is repeatedly executed until the designated condition is satisfied (WA-TEST-FIELD is greater than WA-LIMIT):

```
PERFORM 500-PROCESS-RESERVE
    UNTIL WA-TEST-FIELD > WA-LIMIT
```

On the other hand, what happens if the initial value in WA-TEST-FIELD is less than that of WA-LIMIT? The answer is that the 500 module is never executed at

Figure 8-34
An alternate menu control sequence using condition-names.

```
   10   UC-USER-CHOICE            PIC X.
        88  UC-PROCESS-RECORDS     VALUE "E"
        88  UC-DISPLAY-RECORDS     VALUE "D"
        88  UC-CREATE-FORM-LETTERS VALUE "F"
        88  UC-DO-MAINTENANCE      VALUE "M"
        88  UC-EXIT-THE-MENU       VALUE "X"

   10   EXIT-MENU-SWITCH          PIC X.
        88  CONTINUE-IN-MENU       VALUE "Y"
        88  EXIT-MENU              VALUE "N"




   EVALUATE TRUE
       WHEN UC-PROCESS-RECORDS
           PERFORM 300-PROCESS-RECORDS
       WHEN UC-DISPLAY-RECORDS
           PERFORM 320-DISPLAY-RECORDS
       WHEN UC-CREATE-FORM-LETTERS
           PERFORM 330-CREATE-FORM-LETTERS
       WHEN UC-DO-MAINTENANCE
           PERFORM 340-DO-MAINTENANCE
       WHEN UC-EXIT-THE-MENU
           SET EXIT-MENU TO TRUE
       WHEN OTHER
           PERFORM 900-REQUEST-ANOTHER-ENTRY.
   END-EVALUATE
```

Figure 8-35   General format of the EVALUATE.

```
EVALUATE  { identifier-1  }  [ ALSO  { identifier-2  }  ] ...
          { literal-1     }         { literal-2     }
          { expression-1  }         { expression-2  }
          { TRUE          }         { TRUE          }
          { FALSE         }         { FALSE         }


{{WHEN

    { ANY                                                                          }
    { condition-1                                                                  }
    { TRUE                                                                         }
    { FALSE                                                                        }
    {       { identifier-3            } [ { THROUGH } { identifier-4            } ] }
    { [NOT] { literal-3               }   { THRU    } { literal-4               }   }
    {       { arithmetic-expression-1 }              { arithmetic-expression-2 }   }


  [ ALSO

    { ANY                                                                          }
    { condition-2                                                                  }
    { TRUE                                                                         } ... } ...
    { FALSE                                                                        }
    {       { identifier-5            } [ { THROUGH } { identifier-6            } ] }
    { [NOT] { literal-5               }   { THRU    } { literal-6               }   }
    {       { arithmetic-expression-3 }              { arithmetic-expression-4 }   }  ]

  imperative-statement-1} ...

  [WHEN OTHER imperative-statement-2]

  [END-EVALUATE]
```

all; processing immediately continues to the next statement in the sequence. The reason is that the first action of the PERFORM is to make the test. In other words: (1) the test is made and (2) the paragraph is performed if so indicated as a result of the test. This is commonly called a **test before action**.

In most applications, this is the desired form: the paragraph is not performed unless the condition is satisfied. However, what if you want the 500 module of the preceding example to be performed at least once, regardless of the condition? To force this, COBOL-85 includes a clause that causes the PERFORM to carry out the test *after* performing the specified module. This is called a **test after action** and is coded as follows:

```
PERFORM 500-PROCESS-RESERVE
    WITH TEST AFTER
    UNTIL WA-TEST-FIELD > WA-LIMIT
```

With this form, which is new to COBOL-85, (1) the paragraph is performed and (2) the test is made. At first, you might think that the test after will cause a loop to be executed one more time than a test before. This is *not* the case. The only difference between the two is that the test after forces at least one execution, regardless of the test.

Regarding placement of the WITH TEST AFTER phrase, notice that it precedes the UNTIL and follows the name of the paragraph to be performed.

Although this example uses an out-of-line PERFORM, the test after can also be used with the inline PERFORM. For instance, the inline sequence of the following would be executed once, regardless of the test condition:

```
PERFORM WITH TEST AFTER
       UNTIL WA-TEST-FIELD > WA-LIMIT
   ⋮
END-PERFORM
```

Early Exit from a Performed Paragraph

One of structured programming's basic principles is that each module must have a single entry and single exit. That is, execution always begins with the first statement of the module and ends with the last. In some situations, maintaining a strict adherence to the single-exit principle can result in very cumbersome coding. Because of this, many languages have a statement that causes immediate termination of a module and returns control to the calling module. With this book's convention of not using periods within a PROCEDURE DIVISION paragraph, this can be accomplished with the NEXT SENTENCE statement. To illustrate its use, assume that a module consists of the following:

1. Some initial processing
2. An EVALUATE
3. Some final processing that may or may not be executed, depending upon prior actions

Figure 8-36 includes two sample skeletons of this module. If *condition-2* (the second WHEN) is satisfied, then after the *imperative-statements-2* are executed, no further processing in this module is allowed. That is, the statements identified as *Remaining statements of module* are skipped. In Figure 8-36(a), a condition-name is used that is set to true after the *imperative-statements-2* are executed. Then all remaining statements following the END-EVALUATE are executed conditionally. Although this example is reasonably clear, with more complex conditions, this form can become obscure and deceptive.

In Figure 8-36(b), *imperative-statements-2* are followed by the NEXT SENTENCE statement. This causes execution to proceed to the statement following the next period. Since that period is at the end of the module, control progresses to the end of the module (without execution of the statements designated by *Remaining statements of module*). From there, control returns to the calling module.

Chapter Summary

An IF statement can be written as either (1) a simple one-condition statement, (2) a multiple-condition statement combined by logical operators, or (3) a multiple-condition nested IF statement.

Four types of conditions can be tested with an IF statement: relation, class, sign, and condition-name.

■ Relation conditions test whether the subject of the condition IS GREATER THAN, IS EQUAL TO, or IS LESS THAN the object. (COBOL-85 also includes IS GREATER THAN OR EQUAL TO and IS LESS THAN OR EQUAL TO.) When the subject and the object are both numeric items, comparisons are made according to their algebraic values. Alphanumeric comparisons depend upon the collating sequence of the computer used. With alphanumeric fields,

Figure 8-36
Conditionally skipping a
sequence of statements.

```
        400-PROCESS-CALCULATED-RESULTS.
            ⋮
            EVALUATE TRUE
                WHEN (condition-1)
                    (imperative-statements-1)
                WHEN (condition-2)
                    (imperative-statements-2)
                    SET ABNORMAL-CONDITION TO TRUE
                WHEN (condition-3)
                    (imperative-statements-3)
            END-EVALUATE
            IF NOT ABNORMAL-CONDITION
                ⋮ (Remaining statements of module)
            END-IF.


        (a) Setting a switch and testing it.


        400-PROCESS-CALCULATED-RESULTS.
            ⋮
            EVALUATE TRUE
                WHEN (condition-1)
                    (imperative-statements-1)
                WHEN (condition-2)
                    (imperative-statements-2)
*Exit-->        EXIT THIS MODULE
                NEXT SENTENCE
                WHEN (condition-3)
                    (imperative-statements-3)
            END-EVALUATE
            ⋮ (Remaining statements of module)


        (b) Early exit from the module with the NEXT SENTENCE.
```

comparison begins at the leftmost character position and proceeds to the right. If the fields are not the same length, the shorter field is internally extended with spaces to equal the length of the longer field.

- Class conditions test whether a field contains only numeric digits or only alphabetic characters. Fields that contain only numeric digits (0 through 9) are considered NUMERIC; those containing only alphabetic characters (including spaces) are ALPHABETIC.

- Sign conditions test whether a numeric field is POSITIVE, NEGATIVE, or ZERO.

- Condition-name conditions are a special way of writing a relation condition that requires an 88-level entry in the DATA DIVISION.

Each 88-level item requires a condition-name VALUE clause in its data-item description. Condition-name VALUE clauses differ from initializing VALUE clauses because a condition-name VALUE clause:

- Can be used in either the FILE SECTION or the WORKING-STORAGE SECTION

- Can be associated with a REDEFINES clause

- Can be associated with an OCCURS clause

- Can be specified with multiple values or a range of values

A combined IF statement contains multiple conditions connected with the logical operators AND or OR.

- When conditions are joined by the AND operator, all conditions must be true for the true actions to be executed; if one or more conditions are false, the false actions are executed.

- With the OR operator, if one or more conditions are true, the true actions are executed; if all conditions are false, the false actions are executed.

When both the operators AND and OR are used in the same IF statement, the result is termed a complex condition.

An IF statement within another IF is called a nested IF. Use it with caution, if at all; in most cases, the EVALUATE serves the same purpose.

The EVALUATE statement (not part of COBOL-74) provides the case capability of multiple selections based on one or more conditions.

Style Summary

For relation conditions, make the data class of the subject and the object consistent. That is, when the subject is numeric, the object should be numeric; when the subject is alphanumeric, the object should also be alphanumeric (or a nonnumeric literal).

If your program requires that you use complex conditions, use parentheses to explicitly specify the evaluation sequence and to make the condition understandable.

Use implied subjects and relation operators with care, if at all. They tend to cause confusion.

Do not use nested IF statements; use the EVALUATE instead. If you are using COBOL-74, simulate the EVALUATE with your nested IF sequence.

Indent elements of your IF and EVALUATE statements—as illustrated by this chapter's examples—in order to enhance clarity.

Features Not in COBOL-74

The following additional relation conditions are not in COBOL-74:

```
IS GREATER THAN OR EQUAL TO
>=
IS LESS THAN OR EQUAL TO
<=
```

These items are also not included in COBOL-74:

- The EVALUATE statement to handle multiple-condition testing.

- The END-IF scope terminator.

- The class conditions ALPHABETIC-UPPER and ALPHABETIC-LOWER, which test that fields contain only uppercase letters or lowercase letters, respectively.

- Programmer-defined data classes (the CLASS clause).

Exercises

Terms for Definition

boolean diagram
case structure
class condition
collating sequence
combined conditions
complex condition
condition-name condition
condition-name VALUE clause
implied relation operators
implied subject
initializing VALUE clause

logical operators
negated condition
nested IF statement
object
relation condition
selection object
selection subject
sign condition
subject
test after action
test before action

Review Questions

1. Name the four types of conditions that may be expressed with an IF statement.

2. Identify the three basic relation test operators.

3. With a relation condition, the element before the relation operator is called the _____ ; the element after the operator is termed the _____ .

4. When the subject and the object of a relation test are both numeric, comparison of the two values is made according to their _____ values.

5. When the subject and/or object of a relation test are alphanumeric, comparison of the two values is made in accordance with the _____ of the computer system used.

6. When an alphanumeric comparison is made and the subject and object are of different lengths, the shorter field is _____ .

7. Name the two data classes that can be tested with a class condition.

8. Name the three sign conditions that can be tested.

9. A sign test can be performed only upon _____ fields.

10. A condition-name test requires a (n) _____ -level item in the _____ DIVISION.

11. A condition-name VALUE clause may contain one value, _____ values, or a(n) _____ of values.

12. Condition-name VALUE clauses _____ (can/cannot) be specified in the FILE SECTION of the DATA DIVISION.

13. When the logical operator _____ is specified in a combined IF statement, all conditions must be true for the true statements to be executed.

14. When the logical operator _____ is specified, one or more conditions must be true for the true statements to be executed.

15. Assume that each of the following is stored as an alphanumeric field within your computer. Arrange them into ascending sequence (smallest first, largest last), according to the collating sequence of your computer.

```
EGG NOODLES
BRAN CEREAL
7 UP
#1 WHOLE WHEAT
12PM CAKE MIX
Z-BRAN
ZBRAN
 ZBRAN
Z BRAN
Bran Cereal
All-good Crunch
aLL-GOOD CRUNCH
```

16. The following is a list of numeric values stored in your computer. For these, assume the following: (1) they are stored in the appropriate format regarding assumed decimal and sign positioning, and (2) the field length of each is as suggested by the number of digits shown. Arrange them in sequence from the smallest to the largest, as would be determined by the COBOL relation condition. If any two or more are equal, place a bracket around them to indicate this.

```
256
-1
000078.63
-000.95
00000256.000
1000.0
.95
00000.000
-.95
0
```

17. Each of the following IF conditions can be written in a different form (for instance, compare Examples 2 and 5 in Figure 8-3). Write an equivalent form for each.

a.
```
IF FA IS GREATER THAN FB
     ADD 1 TO FA-COUNT
END-IF
```

b.
```
IF FC IS POSITIVE
     ADD 1 TO FC-COUNT
END-IF
```

c.
```
IF NOT FD GREATER FE
     ADD 1 TO FE-COUNT
END-IF
```

Use the following condition-names for d. and e.:

```
05  GENDER        PIC X(1).
    88   MASCULINE    VALUE "M".
    88   FEMININE     VALUE "F".
    88   NEUTER       VALUE "N".
```

d.
```
IF MASCULINE
     ADD 1 TO M-COUNT
END-IF
```

e.
```
IF NOT FEMININE
     ADD 1 TO S-COUNT
END-IF
```

18. Consider the following complex condition (note that the entire condition is written on one line so that you can easily group the parentheses):

```
IF ((FA GREATER 10 OR FB EQUAL 0) AND FC LESS 55) OR FD NOT ZERO
```

For each of the following sets of data values, determine whether this condition will be true or false:

	FA	FB	FC	FD
a.	10	0	0	22
b.	11	0	55	-1
c.	-100	-100	-100	0
d.	-100	-100	-100	-100
e.	0	0	0	0
f.	100	100	100	100

19. Among the functions performed by a citizen survey program is to perform counts of the number of citizens in various categories. One group of counts is the following:

Category	Program counter variable
Males having voted	MALE-VOTERS
Females having voted	FEMALE-VOTERS
Persons not voting	REGISTERED-NONVOTERS
Unregistered persons	NONREGISTERED-PERSONS

Assume that the condition-names REGISTERED (true if person is registered voter), VOTED (true if person has voted), and MALE (true if person is male) were defined in the DATA DIVISION. As each record is read, it must be evaluated and counted into one of the four previous categories. Write an EVALUATE statement to do this.

Syntax/Debug Exercises

1. The following fields are defined in the WORKING-STORAGE SECTION of a program:

```
05  FIELD-A      PIC X(5).
05  FIELD-B      PIC 9(5).
05  FIELD-C      PIC 9(5).
05  FIELD-D      PIC 9(1).
05  FIELD-E      PIC X(1).
    88   VAL-1        VALUE "A".
    88   VAL-2        VALUE "B".
    88   VAL-3        VALUE "C".
```

Some of the following conditions violate the syntax rules. Identify each that is incorrect and the reason.

a. IF FIELD-E LESS "1"

b. IF FIELD-A IS EQUAL TO FIELD-B

c. IF NOT VAL-1

d. IF FIELD-E NOT ALPHABETIC

e. IF FIELD-E IS EQUAL TO VAL-3

f. IF FIELD-D IS NOT ZERO

g. IF   VAL-3
        AND FIELD-B IS GREATER THAN FIELD-D

h. IF FIELD-B NOT EQUAL TO FIELD-D

i. IF NOT VAL-1 AND NOT VAL-2

j. IF FIELD-A NUMERIC

k. IF FIELD-E NOT NUMERIC AND NOT ALPHABETIC

l. IF   FIELD-B GREATER THAN 0
        AND LESS THAN 100

m. IF FIELD-B AND FIELD-C GREATER THAN 10

n. IF FIELD-B - FIELD-C IS NEGATIVE

o. IF FIELD-B - FIELD-C IS NUMERIC

Programming Assignments

Programming Assignment 8-1: Test Grades Report

Background information:

One of the instructors at the Bayview Institute of Computer Technology wants to automate recordkeeping for student examinations. Her file contains one record for each exam taken by each student. It includes the number of questions on the exam and the number missed by the student. The instructor needs a program to determine and print letter grades based on the raw input.

Input file: Student file (STUDENT.DAT)

Student record

	Student last name	Student first name		Section number	Questions asked	Questions missed	
1 2 3 4 5 6 7 8 9 10 11	12 13 14 15 16 17 18 19 20 21 22 23 24 25	26 27 28 29 30 31 32 33 34 35	36 37 38 39 40 41 42 43 44 45 46 47 48 49 50 51	52 53 54 55 56 57	58 59 60 61	62 63 64 65	66 67 68 69 70

Output-report format:

```
              0         1         2         3         4         5         6         7         8
     1234567890123456789012345678901234567890123456789012345678901234567890123456789012345678 9
1
2
3
4                          TEST  GRADES  REPORT  (8-1)
5
6     SECTION  -------STUDENT  NAME--------  QUESTIONS   QUESTIONS   PERCENTAGE    LETTER
7     NUMBER   LAST  NAME       FIRST  NAME    ASKED       MISSED      CORRECT      GRADE
8
9      99999   XXXXXXXXXXXXXX  XXXXXXXXXX      ZZ9         ZZ9         ZZ9%          X
10
11     99999   XXXXXXXXXXXXXX  XXXXXXXXXX      ZZ9         ZZ9         ZZ9%          X
12
```

Program operations:

1. Process each input student record.

2. Print the three heading lines on the first page and on each following page of the report.

3. For each input student record, do the following:
   a. Calculate the percentage of correct answers by subtracting the questions missed from the questions asked and dividing the remainder by the questions asked.
   b. Assign the letter grade in accordance with the percentage correct as follows:

   100% through 90% = A

   89% through 80% = B

   79% through 70% = C

   69% through 60% = D

   59% through 0%   = F

   c. Print an output detail line as specified on the print chart.

4. Program option: Maintain a count of how many students obtained each grade. At the end of the report, print a summary of these grade counts. Do this on a separate page; use appropriate formatting.

5. Double-space each detail line. Provide for a span of 56 lines per page.

Programming Assignment 8-2: Special County Tax Report

Background information:

The payroll supervisor at Silicon Valley Manufacturing must prepare a quarterly summary of Special County tax for all employees. This tax is computed as follows:

Earnings	Tax rate
To $45,000	1.27%
In excess of $45,000	None

Note that tax is calculated for only those earnings up to $45,000. After an employee's year-to-date earnings reach $45,000, tax is no longer withheld.

Input file: Earnings file (EARNINGS.DAT)

Earnings record

	Employee number	Employee last name	Employee first name		Current-period earnings	Year-to-date earnings	
1 2 3 4 5 6 7 8 9 10	11 12 13 14 15 16 17 18 19 20	21 22 23 24 25 26 27 28 29 30 31	32 33 34 35 36 37 38 39 40	41 42 43 44 45 46 47 48 49 50 51 52 53 54 55 56 57 58 59	60 61 62 63 64 65 66	67 68 69 70 71 72 73 74	75 76 77 78 79

Output-report format:

```
         0         1         2         3         4         5         6         7         8
 1234567890123456789012345678901234567890123456789012345678901234567890123456789012345678901
1
2
3
4 SPECIAL COUNTY TAX REPORT (8-2)                                                PAGE ZZ9
5
6 SOC. SEC.        ----EMPLOYEE NAME-----   YEAR-TO-DATE    THIS PERIOD EARNINGS   CNTY TAX
7  NUMBER          LAST        FIRST          EARNINGS         AMOUNT     TAXABLE   THIS PER.
8
9 999-99-9999      XXXXXXXXXXX XXXXXXXXX    ZZZ,ZZZ.99      ZZ,ZZZ.99-  ZZ,ZZZ.99-  Z,ZZZ.99-
10
11 999-99-9999      XXXXXXXXXXX XXXXXXXXX    ZZZ,ZZZ.99      ZZ,ZZZ.99-  ZZ,ZZZ.99-  Z,ZZZ.99-
12
```

Program operations:

1. Process each input employee record.

2. Print the three heading lines on the first page and on each following page of the report.
   a. Accumulate and print the page number on the first heading line as specified on the print chart.

3. For each input employee record, do the following:
   a. Determine the Current-period-taxable-amount as follows:

   - If the input Year-to-date-earnings field is equal to or less than $45,000.00, use the Current-period earnings.

- If the input year-to-date earnings is more than $45,000.00, subtract the Current-period earnings from the Year-to-date-earnings (call this quantity Deficient-amount).

  > If Deficient-amount is less than $45,000, calculate the Current-period-taxable-amount as 45,000 minus Deficient-amount.
  > Else
  >   > Set Current-period-taxable-amount to zero

- Calculate that the Special-county-tax amount will be equal to 1.27% (rounded) of the Current-period-taxable-amount.

b. Print an output Special-county-tax report detail line as specified on the print chart.

4. Double-space each detail line. Provide for a span of 54 lines per page.

Programming Assignment 8-3: Accounts Receivable Register

Background information:

At the first of each month, Silicon Valley Manufacturing calculates the balance owed by each customer from data in the customer file. Included in the calculations are the prior balance (balance forward), new purchases, payments received, finance charges, and late charges. A bill is printed and mailed to each customer. In addition, a summary called an accounts receivable register is printed for use by the accounting department.

Input file: Customer file (CUSTOMER.DAT)

Customer name record

Customer number	Customer name		Balance forward	New purchases		Payments received
1 2	3 4 5 6 7 8 9 10 11 12 13 14 15 16 17 18 19 20 21 22 23 24 25 26 27 28 29 30 31	32 33 34 35 36 37 38	39 40 41 42 43 44 45 46	47 48 49 50 51 52 53 54	55 56 57 58 59 60 61 62 63 64 65 66 67 68 69 70 71 72	73 74 75 76 77 78 79 80

Output-report format:

```
             0         1         2         3         4         5         6         7         8         9         10        11
    1234567890123456789012345678901234567890123456789012345678901234567890123456789012345678901234567890123456789
 1
 2
 3
 4  ACCOUNTS RECEIVABLE REGISTER (8-3)                                                    RUN DATE MM/DD/YY    PAGE ZZ9
 5
 6  CUST.                          BALANCE       PAYMENTS      FINANCE     LATE     NEW               NEW        MINIMUM
 7   NO.      CUSTOMER NAME        FORWARD       RECEIVED      CHARGE      CHARGE   PURCHASES         BALANCE     PAYMENT      STATUS
 8
 9  99999  XXXXXXXXXXXXXXXXXXXXXX ZZZ,ZZZ.99-  ZZZ,ZZZ.99-  ZZ,ZZZ.99  Z,ZZZ.99  ZZZ,ZZZ.99-  ZZZ,ZZZ.99-  ZZ,ZZZ.99  XXXXXXXX
10
11  99999  XXXXXXXXXXXXXXXXXXXXXX ZZZ,ZZZ.99-  ZZZ,ZZZ.99-  ZZ,ZZZ.99  Z,ZZZ.99  ZZZ,ZZZ.99-  ZZZ,ZZZ.99-  ZZ,ZZZ.99  XXXXXXXX
12
13
14              REPORT TOTALS   Z,ZZZ,ZZZ.99-*             ZZZ,ZZZ.99 *          Z,ZZZ,ZZZ.99-*             ZZZ,ZZZ.99 *
15                                             Z,ZZZ,ZZZ.99-*          ZZ,ZZZ.99 *          Z,ZZZ,ZZZ.99-*
16
17
```

Program operations:

1. Process each input customer record.

2. Print the three heading lines on the first page and on each following page of the report.
   a. Print the run date on the first heading line as specified on the print chart.
   b. Accumulate and print the page number on the first heading line as specified on the print chart.

3. For each input customer record, do the following:
   a. Calculate the finance charge by subtracting the Payments-received amount from the Balance-forward amount and multiplying the remainder by 1.5% (the monthly service charge applicable to the unpaid balance).
   b. If the Payments-received amount is less than 10% of the Balance-forward amount, apply a late charge equal to 1% of the difference. If a late charge is applicable and the Late-charge amount is less than $5.00, apply a minimum late charge of $5.00.
   c. Calculate the new balance by subtracting the Payments-received amount from the Balance-forward amount and adding to the remainder the finance charge, late charge, and New-purchases amounts.
   d. Calculate the minimum-payment amount equal to 10% of the New-balance amount.
   e. Print an output Accounts-receivable register detail line as specified on the print chart.
   f. Accumulate the following totals:
      - Balance forward
      - Payments received
      - Finance charge
      - Late charge
      - New purchases
      - New balance
      - Minimum payment
   g. Print the account status as follows:
      - If the New-balance amount is zero or negative, leave the status field blank.
      - If the Payments-received amount is equal to or greater than 10% of the Balance-forward amount, print "CURRENT."
      - If the Balance-forward amount is not equal to zero and the Payments-received amount is not equal to zero but less than 10% of the Balance-forward amount, print "OVERDUE."
      - If the Balance-forward amount is not equal to zero and the Payments-received amount is equal to zero, print "PAST DUE."

4. Double-space each detail line. Provide for a span of 54 lines per page.

5. After all input customer records are processed, print the two output-report total lines (triple-spaced from the last detail line) as specified on the print chart.

Programming Assignment 8-4: Inventory Reorder Report

Background information:

An inventory reorder report is to be printed from the parts file.

Input file: Inventory file (INVEN.DAT)

Inventory record

Product identification	Product description	Inventory class	Unit cost	Reorder point	Quanity on hand	Quanity on order		Order quantity	

```
1 2 3 4 5 6 7 8 9 10 11 12 13 14 15 16 17 18 19 20 21 22 23 24 25 26 27 28 29 30 31 32 33 34 35 36 37 38 39 40 41 42 43 44 45 46 47 48 49 50 51 52 53 54 55 56 57 58 59 60 61 62 63 64 65 66 67 68 69 70 71 72 73 74 75 76 77 78 79 80
```

Output-report format:

```
INVENTORY  REORDER  REPORT  (8-4)                                    RUN  TIME  HH:MM    RUN  DATE  MM/DD/YY
                                                                                                  PAGE  ZZ9

  PRODUCT                        QUANTITY   QUANTITY   INV.   REORDER    REORDER    QUANTITY       UNIT      INVENTORY               REORDER
  IDENT       PRODUCT DESCRIPTION ON HAND   ON ORDER  CLASS   POINT     QUANTITY    TO ORDER       COST        VALUE                    COST

XXXXXXXXX  XXXXXXXXXXXXXXXXXXXXXXXXXXX Z.ZZ9    Z.ZZ9      X    Z.ZZ9      Z.ZZZ       Z.ZZZ   Z.ZZZ.99  ZZ.ZZZ.ZZZ.99    ZZ.ZZZ.ZZZ.99

XXXXXXXXX  XXXXXXXXXXXXXXXXXXXXXXXXXXX Z.ZZ9    Z.ZZ9      X    Z.ZZ9      Z.ZZZ       Z.ZZZ   Z.ZZZ.99  ZZ.ZZZ.ZZZ.99    ZZ.ZZZ.ZZZ.99



                                                          TOTAL FOR INVENTORY CLASS A ITEMS   ZZZ.ZZZ.ZZZ.99*  ZZZ.ZZZ.ZZZ.99
                                                                                    B ITEMS   ZZZ.ZZZ.ZZZ.99*  ZZZ.ZZZ.ZZZ.99
                                                                                    C ITEMS   ZZZ.ZZZ.ZZZ.99*  ZZZ.ZZZ.ZZZ.99
                                                                                    X ITEMS   ZZZ.ZZZ.ZZZ.99*  ZZZ.ZZZ.ZZZ.99

                                                       TOTALS FOR ALL INVENTORY ITEMS Z.ZZZ.ZZZ.ZZZ.99**
                                                                                                  Z.ZZZ.ZZZ.ZZZ.99
```

Program operations:

1. Process each input inventory record.

2. Print the four heading lines on the first page and on each following page of the report.
   a. Print the run time and run date on the first heading line as specified on the print chart.
   b. Accumulate and print the page number on the second heading line as specified on the print chart.

3. For each input part record, do the following:
   a. If the input Inventory-class code is not equal to A, B, C, or X, print an asterisk (*) in the inventory-class field on the output-report line, but treat the part as an inventory-class C item.
   b. Calculate the Quantity-available amount by adding the Quantity-on-hand amount to the Quantity-on-order amount.
   c. If the Quantity-available amount is less than the Reorder-point amount, calculate the Quantity-to-order amount. The Quantity-to-order amount should be the Order-quantity amount—unless the Quantity-to-order amount is greater. In that case, it should be the next higher multiple of the Order-quantity amount.
   d. If the Quantity-available amount is not less than the Reorder-point amount, set the Quantity-to-order amount to zero.
   e. When the Quantity-to-order amount is not equal to zero, print an asterisk in print position 1, as shown on the print chart. Otherwise, leave print position 1 blank.

f. Calculate the Inventory-value amount by multiplying the Unit-cost amount by the Quantity-on-hand amount.

g. Calculate the Reorder-cost amount by multiplying the Unit-cost amount by the Quantity-to-order amount.

h. Print an output inventory reorder report detail line as specified on the print chart.

i. Accumulate the following totals:

- Inventory value (for each inventory class and for all items, as specified on the print chart)

- Reorder cost (for each inventory class and for all items, as specified on the print chart)

4. Double-space each detail line. Provide for a span of 53 lines per page.

5. After all input part records are processed, print the six output-report total lines (triple-spaced from the last detail line) as specified on the print chart.

Programming Assignment 8-5: Nurses' Salary Increase Projection

Background information:

After meeting with the union, the Brooklawn Hospital management found the report of Assignment 7-5 inadequate to cope with some of the union proposals. These include adjusting pay based on various factors—including seniority, part-time/fulltime status, and supervisory responsibility—in addition to shift differential. Although the hospital board of trustees agrees with management, the press has supported most of the union proposals as reasonable. The report of Assignment 7-5 must be expanded further.

Input file: Nurses file (NURSES.DAT)

Nurses record

Employment code ⌐ ⌐ Supervisory code   Shift code (1, 2, or 3) ⌐

| Name | | Prof. specialty | Date hired (yymmdd) | | | Base monthly salary | | Shift code |

Output-report format:

Program operations:

1. Process each input record.

2. Calculated quantities for detail output are
    a. Projected-base-salary is the Input-base-salary times 1.09.
    b. Benefits-adjustment is to be calculated as:

    If Employment-code = F, use 30% of Projected-base-salary otherwise use 15% of Projected-base-salary.

    c. Seniority is to be determined as of 1/1/95. To calculate Years-seniority, subtract the year subfield of Date-hired from 95. Then calculate Seniority-adjustment as the following percentage of the Projected-base-salary:

    None if Years-seniority is less than 10

    3% if the Years-seniority is between 10 and 19 (inclusive)

    7% if the Years-seniority is 20 or greater

    d. Supervisory-adjustment is 10% of the Projected-base-salary if the Supervisory-code contains Y.
    e. Shift-adjustment is calculated as the following percentage of the Projected-base-salary:

    None if Shift-code = 1

    5% if Shift-code   = 2

    10% if Shift-code   = 3

    f. Total-salary is the sum of Projected-base-salary and all salary adjustments.

3. Accumulate the following totals:

    Projected-base-salary

    Benefits-adjustment

    Seniority-adjustment

    Supervisory-adjustment

    Shift-adjustment

    Total-salary

4. Double-space each detail line. Provide for a span of 53 lines per page.

5. After all input records are processed, print the three output-report total lines (triple-spaced from the last detail line) as specified on the print chart.

Programming Assignment 8-6: Vehicle Rental Discounts

Background information:

The basic daily rental fee advertised by Rent-Ur-Wheels is only one element of determining the actual daily rate. Customers can receive a variety of discounts—or none at all. Two types of insurance are available and must be factored into the rate. This program prints a list of all rented vehicles together with the actual daily rate (including any discounts or insurance charges).

Input file: Vehicle file (VEHICLE.DAT)

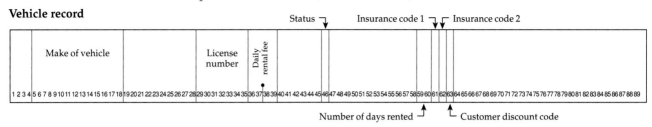

Vehicle record

Output-report format:

```
     0         1         2         3         4         5         6         7         8         9
     1234567890123456789012345678901234567890123456789012345678901234567890123456789012345678901234567890123456789
 1
 2
 3
 4  RENT-UR-WHEELS                                                              RUN DATE MM/DD/YY
 5  DAILY RENTAL SUMMARY (8-6)                                                          PAGE ZZ9
 6
 7  LICENSE                    BASIC          C1 INSUR.      NET     C2 INSUR.   SCHED.   PROJECTED
 8  NUMBER   MAKE              RATE     DISC     RATE       RATE     AMOUNT      DAYS      AMOUNT
 9
10  XXXXXXX  XXXXXXXXXXXXXXX   ZZ.99   ZZ.ZZ   ZZ.ZZ      ZZ.ZZ      ZZ.ZZ       Z9     Z,ZZZ.99
11
12  XXXXXXX  XXXXXXXXXXXXXXX   ZZ.99   ZZ.ZZ   ZZ.ZZ      ZZ.ZZ      ZZ.ZZ       Z9     Z,ZZZ.99
13
14
15                            RENTAL SUMMARY TOTALS:  VEHICLES RENTED    ZZ9
16                                                    VEHICLE DAYS       Z,ZZ9
17                                                    PROJECTED GROSS    ZZ,ZZZ.99
18
```

Program operations:

1. Process only those input records with a value R (rented) in the Status field.

2. Calculated quantities for detail output are
   a. Calculate a discount on the Daily-rental-fee (the Basic Rate on the output report) based on the Customer-discount-code and Number-of-days-rented, as follows:

Discount code	Number-of-Days-Rented	
	Less than 14	**14 or greater**
1	4%	4%
2	6%	7%
3	10%	12%
Blank	No discount	No discount

   b. If the Insurance-code-1 field contains Y, calculate a C1-insurance-rate fee of 6.5% the Daily-rental-fee.
   c. Calculate the Net-rate as:

   Daily-rental-fee – Discount + C1-insurance-rate

   d. If the Insurance-code-2 field contains Y, use a C2-insurance-amount of 7.50; otherwise, use zero.

   e. Calculate the Projected-amount as:

   Number-of-days-rented × Net-rate + C2-insurance-amount

   Note: Number-of-days-rented is to be printed as Scheduled Days.

3. Accumulate the following totals:

    Number of vehicles currently rented

    Total number of vehicle days (total of Number-of-days-rented fields)

    Projected gross income (total of Projected-amount fields)

4. Double-space each detail line. Provide for a span of 36 lines per page.

5. After all input records are processed, print the three output-report total lines (triple-spaced from the last detail line) as specified on the print chart.

Programming Assignment 8-7: Screen Record Display

Background information:

Your supervisor requires a program to display records from a data file in either of two forms: (1) single-record display on full screen, or (2) listing form with 18 records per screen.

Input file:

Select whichever file you've used in past assignments.

Output-screen format:

You design. For full-screen display of a single record, use a balanced layout and appropriate descriptions. For the listing form, display a one- or two-line column heading followed by a group of 18 records. You do not need to display all fields from the record if the line length will exceed 80 positions (the screen width). If a problem, you select the fields to display.

Program operations:

1. Display an announcement screen that provides the user with the following three options: (1) full-screen, single-record display, (2) listing display, and (3) terminate the program.

2. For the single-record display, after each record, give the user the option of terminating single-record display or viewing the next record.

3. For the listing display, after each group of 18 records is listed on the screen, give the user the option of terminating listing display or viewing the next 18 records.

4. After terminating either the single-record or the listing option, display the announcement screen and the three user options.

5. If the end-of-file is reached from either screen, notify the user and then return to the announcement screen.

6. Terminate the program only from the announcement screen.

Note: Think carefully about the need for opening and closing the input file.

Programming Assignment 8-8: Searching a File

Background information:

The Century-21 Marketing Agency wants interactive access to individual employee data in their employee file. The user must be able to enter either (1) the employee number or (2) the employee last name, and obtain a full-screen display of the employee data.

Note: This assignment is virtually two programs in one. As an option (if a shorter assignment is desired), you can do either the employee-number search or the employee-name search as a complete program.

Input file: Employee file (EMPLOYEE.DAT)

Employee record   Middle initial ⌐

Employee number	Last name	First name		Employee address	Employee city/state/zip	Telephone ext.
1 2	3 4 5 6 7	8 9 10 11 12 13 14 15 16 17 18	19 20 21 22 23 24 25 26 27 28	29 30 31 32 33 34 35 36 37 38 39 40 41 42 43 44 45 46 47 48 49 50 51	52 53 54 55 56 57 58 59 60 61 62 63 64 65 66 67 68 69 70 71 72 73 74	75 76 77 78

Note: Records of this file are in sequence based on the employee number field. That is, the record with the lowest employee number is first in the file; higher numbers follow, in order.

Output-screen format:

Design a full-screen, single-record display using a balanced layout and appropriate descriptions. Include every field from the record.

Program operations:

1. Display an announcement screen that provides the user with the following three options: (1) search on employee number, (2) search on employee last name, and (3) terminate the program. If you are programming only one of the search options, then the announcement screen should give the user the option of continuing or aborting.

2. For the employee number option:
   a. Accept the employee number from the keyboard of the desired employee.
   b. Search the file by reading one record at a time and comparing the input employee to the employee number of the input record.

      ■ If the fields are equal (record found), display the record.

      ■ If the requested employee number is greater than the input record employee number, read and check the next record.

      ■ If the requested employee number is greater than the input record employee number (or if the end-of-file is detected), display the message RECORD NOT IN FILE.

   c. After a search for an individual record is complete, give the user the option of terminating employee number search or searching for another record.
   d. Upon terminating the search, return control to the announcement screen.

3. For the employee last-name field, proceed as with the employee number field—except take the following steps for item 2(b).
   a. If the fields are equal (record found), display the record.
   b. Ask the user if this is the correct record. If it is not, continue the search (more than one person in the file may have the same last name).
   c. When the end-of-file is detected, display the message END OF FILE ENCOUNTERED.

4. If you are programming both display options, terminate the program only from the announcement screen.

Note: Think carefully about the need for opening and closing the input file.

DESIGNING AND WRITING CONTROL-BREAK PROGRAMS

CHAPTER OUTLINE

CHAPTER OBJECTIVES

In this text's previous programs, we were concerned only with individual records of a file; the relationship of one record to another record within the file was not a factor. Control-break programs require that the records be in proper sequence based on a particular field of the record (called the control field). Furthermore, program logic must compare the control field of each record to the control field of the previous record. From this chapter, you will learn the following:

- The similarity of control-break processing to page-break techniques studied in Chapter 7.

- Single-level control breaks.

- Multiple levels of control breaks.

TOPIC	

A Single-Level Control-Break Program

Introduction to Control-Break Processing

Assume that the Pyramid Sales Company maintains a sales file with one record for each sale made by each sales representative (sales rep) of the company. The sales manager wants a detail listing with a report total showing the total number of units sold by the sales force. To illustrate, consider the abbreviated file of Figure 9-1(a). Calculating the total involves the simple task of accumulating values in the second column.

On the other hand, what if the manager wants the report to also include the total number of units sold by each sales representative? As you can see by looking at the records for representative 10006, this is clumsy because the records for any given representative are scattered throughout the file.

On the other hand, the task is much simpler if records of the file are *sorted* (that is, arranged in sequence) based on the representative number. As you can see in Figure 9-1(b), when the records are in order by representative number, the records for each representative are grouped together. Manually, it is simple to compute the total for each representative. Fortunately, writing a program to compute the individual totals is similar to the mental task you follow when performing a manual calculation.

Here, grouping the records is controlled by one of the data-record fields: the representative number. This field is called the **control field** for the application. As you can see in Figure 9-2, each set of records with the same control field value is called a **control group**. A **control break** occurs whenever a change occurs in the value of the control field. This example is called a **single-level control break** because the control break is based on a single control field. Another example in this chapter illustrates a multiple-level control break.

Actually, you have already studied control groups and control-group processing in its simplest form in Chapter 7. That is, the PATLIST3 program prints a total for each group of records on the printed page. In this simple form of group-total processing, each group was determined by the number of detail lines that fit on a page. Its logic involved:

1. Read the next record.
2. If the page is full (a page break), perform the following page-break operations.
   a. Print the page-total line.
   b. Add the page-total accumulators to the report-total accumulators.
   c. Set the page-total accumulators to zero.
   d. Progress to the next page and print headings.
3. Process the record.

On a broad basis, the logic for control-break processing is similar:

1. Read the next record.
2. If the control-field value for this record is different from that of the preceding record, perform the following control-break operations.
   a. Print the control-group-total line.
   b. Add the control-group-total accumulators to the report-total accumulators.

Figure 9-1
Records in a file.

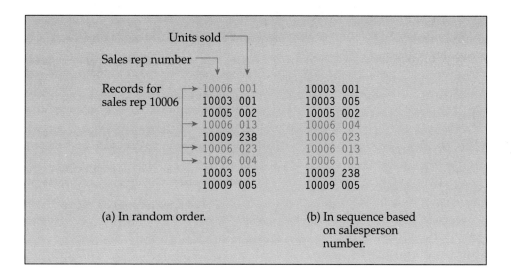

Units sold

Sales rep number

Records for sales rep 10006	10006 001	10003 001
	10003 001	10003 005
	10005 002	10005 002
	10006 013	10006 004
	10009 238	10006 023
	10006 023	10006 013
	10006 004	10006 001
	10003 005	10009 238
	10009 005	10009 005

(a) In random order.

(b) In sequence based on salesperson number.

Figure 9-2
Control groups.

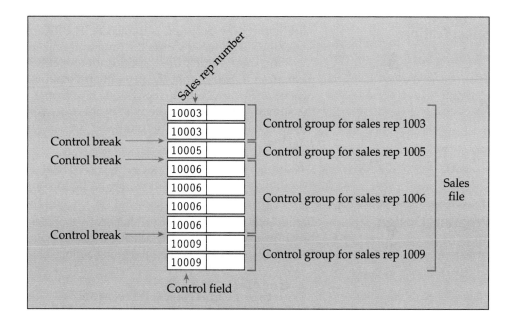

Sales rep number

10003		Control group for sales rep 1003
10003		
10005		Control group for sales rep 1005
10006		
10006		Control group for sales rep 1006
10006		
10006		
10009		Control group for sales rep 1009
10009		

Control break

Control break

Control break

Control field

Sales file

    c. Set the control-group-total accumulators to zero.
    d. Save the control-group value of the record just read.
  3. Process the record.

Essential to control-break processing is the ability to compare the control-field value of the record just read to the value of the preceding record. Step 2d provides for this: the control-group value of the record just read (the one triggering the control break) is saved.

You know from page-control processing that the actual program logic is more complicated than the simple representation here. The added complexity arises from the fact that three pseudo-break conditions require attention: the first record, an actual control break, and the end of the data file. The needs for control-break processing are similar. Figure 9-3's pseudocode illustrates the control-break logic used in this book. This pseudocode represents the control-break test module that will be performed after each record is read.

Figure 9-3
Control-break
processing logic.

```
Evaluate the following case:
  When first record
    Set the control-group accumulators to zero
    Save the control field of the record just read
  When control field is not equal previous control field
    Print the control-group-total line
    Add the control-group accumulators to the report
                                       accumulators
    Set the control-group accumulators to zero
    Save the control field of the record just read
  When end of file
    Print the control-group-total line
    Add the control-group accumulators to the report
                                       accumulators

    Print the report-total line
  Otherwise
    Take no action
```

Programming Specifications

Pyramid Sales Company needs a single-level control-break program to print its sales report. The program is named SCTLBRK, for Single-level ConTroL-BReaK sales report. Figure 9-4 shows the programming specifications.

You should study these specifications carefully before proceeding to the program design. Notice that the print chart contains four heading-line formats, one detail-line format, and one report-total line format. The sales rep-total line includes the sum of the sales of all records for this sales rep; that is, for this control group. As such, it is called a **control total**, and the sales rep-total line is called a **control-total line**.

Program Design

Single-Level Control-Break Structure

Before laying out the structure chart, let's consider how this book handles control-break processing. As with other programs you studied (for instance, refer to PATLIST3 on page 213), the processing actions of the main module include:

```
Open files
Perform Initialize-variable-fields
Repeat the following until end of file
  Read next data record
    If not end of file
      Process data record
Perform needed finish-up actions
Close files
Stop
```

However, with a control-break application, processing requires that special processing be performed when a break occurs. As described earlier, you will use a separate control-break processing module that will fit in as follows:

```
Open files
Perform Initialize-variable-fields
Repeat the following until end of file
  Read next data record
    If not end of file
      Perform module to process control break
      Perform module to process data record
Perform needed finish-up actions
Close files
Stop
```

Figure 9-4   Programming specifications, record layout, print chart, and sample report outline: single-level control-break sales report program—SCTLBRK.

PROGRAMMING SPECIFICATIONS

Program Name: SINGLE-LEVEL CONTROL-BREAK SALES REPORT   Program ID: SCTLBRK

Program Description:

This program is to read input sales records, compute the sales revenue for each record, and print a sales-report detail-line for each sales record.

When the sales-representative number changes, a sales-representative control-total line is to be printed. After all input sales records are processed, a report-total line is to be printed.

Input File:

Sales File

Output File:

Sales Report (single-level)

List of Program Operations:

A. Read each input sales record.

B. For each sales record, the program is to:

    1. Compute the sales-revenue amount by multiplying the unit-price field by the quantity-sold field.

    2. Print a detail-line that contains the following fields in accordance with the format shown on the print chart.
    -Sales-representative number
    -State
    -Branch
    -Date-of-sale
    -Product-code
    -Product-description
    -Unit-price
    -Quantity-sold
    -Sales-revenue

    3. Accumulate the following totals:
    -Total sales-revenue for each sales-representative
    -Total sales-revenue for all sales-representatives

C. Whenever the sales-representative number changes, the program is to print a sales-representative control-total line containing the following fields in accordance with the format shown on the print chart:
-Sales-representative number
-The words "SALES REP. TOTAL"
-Total sales-revenue for that sales-representative
-One asterisk (*)

D. After all the input sales records are processed, the program is to print the following total fields on the report-total line in accordance with the format shown on the print chart:
-The words "REPORT TOTAL"
-Total sales-revenue for all sales-representatives
-Two asterisks (**)

E. Headings are to be printed on each page of the report. After 54 lines have been printed on a page, the program should skip to the next page.

    1. The page number is to be incremented each time the heading is printed and displayed on the first heading-line in accordance with the format shown on the print chart.

    2. The run date is to be obtained from the operating system and printed on the second heading-line in accordance with the format shown on the print chart.

F. Line-spacing is to be handled as follows:

    1. The first detail-line printed after the headings is to be double-spaced from the last heading-line.

    2. Detail-lines for the same sales-representative are to be single-spaced from one another.

    3. Each sales-representative control-total line is to be double-spaced from the previous detail-line.

    4. The first detail-line for each sales-representative is to be triple-spaced from the previous control-total line.

    5. The report-total line is to be triple-spaced from the last sales-representative control-total line.

So, the first-level modules are

Initialize-variable-fields
Process-control-break
Process-detail-record

Figure 9-4 (continued)

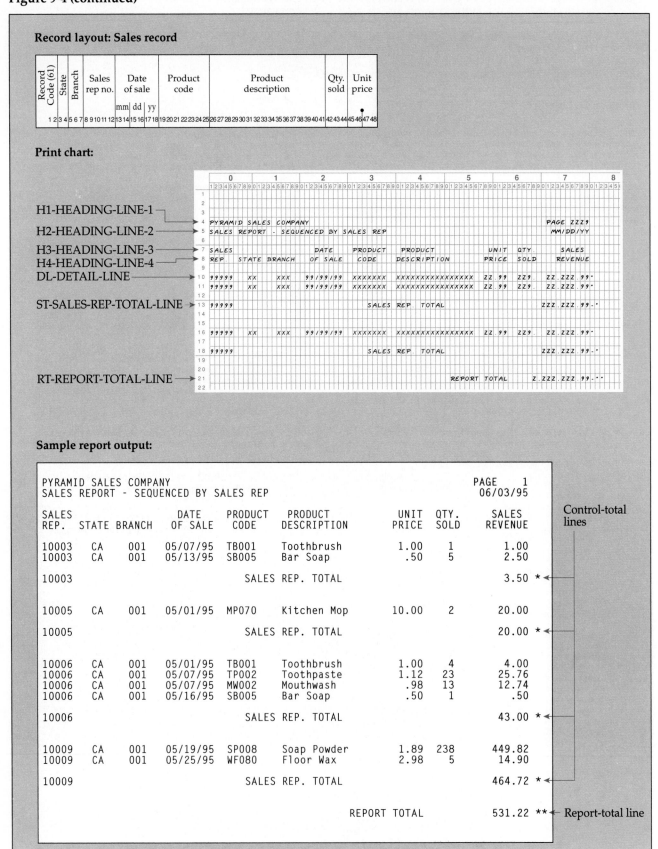

At the second level, modules performed from the Process-control-break module are

```
Print-report-headings (performed on first-record condition)
Print-sales-rep-total-line
Print-report-total-line (performed on end-of-file condition)
```

We must not forget page control: When the printed page is full, the print form must be moved to a new page and page headings printed. The Process-detail-record module will include page-control actions. In a deviation from the structures in earlier programs, detail-line printing is moved to a separate module. So, the Process-detail-record module performs the following subordinate modules:

```
Print-report-headings (performed when a page becomes full)
Print-detail-line
```

The result of filling in the missing pieces is the structure chart of Figure 9-5.

Program Logic— Pseudocode

The overall program logic for this program is relatively straightforward, but it includes two tricky items, both relating to printing.

Line-Spacing Logic

From Chapter 7, remember that the sample programs used single-spacing for detail lines. However, an exception occurred: The first line after the heading lines was double-spaced. This spacing was accomplished by simply printing a blank after the last heading line (and before the first detail line).

If you look at Figure 9-4's print chart and sample output, you will see that line-spacing requirements for this program are even more complicated than

Figure 9-5
Structure chart: Single-level control-break sales report program.

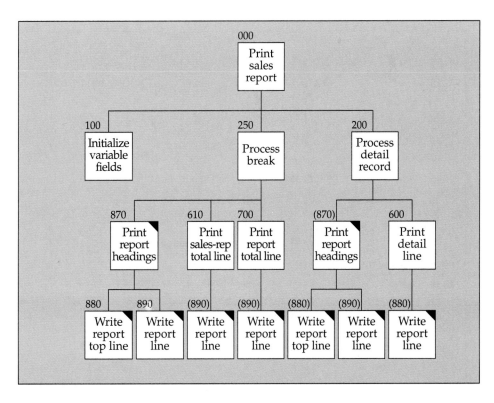

that coded in Chapter 7's programs. That is, detail-line spacing for this single-level control-break application is as follows:

```
Double-space after report headings (one blank line)
Triple-space after control-total lines (two blank lines)
Single-space for all other lines
```

The line-spacing technique introduced in PATLIST3 (Figure 7-12) is readily adapted to these needs. Remember, it involves the following three-step sequence:

Move the detail-line record to the output-line-area

Move the line-spacing value to the line-spacing-variable

Perform the module to write the line after advancing line-spacing-variable lines

Figure 9-6 illustrates a minor variation on this technique. You know that a detail line is printed after the last heading line, so set the line-spacing variable to 2 immediately after printing the heading line. This establishes the line-spacing requirement of the first detail line on the page. Also, you know that a detail line is printed after the group-total line—so after printing this line, set the line-spacing-variable to 3, as required by the next detail line. In other words, print and then set the line spacing for the next print operation. You will see this technique in the pseudocode and the program.

Figure 9-6 Variable line spacing for detail lines.

Write this line, then move 2 to the line-spacing variable.

```
PYRAMID SALES COMPANY                                              PAGE    1
SALES REPORT - SEQUENCED BY SALES REP                             06/03/95

SALES              DATE     PRODUCT   PRODUCT           UNIT  QTY.    SALES
REP.  STATE BRANCH OF SALE  CODE      DESCRIPTION       PRICE SOLD  REVENUE
10003  CA   001    05/07/95 TB001     Toothbrush        1.00   1       1.00
10003  CA   001    05/13/95 SB005     Bar Soap           .50   5       2.50

10003                             SALES REP. TOTAL                    3.50 *

10005  CA   001    05/01/95 MP070     Kitchen Mop      10.00   2      20.00

10005                             SALES REP. TOTAL                   20.00 *

10006  CA   001    05/01/95 TB001     Toothbrush        1.00   4       4.00
10006  CA   001    05/07/95 TP002     Toothpaste        1.12  23      25.76
10006  CA   001    05/07/95 MW002     Mouthwash          .98  13      12.74
10006  CA   001    05/16/95 SB005     Bar Soap           .50   1        .50

10006                             SALES REP. TOTAL                   43.00 *

10009  CA   001    05/19/95 SP008     Soap Powder       1.89 238     449.82
10009  CA   001    05/25/95 WF080     Floor Wax         2.98   5      14.90

10009                             SALES REP. TOTAL                  464.72 *

                                  REPORT TOTAL                      531.22 **
```

Write a detail line, then move 1 to the line-spacing variable.

Write this line, then move 3 to the line-spacing variable.

Test for End-of-Page

This sales report program has two different line formats printed in the body of the report: a detail line and a control-total line. Whenever more than one type of line is printed in the body of a report, a question arises regarding when to test for the full-page condition. For a control-break program, it is usually best to test for headings only when a detail line is printed. So, a test for headings should be omitted when the control-total line is printed. Such processing ensures that control totals are not printed by themselves on a separate page. It is easier to read a report when the totals are together on the same page with the last detail line for the control group.

However, when designing the report, you must ensure that enough room is available to print required control totals when the bottom of the page is reached. So, although the programming specifications state that a line span of up to 57 lines is available, we will design the program to test—before each detail line is printed—whether 54 lines or more were used on the page. If so, a new page is started. If not, that detail line—plus a possible double-spaced total line—will still fit within the 57-line page span (54 lines used plus 1 single-spaced detail line plus 2 lines for the double-spaced control-total line equals 57 lines).

Pseudocode Solution

The pseudocode solution for this control-break application is shown in Figure 9-7. Notice the processing logic: After either a data record is read or the end-of-file is detected (at step 3 of the 000 module), the 250-Process-Break module is executed. Each of the three pseudobreak conditions is checked: first record, change in Sales-rep number, or end of file. Appropriate action is taken in each case. If none of the conditions is true—meaning no control break occurred—nothing happens and control returns to the 000 module.

Another feature evident in the pseudocode is the spacing control for detail-line printing. As described earlier, detail-line spacing is set after the preceding print operation. For instance, steps 11–13 of the 870 module print the last heading line. Then the line-spacing indicator is set for double-spacing (step 14). In the 600 module to print the detail line, that line-spacing value is used unchanged, thereby resulting in double-spacing of the first detail line following the heading. You can see (at step 4) that, after printing the line, the line-spacing value is set to single-spacing for subsequent detail lines. Similarly, in the 610 module to print the group-total line, the line spacing is set to triple-spacing after the group-total line is printed (step 6).

Program Coding

The WORKING-STORAGE SECTION

The complete SCTLBRK program is shown in Figure 9-8. If you check the WORKING-STORAGE SECTION of this program, you see relatively minor differences over that of PATLIST3 from Chapter 7. One of the differences is the use of condition-names for the program switches—for instance:

```
05  S1-END-OF-FILE-SWITCH    PIC X(1).
    88  S1-END-OF-FILE            VALUE "E".
    88  S1-NOT-END-OF-FILE        VALUE "N".
```

The statement

```
SET S1-END-OF-FILE TO TRUE
```

moves a value of E into the switch. Correspondingly, the statement

```
SET S1-NOT-END-OF-FILE TO TRUE
```

Figure 9-7
Pseudocode: single-level control-break sales report program—SCTLBRK.

```
000-Print-Sales-Report module
1.  Open the files.
2.  Perform 100-Initialize-Variable-Fields.
3.  Perform until end of file:
        Read a record from the Sales file
        at end
            Set end-of-file to true
            Perform 250-Process-Break
        not at end
            Perform 250-Process-Break
            Perform 200-Process-Detail-Record.
4.  Close the files.
5.  Stop the run.
100-Initialize-Variable-Fields module
1.  Set the Not-end-of-file switch to true.
2.  Set First-record switch to true.
3.  Set the Page-count and Lines-used fields to zero.
4.  Set the Total-accumulator fields to zero.
5.  Obtain the date from the operating system and move it to
    the heading-line area.
200-Process-Detail-Record module
1.  If page is full
        Perform 870-Print-Report-Headings.
2.  Multiply the input Unit-price by the input Quantity-sold
    to equal the Sales-revenue.
3.  Perform 600-Print-Detail-Line.
4.  Add the Sales-revenue for this record to the Total-sales-
    rep-sales-revenue.
250-Process-Break module
1.  Evaluate the following case:
        When first record
            Move the input Sales-rep field to the
            Previous-sales-rep field.
            Perform 870-Print-Report-Headings.
            Set Not-first-record switch to True.
        When the input Sales-rep field is not equal
        to the Previous-sales-rep field
            Perform 610-Process-End-Of-Sales-Rep.
        When end of file
            Perform 610-Print-Sales-Rep-Total-Line.
            Perform 700-Print-Report-Total-Line.
600-Print-Detail-Line module
1.  Move following input/calculated fields to output area:
        Sales-rep
        State
        Branch
        Date-of-sale
        Product-code
        Product-description
        Quantity-sold
        Unit-price
        Sales-Revenue
2.  Move the detail-line to the output print-line area.
3.  Perform 890-Write-Report-Line.
4.  Set Line-spacing to single-spacing.
610-Process-End-Of-Sales-Rep module
1.  Move the Previous-sales-rep field to the Sales-rep-total-
    line.
2.  Move the Total-sales-rep-sales-revenue to the Sales-rep-
    total-line Sales-revenue.
3.  Move the Sales-rep-total-line to the output print-line
    area.
4.  Set Line-spacing to double-spacing.
```

Figure 9-7 (continued)

```
    5. Perform 880-Write-Report-Line.
    6. Set Line-spacing to triple-spacing.
    7. Add the Total-sales-rep-sales-revenue to the Total-report-
       sales-revenue.
    8. If not end of file
          Move the input Sales-rep field to the Previous-sales-
          rep field.
          Set the Total-sales-rep-sales-revenue to 0.
  700-Print-Report-Total-Line module
    1. Move the Total-report-sales-revenue to the Report-total-
       line.
    2. Move the Report-total-line to the output print-line area.
    3. Set Line-spacing to triple-spacing.
    4. Perform 890-Write-Report-Line.
  870-Print-Report-Headings module
    1.  Add 1 to the Page-count.
    2.  Move the Page-count to the Page-number field in the first
        heading-line.
    3.  Move Heading-line-1 to the output print-line area.
    4.  Perform 880-Write-Report-Top-Line.
    5.  Move Heading-line-2 to the output print-line area.
    6.  Set Line-spacing to single-spacing.
    7.  Perform 890-Write-Report-Line.
    8.  Move Heading-line-3 to the output print-line area.
    9.  Set Line-spacing to double-spacing.
   10.  Perform 890-Write-Report-Line.
   11.  Move Heading-line-4 to the output print-line area.
   12.  Set Line-spacing to single-spacing.
   13.  Perform 890-Write-Report-Line.
   14.  Set Line-spacing to double-spacing.
  880-Print-Report-Top-Line module
    1.  Advance to the top of the next report page and write out
        the output print-line area.
    2.  Set the Lines-used indicator to 1.
  890-Write-Report-Line module
    1.  Advance the forms in accordance with the value in the
        Line-spacing indicator field and write the output print-
        line area.
    2.  Add the Line-spacing indicator to the Lines-used field.
```

moves a value of N into the switch. Notice the values used: E to indicate End-of-file and N to indicate Not end-of-file. Any entries could be used because the program refers only to the condition-names.

The other switch defined in this switch record indicates the first record (S2-FIRST-RECORD/S2-NOT-FIRST-RECORD). You will see how this is used in the PROCEDURE DIVISION description.

Accumulators and other working variables are almost identical to their counterparts in PATLIST3. The significant addition is the field RC-PREV-SALES-REP (line 58). This field is used to save the sales representative number when looking for a control break (change in sales representative number).

The input record description, the heading lines, the detail line, the group-total line, and the report-total line are all coded in accordance with the programming specifications.

Stepping Through the PROCEDURE DIVISION

At a glance, the PROCEDURE DIVISION looks much like that of the page-break program PATLIST3 from Chapter 7. The significant difference, of course, is the way in which the control-break condition is handled. Each of the two pseudo-breaks is controlled by a program switch (S1-END-OF-FILE/S1-NOT-END-OF-FILE

Figure 9-8   SCTLBRK: single-level control-break sales report program.

```
 1    IDENTIFICATION DIVISION.                          71    01  SR-SALES-RECORD.
 2    PROGRAM-ID.    SCTLBRK.                           72        05  SR-RECORD-CODE          PIC X(2).
 3                                                      73        05  SR-STATE                PIC X(2).
 4  * Written by T. Welburn 2-27-86.                    74        05  SR-BRANCH               PIC X(3).
 5  * Revised 9-18-89 & 1-17-95 by W. Price.            75        05  SR-SALES-REP            PIC X(5).
 6  * PYRAMID SALES COMPANY.                            76        05  SR-DATE-OF-SALE         PIC X(6).
 7                                                      77        05  SR-PRODUCT-CODE         PIC X(7).
 8  * This program reads sales records, computes the sales  78    05  SR-PRODUCT-DESCRIPTION  PIC X(16).
 9  * revenue for each sales record, and prints a sales 79        05  SR-QUANTITY-SOLD        PIC S9(3).
10  * detail line for each sales record.                80        05  SR-UNIT-PRICE           PIC 9(2)V99.
11                                                      81
12  * When the Sales Rep number changes, a Sales-Rep    82    01  H1-HEADING-LINE-1.
13  * total line is printed.                            83        05          PIC X(70)  VALUE "PYRAMID SALES COMPANY".
14                                                      84        05          PIC X(5)   VALUE "PAGE ".
15  * After all records are processed, a report total line 85    05  H1-PAGE-NBR PIC ZZZ9.
16  * is printed.                                       86
17                                                      87    01  H2-HEADING-LINE-2.
18                                                      88        05          PIC X(71)
19    ENVIRONMENT DIVISION.                             89            VALUE "SALES REPORT - SEQUENCED BY SALES REP".
20                                                      90        05  H2-RUN-MONTH PIC Z9.
21    INPUT-OUTPUT SECTION.                             91        05          PIC X(1)   VALUE "/".
22                                                      92        05  H2-RUN-DAY   PIC 9(2).
23    FILE-CONTROL.                                     93        05          PIC X(1)   VALUE "/".
24        SELECT SALES-FILE                             94        05  H2-RUN-YEAR PIC 9(2).
25            ASSIGN TO (system dependent).             95
26        SELECT SALES-REPORT                           96    01  H3-HEADING-LINE-3.
27            ASSIGN TO (system dependent).             97        05          PIC X(22)  VALUE "SALES".
28                                                      98        05          PIC X(36)
29                                                      99            VALUE "DATE     PRODUCT    PRODUCT".
30    DATA DIVISION.                                    100       05          PIC X(20)  VALUE "UNIT QTY.      SALES".
31                                                      101
32    FILE SECTION.                                     102   01  H4-HEADING-LINE-4.
33                                                      103       05          PIC X(39)
34    FD  SALES-FILE.                                   104           VALUE "REP.  STATE BRANCH   OF SALE   CODE".
35    01  SALES-RECORD.                                 105       05          PIC X(40)
36        05  PIC X(48).                                106           VALUE "DESCRIPTION       PRICE  SOLD    REVENUE".
37                                                      107
38    FD  SALES-REPORT.                                 108   01  DL-DETAIL-LINE.
39    01  SALES-REPORT-LINE.                            109       05  DL-SALES-REP            PIC X(5).
40        05  PIC X(132).                               110       05                          PIC X(3)   VALUE SPACES.
41                                                      111       05  DL-STATE                PIC X(2).
42    WORKING-STORAGE SECTION.                          112       05                          PIC X(4)   VALUE SPACES.
43                                                      113       05  DL-BRANCH               PIC X(3).
44    01  PROGRAM-SWITCHES.                             114       05                          PIC X(3)   VALUE SPACES.
45        05  S1-END-OF-FILE-SWITCH   PIC X(1).         115       05  DL-DATE-OF-SALE         PIC XX/XX/XX.
46            88  S1-END-OF-FILE          VALUE "E".    116       05                          PIC X(2)   VALUE SPACES.
47            88  S1-NOT-END-OF-FILE      VALUE "N".    117       05  DL-PRODUCT-CODE         PIC X(7).
48        05  S2-FIRST-RECORD-SWITCH  PIC X(1).         118       05                          PIC X(2)   VALUE SPACES.
49            88  S2-FIRST-RECORD         VALUE "F".    119       05  DL-PRODUCT-DESCRIPTION  PIC X(16).
50            88  S2-NOT-FIRST-RECORD     VALUE "N".    120       05                          PIC X(2)   VALUE SPACES.
51                                                      121       05  DL-UNIT-PRICE           PIC ZZ.99.
52                                                      122       05                          PIC X(2)   VALUE SPACES.
53    01  RC-REPORT-CONTROLS.                           123       05  DL-QUANTITY-SOLD        PIC ZZ9-.
54        05  RC-PAGE-COUNT           PIC 9(4).         124       05                          PIC X(2)   VALUE SPACES.
55        05  RC-LINES-PER-PAGE       PIC 9(2)  VALUE 54. 125     05  DL-SALES-REVENUE        PIC ZZ,ZZZ.99-.
56        05  RC-LINES-USED           PIC 9(2).         126
57        05  RC-LINE-SPACING         PIC 9(2).         127   01  ST-SALES-REP-TOTAL-LINE.
58        05  RC-PREV-SALES-REP       PIC X(5).         128       05  ST-SALES-REP            PIC X(5).
59                                                      129       05                          PIC X(28)  VALUE SPACES.
60    01  WA-WORK-AREAS.                                130       05                          PIC X(16)  VALUE "SALES REP. TOTAL".
61        05  WA-RUN-DATE.                              131       05                          PIC X(20)  VALUE SPACES.
62            10  WA-RUN-YEAR         PIC 9(2).         132       05  ST-SALES-REVENUE        PIC ZZZ,ZZZ.99-.
63            10  WA-RUN-MONTH        PIC 9(2).         133       05                          PIC X(1)   VALUE "*".
64            10  WA-RUN-DAY          PIC 9(2).         134
65        05  WA-SALES-REVENUE        PIC S9(5)V99.     135   01  RT-REPORT-TOTAL-LINE.
66                                                      136       05                          PIC X(50)  VALUE SPACES.
67    01  TA-TOTAL-ACCUMULATORS.                        137       05                          PIC X(12)  VALUE "REPORT TOTAL".
68        05  TA-TOTAL-SALES-REP-ACCUM PIC S9(6)V99.    138       05                          PIC X(5)   VALUE SPACES.
69        05  TA-TOTAL-REPORT-ACCUM   PIC S9(7)V99.     139       05  RT-SALES-REVENUE        PIC Z,ZZZ,ZZZ.99-.
70                                                      140       05                          PIC X(2)   VALUE "**".
```

and S2-FIRST-RECORD/S2-NOT-FIRST-RECORD). To give you a better insight into this program, consider what takes place if the input file contains three data records with the following sales representative numbers:

    1003
    1003
    1005
    end-of-file

Figure 9-8 (continued)

```
141                                                    208    600-PRINT-DETAIL-LINE.
142                                                    209        MOVE SR-SALES-REP TO DL-SALES-REP
143    PROCEDURE DIVISION.                             210        MOVE SR-STATE TO DL-STATE
144                                                    211        MOVE SR-BRANCH TO DL-BRANCH
145    000-PRINT-SALES-REPORT.                         212        MOVE SR-DATE-OF-SALE TO DL-DATE-OF-SALE
146                                                    213        MOVE SR-PRODUCT-CODE TO DL-PRODUCT-CODE
147    ************Initialization Sequence************ 214        MOVE SR-PRODUCT-DESCRIPTION TO DL-PRODUCT-DESCRIPTION
148        OPEN INPUT SALES-FILE                       215        MOVE SR-UNIT-PRICE TO DL-UNIT-PRICE
149             OUTPUT SALES-REPORT                    216        MOVE SR-QUANTITY-SOLD TO DL-QUANTITY-SOLD
150        PERFORM 100-INITIALIZE-VARIABLE-FIELDS      217        MOVE WA-SALES-REVENUE TO DL-SALES-REVENUE
151                                                    218        MOVE DL-DETAIL-LINE TO SALES-REPORT-LINE
152    ************Processing Sequence************     219        PERFORM 890-WRITE-REPORT-LINE
153        PERFORM UNTIL S1-END-OF-FILE                220        MOVE 1 TO RC-LINE-SPACING
154            READ SALES-FILE INTO SR-SALES-RECORD    221        .
155                AT END                              222    610-PROCESS-END-OF-SALES-REP.
156                    SET S1-END-OF-FILE TO TRUE      223        MOVE RC-PREV-SALES-REP TO ST-SALES-REP
157                    PERFORM 250-PROCESS-BREAK       224        MOVE TA-TOTAL-SALES-REP-ACCUM TO ST-SALES-REVENUE
158                NOT AT END                          225        MOVE ST-SALES-REP-TOTAL-LINE TO SALES-REPORT-LINE
159                    PERFORM 250-PROCESS-BREAK       226        MOVE 2 TO RC-LINE-SPACING
160                    PERFORM 200-PROCESS-DETAIL-RECORD 227      PERFORM 890-WRITE-REPORT-LINE
161            END-READ                                228        MOVE 3 TO RC-LINE-SPACING
162        END-PERFORM                                 229    *   Sales-Rep break housekeeping
163                                                    230        ADD TA-TOTAL-SALES-REP-ACCUM TO TA-TOTAL-REPORT-ACCUM
164    ************Termination Sequence************    231        IF S1-NOT-END-OF-FILE
165        CLOSE SALES-FILE                            232            MOVE SR-SALES-REP TO RC-PREV-SALES-REP
166              SALES-REPORT                          233            MOVE ZEROS TO TA-TOTAL-SALES-REP-ACCUM
167        STOP RUN                                    234        END-IF
168        .                                           235        .
169    **************************************************  236    700-PRINT-REPORT-TOTAL-LINE.
170                                                    237        MOVE TA-TOTAL-REPORT-ACCUM TO RT-SALES-REVENUE
171    100-INITIALIZE-VARIABLE-FIELDS.                 238        MOVE RT-REPORT-TOTAL-LINE TO SALES-REPORT-LINE
172        SET S1-NOT-END-OF-FILE TO TRUE              239        MOVE 3 TO RC-LINE-SPACING
173        SET S2-FIRST-RECORD TO TRUE                 240        PERFORM 890-WRITE-REPORT-LINE
174        INITIALIZE TA-TOTAL-ACCUMULATORS            241        .
175        MOVE ZERO TO RC-PAGE-COUNT                  242    870-PRINT-REPORT-HEADINGS.
176                   RC-LINES-USED                    243        ADD 1 TO RC-PAGE-COUNT
177        ACCEPT WA-RUN-DATE FROM DATE                244        MOVE RC-PAGE-COUNT TO H1-PAGE-NBR
178        MOVE WA-RUN-MONTH TO H2-RUN-MONTH           245        MOVE H1-HEADING-LINE-1 TO SALES-REPORT-LINE
179        MOVE WA-RUN-DAY TO H2-RUN-DAY               246        PERFORM 880-WRITE-REPORT-TOP-LINE
180        MOVE WA-RUN-YEAR TO H2-RUN-YEAR             247        MOVE H2-HEADING-LINE-2 TO SALES-REPORT-LINE
181        .                                           248        MOVE 1 TO RC-LINE-SPACING
182    200-PROCESS-DETAIL-RECORD.                      249        PERFORM 890-WRITE-REPORT-LINE
183        IF RC-LINES-USED IS NOT LESS THAN RC-LINES-PER-PAGE 250 MOVE H3-HEADING-LINE-3 TO SALES-REPORT-LINE
184            PERFORM 870-PRINT-REPORT-HEADINGS       251        MOVE 2 TO RC-LINE-SPACING
185        END-IF                                      252        PERFORM 890-WRITE-REPORT-LINE
186        MULTIPLY SR-UNIT-PRICE BY SR-QUANTITY-SOLD  253        MOVE H4-HEADING-LINE-4 TO SALES-REPORT-LINE
187            GIVING WA-SALES-REVENUE                 254        MOVE 1 TO RC-LINE-SPACING
188        PERFORM 600-PRINT-DETAIL-LINE               255        PERFORM 890-WRITE-REPORT-LINE
189        ADD WA-SALES-REVENUE TO TA-TOTAL-SALES-REP-ACCUM 256    MOVE 2 TO RC-LINE-SPACING
190        .                                           257        .
191    250-PROCESS-BREAK.                              258    880-WRITE-REPORT-TOP-LINE.
192        EVALUATE TRUE                               259        WRITE SALES-REPORT-LINE
193                                                    260            AFTER ADVANCING PAGE
194            WHEN S2-FIRST-RECORD                    261        MOVE 1 TO RC-LINES-USED
195                MOVE SR-SALES-REP TO RC-PREV-SALES-REP 262     .
196                PERFORM 870-PRINT-REPORT-HEADINGS   263    890-WRITE-REPORT-LINE.
197                SET S2-NOT-FIRST-RECORD TO TRUE     264        WRITE SALES-REPORT-LINE
198                                                    265            AFTER ADVANCING RC-LINE-SPACING
199            WHEN SR-SALES-REP NOT EQUAL TO RC-PREV-SALES-REP 266  ADD RC-LINE-SPACING TO RC-LINES-USED
200                PERFORM 610-PROCESS-END-OF-SALES-REP 267        .
201
202            WHEN S1-END-OF-FILE
203                PERFORM 610-PROCESS-END-OF-SALES-REP
204                PERFORM 700-PRINT-REPORT-TOTAL-LINE
205
206        END-EVALUATE
207        .
```

1. In the 100 module, the two switches are set: S1-NOT-END-OF-FILE to True and S2-FIRST-RECORD to True, reflecting the beginning conditions.
2. When the first record is read (line 154), the NOT AT END option is exercised and the 250 module is performed (from line 159).
3. In the EVALUATE of the 250 module, the S2-FIRST-RECORD condition is true, so that option is executed (this is the first-record pseudo-break), resulting in:

   a. The first sales representative number (1003) is moved to the save area (RC-PREV-SALES-REP).

   b. The first-page headings are printed.

    c. The first-record switch is turned off by setting S2-NOT-FIRST-RECORD to true.

    d. Execution of this module is completed and control is returned to the calling 000 module to resume at line 160.

4. The input record is processed in the 200 module.

5. The second record with a sales representative number 1003 is read (line 154), the NOT AT END option is exercised, and the 250 module is performed (from line 159).

6. In the EVALUATE of the 250 module, all three conditions are false. Remember, both SR-SALES-REP (the input sales representative number) and RC-PREV-SALES-REP (the previous sales representative number) contain 1003. Therefore, no action occurs in this module and control returns to the 000 module.

7. The second record is processed.

8. The third record with a sales representive number 1005 is read (line 154), the NOT AT END option is exercised, and the 250 module is performed (from line 159).

9. In the EVALUATE of the 250 module, the second WHEN option (line 199)

```
SR-SALES-REP NOT EQUAL TO RC-PREV-SALES-REP
```

is true because SR-SALES-REP (the input sales representative number) contains 1005 and RC-PREV-SALES-REP (the previous sales representative number) contains 1003. So, the 610 module is performed (from line 200).

10. In the 610 module, the group-total line is printed and the group total is added to the report total. Since S1-NOT-END-OF-FILE is true, the latest sales representative number is saved and the group-total accumulator is set to zero. Control returns to the 250 module and immediately to the 000 module to resume at line 160.

11. The third record is processed.

12. The READ is executed a fourth time, thereby reading the end-of-file, which causes the AT END sequence to be executed.

13. S1-END-OF-FILE is set to True (line 156) and the 250 module is performed (from line 157). This represents the end-of-file pseudo-break.

14. In the EVALUATE, the first two conditions are false, but the S1-END-OF-FILE condition is true. So, the 610 and 700 modules are performed (from lines 203 and 204), printing the final sales representative total line and the report-total line.

15. Upon return to the 000 module, the inline PERFORM is completed and execution falls through—closing the files and terminating the program.

Other Factors Relating to SCTLBRK

The preceding sequence of steps should give you a good insight into the nature of this program, and to control-break processing in general. However, you should notice several other elements. In the 610 module to print the group-total line (including the sales representative number for that group), look at the following MOVE statement (line 223):

```
MOVE RC-PREV-SALES-REP TO ST-SALES-REP
```

Notice that RC-PREV-SALES-REP, *not* RC-SALES-REP, is moved to the group-total line for printing. Remember, the control break is caused by detection of a new sales representative number. RC-SALES-REP contains this new number; RC-PREV-SALES-REP contains the number of the sales representive whose group total is being printed.

In the 610 module, saving the sales representative number and zeroing the accumulator are done conditionally; they are not done if an end-of-file condition has occurred. What if the IF statement were deleted and these two actions were carried out on the end-of-file condition? The answer is that it makes no difference because these fields are not used in the program's "finish-up" sequence. Since no record is read into the input area SR-SALES-RECORD upon detecting the end-of-file, the sales representative number from the last data record remains and is moved. However, think of the documentation implication. That is, if the actions are carried out at this point, you might forget the reason during later program maintenance. Generally, this is not good programming practice. The IF statement avoids any misunderstanding.

One other element of this program is critical to its proper functioning: the sequencing of the WHEN clauses in the EVALUATE. The sequence in SCTLBRK is

> When first record
>> do first-record actions
> When control break
>> do control-break actions
> When end of file
>> do end-of-file actions

Technically, the first and second conditions are not mutually exclusive. That is, on the first record condition, the control-break condition *is also true*. Of course, the latter is not executed because the first-record condition is encountered first. However, if this sequence were changed to the following, the program would not function properly:

> When control break
>> do control-break actions
> When first record
>> do first-record actions
> When end of file
>> do end-of-file actions

When the first record is read, the value in the save area RC-PREV-SALES-REP is undefined. The control-break condition (new number different from the old one) occurs, treating this as a full control break.

As a rule, conditions that are not mutually exclusive (and thereby depend on sequencing within the EVALUATE) are risky to use. However, that approach in control-break processing is not unreasonable because the required sequencing is a logical one that is easily carried over to multiple-level control-break programming.

Two Alternate Forms of the EVALUATE

If you feel uncomfortable with the sequencing requirement of this application of the EVALUATE, Figure 9-9's form avoids its potential problem. Recall that single-level break processing involves three pseudo-breaks: first-record, normal break, and end-of-file. A normal break occurs when

> First-record is false
> The control-field value changes
> End-of-file is false

Corresponding to this, in Figure 9-9, you see that a sales-representative break explicitly requires: (1) a change in the sales representative number, *and* (2) no first-record condition, *and* (3) no end-of-file condition.

Figure 9-9
Alternate coding for the
EVALUATE statement—
multiple-condition test.

```
      EVALUATE TRUE

  *     No records in file
        WHEN S2-FIRST-RECORD
          AND S1-END-OF-FILE
            PERFORM 990-EMPTY-FILE-ERROR

  *     Process first record
        WHEN S2-FIRST-RECORD
          AND S1-NOT-END-OF-FILE
            MOVE SR-SALES-REP TO RC-PREV-SALES-REP
            PERFORM 870-PRINT-REPORT-HEADINGS
            SET S2-NOT-FIRST-RECORD TO TRUE

  *     Sales-representative break
        WHEN SR-SALES-REP NOT EQUAL TO RC-PREV-SALES-REP
          AND S2-NOT-FIRST-RECORD
          AND S1-NOT-END-OF-FILE
            PERFORM 610-PROCESS-END-OF-SALES-REP

  *     End of file
        WHEN S1-END-OF-FILE
          AND S2-NOT-FIRST-RECORD
            PERFORM 610-PRINT-SALES-REP-TOTAL-LINE
            PERFORM 700-PRINT-REPORT-TOTAL-LINE

      END-EVALUATE
```

This example sequence also illustrates another feature. What if you want to perform an error routine on a file containing no records? The first WHEN takes care of this possibility since, for an empty file, the first record read is the end-of-file record. So, both S2-FIRST-RECORD and S1-END-OF-FILE are true and the error-processing sequence is performed.

With this complete set of test conditions, you can see that the options are all mutually exclusive and the order of the WHENs has no bearing on execution of the program.

Still another form exists that presents the conditions in a tabular form and provides excellent documentation. Remember from Chapter 7 that the ALSO feature of the EVALUATE allows you to set up multiple subjects (tests listed following EVALUATE) and corresponding objects (conditions following the WHEN). Four of Figure 9-10's five WHEN clauses correspond to those of Figure 9-9. For instance, compare the control break WHEN forms of the two examples (the second WHEN in Figure 9-10 and the third in Figure 9-9). They both require the following:

S2-FIRST-RECORD condition FALSE (S2-NOT-FIRST-RECORD condition TRUE)

SR-SALES-REP NOT = RC-PREV-SALES-REP condition TRUE

S1-END-OF-FILE condition FALSE (S1-NOT-END-OF-FILE condition TRUE)

Also, in the first-record test of Figure 9-10 (the third WHEN), you can see that S2-FIRST-RECORD is tested for TRUE and S1-END-OF-FILE is tested for FALSE. Including the word ANY as the object for the sales representative number compare means that particular test is not even made, which is correct on the first-record test. Note that the same is true for the end-of-file condition.

Another advantage of Figure 9-10's form is that the first WHEN immediately terminates execution of the EVALUATE if no break has occurred.

**Alternate Forms
for COBOL-74**

Unfortunately, the powerful EVALUATE statement is not part of COBOL-74, so nested IF statements must be used. The code segment of Figure 9-11(a) is equivalent to the EVALUATE used in the program of Figure 9-8 (lines 192–206). It is sequence dependent and does not test for the empty file condition.

Figure 9-10
Alternate coding for the
EVALUATE statement—
using the ALSO clause.

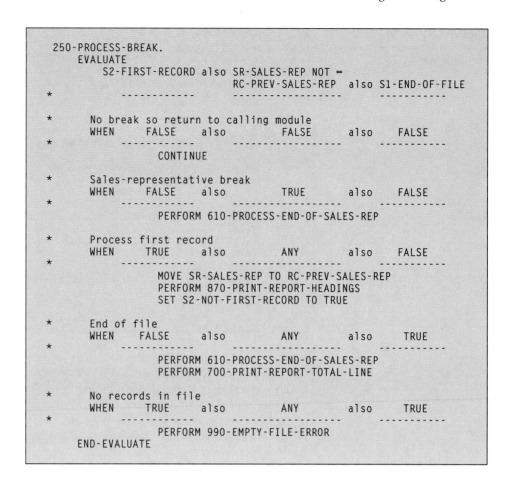

```
250-PROCESS-BREAK.
    EVALUATE
        S2-FIRST-RECORD also SR-SALES-REP NOT =
                              RC-PREV-SALES-REP  also S1-END-OF-FILE
*        ------------      ------------------      -----------

*      No break so return to calling module
       WHEN     FALSE   also        FALSE      also   FALSE
*        ------------      ------------------      -----------
                    CONTINUE

*      Sales-representative break
       WHEN     FALSE   also         TRUE      also   FALSE
*        ------------      ------------------      -----------
                    PERFORM 610-PROCESS-END-OF-SALES-REP

*      Process first record
       WHEN     TRUE    also         ANY       also   FALSE
*        ------------      ------------------      -----------
                    MOVE SR-SALES-REP TO RC-PREV-SALES-REP
                    PERFORM 870-PRINT-REPORT-HEADINGS
                    SET S2-NOT-FIRST-RECORD TO TRUE

*      End of file
       WHEN     FALSE   also         ANY       also   TRUE
*        ------------      ------------------      -----------
                    PERFORM 610-PROCESS-END-OF-SALES-REP
                    PERFORM 700-PRINT-REPORT-TOTAL-LINE

*      No records in file
       WHEN     TRUE    also         ANY       also   TRUE
*        ------------      ------------------      -----------
                    PERFORM 990-EMPTY-FILE-ERROR
    END-EVALUATE
```

Figure 9-11
Alternate coding for
COBOL-74.

```
**************Processing Sequence**************
     PERFORM 150-READ-INPUT-RECORD
              UNTIL S1-END-OF-FILE.
     :
 150-READ-INPUT-RECORD
       READ SALES-FILE INTO SR-SALES-RECORD
         AT END
             MOVE "E" TO S1-END-OF-FILE-SWITCH
             PERFORM 250-PROCESS-BREAK.
         IF NOT END-OF-FILE
             PERFORM 250-PROCESS-BREAK
             PERFORM 200-PROCESS-DETAIL-RECORD.
     :
 250-PROCESS-BREAK.
     IF FIRST-RECORD
         MOVE SR-SALES-REP TO RC-PREV-SALES-REP
         PERFORM 870-PRINT-REPORT-HEADINGS
         MOVE "N" TO S2-FIRST-RECORD-SWITCH
     ELSE
     IF SR-SALES-REP NOT = RC-PREV-SALES-REP
         PERFORM 610-PROCESS-END-OF-SALES-REP
     ELSE
     IF END-OF-FILE
         PERFORM 610-PROCESS-END-OF-SALES-REP
         PERFORM 700-PRINT-REPORT-TOTAL-LINE.  ⟵ Period is only here
```

(a) Substitute for EVALUATE of Figure 9-8.   (continues)

Figure 9-11 (continued)

```
250-PROCESS-BREAK.
    IF  S2-FIRST-RECORD
    AND S1-END-OF-FILE
        PERFORM 990-EMPTY-FILE-ERROR
    ELSE
    IF  FIRST-RECORD
    AND S2-NOT-END-OF-FILE
        MOVE SR-SALES-REP TO RC-PREV-SALES-REP
        PERFORM 870-PRINT-REPORT-HEADINGS
        MOVE "N" TO S2-FIRST-RECORD-SWITCH
    ELSE
    IF  SR-SALES-REP NOT = RC-PREV-SALES-REP
    AND S1-NOT-FIRST-RECORD
    AND S2-NOT-END-OF-FILE
        PERFORM 610-PROCESS-END-OF-SALES-REP
    ELSE
    IF  END-OF-FILE
    AND S2-NOT-FIRST-RECORD
        PERFORM 610-PROCESS-END-OF-SALES-REP
        PERFORM 700-PRINT-REPORT-TOTAL-LINE.  ⟵ Period is only here
```

(b) Substitute for EVALUATE of Figure 9-9.

On the other hand, the nested IF conditions are expanded in Figure 9-11(b) so that it is equivalent to the form of Figure 9-9. In both cases, notice the use of periods to indicate the scope of each of the conditional components. Since the nested IF of the 250 module is to be treated as a single case statement, a period is included only at the end of the last statement (the end of the paragraph, in this case).

<hr>

TOPIC

A Multiple-Level Control-Break Program

In the preceding program example, group totals were printed after each change in the sales representative number; this is single-level control-break processing. If you refer to the record layout of Figure 9-4 (page 284), you will see that positions 5–7 contain the Branch—the branch office to which each sales representative is assigned. This gives the capability to generate a sales report in which group totals are printed for each sales representative and—on a broader basis—for each branch office. The branch totals are the sum of all the sales representative totals for that branch. This is a *two-level* control-break application. If you look at the input record again, you see that positions 3–4 contain the State field. From this, you can produce a *three-level* report in which sales representative totals within branch totals within state totals are printed.

Figure 9-12 illustrates the concept of multiple-level control groups (three levels, in this case). Generally, **multiple-level control-break** processing requires one control field for each control-break level. The most inclusive control field—the State field in this case—is called the **major control field**. The next control-level field—the Branch field in this case—is called the **intermediate control field**. Finally, the lowest control-level field—the Sales representative number field—is called the **minor control field**.

Obviously, in order to generate a multiple-level control-break report, records of the file must be grouped within their respective control groups. If they are not

Figure 9-12
Example of multiple-level
control groups.

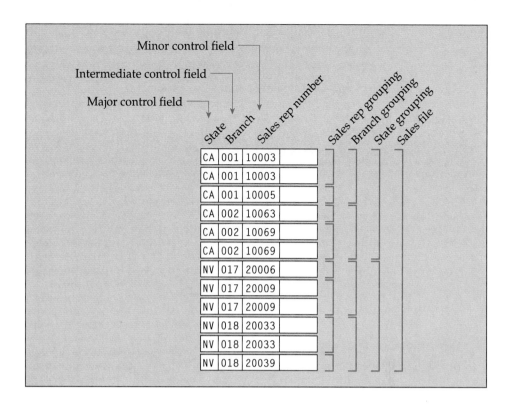

already in the proper order, they can be rearranged by sorting based on the respective control fields. Chapter 13 describes COBOL sorting.

To illustrate a multiple-level control-break program, the single-level sales report program is used as a base. Since most of the programming specifications, design documentation, and coding for this multiple-level control-break sales report program duplicates that of the single-level program, all modifications and new material are highlighted in the applicable illustrations.

Programming Specifications/Input-Record Layout

Instead of printing only sales representative control totals—as was done in the single-level SCTLBRK program—this program prints sales representative totals within branch office totals within state totals. A report total is also printed. The name of the program is MCTLBRK (for Multiple-level ConTroL-BReaK sales report). Figure 9-13 shows the programming specifications. As you can see, the input sales record format is exactly the same as it is for the single-level sales report program.

Print Chart

In the single-level program report, the control field—Sales-representative-number—is printed on the left for convenient reference (see Figure 9-4's print chart, page 284). The State, Branch, and other fields follow.

On the other hand, a multiple-level control-break report is usually easier to read and understand when control fields are arranged in major-field to minor-field order across the line. As you can see by referring to Figure 9-13's print chart, the field sequence is State, Branch, and Sales-representative-number.

In the print chart, you can also see the additional control-total lines for branch and state totals. Notice that on the sales representative control-total line, the applicable state, branch, and sales representative number are printed. Similarly, on the branch control-total line, the state and branch are displayed. (A sales representative number is not displayed for obvious reasons: This level does

Figure 9-13 Programming specifications: multiple-level control-break sales report program.

PROGRAMMING SPECIFICATIONS

Program Name: **MULTIPLE-LEVEL CONTROL-BREAK SALES REPORT**   Program ID: **MCTLBRK**

Program Description:

This program is to read input sales records, compute the sales revenue for each record, and print a sales-report detail-line for each sales record.

Sales-representative control-total lines are printed for each sales-representative within each branch within each state. Branch control-total lines are printed for each branch within each state. A state control-total line is printed for each state. After all input-sales records are processed, a report-total line is to be printed.

Input File:

Sales File

Output File:

Sales Report (multiple-level)

List of Program Operations:

A. **Read each input sales record.**

B. **For each sales record, the program is to:**
   1. **Compute the sales-revenue amount by multiplying the unit-price field by the quantity-sold field.**
   2. **Print a detail-line that contains the following fields in accordance with the format shown on the print chart.**
     -State
     -Branch
     -Sales-representative number
     -Date-of-sale
     -Product-code
     -Product-description
     -Unit-price
     -Quantity-sold
     -Sales-revenue
   3. **Accumulate the following totals:**
     -Total sales-revenue for each sales-representative
     -Total sales-revenue for each branch
     -Total sales-revenue for each state
     -Total sales-revenue for all sales-representatives

C. **Whenever the sales-representative number (within branch and within state) changes, the program is to print a sales-representative control-total line containing the following fields in accordance with the format shown on the print chart:**
   -State
   -Branch
   -Sales-representative number
   -The words "SALES REP. TOTAL"
   -Total sales-revenue for that sales-representative
   -One asterisk (*)

D. Whenever the branch (within state) changes, the program is to print a branch control-total line containing the following fields in accordance with the format shown on the print chart:
   -State
   -Branch
   -The words "BRANCH TOTAL"
   -Total sales-revenue for that branch
   -Two asterisks (**)

E. Whenever the state changes, the program is to print a state control-total line containing the following fields in accordance with the format shown on the print chart:
   -State
   -The words "STATE TOTAL"
   -Total sales-revenue for that state
   -Three asterisks (***)

F. **After all the input sales records are processed, the program is to print the following total fields on the report-total line in accordance with the format shown on the print chart:**
   -The words "REPORT TOTAL"
   -Total sales-revenue for all sales-representatives
   -Four asterisks (****)

G. Headings are to be printed on each page of the report. After 54 lines have been printed on a page, the program should skip to the next page.
   1. The page number is to be incremented each time the heading is printed and displayed on the first heading-line in accordance with the format shown on the print chart.
   2. The run date is to be obtained from the operating system and printed on the second heading-line in accordance with the format shown on the print chart.

H. Line-spacing is to be handled as follows:
   1. The first detail-line printed after the headings is to be double-spaced from the last heading-line.
   2. Detail-lines for the same sales-representative are to be single-spaced from one another.
   3. Each control-total line is to be double-spaced from the previous line.
   4. The first detail-line for each sales-representative is to be triple-spaced from the previous control-total.
   5. The report-total line is to be triple-spaced from the last state-control-total line.

Record layout: Sales record

Record Code (61)	State	Branch	Sales rep no.	Date of sale (mm dd yy)	Product code	Product description	Qty. sold	Unit price
1 2	3	4 5 6 7	8 9 10 11 12	13 14 15 16 17 18	19 20 21 22 23 24 25	26 27 28 29 30 31 32 33 34 35 36 37 38 39 40 41	42 43 44	45 46 47 48

Figure 9-13 (continued)

Print chart:

H1-HEADING-LINE-1
H2-HEADING-LINE-2
H3-HEADING-LINE-3
H4-HEADING-LINE-4
DL-DETAIL-LINE

CT-CONTROL-TOTAL-LINE

RT-REPORT-TOTAL-LINE

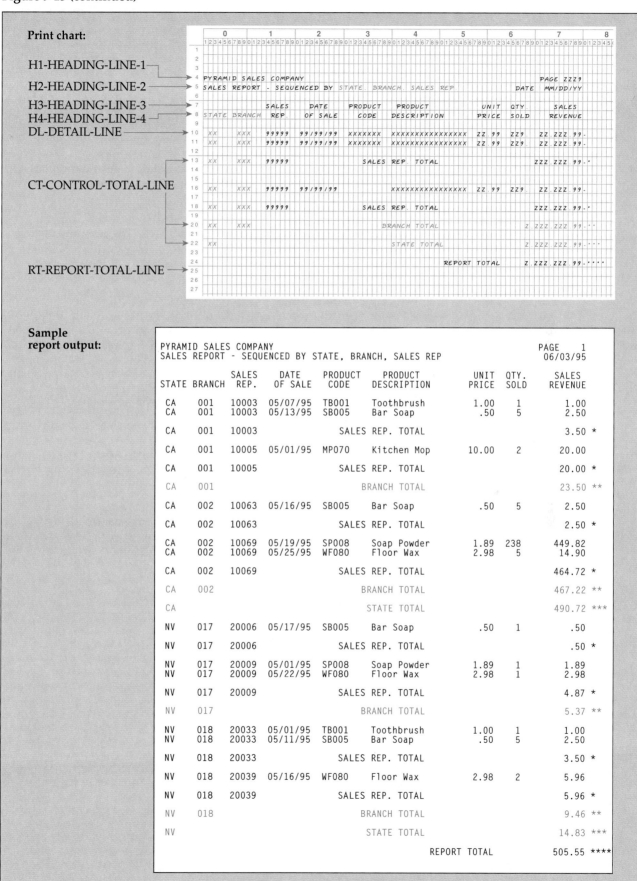

Sample
report output:

```
PYRAMID SALES COMPANY                                    PAGE   1
SALES REPORT - SEQUENCED BY STATE, BRANCH, SALES REP           06/03/95

              SALES    DATE     PRODUCT   PRODUCT           UNIT   QTY.      SALES
STATE BRANCH  REP.     OF SALE  CODE      DESCRIPTION       PRICE  SOLD     REVENUE

CA    001     10003    05/07/95  TB001    Toothbrush        1.00    1        1.00
CA    001     10003    05/13/95  SB005    Bar Soap           .50    5        2.50

CA    001     10003             SALES REP. TOTAL                             3.50 *

CA    001     10005    05/01/95  MP070    Kitchen Mop      10.00    2       20.00

CA    001     10005             SALES REP. TOTAL                            20.00 *

CA    001                       BRANCH TOTAL                                23.50 **

CA    002     10063    05/16/95  SB005    Bar Soap           .50    5        2.50

CA    002     10063             SALES REP. TOTAL                             2.50 *

CA    002     10069    05/19/95  SP008    Soap Powder       1.89  238      449.82
CA    002     10069    05/25/95  WF080    Floor Wax         2.98    5       14.90

CA    002     10069             SALES REP. TOTAL                           464.72 *

CA    002                       BRANCH TOTAL                               467.22 **

CA                              STATE TOTAL                                490.72 ***

NV    017     20006    05/17/95  SB005    Bar Soap           .50    1         .50

NV    017     20006             SALES REP. TOTAL                              .50 *

NV    017     20009    05/01/95  SP008    Soap Powder       1.89    1        1.89
NV    017     20009    05/22/95  WF080    Floor Wax         2.98    1        2.98

NV    017     20009             SALES REP. TOTAL                             4.87 *

NV    017                       BRANCH TOTAL                                 5.37 **

NV    018     20033    05/01/95  TB001    Toothbrush        1.00    1        1.00
NV    018     20033    05/11/95  SB005    Bar Soap           .50    5        2.50

NV    018     20033             SALES REP. TOTAL                             3.50 *

NV    018     20039    05/16/95  WF080    Floor Wax         2.98    2        5.96

NV    018     20039             SALES REP. TOTAL                             5.96 *

NV    018                       BRANCH TOTAL                                 9.46 **

NV                              STATE TOTAL                                 14.83 ***

                                REPORT TOTAL                               505.55 ****
```

not represent any single sales representative.) On the state control-break line, only the state is printed. You should compare the print chart to the sample output to get a good feel for the report's overall form.

Program Design

Multiple-Level Control-Break Logic

One of the important characteristics of multiple-level control-break processing is that detecting a control break at one level implies control breaks at all lower levels. So, when a control-break is detected, control-total lines must be printed as follows:

1. A major field (State) control break triggers minor (Sales-representative), intermediate (Branch), and then major (State) control totals.
2. An intermediate field (Branch) control break triggers minor (Sales-representative) and then intermediate (Branch) control totals.
3. A minor field (Sales-representative) control break triggers only minor (Sales-representative) totals.

You can see this by inspecting Figure 9-13's sample output.

Although this might sound like it is complicated to program, the logic is a relatively simple extension of single-level control-break logic. That is, the control-break processing module expands as shown in Figure 9-14's pseudocode. Compare this to the single-level pseudocode of Figure 9-3 (page 282).

Design Documentation

As you might anticipate from the relatively minor changes to the break-processing logic, the structure chart for the multiple-level sales report of Figure 9-15 is a minor expansion of that for SCTLBRK (Figure 9-5, page 285). That is, the addition of two more control levels requires two more modules (branch and state) to be performed by the 250-Process-Break module.

In the pseudocode of Figure 9-16, the changes over that of SCTLBRK are highlighted. The 250 module sees additions reflecting the two additional control levels illustrated in Figure 9-14.

1. The first-record processing must now save all three control fields: state and branch, as well as sales representative.
2. Both state and branch breaks are tested.

Figure 9-14 Summary of multiple-level control-break logic.

```
Evaluate the following case:
  When first record
    Set the control-group accumulators to zero
    Save the control fields of the record just read
  When state control field is not equal previous state control field
    Process the sales-rep-group-total
    Process the branch-group-total
    Process the state-group-total
  When branch control field is not equal previous branch control field
    Process the sales-rep-group-total
    Process the branch-group-total
  When sales-rep control field is not equal previous sales-rep control field
    Process the sales-rep-group-total
  When end of file
    Process the sales-rep-group-total
    Process the branch-group-total
    Process the state-group-total
    Print the report-total line
  Otherwise
    Take no action
```

Figure 9-15 Structure chart: multiple-level control-break sales report program.

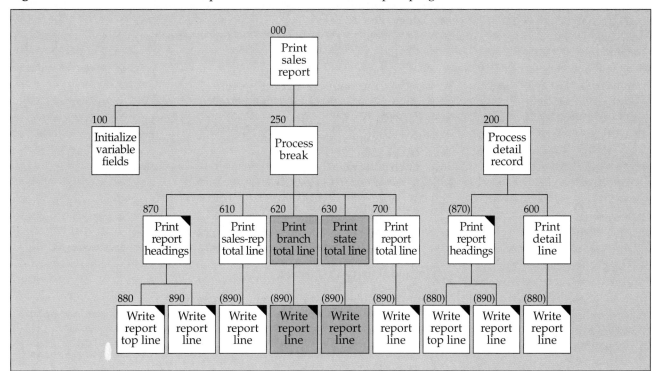

3. The end-of-file condition triggers control lines printed at all control levels.

In the 610 module (Print the sales representative-total line), the branch and state fields—as well as the sales representative field—are moved to the output area. Step 3 sets up the control-total line and involves a technique you will see when studying the program. In step 8, the Total-sales-representative-revenue is added to the branch total (the next higher level total)—rather than the report total, as done in SCTLBRK.

The two additional modules, 620 and 630, process the branch break and state break, respectively. They are identical in form to the 610 module for processing the sales representative break.

Program Coding

The complete MCTLBRK program is shown in Figure 9-17. As with the pseudocode, differences from SCTLBRK (Figure 9-8, page 290) are highlighted.

The WORKING-STORAGE SECTION

As you can see, the changes/additions in the WORKING-STORAGE SECTION over that of SCTLBRK are relatively few.

Control Fields

Because this program has three control fields, two additional fields must be added to the report-control group item (line 53). So, the RC-PREV-BRANCH and RC-PREV-STATE fields are specified to hold the branch and state fields, respectively, from the previous record.

Figure 9-16
Pseudocode: multiple-level control-break sales report program.

```
000-Print-Sales-Report module
1.   Open the files.
2.   Perform 100-Initialize-Variable-Fields.
3.   Perform until end of file:
         Read a record from the Sales file
         at end
             Set end-of-file to true
             Perform 250-Process-Break
         not at end
             Perform 250-Process-Break
             Perform 200-Process-Detail-Record.
4.   Close the files.
5.   Stop the run.
100-Initialize-Variable-Fields module
1.   Set the Not-end-of-file switch to true.
2.   Set First-record switch to true.
3.   Set the Page-count and Lines-used fields to zero.
4.   Set the Total-accumulator fields to zero.
5.   Obtain the date from the operating system and move it to
     the heading-line area.
200-Process-Detail-Record module
1.   If page is full
         Perform 870-Print-Report-Headings.
2.   Multiply the input Unit-price by the input Quantity-sold
     to equal the Sales-revenue.
3.   Perform 600-Print-Detail-Line.
4.   Add the Sales-revenue for this record to the Total-sales-
     rep-sales-revenue.
250-Process-Break module
1.   Evaluate the following case:
         When first record
             Move input Sales-rep field to the Previous-sales-
             rep field.
             Move input Branch field to Previous-branch field.
             Move input State field to Previous-state field.
             Perform 870-Print-Report-Headings.
             Set Not-first-record switch to True.
         When the input State field is not equal to the
         Previous-state field
             Perform 610-Process-End-Of-Sales-Rep
             Perform 620-Process-End-of-Branch
             Perform 630-Process-End-of-State.
         When the input Branch field is not equal to the
         Previous-branch field
             Perform 610-Process-End-of-Sales-Rep
             Perform 620-Process-End-of-Branch.
         When the input Sales-rep field is not equal to the
         Previous-sales-rep field
             Perform 610-Process-End-of-Sales-Rep
         When end of file
             Perform 610-Process-End-of-Sales-Rep.
             Perform 620-Process-End-of-Branch.
             Perform 630-Process-End-of-State.
             Perform 700-Print-Report-Total-Line.
600-Print-Detail-Line module
1.   Move following input/calculated fields to output area:
         Sales-rep
         State
         Branch
         Date-of-sale
         Product-code
         Product-description
         Quantity-sold
         Unit-price
         Sales-revenue
```

Figure 9-16 (continued)

```
   2.  Move the detail-line to the output print-line area.
   3.  Perform 890-Write-Report-Line.
   4.  Set Line-spacing to single-spacing.
610-Process-End-Of-Sales-Rep module
   1.  Move the Previous-sales-rep, Previous-branch, and
       Previous-state fields to the Control-total-line.
   2.  Move the Total-sales-rep-sales-revenue to the Control-
       total-line.
   3.  Move "SALES REP" and "*" to the Control-total-line.
   4.  Move the Control-total-line to the output print-line
       area.
   5.  Set Line-spacing to double-spacing.
   6.  Perform 880-Write-Report-Line.
   7.  Set Line-spacing to triple-spacing.
   8.  Add the Total-sales-rep-sales-revenue to the Total-
       branch-sales-revenue.
   9.  If not end of file
           Move the input Sales-rep field to the Previous-sales-
           rep field.
           Set the Total-sales-rep-sales-revenue to 0.
620-Process-End-of-Branch module
   1.  Move spaces to the Sales-rep field of the Control-total-
       line.
   2.  Move the Total-sales-rep-sales-revenue to the Control-
       total-line.
   3.  Move "BRANCH" and "**" to the Control-total-line.
   4.  Move the Control-total-line to the output print-line
       area.
   5.  Set Line-spacing to double-spacing.
   6.  Perform 880-Write-Report-Line.
   7.  Set Line-spacing to triple-spacing.
   8.  Add the Total-branch-sales-revenue to the Total-state-
       sales-revenue.
   9.  If not end of file
           Move the input Branch field to the Previous-branch
           field.
           Set the Total-branch-sales-revenue to 0.
630-Process-End-of-State module
   1.  Move spaces to the Branch field of the Control-total-
       line.
   2.  Move the Total-sales-rep-sales-revenue to the Control-
       total-line.
   3.  Move "STATE" and "***" to the Control-total-line.
   4.  Move the Control-total-line to the output print-line
       area.
   5.  Set Line-spacing to double-spacing.
   6.  Perform 880-Write-Report-Line.
   7.  Set Line-spacing to triple-spacing.
   8.  Add the Total-state-sales-revenue to the Total-report-
       sales-revenue.
   9.  If not end of file
           Move the input State field to the Previous-state
           field.
           Set the Total-sales-rep-sales-revenue to 0.
700-Print-Report-Total-Line module
   1.  Move the Total-report-sales-revenue to the Report-total-
       line.
   2.  Move the Report-total-line to the output print-line
       area.
   3.  Set Line-spacing to triple-spacing.
   4.  Perform 890-Write-Report-Line
```

(continues)

Figure 9-16 (continued)

```
870-Print-Report-Headings module
   1.   Add 1 to the Page-count.
   2.   Move the Page-count to the Page-number field in the
        first heading-line.
   3.   Move Heading-line-1 to the output print-line area.
   4.   Perform 880-Write-Report-Top-Line.
   5.   Move Heading-line-2 to the output print-line area.
   6.   Set Line-spacing to single-spacing.
   7.   Perform 890-Write-Report-Line.
   8.   Move Heading-line-3 to the output print-line area.
   9.   Set Line-spacing to double-spacing.
  10.   Perform 890-Write-Report-Line.
  11.   Move Heading-line-4 to the output print-line area.
  12.   Set Line-spacing to single-spacing.
  13.   Perform 890-Write-Report-Line.
  14.   Set Line-spacing to double-spacing.
880-Print-Report-Top-Line module
   1.   Advance to the top of the next report page and write out
        the output print-line area.
   2.   Set the Lines-used indicator to 1.
890-Write-Report-Line module
   1.   Advance the forms in accordance with the value in the
        Line-spacing field and write the output print-line area.
   2.   Add the Line-spacing field to the Lines-used field.
```

Accumulator Fields

Similarly, two corresponding entries are included in the accumulators record (line 69) to accumulate the branch and state totals, respectively.

In both the control and accumulator records, notice that the control fields are specified in minor to major order. Although a specific order is not necessary, arrangement in minor to major sequence aids program readability because it depicts the hierarchy of totals as they will be printed on the report.

Detail Line

Although not highlighted in Figure 9-17, the relative placement of the state, branch, and sales representative fields has changed to reflect the arrangement specified on the print chart.

Control-Total Line

SCTLBRK prints a single control-break line—that for the sales representative. On the other hand, MCTLBRK prints three—one for each of the three break levels. However, if you refer to the print chart and sample output of Figure 9-13 (page 299), you will see that they have the same overall format. The differences are (1) the printed description and (2) the printing or not printing of the branch and sales representative fields, depending upon the level. CT-CONTROL-TOTAL-LINE (line 133) provides for these needs; it is designed for use on all three levels of control-line printing. You will see how this is accomplished in the PROCEDURE DIVISION code.

Further, the CT-ASTERISKS field (line 145) was established so that either one, two, or three asterisks can be displayed on the control-total line in accordance with the level of the total (sales representative, branch, or state, respectively).

The use of a single control-total line is both practical and convenient because the lines are sufficiently similar. However, if the three total lines were significantly different in format, it would be necessary to describe each line as a separate 01-level item.

Report-Total Line

Although not highlighted, the number of asterisks following the report total (line 152) was increased from two to four in accordance with the print-chart specifications.

Figure 9-17   Multiple-level control break program—MCTLBRK.

```
  1     IDENTIFICATION DIVISION.                              75    01  SR-SALES-RECORD.
  2     PROGRAM-ID.   MCTLBRK.                                76        05  SR-RECORD-CODE          PIC X(2).
  3                                                           77        05  SR-STATE                PIC X(2).
  4   * Written by T. Welburn 2-27-86.                        78        05  SR-BRANCH               PIC X(3).
  5   * Revised 9-18-89 & 1-17-95 by W. Price.                79        05  SR-SALES-REP            PIC X(5).
  6   * PYRAMID SALES COMPANY.                                80        05  SR-DATE-OF-SALE         PIC X(6).
  7                                                           81        05  SR-PRODUCT-CODE         PIC X(7).
  8   * This program reads sales records, computes the sales  82        05  SR-PRODUCT-DESCRIPTION  PIC X(16).
  9   * revenue for each sales record, and prints a sales     83        05  SR-QUANTITY-SOLD        PIC S9(3).
 10   * detail line for each sales record.                    84        05  SR-UNIT-PRICE           PIC 9(2)V99.
 11                                                           85
 12   * Total lines are printed by Sales-Rep within Branch    86    01  H1-HEADING-LINE-1.
 13   * within State.                                         87        05              PIC X(70) VALUE "PYRAMID SALES COMPANY".
 14                                                           88        05              PIC X(5)  VALUE "PAGE ".
 15   * After all records are processed, a report-total line  89        05  H1-PAGE-NBR PIC ZZZ9.
 16   * is printed.                                           90
 17                                                           91    01  H2-HEADING-LINE-2.
 18                                                           92        05              PIC X(15) VALUE "SALES REPORT - ".
 19     ENVIRONMENT DIVISION.                                 93        05              PIC X(56)
 20                                                           94                        VALUE "SEQUENCED BY STATE, BRANCH, SALES REP".
 21     INPUT-OUTPUT SECTION.                                 95        05  H2-RUN-MONTH PIC Z9.
 22                                                           96        05              PIC X(1)  VALUE "/".
 23     FILE-CONTROL.                                         97        05  H2-RUN-DAY  PIC 9(2).
 24         SELECT SALES-FILE                                 98        05              PIC X(1)  VALUE "/".
 25             ASSIGN TO (system dependent).                 99        05  H2-RUN-YEAR PIC 9(2).
 26         SELECT SALES-REPORT                              100
 27             ASSIGN TO (system dependent).                101    01  H3-HEADING-LINE-3.
 28                                                          102        05              PIC X(41)
 29                                                          103                        VALUE "          SALES     DATE     PRODUCT".
 30     DATA DIVISION.                                       104        05              PIC X(37)
 31                                                          105                        VALUE "PRODUCT            UNIT   QTY.     SALES".
 32     FILE SECTION.                                        106
 33                                                          107    01  H4-HEADING-LINE-4.
 34     FD  SALES-FILE.                                      108        05              PIC X(39)
 35     01  SALES-RECORD.                                    109                        VALUE "STATE BRANCH   REP. OF SALE    CODE".
 36         05  PIC X(48).                                   110        05              PIC X(40)
 37                                                          111                        VALUE "DESCRIPTION      PRICE   SOLD    REVENUE".
 38     FD  SALES-REPORT.                                    112
 39     01  SALES-REPORT-LINE.                               113    01  DL-DETAIL-LINE.
 40         05 PIC X(132).                                   114        05              PIC X(1)  VALUE SPACE.
 41                                                          115        05  DL-STATE                PIC X(2).
 42     WORKING-STORAGE SECTION.                             116        05              PIC X(4)  VALUE SPACES.
 43                                                          117        05  DL-BRANCH               PIC X(3).
 44     01  PROGRAM-SWITCHES.                                118        05              PIC X(3)  VALUE SPACES.
 45         05  S1-END-OF-FILE-SWITCH   PIC X(1).            119        05  DL-SALES-REP            PIC X(5).
 46             88  S1-END-OF-FILE          VALUE "E".       120        05              PIC X(2)  VALUE SPACES.
 47             88  S1-NOT-END-OF-FILE      VALUE "N".       121        05  DL-DATE-OF-SALE         PIC XX/XX/XX.
 48         05  S2-FIRST-RECORD-SWITCH  PIC X(1).            122        05              PIC X(2)  VALUE SPACES.
 49             88  S2-FIRST-RECORD         VALUE "F".       123        05  DL-PRODUCT-CODE         PIC X(7).
 50             88  S2-NOT-FIRST-RECORD     VALUE "N".       124        05              PIC X(2)  VALUE SPACES.
 51                                                          125        05  DL-PRODUCT-DESCRIPTION  PIC X(16).
 52                                                          126        05              PIC X(2)  VALUE SPACES.
 53     01  RC-REPORT-CONTROLS.                              127        05  DL-UNIT-PRICE           PIC ZZ.99.
 54         05  RC-PAGE-COUNT           PIC 9(3).            128        05              PIC X(2)  VALUE SPACES.
 55         05  RC-LINES-PER-PAGE       PIC 9(2)  VALUE 54.  129        05  DL-QUANTITY-SOLD        PIC ZZ9-.
 56         05  RC-LINES-USED           PIC 9(2).            130        05              PIC X(2)  VALUE SPACES.
 57         05  RC-LINE-SPACING         PIC 9(2).            131        05  DL-SALES-REVENUE        PIC ZZ,ZZZ.99-.
 58         05  RC-PREV-SALES-REP       PIC X(5).            132
 59         05  RC-PREV-BRANCH          PIC X(3).            133    01  CT-CONTROL-TOTAL-LINE.
 60         05  RC-PREV-STATE           PIC X(2).            134        05              PIC X(1)  VALUE SPACES.
 61                                                          135        05  CT-STATE                PIC X(2).
 62     01  WA-WORK-AREAS.                                   136        05              PIC X(4)  VALUE SPACES.
 63         05  WA-RUN-DATE.                                 137        05  CT-BRANCH               PIC X(3).
 64             10  WA-RUN-YEAR         PIC 9(2).            138        05              PIC X(3)  VALUE SPACES.
 65             10  WA-RUN-MONTH        PIC 9(2).            139        05  CT-SALES-REP            PIC X(5).
 66             10  WA-RUN-DAY          PIC 9(2).            140        05              PIC X(15) VALUE SPACES.
 67         05  WA-SALES-REVENUE        PIC S9(5)V99.        141        05  CT-TOTAL-DESCRIPTION    PIC X(10) JUSTIFIED RIGHT.
 68                                                          142        05              PIC X(6)  VALUE " TOTAL".
 69     01  TA-TOTAL-ACCUMULATORS.                           143        05              PIC X(20) VALUE SPACES.
 70         05  TA-TOTAL-SALES-REP-ACCUM PIC S9(6)V99.       144        05  CT-SALES-REVENUE        PIC ZZZ,ZZZ.99-.
 71         05  TA-TOTAL-BRANCH-ACCUM   PIC S9(6)V99.        145        05  CT-ASTERISKS            PIC X(3).
 72         05  TA-TOTAL-STATE-ACCUM    PIC S9(6)V99.        146
 73         05  TA-TOTAL-REPORT-ACCUM   PIC S9(7)V99.        147    01  RT-REPORT-TOTAL-LINE.
 74                                                          148        05              PIC X(50) VALUE SPACES.
                                                             149        05              PIC X(12) VALUE "REPORT TOTAL".
                                                             150        05              PIC X(5)  VALUE SPACES.
                                                             151        05  RT-SALES-REVENUE        PIC Z,ZZZ,ZZZ.99-.
                                                             152        05              PIC X(4)  VALUE "****".
                                                             153
                                                             154
```

(continues)

Figure 9-17 (continued)

```
155     PROCEDURE DIVISION.                                    246     610-PROCESS-END-OF-SALES-REP.
156                                                           247         MOVE RC-PREV-STATE TO CT-STATE
157     000-PRINT-SALES-REPORT.                               248         MOVE RC-PREV-BRANCH TO CT-BRANCH
158                                                           249         MOVE RC-PREV-SALES-REP TO CT-SALES-REP
159     ************Initialization Sequence************       250         MOVE TA-TOTAL-SALES-REP-ACCUM TO CT-SALES-REVENUE
160         OPEN INPUT SALES-FILE                             251         MOVE "SALES REP." TO CT-TOTAL-DESCRIPTION
161              OUTPUT SALES-REPORT                          252         MOVE "*" TO CT-ASTERISKS
162         PERFORM 100-INITIALIZE-VARIABLE-FIELDS            253         MOVE CT-CONTROL-TOTAL-LINE TO SALES-REPORT-LINE
163                                                           254         MOVE 2 TO RC-LINE-SPACING
164     **************Processing Sequence**************       255         PERFORM 890-WRITE-REPORT-LINE
165         PERFORM UNTIL S1-END-OF-FILE                      256         MOVE 3 TO RC-LINE-SPACING.
166             READ SALES-FILE INTO SR-SALES-RECORD          257     *   Sales-Rep break housekeeping
167                 AT END                                    258         ADD TA-TOTAL-SALES-REP-ACCUM TO TA-TOTAL-BRANCH-ACCUM
168                     SET S1-END-OF-FILE TO TRUE            259         IF S1-NOT-END-OF-FILE
169                     PERFORM 250-PROCESS-BREAK             260             MOVE ZEROS TO TA-TOTAL-SALES-REP-ACCUM
170                 NOT AT END                                261             MOVE SR-SALES-REP TO RC-PREV-SALES-REP
171                     PERFORM 250-PROCESS-BREAK             262         END-IF
172                     PERFORM 200-PROCESS-DETAIL-RECORD     263         .
173             END-READ                                      264     620-PROCESS-END-OF-BRANCH.
174         END-PERFORM                                       265         MOVE SPACES TO CT-SALES-REP
175                                                           266         MOVE TA-TOTAL-BRANCH-ACCUM TO CT-SALES-REVENUE
176     **************Termination Sequence*************       267         MOVE "BRANCH" TO CT-TOTAL- DESCRIPTION
177         CLOSE SALES-FILE                                  268         MOVE "**" TO CT-ASTERISKS
178               SALES-REPORT                                269         MOVE CT-CONTROL-TOTAL-LINE TO SALES-REPORT-LINE
179         STOP RUN                                          270         MOVE 2 TO RC-LINE-SPACING
180         .                                                 271         PERFORM 890-WRITE-REPORT-LINE
181     ***********************************************       272         MOVE 3 TO RC-LINE-SPACING.
182                                                           273     *   Branch break housekeeping
183     100-INITIALIZE-VARIABLE-FIELDS.                       274         ADD TA-TOTAL-BRANCH-ACCUM TO TA-TOTAL-STATE-ACCUM
184         SET S1-NOT-END-OF-FILE TO TRUE                    275         IF S1-NOT-END-OF-FILE
185         SET S2-FIRST-RECORD TO TRUE                       276             MOVE ZEROS TO TA-TOTAL-BRANCH-ACCUM
186         MOVE ZERO TO RC-PAGE-COUNT                        277             MOVE SR-BRANCH TO RC-PREV-BRANCH
187                     RC-LINES-USED                         278         END-IF
188         INITIALIZE TA-TOTAL-ACCUMULATORS                  279         .
189         ACCEPT WA-RUN-DATE FROM DATE                      280     630-PROCESS-END-OF-STATE.
190         MOVE WA-RUN-MONTH TO H2-RUN-MONTH                 281         MOVE SPACES TO CT-BRANCH
191         MOVE WA-RUN-DAY TO H2-RUN-DAY                     282         MOVE TA-TOTAL-STATE-ACCUM TO CT-SALES-REVENUE
192         MOVE WA-RUN-YEAR TO H2-RUN-YEAR                   283         MOVE "STATE" TO CT-TOTAL-DESCRIPTION
193         .                                                 284         MOVE "***" TO CT-ASTERISKS
194     200-PROCESS-DETAIL-RECORD.                            285         MOVE CT-CONTROL-TOTAL-LINE TO SALES-REPORT-LINE
195         IF RC-LINES-USED IS NOT LESS THAN RC-LINES-PER-PAGE 286       MOVE 2 TO RC-LINE-SPACING
196             PERFORM 870-PRINT-REPORT-HEADINGS             287         PERFORM 890-WRITE-REPORT-LINE
197         END-IF                                            288         MOVE 3 TO RC-LINE-SPACING.
198         MULTIPLY SR-UNIT-PRICE BY SR-QUANTITY-SOLD        289     *   State break housekeeping
199             GIVING WA-SALES-REVENUE                       290         ADD TA-TOTAL-STATE-ACCUM TO TA-TOTAL-REPORT-ACCUM
200         PERFORM 600-PRINT-DETAIL-LINE                     291         IF S1-NOT-END-OF-FILE
201         ADD WA-SALES-REVENUE TO TA-TOTAL-SALES-REP-ACCUM  292             MOVE ZEROS TO TA-TOTAL-STATE-ACCUM
202         .                                                 293             MOVE SR-STATE TO RC-PREV-STATE
203     250-PROCESS-BREAK.                                    294         END-IF
204         EVALUATE TRUE                                     295         .
205             WHEN S2-FIRST-RECORD                          296     700-PRINT-REPORT-TOTAL-LINE.
206                 MOVE SR-SALES-REP TO RC-PREV-SALES-REP    297         MOVE TA-TOTAL-REPORT-ACCUM TO RT-SALES-REVENUE
207                 MOVE SR-BRANCH TO RC-PREV-BRANCH          298         MOVE RT-REPORT-TOTAL-LINE TO SALES-REPORT-LINE
208                 MOVE SR-STATE TO RC-PREV-STATE            299         MOVE 3 TO RC-LINE-SPACING
209                 PERFORM 870-PRINT-REPORT-HEADINGS         300         PERFORM 890-WRITE-REPORT-LINE
210                 SET S2-NOT-FIRST-RECORD TO TRUE           301         .
211                                                           302     870-PRINT-REPORT-HEADINGS.
212             WHEN SR-STATE NOT EQUAL TO RC-PREV-STATE      303         ADD 1 TO RC-PAGE-COUNT
213                 PERFORM 610-PROCESS-END-OF-SALES-REP      304         MOVE RC-PAGE-COUNT TO H1-PAGE-NBR
214                 PERFORM 620-PROCESS-END-OF-BRANCH         305         MOVE H1-HEADING-LINE-1 TO SALES-REPORT-LINE
215                 PERFORM 630-PROCESS-END-OF-STATE          306         PERFORM 880-WRITE-REPORT-TOP-LINE
216                                                           307         MOVE H2-HEADING-LINE-2 TO SALES-REPORT-LINE
217             WHEN SR-BRANCH NOT EQUAL TO RC-PREV-BRANCH    308         MOVE 1 TO RC-LINE-SPACING
218                 PERFORM 610-PROCESS-END-OF-SALES-REP      309         PERFORM 890-WRITE-REPORT-LINE
219                 PERFORM 620-PROCESS-END-OF-BRANCH         310         MOVE H3-HEADING-LINE-3 TO SALES-REPORT-LINE
220                                                           311         MOVE 2 TO RC-LINE-SPACING
221             WHEN SR-SALES-REP NOT EQUAL TO RC-PREV-SALES-REP 312       PERFORM 890-WRITE-REPORT-LINE
222                 PERFORM 610-PROCESS-END-OF-SALES-REP      313         MOVE H4-HEADING-LINE-4 TO SALES-REPORT-LINE
223                                                           314         MOVE 1 TO RC-LINE-SPACING
224             WHEN S1-END-OF-FILE                           315         PERFORM 890-WRITE-REPORT-LINE
225                 PERFORM 610-PROCESS-END-OF-SALES-REP      316         MOVE 2 TO RC-LINE-SPACING
226                 PERFORM 620-PROCESS-END-OF-BRANCH         317         .
227                 PERFORM 630-PROCESS-END-OF-STATE          318     880-WRITE-REPORT-TOP-LINE.
228                 PERFORM 700-PRINT-REPORT-TOTAL-LINE       319         WRITE SALES-REPORT-LINE
229                                                           320             AFTER ADVANCING PAGE
230         END-EVALUATE                                      321         MOVE 1 TO RC-LINES-USED
231         .                                                 322         .
232     600-PRINT-DETAIL-LINE.                                323     890-WRITE-REPORT-LINE.
233         MOVE SR-SALES-REP TO DL-SALES-REP                 324         WRITE SALES-REPORT-LINE
234         MOVE SR-STATE TO DL-STATE                         325             AFTER ADVANCING RC-LINE-SPACING
235         MOVE SR-BRANCH TO DL-BRANCH                       326         ADD RC-LINE-SPACING TO RC-LINES-USED.
236         MOVE SR-DATE-OF-SALE TO DL-DATE-OF-SALE           327         .
237         MOVE SR-PRODUCT-CODE TO DL-PRODUCT-CODE
238         MOVE SR-PRODUCT-DESCRIPTION TO DL-PRODUCT-DESCRIPTION
239         MOVE SR-UNIT-PRICE TO DL-UNIT-PRICE
240         MOVE SR-QUANTITY-SOLD TO DL-QUANTITY-SOLD
241         MOVE WA-SALES-REVENUE TO DL-SALES-REVENUE
242         MOVE DL-DETAIL-LINE TO SALES-REPORT-LINE
243         PERFORM 890-WRITE-REPORT-LINE
244         MOVE 1 TO RC-LINE-SPACING
245         .
```

**Coding the
PROCEDURE
DIVISION**

Most of the PROCEDURE DIVISION modules of MCTLBRK are unchanged from SCTLBRK; others have some basic changes. Also, some new modules were added. However, you should recognize most of these changes and additions from your study of the pseudocode changes.

Sequencing in the EVALUATE

At lines 212–219, you see the addition of tests for the branch and state control breaks. The sequencing of these WHEN options is critical: They must be included in major to minor order or the program will not function properly. For instance, assume that the order were reversed as follows:

```
EVALUATE TRUE
  WHEN FIRST-RECORD
    ⋮

  WHEN SR-SALES-REP NOT EQUAL TO RC-PREV-SALES-REP
    ⋮

  WHEN SR-BRANCH NOT EQUAL TO RC-PREV-BRANCH
    ⋮

  WHEN SR-STATE NOT EQUAL TO RC-PREV-STATE
    ⋮

  WHEN END-OF-FILE
    ⋮
```

Consider what would occur between records six and seven (Figure 9-12, page 297), which include the following state, branch, and sales representative fields:

CA 002 10069

NV 017 20006

Upon reading the NV record, the difference in sales representative numbers produces a true condition in the sales representative compare. The break is processed as a sales representative break, with no state or branch break processing. Note that this problem is similar to that expressed for SCTLBRK, in which the first-record test must precede the control-break test.

If you are uncomfortable with a sequence-dependent test, you can use the alternate EVALUATE form presented later.

The Control-Total Line

As you saw in the WORKING-STORAGE SECTION, a single control-total line prints each of the three levels of control totals. The sales representative line must include the state, branch, and sales representative number so they are moved to the total line (program lines 247–249). Also, the total-line title "SALES REP" and the single asterisk are moved (lines 251 and 252).

Next, consider the 620 module to print the branch totals. Since printing a branch total is always preceded by printing a sales representative total, it is only necessary to blank the previously printed sales representative number (line 265). Then the needed title and asterisks are moved as in the 610 module (lines 267 and 268).

The same action takes place in the state-total module (630), as you can see by inspecting lines 281, 283, and 284.

The only other difference among these three modules (610, 620, and 630) involves the fields used in the housekeeping actions. For this, refer to lines 258–262 of the 610 module and corresponding lines of the other two modules.

**An Alternate Form
of the EVALUATE**

If you feel uncomfortable with the sequencing requirements of the EVALUATE, you can introduce multiple-test conditions, as done for SCTLBRK in Figure 9-9 (page 294). (If you try it, you will find that using the multiple conditions related by ANDs is very clumsy and tends to introduce mistakes.) Instead, you could use the tabular form of Figure 9-18, which is equivalent to the EVALUATE of Figure 9-10 of SCTLBRK. With the inclusion of comment lines, the workings of this

Figure 9-18
Alternate coding for the
EVALUATE statement.

```
      250-PROCESS-BREAK.
          EVALUATE
            S2-FIRST-RECORD
                    also
                        SR-SALES-REP NOT =
                        RC-PREV-SALES-REP
                                also
                                    SR-BRANCH NOT =
                                    RC-PREV-BRANCH
                                            also
                                                SR-STATE NOT =
                                                RC-PREV-STATE
                                                        also
                                                            S1-END-OF-FILE
    *      ----------  ---------  ---------  ---------  ---------
    *      No break so return to calling module
           WHEN FALSE also FALSE also FALSE also FALSE also FALSE
    *      ----------  ---------  ---------  ---------  ---------
               CONTINUE

    *      Sales-representative break
           WHEN FALSE also TRUE  also FALSE also FALSE also FALSE
    *      ----------  ---------  ---------  ---------  ---------
               PERFORM 610-PRINT-SALES-REP-TOTAL-LINE

    *      Branch break
           WHEN FALSE also  ANY  also TRUE  also FALSE also FALSE
    *      ----------  ---------  ---------  ---------  ---------
               PERFORM 610-PRINT-SALES-REP-TOTAL-LINE
               PERFORM 620-PRINT-BRANCH-TOTAL-LINE

    *      State break
           WHEN FALSE also  ANY  also  ANY  also TRUE  also FALSE
    *      ----------  ---------  ---------  ---------  ---------
               PERFORM 610-PRINT-SALES-REP-TOTAL-LINE
               PERFORM 620-PRINT-BRANCH-TOTAL-LINE
               PERFORM 630-PRINT-STATE-TOTAL-LINE

    *      Process first record
           WHEN TRUE  also FALSE also  ANY  also  ANY  also  ANY
    *      ----------  ---------  ---------  ---------  ---------
               MOVE SR-SALES-REP TO RC-PREV-SALES-REP
               MOVE SR-BRANCH TO RC-PREV-BRANCH
               MOVE SR-STATE TO RC-PREV-STATE
               PERFORM 870-PRINT-REPORT-HEADINGS
               SET S2-NOT-FIRST-RECORD TO TRUE

    *      End of file
           WHEN FALSE also  ANY  also  ANY  also  ANY  also TRUE
    *      ----------  ---------  ---------  ---------  ---------
               PERFORM 610-PRINT-SALES-REP-TOTAL-LINE
               PERFORM 620-PRINT-BRANCH-TOTAL-LINE
               PERFORM 630-PRINT-STATE-TOTAL-LINE
               PERFORM 700-PRINT-REPORT-TOTAL-LINE

    *      No records in file
           WHEN TRUE  also  ANY  also  ANY  also  ANY  also TRUE
    *      ----------  ---------  ---------  ---------  ---------
               PERFORM 990-PROCESS-EMPTY-FILE-ERROR

          END-EVALUATE
          .
```

statement are very clear. Notice that Sales-representative break includes requirements that both the branch-break and state-break conditions be false. So, the CA to NV break illustrated previously is only processed by the state-break condition.

With the combination of TRUE and FALSE selection subjects, the conditions are all mutually exclusive and the order of the WHENs has no bearing on the program's execution.

With the five selection objects in the EVALUATE, the code must be "squashed together" to conform to the column 72 limitation on COBOL statements. However, the elimination of this restriction in COBOL-9X will enable you to spread out the statement from left to right, making it easier to read.

An Alternate Form for COBOL-74

As with the SCTLBRK program, if you are using COBOL-74, you must replace the EVALUATE with a nested IF. If you are comfortable with sequence-dependent code, then you can use Figure 9-19's coding, which includes a test for a file with no records. Recognize that the sequencing of these respective IFs is critical. That is, the tests must be made in the order: empty file, first record, major to minor control breaks, and end-of-file. You can make it sequence independent by multiple test conditions interrelated with the AND (as in Figure 9-11(a), page 295), but you will probably find that the form is clumsy and tends to introduce mistakes.

As with SCTLBRK, since the nested IF is to be treated as a single case statement, a period is only at the end of the last statement (the end of the paragraph, in this case).

Figure 9-20 is a complete COBOL-74 multiple-level control-break program using the priming READ. The first record is read by line 165 and successive records are read by line 203, following the processing of a detail record.

Chapter Summary

Control-break programs require that the input records be in proper control-field sequence for the control breaks. The program logic must compare the control fields of the current record to those of the previous record. When the values are different, a control break occurs. As the result of a control break, a control-total line is typically printed, which contains accumulations—control totals—of certain detail-line fields for that control group of records.

Figure 9-19
Alternate coding for COBOL-74.

```
250-PROCESS-BREAK.
    IF S2-FIRST-RECORD AND S1-END-OF-FILE
        PERFORM 990-PROCESS-EMPTY-FILE-ERROR
    ELSE IF S2-FIRST-RECORD
        MOVE SR-SALES-REP TO RC-PREV-SALES-REP
        MOVE SR-BRANCH TO RC-PREV-BRANCH
        MOVE SR-STATE TO RC-PREV-STATE
        PERFORM 870-PRINT-REPORT-HEADINGS
        MOVE "N" TO S1-FIRST-RECORD-SWITCH
    ELSE IF SR-STATE NOT = RC-PREV-STATE
        PERFORM 610-PRINT-SALES-REP-TOTAL-LINE
        PERFORM 620-PRINT-BRANCH-TOTAL-LINE
        PERFORM 630-PRINT-STATE-TOTAL-LINE
    ELSE IF SR-BRANCH NOT = RC-PREV-BRANCH
        PERFORM 610-PRINT-SALES-REP-TOTAL-LINE
        PERFORM 620-PRINT-BRANCH-TOTAL-LINE
    ELSE IF SR-SALES-REP NOT = RC-PREV-SALES-REP
        PERFORM 610-PRINT-SALES-REP-TOTAL-LINE
    ELSE IF S1-END-OF-FILE
        PERFORM 610-PRINT-SALES-REP-TOTAL-LINE
        PERFORM 620-PRINT-BRANCH-TOTAL-LINE
        PERFORM 630-PRINT-STATE-TOTAL-LINE
        PERFORM 700-PRINT-REPORT-TOTAL-LINE.
```

Figure 9-20   COBOL-74 multiple-level control-break program using priming READ.

```
1       IDENTIFICATION DIVISION.
2       PROGRAM-ID.   MCTLBRK.
3
4    *  Written by T. Welburn 2-27-86.
5    *  Revised 9-18-89 & 1-17-95 by W. Price.
6    *  PYRAMID SALES COMPANY.
7    *  Written for COBOL-74.
8
9    *  This program reads sales records, computes the sales
10   *  revenue for each sales record, and prints a sales
11   *  detail line for each sales record.
12
13   *  Total lines are printed by Sales-Rep within Branch
14   *  within State.
15
16   *  After all records are processed, a report-total line
17   *  is printed.
18
19
20      ENVIRONMENT DIVISION.
21
22      CONFIGURATION SECTION.
23
24         SOURCE-COMPUTER. (system dependent).
25         OBJECT-COMPUTER. (system dependent).
26
27      INPUT-OUTPUT SECTION.
28
29      FILE-CONTROL.
30         SELECT SALES-FILE
31            ASSIGN TO (system dependent).
32         SELECT SALES-REPORT
33            ASSIGN TO (system dependent).
34
35
36      DATA DIVISION.
37
38      FILE SECTION.
39
40      FD  SALES-FILE.
41      01  SALES-RECORD.
42          05  PIC X(48).
43
44      FD  SALES-REPORT.
45      01  SALES-REPORT-LINE.
46          05  PIC X(132).
47
48      WORKING-STORAGE SECTION.
49
50      01  PROGRAM-SWITCHES.
51          05  S1-END-OF-FILE-SWITCH    PIC X(1).
52              88  S1-END-OF-FILE           VALUE "E".
53              88  S1-NOT-END-OF-FILE       VALUE "N".
54
55
56      01  RC-REPORT-CONTROLS.
57          05  RC-PAGE-COUNT        PIC 9(3).
58          05  RC-LINES-PER-PAGE    PIC 9(2)    VALUE 54.
59          05  RC-LINES-USED        PIC 9(2).
60          05  RC-LINE-SPACING      PIC 9(2).
61          05  RC-PREV-SALES-REP    PIC X(5).
62          05  RC-PREV-BRANCH       PIC X(3).
63          05  RC-PREV-STATE        PIC X(2).
64
65      01  WA-WORK-AREAS.
66          05  WA-RUN-DATE.
67              10  WA-RUN-YEAR      PIC 9(2).
68              10  WA-RUN-MONTH     PIC 9(2).
69              10  WA-RUN-DAY       PIC 9(2).
70          05  WA-SALES-REVENUE     PIC S9(5)V99.
71
72      01  TA-TOTAL-ACCUMULATORS.
73          05  TA-TOTAL-SALES-REP-ACCUM  PIC S9(6)V99.
74          05  TA-TOTAL-BRANCH-ACCUM     PIC S9(6)V99.
75          05  TA-TOTAL-STATE-ACCUM      PIC S9(6)V99.
76          05  TA-TOTAL-REPORT-ACCUM     PIC S9(7)V99.
77
78      01  SR-SALES-RECORD.
79          05  SR-RECORD-CODE           PIC X(2).
80          05  SR-STATE                 PIC X(2).
81          05  SR-BRANCH                PIC X(3).
82          05  SR-SALES-REP             PIC X(5).
83          05  SR-DATE-OF-SALE          PIC X(6).
84          05  SR-PRODUCT-CODE          PIC X(7).
85          05  SR-PRODUCT-DESCRIPTION   PIC X(16).
86          05  SR-QUANTITY-SOLD         PIC S9(3).
87          05  SR-UNIT-PRICE            PIC 9(2)V99.
88
89      01  H1-HEADING-LINE-1.
90          05  FILLER      PIC X(70)  VALUE "PYRAMID SALES COMPANY".
91          05  FILLER      PIC X(5)   VALUE "PAGE ".
92          05  H1-PAGE-NBR PIC ZZZ9.
93
94      01  H2-HEADING-LINE-2.
95          05  FILLER      PIC X(15)  VALUE "SALES REPORT - ".
96          05  FILLER      PIC X(56)
97                          VALUE "SEQUENCED BY STATE, BRANCH, SALES REP".
98          05  H2-RUN-MONTH PIC Z9.
99          05  FILLER      PIC X(1)   VALUE "/".
100         05  H2-RUN-DAY   PIC 9(2).
101         05  FILLER      PIC X(1)   VALUE "/".
102         05  H2-RUN-YEAR  PIC 9(2).
103
104     01  H3-HEADING-LINE-3.
105         05  FILLER      PIC X(41)
106                    VALUE "                 SALES     DATE      PRODUCT".
107         05  FILLER      PIC X(37)
108                    VALUE "PRODUCT              UNIT   QTY.     SALES".
109
110     01  H4-HEADING-LINE-4.
111         05  FILLER      PIC X(39)
112                    VALUE "STATE BRANCH    REP.  OF SALE    CODE".
113         05  FILLER      PIC X(40)
114                    VALUE "DESCRIPTION        PRICE    SOLD     REVENUE".
115
116     01  DL-DETAIL-LINE.
117         05  FILLER                   PIC X(1)   VALUE SPACES.
118         05  DL-STATE                 PIC X(2).
119         05  FILLER                   PIC X(4)   VALUE SPACES.
120         05  DL-BRANCH                PIC X(3).
121         05  FILLER                   PIC X(3)   VALUE SPACES.
122         05  DL-SALES-REP             PIC X(5).
123         05  FILLER                   PIC X(2)   VALUE SPACES.
124         05  DL-DATE-OF-SALE          PIC XX/XX/XX.
125         05  FILLER                   PIC X(2)   VALUE SPACES.
126         05  DL-PRODUCT-CODE          PIC X(7).
127         05  FILLER                   PIC X(2)   VALUE SPACES.
128         05  DL-PRODUCT-DESCRIPTION   PIC X(16).
129         05  FILLER                   PIC X(2)   VALUE SPACES.
130         05  DL-UNIT-PRICE            PIC ZZ.99.
131         05  FILLER                   PIC X(2)   VALUE SPACES.
132         05  DL-QUANTITY-SOLD         PIC ZZ9-.
133         05  FILLER                   PIC X(2)   VALUE SPACES.
134         05  DL-SALES-REVENUE         PIC ZZ,ZZZ.99-.
135
136     01  CT-CONTROL-TOTAL-LINE.
137         05  FILLER                   PIC X(1)   VALUE SPACES.
138         05  CT-STATE                 PIC X(2).
139         05  FILLER                   PIC X(4)   VALUE SPACES.
140         05  CT-BRANCH                PIC X(3).
141         05  FILLER                   PIC X(3)   VALUE SPACES.
142         05  CT-SALES-REP             PIC X(5).
143         05  FILLER                   PIC X(15)  VALUE SPACES.
144         05  CT-TOTAL-DESCRIPTION     PIC X(10)  JUSTIFIED RIGHT.
145         05  FILLER                   PIC X(6)   VALUE " TOTAL".
146         05  FILLER                   PIC X(20)  VALUE SPACES.
147         05  CT-SALES-REVENUE         PIC ZZZ,ZZZ.99-.
148         05  CT-ASTERISKS             PIC X(3).
149
150     01  RT-REPORT-TOTAL-LINE.
151         05  FILLER          PIC X(50)  VALUE SPACES.
152         05  FILLER          PIC X(12)  VALUE "REPORT TOTAL".
153         05  FILLER          PIC X(5)   VALUE SPACES.
154         05  RT-SALES-REVENUE PIC Z,ZZZ,ZZZ.99-.
155         05  FILLER          PIC X(4)   VALUE "****".
```

Figure 9-20 (continued)

```
156                                                          236       610-PROCESS-END-OF-SALES-REP.
157                                                          237           MOVE RC-PREV-STATE TO CT-STATE
158     PROCEDURE DIVISION.                                  238           MOVE RC-PREV-BRANCH TO CT-BRANCH
159                                                          239           MOVE RC-PREV-SALES-REP TO CT-SALES-REP
160     000-PRINT-SALES-REPORT.                              240           MOVE TA-TOTAL-SALES-REP-ACCUM TO CT-SALES-REVENUE
161                                                          241           MOVE "SALES REP." TO CT-TOTAL-DESCRIPTION
162  *************Initialization Sequence************        242           MOVE "*" TO CT-ASTERISKS
163         OPEN INPUT SALES-FILE                            243           MOVE CT-CONTROL-TOTAL-LINE TO SALES-REPORT-LINE
164              OUTPUT SALES-REPORT                          244           MOVE 2 TO RC-LINE-SPACING
165         PERFORM 800-READ-SALES-RECORD                    245           PERFORM 890-WRITE-REPORT-LINE
166         PERFORM 100-INITIALIZE-VARIABLE-FIELDS           246           MOVE 3 TO RC-LINE-SPACING
167         PERFORM 870-PRINT-REPORT-HEADINGS                247  *        Sales-Rep break housekeeping
168                                                          248           ADD TA-TOTAL-SALES-REP-ACCUM TO TA-TOTAL-BRANCH-ACCUM
169  **************Processing Sequence***************        249           IF S1-NOT-END-OF-FILE
170         PERFORM 150-EVALUATE-CONDITION                   250              MOVE ZEROS TO TA-TOTAL-SALES-REP-ACCUM
171              UNTIL S1-END-OF-FILE                         251              MOVE SR-SALES-REP TO RC-PREV-SALES-REP.
172                                                          252
173  **************Termination Sequence*************         253       620-PROCESS-END-OF-BRANCH.
174         PERFORM 610-PROCESS-END-OF-SALES-REP             254           MOVE SPACES TO CT-SALES-REP
175         PERFORM 620-PROCESS-END-OF-BRANCH                255           MOVE TA-TOTAL-BRANCH-ACCUM TO CT-SALES-REVENUE
176         PERFORM 630-PROCESS-END-OF-STATE                 256           MOVE "BRANCH" TO CT-TOTAL-DESCRIPTION
177         PERFORM 700-PRINT-REPORT-TOTAL-LINE              257           MOVE "**" TO CT-ASTERISKS
178         CLOSE SALES-FILE                                 258           MOVE CT-CONTROL-TOTAL-LINE TO SALES-REPORT-LINE
179              SALES-REPORT                                 259           MOVE 2 TO RC-LINE-SPACING
180         STOP RUN.                                        260           PERFORM 890-WRITE-REPORT-LINE
181                                                          261           MOVE 3 TO RC-LINE-SPACING.
182  ***********************************************         262  *        Branch break housekeeping
183                                                          263           ADD TA-TOTAL-BRANCH-ACCUM TO TA-TOTAL-STATE-ACCUM
184     100-INITIALIZE-VARIABLE-FIELDS.                      264           IF S1-NOT-END-OF-FILE
185         MOVE SR-SALES-REP TO RC-PREV-SALES-REP           265              MOVE ZEROS TO TA-TOTAL-BRANCH-ACCUM
186         MOVE SR-BRANCH TO RC-PREV-BRANCH                 266              MOVE SR-BRANCH TO RC-PREV-BRANCH.
187         MOVE SR-STATE TO RC-PREV-STATE                   267
188         MOVE "N" TO S1-END-OF-FILE-SWITCH                268       630-PROCESS-END-OF-STATE.
189         MOVE ZERO TO TA-TOTAL-SALES-REP-ACCUM            269           MOVE SPACES TO CT-BRANCH
190                     TA-TOTAL-BRANCH-ACCUM                270           MOVE TA-TOTAL-STATE-ACCUM TO CT-SALES-REVENUE
191                     TA-TOTAL-STATE-ACCUM                 271           MOVE "STATE" TO CT-TOTAL-DESCRIPTION
192                     TA-TOTAL-REPORT-ACCUM                272           MOVE "***" TO CT-ASTERISKS
193                     RC-PAGE-COUNT                        273           MOVE CT-CONTROL-TOTAL-LINE TO SALES-REPORT-LINE
194                     RC-LINES-USED                        274           MOVE 2 TO RC-LINE-SPACING
195         ACCEPT WA-RUN-DATE FROM DATE                     275           PERFORM 890-WRITE-REPORT-LINE
196         MOVE WA-RUN-MONTH TO H2-RUN-MONTH                276           MOVE 3 TO RC-LINE-SPACING.
197         MOVE WA-RUN-DAY TO H2-RUN-DAY                    277  *        State break housekeeping
198         MOVE WA-RUN-YEAR TO H2-RUN-YEAR.                 278           ADD TA-TOTAL-STATE-ACCUM TO TA-TOTAL-REPORT-ACCUM
199                                                          279           IF S1-NOT-END-OF-FILE
200     150-EVALUATE-CONDITION.                              280              MOVE ZEROS TO TA-TOTAL-STATE-ACCUM
201         IF SR-SALES-REP = RC-PREV-SALES-REP              281              MOVE SR-STATE TO RC-PREV-STATE.
202             PERFORM 200-PROCESS-DETAIL-RECORD            282
203             PERFORM 800-READ-SALES-RECORD                283       700-PRINT-REPORT-TOTAL-LINE.
204         ELSE IF SR-STATE NOT EQUAL TO RC-PREV-STATE      284           MOVE TA-TOTAL-REPORT-ACCUM TO RT-SALES-REVENUE
205             PERFORM 610-PROCESS-END-OF-SALES-REP         285           MOVE RT-REPORT-TOTAL-LINE TO SALES-REPORT-LINE
206             PERFORM 620-PROCESS-END-OF-BRANCH            286           MOVE 3 TO RC-LINE-SPACING
207             PERFORM 630-PROCESS-END-OF-STATE             287           PERFORM 890-WRITE-REPORT-LINE.
208         ELSE IF SR-BRANCH NOT EQUAL TO RC-PREV-BRANCH    288
209             PERFORM 610-PROCESS-END-OF-SALES-REP         289       800-READ-SALES-RECORD.
210             PERFORM 620-PROCESS-END-OF-BRANCH            290           READ SALES-FILE INTO SR-SALES-RECORD
211         ELSE                                             291              AT END MOVE "E" TO S1-END-OF-FILE-SWITCH.
212             PERFORM 610-PROCESS-END-OF-SALES-REP.        292
213                                                          293       870-PRINT-REPORT-HEADINGS.
214     200-PROCESS-DETAIL-RECORD.                           294           ADD 1 TO RC-PAGE-COUNT
215         IF RC-LINES-USED IS NOT LESS THAN RC-LINES-PER-PAGE  295       MOVE RC-PAGE-COUNT TO H1-PAGE-NBR
216             PERFORM 870-PRINT-REPORT-HEADINGS.           296           MOVE H1-HEADING-LINE-1 TO SALES-REPORT-LINE
217         MULTIPLY SR-UNIT-PRICE BY SR-QUANTITY-SOLD       297           PERFORM 880-WRITE-REPORT-TOP-LINE
218             GIVING WA-SALES-REVENUE                      298           MOVE H2-HEADING-LINE-2 TO SALES-REPORT-LINE
219         PERFORM 600-PRINT-DETAIL-LINE                    299           MOVE 1 TO RC-LINE-SPACING
220         ADD WA-SALES-REVENUE TO TA-TOTAL-SALES-REP-ACCUM. 300          PERFORM 890-WRITE-REPORT-LINE
221                                                          301           MOVE H3-HEADING-LINE-3 TO SALES-REPORT-LINE
222     600-PRINT-DETAIL-LINE.                               302           MOVE 2 TO RC-LINE-SPACING
223         MOVE SR-SALES-REP TO DL-SALES-REP                303           PERFORM 890-WRITE-REPORT-LINE
224         MOVE SR-STATE TO DL-STATE                        304           MOVE H4-HEADING-LINE-4 TO SALES-REPORT-LINE
225         MOVE SR-BRANCH TO DL-BRANCH                      305           MOVE 1 TO RC-LINE-SPACING
226         MOVE SR-DATE-OF-SALE TO DL-DATE-OF-SALE          306           PERFORM 890-WRITE-REPORT-LINE
227         MOVE SR-PRODUCT-CODE TO DL-PRODUCT-CODE          307           MOVE 2 TO RC-LINE-SPACING.
228         MOVE SR-PRODUCT-DESCRIPTION TO DL-PRODUCT-DESCRIPTION  308
229         MOVE SR-UNIT-PRICE TO DL-UNIT-PRICE              309       880-WRITE-REPORT-TOP-LINE.
230         MOVE SR-QUANTITY-SOLD TO DL-QUANTITY-SOLD        310           WRITE SALES-REPORT-LINE
231         MOVE WA-SALES-REVENUE TO DL-SALES-REVENUE        311              AFTER ADVANCING PAGE
232         MOVE DL-DETAIL-LINE TO SALES-REPORT-LINE         312           MOVE 1 TO RC-LINES-USED.
233         PERFORM 890-WRITE-REPORT-LINE                    313
234         MOVE 1 TO RC-LINE-SPACING.                       314       890-WRITE-REPORT-LINE.
235                                                          315           WRITE SALES-REPORT-LINE
                                                             316              AFTER ADVANCING RC-LINE-SPACING
                                                             317           ADD RC-LINE-SPACING TO RC-LINES-USED.
```

A single-level control-break program has one control field that triggers one type of control break. The SCTLBRK program is an example of a single-level control-break program.

A multiple-level control-break program has two or more control fields that trigger two or more control-break levels. The MCTLBRK program is an example of a three-level control-break program.

An important element of this book's control-break technique is to check for a control-break occurrence immediately upon reading a record. This is done in a separate control-break processing module. If a control break has occurred, appropriate processing takes place.

Processing a control break involves the following actions: (1) set up and print the control line, (2) add the current-level control-total fields to the next higher-level control-total accumulators, (3) zero the current-level control-total fields, and (4) save the current-level control-field value.

Exercises

Terms for Definition

control break
control field
control group
control total
control-total line

intermediate control field
major control field
minor control field
multiple-level control-break program
single-level control break

Review Questions

1. Control-break programs require that the input records be _____.

2. Control-break program logic requires that the _____ field(s) of the _____ record be compared to that (those) of the _____ record.

3. A single-level control-break program has _____ control field(s).

4. A two-level control-break program has _____ control field(s).

5. For two-level control breaks, the _____ control field must be tested first; the _____ control field must be tested last.

Questions About the Example Programs

1. Assume that the following statement from SCTLBRK (Figure 9-8, line 195) was accidentally omitted:

    ```
    MOVE SR-SALES-REP TO RC-PREV-SALES-REP
    ```

    Describe how this will affect the running and/or the output of the program.

2. Assume that the following statement from MCTLBRK (Figure 9-17, line 207) was accidentally omitted:

    ```
    MOVE SR-BRANCH TO RC-PREV-BRANCH
    ```

    Describe how this will affect the running and/or the output of the program.

3. Assume that the Sales file of the SCTLBRK program (Figure 9-8) is not correctly sorted and that in one portion of the file, the sequence of the Sales-representative field is as follows:

    10006
    10006
    10009
    10006
    10009
    10009
    10014

    Describe the output relative to the group-total lines that will be printed.

4. In the 250 module of the MCTLBRK program, assume that the statement (Figure 9-17, line 292)

    ```
    MOVE ZEROS TO TA-TOTAL-STATE-ACCUM
    ```

    was omitted. How would this affect the program's output?

5. For the MCTLBRK program, the Sales file must be sorted by Sales-representative-number within Branch within State. However, assume it was incorrectly sorted within State within Branch within Sales-representative-number. In other words, the records are exactly reversed. Also, assume that each salesperson has at least two records. Describe the appearance of the report, especially relating to the group-total lines.

6. In the 250 module of the MCTLBRK program, assume that the sales-representative control-break test (Figure 9-17, lines 221 and 222) were moved so that they precede the state-break test (line 212). Explain the consequences of this change.

Programming Assignments

Programming Assignment 9-1: Account Balance Report

Background information:

In any business, keeping an accurate record of money coming in and going out of the company is critical to that company's operation. Such data is commonly kept in file called a general ledger file. In a general ledger system, separate accounts are defined for the variety of fiscal activity. Typical accounts are salaries, travel, building rental, and petty cash. As financial transactions occur, each is combined with summary data in the appropriate account. For a particular application, Silicon Valley Manufacturing requires an account balance report. Single-level control totals should be printed whenever the first (leftmost) digit of the account number changes. A report total should also be printed.

Input file: Ledger file (LEDGER.DAT)

Ledger record

	Account number	Account description		Account balance
1 2 3	4 5 6 7 8 9 10 11	12 13 14 15 16 17 18 19 20 21 22 23 24 25 26 27 28 29 30 31 32 33 34 35 36 37 38 39	40 41 42 43 44 45 46	47 48 49 50 51 52 53 54 55 56

Output-report format:

```
        0         1         2         3         4         5         6         7
1234567890123456789012345678901234567890123456789012345678901234567890123456789

4       . . . .              ACCOUNT  BALANCE  REPORT  (9-1)              . . . .

6          ACCOUNT  NUMBER        ACCOUNT  DESCRIPTION        ACCOUNT  BALANCE

8              9999.9999      XXXXXXXXXXXXXXXXXXXXXXXXXXXX  ZZ.ZZZ.ZZZ.99-
9              9999.9999      XXXXXXXXXXXXXXXXXXXXXXXXXXXX  ZZ.ZZZ.ZZZ.99-

11                              TOTAL  FOR  ACCOUNT  9XXX     ZZZ.ZZZ.ZZZ.99-.

14             9999.9999      XXXXXXXXXXXXXXXXXXXXXXXXXXXX  ZZ.ZZZ.ZZZ.99-

16                              TOTAL  FOR  ACCOUNT  9XXX     ZZZ.ZZZ.ZZZ.99-.

19                              REPORT  TOTAL                 ZZZ.ZZZ.ZZZ.99-..
```

Program operations:

1. Process each input ledger record.

2. Print the two heading lines on the first page and on each following page of the report.

3. The input ledger records are already sequenced by the account-number field. For each input ledger record, do the following:
   a. Print an output detail line as specified on the print chart.
   b. Accumulate the account balance.

4. Whenever the first (leftmost) digit of the account-number field changes, print a control-total line as shown on the print chart. The following fields should be printed on the control-total line:
   a. The words TOTAL FOR ACCOUNT.
   b. The first digit of the account number followed by the letters XXX (to indicate that this total applies to all accounts beginning with that number).
   c. The total account balance for such account numbers (followed by a single asterisk).

5. Accumulate the control totals into a report total. After all input records are processed, print the report-total line.

6. Provide for a span of 55 lines per page. Do not permit a control-total line to be printed at the top of a new page. (That is, do not print a control-total line on a report page that does not contain at least one detail line for the control group to which it applies.) Line spacing should be handled as follows:
   a. Single-space each detail line, with the following exceptions: (1) double-space between the last heading line and the first detail of a page, and (2) triple-space between the control-total line and the first detail line for the next control group.
   b. Triple-space the report-total line from the preceding control-total line.

Programming Assignment 9-2: Daily Cash Requirements Report

Background information:

In the vendor file of Tools Unlimited, each vendor record will contain the amount owed to that vendor and the date that it is due. In order for Tools Unlimited to manage its resources efficiently, the financial officer needs a report showing how much money owed comes due each day. This gives management a picture of how much cash is required daily. To produce the report, the vendor file is sorted on the Date-due field. Multiple-level control totals are printed whenever the Date-due field changes. The totals reflect the amount due for each day, each month, and each year. A report total is also printed.

Input file: Vendor file (VENDOR.DAT)

Vendor record

	Vendor number	Date due (yymmdd)	Vendor name		Amount due

1 2 3 4 5 6 7 8 9 10 11 12 13 14 15 16 17 18 19 20 21 22 23 24 25 26 27 28 29 30 31 32 33 34 35 36 37 38 39 40 41 42 43 44 45 46 47 48 49 50 51 52 53 54 55 56 57 58 59 60 61 62 63 64 65 66 67 68 69 70 71 72 73 74

Output-report format:

```
         0         1         2         3         4         5         6         7         8
1234567890123456789012345678901234567890123456789012345678901234567890123456789
 1
 2
 3
 4  DAILY CASH REQUIREMENTS REPORT (9-2)                              PAGE ZZ9
 5
 6         DATE DUE      VENDOR                          AMOUNT
 7         YY MO DA      NUMBER        VENDOR NAME          DUE
 8
 9         YY MM DD      99999999   XXXXXXXXXXXXXXXXXXXX  ----,---.99
10               DD      99999999   XXXXXXXXXXXXXXXXXXXX  ----,---.99
11                       TOTAL DUE ON YY-MM-DD          Z,ZZZ,ZZZ.99*
12
13                       TOTAL DUE IN YY-MM           ZZ,ZZZ,ZZZ.99**
14
15                       TOTAL DUE IN 19YY           ZZZ,ZZZ,ZZZ.99***
16
17                       TOTAL DUE                   ZZZ,ZZZ,ZZZ.99****
18
```

Program operations:

1. Process each input vendor record.

2. Print the three heading lines on the first page and on each following page of the report.
   a. Accumulate and print the page number on the first heading line as shown on the print report.

3. The input vendor records are already sequenced by the Date-due field. For each input vendor record, do the following:
   a. On the detail line, provide group indication for the year and month of the Date-due field. That is, print the year only on the first detail line of each page and on the first detail line when the year changes. Print the month only on the first detail line of each page and on the first detail line when the month and/or year changes.
   b. Print an output detail line as specified on the print chart.
   c. Accumulate the Amount-due field.

4. Print control-total lines as follows:
    a. Whenever the Date-due changes, print a day control-total line (one-asterisk total) as shown on the print chart.
    b. Whenever the month and/or year of the Date-due changes, print a month control-total line (two-asterisk total) as shown on the print chart.
    c. Whenever the year of the Date-due changes, print a year control-total line (three-asterisk total) as shown on the print chart.

5. Accumulate the year control-totals into a report-total. After all input records are processed, print the report-total line.

6. Provide for a span of 54 lines per page. Do not permit control-total lines to be printed at the top of a new page. (That is, do not print a control-total line on a report page that does not contain at least one detail line for the control group to which it applies.) Line spacing is handled as follows:
    a. Single-space each detail line, with the following exceptions: (1) double-space between the last heading line and the first detail line on each page, and (2) double-space between the control-total line and the first detail line for the next control group.
    b. Single-space the day control-total line from the preceding detail line, as shown on the print chart.
    c. Double-space the month control-total line from the preceding day control-total line, as shown on the print chart.
    d. Double-space the year control-total line from the preceding month control-total line, as shown on the print chart.
    e. Triple-space the report-total line from the preceding year control-total line.

Programming Assignment 9-3: Departmental Earnings Report

Background information:

The employee earnings file of Silicon Valley Manufacturing was used for various programming assignments in preceding chapters. Since each employee earnings record includes a Plant-code and a Department-number, group-total reports can be prepared. In particular, the payroll department supervisor needs a multiple-level control-total report in which totals are printed whenever the plant or department number changes. A report total is also required.

Input file: Earnings file (EARNINGS.DAT)

Earnings record

Plant code	Dept. number	Employee number	Employee last name	Employee first name		Current-period earnings	Year-to-date earnings	
1 2 3	4 5 6	7 8 9 10	11 12 13 14 15 16 17 18 19	20 21 22 23 24 25 26 27 28 29 30 31	32 33 34 35 36 37 38 39 40 41 42 43 44 45 46 47 48 49 50 51 52 53 54 55 56 57 58 59	60 61 62 63 64 65 66	67 68 69 70 71 72 73 74	75 76 77 78 79

Output-report format:

```
             0         1         2         3         4         5         6         7         8
    1234567890123456789012345678901234567890123456789012345678901234567890123456789012345678 9
 1
 2
 3
 4  DEPARTMENTAL EARNINGS REPORT (9-3)                                        PAGE ZZ9
 5  SEQUENCED BY EMPLOYEE NUMBER                                              MM/DD/YY
 6    WITHIN DEPARTMENT WITHIN PLANT
 7
 8                                        XXXXXXX PLANT
 9
10  PLANT   DEPT    EMPL NUMBER    LAST NAME      FIRST NM      CURR PER     YEAR-TO-DT
11
12  XXX     9999    999-99-9999    XXXXXXXXXXX XXXXXXXXX     ZZ,ZZZ.99     ZZZ,ZZZ.99
13                  999-99-9999    XXXXXXXXXXX XXXXXXXXX     ZZ,ZZZ.99     ZZZ,ZZZ.99
14
15                          TOTAL FOR DEPT 9999            ZZZ,ZZZ.99  Z,ZZZ,ZZZ.99*
16
17                          TOTAL FOR PLANT XXXXXXX     Z,ZZZ,ZZZ.99 ZZ,ZZZ,ZZZ.99**
18
19
20                          REPORT TOTAL                Z,ZZZ,ZZZ.99 ZZ,ZZZ,ZZZ.99***
21
22
```

Program operations:

1. Process each input record.

2. Print the five heading lines on the first page and on each following page of the report.
   a. Accumulate and print the page number on the first heading line as shown on the print chart.
   b. Print the run date on the second heading line as shown on the print chart.
   c. Print the plant identification (as explained in step 3) on the fourth heading line.

3. The input earnings records are already sequenced by Employee-number within Department within Plant within Record-code. Whenever a new Plant control group starts, skip to a new report page. In other words, the first Plant control group begins on the first page; each following Plant control group should also begin on a new page.
   a. The abbreviation stored in the Plant field should be converted to the complete plant identification as follows:

   ATL = ATLANTIC
   CTL = CENTRAL
   MTN = MOUNTAIN
   PAC = PACIFIC

   b. The applicable plant identification should be printed on the fourth heading line of each page.

4. For each input earnings record, do the following:
   a. On the detail line, provide group indication for the Plant and Department-number fields. That is, print the Plant field only on the first detail line of each page and on the first detail line when the Plant changes. Print the Department-number field only on the first detail line of each page and on the first detail line when the value of the Department-number and/or plant field changes.
   b. Print an output detail line as specified on the print chart.
   c. Accumulate the This-period-earnings and Year-to-date-earnings fields.

5. Print control-total lines as follows:
   a. Whenever the Department-number and/or Plant changes, print a Department-number control-total line (one-asterisk total) as shown on the print chart.
   b. Whenever the Plant changes, print a Plant control-total line (two-asterisk total) as shown on the print chart. Print the Plant identification on this line as explained previously in step 3a.

6. Accumulate the Plant control totals into a report total. After all input records are processed, print the report-total line.

7. Provide for a span of 54 lines per page. Do not permit control-total lines to be printed at the top of a new page. (That is, do not print a control-total line on a report page that does not contain at least one detail line for the control group to which it applies.) Line spacing is handled as follows:
   a. Single-space each detail line, with the following exceptions: (1) double-space between the last heading line and the first detail line on each page, and (2) double-space between the control-total line and the first detail line for the next control group.
   b. Double-space the Department-number control-total line from the preceding detail line, as shown on the print chart.
   c. Double-space the Plant control-total line from the preceding department-number control-total line, as shown on the print chart.
   d. Triple-space the report-total line from the preceding Plant control-total line.

Programming Assignment 9-4: Territory Sales Report

Background information:

The Salesperson file of Follow-the-Sun Sales was used in various programming assignments, beginning in Chapter 2. Since each salesperson record includes fields for the territory and region to which the salesperson belongs, you might guess that the sales manager wants a report with appropriate breakdowns. To do this, a multiple-level report is needed that prints control totals whenever the region or territory changes. A report total should also be printed.

Input file: Salesperson file (SALESPER.DAT)

Salesperson record

Region	Territory	Number	Salesperson name		Sales revenue	Sales quota
1 2	3 4	5 6 7 8	9 10 11 12 13 14 15 16 17 18 19 20 21 22 23 24 25 26 27 28 29 30 31 32 33 34 35 36 37	38 39 40 41 42 43 44 45 46 47 48 49 50 51 52 53 54 55 56 57 58 59 60	61 62 63 64 65 66 67 68 69 70	71 72 73 74 75 76 77 78 79

Output-report format:

```
          0         1         2         3         4         5         6         7         8
 1234567890123456789012345678901234567890123456789012345678901234567890123456789012345678901

 4  TERRITORY SALES REPORT (9-4)                                                    PAGE ZZ9
 5  SEQUENCED BY SALESPERSON                XXXXXXXXXXX REGION                       MM/DD/YY
 6    WITHIN TERRITORY WITHIN REGION

 8     NBR   SALESPERSON                SALES REVENUE     SALES QUOTA   PCTG        VARIANCE

10  REGION-XX TERRITORY 9999   (CONTINUED)

12     999 XXXXXXXXXXXXXXXXXXXXXXXXX  ZZ,ZZZ,ZZZ.99  ZZ,ZZZ,ZZZ.99 ZZZ.9%   ZZ,ZZZ,ZZZ.99-
13     999 XXXXXXXXXXXXXXXXXXXXXXXXX  ZZ,ZZZ,ZZZ.99  ZZ,ZZZ,ZZZ.99 ZZZ.9%   ZZ,ZZZ,ZZZ.99-

15            TERRITORY 9999 TOTAL   ZZZ,ZZZ,ZZZ.99 ZZZ,ZZZ,ZZZ.99 ZZZ.9%  ZZZ,ZZZ,ZZZ.99-*

17               REGION XX TOTAL     ZZZ,ZZZ,ZZZ.99 ZZZ,ZZZ,ZZZ.99 ZZZ.9%  ZZZ,ZZZ,ZZZ.99-**

20                REPORT TOTAL       ZZZ,ZZZ,ZZZ.99 ZZZ,ZZZ,ZZZ.99 ZZZ.9%  ZZZ,ZZZ,ZZZ.99-***
```

Program operations:

1. Process each input record.

2. Print the four heading lines on the first page and on each following page of the report.
   a. Accumulate and print the page number on the first heading line as shown on the print chart.
   b. Print the run date on the second heading line as shown on the print chart.
   c. Print the name of the Region (as explained in step 3) on the second heading line.

3. The input salesperson records are already sequenced by Salesperson-number within Territory within Region within Record-code. Whenever a new Region control group starts, skip to a new report page. In other words, the first Region control group begins, of course, on the first page; each following Region control group should also begin on a new page.
   a. The abbreviation stored in the Region field should be converted to the complete region name as follows:

      NE = NORTHEASTERN
      SE = SOUTHEASTERN
      MW = MIDWESTERN
      NW = NORTHWESTERN
      SW = SOUTHWESTERN

   b. The applicable region name should be printed on the second heading line of each page.

4. Whenever a new Territory control group starts, a control-heading line should print out the Region and Territory as shown on the print chart. If a Territory is continued from one report page to another, print the word (CONTINUED), as shown on the print chart.

5. For each input salesperson record, do the following:
   a. Print an output detail line as specified on the print chart.
   b. Calculate the Variance as the Sales-quota minus the Sales-revenue.
   c. Accumulate the Sales-revenue, Sales-quota, and Variance fields.

6. Print control-total lines as follows:
   a. Whenever the Region and/or Territory changes, print a Territory control-total line (one-asterisk total) as shown on the print chart.
   b. Whenever the Region changes, print a Region control-total line (two-asterisk total) as shown on the print chart.

7. Accumulate the Region control totals into a report total. After all input records are processed, print the report-total line.

8. Provide for a span of 54 lines per page.
   a. Do not permit control-heading lines (see line 10 of the print chart) to be printed at the bottom of a page. That is, do not print a control-heading line unless room also exists for at least two detail lines to be printed for that control group.
   b. Do not permit control-total lines to be printed at the top of a new page. That is, do not print a control-total line on a report page that does not contain at least one detail line for the control group to which it applies.

9. Line spacing is handled as follows:
   a. Single-space each detail line, except double-space after each control-heading line.
   b. Double-space the Territory control-total line from the preceding detail line, as shown on the print chart.
   c. Double-space the Region control-total line from the preceding Territory control-total line, as shown on the print chart.
   d. Triple-space the report-total line from the preceding Region control-total line, as shown on the print chart.

Programming Assignment 9-5: Budget Summary for Nurses—Single-Level Control Break

Background information:

As in most organizations, Brooklawn Hospital controls expenditures through budget codes that define categories to which each expenditure is charged. For budgetary purposes, each employee is charged to a cost center (depending upon the employee's manager) and each is given a budget code depending on the type of function performed. Management needs a report that summarizes by cost center.

Input file: Nurses file (NURSES.DAT)

Nurses record

Name		Prof. specialty	Date hired (yymmdd)	Cost center	Base monthly salary	

1 2 3 4 5 6 7 8 9 10 11 12 13 14 15 16 17 18 19 20 21 22 23 24 25 26 27 28 29 30 31 32 33 34 35 36 37 38 39 40 41 42 43 44 45 46 47 48 49 50 51 52 53 54 55 56 57 58 59 60 61 62 63 64 65 66 67 68 69 70 71 72 73 74 75 76 77 78 79 80 81 82 83 84 85 86 87 88 89 90 91 92 93 94 95 96 97

Output-report format:

```
        0             1             2             3             4             5             6
     1234567890123456789012345678901234567890123456789012345678901234567890123456789
 1
 2
 3
 4  BROOKLAWN COST CENTER SUMMARY (9-5)                              PAGE ZZ9
 5
 6  COST                                DATE                              BASE
 7  CTR   EMPLOYEE NAME                 HIRED    SPECIALTY                SALARY
 8
 9  XXX   XXXXXXXXXXXXXXXXXXXXXXXX  XX/XX/XX  XXXXXXXXXXXXX      Z,ZZZ.99
10        XXXXXXXXXXXXXXXXXXXXXXXX  XX/XX/XX  XXXXXXXXXXXXX      Z,ZZZ.99
11
12
13
14         TOTAL FOR COST CENTER XXX                      ZZZ,ZZZ.99*
15
16
17         REPORT TOTAL                               Z,ZZZ,ZZZ.99**
18
```

Program operations:

1. Process each input record.

2. Print the three heading lines on the first page and on each following page of the report.

3. The input records are in sequence by the Cost-center field. For each record, do the following:

   a. Print an output detail line as specified on the print chart. On the detail line, provide group indication for the cost center. That is, print the Cost-center field only on the first detail line for that cost center or on the first detail line of each page.

   b. Accumulate the Base-monthly-salary field.

4. Whenever the cost center changes, print a control-total line (one-asterisk total) as shown on the print chart.

5. Accumulate the cost center control totals into a report total. After all input records are processed, print the report-total line.

6. Provide for a span of 54 lines per page. Do not permit control-total lines to be printed at the top of a new page. (That is, do not print a control-total line on a report page that does not contain at least one detail line for the control group to which it applies.) Line spacing is handled as follows:

   a. Single-space each detail line, with the following exceptions: (1) double-space between the last heading line and the first detail line on each page, and (2) double-space between the control-total line and the first detail line for the next control group.

   b. Triple-space the report-total line from the preceding year control-total line.

Programming Assignment 9-6: Budget Summary for Nurses—Two-Level Control Break

Background information:

Instead of a single-level grouping by cost center, Brooklawn Hospital's management requires a two-level grouping by cost center, then by budget code.

Input file: Nurses file (NURSES.DAT)

Nurses record

Name		Professional specialty	Date hired (yymmdd)	Cost center	Budget code	Base monthly salary	

1 2 3 4 5 6 7 8 9 10 11 12 13 14 15 16 17 18 19 20 21 22 23 24 25 26 27 28 29 30 31 32 33 34 35 36 37 38 39 40 41 42 43 44 45 46 47 48 49 50 51 52 53 54 55 56 57 58 59 60 61 62 63 64 65 66 67 68 69 70 71 72 73 74 75 76 77 78 79 80 81 82 83 84 85 86 87 88 89 90 91 92 93 94 95 96 97

Output-report format:

```
             0         1         2         3         4         5         6
      1234567890123456789012345678901234567890123456789012345678901234567890123456789

 1
 2
 3
 4    BROOKLAWN COST CENTER SUMMARY (9-6)              RUN DATE MM/DD/YY
 5    BUDGET SUMMARY                                            PAGE ZZ9
 6    COST CENTER XXX -- XXXXXXXXX
 7
 8         EMPLOYEE NAME                HIRED   SPECIALTY            SALARY
 9
10    BUDGET CODE XXXX   (CONTINUED)
11
12         XXXXXXXXXXXXXXXXXXXXXXXX XX/XX/XX XXXXXXXXXXXXXXX      Z,ZZZ.99
13         XXXXXXXXXXXXXXXXXXXXXXXX XX/XX/XX XXXXXXXXXXXXXXX      Z,ZZZ.99
14
15
16         BUDGET TOTAL FOR BUDGET CODE XXXX             ZZZ,ZZZ.99*
17
18         BUDGET TOTAL FOR COST CENTER XXX              ZZZ,ZZZ.99**
19
20
21         REPORT TOTAL                               Z,ZZZ,ZZZ.99***
22
23
24
```

Program operations:

1. Process each input record.

2. Print the four heading lines on the first page and on each following page of the report.
   a. Print the run date on the first heading line as shown on the print chart.
   b. Accumulate and print the page number on the second heading line as shown on the print chart.
   c. On the third heading line, print the Cost-center value and the name of that cost center's manager (as explained in step 3).

3. The input records are in sequence by budget code within cost center. Whenever a new cost center control goup starts, skip to a new report page. In other words, the first cost center control group begins on the first page; each following cost center control group should also begin on a new page.
   a. The cost center code on the third heading line must be supplemented by the manager's name. Normally, this is available from another file. For this program, use the following:

Cost center	Manager
100	JOHNSON
104	STEVENS
112	HAMILTON
199	MORALES

4. Whenever a new budget code control group starts, a control-heading line should print out the budget code as shown on the print chart. If a budget code is continued from one report page to another, print the word (CONTINUED), as shown on the print chart.

5. For each input record, do the following:
   a. Print an output detail line as specified on the print chart.
   b. Accumulate the Base-monthly-salary field.

6. Print control-total lines as follows:
   a. Whenever the cost center and/or budget code changes, print a budget code control-total line (one-asterisk total) as shown on the print chart.
   b. Whenever the cost center changes, print a cost center control-total line (two-asterisk total) as shown on the print chart.

7. Accumulate the cost center control totals into a report total. After all input records are processed, print the report-total line.

8. Provide for a span of 54 lines per page.
   a. Do not permit control-heading lines (see line 10 of the spacing chart) to be printed at the bottom of a page. That is, do not print a control-heading line unless room also exists for at least two detail lines to be printed for that control group.
   b. Do not permit control-total lines to be printed at the top of a new page. That is, do not print a control-total line on a report page that does not contain at least one detail line for the control group to which it applies.

9. Line spacing is handled as follows:
   a. Single-space each detail line, except double-space after each control-heading line.
   b. Triple-space the budget code control-total line from the preceding detail line, as shown on the print chart.
   c. Double-space the cost center control-total line from the preceding budget code control total line, as shown on the print chart.
   d. Triple-space the report-total line from the preceding cost center control-total line, as shown on the print chart.

DATA VALIDATION CONCEPTS

MODULE OBJECTIVES

One of a data-processing department's important functions is to protect the integrity of a valuable company asset: the company's data. After data is entered into the computer, numerous techniques are used to ensure that it does not become corrupted. One of the principal keys to ensuring error-free data is making certain that all data is correct before it is introduced into the files. This is called data validation, the topic of this module. From this module, you will learn the following:

- The nature of character testing—testing for validity of individual characters of fields.

- The various methods for field checking, including checking to ensure that a field is present, checking allowable ranges of numeric fields, checking to ensure that values entered are reasonable, and checking dates.

- Data validation programs for checking input data. This can be done on-line (data checked as it is entered) or by a batch process in which all data is entered and then checked in a batch.

MODULE OUTLINE

About Garbage

Character Testing
    Class Test
    Sign Test

Field Checking
    Presence Check
    Absence Check
    Range Check
    Limit Check
    Reasonableness Check
    Consistency Check
    Justification Check
    Embedded-Blank Check
    Date Check
    Code-Existence Check

Data Validation Programs
    On-Line vs. Batch Data Validation

About Garbage

That cliché "G.I.G.O." (garbage in—garbage out!) is all too familiar to data-processing personnel and users. Although some may lamely try to enlist the phrase as a defense against an input data deviation, a professional programmer/analyst should never utter these words. Instead, the motto should be "G.D.G.I." (garbage doesn't get in). It is the programmer/analyst's responsibility to specify the safeguards and controls necessary to ensure data integrity within the system. This module discusses such aspects of control as they relate to data validation during initial input of data into a computer system.

One of the most common mistakes made by a beginning programmer/analyst is the failure to validate data completely during its initial entry into the system. This is known as letting "garbage" or "dirty data" into the system. The consequences are severe. For instance, consider a customer order-processing system in which data for each item is taken from an inventory file. Assume that an incorrect price has been entered into the record of one inventory item. For each customer order that includes this item, the price in the resulting invoice record and the invoice total will be incorrect. Furthermore, the balance-owed field in the customer's record will be updated with an incorrect amount. In other words, any processing that uses this incorrect data will produce other incorrect entries in the system.

It is critical that the programmer/analyst incorporate programmed validation checks on data at initial input. This module focuses on two general categories of programmed input validation checks: character testing and field checking.

Character Testing

The most basic form of data validation control is testing individual character positions within a field. The two forms of character tests are class and sign.

Class Test

Class tests determine whether data values within a field fall into the numeric, alphabetic, or alphanumeric class. Figure D-1 categorizes character representations according to their class.

Generally, numeric fields should be validated to ensure that each digit position is purely numeric. When alphabetic or special characters are present in a numeric field, the data is erroneous. So, a numeric class test helps to ensure the data integrity of the validated numeric field—and also of any fields that hold the results of computations involving the field.

Don't assume that declaring a field as numeric with PIC 9 guarantees that the data will always be numeric. Remember from earlier discussions that the picture

Figure D-1
Classes of data.

Data class	Valid characters
Numeric	Digits 0–9 and an operational sign
Alphabetic	Letters A–Z, space
	Letters a–z (COBOL-85 only)
Alphanumeric	Digits 0–9
	Letters A–Z, space
	Letters a–z (COBOL-85 only)
	Special characters

only tells the compiler the types of actions that can be performed on the data. No restrictions exist on the data that can be entered into a PIC 9 field from, for instance, a READ statement. Also, remember that an alphanumeric field (PIC X) can be tested (using the NUMERIC class test) to determine if it is numeric—that is, contains only digits. It is *not* necessary to define a field as numeric in order to perform a numeric class check on it.

A two-letter state code—such as CA for California, NY for New York, or TX for Texas—is an example of a data element that may be checked to ensure that it is alphabetic. In practice, fields are checked to ensure an alphabetic class much less frequently than they are to validate a numeric class. This is because purely alphabetic-character fields seldom occur. An individual's name, for example, may validly contain an apostrophe or a hyphen. The apostrophe and the hyphen are not alphabetic characters, but instead are special characters of the alphanumeric class.

The term *alphanumeric* encompasses both the numeric and alphabetic data classes and all special characters. By definition, all fields can be considered alphanumeric. So, there is no need—and no COBOL reserved word available—to test for an alphanumeric class.

Sign Test

A **sign test** is performed only on fields defined in the DATA DIVISION as numeric (PIC 9). Numeric data can be considered in two categories. Data quantities that actually represent numeric values (such as a quantity-on-hand or a sale-price) are algebraic because technically they can have a plus or minus sign and can be operated on arithmetically. (Whether or not a given quantity is actually involved in a specific program's arithmetic is unimportant). On the other hand, numeric codes such as Social Security numbers, telephone numbers, and zip codes are examples of absolute values. For them, a sign has no meaning. Within your program, you may code these as either PIC 9 or PIC X fields. However, in some instances, you may find that coding them PIC 9 simplifies the validation.

Three normal arithmetic sign configurations exist: positive, negative, and unsigned. (Sometimes a positive sign is used in place of an unsigned representation, and vice versa.) The location and coding method used to represent the sign varies depending upon the computer hardware and software.

Field Checking

In addition to the basic character testing of input data fields, most data elements should be subjected to further, more rigorous checks. These are called **field checks**.

Presence Check

A **presence check** detects missing values in fields. Most input records contain both required and optional fields. For instance, in an employee file, each employee's record is probably identified by his or her Social Security number. Obviously, an employee should not be entered into the employee file without a value for this identifying field.

A test for presence should normally be applied to all required fields. Its power is limited, however, since a presence check establishes only that data is in the field; it does not address the quality or accuracy of the data. So, whenever possible, additional field checks should be applied to each field to help ensure that the data is correct.

Absence Check

The converse of a presence check is an **absence check**, which ensures that a field or record area is blank. The absence check is typically limited to situations in which an unused or unassigned area of an input record exists. For example, assume that positions 52 through 57 of a record should not be used, but data is keyed in position 57. The unexplained data probably belongs in the adjacent field, starting in position 58. An absence check can signal such possible field-alignment errors. Figure D-2 provides examples of presence and absence tests.

Figure D-2   Presence/absence check examples.

Employee-salary record:

	SMITH	JOHN			2/000000b
	Last name	First name	Middle name	Unassigned area	Monthy salary

Data element	Validation	Result of test on above data
Last name	Must be present	Passes presence test
First name	Must be present	Passes presence test
Middle name	Optional	Untested
Unassigned area	Must be blank	Fails absence test
Monthly salary	Must be present	Passes presence test
	Must be numeric	Fails numeric class test (because of blank space)

Range Check

A **range check** is applied to code numbers to verify that they exist in the coding system used. For example, the area identification codes assigned to the first three digits of Social Security numbers range from 001–626 and from 700–799. A range check applied to these digits can identify certain transposed or otherwise erroneously coded entries. The following are some typical range-check examples:

Data element	Allowable range
Month number	01–12
Invoice numbers	10001–10599 and 11001–12999
U.S. telephone prefixes	221–998

Although these examples suggest that the fields are defined as numeric, such tests can be performed with either numeric or alphanumeric defined data. For instance, *assuming that the fields were already verified to contain only digits*, the following two sets of code perform exactly the same function:

```
05  TELE-PREFIX      PIC 9(3).        05  TELE-PREFIX          PIC X(3).
    :                                     :
    :                                     :
IF  TELE-PREFIX LESS THAN 221         IF  TELE-PREFIX LESS THAN "221"
OR  GREATER THAN 299...               OR  GREATER THAN "299"...
```

Limit Check

A **limit check** tests a field against maximum and/or minimum values. The limits can be either absolute amounts or percentages. An example of an absolute limit is when all expenditure transactions processed through a petty cash account must be less than $35.00. Similarly, product price changes may be validated against a percentage limit to ensure that a new price is not more than, for example, 15 percent above or below the corresponding old price.

Reasonableness Check

A **reasonableness check** identifies abnormal data values. In a department store, for instance, a unit sales price of $800 in the notions department or a sales tag indicating a purchase quantity of 10 diamond rings could be identified as an exception condition. As another example, any discount greater than 20 percent of the corresponding list price can be flagged for investigation. The reasonableness check is similar to the limit check because it requires the establishment of parameters against which data is tested. It differs, however, because the parameters are norms, rather than rigid limits. The following are other examples of typical parameters for reasonableness checks:

Data element	Reasonable Value	
	Minimum	Maximum
Number of dependents	0	12
Adult height	58 inches	82 inches
Adult weight	90 pounds	299 pounds
Annuity withholding	$.00	$1,500.00

It is important to remember that certain values identified as exceptions will, in fact, be valid. So, any program must include provisions to override reasonableness checks to force acceptance of the data into the system. For instance, a data-entry program might display a warning message for an input value that does not meet the reasonableness check. However, the program would be designated to allow the operator to override and enter the data anyway.

Consistency Check

A **consistency check** (sometimes called a **relationship check** or a **combination check**) is the consideration of two or more data elements in relation to one another. It can be a powerful way to detect erroneous data. Suppose that patient diagnosis data is input to a medical-records application and is then checked. If the diagnosis code indicates pregnancy and the gender code specifies male, a prime example of inconsistent data exists. Note that the consistency check does not indicate which of the involved fields is incorrect. It does, though, identify a discrepancy that requires resolution.

Consistency checks are used not only in uncovering data recording errors, but also in monitoring processing operations. Consider a charge account system that uses credit limits of dollar amounts, beyond which the customer may not incur further debts. Suppose a customer's current balance is $1,900 and credit limit is $2,000. If the customer makes a purchase of $200, an over-limit condition will be detected by checking the relationship of one field to another.

Justification Check

A **justification check** ensures proper alignment of data within a field. Alphabetic and alphanumeric fields are usually left-justified (the first character is in the leftmost position of the field), numeric-integer fields are normally right-justified, and numeric fields with decimal places are decimal-point aligned. An alphanumeric field that is present but has a space in the leftmost character position fails a normal justification check.

Justification checks are rarely performed on numeric fields. Instead, a numeric field with blank positions is flagged as erroneous by a numeric class test. The numeric class test is more powerful because it (1) detects both blank and non-numeric characters and (2) checks all positions of the field.

Embedded-Blank Check

An **embedded-blank check** checks certain key alphanumeric fields to ensure that blank positions were not entered inadvertently. An embedded blank is one that has data characters within the field both to the left and to the right of the blank position.

For example, consider a part number field (alphanumeric) serving as a key field for inventory records. As a rule, it is poor practice to allow embedded blanks in key fields because the blanks cause confusion when entering and retrieving records. So, if embedded blanks are prohibited, detection of an embedded blank identifies an erroneous entry.

As with justification checks, embedded-blank tests are not typically made on numeric fields. Since blanks are not numeric digits, a numeric class test detects embedded blanks. Also, the class test is much easier to code.

Date Check

A **date check** ensures the validity of calendar dates recorded in input transactions. Two basic formats express dates in data-processing systems: Gregorian and Julianized.

A Gregorian date is the one we use daily. The date July 4, 1776, is an example of a Gregorian date representation; it is a date based upon the Gregorian calendar. You will encounter two formats: *mmddyy* and *yymmdd* (for instance, 070476 and 760704, respectively). Although less familiar to us, the format *yymmdd* is commonly used within the computer because the elements of the data progress from most significant to least significant, making it amenable to sorting. With the upcoming need for years in both the 1900s and the 2000s, it is a good idea to expand the year to four positions: *yyyymmdd*.

With a Julianized date, the day is assigned a sequential day number within the year, giving the *yyddd* or *yyyyddd* format (where *ddd* represents the day number of the year from 001 to 365, or 366 for leap year). Represented in Julianized format, Independence Day appears as 76186.

Gregorian dates are used most frequently for input and output because they are common to our everyday lives and therefore much easier for us to understand. Julianized dates are often used internally with data-processing systems. The advantage of a Julianized date is that date-span computations can be made arithmetically without need for adjustments when the dates are not within the same month. However, the Intrinsic Function Module of 1989 for COBOL-85 adds the date functions DATE-OF-INTEGER and DAY-OF-INTEGER to COBOL-85. These make date-span computations almost trivial.

For Gregorian dates, month numbers are checked to ensure that they are within the range 01–12. Day numbers are, as a minimum, validated against the range 01–31. If increased data integrity is required, a consistency check of day in relation to month can be made (for example, the day range of April, June, September, and November is limited to the span 01–30).

February presents a special day-range problem. A precise date check for February involves dividing the year by four. If the remainder is zero, the year is a leap year and the acceptable range is then, of course, 01–29, rather than 01–28. This rule has one exception, however. If the year ends in 00 (for example, 2000), the year is not a leap year unless the four-digit year number is evenly divisible by 400. So, 1600 was a leap year and 2000 is a leap year—but 1700, 1800, and 1900 were not.

Besides checking for valid month/day combinations, it is generally advisable to validate dates for recency. Input transactions to be processed usually have a recent date. The further in the past or future the date, the greater the likelihood that a date error was made. So, it is wise to establish a reasonableness check regarding how much variance is permitted before the distant date is identified as an exception condition. Remember that, with all reasonableness checks, a re-entry override must be provided to allow the system to accept exception conditions.

Code-Existence Check

A **code-existence check** ensures that a particular code is valid. Many numeric codes can be validated through the use of range checks or techniques appropriate to a specific application. However, certain codes—particularly those that are alphanumeric or have a relatively low number of entries—require positive matches against a table of valid codes maintained within a program or data file. For example, a food processor may use only the following units of measure.

Code	Meaning
HP	Half-pint
PT	Pint
QT	Quart
HG	Half-gallon
GL	Gallon

Each input code value is then matched by the program against this table. (This function is called a table-lookup and is covered in Module E and Chapters 11 and 12.) If a match is made, the input code is assumed to be valid; if not, the code is identified as erroneous.

Data Validation Programs

The programmer/analyst must study actual conditions carefully before establishing a data validation plan. The class of each field within the record to be validated must be identified. Numeric class tests should be applied to each numeric field; alphabetic class tests should be performed on any purely alphabetic fields. Additional field checks should be chosen, as appropriate, for each field. When applicable, the order and set requirements of each record within the file should also be validated.

The checks instituted should be rigorous enough to reject a high proportion of the invalid data, but flexible enough to accept all legitimate values.

On-Line vs. Batch Data Validation

Most data entry is done through terminals connected to a computer or into a personal computer. The entered data can be validated in two ways: on-line and batch. When data is entered directly into a system through a terminal, it is commonly checked for validity as it is entered; this is on-line validation. For instance, if you are an order-entry clerk and enter a product code as G1557 instead of H1557, there are two possibilities. One is that there is no product with the incorrect code—the computer can alert you immediately. The other is that the incorrect product record will be accessed and displayed. By inspecting the product description, you can recognize the error. In either case, an appropriate correction can be made. In on-line applications in which data goes directly into the system, it is imperative that validation is completed immediately— before that transaction is stored.

Other applications are not amenable to validation during data entry. For instance, a company might send its weekly payroll source data (perhaps handwritten) to a service bureau for keying. The service bureau returns one or more cartridges, tapes, or disks containing the keyed data. Usually some validation was performed during entry—for instance, the data-entry program might be designed to allow only digits to be entered into numeric fields. However, a data-entry person—who is usually unfamiliar with the application—simply does not have the knowledge to correct many other types of errors. For instance, data incorrectly recorded on the source document—yet accurately keyed—might fail range, reasonableness, or code-existence checks. As a result, in this type of data entry, all data is accepted with the intent of validating it later. A special **data validation program** has the sole purpose of checking to ensure that only valid data is entered into the system. Once detected, erroneous data can be corrected by individuals familiar with the application. This is called batch validation.

Most batch data validation programs read an input transaction file and write an audit list and an error list. An **audit list** is a report that shows the contents of each record that was input into the system. An **error list** is an action document that reports what error or exception conditions have entered the system. Error lists require action to correct or confirm the identified conditions, whereas audit lists only need to be retained for reference over a specified period of time. The combined audit/error list serves both functions.

An error list is usually designed with the fields of the input records displayed on the left-hand side of the report; this is referred to as the **record-image area**. To the right of the record-image area, error messages that apply to that record are printed.

In the next chapter, you will study a sample sales-transaction validation program. You may think of it as a model data validation program for batch processing. That is, the general program logic used in this example can apply to practically any data validation program—regardless of the specific application or type of record being validated. Later in Chapter 10, the same validation techniques are applied to a data-entry program.

Module Summary

Data-processing systems should have safeguards and controls to help ensure the integrity of data within the system. Two general categories of programmed validation of input data are described in this chapter: character testing and field checking.

Character Testing

Class tests determine whether positions within a field contain numeric or alphabetic data. A sign test checks whether the value of a numeric field is positive, negative, or unsigned.

Field Checking

Presence checks are used to detect missing fields. Absence checks identify extraneous data and misaligned fields. Range checks are applied to code numbers to verify that a number is valid. The limit check tests a field against maximum and/or minimum values. Reasonableness checks identify abnormal (though not necessarily incorrect) values. A consistency check is the consideration of two or more data elements in relation to one another. Proper alignment of data within alphanumeric fields is tested by justification and embedded-blank checks. A date check tests the validity of calendar dates. To ensure that a particular code is valid, code-existence checks are used.

Data Validation Programs

Data validation programs check input record fields to help ensure that only valid data enters the system. Data validation can be done in either the on-line or batch mode. Most on-line data validation requires the operator to re-enter erroneous data before progressing to the next data-item. Most batch data validation programs read an input transaction file and write an audit list and an error list; combined audit/error lists are sometimes produced.

Exercises

Terms for Definition

absence check
alphabetic class
alphanumeric class
audit list
class test
code-existence check
combination check
consistency check
data validation program
date check
embedded-blank check

error list
field check
justification check
limit check
numeric class
presence check
range check
reasonableness check
record-image area
relationship check
sign test

Matching Exercise

The following is the Nurses record format.

Match the data validation check type with a corresponding validation need by writing the letter of the validation check in the space provided.

Nurses record

Employment code ¬
F - Fulltime employee
P - Parttime employee

Supervisory code
Y - Yes
N - No

Shift code ¬
Value: 1, 2, or 3

Record code	Name		Home telephone number	Professional specialty	Date hired	Salary schedule		Cost center	Budget code		Base monthly salary	Annuity code	Annuity withholding			Ward/duty station
	Last name	Middle initial / First name														

1 2|3 4 5 6 7 8 9 10 11 12 13|14 15 16 17 18 19 20 21 22 23 24|25|26 27 28 29 30 31 32|33 34 35 36 37 38 39 40 41 42 43 44 45 46|47 48 49 50 51 52|53 54 55|56 57|58 59 60|61 62 63 64|65 66 67|68 69 70 71|72 73|74 75 76 77 78|79 80|81 82 83 84 85 86 87 88 89 90 91 92 93|94 95 96|97

└ Value NU

a. presence check   g. justification check

b. absence check   h. embedded-blank check

c. range check   i. date check

d. limit check   j. class test

e. reasonableness check   k. sign test

f. consistency check   l. code-existence check

____ The Ward/duty-station field must not include any spaces.

____ The Cost-center field must be numeric.

____ The Annuity field must not be more than 10 percent of the Base-monthly-salary field.

____ All supervisors are fulltime employees.

____ Each new record entered must include entries for the Name.

____ The Ward/duty-station and Shift-code fields must be blank when a new record is created.

____ The Cost-center code must be within 001–199 or 201–449.

____ The Date-hired field must not be later than the date the entry is made.

____ The Professional-specialty entry begins in column 33.

____ Reject any entry for the Employment field that is not F or P.

____ The Annuity-withholding field must not be negative.

____ Ensure that the day and month hired are valid entries.

Data Validation Design and Coding

CHAPTER

10

CHAPTER OBJECTIVES

In Module D, you learned about basic data validation operations. Now it's time to apply these principles. From this chapter, you will learn the following:

- The two forms of the INSPECT statement, which allow you to process a field character by character: INSPECT/REPLACING and INSPECT/ TALLYING.

- Using alphanumeric definition of numeric fields to avoid error conditions that could terminate execution of the program.

- Data validation techniques that check for:

    - A given value or a group of values

    - The presence of an entry in a field

    - The data class

    - A range of values

    - Field justification

    - Consistency between fields

- On-line data validation during data entry.

The Elements of an Editing Task

Before learning the techniques of data validation, you need to know about the INSPECT statement. With the INSPECT, you can examine a field on a character-by-character basis, an essential task for ensuring the validity of data. The two primary forms of INSPECT are INSPECT/REPLACING and INSPECT/TALLYING. (This chapter discusses only commonly used forms of the INSPECT statement. Appendix D includes additional forms.)

The INSPECT/ REPLACING Statement

You use the INSPECT statement with the REPLACING phrase for character translation tasks. It allows you to convert characters within a field from one value to another. For instance, assume that a record's field may contain one or more asterisks and that you need to change each asterisk to a slash character. The INSPECT/REPLACING statement you use would designate three data-items:

1. The field being inspected in which the asterisks are changed to slashes. This is called the **inspected field**.
2. The asterisk character. Since the inspected field is searched for each occurrence of this character, it is called the **search-field value**.
3. The slash character. This is the character that replaces each asterisk. So, it is called the **replacement-field value**.

As shown in Figure 10-1's INSPECT/REPLACING format, the three commonly used options are REPLACING ALL, REPLACING LEADING, and REPLACING FIRST. In each of Figure 10-1's examples, both the search-field value and the replacement-field value are one character in length. However, these two fields can be any length—as long as they are both the same length.

REPLACING ALL Option

The INSPECT statement with the REPLACING ALL option causes all occurrences of a specified character to be replaced by another character. Suppose that you have a date field with the month, day, and year separated by slashes—but the programming specifications call for hyphen separators. The INSPECT/REPLACING ALL statement shown in Example A of Figure 10-1 handles this conversion. Each character of the SALE-DATE field is examined starting from the left. When a character that is identical to the search-field value (a slash, in this case) is found, that character is changed to the replacement-field value (a hyphen, in this case).

The inspected field can be either an elementary or a group data-item. Both the search-field value and the replacement-field value can be expressed as either a literal, a figurative constant, or as the data-name of an elementary field. Also, as covered later in this chapter, it is important to recognize that the data class of the search-field and replacement-field values must be consistent with that of the inspected field.

Example B of Figure 10-1 shows a situation in which the INSPECT/REPLACING statement changes spaces to hyphens within a Social Security number. Here, the search-field value is expressed as a figurative constant and the replacement field value is a data-name.

REPLACING LEADING Option

With the REPLACING LEADING option, only leftmost occurrences of the search-field value are converted to the replacement-field value. This option is commonly used in data validation programs to force unused positions of a numeric field to zeros. When numeric fields are initially entered into a system, the unused leading positions sometimes contain spaces. To use the field for arithmetic operations or numeric editing, however, the field should contain no spaces. As Example C of Figure 10-1 illustrates, the REPLACING LEADING option can be used for this application. (This form of the REPLACING is used several times in the data validation program shown later.)

Figure 10-1
The INSPECT/
REPLACING statement.

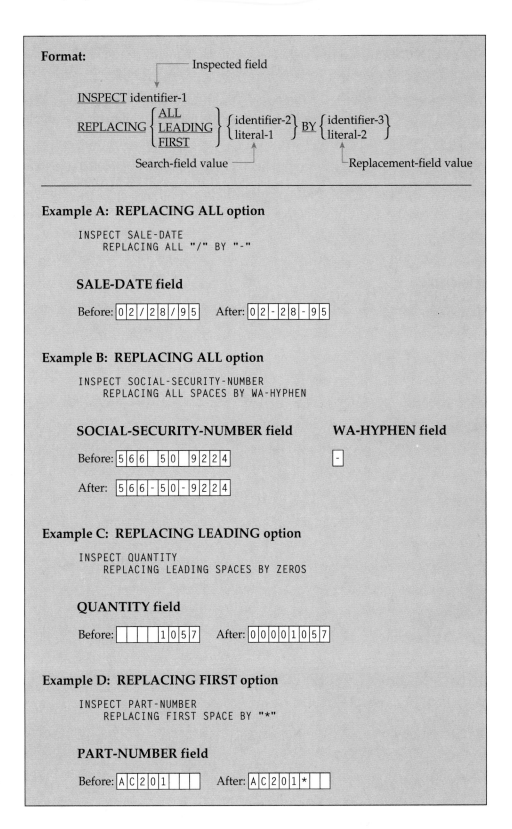

Format:

```
                        Inspected field
INSPECT identifier-1
REPLACING { ALL / LEADING / FIRST } { identifier-2 / literal-1 } BY { identifier-3 / literal-2 }
              Search-field value                          Replacement-field value
```

Example A: REPLACING ALL option

```
INSPECT SALE-DATE
    REPLACING ALL "/" BY "-"
```

SALE-DATE field

Before: `0 2 / 2 8 / 9 5`   After: `0 2 - 2 8 - 9 5`

Example B: REPLACING ALL option

```
INSPECT SOCIAL-SECURITY-NUMBER
    REPLACING ALL SPACES BY WA-HYPHEN
```

SOCIAL-SECURITY-NUMBER field   WA-HYPHEN field

Before: `5 6 6   5 0   9 2 2 4`   `-`

After: `5 6 6 - 5 0 - 9 2 2 4`

Example C: REPLACING LEADING option

```
INSPECT QUANTITY
    REPLACING LEADING SPACES BY ZEROS
```

QUANTITY field

Before: `      1 0 5 7`   After: `0 0 0 0 1 0 5 7`

Example D: REPLACING FIRST option

```
INSPECT PART-NUMBER
    REPLACING FIRST SPACE BY "*"
```

PART-NUMBER field

Before: `A C 2 0 1    `   After: `A C 2 0 1 *  `

REPLACING
FIRST Option

With the REPLACING FIRST option of the INSPECT statement, only the first occurrence of the search-field value is replaced by the replacement-field value. Example D of Figure 10-1 provides an example. This FIRST option has considerably fewer uses than the ALL and LEADING options.

The INSPECT/
TALLYING Statement

The INSPECT statement with the TALLYING phrase counts the occurrences of certain characters within a field. Its format is shown in Figure 10-2. The two commonly used INSPECT/TALLYING options are TALLYING ALL and TALLYING LEADING.

TALLYING ALL Option

An INSPECT statement with the TALLYING ALL option counts all occurrences of a character within the inspected field. The count is kept in a field called the **tallying field**.

Suppose a program permits entry of a numeric quantity into an alphanumeric field. The field must be validated to ensure that not more than one decimal point was keyed. The INSPECT/TALLYING ALL statement shown in Example A of Figure 10-2 handles this task. Each character of the DOLLAR-AMOUNT field is examined from left to right. Whenever a decimal point is found, the tallying field—WA-TALLY—is incremented by one.

Figure 10-2
The INSPECT/TALLYING
statement.

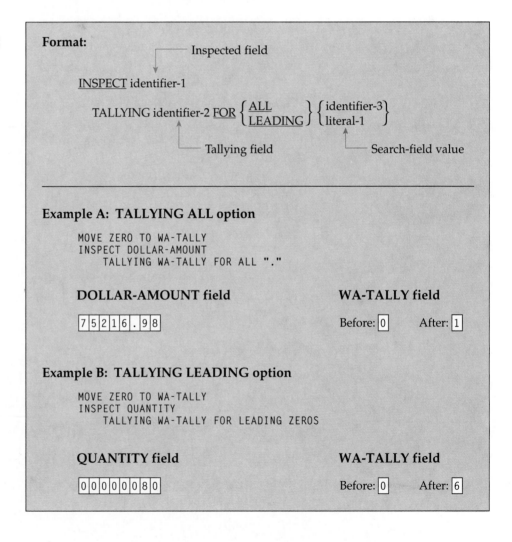

Format:

```
                          ┌──── Inspected field
                          ▼
INSPECT identifier-1

    TALLYING identifier-2 FOR ⎧ ALL     ⎫ ⎧ identifier-3 ⎫
                              ⎩ LEADING ⎭ ⎩ literal-1    ⎭
                    ▲                              ▲
                    └── Tallying field             └── Search-field value
```

Example A: TALLYING ALL option

```
MOVE ZERO TO WA-TALLY
INSPECT DOLLAR-AMOUNT
    TALLYING WA-TALLY FOR ALL "."
```

DOLLAR-AMOUNT field   **WA-TALLY field**

| 7 | 5 | 2 | 1 | 6 | . | 9 | 8 | Before: [0]   After: [1]

Example B: TALLYING LEADING option

```
MOVE ZERO TO WA-TALLY
INSPECT QUANTITY
    TALLYING WA-TALLY FOR LEADING ZEROS
```

QUANTITY field   **WA-TALLY field**

| 0 | 0 | 0 | 0 | 0 | 0 | 8 | 0 | Before: [0]   After: [6]

The tallying field must be an elementary numeric-integer field. You should note that it is your responsibility to properly initialize the tallying field. Such initialization typically takes the form of an immediately preceding statement that moves zeros to the tallying field, as shown in the examples.

TALLYING LEADING Option

With the TALLYING LEADING option of the INSPECT statement, only leftmost occurrences of the search-field value are counted. Example B of Figure 10-2 shows how leading zeros can be tallied within a field.

Definition of the Editing Task

The Overall Job

Now that you've seen what the INSPECT statement can do for you, let's consider a typical assignment that you might be given as a programmer. Your employer, General Merchandise Supply Company, is setting up a new sales transaction system. At the end of each day, sales transaction data will be entered into a file unedited. Before loading it into the sales transaction file, it must be validated. Your programming supervisor has designed a data validation program (called DATAVAL) to do the following:

- Read each record from a "raw" data file.

- For each record, test and validate each field.

- Write each valid record to a new file.

- Prepare a report that lists each invalid record, together with appropriate error messages.

Working as a programming team member, you are assigned the task of writing the modules to perform the validation.

The Validation Portion of the Job

You now know where your portion of the task fits into the overall plan; in order to complete your assignment, you also need to know:

- The input to each module

- The actions to be taken

Input: Alphanumeric Definition of All Input Fields

The input to data validation modules consists of the input record itself. So, your supervisor gives you a copy of the input record description shown in Figure 10-3.

In this description, two fields—Quantity and Price (SR-QUANTITY-X and SR-PRICE-X)—are defined as alphanumeric and then redefined as numeric. You will see the reason for this when you view the validation routines themselves.

Observe that each field is defined as alphanumeric with the symbol X, even if it is actually numeric and might normally be defined with the symbol 9. In a data validation program, it is a good practice to define numeric fields as alphanumeric, rather than numeric. The reason is that many computer systems cause program processing to be abnormally terminated—the program "blows up"—when arithmetic operations or relation tests are performed on a field that is defined as numeric, but contains nonnumeric data. This type of program interruption is called a **data exception** or a **numeric-field error**. Data exceptions are the COBOL programmer's nemesis; one of a data validation program's prime functions is editing numeric fields to ensure that they do not occur.

Figure 10-3
Record description for the
DATAVAL program.

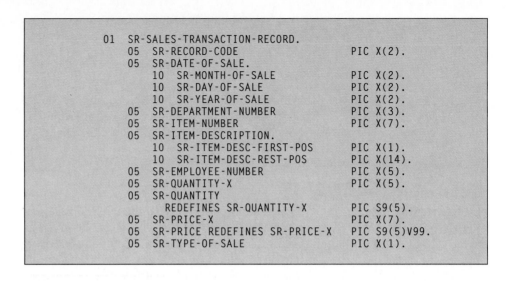

```
        01  SR-SALES-TRANSACTION-RECORD.
            05  SR-RECORD-CODE                 PIC X(2).
            05  SR-DATE-OF-SALE.
                10   SR-MONTH-OF-SALE          PIC X(2).
                10   SR-DAY-OF-SALE            PIC X(2).
                10   SR-YEAR-OF-SALE           PIC X(2).
            05  SR-DEPARTMENT-NUMBER           PIC X(3).
            05  SR-ITEM-NUMBER                 PIC X(7).
            05  SR-ITEM-DESCRIPTION.
                10   SR-ITEM-DESC-FIRST-POS    PIC X(1).
                10   SR-ITEM-DESC-REST-POS     PIC X(14).
            05  SR-EMPLOYEE-NUMBER             PIC X(5).
            05  SR-QUANTITY-X                  PIC X(5).
            05  SR-QUANTITY
                   REDEFINES SR-QUANTITY-X     PIC S9(5).
            05  SR-PRICE-X                     PIC X(7).
            05  SR-PRICE REDEFINES SR-PRICE-X  PIC S9(5)V99.
            05  SR-TYPE-OF-SALE                PIC X(1).
```

Actions to Be Taken

Each of the input fields must be tested; the logic of the test module (it will be applicable to each field) is shown in Figure 10-4. Notice that for each record found to be invalid, you must:

- Move a descriptive error message identifying the type of error to an output message area. The error message receiving field (in WORKING-STORAGE) is defined as AL-ERROR-MESSAGE with a length of 25.

- Perform the procedure 410-Print-Audit-Error-Line.

Although not illustrated by this flowchart segment, some fields have more than one potential error condition. Each should be identified and processed by the preceding two-step action.

Figure 10-4
Test module logic.

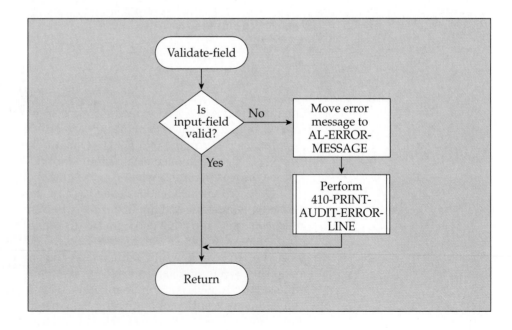

Field Validation Specifications

Figure 10-5 summarizes the validation operations you must perform on each field of this sales transaction record and the error messages to be printed. Notice that the tests range from relatively simple (Record-code equal to 27) to fairly extensive (Price subjected to four tests).

To obtain modular independence, the validation for each field is coded as an independent module. Let's consider these modules.

Figure 10-5 Field validation specifications.

Field	Validation type	Validation	Error message
Record-code	Code-existence	Equal to 27	INVALID RECORD CODE
Date-of-sale	Date/range	Month: range 01–12	INVALID MONTH
	Date/range	Day: range 01–31	INVALID DAY
	Date/class	Year: numeric	YEAR NOT NUMERIC
Department-number	Class	Numeric	DEPT NO. NOT NUMERIC
	Presence	Not equal to zero	DEPT NO. NOT PRESENT
Item-number	Class	Numeric	ITEM NO. NOT NUMERIC
	Presence	Not equal to zero	ITEM NO. NOT PRESENT
Item-description	Presence	Not equal to spaces	ITEM DESC. NOT PRESENT
	Justification	If present, first position not equal to a space	ITEM DESC. NOT LEFT JUST.
Employee-number	Class	Numeric	EMPLOYEE NUMBER NOT NUMERIC
	Range	10001 through 79999	INVALID EMPLOYEE NUMBER
Quantity	Class	Numeric	QUANTITY NOT NUMERIC
	Presence	Not equal to zero	QUANTITY NOT PRESENT
Price	Class	Numeric	PRICE NOT NUMERIC
	Presence	Not equal to zero	PRICE NOT PRESENT
	Sign	Not negative	PRICE NOT POSITIVE
	Consistency	If dept. num. is less than 500, price must be less than $1,000.00	PRICE NOT CONSISTENT
Type-of-sale	Code-existence	Equal to "$", "C", or "R"	INVALID TYPE OF SALE CODE

Validating Numeric Fields

Blanks in Numeric Fields

You will encounter two general categories of numeric fields in data validation: calculational and noncalculational. A numeric field on which arithmetic, numeric editing, or numeric-conditional tests are required—a *calculational numeric* field—must be defined with 9 PICTURE elements. These fields must contain digits 0–9 only and always must be checked to ensure that they do.

Upon initial data entry, unused positions of calculational numeric fields sometimes contain spaces. Remember that spaces are not numeric digits. A numeric field must contain only valid digits when it is operated on arithmetically; otherwise, a data exception might occur.

You will also encounter numeric fields on which no arithmetic type operations will be performed; these can be defined with either X or 9 PICTURE elements. A Social Security number is a typical example. Frequently, these fields can contain digits or can be entirely blank (for example, if a person's Social Security number is not available when the data is entered).

Zero-Filling of Numeric Fields

To ensure that numeric fields contain no spaces, COBOL programmers use the INSPECT statement to force the spaces to be replaced by zeros. As shown in Example A of Figure 10-6, an INSPECT statement can be coded to replace ALL spaces within the field by zeros. Although this technique is often used, you should recognize that it successfully handles only those situations in which the numeric field is completely blank or has only leftmost leading spaces.

Suppose the numeric data within the field is misaligned or inadvertently contains a space—either embedded within the digits or to the right of the value. After all spaces within the field are replaced by zeros, an incorrect value results. For example, consider that the value 1856 is misaligned within its field, as shown below:

| | | 1 | 8 | 5 | 6 | Incorrectly aligned as: | | 1 | 8 | 5 | 6 | |

The ALL operator will erroneously convert it to 18560.

Example B of Figure 10-6 shows a simple way to counter this problem: code the operator LEADING instead of ALL. Then only leading, nonsignificant spaces will convert to zeros. Any additional spaces embedded within the digits or to the left of the digits can then be detected by a NUMERIC class test.

When using the INSPECT, you should guard against a common coding error—the failure to maintain consistency between the data class of the field being inspected and the data class of the character being replaced. Example C of Figure 10-6 shows an invalid statement in which the programmer specified a numeric field and wants to replace the spaces. Recognize that SPACE is a nonnumeric character. For a SPACE to be present in a field, the field should be of alphanumeric data class. A syntax error occurs when a numeric field is coded and a nonnumeric character such as SPACE is specified as the value to be replaced. If the value to be replaced is a nonnumeric character, the field specified in the INSPECT statement must be alphanumeric (defined with the X).

Numeric Class Tests

Even after replacing spaces in a numeric field with zeros, the field may still contain nonnumeric data. A space is only one nonnumeric character. Other garbage characters—such as letters, asterisks, and hyphens—must be guarded against. To ensure that a field contains only valid numeric digits, a numeric class test must be made after the zero-filling operation. You will see this in the data validation modules that follow.

Figure 10-6
Replacing spaces
with zeros.

Part 1: Quantity-field input example values

Full field	1 7 3 0 5
Leading zeros	0 0 0 0 3
Zero value	0 0 0 0 0
Leading spaces	1 2
Blank field	

Part 2: Coding to replace spaces with zeros

Example A:
A commonly used technique to replace spaces with zeros in numeric fields
(which may result in erroneous values for miskeyed data)

```
INSPECT SR-QUANTITY-X
     REPLACING ALL SPACES BY ZEROS
```

Example B:
A better technique to replace spaces with zeros in numeric fields

```
INSPECT SR-QUANTITY-X
     REPLACING LEADING SPACES BY ZEROS
```

Example C:
A syntactically invalid INSPECT statement
(a numeric field cannot be inspected for nonnumeric values)

```
INSPECT SR-QUANTITY
     REPLACING LEADING SPACES BY ZEROS
```

Validation Modules

Record-Code Validation

To validate the Record-code field, you only need to ensure that it contains a value of 27. Figure 10-7 shows the needed module for this action. Notice that if the code is not 27, two actions are taken: The appropriate message is moved to AL-ERROR-MESSAGE and the module 410-PRINT-AUDIT-ERROR-LINE is performed.

Date-of-Sale Validation

Referring back to Figure 10-5, you see that validation of the date field is much more extensive. All fields must be numeric and the month and day are restricted to their ranges. This added complexity is evident in Figure 10-8's 320 module.

Here you see that the first action is to replace leading spaces with zeros. Then each component of the date (month, day, and year) is tested separately. The tests for both the month and day involve a numeric test, as well as a range test. At first

Figure 10-7
Record-code validation.

```
310-VAL-RECORD-CODE.
    IF SR-RECORD-CODE IS NOT EQUAL TO "27"
        MOVE "INVALID RECORD CODE" TO AL-ERROR-MESSAGE
        PERFORM 410-PRINT-AUDIT-ERROR-LINE
    END-IF
    .


        For COBOL-74, delete END-IF.
```

Figure 10-8
Date-of-sale validation.

```
                                                        For COBOL-74, delete all
                                                        END-IFs and insert
                                                        periods here.

320-VAL-DATE-OF-SALE.
    INSPECT SR-MONTH-OF-SALE
        REPLACING LEADING SPACES BY ZERO
    IF SR-MONTH-OF-SALE IS NOT NUMERIC
    OR SR-MONTH-OF-SALE IS LESS THAN "01"
    OR SR-MONTH-OF-SALE IS GREATER THAN "12"
        MOVE "INVALID MONTH" TO AL-ERROR-MESSAGE
        PERFORM 410-PRINT-AUDIT-ERROR-LINE
    END-IF
    IF SR-DAY-OF-SALE IS NOT NUMERIC
    OR SR-DAY-OF-SALE IS LESS THAN "01"
    OR SR-DAY-OF-SALE IS GREATER THAN "31"
        MOVE "INVALID DAY" TO AL-ERROR-MESSAGE
        PERFORM 410-PRINT-AUDIT-ERROR-LINE
    END-IF
    IF SR-YEAR-OF-SALE IS NOT NUMERIC
        MOVE "YEAR NOT NUMERIC" TO AL-ERROR-MESSAGE
        PERFORM 410-PRINT-AUDIT-ERROR-LINE
    END-IF
    .
```

glance, you might feel that the numeric test is not necessary because any quantity with a valid range (between "01" and "12") must therefore be numeric. However, this is *not* necessarily the case because in an alphanumeric field, the digit 0 followed by any letter falls between 09 and 10 (this is a result of the collating sequence). So, the range check would not detect an incorrect month entry of, for instance, 0P.

If the numeric class tests were not coupled with the nonnumeric range tests and if an invalid character within the range happened to be recorded in that date-of-sale field, the erroneous data would not be detected. So, whenever a numeric range test is handled by an alphanumeric comparison, a numeric class test must also be specified.

Department-Number and Item-Number Validation

The Department-number and Item-number checks both require that the fields be present and that they be numeric. Figure 10-9 shows the corresponding code for the Department-number check. Here you can see that leading spaces are first changed to zeros. Then two tests are performed: numeric and zero. If the field were empty (filled with spaces), the INSPECT statement would replace them all with zeros. So, the second test checks for existence of an entry in this field.

Notice that, as tested, these two error conditions are mutually exclusive; that is, a field cannot be both not-numeric and not-present. So the EVALUATE statement is used for the tests; the COBOL-74 version uses a nested IF.

Figure 10-9 Department-number and Item-number validation.

```
COBOL-85                                     COBOL-74

330-VAL-DEPT-NUMBER.                         330-VAL-DEPT-NUMBER.
    INSPECT SR-DEPARTMENT-NUMBER                 INSPECT SR-DEPARTMENT-NUMBER.
        REPLACING LEADING SPACES BY ZEROS            REPLACING LEADING SPACES BY ZEROS.
    EVALUATE TRUE                                IF SR-DEPARTMENT-NUMBER IS NOT NUMERIC
      WHEN SR-DEPARTMENT-NUMBER IS NOT NUMERIC       MOVE "DEPT. NO. NOT NUMERIC" TO AL-ERROR-MESSAGE
        MOVE "DEPT. NO. NOT NUMERIC" TO AL-ERROR-MESSAGE   PERFORM 410-PRINT-AUDIT-ERROR-LINE
        PERFORM 410-PRINT-AUDIT-ERROR-LINE     ELSE IF SR-DEPARTMENT-NUMBER IS EQUAL TO ZERO
      WHEN SR-DEPARTMENT-NUMBER IS EQUAL TO ZERO       MOVE "DEPT. NO. NOT PRESENT" TO AL-ERROR-MESSAGE
        MOVE "DEPT. NO. NOT PRESENT" TO AL-ERROR-MESSAGE   PERFORM 410-PRINT-AUDIT-ERROR-LINE.
        PERFORM 410-PRINT-AUDIT-ERROR-LINE
    END-EVALUATE
    .
```

The code for the 340-VAL-ITEM-NUMBER paragraph is the same as that in Figure 10-9, except the field SR-ITEM-NUMBER is used where appropriate and the message refers to the item field.

Item-Description Validation

The validation specifications require that two tests be made on the Item-description field: an entry must exist (the field must not be empty), and it must be justified (the description must begin in the field's first position). This is done by breaking the field into two elements, as Figure 10-10 shows. Alternately, with COBOL-85 you can define SR-ITEM-DESCRIPTION as a 15-character elementary item, then use reference modification as follows:

```
WHEN SR-ITEM-DESCRIPTION (1:1) IS EQUAL TO SPACE
```

The 350 module illustrates an easy, efficient way to ensure that an alphanumeric field is properly left-justified. The first test (WHEN) checks to ensure that the entire field is not empty. If not, the second test (WHEN) checks the first position for left justification.

Employee-Number Validation

The Employee-number validation is identical to the validation of sales month and day: it must be checked for numeric, and to ensure that it lies within the allowable range. This is done in Figure 10-11's 360 module.

Figure 10-10
Item-description validation.

```
        05  SR-ITEM-DESCRIPTION.
            10 SR-ITEM-DESC-FIRST-POS      PIC X(1).
            10 SR-ITEM-DESC-REST-POS       PIC X(14).


        350-VAL-ITEM-DESCRIPTION.
            EVALUATE TRUE
              WHEN SR-ITEM-DESCRIPTION IS EQUAL TO SPACES
                MOVE "ITEM DESC. NOT PRESENT" TO AL-ERROR-MESSAGE
                PERFORM 410-PRINT-AUDIT-ERROR-LINE
              WHEN SR-ITEM-DESC-FIRST-POS IS EQUAL TO SPACE
                MOVE "ITEM DESC. NOT LEFT JUST." TO AL-ERROR-MESSAGE
                PERFORM 410-PRINT-AUDIT-ERROR-LINE
            END-EVALUATE
            .

    For COBOL-74, use a nested IF, as in Figure 10-9.
```

Figure 10-11
Employee-number
validation.

```
360-VAL-EMPLOYEE-NUMBER.
    INSPECT SR-EMPLOYEE-NUMBER
        REPLACING LEADING SPACES BY ZEROS
    IF SR-EMPLOYEE-NUMBER IS NOT NUMERIC
    OR SR-EMPLOYEE-NUMBER IS LESS THAN "10001"
    OR SR-EMPLOYEE-NUMBER IS GREATER THAN "79999"
        MOVE "INVALID EMPLOYEE NUMBER" TO AL-ERROR-MESSAGE
        PERFORM 410-PRINT-AUDIT-ERROR-LINE
    END-IF
    .

For COBOL-74, delete END-IF.
```

Quantity Validation

The Quantity field is the first of two that are calculational numeric fields. Although it cannot be zero (it must be present), it can be negative. So, in Figure 10-12, you can see that the NOT NUMERIC test is performed on SR-QUANTITY (defined with a 9 PICTURE)—refer back to the record definition of Figure 10-3 (page 340). If the test were on SR-QUANTITY-X (defined with an X PICTURE), the sign would give a nonnumeric indication.

The second WHEN, the test for a zero value, uses the numeric definition for this field (SR-QUANTITY). Actually, either SR-QUANTITY or SR-QUANTITY-X could be used since the figurative constant ZERO is interpreted as numeric or alphanumeric by the compiler, depending upon the context.

You might have noticed that the leading spaces are not replaced with zeros in this module. The reason, as you will see, is that zero replacement is done in a module preceding this one to satisfy other needs of the program.

Price Validation

The Price field includes a variety of checking. First, it must be checked to determine if it is numeric. If not, an appropriate message must be printed. If it is numeric, then it must be checked to determine if it is less than zero, not present, or consistent with the department number. In the 380 module of Figure 10-13, this is accomplished by including an EVALUATE as the ELSE option of an IF. For the consistency check, if the Department-number is less than 500, then the value in this field must be less than $1,000. You see this test in the third WHEN of the EVALUATE.

This particular test illustrates a serious problem in creating nested-IF forms with COBOL-74. That is, the first period detected within a nested-IF terminates the outermost IF—and all those that are nested. Figure 10-14 shows the safest COBOL-74 form to use for the Price validation.

Type-of-Sale Validation

The only three allowable values for the Type-of-sale field are $, R, and C; any other entry must be identified as an error. This is done in the 390 module, as Figure 10-15 shows.

Figure 10-12
Quantity validation.

```
370-VAL-QUANTITY.
    EVALUATE TRUE
        WHEN SR-QUANTITY-X IS NOT NUMERIC
            MOVE "QUANTITY NOT NUMERIC" TO AL-ERROR-MESSAGE
            PERFORM 410-PRINT-AUDIT-ERROR-LINE
        WHEN SR-QUANTITY IS EQUAL TO ZERO
            MOVE "QUANTITY NOT PRESENT" TO AL-ERROR-MESSAGE
            PERFORM 410-PRINT-AUDIT-ERROR-LINE
    END-EVALUATE
    .

For COBOL-74, use a nested IF, as in Figure 10-9.
```

Figure 10-13
Price validation.

```
380-VAL-PRICE.
    IF SR-PRICE IS NOT NUMERIC
        MOVE "PRICE NOT NUMERIC" TO AL-ERROR-MESSAGE
        PERFORM 410-PRINT-AUDIT-ERROR-LINE
    ELSE
        EVALUATE TRUE
            WHEN SR-PRICE IS LESS THAN ZERO
                MOVE "PRICE NOT POSITIVE" TO AL-ERROR-MESSAGE
                PERFORM 410-PRINT-AUDIT-ERROR-LINE
            WHEN SR-PRICE IS EQUAL TO ZERO
                MOVE "PRICE NOT PRESENT" TO AL-ERROR-MESSAGE
                PERFORM 410-PRINT-AUDIT-ERROR-LINE
            WHEN SR-PRICE IS GREATER THAN 999.99
            AND SR-DEPARTMENT-NUMBER IS LESS THAN "500"
                MOVE "PRICE NOT CONSISTENT" TO AL-ERROR-MESSAGE
                PERFORM 410-PRINT-AUDIT-ERROR-LINE
        END-EVALUATE
    END-IF
    .
```

Figure 10-14
Price validation—
COBOL-74.

```
380-VAL-PRICE.
    IF SR-PRICE IS NOT NUMERIC
        MOVE "PRICE NOT NUMERIC" TO AL-ERROR-MESSAGE
        PERFORM 410-PRINT-AUDIT-ERROR-LINE.
    IF SR-PRICE IS NUMERIC
        IF SR-PRICE IS LESS THAN ZERO
            MOVE "PRICE NOT POSITIVE" TO AL-ERROR-MESSAGE
            PERFORM 410-PRINT-AUDIT-ERROR-LINE.
    IF SR-PRICE IS NUMERIC
        IF SR-PRICE IS EQUAL TO ZERO
            MOVE "PRICE NOT PRESENT" TO AL-ERROR-MESSAGE
            PERFORM 410-PRINT-AUDIT-ERROR-LINE.
    IF SR-PRICE IS NUMERIC
        IF SR-PRICE IS GREATER THAN 999.99
        AND SR-DEPARTMENT-NUMBER IS LESS THAN "500"
            MOVE "PRICE NOT CONSISTENT" TO AL-ERROR-MESSAGE
            PERFORM 410-PRINT-AUDIT-ERROR-LINE.
```

Figure 10-15
Type-of-sale validation.

```
390-VAL-TYPE-OF-SALE.
    IF SR-TYPE-OF-SALE IS NOT EQUAL TO "$"
    AND SR-TYPE-OF-SALE IS NOT EQUAL TO "C"
    AND SR-TYPE-OF-SALE IS NOT EQUAL TO "R"
        MOVE "INVALID TYPE OF SALE CODE" TO AL-ERROR-MESSAGE
        PERFORM 410-PRINT-AUDIT-ERROR-LINE
    END-IF
    .
```

For COBOL-74, delete END-IF.

Alternate Coding Techniques

The coding presented in the DATAVAL program we're developing was written to best explain the logic of a data validation program, together with a variety of methods. However, some alternative coding techniques could be incorporated into such a program.

88-Level Condition-Names for Applicable Validations

The IF statement relation-condition tests used for the field validations could be replaced by condition-name tests. This would require specification of 88-level condition-name entries in the input SR-SALES-TRANSACTION-RECORD, as Figure 10-16 shows.

Figure 10-16
Specification of condition-
names for field validations.

```
01 SR-SALES-TRANSACTION-RECORD.
    05  SR-RECORD-CODE                     PIC X(2).
        88 VALID-RECORD-CODE                    VALUE "27".
    05  SR-DATE-OF-SALE.
        10  SR-MONTH-OF-SALE               PIC X(2).
            88 VALID-MONTH                       VALUE "01" THRU "12".
        10  SR-DAY-OF-SALE                 PIC X(2).
            88 VALID-DAY                         VALUE "01" THRU "31".
        10  SR-YEAR-OF-SALE                PIC X(2).
    05  SR-DEPARTMENT-NUMBER               PIC X(3).
            88 DEPT-NO-NOT-PRESENT              VALUE ZERO.
            88 DEPT-NO-LESS-THAN-500           VALUE "001"
                                                    THRU "499".
    05  SR-ITEM-NUMBER                     PIC X(7).
            88 ITEM-NO-NOT-PRESENT              VALUE ZERO.
    05  SR-ITEM-DESCRIPTION.
            88 ITEM-DESC-NOT-PRESENT           VALUE SPACES.
        10  SR-ITEM-DESC-FIRST-POS         PIC X(1).
            88 ITEM-DESC-FIRST-POS-BLANK   VALUE SPACE.
        10  SR-ITEM-DESC-REST-POS          PIC X(14).
            88 ITEM-DESC-REST-POS-BLANK    VALUE SPACES.
    05  SR-EMPLOYEE-NUMBER                 PIC   X(5).
            88  VALID-EMPLOYEE-NUMBER          VALUE "10001"
                                                    THRU "79999".
    05  SR-QUANTITY-X                      PIC X(5).
            88  QUANTITY-NOT-PRESENT           VALUE ZERO.
    05  SR-QUANTITY REDEFINES SR-QUANTITY-X
                                           PIC  S9(5).
    05  SR-PRICE-X                         PIC  X(7).
            88 PRICE-NOT-PRESENT               VALUE ZEROS.
    05  SR-PRICE REDEFINES SR-PRICE-X      PIC S9(5)V99.
            88 PRICE-1000-DLRS-OR-MORE         VALUE 01000.00
                                                    THRU 99999.99.
    05  SR-TYPE-OF-SALE                    PIC X(1).
            88 VALID-TYPE-OF-SALE              VALUE "$"
                                                    "C"
                                                    "R"
```

Error Messages in WORKING-STORAGE

Instead of coding the error messages as nonnumeric literals in the PROCEDURE DIVISION, they could be established as data-items in the WORKING-STORAGE SECTION, as Figure 10-17 shows. This technique groups all the error messages into one area of the program listing for easy access.

As a reference aid, observe that the data-names for each error message incorporate the module number in which the applicable error condition is tested.

Figure 10-17
Specification of error
messages in the
WORKING-STORAGE
SECTION.

```
01  EM-ERROR-MESSAGES.
    05  EM-310-ERR-1 PIC X(25) VALUE "INVALID RECORD CODE".
    05  EM-320-ERR-1 PIC X(25) VALUE "INVALID MONTH".
    05  EM-320-ERR-2 PIC X(25) VALUE "INVALID DAY".
    05  EM-320-ERR-3 PIC X(25) VALUE "YEAR NOT NUMERIC".
    05  EM-330-ERR-1 PIC X(25) VALUE "DEPT. NO. NOT NUMERIC".
    05  EM-330-ERR-2 PIC X(25) VALUE "DEPT. NO. NOT PRESENT".
    05  EM-340-ERR-1 PIC X(25) VALUE "ITEM NO. NOT NUMERIC".
    05  EM-340-ERR-2 PIC X(25) VALUE "ITEM NO. NOT PRESENT".
    05  EM-350-ERR-1 PIC X(25) VALUE "ITEM DESC. NOT PRESENT".
    05  EM-350-ERR-2 PIC X(25) VALUE "ITEM DESC. NOT LEFT JUST".
    05  EM-360-ERR-1 PIC X(25) VALUE "INVALID EMPLOYEE NUMBER".
    05  EM-370-ERR-1 PIC X(25) VALUE "QUANTITY NOT NUMERIC".
    05  EM-370-ERR-2 PIC X(25) VALUE "QUANTITY NOT PRESENT".
    05  EM-380-ERR-1 PIC X(25) VALUE "PRICE NOT NUMERIC".
    05  EM-380-ERR-2 PIC X(25) VALUE "PRICE NOT POSITIVE".
    05  EM-380-ERR-3 PIC X(25) VALUE "PRICE NOT PRESENT".
    05  EM-380-ERR-4 PIC X(25) VALUE "PRICE NOT CONSISTENT".
    05  EM-390-ERR-1 PIC X(25) VALUE "INVALID TYPE OF SALE CODE".
```

Figure 10-18   Field-validation coding using condition-names and WORKING-STORAGE error messages.

```
310-VAL-RECORD-CODE.
    IF NOT VALID-RECORD-CODE
        MOVE EM-310-ERR-1 TO AL-ERROR-MESSAGE
        PERFORM 410-PRINT-AUDIT-ERROR-LINE
    END-IF
    .
320-VAL-DATE-OF-SALE.
    INSPECT SR-MONTH-OF-SALE
        REPLACING LEADING SPACES BY ZERO
    IF ST-MONTH-OF-SALE IS NOT NUMERIC
    OR NOT VALID-MONTH
        MOVE EM-320-ERR-1 TO AL-ERR
        PERFORM 410-PRINT-AUDIT-ERROR-LINE
    END-IF
    IF ST-DAY-OF-SALE IS NOT NUMERIC
    OR NOT VALID-DAY
        MOVE EM-320-ERR-2 TO AL-ERROR-MESSAGE
        PERFORM 410-PRINT-AUDIT-ERROR-LINE
    END-IF
    IF SR-YEAR-OF-SALE IS NOT NUMERIC
        MOVE EM-320-ERR-3 TO AL-ERROR-MESSAGE
        PERFORM 410-PRINT-AUDIT-ERROR-LINE
    END-IF
    .
330-VAL-DEPT-NUMBER.
    INSPECT SR-DEPARTMENT-NUMBER
        REPLACING LEADING SPACES BY ZEROS
    EVALUATE TRUE
        WHEN SR-DEPARTMENT-NUMBER IS NOT NUMERIC
            MOVE EM-330-ERR-1 TO AL-ERROR-MESSAGE
            PERFORM 410-PRINT-AUDIT-ERROR-LINE
        WHEN DEPT-NO-NOT-PRESENT
            MOVE EM-330-ERR-2 TO AL-ERROR-MESSAGE
            PERFORM 410-PRINT-AUDIT-ERROR-LINE
    END-EVALUATE
    .
340-VAL-ITEM-NUMBER.
    INSPECT SR-ITEM-NUMBER
        REPLACING LEADING SPACES BY ZEROS
    EVALUATE TRUE
        WHEN SR-ITEM-NUMBER IS NOT NUMERIC
            MOVE EM-340-ERR-1 TO AL-ERROR-MESSAGE
            PERFORM 410-PRINT-AUDIT-ERROR-LINE
        WHEN ITEM-NO-NOT-PRESENT
            MOVE EM-340-ERR-2 TO AL-ERROR-MESSAGE
            PERFORM 410-PRINT-AUDIT-ERROR-LINE
    END-EVALUATE
    .

350-VAL-ITEM-DESCRIPTION.
    EVALUATE TRUE
        WHEN ITEM-DESC-NOT-PRESENT
            MOVE EM-350-ERR-1 TO AL-ERROR-MESSAGE
            PERFORM 410-PRINT-AUDIT-ERROR-LINE
        WHEN ITEM-DESC-FIRST-POS-BLANK
            MOVE EM-350-ERR-2 TO AL-ERROR-MESSAGE
            PERFORM 410-PRINT-AUDIT-ERROR-LINE
    END-EVALUATE
    .
360-VAL-EMPLOYEE-NUMBER.
    INSPECT SR-EMPLOYEE-NUMBER
        REPLACING LEADING SPACES BY ZEROS
    IF SR-EMPLOYEE-NUMBER IS NOT NUMERIC
    OR NOT VALID-EMPLOYEE-NUMBER
        MOVE EM-360-ERR-1 TO AL-ERROR-MESSAGE
        PERFORM 410-PRINT-AUDIT-ERROR-LINE
    END-IF
    .
370-VAL-QUANTITY.
    EVALUATE TRUE
        WHEN SR-QUANTITY-X IS NOT NUMERIC
            MOVE EM-370-ERR-1 TO AL-ERROR-MESSAGE
            PERFORM 410-PRINT-AUDIT-ERROR-LINE
        WHEN QUANTITY-NOT-PRESENT
            MOVE EM-370-ERR-2 TO AL-ERROR-MESSAGE
            PERFORM 410-PRINT-AUDIT-ERROR-LINE
    END-EVALUATE
    .
380-VAL-PRICE.
    IF SR-PRICE IS NOT NUMERIC
        MOVE EM-380-ERR-1 TO AL-ERROR-MESSAGE
        PERFORM 410-PRINT-AUDIT-ERROR-LINE
    ELSE
        EVALUATE TRUE
            WHEN SR-PRICE IS LESS THAN ZERO
                MOVE EM-380-ERR-2 TO AL-ERROR-MESSAGE
                PERFORM 410-PRINT-AUDIT-ERROR-LINE
            WHEN PRICE-NOT-PRESENT
                MOVE EM-380-ERR-3 TO AL-ERROR-MESSAGE
                PERFORM 410-PRINT-AUDIT-ERROR-LINE
            WHEN DEPT-NO-LESS-THAN-500
            AND PRICE-1000-DLRS-OR-MORE
                MOVE EM-380-ERR-4 TO AL-ERROR-MESSAGE
                PERFORM 410-PRINT-AUDIT-ERROR-LINE
        END-EVALUATE
    END-IF
    .
390-VAL-TYPE-OF-SALE.
    IF NOT VALID-TYPE-OF-SALE
        MOVE EM-390-ERR-1 TO AL-ERROR-MESSAGE
        PERFORM 410-PRINT-AUDIT-ERROR-LINE
    END-IF
    .
```

Figure 10-18 shows the PROCEDURE DIVISION coding for the validation modules, which incorporates the condition-name tests and WORKING-STORAGE SECTION error messages.

TOPIC

The Complete Data Validation Program

In any computer application, special attention is given to ensuring that data entered into the system is accurate. The preceding portion of this chapter illustrated some of the programming techniques used to achieve this. New data is available for entry into a system in two ways. One is in the form of a raw, unvalidated file that must first be checked by a data validation program using this chapter's techniques. This is called **batch validation**.

The other is through a data entry/validation program that checks each field as it is entered from a keyboard. For instance, assume that such a program is used to enter the sales-transaction information and that the user types a price that is not consistent with the department number. After detecting the inconsistency, the program displays an error message and waits for the user to re-enter a correct value. In other words, the program will not accept an incorrect value. This approach to data validation is called **interactive validation**. With the prevalence of "smart" computer terminals and of personal computers, almost all data is validated interactively.

The next part of this chapter describes a batch data validation program using the validation modules described earlier. The rest of this chapter describes using those same modules for interactive data validation.

Programming Specifications for the Sales-Transaction Validation Program

So far, you've looked at one perspective of the data validation report program: the routines to perform the actual verification of data. Let's see how those modules fit into the overall picture. The program has two main purposes: (1) to create a new file consisting of valid records from the input file and (2) to identify incorrect records and state reasons why they are not correct.

Figure 10-19 shows programming specifications for the sales-transaction validation program. Observe that the system flowchart contains one input sales-transaction file and two output files: an audit/error list and a valid sales-transaction file on disk.

The program will produce a combined audit/error list. Notice on the print chart that the field values for each input record processed should be printed in the record-image area on the left-hand side of the report. If any fields of the record are in error, an error message should be printed to the right in the error-message area. In Figure 10-20's output example, observe that when an input record contains more than one error, the second error and all additional errors are printed on a separate line following each preceding error. The record-image area is not repeated. After all input records are processed, record counts are printed at the end of the report.

Input records that pass all validation checks are written to the output disk file. The output logical record format is exactly the same as the input record format.

Design Documentation for the Sales-Transaction Validation Program

Structure Chart

Each of this book's example programs—including the data validation program—introduces you to one or more techniques familiar to good programmers. So before progressing to the structure chart, let's consider some of the methods used in this program.

First, consider what takes place after a record is read. Each field is checked for validity. As each error is found, an appropriate detail line—including an error message—is printed. If the record is error free, the record image is printed. Figure 10-20's sample output shows the different types of detail lines that can be printed.

1. The first record (DISHWASHER) is error free, so the output line contains only fields from the input record. You can assume that this line is printed only after all the error checks are complete.
2. In the second record (VCR), the year is found to be invalid (A5). In this case, the input record and the error message are printed. Remember that each validation module performs the 410-Print-Audit-Error-Line module if an error is detected.
3. In the third record, four fields are found to be in error. Only the first line of output includes the record itself; the other three include only the error message.

Figure 10-19 Programming specifications: sales-transaction validation program (DATAVAL).

PROGRAMMING SPECIFICATIONS

Program Name: SALES-TRANSACTION VALIDATION   **Program ID:** DATAVAL

Program Description:

This program must read input sales-transaction records and perform designated field validations on each record. An audit/error list must be printed that lists each record and each error detected. Validated records are written to a disk file of validated-sales-transaction records. At the conclusion of the run, record-count totals should be printed.

Input File: Sales-Transaction File

Output Files: Audit/Error List
Validated Sales-Transaction File

List of Program Operations:

A. Read each input sales-transaction record.
   1. Validate each of the fields within the record as designated in the field validation specifications.
B. For each record that passes all the validation tests, the program is to:
   1. Write the record to the validated-sales-transaction file. The sales-transaction record format remains the same.
   2. Write an audit-line that contains the record image on the audit/error list.
C. For each record that has one or more errors, write an error-line on the audit/error list for each error detected in that record.
   1. The first error-line for each record must contain the record image and the error message.
   2. Successive error-lines (if any) for the same record should contain only the error message.

3. Do not write the record to the disk file.
D. Accumulate the following record counts and, after all input sales-transaction records are processed, print each count on a separate line in accordance with the format shown on the print chart.
   - Total number of records read
   - Total number of valid records
   - Total number of error records
E. Headings must be printed on each page of the report.
   1. The run date must be obtained from the operating system and printed on the first heading-line in accordance with the print chart.
   2. The page number should be printed on the second heading-line in accordance with the print chart.
F. Line-spacing must be handled as follows:
   1. The first audit/error-line printed after the headings must be double-spaced from the last heading-line.
   2. Second and successive error-lines for the same sales-transaction record must be single-spaced from one another.
   3. The first audit or error line for each sales transaction record should be double-spaced from the previous line.
   4. The record-count total lines must be single-spaced from one another. The first record-count total-line must be double-spaced from the last detail-line.

System flowchart:

Record layout: Sales-transaction record

Print chart:

Figure 10-20   Sample report output.

```
GENERAL MERCHANDISE SUPPLY COMPANY                                    11-28-95
SALES TRANSACTION DATA VALIDATION - AUDIT/ERROR LIST                  PAGE   1

RCD  DATE  DEPT  ITEM        ITEM         EMP                T
COD  SALE  NBR   NUMBER   DESCRIPTION     NBR                S   E R R O R   M E S S A G E

27  112795  310  4580013 DISHWASHER      50781  00001  0049800  C

27  1127A5  300  4575510 VCR             25777  00001  0059800  C   YEAR NOT NUMERIC

28  112795  000  4598217                 33937  00012  0000398- $   INVALID RECORD CODE
                                                                    DEPT. NO. NOT PRESENT
                                                                    ITEM DESC. NOT PRESENT
                                                                    PRICE NOT POSITIVE

27  112795  310  5584383 MICROWAVE OVEN  50781  00001  0031998  C

27  112795  310  5584383 MICROWAVE OVEN  80781  00001  0031998  X   INVALID EMPLOYEE NUMBER
                                                                    INVALID TYPE OF SALE CODE

27  112795  320  3475968 COMFORTER       45873  00001  0012995  R

                                                                6 RECORDS READ
                                                                3 VALID RECORDS
                                                                3 ERROR RECORDS
```

As you will see, the structure chart for the sales-transaction validation program conforms to the general patterns set by this text's previous programs. However, one significant difference exists. Until now, in the Process-record module, you moved fields to the output area and printed. In this program, the record is read and fields moved to the output area, but the record is not yet printed. The reason is that it may be necessary to print an error message together with the record.

So, the second level in the structure chart will include the same general modules as previous report generation programs:

> 000-Validate-Sales-Transactions
>> 100-Initialize-Variable-Fields
>> 870-Print-Report-Headings
>> 200-Process-Sales-Transaction
>> 700-Print-Report-Totals

The largest of these second-level modules is the 200 module, which (1) prepares for record-image printing (including page control), (2) performs validation on each field (including writing a line if an error is detected), and (3) writes a line for a valid record case. So, it includes the following modules:

> 200-Process-Sales-Transaction
>> 210-Format-Record-Image
>> 310 through 390 (data validation)
>> 890-Write-Report-Line

This leads to the structure chart shown in Figure 10-21. Although it contains quite a few more modules, it is no more complex than those you have already considered. Notice that the 200 module includes one additional module not already described: 830-Write-Valid-Sales-Trans. Recall that the program specifications require that each valid record be written to a validated sales-transaction file. This module accomplishes that task.

Figure 10-21
Structure chart:
sales-transaction
validation program.

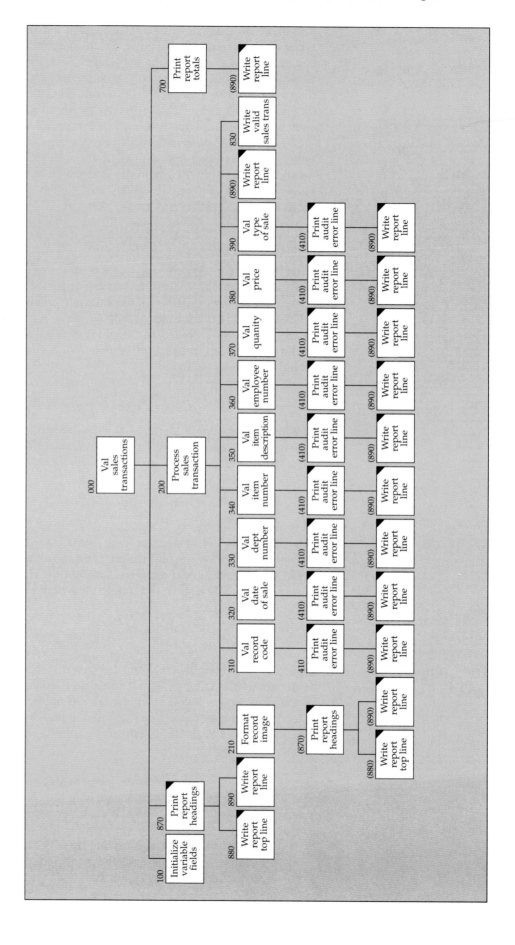

Pseudocode

The trickiest aspect of this program is printing the detail line. Remember, three types of lines should be printed: the record image with no error message, the record image with an error message, and an error message only. A program switch to indicate a valid/invalid record is commonly employed. As each record is read, the switch is set to indicate a valid record. Detection of an error in any of the validation modules causes the switch to be set to indicate an invalid record. This switch controls detail line printing and line spacing.

Figure 10-22 presents pseudocode for the program. You are already familiar with the data validation modules (310 through 390). Most of the others are almost identical to corresponding modules you saw in other report generation programs. However, three of them (200, 210, and 410) illustrate the primary differences between this and earlier programs.

200-Process-Transaction-Record Module

After the record is read, this module sets up the record-image output area (through module 210), sets the Valid-record switch to True, and performs the nine validation routines. If an error is detected, the Valid-record switch is set to False; you will see this later in the 410 module. At step 12, if the record contains no errors (as indicated by the record switch), the record is counted and its image is printed. A copy of the record is also written to the new file. If an error was detected, the invalid record count is incremented.

210-Format-Record-Image Module

This module is almost identical to corresponding report generation modules in that it performs page control and sets up the output area. However, it does not print the output line because validation operations must be performed first.

410-Print-Audit-Error-Line Module

This module controls record-image area printing for each error line. The first time this module is performed for each record, the record-image area is printed. However, if additional error lines are printed for the same record, the record-image area is not reprinted and must be blanked out. The logic of this module controls such processing by testing and setting the record switch.

The Complete DATAVAL Program

Figure 10-23 shows the complete DATAVAL program. From earlier studies, you know about all of the COBOL principles used in this program; however, some of the applications involve new twists. Do not be intimidated by this program's size. Although larger than any previous examples, it is simply a report generation program similar to those studied in Chapter 7—plus some new data validation elements.

Redefinition of the Quantity and Price Fields

For the purpose of data validation, input fields are commonly defined as alphanumeric, as you already know. However, both the Quantity and Price fields are redefined (lines 87 and 89 of DATAVAL) as numeric for two reasons:

1. The output report requires that these fields show a sign indication if negative (for instance, see the print chart of Figure 10-19, page 351). So, numeric editing is required.

Figure 10-22 Pseudocode: sales-transaction validation program.

```
000-Val-Sales-Transactions module
 1. Open the files.
 2. Perform 100-Initialize-Variable-Fields.
 3. Perform 870-Print-Report-Headings.
 4. Perform until end of file:
        Read a record from Sales file
          at end
              Set end-of-file to true
          not at end
              Add 1 to the Records-read count
              Perform 200-Process-
                Transaction-Record.
 5. Perform 700-Print-Report-Totals.
 6. Close the files.
 7. Stop the run.
100-Initialize-Variable-Fields module
 1. Set the Not-end-of-file indicator to True.
 2. Initialize the Page-count, Lines-used,
    Accumulator fields, and Output-line.
 3. Obtain the date from the operating system and
    move it to the first heading-line.
200-Process-Transaction-Record module
 1. Perform 210-Format-Record-Image.
 2. Set Valid-record to True.
 3. Perform 310-Val-Record-Code.
 4. Perform 320-Val-Date-Of-Sale.
 5. Perform 330-Val-Dept-Number.
 6. Perform 340-Val-Item-Number.
 7. Perform 350-Val-Item-Description.
 8. Perform 360-Val-Employee-Number.
 9. Perform 370-Val-Quantity.
10. Perform 380-Val-Price.
11. Perform 390-Val-Type-Of-Sale.
12. If no errors were detected in the input record
        Add 1 to the Valid-Record count
        Move the input-record image
          to the print-line area.
        Set for double-spacing.
        Perform 890-Write-Report-Line
        Move the input Sales-transaction
          record to the output
          Validated-sales-transaction
          record area
        Perform 830-Write-Valid-Sales-
          Trans module
    Else
        Add 1 to the Error-record count.
210-Format-Record-Image module
 1. If the report-page is full,
      Perform 870-Print-Report-Headings.
 2. Move Spaces to the Audit-line area.
 3. Move each input field to its respective
    Audit-line field.
310-Val-Record-Code module
320-Val-Date-Of-Sale module
330-Val-Dept-Number module
340-Val-Item-Number module
350-Val-Item-Description module
360-Val-Employee-Number module
370-Val-Quantity module
380-Val-Price module
390-Val-Type-Of-Sale module
For each of the previous modules (310- through
390-), the general logic outlined below is used:
 1. The validation for that field as designated in
    the field validation specifications are made.
```

```
 2. If an error is detected,
        Move the respective error-message
        to the Error-message field in
          the Audit-line.
        Perform 410-Print-Audit-Error-Line.
410-Print-Audit-Error-Line module
 1. If this is not the first error-line for this
    Sales-transaction record
        Move Spaces to the Record-image-area
        Set Line-spacing to single-spacing
    Else
        Set Line-spacing to double-spacing
 2. Move the Audit-line to the output print-
    line area.
 3. Perform 890-Write-Report-Line.
 4. Set Invalid-record to True.
700-Print-Report-Totals module
 1. Move spaces to the Total-line area.
 2. Move the Records-read count field and
    descriptive title to the Total-line.
 3. Move the Total-line to the output print-
    line area.
 4. Set Line-spacing to double-spacing.
 5. Perform 890-Write-Report-Line.
 6. Move the Valid-records count field and
    descriptive title to the Total-line.
 7. Move the Total-line to the output print-
    line area.
 8. Set Line-spacing to single-spacing.
 9. Perform 890-Write-Report-Line.
10. Move the Error-record count field and
    descriptive title to the Total-line.
11. Move the Total-line to the output print-
    line area.
12. Perform 890-Write-Report-Line.
830-Write-Valid-Sales-Trans module
 1. Write the output Valid-sales-transaction
    record area.
870-Print-Report-Headings module
 1. Add 1 to the Page-count field.
 2. Move the Page-count to Heading-line-1.
 3. Move Heading-line-1 to the output print-
    line area.
 4. Perform 880-Write-Report-Top-Line.
 5. Move Heading-line-2 to the output print-
    line area.
 6. Set Line-spacing to single-spacing.
 7. Perform 890-Write-Report-Line.
 8. Move Heading-line-3 to the output print-
    line area.
 9. Set Line-spacing to double-spacing.
10. Perform 890-Write-Report-Line.
11. Move Heading-line-4 to the output print-
    line area.
12. Set Line-spacing to single-spacing.
13. Perform 890-Write-Report-Line.
880-Write-Report-Top-Line module
 1. Advance to the top of the next report page
    and write the output print-line area.
 2. Set the Lines-used indicator to 1.
890-Write-Report-Line module
 1. Advance the forms in accordance with the
    value in the Line-spacing indicator field.
 2. Add the Line-spacing indicator to the
    Lines-used field.
```

2. For the Price field, program requirements call for a validation of the Price field to ensure that it is positive. A convenient way to make this validation is to use the sign test, which requires a numeric data-item.

Corresponding to these input redefinitions, you can see that the output versions of these fields are similarly redefined on the printer output area (lines 133

Figure 10-23   The sales-transaction validation program DATAVAL.

```
1      IDENTIFICATION DIVISION.                              73    01  SR-SALES-TRANSACTION-RECORD.
2                                                            74        05  SR-RECORD-CODE                    PIC X(2).
3      PROGRAM-ID.    DATAVAL.                               75        05  SR-DATE-OF-SALE.
4                                                            76            10  SR-MONTH-OF-SALE              PIC X(2).
5    *    GENERAL MERCHANDISE SUPPLY COMPANY.                77            10  SR-DAY-OF-SALE               PIC X(2).
6    *    Written by T. Welburn.                             78            10  SR-YEAR-OF-SALE              PIC X(2).
7    *    Mar  5, 1986.                                      79        05  SR-DEPARTMENT-NUMBER             PIC X(3).
8    *    Revised 9-22-89, 1-19-95 by W. Price.              80        05  SR-ITEM-NUMBER                   PIC X(7).
9                                                            81        05  SR-ITEM-DESCRIPTION.
10   *    This program reads input sales transaction records and  82        10  SR-ITEM-DESC-FIRST-POS       PIC X(1).
11   *    performs certain validations on selected fields of each 83        10  SR-ITEM-DESC-REST-POS        PIC X(14).
12   *    record.  Each validated record is written to a disk file. 84    05  SR-EMPLOYEE-NUMBER            PIC X(5).
13                                                           85        05  SR-QUANTITY-X                    PIC X(5).
14   *    Each record is printed on an audit record list with 86     05  SR-QUANTITY
15   *    identifying errors, if any.  At the conclusion of the 87           REDEFINES SR-QUANTITY-X       PIC S9(5).
16   *    run, record-count totals are printed.              88        05  SR-PRICE-X                       PIC X(7).
17                                                           89        05  SR-PRICE REDEFINES SR-PRICE-X    PIC S9(5)V99.
18                                                           90        05  SR-TYPE-OF-SALE                  PIC X(1).
19     ENVIRONMENT DIVISION.                                 91
20                                                           92    01  H1-HEADING-LINE-1.
21     INPUT-OUTPUT SECTION.                                 93        05                PIC X(87)
22                                                           94              VALUE "GENERAL MERCHANDISE SUPPLY COMPANY".
23     FILE-CONTROL.                                         95        05  H1-MONTH    PIC X(2).
24         SELECT SALES-TRANSACTION-FILE                     96        05                PIC X(1)    VALUE "-".
25             ASSIGN TO (system dependent).                 97        05  H1-DAY      PIC X(2).
26         SELECT AUDIT-REPORT                               98        05                PIC X(1)    VALUE "-".
27             ASSIGN TO (system dependent).                 99        05  H1-YEAR     PIC X(2).
28         SELECT VALID-SALES-TRANSACTION-FILE              100
29             ASSIGN TO (system dependent).                101    01  H2-HEADING-LINE-2.
30                                                          102        05                PIC X(87)
31                                                          103        VALUE "SALES TRANSACTION DATA VALIDATION - AUDIT/ERROR LIST".
32     DATA DIVISION.                                       104        05              PIC X(5)    VALUE "PAGE".
33                                                          105        05  H2-PAGE-NBR PIC ZZ9.
34     FILE SECTION.                                        106
35                                                          107    01  H3-HEADING-LINE-3.
36     FD  SALES-TRANSACTION-FILE.                          108        05                PIC X(66)
37     01  SALES-TRANSACTION-RECORD          PIC X(51).     109              VALUE "RCD  DATE DEPT   ITEM        ITEM         EMP".
38                                                          110        05              PIC X       VALUE "T".
39     FD  AUDIT-REPORT.                                    111
40     01  AUDIT-LINE                        PIC X(132).    112    01  H4-HEADING-LINE-4.
41                                                          113        05                PIC X(52)
42     FD  VALID-SALES-TRANSACTION-FILE.                    114              VALUE "COD  SALE NBR  NUMBER   DESCRIPTION      NBR".
43     01  VALID-SALES-TRANSACTION-RECORD    PIC X(51).     115        05                PIC X(43)
44                                                          116              VALUE "QTY   PRICE  S   E R R O R   M E S S A G E".
45     WORKING-STORAGE SECTION.                             117
46                                                          118    01  AL-AUDIT-DETAIL-LINE.
47     01  PROGRAM-SWITCHES.                                119        05  AL-RECORD-IMAGE-AREA.
48         05  END-OF-FILE-SW               PIC X.          120            10  AL-RECORD-CODE               PIC X(2).
49             88  END-OF-FILE                 VALUE "E".   121            10                               PIC X(2).
50             88  NOT-END-OF-FILE             VALUE "N".   122            10  AL-DATE-OF-SALE              PIC X(6).
51         05  VALID-SALES-TRANS-SW         PIC X.          123            10                               PIC X(2).
52             88  VALID-SALES-TRANS           VALUE "V".   124            10  AL-DEPARTMENT-NUMBER         PIC X(3).
53             88  INVALID-SALES-TRANS         VALUE "I".   125            10                               PIC X(2).
54                                                          126            10  AL-ITEM-NUMBER               PIC X(7).
55     01  RC-REPORT-CONTROLS.                              127            10                               PIC X(2).
56         05  RC-PAGE-COUNT                PIC S9(3).      128            10  AL-ITEM-DESCRIPTION          PIC X(15).
57         05  RC-LINES-PER-PAGE            PIC S9(2) VALUE 54. 129        10                               PIC X(2).
58         05  RC-LINES-USED                PIC S9(2).      130            10  AL-EMPLOYEE-NUMBER           PIC X(5).
59         05  RC-LINE-SPACING              PIC S9(2).      131            10                               PIC X(2).
60                                                          132            10  AL-QUANTITY                  PIC 99999-.
61     01  WA-WORK-AREAS.                                   133            10  AL-QUANTITY-X REDEFINES AL-QUANTITY
62         05  WA-DATE-WORK                 PIC 9(6).       134                                             PIC X(5).
63         05  WA-DATE-CONVERSION REDEFINES WA-DATE-WORK.   135            10                               PIC X(1).
64             10  WA-YEAR                  PIC 9(2).       136            10  AL-PRICE                     PIC 99999V99-.
65             10  WA-MONTH                 PIC 9(2).       137            10  AL-PRICE-X REDEFINES AL-PRICE
66             10  WA-DAY                   PIC 9(2).       138                                             PIC X(7).
67                                                          139            10                               PIC X(1).
68     01  WA-TOTAL-ACCUMULATORS.                           140            10  AL-TYPE-OF-SALE              PIC X(1).
69         05  WA-RECORDS-READ              PIC S9(4).      141        05                                   PIC X(3).
70         05  WA-VALID-RECORDS             PIC S9(4).      142        05  AL-ERROR-MESSAGE                 PIC X(25).
71         05  WA-ERROR-RECORDS             PIC S9(4).      143
72                                                          144    01  TL-TOTAL-LINE.
                                                            145        05                                   PIC X(76).
                                                            146        05  TL-RECORD-COUNT                  PIC Z,ZZ9.
                                                            147        05                                   PIC X(1).
                                                            148        05  TL-RECORD-COUNT-DESCRIPTION      PIC X(13).
                                                            149
                                                            150
```

Figure 10-23 (continued)

```
151    PROCEDURE DIVISION.                              221    210-FORMAT-RECORD-IMAGE.
152                                                     222        IF RC-LINES-USED IS NOT LESS THAN RC-LINES-PER-PAGE
153    000-VALIDATE-SALES-RECORDS.                      223            PERFORM 870-PRINT-REPORT-HEADINGS
154                                                     224        END-IF
155    ***********Initialization Sequence***********    225        MOVE SR-RECORD-CODE TO AL-RECORD-CODE
156        OPEN INPUT SALES-TRANSACTION-FILE            226        MOVE SR-DATE-OF-SALE TO AL-DATE-OF-SALE
157             OUTPUT AUDIT-REPORT                      227        MOVE SR-DEPARTMENT-NUMBER TO AL-DEPARTMENT-NUMBER
158                    VALID-SALES-TRANSACTION-FILE      228        MOVE SR-ITEM-NUMBER TO AL-ITEM-NUMBER
159        PERFORM 100-INITIALIZE-VARIABLE-FIELDS       229        MOVE SR-ITEM-DESCRIPTION TO AL-ITEM-DESCRIPTION
160        PERFORM 870-PRINT-REPORT-HEADINGS            230        MOVE SR-EMPLOYEE-NUMBER TO AL-EMPLOYEE-NUMBER
161                                                     231        INSPECT SR-QUANTITY-X
162    **************Processing Sequence**************   232            REPLACING LEADING SPACES BY ZEROS
163        PERFORM UNTIL END-OF-FILE                     233        IF SR-QUANTITY IS NUMERIC
164            READ SALES-TRANSACTION-FILE               234            MOVE SR-QUANTITY TO AL-QUANTITY
165                    INTO SR-SALES-TRANSACTION-RECORD  235        ELSE
166                AT END                                236            MOVE SR-QUANTITY-X TO AL-QUANTITY-X
167                    SET END-OF-FILE TO TRUE           237        END-IF
168                NOT AT END                            238        INSPECT SR-PRICE-X
169                    ADD 1 TO WA-RECORDS-READ          239            REPLACING LEADING SPACES BY ZEROS
170                    PERFORM 200-PROCESS-TRANSACTION-RECORD  240   IF SR-PRICE IS NUMERIC
171            END-READ                                  241            MOVE SR-PRICE TO AL-PRICE
172        END-PERFORM                                   242        ELSE
173                                                     243            MOVE SR-PRICE-X TO AL-PRICE-X
174    ***************Termination Sequence*************  244        END-IF
175        PERFORM 700-PRINT-REPORT-TOTALS              245        MOVE SR-TYPE-OF-SALE TO AL-TYPE-OF-SALE
176        CLOSE SALES-TRANSACTION-FILE                 246        .
177              AUDIT-REPORT                            247    310-VAL-RECORD-CODE.
178              VALID-SALES-TRANSACTION-FILE            248        IF SR-RECORD-CODE IS NOT EQUAL TO "27"
179        STOP RUN                                      249            MOVE "INVALID RECORD CODE" TO AL-ERROR-MESSAGE
180        .                                            250            PERFORM 410-PRINT-AUDIT-ERROR-LINE
181    *************************************************  251        END-IF
182    100-INITIALIZE-VARIABLE-FIELDS.                  252        .
183        SET NOT-END-OF-FILE TO TRUE                  253    320-VAL-DATE-OF-SALE.
184        INITIALIZE RC-PAGE-COUNT                     254        INSPECT SR-MONTH-OF-SALE
185                   RC-LINES-USED                     255            REPLACING LEADING SPACES BY ZERO
186                   WA-TOTAL-ACCUMULATORS             256        IF SR-MONTH-OF-SALE IS NOT NUMERIC
187                   AL-AUDIT-DETAIL-LINE              257        OR SR-MONTH-OF-SALE IS LESS THAN "01"
188        ACCEPT WA-DATE-WORK FROM DATE               258        OR SR-MONTH-OF-SALE IS GREATER THAN "12"
189            MOVE WA-MONTH TO H1-MONTH                259            MOVE "INVALID MONTH" TO AL-ERROR-MESSAGE
190            MOVE WA-DAY TO H1-DAY                     260            PERFORM 410-PRINT-AUDIT-ERROR-LINE
191            MOVE WA-YEAR TO H1-YEAR                   261        END-IF
192        .                                            262        IF SR-DAY-OF-SALE IS NOT NUMERIC
193    200-PROCESS-TRANSACTION-RECORD.                  263        OR SR-DAY-OF-SALE IS LESS THAN "01"
194  * Move input fields to output area                 264        OR SR-DAY-OF-SALE IS GREATER THAN "31"
195        PERFORM 210-FORMAT-RECORD-IMAGE              265            MOVE "INVALID DAY" TO AL-ERROR-MESSAGE
196  * Validate sales transaction fields               266            PERFORM 410-PRINT-AUDIT-ERROR-LINE
197        SET VALID-SALES-TRANS TO TRUE               267        END-IF
198        PERFORM 310-VAL-RECORD-CODE                 268        IF SR-YEAR-OF-SALE IS NOT NUMERIC
199        PERFORM 320-VAL-DATE-OF-SALE                269            MOVE "YEAR NOT NUMERIC" TO AL-ERROR-MESSAGE
200        PERFORM 330-VAL-DEPT-NUMBER                 270            PERFORM 410-PRINT-AUDIT-ERROR-LINE
201        PERFORM 340-VAL-ITEM-NUMBER                 271        END-IF
202        PERFORM 350-VAL-ITEM-DESCRIPTION            272        .
203        PERFORM 360-VAL-EMPLOYEE-NUMBER             273    330-VAL-DEPT-NUMBER.
204        PERFORM 370-VAL-QUANTITY                    274        INSPECT SR-DEPARTMENT-NUMBER
205        PERFORM 380-VAL-PRICE                       275            REPLACING LEADING SPACES BY ZEROS
206        PERFORM 390-VAL-TYPE-OF-SALE                276        EVALUATE TRUE
207        IF VALID-SALES-TRANS                        277            WHEN SR-DEPARTMENT-NUMBER IS NOT NUMERIC
208  *         Write record to output audit report     278                MOVE "DEPT. NO. NOT NUMERIC" TO AL-ERROR-MESSAGE
209            ADD 1 TO WA-VALID-RECORDS                279                PERFORM 410-PRINT-AUDIT-ERROR-LINE
210            MOVE AL-RECORD-IMAGE-AREA TO AUDIT-LINE  280            WHEN SR-DEPARTMENT-NUMBER IS EQUAL TO ZERO
211            MOVE 2 TO RC-LINE-SPACING                281                MOVE "DEPT. NO. NOT PRESENT" TO AL-ERROR-MESSAGE
212            PERFORM 890-WRITE-REPORT-LINE            282                PERFORM 410-PRINT-AUDIT-ERROR-LINE
213  *         Write record to validated file          283        END-EVALUATE
214            MOVE SR-SALES-TRANSACTION-RECORD        284        .
215                 TO VALID-SALES-TRANSACTION-RECORD
216            PERFORM 830-WRITE-VALID-SALES-TRANS
217        ELSE
218            ADD 1 TO WA-ERROR-RECORDS
219        END-IF
220        .
                                                                                              (continues)
```

and 137). Notice that, in both cases, the numeric field is redefined as alphanumeric. As you see, the numeric fields are one position longer because of the sign. They are defined/redefined in this order because in COBOL-74, a field with a REDEFINES clause must be equal to or shorter in length than the field that it is redefining. In COBOL-85, it makes no difference.

You can see how moving these two fields is handled in the 210 module (lines 233–244). In each case (Quantity and Price), if the field is numeric, the numeric definitions are referenced (for instance, SR-QUANTITY to AL-QUANTITY). If the field is not numeric, the alphanumeric definitions are referenced (for instance, SR-QUANTITY-X to AL-QUANTITY-X).

Figure 10-23 (continued)

```
285   340-VAL-ITEM-NUMBER.                                    354   410-PRINT-AUDIT-ERROR-LINE.
286       INSPECT SR-ITEM-NUMBER                              355       IF INVALID-SALES-TRANS
287           REPLACING LEADING SPACES BY ZEROS              356           MOVE SPACES TO AL-RECORD-IMAGE-AREA
288       EVALUATE TRUE                                       357           MOVE 1 TO RC-LINE-SPACING
289           WHEN SR-ITEM-NUMBER IS NOT NUMERIC             358       ELSE
290               MOVE "ITEM NO. NOT NUMERIC" TO AL-ERROR-MESSAGE  359           MOVE 2 TO RC-LINE-SPACING
291               PERFORM 410-PRINT-AUDIT-ERROR-LINE         360       END-IF
292           WHEN SR-ITEM-NUMBER IS EQUAL TO ZERO           361       MOVE AL-AUDIT-DETAIL-LINE TO AUDIT-LINE
293               MOVE "ITEM NO. NOT PRESENT" TO AL-ERROR-MESSAGE  362       PERFORM 890-WRITE-REPORT-LINE
294               PERFORM 410-PRINT-AUDIT-ERROR-LINE         363       SET INVALID-SALES-TRANS TO TRUE
295       END-EVALUATE                                        364       .
296       .                                                   365   700-PRINT-REPORT-TOTALS.
297   350-VAL-ITEM-DESCRIPTION.                               366       MOVE SPACES TO TL-TOTAL-LINE
298       EVALUATE TRUE                                       367       MOVE WA-RECORDS-READ TO TL-RECORD-COUNT
299           WHEN SR-ITEM-DESCRIPTION IS EQUAL TO SPACES    368       MOVE "RECORDS READ" TO TL-RECORD-COUNT-DESCRIPTION
300               MOVE "ITEM DESC. NOT PRESENT" TO AL-ERROR-MESSAGE  369       MOVE TL-TOTAL-LINE TO AUDIT-LINE
301               PERFORM 410-PRINT-AUDIT-ERROR-LINE         370       MOVE 2 TO RC-LINE-SPACING
302           WHEN SR-ITEM-DESC-FIRST-POS IS EQUAL TO SPACE  371       PERFORM 890-WRITE-REPORT-LINE
303               MOVE "ITEM DESC. NOT LEFT JUST." TO AL-ERROR-MESSAGE  372       MOVE WA-VALID-RECORDS TO TL-RECORD-COUNT
304               PERFORM 410-PRINT-AUDIT-ERROR-LINE         373       MOVE "VALID RECORDS" TO TL-RECORD-COUNT-DESCRIPTION
305       END-EVALUATE                                        374       MOVE TL-TOTAL-LINE TO AUDIT-LINE
306       .                                                   375       MOVE 1 TO RC-LINE-SPACING
307   360-VAL-EMPLOYEE-NUMBER.                                376       PERFORM 890-WRITE-REPORT-LINE
308       INSPECT SR-EMPLOYEE-NUMBER                          377       MOVE WA-ERROR-RECORDS TO TL-RECORD-COUNT
309           REPLACING LEADING SPACES BY ZEROS              378       MOVE "ERROR RECORDS" TO TL-RECORD-COUNT-DESCRIPTION
310       IF SR-EMPLOYEE-NUMBER IS NOT NUMERIC               379       MOVE TL-TOTAL-LINE TO AUDIT-LINE
311       OR SR-EMPLOYEE-NUMBER IS LESS THAN "10001"         380       PERFORM 890-WRITE-REPORT-LINE
312       OR SR-EMPLOYEE-NUMBER IS GREATER THAN "79999"      381       .
313           MOVE "INVALID EMPLOYEE NUMBER" TO AL-ERROR-MESSAGE  382   830-WRITE-VALID-SALES-TRANS.
314           PERFORM 410-PRINT-AUDIT-ERROR-LINE             383       WRITE VALID-SALES-TRANSACTION-RECORD
315       END-IF                                              384       .
316       .                                                   385   870-PRINT-REPORT-HEADINGS.
317   370-VAL-QUANTITY.                                       386       ADD 1 TO RC-PAGE-COUNT
318       EVALUATE TRUE                                       387       MOVE RC-PAGE-COUNT TO H2-PAGE-NBR
319           WHEN SR-QUANTITY IS NOT NUMERIC                388       MOVE H1-HEADING-LINE-1 TO AUDIT-LINE
320               MOVE "QUANTITY NOT NUMERIC" TO AL-ERROR-MESSAGE  389       PERFORM 880-WRITE-REPORT-TOP-LINE
321               PERFORM 410-PRINT-AUDIT-ERROR-LINE         390       MOVE H2-HEADING-LINE-2 TO AUDIT-LINE
322           WHEN SR-QUANTITY IS EQUAL TO ZERO              391       MOVE 1 TO RC-LINE-SPACING
323               MOVE "QUANTITY NOT PRESENT" TO AL-ERROR-MESSAGE  392       PERFORM 890-WRITE-REPORT-LINE
324               PERFORM 410-PRINT-AUDIT-ERROR-LINE         393       MOVE H3-HEADING-LINE-3 TO AUDIT-LINE
325       END-EVALUATE                                        394       MOVE 2 TO RC-LINE-SPACING
326       .                                                   395       PERFORM 890-WRITE-REPORT-LINE
327   380-VAL-PRICE.                                          396       MOVE H4-HEADING-LINE-4 TO AUDIT-LINE
328       IF SR-PRICE IS NOT NUMERIC                          397       MOVE 1 TO RC-LINE-SPACING
329           MOVE "PRICE NOT NUMERIC" TO AL-ERROR-MESSAGE   398       PERFORM 890-WRITE-REPORT-LINE
330           PERFORM 410-PRINT-AUDIT-ERROR-LINE             399       .
331       ELSE                                                400   880-WRITE-REPORT-TOP-LINE.
332           EVALUATE TRUE                                   401       WRITE AUDIT-LINE
333               WHEN SR-PRICE IS LESS THAN ZERO            402           AFTER ADVANCING PAGE
334                   MOVE "PRICE NOT POSITIVE" TO AL-ERROR-MESSAGE  403       MOVE 1 TO RC-LINES-USED
335                   PERFORM 410-PRINT-AUDIT-ERROR-LINE     404       .
336               WHEN SR-PRICE IS EQUAL TO ZERO             405   890-WRITE-REPORT-LINE.
337                   MOVE "PRICE NOT PRESENT" TO AL-ERROR-MESSAGE  406       WRITE AUDIT-LINE
338                   PERFORM 410-PRINT-AUDIT-ERROR-LINE     407           AFTER ADVANCING RC-LINE-SPACING
339               WHEN SR-PRICE IS GREATER THAN 999.99       408       ADD RC-LINE-SPACING TO RC-LINES-USED
340                   AND SR-DEPARTMENT-NUMBER IS LESS THAN "500"  409       .
341                       MOVE "PRICE NOT CONSISTENT" TO AL-ERROR-MESSAGE
342                       PERFORM 410-PRINT-AUDIT-ERROR-LINE
343           END-EVALUATE
344       END-IF
345       .
346   390-VAL-TYPE-OF-SALE.
347       IF SR-TYPE-OF-SALE IS NOT EQUAL TO "$"
348       AND SR-TYPE-OF-SALE IS NOT EQUAL TO "C"
349       AND SR-TYPE-OF-SALE IS NOT EQUAL TO "R"
350           MOVE "INVALID TYPE OF SALE CODE" TO AL-ERROR-MESSAGE
351           PERFORM 410-PRINT-AUDIT-ERROR-LINE
352       END-IF
353       .
```

Valid/Invalid Record Control

Valid/invalid record control is accomplished through the program switch defined at lines 51–53 with the condition-names VALID-SALES-TRANS and INVALID-SALES-TRANS. After each record is read, VALID-SALES-TRANS is set to TRUE (in the 200 module at line 197). This switch is both tested and reset in the 410 module; it is also tested in the 200 module after all validation checks are complete.

410-PRINT-AUDIT-ERROR-LINE Paragraph

The 410 module (repeated in Figure 10-24) is performed from any of the validation modules (310–390) that detect an error. The first time this module is executed for

Figure 10-24
Error processing—
the 410 module.

```
410-PRINT-AUDIT-ERROR-LINE.
    IF INVALID-SALES-TRANS
        MOVE SPACES TO AL-RECORD-IMAGE-AREA
        MOVE 1 TO RC-LINE-SPACING
    ELSE
        MOVE 2 TO RC-LINE-SPACING
    END-IF
    MOVE AL-AUDIT-DETAIL-LINE TO AUDIT-LINE
    PERFORM 890-WRITE-REPORT-LINE
    SET INVALID-SALES-TRANS TO TRUE
    .
```

each record, VALID-SALES-TRANS is TRUE as originally set. (So, INVALID-SALES-TRANS is FALSE.) Consequently, the input record image (moved in the 210 module) remains and is printed together with the error message. In this module's last action, INVALID-SALES-TRANS is set to TRUE. Therefore, when another error is detected for the current record, spaces are moved to the record-image area and only the error message is printed. So, the keys to using this switch to control the processing are

1. Setting VALID-SALES-TRANS to TRUE after an input record is read.
2. Setting INVALID-SALES-TRANS to TRUE when an error is detected.

200-PROCESS-TRANSACTION-RECORD—The IF Statement

In lines 207–219 of the 200 module, repeated in Figure 10-25, the record switch is again used to control processing. That is, if no errors are detected for this record, VALID-SALES-TRANS remains true. This causes the record to be printed and a copy written to the new validated file.

Testing for End-of-Page

The placement of this program's page-full test has an important and subtle feature. Notice that the test is made only when a new record is processed, and *not* before printing each line. If a record contains two or more errors, the additional error lines can be printed beyond the allowable line count limit (54, as defined at line 57). The reason is that splitting part of the error messages from the record image—because of starting a new page—creates clumsy reading. In this sense, the rationale is the same as that of keeping the group totals on the same page as their corresponding detail lines.

An alternative technique is to print, at the bottom of the page, a continuation note indicating that additional error lines continue on the next page. Then, on the next page, the record-image area is reprinted on the first line. A continued indication might also appear on the new page. If each field could include many error

Figure 10-25
Conditional output of
a valid record—from
the 200 module.

```
        IF VALID-SALES-TRANS
*           Write record to output audit report
            ADD 1 TO WA-VALID-RECORDS
            MOVE AL-RECORD-IMAGE-AREA TO AUDIT-LINE
            MOVE 2 TO RC-LINE-SPACING
            PERFORM 890-WRITE-REPORT-LINE
*           Write record to validated file
            MOVE SR-SALES-TRANSACTION-RECORD
                TO VALID-SALES-TRANSACTION-RECORD
            PERFORM 830-WRITE-VALID-SALES-TRANS
        ELSE
            ADD 1 TO WA-ERROR-RECORDS
        END-IF
```

messages (for instance, 10 or 12), you would probably want to use this method. As you can appreciate, this approach requires more program logic.

Writing Output Records

This text's previous program examples were limited to two files: one input file and one output file. DATAVAL is an example with multiple (two) output files. So, lines 24–29 of Figure 10-23 contain three file-control entries—three SELECT sentences—in the FILE-CONTROL paragraph. Having three file-control entries means, of course, that three FD entries must be specified in the FILE SECTION of the DATA DIVISION.

The WRITE statement coded in the 830 module (line 383) is identical to that for writing to a printer, except that no ADVANCING phrase is included. Whether the output goes to a fixed or removable disk, floppy disk, magnetic tape, or a tape cartridge depends upon entries in the SELECT statement—and, in some cases, operating system commands.

COBOL-74

The following changes to DATAVAL are necessary to obtain a COBOL-74–compatible program:

1. Insert the CONFIGURATION SECTION.

2. Insert LABEL RECORDS clauses.

3. Include the reserved word FILLER in the output line areas.

4. Modify the processing sequence of module 000; use the technique of either Figure 3-16 (page 86—priming READ) or Figure 3-17. Do not forget to follow the READ/AT END with a period to terminate the AT END scope.

5. Remove all END-IFs and insert periods as appropriate.

6. Modify each validation module 310–390, as described in earlier sections.

7. Change all SET statements operating on condition-names to corresponding MOVE statements moving to data-names.

8. Replace the INITIALIZE statement with appropriate MOVE statements.

TOPIC

Interactive Data Validation

The DATAENT Program

Program Specifications

The DATAVAL program illustrates techniques for validating data already stored in a file. As indicated earlier, with the wide use of on-line systems, data validation at data entry is much more common. The next example program demonstrates this by performing exactly the same validation operations as DATAVAL.

Programming specifications for this application are shown in Figure 10-26; the input record format and data validation requirements are identical to those

Figure 10-26
Programming
specifications—
data entry with
validation.

> **PROGRAMMING SPECIFICATIONS**
>
> Program Name: SALES-TRANSACTION ENTRY   Program ID: DATAENT
> _____
>
> **Program Description:**
>
> This program allows a user to add new records to the Sales-transaction
> file via the keyboard. Each field is validated as it is entered.
>
> **Input File:**
>
> Keyboard
>
> **Output File:**
>
> Sales-Transaction File (TRANS1.DAT)
>
> **List of Program Operations:**
>
> A. Accept each input sales-transaction record from the keyboard.
>   1. After each field is entered, validate it as designated in the
>   field validation specifications.
>   2. If a field is not valid, display an appropriate error message
>   and allow for re-entry of that field.
>   3. Do not allow data entry to progress to the next field unless
>   the current field value is valid.
>
> B. When data entry for a record is complete, provide the user with
>   the following options:
>   1. Write the on-screen record to disk.
>   2. Make changes to the on-screen record.
>   3. Erase the on-screen record.
>
> C. Query the user about entering another record. If the user does
>   not want to continue, terminate processing.

of DATAVAL. (See Figure 10-5, page 341, for the validation requirements and Figure 10-19, page 351, for the output record format.) Figure 10-27 shows the data-entry screen layout.

The list of program operations describes the three-step approach to accepting each field (step A of Figure 10-26). After entry, the field is validated. If an error is found, an error message must be displayed and the user required to re-enter the field. After all fields are entered and validated, the user is given three options: save the on-screen record, make changes to it, or erase it.

As you will see, the data validation principles incorporated in the program are nearly identical to DATAVAL's. This program's primary feature is the way it handles interaction with the user. One very important characteristic of any interactive program is that it is user-friendly. You want the program to be easy to use; you do not want the user's slightest miscue to have unpleasant consequences.

Sample Screen Displays

Generally, you will find it much easier to understand the code of an interactive program if you spend some time running it. This interactive program's name is DATAENT; it is stored on one of the diskettes accompanying this book. Run it and enter some records; try all of the options. Figure 10-28 shows two forms of the screen that you will see. In the first screen, the Price entry is 1259.95, rather than the correct value 259.95. Since this is not consistent with the validation requirements, an error message is displayed and the cursor is positioned at the Price field, awaiting a correction. In the second screen, the Price entry was corrected and the user is given the choice of saving the screen record, making changes, or aborting it. To ensure that a correct response is made, the entry is checked. If the response is not S, M, or A, the prompt line (last line) would change to

    Invalid entry, try again. Your choice <S, M, or A>?

You should try each of the options to see how it works.

Figure 10-27 Screen format.

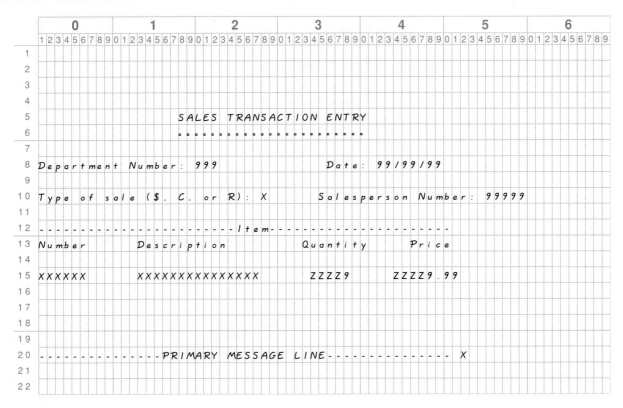

Program Planning

Because the features of this chapter's two programs are so similar, you don't need to work from detailed pseudocode. However, the two programs differ in a few general areas, as the broad pseudocode of Figure 10-29 shows.

In the Typical Accept-Field module, you can see that execution is controlled by the valid-field switch and an inline PERFORM. Exit from the module only occurs when the entered field is valid.

From the Main module, input of records is repeated under control of the inline PERFORM at step 3. First, input for the record is accepted through the Build-a-Record module. Next, the module to determine the desired user action is performed (you saw this in Figure 10-28(b)'s screen). The IF statement at step 3c is incorporated in order to allow the previously entered screen record to be changed. You will see how the program implements this

Before proceeding to the program, let's give some thought to the nature of this record's fields:

Date-of-sale
Department-number
Employee-number
Type-of-sale
Item-number
Item-description
Quantity
Price

In this type of program, it is likely that any given salesperson will have two or more consecutive entries. In fact, each source document may include several items under a given salesperson. That means that the first four of these fields will probably have the same values for two or more records. Only the last four will change from one record to another. So, data-entry speed is improved by offering the first four fields as default values.

Figure 10-28   Sample screen displays.

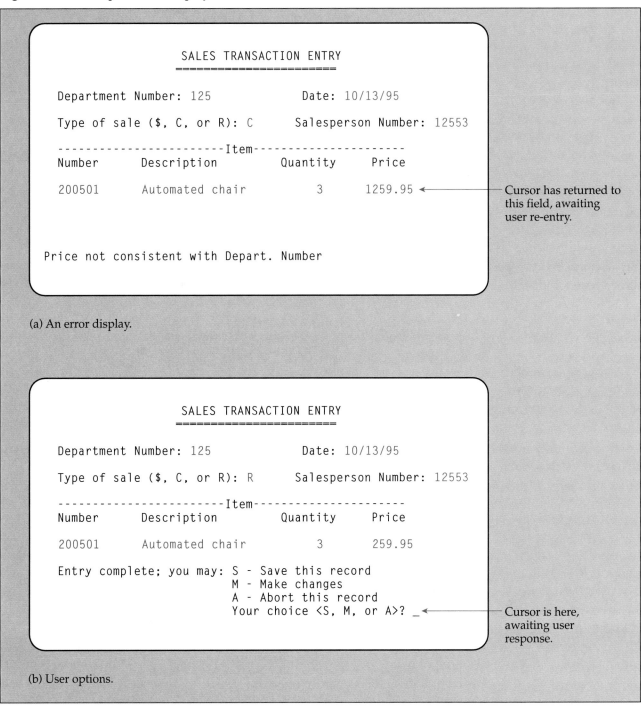

(a) An error display.

(b) User options.

The complete validating data-entry program prepared using Micro Focus DISPLAY/ACCEPT features is shown in Figure 10-30.

The DATA DIVISION of the Data-Entry Program—DATAENT

Two program switches and one flag are used in this program. They are

S1-FIELD-VALID-SWITCH	This switch ensures that data entered for a given field is valid. If not, it keeps control within the accept-field module until a correct entry is made.
S2-CONTINUE-SWITCH	This switch controls access to the program and repetition of the primary processing loop.
S3-RESPONSE-OPTION	This field accepts user responses to Yes/No and menu selection entries. Its condition-name (88-level) entries designate acceptable entries.

The output record definition (lines 56–75) contains three items that are important to you:

- The record code is defined with a VALUE clause. Since a value of 27 is required for the sales record, you do not need to request an entry from the user.

Figure 10-29
Broad pseudocode.

```
Main-module
    Query user to continue.
    If yes
        1.  Perform initialize.
        2.  Open output file for extend.
        3.  Perform until no more records to add.
            a.  Perform Build-a-Record module.
            b.  Perform Determine-Record-Action.
            c.  If No record to be changed
                Query user about more records to add.
        4.  Close file.
    Stop run.


Build-a-Record module
    1.  Perform modules to accept each field.


Determine-Record-Action module
    1.  Query user regarding action to take.
        Options are
            Save screen record
            Make changes to screen record
            Erase screen record.
        a.  If save record
            Write record to disk.
        b.  If save record or erase record
            Repaint screen and initialize input fields.


Typical Accept-Field module
    1.  Set valid-field switch to false.
    2.  Perform until valid-field is true.
        a.  Accept field.
        b.  If field is not valid
                move error message to message line
            else
                set valid-field switch to true.
        c.  Display message line.
```

- Allowable values and value ranges are designated for appropriate fields with condition-name entries—these will be used in the validation modules.

- All fields that require numeric validation are defined as numeric data-items. The Micro Focus extension of the ACCEPT statement allows the entry of only numeric quantities. So, it will not be necessary to perform a numeric check on the input values.

Two fields are defined as numeric-edited to facilitate input of truly numeric quantities: SI-QUANTITY and SI-PRICE (lines 53 and 54). These are used to accept input data for quantity and price, respectively.

PROCEDURE DIVISION Features

The 050 module displays the announcement screen and queries the user regarding continuing. Any response except Y (or y) causes the entire program sequence (lines 83–100) to be skipped and the program terminated.

In the 100 module, all fields except SR-RECORD-CODE are initialized in preparation for input of the first record. The screen template is also displayed (see the 825 module).

From line 86, the 200 module is performed—which, in turn, accepts entries into each of the input fields. Because it is typical of the input modules, let's consider the 830 module to accept the department number field.

- The first action is to set S1-VALID-FIELD-SWITCH to False (SET S1-INVALID-FIELD TO TRUE at line 190). This forces execution of the PERFORM loop that follows.

- The department number is accepted via the statement at line 192.

- If the entry is not valid (is zero), an error message is moved to the message line—lines 195 and 196. The controlling switch S1 is not changed.

- Execution of the PERFORM at line 200 causes the 845 module to be performed—which, in this case, displays the error message.

- Upon return to the controlling PERFORM in the 830 module (line 191), the loop is repeated because the condition (S1-VALID-FIELD) is not met.

- A valid entry causes the S1 switch to be set to true at line 198.

- When the 845 module is performed from line 200, the message line will be cleared to blanks.

- Upon return to the controlling PERFORM at line 191, the true condition causes execution to fall through to the end of the module, thereby returning control to the 200 module.

One of this program's trickier elements is responding to the user request to save the record (S), make changes (M), or abort the record (A). Unlike the Yes/No responses where any entry other than Y (or y) is treated as No, the user must respond with one of the three allowable entries. This is controlled by the inline PERFORM of line 145. This statement will not allow exit from the loop until a valid selection is made.

The save-record option occurs at lines 156–160. At lines 163–167, the sequence to repaint the screen and initialize the four data field values is *not* executed if the user selected the Make changes (M) option. Also, after returning to the 000 module, the user is not questioned about entering another record under the change condition (see line 88). The existing screen record must be modified first.

Figure 10-30 The DATAENT program.

```
1    IDENTIFICATION DIVISION.                              78   PROCEDURE DIVISION.
2    PROGRAM-ID. DATAENT.                                  79
3                                                          80   000-BUILD-DATA-FILE.
4    *   General Merchandise Supply Company                81       PERFORM 050-QUERY-TO-EXECUTE
5    *   Written by W. Price  9-30-89                      82       IF S3-YES-RESPONSE
6    *              modified 1-19-95                        83           PERFORM 100-INITIALIZE-VARIABLE-FIELDS
7                                                          84           OPEN EXTEND SALES-TRANSACTION-FILE
8    *   This program allows records to be added to the    85           PERFORM UNTIL NOT S2-MORE-RECORDS-TO-ADD
9    *   sales transaction file. Data entered from the     86               PERFORM 200-BUILD-A-RECORD
10   *   keyboard is fully validated as it is entered.     87               PERFORM 250-DETERMINE-RECORD-ACTION
11                                                         88               IF NOT S3-MAKE-CHANGES-OPTION
12                                                         89                   MOVE
13   ENVIRONMENT DIVISION.                                 90                   "        Do you want to enter another record <Y/N>?"
14                                                         91                       TO WA-USER-MESSAGE
15   INPUT-OUTPUT SECTION.                                 92                   SET S3-YES-RESPONSE TO TRUE
16                                                         93                   PERFORM 840-GET-RESPONSE
17   FILE-CONTROL.                                         94                   IF NOT S3-YES-RESPONSE
18       SELECT SALES-TRANSACTION-FILE                     95                       SET S2-NO-MORE-RECORDS-TO-ADD TO TRUE
19           ASSIGN TO DISK "SALES_T.DAT"                  96                   END-IF
20           ORGANIZATION LINE SEQUENTIAL.                 97               END-IF
21                                                         98           END-PERFORM
22                                                         99           CLOSE SALES-TRANSACTION-FILE
23   DATA DIVISION.                                        100      END-IF
24                                                         101      STOP RUN
25   FILE SECTION.                                         102      .
26                                                         103  050-QUERY-TO-EXECUTE.
27   FD  SALES-TRANSACTION-FILE.                           104      DISPLAY "This program allows you to enter new"
28   01  SALES-TRANSACTION-RECORD        PIC X(51).        105                                        LINE 14 COL 20
29                                                         106                                        WITH BLANK SCREEN
30   WORKING-STORAGE SECTION.                              107      DISPLAY "sales transaction records into the sales file:"
31                                                         108                                        LINE 15 COL 20
32   01  SW-SWITCHES.                                      109      MOVE "                Do you want to continue <Y/N>?"
33       05  S1-FIELD-VALID-SWITCH       PIC X(1).         110          TO WA-USER-MESSAGE
34           88  S1-VALID-FIELD              VALUE "T".    111      SET S3-YES-RESPONSE TO TRUE
35           88  S1-INVALID-FIELD            VALUE "F".    112      PERFORM 840-GET-RESPONSE
36       05  S2-CONTINUE-SWITCH          PIC X(1).         113      IF S3-YES-RESPONSE
37           88  S2-MORE-RECORDS-TO-ADD      VALUE "T".    114          SET S2-MORE-RECORDS-TO-ADD TO TRUE
38           88  S2-NO-MORE-RECORDS-TO-ADD   VALUE "F".    115      ELSE
39       05  S3-RESPONSE-OPTION          PIC X(1).         116          SET S2-NO-MORE-RECORDS-TO-ADD TO TRUE
40           88  S3-YES-RESPONSE             VALUE "Y" "y".117      END-IF
41           88  S3-NO-RESPONSE              VALUE "N".    118
42           88  S3-SAVE-RECORD-OPTION       VALUE "S" "s".119  100-INITIALIZE-VARIABLE-FIELDS.
43           88  S3-MAKE-CHANGES-OPTION      VALUE "M" "m".120      INITIALIZE SR-SALES-TRANSACTION-RECORD
44           88  S3-ABORT-RECORD-OPTION      VALUE "A" "a".121          REPLACING NUMERIC DATA BY 0.
45           88  S3-VALID-OPTION             VALUE "S" "M" "A"122      MOVE SPACE TO SR-TYPE-OF-SALE
46                                              "s" "m" "a".123      PERFORM 825-PAINT-SCREEN-TEMPLATE
47           88  S3-BLANK-OPTION             VALUE " ".    124
48                                                         125  200-BUILD-A-RECORD.
49   01  WA-WORK-VARIABLES.                                126      PERFORM 830-OBTAIN-DEPARTMENT-NUMBER
50       05  WA-USER-MESSAGE             PIC X(50).        127      PERFORM 831-OBTAIN-MONTH-OF-SALE
51                                                         128      PERFORM 832-OBTAIN-DAY-OF-SALE
52   01  SI-SCREEN-INPUT-ITEMS.                            129      PERFORM 833-OBTAIN-YEAR-OF-SALE
53       05  SI-QUANTITY                 PIC ZZZZ9.        130      PERFORM 834-OBTAIN-TYPE-OF-SALE
54       05  SI-PRICE                    PIC ZZZZ9.99.     131      PERFORM 835-OBTAIN-EMPLOYEE-NUMBER
55                                                         132      PERFORM 836-OBTAIN-ITEM-NUMBER
56   01  SR-SALES-TRANSACTION-RECORD.                      133      PERFORM 837-OBTAIN-ITEM-DESCRIPTION
57       05  SR-RECORD-CODE              PIC X(2)          134      PERFORM 838-OBTAIN-QUANTITY
58                                       VALUE "27".       135      PERFORM 839-OBTAIN-PRICE
59       05  SR-DATE-OF-SALE.                              136
60           10  SR-MONTH-OF-SALE        PIC 9(2).         137  250-DETERMINE-RECORD-ACTION.
61               88  VALID-MONTH     VALUE 01 THRU 12.     138      DISPLAY "Entry complete; you may: S - Save this record"
62           10  SR-DAY-OF-SALE          PIC 9(2).         139                                        LINE 17 COL 1
63               88  VALID-DAY       VALUE 01 THRU 31.     140      DISPLAY "M - Make changes"        LINE 18 COL 26
64           10  SR-YEAR-OF-SALE         PIC 9(2).         141      DISPLAY "A - Abort this record"   LINE 19 COL 26
65       05  SR-DEPARTMENT-NUMBER        PIC 9(3).         142      MOVE "                  Your choice <S, M, or A>?"
66       05  SR-ITEM-NUMBER              PIC 9(7).         143          TO WA-USER-MESSAGE
67       05  SR-ITEM-DESCRIPTION         PIC X(15).        144      SET S3-BLANK-OPTION TO TRUE
68       05  SR-EMPLOYEE-NUMBER          PIC 9(5).         145      PERFORM UNTIL S3-VALID-OPTION
69           88  VALID-EMPLOYEE-NUMBER VALUE 10001 THRU 79999.146          PERFORM 840-GET-RESPONSE
70       05  SR-QUANTITY                 PIC S9(5).        147          IF S3-VALID-OPTION
71       05  SR-PRICE                    PIC 9(5)V99.      148              DISPLAY " " LINE 17 COL 1   WITH BLANK LINE
72       05  SR-TYPE-OF-SALE             PIC X(1).         149              DISPLAY " " LINE 18 COL 26  WITH BLANK LINE
73           88  VALID-TYPE-OF-SALE  VALUES "S"           150              DISPLAY " " LINE 19 COL 26  WITH BLANK LINE
74                                          "C"            151          ELSE
75                                          "R".           152              MOVE "Invalid entry, try again. Your choice<S, M, or A>?"
76                                                         153                  TO WA-USER-MESSAGE
77                                                         154          END-IF
                                                           155      END-PERFORM
                                                           156      IF S3-SAVE-RECORD-OPTION
                                                           157          MOVE SR-SALES-TRANSACTION-RECORD
                                                           158              TO SALES-TRANSACTION-RECORD
                                                           159          PERFORM 800-WRITE-SALES-TRANS-RECORD
                                                           160      END-IF
                                                           161      IF S3-ABORT-RECORD-OPTION
                                                           162      OR S3-SAVE-RECORD-OPTION
                                                           163          PERFORM 825-PAINT-SCREEN-TEMPLATE
                                                           164          INITIALIZE SR-ITEM-NUMBER
                                                           165                     SR-ITEM-DESCRIPTION
                                                           166                     SI-QUANTITY
                                                           167                     SI-PRICE
                                                           168      END-IF
                                                           169      .
```

Figure 10-30 (continued)

```
170    800-WRITE-SALES-TRANS-RECORD.
171        WRITE SALES-TRANSACTION-RECORD
172        .
173    825-PAINT-SCREEN-TEMPLATE.
174        DISPLAY "SALES TRANSACTION ENTRY"        LINE 5  COL 18
175                                                 WITH BLANK SCREEN
176        DISPLAY "═══════════════════════"        LINE 6  COL 18
177        DISPLAY "Department Number: "            LINE 8  COL 1
178        DISPLAY "Date: "                         LINE 8  COL 36
179        DISPLAY "/  /"                           LINE 8  COL 44
180        DISPLAY "Type of sale ($, C, or R):"     LINE 10 COL 1
181        DISPLAY "Salesperson Number:"            LINE 10 COL 35
182        DISPLAY
183            "----------------------Item----------------------"
184                                                 LINE 12 COL 1
185        DISPLAY "Number      Description         Quantity      Price"
186
187                                                 LINE 13 COL 1
188        .
189    830-OBTAIN-DEPARTMENT-NUMBER.
190        SET S1-INVALID-FIELD TO TRUE
191        PERFORM UNTIL S1-VALID-FIELD
192            ACCEPT SR-DEPARTMENT-NUMBER          LINE 8  COL 20
193                                                 WITH REVERSE-VIDEO
194            IF SR-DEPARTMENT-NUMBER = ZERO
195                MOVE "Department number must not be zero"
196                    TO WA-USER-MESSAGE
197            ELSE
198                SET S1-VALID-FIELD TO TRUE
199            END-IF
200            PERFORM 845-DISPLAY-MESSAGE-LINE
201        END-PERFORM
202        .
203    831-OBTAIN-MONTH-OF-SALE.
204        SET S1-INVALID-FIELD TO TRUE
205        PERFORM UNTIL S1-VALID-FIELD
206            ACCEPT SR-MONTH-OF-SALE             LINE 8  COL 42
207                                                WITH REVERSE-VIDEO
208            IF NOT VALID-MONTH
209                MOVE "Month number must be between 01 and 12"
210                    TO WA-USER-MESSAGE
211            ELSE
212                SET S1-VALID-FIELD TO TRUE
213            END-IF
214            PERFORM 845-DISPLAY-MESSAGE-LINE
215        END-PERFORM
216        .
217    832-OBTAIN-DAY-OF-SALE.
218        SET S1-INVALID-FIELD TO TRUE
219        PERFORM UNTIL S1-VALID-FIELD
220            ACCEPT SR-DAY-OF-SALE               LINE 8  COL 45
221                                                WITH REVERSE-VIDEO
222            IF NOT VALID-DAY
223                MOVE "Day number must be between 01 and 31"
224                    TO WA-USER-MESSAGE
225            ELSE
226                SET S1-VALID-FIELD TO TRUE
227            END-IF
228            PERFORM 845-DISPLAY-MESSAGE-LINE
229        END-PERFORM
230        .
231    833-OBTAIN-YEAR-OF-SALE.
232        ACCEPT SR-YEAR-OF-SALE                  LINE 8  COL 48
233                                                WITH REVERSE-VIDEO
234        .
235    834-OBTAIN-TYPE-OF-SALE.
236        SET S1-INVALID-FIELD TO TRUE
237        PERFORM UNTIL S1-VALID-FIELD
238            ACCEPT SR-TYPE-OF-SALE              LINE 10 COL 28
239                                                WITH REVERSE-VIDEO
240            IF NOT VALID-TYPE-OF-SALE
241                MOVE "Sale code must be $, C, or R"
242                    TO WA-USER-MESSAGE
243            ELSE
244                SET S1-VALID-FIELD TO TRUE
245            END-IF
246            PERFORM 845-DISPLAY-MESSAGE-LINE
247        END-PERFORM
248        .
249    835-OBTAIN-EMPLOYEE-NUMBER.
250        SET S1-INVALID-FIELD TO TRUE
251        PERFORM UNTIL S1-VALID-FIELD
252        ACCEPT SR-EMPLOYEE-NUMBER               LINE 10 COL 55
253                                                WITH REVERSE-VIDEO
254            IF NOT VALID-EMPLOYEE-NUMBER
255                MOVE "Salesperson number must be between 10001 and 79999"
256                    TO WA-USER-MESSAGE
257            ELSE
258                SET S1-VALID-FIELD TO TRUE
259            END-IF
260            PERFORM 845-DISPLAY-MESSAGE-LINE
261        END-PERFORM
262        .
263    836-OBTAIN-ITEM-NUMBER.
264        SET S1-INVALID-FIELD TO TRUE
265        PERFORM UNTIL S1-VALID-FIELD
266            ACCEPT SR-ITEM-NUMBER               LINE 15 COL 1
267                                                WITH REVERSE-VIDEO
268
269            IF SR-ITEM-NUMBER IS EQUAL TO ZERO
270                MOVE "Non-zero item number is required"
271                    TO WA-USER-MESSAGE
272            ELSE
273                SET S1-VALID-FIELD TO TRUE
274            END-IF
275            PERFORM 845-DISPLAY-MESSAGE-LINE
276        END-PERFORM
277        .
278    837-OBTAIN-ITEM-DESCRIPTION.
279        SET S1-INVALID-FIELD TO TRUE
280        PERFORM UNTIL S1-VALID-FIELD
281            ACCEPT SR-ITEM-DESCRIPTION          LINE 15 COL 13
282                                                WITH REVERSE-VIDEO
283            IF SR-ITEM-DESCRIPTION (1:1) IS EQUAL TO SPACE
284                MOVE "First position must not be blank"
285                    TO WA-USER-MESSAGE
286            ELSE
287                SET S1-VALID-FIELD TO TRUE
288            END-IF
289            PERFORM 845-DISPLAY-MESSAGE-LINE
290        END-PERFORM
291        .
292
293    838-OBTAIN-QUANTITY.
294        SET S1-INVALID-FIELD TO TRUE
295        PERFORM UNTIL S1-VALID-FIELD
296            ACCEPT SI-QUANTITY                  LINE 15 COL 34
297                                                WITH REVERSE-VIDEO
298            MOVE SI-QUANTITY TO SR-QUANTITY
299            IF SR-QUANTITY IS EQUAL TO ZERO
300                MOVE "Entry must be greater than zero"
301                    TO WA-USER-MESSAGE
302            ELSE
303                SET S1-VALID-FIELD TO TRUE
304            END-IF
305            PERFORM 845-DISPLAY-MESSAGE-LINE
306        END-PERFORM
307        .
308    839-OBTAIN-PRICE.
309        SET S1-INVALID-FIELD TO TRUE
310        PERFORM UNTIL S1-VALID-FIELD
311            ACCEPT SI-PRICE                     LINE 15 COL 44
312                                                WITH REVERSE-VIDEO
313            MOVE SI-PRICE TO SR-PRICE
314            EVALUATE TRUE
315                WHEN SR-PRICE IS EQUAL TO ZERO
316                    MOVE "Entry must be greater than zero"
317                        TO WA-USER-MESSAGE
318                WHEN   SR-DEPARTMENT-NUMBER IS LESS THAN "500"
319                    AND SR-PRICE IS GREATER THAN 999.99
320                    MOVE "Price not consistent with Depart. Number"
321                        TO WA-USER-MESSAGE
322                WHEN OTHER
323                    SET S1-VALID-FIELD TO TRUE
324            END-EVALUATE
325            PERFORM 845-DISPLAY-MESSAGE-LINE
326        END-PERFORM
327        .
328    840-GET-RESPONSE.
329        DISPLAY WA-USER-MESSAGE                 LINE 20 COL 1
330        ACCEPT S3-RESPONSE-OPTION               LINE 20 COL 52
331        DISPLAY " "                             LINE 20 COL 1
332                                                WITH BLANK LINE
333
334    845-DISPLAY-MESSAGE-LINE.
335        IF S1-VALID-FIELD
336            DISPLAY " "                         LINE 20 COL 1
337                                                WITH BLANK LINE
338        ELSE
339            DISPLAY WA-USER-MESSAGE             LINE 20 COL 1
340        END-IF
341        .
```

COBOL-9X

Currently, considerable code is required to verify each of the fields. It is likely that this task will be greatly simplified by COBOL-9X, which will probably include a VALIDATE statement. The VALIDATE will check data-items to ensure that values they contain are consistent with specifications included with their definition in the DATA DIVISION.

COBOL-74

DATAENT uses numerous COBOL-85 features that are not compatible with COBOL-74. For instance, the 000 module must be broken into two modules (as required by the out-of-line PERFORM). Figure 10-31(a) shows this change. In addition, each of the other modules containing an inline PERFORM must be rewritten; Figure 10-31(b) gives a sample. This same change is required of each module 831–839. The following other changes are also required:

1. Insert the CONFIGURATION SECTION.

2. Insert LABEL RECORDS clauses.

3. Include the reserved word FILLER in the output line areas.

4. Remove all END-IFs and insert periods as appropriate.

5. Modify each validation 830 through 839, as described for modules 310 through 390 of DATAVAL.

6. Change all SET statements operating on condition-names to corresponding MOVE statements moving to data-names.

7. Replace the INITIALIZE statement with appropriate MOVE statements.

Figure 10-31 COBOL-74 modifications to DATAENT.

```
000-BUILD-DATA-FILE.                              250-DETERMINE-RECORD-ACTION.
    PERFORM 050-QUERY-TO-EXECUTE                      DISPLAY "Entry complete; you may: S - Save this record"
    IF S3-YES-RESPONSE                                                                LINE 17 COL 1
       PERFORM 100-INITIALIZE-VARIABLE-FIELDS         DISPLAY "M - Make changes"      LINE 18 COL 26
       OPEN EXTEND SALES-TRANSACTION-FILE             DISPLAY "A - Abort this record" LINE 19 COL 26
       PERFORM 150-PROCESS-INPUT-REQUEST              MOVE "                    Your choice <S, M, or A>?"
           UNTIL NOT S2-MORE-RECORDS-TO-ADD                TO WA-USER-MESSAGE
       CLOSE SALES-TRANSACTION-FILE                   MOVE SPACE TO S3-RESPONSE-OPTION
    END-IF                                            PERFORM 250-ACCEPT-RECORD-OPTION
    STOP RUN.                                             UNTIL S3-VALID-OPTION
    .                                                 IF S3-SAVE-RECORD-OPTION
    .                                                    MOVE SR-SALES-TRANSACTION-RECORD
    .                                                        TO SALES-TRANSACTION-RECORD
150-PROCESS-INPUT-REQUEST.                               PERFORM 800-WRITE-SALES-TRANS-RECORD.
    PERFORM 200-BUILD-A-RECORD                        IF S3-ABORT-RECORD-OPTION
    PERFORM 250-DETERMINE-RECORD-ACTION               OR S3-SAVE-RECORD-OPTION
    IF NOT S3-MAKE-CHANGES-OPTION                        PERFORM 825-PAINT-SCREEN-TEMPLATE
       MOVE                                              MOVE ZERO TO SR-ITEM-NUMBER
       "        Do you want to enter another record <Y/N>?"                SI-QUANTITY
          TO WA-USER-MESSAGE                                               SI-PRICE
       MOVE "Y" TO S3-RESPONSE-OPTION                    MOVE SPACES TO SR-ITEM-DESCRIPTION.
       PERFORM 840-GET-RESPONSE
       IF NOT S3-YES-RESPONSE                       250-ACCEPT-RECORD-OPTION.
          MOVE "F" TO S2-CONTINUE-SWITCH.              PERFORM 840-GET-RESPONSE
                                                       IF S3-VALID-OPTION
                                                          DISPLAY " "  LINE 17 COL 1    WITH BLANK LINE
                                                          DISPLAY " "  LINE 18 COL 26   WITH BLANK LINE
                                                          DISPLAY " "  LINE 19 COL 26   WITH BLANK LINE
                                                       ELSE
                                                          MOVE "Invalid entry, try again. Your choice<S, M, or A>?"
                                                              TO WA-USER-MESSAGE.
```

(a) To the 000 module.   (b) To the 250 module.

Chapter Summary

The INSPECT/REPLACING statement is used for character-translation applications; it has the following options:

- REPLACING ALL: Causes all occurrences of the search-field value within the inspected field to be converted to the replacement-field value.

- REPLACING LEADING: Only leftmost occurrences of the search-field value are converted to the replacement-field value.

- REPLACING FIRST: Causes only the first occurrence of the search-field value to be converted to the replacement-field value.

The INSPECT/TALLYING statement is used for character-counting applications; it has the following options:

- TALLYING ALL: Counts all occurrences of the search-field value within the inspected field.

- TALLYING LEADING: Only leftmost occurrences of the search-field value are counted.

For data validation, define all fields as alphanumeric. If operations must be performed on numeric fields requiring numeric definitions, then redefine those fields with the appropriate numeric descriptions.

Before validating numeric fields, use the INSPECT/REPLACING to replace leading spaces with zeros.

When validating a numeric field defined with a 9 PICTURE, always perform a numeric test before performing actions that might give a data exception.

Define nonarithmetic numeric fields as alphanumeric, rather than numeric. On some computer systems, numeric fields introduce the possibility that data exceptions may occur, causing abnormal program termination. In certain cases, however, the alphanumeric field requires redefinition as a numeric field (PIC 9 or S9). Such situations are as follows:

1. The input field is a signed numeric field. The input field must be redefined and the signed numeric data-name must be used in the NUMERIC class test. Testing the alphanumeric data-name results in an incorrect NOT NUMERIC result for a valid numeric value that carries an arithmetic sign.

2. A sign test (IF POSITIVE, IF NEGATIVE, or IF ZERO) will be made on the input field. The input field must be redefined and the numeric data-name must be used in the sign test. (Remember that COBOL syntax requires a numeric data-name to be referenced in a sign test.) However, recognize that if the data does not pass a NUMERIC class test, that particular field value must not be tested with the sign test because a data exception might occur.

3. The input field will be moved to a numeric-edited field (such as on the audit/error list). The input field must be redefined and the numeric data-name must be used as the sending field of the MOVE operation. However, recognize that if the data does not pass a NUMERIC class test, that particular field value must not be moved to the numeric-edited field because a data exception might occur.

4. An input numeric field with decimal positions will be moved to a numeric field that contains the PICTURE symbol V. The input field must be redefined and the numeric data-name must be used in the MOVE operation. (Remember that COBOL syntax does not permit an alphanumeric field to be moved to a numeric field with decimal positions.) However, recognize that if the data does not pass a NUMERIC class test, that particular field value must not be moved to the numeric field because an incorrect numeric value might result.

5. You prefer to use a numeric range test (rather than the alphanumeric range test coupled with a numeric class test described in this chapter). The input field must be redefined and the numeric data-name must be used in the range test. However, recognize that if the data does not pass a NUMERIC class test, the numeric data-name must not be tested because a data exception might occur.

Exercises

Terms for Definition

batch validation
data exception
inspected field
interactive validation

numeric-field error
replacement-field value
search-field value
tallying field

Review Questions

1. What are the three INSPECT/REPLACING statement options?

2. What are the two INSPECT/TALLYING statement options?

3. Why should nonarithmetic numeric-integer fields generally be specified as alphanumeric—rather than as numeric—fields?

4. For numeric fields that are not zero-filled, why is it advisable to replace LEADING SPACES BY ZEROS rather than ALL SPACES BY ZEROS?

5. Explain why a numeric field should be tested for NUMERIC even though all SPACES were replaced by ZEROS.

6. Explain why a numeric range test made with nonnumeric literals also requires a NUMERIC class test.

Questions About the DATAVAL Program

1. What is the maximum number of output lines that can be printed on a single page by DATAVAL?

2. Assume that the system designer and the programmer had a misunderstanding and the first three fields of the input record were defined as follows:

Field	Positions
Record code	1
Date of sale	2–7
Department number	9–11

These definitions were used in writing the program. Notice that the Department-number and fields that follow will be correctly defined. Also assume that no Record-code validation exists (the 310 module is not included in the program). Would any records be written to the file VALID-SALES-TRANSACTION-FILE? Explain your answer.

3. The statement

```
SET VALID-SALES-TRANS TO TRUE
```

was placed in the 100 module, instead of the 200 module. Describe what will happen because of this error.

Programming Assignments

Programming Assignment 10-1: Ledger-Record Validation

Background information:

Silicon Valley Manufacturing requires that records of their general ledger file (see Assignment 9-1) be validated. An audit/error list is to be printed that lists each record and identifies, by error code, each error detected.

Input file: Ledger file (LEDGER.ERR)

Ledger record

Record code		Account number	Account description			Account type	Account balance	

```
1 2 3 4 5 6 7 8 9 10 11 12 13 14 15 16 17 18 19 20 21 22 23 24 25 26 27 28 29 30 31 32 33 34 35 36 37 38 39 40 41 42 43 44 45 46 47 48 49 50 51 52 53 54 55 56 57 58 59 60 61 62 63 64 65 66 67 68 69 70 71 72 73 74 75 76 77 78 79
```

Output-report format:

```
          0         1         2         3         4         5         6         7         8
 1234567890123456789012345678901234567890123456789012345678901234567890123456789
 1
 2
 3
 4 LEDGER RECORD VALIDATION (10-1)                                    AUDIT/ERROR LIST
 5
 6 RC   ACCT NBR      ACCOUNT NAME              AT       BALANCE       ERROR CODES
 7
 8 XX   99999.999   XXXXXXXXXXXXXXXXXXXXXXXXXX   9   ZZ,ZZZ,ZZZ.99-      A B C D E F
 9
10 XX   99999.999   XXXXXXXXXXXXXXXXXXXXXXXXXX   9   ZZ,ZZZ,ZZZ.99-      A B C D E F
11
12
```

Program operations:

1. Process each input ledger record.

2. Print the two report-heading lines on each following page of the audit/ error list.

3. For each input ledger record, print each field of the record and make field validations as follows. When a field value does not pass the validation, print the applicable error code (shown in parentheses) at the location specified on the print chart.
   a. (Error code A) Validate the record-code field to ensure that it is equal to LM.
   b. (Error code B) Validate the account-number field to ensure that it is present.
   c. (Error code C) Validate the account-number field to ensure that it is numeric.
   d. (Error code D) If the account-name field is present (not equal to spaces), validate it to ensure that it is left-justified.
   e. (Error code E) Validate the account-type field to ensure that the account-type field contains either a space or a numeric digit within the range 1–6.

f. (Error code F) After replacing any leading spaces with zeros, validate it to ensure that it is numeric.

4. Double-space each audit/error list detail line as specified on the print chart. Provide for a span of 57 lines per page.

Programming Assignment 10-2: Vendor-Record Validation

Background information:

Tools Unlimited has many vendors from whom it makes a wide variety of purchases. A favorite project of the purchasing agent is maintaining data about vendors on a personal computer, using a BASIC program that a friend wrote. This data now needs to integrate with other systems. A program was written to convert the data file to a form compatible with the vendor-control program in COBOL. These records must be validated. An audit/error list should be printed that lists each record and identifies, by error code, each error detected. The erroneous field should also be highlighted by marking asterisks beneath it in the record-image area of the audit/error list.

Input file: Vendor file (VENDOR.ERR)

Vendor record

Record code	Vendor number	Date due (yymmdd)	Vendor name		Amount due
1 2	3 4 5 6 7 8 9 10 11	12 13 14 15 16 17	18 19 20 21 22 23 24 25 26 27 28 29 30 31 32 33 34 35 36 37	38 39 40 41 42 43 44 45 46 47 48 49 50 51 52 53 54 55 56 57 58 59 60 61 62 63 64 65 66	67 68 69 70 71 72 73 74

Output-report format:

```
                0              1              2              3              4              5              6              7              8
   1234567890123456789012345678901234567890123456789012345678901234567890123456789012345678901
 1
 2
 3
 4 VENDOR RECORD VALIDATION - AUDIT ERROR LIST (10-2)                              PAGE ZZ9
 5
 6 RC   VENDOR-#   DATE DUE    VENDOR NAME          AMOUNT DUE        ---ERROR CODES---
 7
 8 XX   99999999   99/99/99  XXXXXXXXXXXXXXXXXXXX   ZZ.ZZZ.99-       A  B  C  D  E  F  G  H  I
 9 ..   ........   .. .. ..   .                     .........        
10
11 XX   99999999   99/99/99  XXXXXXXXXXXXXXXXXXXX   ZZ.ZZZ.99-       A  B  C  D  E  F  G  H  I
12
```

Program operations:

1. Read each input vendor-transaction record.

2. Print the two report-heading lines on each page of the audit/error list. Include a page number as shown on the print chart.

3. For each input vendor record, print each field of the record and make field validations as follows. When a field value does not pass the validation, then (a) print the applicable error code (shown in the following list in parentheses) at the location specified on the print chart, and (b) print a row of asterisks (error code H takes only one asterisk) beneath the respective field in the record-image area of the audit/error list.

    a. (Error code A) Validate the record-code field to ensure that is equal to VM.

    b. (Error code B) Validate the vendor-number field to ensure that it is present.

    c. (Error code C) Validate the vendor-number field to ensure that it is numeric.

    d. (Error code D) If the date-due field is equal to zero, validate the amount-due field to ensure that it is a negative value (credit balance). If the date due is zero and the amount due is negative, make no further date-due validations (error codes E, F, and G).

    e. (Error code E) Validate the date-due field to ensure that the month number is within the range 01–12.

    f. (Error code F) Validate the date-due field to ensure that the day number is within the range 01–31.

    g. (Error code G) Validate the date-due field to ensure that the date is not later than the current date plus one year.

    h. (Error code H) If the vendor-name field is present (not equal to spaces), validate it to ensure that it is left-justified.

    i. (Error code I) After replacing any leading spaces with zeros, validate the amount-due field to ensure that it is numeric.

4. Space each audit/error list detail line as specified on the print chart.

    a. Double-space each audit/error line from the previous audit line or error line with asterisks.

    b. Single-space each error line with asterisks from its previous audit/error line. Always print the error line with asterisks on the same report page as its respective audit/error line.

    c. Provide for a span of not more than 57 lines per page.

Programming Assignment 10-3: Earnings-Record Validation

Background information:

Silicon Valley Manufacturing was the victim of a computer virus intended to destroy the payroll system. Fortunately, a programmer detected it before much damage was done. However, before processing can resume, all records of the earnings file must be validated. An audit/error list should be printed that lists each record and identifies, by error message, each error detected. Record-count totals should be printed at the end of the listing.

Input file: Earnings file (EARNINGS.ERR)

Earnings record

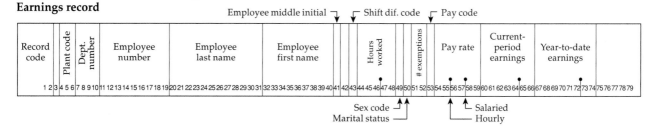

Output-report format:

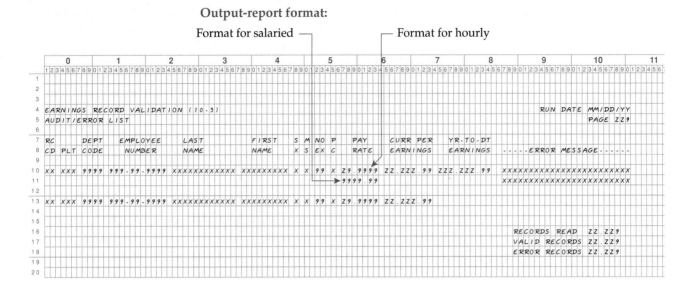

Program operations:

1. Process each input earnings record.

2. Print the four heading lines on each first page of the audit/error list. Include the run date and page number as shown on the print chart.

3. For each input earnings record, print each field of the record and make field validations as follows. When a field value does not pass the validation, print the applicable error message.

   a. Validate the Record-code field to ensure that it is equal to EM. If it is not, print the error message RECORD CODE INVALID.

   b. Validate the Plant-code field to ensure that it is equal to ATL (Atlantic), CTL (Central), MTN (Mountain), or PAC (Pacific). If it is not, print the error message PLANT CODE INVALID.

   c. After replacing any leading spaces with zeros, validate the Department-number field to ensure that it is numeric. If it is not, print the error message DEPT NUMBER NOT NUMERIC.

   d. Validate the Department-number field to ensure that it is not equal to zero. If it is, print the error message DEPT NUMBER MISSING.

   e. After replacing any leading spaces with zeros, validate the Employee-number field to ensure that it is numeric. If it is not, print the error message EMP NUMBER NOT NUMERIC.

   f. Validate the Employee-number field to ensure that it is not equal to zero. If it is, print the error message EMP NUMBER MISSING.

   g. Validate the employee Last-name field to ensure that it is present. If it is not, print the error message LAST NAME MISSING.

   h. If data is in the employee Last-name field, validate to ensure that it is left-justified. If it is not, print the error message LAST NAME NOT LEFT JUST.

   i. Validate the employee First-name field to ensure that it is present. If it is not, print the error message FIRST NAME MISSING.

   j. If data is in the employee First-name field, validate to ensure that it is left-justified. If it is not, print the error message FIRST NAME NOT LEFT JUST.

   k. Validate the Sex-code field to ensure that it contains either the letter M (male) or F (female). If it does not, print the error message SEX CODE INVALID.

l. Validate the Marital-status field to ensure that it contains either the letter M (married), S (single), or H (head of household). If it does not, print the error message MARITAL STATUS INVALID.

m. After replacing leading spaces with zeros, validate the Number-of-exemptions field to ensure that it is numeric. If it is not, print the error message NBR EXEMPTS NOT NUMERIC.

n. Validate the Pay-code field to ensure that it contains either the letter H (hourly) or the letter S (salaried). If it does not, print the error message PAY CODE INVALID.

o. After replacing any leading spaces with zeros, validate the Pay-rate field to ensure that it is numeric. If it is not, print the error message PAY RATE NOT NUMERIC.

p. If the Pay-code field indicates an hourly employee and the Pay-rate field is numeric, validate the Pay-rate field to ensure that the value is not less than four dollars (04.0000) and not greater than twenty dollars (20.0000). If it is not, print the error message HOURLY RATE INVALID.

q. If the Pay-code field indicates a salaried employee and the Pay-rate field is numeric, validate the Pay-rate field to ensure that the value is equal to or greater than one thousand dollars (1000.00). If it is not, print the error message SALARY AMOUNT INVALID.

r. After replacing leading spaces with zeros, validate the Current-period-earnings field to ensure that it is numeric. If it is not, print the error message CURR-PR EARN NOT NUMERIC.

s. After replacing leading spaces with zeros, validate the Year-to-date earnings field to ensure that it is numeric. If it is not, print the error message YR-DT EARN NOT NUMERIC.

t. If both the Current-period-earnings and the Year-to-date-earnings fields are numeric, validate the Year-to-date-earnings field to ensure that it is not less than the Current-period-earnings field. If it is, print the error message EARNING RELATION INVALID.

4. Accumulate the following record-count totals:
   a. Total number of records read.
   b. Total number of valid records (those that contain no errors).
   c. Total number of error records (those that contain one or more errors).

5. Print audit/error lines as follows:
   a. For each record that passes all the validation tests, write an audit line containing the record-image area on the audit/error list. This line is to be double-spaced from the previous line.
   b. For each record with one or more errors, write one line for each error detected. The first error line for each record should contain the record-image area and the first error detected. This line should be double-spaced from the previous line. Successive error lines for each record should be single-spaced from the previous line and contain only the error message (except as specified in item 6, below).

6. Provide for a span of not more than 57 lines per page.
   a. When it is necessary to continue error messages from one page to another, repeat the record image on the first audit/error line printed on the new page. Print the continuation message (CONTINUED) on that first line.
   b. If a record has two or more errors, print at least two lines before skipping to a new page. In other words, do not continue to a new page immediately after just one error line is printed for a record with multiple errors.

7. After all input earnings records are processed, print the three output-report total lines (triple-spaced from the last detail line) as specified on the print chart.

Programming
Assignment 10-4:
Nurses File Validation

Background information:

Several programming assignments in preceding chapters used Brooklawn Hospital's nurses file. The original program for data entry was written with limited data-checking capabilities. Consequently, this file's data contains many errors and inconsistencies. The Brooklawn data-processing staff is rewriting the data-entry programs to include strict data control. Before the new programs are implemented, a data validation program is required to validate the existing file and prepare a report that lists each record and identifies, by error code, each error detected.

Input file: Nurses file (NURSES.ERR)

Nurses record

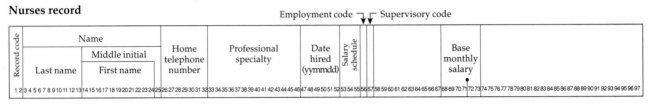

Output-report format:

```
     0         1         2         3         4         5         6         7         8         9         10        11
    1234567890123456789012345678901234567890123456789012345678901234567890123456789012345678901234567890123456789012345678
 1
 2
 3
 4  NURSES FILE RECORD VALIDATION (10-4)                                                            RUN DATE MM/DD/YY
 5  AUDIT/ERROR LIST                                                                                          PAGE ZZ9
 6
 7  RC  LAST        FIRST        M    PROFESSIONAL     TELE     DATE     SAL   EMP  SUP  BASE
 8  CD  NAME        NAME         I    SPECIALTY        NUMBER   HIRED    SCHED CDE  CDE  SALARY  ------ERROR MESSAGE------
 9
10  XX  XXXXXXXXXX  XXXXXXXXXXX  X    XXXXXXXXXXXXXX   XXXXXXX  XXXXXX   XXX   X    X    XXXXXX  XXXXXXXXXXXXXXXXXXXXXXXXXX
11                                                                                              XXXXXXXXXXXXXXXXXXXXXXXXX
12
13  XX  XXXXXXXXXX  XXXXXXXXXXX  X    XXXXXXXXXXXXXX   XXXXXXX  XXXXXX   XXX   X    X    XXXXXX
14
15
16                                                                                              RECORDS PROCESSED  ZZ,ZZ9
17                                                                                              VALID RECORDS      ZZ,ZZ9
18                                                                                              ERROR RECORDS      ZZ,ZZ9
19
20
21
22
```

Program operations:

1. Process each record.

2. Print the four heading lines on each page of the audit/error list. Include the run date and the page number as shown on the print chart.

3. For each input record, print each field of the record and make field validations as follows. When a field value does not pass the validation, print the applicable error message. Fields not identified for validation do not need to be tested because they will be replaced when the new system is implemented.

   a. Validate the Record-code field to ensure that it is equal to NU. If it is not, print the error message RECORD CODE INVALID.

   b. Validate the Last-name field to ensure that it is present. If it is not, print the error message LAST NAME MISSING.

   c. If data is in the employee Last-name field, validate to ensure that it is left-justified. If it is not, print the error message LAST NAME NOT LEFT JUST.

   d. Validate the employee First-name field to ensure that it is present. If it is not, print the error message FIRST NAME MISSING.

   e. If data is in the employee First-name field, validate to ensure that it is left-justified. If it is not, print the error message FIRST NAME NOT LEFT JUST.

f. Validate the Middle-initial field to ensure that it is a letter or blank. If it is not, print the error message MIDDLE INITIAL NOT ALPHA.

g. If an entry is in the Telephone-number field, check to ensure that it is numeric. If it is not numeric, print the error message TELE NUM NOT NUMERIC.

h. Validate the Professional-specialty field to ensure that it is present. If it is not, print the error message PROF SPECIALTY MISSING.

i. Validate the Date-hired field to ensure that it is present. If it is not, print the error message DATE HIRED MISSING.

j. If data is in the Date-hired field, check to ensure that it is numeric. If it is not, print the error message DATE HIRED NOT NUM.

k. If the Date-hired field is numeric, check to ensure that the Year is between 50 (1950) and the current year, inclusive. If it is not, print the error message HIRE YEAR OUT OF RANGE.

l. If the Date-hired field is numeric, check to ensure that the Month is between 1 and 12. If it is not, print the error message HIRE MONTH INVALID.

m. If the Date-hired field is numeric, check to ensure that the Day meets the following conditions:
- If month is February and the year is not a leap year, the day number must not be greater than 28; if a leap year, the day number must not be greater than 29. (Note: Leap years occur every four years and are evenly divisible by four; for example, 1996 is a leap year.)
- If the month is April, June, September, or November, the day number must not be greater than 30.
- For any other month, the day number must not be greater than 31.

If the Day number does not meet these criterion, print the error message HIRE DAY INVALID.

n. Validate the Salary-schedule field to ensure that it is present. If it is not, print the error message SALARY SCHEDULE MISSING.

o. Check to ensure that the Employment-code contains either F or P. If it does not, print the error message INVALID EMPLOYMENT CODE.

p. Check to ensure that the Supervisory-code contains either Y or N. If it does not, print the error message INVALID SUPER CODE.

q. After replacing any leading spaces with zeros, validate the Base-monthly-salary field to ensure that it is numeric. If it is not, print the error message SALARY NOT NUMERIC.

4. Accumulate the following record-count totals:
a. Total number of records read.
b. Total number of valid records (those that contain no errors).
c. Total number of error records (those that contain one or more errors).

5. Print audit/error lines as follows:
a. For each record that passes all the validation tests, write an audit line containing the record-image area on the audit/error list. This line should be double-spaced from the previous line.
b. For each record with one or more errors, write one line for each error detected. The first error line for each record should contain the record-image area and the first error detected. This line should be double-spaced from the previous line. Successive error lines for each record should be single-spaced from the previous line and should contain only the error message (except as specified in item 6, next).

6. Provide for a span of not more than 57 lines per page.
a. When it is necessary to continue error messages from one page to another, repeat the record image on the first audit/error line printed on the new page. Print the continuation message (CONTINUED) on that first line.

b. If a record has two or more errors, print at least two lines before skipping to a new page. In other words, do not continue to a new page immediately after just one error line is printed for a record with multiple errors.

7. After all input earnings records are processed, print the three output-report total lines (triple-spaced from the last detail line) as specified on the print chart.

Programming Assignment 10-5: Data Validation/ Data Entry

For any of the four preceding assignments, write a data-entry program that includes the designated record checking. Include all the features of DATAENT, plus any that you feel will make the program more user-friendly. Optionally, print a summary report of all records entered during a given session. Use appropriate report and column headings.

Processing Arrays/Tables

CHAPTER

11

CHAPTER OBJECTIVES

Array/table processing is an important COBOL subject that has many aspects. This chapter describes fundamental array/table-processing concepts; Chapter 12 covers more advanced table-processing considerations. From this chapter, you will learn the following:

- Accessing an array using subscripts to identify the particular element that is desired.

- The OCCURS clause, which specifies how many times a field or group of fields is repeated.

- Defining a table in the WORKING-STORAGE SECTION using VALUE clauses.

- The PERFORM/VARYING statement, which uses automatic counting for the control of a processing loop.

- Storing data from an input file into an array for later processing.

- The Format-1 (serial) SEARCH statement, which is specifically designed for a serial search.

- Performing a binary search using the Format-2 (binary) SEARCH ALL statement.

Calculating an Average

Let's consider a current need of Pyramid Sales Company (used in Chapter 9 for control-break processing). Recall the following about Pyramid's sales file:

1. It contains one record for each sale made. Each sales representative has one or more records in the file.
2. The record format includes the sales representative number.
3. Since the file is in sequence based on this number, the records for each sales representative are grouped together.

The sales manager intends to study sales patterns, so he begins by looking at the average sales of his sales force. As you might anticipate, the required programming is a relatively simple task, you need only:

1. Read each record in the sales file, calculate the sales revenue (Quantity-sold times Unit-price), and add the sales revenue to a total accumulator.
2. With each break in the sales representative number, add 1 to a sales representative counter.
3. After the last record is read, calculate the average (divide the total accumulator by the counter).

Figure 11-1 Calculating an average—The AVERAGE program.

```
1        IDENTIFICATION DIVISION.                              54        PROCEDURE DIVISION.
2        PROGRAM-ID.    AVERAGE.                               55
3                                                              56        000-PRINT-SALES-REPORT.
4      * Written by W. Price 1-23-95                           57
5      * PYRAMID SALES COMPANY.                                58      ************Initialization Sequence************
6                                                              59            OPEN INPUT SALES-FILE
7      * This program calculates the average sales             60            PERFORM 100-INITIALIZE-VARIABLE-FIELDS
8      * for sales representatives.                            61
9                                                              62      **************Processing Sequence**************
10                                                             63      *    Read file and load array
11       ENVIRONMENT DIVISION.                                 64            PERFORM UNTIL SW-END-OF-FILE
12                                                             65               READ SALES-FILE INTO SR-SALES-RECORD
13       INPUT-OUTPUT SECTION.                                 66                  AT END
14                                                             67                     SET SW-END-OF-FILE TO TRUE
15       FILE-CONTROL.                                         68                  NOT AT END
16           SELECT SALES-FILE                                 69                     PERFORM 200-PROCESS-DETAIL-RECORD
17               ASSIGN TO (system dependent).                 70               END-READ
18                                                             71            END-PERFORM
19                                                             72            DIVIDE WA-SALES-REVENUE-TOTAL BY WA-REP-COUNT
20       DATA DIVISION.                                        73               GIVING WA-SALES-REVENUE-AVERAGE ROUNDED
21                                                             74            PERFORM 850-DISPLAY-RESULTS
22       FILE SECTION.                                         75
23                                                             76      *************Termination Sequence*************
24       FD  SALES-FILE.                                       77            CLOSE SALES-FILE
25       01  SALES-RECORD.                                     78            STOP RUN
26           05  PIC X(48).                                    79            .
27                                                             80      **********************************************
28       WORKING-STORAGE SECTION.                              81
29                                                             82        100-INITIALIZE-VARIABLE-FIELDS.
30       01  PROGRAM-SWITCHES.                                 83            SET SW-NOT-END-OF-FILE TO TRUE
31           05  SW-END-OF-FILE-SWITCH    PIC X(1).            84            INITIALIZE WA-REP-COUNT
32               88  SW-END-OF-FILE           VALUE "E".       85                       WA-SALES-REVENUE-TOTAL
33               88  SW-NOT-END-OF-FILE       VALUE "N".       86            MOVE LOW-VALUES TO WA-PREV-SALES-REP
34                                                             87            .
35       01  WA-WORK-AREAS.                                    88        200-PROCESS-DETAIL-RECORD.
36           05  WA-SALES-REVENUE-1-REC   PIC S9(5)V99.        89            IF SR-SALES-REP NOT = WA-PREV-SALES-REP
37           05  WA-SALES-REVENUE-TOTAL   PIC S9(6)V99.        90               MOVE SR-SALES-REP TO WA-PREV-SALES-REP
38           05  WA-SALES-REVENUE-AVERAGE PIC S9(5)V99.        91               ADD 1 TO WA-REP-COUNT
39           05  WA-REP-COUNT             PIC 9(3).            92            END-IF
40           05  WA-PREV-SALES-REP        PIC X(5).            93            MULTIPLY SR-UNIT-PRICE BY SR-QUANTITY-SOLD
41                                                             94               GIVING WA-SALES-REVENUE-1-REC
42       01  SR-SALES-RECORD.                                  95            ADD WA-SALES-REVENUE-1-REC
43           05                           PIC X(7).            96                       TO WA-SALES-REVENUE-TOTAL
44           05  SR-SALES-REP             PIC X(5).            97            .
45           05                           PIC X(29).           98        850-DISPLAY-RESULTS.
46           05  SR-QUANTITY-SOLD         PIC S9(3).           99            MOVE WA-SALES-REVENUE-AVERAGE
47           05  SR-UNIT-PRICE            PIC 9(2)V99.        100                       TO DI-HIGH-SALES-REVENUE
48                                                            101            DISPLAY DI-HIGH-SALES-REVENUE
49       01  DISPLAY-ITEMS.                                   102            DISPLAY " "
50           05  DI-HIGH-SALES-REVENUE    PIC ZZ,ZZ9.99.      103            DISPLAY "Press the Enter key to terminate "
51           05  DI-DUMMY                 PIC X.              104            ACCEPT DI-DUMMY
52                                                            105            .
53
```

A program to do this—and display the result on the screen—is shown in Figure 11-1. In the DATA DIVISION, you see the following:

- The input record definition SR-SALES-RECORD, which begins on line 42. Only those fields needed for this application are named; other positions are designated as filler.

- The DISPLAY-ITEMS (lines 49–51) display the computed result.

- Usual arithmetic work areas are defined in WA-WORK-AREAS, beginning on line 35.

- As with conventional control-break programming, it is necessary to define a save area to hold the current sales representative number in order to count the number of sales representatives. This need is served by WA-PREV-SALES-REP, defined on line 40.

Most of the PROCEDURE DIVISION is reasonably straightforward. After each record is read, the sales amount is calculated (lines 93 and 94), then added to the accumulator (lines 95 and 96). The only tricky aspect is counting the number of sales representatives. For this, a simplified control-break logic is used. At lines 89–92, you can see that whenever a new sales representative is detected, 1 is added to the counter WA-REP-COUNT. The first record triggers this count because LOW-VALUES was moved into WA-PREV-SALES-REP in the 100 module (line 86). LOW-VALUES is a literal that represents the lowest possible value in the collating sequence.

COBOL-74

The necessary COBOL-74 changes for the AVERAGE program are
1. Insert the CONFIGURATION SECTION and LABEL RECORDS clauses.
2. Include the reserved word FILLER in the record description.
3. Change each SET statement to a corresponding MOVE.
4. Modify the processing sequence (lines 64–71), using either the priming READ or the COBOL-74 equivalent of this code.
5. Remove the END-IF scope terminators and terminate the IF scope with a period.
6. Replace the INITIALIZE with an appropriate MOVE.
7. If necessary, move separate-line paragraph-ending periods to the end of the preceding line.

Basic Principles of Arrays

Subscripting

The AVERAGE program—like all examples and techniques until now—involves reading a record, operating on its data, printing results, then reading the next record, and so on. In other words, each data record is read, processed, and then discarded for the next one. However, some applications require that data values be read *and saved* for later processing. Let's examine an expansion of the preceding example.

The sales manager wants a special incentive program that gives special benefits to the most profitable sales representatives. As part of his study, he needs to know how many sales representatives have sales exceeding the average by more than 20 percent. This processing sequence involves the following operations.

1. Read each record in the sales file, calculate the sales revenue (Quantity-sold times Unit-price), and add the sales revenue to sales representative and total accumulators.
2. With each break in the sales representative number, add 1 to a sales representative counter *and save the sales representative total.*
3. After the last record is read, calculate the average (divide the total accumulator by the counter).
4. Compare each of the previously calculated sales representative totals to 1.2 times the calculated average.

The question now is, "How do we store the sales for each representative so that we have access to it after processing the file?" The answer is to take a mathematician's approach and use **subscripts** (the word *subscript* comes from a Latin word meaning "to write below"). To illustrate, assume that the file contains data on five sales representatives. With the standard subscript notation, you could refer to the sales figures for those five representatives as s_1, s_2, s_3, s_4, and s_5. In other words, you refer to any individual entry by including the appropriate subscript (1–5) with the variable name (s). For instance, the fourth representative is represented by s_4 (called "s subfour" or simply "s four").

To further generalize, you can refer to any desired entry as s_i, where i is limited to the range 1–5. A variable that includes a subscript—such as s_i, in this case—is known as a *subscripted variable*. The entire set s of sales figures (consisting of all five s_i subscripted variables) is called an **array**.

Subscripting is so powerful that most computers have special hardware features for implementing subscripted quantities. Also, most high-level languages include extensive provisions for using subscripting. In algebra, a subscripted variable takes a form such as s_3; in most programming languages, the form is S(3). Because it is impractical to enter subscripted characters through a terminal in the usual sense, a subscripted quantity consists of a data-name followed by a pair of parentheses enclosing a data-item (the subscript). In COBOL, as in most languages, the subscript can be a data-name (a variable) or a numeric literal. So, S(I) is equivalent to s_i and S(3) to s_3; this capability represents a powerful COBOL feature.

Defining a Table in the WORKING-STORAGE SECTION

To define a data-item array or **table**, as it is commonly called in COBOL, you must use the OCCURS clause, as shown in Figure 11-2. The OCCURS clause specifies how many times a particular field or group of fields is repeated. The integer number specified in the OCCURS clause identifies the number of repetitions.

Figure 11-2
The OCCURS clause.

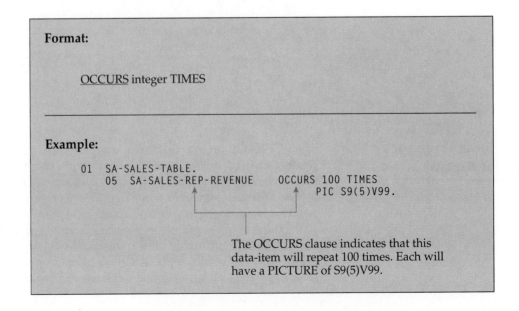

Format:

    OCCURS integer TIMES

Example:

    01 SA-SALES-TABLE.
        05 SA-SALES-REP-REVENUE   OCCURS 100 TIMES
                                          PIC S9(5)V99.

The OCCURS clause indicates that this data-item will repeat 100 times. Each will have a PICTURE of S9(5)V99.

In many applications, an array's size is specifically determined by its nature. For instance, if you create an array of work days in each month of the year, you specify 12 in the OCCURS because each year contains 12 months. On the other hand, in some applications, you will not have an exact figure. For instance, how many sales representatives does Pyramid Sales employ? Perhaps it is 82 today, but the firm plans to hire more soon. In such a case, you select a value that is large enough to accommodate whatever is likely to occur. In Figure 11-2's example, it is assumed that Pyramid will never have more than 100 sales representatives.

The OCCURS clause can be used with any data-item that has a level-number from 02–49. Because each of the elements of the array will contain different values, using a VALUE clause with the OCCURS is not practical.

Accessing the Array Data Using Subscripts

Whenever an OCCURS clause is associated with a data-item, either a subscript or an index (covered later in this chapter) must be used when referring to that item in the PROCEDURE DIVISION.

Elements of the sales-amount array are easily accessible by using a subscript on the variable whose name is defined with the OCCURS clause. For instance, if you want to display the sales for the seventh sales representative on the screen, you use a literal subscript and code:

```
DISPLAY SA-SALES-REP-REVENUE (7)
```

Notice the spacing in the subscript form. Some compilers require that a space precede the open parenthesis and that no spaces be included inside the parentheses. However, COBOL-85 places no such restrictions on the use of spaces.

Similarly, if you want to display the sales for the sales representative whose array position is stored in the variable SC-SUBSCRIPT, you use a **variable subscript** and code:

```
DISPLAY SA-SALES-REP-REVENUE (SC-SUBSCRIPT)
```

Variable subscripts must be elementary numeric-integer fields defined in the DATA DIVISION. The length of a field used for a subscript must be sufficient to contain the number of occurrences specified in the OCCURS clause.

With a few specialized exceptions, any reference in the PROCEDURE DIVISION to SA-SALES-REP-REVENUE *must include a subscript*. That is, you *cannot* use the statement:

```
DISPLAY SA-SALES-REP-REVENUE
```

You must specify which array element you want by including a subscript.

Varying the Subscript

Assume that you want to display the sales amounts from the first ten array entries. The simplest way, of course, is to write ten separate DISPLAY statements. The first three are

```
DISPLAY SA-SALES-REP-REVENUE (1)
DISPLAY SA-SALES-REP-REVENUE (2)
DISPLAY SA-SALES-REP-REVENUE (3)
```

However, this might be clumsy if you need to display 50 sales amounts, instead of only 10. The best way to handle this is by using a variable subscript whose value is changed within a loop, as Figure 11-3 shows. Significant features of this example are

1. The variable used as the subscript, SC-SUBSCRIPT, is *initialized* to 1 before entering the PERFORM loop.
2. This subscript is *incremented* by 1 with each execution of the loop.

Figure 11-3 A loop to display exactly 50 table items.

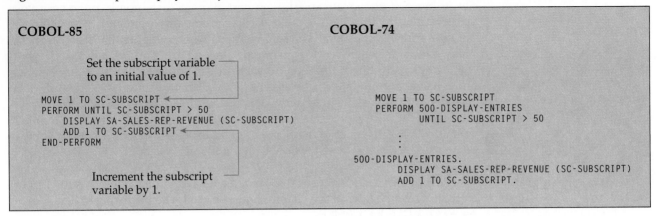

3. Repetition of the loop is *controlled* by comparing the value of the sub-script to the desired number of entries to be displayed. Be aware that this is not the only way to control repetition of an array processing loop.

The first time through the loop, the subscript will be 1 and the value from SA-SALES-REP-REVENUE (1) will be displayed. The second time through the loop, the subscript will be 2—and so on. You should pay particular attention to the way in which the loop executes. That is, the subscript is initialized to 1 before entering the loop, then is incremented by 1 *after* processing (displaying) the current array element. For this reason, the UNTIL test in the PERFORM is IS GREATER THAN, rather than IS EQUAL TO. An implication of this is that after execution of the loop is finished, the value in the subscript variable (SC-SALES-REP, in this case) is 1 greater than the last value used within the loop.

COBOL-74

The consequence of not having an inline PERFORM in COBOL-74 is evident in Figure 11-3 where, in order to repeat two statements, they must be moved to a separate paragraph.

The VARYING Option of the PERFORM Statement

In many programming applications, looping requires an incrementing action such as that in Figure 11-3. In fact, the activity is sufficiently common that most programming languages provide special statements for its implementation. In COBOL, the PERFORM/UNTIL statement with the VARYING phrase serves the purpose; Figure 11-4(a) shows its format and examples. The three elements of the VARYING function are as follows:

VARYING   Identifies the variable (or index, as you will learn later) that will be incremented within the loop.

FROM   Designates the initial value to be assigned to the variable before entering the loop.

BY   Designates the amount to be added to the variable with each execution of the loop.

Figure 11-4(b) shows the logic of the PERFORM/VARYING. As with Figure 11-3's loop, the variable is incremented at the end of the loop. So after the loop is executed 50 times, the value in the variable is 51, not 50. Later, you will see how you must account for this in certain applications.

Figure 11-4   PERFORM/VARYING statement.

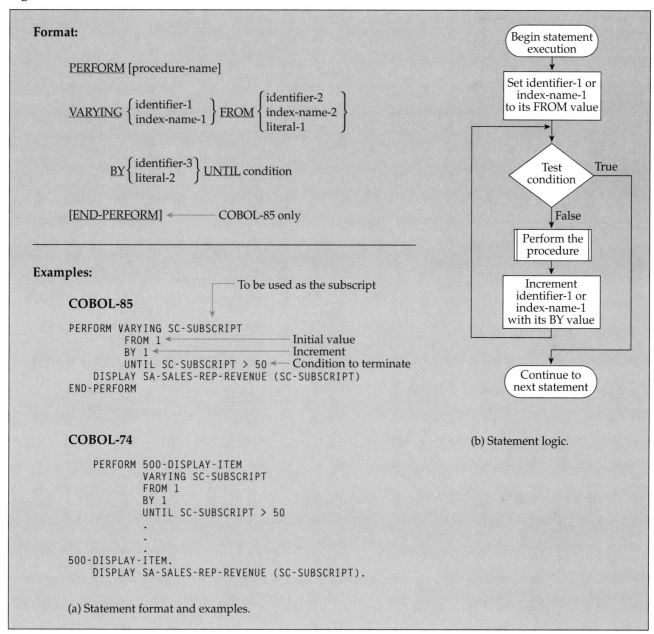

Format:

PERFORM [procedure-name]

$$\underline{VARYING} \begin{Bmatrix} \text{identifier-1} \\ \text{index-name-1} \end{Bmatrix} \underline{FROM} \begin{Bmatrix} \text{identifier-2} \\ \text{index-name-2} \\ \text{literal-1} \end{Bmatrix}$$

$$\underline{BY} \begin{Bmatrix} \text{identifier-3} \\ \text{literal-2} \end{Bmatrix} \underline{UNTIL} \text{ condition}$$

[END-PERFORM] ◄———— COBOL-85 only

Examples:

To be used as the subscript

COBOL-85

```
PERFORM VARYING SC-SUBSCRIPT
        FROM 1  ◄————————— Initial value
        BY 1  ◄——————————— Increment
        UNTIL SC-SUBSCRIPT > 50  ◄—— Condition to terminate
    DISPLAY SA-SALES-REP-REVENUE (SC-SUBSCRIPT)
END-PERFORM
```

COBOL-74

```
    PERFORM 500-DISPLAY-ITEM
            VARYING SC-SUBSCRIPT
            FROM 1
            BY 1
            UNTIL SC-SUBSCRIPT > 50
            .
            .
            .
    500-DISPLAY-ITEM.
        DISPLAY SA-SALES-REP-REVENUE (SC-SUBSCRIPT).
```

(a) Statement format and examples.

Flowchart (right side):

Begin statement execution → Set identifier-1 or index-name-1 to its FROM value → Test condition → (True) Continue to next statement → (False) Perform the procedure → Increment identifier-1 or index-name-1 with its BY value → (loops back to Test condition)

(b) Statement logic.

Loading and Using a Data Set—HIGHREP1

The array concepts that you have just learned are incorporated into Figure 11-5's HIGHREP1 program. If you compare it to Figure 11-1's AVERAGE program, you will see that HIGHREP1 is simply an extension of AVERAGE.

DATA DIVISION Features

At lines 46–48, you see the array defined (as previously illustrated in Figure 11-2). Immediately following is the 01-level entry SC-SALES-REP-ARRAY-CONTROLS. It contains the following fields that are used for processing and accessing the array:

SC-ENTRY-MAXIMUM   Given a value of 100, the size of the array (the maximum number of sales representatives that can be handled).

Figure 11-5   Processing an array—The HIGHREP1 program.

```
1        IDENTIFICATION DIVISION.                              84   *************Processing Sequence**************
2        PROGRAM-ID.    HIGHREP1.                              85   *    Read file and load array
3                                                              86        PERFORM UNTIL S1-END-OF-FILE
4     *  Written by W. Price  1-23-95                          87                OR S3-ARRAY-FULL
5     *  PYRAMID SALES COMPANY.                                88            READ SALES-FILE INTO SR-SALES-RECORD
6                                                              89                AT END
7     *  This program processes the sales representative file  90                    SET S1-END-OF-FILE TO TRUE
8     *  as follows:                                           91                NOT AT END
9     *  1. Sales revenue for each sales representative is     92                    PERFORM 200-LOAD-ARRAY-ELEMENT
10    *     accumulated and stored in one element of an array. 93            END-READ
11    *  2. After the last record is processed, the average    94        END-PERFORM
12    *     sales for the sales reps is calculated.            95        SET S2-OKAY-TO-CONTINUE TO TRUE
13    *  3. The number of sales reps whose sales exceed the    96        IF S3-ARRAY-FULL
14    *     average by more than 20% is determined.            97            PERFORM 900-QUERY-TO-CONTINUE
15                                                             98        END-IF
16                                                             99   *    Process array
17       ENVIRONMENT DIVISION.                                100        IF S2-OKAY-TO-CONTINUE
18                                                            101            PERFORM 220-CALCULATE-THE-AVERAGE
19       INPUT-OUTPUT SECTION.                                102            PERFORM 240-SCAN-THE-ARRAY
20                                                            103            PERFORM 850-DISPLAY-RESULTS
21       FILE-CONTROL.                                        104        END-IF
22           SELECT SALES-FILE                                105
23               ASSIGN TO (system dependent).                106   *************Termination Sequence*************
24                                                            107        CLOSE SALES-FILE
25                                                            108        STOP RUN
26       DATA DIVISION.                                       109        .
27                                                            110   ****************************************************
28       FILE SECTION.                                        111
29                                                            112   100-INITIALIZE-VARIABLE-FIELDS.
30       FD  SALES-FILE.                                      113        SET S1-NOT-END-OF-FILE TO TRUE
31       01  SALES-RECORD.                                    114        SET S3-ARRAY-NOT-FULL TO TRUE
32           05  PIC X(48).                                   115        INITIALIZE SA-SALES-ARRAY
33                                                            116                SC-ENTRY-COUNT
34       WORKING-STORAGE SECTION.                             117                WA-COUNT-EXCEEDING-HI
35                                                            118                WA-SALES-REVENUE-TOTAL
36       01  PROGRAM-SWITCHES.                                119                SC-SUBSCRIPT
37           05  S1-END-OF-FILE-SWITCH      PIC X(1).         120        MOVE LOW-VALUES TO SC-PREV-SALES-REP
38               88  S1-END-OF-FILE         VALUE "E".        121
39               88  S1-NOT-END-OF-FILE     VALUE "N".        122   200-LOAD-ARRAY-ELEMENT.
40           05  S2-OVERFLOW-CONTINUE-SWITCH PIC X(1).        123        IF SR-SALES-REP NOT = SC-PREV-SALES-REP
41               88  S2-OKAY-TO-CONTINUE    VALUE "Y" "y".    124            MOVE SR-SALES-REP TO SC-PREV-SALES-REP
42           05  S3-ARRAY-FULL-SWITCH       PIC X.            125            ADD 1 TO SC-SUBSCRIPT
43               88  S3-ARRAY-NOT-FULL      VALUE "N".        126        END-IF
44               88  S3-ARRAY-FULL          VALUE "F".        127        IF SC-SUBSCRIPT > SC-ENTRY-MAXIMUM
45                                                            128            SET S3-ARRAY-FULL TO TRUE
46       01  SA-SALES-ARRAY.                                  129            SUBTRACT 1 FROM SC-SUBSCRIPT
47           05  SA-SALES-REP-REVENUE       OCCURS 100 TIMES  130        ELSE
48                                          PIC S9(5)V99.     131            MULTIPLY SR-UNIT-PRICE BY SR-QUANTITY-SOLD
49                                                            132                GIVING WA-SALES-REVENUE-1-REP
50       01  SC-SALES-REP-ARRAY-CONTROLS.                     133            ADD WA-SALES-REVENUE-1-REP TO
51           05  COMP-FIELDS    USAGE COMP.                   134                SA-SALES-REP-REVENUE(SC-SUBSCRIPT)
52               10  SC-ENTRY-MAXIMUM  PIC 9(3) VALUE 100.    135                WA-SALES-REVENUE-TOTAL
53               10  SC-ENTRY-COUNT    PIC 9(3).              136        END-IF
54               10  SC-SUBSCRIPT      PIC 9(3).              137        .
55           05  SC-PREV-SALES-REP     PIC X(5).             138   220-CALCULATE-THE-AVERAGE.
56                                                           139        MOVE SC-SUBSCRIPT TO SC-ENTRY-COUNT
57       01  WA-WORK-AREAS.                                  140        DIVIDE WA-SALES-REVENUE-TOTAL BY SC-ENTRY-COUNT
58           05  WA-SALES-REVENUE-1-REP  PIC S9(5)V99.       141            GIVING WA-SALES-REVENUE-AVERAGE ROUNDED
59           05  WA-SALES-REVENUE-TOTAL  PIC S9(6)V99.       142        MULTIPLY WA-SALES-REVENUE-AVERAGE BY 1.2
60           05  WA-SALES-REVENUE-AVERAGE PIC S9(5)V99.      143            GIVING WA-HIGH-SALES-REVENUE
61           05  WA-HIGH-SALES-REVENUE   PIC S9(5)V99.       144        .
62           05  WA-COUNT-EXCEEDING-HI   PIC 9(2) USAGE COMP.145   240-SCAN-THE-ARRAY.
63                                                           146        PERFORM VARYING SC-SUBSCRIPT
64       01  SR-SALES-RECORD.                                147            FROM 1
65           05                          PIC X(7).           148            BY 1
66           05  SR-SALES-REP            PIC X(5).           149            UNTIL SC-SUBSCRIPT > SC-ENTRY-COUNT
67           05                          PIC X(29).          150        IF SA-SALES-REP-REVENUE(SC-SUBSCRIPT)
68           05  SR-QUANTITY-SOLD        PIC S9(3).          151            > WA-HIGH-SALES-REVENUE
69           05  SR-UNIT-PRICE           PIC 9(2)V99.        152            ADD 1 TO WA-COUNT-EXCEEDING-HI
70                                                           153        END-IF
71       01  DISPLAY-ITEMS.                                  154        END-PERFORM
72           05  DI-HIGH-SALES-REVENUE   PIC ZZ,ZZ9.99.      155        .
73           05  DI-DUMMY                PIC X.              156   850-DISPLAY-RESULTS.
74                                                           157        MOVE WA-HIGH-SALES-REVENUE TO DI-HIGH-SALES-REVENUE
75                                                           158        DISPLAY WA-COUNT-EXCEEDING-HI
76       PROCEDURE DIVISION.                                 159            " sales reps exceeded the high-sales revenue amount: "
77                                                           160            DI-HIGH-SALES-REVENUE
78       000-PRINT-SALES-REPORT.                             161        DISPLAY " "
79                                                           162        DISPLAY "Press the Enter key to terminate "
80    ***********Initialization Sequence***********          163            WITH NO ADVANCING
81       OPEN INPUT SALES-FILE                               164        ACCEPT DI-DUMMY
82       PERFORM 100-INITIALIZE-VARIABLE-FIELDS              165        .
83                                                           166   900-QUERY-TO-CONTINUE.
                                                             167        DISPLAY "Unable to process all sales representatives."
                                                             168        DISPLAY "You can proceed and process only those that "
                                                             169        DISPLAY "have been loaded or you can abort."
                                                             170        DISPLAY " "
                                                             171        DISPLAY "Do you want to proceed <Y/N>? "
                                                             172            WITH NO ADVANCING
                                                             173        ACCEPT S2-OVERFLOW-CONTINUE-SWITCH
                                                             174        .
```

SC-ENTRY-COUNT	Will contain a count of the number of entries (the number of sales representatives) in the array after it is loaded.
SC-SUBSCRIPT	As the name suggests, it is used as the variable subscript when accessing elements of the array.
SC-PREV-SALES-REP	The save variable for the sales representative number.

Establishment of a dedicated area—near the array—for these fields helps with good program organization and facilitates program maintenance.

Work area variables include the two additions at lines 61 and 62: WA-HIGH-SALES-REVENUE and WA-COUNT-EXCEEDING-HI. You will see how these are used in the PROCEDURE DIVISION.

At lines 51 and 62, you can see that some of the fields are defined as USAGE COMP. The USAGE clause can control the internal format in which data is stored. For whole number quantities, USAGE COMP results in a pure binary form that is very efficient for arithmetic operations. Although program efficiency should not be a primary consideration in program design, in this case, subscripting operations can be sped up with no sacrifice of program quality.

In addition, the switch S3-ARRAY-FULL-SWITCH (lines 42–44) is used to ensure that an attempt is not made to enter more than 100 entries in the array. S2-OVERFLOW-CONTINUE-SWITCH (lines 40–41) is used to query the user if this condition occurs.

PROCEDURE DIVISION Features

Initialization Actions

Notice the list of data-items that are initialized in HIGHREP1's 100 module. These include all accumulators, plus the entire array (line 115). The latter is necessary because each array element is used as an accumulator when data is read from the file. (You will see this in descriptions of the 200 module.) At line 115, the record name assigned to the array SA-SALES-ARRAY is designated. The INITIALIZE causes all subordinate items (array entries, in this case) to be initialized.

Loading Data Into the Array

As each record is read, the 200 module (beginning line 122) is performed. As with AVERAGE, a change in the sales representative number causes the new number to be saved and the subscript to be incremented by 1. (The subscript was initialized to 0 at line 119.)

At line 127, a test is made to ensure that processing does not go beyond the end of the array. If the input file includes more than 100 sales representatives, only the first 100 are processed.

The ADD at lines 133–135 adds the calculated sales amount for the input record to both the sales representative array element and to the total accumulator.

Checking for Table Overflow

At line 95, the S2-OVERFLOW-CONTINUE-SWITCH data-item is initialized by setting S2-OKAY-TO-CONTINUE to true. Through the IF at line 96, module 900 is performed if an excess of input records occurs. The user is queried about continuing (lines 167–173), with the response accepted into the switch S2-OVERFLOW-CONTINUE-SWITCH. Any entry except "Y" or "y" causes the program to be terminated through the IF at line 100.

Scanning the Array

After calculating the average and then the high-sales value (1.2 times the average) in the 220 module, the array scan begins. For the scan, you can see that the PER-FORM/VARYING starting at line 146 (previously illustrated in Figure 11-4) controls the loop. Each array entry is compared to the high-sales value (lines 150 and 151). Only if the entry is larger is the counter incremented (line 152).

At line 102, the 240 module is executed through a PERFORM. Since the 240 module consists only of the PERFORM/VARYING statement, you could change the code at line 102 to:

```
PERFORM 240-SCAN-THE-ARRAY
    VARYING SC-SUBSCRIPT
        FROM 1
        BY 1
        UNTIL SC-SUBSCRIPT IS GREATER THAN SC-ENTRY-COUNT
```

Then you could eliminate the PERFORM/VARYING from the 240 module. However, Figure 11-5's form is better practice because the subscript control elements are together with the code that uses them. It provides less opportunity for error and produces more maintainable code.

COBOL-74

The COBOL-74 changes for HIGHREP1 are

1. Insert the CONFIGURATION SECTION and LABEL RECORDS clauses.
2. Include the reserved word FILLER in the record description.
3. Change each SET statement to a corresponding MOVE.
4. Modify the processing sequence (lines 86–94), using either the priming READ or the COBOL-74 equivalent of this code.
5. In contrast to the COBOL-85 version, include the VARYING option in the out-of-line PERFORM at line 102. Then delete the inline PERFORM from the 240 module.
6. Remove the END-IF scope terminators and terminate the IF scope with a period.
7. Replace the INITIALIZE with appropriate MOVE statements.
8. If necessary, move separate-line paragraph-ending periods to the end of the preceding line.

An Array with Two Columns

After one look at HIGHREP1's output, the sales manager of Pyramid Sales decides that he wants a list of the sales representatives who exceed the high-sales amount. So, it is necessary to store not only the total sales for each representative, but also his or her number. You can envision this as the two-column array of Figure 11-6. Again, the necessary modifications to expand the program are relatively simple, as you can see in Figure 11-7.

Figure 11-6
Two-column array.

```
Number      Amount
------      ------
1003        88,641.63
1005        72,711.91
1041        91,094.82
1060        77,984.39
1091        82,881.02
1096        85,482.09
```

Figure 11-7   Processing a two-column array—HIGHREP2.

```
1        IDENTIFICATION DIVISION.                          83    ***************Processing Sequence**************
2        PROGRAM-ID.   HIGHREP2.                           84    *  Read file and load array
3                                                          85       PERFORM UNTIL S1-END-OF-FILE
4     *  Written by W. Price  1-23-95                      86            OR S3-ARRAY-FULL
5     *  PYRAMID SALES COMPANY.                            87          READ SALES-FILE INTO SR-SALES-RECORD
6                                                          88             AT END
7     *  This program processes the sales representative file 89          SET S1-END-OF-FILE TO TRUE
8     *  as follows:                                       90             NOT AT END
9     *  1. Sales revenue for each sales representative is  91             PERFORM 200-LOAD-ARRAY-ELEMENT
10    *     accumulated and stored in one element of an array. 92         END-READ
11    *     The sales-rep number is also stored.           93       END-PERFORM
12    *  2. After the last record is processed, the average 94       SET S2-OKAY-TO-CONTINUE TO TRUE
13    *     sales for the sales reps is calculated.        95       IF S3-ARRAY-FULL
14    *  3. The sales reps whose sales exceed the average  96          PERFORM 900-QUERY-TO-CONTINUE
15    *     by more than 20% are listed.                   97       END-IF
16                                                         98    *  Process array
17                                                         99       IF S2-OKAY-TO-CONTINUE
18       ENVIRONMENT DIVISION.                             100         PERFORM 220-CALCULATE-THE-AVERAGE
19                                                         101         PERFORM 850-DISPLAY-HIGH-REPS
20       INPUT-OUTPUT SECTION.                             102      END-IF
21       FILE-CONTROL.                                     103
22          SELECT SALES-FILE                              104    ***************Termination Sequence*************
23             ASSIGN TO (system dependent).               105      CLOSE SALES-FILE
24                                                         106      STOP RUN
25                                                         107      .
26       DATA DIVISION.                                    108    **************************************************
27       FILE SECTION.                                     109
28                                                         110    100-INITIALIZE-VARIABLE-FIELDS.
29       FD  SALES-FILE.                                   111      SET S1-NOT-END-OF-FILE TO TRUE
30       01  SALES-RECORD.                                 112      SET S3-ARRAY-NOT-FULL TO TRUE
31           05  PIC X(48).                                113      INITIALIZE SA-SALES-ARRAY
32                                                         114               SC-ENTRY-COUNT
33       WORKING-STORAGE SECTION.                          115               WA-SALES-REVENUE-TOTAL
34                                                         116               SC-SUBSCRIPT
35       01  PROGRAM-SWITCHES.                             117      MOVE LOW-VALUES TO SC-PREV-SALES-REP
36           05  S1-END-OF-FILE-SWITCH    PIC X(1).        118      .
37               88  S1-END-OF-FILE       VALUE "E".       119    200-LOAD-ARRAY-ELEMENT.
38               88  S1-NOT-END-OF-FILE   VALUE "N".       120      IF SR-SALES-REP NOT EQUAL TO SC-PREV-SALES-REP
39           05  S2-OVERFLOW-CONTINUE-SWITCH PIC X(1).     121         MOVE SR-SALES-REP TO SC-PREV-SALES-REP
40               88  S2-OKAY-TO-CONTINUE  VALUE "Y" "y".   122         ADD 1 TO SC-SUBSCRIPT
41           05  S3-ARRAY-FULL-SWITCH     PIC X.           123      END-IF
42               88  S3-ARRAY-NOT-FULL    VALUE "N".       124      IF SC-SUBSCRIPT IS GREATER THAN SC-ENTRY-MAXIMUM
43               88  S3-ARRAY-FULL        VALUE "F".       125         SET S3-ARRAY-FULL TO TRUE
44                                                         126         SUBTRACT 1 FROM SC-SUBSCRIPT
45       01  SA-SALES-ARRAY.                               127      ELSE
46           05                       OCCURS 100 TIMES.    128         MULTIPLY SR-UNIT-PRICE BY SR-QUANTITY-SOLD
47               10  SA-SALES-REP         PIC X(5).        129            GIVING WA-SALES-REVENUE-1-REC
48               10  SA-SALES-REP-REVENUE PIC S9(5)V99.    130         MOVE SR-SALES-REP TO SA-SALES-REP (SC-SUBSCRIPT)
49                                                         131         ADD WA-SALES-REVENUE-1-REC TO
50       01  SC-SALES-REP-ARRAY-CONTROLS.                  132            SA-SALES-REP-REVENUE (SC-SUBSCRIPT)
51           05  COMP-FIELDS    USAGE COMP.                133            WA-SALES-REVENUE-TOTAL
52               10  SC-ENTRY-MAXIMUM  PIC 9(3) VALUE 100. 134      END-IF
53               10  SC-ENTRY-COUNT    PIC 9(3).           135      .
54               10  SC-SUBSCRIPT      PIC 9(3).           136
55           05  SC-PREV-SALES-REP     PIC X(5).           137    220-CALCULATE-THE-AVERAGE.
56                                                         138      MOVE SC-SUBSCRIPT TO SC-ENTRY-COUNT
57       01  WA-WORK-AREAS.                                139      DIVIDE WA-SALES-REVENUE-TOTAL BY SC-ENTRY-COUNT
58           05  WA-SALES-REVENUE-1-REC   PIC S9(5)V99.    140         GIVING WA-SALES-REVENUE-AVERAGE ROUNDED
59           05  WA-SALES-REVENUE-TOTAL   PIC S9(6)V99.    141      MULTIPLY WA-SALES-REVENUE-AVERAGE BY 1.2
60           05  WA-SALES-REVENUE-AVERAGE PIC S9(5)V99.    142         GIVING WA-HIGH-SALES-REVENUE
61           05  WA-HIGH-SALES-REVENUE    PIC S9(5)V99.    143      .
62                                                         144    850-DISPLAY-HIGH-REPS.
63       01  SR-SALES-RECORD.                              145      MOVE WA-HIGH-SALES-REVENUE TO DI-HIGH-SALES-REVENUE
64           05                       PIC X(7).            146      DISPLAY "High-sales revenue amount: "
65           05  SR-SALES-REP         PIC X(5).            147               DI-HIGH-SALES-REVENUE
66           05                       PIC X(29).           148      DISPLAY " "
67           05  SR-QUANTITY-SOLD     PIC S9(3).           149      DISPLAY "High-sales Sales Representatives"
68           05  SR-UNIT-PRICE        PIC 9(2)V99.         150      PERFORM VARYING SC-SUBSCRIPT
69                                                         151               FROM 1
70       01  DISPLAY-ITEMS.                                152               BY 1
71           05  DI-HIGH-SALES-REVENUE  PIC ZZ,ZZ9.99.     153               UNTIL SC-SUBSCRIPT IS GREATER THAN SC-ENTRY-COUNT
72           05  DI-DUMMY               PIC X.             154         IF SA-SALES-REP-REVENUE (SC-SUBSCRIPT)
73                                                         155               IS GREATER THAN WA-HIGH-SALES-REVENUE
74                                                         156            DISPLAY SA-SALES-REP (SC-SUBSCRIPT)
75       PROCEDURE DIVISION.                               157         END-IF
76                                                         158      END-PERFORM
77       000-PRINT-SALES-REPORT.                           159      DISPLAY " "
78                                                         160      DISPLAY "Press the Enter key to terminate "
79       ************Initialization Sequence************   161               WITH NO ADVANCING
80          OPEN INPUT SALES-FILE                          162      ACCEPT DI-DUMMY
81          PERFORM 100-INITIALIZE-VARIABLE-FIELDS         163      .
82                                                         164    900-QUERY-TO-CONTINUE.
                                                           165      DISPLAY "Unable to process all sales representatives."
                                                           166      DISPLAY "You can proceed and process only those that "
                                                           167      DISPLAY "have been loaded or you can abort."
                                                           168      DISPLAY " "
                                                           169      DISPLAY "Do you want to proceed <Y/N>? "
                                                           170               WITH NO ADVANCING
                                                           171      ACCEPT S2-OVERFLOW-CONTINUE-SWITCH
                                                           172      .
```

At lines 45–48, you see the two-column array defined. The pair of entries defined at the 10 level specify the data elements themselves. The 05 entry contains the OCCURS clause, which causes the array of 100 pairs of elements to be established. Because this entry is never referenced in the program, it does not need to be given a name.

In the 200 module to load the array, the sales representative number is moved into the array (line 130) and the sales record revenue is added to the array element. (Note: If a sales representative has, for instance, ten records, then the representative number is moved into the same array element ten times. Obviously, the last nine moves are not necessary. Although not erroneous, this method is not particularly elegant. It could be avoided with a first-record switch for each representative.)

After the array is loaded and the high-sales figure is calculated, the array can be scanned and the qualifying representatives' numbers displayed. This is done with an inline PERFORM in the 850 module. Notice that the subscript variable SC-SUBSCRIPT "points to" the representative number (line 156) corresponding to the qualifying representative sales revenue (line 154).

Wrap-Up

A key element of the HIGHREP programs is that the input file records were in order based on the sales representative number. Interestingly, this does not need to be the case. In fact, one of the primary features of arrays is that they are easily searched. The last example in this chapter will show you how to use the special COBOL SEARCH statement in conjunction with loading an array.

COBOL-74

The COBOL-74 changes for HIGHREP2 are the same as those for HIGHREP1—except for item 5. Instead, change the inline PERFORM at line 150 to an out-of-line PERFORM and move the IF statement (lines 154–156) to a separate paragraph (name it 851-SCAN-ARRAY).

Principles of Tables

In the preceding examples, a set of data values was created, stored in an array, and then processed. The COBOL array was used as a temporary storage area for data that was to be used again later during program execution.

Arrays are used in another way, which is best illustrated by an example. Suppose you work for a soft-drink vendor who has a system in which each soft drink is identified by its three-digit product number. For instance, ginger ale might be represented by the product number 300. In most of the processing programs, a desired soft drink is identified by its product number (input). However, for output (screen display and printed reports), you want the soft-drink description. This is a classic table application in which Figure 11-8(a)'s table provides the needed information.

This table contains 11 table entries, each consisting of a **table argument** and a **table function**. The product number is the table argument and the product description is the table function. To illustrate using this table, assume that you need to find the description for soft-drink number 100. (Since you will be searching the table for the entry with this product number, it is commonly called the **search argument**.) You would scan the list of table arguments, comparing each to the search argument until you found a match. Then you would read across to the desired table function.

Some tables have more than one table function. For example, each soft drink might have an inventory code that differs from the product number. This becomes

Figure 11-8
Table components.

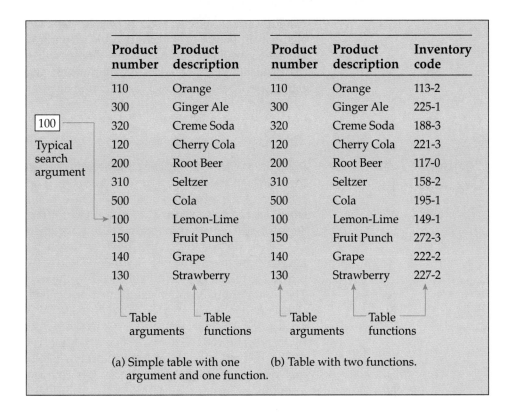

Product number	Product description	Product number	Product description	Inventory code
110	Orange	110	Orange	113-2
300	Ginger Ale	300	Ginger Ale	225-1
320	Creme Soda	320	Creme Soda	188-3
120	Cherry Cola	120	Cherry Cola	221-3
200	Root Beer	200	Root Beer	117-0
310	Seltzer	310	Seltzer	158-2
500	Cola	500	Cola	195-1
100	Lemon-Lime	100	Lemon-Lime	149-1
150	Fruit Punch	150	Fruit Punch	272-3
140	Grape	140	Grape	222-2
130	Strawberry	130	Strawberry	227-2

100 — Typical search argument

Table arguments   Table functions   Table arguments   Table functions

(a) Simple table with one argument and one function.

(b) Table with two functions.

available to processing by expanding the table to include two functions, as Figure 11-8(b) shows.

In other tables, the table arguments are consecutive integers, as shown in Figure 11-9's month number/name abbreviation table. You will see how this results in a very efficient method of storing and accessing the table data.

If you compare the tables of Figures 11-8 and 11-9, you will see that Figure 11-8's entries are arranged randomly. That is, it appears to make little difference whether

Figure 11-9
Table adaptable to positional organization.

Month number	Month name abbreviation
01	JAN
02	FEB
03	MAR
04	APR
05	MAY
06	JUN
07	JUL
08	AUG
09	SEP
10	OCT
11	NOV
12	DEC

Table arguments correspond to the position of the entry in the table.

Ginger Ale is positioned second, first, or last. On the other hand, the positioning of elements in Figure 11-9's month table is important. This brings us to the topic of table organization. Examples in this chapter will deal with three methods of arranging table-entry elements: positional, random, and sequential. Let's begin with the rather specialized positional organization illustrated by the month table.

Positional Table Organization

Establishing a Table

In Figure 11-9, notice that the table arguments correspond exactly to the position of the entries in the table. That is, for instance, month number 03 occupies the third position of the table. Because of this correspondence, the argument need not be stored in the table. This is an example of a table with **positional organization** because each entry's position implies its argument value.

How do you make this table available to a program for processing? The answer is that you can either **hard-code** it in the WORKING-STORAGE SECTION or you can read it from a file. Hard-coding the month table is shown in Figure 11-10. The 12-month abbreviation values are first defined as elementary items with VALUE clauses under the record MT-MONTH-ABBREVIATION-DATA. This record is redefined as MT-MONTH-ABBREVIATION-TABLE, consisting of 12 occurrences of MT-MONTH-ABBREVIATION. Then MT-MONTH-ABBREVIATION (1) contains JAN—the first entry under MT-MONTH-ABBREVIATION-DATA—and so on for each of the remaining 11 occurrences. It is necessary to use the REDEFINES because individual elements of MT-MONTH-ABBREVIATION cannot be given separate values by including a VALUE clause together with the OCCURS.

You should recognize that the month table is well suited to hard-coding because the months of the year are (1) stable—rather than volatile—data entities and (2) the number of table entries is limited (to 12).

Although in the month table, the arguments are consecutive integers beginning with 1, this does not need to be the case. Any table in which the relative position in the table can be determined either directly (search argument identical to the table argument) or by calculation using the search argument can use positional organization.

Accessing a Positionally Organized Table

Assume that you are working on a program in which one of the input fields (SR-MONTH-NUM) is the month number. From that, you must place the corresponding month abbreviation in the report line field RL-MONTH. Accessing the desired month abbreviation is simple because the month number designates the exact table entry you want. The MOVE statement takes the following form:

```
MOVE MT-MONTH-ABBREVIATION (SR-MONTH-NUM) TO RL-MONTH
```

Figure 11-10
Hard-coding
the month table.

```
01  MT-MONTH-ABBREVIATION-DATA.
    05          PIC X(3)     VALUE "JAN".
    05          PIC X(3)     VALUE "FEB".
    05          PIC X(3)     VALUE "MAR".
    05          PIC X(3)     VALUE "APR".
    05          PIC X(3)     VALUE "MAY".
    05          PIC X(3)     VALUE "JUN".
    05          PIC X(3)     VALUE "JUL".
    05          PIC X(3)     VALUE "AUG".
    05          PIC X(3)     VALUE "SEP".
    05          PIC X(3)     VALUE "OCT".
    05          PIC X(3)     VALUE "NOV".
    05          PIC X(3)     VALUE "DEC".
01  MT-MONTH-ABBREVIATION-TABLE
        REDEFINES MT-MONTH-ABBREVIATION-DATA.
    05  MT-MONTH-ABBREVIATION          OCCURS 12 TIMES
                                       PIC X(3).
```

As you can see, no searching is required; this technique of accessing data from a file is sometimes called **direct lookup**. However, before attempting to do a direct lookup access, it is imperative that the search argument be validated to ensure that it is within the table's range. For example, with the month table, it is mandatory that the search argument value be checked to ensure that it is (1) numeric, (2) greater than 0, and (3) less than 13. If a nonnumeric or out-of-range value is used, erroneous processing occurs.

A Table with Arguments and Functions

Establishing the Table

Let's reconsider the beverage table of Figure 11-8(a). Unlike the month table, the beverage table is probably not a good candidate for hard-coding. The reason is that the table will change. That is, beverages will be added to and deleted from the table; perhaps even one or more of the codes might change. Hard-coding the table would require that the program be modified and recompiled with each table change. So, this table would likely be stored as a data file and loaded before using it.

For the sake of simplicity in the following examples, hard-coding is used. This provides you with a table that you can see and relate its values to elements of the array defined following it. Techniques for processing the table are completely independent of whether it is hard-coded or file-loaded.

Because no direct relationship exists in the beverage table between the arguments and their corresponding functions, both must be stored in the table. Establishing it as the hard-coded table of Figure 11-11, you see that:

■ The table argument is defined with a length of 3, corresponding to the beverage number field size.

■ The table function is defined with a length of 11 in order to accommodate the longest beverage name.

■ Entries of the hard-coded table are specified in number/name (argument/function) pairs. This corresponds to the redefinition for the table elements BT-BEVERAGE-NUMBER and BT-BEVERAGE-NAME.

Figure 11-11
Defining a table with functions and arguments.

```
                        Beverage number                Beverage name
                        (table arguments)              (table functions)

        01   BEVERAGE-DATA.
             05      PIC X(14) VALUE "110Orange".
             05      PIC X(14) VALUE "300Ginger Ale".
             05      PIC X(14) VALUE "320Creme Soda".
             05      PIC X(14) VALUE "120Cherry Cola".
             05      PIC X(14) VALUE "200Root Beer".
             05      PIC X(14) VALUE "310Seltzer".
             05      PIC X(14) VALUE "500Cola".
             05      PIC X(14) VALUE "100Lemon-Lime".
             05      PIC X(14) VALUE "150Fruit Punch".
             05      PIC X(14) VALUE "140Grape".
             05      PIC X(14) VALUE "130Strawberry".
        01   BT-BEVERAGE-TABLE REDEFINES BEVERAGE-DATA.
             05        BT-BEVERAGE-ENTRY  OCCURS 11 TIMES.
                  10   BT-BEVERAGE-NUMBER PIC X(3).
                  10   BT-BEVERAGE-NAME   PIC X(11).

        Redefines
        table argument

              Redefines
              table function
```

Random Table
Organization

Entries in the tables of Figure 11-8 are randomly arranged. That is, the table entries are listed in random product number order. Searching a randomly ordered table for a desired entry requires a serial search. A **serial search** compares the search argument to consecutive table arguments until either (1) a table argument that matches the search argument is found or (2) the end of the table is reached. Scanning the sales representative revenue array of HIGHREP1 and HIGHREP2 is a serial activity. If the table organization is truly random, then on the average, you can expect to search half the table before finding a desired entry. If the search argument does not have a corresponding entry in the array, the entire array must be searched to determine this. For very large tables, the search can be time-consuming.

Searching the Table

The two sales program examples earlier in this chapter scanned the entire array to find all entries meeting a particular condition. In contrast, the term *table searching* commonly means searching a table (an array) for a particular entry. For instance, assume that you are working on a program with the following parameters:

1. One of the input items is a beverage number contained in the data-item WV-BEVERAGE-NUMBER.
2. You must search the table to find the input beverage number.
   a. If found, move the corresponding beverage name to the data-item WV-BEVERAGE-NAME.
   b. If not found, move the message "Bad number" to the data-item WV-BEVERAGE-NAME.
3. The data-item BT-SUBSCRIPT is defined for use as the subscript.

The segment of code in Figure 11-12 performs the required action. Its significant points are

1. The VARYING component of this PERFORM uses the data-item BT-SUBSCRIPT, which is initialized to 1 and incremented by 1 for each pass through the loop.

Figure 11-12   Searching a table.

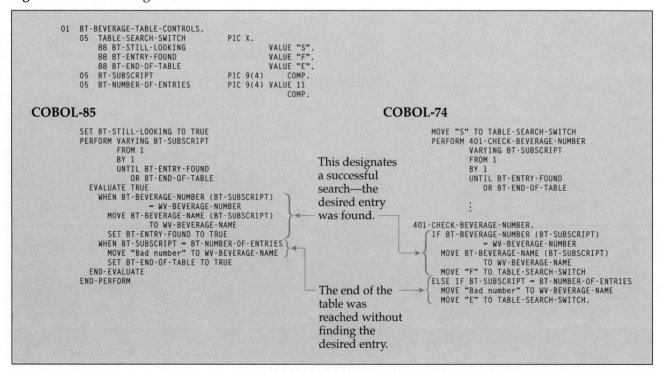

2. BT-SUBSCRIPT is used as the subscript to access successive table arguments—BT-BEVERAGE-NUMBER (BT-SUBSCRIPT)—and the corresponding function—BT-BEVERAGE-NAME (BT-SUBSCRIPT)—when a match is found.

3. If the desired entry is found, the corresponding argument is moved to the designated work area and the switch BT-ENTRY-FOUND is set to true. This is done under the first WHEN of the EVALUATE.

4. Reaching the end of the table (when the subscript equals the number of entries) without finding the desired search argument discontinues the search by setting the switch BT-END-OF-TABLE to true. This is done under the second WHEN of the EVALUATE.

Using an Index

Table processing is such a common type of operation in business programming that COBOL includes a special SEARCH statement to simplify the searching operation. However, in contrast to previous programs that use a subscript to identify the particular table element, the SEARCH statement requires use of an index.

Index Versus Subscript

An **index** is merely another way of accessing elements from a table. To specify an index for a table, you must include an INDEXED BY phrase in the OCCURS clause, as Figure 11-13 illustrates. Three differences exist between indexes and subscripts:

1. When an index-name is specified in the INDEXED BY clause, the compiler automatically provides for the index variable. The programmer does not code a separate data-item in the DATA DIVISION, as is done for a variable subscript. So, for instance, the index BT-INDEX of Figure 11-13 would replace the subscript variable BT-SUBSCRIPT of Figure 11-12.

2. A subscript is a conventional numeric quantity defined with a 9 PICTURE element and is used for the storage of **occurrence numbers**. That is, when used as a subscript, it will contain a number between 1 and the maximum defined in the OCCURS. An index is a special quantity whose precise form is implementor dependent. However, its contents will correspond to the equivalent occurrence number.

3. Since index values may differ from normal occurrence values, an index cannot be initialized with the MOVE statement as done with a subscript. Similarly, arithmetic statements—such as ADD and SUBTRACT—cannot be used to increment or decrement an index. Instead, the SET statement is provided to initialize, increment, and decrement the index.

Figure 11-13
The INDEX format.

INDEXED BY phrase format:

OCCURS integer TIMES

[INDEXED BY index-name-1 [index-name-2] ...]

Examples:

```
01  BT-BEVERAGE-TABLE REDEFINES BEVERAGE-DATA.
    05  BT-BEVERAGE-ENTRY        OCCURS 11 TIMES
                                 INDEXED BY BT-INDEX.
        10   BT-BEVERAGE-NUMBER PIC X(3).
        10   BT-BEVERAGE-NAME   PIC X(11).
```

Although indexes differ from subscripts and cannot be changed with the MOVE and ADD statements, COBOL includes special provisions for using them in relational expressions. To illustrate, consider the following WHEN from the EVALUATE of Figure 11-12:

```
WHEN BT-SUBSCRIPT = BT-NUMBER-OF-ENTRIES
```

Here the occurrence value stored in BT-SUBSCRIPT is compared to a data-item containing the maximum number of entries. The following form is equally valid when using an index:

```
WHEN BT-INDEX = BT-NUMBER-OF-ENTRIES
```

The SET Statement

Figure 11-14 shows the SET statement format. Format-1 is used for initializing an index. This format converts occurrence numbers to index displacement values, and vice versa. Format-2 is used for incrementing and decrementing an index.

The Format-1 (Serial) SEARCH Statement

The SEARCH statement has two versions. Format-1 is used for a serial search; its partial format is shown in Figure 11-15. When a SEARCH statement is executed, the table specified as identifier-1 is stepped through, entry by entry, until one of the designated conditions is satisfied. These conditions are specified under the following:

AT END   If end-of-table is reached (no other condition was satisfied), the action or actions specified in the AT END phrase are executed.

WHEN   If a condition designated in a WHEN phrase is found to be true, the action or actions specified in the WHEN phrase are executed.

Notice in the format that the WHEN entry can be repeated. So, the SEARCH statement is like the EVALUATE/TRUE in this respect. That is, if multiple WHEN phrases are specified, the search ends whenever any one of the WHEN conditions is satisfied.

Figure 11-14
SET statement format.

Format-1:

$$\underline{SET} \left\{ \begin{array}{l} \text{identifier-1 [identifier-2] ...} \\ \text{index-name-1 [index-name-2] ...} \end{array} \right\} \underline{TO} \left\{ \begin{array}{l} \text{identifier-3} \\ \text{index-name-3} \\ \text{integer-1} \end{array} \right\}$$

Format-2:

$$\underline{SET} \text{ index-name-1 [index-name-2] ...} \left\{ \begin{array}{l} \underline{UP}\ \underline{BY} \\ \underline{DOWN}\ \underline{BY} \end{array} \right\} \left\{ \begin{array}{l} \text{identifier-2} \\ \text{integer-1} \end{array} \right\}$$

Examples:

```
SET ST-INDEX TO 1          ── Initializes index
SET ST-INDEX UP BY 1       ── Increments index
SET ST-INDEX DOWN BY 1     ── Decrements index
```

Figure 11-17   Alternative search forms.

```
000-SEARCH-TABLE.

    SET REPEAT-LOOP TO TRUE
    PERFORM UNTIL NOT REPEAT-LOOP
        MOVE SPACES TO WV-BEVERAGE-NUMBER
        DISPLAY " "
        DISPLAY  "Enter beverage number " WITH NO ADVANCING
        ACCEPT WV-BEVERAGE-NUMBER
        PERFORM 500-LOOKUP-BEVERAGE-NAME
        DISPLAY "                      ", WV-BEVERAGE-NAME
        DISPLAY " "
        DISPLAY " "
        DISPLAY "Do you want to access another entry <Y/N>? "
                WITH NO ADVANCING
        ACCEPT S2-YES-NO-QUERY
    END-PERFORM
    STOP RUN
    .
500-LOOKUP-BEVERAGE-NAME.
    SET BT-INDEX TO 1
    SEARCH BT-BEVERAGE-ENTRY
      AT END
          MOVE "Bad number" TO WV-BEVERAGE-NAME
          SET BT-END-OF-TABLE TO TRUE
      WHEN WV-BEVERAGE-NUMBER
          = BT-BEVERAGE-NUMBER (BT-INDEX)
          MOVE BT-BEVERAGE-NAME (BT-INDEX)
              TO WV-BEVERAGE-NAME
          SET BT-ENTRY-FOUND TO TRUE
    END-SEARCH
    .
```

```
000-SEARCH-TABLE.

    SET REPEAT-LOOP TO TRUE
    PERFORM UNTIL NOT REPEAT-LOOP
        MOVE SPACES TO WV-BEVERAGE-NUMBER
        DISPLAY " "
        DISPLAY  "Enter beverage number " WITH NO ADVANCING
        ACCEPT WV-BEVERAGE-NUMBER
        SET BT-INDEX TO 1
        SEARCH BT-BEVERAGE-ENTRY
          AT END
              DISPLAY "                Bad beverage number"
          WHEN WV-BEVERAGE-NUMBER
              = BT-BEVERAGE-NUMBER (BT-INDEX)
              DISPLAY "         ",
                    BT-BEVERAGE-NAME (BT-INDEX)
        END-SEARCH
        DISPLAY " "
        DISPLAY " "
        DISPLAY "Do you want to access another entry <Y/N>? "
                WITH NO ADVANCING
        ACCEPT S2-YES-NO-QUERY
    END-PERFORM
    STOP RUN
    .
```

(a) The SEARCH in a separate module.   (b) The SEARCH in the main module.

of sequential organization is that it allows you to use very efficient searching methods.

Principles of the Binary Search

When a table contains numerous table entries, a serial search for arguments whose entries are located deep in the table becomes time-consuming. For sequentially organized tables, a binary search can be used instead of a serial search. With longer tables, a binary search will substantially reduce the average amount of time required to locate a table entry.

Figure 11-19 diagrams a **binary search** technique in which the entry for product number 200 is desired. Notice that the first comparison is made against the

Figure 11-18
Sequential organization of a table.

Product number	Product description
100	Lemon-Lime
110	Orange
120	Cherry Cola
130	Strawberry
140	Grape
150	Fruit Punch
200	Root Beer
300	Ginger Ale
310	Seltzer
320	Creme Soda
500	Cola

Figure 11-19
A binary search.

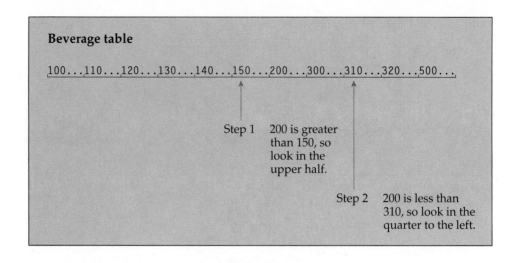

Beverage table

100...110...120...130...140...150...200...300...310...320...500...

Step 1   200 is greater
          than 150, so
          look in the
          upper half.

Step 2   200 is less than
          310, so look in the
          quarter to the left.

table argument in the middle of the table (rather than the first argument, as is done with the serial search). Three possibilities can occur:

- If the search argument is equal to the table argument, the search is complete.
- If the search argument is greater than the middle table argument, the desired entry is in the upper half of the table (as Figure 11-19 illustrates).
- If the search argument is less than the middle table argument, the desired entry is in the lower half of the table.

Because the search argument 200 is greater than the middle table argument (150), the desired entry must be in the upper half of the table. So, the next comparison is made at the middle of the upper half. Since the search argument 200 is less than the selected table argument (310), the desired entry must be in the quarter of the table to the left. This process of halving the table continues until either the desired entry is found or it is determined that the search argument is not in the table.

A binary search receives its name from the fact that the maximum number of searches required to find an entry in a sequentially organized table is a power of 2. It is the lowest power to which 2 must be raised in order to exceed the number of entries in the table. So, a table with 1,000 entries could be searched with a maximum of 10 comparisons. (2 raised to the power 10 equals 1,024.) For a sequential search, that same 1,000-entry table requires (on the average) 500 searches. However, since a binary search requires some "overhead" for initialization and execution, it is not as efficient for smaller tables.

The Format-2 (Binary) SEARCH Statement

When a table will be used in a binary search, the KEY clause must be specified to indicate whether the table arguments are arranged in ASCENDING or DESCENDING sequence. Figure 11-20 shows the KEY clause format and an example for the beverage table.

Recognize that specification of the KEY clause does not actually cause the table arguments to be arranged in ascending or descending order. It is the programmer's responsibility to make sure that the table is actually arranged in accordance with the KEY clause specifications.

The Format-2 SEARCH (SEARCH ALL) statement provides a binary search. Figure 11-21 (page 404) shows its format and an example. Specification of the reserved word ALL in the SEARCH statement triggers the binary search logic. Because a binary search is more complicated than a serial search, the Format-2 SEARCH statement imposes some coding restrictions that do not apply to the

Figure 11-20
KEY clause format.

Format:

OCCURS integer TIMES

$\begin{bmatrix} \underline{ASCENDING} \\ \underline{DESCENDING} \end{bmatrix}$ KEY IS data-name-1 [data-name-2] …

[$\underline{INDEXED}$ BY index-name-1 [index-name-2] …]

Example:

```
01  BT-BEVERAGE-TABLE REDEFINES BEVERAGE-DATA.
    05        BT-BEVERAGE-ENTRY   OCCURS 11 TIMES
                                  ASCENDING KEY
                                    BT-BEVERAGE-NUMBER
                                  INDEXED BY BT-INDEX.
        10    BT-BEVERAGE-NUMBER PIC X(3).
        10    BT-BEVERAGE-NAME   PIC X(11).
```

Format-1 SEARCH: (1) the WHEN phrase requires specification of the indexed-key field as the first entry and (2) the condition test is limited to an EQUAL relationship. Here you see that, unlike the Format-1 SEARCH, multiple WHENs cannot be used. However, compound conditions can be formulated by using the AND operator.

When ALL is specified to obtain a binary search, index initialization is handled automatically by the SEARCH statement. So, the programmer does not need to code a SET statement as for the Format-1 (serial) SEARCH statement.

Additional Topics

Tables with Range-Step Arguments

Sometimes, a one-to-one correspondence will not exist between the search and table argument values. This situation occurs when one table function (or a set of table functions) applies to a range of argument values. A common example of this is an income tax table in which a range of earned-income dollar amounts pertains to a specific tax bracket. Similarly, a range of birth dates applies to each one of the 12 zodiac signs. A zodiac-sign table used for a lookup of a given birthdate's sun-sign is an example of a **range-step table**.

Suppose you want to use the month and day of the birthdate field to look up the applicable zodiac sign using Figure 11-22(a)'s table. One way to find a particular entry is to scan the ending-date column, comparing each to your desired date. For instance, consider May 10. It "exceeds" April 19, so continue to the next entry. Since it is less than May 20, the desired entry is found under Taurus.

The best way to handle the sunsign table is to use the highest numerical value for each sunsign date range as the table argument. The table function is, of course, the sunsign name. Also, since the date range for Capricorn spans from one year to the next, it requires two entries: one for the last day of the sunsign period and one for the last day of December. When establishing the table, the 13 entries must be listed in numerical order according to the four-digit *mmdd* date value. The table is rearranged accordingly in Figure 11-22(b).

Instead of testing just for an equal condition in the lookup module, the correspondence test looks for a search argument that is less than or equal to the table argument value.

Figure 11-21
Format-2 (binary) SEARCH
statement format.

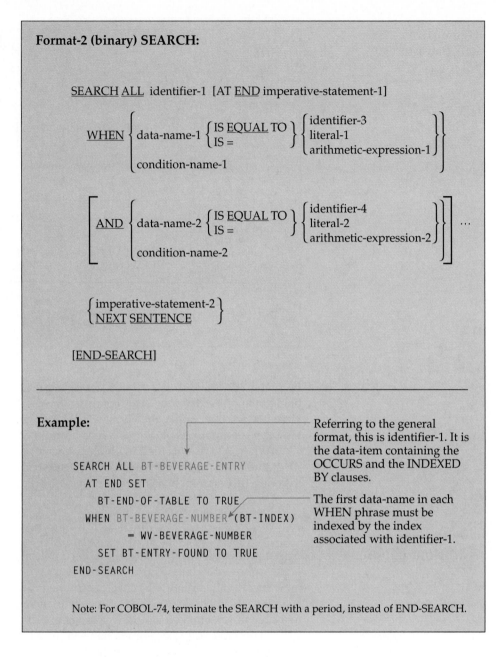

Format-2 (binary) SEARCH:

SEARCH ALL identifier-1 [AT END imperative-statement-1]

$$\text{WHEN} \begin{Bmatrix} \text{data-name-1} \begin{Bmatrix} \text{IS EQUAL TO} \\ \text{IS} = \end{Bmatrix} \begin{Bmatrix} \text{identifier-3} \\ \text{literal-1} \\ \text{arithmetic-expression-1} \end{Bmatrix} \\ \text{condition-name-1} \end{Bmatrix}$$

$$\left[\text{AND} \begin{Bmatrix} \text{data-name-2} \begin{Bmatrix} \text{IS EQUAL TO} \\ \text{IS} = \end{Bmatrix} \begin{Bmatrix} \text{identifier-4} \\ \text{literal-2} \\ \text{arithmetic-expression-2} \end{Bmatrix} \\ \text{condition-name-2} \end{Bmatrix} \right] \dots$$

$$\begin{Bmatrix} \text{imperative-statement-2} \\ \text{NEXT SENTENCE} \end{Bmatrix}$$

[END-SEARCH]

Example:

```
SEARCH ALL BT-BEVERAGE-ENTRY
    AT END SET
      BT-END-OF-TABLE TO TRUE
    WHEN BT-BEVERAGE-NUMBER (BT-INDEX)
        = WV-BEVERAGE-NUMBER
      SET BT-ENTRY-FOUND TO TRUE
END-SEARCH
```

Referring to the general format, this is identifier-1. It is the data-item containing the OCCURS and the INDEXED BY clauses.

The first data-name in each WHEN phrase must be indexed by the index associated with identifier-1.

Note: For COBOL-74, terminate the SEARCH with a period, instead of END-SEARCH.

Figure 11-23 shows the appropriate code to define the table and to search it using the search argument IN-BIRTH-MONTH-DAY. Notice the following about this example:

1. The search argument must be validated. The numeric test protects against an entry such as 021A, which is less than 0218 (the second entry). The "less than 0101" protects against values such as 0000, which would be less than 0119 (the first entry). A high-value test is not required because it is handled automatically by the AT END of the SEARCH.
2. A sunsign match occurs when IN-BIRTH-MONTH-DAY is less than or equal to the ZT-SIGN-END-DATE table element being tested. Observe that this less than or equal to relationship is coded with the NOT GREATER THAN operator in the WHEN phrase.

Figure 11-22
Zodiac-sign tables.

Birthdate		Sunsign	Ending date	Sunsign
Mar. 21 – Apr. 19		Aries	01/19	Capricorn
Apr. 20 – May 20		Taurus	02/18	Aquarius
May 21 – Jun. 20		Gemini	03/20	Pisces
Jun. 21 – Jul. 22		Cancer	04/19	Aries
Jul. 23 – Aug. 22		Leo	05/20	Taurus
Aug. 23 – Sep. 22		Virgo	06/20	Gemini
Sep. 23 – Oct. 22		Libra	07/22	Cancer
Oct. 23 – Nov. 21		Scorpio	08/22	Leo
Nov. 22 – Dec. 21		Sagittarius	09/22	Virgo
Dec. 22 – Jan. 19		Capricorn	10/22	Libra
Jan. 20 – Feb. 18		Aquarius	11/21	Scorpio
Feb. 19 – Mar. 20		Pisces	12/21	Sagittarius
			12/31	Capricorn

(a) Sunsign date ranges.   (b) Sunsign ending dates.

One final note about range-step tables is that you cannot use the SEARCH ALL. Because its condition test is limited to the equal relationship, you must use the SEARCH as in Figure 11-23.

Loading a Table from a Randomly Arranged Input File

A key element of the HIGHREP programs is that file records must be in sequence by sales representative number. Because these programs use the control-break technique, they will not function properly if the records are in random order. However, only a simple modification is required to make the HIGHREP2 program process an input file with the records in random order. The broad sequence of steps is

1. Read an input record.
2. Search the array for the sales representative number of this record (the search argument).
   a. If the number is not found, this is the file's first occurrence of this sales representative number. Save the number and the sales revenue for this record in the array.
   b. If the number is found, a record for this sales representative was already processed and, therefore, an array entry already exists. So add the sales revenue for this record to the corresponding array function.
3. After the array is loaded, process as in the HIGHREP2 program.

Figure 11-24 shows a complete program. The only new concept is the DEPENDING ON phrase at line 47. You know from preceding descriptions that the SEARCH statement searches an array (table) until a match is found or until the end of the table is reached (the AT END). From the OCCURS at line 46, you consider the end of the table to be the 100th entry. However, for the purpose of the SEARCH, this is not necessarily the case. For instance, assume that you loaded the

Figure 11-23
Range-step zodiac-sign
lookup.

```
        01  ZT-ZODIAC-SIGN-DATA.
            05  FILLER          PIC X(15)      VALUE "0119CAPRICORN".
            05  FILLER          PIC X(15)      VALUE "01218AQUARIUS".
             .
             .
             .
            05  FILLER          PIC X(15)      VALUE "1221SAGITTARIUS".
            05  FILLER          PIC X(15)      VALUE "1231CAPRICORN".
        01  ZT-ZODIAC-SIGN-TABLE REDEFINES ZT-ZODIAC-SIGN-DATA.
            05  ZT-ZODIAC-SIGN-ENTRY          OCCURS 13 TIMES
                                              INDEXED BY ZT-INDEX.
                10  ZT-SIGN-END-DATE              PIC X(4).
                10  ZT-SIGN-NAME                 PIC X(11).

        01  ZT-TABLE-CONTROLS
            05  ZT-ENTRY-FOUND-SWITCH            PIC X(1).
                88  ZODIAC-ENTRY-FOUND               VALUE "F".
                88  ZODIAC-ENTRY-NOT-FOUND           VALUE "N".
             .
             .
             .
        IF IN-BIRTH-MONTH-DAY IS NOT NUMERIC
        OR IN-BIRTH-MONTH-DAY < "0101"
           SET ZODIAC-ENTRY-NOT-FOUND TO TRUE
        ELSE
           SET ZT-INDEX TO 1.
           SEARCH ZT-ZODIAC-SIGN-ENTRY
               AT END
                   SET ZODIAC-ENTRY-NOT-FOUND TO TRUE
               WHEN IN-BIRTH-MONTH-DAY NOT > ZT-SIGN-END-DATE (ZT-INDEX)
                   SET ZODIAC-ENTRY-FOUND TO TRUE
           END-SEARCH
        END-IF
```

Note: For COBOL-74, remove both scope terminators. A period following the
reserved word TRUE terminates both the IF and the SEARCH. Also, use the MOVE
to change program switch values.

first 57 elements of the array. Then in a SEARCH, element number 57 should be
treated as the end of the array. You can do exactly that with the DEPENDING ON
phrase at line 47. Notice that it identifies a numeric item—SC-ENTRY-COUNT—
defined at line 55. Whatever value is contained in SC-ENTRY-COUNT signals the
end of the array to the SEARCH statement.

Now, let's consider what takes place with the SEARCH statement during
execution of the program:

1. When a data record is read (line 87), execution proceeds to the 200
   module, where the record revenue is calculated (lines 118 and 119).
2. The array index is set to 1 (line 120) and the search initiated (line 121).
   Remember, encountering the end of the array means that a record was
   read that contained a sales representative number not yet in the array.
3. If the end of the array was reached (AT END), the index is compared
   to the maximum number of entries (line 123).
   a. If the index exceeds the maximum, the array is already full, so
      the switch is set accordingly.
   b. If the index does not exceed the maximum, the active array size
      variable (SC-ENTRY-COUNT) is incremented by 1 (line 126).
      Then the new sales representative number and the sales amount
      are moved into the array.
4. If the sales representative number is found in the table (WHEN at line
   133), the sales amount is added to the existing table entry function (lines
   134 and 135).

Figure 11-24   The HIGHREP3 program.

```
1        IDENTIFICATION DIVISION.
2        PROGRAM-ID.   HIGHREP3.
3
4     *  Written by W. Price  1-23-95
5     *  PYRAMID SALES COMPANY.
6
7     *  This program processes the sales representative file
8     *  as follows:
9     *  1. Sales revenue for each sales representative is
10    *     accumulated and stored in one element of an array.
11    *     The sales rep number is also stored.
12    *  2. After the last record is processed, the average
13    *     sales for the sales reps is calculated.
14    *  3. The sales reps whose sales exceed the average
15    *     by more than 20% are listed.
16
17
18       ENVIRONMENT DIVISION.
19
20       INPUT-OUTPUT SECTION.
21       FILE-CONTROL.
22           SELECT SALES-FILE
23               ASSIGN TO (system dependent).
24
25
26       DATA DIVISION.
27       FILE SECTION.
28
29       FD  SALES-FILE.
30       01  SALES-RECORD.
31           05  PIC X(48).
32
33       WORKING-STORAGE SECTION.
34
35       01  PROGRAM-SWITCHES.
36           05  S1-END-OF-FILE-SWITCH      PIC X(1).
37               88  S1-END-OF-FILE            VALUE "E".
38               88  S1-NOT-END-OF-FILE        VALUE "N".
39           05  S2-OVERFLOW-CONTINUE-SWITCH PIC X(1).
40               88  S2-OKAY-TO-CONTINUE       VALUE "Y" "y".
41           05  S3-ARRAY-FULL-SWITCH      PIC X.
42               88  S3-ARRAY-NOT-FULL         VALUE "N".
43               88  S3-ARRAY-FULL             VALUE "F".
44
45       01  SA-SALES-ARRAY.
46           05  SA-SALES-ENTRY   OCCURS 100 TIMES
47                              DEPENDING ON SC-ENTRY-COUNT
48                              INDEXED BY SC-INDEX.
49               10  SA-SALES-REP        PIC X(5).
50               10  SA-SALES-REP-REVENUE PIC S9(5)V99.
51
52       01  SC-SALES-REP-ARRAY-CONTROLS.
53           05  COMP-FIELDS    USAGE COMP.
54               10  SC-ENTRY-MAXIMUM     PIC 9(3) VALUE 100.
55               10  SC-ENTRY-COUNT       PIC 9(3).
56
57       01  WA-WORK-AREAS.
58           05  WA-SALES-REVENUE-1-REC  PIC S9(5)V99.
59           05  WA-SALES-REVENUE-TOTAL  PIC S9(6)V99.
60           05  WA-SALES-REVENUE-AVERAGE PIC S9(5)V99.
61           05  WA-HIGH-SALES-REVENUE   PIC S9(5)V99.
62
63       01  SR-SALES-RECORD.
64           05                          PIC X(7).
65           05  SR-SALES-REP            PIC X(5).
66           05                          PIC X(29).
67           05  SR-QUANTITY-SOLD        PIC S9(3).
68           05  SR-UNIT-PRICE           PIC 9(2)V99.
69
70       01  DISPLAY-ITEMS.
71           05  DI-HIGH-SALES-REVENUE   PIC ZZ,ZZ9.99.
72           05  DI-DUMMY                PIC X.
73
74
75       PROCEDURE DIVISION.
76
77       000-PRINT-SALES-REPORT.
78
79       ************Initialization Sequence************
80           OPEN INPUT SALES-FILE
81           PERFORM 100-INITIALIZE-VARIABLE-FIELDS
82
83       *************Processing Sequence*************
84       *   Read file and load array
85           PERFORM UNTIL S1-END-OF-FILE
86                     OR S3-ARRAY-FULL
87               READ SALES-FILE INTO SR-SALES-RECORD
88                   AT END
89                       SET S1-END-OF-FILE TO TRUE
90                   NOT AT END
91                       PERFORM 200-LOAD-ARRAY-ELEMENT
92               END-READ
93           END-PERFORM
94           SET S2-OKAY-TO-CONTINUE TO TRUE
95           IF S3-ARRAY-FULL
96               PERFORM 900-QUERY-TO-CONTINUE
97           END-IF
98       *   Process array
99           IF S2-OKAY-TO-CONTINUE
100              PERFORM 220-CALCULATE-THE-AVERAGE
101              PERFORM 850-DISPLAY-HIGH-REPS
102          END-IF
103
104      *************Termination Sequence*************
105          CLOSE SALES-FILE
106          STOP RUN
107          .
108      *************************************************
109
110      100-INITIALIZE-VARIABLE-FIELDS.
111          SET S1-NOT-END-OF-FILE TO TRUE
112          SET S3-ARRAY-NOT-FULL TO TRUE
113          INITIALIZE SA-SALES-ARRAY
114                     SC-ENTRY-COUNT
115                     WA-SALES-REVENUE-TOTAL
116          .
117      200-LOAD-ARRAY-ELEMENT.
118          MULTIPLY SR-UNIT-PRICE BY SR-QUANTITY-SOLD
119              GIVING WA-SALES-REVENUE-1-REC
120          SET SC-INDEX TO 1
121          SEARCH SA-SALES-ENTRY
122              AT END
123                  IF SC-INDEX > SC-ENTRY-MAXIMUM
124                      SET S3-ARRAY-FULL TO TRUE
125                  ELSE
126                      ADD 1 TO SC-ENTRY-COUNT
127                      MOVE SR-SALES-REP TO SA-SALES-REP (SC-INDEX)
128                      MOVE WA-SALES-REVENUE-1-REC TO
129                          SA-SALES-REP-REVENUE (SC-INDEX)
130                      ADD WA-SALES-REVENUE-1-REC TO
131                          WA-SALES-REVENUE-TOTAL
132                  END-IF
133              WHEN  SR-SALES-REP = SA-SALES-REP (SC-INDEX)
134                  ADD WA-SALES-REVENUE-1-REC TO
135                      SA-SALES-REP-REVENUE (SC-INDEX)
136                      WA-SALES-REVENUE-TOTAL
137          END-SEARCH
138          .
139
140      220-CALCULATE-THE-AVERAGE.
141          DIVIDE WA-SALES-REVENUE-TOTAL BY SC-ENTRY-COUNT
142              GIVING WA-SALES-REVENUE-AVERAGE ROUNDED
143          MULTIPLY WA-SALES-REVENUE-AVERAGE BY 1.2
144              GIVING WA-HIGH-SALES-REVENUE
145          .
146      850-DISPLAY-HIGH-REPS.
147          MOVE WA-HIGH-SALES-REVENUE TO DI-HIGH-SALES-REVENUE
148          DISPLAY "High-sales revenue amount: "
149              DI-HIGH-SALES-REVENUE
150          DISPLAY " "
151          DISPLAY "High-sales Sales Representatives"
152          PERFORM VARYING SC-INDEX
153              FROM 1
154              BY 1
155              UNTIL SC-INDEX > SC-ENTRY-COUNT
156          IF SA-SALES-REP-REVENUE (SC-INDEX)
157              > WA-HIGH-SALES-REVENUE
158              DISPLAY SA-SALES-REP (SC-INDEX)
159          END-IF
160          END-PERFORM
161          DISPLAY " "
162          DISPLAY "Press the Enter key to terminate "
163              WITH NO ADVANCING
164          ACCEPT DI-DUMMY
165          .
166      900-QUERY-TO-CONTINUE.
167          DISPLAY "Unable to process all sales representatives."
168          DISPLAY "You can proceed and process only those that "
169          DISPLAY "have been loaded or you can abort."
170          DISPLAY " "
171          DISPLAY "Do you want to proceed <Y/N>? "
172              WITH NO ADVANCING
173          ACCEPT S2-OVERFLOW-CONTINUE-SWITCH
174          .
```

The rest of the program is the same as HIGHREP2. Notice that the array does not need to be initialized (at line 113). The reason is that each time a new sales representative is encountered, the sales amount is moved into the table function field (lines 128 and 129)—rather than accumulated, as in HIGHREP2. However, it is a good idea to initialize arrays, as done here. Then—if for some reason during debugging, you must look at array contents—you know that they were initially zero (or blank for alphanumeric fields).

USAGE INDEX and the SEARCH/VARYING

Occasionally, you will need a data-item defined as an INDEX variable. For instance, the following defines WA-INDEX-VARIABLE in this way:

```
05  WA-INDEX-VARIABLE    PIC 9(3)  USAGE INDEX.
```

Note that this is not the index designated in the OCCURS clause, but a separate index altogether. You can, for instance, move a value into it from the index field of an array if you need to save a selected index value.

Also, the SEARCH allows you to cause a second index variable to be incremented during the search with the VARYING phrase. For instance, the SEARCH of Figure 11-24 (HIGHREP3), line 121, could be written:

```
SEARCH SA-SALES-ENTRY VARYING WA-INDEX-VARIABLE
```

Both the index associated with the array (SC-INDEX) and WA-INDEX-VARIABLE would be incremented during the search.

The VALUE Clause Use with the OCCURS Clause

In COBOL-85, you can include a VALUE clause with an OCCURS clause or with any entry subordinate to the OCCURS. This results in every occurrence of the associated data-item being assigned the specified value. For example, the sales representative revenue array could be initialized in WORKING-STORAGE as follows:

```
05  SA-SALES-ENTRY   OCCURS 100 TIMES
                        DEPENDING ON SC-ENTRY-COUNT
                        INDEXED BY SC-INDEX.
    10  SA-SALES-REP        PIC X(5).
    10  SA-SALES-REP-REVENUE  PIC S9(5)V99
                              VALUE ZERO.
```

However, in keeping with this book's standard of using the VALUE clause only to assign constant values, the array is initialized in the PROCEDURE DIVISION.

Relative Subscripting

COBOL-85 also provides for relative subscripting; a variable subscript can be augmented or decremented by a literal. For example, (SC-SALES-REP + 1) can be coded to reference the next table entry; (SC-SALES-REP – 1) can be coded to reference the immediately prior table entry. This is useful in certain programming circumstances.

> **COBOL-74**
> The COBOL-74 change requirements for HIGHREP3 are the same as those for HIGHREP1 and HIGHREP2 (see pages 390 and 392).

Chapter Summary

Tables are defined in the WORKING-STORAGE SECTION of the DATA DIVISION and are accessed in the PROCEDURE DIVISION. Hard-coded table data is specified with VALUE clauses and then redefined with an OCCURS clause.

Whenever an OCCURS clause is associated with a data-item, either a sub-script or an index must be used when referring to that item in the PROCEDURE DIVISION. The subscript or index references a specific occurrence of a repeated field defined with the OCCURS clause.

A variable subscript is a programmer-defined data-item; its value identifies the occurrence number. An index is defined in an INDEXED BY clause coded in conjunction with an OCCURS clause.

The PERFORM/VARYING statement can be used to scan an array. It is especially useful because it provides for initializing and incrementing the subscript.

The two formats of the SEARCH are Format-1 (serial) SEARCH and Format-2 (binary) SEARCH ALL. Both require the use of an index, rather than a subscript.

A serial search, used to retrieve data from a randomly organized table, is best performed using the Format-1 (serial) SEARCH statement. This statement requires that the index be initialized to its starting value before its execution. Incrementing is done automatically by the statement.

A binary search, used to retrieve data from a sequentially organized table, is best performed using the Format-2 (binary) SEARCH ALL statement.

When a one-to-one correspondence does not exist between the search argument value and the table argument value, a range-step table results. A range-step table must be of sequential organization; the table arguments are usually arranged in ascending sequence. Typically, only the highest argument value for each range step is stored in the table. So, in the table lookup, the test for correspondence must check for a less than or equal to condition.

COBOL Language Element Summary

The OCCURS clause indicates how many times a particular field, or group of fields, is repeated. The integer specified in the OCCURS clause indicates the number of repetitions. The OCCURS clause can be used with any data-item description that has a level-number from 02–49.

A literal subscript is an integer numeric literal coded within parentheses to identify a specific occurrence of a repeated field. The literal's value must not be less than 1 or greater than the number of occurrences specified in the OCCURS clause for the field being referenced.

A variable subscript is a programmer-defined field; the value contained within it is used to identify a specific occurrence of a repeated field. A field used for a subscript must:

- Be an elementary numeric-integer field defined in the DATA DIVISION.

- Contain enough digit positions to accommodate the number of occurrences specified in the OCCURS clause for the field being referenced.

At execution time, the subscript field must contain a value not less than 1 or greater than the number of occurrences specified in the OCCURS clause for the field being referenced.

An index is used much like a subscript, except for three important differences:

- The index-field area is automatically provided by the compiler when an index-name is specified in the INDEXED BY clause. The programmer does not code a separate data-item, as is done for a subscript field.

- A subscript is a numeric quantity defined with a 9 PICTURE; an index is a special quantity whose precise form is implementor dependent.

- Initializing, incrementing, and decrementing an index must be done with a SET statement. Subscripts are modified by MOVE, ADD, and SUBTRACT statements.

Style Summary

In a hard-coded table, arrange the table arguments adjacent to the table function(s) to ease programmer checking, debugging, and maintenance tasks.

Indexes usually provide more efficient processing than subscripts. So, in most cases, the INDEXED BY clause should be specified and the index should be used in the PROCEDURE DIVISION.

For easier reference, establish table control fields immediately before the table. Fields to be specified in this area include (1) an entry-found switch, (2) a subscript field (when an index is not used), and (3) a number-of-table-entries field (unless the SEARCH statement or a dummy end-of-table entry is used).

Processing efficiency is usually enhanced by specifying USAGE COMP for subscripts.

Exercises

Terms for Definition

array
binary search
direct lookup
hard-coded table
index
occurrence number
positionally organized table
randomly organized table
range-step table

search argument
sequentially organized table
serial search
subscript
table
table argument
table function
variable subscript

Review Questions

1. After establishing hard-coded table data, it must be _____ with a data-item description entry containing a(n) _____ clause.

2. The OCCURS clause can be specified only with level-numbers _____ through _____.

3. When an OCCURS clause is associated with a data-item, either a(n) _____ or a(n) _____ must be used when referring to that data-name in the PROCEDURE DIVISION.

4. When a statement containing a subscript is being executed, the value contained within the subscript field should not be less than _____ or greater than _____.

5. What results from the specification of an OCCURS clause at the group level?

6. Index-names are defined in the _____ clause.

7. Subscripts are usually initialized by a(n) _____ statement; indexes are initialized by a(n) _____ statement.

8. When a SEARCH statement reaches the end of the table and the condition expressed in the WHEN phrase was not satisfied, the _____ phrase is executed.

9. Execution of a SEARCH statement ends when either _____ or _____.

10. Identifier-1 specified immediately after the SEARCH verb must be the name of a data-item that contains both a(n) _____ clause and a(n) _____ clause in its data-item description.

11. For a binary search, the _____ clause must be specified for the table in the DATA DIVISION and the _____ phrase must be coded in the SEARCH statement of the PROCEDURE DIVISION.

Syntax/Debug Exercises

```
01  RT-REGION-DATA.
    05  FILLER      PIC X(14)   VALUE "GSGREAT SMOKEY".
    05  FILLER      PIC X(14)   VALUE "RVRIM VIEW".
    05  FILLER      PIC X(14)   VALUE "MEMETROPOLITAN".
    05  FILLER      PIC X(14)   VALUE "HIHINTERLANDS".
    05  FILLER      PIC X(14)   VALUE "LVLAKE VIEW".
01  RT-REGION-TABLE REDEFINES RT-REGION-DATA.
    05  RT-REGION-ENTRY         OCCURS 5 TIMES
        10  RT-REGION-ABBR         PIC X(2).
        10  RT-REGION-NAME         PIC X(12).
```

The statements that follow refer to the preceding table definition. Identify each statement as valid or invalid—if invalid, give the reason. In all cases, assume that other fields referenced are properly defined (for instance, assume that HOLD-AREA is appropriately defined in WORKING-STORAGE).

1. `MOVE RT-REGION-ENTRY TO HOLD-AREA`

2. `MOVE RT-REGION-NAME TO OUT-AREA`

3. `MOVE "NEW VIEW" TO RT-REGION-NAME (5)`

4. `MOVE RT-REGION-DATA TO SAVE-TABLE`

5. `MOVE RT-REGION-NAME (RT-REGION-ABBR) TO OUT-AREA`

6. `MOVE RT-REGION-NAME (HIGH-VALUES) TO ERROR-MESSAGE`

7. `MOVE RT-REGION-NAME ("HI") TO OUT-AREA`

8. `MOVE RT-REGION-NAME (6) TO OUT-AREA`

9. `MOVE RT-REGION-NAME (ITEM) TO OUT-AREA`

10. `MOVE RT-REGION-NAME (COUNTER) TO OUT-AREA1`
    `ADD 5 TO COUNTER`
    `MOVE RT-REGION-NAME (COUNTER) TO OUT-AREA2`

11. `SET RT-INDEX TO 1`
    `MOVE RT-REGION-NAME (RT-INDEX) TO OUT-AREA`

Programming Assignments

Programming Assignment 11-1: Department-Name Lookup

Background information:

The personnel manager at Silicon Valley Manufacturing wants an employee listing that includes each employee's name, department number, and department name. This can be generated from the Earnings file, but—since the record includes only the department number—a table lookup is required.

Input file: Earnings file (EARNINGS.DAT)

Earnings record

	Dept. number	Employee number	Employee last name	Employee first name	
1 2 3 4 5 6	7 8 9 10	11 12 13 14 15 16 17 18 19	20 21 22 23 24 25 26 27 28 29 30 31	32 33 34 35 36 37 38 39 40	41 42 43 44 45 46 47 48 49 50 51 52 53 54 55 56 57 58 59 60 61 62 63 64 65 66 67 68 69 70 71 72 73 74 75 76 77 78 79

Table data:

Department number	Department name
1000	Administration
1100	Purchasing
1200	Personnel
1300	Advertising
1350	Public Relations
1900	Training
2000	Research /Devel.
3000	Finance
3500	Data Processing
4000	Manufacturing

Output-report format:

```
        0         1         2         3         4         5         6         7
   1234567890123456789012345678901234567890123456789012345678901234567890123456789012345
 1
 2
 3
 4 (11-1)    LAST NAME       FIRST NAME              DEPT    DEPARTMENT NAME
 5
 6           XXXXXXXXXXX     XXXXXXXXX               9999    XXXXXXXXXXXXXXXXX
 7
 8           XXXXXXXXXXX     XXXXXXXXX               9999    XXXXXXXXXXXXXXXXX
 9
10
```

Program operations:

1. Process each input earnings record.

2. Print the heading line on each page of the report.

3. For each earnings record, do the following:

a. Use the input department-number field to look up the department name. If the input department number cannot be located in the table, print NO SUCH DEPT NBR in the department-name field of the output report.

b. Print the detail line in accordance with the print-chart specifications.

4. Double-space each detail line. Provide for a span of 57 lines per page.

Programming Assignment 11-2: Degree-Program Lookup

Background information:

The registrar at the Bayview Institute of Computer Technology wants a list of students and their degree programs. Since the Student file only includes the student's major code (not the degree program), the major code should be used for lookup to determine the degree program.

Input file: Student file (STUDENT.DAT)

Student record

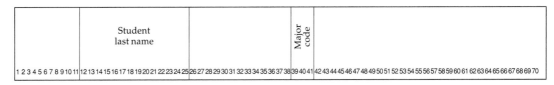

Table data:

Major code	Degree program and degree	Major code	Degree program and degree
100	Accounting (B.S.)	200	Prelegal Studies (B.A.)
110	Administrative Management (B.S.)	250	Administration of Justice (B.A.)
120	Business & Humanities (B.A.)	300	Health Services Mgmt. (B.S.)
130	Business Economics (B.A.)	400	Hotel & Rest. Mgmt. (B.S.)
140	Finance (B.S.)	500	Information Systems (B.S.)
150	Human Relations (B.A.)	510	Telecommunications Mgmt. (B.S.)
160	International Management (B.S.)	600	Medical Record Mgmt. (B.S.)
170	Industrial Management (B.S.)	700	Political Science (B.A.)
180	Marketing (B.S.)	750	Public Administration (B.A.)
190	Transportation (B.S.)	800	Security Management (B.S.)

Output-report format:

```
        0         1         2         3         4         5         6         7         8
 1234567890123456789012345678901234567890123456789012345678901234567890123456789012345 67
 1
 2
 3
 4 (11-2)   STUDENT LAST NAME   MAJOR    DEGREE PROGRAM                DEGREE  PG.ZZ9
 5
 6          XXXXXXXXXXXXXX      999      XXXXXXXXXXXXXXXXXXXXXXXXX     XXXX
 7
 8          XXXXXXXXXXXXXX      999      XXXXXXXXXXXXXXXXXXXXXXXXX     XXXX
 9
10
```

Program operations:

1. Process each input student record.

2. Print the heading line on each page of the report.
   a. Accumulate and print the page number on the heading line as specified on the print chart.

3. For each student record, do the following:
   a. Use the input major-code field to look up the degree program and the degree. If the input major code cannot be located in the table, print MAJOR CODE NOT IN TABLE in the degree-program field of the output report and print asterisks in the degree field of the output report.
   b. Print the detail line in accordance with the print-chart specifications.

4. Double-space each detail line. Provide for a span of 57 lines per page.

Programming Assignment 11-3: Region- and Territory-Name Lookup

Background information:

Many Follow-the-Sun Sales employees complain because the reports concerning sales representatives list only computer codes for Region and Territory. The Region is not bad because the codes are easy to recognize; for example, NE means Northeastern. On the other hand, the Territory codes are confusing; no one ever remembers, for instance, that 1300 is the code for Hawkeye or that 4900 is the code for Badger. To satisfy this complaint, a program is required that will print the region name and territory name for each salesperson. The staff hopes that this program's new structure will be incorporated into other salesperson and territory assignment programs.

Input file: Salesperson file (SALESPER.DAT)

Salesperson record

Region	Territory	Salesperson name	
1 2	3 4	5 6 7 8	9 10 11	12 13 14 15 16 17 18 19 20 21 22 23 24 25 26 27 28 29 30 31 32 33 34 35 36 37	38 39 40 41 42 43 44 45 46 47 48 49 50 51 52 53 54 55 56 57 58 59 60 61 62 63 64 65 66 67 68 69 70 71 72 73 74 75 76 77 78 79

Table data:

Region

Code	Name
NE	Northeastern
NW	Northwestern
MW	Midwestern
SE	Southeastern
SW	Southwestern

Territory			Territory			Territory	
Code	**Name**		**Code**	**Name**		**Code**	**Name**
0100	Midnight Sune		1800	Bluegrass		3500	Empire
0200	Yellowhammer		1900	Pelican		3600	Buckeye
0300	Opportunity		2000	Bay		3700	Sooner
0400	Grand Canyon		2100	Old Line		3800	Beaver
0500	Golden		2200	Pine Tree		3900	Keystone
0600	Centennial		2300	Wolverine		4000	Ocean
0700	Constitution		2400	North Star		4100	Palmetto
0800	Capitol		2500	Show-Me		4200	Coyote
0900	Diamond		2600	Magnolia		4300	Volunteer
1000	Sunshine		2700	Treasure		4400	Lone Star
1100	Peach		2800	Tarheel		4500	Beehive
1200	Aloha		2900	Sioux		4600	Old Dominion
1300	Hawkeye		3000	Cornhusker		4700	Green Mountain
1400	Gem		3100	Granite		4800	Evergreen
1500	Prairie		3200	Garden		4900	Badger
1600	Hoosier		3300	Enchantment		5000	Mountain
1700	Sunflower		3400	Sagebrush		5100	Equality

Output-report format:

```
          0         1         2         3         4         5         6         7         8
   1234567890123456789012345678901234567890123456789012345678901234567890123456789012345 67
 1
 2
 3
 4 SALESPERSON REGION/TERRITORY LIST (11-3)                        MM/DD/YY   PAGE ZZ9
 5
 6      SALESPERSON NAME              REGION            TERRITORY
 7
 8      XXXXXXXXXXXXXXXXXXXXXXXXX     XX  XXXXXXXXXXX   9999  XXXXXXXXXXXXXX
 9
10      XXXXXXXXXXXXXXXXXXXXXXXXX     XX  XXXXXXXXXXX   9999  XXXXXXXXXXXXXX
11
12
```

Program operations:

1. Process each input salesperson record.

2. Print the two heading lines on each page of the report.
   a. Print the run date on the first heading line as specified on the print chart.
   b. Accumulate and print the page number on the first heading line as specified on the print chart.

3. For each salesperson record, do the following:
   a. Use the input region field to look up the region's name. If the input region code cannot be located in the table, print asterisks in the region-name field of the output report.
   b. Use the input territory field to look up the name of the territory. If the input territory code cannot be located in the table, print asterisks in the territory-name field of the output report.
   c. Print the detail line in accordance with the print-chart specifications.

4. Double-space each detail line. Provide for a span of 57 lines per page.

Programming
Assignment 11-4:
Nurses Annuity
Lookup

Background information:

Brooklawn Hospital's employees can participate in a special annuity program for long-term savings. To provide each employee with maximum flexibility, Brooklawn has an approved list of institutions with which it does business. Each employee's participation is indicated by an Annuity-fund field in the data record. The personnel manager of Brooklawn needs a report listing the participation of each employee.

Input file: Nurses file (NURSES.DAT)

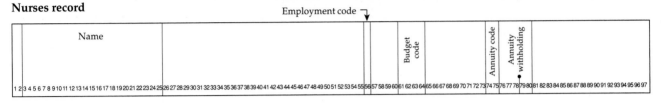

Nurses record

Table data:

Annuity Company		Annuity Company	
Code	**Name**	**Code**	**Name**
AF	Ace High Income Fund	IB	International Brokers
AM	AmWest	IE	Integrated Equity
AP	Associated Planners	JA	Johnson and Associates
CI	Century Investments	LN	Lincoln National Investment
DF	Drexel, Drexel, & Fox	MF	Monarch Insurance
DI	Dewey, Cheatum, & Howe	MI	Mutual Fund of Idaho
FF	Future Fund	RP	Research Plus
FS	Futura Securities	SS	Soyanora Securities
GA	Golden Age Securities	TB	Tres Bien Fund
HM	Hawkeye Mutual	TE	Transportations Equities

Output-report format:

```
          0         1         2         3         4         5         6         7         8
 1234567890123456789012345678901234567890123456789012345678901234567890123456789012345678901234567890
 1
 2
 3
 4 BROOKLAWN HOSPITAL ANNUITY SUMMARY (11-4)                              PAGE ZZ9
 5
 6
 7    EMPLOYEE NAME             B/C   ANNUITY SELECTION                   AMOUNT
 8
 9    XXXXXXXXXXXXXXXXXXXXXXXX  XXXX  XXXXXXXXXXXXXXXXXXXXXXXXXXXXX       ZZZ.ZZ PARTTIME
10
11    XXXXXXXXXXXXXXXXXXXXXXXX  XXXX  XXXXXXXXXXXXXXXXXXXXXXXXXXXXX       ZZZ.ZZ
12
```

Program operations:

1. Process each input record.

2. Print the two heading lines on each page of the report.

   a. Accumulate and print the page number on the first heading line as specified on the print chart.

3. For each employee record, use the input annuity-program field to look up the name of the annuity company. Print the detail line in accordance with the print-chart specifications.

   a. If the input annuity program code cannot be located in the table, print the words INVALID ANNUITY CODE in the annuity selection positions of the output report. Leave the amount entry blank.

   b. If the employee has no entry for the annuity-program field, then that employee is not participating—so leave both the annuity selection and amount fields blank.

   c. If the employee is parttime (employment-code field contains P), print PARTTIME as shown in the print chart; otherwise, leave these positions blank.

4. Double-space each detail line. Provide for a span of 57 lines per page.

Programming Assignment 11-5: Complete Computers Corporation Vendor Lookup

Background information:

In their inventory file, the Complete Computers Corporation of Chapter 2 stores data designating up to three vendors from whom each product can be obtained. The Smiths—the company's owners—want a report indicating the vendor with the best price for each product.

Input file: CCC Inventory file (CCCINVEN.DAT)

CCC Inventory record

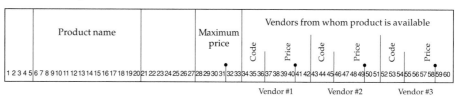

Table data:

Vendor			Vendor	
Code	**Name**		**Code**	**Name**
ABA	Abacus Systems		NAT	National Telecom Systems
ASP	Aspen, Incorporated		NPC	National Partial Conductor
BIC	Burlington International		OH	OH Products
DIA	Diamond Hardware		OPM	Optical Memory
EVH	Everhope Corporation		QUI	Quicksilver Accelerator
GAT	Gates Supply		RWI	Raleigh Wilson, Inc.
GCS	General Computer Supply		SCS	Specific Computer Supply
GS	General Supply		SGM	Shortgrass Memories
HAR	Harbor Circuits		SKS	Standby Keypunch Systems
HFC	High Flyers Disk		STD	Standard Keyboards
MEG	Mega-Systems, Incorporated		UPS	Universal Power Systems
MFM	MicroFine Monitors		VAC	Vacuum Tubes, Anonymous

Output-report format:

If lowest price exceeds maximum allowable price, print three asterisks.

		0		1		2		3		4		5		6		7		8

```
      0         1         2         3         4         5         6         7         8
 12345678901234567890123456789012345678901234567890123456789012345678901234567
1
2
3
4 COMPLETE COMPUTERS BEST PRICE SUMMARY (11-5)                    PAGE  ZZ9
5
6    PRODUCT           VENDOR                              PRICE     MAXIMUM
7                                                                          ↓
8    XXXXXXXXXXXXXX    XXXXXXXXXXXXXXXXXXXXXXXXXXX    Z,ZZZ.99   Z,ZZZ.99  ***
9
10   XXXXXXXXXXXXXX    XXXXXXXXXXXXXXXXXXXXXXXXXXX    Z,ZZZ.99   Z,ZZZ.99
11
12
```

Program operations:

1. Process each input record.

2. Print the two heading lines on each page of the report.
   a. Accumulate and print the page number on the first heading line as specified on the print chart.

3. For each inventory record, do the following:
   a. Find the vendor with the lowest price of the three. This one will be used for report output. You must be aware that some records will not have entries for all three vendors. However, every record will have at least one vendor and an associated price that is greater than zero.
   b. Look up the name of the lowest price vendor in the table.
   c. Print the detail line as shown in the print chart. Use the lowest priced vendor name and price.
   d. If the price exceeds the maximum-price field, print three asterisks to the right on the output line as shown in the print chart.

4. Double-space each detail line. Provide for a span of 57 lines per page.

Programming Assignment 11-6: Load and Search Temperature Log

Background information:

The computer center manager of Coastaltown, U.S.A., is a meteorology buff and keeps an accurate record of daily high and low temperatures. He wants an interactive program that displays statistics for any selected period of time.

Input file: Temperature file (TEMPER.DAT)

Temperature record

Date (mmdd)	High temp	Low temp
1 2 3 4	5 6 7 8 9 10 11	12 13 14 15

Keyboard input:

Beginning date and ending date (month and day).

Screen display:

Design a neat, balanced screen with descriptions and display the following items:

Beginning and ending dates with appropriate editing

Number of elapsed days

The low temperature for the period

The high temperature for the period

The average low temperature for the period

The average high temperature for the period

Program operations:

1. Load the temperature file into an array consisting of one argument (month/day) and two functions (low temperature and high temperature).

2. Accept the beginning month and day and the ending month and day from the keyboard.
   a. Verify the day number against the month number. For April, June, September, and November, the day number cannot be greater than 30; other months are 31—except use 29 for February. (You can do this with condition-names associated with the month.) Display an error message for an invalid entry and allow the user to re-enter.

3. Search the array for the desired beginning month/day.

4. Process each array entry until the ending month/day entry is encountered.
   a. Compare the current entry high and low temperatures to previously saved high and low temperatures. If new high or low, replace the previous high or low.
   b. Accumulate the high temperature and the low temperature for the later average calculations.
   c. Count the entry (this count is needed for the average calculations).

5. After the last entry is accessed, calculate the average high and average low for the time period by dividing the accumulated high temperatures and the accumulated low temperatures by the count.

6. Display the results.

7. Provide the user with the option of entering another set of ranges or terminating.

Programming Assignment 11-7: Screen Display of Report

Program operations:

For any of the preceding assignments (except 11-6), write a display program that functions as follows:

1. Display the output on the screen according to the format of the print chart.

2. After each group of 18 records, temporarily stop processing so the user can view the screen.

3. Provide the user with the option of viewing the next 18 records or terminating processing.

4. Include headings on each screen page of display.

5. When the end of file is reached, inform the user and display a count of the number of records viewed.

PROCESSING MULTI-DIMENSION TABLES

CHAPTER OBJECTIVES

Chapter 11 presented basic array/table-processing operations. This chapter introduces more advanced table-handling concepts and techniques that you, as a COBOL programmer, should know. From this chapter, you will learn the following:

- Creating multiple-level tables.

- Processing multiple-level tables.

- Loading a table from an input file and precautions to ensure that it is valid.

- Using the PERFORM/VARYING/AFTER statement for processing multiple-level tables.

Introduction to Multiple-Level Tables

All the array/tables examples presented in Chapter 11 were examples of **single-level tables**. Although single-level tables are commonly used, many applications require the use of **multiple-level tables**. COBOL-85 can handle multiple-level tables of up to seven levels. (COBOL-74 is limited to three levels.) Multiple-level tables have table entries within table entries. As you will see, a **two-level table** contains two OCCURS clauses—one nested within the other. A **three-level table** has three nested OCCURS clauses—and so on. Let's begin by looking at a two-level table example.

Example Definition

The Programming Task

Assume that your employer wants to rewrite the company payroll system. The part of the new system assigned to you must access the hourly rate from a table such as that shown in Figure 12-1. The specifications of your task are as follows:

Input: Accept from the keyboard:
          Job classification code
          Shift code

Output: Pay rate from table

Actions: Validate the input items:
          If invalid, display appropriate error message
          If valid, access pay rate from table

To explore all possibilities, you must code the table in three different forms:

1. Positional organization for both the Job classification code and the Shift code. Input will be Job classification number (1–7) and Shift number (1–3).
2. Explicit argument for Job classification and positional organization for Shift code.
3. Explicit arguments for both Job classification and Shift code.

General Pseudocode Solution

Figure 12-2 shows a pseudocode solution that will be applicable to all three example programs. As you can see, the logic is relatively simple. The user enters the desired Job classification and Shift code from the keyboard. Either of three program responses are displayed on the screen: (1) an error message for an invalid Job classification, (2) an error message for an invalid Shift code, or (3) the desired Pay rate from the table. The user can repeat the sequence as many times as desired.

Figure 12-1
Pay rate table.

| | Rate of Pay | | |
Job classification	Shift 1 (day)	Shift 2 (swing)	Shift 3 (grave)
1	10.64	11.60	12.09
2	9.93	10.82	11.27
3	8.12	8.83	9.19
4	7.80	8.48	8.82
5	7.07	7.68	7.98
6	6.41	6.95	7.22
7	5.39	5.83	6.04

Figure 12-2
General pseudocode
solution for Pay rate
table examples.

```
000-Table-Test-Program
   1.  Perform until user finished
       a.  Perform 200-Lookup-Pay-Rate
       b.  If Pay-rate found in table
              display Pay-rate
       c.  Query user about repeating

200-Lookup-Pay-Rate
   1.  Accept user selected Job classification
   2.  If invalid Job classification
          Display error message
       else
          Accept user selected Shift
          If invalid Shift
             Display error message
          else
             Move desired Pay rate from table to edited field
```

Hard-Coded and File-Loaded Tables

You know from Chapter 11 that hard-coding tables is reasonable only if the table entries are fixed and unchanging. If the table entries are likely to change, then the table should be stored on disk and loaded by the program. Since pay rates frequently change, this example's table would normally be stored on disk. However, to focus on table-processing principles, the table will be hard-coded in most of the Pay rate table examples. But—to give you an insight into how multi-level table file loading is done—two file-loaded examples are also included.

Positionally Organized Table

Establishing a Two-Level Table

As you inspect Figure 12-1's table, notice that this is a positional table application. Remember, a positional table is one consisting only of table functions (no table arguments). For instance, to obtain a desired Pay rate for Job classification 4 and Shift code 3, you look across row 4 to column 3 for the amount 8.82.

Consider the code example of Figure 12-3, which corresponds to Figure 12-1's table. Each element of RT-JOB-CLASS includes the Pay rates for all three Shift codes. For instance, RT-JOB-CLASS(1) contains the three rates for Job classification 1, RT-JOB-CLASS(2) for Job classification 2, and so on, as Figure 12-4 illustrates.

Of course, in actual processing, we want a single Pay rate, not a collection of rates for a given group. Since each element of RT-JOB-CLASS contains, in order, the three Shift code values, we must define another OCCURS subordinate to RT-JOB-CLASS, as in Figure 12-5. This effectively says that each of the seven RT-JOB-CLASS entries consists of three RT-PAY-RATE entries, corresponding to

Figure 12-3
Grouping of Pay rates
by Shift code.

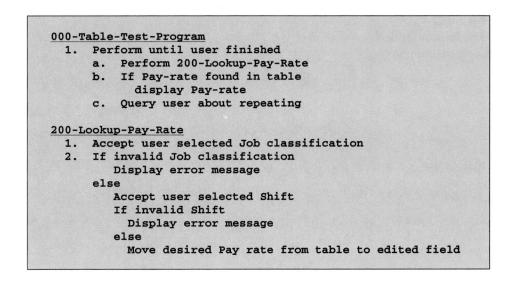

```
                                                 Pay rates for Shift codes

                                              1     2     3
        01   RT-RATE-DATA.
             05   PIC X(12)   VALUE  "106411601209"
             05   PIC X(12)   VALUE  "099310821127"
             05   PIC X(12)   VALUE  "081208830919"
             05   PIC X(12)   VALUE  "078008480882"        Seven Job
             05   PIC X(12)   VALUE  "070707680798"        classifications
             05   PIC X(12)   VALUE  "064106950722"
             05   PIC X(12)   VALUE  "053905830604"
        01   RT-RATE-TABLE REDEFINES RT-RATE-DATA.
             05   RT-JOB-CLASS              OCCURS 7 TIMES
                                           PIC 9(12).
```

Figure 12-4
The Pay rate table in
computer memory.

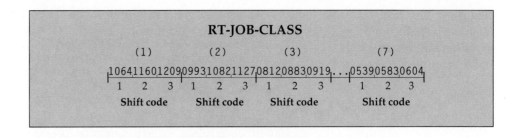

Figure 12-5
A two-level table definition.

```
01  RT-RATE-TABLE REDEFINES RT-RATE-DATA.
    05  RT-JOB-CLASS              OCCURS 7 TIMES.
        10  RT-PAY-RATE           OCCURS 3 TIMES
                                  PIC 99V99.
```

the three Shift codes. To access a desired rate, you must use two subscripts: one for RT-JOB-CLASS and a second for RT-PAY-RATE. For instance, assume you must move the Pay rate for Job classification 4, Shift code 3 to RL-RATE-OF-PAY. The subscripting takes the form shown in Figure 12-6. Notice that a comma and a space were used to separate the two entries within the parentheses. (Earlier versions of COBOL required the comma; for COBOL-74 and COBOL-85, it is optional. However, it serves as good documentation in this case.)

When using multiple-level tables, simply remember that the subscripts appear within the parentheses in the same order as the corresponding OCCURS clauses are included within the table definition.

Accessing a Two-Level Positionally Organized Table—PAYTBLE1

The PAYTBLE1 program shown in Figure 12-7 provides the user with access to data in the Pay rate table. Its significant features are

1. Table data is defined in lines 40–46 and the table (array) itself in lines 47–50. If the table were loaded from a file, the table-data code (lines 39–46) and the REDEFINES in line 47 would not be required.
2. Repetition is controlled through the program switch S2-REPEAT-TEST-SWITCH defined with appropriate condition-names (lines 26–28).
3. The loop-control PERFORM statement (lines 60–61) employs the WITH TEST AFTER phrase. By using this, the switch does not need to be initialized. Its value is established by the user response at line 68.
4. The user input and value verification is accomplished within a nested IF sequence (beginning line 79). If the Job classification is not valid, an error message is displayed and the S1-PAY-RATE-FOUND-SWITCH is set accordingly. Execution then proceeds to the outer END-IF (the end of the procedure), thereby returning control to the main module.
5. If the Job classification is valid, the ELSE sequence (beginning line 83) is executed. The Shift code entry is accepted and tested in the same way as the Job classification. A valid entry causes the pay-rate value from the table to be moved to DI-PAY-RATE.

Figure 12-6
Using two subscripts.

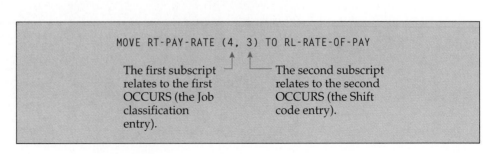

Figure 12-7   Two-level Pay rate table lookup (positional addressing at both levels)—PAYTBLE1.

```
 1        IDENTIFICATION DIVISION.                    51
 2        PROGRAM-ID. PAYTBLE1.                        52
 3                                                     53        PROCEDURE DIVISION.
 4      * Interplanetary Transport, Inc.              54
 5      * Pay Table Lookup Test Program #1            55        000-TABLE-TEST-PROGRAM.
 6      * Written by W. Price    1-23-95              56        ************Initialization Sequence************
 7                                                     57            DISPLAY "Look up a table entry"
 8      * Input:   Keyboard entry of                  58            DISPLAY " "
 9      *              Job classification number       59        **************Processing Sequence**************
10      *              Shift number                    60            PERFORM WITH TEST AFTER
11      * Output:  Pay rate accessed from Pay rate table  61                UNTIL S2-DO-NOT-REPEAT-TEST
12      * Comment: The Pay rate table is two level and is 62            PERFORM 200-LOOKUP-PAY-RATE
13      *          organized positionally. Direct lookup  63            IF S1-PAY-RATE-FOUND
14      *          is used for table access.          64                DISPLAY "Pay rate: ", DI-PAY-RATE
15                                                     65            END-IF
16                                                     66            DISPLAY " "
17        DATA DIVISION.                               67            DISPLAY "Do you want to make another test <Y/N>? "
18                                                     68            ACCEPT S2-REPEAT-TEST-SWITCH
19        WORKING-STORAGE SECTION.                     69        END-PERFORM
20                                                     70        **************Termination Sequence**************
21        01  PROGRAM-SWITCHES.                        71            DISPLAY "Processing complete"
22            05  S1-PAY-RATE-FOUND-SWITCH  PIC X.     72            STOP RUN
23                88  S1-PAY-RATE-FOUND      VALUE "F". 73            .
24                88  S1-PAY-RATE-NOT-FOUND  VALUE "N". 74        ***********************************************
25                                                     75        200-LOOKUP-PAY-RATE.
26            05  S2-REPEAT-TEST-SWITCH     PIC X.     76            DISPLAY " "
27                88  S2-REPEAT-TEST        VALUE "Y" "y". 77            DISPLAY "Please enter the job classification <1-7> "
28                88  S2-DO-NOT-REPEAT-TEST VALUE "N". 78            ACCEPT WA-CLASS-CODE
29                                                     79            IF WA-CLASS-CODE NOT NUMERIC
30        01  WORK-FIELDS.                             80            OR NOT WA-VALID-CLASS-CODE
31            05  WA-CLASS-CODE             PIC 9.     81                SET S1-PAY-RATE-NOT-FOUND TO TRUE
32                88  WA-VALID-CLASS-CODE  VALUE 1 THRU 7. 82                DISPLAY "Job classification code must be 1-7"
33            05  WA-SHIFT-CODE             PIC 9.     83            ELSE
34                88  WA-VALID-SHIFT-CODE  VALUE 1 THRU 3. 84                DISPLAY "Please enter the shift number <1-3> "
35                                                     85                ACCEPT WA-SHIFT-CODE
36        01  DISPLAY-FIELDS.                          86                IF WA-SHIFT-CODE NOT NUMERIC
37            05  DI-PAY-RATE               PIC $$Z.99. 87                OR NOT WA-VALID-SHIFT-CODE
38                                                     88                    SET S1-PAY-RATE-NOT-FOUND TO TRUE
39        01  RT-RATE-DATA.                            89                    DISPLAY "Shift number must be 1, 2, or 3"
40            05      PIC X(12)  VALUE "106411601209". 90                ELSE
41            05      PIC X(12)  VALUE "099310821127". 91                    SET S1-PAY-RATE-FOUND TO TRUE
42            05      PIC X(12)  VALUE "081208830919". 92                    MOVE RT-PAY-RATE (WA-CLASS-CODE,
43            05      PIC X(12)  VALUE "078008480882". 93                                      WA-SHIFT-CODE)
44            05      PIC X(12)  VALUE "070707680798". 94                                      TO DI-PAY-RATE
45            05      PIC X(12)  VALUE "064106950722". 95                END-IF
46            05      PIC X(12)  VALUE "053905830604". 96        END-IF
47        01  RT-RATE-TABLE REDEFINES RT-RATE-DATA.    97            .
48            05  RT-JOB-CLASS-ENTRY   OCCURS 7 TIMES.
49                10  RT-PAY-RATE          OCCURS 3 TIMES
50                                        PIC 99V99.
```

6. Notice that the subscripts for RT-PAY-RATE (lines 92–93) are listed in the same order as they appear in the OCCURS clauses: Job classification first and Shift code next.

COBOL-74

The necessary COBOL-74 changes for PAYTBLE1 are

1. Insert the CONFIGURATION SECTION and LABEL RECORDS clauses.
2. Include the reserved word FILLER in the Pay rate table entries.
3. Change each SET statement to a corresponding MOVE.
4. Move the inline PERFORM code of lines 62–68 to a separate module and change the PERFORM to execute that module.
5. The TEST AFTER is not part of COBOL-74; delete it from line 60. With this, you will need to initialize the S2 switch to Y.
6. Remove the END-IF scope terminators at lines 95–96. A single period ending line 94 will terminate the IF statements at lines 79 and 86.
7. If necessary, move separate-line paragraph-ending periods to the end of the preceding line.

A Two-Level Table with One (First-Level) Explicit Argument

The Table

As previously mentioned, only certain applications can employ positionally organized tables. For instance, assume that the seven Job classification codes are A1, A2, B1, C1, C2, C3, and C4—rather than 1–7. Then these codes (table arguments) must be explicitly represented within the table data. This situation requires a two-level table with an explicit table argument at one level. Many two-level tables fall into this category.

Figure 12-8(a) defines a two-level table to accommodate this. The first level (Job classification) includes the INDEXED BY phrase to allow use of the SEARCH statement in accessing at this level. This phrase is not necessary at the second level because positional access is used at this level.

Within the table, each first-level entry (RT-JOB-CLASS-ENTRY) is composed of the following:

- One RT-JOB-CLASS entry

- Three RT-PAY-RATE entries

You can see this in the representation of the table data in Figure 12-8(b).

In the following examples, assume that RT-CLASS-INDEX contains an occurrence value of 3 and WA-SHIFT-CODE contains a value of 2. Data can be accessed from this table in three ways.

Figure 12-8 Two-level table—explicit argument at first level and positional addressing at second level.

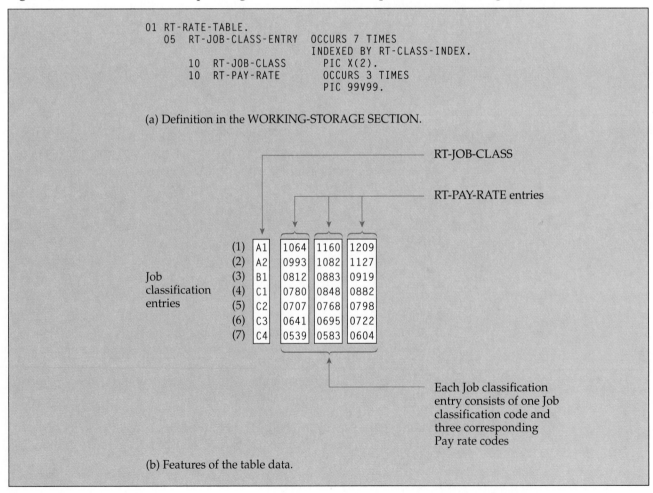

```
01 RT-RATE-TABLE.
   05  RT-JOB-CLASS-ENTRY   OCCURS 7 TIMES
                            INDEXED BY RT-CLASS-INDEX.
       10  RT-JOB-CLASS     PIC X(2).
       10  RT-PAY-RATE      OCCURS 3 TIMES
                            PIC 99V99.
```

(a) Definition in the WORKING-STORAGE SECTION.

RT-JOB-CLASS

RT-PAY-RATE entries

Job classification entries

(1)	A1	1064	1160	1209
(2)	A2	0993	1082	1127
(3)	B1	0812	0883	0919
(4)	C1	0780	0848	0882
(5)	C2	0707	0768	0798
(6)	C3	0641	0695	0722
(7)	C4	0539	0583	0604

Each Job classification entry consists of one Job classification code and three corresponding Pay rate codes

(b) Features of the table data.

1. Accessing RT-JOB-CLASS-ENTRY. Since RT-CLASS-INDEX has an occurrence value of 3,

   ```
   RT-JOB-CLASS-ENTRY (RT-CLASS-INDEX)
   ```

   is equivalent to

   ```
   RT-JOB-CLASS-ENTRY (3).
   ```

   This refers to the entire third row, consisting of RT-JOB-CLASS (value B1) and the corresponding three sets of Pay rate. It is a group item. Its length is 14 (2 + 3 × 4). Only one entry designator (an index or occurrence number) can be used within the parentheses when designating this item.

2. Accessing RT-JOB-CLASS. With the specified value for RT-CLASS-INDEX,

   ```
   RT-JOB-CLASS (RT-CLASS-INDEX)
   ```

   is equivalent to

   ```
   RT-JOB-CLASS (3).
   ```

   This refers to a single elementary item, B1: the third Job classification entry. Like RT-JOB-CLASS-ENTRY, it falls under a single OCCURS, so only one entry designator (an index or occurrence number) may be used with it.

3. Accessing RT-PAY-RATE. With the specified values for RT-CLASS-INDEX and WA-SHIFT-CODE,

   ```
   RT-PAY-RATE (RT-CLASS-INDEX, WA-SHIFT-CODE)
   ```

   is equivalent to

   ```
   RT-PAY-RATE (3, 2).
   ```

   This refers to a single Pay rate entry—0883—which is in the third table entry (row) and the second Pay rate entry (column). Because its definition falls under two OCCURS, it requires two entry designators: the first, an index and the second, a subscript.

The PAYTBLE2 Program   Figure 12-9's PAYTBLE2 program displays the coding required to look up the Pay rate with an explicit table argument at the first level. As you study this, you must remember exactly how the SEARCH statement works. The SEARCH simply progresses from one table entry (at the level designated in the SEARCH) to the next until:

1. The end of the table is reached (the AT END phrase) or
2. A condition designated in the WHEN becomes true

Keeping this in mind, look at line 86's SEARCH, in which RT-JOB-CLASS-ENTRY is designated. This is a *single-level table search*. It is looking for the Job classification entry (full row in Figure 12-8), in which the Job classification code is equal to the input Job classification code value (line 90). If found, then execution can continue to the next statement to accept the Shift code number (beginning line 91). Once verified, that entry can be used—together with the previous search index value—to access the desired Pay rate (lines 99–101).

As you can see, the lookup for this two-level table with one explicit argument is a single-level search followed by positional addressing of the column within the row. This type of table, using this lookup method, is commonly encountered.

Figure 12-9 Two-level Pay rate table lookup (serial SEARCH at first level)—PAYTBLE2.

```
1       IDENTIFICATION DIVISION.                          57
2       PROGRAM-ID. PAYTBLE2.                             58
3                                                         59      PROCEDURE DIVISION.
4     * Interplanetary Transport, Inc.                    60
5     * Pay Table Lookup Test Program #2                  61      000-TABLE-TEST-PROGRAM.
6     * Written by W. Price    1-23-95                    62    *************Initialization Sequence************
7                                                         63          DISPLAY "Look up a table entry"
8     * Input:    Keyboard entry of                       64          DISPLAY " "
9     *                Job classification code            65    *************Processing Sequence**************
10    *                Shift number                       66          PERFORM WITH TEST AFTER
11    * Output:  Pay rate accessed from Pay rate table    67              UNTIL S2-DO-NOT-REPEAT-TEST
12    * Comment: Pay rate table is two level. The first   68          PERFORM 200-LOOKUP-PAY-RATE
13    *          level includes the Job classification    69          IF S1-PAY-RATE-FOUND
14    *          as the argument (it is indexed). The     70              DISPLAY "Pay rate: ", DI-PAY-RATE
15    *          second level (shift number) is organized 71          END-IF
16    *          positionally. The SEARCH statement is    72          DISPLAY " "
17    *          used for first-level (classification)    73          DISPLAY "Do you want to make another test <Y/N>? "
18    *          access and direct for second-level       74          ACCEPT S2-REPEAT-TEST-SWITCH
19    *          (shift) access.                          75          END-PERFORM
20                                                        76    *************Termination Sequence*************
21                                                        77          DISPLAY "Processing complete"
22      DATA DIVISION.                                    78          STOP RUN
23                                                        79          .
24      WORKING-STORAGE SECTION.                          80    ************************************************
25                                                        81      200-LOOKUP-PAY-RATE.
26      01  PROGRAM-SWITCHES.                             82          DISPLAY " "
27          05  S1-PAY-RATE-FOUND-SWITCH PIC X.           83          DISPLAY "Please enter the job classification "
28              88  S1-PAY-RATE-FOUND      VALUE "F".     84          ACCEPT WA-CLASS-CODE
29              88  S1-PAY-RATE-NOT-FOUND  VALUE "N".     85          SET RT-CLASS-INDEX TO 1
30                                                        86          SEARCH RT-JOB-CLASS-ENTRY
31          05  S2-REPEAT-TEST-SWITCH   PIC X.            87              AT END
32              88  S2-REPEAT-TEST         VALUE "Y" "y". 88                  SET S1-PAY-RATE-NOT-FOUND TO TRUE
33              88  S2-DO-NOT-REPEAT-TEST  VALUE "N".     89                  DISPLAY "Invalid job classification code"
34                                                        90              WHEN RT-JOB-CLASS (RT-CLASS-INDEX) = WA-CLASS-CODE
35      01  WORK-FIELDS.                                  91                  DISPLAY "Please enter the shift number <1-3> "
36          05  WA-CLASS-CODE       PIC XX.               92                  ACCEPT WA-SHIFT-CODE
37          05  WA-SHIFT-CODE       PIC 9.                93                  IF WA-SHIFT-CODE NOT NUMERIC
38              88  WA-VALID-SHIFT-CODE  VALUE 1 THRU 3.  94                  OR NOT WA-VALID-SHIFT-CODE
39                                                        95                      SET S1-PAY-RATE-NOT-FOUND TO TRUE
40      01  DISPLAY-FIELDS.                               96                      DISPLAY "Shift number must be 1, 2, or 3"
41          05  DI-PAY-RATE         PIC $$Z.99.           97                  ELSE
42                                                        98                      SET S1-PAY-RATE-FOUND TO TRUE
43      01  RT-RATE-DATA.                                 99                      MOVE RT-PAY-RATE (RT-CLASS-INDEX,
44          05      PIC X(14)   VALUE  "A1106411601209". 100                                     WA-SHIFT-CODE)
45          05      PIC X(14)   VALUE  "A2099310821127". 101                           TO DI-PAY-RATE
46          05      PIC X(14)   VALUE  "B1081208830919". 102                  END-IF
47          05      PIC X(14)   VALUE  "C1078008480882". 103          END-SEARCH
48          05      PIC X(14)   VALUE  "C2070707680798". 104          .
49          05      PIC X(14)   VALUE  "C3064106950722".
50          05      PIC X(14)   VALUE  "C4053905830604".
51      01 RT-RATE-TABLE REDEFINES RT-RATE-DATA.
52          05  RT-JOB-CLASS-ENTRY  OCCURS 7 TIMES
53                              INDEXED BY RT-CLASS-INDEX.
54              10  RT-JOB-CLASS    PIC X(2).
55              10  RT-PAY-RATE     OCCURS 3 TIMES
56                              PIC 99V99.
```

COBOL-74

The necessary COBOL-74 changes for PAYTBLE2 are identical to those of PAYTBLE1 (Figure 12–7). The paragraph-ending period at line 104 will terminate both the SEARCH and its contained IF.

A Two-Level Table with Two Explicit Arguments

The Table

Sometimes, a two-level table has two explicit arguments. For example, assume that the Shift codes—instead of being coded 1–3—are represented by the alphanumeric codes of D for day shift, S for swing shift, and G for graveyard shift. Here we have an example of a two-level table with explicit table arguments at both levels. Figure 12–10(a) shows DATA DIVISION coding to establish this table. You can see that seven Job classification entries still exist—nothing has changed there. However, a

Shift code entry (RT-SHIFT-ENTRY) is inserted. It occurs three times and is composed of Shift code/Pay rate pairs. The INDEXED BY clause is specified at both the Job classification and the Shift levels. Figure 12-10(b) shows how the table data must be laid out in order to conform to the table definition. Although the entries of this table—with their interspersed Shift code values—appear very clumsy, it would likely be stored on disk and be accompanied by an appropriate program for updating it. Later in this chapter, you will see an alternative to this technique.

Data can be accessed from this table in four ways. The following examples use occurrence numbers of 3 for Job classification and 2 for Shift code to illustrate this:

RT-JOB-CLASS-ENTRY (3)	As in the preceding example (Figure 12-8), this refers to the entire third row. Its length is 17 $(2 + 3 \times 5)$. Only one index may be used when designating this item.
RT-JOB-CLASS (3)	This is identical to the preceding example of Figure 12-8.
RT-SHIFT-CODE (3, 2)	This refers to the single argument of the Shift code/Pay rate pair. It requires two indexes or occurrence numbers.
RT-PAY-RATE (3, 2)	This refers to a single function of the Shift code/Pay rate pair. It requires two indexes or occurrence numbers.

Figure 12-10
Two-level table—explicit arguments at both levels.

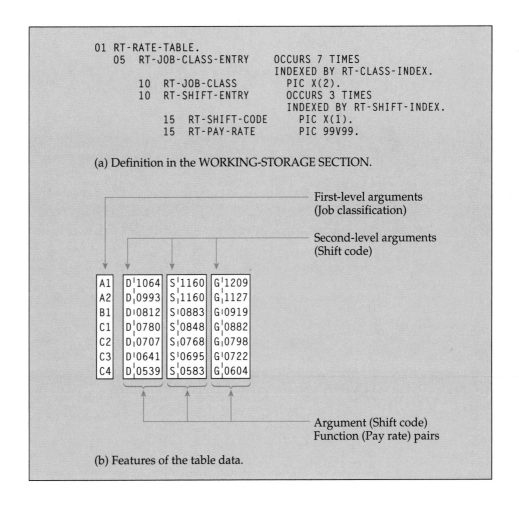

```
01 RT-RATE-TABLE.
   05  RT-JOB-CLASS-ENTRY     OCCURS 7 TIMES
                              INDEXED BY RT-CLASS-INDEX.
       10  RT-JOB-CLASS       PIC X(2).
       10  RT-SHIFT-ENTRY     OCCURS 3 TIMES
                              INDEXED BY RT-SHIFT-INDEX.
           15  RT-SHIFT-CODE  PIC X(1).
           15  RT-PAY-RATE    PIC 99V99.
```

(a) Definition in the WORKING-STORAGE SECTION.

First-level arguments
(Job classification)

Second-level arguments
(Shift code)

A1	D'1064	S'1160	G'1209
A2	D'0993	S'1160	G'1127
B1	D'0812	S'0883	G'0919
C1	D'0780	S'0848	G'0882
C2	D'0707	S'0768	G'0798
C3	D'0641	S'0695	G'0722
C4	D'0539	S'0583	G'0604

Argument (Shift code)
Function (Pay rate) pairs

(b) Features of the table data.

The PAYTBLE3 Program

Figure 12-11's PAYTBLE3 program has only minor differences from PAYTBLE2. During execution, the following takes place:

1. After accepting the Job classification code, the RT-JOB-CLASS-ENTRY is searched (as with PAYTBLE2). If a matching Job classification code is found (line 91), execution continues to line 92.
2. The Shift code entry is accepted (line 93).
3. Then the group of Shift code entries of the selected row is searched (RT-SHIFT-ENTRY at line 95). If a matching Shift code is found (lines 99–100), the selected entry is moved to the display item (lines 102–104).

COBOL-74

The necessary COBOL-74 changes for PAYTBLE3 are identical to those of PAYTBLE2 (Figure 12–9). The paragraph-ending period at line 107 will terminate both SEARCH statements.

Figure 12-11 Two-level Pay rate table lookup (serial SEARCH at both levels)—PAYTBLE3.

```
1       IDENTIFICATION DIVISION.                              58
2       PROGRAM-ID. PAYTBLE3.                                 59
3                                                             60      PROCEDURE DIVISION.
4     * Interplanetary Transport, Inc.                        61
5     * Pay Table Lookup Test Program #3                      62      000-TABLE-TEST-PROGRAM.
6     * Written by W. Price    1-23-95                        63    ************Initialization Sequence***********
7                                                             64          DISPLAY "Look up a table entry"
8     * Input:    Keyboard entry of                           65          DISPLAY " "
9     *                 Job classification code               66    ************Processing Sequence**************
10    *                 Shift code                            67          PERFORM WITH TEST AFTER
11    * Output: Pay rate accessed from Pay rate table         68              UNTIL S2-DO-NOT-REPEAT-TEST
12    * Comment: Pay rate table is two level. The first       69          PERFORM 200-LOOKUP-PAY-RATE
13    *          level includes the Job classification        70          IF S1-PAY-RATE-FOUND
14    *          as the argument (it is indexed). The         71              DISPLAY "Pay rate: ", DI-PAY-RATE
15    *          second level includes the Shift code         72          END-IF
16    *          as the argument (it is indexed).             73          DISPLAY " "
17    *          Nested SEARCH statements are used            74          DISPLAY "Do you want to make another test <Y/N>? "
18    *          for first-level (classification)             75          ACCEPT S2-REPEAT-TEST-SWITCH
19    *          and second-level (shift) access.             76      END-PERFORM
20                                                            77    ************Termination Sequence*************
21                                                            78          DISPLAY "Processing complete"
22      DATA DIVISION.                                        79          STOP RUN
23                                                            80          .
24      WORKING-STORAGE SECTION.                              81    ******************************************
25                                                            82      200-LOOKUP-PAY-RATE.
26      01  PROGRAM-SWITCHES.                                 83          DISPLAY " "
27          05  S1-PAY-RATE-FOUND-SWITCH PIC X.              84          DISPLAY "Please enter the job classification "
28              88  S1-PAY-RATE-FOUND     VALUE "F".         85          ACCEPT WA-CLASS-CODE
29              88  S1-PAY-RATE-NOT-FOUND VALUE "N".         86          SET RT-CLASS-INDEX TO 1
30                                                            87          SEARCH RT-JOB-CLASS-ENTRY
31          05  S2-REPEAT-TEST-SWITCH    PIC X.              88              AT END
32              88  S2-REPEAT-TEST        VALUE "Y" "y".      89                  SET S1-PAY-RATE-NOT-FOUND TO TRUE
33              88  S2-DO-NOT-REPEAT-TEST VALUE "N".         90                  DISPLAY "Invalid job classification code"
34                                                            91              WHEN RT-JOB-CLASS (RT-CLASS-INDEX) = WA-CLASS-CODE
35      01  WORK-FIELDS.                                      92                  DISPLAY "Please enter the shift code "
36          05  WA-CLASS-CODE        PIC XX.                 93                  ACCEPT WA-SHIFT-CODE
37          05  WA-SHIFT-CODE        PIC X.                  94                  SET RT-SHIFT-INDEX TO 1
38                                                            95                  SEARCH RT-SHIFT-ENTRY
39      01  DISPLAY-FIELDS.                                   96                      AT END
40          05  DI-PAY-RATE         PIC $$Z.99.              97                          SET S1-PAY-RATE-NOT-FOUND TO TRUE
41                                                            98                          DISPLAY "Invalid shift code"
42      01  RT-RATE-DATA.                                     99                      WHEN RT-SHIFT-CODE (RT-CLASS-INDEX, RT-SHIFT-INDEX)
43          05      PIC X(17)  VALUE "A1D1064S1160G1209".   100                          = WA-SHIFT-CODE
44          05      PIC X(17)  VALUE "A2D0993S1082G1127".   101                          SET S1-PAY-RATE-FOUND TO TRUE
45          05      PIC X(17)  VALUE "B1D0812S0883G0919".   102                          MOVE RT-PAY-RATE (RT-CLASS-INDEX,
46          05      PIC X(17)  VALUE "C1D0780S0848G0882".   103                                            RT-SHIFT-INDEX)
47          05      PIC X(17)  VALUE "C2D0707S0768G0798".   104                          TO DI-PAY-RATE
48          05      PIC X(17)  VALUE "C3D0641S0695G0722".   105                  END-SEARCH
49          05      PIC X(17)  VALUE "C4D0539S0583G0604".   106          END-SEARCH
50      01 RT-RATE-TABLE REDEFINES RT-RATE-DATA.            107          .
51          05  RT-JOB-CLASS-ENTRY   OCCURS 7 TIMES
52                                   INDEXED BY RT-CLASS-INDEX.
53              10  RT-JOB-CLASS      PIC X(2).
54              10  RT-SHIFT-ENTRY    OCCURS 3 TIMES
55                                    INDEXED BY RT-SHIFT-INDEX.
56                  15  RT-SHIFT-CODE   PIC X(1).
57                  15  RT-PAY-RATE     PIC 99V99.
```

A Three-Level Table Loaded from a File

Table-File Loading Concepts

As indicated earlier, instead of hard-coding the Pay rate table data with VALUE clauses, table data would probably be loaded into the program at run time from records stored on tape or disk. When tables are loaded from input records, each record typically contains the data for one table entry. A program to load a table file to be used for processing a data file essentially becomes "a program within another program." That is, you need a complete set of definition and processing statements for the table file. You must code appropriate SELECT, FD, OPEN, READ, and CLOSE statements strictly for the table file.

With an input-loaded table, the chance always exists that—because of additions to the table—the number of table entries will exceed the number of occurrences provided for the table as specified in the OCCURS clause. When designing the program, therefore, you must be certain to specify an OCCURS value large enough to accommodate a reasonable number of table-entry additions.

Then, in the table-loading routine, your program logic must check the table limits before adding each entry. For example, if 105 entries were present for a table defined with an OCCURS clause specifying 100 occurrences, severe processing bugs would occur unless the program logic diagnosed and reported the error.

Three-Level Table Definition

As an example of three-level table processing, assume that your company decides to break the pay structure into two other categories: Temporary (code TE) and Permanent (code PE). Responding to this need, the systems manager sets up the table with three levels:

Job classification

Job status (Temporary or Permanent)

Shift

Figure 12–12(a) shows a DATA DIVISION entry to establish the table. You can see that it is a simple progression from the two-level definition of Figure 12-10(a): a Status code entry was inserted preceding the Shift code entry. Figure 12–12(b) shows a schematic representation of how the COBOL table can be constructed. Now, to obtain a selected Pay rate, you need: (1) the Job classification, (2) the Status code, and (3) the Shift code.

For the next example program, the table data shown in Figure 12-12(b) is stored in the table file PAY-RATE.TBL. It is stored as shown (without spaces between items), one record per Job classification entry (row). So, its format conforms exactly to Figure 12–12(a)'s table definition.

The table program using explicit table arguments is expanded to include: (1) processing a three-level table and (2) loading the table data from a disk file. The program, PAYTBLE4, is shown in Figure 12-13 (pages 434 and 435).

Loading the Pay Rate Table

The broad sequence of table-loading actions is as follows:

```
Open table file
Initialize
Repeat until table loaded or load error
   Read table file record
   Check loading conditions
   If okay
      Move table record to table
   If not okay
      Indicate load error
Close table file
```

Lines 119–122 of Figure 12-13 contain the table-load initialization sequence. The data-item WA-TABLE-ENTRY-COUNT (defined at line 64 and initialized at line 122) counts the number of records read. It is assigned a condition-name (line 65) designating the allowable number of table entries.

Figure 12-12   Three-level table—explicit arguments at all levels.

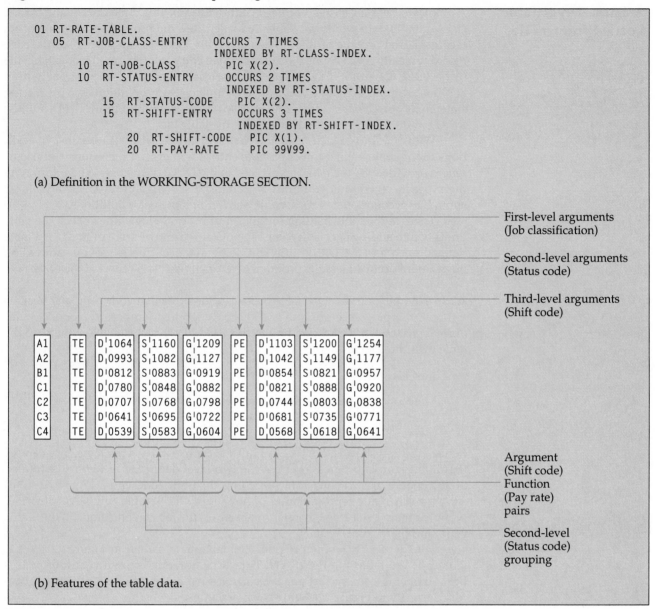

```
01 RT-RATE-TABLE.
   05  RT-JOB-CLASS-ENTRY      OCCURS 7 TIMES
                               INDEXED BY RT-CLASS-INDEX.
      10   RT-JOB-CLASS        PIC X(2).
      10   RT-STATUS-ENTRY     OCCURS 2 TIMES
                               INDEXED BY RT-STATUS-INDEX.
         15   RT-STATUS-CODE   PIC X(2).
         15   RT-SHIFT-ENTRY   OCCURS 3 TIMES
                               INDEXED BY RT-SHIFT-INDEX.
            20   RT-SHIFT-CODE PIC X(1).
            20   RT-PAY-RATE   PIC 99V99.
```

(a) Definition in the WORKING-STORAGE SECTION.

(b) Features of the table data.

The loop is controlled by the PERFORM VARYING at lines 125–128, which increments the first-level table index RT-CLASS-INDEX. The S4 switch, initialized at line 121, controls repetition (lines 127 and 128). At line 129, the table record is read.

Let's consider the error possibilities in loading this table. With seven Job classification codes, seven records must be in the Pay rate file; the program must ensure that it has no more and no less. If—as each input table record is moved into the table—it is counted, then the following four conditions might occur.

1. End-of-file not detected and record count is not 7.
   Implication: Valid condition—table loading not complete.
   Action: Continue loading table (increment to next table entry).
2. End-of-file not detected and record count is 7.
   Implication: Invalid condition—file contains more than seven records.
   Action: Print error message and terminate processing.
3. End-of-file detected and record count is not 7.
   Implication: Invalid condition—file contains fewer than seven records.
   Action: Print error message and terminate processing.
4. End-of-file detected and record count is 7.
   Implication: Valid condition—table is properly loaded.
   Action: Proceed to next part of the program.

Note that these four possibilities are mutually exclusive (only one can occur for any given pass through the loop).

The decision-table format of the EVALUATE at lines 132–158 corresponds exactly to the preceding four possibilities. At lines 139–140, the input table record is moved to its proper table entry (controlled by the index RT-CLASS-INDEX). At line 141, the entry is counted.

Notice that the table file is closed as soon as the loading action is complete (or a load error is detected). After the table is loaded, access to the file is no longer required, so the file is closed. Whenever a file is required at only a certain point in a program, it is good programming practice to open it at the point required and close it when it is no longer needed.

Accessing the Three-Level Table

Three-level table processing is similar to two-level table processing—except that it requires three subscripts and/or indexes to reference the elementary occurrences within the table. The only difference between the 200 module of PAYTBLE4 and that of PAYTBLE3 (two-level search) is the insertion of another SEARCH statement. This set of nested SEARCH statements has the following form—which, as you can see, is essentially that of a nested IF:

Search for Job-classification	Line 169
If unsuccessful	
Display error message	
Fall through to end of module	
If successful	
Search for Status-code	Line 177
If unsuccessful	
Display error message	
Fall through to end of module	
If successful	
Search for Shift-code	Line 187
If unsuccessful	
Display error message	
Fall through to end of module	
If successful	
Access table entry	Line 197

Figure 12-13 Three-level Pay rate table lookup with file-loaded table—PAYTBLE4.

```
 1        IDENTIFICATION DIVISION.                               59     01  WORK-FIELDS.
 2        PROGRAM-ID. PAYTBLE4.                                  60         05  WA-CLASS-CODE              PIC X(2).
 3                                                               61         05  WA-STATUS-CODE             PIC X(2).
 4      * Interplanetary Transport, Inc.                         62         05  WA-SHIFT-CODE              PIC X.
 5      * Pay Table Lookup Test Program #4                       63         05  WA-DUMMY-RESPONSE-FIELD    PIC X.
 6      * Written by W. Price    1-23-95                         64         05  WA-TABLE-ENTRY-COUNT       PIC 9.
 7                                                               65             88  CORRECT-TABLE-COUNT        VALUE 7.
 8      * Table:   Loaded from a file.                           66
 9      * Input:   Keyboard entry of                             67     01  DISPLAY-FIELDS.
10      *              Job classification code                   68         05  DI-PAY-RATE                PIC $$Z.99.
11      *              Job status code                           69
12      *              Shift code                                70     01  RT-RATE-TABLE.
13      * Output:  Pay rate accessed from Pay rate table         71         05  RT-JOB-CLASS-ENTRY     OCCURS 7 TIMES
14      * Comment: Pay rate table is three level                 72                                    INDEXED BY RT-CLASS-INDEX.
15      *             including arguments as follows             73             10  RT-JOB-CLASS       PIC X(2).
16      *             (all three levels indexed):                74             10  RT-STATUS-ENTRY    OCCURS 2 TIMES
17      *                Job classification                      75                                    INDEXED BY RT-STATUS-INDEX.
18      *                Job status                              76                 15  RT-STATUS-CODE     PIC X(2).
19      *                Shift code                              77                 15  RT-SHIFT-ENTRY     OCCURS 3 TIMES
20      *             Nested SEARCH statements are used          78                                        INDEXED BY RT-SHIFT-INDEX.
21      *             for first level (classification),          79                     20  RT-SHIFT-CODE    PIC X(1).
22      *             second level (status), and                80                     20  RT-PAY-RATE      PIC 99V99.
23      *             third level (shift) access.                81
24                                                               82
25                                                               83     PROCEDURE DIVISION.
26        ENVIRONMENT DIVISION.                                  84
27                                                               85     000-TABLE-TEST-PROGRAM.
28        INPUT-OUTPUT SECTION.                                  86
29                                                               87     ************Initialization Sequence************
30        FILE-CONTROL.                                          88         DISPLAY "Look up a table entry"
31            SELECT PAY-RATE-TABLE-FILE                         89         DISPLAY " "
32                ASSIGN TO (system dependent).                  90         PERFORM 110-LOAD-PAY-RATE-TABLE
33                                                               91
34                                                               92     ***************Processing Sequence**************
35        DATA DIVISION.                                         93         IF S4-TABLE-LOAD-ERROR
36                                                               94             DISPLAY "TABLE LOAD ERROR - RUN ABORTED"
37        FILE SECTION.                                          95             DISPLAY "Press ENTER to exit"
38                                                               96             ACCEPT WA-DUMMY-RESPONSE-FIELD
39        FD  PAY-RATE-TABLE-FILE.                               97             SET S2-DO-NOT-REPEAT-TEST TO TRUE
40        01  PAY-RATE-TABLE-RECORD    PIC X(36).                98         ELSE
41                                                               99             SET S2-REPEAT-TEST TO TRUE
42        WORKING-STORAGE SECTION.                              100         END-IF
43                                                              101
44        01  PROGRAM-SWITCHES.                                 102         PERFORM UNTIL S2-DO-NOT-REPEAT-TEST
45            05  S1-PAY-RATE-FOUND-SWITCH    PIC X.            103             PERFORM 200-LOOKUP-PAY-RATE
46                88  S1-PAY-RATE-FOUND         VALUE "F".      104             IF S1-PAY-RATE-FOUND
47                88  S1-PAY-RATE-NOT-FOUND     VALUE "N".      105                 DISPLAY "Pay rate: ", DI-PAY-RATE
48            05  S2-REPEAT-TEST-SWITCH       PIC X.            106             END-IF
49                88  S2-REPEAT-TEST            VALUE "Y" "y".  107             DISPLAY " "
50                88  S2-DO-NOT-REPEAT-TEST     VALUE "N".      108             DISPLAY "Do you want to make another test <Y/N>? "
51            05  S3-TABLE-FILE-SWITCH        PIC X.            109             ACCEPT S2-REPEAT-TEST-SWITCH
52                88  S3-END-OF-TABLE-FILE      VALUE "E".      110         END-PERFORM
53                88  S3-NOT-END-OF-TABLE-FILE  VALUE "N".      111
54            05  S4-TABLE-LOADED-SWITCH      PIC X.            112     **************Termination Sequence*************
55                88  S4-TABLE-LOAD-COMPLETE    VALUE "C".      113         STOP RUN
56                88  S4-TABLE-LOAD-ERROR       VALUE "E".      114         .
57                88  S4-TABLE-LOAD-NOT-COMPLETE VALUE "N".     115     ************************************************
58
```

COBOL-74

The necessary COBOL-74 changes for PAYTBLE4 are

1. Insert the CONFIGURATION SECTION and LABEL RECORDS clauses.
2. Change each SET statement to a corresponding MOVE.
3. Move the inline PERFORM code of lines 103–109 to a separate module and change the PERFORM to execute that module.
4. Move the inline PERFORM code of lines 129–156 to a separate module and change the PERFORM to execute that module. At the same time, replace the EVALUATE with a nested IF. Also, replace the END-READ (line 131) with a scope-ending period.
5. Delete the three END-SEARCH scope terminators at lines 201–203.
6. If necessary, move separate-line paragraph-ending periods to the end of the preceding line.

Figure 12-13 (continued)

```
116                                                        164        200-LOOKUP-PAY-RATE.
117        110-LOAD-PAY-RATE-TABLE.                         165            DISPLAY " "
118    *      Table-load initialization                     166            DISPLAY "Please enter the job classification "
119           OPEN INPUT PAY-RATE-TABLE-FILE                167            ACCEPT WA-CLASS-CODE
120           SET S3-NOT-END-OF-TABLE-FILE TO TRUE          168            SET RT-CLASS-INDEX TO 1
121           SET S4-TABLE-LOAD-NOT-COMPLETE TO TRUE        169            SEARCH RT-JOB-CLASS-ENTRY
122           INITIALIZE WA-TABLE-ENTRY-COUNT               170               AT END
123                                                         171                  SET S1-PAY-RATE-NOT-FOUND TO TRUE
124    *      Table-load sequence                           172                  DISPLAY "Invalid Job classification code"
125           PERFORM VARYING RT-CLASS-INDEX                173               WHEN RT-JOB-CLASS (RT-CLASS-INDEX) = WA-CLASS-CODE
126                 FROM 1 BY 1                              174                  DISPLAY "Please enter the Status code "
127                    UNTIL S4-TABLE-LOAD-COMPLETE         175                  ACCEPT WA-STATUS-CODE
128                    OR S4-TABLE-LOAD-ERROR               176                  SET RT-STATUS-INDEX TO 1
129              READ PAY-RATE-TABLE-FILE                   177                  SEARCH RT-STATUS-ENTRY
130                 AT END SET S3-END-OF-TABLE-FILE TO TRUE 178                     AT END
131              END-READ                                   179                        SET S1-PAY-RATE-NOT-FOUND TO TRUE
132              EVALUATE                                   180                        DISPLAY "Invalid Status code"
133                 S3-END-OF-TABLE-FILE also CORRECT-TABLE-COUNT  181                    WHEN RT-STATUS-CODE (RT-CLASS-INDEX,
134    *          --------------------    --------------------  182                                       RT-STATUS-INDEX)
135                                                         183                              = WA-STATUS-CODE
136    *          Valid table entry so store it            184                        DISPLAY "Please enter the shift code "
137                 WHEN     FALSE      also      FALSE     185                        ACCEPT WA-SHIFT-CODE
138    *          --------------------    --------------------  186                        SET RT-SHIFT-INDEX TO 1
139                    MOVE PAY-RATE-TABLE-RECORD           187                        SEARCH RT-SHIFT-ENTRY
140                       TO RT-JOB-CLASS-ENTRY (RT-CLASS-INDEX)  188                           AT END
141                    ADD 1 TO WA-TABLE-ENTRY-COUNT        189                              SET S1-PAY-RATE-NOT-FOUND TO TRUE
142                                                         190                              DISPLAY "Invalid shift code"
143    *          Table file contains too many entries      191                           WHEN RT-SHIFT-CODE (RT-CLASS-INDEX,
144                 WHEN     FALSE      also      TRUE      192                                             RT-STATUS-INDEX,
145    *          --------------------    --------------------  193                                             RT-SHIFT-INDEX)
146                    SET S4-TABLE-LOAD-ERROR TO TRUE      194                                    = WA-SHIFT-CODE
147                                                         195
148    *          Table file contains insufficient entries  196                              SET S1-PAY-RATE-FOUND TO TRUE
149                 WHEN     TRUE       also      FALSE     197                              MOVE RT-PAY-RATE (RT-CLASS-INDEX,
150    *          --------------------    --------------------  198                                                RT-STATUS-INDEX,
151                    SET S4-TABLE-LOAD-ERROR TO TRUE      199                                                RT-SHIFT-INDEX)
152                                                         200                                 TO DI-PAY-RATE
153    *          Table file is properly loaded            201                           END-SEARCH
154                 WHEN     TRUE       also      TRUE      202               END-SEARCH
155    *          --------------------    --------------------  203        END-SEARCH
156                    SET S4-TABLE-LOAD-COMPLETE TO TRUE   204            .
157
158              END-EVALUATE
159           END-PERFORM
160
161    *      Table-load termination
162           CLOSE PAY-RATE-TABLE-FILE
163           .
```

Using Argument Tables to Access a Multiple-Level Table Directly

Let's consider an alternate technique for PAYTBLE2's table (Figure 12-8, page 426), which consists of an explicit argument at the first level and positional addressing at the second level. In Figure 12-14, the arguments (Job classification codes) are defined as a separate, independent table. Notice the following:

1. The Pay rate table is positionally organized—it contains no arguments.
2. The table CT-CLASS-TABLE consists only of a table of Job classification codes corresponding to the entries of the Job classification table.
3. A positional correspondence exists between the two tables. For instance, entry 4 of CT-CLASS-ENTRY (value C1) corresponds to entry 4 of RT-JOB-CLASS-ENTRY.

In a program, you can search CT-CLASS-TABLE for a desired Job classification value, then use the resulting positional value to directly access the Pay rate table. To illustrate, assume the following:

1. WA-CLASS-CODE contains the desired input Job classification code.
2. WA-SHIFT-NUMBER contains a validated Shift number.
3. RT-CLASS-SUBSCR is defined as PIC 9(1).

In the code segment of Figure 12-15(a), you can see how the Pay rate table is accessed through the Job classification table. The Job classification table is searched for the input Job classification code. If found, the occurrence number of its index

Figure 12-14
Using a separate
argument table.

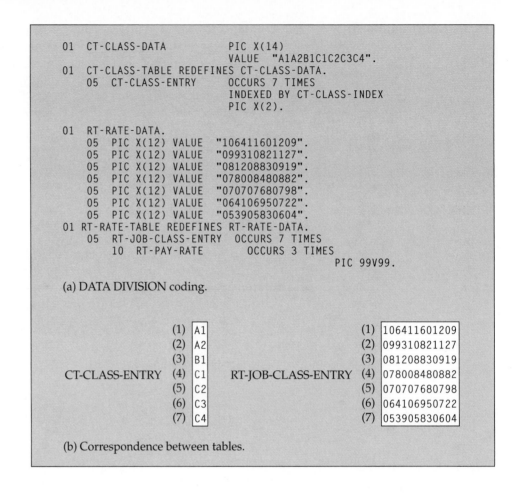

```
        01  CT-CLASS-DATA           PIC X(14)
                                    VALUE  "A1A2B1C1C2C3C4".
        01  CT-CLASS-TABLE REDEFINES CT-CLASS-DATA.
            05  CT-CLASS-ENTRY      OCCURS 7 TIMES
                                    INDEXED BY CT-CLASS-INDEX
                                    PIC X(2).

        01  RT-RATE-DATA.
            05  PIC X(12) VALUE  "106411601209".
            05  PIC X(12) VALUE  "099310821127".
            05  PIC X(12) VALUE  "081208830919".
            05  PIC X(12) VALUE  "078008480882".
            05  PIC X(12) VALUE  "070707680798".
            05  PIC X(12) VALUE  "064106950722".
            05  PIC X(12) VALUE  "053905830604".
        01  RT-RATE-TABLE REDEFINES RT-RATE-DATA.
            05  RT-JOB-CLASS-ENTRY  OCCURS 7 TIMES
                10  RT-PAY-RATE         OCCURS 3 TIMES
                                    PIC 99V99.
```

(a) DATA DIVISION coding.

	CT-CLASS-ENTRY		RT-JOB-CLASS-ENTRY	
(1)	A1	(1)	106411601209	
(2)	A2	(2)	099310821127	
(3)	B1	(3)	081208830919	
(4)	C1	(4)	078008480882	
(5)	C2	(5)	070707680798	
(6)	C3	(6)	064106950722	
(7)	C4	(7)	053905830604	

(b) Correspondence between tables.

(CT-CLASS-INDEX) corresponds to the RT-JOB-CLASS-ENTRY subscript number. Before the MOVE statement, RT-CLASS-SUBSCR receives the occurrence number of CT-CLASS-INDEX through the SET statement. Note that the SET is used—rather than a MOVE—because one of the fields is an index.

An equivalent code sequence is shown in Figure 12-15(b), using the VARYING phrase with the SEARCH. The action of this SEARCH is identical to that of the SEARCH in Figure 12-15(a), except for its treatment of the variable named following VARYING. That is, each time the index of the SEARCH statement

Figure 12-15   Direct lookup through an argument table.

```
SET ST-CLASS-INDEX TO 1                    SET ST-CLASS-INDEX TO 1
SEARCH CT-CLASS-ENTRY                       MOVE 1 TO RT-CLASS-SUBSCR
    AT END                                  SEARCH CT-CLASS-ENTRY VARYING RT-CLASS-SUBSCR
       SET S1-PAY-RATE-NOT-FOUND TO TRUE       AT END
       DISPLAY "Invalid Job classification code"  SET S1-PAY-RATE-NOT-FOUND TO TRUE
    WHEN CT-CLASS-ENTRY (CT-CLASS-INDEX)          DISPLAY "Invalid Job classification code"
              = WA-CLASS-CODE               WHEN CT-CLASS-ENTRY (CT-CLASS-INDEX)
       SET RT-CLASS-SUBSCR TO CT-CLASS-INDEX          = WA-CLASS-CODE
       MOVE RT-RATE-TABLE (RT-CLASS-SUBSCR,       MOVE RT-RATE-TABLE (RT-CLASS-SUBSCR,
                  WA-SHIFT-NUMBER)                          WA-SHIFT-NUMBER)
           TO DI-PAY-RATE                             TO DI-PAY-RATE
END-SEARCH                                  END-SEARCH
```

(a) Setting the table subscript after the   (b) Using the SEARCH/VARYING.
    argument table search.

Note: For COBOL-74, replace END-SEARCH with period to end scope of SEARCH.

(CT-CLASS-INDEX) is incremented to the next table element, the VARYING data-item (RT-CLASS-SUBSCR) is incremented by 1. If the VARYING data-item is another index, its occurrence number is incremented by 1.

Note: Included on the diskette accompanying this book is an alternate version of the three-level program PAYTBLE4. The program, PAYTBLE6, uses a positional table for the Pay rate data and separate tables for each of the three codes.

Another Table-Accessing Technique

Printing a Table

When learning about multiple-level tables, it is easy to assume that table searching or processing must begin with the highest level index and progress to lower levels. This is not true. You can work through a multiple-level table by varying the indexes (or subscripts) as appropriate to your application. To illustrate, consider Figure 12-16, which is a simple printed summary of the Pay rate table used in PAYTBLE4. Headings and other descriptive information are minimized to focus on this program's table-processing aspects.

In the report, you see that the printed output is grouped first by the Job status code, next by the Shift code, and finally by the Job classification code. Obviously, this grouping does not correspond to the table levels (Job classification/Status/ Shift).

Figure 12-17 shows the program that generated this report. Let's first consider the DATA DIVISION entries.

DATA DIVISION Entries—PAYTBLE5

Figure 12-16's report includes three different line formats: two heading lines and one detail line. This is reflected in the code of lines 70–82 of Figure 12–17's program. The Status code line contains only the Status description (Permanent or Temporary). It is described by the record defined in lines 76–77.

As you see by referring to Figure 12-16, the detail line includes a Shift description and the seven Pay rates (for the seven Job classifications). Line 72 of the program reserves space for the Shift description. Lines 73–74, because of the OCCURS, reserves space for the seven Pay rates with numeric editing. The PICTURE—ZZZZZ.99—provides width for the rate field *and* spacing between respective Pay rates.

The Job classification description line is defined in lines 79–82. The filler of 14 and the H2-CLASS field width of 8 were selected so that the Job classification codes are printed directly above the corresponding Pay rates.

The needed report titles are defined—as tables—at lines 29–35 and lines 37–43. They are listed in exactly the same sequence as the corresponding entries in the Pay rate table. For instance, Temporary is the first entry at line 30 and TE is the first argument entry of the table's second level (see table entries, lines 50–56). This feature is utilized when printing the report.

Figure 12-16
A printout of the Pay rate table.

```
Permanent
             A1      A2      B1      C1      C2      C3      C4
     Day   11.03   10.42    8.54    8.21    7.44    6.81    5.68
   Swing   12.00   11.49    8.21    8.88    8.03    7.35    6.18
   Grave   12.54   11.77    9.57    9.20    8.38    7.71    6.41

Temporary
             A1      A2      B1      C1      C2      C3      C4
     Day   10.64    9.93    8.12    7.80    7.07    6.41    5.39
   Swing   11.60   10.82    8.83    8.48    7.68    6.95    5.83
   Grave   12.09   11.27    9.19    8.82    7.98    7.22    6.04
```

Looking at Figure 12-16's output, you can surmise that the program logic necessary to produce this report is similar to the following:

```
Repeat for 2 Status-codes
   Print Status-description
   Repeat for 7 Job-description codes
      Move Job-description code to output line
   Print Job-description code line
   Repeat for 3 Shifts
      Move Shift-description to output line
      Repeat for 7 Pay-rates
      Move Pay-rate to output line
   Print Shift-description/Pay-rate line
```

The PROCEDURE DIVISION of Figure 12-17 illustrates several new twists of previously encountered techniques:

1. The outermost PERFORM (lines 99–101), which controls the status loop, uses a beginning value of 2 and an increment of –1. This causes the permanent status group to be printed first, even though it is the second entry in the table.
2. At line 102, the Status description entry is tied to the loop controlling index with a SET statement. So, the desired description table entry can be moved to the output line at line 103.
3. The Job classification codes are moved to the output line by the code of lines 107–113.
4. Printing the detail line is controlled by the loop of lines 117–131. First, the Shift description is moved (using the same technique as for the Status description) at lines 120–121. Then the seven Pay rates are moved under control of the loop (lines 123–131).

If you look at the 200 module, you'll see that the outer loop encompasses every statement in the module. So, it would be possible to remove the PERFORM (lines 99–101) and the END-PERFORM (line 137) and insert the repetition in the out-of-line PERFORM at line 93. That is, this PERFORM becomes

```
PERFORM 200-PRINT-TABLE-LINES
   VARYING RT-STATUS-INDEX
        FROM 2 BY -1
        UNTIL RT-STATUS-INDEX < 1
```

However, Figure 12-17's form is better programming practice because of the documentation value. That is, the statement that causes the value of the index RT-STATUS-INDEX to change is located within the module that uses it. In a large program, the module to be performed could be far removed from the module with the out-of-line PERFORM statement. This modification is necessary for COBOL-74.

Note: Another version of this program is included on the diskette accompanying this book. It is named PAYTBLE7 and prints the Pay rate table defined with positional entries (used in PAYTBLE6, which is also on the diskette).

COBOL-74

The modifications required by COBOL-74 are extensive because of the lack of the inline PERFORM. Figure 12–18 shows the COBOL-74 PROCEDURE DIVISION.

Figure 12-17   Printing a table—PAYTBLE5.

```
1      IDENTIFICATION DIVISION.
2      PROGRAM-ID. PAYTBLE5.
3
4    * Interplanetary Transport, Inc.
5    * Pay Table List Program
6    * Written by W. Price    1-23-95
7
8    * This program prints a copy of the
9    * Pay rate table.
10
11     ENVIRONMENT DIVISION.
12
13     INPUT-OUTPUT SECTION.
14
15     FILE-CONTROL.
16        SELECT TABLE-LIST
17           ASSIGN TO (system dependent).
18
19
20     DATA DIVISION.
21
22     FILE SECTION.
23
24     FD  TABLE-LIST.
25     01  TABLE-LINE              PIC X(65).
26
27     WORKING-STORAGE SECTION.
28
29     01  ST-STATUS-DESCR-DATA.
30         05    PIC X(9)          VALUE "Temporary".
31         05    PIC X(9)          VALUE "Permanent".
32     01  ST-STATUS-DESCR-TABLE
33               REDEFINES ST-STATUS-DESCR-DATA.
34         05  ST-STATUS-DESCR    OCCURS 2 TIMES
35                                PIC X(9).
36
37     01  SH-SHIFT-DESCR-DATA.
38         05    PIC X(5)          VALUE "Day".
39         05    PIC X(5)          VALUE "Swing".
40         05    PIC X(5)          VALUE "Grave".
41     01  SH-SHIFT-DESCR-TABLE REDEFINES SH-SHIFT-DESCR-DATA.
42         05  SH-SHIFT-DESCR     OCCURS 3 TIMES
43                                PIC X(5).
44
45     01  DS-DESCRIPTION-SUBSCRIPTS.
46         05  DS-STATUS-SUBSCR   PIC 9(1).
47         05  DS-SHIFT-SUBSCR    PIC 9(1).
48
49     01  RT-RATE-DATA.
50         05  PIC X(36) VALUE "A1TED1064S1160G1209PED1103S1200G1254".
51         05  PIC X(36) VALUE "A2TED0993S1082G1127PED1042S1149G1177".
52         05  PIC X(36) VALUE "B1TED0812S0883G0919PED0854S0821G0957".
53         05  PIC X(36) VALUE "C1TED0780S0848G0882PED0821S0888G0920".
54         05  PIC X(36) VALUE "C2TED0707S0768G0798PED0744S0803G0838".
55         05  PIC X(36) VALUE "C3TED0641S0695G0722PED0681S0735G0771".
56         05  PIC X(36) VALUE "C4TED0539S0583G0604PED0568S0618G0641".
57
58     01 RT-RATE-TABLE REDEFINES RT-RATE-DATA.
59         05  RT-JOB-CLASS-ENTRY    OCCURS 7 TIMES
60                              INDEXED BY RT-CLASS-INDEX.
61            10  RT-JOB-CLASS    PIC X(2).
62            10  RT-STATUS-ENTRY    OCCURS 2 TIMES
63                              INDEXED BY RT-STATUS-INDEX.
64               15  RT-STATUS-CODE  PIC X(2).
65               15  RT-SHIFT-ENTRY   OCCURS 3 TIMES
66                              INDEXED BY RT-SHIFT-INDEX.
67                  20  RT-SHIFT-CODE  PIC X(1).
68                  20  RT-PAY-RATE    PIC 99V99.
69

70     01  DL-DETAIL-LINE.
71         05                     PIC X(4) VALUE SPACES.
72         05   DL-SHIFT          PIC X(5).
73         05   DL-PAY-RATE       OCCURS 7 TIMES
74                                PIC ZZZZZ.99.
75
76     01  H1-STATUS-HEADING-LINE.
77         05  H1-STATUS          PIC X(9).
78
79     01  H2-CLASS-HEADING-LINE.
80         05                     PIC X(14) VALUE SPACES.
81         05  H2-CLASS           OCCURS 7 TIMES
82                                PIC X(8).
83
84     01  PR-PRINT-LINE-SUBSCRIPTS.
85         05  PR-CLASS-SUBSCR    PIC 9(1).
86         05  PR-PAY-RATE-SUBSCR PIC 9(1).
87
88
89     PROCEDURE DIVISION.
90
91     000-PRINT-TABLE.
92         OPEN OUTPUT TABLE-LIST
93         PERFORM 200-PRINT-TABLE-LINES
94         CLOSE TABLE-LIST
95         STOP RUN
96         .
97     200-PRINT-TABLE-LINES.
98    *    Print the status group
99         PERFORM VARYING RT-STATUS-INDEX
100                    FROM 2 BY -1
101                    UNTIL RT-STATUS-INDEX < 1
102            SET DS-STATUS-SUBSCR TO RT-STATUS-INDEX
103            MOVE ST-STATUS-DESCR (DS-STATUS-SUBSCR) TO H1-STATUS
104            MOVE H1-STATUS-HEADING-LINE TO TABLE-LINE
105            PERFORM 800-WRITE-TABLE-LINE
106    *       Print the Classification heading line
107            PERFORM VARYING RT-CLASS-INDEX
108                       FROM 1 BY 1
109                       UNTIL RT-CLASS-INDEX > 7
110               SET PR-CLASS-SUBSCR TO RT-CLASS-INDEX
111               MOVE RT-JOB-CLASS (RT-CLASS-INDEX)
112                       TO H2-CLASS (PR-CLASS-SUBSCR)
113            END-PERFORM
114            MOVE H2-CLASS-HEADING-LINE TO TABLE-LINE
115            PERFORM 800-WRITE-TABLE-LINE
116    *       Print the detail line w/Shift descr & 7 Pay rates
117            PERFORM VARYING RT-SHIFT-INDEX
118                       FROM 1 BY 1
119                       UNTIL RT-SHIFT-INDEX > 3
120               SET DS-SHIFT-SUBSCR TO RT-SHIFT-INDEX
121               MOVE SH-SHIFT-DESCR (DS-SHIFT-SUBSCR) TO DL-SHIFT
122    *          Move the seven Pay rates to the output line
123               PERFORM VARYING RT-CLASS-INDEX
124                          FROM 1 BY 1
125                          UNTIL RT-CLASS-INDEX > 7
126                  SET PR-CLASS-SUBSCR TO RT-CLASS-INDEX
127                  MOVE RT-PAY-RATE (RT-CLASS-INDEX,
128                             RT-STATUS-INDEX,
129                             RT-SHIFT-INDEX)
130                          TO DL-PAY-RATE (PR-CLASS-SUBSCR)
131               END-PERFORM
132               MOVE DL-DETAIL-LINE TO TABLE-LINE
133               PERFORM 800-WRITE-TABLE-LINE
134            END-PERFORM
135            MOVE SPACES TO TABLE-LINE
136            PERFORM 800-WRITE-TABLE-LINE
137         END-PERFORM
138         .
139     800-WRITE-TABLE-LINE.
140         WRITE TABLE-LINE
141             AFTER ADVANCING 1 LINE
142         .
```

The PERFORM/ VARYING/AFTER Statement

As you learned, the PERFORM with a VARYING phrase is a powerful tool for table processing. Another phrase can also be used with this form to simplify tasks such as multiple-level table initializing, copying, totaling, and printing. To illustrate, assume that you must add $1.00 to every entry of the three-level Pay rate

Figure 12-18   COBOL-74 PROCEDURE DIVISION for PAYTBLE5.

```
PROCEDURE DIVISION.                                    210-SET-UP-HEADING-LINE.
                                                          SET PR-CLASS-SUBSCR TO RT-CLASS-INDEX
000-PRINT-TABLE.                                          MOVE RT-JOB-CLASS (RT-CLASS-INDEX)
   OPEN OUTPUT TABLE-LIST                                          TO H2-CLASS (PR-CLASS-SUBSCR).
   PERFORM 200-PRINT-TABLE-LINES
        VARYING RT-STATUS-INDEX                        220-PRINT-UP-DETAIL-LINE.
              FROM 2 BY -1                                SET DS-SHIFT-SUBSCR TO RT-SHIFT-INDEX
              UNTIL RT-STATUS-INDEX < 1                   MOVE SH-SHIFT-DESCR (DS-SHIFT-SUBSCR) TO DL-SHIFT
   CLOSE TABLE-LIST                                    *  Move the seven Pay rates to the output line
   STOP RUN.                                              PERFORM 230-SET-UP-PAY-RATES
                                                              VARYING RT-CLASS-INDEX
200-PRINT-TABLE-LINES.                                             FROM 1 BY 1
*  Print the status group                                          UNTIL RT-CLASS-INDEX > 7
   SET DS-STATUS-SUBSCR TO RT-STATUS-INDEX               MOVE DL-DETAIL-LINE TO TABLE-LINE
   MOVE ST-STATUS-DESCR (DS-STATUS-SUBSCR) TO H1-STATUS  PERFORM 800-WRITE-TABLE-LINE.
   MOVE H1-STATUS-HEADING-LINE TO TABLE-LINE
   PERFORM 800-WRITE-TABLE-LINE                        230-SET-UP-PAY-RATES.
*  Print the Classification heading line                  SET PR-CLASS-SUBSCR TO RT-CLASS-INDEX
   PERFORM 210-SET-UP-HEADING-LINE                        MOVE RT-PAY-RATE (RT-CLASS-INDEX,
        VARYING RT-CLASS-INDEX                                          RT-STATUS-INDEX,
              FROM 1 BY 1                                                RT-SHIFT-INDEX)
              UNTIL RT-CLASS-INDEX > 7                             TO DL-PAY-RATE (PR-CLASS-SUBSCR).
   MOVE H2-CLASS-HEADING-LINE TO TABLE-LINE
   PERFORM 800-WRITE-TABLE-LINE                        800-WRITE-TABLE-LINE.
*  Print the detail line w/Shift descr & 7 Pay rates      WRITE TABLE-LINE
   PERFORM 220-PRINT-UP-DETAIL-LINE                             AFTER ADVANCING 1 LINE.
        VARYING RT-SHIFT-INDEX
              FROM 1 BY 1
              UNTIL RT-SHIFT-INDEX > 3
   MOVE SPACES TO TABLE-LINE
   PERFORM 800-WRITE-TABLE-LINE.
```

table. One way is to use nested PERFORM/VARYING statements, as Figure 12-19(a) shows. The sequence of actions is

RT-CLASS-INDEX is initialized to 1
RT-STATUS-INDEX is initialized to 1
RT-SHIFT-INDEX is initialized to 1
1.00 is added to RT-PAY-RATE (1, 1, 1)
RT-SHIFT-INDEX is incremented to 2
1.00 is added to RT-PAY-RATE (1, 1, 2)
RT-SHIFT-INDEX is incremented to 3
1.00 is added to RT-PAY-RATE (1, 1, 3)
RT-STATUS-INDEX is incremented to 2
RT-SHIFT-INDEX is initialized to 1
1.00 is added to RT-PAY-RATE (1, 2, 1)
$\vdots$

So, the ADD statement is executed exactly 42 times—once for each table Pay rate entry.

Figure 12-19   Accessing all elements of a three-level table.

```
PERFORM VARYING RT-CLASS-INDEX                    PERFORM  500-ADD-TO-TABLE-ENTRIES
        FROM 1 BY 1                                       VARYING RT-CLASS-INDEX
        UNTIL RT-CLASS-INDEX > 7                          FROM 1 BY 1
   PERFORM VARYING RT-STATUS-INDEX                        UNTIL RT-CLASS-INDEX > 7
        FROM 1 BY 1                                    AFTER RT-STATUS-INDEX
        UNTIL RT-STATUS-INDEX < 2                         FROM 1 BY 1
      PERFORM VARYING RT-SHIFT-INDEX                      UNTIL RT-STATUS-INDEX < 2
        FROM 1 BY 1                                    AFTER RT-SHIFT-INDEX
        UNTIL RT-SHIFT-INDEX > 3                          FROM 1 BY 1
      ADD 1.00 TO RT-PAY-RATE (RT-CLASS-INDEX,          UNTIL RT-SHIFT-INDEX > 3
                    RT-STATUS-INDEX,
                    RT-SHIFT-INDEX)                          :
                                                           :
   END-PERFORM
   END-PERFORM                                    500-ADD-TO-TABLE-ENTRIES
END-PERFORM                                          ADD 1.00 TO RT-PAY-RATE (RT-CLASS-INDEX,
                                                                  RT-STATUS-INDEX,
                                                                  RT-SHIFT-INDEX).
```

(a) Using nested PERFORM/VARYING statements.   (b) Using the PERFORM/VARYING/AFTER statement.

Exactly the same action results from the code of Figure 12-19(b), which uses the AFTER phrase. You should notice two items here:

1. The PERFORM/VARYING/AFTER may only be used in the out-of-line form; that is, it must reference a separate procedure. As you can see by referring to Figure 12-20's statement form, it therefore does not use an END-PERFORM scope terminator.

2. The code following the word AFTER has the same form as that following the word VARYING. Although not allowed in the statement, you can think of the AFTER phrase as equivalent to, for instance, AFTER *VARYING* RT-STATUS-INDEX.

As it is with the VARYING phrase, all identifiers, data-names, and literals specified in the AFTER phrase must be numeric or index items. The condition specified after the reserved word UNTIL can be any valid relation, class, sign, or condition-name condition.

Program Example— Processing Using an Input-Loaded Table

Introduction to the COBOL Institute of Technology

As a final table-processing example, let's consider the room-scheduling needs of the COBOL Institute of Technology. The Institute operates five days a week, with each day consisting of eight periods. Classes offered are scheduled (1) daily, (2) Monday, Wednesday, and Friday, and (3) Tuesday and Thursday. The Institute has 20 classrooms of various sizes. The dean of instruction maintains a manual room chart to keep track of room usage and scheduling. Figure 12–21 shows the programming specifications to computerize this application.

Each record of the input table file contains one room entry (first level) of the room table. The room-availability portion of the record is divided into five parts: one for each of the five days. Each day consists of eight positions: one for each period. If any period of a day is scheduled for use, the corresponding position contains a value X; otherwise, it is blank.

Remembering the principles you already studied from previous example programs, let's consider the program's modular organization. Assuming that the mainline module controls repeated execution of the program (as required by the user), the following first-level modules are probably necessary.

Figure 12-20
Format of PERFORM/ VARYING/AFTER statement.

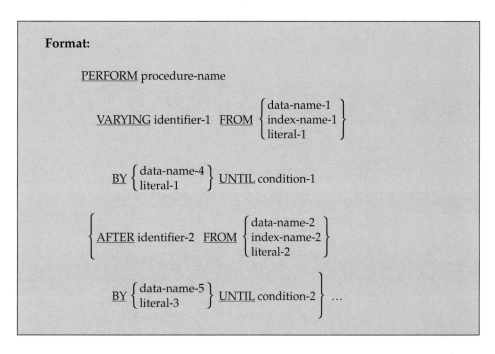

General announcement to the user

Table load

Accept user keyboard request (room number, days, and period)

Search the table for an acceptable room

Update the table as requested by the user

Write the updated table to a disk file

This program structure is illustrated by the structure chart of Figure 12-22 and the logic in the pseudocode of Figure 12-23. The completed program is in Figure 12-24.

Figure 12-21
Program specifications:
ROOMS program.

PROGRAMMING SPECIFICATIONS

Program Name: ROOM CHART PROCESSING   **Program ID:** ROOMS

Program Description:

This is to search a room chart for room availability. If a room is found meeting the specified needs of the user, it can be reserved.

Input File:

Room chart (table)

Input File Format:

Positions	Field	Description
1-5	Room number	
6-8	Room capacity	Whole number
9-48	Room availability	Space if period free, X if period not free

In the Room-availability portion of the record, each hour of each day is allocated one position, as illustrated by the following:

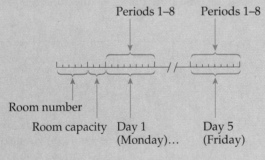

Periods 1–8   Periods 1–8

Room number

Room capacity   Day 1   Day 5
                (Monday)…   (Friday)

Output File:

Updated room chart

List of Program Operations:

A. Load the room-chart file into the program table.
    1. If the number of records in the table file exceeds the capacity of the program table, terminate processing.
B. Process each user room request of (1) minimum room size, (2) period, and (3) days required.
    1. Scan room table for first room meeting user's needs.
        a. If room found, display room information.
    2. Allow user to reserve the found room.
C. Write the updated table to disk.

Figure 12-22
Structure chart:
ROOMS program.

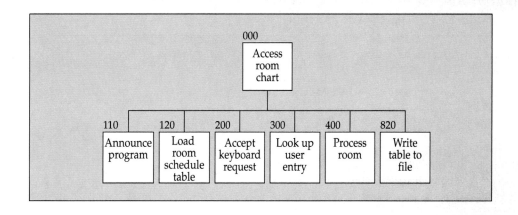

Figure 12-23   Pseudocode: ROOMS program.

PSEUDOCODE

Program Name: **ROOM CHART PROCESSING**   Program ID: **ROOMS**

000-Access-Room-Chart module
1. Perform 110-Announce-Program module.
2. Perform 110-Load-Room-Schedule-Table module.
3. If table loaded
      Repeat until No-more-assignments
        Perform 200-Accept-Keyboard-Request
        Perform 300-Lookup-User-Request
        If Room-found
            Perform 400-Process-Room
        Else
            Display "No space" message
        Query user about continuing
        Accept response to
            "More assignments" query
        Perform 820-Write-Table-To-File
   Else
      Display "Table overflow" message.
4. Stop run.

110-Announce-Program module
1. Display a description of the program.
2. Accept user response to proceed.
120-Load-Room-Schedule-Table module
1. Open room-schedule file.
2. Initialize Table-loaded switch to not
   loaded.
3. Perform the following varying Room-index
   until Table-loaded or Table-error.
      Read table record
      at end
        Set Table-loaded switch to True
      not at end
        If index value exceeds maximum
            Set Table-error switch to True
        Else
            Move record to table
4. Save room count from Room-index.
5. Close room-schedule file.
200-Accept-Keyboard-Request module
1. Repeat until Valid-seats-requested.
      Accept Seats-required
      If Seats-requested numeric and
      within limits
        Set Valid-seats-requested to True
      Else
        Set Invalid-seats-requested to True
        Display error message.

2. Repeat until Valid-days-requested.
      Display three choices:
        MWF
        TTh
        Daily
      Accept Days-required
      If Valid-day
        Initialize day-control variables
        Set Valid-days-requested to True
      Else
        Set Invalid-days-requested to True
3. Repeat until Valid-period-requested.
      Accept Period-required
      If Period-required numeric and
      within limits
        Set Valid-period-requested to True
      Else
        Set Invalid-period-requested to True
        Display error message.
300-Lookup-User-Request module
1. Move 1 to Start-search
2. Set Not-end-of-table to True
3. Set Room-not-found to True
4. Perform until End-of-table
        or Room-found
      Set Room-index to Start-search
      Search Room-entry
      at end
        Set End-of-table to True
      when
        Room capacity sufficient
            Set Room-found to True
            Check room availability
            If room not available
                Set Room-not-found to True
      Update Start-search from Room-index.
400-Process-Room module
1. Query user to reserve found room.
2. If user response yes
      Move X to Room/Days/Hours
820-Write-Table-To-File module
1. Open room-schedule file.
2. Perform the following varying Room-index
   until all table entries written.
        Move table entry to output area
        Write the record
3. Close room-schedule file.

Figure 12-24   The ROOMS program.

```
1        IDENTIFICATION DIVISION.                              79
2        PROGRAM-ID. ROOMS.                                    80      01  TC-TABLE-CONTROLS.
3                                                              81          05  TC-ROOM-COUNT              PIC 9(2).
4        *      Written by W. Price                            82          05  TC-START-SEARCH           PIC 9(2).
5        *      COBOL Institute of Technology                  83          05  TC-DAY-SUB                PIC 9(1).
6        *      1-23-95                                        84          05  TC-PERIOD-SUB             PIC 9(1).
7                                                              85          05  TC-MAXIMUM-ROOM-COUNT     PIC 9(2) VALUE 20.
8        * ROOM SCHEDULING SYSTEM                              86
9        *                                                     87
10       * This system processes a room chart stored in a     88      PROCEDURE DIVISION.
11       * data file. The chart accommodates up to            89
12       * 20 classes, 5 days/week, 8 periods per day.        90      000-ACCESS-ROOM-CHART.
13       * It is loaded into an array and accessed from       91
14       * the array. When a session is completed, the        92      ************Initialization Sequence************
15       * updated array is written back to the file.         93          PERFORM 110-ANNOUNCE-PROGRAM
16                                                             94          PERFORM 120-LOAD-ROOM-SCHEDULE-TABLE
17                                                             95
18       ENVIRONMENT DIVISION.                                 96      **************Processing Sequence**************
19                                                             97          IF S5-TABLE-LOAD-COMPLETE
20       INPUT-OUTPUT SECTION.                                 98              SET S4-MORE-ROOM-ASSIGNMENTS TO TRUE
21                                                             99              PERFORM UNTIL S4-NO-MORE-ROOM-ASSIGNMENTS
22       FILE-CONTROL.                                        100                  PERFORM 200-ACCEPT-KEYBOARD-REQUEST
23           SELECT ROOM-SCHEDULE-FILE                        101                  PERFORM 300-LOOKUP-USER-ENTRY
24               ASSIGN TO (system dependent).                102                  IF S6-ROOM-FOUND
25                                                            103                      PERFORM 400-PROCESS-ROOM
26                                                            104                  ELSE
27       DATA DIVISION.                                       105                      DISPLAY "No room available"
28                                                            106                  END-IF
29       FILE SECTION.                                        107                  DISPLAY "Search for another room <Y/N>? "
30                                                            108                  ACCEPT S4-MORE-ROOM-ASSIGNMENTS-SW
31       FD  ROOM-SCHEDULE-FILE.                              109              END-PERFORM
32       01  ROOM-SCHEDULE-RECORD          PIC X(48).         110              PERFORM 820-WRITE-TABLE-TO-FILE
33                                                            111          ELSE
34       WORKING-STORAGE SECTION.                             112              DISPLAY "***ROOM TABLE TOO SMALL***"
35                                                            113              DISPLAY "Press ENTER to abort: "
36       01  PROGRAM-SWITCHES.                                114              ACCEPT WA-DUMMY
37           05  S1-TABLE-SWITCH           PIC X.             115          END-IF
38               88  S1-END-OF-TABLE           VALUE "E".     116          STOP RUN
39               88  S1-NOT-END-OF-TABLE       VALUE "N".     117          .
40           05  S2-QUERY-RESPONSE-SWITCH  PIC X.             118      **************************************************
41               88  S2-VALID-QUERY-RESPONSE   VALUE "V".     119
42               88  S2-INVALID-QUERY-RESPONSE VALUE "I".     120      110-ANNOUNCE-PROGRAM.
43           05  S3-YES-NO-QUERY           PIC X.             121          DISPLAY "    ROOM CHART PROCESSOR"
44               88  S3-YES-RESPONSE           VALUE "Y" "y". 122          DISPLAY " "
45           05  S4-MORE-ROOM-ASSIGNMENTS-SW PIC X.           123          DISPLAY "This is the room-chart processor."
46               88  S4-MORE-ROOM-ASSIGNMENTS   VALUE "Y" "y".124          DISPLAY "It allows you to access the room "
47               88  S4-NO-MORE-ROOM-ASSIGNMENTS VALUE "N".   125          DISPLAY "database in order to schedule"
48           05  S5-TABLE-LOAD-SWITCH      PIC X.             126          DISPLAY "room usage for classes."
49               88  S5-TABLE-LOAD-COMPLETE    VALUE "C".     127          DISPLAY " "
50               88  S5-TABLE-LOAD-ERROR       VALUE "E".     128          DISPLAY "Press ENTER when ready to proceed. "
51               88  S5-TABLE-LOAD-NOT-COMPLETE VALUE "N".    129          ACCEPT WA-DUMMY
52           05  S6-ROOM-FOUND-SWITCH      PIC X.             130          .
53               88  S6-ROOM-FOUND             VALUE "F".     131      120-LOAD-ROOM-SCHEDULE-TABLE.
54               88  S6-ROOM-NOT-FOUND         VALUE "N".     132      *   Initialization sequence for LOAD module
55                                                            133          OPEN INPUT ROOM-SCHEDULE-FILE
56       01  WA-WORK-AREAS.                                   134          SET S5-TABLE-LOAD-NOT-COMPLETE TO TRUE
57           05  WA-DUMMY             PIC X VALUE SPACE.       135      *   Load the table
58           05  WA-SEATS-REQUIRED    PIC 9(3).               136          PERFORM VARYING RT-ROOM-INDEX
59               88  WA-VALID-SEAT-COUNT  VALUE 1 THRU 150.   137              FROM 1 BY 1
60           05  WA-DAY-REQUIRED      PIC X(1).               138                  UNTIL S5-TABLE-LOAD-COMPLETE
61               88  WA-VALID-DAY         VALUE "1" THRU "3". 139                  OR S5-TABLE-LOAD-ERROR
62           05  WA-START-DAY         PIC 9(1).               140              READ ROOM-SCHEDULE-FILE
63           05  WA-INCR-DAY          PIC 9(1).               141              AT END
64           05  WA-PERIOD-REQUIRED   PIC 9(1).               142                  SET S5-TABLE-LOAD-COMPLETE TO TRUE
65               88  WA-VALID-PERIOD      VALUE 1 THRU 8.     143              NOT AT END
66           05  WA-NUMBER-OF-PERIODS PIC 9(1) VALUE 8.       144                  IF RT-ROOM-INDEX > TC-MAXIMUM-ROOM-COUNT
67           05  WA-NUMBER-OF-DAYS    PIC 9(1) VALUE 5.       145                      SET S5-TABLE-LOAD-ERROR TO TRUE
68                                                            146                  ELSE
69       01  RT-ROOM-TABLE.                                   147                      MOVE ROOM-SCHEDULE-RECORD
70           05  RT-ROOM-ENTRY        OCCURS 20 TIMES         148                          TO RT-ROOM-ENTRY (RT-ROOM-INDEX)
71                                    DEPENDING ON TC-ROOM-COUNT 149                  END-IF
72                                    INDEXED BY RT-ROOM-INDEX.150              END-READ
73               10  RT-ROOM-NUMBER   PIC X(5).               151          END-PERFORM
74               10  RT-ROOM-CAPACITY PIC 9(3).               152      *   Termination sequence for LOAD module
75               10  RT-DAY-PERIOD-TABLE.                     153          SET TC-ROOM-COUNT TO RT-ROOM-INDEX
76                   15  RT-DAY       OCCURS 5 TIMES.         154          SUBTRACT 2 FROM TC-ROOM-COUNT
77                       20  RT-DAY-PERIOD  OCCURS 8 TIMES    155          CLOSE ROOM-SCHEDULE-FILE
78                              PIC X.                        156          .
```

Figure 12-24   (continued)

```
157   200-ACCEPT-KEYBOARD-REQUEST.                    208   300-LOOKUP-USER-ENTRY.
158       PERFORM WITH TEST AFTER                     209       MOVE 1 TO TC-START-SEARCH
159             UNTIL S2-VALID-QUERY-RESPONSE         210       SET S1-NOT-END-OF-TABLE TO TRUE
160         DISPLAY "Enter the number of seats <max 150>: " 211  SET S6-ROOM-NOT-FOUND TO TRUE
161         ACCEPT WA-SEATS-REQUIRED                  212       PERFORM UNTIL S1-END-OF-TABLE
162         IF  WA-SEATS-REQUIRED NUMERIC             213             OR S6-ROOM-FOUND
163         AND WA-VALID-SEAT-COUNT                   214           SET RT-ROOM-INDEX TO TC-START-SEARCH
164             SET S2-VALID-QUERY-RESPONSE TO TRUE   215           SEARCH RT-ROOM-ENTRY
165         ELSE                                      216             AT END
166             SET S2-INVALID-QUERY-RESPONSE TO TRUE 217               SET S1-END-OF-TABLE TO TRUE
167             DISPLAY "Invalid entry, try again "   218             WHEN RT-ROOM-CAPACITY (RT-ROOM-INDEX)
168         END-IF                                    219                   NOT < WA-SEATS-REQUIRED
169       END-PERFORM                                 220   *         Room size okay so check days and period
170                                                   221               SET S6-ROOM-FOUND TO TRUE
171       PERFORM WITH TEST AFTER                     222               PERFORM VARYING TC-DAY-SUB
172             UNTIL S2-VALID-QUERY-RESPONSE         223                   FROM WA-START-DAY BY WA-INCR-DAY
173         DISPLAY "The class days can be:"          224                   UNTIL TC-DAY-SUB > WA-NUMBER-OF-DAYS
174         DISPLAY "  1 - MWF"                        225                     OR S6-ROOM-NOT-FOUND
175         DISPLAY "  2 - TTh"                        226                 IF RT-DAY-PERIOD (RT-ROOM-INDEX,
176         DISPLAY "  3 - Daily"                      227                                   TC-DAY-SUB,
177         DISPLAY "Enter your choice <1,2,3> "       228                                   WA-PERIOD-REQUIRED)
178         ACCEPT WA-DAY-REQUIRED                     229                     NOT = SPACES
179         IF WA-VALID-DAY                            230                   SET S6-ROOM-NOT-FOUND TO TRUE
180           EVALUATE WA-DAY-REQUIRED                 231                   SET TC-START-SEARCH TO RT-ROOM-INDEX
181             WHEN 1  MOVE 1 TO WA-START-DAY         232                   ADD 1 TO TC-START-SEARCH
182                     MOVE 2 TO WA-INCR-DAY          233                 END-IF
183             WHEN 2  MOVE 2 TO WA-START-DAY         234               END-PERFORM
184                     MOVE 2 TO WA-INCR-DAY          235           END-SEARCH
185             WHEN 3  MOVE 1 TO WA-START-DAY         236       END-PERFORM
186                     MOVE 1 TO WA-INCR-DAY          237       .
187           END-EVALUATE                             238   400-PROCESS-ROOM.
188           SET S2-VALID-QUERY-RESPONSE TO TRUE      239       DISPLAY " "
189         ELSE                                       240       DISPLAY "The following room is available: "
190           SET S2-INVALID-QUERY-RESPONSE TO TRUE    241               RT-ROOM-NUMBER (RT-ROOM-INDEX)
191           DISPLAY "Invalid entry, try again "      242       DISPLAY "Do you want to reserve it <Y/N>? "
192         END-IF                                     243       ACCEPT S3-YES-NO-QUERY
193       END-PERFORM                                  244       IF S3-YES-RESPONSE
194                                                    245         PERFORM VARYING TC-DAY-SUB
195       PERFORM  WITH TEST AFTER                     246               FROM WA-START-DAY BY WA-INCR-DAY
196             UNTIL S2-VALID-QUERY-RESPONSE          247               UNTIL TC-DAY-SUB > WA-NUMBER-OF-DAYS
197         DISPLAY "Enter the class period <1-8>: "   248           MOVE "X" TO RT-DAY-PERIOD (RT-ROOM-INDEX,
198         ACCEPT WA-PERIOD-REQUIRED                  249                                   TC-DAY-SUB,
199         IF  WA-PERIOD-REQUIRED NUMERIC             250                                   WA-PERIOD-REQUIRED)
200         AND WA-VALID-PERIOD                        251         END-PERFORM
201             SET S2-VALID-QUERY-RESPONSE TO TRUE    252       END-IF
202         ELSE                                       253       .
203             SET S2-INVALID-QUERY-RESPONSE TO TRUE  254   820-WRITE-TABLE-TO-FILE.
204             DISPLAY "Invalid entry, try again "    255       OPEN OUTPUT ROOM-SCHEDULE-FILE
205         END-IF                                     256       PERFORM VARYING RT-ROOM-INDEX
206       END-PERFORM                                  257             FROM 1 BY 1
207       .                                            258             UNTIL RT-ROOM-INDEX > TC-ROOM-COUNT
                                                       259         MOVE RT-ROOM-ENTRY (RT-ROOM-INDEX)
                                                       260             TO ROOM-SCHEDULE-RECORD
                                                       261         WRITE ROOM-SCHEDULE-RECORD
                                                       262       END-PERFORM
                                                       263       CLOSE ROOM-SCHEDULE-FILE
                                                       264       .
```

DATA DIVISION Coding—ROOMS

Inspecting the first three divisions in Figure 12-24, you can see that nothing is really new to you. Some points that you might notice are

- Six program switches are defined (lines 37–54); you will see how each of them is used in the PROCEDURE DIVISION.

- Condition-names are associated with user input items (required seats, days, and period)—see lines 59, 61, and 65. These will be used for input data verification.

- The first-level table entry is defined with: (1) the DEPENDING ON phrase to control the SEARCH since the table will not necessarily be loaded to capacity and (2) an index to allow use of the SEARCH. See lines 71 and 72.

- The second- and third-level table entries use subscripts.

Loading the Table

This program's table-loading module is similar to that of PAYTBLE4 in Figure 12-13 (page 434). However, unlike the Pay rate table, this table is not required to have exactly 20 entries. The check is that the file does not have more records than the table allocation. So, the overflow test is done by comparing the index RT-ROOM-INDEX to TC-MAXIMUM-ROOM-COUNT (defined at line 85) at line 144. The table load loop is terminated when the S5 switch is changed either at line 142 (end of the table file—a successful load) or line 145 (more table records than allocated table entries—unsuccessful load).

Perhaps the trickiest part of this module is setting the number of table entries, TC-ROOM-COUNT. Notice that at line 154, it is decremented by 2. To illustrate the reason, assume that 16 table records are processed. Then the loop is executed 17 times in order to read the 16 records *and* the EOF record. At the end of the loop, the PERFORM/VARYING automatically increments the designated variable to the next value. So, the occurrence number in RT-ROOM-INDEX will be 18, 2 greater than the number of table records processed.

Accepting a User Request

Three input values must be accepted from the user: the required number of seats, the days, and the period. By using a PERFORM WITH TEST AFTER (for instance, see line 158), each input entry is validated before going on to the next. The code for accepting the number of seats required (lines 158–169) is typical of the three. You can see the validation at lines 162–168. The requested days' input is handled a little differently. At lines 173–177, the user is given a menu of the three day options. The two data-items WA-START-DAY and WA-INCR-DAY are assigned values that will control day processing, as you will see in the 300 module.

Searching the Table

The table search element of this program involves finding a room meeting the following criterion:

- Its capacity is equal to or greater than the number of seats requested.

- The room is not already in use on the requested days during the requested period.

Pseudocode to do this is as follows:

```
Move 1 to Start-search
Repeat the following until Room-found or End-of-table
   Set Room-index to Start-search
   Search the Room-table
      At end
         Set End-of-table to True
      Not at end
         Set Room-found to True
         Check Day/Period entries of table
         If not available
            Set Room-not-found to True
            Set Start-search to Room-index plus 1
```

Notice that if a room of sufficient size is found—but it is not free at the desired day/time—the search must be resumed. So, the next search sequence must start at the point where the preceding search ended. You can see this implemented in the code of lines 214–235.

1. The starting value of the index (RT-ROOM-INDEX) for the search is set to 1 from the variable TC-START-SEARCH, which itself was initialized to 1. (Refer to lines 209 and 214.)
2. If a room of sufficient capacity is found (lines 218–219), the period/days are checked for availability (lines 222–234). A detailed description of this technique follows.

3. If the room is not available, the room search must continue from the room following the current room. This is accomplished by setting the variable TC-START-SEARCH to the current occurrence value of RT-ROOM-INDEX, then increasing it by 1 (lines 231–232). Notice also that the S6 switch is set accordingly (line 230).

4. If the room was not available, the outer loop (starting line 212) is repeated. The room search at line 215 begins at the entry indicated by the value in the variable TC-START-SEARCH.

The check to determine if the day/period slots are available is done by the IF of lines 226–233. Remember, the required period is fixed (the input value WA-PERIOD-REQUIRED). The days are checked through the PERFORM at line 222 under control of the fields WA-START-DAY and WA-INCR-DAY (whose values were set at lines 181–186).

To illustrate how this works, assume the request is for Monday, Wednesday, and Friday; the value of WA-START-DAY would be 1 and of WA-INCR-DAY would be 2. Then the PERFORM at line 222 would execute using values for the subscript TC-DAY-SUB of 1, 3, and 5.

Other Modules

The remaining two modules are reasonably straightforward. The 400 module queries the user to determine if the room should be reserved for the requested days and period. If so, the X character is moved to the appropriate entries.

When processing is complete, the table is written back to disk. Be aware that this erases the previous copy of the table. In an actual work environment, strict controls are implemented to ensure that a "bad" copy does not replace a "good" copy—perhaps the result of erroneous entries. One method assigns a different file-name and keeps the last several copies for backup. Another creates a separate file in which all changes to the table are recorded. This is called an *audit trail* and provides data to reconstruct a file that somehow became corrupted.

Chapter Summary

Multiple-level tables contain tables within table entries. A two-level table contains two OCCURS clauses, one nested inside the other. A three-level table has three nested OCCURS clauses. COBOL-85 allows tables of up to seven levels; COBOL-74 allows tables of up to three levels.

Whenever a multiple-level table is accessed, the name of the table entry must be followed by multiple subscripts or indexes. A two-level table requires two subscripts and/or indexes within the parentheses; a three-level table needs three.

The PERFORM/VARYING/AFTER statement can be used to handle multiple-level table initialization, copying, totaling, and printing tasks.

Sometimes, table arguments and table functions are defined in separate tables. When subscripts are employed in the table lookup, the same subscript can be used for both tables. However, if the tables are processed with indexes, separate index-names must be defined and used for each table. The SEARCH/VARYING statement can be used to conveniently handle table lookups for separately defined indexed arguments and functions.

Rather than hard-coding table data directly into the program, input-loaded tables are often used. When tables are loaded from input records, each record typically contains the data for one table entry. When processing input-loaded tables, the programmer must provide appropriate logic to handle table-checking and limit considerations.

Exercises

Terms for Definition

multiple-level table
single-level table
three-level table
two-level table

Review Questions

1. To provide for lookup and retrieval from tables with separately defined arguments and functions, a SEARCH statement with the _____ phrase can be used.

2. COBOL-85 can handle multiple-level tables with up to _____ levels.

3. A three-level table contains _____ nested OCCURS clauses.

4. When an elementary field—whose own data-item description does not contain an OCCURS clause—is subordinate to two group fields that do contain OCCURS clauses, _____ subscripts and/or indexes must be coded within parentheses in the PROCEDURE DIVISION to identify the specific occurrence.

5. Instead of hard-coding table data into a program, the table data can be

    _____ .

Questions About Chapter Examples

1. In the PAYTBLE1 program (Figure 12-7), how would the table entries appear in memory if the PICTURE clauses were coded as X(13) instead of X(12)? (Also refer to Figure 12-4.) Would the program function properly?

2. In the PAYTBLE1 program (Figure 12-7), what would happen if the clause OCCURS 7 TIMES were coded as OCCURS 6 TIMES?

3. The DATA DIVISION in Figure 12-7's program segment was changed as follows. Study it carefully and compare it to Figure 12-7's code.

```
01  RT-RATE-DATA.
    05      PIC X(12)    VALUE  "10640993081207800707064105391".
    05      PIC X(12)    VALUE  "11601082088308480768069505831".
    05      PIC X(12)    VALUE  "12091127091908820798072206041".
01  RT-RATE-TABLE REDEFINES RT-RATE-DATA.
    05  RT-SHIFT-ENTRY              OCCURS 3 TIMES.
        10  RT-JOB-CLASS               OCCURS 7 TIMES
                                       PIC 99V99.
```

What changes are needed in the PROCEDURE DIVISION code to process the table in this form?

4. The PAYTBLE4 program (Figure 12-13) is designed to load a table of a set size from disk: seven Job classifications and three Pay codes. What changes must be made to the program if the number of Job classifications were changed from seven to eight?

5. What changes must be made to the PAYTBLE4 program if the number of Job classifications could be up to 20—but not necessarily 20?

6. How would the report of Figure 12-16 be changed if lines 100 and 101 of the PAYTBLE5 program (Figure 12-17) were changed to the following?

```
FROM 2 BY -1
UNTIL RT-STATUS-INDEX > 3
```

7. What would happen in the ROOMS program (Figure 12-24) if the ADD statement at line 232 were omitted?

Programming Assignments

Programming Assignment 12-1: Load Parts Table

Background information:

For certain activities, Tools Unlimited wants to build a table in memory from their inventory file. Each table entry should consist of the Product definition as an argument and the Product description and Price as corresponding functions. The table produced by this program will be used in conjunction with other programs.

Input file: Inventory file (INVEN.DAT)

Inventory record

Output-report format:

Program operations:

1. Process each input inventory record.

2. Print the two heading lines on the first page and on each following page of the report.
   a. Accumulate and print the page number on the first heading line as specified on the print chart.

3. Load the appropriate fields from each record into a parts table that contains 75 table entries. The table argument is the product identification. The table functions are the product description and price.

    a. Check the sequence of each record to ensure that the product identifications are not duplicated and are in ascending sequence. If the records are out of sequence, print an error message TABLE RECS OUT OF SEQUENCE.

    b. Check to ensure that not more than 75 parts table records are in the file. If there are, print an error message OVER 75 TABLE RECORDS in the product description field on the output report.

    c. Check to ensure that at least 15 parts table records are in the file. If there are not, print an error message LESS THAN 15 TABLE RECORDS in the product description field on the output report.

4. After all the table records are loaded, print the parts table list as specified on the print chart.

    a. Print the table occurrence number at which each entry is loaded.

    b. Print the detail line in accordance with the print-chart specifications.

5. Double-space each detail line. Provide for a span of 57 lines per page.

Interactive test option:

As an interactive option to this assignment, you should include the ability for the user to test table access in your table-load program.

1. The prompt displayed to the user should be

```
Enter the desired product identification (type END to terminate):
```

2. Accept the request from the keyboard.

3. If the user enters END, terminate execution of the program.

4. If the user enters other than END, access and display the description and price for that part.

5. If the product identification is not in the table, display an appropriate error message.

Programming Assignment 12-2: Federal Income Tax Computation

Background information:

A federal income tax register report must be printed. To determine the tax amount, the taxable income for each employee must be used as the search argument in a table lookup.

Input file: Earnings file (EARNINGS.DAT)

Earnings record

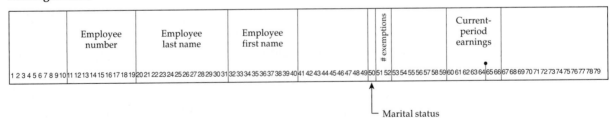

Table data:

Note: The following tax table, to be used for this assignment, is for the year 1985. Changes to the tax laws since then have reduced the number of categories. The 1985 table is better as a COBOL application.

If the amount of wages is:		The amount of income tax to be withheld shall be:	
Not over $1,420		0	

Over—	But not over—		of excess over—
$1,420	—$4,370	12%	—$1,420
$4,370	—$9,600	$354.00 plus 15%	—$4,370
$9,600	—$15,200	$1,138.50 plus 19%	—$9,600
$15,200	—$22,900	$2,202.50 plus 25%	—$15,200
$22,900	—$28,930	$4,127.50 plus 30%	—$22,900
$28,930	—$34,450	$5,936.50 plus 34%	—$28,930
$34,450		$7,813.30 plus 37%	—$34,450

(a) SINGLE person—including head of household.

If the amount of wages is:		The amount of income tax to be withheld shall be:	
Not over $2,500		0	

Over—	But not over—		of excess over—
$2,500	—$10,000	12%	—$2,500
$10,000	—$19,950	$900.00 plus 17%	—$10,000
$19,950	—$24,560	$2,591.50 plus 22%	—$19,950
$24,560	—$30,080	$3,605.70 plus 25%	—$24,560
$30,080	—$35,590	$4,985.70 plus 28%	—$30,080
$35,590	—$46,620	$6,528.50 plus 33%	—$35,590
$46,620		$10,168.40 plus 37%	—$46,620

(b) MARRIED person.

Output-report format:

```
          0          1          2          3          4          5          6          7          8          9
 1234567890123456789012345678901234567890123456789012345678901234567890123456789012345678901234567890123456
 1
 2
 3
 4 FEDERAL INCOME TAX REGISTER (12-2)                                            MM/DD/YY    PAGE ZZ9
 5
 6    EMPLOYEE     ------EMPLOYEE-NAME----   M   NO.   CURR PER.   ANNUALIZED     TAXABLE          TAX
 7     NUMBER    LAST          FIRST         S   EX.   EARNINGS     EARNINGS      EARNINGS       AMOUNT
 8
 9 999-99-9999  XXXXXXXXXXX XXXXXXXXX        X   99   ZZ,ZZZ.99   ZZZ,ZZZ.99   ZZZ,ZZZ.99   ZZ,ZZZ.99
10
11 999-99-9999  XXXXXXXXXXX XXXXXXXXX        X   99   ZZ,ZZZ.99   ZZZ,ZZZ.99   ZZZ,ZZZ.99   ZZ,ZZZ.99
12
13
14
```

Program operations:

1. You should either hard-code this table or create a separate table file and load it, as directed by your instructor.

2. Process each input earnings record.

3. Print the three heading lines on the first page and on each following page of the report.
   a. Print the run date on the first heading line as specified on the print chart.
   b. Accumulate and print the page number on the first heading line as specified on the print chart.

4. For each earnings record, do the following:
   a. Calculate the annualized earnings by multiplying the current-period-earnings field by 12 (the pay periods are monthly; 12 monthly pay periods per year).
   b. Calculate the taxable earnings by multiplying the number of withholding exemptions by $1,000.00 (the standard deduction) and subtract the product from the annualized earnings.
   c. Calculate the annualized federal tax amount from the tax table in accordance with the value of the marital status field. (An S in the marital status field indicates single; an H means head of household; M indicates married.)
   d. Divide the annualized federal tax amount by 12 to equal the federal tax withholding amount for this-period earnings.
   e. Print the detail line in accordance with the print-chart specifications.

5. Double-space each detail line. Provide for a span of 57 lines per page.

Programming Assignment 12-3: Load, Analyze, and Print Temperature Log

Background information:

The computer center manager of Coastaltown, U.S.A., likes the interactive access he has to his temperature data (Assignment 11-6), but now he wants more. In particular, he needs a report listing daily temperature highs and lows, monthly highs and lows, and the yearly high and low.

Input file: Temperature file (TEMPER.DAT)

Temperature record

Output-report format:

```
          0         1         2         3         4         5         6         7         8         9
   1234567890123456789012345678901234567890123456789012345678901234567890123456789012345678901234567890 1
 4 ANNUAL TEMPERATURE LOG - BY DAY (12-3)                                          MM/DD/YY   PAGE 9      ← Low-temperature line
 7 JANUARY      1-XXX   2-XXX   3-XXX   4-XXX   5-XXX   6-XXX   7-XXX   8-XXX   9-XXX  10-XXX ←
 8               XXX     XXX     XXX     XXX     XXX     XXX     XXX     XXX     XXX     XXX  ←            High-temperature line
10             11-XXX  12-XXX  13-XXX  14-XXX  15-XXX  16-XXX  17-XXX  18-XXX  19-XXX  20-XXX
11               XXX     XXX     XXX     XXX     XXX     XXX     XXX     XXX     XXX     XXX
13             21-XXX  22-XXX  23-XXX  24-XXX  25-XXX  26-XXX  27-XXX  28-XXX  29-XXX  30-XXX  31-XXX     Example of month-highest indication
14               XXX     XXX     XXX     XXX     XXX     XXX     XXX     XXX     XXX     XXX     XXX
19 DECEMBER     1-XXX   2-XXX   3-XXX   4-XXX   5-XXX   6-XXX   7-XXX   8-XXX   9-XXX  10-XXXH ←
20               XXX     XXX     XXX     XXX     XXX     XXX     XXX     XXX     XXX     XXX
22             11-XXX  12-XXX  13-XXX  14-XXX  15-XXX  16-XXX  17-XXX  18-XXX  19-XXX  20-XXX
23               XXX     XXX     XXX     XXX     XXX     XXX     XXX     XXX     XXX    XXXL ←             Example of month-lowest indication
25             21-XXX  22-XXX  23-XXX  24-XXX  25-XXX  26-XXX  27-XXX  28-XXX  29-XXX  30-XXX  31-XXX
26               XXX     XXX     XXX     XXX     XXX     XXX     XXX     XXX     XXX     XXX     XXX
31                             HOTTEST DAY OF THE YEAR   ZZ9- MM/DD
32                             COLDEST DAY OF THE YEAR   ZZ9- MM/DD
34                             TEMPERATURES RECORDED FOR ZZ9 DAYS
```

Program operations:

1. Read each input temperature record. Load the high and low temperatures into a table at the appropriate date location.
   a. If a record has an invalid date, bypass that record; no error message needs to be printed.
   b. If any one date has more than one record, identify the error condition by storing asterisks (***) for that day's temperatures.

2. After all temperatures are loaded, determine the following:
   a. The highest high temperature for each month.
   b. The lowest low temperature for each month.

3. Print the annual temperature log as specified on the print chart.
   a. Print the heading line on the first page and on each following page of the report.
      ■ Print the run-date on the first heading line as specified on the print chart.
      ■ Accumulate and print the page number on the first heading line as specified on the print chart.

b. Print the set of six detail lines for each of the 12 months in accordance with the print-chart specifications.

- Left-justify the zero-suppressed temperature adjacent to the hyphen that separates the day number from the temperature. For example, a temperature of 9 degrees on January 1st should be printed as 1-9; a temperature of 32 degrees on January 1st should be printed as 1-32.
- Print the letter H immediately to the right of the highest temperature for each month. Print the letter L immediately to the left of the lowest temperature for each month.
- If the temperatures are missing for a given date, print hyphens in the temperature areas for that date.

c. Print the following information at the end of the report:

- The temperature and date for the hottest day of the year.
- The temperature and date for the coldest day of the year.
- The total number of days for which valid temperature readings are present within the table.

d. Line spacing should be handled as specified on the print chart. Print four months per page; quintuple-space (five) between month entries. Print the report footing data on the last page.

Programming Assignment 12-4: Vehicle Insurance Lookup

Background information:

The management of Rent-Ur-Wheels has decided to require a special surcharge that is based on the vehicle type and make. They desire a report listing the daily rental rate and surcharge rate for each vehicle.

Input file: Vehicle file (VEHICLE.DAT)

Vehicle record

Vehicle surcharge table:

Make	Type				
	STD	LUX	VAN	SPTS	TRCK
CHEVROLET	2.35	2.97	2.62	2.88	2.61
CHRYSLER	2.50	3.03	2.85	2.99	2.87
FORD	2.38	3.02	2.81	3.02	2.85
OLDSMOBILE	2.62	3.14	2.75	2.92	2.72
NISSAN	2.89	3.26	3.00	3.07	2.99
TOYOTA	2.21	2.82	2.61	2.75	2.63
BMW	2.92	3.31	3.15	3.20	3.14
MERCEDES	3.12	3.57	3.33	3.40	3.32

Output-report format:

```
        0                 1                 2                 3                 4                 5                 6
   1 2 3 4 5 6 7 8 9 0 1 2 3 4 5 6 7 8 9 0 1 2 3 4 5 6 7 8 9 0 1 2 3 4 5 6 7 8 9 0 1 2 3 4 5 6 7 8 9 0 1 2 3 4 5 6 7 8 9 0 1 2 3 4 5 6 7 8 9

 1
 2
 3
 4  RENT-UR-WHEELS  VEHICLE  SURCHARGE  RATES  (12-4)                    PAGE  ZZ9
 5
 6
 7      LICENSE          MAKE                TYPE     RATE      SUR.        TOTAL
 8
 9      XXXXXXX          XXXXXXXXXXXXX       XXXX     ZZ.99     Z.99        ZZ.99
10
11      XXXXXXX          XXXXXXXXXXXXX       XXXX     ZZ.99     Z.99        ZZ.99
12
13
```

Program operations:

1. You should either hard-code this table or create a separate table file and load it, as directed by your instructor.

2. Process each input record.

3. Print the two heading lines on the first page and on each following page of the report.
   a. Accumulate and print the page number on the first heading line as specified on the print chart.

4. For each vehicle record, do the following:
   a. Use the vehicle Make and Type to look up the surcharge. If either field is not found in the table, print four asterisks in place of the surcharge output field; do not print a total for that record.
   b. Print the detail line in accordance with the print-chart specifications.

5. Double-space each detail line. Provide for a span of 57 lines per page.

Programming Assignment 12-5: Screen Display of Report

Program operations:

For either Assignment 12-2 or 12-4, write a display program that functions as follows:

1. Display the output on the screen according to the format of the print chart.

2. After each group of 18 records, temporarily stop processing so the user can view the screen.

3. Provide the user with the option of viewing the next 18 records or terminating processing.

4. Include headings on each screen page of display.

5. When the end of file is reached, inform the user and display a count of the number of records viewed.

**Programming
Assignment 12-6:
Adding Class Codes
to the ROOMS Table**

Background information:

The dean of instruction at the COBOL Institute of Technology is delighted with the room-chart program ROOMS. In fact, she is so pleased that she wants the program expanded to provide more versatility.

Input table file: Rooms table file (ROOMS2.DAT)

Table format:

Positions	Field	Description
1–5	Room number	
6–8	Room capacity	Whole number
9–128	Room availability	Value: Space if period free
		3-digit class code if period not free

Room availability field:
Consists of 5 day groups (Monday through Friday)—24 positions each
Each day group consists of 8 period groups—3 positions each

Program modifications:

1. Change the Room-available table entries from 1 position per day/period to 3 positions. These will be used to store a 3-digit class code, rather than the letter X.

2. After finding an available room, display the room number and seating capacity.

3. Provide the user with the option of:
   a. Reserving this room.
   b. Continuing the search for the next available room.

4. If the user wants to reserve a room, request the class code (3 positions) for the course. Accept it from the keyboard and move it into the day/period table entries for this room.

**Programming
Assignment 12-7:
Displaying a
Room Chart**

Background information:

The room-chart program must be modified to display the room chart for a selected room. The modification can be done by working from the original version of ROOMS or from Assignment 12-6.

Room-chart partial screen sample display:

```
Room: A112

Period  MON  TUE  WED  THU  FRI

   1    157       157       157
   2    200  200  200  200  200
   3    087  112  087  112  087
   :
   :
```

This partial sample display shows the following about the first three periods for room A112:

Period 1   Class-code 157 scheduled Monday, Wednesday, and Friday. Room not used Tuesday and Thursday.

Period 2   Class-code 200 scheduled daily.

Period 3   Class-code 087 scheduled Monday, Wednesday, and Friday. Class-code 112 scheduled Tuesday and Thursday.

Note: If the Assignment 12-6 modification is not made to the original ROOMS program, then the letter X will be displayed in place of the class code.

Program operations:

1. Request the room number from the user; accept the user response.

2. Search the table for the desired room.
   a. If not found, display an appropriate error message.
   b. If found, display the room table (include all eight periods).

3. Provide the user with the option of displaying the room chart for another room.

4. Optionally, combine the room-chart display program with the room-scheduling program. After entering the combined program, the user must be given the option of room scheduling or room-chart display.

PRINCIPLES OF FILE PROCESSING

MODULE OBJECTIVES

The focus of this module is to provide you with some of the basic file-processing principles that you will apply in the next three chapters. From this module, you will learn about the following:

- Types of files as categorized by the type of data stored in the file and its usage.

- File-organization methods: sequential, relative, and indexed.

- File-processing modes: sequential, random, and dynamic.

- Principles of master-transaction file processing: batch processing for sequential files, and batch and on-line processing for random-access files.

MODULE OUTLINE

Types of Files
Master File
Transaction File
Summary File
Table File
Control File
History File
Journal File

File-Organization Principles
Some Elementary File-Access Concepts
Sequential File Organization
Relative File Organization
Indexed File Organization

Access Mode

Master-Transaction Processing
Master File Updating—Batch
Master File Updating—On-Line
File Maintenance

Types of Files

Until Chapter 11, each input file you used for programming assignments supplied data to be processed. The files were always referred to simply as "data files." However, Chapters 11 and 12 mentioned files containing table data—table files. Although the table file does indeed store data, it is common to categorize it by its predominant usage. In that sense, the classifications described next are commonly utilized.

Master File

A **master file** contains permanent and semipermanent data pertaining to a particular application. Most of the files used in your programming assignments are essentially master files. For instance, each employee record of EARNINGS.DAT (an example of a payroll master file) includes the following types of data:

Permanent	For instance, the employee's Social Security number.
Semipermanent	For instance, marital status and number of exemptions.
Cumulative	Total earnings for the current period and year-to-date.

These data types are common to master files.

Example data files used in this book suggest other types of master files. For instance, each record of an inventory file contains the product number, description, unit price, and quantity on hand. Each record of a student file contains the student number, name, and units completed.

Transaction File

In contrast, a **transaction file** is one containing data that is relatively transient. For example, in the payroll example, a transaction file contains records that reflect how many hours an employee worked during a given pay period. Transaction records for employees are processed against their respective master records to generate pay checks and reports required by the employer. At the same time, money earned and deductions for that pay period are usually posted to the master file.

Summary File

A file containing data that is extracted and reduced from the records of another file is called a **summary file**. Again, using the payroll example, departmental-earnings figures can be accumulated, summarized, and used to produce a departmental labor-cost summary file. Notice that in the payroll master and transaction files, the data entity is the employee. However, in the summary file, the department is the data entity.

Table File

From Chapters 11 and 12, you are basically familiar with **table files**. When table entries are stored in a table file, your program must include a table-load routine. Sometimes, large tables remain on disk during processing, which requires a table record-retrieval routine to access the desired table entries. As you will learn later in this chapter, another method besides sequential access to the file's records is required.

Control File

A file that contains a limited number of records to be used for program control or to run accumulative statistics is called a **control file**. For example, a control file for an order-entry system might include the next available order number. As a new order is entered, the order number would be accessed from the control file (for the current order), incremented by 1, then written back to the control file.

History File

A **history file** is maintained either to facilitate reconstruction of a master file or to permit retrieval of past transaction data. As you will learn, master-transaction processing produces a new master file from the posting of transaction data to the previous master. Both the previous master and the transaction become history files.

Journal File

A special-purpose chronologically sequenced history or audit file for on-line systems is called a **journal file**. A journal file contains the data that is needed to handle the subsequent reconstruction of events or data changes when such actions are necessary. As an audit trail, journal files usually contain "before" and "after" images of each master record updated and/or a record of each transaction passing through the system. A journal that contains only transaction images is alternately termed a **log file**.

File-Organization Principles

The way in which records are stored in a file and are accessible from the file is called **file organization**. The COBOL standards specify three file organization methods: sequential, relative, and indexed.

Some Elementary File-Access Concepts

Before considering file organization, let's briefly view the two broad ways in which data stored on disk is accessed. In all of your programming assignments, you read and processed records one by one—beginning with the first and proceeding to the last. This is sequential access because records of the file are processed, in sequence, beginning with the first file record.

On the other hand, what if you had to write a program in which a bank teller needed to obtain account information for each customer after he or she approached the window? Sequential access is totally impractical. You need the ability to access records from the file at random. So, you need random access to a particular record without looking at all of those preceding.

Sequential File Organization

Actually, the term *sequential* is somewhat of a misnomer because it implies that the records are in some type of sequence. Sequential file organization really means that the records are stored in such a manner that the only way they are available to you is one after the other—beginning with the first and proceeding to the last. All of the sample data files in this book so far are sequentially organized.

Usually records of a sequential file are, in fact, arranged in sequence—either on a key field or chronologically. For instance, a payroll master file is probably in sequence on the employee's Social Security number. A transaction history file is probably in sequence based on the date entered (chronological). Sequencing of the records depends upon the way the file is normally processed. However, even if the record sequencing within the file is completely random, the file is still considered a sequential file.

The major drawback to sequential files is that it is not possible to access a selected record directly without reading all records preceding it. However, for applications in which direct access is not required, the sequential file is effective. It is simple, usually requires the least storage of the three methods, and requires a minimum of processing overhead. Also, it is the only organization method that can be used with magnetic tape.

Relative File Organization

In Chapter 11, you were introduced to positional table organization. (Refer to the table of month names, Figures 11-9 and 11-10, pages 393 and 394.) Data from the table was accessible because the table argument (month number) corresponded to the relative entry number of the table name.

This exact principle is used with **relative file organization**, in which access to file records is by the relative position that each record occupies in the file. In a sense, a relative file is simply a disk-oriented table. The "slots" of the file, like the entries of a table, are numbered beginning with 1 and progressing to 2, 3, and so on. The file can be accessed sequentially by reading the records one after the other, or it can be accessed directly by specifying the slot, or **relative record number**, of the desired record—much as you specify the subscript of an array's desired element.

A relative file is best used when the record's key value is the same as its position in the file (its relative record number) or can be adjusted by simple arithmetic. For instance, assume that a company assigns each employee a number beginning with 1001 and progresses by 1 for each employee. Then 1001 is the first record in the file, 1002 the second, and so on. Note that the relative record number can be obtained by subtracting 1000 from the employee number. So if you need the record for employee 1837, you directly access record 837—without looking at any of the records preceding it.

The relative organization can be used whenever the record key field either corresponds to the relative record number or can be converted to it by a simple calculation. The advantage of relative organization is that it is efficient storagewise—unless the file's key-field values have a lot of gaps—and it provides extremely fast access with little overhead. One disadvantage is that it is only practical for applications in which key field values are issued consecutively (or nearly so). Most applications are simply not that way. For instance, an employee file in which the key field is the employee's Social Security number will have large gaps between the numbers of consecutive employees. Another disadvantage is that there are no provisions for alternate key fields, a topic you will study next.

Indexed File Organization

You encounter many types of indexes every day. For example, the directory of a large building is an index. To find the office of, for instance, Dr. Hargrove, you look up the name in the directory (index) and read the corresponding office number. Then you go to the office based on the indicated floor and room numbers.

Indexed files use exactly the same principle. That is, stored on disk are the data records *and* an index to the records. As an example, consider the payroll file containing one payroll record for each employee. The key field for the file is the Social Security number. The index is actually a table with one entry for each record of the file. Each table entry contains a Social Security number (key field value) and the disk location of the record. Figure E-1 illustrates this. So, if your program requires the record corresponding to the Social Security number 133 44 1121, the action is (1) load the index into memory, (2) search the index for the entry 133 44 1121, (3) obtain the corresponding record location or relative record number, and (4) read the desired record.

In Figure E-1, you can see that the records are in no particular sequence. This may or may not be the case; in some systems, the data records are also in sequence based on the key field. However, the index is in sequence based on the key field. This allows fast table-search techniques to be used when searching for the desired entry.

Figure E-1 A file index.

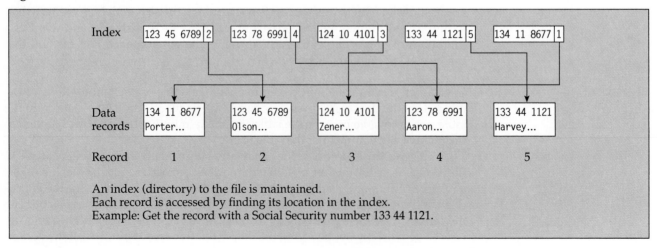

An index (directory) to the file is maintained.
Each record is accessed by finding its location in the index.
Example: Get the record with a Social Security number 133 44 1121.

An important feature of an indexed file is that no two records of the file can have the same key field value. This is necessary so that each record can be uniquely accessed through its key field value.

In many applications, the primary access to file records is through the designated key. However, in some cases, it may also be necessary to have direct access via another field of the record. For example, although primary access to the payroll file is through the Social Security number, some processing needs may require access via the last-name field. For this type of need, you can create one or more alternate key indexes. **Alternate key fields** can be designated to allow duplicate key values (more than one record with the same alternate key field value).

The advantage of the indexed organization is its versatility. Records can be processed sequentially—through any of the keys defined for the file—or directly. The disadvantage is the overhead, both in disk space required and processing speed.

Access Mode

The preceding section described methods of file organization. **Access mode** is a related topic that refers to the way in which file records are retrieved from or placed in the file. Three access modes can be specified with COBOL: sequential, random, and dynamic. With **sequential access**, logical records are obtained from or placed into a file consecutively in a sequence that is determined by the physical order of the records within the file. Sequential access can be used with any of the three file-organization methods.

Random access allows a program-specified key value to identify the record that is to be accessed from or added to the file. That is, a single, selected record can be accessed from anywhere in the file. **Dynamic access** combines random and sequential features. With dynamic access, you can access a particular record randomly—then access records following it sequentially. (You will see an example of dynamic access in Chapter 15.) Neither random access nor dynamic access is possible with sequential file organization.

Master-Transaction Processing

One of the most basic operations of business data-processing applications is updating data stored in master records as a result of transactions. This is commonly called **master-transaction processing** because data in a master file is brought up-to-date from transaction data. The way in which master-transaction processing is implemented depends upon the file organization and the particular needs of the application. To illustrate, let's consider an example.

Master File Updating—Batch

A typical student record-processing system includes a student master file that consists of one record for each student. The record includes permanent data such as the student's number (the key field), semipermanent data such as the student's last name or address, and summary data such as total units completed and total points earned. At the end of each semester, a transaction file is created that consists of one record for each course in which each student is enrolled. The transaction record includes the student number (the key field), the course information, and the grade. Figure E-2 shows segments of a student master and its corresponding transaction records. You know that these transaction records are associated with the master record because they both have the same key field value.

Master-transaction processing is the action of combining data from the transaction records with that of the corresponding master records to produce an

Figure E-2
A master record
and corresponding
transaction records.

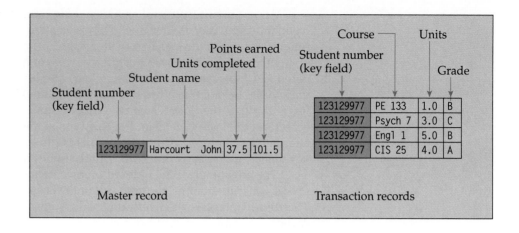

updated master record. For instance, in this example, total units for the four transaction records in Figure E-2 is 13.0. This is added to the units completed field of the master, giving an updated total of 50.5.

If both the master and transaction files are sequentially organized (as is always done with tape files), the updating process normally involves: (1) updating the summary data on each master from data in the corresponding transaction records and (2) writing an updated record to a new master file. Figure E-3 illustrates this process. The old master file then serves as a backup if erroneous processing occurs during the update procedure. The new master serves as the input file for the next processing cycle. This type of updating requires that both files must be in sequence on the same field.

If the master file is indexed, the file can be updated in place without regard to sequencing of either file. However, normally the transaction file is in sequence so that all the records for a given master are grouped together. This can have a significant effect on the processing speed. The updating process then becomes as follows: (1) read a transaction record (sequentially), (2) read the corresponding master record (randomly), (3) update the master record, (4) read subsequent corresponding transactions and update the master from each, and (5) when a transaction

Figure E-3
Sequential master-
transaction processing.

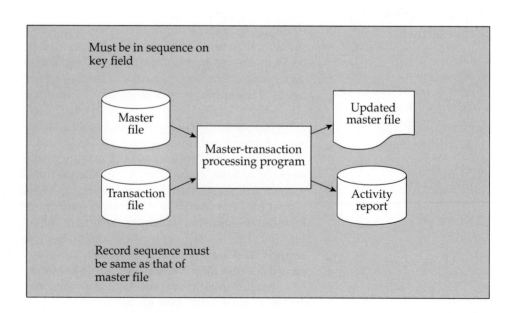

record is read with a different key field value, write the master back to disk. In the system flowchart of Figure E-4, you can see that the updated record replaces the original on disk. The simplest way of providing backup is to make a copy of the original file before processing begins.

In both of the preceding examples, transaction data is accumulated over a period of time and then processed in a single batch. This type of processing is commonly called batch processing.

Master File Updating—On-Line

Many applications simply are not amenable to batch updating. For instance, assume that you are a manufacturer and the wombat breaks on your zilching machine. So you call your supplier and ask, "Do you have a wombat in inventory?" If the supplier responds with, "We won't know until we make an inventory update run tomorrow," you will probably look for another supplier. Applications such as this need **on-line transaction processing**. Then the sequence of events becomes (1) the salesperson enters the product identification (key field value) for the wombat, (2) the program randomly accesses the desired record and displays it, (3) if the display shows that the item is in stock, the salesperson takes your order, and (4) the program updates the inventory by subtracting 1 from the quantity-on-hand field, then writes the record back to disk.

Obviously, on-line transaction processing requires: (1) a direct-access storage device (commonly a disk) and (2) a file organization that allows random access.

File Maintenance

The preceding examples all illustrate master-transaction processing in which one or more master summary fields are brought up-to-date from data in a transaction file. These are fields that change with each processing cycle (batch) or each transaction (on-line). This is a file *updating* process. In addition, master files must be *maintained*. The basic **file maintenance** actions performed on master records are (1) deletion of an existing master, (2) addition of a new master, and (3) changing field entries of a master. For instance, an employer might add a new employee or terminate an existing one. Or an employee might change her last name through marriage.

Although exactly the same program logic can be used for updating and maintenance, they are conceptually different. Updating summary data in the master means updating data that normally changes from one processing cycle to the next. Maintenance, in addition to adding and deleting records, changes fields of the master that do not normally change. Like updating, maintenance can be done either by batch or on-line processing.

Figure E-4
Master-transaction processing with an indexed master.

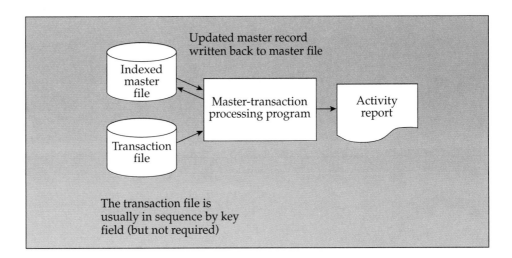

Module Summary

Common file classifications include master file, transaction file, summary file, control file, history file, and journal file.

The way in which records are stored in a file and are accessible from the file is called file organization. Three organizations are sequential, relative, and indexed. Sequentially organized files can only be processed sequentially (one after the other). Indexed and relative files can be processed sequentially or randomly.

Record retrieval falls into either of two categories: sequential or random (dynamic combines features of the two).

Master-transaction processing is the updating of data in a master file from transaction data. In batch processing, transaction records are accumulated over a period of time, then the master is updated from data in the "batch" of records. In on-line processing, transaction data updates the master data as the transaction is taking place.

Exercises

Terms for Definition

alternative key field	master file
access mode	master-transaction processing
control file	on-line transaction processing
dynamic access	random access
file maintenance	relative file organization
file organization	relative record number
history file	sequential access
indexed files	summary file
journal file	table files
log file	transaction file

SORTING

CHAPTER 13

CHAPTER OBJECTIVES

In Chapter 9, you learned how to write control-break programs. Recall that in order to do control-break processing, file records must be in sequence on the control-break fields. For instance, the MCTLBRK program processes a file of sales records, each containing information about one sale—including the product sold, the salesperson number, the branch office, and the state. However, before this report can be run, file records must be in sequence by state, then within each state group by branch office, and finally within each branch office group by salesperson.

This chapter's purpose is to teach you how to use the SORT statement to arrange file records into a desired sequence. From this chapter, you will learn the following:

- Basic principles of the SORT statement and its format.

- How to use the SORT statement to sort a file, without taking any other actions (sort only).

- How to use the SORT statement to preprocess records of the file before sorting it (sort with preprocessing).

- How to use the SORT statement to sort a file and then execute processing actions on records of the sort file (sort with postprocessing).

- How to use the SORT statement to preprocess the file before sorting it and then execute processing actions on the sort file (sort with preprocessing and postprocessing).

- How to use the MERGE statement to combine two files.

Sorting Concepts

Field Type

Fields can be classified as either indicative or control, in accordance with the function served within the record. Typically, most fields within a record are of the indicative type; they contain descriptive, reference-type, or quantitative data about the data entity to which they apply. Fields used to store an address, an inventory code, or a rate-of-pay are examples of indicative fields.

Control fields, as you learned in Chapter 9, are used either to explicitly identify a data entity or to sequence the data for a record within a report or list. An important type of control field is a key field. The key field is used to explicitly identify a logical record and to relate it to a data entity. For example, if a record contains information about a machine part, its key field is the part number. A record for an employee will probably use a Social Security or employee number field as its key field.

The key field usually serves as the basis for the file's organization. That is, records are arranged in sequence according to the value of the key field. In the patron list example of earlier chapters, the name field uniquely identifies the data entity and so can be considered the key field. (Although, in general, the name is a poor choice as a key field because two people can have the same name.)

Sometimes indicative fields are used as a control field for certain record-sequencing applications. For example, a zip code might be used as a control field when preparing output to be mailed.

What Is Sorting?

Sorting is the process of arranging items according to a certain order or sequence. File records are generally stored according to the value of a predefined field or set of fields. For example, Programming Assignments in earlier chapters used the Silicon Valley Manufacturing employee earnings file. The key field of this file is the employee Social Security number. Records in that file are normally arranged in order by the Social Security number, with the smallest number first in the file and the largest number last.

The Sort Key

The field, or group of fields, that contains the value used to sequence the file is called the **sort key**. In the employee earnings file, the sort key is the employee Social Security number field.

Often, files must be sorted based on two or more fields. For instance, the multiple-level control-break example of Chapter 9 requires that the records be in sequence by state, and within each state by sales region branch, and within each branch by sales representative number. This is an example of a **multiple-field sort key**; it contains more than one field.

As first mentioned in Chapter 9, when a sort key contains numerous fields, the most-significant field—the one that determines the overall order of the file—is termed the major field. The least-significant field is called the minor field. Others are called intermediate fields. So, in the multiple-level control-break example, the state, branch, and sales representative number are the major, intermediate, and minor fields, respectively.

Each sort-key field can be classified as to whether it is ordered in **ascending** value (smallest first, largest last) or **descending** value (largest first, smallest last) sequence. It is far more common to arrange sort-key fields in ascending value sequence, since that pertains to our normal numerical and alphabetical orders. In certain instances, though, it is more convenient to use outputs arranged in descending order. For example, a business might prepare a list of customers with overdue bills, arranging the customers in descending sequence on the amount due. This way, customers owing the most money are listed first.

Sometimes, records are sorted on multiple fields with one or more fields in ascending sequence and one or more fields in descending sequence. For instance, a student scholarship report might require that the output be in descending sequence on grade-point average (GPA), and ascending sequence on student last name. This way, students with identical grade-point averages are in alphabetic sequence within their GPA grouping.

The File to Be Sorted

To keep this chapter's primary focus on sort-program coding, the same file is used for two sample programs. It is an inventory file and has a record format shown in Figure 13-1. In both examples, the sorting is on three fields as follows:

Major field	Warehouse code (columns 3–4)
Intermediate field	Inventory value (columns 46–54)
Minor field	Part number (columns 5–19)

Remember, this means that all records with the same warehouse code (major field) are grouped together. Within each group, the records are in sequence by inventory value (intermediate field), and so on. If you need to clarify this, refer to Figure 13-2.

Basic Principles of the SORT Verb

The SORT verb provides the COBOL programmer with the ability to sort an entire file with a single statement. This statement requires three files:

1. The input file containing the records to be sorted.
2. The output file into which the sorted records of the input file will be written.
3. A work file that is used by the SORT as an area in which to rearrange the records during the sorting process. This **sort-work file** must be specified in the COBOL program.

Figure 13-1
Format for the
Inventory record.

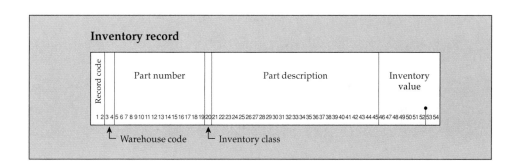

Figure 13-2   Inventory records sorted on Warehouse code, Inventory value, and Part number.

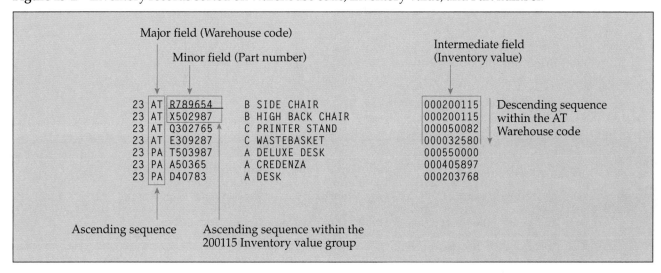

In its most basic form, the SORT statement followed by a STOP RUN can compose a two-statement program. The input is the unsorted file and the output is the corresponding sorted file. In practice, the SORT is most commonly used together with an input procedure to perform preprocessing on the input file, and/or an output procedure to perform postprocessing of the sorted output. First, let's consider the simplest form—sorting only.

All of the preceding example programs were introduced with complete program documentation in order to lay a solid foundation for overall program design and coding. This served as a consistent example of how you should design and code your own programs. By now, you should be experienced with these concepts. So in order to concentrate on sort-related topics, the inventory program documentation is somewhat abbreviated.

A Sort-Only Program

Figure 13-3 shows programming specifications and a system flowchart for a program to sort an inventory file. Observe that the only function of this program is to sort the records of the file into sequence in accordance with the values contained in the Warehouse-code, Inventory-value, and Part-number fields.

Figure 13-3   Programming documentation: Sort-only inventory-record program.

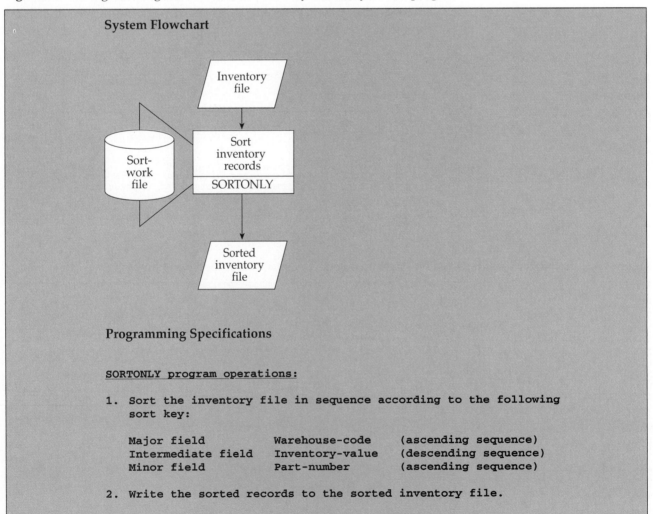

System Flowchart

Programming Specifications

<u>SORTONLY program operations:</u>

1. Sort the inventory file in sequence according to the following sort key:

Major field	Warehouse-code	(ascending sequence)
Intermediate field	Inventory-value	(descending sequence)
Minor field	Part-number	(ascending sequence)

2. Write the sorted records to the sorted inventory file.

This program is named SORTONLY to indicate that it is an example of a sort-only program. The program coding is shown in Figure 13-4. Let's consider this program's components.

ENVIRONMENT and DATA DIVISION Coding

SELECT Statement for the Sort-Work File

To the extent that the SELECT statement is used in this book, the sort-work SELECT is coded exactly like that for any other type of file (refer to lines 25 and 26 of SORTONLY). However, some computer-operating systems have a special implementor-name that must be specified in the ASSIGN clause. (For this requirement, you should check your specific compiler's reference manual.) Because most COBOL programs contain only one sort-work file per program, and because an application-dependent file-name does not offer much meaning for this file, the user-defined file-name of SORT-FILE is often chosen for the sort-work file.

The SD Entry and Corresponding Record-Description Entry

Like other files, the sort-work file must be described in the FILE SECTION of the DATA DIVISION. However, while an FD entry is used for regular files, an SD (Sort-File description) entry is required to describe a sort-work file. As with the SELECT, the form of the SD and its corresponding record definition—as used in this book—is identical to that of the FD.

Just as one or more 01-level record-description entries follow an FD entry, record-description entries for the records to be sorted follow the SD entry. Unless a special input procedure is used, the sort record must be the same length as the input file record. Within the record-description entry for the sort-file record, you need to specify only those fields that will be used to determine the record sequence. That is, you must name the sort-key fields (SR-WAREHOUSE-CODE, SR-INVENTORY-VALUE and SR-PART NUMBER, for the SORTONLY program). Definitions for fields that are not part of the sort key are not required and serve little purpose. So, all other areas of the record are simply designated filler.

Figure 13-4   COBOL coding: SORTONLY program.

```
 1        IDENTIFICATION DIVISION.              27
 2        PROGRAM-ID.    SORTONLY.              28
 3                                              29    DATA DIVISION.
 4      * WRITTEN BY T. WELBURN.                30
 5      * SILICON VALLEY MANUFACTURING COMPANY. 31    FILE SECTION.
 6      * MAR 28, 1986.                         32
 7      * REVISED 10/3/89 & 2/3/95 BY W. PRICE. 33    FD  INVENTORY-FILE.
 8                                              34    01  IR-INVENTORY-RECORD      PIC X(54).  } ← Input file to
 9      * THIS IS A SORT-ONLY PROGRAM.          35                                                    be sorted
10                                              36    FD  SORTED-INVENTORY-FILE.
11      * SORT STATEMENT PHRASES SPECIFIED ARE: 37    01  SI-INVENTORY-RECORD      PIC X(54).  } ← Sorted output file
12      *      USING                            38
13      *      GIVING                           39    SD  SORT-FILE.
14                                              40    01  SR-SORT-RECORD.
15                                              41        05                       PIC X(2).
16        ENVIRONMENT DIVISION.                 42        05  SR-WAREHOUSE-CODE    PIC X(2).   } ← Sort-work file
17                                              43        05  SR-PART-NUMBER       PIC X(15).
18        INPUT-OUTPUT SECTION.                 44        05                       PIC X(26).
19                                              45        05  SR-INVENTORY-VALUE   PIC S9(7)V99.
20        FILE-CONTROL.                         46
21            SELECT INVENTORY-FILE             47
22                ASSIGN TO (system dependent). 48    PROCEDURE DIVISION.
23            SELECT SORTED-INVENTORY-FILE      49
24                ASSIGN TO (system dependent). 50    000-SORT-INVENTORY-RECORDS.
25            SELECT SORT-FILE                  51        SORT SORT-FILE
26                ASSIGN TO (system dependent). 52            ASCENDING KEY  SR-WAREHOUSE-CODE
                                                53            DESCENDING KEY SR-INVENTORY-VALUE
                                                54            ASCENDING KEY  SR-PART-NUMBER   } ← SORT statement
                                                55                USING  INVENTORY-FILE
                                                56                GIVING SORTED-INVENTORY-FILE.
                                                57        STOP RUN.
```

PROCEDURE DIVISION Coding

The PROCEDURE DIVISION for the SORTONLY program is very short. It contains only two statements: SORT and STOP.

The SORT Statement

SORTONLY's version of the SORT statement includes, in addition to the SORT verb itself, four components: (1) the name of the sort-work file, (2) the sort-key fields, (3) the input file, and (4) the output file. These are illustrated by the SORT verb shown in Figure 13-5. Figure 13-6 depicts the SORT action.

After the sort-work file-name, you must designate the fields on which the sort must be performed (the sort keys). This is done with the phrase ASCENDING KEY or DESCENDING KEY, depending upon whether the sort-key field will be arranged in ascending or descending sequence. In this phrase, you list each of the sort-key fields in major through minor field order.

The reserved words ASCENDING KEY and DESCENDING KEY may be specified for each field or merely coded only for the first field and whenever a

Figure 13-5
The SORT statement from SORTONLY.

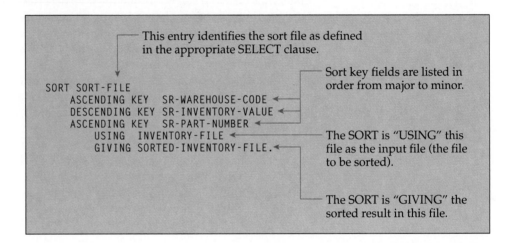

Figure 13-6   The SORT action.

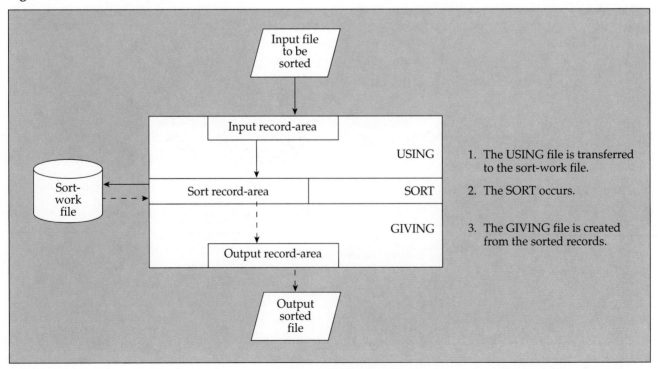

Figure 13-7
KEY phrase examples.

```
        SORT SORT-FILE
             ASCENDING KEY  DEPARTMENT-NUMBER
                            EMPLOYEE-NUMBER
             ⋮


        (a) ASCENDING KEY specified once.



        SORT SORT-FILE
             ASCENDING KEY  TERRITORY-CODE
             ASCENDING KEY  SALES-REP-NUMBER
             ASCENDING KEY  PRODUCT-CODE
             ⋮

        (b) ASCENDING KEY specified for each sort-key field.



        SORT SORT-FILE
             DESCENDING KEY  GRADE-POINT-AVERAGE
             ASCENDING KEY   LAST-NAME
                             FIRST-NAME
                             MIDDLE-NAME
             ⋮

        (c) Both ASCENDING KEY and DESCENDING KEY phrases specified.
```

change occurs from ASCENDING to DESCENDING or vice versa. Figure 13-7 includes three KEY phrase examples.

If you are sorting on a numeric field, the sorted result will be correct whether the field is defined as numeric or alphanumeric, unless the field may contain both positive and negative numbers. If so, then the field must be defined as an elementary item with a signed numeric PICTURE in the sort record. Then correct sequencing will result in which the records will be arranged in sequence—taking into account negative, zero, and positive values. Remember that if you define two or more numeric fields as a group item, the group item is treated as an alphanumeric field, exactly as with the MOVE statement.

The USING and GIVING Phrases

After the KEY phrase is coded, the USING phrase is specified to name the input file that will be sorted. When the USING phrase is coded, the SORT statement causes the named file to be opened, transferred to the sort-work file, and closed. Because this is handled automatically, you must not include an OPEN and/or a CLOSE for the input file. In the SORTONLY program, the INVENTORY-FILE is named in the USING phrase as the input file to be sorted.

Actually, the COBOL Standard allows you to include more than one file for input to the sort, as the following USING illustrates:

```
USING INVENTORY-FILE-1
      INVENTORY-FILE-2
      INVENTORY-FILE-3
```

In this case, the records from each of the three files will be combined and sorted. Of course, each of these files must be identified and defined in the ENVIRONMENT and PROCEDURE divisions.

The GIVING phrase provides you with the ability to name the sorted output file that will be created. When it is coded, the SORT statement causes the named file to be opened, handles the transfer of records from the sort-work file to it, and provides for the file's closing. As with the USING file, you must not code OPEN and CLOSE statements for a GIVING file. In the SORTONLY program, the file SORTED-INVENTORY-FILE will be created as the sorted output file.

Other SORT Considerations

Format of the SORT Statement

In the format of Figure 13-8's SORT, you can see the basic elements used in SORTONLY: ASCENDING/DESCENDING, USING, and GIVING. From the example, you know that:

- The sort-work file is identified as file-name-1.
- ASCENDING and DESCENDING designate the sequence of the sort key data-name-1. One or more sort keys can be included.
- USING identifies the input file file-name-2 or files. If two or more files are listed, the merged records from the files serve as input to the sort.
- GIVING identifies the input file file-name-3 or files. If two or more files are listed, their contents will be identical.

The DUPLICATES Phrase

The DUPLICATES phrase (not available in COBOL-74) indicates the action to be taken with duplicate values of the sort key. To illustrate, assume that you work for a mail-order company and you receive two prospective customer lists—File-A and File-B. You know that File-A contains some of the same names (duplicates) as those in File-B. Also, some duplicate records exist even within each of the files. In order to check for duplicates, you want to combine them into a single file in sequence on the name. For your particular needs, each duplicate from File-A must precede its corresponding record(s) from File-B. Furthermore, duplicates within File-A and within File-B must remain in the same relative order as in the original files. Figure 13-9, which includes two records for Tony Anthony in File-A and three in File-B, illustrates this requirement.

If the DUPLICATES phrase is included and File-A is listed first in the USING, then the order of duplicates is as illustrated in the "As required" example of the sorted file in Figure 13-9. Without the DUPLICATES phrase, their relative order is not guaranteed—it is up to the implementor.

The Collating Sequence

The sequencing order of characters in a character set is called the collating sequence and is commonly determined by a particular character's binary value. For alphabetic characters, the collating sequence corresponds to the alphabetic sequence. For example, "A" is sequenced before "B" (or "A" is "smaller" than "B").

Figure 13-8
SORT statement format.

```
SORT file-name-1 { ON { ASCENDING  } KEY { data-name-1 } ... } ...
                       { DESCENDING }

     [ WITH DUPLICATES IN ORDER ]

     [ COLLATING SEQUENCE IS alphabet-name-1 ]

     { INPUT PROCEDURE IS procedure-name-1 }
     { USING { file-name-2 } ...           }

     { OUTPUT PROCEDURE IS procedure-name-3 }
     { GIVING { file-name-3 } ...           }
```

Figure 13-9
Sequencing of duplicate
sort-key entries.

Input Files	
File-A	**File-B**
Tony Anthony (FA-1)	Tony Anthony (FB-1)
Tony Anthony (FA-2)	Tony Anthony (FB-2)
	Tony Anthony (FB-3)

Sorted Files	
As required	**Incorrect—not desired**
Tony Anthony (FA-1)	Tony Anthony (FB-1)
Tony Anthony (FA-2)	Tony Anthony (FB-3)
Tony Anthony (FB-1)	Tony Anthony (FB-2)
Tony Anthony (FB-2)	Tony Anthony (FA-2)
Tony Anthony (FB-3)	Tony Anthony (FA-1)

Unfortunately, the pitfall to this is that uppercase letters have a different sort value than lowercase letters. Even worse, uppercase letters are sequenced *before* lowercase letters with personal computers, but *after* with IBM-compatible mainframe computers. The following table is typical of what you might encounter with fields containing both upper- and lowercase letters; the alphabetic sequence is usually the desired form.

Sequencing of Alphabetic Fields		
Personal computer	**IBM mainframe**	**Alphabetic**
Alberts John	deHate Mike	Alberts John
DeHate Mike	Alberts John	deHate Mike
Dunlop Howard	DeHate Mike	DeHate Mike
MARTINI EMMI	Dunlop Howard	Dunlop Howard
MORTON JEAN	Martini Emmi	Martini Emmi
Martini Emmi	Morton Jean	MARTINI EMMI
Morton Jean	MARTINI EMMI	Morton Jean
deHate Mike	MORTON JEAN	MORTON JEAN

The SEQUENCE phrase of the SORT allows the programmer to control character sequencing when used in conjunction with an ENVIRONMENT DIVISION entry.

Designating a Collating Sequence

In order to use the SEQUENCE phrase in the SORT statement, the sequence must first be defined. This is done in the CONFIGURATION SECTION of the ENVIRONMENT DIVISION. The element of this section of interest to us is the ALPHABETIC clause of the SPECIAL-NAMES paragraph. It allows the programmer to designate any desired collating sequence for SORT statement use. Although this book focuses little attention on it, the example program of Figure 13-10 (to merge and sort the preceding File-A and File-B) sufficiently illustrates the techniques.

The key word ALPHABET precedes a user-selected name by which this sequencing list will be identified. Then the characters are listed, in the desired sequencing order. The word ALSO indicates that two characters have the same collating sequence value. So, "A" will be seen by SORT as equivalent to "a"—and so on. Sequencing of the digits is defined at line 43, where the word THRU indicates a consecutive sequence of the smallest through the largest. All characters not explicitly designated fall at the bottom of the list in their natural collating sequence order. Notice that the blank is included at the top of the list. If it were omitted, the blank would be placed after the last entry in this list, resulting in an undesirable sequencing of name fields in which names entries shorter than the allotted field are padded with spaces.

Sorting with Input File Preprocessing and Output File Postprocessing

Programming Specifications

As you saw, a sort-only program utilizes the USING and GIVING phrases of the SORT statement. Although SORTONLY is convenient for illustrating the SORT statement, you probably won't encounter a program that does nothing but sort; usually, other processing must be done. The processing may be entirely independent of the sort, on the input data to the sort, or on the output coming from the sort. If related to the sort input or output, then the special USING and GIVING phrases may be used.

Next, the inventory file sort will be expanded to process only selected records from the input file. Also, the program output will include an abbreviated report

Figure 13-10   Creating an alphabetic sequenced sort—SORTALPH.

```
 1        IDENTIFICATION DIVISION.                      45        INPUT-OUTPUT SECTION.
 2        PROGRAM-ID.    SORTALPH.                       46
 3                                                       47        FILE-CONTROL.
 4        *  W. Price  2/3/95                            48            SELECT PROSPECTS-FILE-A
 5                                                       49                ASSIGN TO
 6        *  Illustrating the ALPHABETIC phrase          50
 7        *  to control a sort sequence.                 51            SELECT PROSPECTS-FILE-B
 8                                                       52                ASSIGN TO (system dependent).
 9                                                       53
10        ENVIRONMENT DIVISION.                          54            SELECT SORTED-PROSPECTS-FILE
11                                                       55                ASSIGN TO (system dependent).
12        CONFIGURATION SECTION.                         56
13                                                       57            SELECT SORT-FILE
14        SPECIAL-NAMES.                                 58                ASSIGN TO (system dependent).
15            ALPHABET CASE-INSENSITIVE  ← User-selected name  59
16                " "                    is referenced in the  60
17                "A" ALSO "a"           SORT statement.       61        DATA DIVISION.
18                "B" ALSO "b"                                 62
19                "C" ALSO "c"                                 63        FILE SECTION.
20                "D" ALSO "d"                                 64
21                "E" ALSO "e"                                 65        FD  PROSPECTS-FILE-A.
22                "F" ALSO "f"                                 66        01  PA-FILE-A-RECORD         PIC X(93).
23                "G" ALSO "g"                                 67
24                "H" ALSO "h"                                 68        FD  PROSPECTS-FILE-B.
25                "I" ALSO "i"           Designated collating  69        01  PB-FILE-B-RECORD         PIC X(93).
26                "J" ALSO "j"           sequence for this     70
27                "K" ALSO "k"           program.             71        FD  SORTED-PROSPECTS-FILE.
28                "L" ALSO "l"                                 72        01  SP-PROSPECTS-RECORD      PIC X(93).
29                "M" ALSO "m"                                 73
30                "N" ALSO "n"                                 74        SD  SORT-FILE.
31                "O" ALSO "o"                                 75        01  SR-SORT-RECORD.
32                "P" ALSO "p"                                 76            05  SR-LAST-NAME         PIC X(13).
33                "Q" ALSO "q"                                 77            05  SR-FIRST-NAME        PIC X(10).
34                "R" ALSO "r"                                 78            05                       PIC X(70).
35                "S" ALSO "s"                                 79
36                "T" ALSO "t"                                 80
37                "U" ALSO "u"                                 81        PROCEDURE DIVISION.
38                "V" ALSO "v"                                 82
39                "W" ALSO "w"                                 83        000-SORT-INVENTORY-RECORDS.
40                "X" ALSO "x"                                 84            SORT SORT-FILE
41                "Y" ALSO "y"                                 85                ASCENDING KEY   SR-LAST-NAME
42                "Z" ALSO "z"                                 86                                SR-FIRST-NAME
43                "0" THRU "9".                               87                WITH DUPLICATES IN ORDER
44                                                            88                COLLATING SEQUENCE IS CASE-INSENSITIVE
                                                              89                USING PROSPECTS-FILE-A
                                                              90                      PROSPECTS-FILE-B
                                                              91                GIVING SORTED-PROSPECTS-FILE.
                                                              92            STOP RUN.
```

that lists each processed record. This requires preprocessing the input file and postprocessing the output file.

Figure 13-11 shows programming documentation for a sort program with input file preprocessing and output file postprocessing. Here, the preprocessing action is merely selecting records according to the contents of one of the fields. However, the preprocessing requirements could include any of the principles you studied in previous chapters. You could reformat the input records, summarize the data from multiple records into a single record, validate the input fields, and so on. Similarly, the postprocessing requirements could be every bit as complex—including control-break report generation, summarizing, and so on.

To accomplish these tasks, the SORT statement allows you to designate preprocessing and postprocessing procedures. Without focusing explicitly on the SORT statement, let's consider the logic of how this might be done.

Figure 13-12's pseudocode gives you a broad idea of what to expect in this type of program. Basically, you can think of the input and output procedures

Figure 13-11   Programming documentation: Sort with preprocessing of the input-inventory file and postprocessing of the sorted file.

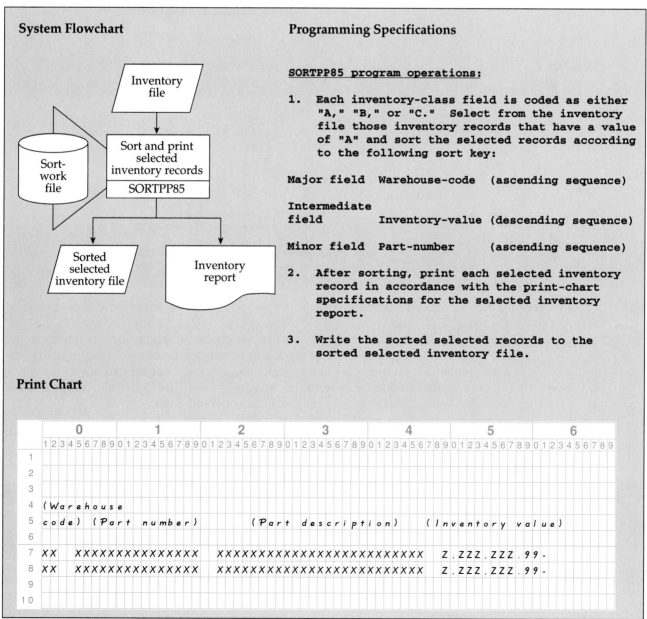

System Flowchart

Inventory file

Sort-work file

Sort and print selected inventory records

SORTPP85

Sorted selected inventory file

Inventory report

Programming Specifications

SORTPP85 program operations:

1. Each inventory-class field is coded as either "A," "B," or "C." Select from the inventory file those inventory records that have a value of "A" and sort the selected records according to the following sort key:

Major field   Warehouse-code   (ascending sequence)

Intermediate
field   Inventory-value (descending sequence)

Minor field   Part-number   (ascending sequence)

2. After sorting, print each selected inventory record in accordance with the print-chart specifications for the selected inventory report.

3. Write the sorted selected records to the sorted selected inventory file.

Print Chart

```
              0                1                2                3                4                5                6
    1 2 3 4 5 6 7 8 9 0 1 2 3 4 5 6 7 8 9 0 1 2 3 4 5 6 7 8 9 0 1 2 3 4 5 6 7 8 9 0 1 2 3 4 5 6 7 8 9 0 1 2 3 4 5 6 7 8 9 0 1 2 3 4 5 6 7 8 9
 1
 2
 3
 4  (Warehouse
 5  code)  (Part  number)              (Part  description)      (Inventory  value)
 6
 7  XX    XXXXXXXXXXXXXXX    XXXXXXXXXXXXXXXXXXXXXXXXXXX    Z.ZZZ.ZZZ.99-
 8  XX    XXXXXXXXXXXXXXX    XXXXXXXXXXXXXXXXXXXXXXXXXXX    Z.ZZZ.ZZZ.99-
 9
10
```

Figure 13-12
Generalization of the pseudocode for sort with input-file preprocessing and output-file postprocessing.

```
              Sort-procedure.
                Sort sort-file
                  Keys as required
                  Perform Input-procedure
                  Perform Output-procedure
                Stop run.

              Input-procedure.
                Main module.
                  Open input-file.
                  Perform while not EOF.
                    Read input-file
                      At end
                        Set EOF to true
                      Not at end
                        Perform Check-record.
                  Close input-file.

                Check-record module.
                  If Class = A
                    Move input record to sort area.
                    Write record to sort-file.

              Output-procedure.
                Main module.
                  Open report-file.
                  Open output-file.
                  Perform while not EOF
                    Read sort-file
                      At end
                        Set EOF to true
                      Not at end
                        Perform Process-record.
                  Close input-file.
                  Close output-file.

                Process-record module.
                  Move fields to report-line.
                  Write report-line.
                  Move record to output-file area.
                  Write output-record.
```

almost as independent programs within the main program. For example, the input procedure includes the three major components: initialization, processing, and termination. Records are read from the input file, the appropriate field is checked, and qualifying records are written to the sort file. The output procedure is much like simple report generation programs you wrote earlier.

There are four new elements needed for using procedures with the SORT: the INPUT PROCEDURE phrase, the OUTPUT PROCEDURE phrase, the RELEASE statement, and the RETURN statement. Let's first consider these two statements.

The RELEASE and RETURN Statements

In the last statement of the pseudocode input-procedure, the selected input record is written to the sort file. However, the action is not performed with a WRITE statement: COBOL includes the special statement RELEASE. It is used to transfer a record from the sort-work file record-area to the sort-work file. Its function is identical to that of a WRITE operation to an output file. This statement can be specified only within an INPUT PROCEDURE.

For input, the RETURN statement corresponds to the READ. It causes a record to be retrieved from the sort-work file and placed in the sort-work file record-area. Like the READ statement, it requires an AT END clause and can include NOT AT END and END-RETURN. The RETURN statement can be specified only within an OUTPUT PROCEDURE.

The overall process is illustrated in Figure 13-13.

The Sort Program

The complete COBOL-85 version of the preprocessing/postprocessing sort program (SORTPP85) is shown in Figure 13-14. Because of this program's record-checking and report-creation needs, its ENVIRONMENT and DATA DIVISION entries differ slightly from those of SORTONLY. Specifically, an additional file must be defined for the report output. More of the individual fields of the input and sort file must be explicitly indicated as they are needed for the input filtering and the report generation. Also, a program switch must be established.

Although WORKING-STORAGE SECTION definition of input and output records is generally recommended in this text, notice that FILE SECTION definition was used in this chapter. This is done to keep these sort programs shorter and more straightforward so that you can focus upon the sort-related processing. However, WORKING-STORAGE SECTION record-definition is recommended for more complex sort programs.

At lines 88 and 89, the input and output procedures are designated. During execution of the sort, the following action takes place:

1. The input procedure is performed (thereby creating the sort-work file from the input inventory file). You can think of the INPUT PROCEDURE

Figure 13-13
Schematic representation of sort with input-file preprocessing and output-file postprocessing.

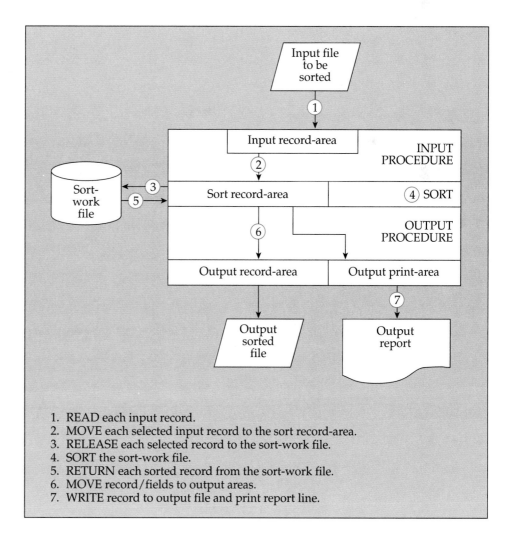

1. READ each input record.
2. MOVE each selected input record to the sort record-area.
3. RELEASE each selected record to the sort-work file.
4. SORT the sort-work file.
5. RETURN each sorted record from the sort-work file.
6. MOVE record/fields to output areas.
7. WRITE record to output file and print report line.

Figure 13-14   Sort with preprocessing of the input-inventory file and postprocessing of the sorted file—
SORTPP85.

```
1        IDENTIFICATION DIVISION.
2        PROGRAM-ID.    SORTPP85.
3
4     *    Written by T. Welburn.
5     *    Silicon Valley Manufacturing Company.
6     *    MAR 28, 1986.
7     *    Revised 10/3/89, 2/3/95 by W. Price.
8
9     *    This is a sort program with preprocessing
10    *       of the input file and postprocessing
11    *       of the sorted output file
12    *       Using 1985 Standard
13    *    Sort statement phrases specified are:
14    *       INPUT PROCEDURE
15    *       OUTPUT PROCEDURE
16
17
18       ENVIRONMENT DIVISION.
19
20       INPUT-OUTPUT SECTION.
21
22       FILE-CONTROL.
23          SELECT INVENTORY-FILE
24             ASSIGN TO (system dependent).
25
26          SELECT INVENTORY-REPORT-FILE
27             ASSIGN TO (system dependent).
28
29          SELECT SORTED-INVENTORY-FILE
30             ASSIGN TO (system dependent).
31
32          SELECT SORT-FILE
33             ASSIGN TO (system dependent).
34
35       DATA DIVISION.
36
37       FILE SECTION.
38
39       FD  INVENTORY-FILE.
40       01  IR-INVENTORY-RECORD.
41           05                          PIC X(19).
42           05    IR-INVENTORY-CLASS-CODE  PIC X(1).
43           05                          PIC X(34).
44
45       FD  INVENTORY-REPORT-FILE.
46       01  RL-REPORT-LINE.
47           05  RL-WAREHOUSE-CODE       PIC X(2).
48           05                          PIC X(2).
49           05  RL-PART-NUMBER          PIC X(15).
50           05                          PIC X(2).
51           05  RL-PART-DESCRIPTION     PIC X(25).
52           05                          PIC X(2).
53           05  RL-INVENTORY-VALUE      PIC Z,ZZZ,ZZZ.99-.
54
55       FD  SORTED-INVENTORY-FILE.
56       01  SI-INVENTORY-RECORD.
57           05  SI-RECORD-CODE          PIC X(2).
58           05  SI-WAREHOUSE-CODE       PIC X(2).
59           05  SI-PART-NUMBER          PIC X(15).
60           05  SI-INVENTORY-CLASS-CODE PIC X(1).
61           05  SI-PART-DESCRIPTION     PIC X(25).
62           05  SI-INVENTORY-VALUE      PIC S9(7)V99.
63
64       SD  SORT-FILE.
65       01  SR-SORT-RECORD.
66           05                          PIC X(2).
67           05  SR-WAREHOUSE-CODE       PIC X(2).
68           05  SR-PART-NUMBER          PIC X(15).
69           05                          PIC X(26).
70           05  SR-INVENTORY-VALUE      PIC S9(7)V99.
71
72       WORKING-STORAGE SECTION.
73
74       01  SW-SWITCHES.
75           05  SW-END-OF-FILE-SWITCH   PIC X(1).
76               88 SW-END-OF-FILE          VALUE "Y".
77               88 SW-NOT-END-OF-FILE      VALUE "N".
78
79
80       PROCEDURE DIVISION.
81
82       0000-SORT-INV-RECORDS.
83
84           SORT SORT-FILE
85               ASCENDING KEY  SR-WAREHOUSE-CODE
86               DESCENDING KEY SR-INVENTORY-VALUE
87               ASCENDING KEY  SR-PART-NUMBER
88               INPUT PROCEDURE IS  2000-SELECT-INVENTORY-RECORDS
89               OUTPUT PROCEDURE IS 3000-PROCESS-SORTED-RECORDS
90
91           STOP RUN
92           .
93       ************INPUT PROCEDURE***************
94
95       2000-SELECT-INVENTORY-RECORDS.
96       *    ** Initialize **
97           OPEN INPUT INVENTORY-FILE
98           SET SW-NOT-END-OF-FILE TO TRUE
99       *    ** Process **
100          PERFORM UNTIL SW-END-OF-FILE
101             READ INVENTORY-FILE
102                AT END
103                   SET SW-END-OF-FILE TO TRUE
104                NOT AT END
105                   PERFORM 2200-SELECT-INVENTORY-RECORD
106             END-READ
107          END-PERFORM
108      *    ** Terminate **
109          CLOSE INVENTORY-FILE
110          .
111      2200-SELECT-INVENTORY-RECORD.
112          IF IR-INVENTORY-CLASS-CODE IS EQUAL TO "A"
113             PERFORM 2830-RELEASE-INVENTORY-RECORD
114          END-IF
115          .
116      2830-RELEASE-INVENTORY-RECORD.
117          MOVE IR-INVENTORY-RECORD TO SR-SORT-RECORD
118          RELEASE SR-SORT-RECORD
119          .
120      ************OUTPUT PROCEDURE***************
121
122      3000-PROCESS-SORTED-RECORDS.
123      *    ** Initialize **
124          OPEN OUTPUT INVENTORY-REPORT-FILE
125                      SORTED-INVENTORY-FILE
126          SET SW-NOT-END-OF-FILE TO TRUE
127      *    ** Process **
128          PERFORM UNTIL SW-END-OF-FILE
129             RETURN SORT-FILE
130                AT END
131                   SET SW-END-OF-FILE TO TRUE
132                NOT AT END
133                   PERFORM 3200-PROCESS-SORTED-INV-RECORD
134             END-RETURN
135          END-PERFORM
136      *    ** Terminate **
137          CLOSE INVENTORY-REPORT-FILE
138                SORTED-INVENTORY-FILE
139          .
140      3200-PROCESS-SORTED-INV-RECORD.
141          MOVE SR-SORT-RECORD TO SI-INVENTORY-RECORD
142          MOVE SPACES TO RL-REPORT-LINE
143          MOVE SI-WAREHOUSE-CODE TO RL-WAREHOUSE-CODE
144          MOVE SI-PART-NUMBER TO RL-PART-NUMBER
145          MOVE SI-PART-DESCRIPTION TO RL-PART-DESCRIPTION
146          MOVE SI-INVENTORY-VALUE TO RL-INVENTORY-VALUE
147          PERFORM 3830-WRITE-SORTED-INV-RECORD
148          PERFORM 3890-WRITE-REPORT-LINE
149          .
150      3830-WRITE-SORTED-INV-RECORD.
151          WRITE SI-INVENTORY-RECORD.
152
153      3890-WRITE-REPORT-LINE.
154          WRITE RL-REPORT-LINE
155              AFTER ADVANCING 1 LINE
156          .
```

phrase at line 88 as operating like a PERFORM statement. That is, control is passed to the procedure and then returned when execution of the procedure is complete.

2. The sort-work file is sorted.
3. The output procedure is performed (thereby copying the sort-work file to the sorted inventory file).

In each of the two procedures (2000 and 3000), you can see the program-within-a-program form described in the pseudocode discussion. For instance, in the 2000 procedure:

1. The input file is opened.
2. The end-of-file switch is set.
3. Records are processed within a loop (until the EOF).
4. The file is closed.

Upon completion of the input procedure, control is returned to the SORT statement where the sort takes place. When the sort finishes, control is given to the 3000 procedure.

Although the statements of the 2200 and 2830 modules could be incorporated directly within the READ (under NOT AT END), they are written as separate modules to illustrate the broad concepts.

Observe that the same end-of-file program switch is used for both the input INVENTORY-FILE and the sort-work SORT-FILE. Normally, a separate switch should be established for each input file. For this program, due to SORT statement handling, it is impossible to process both of these files simultaneously. Therefore, such multiple use is acceptable. Of course, it is initialized before use in each of the procedures.

Module Numbering

Because the input and output procedures are virtually independent programs, a four-digit module-numbering system is implemented. The first digit—0, 2, or 3—signifies the particular component of the program: the mainline elements, the input procedure, and the output procedure, respectively. The other three digits conform to this book's previously established standards.

Special Needs of Sorting with COBOL-74

This portion of the chapter describes three topics necessary to use SORT with COBOL-74: PROCEDURE DIVISION sections, the GO TO statement, and the EXIT statement. If you work exclusively with COBOL-85, you can ignore the GO TO and EXIT descriptions. However, you should read the description of PROCEDURE DIVISION sections because sections are required for the implementation of certain error-recovery techniques in Chapter 15.

Sections in the PROCEDURE DIVISION

As you observed, a *program module* can be defined as a contiguous group of statements referred to as a unit. Throughout this book, the word *module* is synonymous with COBOL paragraph. COBOL identifies the beginning of a paragraph by the paragraph header and its end by the paragraph header of the next paragraph. If a module (paragraph) will be performed, you code a statement such as:

```
PERFORM 100-INITIALIZE-VARIABLE-FIELDS
```

This statement causes control to be transferred to a paragraph; when execution of that paragraph is complete, control is returned.

Actually, COBOL includes the PROCEDURE DIVISION section, a means by which two *or more* paragraphs can be treated as a module and performed by a single PERFORM statement. The beginning of a COBOL section is indicated by a section header; the end of a section is indicated by the section header of the next section.

To illustrate, in Figure 13-15(a), you can see that printing an address label is done in three consecutive paragraphs executed with three consecutive PERFORM statements. In the equivalent code of Figure 13-15(b), the three paragraphs are defined as PRINT-MAILING-LABEL SECTION and are executed by a single PERFORM. When a section is designated in the PERFORM, execution begins with the first paragraph of the section and progresses through each paragraph until the next section header is encountered.

Sections were not introduced earlier in this book because their use tends to be inconsistent with good structured programming practices. However, in certain instances, COBOL requires the use of sections. In this chapter, sections must be used in conjunction with particular applications of the COBOL-74 SORT statement. Sections are also used in Chapter 15.

If you refer to the general format in Figure 13-8, you will see that two clauses refer to procedures: INPUT PROCEDURE and OUTPUT PROCEDURE. COBOL-74 requires that these procedure-names be the names of sections, not paragraphs. So, if you are to use the SORT statement with COBOL-74, you need to know about PROCEDURE DIVISION sections—and also about the GO TO and EXIT statements.

The GO TO Statement

The GO TO statement allows you to transfer control of the program in much the same way as a PERFORM. That is, you could code

```
GO TO 250-CHECK-CONTROL-FIELDS
```

much as you would code

```
PERFORM 250-CHECK-CONTROL-FIELDS
```

However, the significant difference is that no provisions exist for returning to the paragraph from which the transfer is made. After control is transferred to a paragraph, execution continues from that point on. The overuse of this statement is considered *the* taboo in structured COBOL programming. (Other structured languages do not even include a GO TO type of statement.) However, as you will see, the nature of the COBOL-74 SORT statement requires use of the GO TO for certain actions.

Figure 13-15   Paragraphs and sections.

```
    :                                          PERFORM PRINT-MAILING-LABEL
    :                                              :
PERFORM PRINT-NAME-LINE
PERFORM PRINT-ADDRESS-LINE                     PRINT-MAILING-LABEL SECTION.
PERFORM PRINT-CITY-STATE-LINE
    :                                          850-WRITE-NAME-LINE.
    :                                              MOVE SS-NAME TO LB-LINE
850-WRITE-NAME-LINE.                               PERFORM 880-WRITE-LABEL-LINE.
    MOVE SS-NAME TO LB-LINE                    851-WRITE-ADDRESS-LINE.
    PERFORM 880-WRITE-LABEL-LINE.                  MOVE SS-ADDRESS TO LB-LINE
851-WRITE-ADDRESS-LINE.                            PERFORM 880-WRITE-LABEL-LINE.
    MOVE SS-ADDRESS TO LB-LINE                 852-WRITE-CITY-STATE-LINE.
    PERFORM 880-WRITE-LABEL-LINE.                  MOVE SS-CITY-STATE TO LB-LINE
852-WRITE-CITY-STATE-LINE.                         PERFORM 880-WRITE-LABEL-LINE.
    MOVE SS-CITY-STATE TO LB-LINE
    PERFORM 880-WRITE-LABEL-LINE.              WRITE-LABEL SECTION.
    :
    :                                              :
                                                   :

(a) Performing individual paragraphs.          (b) Performing multiple paragraphs composing a section.
```

The EXIT Statement

Right now, it's probably difficult for you to imagine a situation in which it is useful to have a paragraph that does nothing: a **null paragraph**. However, a need does exist for such a paragraph with the COBOL-74 SORT statement. The reserved word EXIT provides a null statement for a dummy PROCEDURE DIVISION paragraph—one that contains no other statements. When EXIT is used, it must be the only statement in the paragraph and must be followed by a period. Such a paragraph takes the following form:

```
400-PARAGRAPH-TO-DO-NOTHING.
    EXIT.
```

The word EXIT is partly a misnomer because it suggests that an exiting action takes place. However, the COBOL standards indicate that it serves only to enable the user to assign a procedure-name to a given point in a program.

Limitations on the COBOL-74 SORT Statement

The preceding features are required for COBOL-74 programs using the SORT statement because of the following restrictions on the COBOL-74 version of the statement:

1. The INPUT and OUTPUT PROCEDURE phrases must refer to section-names; paragraph-names are not permitted in the SORT statement.
2. Within an input or output procedure, program control cannot be transferred to procedures outside it. In other words, PERFORM or GO TO statements within the input procedure (section) cannot name a section or a paragraph that is not itself within the input or output section.

COBOL-74 Sort Program

The COBOL-74 version of this sort program, Figure 13-16, is organized into three sections. Because the sort procedures must be sections, it is logical (and often necessary) to also group the other paragraphs of the program into sections. The abbreviations ML, IP, and OP following the module numbers are used to identify these sections as mainline, input procedure, and output procedure, respectively.

Observe that each procedure includes a GO TO statement at the end of the procedure mainline paragraph. This GO TO statement is required so that, after end-of-file is reached, the remainder of the modules in the section are skipped for a proper return to the SORT statement. The need to get to the end of the section means that a paragraph, 2999-EXIT, must be established to provide a procedure-name for the GO TO statement. Because it is a dummy module—no program operations will be executed—the null statement EXIT is specified within the paragraph.

Recap of Sort Programs with the Input File Preprocessing and/or Sorted File Postprocessing

The previous example program illustrated the SORT statement using both preprocessing and postprocessing. As you observed, the two actions are totally independent of each other. You might have a sort need in which only preprocessing or only postprocessing is required.

Preprocessing of an input file is used when any one of the following program functions is required:

1. To select certain records from the input file and to sort only those selected records (as is done in the SORTPP85 program).
2. To create additional records to be included in the sorted file.
3. To change any characteristics of the input record (record length, field size, field location, field values, and so on) before the sort.
4. To validate, or edit, the records before sorting.
5. To list the input records before sorting.
6. To count the records of the input file.

Figure 13-16   Sort with preprocessing of the input-inventory file and postprocessing of the sorted file—
SORTPP74.

```
  1     IDENTIFICATION DIVISION.                        83     PROCEDURE DIVISION.
  2     PROGRAM-ID.    SORTPP74.                         84
  3                                                      85     0000-ML-SORT-INV-RECORDS SECTION.
  4     *   Written by T. Welburn.                       86
  5     *   Silicon Valley Manufacturing Company.       87     0000-SORT-INV-RECORDS.
  6     *   MAR 28, 1986.                                88
  7     *   Revised 10/3/89, 2/3/95 by W. Price.        89         SORT SORT-FILE
  8                                                      90             ASCENDING KEY   SR-WAREHOUSE-CODE
  9     *   This is a sort program with preprocessing    91             DESCENDING KEY  SR-INVENTORY-VALUE
 10     *      of the input file and postprocessing      92             ASCENDING KEY   SR-PART-NUMBER
 11     *      of the sorted output file                 93             INPUT PROCEDURE IS   2000-IP-SELECT-INV-RECORDS
 12     *      Using 1974 Standard                       94             OUTPUT PROCEDURE IS 3000-OP-PROCESS-SORTED-RECORDS.
 13     *   Sort statement phrases specified are:        95
 14     *       INPUT PROCEDURE                          96         STOP RUN.
 15     *       OUTPUT PROCEDURE                         97
 16                                                      98     ************INPUT PROCEDURE***************
 17                                                      99
 18     ENVIRONMENT DIVISION.                           100     2000-IP-SELECT-INV-RECORDS SECTION.
 19                                                     101
 20     INPUT-OUTPUT SECTION.                           102     2000-SELECT-INVENTORY-RECORDS.
 21                                                     103     *   ** Initialize **
 22     FILE-CONTROL.                                   104         OPEN INPUT INVENTORY-FILE.
 23         SELECT INVENTORY-FILE                       105         MOVE "N" TO SW-END-OF-FILE-SWITCH.
 24             ASSIGN TO DISK "INVEN-U.DAT"            106         PERFORM 2800-READ-INVENTORY-RECORD.
 25             ORGANIZATION IS LINE SEQUENTIAL.        107     *   ** Process **
 26         SELECT INVENTORY-REPORT-FILE                108         PERFORM 2200-SELECT-INVENTORY-RECORD
 27             ASSIGN TO PRINTER "PRN-FILE".           109             UNTIL SW-END-OF-FILE.
 28         SELECT SORTED-INVENTORY-FILE                110     *   ** Terminate **
 29             ASSIGN TO DISK "INVEN-S.DAT"            111         CLOSE INVENTORY-FILE.
 30             ORGANIZATION IS LINE SEQUENTIAL.        112         GO TO 2999-EXIT.
 31         SELECT SORT-FILE                            113
 32             ASSIGN TO DISK "INVEN-W.DAT".           114     2200-SELECT-INVENTORY-RECORD.
 33                                                     115         IF  IR-INVENTORY-CLASS-CODE IS EQUAL TO "A"
 34                                                     116             PERFORM 2830-RELEASE-INVENTORY-RECORD.
 35     DATA DIVISION.                                  117         PERFORM 2800-READ-INVENTORY-RECORD.
 36                                                     118
 37     FILE SECTION.                                   119     2800-READ-INVENTORY-RECORD.
 38                                                     120         READ INVENTORY-FILE
 39     FD  INVENTORY-FILE                              121             AT END
 40         LABEL RECORDS ARE STANDARD.                 122                 MOVE "Y" TO SW-END-OF-FILE-SWITCH.
 41     01  IR-INVENTORY-RECORD.                        123
 42         05  FILLER                 PIC X(19).       124     2830-RELEASE-INVENTORY-RECORD.
 43         05  IR-INVENTORY-CLASS-CODE PIC X(1).       125         MOVE IR-INVENTORY-RECORD TO SR-SORT-RECORD.
 44         05  FILLER                 PIC X(34).       126         RELEASE SR-SORT-RECORD.
 45                                                     127
 46     FD  INVENTORY-REPORT-FILE                       128     2999-EXIT.
 47         LABEL RECORDS ARE OMITTED.                  129         EXIT.
 48     01  RL-REPORT-LINE.                             130
 49         05  RL-WAREHOUSE-CODE      PIC X(2).        131     ************OUTPUT PROCEDURE***************
 50         05  FILLER                 PIC X(2).        132
 51         05  RL-PART-NUMBER         PIC X(15).       133     3000-OP-PROCESS-SORTED-RECORDS SECTION.
 52         05  FILLER                 PIC X(2).        134
 53         05  RL-PART-DESCRIPTION    PIC X(25).       135     3000-PROCESS-SORTED-RECORDS.
 54         05  FILLER                 PIC X(2).        136     *   ** Initialize **
 55         05  RL-INVENTORY-VALUE     PIC Z,ZZZ,ZZZ.99-. 137       OPEN OUTPUT INVENTORY-REPORT-FILE
 56                                                     138                    SORTED-INVENTORY-FILE.
 57     FD  SORTED-INVENTORY-FILE                       139         MOVE "N" TO SW-END-OF-FILE-SWITCH.
 58         LABEL RECORDS ARE STANDARD.                 140         PERFORM 3800-RETURN-SORTED-INV-RECORD.
 59     01  SI-INVENTORY-RECORD.                        141     *   ** Process **
 60         05  SI-RECORD-CODE         PIC X(2).        142         PERFORM 3200-PROCESS-SORTED-INV-RECORD
 61         05  SI-WAREHOUSE-CODE      PIC X(2).        143             UNTIL SW-END-OF-FILE.
 62         05  SI-PART-NUMBER         PIC X(15).       144     *   ** Terminate **
 63         05  SI-INVENTORY-CLASS-CODE PIC X(1).       145         CLOSE INVENTORY-REPORT-FILE
 64         05  SI-PART-DESCRIPTION    PIC X(25).       146                     SORTED-INVENTORY-FILE.
 65         05  SI-INVENTORY-VALUE     PIC S9(7)V99.    147         GO TO 3999-EXIT.
 66                                                     148
 67     SD  SORT-FILE                                   149     3200-PROCESS-SORTED-INV-RECORD.
 68         LABEL RECORDS ARE STANDARD.                 150         MOVE SR-SORT-RECORD TO SI-INVENTORY-RECORD.
 69     01  SR-SORT-RECORD.                             151         MOVE SPACES TO RL-REPORT-LINE.
 70         05  FILLER                 PIC X(2).        152         MOVE SI-WAREHOUSE-CODE TO RL-WAREHOUSE-CODE.
 71         05  SR-WAREHOUSE-CODE      PIC X(2).        153         MOVE SI-PART-NUMBER TO RL-PART-NUMBER.
 72         05  SR-PART-NUMBER         PIC X(15).       154         MOVE SI-PART-DESCRIPTION TO RL-PART-DESCRIPTION.
 73         05  FILLER                 PIC X(26).       155         MOVE SI-INVENTORY-VALUE TO RL-INVENTORY-VALUE.
 74         05  SR-INVENTORY-VALUE     PIC S9(7)V99.    156         PERFORM 3830-WRITE-SORTED-INV-RECORD.
 75                                                     157         PERFORM 3890-WRITE-REPORT-LINE.
 76     WORKING-STORAGE SECTION.                        158         PERFORM 3800-RETURN-SORTED-INV-RECORD.
 77                                                     159
 78     01  SW-SWITCHES.                                160     3800-RETURN-SORTED-INV-RECORD.
 79         05  SW-END-OF-FILE-SWITCH  PIC X(1).        161         RETURN SORT-FILE
 80             88  SW-END-OF-FILE         VALUE "Y".   162             AT END
 81                                                     163                 MOVE "Y" TO SW-END-OF-FILE-SWITCH.
 82                                                     164
                                                        165     3830-WRITE-SORTED-INV-RECORD.
                                                        166         WRITE SI-INVENTORY-RECORD.
                                                        167
                                                        168
                                                        169     3890-WRITE-REPORT-LINE.
                                                        170         WRITE RL-REPORT-LINE
                                                        171             AFTER ADVANCING 1 LINE.
                                                        172
                                                        173     3999-EXIT.
                                                        174         EXIT.
```

The INPUT PROCEDURE phrase must be coded within the SORT statement to provide for preprocessing of the input file.

Postprocessing of the sorted file is needed when any one of the following program functions is required:

1. To create more than one sorted output file.
2. To select or summarize records after sorting and before writing them to a sorted output file.
3. To create additional records after sorting to be included in the sorted output file.
4. To change any characteristics of the sorted record (record length, field size, field location, field values, and so on) after the sort.
5. To validate, or edit, the records after sorting.
6. To list the sorted records (as is done in SORTPP85 and SORTPP74).
7. To count the sorted records.

The OUTPUT PROCEDURE phrase must be coded within the SORT statement to provide for postprocessing of the sorted file.

The MERGE Statement

Merging is the action of combining two or more files currently in the same sequence into one sequenced file. For instance, two sales transaction files might be combined into a single file. Or a department store's accounts-receivable application might require the merging of the month's charge transaction file and the cash-payments transaction file before preparing customer statements. (With the wide use of disks and the ease of using multiple files in an application, physical merging of files is not as significant as it was when magnetic tape processing was predominant.)

The format for the MERGE statement is shown in Figure 13-17. To merge two or more files, remember that each file must already be in correct sequence according to the merge-key fields (those fields specified in the ASCENDING/DESCENDING KEY phrase of the MERGE statement). As can be inferred from the similarity of the SORT and MERGE statements, merge programs follow the same general pattern as sort programs. However, two differences exist. Because a merge operation will always require at least two files, observe in the format notation that at least two files must be specified in the USING phrase. Notice also that the MERGE statement format does not offer an INPUT PROCEDURE phrase—the USING phrase must be specified. However, the OUTPUT PROCEDURE can be used, together with the RETURN statement, as with the SORT.

Figure 13-17
MERGE statement format.

$$\underline{\text{MERGE}} \text{ file-name-1} \left\{ \text{ON} \left\{ \begin{array}{l} \underline{\text{ASCENDING}} \\ \underline{\text{DESCENDING}} \end{array} \right\} \text{KEY} \{ \text{data-name-1} \} \dots \right\} \dots$$

$$[\text{ COLLATING } \underline{\text{SEQUENCE}} \text{ IS alphabet-name-1 }]$$

$$\underline{\text{USING}} \text{ file-name-2} \{ \text{ file-name-3} \} \dots$$

$$\left\{ \begin{array}{l} \underline{\text{OUTPUT}} \underline{\text{PROCEDURE}} \text{ IS procedure-name-1} \\ \underline{\text{GIVING}} \{ \text{ file-name-4} \} \dots \end{array} \right\}$$

Chapter Summary

A program using the SORT takes one of four variations: (1) sort only, (2) sort with preprocessing of the input file, (3) sort with preprocessing of the input file and postprocessing of the sorted file, or (4) sort with postprocessing of the sorted file.

A sort-only program is coded by specifying the USING and GIVING phrases of the SORT statement.

A sort program with preprocessing of the input file is coded by specifying the INPUT PROCEDURE phrase (instead of the USING phrase) of the SORT statement. The RELEASE statement transfers records to the sort-work file. This type of sort program is useful to (1) select and sort only certain records from the input file, (2) create additional records to be included in the sorted file, (3) make changes to the input record before sorting, (4) validate records before sorting, (5) list the input records before sorting, and/or (6) count records prior to the sort.

A sort program with postprocessing of the sorted file is coded by specifying the OUTPUT PROCEDURE phrase (instead of the GIVING phrase) of the SORT statement. The RETURN statement retrieves sorted records from the sort-work file. This type of sort program is useful to (1) create more than one sorted output file, (2) select or summarize records after sorting and before writing them to the sorted output file, (3) create additional records after sorting to be included in the sorted output file, (4) make changes to the record after sorting, (5) validate the sorted records, (6) list the sorted records, and/or (7) count the sorted records.

COBOL Language Element Summary

A file-control SELECT entry must be provided for the sort file named in each SORT statement (or for the merge file named in each MERGE statement).

An SD (Sort Definition) entry must be provided for each sort file (or merge file) named in a file-control entry. An SD entry is like an FD entry. Following the SD entry, an 01-level record-description entry describing the record to be sorted is specified.

- The SD-name must match the name of the sort file (or merge file) selected in the ENVIRONMENT DIVISION file-control entry.

- The 01-level record-description entry must contain a data-item description for each sort-key (or merge-key) field named in the KEY phrase(s) of the SORT (or MERGE) statement. The key fields may appear anywhere in the record and in any order.

The SORT statement is used to invoke the sort function; in addition to the key word SORT, it consists of four basic components:

- The name of the sort-work file (identified in the SELECT and SD clauses).

- KEY phrase(s) that specify field(s) upon which the sort will be performed and whether or not the sequencing will be ASCENDING or DESCENDING.

- The USING phrase to designate the input file, or the INPUT PROCEDURE phrase to designate the procedure that provides for preprocessing of the input file.

- The GIVING phrase to designate the output file, or the OUTPUT PROCEDURE phrase to designate the procedure that provides for postprocessing of the sorted sort file.

The RELEASE statement transfers a record to the sort file; it is similar to a WRITE statement. The RELEASE statement can only be specified within an INPUT PROCEDURE. The record to be released must be physically present (that is, moved to) the SD record-description area before issuing the RELEASE. The FROM option of the RELEASE statement may be coded to provide for this.

The RETURN statement retrieves a record from the sort file after the records are sorted; it is similar to a READ statement. The RETURN statement can only be specified within an OUTPUT PROCEDURE.

COBOL-74 restrictions are

- The INPUT PROCEDURE and the OUTPUT PROCEDURE must be formed as sections.

- The INPUT PROCEDURE and the OUTPUT PROCEDURE section-names must not be referenced except by a SORT (or MERGE) statement.

- Within an INPUT PROCEDURE or an OUTPUT PROCEDURE, program control cannot be transferred to procedures outside it.

Exercises

Terms for Definition

ascending
descending
merge
multiple-field sort key

null paragraph
sorting
sort key
sort-work file

Review Questions

1. When a SORT or MERGE statement is specified in a COBOL program, a(n) _____ entry for the sort-work file is required in the ENVIRON-MENT DIVISION.

2. When a SORT or MERGE statement is specified in a COBOL program, a(n) _____ entry for the sort-work file is required in the FILE SECTION of the DATA DIVISION.

3. Sort- and merge-key fields are specified in the _____ phrase of the SORT statement.

4. Specification of an input file to be sorted without preprocessing of the input records is handled by the _____ phrase of the SORT statement.

5. To create a sorted output file without postprocessing of the sorted records, the _____ phrase of the SORT statement is used.

6. To permit preprocessing of the input file to be sorted, the _____ phrase of the SORT statement must be specified.

7. To permit postprocessing of the sorted file, the _____ phrase of the SORT statement must be specified.

8. A RELEASE statement is similar in function to a(n) _____ statement.

9. A RETURN statement is similar in function to a(n)_____ statement.

10. List six sort program requirements that call for specification of an INPUT PROCEDURE.

11. List six sort program requirements that call for specification of an OUTPUT PROCEDURE.

12. When files are merged, each file must already be _____.

13. In contrast to the SORT statement, the MERGE statement does not provide for specification of a(n) _____ phrase.

Programming Assignments

Programming Assignment 13-1: Sort Vendor File

Background information:

For a better idea of how various vendors pay their bills, the financial officer of Tools Unlimited requires some reports in which the vendor file is by amount due within due date within vendor name.

Input file: Vendor file (VENDOR.DAT)

Vendor record

Output file: Sorted vendor file

Program operations:

1. Sort the vendor file.
   a. Arrange the records alphabetically in accordance with the value of the Vendor-name field.
   b. Any records with matching vendor names are to be arranged in accordance with the Date-due field (newest date first; oldest date last).
   c. Any records with matching vendor names and due dates are to be arranged in accordance with the Amount-due field (highest amount first; lowest amount last).

2. Create a file of the sorted vendor records.

Programming Assignment 13-2: Select and Sort Inventory-Reorder Records

Background information:

The production manager of Tools Unlimited wants to minimize her inventory cost. To that end, she needs some reports generated from the inventory file in which the records are sequenced by Product identification within Order cost within Inventory class.

Input file: Inventory file (INVEN.DAT)

Inventory record

Inventory class ⌐

	Product identification		Unit price or Unit cost	Reorder point	Quantity on hand	Quantity on order		Order quantity	

1 2 3│4 5 6 7 8 9 10 11 12 13│14 15 16 17 18 19 20 21 22 23 24 25 26 27 28 29 30 31 32 33 34 35 36 37 38 39│40│41 42 43 44 45 46│47│48 49 50 51│52 53 54 55│56 57 58 59│60 61 62 63 64 65 66 67 68 69 70│71 72 73 74│75 76 77 78 79 80

Output file: Sorted parts file

Program operations:

1. Determine the Reorder cost in accordance with the following:
   a. Calculate the Inventory-deficiency as
      Inventory-deficiency = Quantity-on-hand
                              + Quantity-on-order
                              − Reorder-point
   b. If the Inventory-deficiency is not negative, set the Quantity-to-order amount to zero.
   c. If the Inventory-deficiency is negative, set the Quantity-to-order amount to a multiple of the Order-quantity such that the Quantity-to-order equals or exceeds the absolute value of the Inventory-deficiency.
   d. Multiply the Quantity-to-order amount by the Unit-cost field to equal the Reorder cost.

2. Select and sort those records requiring a reorder (that is, Quantity-to-order greater than zero).
   a. Arrange the records alphabetically in accordance with the value of the Inventory-class field.
   b. Those records with matching inventory-class codes should be arranged in accordance with the Order-cost value (highest cost first; lowest cost last).
   c. Any records with matching inventory-class codes and Order-cost values should be arranged in ascending sequence in accordance with the value of the Part-number field.

3. Create a file of the sorted selected inventory records.

Programming Assignment 13-3: Sort and Print Earnings File

Background information:

The payroll manager of Silicon Valley Manufacturing needs a report with output lines in sequence by employee name within year-to-date earnings within pay rate within pay code. Each record should be printed in its sorted sequence together with the total number of hourly and salaried employees listed on the report. A sorted earnings file must be created on disk.

Input file: Earnings file (EARNINGS.DAT)

Earnings record

Employee middle initial ⌐   ⌐ Pay code

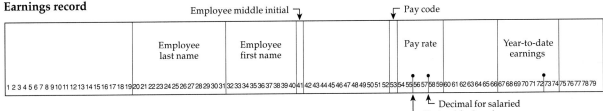

	Employee last name	Employee first name			Pay rate	Year-to-date earnings	

1 2 3 4 5 6 7 8 9 10 11 12 13 14 15 16 17 18 19│20 21 22 23 24 25 26 27 28 29 30 31│32 33 34 35 36 37 38 39 40│41 42 43 44 45 46 47 48 49 50 51 52│53 54 55│56 57 58 59│60 61 62 63 64 65 66│67 68 69 70 71 72 73 74│75 76 77 78 79

⌐ ⌐ Decimal for salaried
⌐ Decimal for hourly

Output files: Sorted earnings file
Earnings by pay-code report

Output-report format:

```
          0             1             2             3             4             5             6             7
 1234567890123456789012345678901234567890123456789012345678901234567890123456
 4 EARNINGS BY PAY CODE REPORT (13-3)                          MM-DD-YY    PAGE ZZ9
 6      P         PAY           YEAR-TO-DT      -------EMPLOYEE NAME------
 7      C        RATE            EARNINGS       LAST          FIRST     MI
 9      X    →ZZ.9999         ZZZ,ZZZ.99   XXXXXXXXXXX XXXXXXXXX X
10      X     ZZZZ.99    ←  ZZZ,ZZZ.99   XXXXXXXXXXX XXXXXXXXX X
12                                             HOURLY EMPLOYEES    Z,ZZ9
13                                            SALARIED EMPLOYEES   Z,ZZ9
```

—— Format for salaried

—— Format for hourly

Program operations:

1. Sort the earnings file.
   a. Arrange the records alphabetically in accordance with the value of the Pay-code field.
   b. Those records with matching Pay-code values should be arranged in accordance with the value of the Pay-rate field (highest rate first; lowest rate last).
   c. Those records with matching Pay-code and Pay-rate values should be arranged in accordance with the value of the Year-to-date-earnings field (highest earnings first; lowest earnings last).
   d. Any records with matching Pay-code, Pay-rate, and Year-to-date-earnings are to be arranged alphabetically by the Employee-name-field.

2. Make these accumulations.
   a. Total number of hourly employees (Pay-code field equal to H).
   b. Total number of salaried employees (Pay-code field equal to S).

3. Create a disk file of the sorted earnings records.

4. Print each sorted earnings record in accordance with the print-chart specifications.
   a. Single-space each detail line.
   b. Provide for a line span of 57 lines per page.

Programming Assignment 13-4: Classify, Sort, and Print Student Records

Background information:

The dean of instruction at Bayview Institute of Computer Technology makes periodic studies of student scholarships. A report is needed in which students are listed in order by student name within grade-point average within college-year status. The report must also include the total number of students in each college year. A disk file of the sorted records must be created.

Input file: Student file (STUDENT.DAT)

Student record

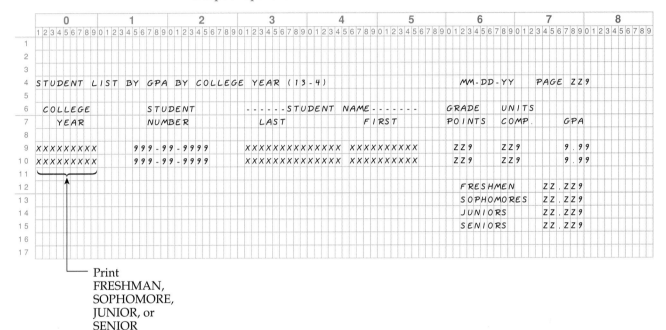

Output files: Student list by GPA by college year
Sorted student file

Output-report format:

```
        0            1            2            3            4            5            6            7            8
 1234567890 1234567890 1234567890 1234567890 1234567890 1234567890 1234567890 1234567890 123456789
 1
 2
 3
 4  STUDENT LIST BY GPA BY COLLEGE YEAR (13-4)                        MM-DD-YY      PAGE ZZ9
 5
 6  COLLEGE          STUDENT       ------STUDENT NAME-------      GRADE     UNITS
 7    YEAR           NUMBER          LAST          FIRST          POINTS    COMP.        GPA
 8
 9  XXXXXXXX      999-99-9999      XXXXXXXXXXXXX XXXXXXXXXX        ZZ9       ZZ9         9.99
10  XXXXXXXX      999-99-9999      XXXXXXXXXXXXX XXXXXXXXXX        ZZ9       ZZ9         9.99
11
12                                                                        FRESHMEN    ZZ,ZZ9
13                                                                        SOPHOMORES  ZZ,ZZ9
14                                                                        JUNIORS     ZZ,ZZ9
15                                                                        SENIORS     ZZ,ZZ9
16
17
```

Print
FRESHMAN,
SOPHOMORE,
JUNIOR, or
SENIOR

Program operations:

1. Determine the College-year-status for each student in accordance with the value of the Units-completed field.
   a. Units completed from 0 to 29 = Freshman
   b. From 30 to 59   = Sophomore
   c. From 60 to 89   = Junior
   d. Over 89   = Senior

2. Calculate each student's Grade-point-average by dividing the Grade-points field by the Units-completed field. Carry the quotient to two decimal places.

3. Sort the student records.
   a. Arrange the records in College-year order (seniors first; freshmen last).
   b. Those records with matching college years should be arranged in accordance with the Grade-point-average (highest GPA first; lowest GPA last).
   c. Any records with matching college years and GPAs should be arranged alphabetically by Student-name (last name first).

4. Accumulate the number of students in each of the four college years.

5. Create a disk file of the sorted student records.

6. Print the student list by GPA by college year in accordance with the print-chart specifications.
   a. Single-space each detail line.
   b. Provide for a line span of 57 lines per page.

Programming
Assignment 13-5:
Sorted Nurses
Telephone Directory

Background information:

The personnel director of Brooklawn Hospital needs a telephone directory of all nonsupervisory nursing personnel in the hospital. The list should be grouped with the parttime employees first, then the fulltime employees. Within these two groupings, the list should be in alphabetic sequence.

Input file: Nurses file (NURSES.DAT)

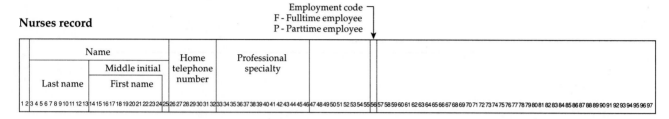

Output-report format:

```
              0             1             2             3             4             5             6
     1234567890 1234567890 1234567890 1234567890 1234567890 1234567890 123456789
 1
 2
 3
 4  BROOKLAWN HOSPITAL NONSUPERV. TELE. DIR. (13-5) PAGE ZZ9
 5  XXXXXXXX EMPLOYEES
 6
 7
 8      EMPLOYEE NAME              PROF. SPECIALTY       TELEPHONE
 9
10      XXXXXXXXXXXXXXXXXXXXXXX    XXXXXXXXXXXXX         XXX-XXXX
11
12      XXXXXXXXXXXXXXXXXXXXXXX    XXXXXXXXXXXXX         XXX-XXXX
13
14
```

Program operations:

1. Select records for nonsupervisory personnel only.

2. Sort the selected records.
   a. Group the records by Employment-code (parttime first, then fulltime).
   b. Within each Employment-code group, sort the records alphabetically by Name.

3. Create a disk file of the sorted records.

4. Print the sorted telephone directory file in accordance with the print-chart specifications.

    a Print two heading lines on the first page and all subsequent pages; accumulate page numbers for the first line.

    b. Start a new page to begin the fulltime employees (after the last parttime employee).

    c. On the second heading line, print PARTTIME or FULLTIME as appropriate.

    d. Double-space each detail line.

    e. Provide for a line span of 25 lines.

SEQUENTIAL MASTER-TRANSACTION FILE PROCESSING

CHAPTER

14

All programs you have studied so far have involved a single input data file, which is adequate for many areas of COBOL programming. However, much business programming requires data from two or more files. For example, a customer charge account system might include one file containing permanent customer records and another file containing records for purchases and payments by the customers. Creating the customer bill would require data from both files. This is called master-transaction processing, which was first covered in Module E and is described more fully in this chapter. From this chapter, you will learn the following:

- The variety of conditions to be encountered when matching transaction and master records.

- The overall structure and logic of processing a transaction file against a master file.

- The importance of record sequencing in master-transaction processing.

- How to change fields in an existing master record.

- How to add new records and delete existing records from a master file.

- How to update a record by making modifications, then rewriting it back to disk—thereby replacing the original copy.

Principles of Master-Transaction Processing

Records Must Be in Sequence

Master-transaction processing—as Figure E-3 (page 464) illustrated—is sequential and so requires that *both* files be in sequence by a common key field. With the wide use of magnetic disk and random-access capabilities, this type of sequential master-transaction processing is much less common than it once was. However, you should be familiar with the programming techniques involved. For an insight to some of the problems of matching records from two different files, let's consider a variety of record sequences. In studying these examples, place them in the context of the student master-transaction example of Module E. Remember that the master record for each student includes the total units earned. Each corresponding transaction record includes data for one completed course. Processing includes updating the master total units from transaction units.

Matching Records from Two Files

In the first record sequence illustrated by Figure 14-1, the next master record to be read has a key field value of 07427. Corresponding to it are three records in the transaction file. Execution proceeds as follows:

1. Read the master record (key field 07427).
2. Read the first transaction record. Since its key field is 07427 (equal to that of the master), process the transaction amount for updating the master.
3. Read the next transaction record. Since its key field is 07427, process the transaction amount for updating the master.
4. Read the next transaction record. Since its key field is 07427, process the transaction amount for updating the master.
5. Read the next transaction record. Since its key field is 10164, processing for master record 07427 is complete, so write the master record to the new master file.
6. Read the next master record. Since its key field (10164) matches that of the previously read transaction record, repeat the cycle for this master record.

You can see that processing involves reading a master, then reading and processing the corresponding transactions—a relatively basic operation. However, two conditions make the programming a little tricky. First, there may be master records for which no transactions have occurred during the processing period; that is, unmatched masters. Usually, these masters are written to the new master file with no change. This is a normal condition. Second, the transaction file might contain one or more transaction records with a key field that does not have a corresponding record in the master file. In the example student system, such an unmatched transaction record probably represents an error condition. In the example inventory system (which allows the addition of master records from the transaction file), this could be a valid situation requiring special handling.

First, let's consider how execution would progress for the unmatched master record of Figure 14-2. Assume that the 15674 transaction record was read and that the new master for 10164 was written. Execution proceeds as follows:

Figure 14-1
Matching transaction records with a corresponding master.

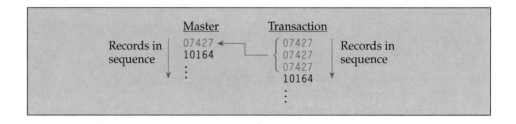

Figure 14-2
An unmatched
master record.

	Master	Transaction	
	10164	10164	
Unmatched master →	15589	10164	
record (it has no	15674	10164	
corresponding	.	15674 ←	If there were a
transactions).	.	.	transaction record
		.	for master 15589, it
			would be here.

1. Read the next master record (15589).
2. Compare the current master record key field value (15589) to the current transaction record key field value (15674). The transaction record value is higher, which indicates that no transaction record exists for this master record. So, the master record is written to the new master file without change.
3. Read the next master record. Since its key field (15674) matches that of the current transaction record, repeat the master-transaction cycle for this master record.

For the second exception condition, an unmatched transaction, consider the record sequence of Figure 14-3. Assume that the 13674 transaction record was read and that the new master for 10164 was written. Execution proceeds as follows:

1. Read the next master record (15589).
2. Compare the current master record key field value (15589) to the current transaction record key field value (13674). The transaction record value is lower, which indicates that no master record exists for this transaction record. The appropriate unmatched-transaction processing is performed.
3. Read the next transaction record. Since its key field (15589) matches that of the current master record, repeat the master-transaction cycle for this master record.

Notice in each of the preceding scenarios, the assumption was made that the records were properly sorted and that none was out of sequence.

Since two files are being read, both must be checked for the EOF condition. Detection of the EOF for *either* file signals the end of the normal master-transaction processing activities. In all previous examples, detection of the EOF meant the end of the file processing. However, for master-transaction processing, more needs to be done. The specific actions depend upon whichever of the following data conditions exist:

- The EOF was detected for the transaction file and no more master records remain.

Figure 14-3
An unmatched
transaction record.

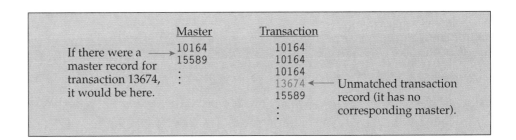

	Master	Transaction	
	10164	10164	
If there were a →	15589	10164	
master record for	.	10164	
transaction 13674,	.	13674 ←	Unmatched transaction
it would be here.		15589	record (it has no
		.	corresponding master).

- The EOF was detected for the transaction file and one or more master records remain.

- The EOF was detected for the master file and one or more transaction records remain.

First, consider how execution would terminate when the transaction file EOF is detected and no more master records remain, as Figure 14-4 illustrates. Assume that the third 91655 transaction record was read and processed. Then reading the next transaction record—EOF, in this case—signals that processing for master record 91655 is complete and it must be written to the new master file. Since no more records need to be processed, the master-transaction update is complete.

However, processing cannot simply end after the last record is updated—as suggested in the example of Figure 14-4—because the master file might contain additional unmatched records, as Figure 14-5 illustrates. So, the execution sequence should be as follows—assuming that the third 91655 transaction record was read and processed:

1. Read the next transaction record—the EOF, in this case.
2. Processing for master record 91655 is complete, so write the master record to the new master file.
3. Complete processing of the master file by reading records and writing to the new master until the master file EOF is detected.

Figure 14-4
Final master-transaction set.

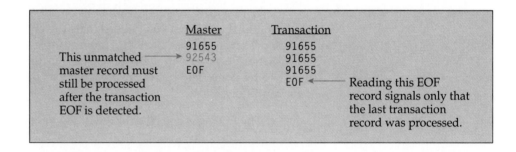

Master	Transaction
91655	91655
EOF	91655
	91655
	EOF ← Reading this EOF record triggers the final processing actions.

Figure 14-5
An unmatched master at the end of the file.

	Master	Transaction
	91655	91655
This unmatched →	92543	91655
master record must	EOF	91655
still be processed		EOF ← Reading this EOF
after the transaction		record signals only that
EOF is detected.		the last transaction
		record was processed.

Figure 14-6
Unmatched transactions at the end of the file.

	Master	Transaction
	91655	91655
Detection of a new →	EOF	91655
transaction number		91655
(92543) causes the		92543 ⎫
master to be read		92543 ⎬ ← These records must be
and this EOF to		EOF processed separately as
be detected.		unmatched transactions.

The other case to consider is one or more unmatched transaction records at the end of the file, as Figure 14-6 illustrates. In this case, assume that the third 91655 transaction record was just read and processed. Execution proceeds as follows:

1. Read the next transaction record—92543, in this case.
2. Processing for master record 91655 is complete, so write the master record to the new master file.
3. Read the next master record. Since this is the EOF, master-transaction processing is complete. The current transaction record and all that follow it must be processed as unmatched transaction records.

Sequential Master-Transaction Processing Logic

Pseudocode and Structure Chart

The possibilities illustrated by Figures 14-1 through 14-6 give you some insight regarding factors to be considered in sequential master-transaction processing. Basically, you are reading from two files "side-by-side" and comparing respective entries. Specific occurrences may be handled in numerous ways, but Figure 14-7's pseudocode shows the essentials of the process. You can tell at a glance that the pseudocode closely parallels COBOL code. It is written this way because it is meaningful, while the pseudocode does avoid some of the fine detail required of COBOL code.

The overall structure is evident in Figure 14-8's structure chart, which displays distinct levels. You will see later that the resulting programs are well modularized and relatively easy to follow.

Referring to the logic of Figure 14-7, let's begin our consideration of this pseudocode with the program switches.

Program Switches

This pseudocode uses five program switches: EOF-master, EOF-trans, Read-master, Read-trans, and Trans-processed. As might be expected, the program requires two end-of-file switches. EOF-master indicates the end of the master file, and EOF-trans indicates the end of the transaction file. Each time through the processing loop, a record must be read from either the master file or the transaction file. Selecting the proper Read is accomplished by the switches Read-master and Read-trans. The one remaining switch is Trans-processed. Its function is to identify unmatched master records.

Reading Input Records

Three different file-read scenarios exist:

- A record is read from both files (the first time through the processing loop).
- The next record read is from the master file.
- The next record read is from the transaction file.

This selection is made in the 200 module, which consists of a single Evaluate—see item ① in Figure 14-7. Both the Read-master and Read-trans switches are set to True in the 100 module. Therefore, the first execution of the 200 module sees the first option (True also True) satisfied. The first record is read from each file by the 800 and 820 modules. After the records are read, the switches Read-master and Read-trans are set to False, indicating that a record was just read. The Trans-processed switch is also set to False.

The other two options of this Evaluate—read the next master or transaction record—are controlled by the switches Read-master and Read-trans.

Figure 14-7 Pseudocode—Sequential master-transaction processing.

```
000-Process-Master-Trans.                    End of transaction file
1.  Open files.                              When    True    also   False  <---- (6)
2.  Perform 100-Initialize-Variable-Fields.  ---------      ----------
3.  Perform until EOF-master & EOF-trans             If Trans-processed
        Perform 200-Get-Next-Record                     Perform 400-Process-Master
        Perform 220-Process-Record.                 Else
4.  Close files.                                        Perform 450-Process-Unmatched-Master
5.  Stop run.                                        Set Read-master to True
100-Initialize-Variable-Fields.
1.  Set Read-master, Read-trans to True.
2.  Set EOF-master, EOF-trans to False.      End of master file
3.  Move low values to Previous-Master       When    False    also   True  <---- (7)
    and Previous-Trans keys                  ---------       ----------
200-Get-Next-Record.                                 Perform 350-Process-Unmatched-Trans
Evaluate                                             Set Read-trans to True
    Read-master also Read-trans  <---- (1)  300-Process-Trans.
    ----------       ----------                  Code as required by application.
      True      also    True                 350-Process-Unmatched-Trans.
    ----------       ----------                  Code as required by application.
            Perform 800-Read-Master-Record   400-Process-Master.
            Perform 820-Read-Trans-Record        Code as required by application.
            Set Read-master to False         450-Process-Unmatched-Master.
            Set Trans-processed to False         Code as required by application.
            Set Read-trans to False          800-Read-Master-Record.
      True      also    False                Read master file
    ----------       ----------                  at end
            Perform 800-Read-Master-Record           Set EOF-master to True
            Set Read-master to False             not at end
            Set Trans-processed to False             If Current-Master key not >
     False     also    True                            Previous-Master key
    ----------       ----------                            Display error message
            Perform 820-Read-Trans-Record                 Perform 950-Abort-Program
            Set Read-trans to False               Else
220-Process-Record.                                       Save Current-Master key
Evaluate                                     820-Read-Trans-Record.
        EOF-trans    also EOF-master         Read transaction file
        ---------        ----------              at end
  No end of file                                     Set EOF-trans to true
  When    False    also    False  <---- (2)      not at end
        ---------        ----------                 If Current-Trans key <
    Evaluate true                                     Previous-Trans key
      When Master = Trans                                Display error message
            Perform 300-Process-Trans  <---- (3)         Perform 950-Abort-Program
            Set Read-trans to True                Else
            Set Trans-processed to True               Save Current-Trans key
      When Master < Trans  <---- (4)           950-Abort-Program.
            If Trans-processed               Set EOF-master, EOF-trans to false
                Perform 400-Process-Master
            Else
                Perform 450-Process-Unmatched-Master
            Set Read-master to True
      When Master > Trans  <---- (5)
            Perform 350-Process-Unmatched-Trans
            Set Read-trans to True
```

Processing Master-Transactions

Processing is broken into three major categories: (1) end-of-file not yet detected on either file, (2) end-of-file detected on the transaction file (but not on the master file), and (3) end-of-file detected on the master file (but not on the transaction file). In the 220 module, this is controlled by the Evaluate with the condition EOF-trans also EOF-master ((2), (6), and (7)). In option (2) (both conditions False), a further

Figure 14-8   Structure chart—Sequential master-transaction processing.

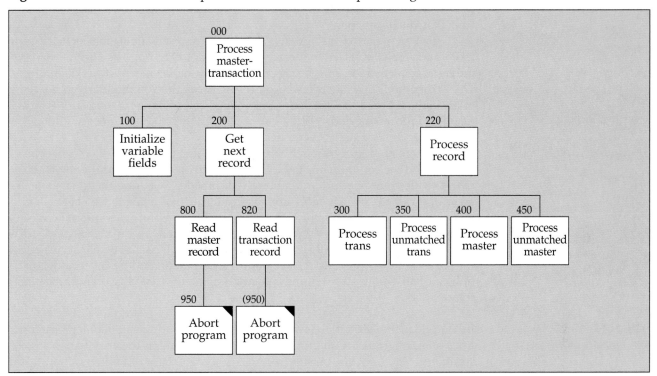

determination is made by comparing the key fields of the current master and transaction records. Three possibilities exist:

1. The master and transaction key fields are equal (③, Master = Trans). This requires that the master be updated from the transaction, represented by the 300 module in Figure 14-7. In the case of a student grade-processing system, one of the actions is to add the units from the course record (transaction) to the units-completed field of the student master record (refer to Figure E-2, page 464).

2. The master key field is less than the transaction key field (④, Master < Trans). This is a valid condition and means that all processing against the current master (if any) is complete and the current master must be written to the new file. Figure 14-1, page 498, demonstrates the scenario in which transaction records were processed against the master; Figure 14-2 demonstrates the unmatched master scenario. These are accommodated under ④ of Figure 14-7. The If is controlled by the switch Trans-processed, which is set to False whenever a master record is read (200 module) and to True whenever the equal key condition is detected under ③.

3. The master key field is greater than the transaction key field (⑤, Master > Trans). This condition signals an unmatched transaction record—the condition illustrated in Figure 14-5. In that case, the 350 module to process an unmatched master is executed.

At the end of each of these options—③, ④, and ⑤—the appropriate Read switch is set to True to read the next master or transaction record, as appropriate.

The End of transaction file option (⑥) of the primary Evaluate sees two possibilities. The first is illustrated by the sequence of Figure 14-4, in which the updating must occur for the last master record. The second occurs when one or more unmatched master records end the master file, as the sequence of Figure 14-5 illustrated. Whether or not the master is processed as matched or unmatched is controlled by the If statement.

The End of master file option ($\widehat{7}$) of the primary Evaluate means that one or more unmatched transaction records exist—refer to Figure 14-6. Then all remaining transaction records must be processed as unmatched records (the 350 module).

When both EOF switches become true (from the 200 module), no action is taken in the 220 module. The loop controlling Perform in the 000 module is terminated and processing ends.

Sequence Checking

With sequential master-transaction processing, it is essential that both files be in sequence on the common key field. If there is any question about the sequencing, then the files must be sorted. Although, in practice, it is rare that a sequencing error occurs, the consequences are so significant that a sequence check should always be performed. Both the 800 and 820 modules perform a sequence check as the *not at end* action. If a sequencing error is detected, an error message is displayed and the 950 module is performed. Control is immediately returned to the 000 module via the calling read module and the 220 module. Since both conditions are satisfied at step 3 of the 000 module, the files are closed and processing terminated.

About Master-Transaction Processing

In Module E, the distinction is made between the updating and maintenance functions of master-transaction processing. That is, updating is the activity of bringing summary fields of the master record up-to-date based on transaction data. Maintenance is the activity of adding and deleting master records, and making changes to semi-permanent fields of the master. From the point of view of logic and structure (illustrated by Figures 14-7 and 14-8), there is no difference between these two functions.

In fact, the logic of Figure 14-7 is equally applicable to master-transaction report generation in which data from master records is combined with data from transaction records to create a report. For instance—referring to the grade reporting example—student grade reports could be run entirely separate from the master updating procedure.

Because all of these applications utilize the same logic—with minor variations—only one example of sequential master-transaction processing is covered: a maintenance activity.

A Budget Control Application

Program Specifications

Preparing an annual budget is a ritual for managers of businesses, both large and small. Generally, the manager breaks expenditures and income into categories—for instance, travel, advertising, supplies, and so on. Each category is identified by a budget code and given a certain amount of money. Throughout the year as expenditures are made (or income received), they are processed against the appropriate budget code—thereby decreasing the amount remaining (expenditure) or increasing it (income). Also, periodic maintenance operations must be performed.

For this example, let's consider a minimal budget control system described by the program specifications of Figure 14-9. As you can see, the transaction record contains the same fields as the master record. The difference is that the transaction record includes a one-position transaction code and a four-position transaction number. The transaction code provides for the three basic maintenance operations: record deletion—code 1, record addition—code 2, and record modification (field changes)—code 3. These program specifications require that the basic structure of Figure 14-8 be expanded as shown in Figure 14-10.

Fields Not Subject
to Change

The addition and deletion actions are reasonably straightforward; changing fields warrants additional comments. In any application, certain fields of a master record are designated as not being able to be modified by change transactions. The best example is the key field—the budget code, in this case. Regardless of the file organization, changing the key field is not allowed because it could corrupt the record sequencing. If, for example, a keystroke error was made in entering a budget master, the correction is made by deleting the incorrect record and adding a new record with the correct code value.

In this example application, the budget balance is another field that probably would not be modified by a change record. As a summary field, it is changed only by charges, credits, and corrections of the updating process. However, if the budget allocation is modified, the balance field must be changed accordingly. For example, if the allocation for a budget is increased by $500, the current balance is also increased by $500.

Sequencing of
Transactions on
Transaction Code

Although both files must be in sequence based on the budget-code field (the key field), the transaction file has the added sequence requirement on the transaction-code field. So, within each group of records with the same budget code, the records are in order by transaction code. In master-transaction processing, this is not an uncommon requirement. The reason for it in this case relates to record deletions and additions. For instance, assume that an existing master record is completely in

Figure 14-9
Programming
specifications—
Sequential master-
transaction maintenance.

```
                    PROGRAMMING SPECIFICATIONS

    Program Name: Sequential Master-Transaction        Program ID: SEQ-MNT
                  Maintenance
    ─────────────────────────────────────────────────────────────────────

    Program Description:

    The budget master file is updated by a transaction file containing
    record additions, changes, and modifications. The transaction file was
    validated prior to this program run. A new, updated budget master file
    is produced; a transaction report is also written.

    Input Files:

    Budget Master File (BUDGET1.DAT)

    Columns          Field                    Description
      1-5            Budget code
      6-20           Description
     21-26           Budget allocation        Dollars and cents
     27-32           Budget balance           Dollars and cents

    Budget Transaction File (BUD-TRAN.DAT)

    Columns          Field                    Description
      1-5            Budget code
       6             Transaction code         Value  1 for record deletion
                                                     2 for record addition
                                                     3 for field changes
      7-10           Transaction number
     11-25           Description
     26-31           Budget allocation        Dollars and cents
     32-37           Budget balance           Dollars and cents

    Common key field: Budget code
    Master file sorted on Budget code
    Transaction file sorted on Budget code + Transaction code

    Output Files:

    Updated Budget master (BUDGET2.DAT)
    Transaction audit/error list (BUD-TRAN.LST)

                                                            (continues)
```

Figure 14-9   (continued)

Program Operations:

A. Read each input budget transaction record.
    1. Validate each transaction code to ensure that it contains a value 1, 2, or 3. If not, write the record to the transaction/error log with the message "INVALID TRANSACTION CODE." Do no further processing of the record.
    2. Check the sequence of the record to ensure that the Budget code + Transaction code is not less than that of the preceding record. If this error condition occurs, display the current and preceding record codes on the screen and terminate processing.
    3. The program logic is to provide for multiple transactions (or none at all) to be processed against the same master.
B. Read each input budget master record.
    1. Check the sequence of the record to ensure that the Budget code is greater than that of the preceding record. If this error condition occurs, display the current and preceding record codes on the screen and terminate processing.
C. Update the budget master record from each corresponding budget transaction record.
    1. Print each transaction record to the transaction/error log.
    2. For each transaction record with a transaction code of 1 (record deletion), delete the corresponding master record by simply failing to write it to the new file. If there is no master record corresponding to this transaction record, include the message "NO MATCHING MASTER" with the printed transaction record. Do no further processing of the record.
    3. For each transaction record with a transaction code of 2 (record addition), write a new master record to the new master file using the following input fields from the transaction record:
            Budget code
            Description
            Budgeted amount
            Budget balance
        If there is already a record with this budget code in the master file, include the message "CANNOT ADD MASTER" with the printed transaction record. Do no further processing of the record.
    4. For each transaction record with a transaction code of 3 (field change), fields of the master must be replaced as follows:
        a. If the input transaction Description field is not blank, replace the master Description field with the transaction Description field.
        b. If the input transaction Budget-allocation field is not blank:
            1. Update the master Budget-balance field by adding the difference between the transaction Budget-balance field and the master Budget-balance to the existing Budget-balance field.
            2. Replace the master Budget-allocation field with the transaction Budget-allocation field. If there is no master record corresponding to this transaction record, include the message "NO MATCHING MASTER" with the printed transaction record. Do no further processing of the record.
    5. When all transactions are processed for a master, write the updated master to the new budget master file. Any master record for which there are no transactions must be written, unchanged, to the updated budget master file.

error and must be replaced (the same budget code). This requires that the existing record first be deleted and then the correct one added.

Data Validation and Report Generation

In any master-transaction processing procedure, it is critical that the transaction data be correct. For instance, you would not want to add a new record to the master file with a budget balance field containing spaces. Obviously, you prevent this by using the data validation techniques of Chapter 10. However, in the example program that follows, data validation is not included solely to reduce the length of the program so that you can more easily focus on the basic master-transaction logic. Following the discussion of the program is an example of data validation for one of the modules.

Figure 14-10   Structure chart—Sequential master-transaction maintenance.

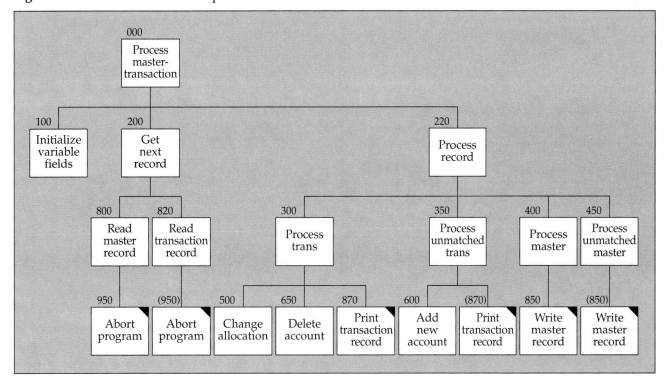

One of the outputs of any master-transaction processing program is a printed report. The report is similar to those you wrote in previous programming assignments—including report and column headings, page control, and a report summary. The summary commonly includes a count of the number of transactions processed and rejected, with a breakdown by type of action. It may also include counts of the number of master records read, added, deleted, changed, and written to the new file. However, report generation in this program is limited to simply printing the transaction record with an appropriate error message for any erroneous transactions.

Master-Transaction Maintenance Program

Figure 14-11 shows the complete master-transaction maintenance program. Let's begin with the DATA DIVISION.

DATA DIVISION Coding

The FILE SECTION includes four FDs, one for each of the four files to be processed: the old and new masters, the transaction, and the transaction report. Corresponding to each of these is a SELECT clause in the ENVIRONMENT DIVISION. The record descriptions are contained in the WORKING-STORAGE records of lines 84–108. Notice the following about them:

1. Only one record area is defined for the master record (MR-MASTER-RECORD, starting line 84). It will be used for both the input from the old master file and the output for the new master file. This is possible because the record is written to the new file with no format change.
2. In the transaction record (lines 90–102), TR-BUDGET-CODE and TR-TRANS-CODE are defined under the group item TR-BUDGET-TRANS-CODE. TR-BUDGET-CODE is the key field needed to match up with the corresponding master record. TR-BUDGET-TRANS-CODE, the

Figure 14-11   Sequential master-transaction processing—SEQ-MNT.

```
1        IDENTIFICATION DIVISION.
2        PROGRAM-ID.   SEQ-MNT.
3
4      * Pyramid Sales Company
5      * Budget File Maintenance
6      * Written by W. Price  2/15/95
7
8      * The program updates the Budget Master file from a
9      * Budget Transaction file. There are 3 trans types:
10     *    1 - Delete a Master record
11     *    2 - Add a Master record
12     *    3 - Change fields of the master record
13     * Output is an updated Budget Master file
14     * and a Transaction activity report
15
16       ENVIRONMENT DIVISION.
17
18       INPUT-OUTPUT SECTION.
19
20       FILE-CONTROL.
21           SELECT OLD-MASTER-FILE
22               ASSIGN TO (system dependent).
23
24           SELECT TRANS-FILE
25               ASSIGN TO (system dependent).
26
27           SELECT NEW-MASTER-FILE
28               ASSIGN TO (system dependent).
29
30           SELECT TRANS-REPORT
31               ASSIGN TO (system dependent).
32
33
34       DATA DIVISION.
35
36       FILE SECTION.
37
38       FD  OLD-MASTER-FILE.
39       01  OLD-MASTER-RECORD              PIC X(32).
40
41       FD  TRANS-FILE.
42       01  TRANS-RECORD                   PIC X(37).
43
44       FD  NEW-MASTER-FILE.
45       01  NEW-MASTER-RECORD              PIC X(32).
46
47       FD  TRANS-REPORT.
48       01  TRANS-LINE                     PIC X(63).
49
50       WORKING-STORAGE SECTION.
51
52       01  PROGRAM-SWITCHES.
53           05  S1-EOF-MASTER-SWITCH      PIC X(1).
54               88  S1-EOF-MASTER              VALUE "T".
55               88  S1-NOT-EOF-MASTER         VALUE "F".
56
57           05  S2-EOF-TRANS-SWITCH       PIC X(1).
58               88  S2-EOF-TRANS              VALUE "T".
59               88  S2-NOT-EOF-TRANS          VALUE "F".
60
61           05  S3-READ-MASTER-SWITCH     PIC X(1).
62               88  S3-READ-MASTER            VALUE "T".
63               88  S3-NOT-READ-MASTER        VALUE "F".
64
65           05  S4-READ-TRANS-SWITCH      PIC X(1).
66               88  S4-READ-TRANS             VALUE "T".
67               88  S4-NOT-READ-TRANS         VALUE "F".
68
69           05  S5-TRANS-PROCESSED-SWITCH PIC X(1).
70               88  S5-TRANS-PROCESSED        VALUE "T".
71               88  S5-NOT-TRANS-PROCESSED    VALUE "F".
72
73           05  S6-RECORD-PENDING-SWITCH  PIC X(1).
74               88  S6-RECORD-PENDING         VALUE "T".
75               88  S6-RECORD-NOT-PENDING     VALUE "F".
76
77       01  WA-WORK-AREAS.
78           05  WA-PREV-MR-BUDGET-CODE        PIC X(5).
79           05  WA-PREV-TR-BUDGET-TRANS-CODE  PIC X(6).
80           05  WA-PENDING-MASTER-RECORD      PIC X(32).
81           05  WA-KEYBOARD-RESPONSE          PIC X(1).
82           05  WA-BALANCE-CORRECTION         PIC S9(4)V99.
83
84       01  MR-MASTER-RECORD.
85           05  MR-BUDGET-CODE            PIC X(5).
86           05  MR-DESCRIPTION            PIC X(15).
87           05  MR-ALLOCATION             PIC 9(4)V99.
88           05  MR-BALANCE                PIC S9(4)V99.
89
90       01  TR-TRANS-RECORD.
91           05  TR-BUDGET-TRANS-CODE.
92               10  TR-BUDGET-CODE            PIC X(5).
93               10  TR-TRANS-CODE             PIC X(1).
94                   88  TR-DELETE-ACCOUNT         VALUE "1".
95                   88  TR-ADD-NEW-ACCOUNT        VALUE "2".
96                   88  TR-CHANGE-FIELDS          VALUE "3".
97           05  TR-TRANS-NUMBER              PIC X(4).
98           05  TR-DESCRIPTION              PIC X(15).
99           05  TR-ALLOCATION              PIC 9(4)V99.
100          05  TR-ALLOCATION-X REDEFINES TR-ALLOCATION
101                                          PIC X(6).
102          05  TR-BALANCE                 PIC S9(4)V99.
103
104      01  TL-TRANS-LINE.
105          05  TL-TRANS-RECORD            PIC X(37).
106          05                             PIC X(2)
107                                          VALUE SPACES.
108          05  TL-ERROR-MESSAGE           PIC X(24).
109
110
111      PROCEDURE DIVISION.
112
113      000-PROCESS-MASTER-TRANS.
114      ************Initialization Sequence************
115          OPEN INPUT OLD-MASTER-FILE
116                     TRANS-FILE
117               OUTPUT NEW-MASTER-FILE
118                      TRANS-REPORT
119          PERFORM 100-INITIALIZE-VARIABLE-FIELDS
120
121      **************Processing Sequence*************
122          PERFORM UNTIL S1-EOF-MASTER
123                    AND S2-EOF-TRANS
124              PERFORM 200-GET-NEXT-RECORD
125              PERFORM 220-PROCESS-RECORD
126          END-PERFORM
127
128      **************Termination Sequence*************
129          CLOSE OLD-MASTER-FILE
130                TRANS-FILE
131                NEW-MASTER-FILE
132                TRANS-REPORT
133          STOP RUN
134          .
135      *************************************************
136
137      100-INITIALIZE-VARIABLE-FIELDS.
138          SET S1-NOT-EOF-MASTER
139              S2-NOT-EOF-TRANS
140              S3-READ-MASTER
141              S4-READ-TRANS
142              S6-RECORD-NOT-PENDING TO TRUE
143          INITIALIZE TL-ERROR-MESSAGE
144          MOVE LOW-VALUES TO WA-PREV-MR-BUDGET-CODE
145                            WA-PREV-TR-BUDGET-TRANS-CODE
146          .
147      200-GET-NEXT-RECORD.
148          EVALUATE
149                  S3-READ-MASTER ALSO S4-READ-TRANS
150      *         --------------      --------------
151
152          WHEN  TRUE       ALSO     TRUE
153      *         --------------           ---------
154                                   PERFORM 800-READ-MASTER-RECORD
155                                   PERFORM 820-READ-TRANS-RECORD
156                                   SET S3-NOT-READ-MASTER
157                                       S4-NOT-READ-TRANS
158                                       S5-NOT-TRANS-PROCESSED TO TRUE
159
160          WHEN  TRUE       ALSO     FALSE
161      *         --------------           ---------
162                                   IF NOT S6-RECORD-PENDING
163                                      PERFORM 800-READ-MASTER-RECORD
164                                   ELSE
165                                      MOVE WA-PENDING-MASTER-RECORD TO
166                                           MR-MASTER-RECORD
167                                      MOVE MR-BUDGET-CODE TO
168                                           WA-PREV-MR-BUDGET-CODE
169                                      SET S6-RECORD-NOT-PENDING TO TRUE
170                                   END-IF
171                                   SET S3-NOT-READ-MASTER
172                                       S5-NOT-TRANS-PROCESSED TO TRUE
173
174          WHEN  FALSE      ALSO     TRUE
175      *         --------------           ---------
176                                   PERFORM 820-READ-TRANS-RECORD
177                                   SET S4-NOT-READ-TRANS TO TRUE
178          END-EVALUATE
179          .
```

Figure 14-11 (continued)

```
180  220-PROCESS-RECORD.
181      EVALUATE
182            S2-EOF-TRANS ALSO S1-EOF-MASTER
183  *        ------------     -------------
184
185  *     No end of file
186      WHEN     FALSE    ALSO    FALSE
187  *        ------------     -------------
188          EVALUATE TRUE
189              WHEN MR-BUDGET-CODE = TR-BUDGET-CODE
190                  PERFORM 300-PROCESS-TRANS
191                  SET S4-READ-TRANS
192                      S5-TRANS-PROCESSED TO TRUE
193              WHEN MR-BUDGET-CODE < TR-BUDGET-CODE
194                  IF S5-TRANS-PROCESSED
195                      PERFORM 400-PROCESS-MASTER
196                  ELSE
197                      PERFORM 450-PROCESS-UNMATCHED-MASTER
198                  END-IF
199                  SET S3-READ-MASTER TO TRUE
200              WHEN MR-BUDGET-CODE > TR-BUDGET-CODE
201                  PERFORM 350-PROCESS-UNMATCHED-TRANS
202                  SET S4-READ-TRANS TO TRUE
203          END-EVALUATE
204
205  *     End of transaction file
206      WHEN     TRUE     ALSO     FALSE
207  *        ------------     -------------
208              IF S5-TRANS-PROCESSED
209                  PERFORM 400-PROCESS-MASTER
210              ELSE
211                  PERFORM 450-PROCESS-UNMATCHED-MASTER
212              END-IF
213              SET S3-READ-MASTER TO TRUE
214
215  *     End of master file
216      WHEN     FALSE    ALSO     TRUE
217  *        ------------     -------------
218                  PERFORM 350-PROCESS-UNMATCHED-TRANS
219                  IF TR-ADD-NEW-ACCOUNT
220                      PERFORM 450-PROCESS-UNMATCHED-MASTER
221                  END-IF
222                  SET S4-READ-TRANS TO TRUE
223
224      END-EVALUATE
225      .
226  ***********************************************************
227  * Record Processing--PERFORMed from 220-PROCESS-RECORD
228  ***********************************************************
229  300-PROCESS-TRANS.
230      EVALUATE TRUE
231          WHEN TR-DELETE-ACCOUNT
232              PERFORM 650-DELETE-ACCOUNT
233          WHEN TR-ADD-NEW-ACCOUNT
234              MOVE "CANNOT ADD MASTER" TO TL-ERROR-MESSAGE
235          WHEN TR-CHANGE-FIELDS
236              PERFORM 500-CHANGE-FIELDS
237          WHEN OTHER
238              MOVE "INVALID TRANSACTION CODE" TO TL-ERROR-MESSAGE
239      END-EVALUATE
240      PERFORM 870-PRINT-TRANS-RECORD
241      .
242  350-PROCESS-UNMATCHED-TRANS.
243      IF TR-ADD-NEW-ACCOUNT
244          PERFORM 600-ADD-NEW-ACCOUNT
245      ELSE
246          MOVE "NO MATCHING MASTER" TO TL-ERROR-MESSAGE
247      END-IF
248      PERFORM 870-PRINT-TRANS-RECORD
249      .
250  400-PROCESS-MASTER.
251      PERFORM 850-WRITE-MASTER-RECORD
252      .
253  450-PROCESS-UNMATCHED-MASTER.
254      PERFORM 850-WRITE-MASTER-RECORD
255      .

256  ***********************************************************
257  * Transaction Processing--PERFORMed from 300 and 350
258  ***********************************************************
259  500-CHANGE-FIELDS.
260      IF TR-DESCRIPTION NOT = SPACES
261          MOVE TR-DESCRIPTION TO MR-DESCRIPTION
262      END-IF
263      IF TR-ALLOCATION-X NOT = SPACES
264          MOVE TR-ALLOCATION TO WA-BALANCE-CORRECTION
265          SUBTRACT MR-ALLOCATION FROM WA-BALANCE-CORRECTION
266          ADD WA-BALANCE-CORRECTION TO MR-BALANCE
267          MOVE TR-ALLOCATION TO MR-ALLOCATION
268      END-IF
269      .
270  600-ADD-NEW-ACCOUNT.
271      IF NOT S1-EOF-MASTER
272          MOVE MR-MASTER-RECORD TO WA-PENDING-MASTER-RECORD
273          SET S6-RECORD-PENDING TO TRUE
274      END-IF
275      MOVE TR-BUDGET-CODE TO MR-BUDGET-CODE
276                             WA-PREV-MR-BUDGET-CODE
277      MOVE TR-DESCRIPTION TO MR-DESCRIPTION
278      MOVE TR-ALLOCATION TO MR-ALLOCATION
279      MOVE TR-BALANCE TO MR-BALANCE
280      SET S4-READ-TRANS TO TRUE
281      .
282  650-DELETE-ACCOUNT.
283      SET S3-READ-MASTER
284          S4-READ-TRANS TO TRUE
285      .
286  ***********************************************************
287  * File Reads--PERFORMed from 200-GET-NEXT-RECORD
288  ***********************************************************
289  800-READ-MASTER-RECORD.
290      READ OLD-MASTER-FILE INTO MR-MASTER-RECORD
291          AT END
292              SET S1-EOF-MASTER TO TRUE
293          NOT AT END
294              IF MR-BUDGET-CODE NOT > WA-PREV-MR-BUDGET-CODE
295                  DISPLAY "MASTER SEQUENCE ERROR; BUDGET CODES:"
296                  DISPLAY WA-PREV-MR-BUDGET-CODE, " ", MR-BUDGET-CODE
297                  PERFORM 950-ABORT-PROGRAM
298              ELSE
299                  MOVE MR-BUDGET-CODE TO WA-PREV-MR-BUDGET-CODE
300              END-IF
301      END-READ
302      .
303  820-READ-TRANS-RECORD.
304      READ TRANS-FILE INTO TR-TRANS-RECORD
305          AT END
306              SET S2-EOF-TRANS TO TRUE
307          NOT AT END
308              IF TR-BUDGET-TRANS-CODE < WA-PREV-TR-BUDGET-TRANS-CODE
309                  DISPLAY "TRANS SEQUENCE ERROR; BUDGET/TRANS CODES:"
310                  DISPLAY WA-PREV-TR-BUDGET-TRANS-CODE, " ",
311                          TR-BUDGET-TRANS-CODE
312                  PERFORM 950-ABORT-PROGRAM
313              ELSE
314                  MOVE TR-BUDGET-TRANS-CODE TO
315                       WA-PREV-TR-BUDGET-TRANS-CODE
316              END-IF
317      END-READ
318      .
319  ***********************************************************
320  * Output/Error Termination Segment
321  ***********************************************************
322  850-WRITE-MASTER-RECORD.
323      MOVE MR-MASTER-RECORD TO NEW-MASTER-RECORD
324      WRITE NEW-MASTER-RECORD
325      .
326  870-PRINT-TRANS-RECORD.
327      MOVE TR-TRANS-RECORD TO TL-TRANS-RECORD
328      MOVE TL-TRANS-LINE TO TRANS-LINE
329      WRITE TRANS-LINE
330      MOVE SPACES TO TL-ERROR-MESSAGE
331      .
332  950-ABORT-PROGRAM.
333      DISPLAY "****** PROGRAM ABORTED ******"
334      DISPLAY "Press ENTER to Exit"
335      ACCEPT WA-KEYBOARD-RESPONSE
336      SET S1-EOF-MASTER
337          S2-EOF-TRANS TO TRUE
338      .
```

combination of the two, is required for sequence checking. Remember, the transaction file must be in sequence based on these two fields.

3. The TR-TRANS-CODE includes three 88-level items to designate the allowable values (as required by the programming specifications).

4. The error record (lines 104–108) provides space for the transaction record and a short error message.

The five program switches described in the general pseudocode form of Figure 14-7 are defined in program lines 53–71. The sixth switch, S6-RECORD-PENDING-SWITCH, will be used to facilitate adding a master record.

The work area (lines 77–82) provides two fields to store the key field values of the preceding records for sequence checking. You will see how the other three work areas are used in the program.

PROCEDURE DIVISION Coding—Input Record Control

One of the features of this program logic is the way in which the switches S3 and S4 control the reading from the two files. Since both S3-READ-MASTER and S4-READ-TRANS are set to True in the initialization module (lines 140 and 141), the first execution of the 200 module causes the WHEN option of line 152 to be exercised. This causes both a master record (line 154) and a transaction record (line 155) to be read. It also turns the Read switches off (by setting S3-NOT-READ-MASTER and S4-NOT-READ-TRANS to True). Basically, this indicates that an unprocessed record is in each of the input record areas.

In subsequent passes, the program will read either a master record (under the WHEN of line 160) or a transaction record (under the WHEN of line 174) as controlled by the S3 and S4 switches. The process of accessing the next master is complicated by the possibility of a record addition transaction. This is described later.

In the 800 and 820 modules to read the records, the sequence check is performed under the NOT AT END phrase. (For the first records, the sequencing test is passed because the save areas were initialized to LOW-VALUES in the 100 module—lines 144 and 145.) If the record is in sequence, its sequence-control field is saved for the next read (line 299 for the master and lines 314 and 315 for the transaction).

As each master or transaction record is processed, the corresponding S3 or S4 switch is set to true (lines 191, 199, 202, 213, or 222). These switches determine whether a master or transaction is read during the next execution of the 200 module.

The 220-PROCESS-RECORD Module

The code of the 220 module corresponds exactly to the pseudocode of Figure 14-7. The three options for the comparison of the budget codes of the master and transaction records begin at lines 189, 193, and 200. It is in this module that the determination of how to process the input record is made.

Record condition	Tested at	Module performed
Matching transaction	Line 189	300-PROCESS-TRANS
Unmatching transaction	Line 200	350-PROCESS-UNMATCHED-TRANS
Matching master	Line 194	400-PROCESS-MASTER
Unmatching master	Line 194	450-PROCESS-UNMATCHED-MASTER

Whenever a transaction record is processed with its budget code equal to that of the current master, S5-TRANS-PROCESSED is set to True—line 192. (S5-NOT-TRANS-PROCESSED was set to False when a new master was read—lines 158 or 172.) So, when a transaction record with a different budget code is read, this switch controls whether the master is processed as an updated master or as an unmatched master (lines 208–212).

Record Processing Modules

The 300 module processes the current transaction record against its corresponding master according to the transaction code; the 350 module processes an unmatched transaction record. Actions of these two modules are best described by the following table, which summarizes the three transaction code possibilities:

Transaction type	Matching master	No matching master
Delete master	Delete existing master (300 module, line 232)	No master to delete—transaction record error (350 module, line 246)
Add master	Transaction error—cannot add master when one already exists (300 module, line 234)	Create new master from the transaction record data (350 module, line 244)
Change fields	Make change (300 module, line 236)	Transaction record error (350 module, line 246)

In each instance, an error condition causes an appropriate error message to be moved to the transaction report line. The transaction record is printed with or without an error message via lines 240 and 248.

The 500-CHANGE-FIELDS Module

A change transaction record can contain new values for the master record description field and the allocation field; a change to the allocation field also changes the balance field, as described earlier. A nonblank transaction description field causes the desired replacement (lines 260–262). In order to test for spaces in the transaction allocation field, that data-item is redefined with the PICTURE symbol X (lines 99–101). Because the budget balance must be adjusted by the same amount as the allocation, a calculation is made in lines 264–266.

Adding a Master— The 600-ADD-NEW-ACCOUNT Module

Adding a new master is considerably more complex than the other two operations. First, the only condition under which a new master can be added is if the transaction record (containing the new master data) has a key field value less than that of the current master. If so, you effectively are dealing with two master records at the same time: one in the master record area and the other in the transaction record area. Handling this is a multi-step process:

1. Move the current master to a temporary save area.
2. Construct the new master in the master record area, using data from the current transaction record.
3. Resume the reading and processing of transaction records. The new master may have one or more transactions to be processed.
4. When a new transaction key field value is detected, write the newly created master to the file.
5. Instead of reading another master from the input master file, move the previously saved master back to the master record area.
6. Continue processing.

You should notice that the 600-ADD-NEW-ACCOUNT module is performed only from the unmatched-transaction module (line 244).

Two additional entries are needed in the DATA DIVISION: a record save area (WA-PENDING-MASTER-RECORD) and a program switch (S6-RECORD-PENDING-SWITCH). These are used in the 600 module as follows:

1. If the master EOF is not detected yet (other master records are still available), the current master is moved to the save area and S6-RECORD-PENDING is set to True (lines 271–274).

2. Values from the transaction record are moved into the master record area, which creates the new master—lines 275 and 277–279.

3. The budget code field of the new master is copied to the previous budget code field for future sequence checking—line 276.

When this action is complete, processing of additional transactions can proceed without regard to this master's source.

With this addition to the program, two sources of master record input exist: the old master file and the record-pending save area. So, new master input is controlled by the S6 switch at line 162. The pending master is accessed at lines 165–168.

Deleting a Master—The 650-DELETE-ACCOUNT Module

As with a budget allocation change, a master can be deleted only under the matching-master condition. The 650 module is performed from the 300 module, line 232. The action of deleting a master simply involves not writing it to the updated file. So, the delete function is almost trivial. At line 283, the S3-READ-MASTER switch is set to True; as with all transaction processing, the S4-READ-TRANS switch is also set to True. Upon completing this module, control is immediately returned via 300—then 220—to the main module. The next pass through the loop causes the read option of lines 154–158 to be executed (both switches are true), thereby reading both a master and a transaction. The previous old master will not be written.

The 400 and 450 Modules

The 400 and 450 modules both consist of a single statement: PERFORM the 850 module. In this simplified version of master-transaction processing, the duplication is not necessary. The 450 module could be omitted and lines 197, 211, and 220 could refer just to the 400 module. In fact, both 400 and 450 could be eliminated and PERFORM statements at lines 195, 197, 209, 211, and 220 could all refer to the 850 module.

However, the general structure of the master-transaction pseudocode (Figure 14-7, page 502) and structure chart (Figure 14-8) can be applied to a wide variety of master-transaction applications. If a program conforms to this general structure, both the overall and the specific of the program are readily recognizable. Modifications—such as eliminating the 400 and 450 modules, as described—can lead to confusion and result in a program more difficult to modify.

The READ Modules

The two READ modules, 800 and 820, are identical in structure. In both, the first action under the NOT AT END condition is to check the record sequence. For the master, the NOT > condition is used to ensure that no two masters have the same key field value. For the transaction, the test is < (less than), which allows more than one transaction record to have the same key field value.

If the records are in sequence, the budget code of the newly read record is moved to the save area for the next time through the cycle (line 299 and lines 314–315).

COBOL-74

The overall logic of the COBOL-74 version of SEQ-MNT shown in Figure 14-12 is almost identical to that of the COBOL-85 version. Perhaps the trickiest aspect is converting EVALUATE statements to corresponding IF forms. The COBOL-74 version contains numerous subtle changes. For example, look at the first condition of the 200 module (lines 147–155)—this code corresponds to lines 160–172 of Figure 14-11. In Figure 14-12, setting of the switches was moved to precede the nested IF statement at line 150. Remember, the period at line 155 terminates both IF statements (lines 147 and 150).

Figure 14-12   COBOL-74 version of SEQ-MNT.

```
1        IDENTIFICATION DIVISION.
2        PROGRAM-ID.   SEQ-MNT.
3
4      * Pyramid Sales Company
5      * Budget File Maintenance
6      * Written by W. Price 2/15/95
7      * COBOL-74
8
9      * The program updates the Budget Master file from a
10     * Budget Transaction file. There are 3 trans types:
11     *    1 - Delete a Master record
12     *    2 - Add a Master record
13     *    3 - Change fields of the master record
14     * Output is an updated Budget Master file
15     * and a Transaction activity report
16
17       ENVIRONMENT DIVISION.
18
19       INPUT-OUTPUT SECTION.
20
21       FILE-CONTROL.
22           SELECT OLD-MASTER-FILE
23               ASSIGN TO (system dependent).
24           SELECT TRANS-FILE
25               ASSIGN TO (system dependent).
26           SELECT NEW-MASTER-FILE
27               ASSIGN TO (system dependent).
28           SELECT TRANS-REPORT
29               ASSIGN TO (system dependent).
30
31
32       DATA DIVISION.
33
34       FILE SECTION.
35
36       FD  OLD-MASTER-FILE.
37       01  OLD-MASTER-RECORD              PIC X(32).
38
39       FD  TRANS-FILE.
40       01  TRANS-RECORD                   PIC X(37).
41
42       FD  NEW-MASTER-FILE.
43       01  NEW-MASTER-RECORD              PIC X(32).
44
45       FD  TRANS-REPORT.
46       01  TRANS-LINE                     PIC X(63).
47
48       WORKING-STORAGE SECTION.
49
50       01  PROGRAM-SWITCHES.
51           05  S1-EOF-MASTER-SWITCH       PIC X(1).
52               88  S1-EOF-MASTER              VALUE "T".
53               88  S1-NOT-EOF-MASTER          VALUE "F".
54
55           05  S2-EOF-TRANS-SWITCH        PIC X(1).
56               88  S2-EOF-TRANS               VALUE "T".
57               88  S2-NOT-EOF-TRANS           VALUE "F".
58
59           05  S3-READ-MASTER-SWITCH      PIC X(1).
60               88  S3-READ-MASTER             VALUE "T".
61               88  S3-NOT-READ-MASTER         VALUE "F".
62
63           05  S4-READ-TRANS-SWITCH       PIC X(1).
64               88  S4-READ-TRANS              VALUE "T".
65               88  S4-NOT-READ-TRANS          VALUE "F".
66
67           05  S5-TRANS-PROCESSED-SWITCH  PIC X(1).
68               88  S5-TRANS-PROCESSED         VALUE "T".
69               88  S5-NOT-TRANS-PROCESSED     VALUE "F".
70
71           05  S6-RECORD-PENDING-SWITCH   PIC X(1).
72               88  S6-RECORD-PENDING          VALUE "T".
73               88  S6-RECORD-NOT-PENDING      VALUE "F".
74
75       01  WA-WORK-AREAS.
76           05  WA-PREV-MR-BUDGET-CODE        PIC X(5).
77           05  WA-PREV-TR-BUDGET-TRANS-CODE  PIC X(6).
78           05  WA-PENDING-MASTER-RECORD      PIC X(32).
79           05  WA-KEYBOARD-RESPONSE          PIC X(1).
80           05  WA-BALANCE-CORRECTION         PIC S9(4)V99.
81
82       01  MR-MASTER-RECORD.
83           05  MR-BUDGET-CODE                PIC X(5).
84           05  MR-DESCRIPTION                PIC X(15).
85           05  MR-ALLOCATION                 PIC 9(4)V99.
86           05  MR-BALANCE                    PIC S9(4)V99.
87
88       01  TR-TRANS-RECORD.
89           05  TR-BUDGET-TRANS-CODE.
90               10  TR-BUDGET-CODE            PIC X(5).
91               10  TR-TRANS-CODE             PIC X(1).
92                   88  TR-DELETE-ACCOUNT         VALUE "1".
93                   88  TR-ADD-NEW-ACCOUNT        VALUE "2".
94                   88  TR-CHANGE-FIELDS          VALUE "3".
95           05  TR-TRANS-NUMBER               PIC X(4).
96           05  TR-DESCRIPTION                PIC X(15).
97           05  TR-ALLOCATION                 PIC 9(4)V99.
98           05  TR-ALLOCATION-X REDEFINES TR-ALLOCATION
99                                             PIC X(6).
100          05  TR-BALANCE                    PIC S9(4)V99.
101
102      01  TL-TRANS-LINE.
103          05  TL-TRANS-RECORD               PIC X(37).
104          05  FILLER                        PIC X(2)
105                                            VALUE SPACES.
106          05  TL-ERROR-MESSAGE              PIC X(24).
107
108
109      PROCEDURE DIVISION.
110
111      000-PROCESS-MASTER-TRANS.
112      *************Initialization Sequence************
113          OPEN INPUT OLD-MASTER-FILE
114                     TRANS-FILE
115               OUTPUT NEW-MASTER-FILE
116                      TRANS-REPORT
117          PERFORM 100-INITIALIZE-VARIABLE-FIELDS
118
119      **************Processing Sequence*************
120          PERFORM 150-PROCESS-RECORDS
121              UNTIL S1-EOF-MASTER
122                AND S2-EOF-TRANS
123
124      **************Termination Sequence************
125          CLOSE OLD-MASTER-FILE
126                TRANS-FILE
127                NEW-MASTER-FILE
128                TRANS-REPORT
129          STOP RUN.
130      *********************************************
131
132      100-INITIALIZE-VARIABLE-FIELDS.
133          MOVE "F" TO S1-EOF-MASTER-SWITCH
134                      S2-EOF-TRANS-SWITCH
135                      S6-RECORD-PENDING-SWITCH
136          MOVE "T" TO S3-READ-MASTER-SWITCH
137                      S4-READ-TRANS-SWITCH
138          MOVE SPACES TO TL-ERROR-MESSAGE
139          MOVE LOW-VALUES TO WA-PREV-MR-BUDGET-CODE
140                             WA-PREV-TR-BUDGET-TRANS-CODE.
141
142      150-PROCESS-RECORDS.
143          PERFORM 200-GET-NEXT-RECORD
144          PERFORM 220-PROCESS-RECORD.
145
```

(continues)

Figure 14-12   (continued)

```
146   200-GET-NEXT-RECORD.
147       IF S3-READ-MASTER
148           MOVE "F" TO S3-READ-MASTER-SWITCH
149           MOVE "F" TO S5-TRANS-PROCESSED-SWITCH
150           IF NOT S6-RECORD-PENDING
151               PERFORM 800-READ-MASTER-RECORD
152           ELSE
153               MOVE WA-PENDING-MASTER-RECORD TO MR-MASTER-RECORD
154               MOVE MR-BUDGET-CODE TO WA-PREV-MR-BUDGET-CODE
155               MOVE "F" TO S6-RECORD-PENDING-SWITCH.
156
157       IF S4-READ-TRANS
158           PERFORM 820-READ-TRANS-RECORD
159           MOVE "F" TO S4-READ-TRANS-SWITCH.
160
161   220-PROCESS-RECORD.
162       IF S2-NOT-EOF-TRANS AND S1-NOT-EOF-MASTER
163           IF MR-BUDGET-CODE = TR-BUDGET-CODE
164               PERFORM 300-PROCESS-TRANS
165               MOVE "T" TO S4-READ-TRANS-SWITCH
166               MOVE "T" TO S5-TRANS-PROCESSED-SWITCH
167           ELSE IF MR-BUDGET-CODE > TR-BUDGET-CODE
168               PERFORM 350-PROCESS-UNMATCHED-TRANS
169               MOVE "T" TO S4-READ-TRANS-SWITCH
170           ELSE IF MR-BUDGET-CODE < TR-BUDGET-CODE
171               MOVE "T" TO S3-READ-MASTER-SWITCH
172               IF S5-TRANS-PROCESSED
173                   PERFORM 400-PROCESS-MASTER
174               ELSE
175                   PERFORM 450-PROCESS-UNMATCHED-MASTER.
176
177   *     End of transaction file
178       IF S2-EOF-TRANS AND S1-NOT-EOF-MASTER
179           MOVE "T" TO S3-READ-MASTER-SWITCH
180           IF S5-TRANS-PROCESSED
181               PERFORM 400-PROCESS-MASTER
182           ELSE
183               PERFORM 450-PROCESS-UNMATCHED-MASTER.
184
185   *     End of master file
186       IF S2-NOT-EOF-TRANS AND S1-EOF-MASTER
187           PERFORM 350-PROCESS-UNMATCHED-TRANS
188           MOVE "T" TO S4-READ-TRANS-SWITCH
189           IF TR-ADD-NEW-ACCOUNT
190               PERFORM 450-PROCESS-UNMATCHED-MASTER.
191
192   ************************************************************
193   * Record Processing--PERFORMed from 220-PROCESS-RECORD
194   ************************************************************
195   300-PROCESS-TRANS.
196       IF TR-DELETE-ACCOUNT
197           PERFORM 650-DELETE-ACCOUNT
198       ELSE IF TR-ADD-NEW-ACCOUNT
199           MOVE "CANNOT ADD MASTER" TO TL-ERROR-MESSAGE
200       ELSE IF TR-CHANGE-FIELDS
201           PERFORM 500-CHANGE-FIELDS
202       ELSE
203           MOVE "INVALID TRANSACTION CODE" TO TL-ERROR-MESSAGE.
204       PERFORM 870-PRINT-TRANS-RECORD.
205       .
206   350-PROCESS-UNMATCHED-TRANS.
207       IF TR-ADD-NEW-ACCOUNT
208           PERFORM 600-ADD-NEW-ACCOUNT
209       ELSE
210           MOVE "NO MATCHING MASTER" TO TL-ERROR-MESSAGE.
211       PERFORM 870-PRINT-TRANS-RECORD.
212
213   400-PROCESS-MASTER.
214       PERFORM 850-WRITE-MASTER-RECORD.
215
216   450-PROCESS-UNMATCHED-MASTER.
217       PERFORM 850-WRITE-MASTER-RECORD.
218
219   ************************************************************
220   * Transaction Processing--PERFORMed from 300 and 350
221   ************************************************************
222   500-CHANGE-FIELDS.
223       IF TR-DESCRIPTION NOT = SPACES
224           MOVE TR-DESCRIPTION TO MR-DESCRIPTION.
225       IF TR-ALLOCATION-X NOT = SPACES
226           MOVE TR-ALLOCATION TO WA-BALANCE-CORRECTION
227           SUBTRACT MR-ALLOCATION FROM WA-BALANCE-CORRECTION
228           ADD WA-BALANCE-CORRECTION TO MR-BALANCE
229           MOVE TR-ALLOCATION TO MR-ALLOCATION.
230
231   600-ADD-NEW-ACCOUNT.
232       IF NOT S1-EOF-MASTER
233           MOVE MR-MASTER-RECORD TO WA-PENDING-MASTER-RECORD
234           MOVE "T" TO S6-RECORD-PENDING-SWITCH.
235       MOVE TR-BUDGET-CODE TO MR-BUDGET-CODE
236                             WA-PREV-MR-BUDGET-CODE
237       MOVE TR-DESCRIPTION TO MR-DESCRIPTION
238       MOVE TR-ALLOCATION TO MR-ALLOCATION
239       MOVE TR-BALANCE TO MR-BALANCE
240       MOVE "T" TO S4-READ-TRANS-SWITCH.
241
242   650-DELETE-ACCOUNT.
243       MOVE "T" TO S3-READ-MASTER-SWITCH
244       MOVE "T" TO S4-READ-TRANS-SWITCH.
245
246   ************************************************************
247   * File Reads--PERFORMed from 200-GET-NEXT-RECORD
248   ************************************************************
249   800-READ-MASTER-RECORD.
250       READ OLD-MASTER-FILE INTO MR-MASTER-RECORD
251           AT END
252               MOVE "T" TO S1-EOF-MASTER-SWITCH.
253       IF S1-NOT-EOF-MASTER
254           IF MR-BUDGET-CODE NOT > WA-PREV-MR-BUDGET-CODE
255               DISPLAY "MASTER SEQUENCE ERROR; BUDGET CODES:"
256               DISPLAY WA-PREV-MR-BUDGET-CODE, " ", MR-BUDGET-CODE
257               PERFORM 950-ABORT-PROGRAM
258           ELSE
259               MOVE MR-BUDGET-CODE TO WA-PREV-MR-BUDGET-CODE.
260
261   820-READ-TRANS-RECORD.
262       READ TRANS-FILE INTO TR-TRANS-RECORD
263           AT END
264               MOVE "T" TO S2-EOF-TRANS-SWITCH.
265       IF S2-NOT-EOF-TRANS
266           IF TR-BUDGET-TRANS-CODE < WA-PREV-TR-BUDGET-TRANS-CODE
267               DISPLAY "TRANS SEQUENCE ERROR; BUDGET/TRANS CODES:"
268               DISPLAY WA-PREV-TR-BUDGET-TRANS-CODE, " ",
269                       TR-BUDGET-TRANS-CODE
270               PERFORM 950-ABORT-PROGRAM
271           ELSE
272               MOVE TR-BUDGET-TRANS-CODE TO
273                    WA-PREV-TR-BUDGET-TRANS-CODE.
274
275   ************************************************************
276   * Output & Error-Termination Segment
277   ************************************************************
278   850-WRITE-MASTER-RECORD.
279       MOVE MR-MASTER-RECORD TO NEW-MASTER-RECORD
280       WRITE NEW-MASTER-RECORD.
281
282   870-PRINT-TRANS-RECORD.
283       MOVE TR-TRANS-RECORD TO TL-TRANS-RECORD
284       MOVE TL-TRANS-LINE TO TRANS-LINE
285       WRITE TRANS-LINE
286       MOVE SPACES TO TL-ERROR-MESSAGE.
287
288   950-ABORT-PROGRAM.
289       DISPLAY "****** PROGRAM ABORTED ******"
290       DISPLAY "Press ENTER to Exit"
291       ACCEPT WA-KEYBOARD-RESPONSE
292       MOVE "T" TO S1-EOF-MASTER-SWITCH
293                   S2-EOF-TRANS-SWITCH.
```

Variations on SEQ-MNT

Data Validation Example for the 500-CHANGE-FIELDS Module

Data validation that normally would be included in the SEQ-MNT program is illustrated by the following validation needs for the change record:

- Balance field blank: the balance cannot be changed by an entry in this field—it must be changed through an update.

- All change fields blank: nothing to change in a change record must be reported.

- Description field not left-justified.

- Allocation field not numeric.

- Allocation field negative.

Program code to perform these functions is shown in Figure 14-13(a), where an additional validation module was added. The validation techniques are familiar to you from Chapter 10. Notice that the field TR-BALANCE-X is used to ensure that this field is blank. The TR-BALANCE field would require a REDEFINES in the DATA DIVISION (as was done with TR-ALLOCATION). If any error is detected in the transaction record, TL-ERROR-MESSAGE will contain an error message. If it contains only spaces, the record is error free and the changes are allowed.

An alternate form is included in Figure 14-13(b), in which validation was incorporated directly into the 500 module under control of an EVALUATE. Which approach is better? The separate module solution is desirable because it separates two distinct functions: validating and changing. On the other hand, the alternate solution—even though it combines two distinct functions—is concise, clear, and not excessively long. In this case, they are both satisfactory.

Figure 14-13   Data validation solutions for change transaction records.

```
500-CHANGE-FIELDS.
    PERFORM 510-VALIDATE-CHANGE-FIELDS
    IF TL-ERROR-MESSAGE = SPACES
      IF TR-DESCRIPTION NOT = SPACES
        MOVE TR-DESCRIPTION TO MR-DESCRIPTION
      END-IF
      IF TR-ALLOCATION-X NOT = SPACES
        MOVE TR-ALLOCATION TO WA-BALANCE-CORRECTION
        SUBTRACT MR-ALLOCATION FROM WA-BALANCE-CORRECTION
        ADD WA-BALANCE-CORRECTION TO MR-BALANCE
        MOVE TR-ALLOCATION TO MR-ALLOCATION
      END-IF
    END-IF
    .
510-VALIDATE-CHANGE-FIELDS.
    EVALUATE TRUE
      WHEN TR-BALANCE-X NOT = SPACES
        MOVE "CANNOT CHANGE BALANCE" TO TL-ERROR-MESSAGE
      WHEN    TR-DESCRIPTION = SPACES
          AND TR-ALLOCATION-X = SPACES
        MOVE "BLANK CHANGE RECORD" TO TL-ERROR-MESSAGE
      WHEN TR-DESCRIPTION NOT = SPACES
          AND TR-DESCRIPTION (1:1) = SPACE
        MOVE "DESCR NOT LEFT-JUST" TO TL-ERROR-MESSAGE
      WHEN TR-ALLOCATION-X NOT = SPACES
        EVALUATE TRUE
          WHEN TR-ALLOCATION-X NOT NUMERIC
            MOVE "NONNUMERIC ALLOCATION" TO TL-ERROR-MESSAGE
          WHEN TR-ALLOCATION < 0
            MOVE "NEGATIVE ALLOCATION" TO TL-ERROR-MESSAGE
        END-EVALUATE
    END-EVALUATE
    .
```

```
500-CHANGE-FIELDS.
    EVALUATE TRUE
*     First, validate fields
      WHEN TR-BALANCE-X NOT = SPACES
        MOVE "CANNOT CHANGE BALANCE" TO TL-ERROR-MESSAGE
      WHEN    TR-DESCRIPTION = SPACES
          AND TR-ALLOCATION-X = SPACES
        MOVE "BLANK CHANGE RECORD" TO TL-ERROR-MESSAGE
      WHEN TR-DESCRIPTION NOT = SPACES
          AND TR-DESCRIPTION (1:1) = SPACE
        MOVE "DESCR NOT LEFT-JUST" TO TL-ERROR-MESSAGE
      WHEN TR-ALLOCATION-X NOT = SPACES
        EVALUATE TRUE
          WHEN TR-ALLOCATION-X NOT NUMERIC
            MOVE "NONNUMERIC ALLOCATION" TO TL-ERROR-MESSAGE
          WHEN TR-ALLOCATION < 0
            MOVE "NEGATIVE ALLOCATION" TO TL-ERROR-MESSAGE
        END-EVALUATE
*     All fields valid, so make changes
      WHEN OTHER
        IF TR-DESCRIPTION NOT = SPACES
          MOVE TR-DESCRIPTION TO MR-DESCRIPTION
        END-IF
        IF TR-ALLOCATION-X NOT = SPACES
          MOVE TR-ALLOCATION TO WA-BALANCE-CORRECTION
          SUBTRACT MR-ALLOCATION FROM WA-BALANCE-CORRECTION
          ADD WA-BALANCE-CORRECTION TO MR-BALANCE
          MOVE TR-ALLOCATION TO MR-ALLOCATION
        END-IF
    END-EVALUATE
    .
```

(a) Separate module solution.

(b) Combined module solution.

No More Than One Transaction Per Master

In most applications, the number of transaction records per master can be none, one, or many. However, what if each master could have no more than one transaction? The general program structure illustrated by SEQ-MNT makes this a simple modification. Referring to the 800 module to read master records, the test (line 294 of Figure 14-11)

```
IF MR-BUDGET-CODE NOT > WA-PREV-MR-BUDGET-CODE
```

ensures that the key field for each master record will be larger than that preceding. This results in no duplication. On the other hand, the test (line 308)

```
IF TR-BUDGET-TRANS-CODE < WA-PREV-TR-BUDGET-TRANS-CODE
```

ensures only that the current key field value is not smaller than the one preceding. The equal condition is allowable. Changing that condition to

```
IF TR-BUDGET-TRANS-CODE NOT > WA-PREV-TR-BUDGET-TRANS-CODE
```

guards against duplicate transaction records—permitting a maximum of one transaction per master. Notice that no other change is required to this program's code.

Matching Records

Occasionally, you will need to ensure that each master has exactly one transaction record. This is almost a trivial application for this master-transaction structure. Each cycle involves reading a record from both files and comparing their key field values. If they are equal, processing can occur—under the WHEN of line 189 in Figure 14-11. If they are not equal, an unmatched master or transaction record was detected and the program run must be aborted via the WHEN options at lines 193 and 200.

Updating In-Place

If the files for master-transaction processing are stored on magnetic disk, it is possible to update the master without writing a new one. This is called **updating in-place**, and it is possible because of the random-access nature of disk storage. The sequence of events in updating in-place processing is (1) read a master record, (2) process against transactions as appropriate, and (3) rewrite the master record. That is, the original master record is replaced by its updated copy.

Only two relatively minor changes are necessary to convert SEQ-MNT to perform the updating in-place: change the OPEN and the WRITE statements. The OPEN becomes as follows:

```
OPEN   I-O OLD-MASTER-FILE
       INPUT TRANS-FILE
       OUTPUT TRANS-ERROR-FILE
```

Here, the original file is now opened for I-O, rather than for INPUT. Also, NEW-MASTER-FILE is removed from the OPEN because no new file is created. (Its SELECT clause and record definition are also deleted from the program.) Whenever a sequential file is opened for I-O, its records can be read in exactly the same way as those of a file opened for INPUT. However, the writing of a record back to the file is limited to rewriting back to the most recent record read. For instance, you cannot read the twentieth record, modify it, and then write it back as the last record in the file.

To write the record back, you must use the REWRITE statement, as the following modified 850 module shows:

```
850-WRITE-MASTER-RECORD.
    MOVE MR-MASTER-RECORD TO OLD-MASTER-RECORD
    REWRITE OLD-MASTER-RECORD
```

Remember, when open for I-O, only the READ and REWRITE statements may be used; the WRITE is not allowed. So it is only possible to write back the record that was just read. Thus, updating in-place is not possible for maintenance functions in which records are added or physically deleted.

Also, do not confuse the I-O mode with the EXTEND mode described in Chapter 4. The EXTEND mode allows you to write new records to the end of an existing sequential file.

With sequential batch-transaction processing in which a new file is created, the old file serves as a backup in case something goes wrong during the processing run. Since updating in-place has no "old file," provisions need to be made for a backup in case the master becomes corrupted during processing.

Chapter Summary

Sequential file processing involves the concurrent reading of two files: a master file and a transaction file. Transaction file records contain data to make changes to master file records. The output is an updated copy of the original master file.

Master-transaction processing requires that (1) the master and transaction files have a field in common—a key field and (2) both files be in sequence based on the key field.

When processing, the transaction record key bears one of three relationships to the master record key: (1) the transaction key is less than the master key, (2) the transaction key is equal to the master key, or (3) the transaction key is greater than the master key.

- A transaction key less means that no matching master exists for that transaction. This is a valid condition only if the transaction signifies a record addition.

- A transaction key equal means that a matching master was found.

- A transaction key greater signals that one or more unmatched master records exist (not an error condition).

Exercises

Terms for Definition   update in-place

Questions About Example Programs   Describe the effect on program execution of each of the following programming errors in the SEQ-MNT program of Figure 14-11.

1. The S4 switch is omitted from the SET statement (line 157).

2. The SET for S6 is omitted (line 273).

3. The SET statements for S5 at lines 158 and 172 are omitted.

Programming Assignments

Programming Assignment 14-1: Vehicle File Maintenance

Background information:

The management of Rent-Ur-Wheels need a sequential maintenance program for the Vehicle file.

Input file 1: Vehicle master file (VEHICLE.DAT)

Vehicle record

Vehicle type	Make of vehicle	Model	License number	Daily rental fee	Daily collision ins.	Daily liability ins.
1 2 3 4	5 6 7 8 9 10 11 12 13 14 15 16 17 18	19 20 21 22 23 24 25 26 27 28	29 30 31 32 33 34 35	36 37 38 39	40 41 42 43	44 45

Input file 2: Vehicle transaction file (VEHICLE.TRA)

Vehicle transaction record

License number	Make of vehicle	Model	Vehicle type	Daily rental fee	Daily collision ins.	Daily liability ins.
1 2 3 4 5 6 7 8	9 10 11 12 13 14 15 16 17 18 19 20 21 22	23 24 25 26 27 28 29 30 31 32	33 34 35 36	37 38 39 40	41 42 43	44 45 46

└ Transaction type

Key field: License number

Output file: Updated Vehicle file

Output-report sample:

```
SEQUENTIAL VEHICLE MASTER FILE MAINTENANCE                    RUN DATE: 11/15/95
AUDIT/ERROR LIST                                                        PAGE    1

C  LICENSE                          TY        COL LIA RECORD/
D  NUMBER  MAKE          MODEL      PE  RATE  INS INS ACTION       ERROR MESSAGE
-  -------  ------------- ---------- --- ---- --- --- ---------    -------------
   1HOE042 CHEVROLET     BLACKWOOD  STD 2995 150 100 OLD MASTER
C  1HOE042                              3145         CHANGE
   1HOE042 CHEVROLET     BLACKWOOD  STD 3145 150 100 NEW MASTER

D  1URL111 CHRYSLER      WHIZZER    STD 3495 200 115 DELETED

D  1VVA188                                          DELETE       NO CORRESPONDING MASTER

A  2AAT268 BMW           SWALLOW    SPTS             ADD          INPUT FIELD NOT VALID

A  20VV230 CHEVROLET     ROMPER     TRCK 3450 240 135 ADD MASTER

Q  300K336 BMW           GALAXY     LUX  4495 265 140              INVALID UPDATE CODE

A  4EGG122 CHEVROLET     FUN WAGON  VAN  3695 235 122 ADD          MASTER ALREADY IN FILE

A  5CDL166 CHEVROLET     BLACKWOOD  STD  2995 150 100 ADD MASTER

   8AGN151 HARLEY        CROW       VAN  3695 235 122 OLD MASTER
C  8AGN151 FORD          SPORT                        CHANGE
   8AGN151 FORD          SPORT      VAN  3695 235 122 NEW MASTER


REPORT SUMMARY

TRANSACTION SUMMARY

              ADDS     DELETES   CHANGES    INVALID CODE
              ----     -------   -------    ------------
PROCESSED       2         1         2
REJECTED        2         1         0            1

MASTER RECORD SUMMARY

MASTERS READ           1,246
MASTERS REWRITTEN      1,245
MASTERS ADDED              2
MASTERS DELETED            1
TOTAL MASTERS WRITTEN  1,247
```

Program operations:

1. Sort the input Vehicle master file on the license number field (it is not already in sorted sequence).

2. Read each input vehicle transaction record.
   a. Validate to ensure that it contains one of the following Transaction-type codes:
      A   (Add record to master file)
      C   (Change fields of existing record)
      D   (Delete record from master file)
   b. Sequence check the input transaction records.

3. For each valid Add transaction, create a new master record.
   a. Validate as follows:
      All numeric fields as numeric and greater than zero.
      Vehicle license number must contain no spaces.
      Vehicle Type, Make, and Model must not be empty.
   b. Fields in master not contained in transaction must be set to 0 (numeric) or spaces (alphanumeric).
   c. For a valid Add, print the transaction record with the message ADD MASTER.

4. For each valid Change transaction, replace fields of the master corresponding to nonblank fields of the transaction.
   a. Validate nonblank numeric fields as numeric and greater than zero.
   b. Only the following fields of the master corresponding to fields of the transaction (excluding the vehicle license number) can be replaced.
   c. For a valid Change, print three lines: the original master, the transaction record, and the changed master. For messages, use OLD MASTER, CHANGE, and NEW MASTER.

5. For each Delete transaction, delete the corresponding master record.
   a. Print the deleted master record with the message DELETED.

6. For each invalid transaction record, print the record with an included error message as follows:

Error condition	Error message
Add—master record already in file	MASTER ALREADY IN FILE
Add/Change—invalid input fields	INPUT FIELD NOT VALID
Delete/Change—no such master in file	NO CORRESPONDING MASTER
Invalid update code	INVALID UPDATE CODE
Transaction file record out of sequence	TRANS SEQUENCE ERROR

7. Print the heading line on the first page and on each following page of the report.
   a. Accumulate and print the page number on the heading line as shown in the sample report.

8. Print a report summary as shown on the sample report.

Programming
Assignment 14-2:
Student Grade
Processing

Background information:

At the conclusion of each semester at Bayview Institute of Computer Technology, student grades are entered into a student transaction file, with one record for each course taken by each student. Semester-end processing involves updating the student master and printing grade reports.

Input file 1: Student master file (STUDENT.DAT)

Student record

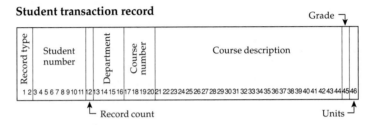

Input file 2: Student course file (STUD-GRA.DAT)

Student transaction record

Key field: Student number

Output file: Updated Student master file

Output-report sample:

```
                    Bayview Institute of Computer Technology
                            Student Grade Report

     Student number: 365-87-0004                      Date:  6/12/95

     Student: BACH        SUZANNE

            Course                                                    Grade
     Dept.  number   Description              Units      Grade        points

     CIS    22B      ADVANCED COBOL             4          A            16
     CIS    121      HYPERVENTILATION CONTROL   3          D             3
     ENGL   22       GUD SPELLING               3          B             9
     PSYC   108      BASIC SOCIAL SKILLS        3          B             9
     PE     33       AEROBICS                   1          A             4

                                                          GPA

                     Current semester totals   14         2.93         41

                     Previous semester totals  88         2.60        229

                     Updated totals            102        2.65        270
```

Program operations:

1. Sort the input student master file on the student number field (it is not already in sorted sequence).

2. Read each input student course record—assume this file is in sequence on the student number field. For each transaction with a corresponding master:
   a. Calculate Grade points by multiplying Units by:
      4 - Grade of A
      3 - Grade of B
      2 - Grade of C
      1 - Grade of D
   b. Add Units to Units-completed of master. Add calculated Grade points to Grade-points of master.
   c. For a grade F, add Units to Units-completed of master, but leave Grade-points of master unchanged.
   d. For a grade W, do no calculations.

3. Write each unmatched transaction record to an error log file.

4. Print a course report for each student, using data from both the input master and course files. Each grade report should be printed on a new page. (Note: The number of records in the course file is deliberately small to minimize the amount of printed output.)

INDEXED FILE PROCESSING

About This Chapter

This chapter differs slightly from previous chapters in two respects. First, in order to maintain continuity in descriptions of example programs, most of the general formats for new statement forms are delayed until the end of the chapter. Second, because the SELECT clause is of special significance for this chapter's examples, all example programs include complete SELECT clauses with the ASSIGN conforming to the Micro Focus implementation.

CHAPTER OUTLINE

CHAPTER OBJECTIVES

Throughout this book, you have worked with sequential data files. The input-output operations you have performed represent a relatively small subset of the file-processing capabilities available to the COBOL programmer. From this chapter, you will learn about the following:

- Indexed and relative file organizations, which allow for both random and sequential access to records of the file.

- Defining and using two or more keys for an indexed file.

- Random access, which allows records of a file to be processed in random order.

- The REWRITE statement, which replaces the record (on disk) just read. The typical processing sequence is to read a record, make changes to it, and rewrite it.

- The DELETE statement, which allows you to remove a record from an indexed or relative file.

- Dynamic access to a file, which allows a file to be processed both randomly and sequentially in the same program.

- The START statement, which allows positioning within a file in order to begin sequential processing at some point other than the beginning of the file.

- Programmer-written error-recovery routines and the COBOL provision for implementing them (declaratives, I-O status, and the USE statement).

Generating a New File

The Employee File

In Chapter 4, you learned that generating a new data file is best done as a two-step process. Through a utility program, you first create a new, empty file. Then through an appropriate data-entry program, you add records. The DATAENT program of Chapter 10 is an example of record addition through keyboard data entry with data validation. The batch-processing sequential maintenance program (SEQ-MNT) of Chapter 14 includes an option to add records to a master file from data input of a transaction file.

Assignments in this chapter use data from sequential files stored on the data diskette included with this book. However, in order to use any of them for this chapter's assignments, you will need to create an indexed equivalent. This is a two-step approach: file creation and record addition. That is, you need to create a random-access file, then load records from the corresponding sequential file.

To illustrate this and other random-access techniques, the starting point for this chapter is the sequential file EMPLOYEE.DAT. (It is stored on the data disk included with this book.) The following is its record format:

Positions	Field	Data class	Comments
1–2	Record code	Numeric	Code "26"
3–7	Employee number	Alphanumeric	
8–18	Employee last name	Alphanumeric	
19–27	First name	Alphanumeric	
28	Middle initial	Alphanumeric	
29–51	Employee address	Alphanumeric	
52–74	Employee city/state/zip	Alphanumeric	
75–78	Telephone extension	Numeric	

The SELECT Clause

As you know, it is in the INPUT-OUTPUT SECTION of the ENVIRONMENT DIVISION that you designate a file to be used in a program. Specifically, the SELECT clause of the FILE-CONTROL paragraph identifies the specific file and its relevant physical attributes. COBOL-85 includes seven clauses that can be used with the SELECT. Only one of them is required: the ASSIGN, which designates the file to use.

It is through the SELECT that you designate the file organization (the ORGANIZATION clause) and the method of record access (the ACCESS clause) for the current program. Both of these topics were described in Module E. If you include neither, then sequential organization and sequential access are both assumed. That is, the following two sample SELECT clauses are equivalent:

```
SELECT EMPLOYEE-FILE
    ASSIGN TO DISK "EMPLOYEE.DAT".

SELECT EMPLOYEE-FILE
    ASSIGN TO DISK "EMPLOYEE.DAT"
    ACCESS IS SEQUENTIAL
    ORGANIZATION IS SEQUENTIAL.
```

In the preceding example, the word IS for both access and organization is optional.

If you are using Micro Focus or Ryan-McFarland COBOL and the data files accompanying this book, then you are already familiar with the ORGANIZATION clause. Because each record on disk is followed by a special end-of-line (record) code, your programs have required ORGANIZATION IS LINE SEQUENTIAL.

This is an implementor extension to the COBOL-85 Standard, but is common to personal computer implementations.

The following are two typical SELECT clauses as you might see them in a program; the first designates an indexed file and the second designates a relative file:

```
SELECT EMPLOYEE-FILE
    ASSIGN TO DISK "EMPLOYEE.DAI"
    ACCESS IS RANDOM
    ORGANIZATION IS INDEXED
    RECORD KEY IS EMPLOYEE-NUMBER.

SELECT EMPLOYEE-FILE
    ASSIGN TO DISK "EMPLOYEE.DAR"
    ACCESS IS RANDOM
    ORGANIZATION IS RELATIVE
    RELATIVE KEY IS WA-EMPLOYEE-POINTER.
```

Significant points regarding these examples are as follows:

- The ORGANIZATION clause designates the file's structure. This is a permanent characteristic of the file that is defined when the file is first created.

- The ACCESS clause designates the type of access to be used within the specific program in which the clause occurs. You can process both of these file organizations randomly and sequentially.

- Access to records of the file is through the record key. The RECORD KEY clause for an indexed file and the RELATIVE KEY clause for a relative file designate the field serving as the record key. As you will learn, the way in which the record key is handled for indexed files is different than that for relative files.

For our first look at indexed and relative files, let's consider a program to create a new, empty file.

Creating a File

The indexed version of the employee file is created by the program EMPCRE8I shown in Figure 15-1(a). Notable items in this program are the following:

- The file is created by the OPEN statement of line 55. Since the file was created and no further action is required, it is immediately closed.

- When the file is created, special information about the file is stored— even though the new file contains no data records. For this, COBOL must know:

  - The record key, designated in line 17, which must be one of the fields of the record—see line 27. This field must be (1) defined as part of the record under the FD and (2) alphanumeric. (Although not standard, most implementations allow numeric.)

  - The length of the record. The exact record format is not needed because individual fields—except for the key field—are not referenced in file creation.

- The ACCESS clause is not included because this program simply creates the file—the program contains no record accessing.

- The particular ASSIGN clause used here is a common implementation; however, the format for other implementations may differ.

Figure 15-1   Creating a new employee file—EMPCRE8I and EMPCRE8R.

```
 1    IDENTIFICATION DIVISION.
 2    PROGRAM-ID.    EMPCRE8I.
 3
 4    *      W. PRICE 3/1/95
 5                                                               1    IDENTIFICATION DIVISION.
 6    *      This program creates an indexed employee file.      2    PROGRAM-ID.    EMPCRE8R.
 7                                                               3
 8                                                               4    *      W. PRICE 3/1/95
 9    ENVIRONMENT DIVISION.                                      5
10                                                               6    *      This program creates a relative employee file.
11    INPUT-OUTPUT SECTION.                                      7
12                                                               8
13    FILE-CONTROL.                                              9    ENVIRONMENT DIVISION.
14        SELECT EMPLOYEE-FILE                                  10
15            ASSIGN TO DISK "EMPLOYEE.DAI"                     11    INPUT-OUTPUT SECTION.
16            ORGANIZATION IS INDEXED                           12
17            RECORD KEY IS EMPLOYEE-NUMBER.                    13    FILE-CONTROL.
18                                                              14        SELECT EMPLOYEE-FILE
19                                                              15            ASSIGN TO DISK "EMPLOYEE.DAR"
20    DATA DIVISION.                                            16            ORGANIZATION IS RELATIVE.
21                                                              17
22    FILE SECTION.                                             18
23                                                              19    DATA DIVISION.
24    FD  EMPLOYEE-FILE.                                        20
25    01  EMPLOYEE-RECORD.                                      21    FILE SECTION.
26        05                          PIC X(2).                 22
27        05  EMPLOYEE-NUMBER         PIC X(5).                 23    FD  EMPLOYEE-FILE.
28        05                          PIC X(71).                24    01  EMPLOYEE-RECORD              PIC X(78)
29                                                              25
30    WORKING-STORAGE SECTION.                                  26    WORKING-STORAGE SECTION.
31                                                              27
32    01  SW-SWITCHES.                                          28    01  SW-SWITCHES.
33        05  SW-RESPONSE-SWITCH      PIC X(1).                 29        05  SW-RESPONSE-SWITCH      PIC X(1).
34            88  SW-YES-RESPONSE     VALUE "Y" "y".            30            88  SW-YES-RESPONSE     VALUE "Y" "y".
35                                                              31
36                                                              32
37    PROCEDURE DIVISION.                                       33    PROCEDURE DIVISION.
38                                                              34
39    000-CREATE-EMPLOYEE-FILE.                                 35    000-CREATE-EMPLOYEE-FILE.
40        DISPLAY "THIS PROGRAM CREATES A NEW EMPLOYEE FILE."   36        DISPLAY "THIS PROGRAM CREATES A NEW EMPLOYEE FILE."
41        DISPLAY " "                                           37        DISPLAY " "
42        DISPLAY "If there is an existing EMPLOYEE file, it will"  38    DISPLAY "If there is an existing EMPLOYEE file, it will"
43        DISPLAY "be erased and replaced with a new, empty file."  39    DISPLAY "be erased and replaced with a new, empty file."
44        DISPLAY " "                                           40        DISPLAY " "
45        DISPLAY "Do you want to create a new EMPLOYEE file <Y/N>? "  41    DISPLAY "Do you want to create a new EMPLOYEE file <Y/N>? "
46                WITH NO ADVANCING                             42                WITH NO ADVANCING
47        ACCEPT SW-RESPONSE-SWITCH                             43        ACCEPT SW-RESPONSE-SWITCH
48        IF SW-YES-RESPONSE                                    44        IF SW-RESPONSE-SWITCH
49            DISPLAY " "                                       45            DISPLAY " "
50            DISPLAY                                           46            DISPLAY
51              "ARE YOU CERTAIN YOU WANT TO CREATE THE FILE <Y/N>? "  47          "ARE YOU CERTAIN YOU WANT TO CREATE THE FILE <Y/N>? "
52                WITH NO ADVANCING                             48                WITH NO ADVANCING
53            ACCEPT SW-RESPONSE-SWITCH                         49            ACCEPT SW-RESPONSE-SWITCH
54            IF SW-YES-RESPONSE                                50            IF SW-RESPONSE-SWITCH
55                OPEN OUTPUT EMPLOYEE-FILE                     51                OPEN OUTPUT EMPLOYEE-FILE
56                CLOSE EMPLOYEE-FILE                           52                CLOSE EMPLOYEE-FILE
57                DISPLAY " "                                   53                DISPLAY " "
58                DISPLAY "File created--Press ENTER key to end."  54              DISPLAY "File created--Press ENTER key to end."
59                ACCEPT SW-RESPONSE-SWITCH                     55                ACCEPT SW-RESPONSE-SWITCH
60            END-IF                                            56            END-IF
61        END-IF                                                57        END-IF
62        STOP RUN.                                             58        STOP RUN.
```

(a) An indexed file.   (b) A relative file.

Because creating a new file destroys an existing one of the same name, extra care is taken to ensure that the program is not run accidentally. Notice that the user is queried twice about continuing: at lines 45–47 and lines 50–53.

Remember from Module E that the relative file is much like a direct lookup table. Access to a given record or table entry is through its relative number within the file or table. So, when creating a relative file, you do not need to designate a key field; you see this in the relative file creation program of Figure 15-1(b). That is, the SELECT clause contains only the ASSIGN and ORGANIZATION clauses. Because a specific field does not need to be identified as the key, the record definition of line 24 does not include a breakdown.

You can see that the PROCEDURE DIVISIONs of the two programs are identical. So, the only way that you can identify the type of file being created is by inspecting the SELECT clause.

COBOL-74

Converting these programs to COBOL-74 requires the following simple changes:

1. Insert the CONFIGURATION SECTION and LABEL RECORDS clauses.
2. Include the reserved word FILLER in filler entries.
3. Remove the two END-IF scope terminators with a period on the preceding line.
4. Change the ASSIGN clause entry as necessary.

Adding Records from a Sequential File

Adding Records to an Indexed File

Figure 15-2's brief programming specifications describe the required actions for adding the records from a sequential employee file to the indexed version. This program's intention is to add new records to an existing indexed file. The existing indexed file may or may not already contain records.

Notice that any record with a key value identical to a record already in the file cannot be added to the file. Recall from Module E that the key field value must be unique—no two records can have the same key field value.

Figure 15-2
Programming specifications—
Indexed file record add.

PROGRAMMING SPECIFICATIONS

Program Name: `Indexed File Record Add`   Program ID: `EMPADDI`

Program Description:

```
This program adds records to the indexed employee file from
the sequential employee file. Records of the sequential file
were previously validated.
```

Input File:

```
Sequential employee file (EMPLOYEE.DAT)
```

Output Files:

```
Indexed employee file (EMPLOYEE.DAI)
Error file (EMPLOYEE.ERR)
```

List of Program Operations:

```
A.  Read each input record from the sequential file.
B.  If there is not already a record in the file with the key
    field value of the current record (duplicate key
    condition)
        Write the input record to the indexed file.
    else
        Write the input record to the error file.
```

The overall logic and structure of Figure 15-3's EMPADDI program is relatively simple. Basically, this is a conventional sequential file process-until-end-of-file program—refer to the processing sequence of lines 68–79. The significant element of this program is the WRITE statement, which—when used for indexed file output—has the format:

Format:

WRITE record-name

[INVALID KEY imperative-statement-1]

[NOT INVALID KEY imperative-statement-2]

[END-WRITE]

If an attempt is made to write a record that will cause a duplicate key, the record is not written and the INVALID KEY condition results. Then imperative-statement-1 is executed. You can see that this works much like the READ/AT END/NOT AT END. Unless other provisions are made for error handling, the INVALID KEY clause is required when writing to an indexed file.

At line 73 of Figure 15-3, the input record is moved to the indexed file record area. Then the WRITE at line 74:

Figure 15-3   Indexed file record add program—EMPADDI.

```
1     IDENTIFICATION DIVISION.                              52          05  S2-ERROR-RECORD-PROCESSED-SW     PIC X(1).
2     PROGRAM-ID.    EMPADDI.                               53              88  S2-ERROR-RECORD-PROCESSED       VALUE "T".
3                                                           54              88  S2-ERROR-RECORD-NOT-PROCESSED VALUE "F".
4     * W. PRICE 3/1/95                                     55
5                                                           56
6     * This program allows records to be added to the     57
7     * indexed employee file from a sequential employee   58     PROCEDURE DIVISION.
8     * Duplicate-key records are written to an error file.59
9                                                           60     000-APPEND-TO-EMPLOYEE-FILE.
10    ENVIRONMENT DIVISION.                                 61
11                                                          62     ************Initialization Sequence***********
12    INPUT-OUTPUT SECTION.                                 63         OPEN INPUT SEQ-EMPLOYEE-FILE
13                                                          64         OPEN I-O IND-EMPLOYEE-FILE
14    FILE-CONTROL.                                         65         PERFORM 100-INITIALIZE-VARIABLE-FIELDS
15        SELECT IND-EMPLOYEE-FILE                          66
16            ASSIGN TO DISK "EMPLOYEE.DAI"                 67     ************Processing Sequence*************
17            ORGANIZATION IS INDEXED                       68         PERFORM UNTIL S1-END-OF-FILE
18            ACCESS IS RANDOM                              69             READ SEQ-EMPLOYEE-FILE
19            RECORD KEY IS IND-EMPLOYEE-NUMBER.            70                 AT END
20                                                          71                     SET S1-END-OF-FILE TO TRUE
21        SELECT SEQ-EMPLOYEE-FILE                          72                 NOT AT END
22            ASSIGN TO DISK "EMPLOYEE.DAT"                 73                     MOVE SEQ-EMPLOYEE-RECORD TO IND-EMPLOYEE-RECORD
23            ORGANIZATION IS LINE SEQUENTIAL.              74                     WRITE IND-EMPLOYEE-RECORD
24                                                          75                         INVALID KEY
25        SELECT EMPLOYEE-ERR-FILE                          76                             PERFORM 950-PROCESS-ERROR-RECORD
26            ASSIGN TO DISK "EMPLOYEE.ERR"                 77                     END-WRITE
27            ORGANIZATION LINE SEQUENTIAL.                 78             END-READ
28                                                          79         END-PERFORM
29                                                          80
30    DATA DIVISION.                                        81     ************Termination Sequence*************
31                                                          82         CLOSE IND-EMPLOYEE-FILE
32    FILE SECTION.                                         83               SEQ-EMPLOYEE-FILE
33                                                          84         IF S2-ERROR-RECORD-PROCESSED
34    FD  IND-EMPLOYEE-FILE.                                85             CLOSE EMPLOYEE-ERR-FILE
35    01  IND-EMPLOYEE-RECORD.                              86         END-IF
36        05                          PIC X(2).            87         STOP RUN
37        05  IND-EMPLOYEE-NUMBER     PIC X(5).            88         .
38        05                          PIC X(71).           89     ***********************************************
39                                                          90     100-INITIALIZE-VARIABLE-FIELDS.
40    FD  SEQ-EMPLOYEE-FILE.                                91         SET S1-NOT-END-OF-FILE
41    01  SEQ-EMPLOYEE-RECORD         PIC X(78).           92             S2-ERROR-RECORD-NOT-PROCESSED TO TRUE
42                                                          93         .
43    FD  EMPLOYEE-ERR-FILE.                                94     950-PROCESS-ERROR-RECORD.
44    01  EMPLOYEE-ERR-RECORD         PIC X(78).           95         IF S2-ERROR-RECORD-NOT-PROCESSED
45                                                          96             OPEN OUTPUT EMPLOYEE-ERR-FILE
46    WORKING-STORAGE SECTION.                              97             SET S2-ERROR-RECORD-PROCESSED TO TRUE
47                                                          98         END-IF
48    01  SW-PROGRAM-SWITCHES.                              99         MOVE SEQ-EMPLOYEE-RECORD TO EMPLOYEE-ERR-RECORD
49        05  S1-EMPLOYEE-EOF-SWITCH  PIC X(1).            100        WRITE EMPLOYEE-ERR-RECORD
50            88  S1-END-OF-FILE      VALUE "T".           101        .
51            88  S1-NOT-END-OF-FILE  VALUE "F".
```

- Obtains the key field value from the key field (line 37) as designated in the RECORD KEY clause (line 19).

- Checks the file index to determine if a record with this key field value already exists in the file.

- If a record does not exist, writes the record to the file and enters the key field value into the index.

- If a record does exist, executes the PERFORM following the INVALID KEY clause.

Backing up for a moment, you can see that the indexed employee file is opened for I-O at line 64. This allows the program to execute output operations via the WRITE. If it were opened for OUTPUT, the existing file would be erased and a new, empty file created.

In the 950 module to write the error record, the error file is created only if an error record is detected (lines 95–98). The S2 switch, initialized at line 92, controls the OPEN—as well as the CLOSE (lines 84–86)—actions.

Code in this program was kept to a minimum in order to focus on file principles. Normally, two reports are generated: one listing the records written and the other listing the records rejected (the error file). Each would include standard report features—such as headings and page control—with which you are familiar from previous programming assignments.

Designating ACCESS IS SEQUENTIAL for Record Addition

At line 18 of EMPADDI, access to this file is designated as RANDOM. This allows records to be entered into the file in random key field order. For example, the record for employee 55017 could be followed by 55002, 55101, 55089, and so on. In an environment in which sequential processing of an indexed file is common, disk operation can be speeded up (significantly, for a large file) if the records are in physical sequence by their key fields. For an application in which this is a requirement, the ACCESS clause of a record input program could be changed to ACCESS IS SEQUENTIAL. Then any input record with a key field not larger than that of the preceding record would be rejected through the INVALID KEY clause of EMPADDI. Of course, this would require that the input sequential file be in sequence by the key field.

Adding Records to a Relative File

Adding records to a relative file is similar to inserting entries into a table. That is, it makes no difference whether you add them beginning with the first record entry and proceeding to the last or add them in random order. Consider two scenarios: One is that the first record added to the employee file is the first relative record of the file. The other is that the first record added is the 500th relative record. In the first case, the size of the file reflects storage of a single record. In the second case, the size of the file reflects 500 records: 499 empty "slots" and the 500th containing the record. Consequently, it is a good idea to monitor the relative record number value to ensure that it is not some unreasonably large value. For instance, a relative record number of 500 accidentally entered as 30500 causes an excessive amount of disk storage space to be set aside for the file.

One of the characteristics of the employee numbers for this application is that they are assigned consecutively, beginning with 55001. So, the relative record number can be calculated by subtracting 55000 from the employee number. If not for this control over the employee number, a relative file would be impractical. In Figure 15-4's programming specifications, you can see that an upper limit is designated for the employee number to prevent an accidentally large value.

Figure 15-5's program to load the relative file is almost identical to the program that loaded the indexed file. In addition to the requirement to check the input

Figure 15-4
Programming
specifications—
Relative file
record add.

PROGRAMMING SPECIFICATIONS

Program Name: **Relative File Record Add**   Program ID: **EMPADDR**

Program Description:

This program adds records to the relative employee file from the sequential employee file. Records of the sequential file were previously validated. Employee numbers are assigned beginning with 55001. The largest permissible employee number is 55500.

Input File:

Sequential employee file (EMPLOYEE.DAT)

Output Files:

Indexed employee file (EMPLOYEE.DAR)
Error file (EMPLOYEE.ERR)

List of Program Operations:

A. Read each input record from the sequential file.
B. Subtract 55000 from the employee number to obtain the relative key for the record.
C. If the relative record key is greater than 500
        Write the input record to the error file.
    else
        If there is not already a record in the file with the relative
        key field value of the current record (duplicate key condition)
            Write the input record to the relative file.
        else
            Write the input record to the error file.

---

employee number (line 79), the important difference is in designating the relative record number. At line 19, you see the clause:

```
RELATIVE KEY IS FK-EMPLOYEE-POINTER.
```

This designates a numeric field, defined in WORKING-STORAGE, that will contain the relative record number for the next output or input operation. So, the sequence of writing or reading a record with a relative file is

1. Place the relative record number in the field designated as the relative key field.
2. WRITE (or READ) the record.

Notice that the relative key field is *not* part of the data record; it is simply a work area defined in WORKING-STORAGE. Referring to the code beginning at line 76, you can see that the relative record number is obtained by moving the employee number of the input record to the relative key field and subtracting 55000. Then the WRITE proceeds exactly as with the indexed file example.

Generally, with the exception of key field handling, relative file statement forms are identical to those for indexed files. Consequently, the rest of this chapter focuses on indexed files.

Sequential Processing of an Indexed File

Listing the Employee Records in Employee Number Sequence

One of the advantages of indexed—and relative—files is that you can process them either sequentially or randomly. As an example, consider the program of Figure 15-6 to print a listing of employees from the employee file. If you look at the PROCEDURE DIVISION, you can see that it's very similar to those of your early programs (for instance, refer to Figure 3-1, page 70). The only difference in the programs lies in the SELECT clause, where the nature of the file is designated:

Figure 15-5   Relative file record add program—EMPADDR.

```
1        IDENTIFICATION DIVISION.                              56       05  S2-ERROR-RECORD-PROCESSED-SW     PIC X(1).
2        PROGRAM-ID.     EMPADDR.                              57           88  S2-ERROR-RECORD-PROCESSED       VALUE "T".
3                                                              58           88  S2-ERROR-RECORD-NOT-PROCESSED VALUE "F".
4        * W. PRICE 3/1/95                                     59
5                                                              60
6        * This program allows records to be added to the     61       PROCEDURE DIVISION.
7        * relative employee file from a sequential employee file. 62
8        * Duplicate-key records are written to an error file. 63       000-APPEND-TO-EMPLOYEE-FILE.
9                                                              64
10       ENVIRONMENT DIVISION.                                 65       ************Initialization Sequence************
11                                                             66           OPEN INPUT SEQ-EMPLOYEE-FILE
12       INPUT-OUTPUT SECTION.                                 67           OPEN I-O REL-EMPLOYEE-FILE
13                                                             68           PERFORM 100-INITIALIZE-VARIABLE-FIELDS
14       FILE-CONTROL.                                         69
15           SELECT REL-EMPLOYEE-FILE                          70       *************Processing Sequence**************
16               ASSIGN TO DISK "EMPLOYEE.DAR"                 71           PERFORM UNTIL S1-END-OF-FILE
17               ORGANIZATION IS RELATIVE                      72               READ SEQ-EMPLOYEE-FILE
18               ACCESS IS RANDOM                              73                   AT END
19               RELATIVE KEY IS FK-EMPLOYEE-POINTER.          74                       SET S1-END-OF-FILE TO TRUE
20                                                             75                   NOT AT END
21           SELECT SEQ-EMPLOYEE-FILE                          76                       MOVE SEQ-EMPLOYEE-RECORD TO REL-EMPLOYEE-RECORD
22               ASSIGN TO DISK "EMPLOYEE.DAX"                 77                       MOVE SEQ-EMPLOYEE-NUMBER TO FK-EMPLOYEE-POINTER
23               ORGANIZATION IS LINE SEQUENTIAL.              78                       SUBTRACT 55000 FROM FK-EMPLOYEE-POINTER
24                                                             79                       IF FK-EMPLOYEE-POINTER > 500
25           SELECT EMPLOYEE-ERR-FILE                          80                           PERFORM 950-PROCESS-ERROR-RECORD
26               ASSIGN TO DISK "EMPLOYEE.ERR"                 81                       ELSE
27               ORGANIZATION LINE SEQUENTIAL.                 82                           WRITE REL-EMPLOYEE-RECORD
28                                                             83                               INVALID KEY
29                                                             84                                   PERFORM 950-PROCESS-ERROR-RECORD
30       DATA DIVISION.                                        85                           END-WRITE
31                                                             86                       END-IF
32       FILE SECTION.                                         87                   END-READ
33                                                             88           END-PERFORM
34       FD  REL-EMPLOYEE-FILE.                                89
35       01  REL-EMPLOYEE-RECORD          PIC X(78).           90       **************Termination Sequence*************
36                                                             91           CLOSE REL-EMPLOYEE-FILE
37       FD  SEQ-EMPLOYEE-FILE.                                92                 SEQ-EMPLOYEE-FILE
38       01  SEQ-EMPLOYEE-RECORD.                              93           IF S2-ERROR-RECORD-PROCESSED
39           05                           PIC X(2).            94               CLOSE EMPLOYEE-ERR-FILE
40           05  SEQ-EMPLOYEE-NUMBER      PIC 9(5).            95           END-IF
41           05                           PIC X(71).           96           STOP RUN
42                                                             97           .
43       FD  EMPLOYEE-ERR-FILE.                                98       *********************************************
44       01  EMPLOYEE-ERR-RECORD          PIC X(78).           99       100-INITIALIZE-VARIABLE-FIELDS.
45                                                             100          SET S1-NOT-END-OF-FILE
46       WORKING-STORAGE SECTION.                              101              S2-ERROR-RECORD-NOT-PROCESSED TO TRUE
47                                                             102          .
48       01  FK-FILE-KEYS.                                     103      950-PROCESS-ERROR-RECORD.
49           05  FK-EMPLOYEE-POINTER      PIC 9(5).            104          IF S2-ERROR-RECORD-NOT-PROCESSED
50                                                             105              OPEN OUTPUT EMPLOYEE-ERR-FILE
51       01  SW-PROGRAM-SWITCHES.                              106              SET S2-ERROR-RECORD-PROCESSED TO TRUE
52           05  S1-EMPLOYEE-EOF-SWITCH   PIC X(1).            107          END-IF
53               88  S1-END-OF-FILE          VALUE "T".        108          MOVE SEQ-EMPLOYEE-RECORD TO EMPLOYEE-ERR-RECORD
54               88  S1-NOT-END-OF-FILE      VALUE "F".        109          WRITE EMPLOYEE-ERR-RECORD
55                                                             110          .
```

- The ORGANIZATION clause specifies that this file uses INDEXED file organization. Remember, this characteristic of the file was established when the file was created.

- The ACCESS clause indicates that the file is processed SEQUENTIALLY in this program. That is, for input operations, records are made available one after the other in key sequence order.

- The RECORD KEY clause identifies the key field of this file, which was established when the file was created. This field determines the sequence in which records are available.

Even though the employee number is defined in the WORKING-STORAGE record ER-EMPLOYEE-RECORD, it still must be identified in the FD record description. The RECORD KEY clause of the SELECT must reference an entry in the FD record description; it is incorrect to specify WORKING-STORAGE field ER-EMPLOYEE-NUMBER in the RECORD KEY clause.

Processing the indexed file sequentially is exactly the same as processing a sequential file. The file is opened for INPUT and the READ/AT END/NOT AT END is used. The PROCEDURE DIVISION gives you no indication of the file organization.

Figure 15-6   Processing an indexed file sequentially—EMPLIST.

```
1        IDENTIFICATION DIVISION.                              54     01  EL-EMPLOYEE-LINE.
2        PROGRAM-ID.    EMPLIST.                               55         05   EL-EMPLOYEE-NUMBER          PIC 9(5).
3                                                              56         05                              PIC X(2).
4      * W. PRICE 3/1/95                                       57         05   EL-FIRST-NAME              PIC X(9).
5                                                              58         05                              PIC X(2).
6      * This program prints a sequential list of records     59         05   EL-LAST-NAME               PIC X(11).
7      * from the indexed employee file.                      60         05                              PIC X(2).
8                                                              61         05   EL-ADDRESS                 PIC X(23).
9        ENVIRONMENT DIVISION.                                 62         05                              PIC X(2).
10                                                             63         05   EL-CITY-STATE-ZIP          PIC X(23).
11       INPUT-OUTPUT SECTION.                                 64
12                                                             65
13       FILE-CONTROL.                                         66
14           SELECT EMPLOYEE-FILE                              67     PROCEDURE DIVISION.
15               ASSIGN TO DISK "EMPLOYEE.DAI"                 68
16               ORGANIZATION IS INDEXED                       69     000-LIST-EMPLOYEE-FILE.
17               ACCESS IS SEQUENTIAL                          70
18               RECORD KEY IS EMPLOYEE-NUMBER.                71     *************Initialization Sequence************
19                                                             72         OPEN  INPUT EMPLOYEE-FILE
20           SELECT EMPLOYEE-LIST                              73               OUTPUT EMPLOYEE-LIST
21               ASSIGN TO DISK "PRN-FILE"                     74         PERFORM 100-INITIALIZE-VARIABLE-FIELDS
22               ORGANIZATION IS LINE SEQUENTIAL.             75
23                                                             76     **************Processing Sequence**************
24                                                             77         PERFORM UNTIL S1-END-OF-FILE
25       DATA DIVISION.                                        78             READ EMPLOYEE-FILE INTO ER-EMPLOYEE-RECORD
26                                                             79             AT END
27       FILE SECTION.                                         80                 SET S1-END-OF-FILE TO TRUE
28                                                             81             NOT AT END
29       FD  EMPLOYEE-FILE.                                    82                 PERFORM 200-PRINT-EMPLOYEE-LINE
30       01  EMPLOYEE-RECORD.                                  83             END-READ
31           05                          PIC X(2).             84         END-PERFORM
32           05  EMPLOYEE-NUMBER         PIC X(5).             85
33           05                          PIC X(71).            86     ***************Termination Sequence*************
34                                                             87         CLOSE EMPLOYEE-FILE
35       FD  EMPLOYEE-LIST.                                    88               EMPLOYEE-LIST
36       01  EMPLOYEE-LINE               PIC X(79).            89         STOP RUN
37                                                             90         .
38       WORKING-STORAGE SECTION.                              91     ***********************************************
39                                                             92     100-INITIALIZE-VARIABLE-FIELDS.
40       01  SW-PROGRAM-SWITCHES.                              93         SET S1-NOT-END-OF-FILE TO TRUE
41           05  S1-EMPLOYEE-EOF-SWITCH  PIC X(1).             94         .
42               88  S1-END-OF-FILE      VALUE "T".            95     200-PRINT-EMPLOYEE-LINE.
43               88  S1-NOT-END-OF-FILE  VALUE "F".            96         MOVE SPACES TO EL-EMPLOYEE-LINE
44                                                             97         MOVE ER-EMPLOYEE-NUMBER TO EL-EMPLOYEE-NUMBER
45       01  ER-EMPLOYEE-RECORD.                               98         MOVE ER-FIRST-NAME TO EL-FIRST-NAME
46           05  ER-RECORD-CODE          PIC 9(2).             99         MOVE ER-LAST-NAME TO EL-LAST-NAME
47           05  ER-EMPLOYEE-NUMBER      PIC 9(5).            100         MOVE ER-CITY-STATE-ZIP TO EL-CITY-STATE-ZIP
48           05  ER-LAST-NAME            PIC X(11).           101         MOVE ER-ADDRESS TO EL-ADDRESS
49           05  ER-FIRST-NAME           PIC X(9).            102         MOVE EL-EMPLOYEE-LINE TO EMPLOYEE-LINE
50           05  ER-MIDDLE-INITIAL       PIC X(1).            103         WRITE EMPLOYEE-LINE
51           05  ER-ADDRESS              PIC X(23).           104         .
52           05  ER-CITY-STATE-ZIP       PIC X(23).
53           05  ER-TELEPHONE-EXT        PIC X(4).
```

To perform the same function with the relative file, the only change to the program is in the SELECT statement. Because of sequential processing, designation of the RELATIVE KEY is not necessary.

Using an Alternate Key

Indexing a file provides direct access to the file for random processing and an ordering of the records in the file for sequential accessing based on the key field. However, what if you need access to the file through another field? For instance, you might want the listing report from the EMPLIST program to print the records in alphabetic sequence based on the employee name. For this, another key is needed: one on the employee name field.

COBOL provides for this by allowing you to define a prime key and one or more alternate keys. The **prime key** is the key whose contents uniquely identify the record. An alternate key is a key, other than the prime key, whose contents identify a record—*but not necessarily uniquely.* For instance, while the employee file has only one employee with a given employee number, two or more employees might have the same name.

The changes to EMPLIST necessary to use an alternate key are highlighted in the revised program of Figure 15-7.

Figure 15-7   Using an alternate key—EMPLISTA.

```
1        IDENTIFICATION DIVISION.                          58
2        PROGRAM-ID.    EMPLISTA.                          59    01  EL-EMPLOYEE-LINE.
3                                                          60        05  EL-EMPLOYEE-NUMBER          PIC 9(5).
4      * W. PRICE 3/1/95                                   61        05                             PIC X(2).
5                                                          62        05  EL-FIRST-NAME              PIC X(9).
6      * This program prints an alphabetically sequenced   63        05                             PIC X(2).
7      * list of records from the indexed employee file    64        05  EL-LAST-NAME              PIC X(11).
8      * using an alternate key.                           65        05                             PIC X(2).
9                                                          66        05  EL-ADDRESS                 PIC X(23).
10       ENVIRONMENT DIVISION.                             67        05                             PIC X(2).
11                                                         68        05  EL-CITY-STATE-ZIP          PIC X(23).
12       INPUT-OUTPUT SECTION.                             69
13                                                         70
14       FILE-CONTROL.                                     71    PROCEDURE DIVISION.
15           SELECT EMPLOYEE-FILE                          72
16               ASSIGN TO DISK "EMPLOYEE.DAA"             73    000-LIST-EMPLOYEE-FILE.
17               ORGANIZATION IS INDEXED                   74
18               ACCESS IS SEQUENTIAL                      75    ***********Initialization Sequence***********
19               RECORD KEY IS EMPLOYEE-NUMBER            76        OPEN  INPUT EMPLOYEE-FILE
20               ALTERNATE RECORD KEY IS EMPLOYEE-FULL-NAME 77            OUTPUT EMPLOYEE-LIST
21                              WITH DUPLICATES.           78        PERFORM 100-INITIALIZE-VARIABLE-FIELDS
22                                                         79
23           SELECT EMPLOYEE-LIST                          80    *************Processing Sequence*************
24               ASSIGN TO DISK "PRN-FILE"                 81        PERFORM UNTIL S1-END-OF-FILE
25               ORGANIZATION IS LINE SEQUENTIAL.          82            READ EMPLOYEE-FILE INTO ER-EMPLOYEE-RECORD
26                                                         83                        KEY IS EMPLOYEE-FULL-NAME
27                                                         84                AT END
28       DATA DIVISION.                                    85                    SET S1-END-OF-FILE TO TRUE
29                                                         86                NOT AT END
30       FILE SECTION.                                     87                    PERFORM 200-PRINT-EMPLOYEE-LINE
31                                                         88            END-READ
32       FD  EMPLOYEE-FILE.                                89        END-PERFORM
33       01  EMPLOYEE-RECORD.                              90
34           05                          PIC X(2).         91    ***************Termination Sequence***********
35           05  EMPLOYEE-NUMBER         PIC X(5).         92        CLOSE EMPLOYEE-FILE
36           05  EMPLOYEE-FULL-NAME      PIC X(21).        93              EMPLOYEE-LIST
37           05                          PIC X(50).        94        STOP RUN
38                                                         95        .
39       FD  EMPLOYEE-LIST.                                96    *********************************************
40       01  EMPLOYEE-LINE               PIC X(79).        97    100-INITIALIZE-VARIABLE-FIELDS.
41                                                         98        SET S1-NOT-END-OF-FILE TO TRUE
42       WORKING-STORAGE SECTION.                          99        .
43                                                         100   200-PRINT-EMPLOYEE-LINE.
44       01  SW-PROGRAM-SWITCHES.                          101       MOVE SPACES TO EL-EMPLOYEE-LINE
45           05  S1-EMPLOYEE-EOF-SWITCH  PIC X(1).         102       MOVE ER-EMPLOYEE-NUMBER TO EL-EMPLOYEE-NUMBER
46               88  S1-END-OF-FILE      VALUE "T".        103       MOVE ER-FIRST-NAME TO EL-FIRST-NAME
47               88  S1-NOT-END-OF-FILE  VALUE "F".        104       MOVE ER-LAST-NAME TO EL-LAST-NAME
48                                                         105       MOVE ER-CITY-STATE-ZIP TO EL-CITY-STATE-ZIP
49       01  ER-EMPLOYEE-RECORD.                           106       MOVE ER-ADDRESS TO EL-ADDRESS
50           05  ER-RECORD-CODE          PIC 9(2).         107       MOVE EL-EMPLOYEE-LINE TO EMPLOYEE-LINE
51           05  ER-EMPLOYEE-NUMBER      PIC 9(5).         108       WRITE EMPLOYEE-LINE
52           05  ER-LAST-NAME            PIC X(11).        109       .
53           05  ER-FIRST-NAME           PIC X(9).
54           05  ER-MIDDLE-INITIAL       PIC X(1).
55           05  ER-ADDRESS              PIC X(23).
56           05  ER-CITY-STATE-ZIP       PIC X(23).
57           05  ER-TELEPHONE-EXT        PIC X(4).
```

- An ALTERNATE KEY clause, included in the SELECT clause, designates the field to be used as the alternate key field. The WITH DUPLICATES phrase indicates that more than one record can have the same value in this field.

- The alternate key field EMPLOYEE-FULL-NAME (as well as the primary key) is defined in the FD record description.

- The READ statement must include the KEY IS clause identifying the key to be used by the READ. This causes access to records of the file to be through the EMPLOYEE-FULL-NAME key. If the KEY IS clause is omitted, then COBOL defaults to the prime key.

You should be aware that you cannot arbitrarily designate any field of an existing file as an alternate key. All alternate keys to be used for processing must be defined as such when the file is originally created. However, if one or more alternate keys are defined for an indexed file—in any given program, you need identify only those that you intend to use for data access. Included on this book's distribution disk are the programs EMPCREA and EMPADDA to create and add records to this version of the indexed employee file.

The alternate key feature is not available with relative file organization.

COBOL-74

To convert the programs EMPADDI, EMPADDR, EMPLIST, and EMPLISTA to COBOL-74, make the following changes:

1. Insert the CONFIGURATION SECTION and LABEL RECORDS clauses.
2. Include the reserved word FILLER in filler entries.
3. Change each SET statement to a corresponding MOVE.
4. Move the inline code of the processing sequence (repetition) to a separate module and change the PERFORM to execute that module.
5. Modify the READ sequence to eliminate the NOT AT END. Do this by using the priming READ form or by replacing the NOT AT END with an appropriate IF statement.
6. Replace the END-IF scope terminators with a period on the preceding line.
7. If necessary, move separate-line paragraph-ending periods to the end of the preceding line.
8. Change the ASSIGN clause entry as necessary.

Interactive File Maintenance

The preceding sample programs were all examples of batch operations with random-access files. To illustrate random processing, let's consider an interactive file maintenance application. This example combines a number of indexed file-processing techniques into a single program.

Programming Specifications

The SEQ-MNT program of Chapter 14 illustrated the sequential file batch maintenance operations of record addition, modification, and deletion. Techniques to perform the same operations on an indexed file are entirely different, as you will learn from the following example. The programming specifications of Figure 15-8 designate the actions. From a menu, the user can select either of the three maintenance options: record addition, modification, or deletion. Within an option, the user must be able to operate on one or more records as needed.

For data entry and record display, a screen is required. The screen layout of Figure 15-9 includes a balanced format for displaying the record contents and two message lines.

The pseudocode of Figure 15-10 illustrates the main module logic. Some of this program's aspects you should focus on are clarified by a careful study of this pseudocode:

- In the outer loop, the user operates from a menu that provides four options: three maintenance and a terminate-execution option.

- After the user selects an option—for example, record addition—the program enters the inner loop, which allows for the entry of one or more records.

- The user enters the employee number of the record to be added, modified, or deleted.

Figure 15-8
File specifications—
Indexed file maintenance.

PROGRAMMING SPECIFICATIONS

Program Name: Indexed File Maintenance   **Program ID:** EMPMNT

Program Description:

This program provides the three basic maintenance functions for the indexed employee file: record addition, modification, and deletion.

Input File:

Indexed employee file (EMPLOYEE.DAI)

Output File:

Updated indexed employee file (EMPLOYEE.DAI)

List of Program Operations:

A. Through menu control, allow the user to select either of three options: record addition, modification, or deletion.
B. Accept the desired employee number from the keyboard.
C. If operation is record addition:
    1. If record already exists for this employee number, display an error message.
    2. Accept input fields from keyboard.
    3. Write record to disk.
D. If operation is record modification:
    1. If no record for this employee number, display an error message.
    2. Accept fields corrections from keyboard.
    3. Write record to disk.
E. If operation is record deletion:
    1. If no record for this employee number, display an error message.
    2. Delete designated record from disk.

Input Record Format:

Positions	Field	Data class	Comments
1-2	Record code	Numeric	Code "26"
3-7	Employee number	Alphanumeric	
8-18	Employee last name	Alphanumeric	
19-27	First name	Alphanumeric	
28	Middle initial	Alphanumeric	
29-51	Address	Alphanumeric	
52-64	City	Alphanumeric	
66-67	State	Alphanumeric	
70-74	Zip	Alphanumeric	
75-78	Telephone extension	Numeric	

Key field: Employee number

- The program attempts to read the record corresponding to the user-entered employee number.

- Desired processing occurs under the following circumstances:

  - For record addition: unsuccessful read (no existing record in the file)—proceed to accept new record entries.

  - For record modification and deletion: successful read— proceed to modify or delete this record.

- Error conditions occur under the following circumstances:

  - For record addition: successful read—means a record with this key field value already exists in the file.

  - For record modification and deletion: unsuccessful read—means the desired record is not in the file.

- After processing of the current record is complete, query the user about remaining in the inner loop (accept another employee number for processing).

Figure 15-9   Screen display format.

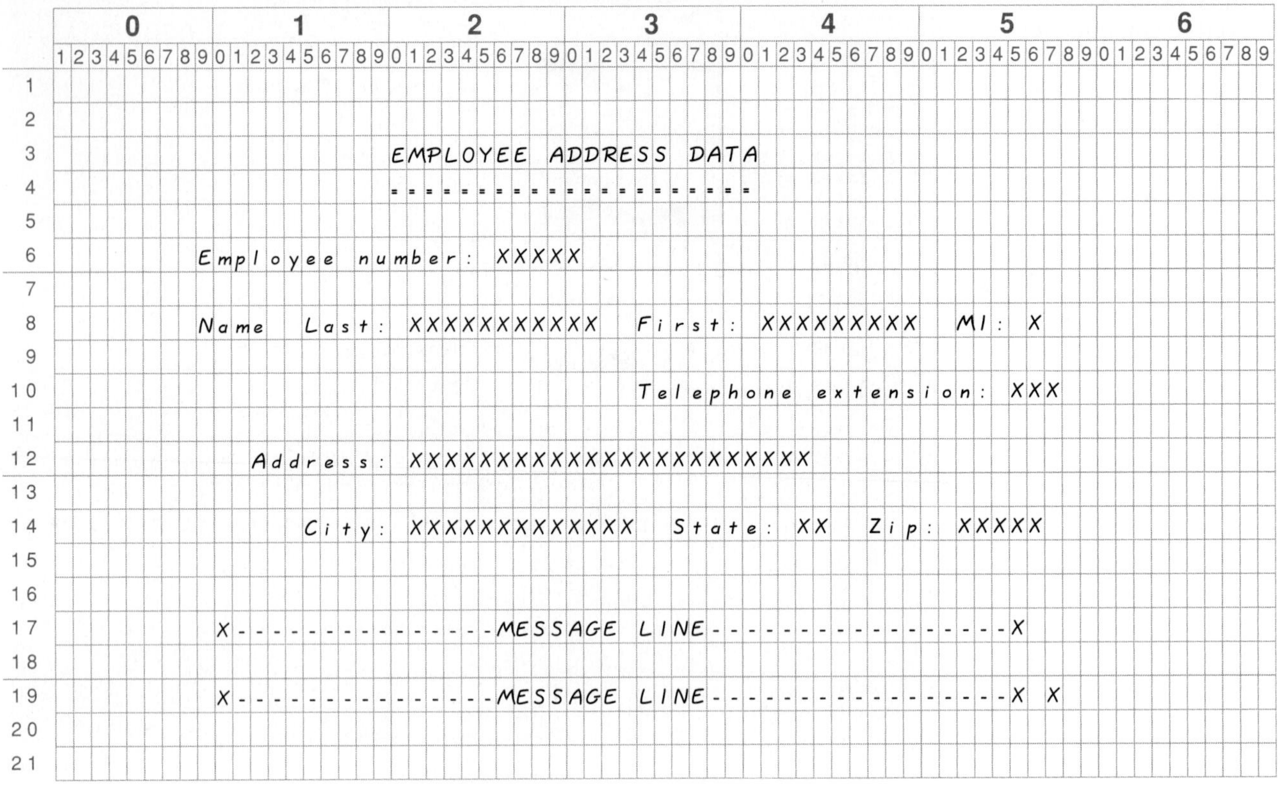

Trial Runs

As with all interactive programs, you will find it much easier to understand the code if you first make some trial runs. The program is stored on disk as EMPMNT. The indexed file it processes, EMPLOYEE.DAI, can be created from the sequential file EMPLOYEE.DAT by running EMPCRE8I, then EMPADDI.

In order to illustrate good screen layouts, Micro Focus nonstandard extensions of the COBOL ACCEPT and DISPLAY statements are used. However, they are kept to a minimum to facilitate converting the program to a form compatible with other implementations. In that respect, the three extensions used in this program are

LINE and COL for screen positioning

WITH BLANK SCREEN to clear the screen

WITH REVERSE-VIDEO for highlighting data entry

Before you attempt your trial runs, you should make any needed changes to the program if you are using another compiler.

When you do run the program, you are first presented with an introduction screen asking if you wish to continue. A yes response produces the menu shown in Figure 15-11, providing you with the three maintenance options and the termination option.

The primary screen (the layout of Figure 15-9) consists of two components: the record display and two message lines. Whenever an action is completed or an error condition occurs, a message is displayed on one or both of these lines. For example, if you attempt to delete a record, you will receive the following messages:

Figure 15-10
Mainline pseudocode for
indexed file maintenance.

```
             Perform until Terminate
               Display menu options:
                        Addition
                        Modification
                        Deletion
                        Terminate
             Accept user response
             Perform until not Repeat-loop
                          or Terminate
               Accept employee number from keyboard
               Read employee record
                 Invalid key
                   If record Addition
                       Perform Addition module
                   If record Modification
                       Display record-not-in-file message
                   If record Deletion
                       Display record-not-in-file message
                 Not invalid key
                   If record Addition
                       Display record-in-file message
                   If record Modification
                       Perform Modification module
                   If record Deletion
                       Perform Deletion module
               End-read
               Query user to Repeat-loop
```

```
DELETING THIS RECORD PERMANENTLY ERASES IT!

Are you certain you want to delete it <Y/N>? _
```

In all cases, the first message line—when displayed—is a description; the second line is a query to which the user must respond.

Your trial runs should test each of the three options: add, modify, and delete. To explore all aspects of the program, try an existing employee number for an add operation and nonexisting numbers for modify and delete. As you try each of the many options, observe the contents of the two message lines.

Figure 15-11
Employee file maintenance
menu screen.

```
EMPLOYEE FILE MAINTENANCE MENU
==================================

The maintenance options are:

A - Add records to file

M - Modify existing records

D - Delete records

X - eXit maintenance

Your choice? _
```

Interactive File Maintenance Program

Mainline Code

In Figure 15-10, you saw the mainline logic in pseudocode form. Before looking at the entire program, let's consider the program code corresponding to the pseudocode; it is included in Figure 15-12(a). While perusing this, be aware that the S3 elements are condition-names representing the various menu options as suggested by the name.

- Repetition of the outer loop is controlled by the S3 option; the menu choice is selected from the 250 module, performed at line 108. (The S3 option was assigned an initial value before line 107.)

- Repetition of the inner loop is controlled by the PERFORM at lines 110 and 111.

- An employee number is accepted from the 800 module, performed from line 112.

- The READ for the desired employee occurs at line 113.

- Under the INVALID KEY, each of the three maintenance options is handled through an EVALUATE (line 115)—refer to the preceding descriptions of the pseudocode.

Figure 15-12 Processing code from mainline module.

```
        Outer loop

              Inner loop

107   PERFORM UNTIL S3-EXIT-OPTION                              PERFORM 200-ACCESS-MENU
108     PERFORM 250-GET-MENU-CHOICE                                 UNTIL S3-EXIT-OPTION
109     SET S2-REPEAT TO TRUE
110     PERFORM UNTIL NOT S2-REPEAT                                     :
111        OR S3-EXIT-OPTION                                           :
112     PERFORM 800-GET-EMPLOYEE-NUMBER              200-ACCESS-MENU.
113     READ EMPLOYEE-FILE INTO ER-EMPLOYEE-RECORD       PERFORM 250-GET-MENU-CHOICE
114       INVALID KEY                                       MOVE "Y" TO S2-CONTINUE-SWITCH
115         EVALUATE TRUE                                   PERFORM 225-PROCESS-RECORD
116           WHEN S3-ADD-RECORD-OPTION                         UNTIL NOT S2-REPEAT
117             PERFORM 300-ADD-RECORD                            OR S3-EXIT-OPTION.
118           WHEN S3-MODIFY-RECORD-OPTION  ◄
119             MOVE ME-NOT-IN-FILE-17 TO ME-MESSAGE-17              :
120           WHEN S3-DELETE-RECORD-OPTION  ◄                        :
121             MOVE ME-NOT-IN-FILE-17 TO ME-MESSAGE-17
122         END-EVALUATE                                225-PROCESS-RECORD.
123       NOT INVALID KEY                                  PERFORM 800-GET-EMPLOYEE-NUMBER
124         PERFORM 855-DISPLAY-EMPLOYEE-TEMPLATE          MOVE "Y" TO S4-MASTER-FOUND-SWITCH
125         PERFORM 860-DISPLAY-EMPLOYEE-RECORD           READ EMPLOYEE-FILE INTO ER-EMPLOYEE-RECORD
126         EVALUATE TRUE                                    INVALID KEY
127           WHEN S3-ADD-RECORD-OPTION  ◄                     MOVE "N" TO S4-MASTER-FOUND-SWITCH.
128             MOVE ME-ALREADY-IN-FILE-17 TO ME-MESSAGE-17  IF NOT S4-MASTER-FOUND
129           WHEN S3-MODIFY-RECORD-OPTION                     IF S3-ADD-RECORD-OPTION
130             PERFORM 400-MODIFY-RECORD                         PERFORM 300-ADD-RECORD
131           WHEN S3-DELETE-RECORD-OPTION           ►      ELSE IF S3-MODIFY-RECORD-OPTION
132             PERFORM 500-DELETE-RECORD                          MOVE ME-NOT-IN-FILE-17 TO ME-MESSAGE-17
133         END-EVALUATE                              ►      ELSE IF S3-DELETE-RECORD-OPTION
134       END-READ                                              MOVE ME-NOT-IN-FILE-17 TO ME-MESSAGE-17.
135       PERFORM 825-QUERY-USER-TO-REPEAT           IF S4-MASTER-FOUND
136     END-PERFORM                                     PERFORM 855-DISPLAY-EMPLOYEE-TEMPLATE
137   END-PERFORM                                       PERFORM 860-DISPLAY-EMPLOYEE-RECORD
                                                     ►  IF S3-ADD-RECORD-OPTION
                                                          MOVE ME-ALREADY-IN-FILE-17 TO ME-MESSAGE-17
                        Error conditions                ELSE IF S3-MODIFY-RECORD-OPTION
                                                          PERFORM 400-MODIFY-RECORD
                                                        ELSE IF S3-DELETE-RECORD-OPTION
                                                          PERFORM 500-DELETE-RECORD.
                                                     PERFORM 825-QUERY-USER-TO-REPEAT.

  (a) COBOL-85.                                       (b) COBOL-74.
```

- The NOT INVALID KEY means that a record was read, so it is first displayed (lines 124 and 125). Then each of the three maintenance options is handled through an EVALUATE (line 126)—refer to the preceding descriptions of the pseudocode.

- Through the PERFORM at line 135, the user is queried about continuing. The response in the 825 module sets the S2 switch, which controls loop repetition at line 110.

- If the S2 switch is false, control is returned to the outer loop.

- Choosing the exit option from the menu (line 108) causes the inner loop to be skipped (the condition at line 111) and control immediately returned to the outer loop. The outer loop is then also terminated.

In the equivalent code of Figure 15-12(b), additional paragraphs are necessary because COBOL-74 does not include the inline PERFORM. You can see how much clearer the resulting code is with the use of scope terminators provided by COBOL-85.

If you understand the mainline code of Figure 15-12, then you have a good grip on the complete program EMPMNT of Figure 15-13. First, let's look at the DATA DIVISION entries.

DATA DIVISION Entries of EMPMNT

Lines 29–32 define the FD record, together with the key field. The corresponding detailed record description is found at lines 84–96. All fields that will contain numeric data are designated with the 9 symbol. This ensures that only numeric data is allowed with the ACCEPT statement.

As you will see, the MO descriptions beginning line 51 are used to query the user for the employee number of the record to be added, modified, or deleted.

Most of the messages and queries for screen lines 17 and 19 (Figure 15-9) are defined as ME descriptions beginning line 60. Notice that each selected data-name designates the message and the screen line on which it is displayed. They are all assigned the same length to ensure that any message remaining from a preceding operation is totally replaced.

From your mainline module consideration (Figure 15-12), you can already anticipate the switches and options defined under line 36. Each of them provides for the entry of both upper- and lowercase letters. You can correlate the menu selection options of Figure 15-11 with the condition-names of lines 43–46.

The Menu and Employee Number Entry

The menu module 250 is performed from line 108 before entering the inner loop. Code for the screen display of Figure 15-11 is obvious in lines 161–169. Ensuring a valid entry is the purpose of the inline PERFORM beginning at line 170. (Notice that the clause WITH TEST AFTER is included to ensure entry into this loop.)

The EVALUATE beginning at line 177 places the appropriate prompt (see lines 53, 55, and 57) into the maintenance option message area (defined at line 58). This prompt is displayed at line 236, where an employee number is requested of the user. At line 238, the field EMPLOYEE-NUMBER is set to spaces (to ensure that the previous employee number is not displayed as a default) prior to the ACCEPT statement.

Adding a Record to the File

With the exception of the first three statements of the record addition module (300), the modules for record addition, modification, and deletion (300, 400, and 500) are almost identical. So, let's consider the 300 module for adding records to the file.

1. Because a new record is being created, individual fields must be initialized (line 187). Then the record code (26) is moved into the record code field, and the employee number is moved from EMPLOYEE-NUMBER to the employee number field of the record.

Figure 15-13   Employee file maintenance program—EMPMNT.

```
1    IDENTIFICATION DIVISION.                                    83    01  ER-EMPLOYEE-RECORD.
2    PROGRAM-ID.    EMPMNT.                                      84        05  ER-RECORD-CODE            PIC 9(2).
3                                                                85        05  ER-EMPLOYEE-NUMBER        PIC 9(5).
4    *  W. PRICE 3/1/95                                          86        05  ER-LAST-NAME              PIC X(11).
5                                                                87        05  ER-FIRST-NAME             PIC X(9).
6    *  Employee file maintenance.                               88        05  ER-MIDDLE-INITIAL         PIC X(1).
7    *  This program allows the user to perform the basic        89        05  ER-ADDRESS                PIC X(23).
8    *  maintenance functions of record addition, deletion,      90        05  ER-CITY                   PIC X(13).
9    *  and modification on an indexed employee file.            91        05                            PIC X(1).
10                                                               92        05  ER-STATE                  PIC X(2).
11                                                               93        05                            PIC X(2).
12    ENVIRONMENT DIVISION.                                      94        05  ER-ZIP                    PIC 9(5).
13                                                               95        05  ER-TELEPHONE-EXT          PIC 9(4).
14    INPUT-OUTPUT SECTION.                                      96
15                                                               97
16    FILE-CONTROL.                                              98
17        SELECT EMPLOYEE-FILE                                   99    PROCEDURE DIVISION.
18            ASSIGN TO DISK "EMPLOYEE.DAI"                     100
19            ORGANIZATION IS INDEXED                           101    000-MAINTAIN-EMPLOYEE-RECORDS.
20            ACCESS IS RANDOM                                  102    ************Initialization Sequence************
21            RECORD KEY IS EMPLOYEE-NUMBER.                    103        OPEN I-O EMPLOYEE-FILE
22                                                              104        PERFORM 050-DISPLAY-ANNOUNCE-SCREEN
23                                                              105
24    DATA DIVISION.                                            106    *************Processing Sequence**************
25                                                              107        PERFORM UNTIL S3-EXIT-OPTION
26    FILE SECTION.                                             108            PERFORM 250-GET-MENU-CHOICE
27                                                              109            SET S2-REPEAT TO TRUE
28    FD  EMPLOYEE-FILE.                                        110            PERFORM UNTIL NOT S2-REPEAT
29    01  EMPLOYEE-RECORD.                                      111                    OR S3-EXIT-OPTION
30        05                            PIC X(2).               112                PERFORM 800-GET-EMPLOYEE-NUMBER
31        05  EMPLOYEE-NUMBER           PIC X(5).               113                READ EMPLOYEE-FILE INTO ER-EMPLOYEE-RECORD
32        05                            PIC X(71).              114                    INVALID KEY
33                                                              115                        EVALUATE TRUE
34    WORKING-STORAGE SECTION.                                  116                            WHEN S3-ADD-RECORD-OPTION
35                                                              117                                PERFORM 300-ADD-RECORD
36    01  SW-SWITCHES.                                          118                            WHEN S3-MODIFY-RECORD-OPTION
37        05  S1-USER-RESPONSE-SWITCH   PIC X(1).               119                                MOVE ME-NOT-IN-FILE-17 TO ME-MESSAGE-17
38            88  S1-YES-RESPONSE           VALUE "Y" "y".      120                            WHEN S3-DELETE-RECORD-OPTION
39        05  S2-CONTINUE-SWITCH        PIC X(1).               121                                MOVE ME-NOT-IN-FILE-17 TO ME-MESSAGE-17
40            88  S2-REPEAT                 VALUE "Y" "y".      122                        END-EVALUATE
41            88  S2-DO-NOT-REPEAT          VALUE "N".          123                    NOT INVALID KEY
42        05  S3-RESPONSE-OPTION        PIC X(1).               124                        PERFORM 855-DISPLAY-EMPLOYEE-TEMPLATE
43            88  S3-ADD-RECORD-OPTION      VALUE "A" "a".      125                        PERFORM 860-DISPLAY-EMPLOYEE-RECORD
44            88  S3-MODIFY-RECORD-OPTION   VALUE "M" "m".      126                        EVALUATE TRUE
45            88  S3-DELETE-RECORD-OPTION   VALUE "D" "d".      127                            WHEN S3-ADD-RECORD-OPTION
46            88  S3-EXIT-OPTION            VALUE "X" "x".      128                                MOVE ME-ALREADY-IN-FILE-17 TO ME-MESSAGE-17
47            88  S3-VALID-OPTION           VALUE "A" "M" "D" "X" 129                          WHEN S3-MODIFY-RECORD-OPTION
48                                              "a" "m" "d" "x". 130                              PERFORM 400-MODIFY-RECORD
49            88  S3-BLANK-OPTION           VALUE " ".          131                            WHEN S3-DELETE-RECORD-OPTION
50                                                              132                                PERFORM 500-DELETE-RECORD
51    01  MO-MAINT-OPTION-DESCRIPTIONS.                         133                        END-EVALUATE
52        05  MO-ADD-OPTION             PIC X(45)               134                END-READ
53            VALUE "  What is the number of the employee to add?". 135            PERFORM 825-QUERY-USER-TO-REPEAT
54        05  MO-MODIFY-OPTION          PIC X(45)               136            END-PERFORM
55            VALUE "What is the number of the employee to change?". 137     END-PERFORM
56        05  MO-DELETE-OPTION          PIC X(45)               138    *************Termination Sequence*************
57            VALUE "What is the number of the employee to delete?". 139     CLOSE EMPLOYEE-FILE
58        05  MO-MAINT-OPTION           PIC X(45).              140        STOP RUN
59                                                              141        .
60    01  ME-MESSAGES.                                          142    ********************************************
61        05  ME-NOT-IN-FILE-17                 PIC X(46)       143    050-DISPLAY-ANNOUNCE-SCREEN.
62            VALUE "No record in file for this employee number  ". 144      DISPLAY "EMPLOYEE FILE MAINTENANCE PROGRAM"
63        05  ME-ALREADY-IN-FILE-17             PIC X(46)       145                                   LINE 7 COL 20
64            VALUE "  The above record is already in the file   ". 146              WITH BLANK SCREEN.
65        05  ME-DELETE-WARNING-17              PIC X(46)       147        DISPLAY "Program provides the maintenance functions:"
66            VALUE "  DELETING THIS RECORD PERMANENTLY ERASES IT! ". 148                             LINE 9 COL 20
67        05  ME-WRITE-ERROR-17                 PIC X(46)       149        DISPLAY "record addition, modification, and deletion."
68            VALUE "Error condition--record not written to disk   ". 150                            LINE 10 COL 20
69        05  ME-DELETE-ERROR-17                PIC X(46)       151        DISPLAY "Do you want to continue <Y/N>?"
70            VALUE "Error condition--record not deleted from disk ". 152                            LINE 12 COL 20
71        05  ME-ADD-MODIFY-WARNING-17          PIC X(46)       153        ACCEPT S1-USER-RESPONSE-SWITCH   LINE 12 COL 51
72            VALUE "You can save this record or abort the entries ". 154     IF S1-YES-RESPONSE
73        05  ME-DELETE-QUERY-19                PIC X(46)       155            SET S3-BLANK-OPTION TO TRUE
74            VALUE "  Are you certain you want to delete it <Y/N>?". 156     ELSE
75        05  ME-SAVE-QUERY-19                  PIC X(46)       157            SET S3-EXIT-OPTION TO TRUE
76            VALUE "Do you want to save this record to disk <Y/N>?". 158     END-IF
77        05  ME-ENTER-TO-CONTINUE-19           PIC X(46)       159        .
78            VALUE "Press the Enter key to continue        ".
79        05  ME-PROCESS-ANOTHER-EMPL-19        PIC X(46)
80            VALUE "Do you want to process another employee <Y/N>?".
81        05  ME-MESSAGE-17                     PIC X(46).
82        05  ME-MESSAGE-19                     PIC X(46).
```

Figure 15-13   (continued)

```
160    250-GET-MENU-CHOICE.
161        DISPLAY "EMPLOYEE FILE MAINTENANCE MENU" LINE 3 COL 20
162             WITH BLANK SCREEN
163        DISPLAY "=================================" LINE  4 COL 20
164        DISPLAY "The maintenance options are:"    LINE  6 COL 20
165        DISPLAY "A - Add records to file"         LINE  8 COL 20
166        DISPLAY "M - Modify existing records"     LINE 10 COL 20
167        DISPLAY "D - Delete records"              LINE 12 COL 20
168        DISPLAY "X - eXit maintenance"            LINE 14 COL 20
169        DISPLAY "Your choice?"                    LINE 16 COL 20
170        PERFORM WITH TEST AFTER
171             UNTIL S3-VALID-OPTION
172          ACCEPT S3-RESPONSE-OPTION               LINE 16 COL 33
173          IF NOT S3-VALID-OPTION
174            DISPLAY "INVALID ENTRY, TRY AGAIN."   LINE 18 COL 20
175          END-IF
176        END-PERFORM
177        EVALUATE TRUE
178          WHEN S3-ADD-RECORD-OPTION
179            MOVE MO-ADD-OPTION TO MO-MAINT-OPTION
180          WHEN S3-MODIFY-RECORD-OPTION
181            MOVE MO-MODIFY-OPTION TO MO-MAINT-OPTION
182          WHEN S3-DELETE-RECORD-OPTION
183            MOVE MO-DELETE-OPTION TO MO-MAINT-OPTION
184        END-EVALUATE
185        .
186    300-ADD-RECORD.
187        INITIALIZE ER-EMPLOYEE-RECORD
188        MOVE 26 TO ER-RECORD-CODE
189        MOVE EMPLOYEE-NUMBER TO ER-EMPLOYEE-NUMBER
190        PERFORM 855-DISPLAY-EMPLOYEE-TEMPLATE
191        PERFORM 860-DISPLAY-EMPLOYEE-RECORD
192        PERFORM 810-ACCEPT-EMPLOYEE-FIELDS
193        MOVE ME-ADD-MODIFY-WARNING-17 TO ME-MESSAGE-17
194        MOVE ME-SAVE-QUERY-19 TO ME-MESSAGE-19
195        PERFORM 850-DISPLAY-MESSAGE-LINES
196        PERFORM 820-QUERY-USER-FOR-ACTION
197        IF S1-YES-RESPONSE
198          MOVE ER-EMPLOYEE-RECORD TO EMPLOYEE-RECORD
199          WRITE EMPLOYEE-RECORD
200            INVALID KEY
201              MOVE ME-WRITE-ERROR-17 TO ME-MESSAGE-17
202          END-WRITE
203        END-IF
204        .
205    400-MODIFY-RECORD.
206        PERFORM 855-DISPLAY-EMPLOYEE-TEMPLATE
207        PERFORM 860-DISPLAY-EMPLOYEE-RECORD
208        PERFORM 810-ACCEPT-EMPLOYEE-FIELDS
209        MOVE ME-ADD-MODIFY-WARNING-17 TO ME-MESSAGE-17
210        MOVE ME-SAVE-QUERY-19 TO ME-MESSAGE-19
211        PERFORM 850-DISPLAY-MESSAGE-LINES
212        PERFORM 820-QUERY-USER-FOR-ACTION
213        IF S1-YES-RESPONSE
214          MOVE ER-EMPLOYEE-RECORD TO EMPLOYEE-RECORD
215          REWRITE EMPLOYEE-RECORD
216            INVALID KEY
217              MOVE ME-WRITE-ERROR-17 TO ME-MESSAGE-17
218          END-REWRITE
219        END-IF
220        .
221    500-DELETE-RECORD.
222        PERFORM 855-DISPLAY-EMPLOYEE-TEMPLATE
223        PERFORM 860-DISPLAY-EMPLOYEE-RECORD
224        MOVE ME-DELETE-WARNING-17 TO ME-MESSAGE-17
225        MOVE ME-DELETE-QUERY-19 TO ME-MESSAGE-19
226        PERFORM 850-DISPLAY-MESSAGE-LINES
227        PERFORM 820-QUERY-USER-FOR-ACTION
228        IF S1-YES-RESPONSE
229          DELETE EMPLOYEE-FILE
230            INVALID KEY
231              MOVE ME-DELETE-ERROR-17 TO ME-MESSAGE-17
232          END-DELETE
233        END-IF
234        .
235    800-GET-EMPLOYEE-NUMBER.
236        DISPLAY MO-MAINT-OPTION                    LINE  6 COL 11
237             WITH BLANK SCREEN
238        MOVE SPACES TO EMPLOYEE-NUMBER
239        ACCEPT EMPLOYEE-NUMBER                     LINE  6 COL 57
240             WITH REVERSE-VIDEO
241        .
242    810-ACCEPT-EMPLOYEE-FIELDS.
243        ACCEPT ER-LAST-NAME       LINE  8 COL 21 WITH REVERSE-VIDEO
244        ACCEPT ER-FIRST-NAME      LINE  8 COL 41 WITH REVERSE-VIDEO
245        ACCEPT ER-MIDDLE-INITIAL  LINE  8 COL 56 WITH REVERSE-VIDEO
246        ACCEPT ER-TELEPHONE-EXT   LINE 10 COL 55 WITH REVERSE-VIDEO
247        ACCEPT ER-ADDRESS         LINE 12 COL 21 WITH REVERSE-VIDEO
248        ACCEPT ER-CITY            LINE 14 COL 21 WITH REVERSE-VIDEO
249        ACCEPT ER-STATE           LINE 14 COL 43 WITH REVERSE-VIDEO
250        ACCEPT ER-ZIP             LINE 14 COL 52 WITH REVERSE-VIDEO
251        .
252    820-QUERY-USER-FOR-ACTION.
253        PERFORM 850-DISPLAY-MESSAGE-LINES
254        MOVE SPACE TO S1-USER-RESPONSE-SWITCH
255        ACCEPT S1-USER-RESPONSE-SWITCH             LINE 19 COL 57
256        MOVE SPACES TO ME-MESSAGE-17
257        .
258    825-QUERY-USER-TO-REPEAT.
259        MOVE ME-PROCESS-ANOTHER-EMPL-19 TO ME-MESSAGE-19
260        PERFORM 850-DISPLAY-MESSAGE-LINES
261        MOVE SPACE TO S2-CONTINUE-SWITCH
262        ACCEPT S2-CONTINUE-SWITCH                  LINE 19 COL 57
263        .
264    850-DISPLAY-MESSAGE-LINES.
265        DISPLAY ME-MESSAGE-17                      LINE 17 COL 10
266        DISPLAY ME-MESSAGE-19                      LINE 19 COL 10
267        .
268    855-DISPLAY-EMPLOYEE-TEMPLATE.
269        DISPLAY "EMPLOYEE ADDRESS DATA"            LINE  3 COL 20
270             WITH BLANK SCREEN
271        DISPLAY "======================="          LINE  4 COL 20
272        DISPLAY "Employee number:"                 LINE  6 COL 9
273        DISPLAY "Name Last:               First:            MI:"
274                                                   LINE  8 COL 9
275        DISPLAY "Telephone extension:"             LINE 10 COL 34
276        DISPLAY "Address:"                         LINE 12 COL 12
277        DISPLAY "City:                State:    Zip:"
278                                                   LINE 14 COL 15
279        .
280    860-DISPLAY-EMPLOYEE-RECORD.
281        DISPLAY ER-EMPLOYEE-NUMBER LINE  6 COL 26 WITH REVERSE-VIDEO
282        DISPLAY ER-FIRST-NAME      LINE  8 COL 41 WITH REVERSE-VIDEO
283        DISPLAY ER-LAST-NAME       LINE  8 COL 21 WITH REVERSE-VIDEO
284        DISPLAY ER-MIDDLE-INITIAL  LINE  8 COL 56 WITH REVERSE-VIDEO
285        DISPLAY ER-TELEPHONE-EXT   LINE 10 COL 55 WITH REVERSE-VIDEO
286        DISPLAY ER-ADDRESS         LINE 12 COL 21 WITH REVERSE-VIDEO
287        DISPLAY ER-CITY            LINE 14 COL 21 WITH REVERSE-VIDEO
288        DISPLAY ER-STATE           LINE 14 COL 43 WITH REVERSE-VIDEO
289        DISPLAY ER-ZIP             LINE 14 COL 52 WITH REVERSE-VIDEO
290        .
```

2. The screen template is displayed (line 190) and then the fields of the current record are displayed (line 191). If you check the 860 module (beginning at line 280), you will see that all fields except the employee number are blank. However, the field areas into which data is ultimately entered are displayed in reverse video. This allows the user to see fields into which data must be entered. Perhaps you noticed this when you ran the program.

3. Input is accepted by the 810 module, performed from line 192. Although the employee number is displayed on the screen during data entry, a new value cannot be entered into it. Its value was obtained in the 800 module—remember, this is the key field.

4. Lines 193–196 provide the two message lines that give the user the option to save this record or to abort it. A response of Y at line 255 means that the condition-name S1-YES-RESPONSE is true.

5. If S1-YES-RESPONSE is true, the record is written to the file (lines 198 and 199).

6. The logic of this program (the NOT INVALID KEY option of the READ) guarantees that no record in the file will have the same employee number as the record to be written. So, an INVALID KEY condition in the WRITE (line 200) is highly unlikely. (It could result from a disk write failure.) However, COBOL requires that this clause be included with the WRITE unless other error handling is invoked.

The Modify Module and the REWRITE Statement

The modify module differs from the add module only in that: (1) the fields of the record are not initialized and (2) the REWRITE statement is used instead of the WRITE. By not initializing the fields, entries from the current record are displayed (by the 860 module), then used as default input values for the 810 module. (Note: When appropriately configured, Micro Focus uses current data-item values for defaults when the LINE/COL options are included with the ACCEPT. If the system you are using does not do this, you will need to include another option with the ACCEPT. This option is commonly named UPDATE.)

You were introduced to the REWRITE at the end of Chapter 14 to update a record in place. Although not commonly used with sequential files, it is a "bread-and-butter" operation in working with indexed files. In this case, the desired record is read, its contents changed, and the record is written back to the file—thereby replacing the previous copy in the file. As you might expect, a record must be read before the REWRITE can be issued because the REWRITE always writes back the record previously read.

The Delete Module and the DELETE Statement

Notice that the record is displayed so that the user can inspect it before going through with the delete. This is important because it is very easy to mistype the employee number and get the wrong record.

The DELETE statement at line 229 deletes the record from the file that is identified by the contents of the FD record description key field value. Although the record was read before deleting (as a precaution) COBOL does not *require* that the record be read before deleting. The INVALID clause is required unless other provisions are made for error handling.

Positioning of Elements on the Screen

Unless you are using special screen-generator software that creates ACCEPT and DISPLAY code for you from a screen layout, determining LINE and COL values is very tedious. In this program, this task is made easier because of two techniques. First, all messages are defined with the same length in a special message area of WORKING-STORAGE. Second, all ACCEPT and DISPLAY statements (they include LINE/COL phrases) pertaining to the primary data screen are executed from input and output modules grouped together—lines 242–290. Keeping all screen-positioning references together—as done in this program—simplifies debugging and changing the screen layout.

COBOL-74

A complete COBOL-74 program—named EMPMNT.C74—is included on the disk that accompanies this book. You will probably need to change optional phrases used with the ACCEPT and DISPLAY statements.

Updating an Indexed Master file from a Sequential Transaction File

Programming Specifications and Pseudocode Solution

The program SEQ-MNT of Chapter 14 updates a sequential file from an input transaction file—a batch operation. At the other extreme, EMPMNT in this chapter allows a user to update records of an indexed file interactively from the keyboard. The next example illustrates batch updating an indexed file (in-place) from a sequential transaction file. Indexed file batch updating differs significantly from sequential file batch updating in that records of the indexed master can be read randomly. While sequential update is constantly reading and comparing masters and transactions, the indexed update can:

1. Read the next transaction.
2. Read the needed master using the key value of the transaction record.
3. Update the master.
4. Rewrite the master to disk.

Although the transaction records can be in random order, they are most commonly in sequence on the key field. In this way, the master needs to be read and rewritten only one time for each group of its transaction records. So, the action becomes one of processing transaction records against a given master until a transaction record with a different key field value is read. If you think back to Chapter 9, you will realize that this is similar to control-break processing. In fact, this application uses Chapter 9's sales representative file, which illustrated single-level control-break processing.

Figure 15-14 shows programming specifications for this application. You can see in the description that report generation is omitted in the interest of focusing on the update process. A normal report would include a control-break type of output with master information, data from each transaction, and summary information for each master record. It would also contain transaction records with no corresponding master (unmatched transactions).

As often happens, the overall program logic to perform a batch indexed file update is very similar to that of another application: control-break processing, in this instance. In fact, you can see that much of the pseudocode in Figure 15-15 for this application is taken from that of Figure 9-7 (page 288) for single-level control-break processing. In the 200 module, a break occurs when a different sales representative is detected in the newly read transaction record. This triggers the updated master to be rewritten and the needed new master to be read.

Sales Master Update Program Solution— SLSUPD

The program solution is included as Figure 15-16 (page 546); the following are some of its features:

1. Repeated processing of transaction records through the PERFORM of line 87 is controlled by the S1 switch. Repetition is ended by the value change resulting from an end-of-file (line 90) or by a REWRITE error (line 157).
2. No action occurs in the 200 module unless a break has occurred (the first record, a different sales representative, or the EOF record).

Figure 15-14
Programming
specifications—Random
master file update.

PROGRAMMING SPECIFICATIONS

Program Name: Random Master File Update   Program ID: SLSUPD

Program Description:

The sales representative master file (indexed) is updated in-place by
a transaction file containing one record for each sales transaction.
The transaction file was validated prior to this program run. This is
a demonstration program, so the normal update report and unmatched
transaction record error log are omitted to minimize the size of the
program.

Input Files:

Sales Representative Master File (SALES_MA.DAI)

Columns	Field	Description
3-7	Sales rep number	
8-20	Rep last name	
21-29	Rep first name	
30-33	Commission rate	V999
34-40	Total sales	Dollars and cents

File is indexed.
Key field is Sales rep number.

Sales File (SALES_S.DAT)

Following are the fields required in this program. The complete
record description is included in the programming specifications for
a single-level control-break program, Figure 9-4.

Columns	Field	Description
8-12	Sales rep number	
42-45	Quantity sold	Whole number
46-49	Unit price	Dollars and cents

Sales file sorted on Sales rep number
Common key field: Sales rep number

Output File:

Updated Sales Representative Master File (SALES_MA.DAI)

List of Program Operations:

A. Read each input sales record.
B. For each sales record, the program is to:
    1. Compute the amount-of-sale by multiplying the unit-price field
        by the quantity-sold field.
    2. Add the amount-of-sale to the master total-sales.
C. Whenever the transaction record sales-representative number
    changes, the program is to:
    1. Rewrite the master record.
    2. Read the master record corresponding to the input sales
        record.
D. Display each unmatched transaction record on the screen and
    continue processing.
E. If an error occurs when rewriting a record, display an error
    message and terminate processing.

---

3. An unmatched transaction record causes a master-record read failure—
   which, in turn, causes the S3 switch to be set at line 145. This triggers
   performing the 300 module (see lines 94–98).
4. Subsequent unmatched transactions are processed through the 300
   module.

Notice that the master record is written conditionally (lines 122–124). To
understand this, assume that three consecutive transaction records have key field
values of 10003 (several records), 10007, 1007, and 10009—and that 10007 has no
matching master. The following occurs:

1. Reading each sales record 10003 causes the corresponding master record to be updated.
2. Reading 10007 triggers the not equal EVALUATE option at line 121. S3-MASTER-FOUND is true (from the preceding master-file read), so the master is rewritten.
3. On attempting to read the master for 10007 (at line 143 performed from line 125), the invalid-key condition occurs and S3-MASTER-NOT-FOUND is set to true.

Figure 15-15
Detailed pseudocode solution—Random master file update.

```
000-Update-Sales-Master-Record module
1.   Open the files.
2.   Perform 100-Initialize-Variable-Fields.
3.   Perform until end of processing:
        Read a transaction record
        at end
            Set end-of-processing to true
            Perform 200-Process-Break
        not at end
            Perform 200-Process-Break
            If Unmatched-transaction
              Perform 300-Process-Unmatched-Trans
            else
              Perform 250-Process-Matched-Trans.
4.   Close the files.
5.   Stop the run.
100-Initialize-Variable-Fields module
1.   Set the Not-end-of-processing switch to true.
2.   Set First-record switch to true.
200-Process-Break module
1.   Evaluate the following case:
        When first record
            Move the input Sales-rep field to the
            Previous-sales-rep field.
            Perform 800-Read-Master-Record.
            Set Not-first-record switch to True.
        When the input Sales-rep field is not equal
        to the Previous-sales-rep field
            Perform 850-Rewrite-Master-Record.
            Perform 800-Read-Master-Record.
        When end of file
            Perform 850-Rewrite-Master-Record.
250-Process-Matched-Trans module
1.   Multiply the input Unit-price by the input Quantity-sold
     to yield the Sales-revenue.
2.   Add the Sales-revenue for this record to the Sales-rep-
     master-revenue.
300-Process-Unmatched-Trans module
1.   Display unmatched transaction record.
800-Read-Master-Record module
1.   Move Trans-sales-rep-number to master Sales-rep key field.
2.   Read Master-file
     Invalid key
        Set Unmatched-record switch to true
     Not invalid key
        Set Unmatched-record switch to false
850-Rewrite-Master-Record module
1.   Move WS-master-record to FD-master-record.
2.   Rewrite master-record
     Invalid key
        Display error message
        Set End-of-processing to true.
```

Figure 15-16   Random master file update program—SLSUPD.

```
  1        IDENTIFICATION DIVISION.                                77     PROCEDURE DIVISION.
  2        PROGRAM-ID.    SLSUPD.                                   78
  3                                                                 79     000-UPDATE-MASTER-FILE.
  4      * W. Price  3/1/95                                         80
  5      * PYRAMID SALES COMPANY.                                   81     ************Initialization Sequence************
  6                                                                 82         OPEN INPUT SALES-FILE
  7      * This program updates sales totals of sales               83              I-O MASTER-FILE
  8      * representative master records.                           84         PERFORM 100-INITIALIZE-VARIABLE-FIELDS
  9      * Input is from a sales transaction file.                  85
 10                                                                 86     **************Processing Sequence**************
 11                                                                 87         PERFORM UNTIL S1-END-OF-PROCESSING
 12        ENVIRONMENT DIVISION.                                    88             READ SALES-FILE INTO SR-SALES-RECORD
 13                                                                 89                 AT END
 14        INPUT-OUTPUT SECTION.                                    90                     SET S1-END-OF-PROCESSING TO TRUE
 15                                                                 91                     PERFORM 200-PROCESS-BREAK
 16        FILE-CONTROL.                                            92                 NOT AT END
 17            SELECT SALES-FILE                                    93                     PERFORM 200-PROCESS-BREAK
 18                ASSIGN TO DISK "SALES_S.DAT"                     94                     IF S3-MASTER-FOUND
 19                ORGANIZATION IS LINE SEQUENTIAL.                 95                         PERFORM 250-PROCESS-MATCHED-TRANS
 20            SELECT MASTER-FILE                                   96                     ELSE
 21                ASSIGN TO DISK "SALES_MA.DAI"                    97                         PERFORM 300-PROCESS-UNMATCHED-TRANS
 22                ORGANIZATION IS INDEXED                          98                     END-IF
 23                ACCESS IS RANDOM                                 99             END-READ
 24                RECORD KEY IS SALES-REP.                        100         END-PERFORM
 25                                                                101
 26                                                                102     **************Termination Sequence*************
 27        DATA DIVISION.                                          103         CLOSE SALES-FILE
 28                                                                104               MASTER-FILE
 29        FILE SECTION.                                           105         STOP RUN
 30                                                                106         .
 31        FD  SALES-FILE.                                         107     **************************************************
 32        01  SALES-RECORD                    PIC X(48).          108
 33                                                                109     100-INITIALIZE-VARIABLE-FIELDS.
 34        FD  MASTER-FILE.                                        110         SET S1-NOT-END-OF-PROCESSING TO TRUE
 35        01  MASTER-RECORD.                                      111         SET S2-FIRST-RECORD TO TRUE
 36            05                              PIC X(2).           112         .
 37            05  SALES-REP                   PIC X(5).           113     200-PROCESS-BREAK.
 38            05                              PIC X(33).          114         EVALUATE TRUE
 39                                                                115
 40        WORKING-STORAGE SECTION.                                116             WHEN S2-FIRST-RECORD
 41                                                                117                 MOVE SR-SALES-REP TO WA-PREV-SALES-REP
 42        01  PROGRAM-SWITCHES.                                   118                 PERFORM 800-READ-MASTER-RECORD
 43            05  S1-END-OF-PROCESSING-SWITCH PIC X(1).           119                 SET S2-NOT-FIRST-RECORD TO TRUE
 44                88  S1-END-OF-PROCESSING       VALUE "E".       120
 45                88  S1-NOT-END-OF-PROCESSING   VALUE "N".       121             WHEN SR-SALES-REP NOT EQUAL TO WA-PREV-SALES-REP
 46            05  S2-FIRST-RECORD-SWITCH      PIC X(1).           122                 IF S3-MASTER-FOUND
 47                88  S2-FIRST-RECORD            VALUE "F".       123                     PERFORM 850-REWRITE-MASTER-RECORD
 48                88  S2-NOT-FIRST-RECORD        VALUE "N".       124                 END-IF
 49            05  S3-MASTER-FOUND-SWITCH      PIC X(1).           125                 PERFORM 800-READ-MASTER-RECORD
 50                88  S3-MASTER-FOUND            VALUE "F".       126
 51                88  S3-MASTER-NOT-FOUND        VALUE "N".       127             WHEN S1-END-OF-PROCESSING
 52                                                                128                 PERFORM 850-REWRITE-MASTER-RECORD
 53        01  WA-WORK-AREAS.                                      129
 54            05  WA-AMOUNT-OF-SALE           PIC S9(5)V99.       130         END-EVALUATE
 55            05  WA-PREV-SALES-REP           PIC X(5).           131         .
 56                                                                132     250-PROCESS-MATCHED-TRANS.
 57        01  SR-SALES-RECORD.                                    133         MULTIPLY SR-UNIT-PRICE BY SR-QUANTITY-SOLD
 58            05  SR-RECORD-CODE              PIC X(2).           134             GIVING WA-AMOUNT-OF-SALE
 59            05  SR-STATE                    PIC X(2).           135         ADD WA-AMOUNT-OF-SALE TO MR-TOTAL-SALES
 60            05  SR-BRANCH                   PIC X(3).           136         .
 61            05  SR-SALES-REP                PIC X(5).           137     300-PROCESS-UNMATCHED-TRANS.
 62            05  SR-DATE-OF-SALE             PIC X(6).           138         DISPLAY "Unmatched transaction record, sales rep: "
 63            05  SR-PRODUCT-CODE             PIC X(7).           139             SR-SALES-REP
 64            05  SR-PRODUCT-DESCRIPTION      PIC X(16).          140         .
 65            05  SR-QUANTITY-SOLD            PIC S9(3).          141     800-READ-MASTER-RECORD.
 66            05  SR-UNIT-PRICE               PIC 9(2)V99.        142         MOVE SR-SALES-REP TO SALES-REP
 67                                                                143         READ MASTER-FILE INTO MR-MASTER-RECORD
 68        01  MR-MASTER-RECORD.                                   144             INVALID KEY
 69            05                              PIC X(2).           145                 SET S3-MASTER-NOT-FOUND TO TRUE
 70            05  MR-SALES-REP                PIC X(5).           146             NOT INVALID KEY
 71            05  MR-LAST-NAME                PIC X(13).          147                 SET S3-MASTER-FOUND TO TRUE
 72            05  MR-FIRST-NAME               PIC X(9).           148         END-READ
 73            05  MR-COMMISSION-RATE          PIC V999.           149         .
 74            05  MR-TOTAL-SALES              PIC S9(6)V99.       150     850-REWRITE-MASTER-RECORD.
 75                                                                151         MOVE MR-MASTER-RECORD TO MASTER-RECORD
 76                                                                152         REWRITE MASTER-RECORD
                                                                   153             INVALID KEY
                                                                   154                 DISPLAY
                                                                   155                     "Error trying to rewrite record for sales rep: "
                                                                   156                     SALES-REP
                                                                   157                 SET S1-END-OF-PROCESSING TO TRUE
                                                                   158         END-REWRITE
                                                                   159         .
```

4. From the main module, the unmatched sales record is processed via the IF (see line 97).
5. The second transaction record for 10007 triggers no action in the 200 module (no break occurs), and is also processed as an unmatched transaction.
6. Reading 10009 is sensed as a break at line 121. Because S3-MASTER-FOUND is not true, no master is written. Remember, the preceding master 10003 was already rewritten.

By this time in your COBOL studies, you have learned a variety of programming techniques that can be incorporated in program solutions. Often, the solution to one application uses almost the same structure and logic as that of a totally different application. At first, you might expect the program logic of an indexed file batch update to be similar to that of a sequential file batch update. However, as you saw, this indexed file batch update is more of a control-break application. Whenever you encounter a new application, view it in terms of techniques and methods you used in other solutions. Reinventing the wheel—or program code—wastes time.

COBOL-74

A complete COBOL-74 program—named SLSUPD.C74—is included on the disk that accompanies this book. You will probably need to change optional phrases used with the ACCEPT and DISPLAY statements.

Dynamic File Access

Accessing a File Both Randomly and Sequentially

From the preceding examples, you saw that the ACCESS clause of the SELECT indicates to COBOL that an indexed or relative file is to be accessed *either* sequentially or randomly during a program's execution. However, consider an application in which processing is as follows:

1. Access a particular record as a starting point—a random access.
2. Access one or more records following the previously accessed record—sequential access.

For example, in a customer billing program, you might want to process all invoices beginning with a particular invoice number. From the employee file, you might want to access an employee by his or her last name, then successively display each employee record with the same last name.

As mentioned in Module E, such a dual-accessing capability is called dynamic access. It involves a two-step process: (1) randomly locating the starting position in the file and (2) sequentially processing records onwards from that point.

The starting position within the file may be located in two ways. One is to use a random-access READ as you saw it used in EMPMNT to access a selected record. The other is to use a much more versatile statement specifically provided for this purpose: the START.

The START Statement

The START allows you to position within an indexed file specifically for subsequent sequential reading. It does not, in itself, read a record. Let's first compare it to the random-access READ statement:

```
MOVE DESIRED-EMPLOYEE-NUMBER TO EMPLOYEE-NUMBER
READ EMPLOYEE-FILE
```

As shown here, before executing the READ, the program must place the desired employee number (the key field value) in the key field defined in the FD record.

The following form of the START operates in the same way, except that no record is read; positioning within the file is to the appropriate record:

```
MOVE DESIRED-EMPLOYEE-NUMBER TO EMPLOYEE-NUMBER
START EMPLOYEE-FILE
```

Then sequential READ statements will read records, beginning with the current file positioning.

If access will be by an alternate key, then for both the READ and START, the alternate key must be specified. For instance, the following READ will access a record based on the contents of the alternate key field EMPLOYEE-FULL-NAME, assuming that this is defined in the SELECT as an alternate key:

```
MOVE DESIRED-EMPLOYEE-NAME TO EMPLOYEE-FULL-NAME
READ EMPLOYEE-FILE KEY IS EMPLOYEE-FULL-NAME
```

In all cases, the preceding example statements search for a record with a key field value equal to that contained in the key field of the FD record description.

On the other hand, the START provides much broader capabilities, as evident from the format:

$$
\underline{\text{START}} \text{ file-name} \left[\underline{\text{KEY}} \left\{ \begin{array}{l} \text{IS } \underline{\text{EQUAL}} \text{ TO} \\ \text{IS =} \\ \text{IS } \underline{\text{GREATER}} \text{ THAN} \\ \text{IS >} \\ \text{IS } \underline{\text{NOT LESS}} \text{ THAN} \\ \text{IS } \underline{\text{NOT}} \text{ <} \\ \text{IS } \underline{\text{GREATER}} \text{ THAN } \underline{\text{OR}} \underline{\text{EQUAL}} \text{ TO} \\ \text{IS >=} \\ \text{IS } \underline{\text{LESS}} \text{ THAN} \\ \text{IS <} \end{array} \right\} \text{data-name} \right]
$$

[INVALID KEY imperative-statement-1]
[NOT INVALID KEY imperative-statement-2]
[END-START]

Execution of the START statement causes positioning within the file according to the contents of the designated key, which affects the READ statement that follows. For relative files, the *data-name* entry must be the relative key as declared in the SELECT clause. For indexed files, it can be the prime key or any alternate key. (It can also be any part of a key field that begins with the first character of that field. This is a significant element of the next example program and is explained later.)

The following two examples illustrate the capabilities of this statement:

```
MOVE "25000" TO EMPLOYEE-NUMBER
START EMPLOYEE-FILE KEY IS GREATER OR EQUAL EMPLOYEE-NUMBER

MOVE "J" TO EMPLOYEE-FULL-NAME
START EMPLOYEE-FILE KEY NOT LESS THAN EMPLOYEE-FULL-NAME
```

In the first example, the file is positioned to the record with a primary key value of 25000. If there is no record with this key value, the file is positioned at the first record with a primary key value greater than 25000. The second example uses the alternate key field defined for the EMPLISTA program of Figure 15-7, page 533. The file is positioned at the first record with the last name beginning with the letter J.

Logic of a Dynamic File-Access Program

The next program demonstrates dynamic access and the START statement through last-name access to the employee file. The employee file used in this example is the version that includes an alternate key on the employee-name field. As with previous programs, understanding the EMPGETA program is easier if you first run it. Be sure to make any needed changes required by your compiler. Search for the last name STEWART because several records have this last name. The three records for ZENER used in the next description are also in the file.

Before looking at the logic of this application, let's investigate the following two data scenarios:

```
ZACHARY HOWARD          ZACHARY HOWARD
ZENER   CLARENCE        ZENER   CLARENCE
ZENER   JUDY            ZENER   JUDY
ZENER   GEORGE          ZENER   GEORGE
ZIEGER  ALICE           EOF
EOF
```

A request for a desired employee record from this file can terminate in any of four ways:

1. The user enters the name ZAMORA. The file contains no such entry, so processing terminates for that employee name upon encountering ZENER.
2. The user enters the name ZENER (desiring the record for LAURA, which has no record in the file). Referring to the data set on the right, after successively accessing records for CLARENCE, JUDY, and GEORGE (at the user's request), the program encounters the EOF (end-of-file). This signals the end of the ZENERs, so processing terminates for that employee name.
3. The user enters the name ZENER (desiring the record for JUDY, which has a record in the file). The record for CLARENCE is displayed on the screen. Progressing to the next record produces the desired display. After inspecting the record, the user terminates for that employee name.
4. The user enters the name ZENER (desiring the record for LAURA, which has no record in the file). Referring to the data set on the left, after successively accessing records for CLARENCE, JUDY, and GEORGE (at the user's request), the program encounters the name ZIEGLER. This signals the end of the ZENERs, so processing terminates for that employee name.

The program to perform this processing uses almost the same screen input/output modules as does the file maintenance program EMPMNT.

Like the EMPMNT program, the most notable element is the processing sequence, which is illustrated by the pseudocode of Figure 15-17(a) for using the START and Figure 15-17(b) for using the READ. In both cases, the portions of the code corresponding to the preceding data scenarios are indicated by numbers. Correlating the preceding descriptions to the pseudocode is reasonably straightforward.

The EMPGETA Program

Figure 15-18 shows the EMPGETA program. The screen input/output components of this program are taken from EMPMNT, so they require little comment. The main processing sequence follows almost directly from the pseudocode of Figure 15-17.

Figure 15-17 Mainline pseudocode for dynamic accessing of records.

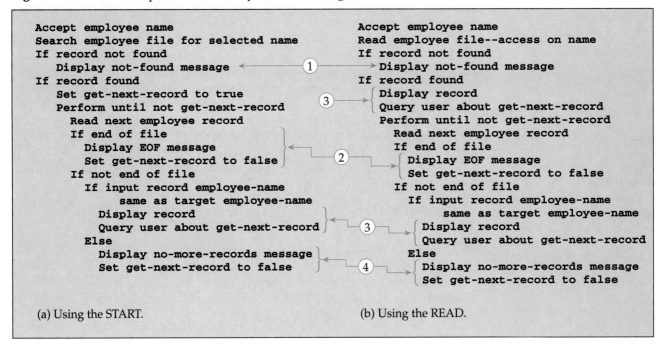

(a) Using the START.   (b) Using the READ.

1. From the 800 module (executed through the PERFORM at line 82), the desired employee last name is accepted and placed in the field LAST-NAME.
2. The START statement (line 83) positions within the file to the first record with the user-entered last-name.
3. The INVALID KEY clause (line 84)—which functions the same as with the READ—indicates that the action was not successful. The not-in-file message is displayed.
4. After positioning within a file with a START, records must be read with a sequential READ. This is accomplished at lines 90 and 91. Whenever the sequential READ is used following a START statement, record access is automatically based on the key field designated in the START statement.
5. When one or more records are in the file for the target last-name, the inline PERFORM (line 89) serves the purpose of sequentially accessing records until: (1) the end-of-file is encountered—lines 92–95, (2) the user chooses not to view more records—line 99, or (3) a record with a different last name is encountered—lines 101–103.

COBOL-74

A complete COBOL-74 program—named EMPGETA.C74—is included on the disk that accompanies this book. You will probably need to change optional phrases used with the ACCEPT and DISPLAY statements.

Figure 15-18   Dynamic accessing of records—EMPGETA.

```
1     IDENTIFICATION DIVISION.
2     PROGRAM-ID.    EMPGETA.
3
4     *      W. PRICE 3/1/95
5
6     *      This program allows the user to display records
7     *      from the indexed employee file based on last name.
8
9
10    ENVIRONMENT DIVISION.
11
12    INPUT-OUTPUT SECTION.
13
14    FILE-CONTROL.
15        SELECT EMPLOYEE-FILE
16            ASSIGN TO DISK "EMPLOYEE.DAA"
17            ORGANIZATION IS INDEXED
18            ACCESS IS DYNAMIC
19            RECORD KEY IS EMPLOYEE-NUMBER
20            ALTERNATE RECORD KEY IS EMPLOYEE-FULL-NAME
21                            WITH DUPLICATES.
22
23
24    DATA DIVISION.
25
26    FILE SECTION.
27
28    FD  EMPLOYEE-FILE.
29    01  EMPLOYEE-RECORD.
30        05                              PIC X(2).
31        05    EMPLOYEE-NUMBER           PIC X(5).
32        05    EMPLOYEE-FULL-NAME.
33            10   LAST-NAME              PIC X(11).
34            10                          PIC X(10).
35        05                              PIC X(50).
36
37    WORKING-STORAGE SECTION.
38
39    01  SW-SWITCHES.
40        05    S1-ANOTHER-EMPLOYEE-SWITCH   PIC X(1).
41            88  S1-ANOTHER-EMPLOYEE       VALUE "Y" "y".
42            88  S1-NOT-ANOTHER-EMPLOYEE   VALUE "N".
43
44        05    S2-GET-NEXT-RECORD-SWITCH    PIC X(1).
45            88  S2-GET-NEXT-RECORD        VALUE "Y" "y".
46            88  S2-NOT-GET-NEXT-RECORD    VALUE "N".
47
48    01  WA-WORK-AREAS.
49        05    WA-EMPLOYEE-LAST-NAME     PIC X(11).
50
51    01  EM-ERROR-MESSAGES.
52        05    EM-RECORD-NOT-FOUND       PIC X(35)
53              VALUE "No record in file for this person".
54        05    EM-NO-MORE-RECORDS        PIC X(35)
55              VALUE "No more records with this last name".
56        05    EM-ERROR-MESSAGE          PIC X(35).
57
58    01  ER-EMPLOYEE-RECORD.
59        05    ER-RECORD-CODE            PIC 9(2).
60        05    ER-EMPLOYEE-NUMBER        PIC X(5).
61        05    ER-LAST-NAME              PIC X(11).
62        05    ER-FIRST-NAME             PIC X(9).
63        05    ER-MIDDLE-INITIAL         PIC X(1).
64        05    ER-ADDRESS                PIC X(23).
65        05    ER-CITY                   PIC X(13).
66        05                              PIC X(1).
67        05    ER-STATE                  PIC X(2).
68        05                              PIC X(2).
69        05    ER-ZIP                    PIC X(5).
70        05    ER-TELEPHONE-EXT          PIC X(4).
71
72
73    PROCEDURE DIVISION.
74
75    000-DISPLAY-PATRON-RECORDS.
76    ************Initialization Sequence************
77        OPEN INPUT EMPLOYEE-FILE
78        PERFORM 050-DISPLAY-ANNOUNCE-SCREEN
79
80    ************Processing Sequence************
81        PERFORM UNTIL S1-NOT-ANOTHER-EMPLOYEE
82            PERFORM 800-GET-EMPLOYEE-LAST-NAME
83            START EMPLOYEE-FILE KEY = LAST-NAME
84                INVALID KEY
85                    MOVE EM-RECORD-NOT-FOUND TO EM-ERROR-MESSAGE
86                    PERFORM 820-DISPLAY-MESSAGE-AND-QUERY
```

```
87                NOT INVALID KEY
88                    SET S2-GET-NEXT-RECORD TO TRUE
89                    PERFORM UNTIL NOT S2-GET-NEXT-RECORD
90                        READ EMPLOYEE-FILE NEXT RECORD
91                              INTO ER-EMPLOYEE-RECORD
92                            AT END
93                                MOVE EM-NO-MORE-RECORDS TO EM-ERROR-MESSAGE
94                                PERFORM 820-DISPLAY-MESSAGE-AND-QUERY
95                                SET S2-NOT-GET-NEXT-RECORD TO TRUE
96                            NOT AT END
97                                IF WA-EMPLOYEE-LAST-NAME = ER-LAST-NAME
98                                    PERFORM 850-DISPLAY-EMPLOYEE-RECORD
99                                    PERFORM 810-QUERY-ABOUT-NEXT-RECORD
100                               ELSE
101                                   MOVE EM-NO-MORE-RECORDS TO EM-ERROR-MESSAGE
102                                   PERFORM 820-DISPLAY-MESSAGE-AND-QUERY
103                                   SET S2-NOT-GET-NEXT-RECORD TO TRUE
104                               END-IF
105                       END-READ
106                   END-PERFORM
107            END-START
108        END-PERFORM
109   ************Termination Sequence************
110        CLOSE EMPLOYEE-FILE
111        STOP RUN
112        .
113   *************************************************
114   050-DISPLAY-ANNOUNCE-SCREEN.
115        DISPLAY "EMPLOYEE FILE RECORD ACCESS"  LINE 5 COL 20
116                WITH BLANK SCREEN
117        DISPLAY
118          "Employee file record access by employee last name."
119                                      LINE 7 COL 20
120        DISPLAY
121          "You enter the employee last name."  LINE 9 COL 20
122        DISPLAY
123          "The record for the first employee with that last"
124                                      LINE 10 COL 20
125        DISPLAY
126          "name is displayed. You can then successively"
127                                      LINE 11 COL 20
128        DISPLAY
129          "display records with the same employee name."
130                                      LINE 12 COL 20
131        DISPLAY "Do you want to continue <Y/N>?"
132                                      LINE 14 COL 20
133        ACCEPT S1-ANOTHER-EMPLOYEE-SWITCH    LINE 14 COL 51
134        .
135   800-GET-EMPLOYEE-LAST-NAME.
136        DISPLAY "Last  Name:"    LINE 8 COL 9
137                WITH BLANK SCREEN
138        MOVE SPACES TO WA-EMPLOYEE-LAST-NAME
139        ACCEPT WA-EMPLOYEE-LAST-NAME     LINE 8  COL 25
140                WITH REVERSE-VIDEO
141        MOVE WA-EMPLOYEE-LAST-NAME TO LAST-NAME
142        .
143   810-QUERY-ABOUT-NEXT-RECORD.
144        DISPLAY " Do you want to see the next record <Y/N>?"
145                                      LINE 17 COL 20
146        ACCEPT S2-GET-NEXT-RECORD-SWITCH    LINE 17 COL 63
147        IF NOT S2-GET-NEXT-RECORD
148            PERFORM 820-DISPLAY-MESSAGE-AND-QUERY
149        END-IF
150        .
151   820-DISPLAY-MESSAGE-AND-QUERY.
152        DISPLAY EM-ERROR-MESSAGE          LINE 16 COL 20
153        DISPLAY "Do you want to get another employee <Y/N>?"
154                                      LINE 17 COL 20
155        ACCEPT S1-ANOTHER-EMPLOYEE-SWITCH    LINE 17 COL 63
156        MOVE SPACES TO EM-ERROR-MESSAGE
157        .
158   850-DISPLAY-EMPLOYEE-RECORD.
159        DISPLAY "EMPLOYEE ADDRESS DATA"    LINE 3 COL 20
160                WITH BLANK SCREEN
161        DISPLAY "--------------------"    LINE 4 COL 20
162        DISPLAY "Employee number:"        LINE 6 COL 9
163        DISPLAY "Name Last:            First:            MI:"
164                                      LINE 8 COL 9
165        DISPLAY "Telephone extension:"    LINE 10 COL 34
166        DISPLAY "Address:"               LINE 12 COL 12
167        DISPLAY "City:            State:      ZIP:"
168                                      LINE 14 COL 15
169        DISPLAY ER-EMPLOYEE-NUMBER LINE 6 COL 26 WITH REVERSE-VIDEO
170        DISPLAY ER-FIRST-NAME      LINE 8 COL 41 WITH REVERSE-VIDEO
171        DISPLAY ER-LAST-NAME       LINE 8 COL 21 WITH REVERSE-VIDEO
172        DISPLAY ER-MIDDLE-INITIAL  LINE 8 COL 56 WITH REVERSE-VIDEO
173        DISPLAY ER-TELEPHONE-EXT   LINE 10 COL 55 WITH REVERSE-VIDEO
174        DISPLAY ER-ADDRESS         LINE 12 COL 21 WITH REVERSE-VIDEO
175        DISPLAY ER-CITY            LINE 14 COL 21 WITH REVERSE-VIDEO
176        DISPLAY ER-STATE           LINE 14 COL 43 WITH REVERSE-VIDEO
177        DISPLAY ER-ZIP             LINE 14 COL 52 WITH REVERSE-VIDEO
178        .
```

Exception Handling During Input and Output Operations

Handling of Common Exception Conditions

During the execution of any input or output operation, conditions may occur that prevent normal completion of the operation. For instance, when reading a sequential file, encountering the end-of-file prevents the normal read from occurring. When writing to an indexed file, the record is not written if its key field value is the same as that of a record already in the file. Any condition like this that prevents normal operation is called an **exception** or **error condition**. (As used in COBOL, exception and error are synonymous.) In your programs, you provided for two types of exception conditions with the phrases AT END and INVALID KEY. If an exception condition exists, statements following these phrases are executed.

The use of an optional phrase in the input or output statement is one of three methods by which exception conditions are communicated to your program. The other two are the I-O status and exception declaratives.

I-O Status

If by this time you have not had a program terminate with an error message, you are an exceptional programmer. For instance, assume that in the SELECT clause, you accidentally designate the filename as EMPLOYEE.DA, instead of EMPLOYEE.DAA. Upon attempting to open the file, you receive an appropriate error message and program execution is terminated. In most implementations, the message includes the error number 35. This two-digit number is called the **I-O status** and is one of many such numbers defined for COBOL to indicate the condition resulting from an input or output operation.

The two digits of the I-O status explicitly identify each status code. The first digit groups the codes by category, as shown in Figure 15-19. Within each category, the second digit identifies individual codes as shown in the status code table of Figure 15-20. Here, each code is identified as being applicable to sequential, indexed, and relative (indicated by S, I, and R) file organizations.

Figure 15-19   I-O status code categories.

	First digit	Condition
Noncritical errors	0	*Successful completion.* The input-output statement was executed successfully and no exception conditions occurred.
	1	*At-end condition.* A sequential READ was not executed successfully because of an at-end condition. These exceptions are detected by the AT END phrase in the READ statement.
	2	*Invalid key* (not meaningful for sequential files). The input-output statement was not executed successfully because of an invalid key condition. These exceptions are detected by the INVALID KEY phrase in the READ or WRITE statement.
Critical errors	3	*Permanent error.* The input-output statement was not executed successfully because of an error that precludes further processing of the file. The problem could be a disk-full or a hardware-error condition.
	4	*Logic error.* The input-output statement was not executed successfully because an improper sequence of input-output statements was performed on the file (for instance, attempting to close a file that was not opened).
	9	*Implementor-defined.* The input-output statement was not executed successfully because of some other type of error. These are conditions defined by the supplier of the COBOL compiler.

Figure 15-20   Common I-O status values.

Code	File type (sequential, indexed, relative)	Description
00	SIR	An input/output operation was successful; no further information available.
02	I	An input/output operation on an indexed file using an alternate index (defined to allow duplicates) was successful. A duplicate key condition occurred.
04	SIR	A READ statement was executed successfully, but the length of the input record being processed does not correspond to the attributes of that file.
10	SIR	A sequential read was attempted and no next logical record exists (the end-of-file occurred).
21	I	A sequencing error occurred for sequential accessing of an indexed file. This can result from changing the prime key value between a READ and a REWRITE for a given file, or from incorrect sequencing of input records during a WRITE operation.
22	IR	An attempt was made to write or rewrite a record that would create a duplicate prime record key.
23	IR	An attempt was made to randomly access a record that does not exist in the file.
24	IR	A write attempted to access storage beyond the limits set by the operating system.
30	SIR	A permanent error occurred for which no further information is available.
34	S	A write attempted to access storage beyond the limits set by the operating system.
35	SIR	An attempt was made to open for INPUT, I-O, or EXTEND a file that does not exist.
37	SIR	An attempted OPEN statement conflicted with file usage designation in the SELECT clause. For instance, you cannot open a printer file for INPUT.
39	SIR	An OPEN was unsuccessful because a conflict existed between the attributes of the file and the attributes designated in the program. For instance, with an indexed file, the program designates an alternate key for a file that does not include an alternate key.
41	SIR	An OPEN was attempted for a file already opened.
42	SIR	A CLOSE was attempted for a file not open.
43	SIR	In the sequential access mode, an attempt was made to execute a DELETE (indexed or relative files only) or REWRITE when a corresponding READ was not successfully executed.
46	SIR	A sequential READ was unsuccessful because the previous START (indexed or relative files only) or READ was not successful.

Noncritical errors (codes 00–24); Critical errors (codes 30–46)

Inspecting the
I-O Status

As a simple illustration of how the I-O status can be used, consider the program EMPADDI (Figure 15-3, page 528) to add records to the indexed employee file from the sequential employee file. As the program is currently written, if an INVALID KEY condition occurs during a WRITE operation, a single error module is performed. Assume that requirements of this program were modified as follows:

1. Records of the input file must be in sequence based on their key field values.
2. If an input record is out of sequence, perform the 950 module.
3. If the key field value of an input record is the same as that of an existing record in the file, perform the 960 module.
4. If any error other than the preceding two occurs, perform the 970 module.

Figure 15-21 shows the necessary code modifications to EMPADDI. These changes are as follows:

1. ACCESS is changed to SEQUENTIAL. This causes COBOL to perform sequence checking before writing each record. (The current record to be written must be larger than the last record of the file.)
2. The FILE STATUS clause is included in the SELECT. It identifies a two-position WORKING-STORAGE field into which the I-O status code is placed after execution of any I/O operation on this file.
3. Under the INVALID KEY clause of the WRITE (to this file), the value in the status field SC-EMPLOYEE-FILE-STATUS determines the module to be performed.

Declarative Procedures
and the USE Statement

The technique of Figure 15-21 can be used only for categories 0, 1, and 2 in Figure 15-19's I-O status codes because they provide for recovery through clauses of the I-O statement. However, the last three categories—status values 3, 4, and 9—are termed **critical error conditions** and require special provisions to avoid immediate termination of a program. If you inspect the list in Figure 15-20, you will see that most of them occur as a result of programming errors. You might expect that after a program is fully debugged, none of those errors is possible. However, most large, complex programs contain at least one programming error—usually in some

Figure 15-21
Testing the I-O status.

```
        FILE-CONTROL.
            SELECT IND-EMPLOYEE-FILE
                ASSIGN TO DISK "EMPLOYEE.DAI"
                ORGANIZATION IS INDEXED
                ACCESS IS SEQUENTIAL
                RECORD KEY IS IND-EMPLOYEE-NUMBER
                FILE STATUS IS SC-EMPLOYEE-FILE-STATUS.
                    ⋮

        01  SC-STATUS-CODES.
            05  SC-EMPLOYEE-FILE-STATUS          PIC X(2).
                    ⋮

                WRITE IND-EMPLOYEE-RECORD
                    INVALID KEY
                        EVALUATE SC-EMPLOYEE-FILE-STATUS
                            WHEN "21"
                                PERFORM 950-PROCESS-SEQUENCE-ERROR
                            WHEN "22"
                                PERFORM 960-PROCESS-DUPLICATE-ERROR
                            WHEN OTHER
                                PERFORM 970-PROCESS-UNEXPECTED-ERROR
                        END-EVALUATE
                END-WRITE
```

obscure corner of the program—that was not detected during testing. When the unlikely combination of conditions occurs that uses that sequence of code, processing is immediately terminated with an obscure error code. Usually, you do not want the program to terminate immediately. You may want the program to perform some cleanup operations before terminating, or perhaps even continue execution. You include such exception/error-processing routines in the program's declarative portion.

Technically, the PROCEDURE DIVISION may contain two types of procedures: **declarative** and **nondeclarative**. All of the program code you have studied so far is nondeclarative. Declarative procedures are those that are executed only under special circumstances, such as after an error condition. The declarative portion of the program, signaled by the key words DECLARATIVES and END DECLARATIVES, must be placed at the beginning of the PROCEDURE DIVISION.

To illustrate using declaratives for exception/error recovery, let's consider a slight modification to the SLSUPD program of Figure 15-16, page 546 (batch update of an indexed file from a sequential file). The user must be able to enter the name of the sequential file containing the records to be added to the indexed file. If the file does not exist, the user must be informed and be given the option to enter another filename or to abort the run.

Existence of a file can be determined by attempting to open it for input. If it does not exist, an I-O status value of 35 is produced (see Figure 15-20). However, because 35 is a critical error, processing terminates unless error-handling provisions are made in the declarative portion of the program. The code fragments of Figure 15-22 illustrate the features necessary to "trap" the error occurrence: DECLARATIVES and the USE statement.

- The DECLARATIVES and END DECLARATIVES entries set error procedures apart from the main program. (Note that technically, END DECLARATIVES is *not* a scope terminator and therefore does not include a hyphen between the words.) Declaratives must precede the code of the main program.

- Each error procedure is identified by a section name followed by a USE statement. The sections contain statements defining the actions to take when exceptions occur. Recall from Chapter 13 that a section in the PROCEDURE DIVISION is a level above a paragraph in that it allows two or more paragraphs to be treated as a unit. A section is identified by the section name followed by the word SECTION. The procedure— subordinate to the section—can consist of zero, one, or more paragraphs. In this example, multiple paragraphs are not needed, so no paragraph header is required.

- The USE statement relates the procedure of its section to a particular file. In this example, the 1000 procedure is related to SALES-FILE. So, any error resulting from an I-O operation on this file causes execution to be transferred to this procedure.

Modifications to the DATA DIVISION include designating the file status fields, the addition of two program switches, and the addition of a field for entry of the filename (FS-SALES-FILE). Also notice that the ASSIGN clause entry is this data-name (rather than a literal). The PROCEDURE DIVISION code includes a loop to accept the keyboard-entered filename. If a valid filename is entered, the file is opened and the loop is not repeated. The following is the sequence if the file does not exist:

1. Upon attempting to open, an error occurs—so control is transferred to the procedure identified for this file (1000).

Figure 15-22 DECLARATIVES and the USE statement for error handling.

```
FILE-CONTROL.
    SELECT SALES-FILE
        ASSIGN TO DISK FS-SALES-FILE
        ORGANIZATION IS LINE SEQUENTIAL
        FILE STATUS IS FS-SALES-FILE-STATUS.
    SELECT MASTER-FILE
        ASSIGN TO DISK "SALES_MA.DAI"
        ORGANIZATION IS INDEXED
        ACCESS IS RANDOM
        RECORD KEY IS SALES-REP
        FILE STATUS IS FS-MASTER-FILE-STATUS.
        :
01  PROGRAM-SWITCHES.
        :
    05  S4-REPEAT-OPEN-SWITCH        PIC X(1).
        88  S4-REPEAT-OPEN               VALUE "Y" "y".
        88  S4-DO-NOT-REPEAT-OPEN        VALUE "N".
    05  S5-QUERY-SWITCH              PIC X(1).
        88  S5-YES-RESPONSE              VALUE "Y" "y".
        88  S5-NO-RESPONSE               VALUE "N".

01  FS-FILE-STATUS-FIELDS.
    05  FS-SALES-FILE-STATUS        PIC X(2).
    05  FS-MASTER-FILE-STATUS       PIC X(2).

01  FN-FILE-NAMES.
    05  FS-SALES-FILE               PIC X(12).
        :
```

```
PROCEDURE DIVISION.                    ← Identifies beginning of declaratives

DECLARATIVES.  ←                          Section header (required)

1000-SALES-FILE-ERROR SECTION.  ←
    USE AFTER ERROR PROCEDURE ON SALES-FILE ←   Relates procedure to
                                                SALES-FILE
    IF FS-SALES-FILE-STATUS = "35"
        DISPLAY "There is no file by this name."
        DISPLAY "Do you want to try another name <Y/N>?"
        ACCEPT S5-QUERY-SWITCH
        IF NOT S5-YES-RESPONSE
            DISPLAY "PROCESSING TERMINATED"
            DISPLAY "Press Enter to exit"
            MOVE SPACE TO S5-QUERY-SWITCH
            ACCEPT S5-QUERY-SWITCH
*           ********
            STOP RUN
*           ********
        END-IF
        SET S4-REPEAT-OPEN TO TRUE
    ELSE
        DISPLAY
         "UNEXPECTED ERROR ON INPUT FILE ", FS-SALES-FILE
        DISPLAY "Error code: ", FS-SALES-FILE-STATUS
        DISPLAY "Following is the last input record read"
        DISPLAY SR-SALES-RECORD
        DISPLAY "Processing terminated"
        DISPLAY "Press Enter to exit"
        MOVE SPACE TO S5-QUERY-SWITCH
        ACCEPT S5-QUERY-SWITCH
*       ********
        STOP RUN
*       ********
    END-IF
    .
2000-MASTER-FILE-ERROR SECTION.  ←         Section header (required)
    USE AFTER ERROR PROCEDURE ON MASTER-FILE
    :  ←                                   Error-handling program code
END DECLARATIVES.  ←                       Identifies end of declaratives


5000-MAIN-PROGRAM SECTION.  ←              Section header to start program

000-UPDATE-MASTER-FILE.

************Initialization Sequence************
    PERFORM WITH TEST AFTER
            UNTIL S4-DO-NOT-REPEAT-OPEN
        SET S4-DO-NOT-REPEAT-OPEN TO TRUE
        DISPLAY "What is the name of the input file?"
        ACCEPT FS-SALES-FILE
        OPEN INPUT SALES-FILE
    END-PERFORM
    OPEN I-O MASTER-FILE
    :
```

Annotations at right of code: "Error-handling program code" (pointing to the SALES-FILE error block), "Error-handling program code" (pointing to MASTER-FILE section).

2. If the file status is 35, the user is informed and queried about continuing.
   a. A No response produces an appropriate message before terminating execution.
   b. A Yes response causes S4-REPEAT-OPEN to be set to true. After encountering the end of this section, control returns to the statement following the statement that caused the error. The input loop for file-name entry is repeated.
3. If the file status is not 35, some other error occurred, either on the OPEN or on a subsequent READ of the file. This is an unexpected error, so an appropriate message is displayed before terminating.

You should notice two other points regarding this example. First, good programming practice dictates using only one program exit—that is, only one STOP RUN. However, in the case of error-handling procedures, program logic is often far too complex to return to the program's nondeclarative portion for program termination. Therefore, it is acceptable practice to include STOP RUN statements within error procedures. However, it is a good idea to make their presence obvious, as done in Figure 15-22.

The second point concerns the COBOL Standard and its distinction between noncritical (categories 0, 1, and 2) and critical (categories 3, 4, and 9) errors. That is, the Standard states that after completion of the error procedure for a noncritical error, control returns to the statement following the statement causing the error. However, the action taken after completion of the error procedure for a critical error is up to the implementor. Although most COBOL compilers return as shown with the noncritical errors, you should check your compiler to be certain because the Standard does not guarantee it.

Optional Clauses on Input and Output Statements

Each file input or output statement—except the WRITE for printer files—has required additional clauses. For instance, the following are two examples taken from the SLSUPD program:

```
READ SALES-FILE INTO SR-SALES-RECORD
  AT END
    SET S1-END-OF-PROCESSING TO TRUE
    :

REWRITE MASTER-RECORD
  INVALID KEY
    DISPLAY
    :
```

If these are left unchanged in the modified EMPADDI program, then the end-of-file and invalid-key conditions are handled as if the error-recovery procedures do not exist. However, if error recovery is specified through a USE statement for a file, then the AT END (or INVALID KEY) clause can be omitted from the input or output statement. Then all error handling—including, for instance, AT END—is through the error procedure defined by the USE.

Chapter Summary

The three file structures available to the programmer are sequential, indexed, and relative.

A file can be opened in any of four modes: input, output, I-O, and extend.

Three input-output statements can be used with sequential files: READ, WRITE, and REWRITE. The permissible uses are summarized in the table of Figure 15-23.

The file-access mode is defined in the SELECT; for relative and indexed files, it can be sequential, random, or dynamic. Five input-output statements can be used with relative and indexed files: READ, WRITE, REWRITE, START, and DELETE. The permissible uses are summarized in the table of Figure 15-24.

COBOL Language Elements

The WRITE statement format is included on page 528 and the START statement format on page 548. Formats of other COBOL statements you studied in this chapter are:

```
DELETE file-name RECORD
  [INVALID KEY imperative-statement-1]
  [NOT INVALID KEY imperative-statement-2]
  [END-DELETE]
```

```
OPEN   ⎧ INPUT {file-name-1}...  ⎫
       ⎨ OUTPUT {file-name-2}... ⎬  ...
       ⎪ I-O {file-name-3}...    ⎪
       ⎩ EXTEND {file-name-4}... ⎭
```

Figure 15-23
Permissible input/output actions—Sequential files.

Statement	Open Mode			
	Input	Output	I-O	Extend
READ	X		X	
WRITE		X		X
REWRITE			X	

Figure 15-24 Permissible input/output actions—Indexed and relative files.

File-Access Mode	Statement	Open Mode			
		Input	Output	I-O	Extend
Sequential	READ	X		X	
	WRITE		X		X
	REWRITE			X	
	START	X		X	
	DELETE			X	
Random	READ	X		X	
	WRITE		X	X	
	REWRITE			X	
	START				
	DELETE			X	
Dynamic	READ	X		X	
	WRITE		X	X	
	REWRITE			X	
	START	X		X	
	DELETE			X	

Sequential Read—Indexed and Relative I-O

READ file-name [NEXT] RECORD [INTO identifier-1]
   [AT END imperative-statement-1]
   [NOT AT END imperative-statement-2]
[END-READ]

Note: The NEXT phrase is used only for files open in dynamic access mode when records are retrieved sequentially.

Random Read—Indexed and Relative I-O

READ file-name RECORD
    [KEY IS data-name-1]
    [INVALID KEY imperative-statement-1]
    [NOT INVALID KEY imperative-statement-2]
[END-READ]

Note: The KEY phrase is applicable only to indexed files and is only required if an alternate key field will be used.

REWRITE record-name
    [INVALID KEY imperative-statement-1]
    [NOT INVALID KEY imperative-statement-2]
[END-REWRITE]

$$
\text{USE AFTER STANDARD ERROR PROCEDURE ON}
\begin{cases}
\{\text{file-name-1}\}\ldots \\
\text{INPUT} \\
\text{OUTPUT} \\
\text{I-O} \\
\text{EXTEND}
\end{cases}
$$

Indexed I-O

SELECT file-name
    ASSIGN TO $\begin{cases} \text{implementor-name-1} \\ \text{literal-1} \end{cases}$

    [ORGANIZATION IS] INDEXED

    $\left[\text{ACCESS MODE IS} \begin{cases} \text{SEQUENTIAL} \\ \text{RANDOM} \\ \text{DYNAMIC} \end{cases} \right]$

    RECORD KEY IS data-name-1
    [ALTERNATE RECORD KEY IS data-name-2 [WITH DUPLICATES]] ...

Relative I-O

SELECT file-name

    ASSIGN TO $\begin{cases} \text{implementor-name-1} \\ \text{literal-1} \end{cases}$

    [ORGANIZATION IS] RELATIVE

    $\left[\text{ACCESS MODE IS} \begin{cases} \text{SEQUENTIAL} & [\text{RELATIVE KEY IS data-name-1}] \\ \begin{cases} \text{RANDOM} \\ \text{DYNAMIC} \end{cases} & \text{RELATIVE KEY IS data-name-1} \end{cases} \right]$

    [FILE STATUS IS data-name-2] .

Exercises

Terms for Definition

critical error condition
declarative
exception (error) condition

I-O status
nondeclarative
prime key

Review Questions

1. Write SELECT statements for each of the following; assume that the input file is named SAMPLE.DTA.
   a. Indexed file, random access, key field is SAMPLE-KEY.
   b. Indexed file, sequential access, key field is SAMPLE-KEY.
   c. Relative file, random access, relative key is WA-SAMPLE-KEY.
   d. Relative file, sequential access, relative key is WA-SAMPLE-KEY.
   e. Indexed file, both random and sequential access, key field is SAMPLE-KEY.
   f. Indexed file, both random and sequential access, key field is SAMPLE-KEY, alternate key is ALT-KEY (duplicates allowable).
   g. Same as f., but must designate the file status as SAMPLE-STATUS.

2. What is the difference between opening a sequential file for OUTPUT and opening one for EXTEND?

3. A programmer is writing a program to add records to an indexed file. He is uncertain whether to designate RANDOM or SEQUENTIAL in the ACCESS clause of the SELECT statement. Explain the difference for this application.

4. A READ statement for an indexed file must include an INVALID KEY clause unless _____ or _____.

5. Describe the way in which records are stored in a relative file.

6. An alternate key of an indexed file may be designated with duplicates; a prime key cannot. Why not?

7. The following code skeleton operates on the indexed file STUDENT-FILE, which has as its key field STUDENT-NUMBER. Describe what occurs with execution of this sequence. There is a danger with this code. What is it?

```
ACCEPT STUDENT-NUMBER
READ STUDENT-FILE
   INVALID KEY
     ....
   NOT INVALID KEY
     DELETE STUDENT-FILE
        INVALID KEY
          .....
        END-DELETE
END-READ
```

8. Describe the action of dynamically accessing records from an indexed file.

9. Identify the three methods for handling exception conditions with input/output operations.

10. Unless a program includes special provisions, what will happen during execution if a critical error condition occurs?

11. Each set of the following consists of a file-access mode, an open mode, and an input or output statement. Identify those in which the input or output statement is not permitted with the corresponding access and open modes.
    a. Sequential, I-O, WRITE
    b. Sequential, Input, START
    c. Sequential, Output, REWRITE
    d. Sequential, Extend, WRITE

e. Random, Input, REWRITE
f. Random, Extend, WRITE
g. Random, Output, START
h. Random, I-O, DELETE
i. Random, Output, DELETE
j. Dynamic, I-O, START
k. Dynamic, Extend, WRITE
l. Dynamic, Input, START
m. Dynamic, Output, WRITE
n. Dynamic, Input, DELETE

Questions About Example Programs

1. In the EMPMNT program (Figure 15-13), what will occur during execution if the MOVE statement at line 214 is omitted?

2. In the EMPMNT program (Figure 15-13), what will occur during execution if the WITH TEST AFTER clause is omitted from the PERFORM at line 170?

3. In the SLSUPD program (Figure 15-16), a programmer accidentally sets S1-END-OF-PROCESSING to True rather than S1-NOT-END-OF-PROCESSING (line 110). What are the consequences of this mistake?

4. In the EMPGETA program (Figure 15-18), the programmer accidentally omits the SET statement at line 103. What will happen during execution of the program because of this omission?

Programming Assignments

Programming Assignment 15-1: Vehicle File Maintenance

Background information:

The management of Rent-Ur-Wheels decided to convert the vehicle record system from batch to on-line processing. The sequential vehicle file must first be converted to indexed, then an update program must be written.

Indexed file creation.

Input file: Vehicle file (VEHICLE.DAT)

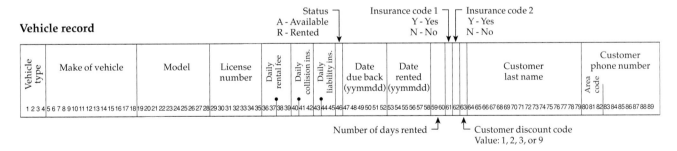

Vehicle record

Output file: Indexed Vehicle file 2 (VEHICLE.DAI)

Key field: License number

File maintenance.

Input file: Indexed Vehicle master file (VEHICLE.DAI)

Key field: License number

Output file: Updated indexed Vehicle file

Program operations:

1. Create an indexed equivalent of the Vehicle file.

2. Present the user with the update option menu:
    A - Add record to master file
    C - Change fields of existing record
    D - Delete record from master file
    X - eXit

3. Accept a request from the user for the license number of the vehicle record to be updated.

4. For each valid Add transaction, create a new master record.
    a. Validate all fields as in Assignment 14-1.
    b. Fields beyond column 45 must be set to 0 (numeric) or spaces (alphanumeric).
    c. If a record already exists, display an appropriate message.

5. For each valid Change transaction, allow for replacement of fields through column 46, except the license number.
    a. Validate all field changes as in Assignment 14-1.
    b. If the requested record does not exist, display an appropriate message.

6. For each Delete transaction, delete the corresponding master record.
    a. If the requested record does not exist, display an appropriate message.

7. For each action (add, change, and delete), give the user the option to complete the action or abort without changes to the record.

8. For each completed action, write a record to a report log file as follows:
    Record addition: The record with the message ADDED
    Record change: The original record with the message ORIGINAL
                          The modified record with the message CORRECTED
    Record deletion: The record with the message DELETED

9. Double-space between each output line, except single-space between the original and the corrected records for a change operation.

10. Use the same detail line format as Assignment 14-1. Headings and page control are optional.

Programming Assignment 15-2: Vehicle File Update

Background information:

This is a continuation of the needs of Assignment 15-1. If you have not also programmed 15-1, you will need to create an indexed version of the Vehicle file.

Input file: Indexed Vehicle master file (VEHICLE.DAI)

For record format, refer to Assignment 15-1.

Key field: License number

Output file: Updated indexed Vehicle file

Program operations:

1. Present the user with the processing option menu:
   1 - Vehicle rental
   2 - Vehicle return
   3 - Terminate

2. Accept a user input for the vehicle license number of the record to be processed.

3. Display the requested record and query user regarding whether or not it is the desired record. If not, allow the user to request another record.

4. For a rental, the Status field must contain "A".
   a. If not, display an error message that the vehicle is already rented.
   b. If so, accept entries for each of these fields. Validate all entries; all fields are mandatory, except the telephone number.

5. For a return, the Status field must contain "R".
   a. If they are, display an error message that the vehicle is not rented.
   b. If so, change alphanumeric fields to blank and numeric fields to zero.

6. If your compiler includes the 1989 Intrinsic Functions (refer to Appendix C), use appropriate data functions to calculate the Number-of days-rented field value.

7. To test your program, you first need to enter returns because all records in the Vehicle file are entered as rented (unless you added records in Assignment 15-1).

Programming Assignment 15-3: Inventory File Update

Background information:

The management of Tools Unlimited decided to convert the tool inventory system from batch to on-line processing. The sequential Inventory file must first be converted to indexed, then an update program must be written.

Indexed file creation.

Input file: Inventory file (INVEN.DAT)

Inventory record

Output file: Indexed inventory file (INVEN.DAI)

Key field: Product identification

File maintenance.

Input file: Indexed inventory file (INVEN.DAI)

Key field: Product identification

Output file: Updated indexed Inventory file

Program operations:

1. Create an indexed equivalent of the inventory file.

2. Present the user with the update option menu:
    1 - Sale
    2 - Return
    3 - Order placed
    4 - Order received
    5 - Inventory adjustment
    9 - Terminate

3. Accept a request from the user for the product identification of the inventory record to be updated.
    a. Allow the user to verify that this is the correct record.
    b. If the record is not in the file, display an appropriate error message.

4. Display a prompt consistent with the update action selected by the user.

5. Accept the user Transaction quantity.
    a. If Sale, subtract Transaction quantity from Quantity-on-hand field.
    b. If Return, add Transaction quantity to Quantity-on-hand field.
    c. If Order-placed, add Transaction quantity to Quantity-on-order field.
    d. If Order-received, add Transaction quantity to Quantity-on-hand field and subtract transaction from Quantity-on-order field.
    e. If Inventory-adjustment (allow for positive or negative entry), add Transaction quantity to Quantity-on-hand field.

6. Reject any transaction (with an appropriate error message) that causes the Quantity-on-hand field to become less than zero.

7. Give the user the option to save the updated record or abort changes.

Programming Assignment 15-4: Student Grade Inquiry

Background information:

The records and admissions office of Bayview Institute of Computer Technology needs an on-line program to display student information from the student master and grade files. The sequential student and grade files must first be converted to indexed, then an inquiry program must be written.

Indexed file creation.

Input file 1: Student master file (STUDENT.DAT)

Student record

Student number	Student last name	Student first name	Major code	Grade points	Units completed		Last update date (mmddyy)
1 2 3 4 5 6 7 8 9 10 11	12 13 14 15 16 17 18 19 20 21 22 23 24 25	26 27 28 29 30 31 32 33 34 35	36 37 38	39 40 41	42 43 44	45 46 47 48 49 50 51 52 53 54 55 56 57 58 59 60 61 62 63 64	65 66 67 68 69 70

Input file 2: Student course file (STUD-GRA.DAT)

Student transaction record

Record type	Student number	Department	Course number	Course description
1 2	3 4 5 6 7 8 9 10 11	12 13 14 15 16	17 18 19 20	21 22 23 24 25 26 27 28 29 30 31 32 33 34 35 36 37 38 39 40 41 42 43 44 45 46

Record count ⌐   Units ⌐

Output file 1: Indexed student master file (STUDENT.DAI)

Key field: Student number

Output file 2: Indexed student grade file (STUD-GRA.DAI)

Key field: Record type + Student number + Record count

Alternate key: Student number

File inquiry

Input files: Indexed files generated by file creation

Typical screen display:

```
        Bayview Institute of Computer Technology
                Student Class Assignments

  Student number: 365-87-0004

  Student: BACH        SUZANNE

           Course
  Dept.    number    Description                Units

  CIS      22B       ADVANCED COBOL               4
  CIS      121       HYPERVENTILATION CONTROL     3
  ENGL     22        GUD SPELLING                 3
  PSYC     108       BASIC SOCIAL SKILLS          3
  PE       33        AEROBICS                     1

  Cumulative summary
  Total units          88
  Earned grade points  229
  Grade point average  2.60

  Do you want to access another student <Y/N>? _
```

Program operations:

1. Create an indexed equivalent of the student master file. Use the Student-number as the key field.

2. Create an indexed equivalent of the grade file. Use the Record type plus the Student-number plus the Record-count field as the primary key field. Use the Student-number as a secondary key (with duplicates).

3. Display an announcement screen.

4. Query the user for the desired student number.

5. Read the student master from disk.
   a. If no master for the request, display an appropriate error message.
   b. Display student master data; calculate Grade point average = Earned grade points/Total units.

6. Read each course record for this student.

7. The screen display must be similar to the sample screen.

8. If the requested student has no course records, display an appropriate message.

9. For testing, inspect the course file. Relatively few student master records have corresponding course records.

PROGRAM MANAGEMENT

CHAPTER OBJECTIVES

The principle of program modularization is one of this book's cornerstones. The PERFORM provides you with the basis for creating your programs as sets of relatively independent modules—each of which is executed (performed) from a higher-level module. This results in programs that are, among other things, easy to write, maintain, and modify—critical traits in a business programming environment.

The business environment also has other needs. For instance, most programs are much larger than those you've encountered and are written by two or more programmers—or even programming teams—working on separate portions of the program. Also, it is very common for particular sections of code to be the same in two or more programs. For instance, any program using the Job code/Pay rate table of Chapter 12 requires the table-load modules. It is through that example (the PAYTBLE4 program, Figure 12-13) that different techniques are examined for separating the table-load operation from the main program. From this chapter, you will learn about the following:

- The COPY statement, which allows source code to be stored as separate files and inserted into the program during the compiling operation.

- The principle of subprograms and techniques by which one program causes a second to be loaded into memory and control is switched between the programs. A subprogram is incorporated into a program with the CALL statement.

- Nested programs, in which a program fully contains one or more subordinate programs.

Introduction to Managing Large Programs

About Data and Data Descriptions

When writing programs to process data, you deal with two major entities: the data to be processed and the programs to process that data. You learned very early in this book that the data file contains data only; it does not contain information about the data. For instance, look at Figure 16-1 and you see one of the records from the patron file in which numeric fields run into each other. Without additional information, you have no idea where one field ends and the next begins; you also do not know anything about the data types. By now, you know that this information is contained in the DATA DIVISION of any program processing this file. Figure 16-2 illustrates the relationship between a COBOL program and the data file it processes. In a broad sense, this is contrary to structured principles. The data—along with information describing the data—should be together.

Think of the application in which a file is used by 50 different programs and some new fields must be added. The data description (DATA DIVISION) must be modified in each of the 50 programs and the programs recompiled. A partial solution to this dilemma is to store the record description as a separate file and copy it into the program whenever the program will be compiled. This serves two useful functions. First, the entire record description does not need to be keyed in for each program, which saves time and reduces the possibility of keying errors. Second, it allows each program to function from a single master description that can be updated as changes are made to the data file.

Uncompiled program code, whether a complete program or a program segment, is called **source code**. (This is as opposed to the compiled version of a program, which is called **object code**.) COBOL compilers include the capability for the automatic inclusion of separately stored source code during the compile operation.

The PAYTBLE4 Program—The Illustration Program

Chapter 12's PAYTBLE series of programs illustrated tables. In PAYTBLE4 (Figure 12-13, page 434), three-level Pay rate data is read from a file into a table for processing. Although the learning focus was on the table-loading process, the primary point of the program was to perform processing. Loading the table was merely a preliminary action necessary before beginning primary processing activities. You can imagine that in a business environment, more than one program would probably use the table and therefore, each would need to load it as part of the initializing procedure. For this chapter's examples, the table load PROCEDURE DIVISION code and the table-description entries are "extracted" from PAYTBLE4. They are used to illustrate the topics of this chapter: the COPY statement, the CALL statement, and nested programs. Figure 16-3 highlights appropriate sections of PAYTBLE4 code.

Figure 16-1
A data record without formatting information.

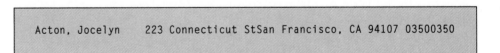

```
Acton, Jocelyn      223 Connecticut StSan Francisco, CA 94107 03500350
```

Figure 16-2
Relationship between a COBOL program and a data file.

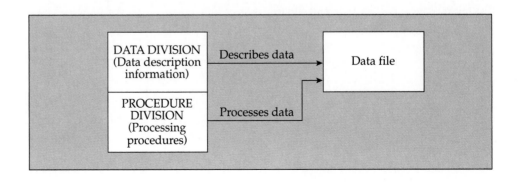

Extracted Source Code   The key to using the COPY statement in an application system is to identify sections of code that will be standardized and to store them as individual source code files. The PAYTBLE4 program will be broken into three parts: the main program and two modules of code, which will be extracted and stored as separate files.

- PAYTBLE8.CBL—The program minus the two sections of code.

- PAYTBLE8.DTA—The table definition together with data-items required during table loading. The extension name DTA indicates that this is the DATA DIVISION portion of the code.

- PAYTBLE8.PRO—The PROCEDURE DIVISION code to load the table. The extension name PRO indicates that this is the PROCEDURE DIVISION portion of the code.

Figure 16-3   The PAYTBLE4 program and code to be extracted.

```
1     IDENTIFICATION DIVISION.                        60      05  S2-REPEAT-TEST-SWITCH        PIC X.
2     PROGRAM-ID. PAYTBLE4.                           61          88  S2-REPEAT-TEST                    VALUE "Y"
3                                                     62                                                       "y".
4   * Interplanetary Transport, Inc.                  63          88  S2-DO-NOT-REPEAT-TEST             VALUE "N".
5   * Pay Table Lookup Test Program #4                64      05  S3-TABLE-FILE-SWITCH        PIC X.
6   * Written by W. Price    1-23-95                  65          88  S3-END-OF-TABLE-FILE              VALUE "E".
7                                                     66          88  S3-NOT-END-OF-TABLE-FILE          VALUE "N".
8   * Table:   Loaded from a file.                    67      05  S4-TABLE-LOADED-SWITCH      PIC X.
9   * Input:   Keyboard entry of                      68          88  S4-TABLE-LOAD-COMPLETE            VALUE "C".
10  *              Job classification code            69          88  S4-TABLE-LOAD-ERROR               VALUE "E".
11  *              Job status code                    70          88  S4-TABLE-LOAD-NOT-COMPLETE        VALUE "N".
12  *              Shift code                         71
13  * Output:  Pay rate accessed from Pay rate table  72   01 RT-RATE-TABLE.
14  * Comment: Pay rate table is three level          73      05  RT-JOB-CLASS-ENTRY      OCCURS 7 TIMES
15  *              including arguments as follows      74                                     INDEXED BY RT-CLASS-INDEX.
16  *              (all three levels indexed):        75          10  RT-JOB-CLASS        PIC X(2).
17  *                 Job classification              76          10  RT-STATUS-ENTRY     OCCURS 2 TIMES
18  *                 Job status                      77                                     INDEXED BY RT-STATUS-INDEX.
19  *                 Shift code                      78              15  RT-STATUS-CODE   PIC X(2).
20  *              Nested SEARCH statements are used   79              15  RT-SHIFT-ENTRY   OCCURS 3 TIMES
21  *              for first level (classification),  80                                     INDEXED BY RT-SHIFT-INDEX.
22  *              second level (status), and         81                  20  RT-SHIFT-CODE   PIC X(1).
23  *              third level (shift) access.        82                  20  RT-PAY-RATE     PIC 99V99.
24                                                    83
25                                                    84
26    ENVIRONMENT DIVISION.                           85      PROCEDURE DIVISION.
27                                                    86
28    INPUT-OUTPUT SECTION.                           87      000-TABLE-TEST-PROGRAM.
29                                                    88
30    FILE-CONTROL.                                   89      ************Initialization Sequence***********
31        SELECT PAY-RATE-TABLE-FILE                  90          DISPLAY "Look up a table entry"
32            ASSIGN TO (system dependent).           91              WITH BLANK SCREEN
33                                                    92          DISPLAY " "
34                                                    93          PERFORM 110-LOAD-PAY-RATE-TABLE
35                                                    94
36    DATA DIVISION.                                  95      ************Processing Sequence*************
37                                                    96          IF S4-TABLE-LOAD-ERROR
38    FILE SECTION.                                   97              DISPLAY "TABLE LOAD ERROR - RUN ABORTED"
39                                                    98              DISPLAY "Press ENTER to exit"
40    FD  PAY-RATE-TABLE-FILE.                        99              ACCEPT WA-DUMMY-RESPONSE-FIELD
41    01  PAY-RATE-TABLE-RECORD       PIC X(36).      100             SET S2-DO-NOT-REPEAT-TEST TO TRUE
42                                                    101         ELSE
43    WORKING-STORAGE SECTION.                        102             SET S2-REPEAT-TEST TO TRUE
44                                                    103         END-IF
45    01  WORK-FIELDS.                                104
46        05  WA-CLASS-CODE           PIC X(2).       105         PERFORM UNTIL S2-DO-NOT-REPEAT-TEST
47        05  WA-STATUS-CODE          PIC X(2).       106             PERFORM 200-LOOKUP-PAY-RATE
48        05  WA-SHIFT-CODE           PIC X.          107             IF S1-PAY-RATE-FOUND
49        05  WA-DUMMY-RESPONSE-FIELD PIC X.          108                 DISPLAY "Pay rate: ", DI-PAY-RATE
50        05  WA-TABLE-ENTRY-COUNT    PIC 9.          109             END-IF
51            88  CORRECT-TABLE-COUNT    VALUE 7.     110             DISPLAY " "
52                                                    111             DISPLAY "Do you want to make another test <Y/N>? "
53    01  DISPLAY-FIELDS.                             112                 WITH NO ADVANCING
54        05  DI-PAY-RATE             PIC $$Z.99.     113             ACCEPT S2-REPEAT-TEST-SWITCH
55                                                    114         END-PERFORM
56    01  PROGRAM-SWITCHES.                           115
57        05  S1-PAY-RATE-FOUND-SWITCH  PIC X.        116     ************Termination Sequence*************
58            88  S1-PAY-RATE-FOUND       VALUE "F".  117         STOP RUN
59            88  S1-PAY-RATE-NOT-FOUND   VALUE "N".  118             .
                                                      119     *************************************************
                                                      120
```

Extract from this program

(continues)

Figure 16-3   (continued)

```
121    110-LOAD-PAY-RATE-TABLE.                          168        200-LOOKUP-PAY-RATE.
122    *      Table-load initialization                  169            DISPLAY " "
123           OPEN INPUT PAY-RATE-TABLE-FILE             170            DISPLAY "Please enter the job classification "
124           SET S3-NOT-END-OF-TABLE-FILE TO TRUE       171                WITH NO ADVANCING
125           SET S4-TABLE-LOAD-NOT-COMPLETE TO TRUE     172            ACCEPT WA-CLASS-CODE
126           INITIALIZE WA-TABLE-ENTRY-COUNT            173            SET RT-CLASS-INDEX TO 1
127                                                      174            SEARCH RT-JOB-CLASS-ENTRY
128    *      Table-load sequence                        175                AT END
129           PERFORM VARYING RT-CLASS-INDEX             176                    SET S1-PAY-RATE-NOT-FOUND TO TRUE
130               FROM 1 BY 1                            177                    DISPLAY "Invalid Job classification code"
131                   UNTIL S4-TABLE-LOAD-COMPLETE       178                WHEN RT-JOB-CLASS (RT-CLASS-INDEX) = WA-CLASS-CODE
132                   OR S4-TABLE-LOAD-ERROR             179                    DISPLAY "Please enter the Status code "
133             READ PAY-RATE-TABLE-FILE                 180                        WITH NO ADVANCING
134                 AT END SET S3-END-OF-TABLE-FILE TO TRUE 181                    ACCEPT WA-STATUS-CODE
135             END-READ                                 182                    SET RT-STATUS-INDEX TO 1
136             EVALUATE                                 183                    SEARCH RT-STATUS-ENTRY
137                 S3-END-OF-TABLE-FILE also CORRECT-TABLE-COUNT 184                        AT END
138    *          --------------------  -------------------- 185                            SET S1-PAY-RATE-NOT-FOUND TO TRUE
139                                                      186                            DISPLAY "Invalid Status code"
140    *          Valid table entry so store it          187                        WHEN RT-STATUS-CODE (RT-CLASS-INDEX,
141                 WHEN    FALSE     also    FALSE       188                                    RT-STATUS-INDEX)
142    *          --------------------  -------------------- 189                                = WA-STATUS-CODE
143                 MOVE PAY-RATE-TABLE-RECORD             190                        DISPLAY "Please enter the Shift code "
144                     TO RT-JOB-CLASS-ENTRY (RT-CLASS-INDEX) 191                            WITH NO ADVANCING
145                 ADD 1 TO WA-TABLE-ENTRY-COUNT          192                        ACCEPT WA-SHIFT-CODE
146                                                      193                        SET RT-SHIFT-INDEX TO 1
147    *          Table file contains too many entries    194                        SEARCH RT-SHIFT-ENTRY
148                 WHEN    FALSE     also    TRUE         195                            AT END
149    *          --------------------  -------------------- 196                                SET S1-PAY-RATE-NOT-FOUND TO TRUE
150                 SET S4-TABLE-LOAD-ERROR TO TRUE        197                                DISPLAY "Invalid Shift code"
151                                                      198                            WHEN RT-SHIFT-CODE (RT-CLASS-INDEX,
152    *          Table file contains insufficient entries 199                                        RT-STATUS-INDEX,
153                 WHEN    TRUE     also    FALSE         200                                        RT-SHIFT-INDEX)
154    *          --------------------  -------------------- 201                                = WA-SHIFT-CODE
155                 SET S4-TABLE-LOAD-ERROR TO TRUE        202
156                                                      203                                SET S1-PAY-RATE-FOUND TO TRUE
157    *          Table file is properly loaded           204                                MOVE RT-PAY-RATE (RT-CLASS-INDEX,
158                 WHEN    TRUE     also    TRUE          205                                        RT-STATUS-INDEX,
159    *          --------------------  -------------------- 206                                        RT-SHIFT-INDEX)
160                 SET S4-TABLE-LOAD-COMPLETE TO TRUE     207                                TO DI-PAY-RATE
161                                                      208                        END-SEARCH
162             END-EVALUATE                              209                    END-SEARCH
163           END-PERFORM                                210            END-SEARCH
164                                                      211            .
165    *      Table-load termination
166           CLOSE PAY-RATE-TABLE-FILE
167           .
```

—— Extract from this program

Figure 16-4 shows the two sections of code extracted from PAYTBLE4. You must recognize that these will be stored as two completely independent files on the disk. Furthermore, they are not complete programs and cannot be compiled by themselves. They are only meaningful when included as part of another program.

Storage and Retrieval of Source Code Segments

If you are using a personal computer, you can store source modules together with the program or in a separate subdirectory specifically defined for the purpose. On a minicomputer or a mainframe (depending on the operating system), they might be cataloged in **source code libraries**, where they are separate from the programs that use them. Each operating system includes its own features, which you use to identify the location of the code required by a program.

Copying Source Components into a Program

In the revised program (PAYTBLE8) of Figure 16-5, the table-loading code was removed and replaced by COPY statements, which are highlighted. You can see that the COPY statement identifies the source code file to be inserted by its filename. For instance,

```
COPY PAYTBLE8.DTA
```

designates the file PAYTBLE8.DTA. The following commentary describes the nature of the COPY as used here:

Figure 16-4   Source code to load a table.

```
* PAYTBLE8.DTA                             * PAYTBLE8.PRO
* Defines work fields and the pay table for  * Loads the pay table from a file into an
* processing, using the Pay rate file as a table.  * in-program table.
 01  TABLE-LOAD-ITEMS.                       110-LOAD-PAY-RATE-TABLE.
     05  WA-TABLE-ENTRY-COUNT      PIC 9.    *     Table-load initialization
         88  CORRECT-TABLE-COUNT       VALUE 7.        OPEN INPUT PAY-RATE-TABLE-FILE
     05  S3-TABLE-FILE-SWITCH      PIC X.          SET S3-NOT-END-OF-TABLE-FILE TO TRUE
         88  S3-END-OF-TABLE-FILE      VALUE "E".      SET S4-TABLE-LOAD-NOT-COMPLETE TO TRUE
         88  S3-NOT-END-OF-TABLE-FILE  VALUE "N".      INITIALIZE WA-TABLE-ENTRY-COUNT
     05  S4-TABLE-LOADED-RESULT    PIC X.
         88  S4-TABLE-LOAD-COMPLETE    VALUE "C".  *     Table-load sequence
         88  S4-TABLE-LOAD-ERROR       VALUE "E".        PERFORM VARYING RT-CLASS-INDEX
         88  S4-TABLE-LOAD-NOT-COMPLETE  VALUE "N".            FROM 1 BY 1
                                                              UNTIL S4-TABLE-LOAD-COMPLETE
                                                                OR S4-TABLE-LOAD-ERROR
 01 RT-RATE-TABLE.                                 READ PAY-RATE-TABLE-FILE
     05  RT-JOB-CLASS-ENTRY   OCCURS 7 TIMES           AT END SET S3-END-OF-TABLE-FILE TO TRUE
                          INDEXED BY RT-CLASS-INDEX.   END-READ
         10  RT-JOB-CLASS      PIC X(2).                EVALUATE
         10  RT-STATUS-ENTRY   OCCURS 2 TIMES                S3-END-OF-TABLE-FILE also CORRECT-TABLE-COUNT
                          INDEXED BY RT-STATUS-INDEX. *     --------------------      --------------------
             15  RT-STATUS-CODE  PIC X(2).
             15  RT-SHIFT-ENTRY  OCCURS 3 TIMES        *     Valid table entry so store it
                          INDEXED BY RT-SHIFT-INDEX. *     WHEN     FALSE        also        FALSE
                 20  RT-SHIFT-CODE  PIC X(1).          *     --------------------      --------------------
                 20  RT-PAY-RATE    PIC 99V99.
                                                            MOVE PAY-RATE-TABLE-RECORD
                                                              TO RT-JOB-CLASS-ENTRY (RT-CLASS-INDEX)
                                                            ADD 1 TO WA-TABLE-ENTRY-COUNT

                                                      *     Table file contains too many entries
                                                            WHEN     FALSE        also         TRUE
                                                      *     --------------------      --------------------

                                                            SET S4-TABLE-LOAD-ERROR TO TRUE

                                                      *     Table file contains insufficient entries
                                                            WHEN     TRUE        also        FALSE
                                                      *     --------------------      --------------------

                                                            SET S4-TABLE-LOAD-ERROR TO TRUE

                                                      *     Table file is properly loaded
                                                            WHEN     TRUE        also         TRUE
                                                      *     --------------------      --------------------

                                                            SET S4-TABLE-LOAD-COMPLETE TO TRUE

                                                           END-EVALUATE
                                                           END-PERFORM

                                                      *     Table-load termination
                                                            CLOSE PAY-RATE-TABLE-FILE
                                                            .
```

(a) The data-definition source code.   (b) The table-load procedure source code.

1. During compilation, as each COPY statement is encountered, the compiler finds the corresponding source code file and inserts it following the COPY statement. This is done in memory during the compilation process. *The original source program—PAYTBLE8—does not change.*

2. The compiled program will be complete in that it will be the result of the original source program plus the copied statements.

3. The post-compile listing will list the inserted statements as if they were included as part of the original program. Some compilers add a special notation (for instance, a + sign) before each copied statement so that it is obvious to the programmer in the listing.

Figure 16-5   Using the COPY statement—PAYTBLE8.

```
1    IDENTIFICATION DIVISION.                         76
2    PROGRAM-ID. PAYTBLE8.                            77   *************Processing Sequence*************
3                                                     78       IF S4-TABLE-LOAD-ERROR
4    * Interplanetary Transport, Inc.                 79           DISPLAY "TABLE LOAD ERROR - RUN ABORTED"
5    * Pay Table Lookup Test Program #4               80           DISPLAY "Press ENTER to exit"
6    * Written by W. Price     3/28/95                81           ACCEPT WA-DUMMY-RESPONSE-FIELD
7                                                     82           SET S2-DO-NOT-REPEAT-TEST TO TRUE
8    * Table:    Loaded from a file with statements   83       ELSE
9    *           inserted using COPY.                 84           SET S2-REPEAT-TEST TO TRUE
10   * Input:    Keyboard entry of                    85       END-IF
11   *              Job classification code           86
12   *              Job status code                   87       PERFORM UNTIL S2-DO-NOT-REPEAT-TEST
13   *              Shift code                        88           PERFORM 200-LOOKUP-PAY-RATE
14   * Output:   Pay rate accessed from Pay rate table 89          IF S1-PAY-RATE-FOUND
15   * Comment:  Pay rate table is three level        90               DISPLAY "Pay rate: ", DI-PAY-RATE
16   *              including arguments as follows     91           END-IF
17   *              (all three levels indexed):       92           DISPLAY " "
18   *                 Job classification             93           DISPLAY "Do you want to make another test <Y/N>? "
19   *                 Job status                      94               WITH NO ADVANCING
20   *                 Shift code                      95           ACCEPT S2-REPEAT-TEST-SWITCH
21   *              Nested SEARCH statements are used  96       END-PERFORM
22   *              for first level (classification), 97
23   *              second level (status), and        98   *************Termination Sequence*************
24   *              third level (shift) access.       99       STOP RUN
25                                                    100      .
26                                                    101  ***************************************************
27   ENVIRONMENT DIVISION.                            102  * Copy the table-load procedure.
28                                                    103      COPY PAYTBLE8.PRO.
29   INPUT-OUTPUT SECTION.                            104
30                                                    105  200-LOOKUP-PAY-RATE.
31   FILE-CONTROL.                                    106      DISPLAY " "
32       SELECT PAY-RATE-TABLE-FILE                   107      DISPLAY "Please enter the job classification "
33           ASSIGN TO (system dependent).            108          WITH NO ADVANCING
34                                                    109      ACCEPT WA-CLASS-CODE
35                                                    110      SET RT-CLASS-INDEX TO 1
36   DATA DIVISION.                                   111      SEARCH RT-JOB-CLASS-ENTRY
37                                                    112        AT END
38   FILE SECTION.                                    113          SET S1-PAY-RATE-NOT-FOUND TO TRUE
39                                                    114          DISPLAY "Invalid Job classification code"
40   FD  PAY-RATE-TABLE-FILE.                         115        WHEN RT-JOB-CLASS (RT-CLASS-INDEX) = WA-CLASS-CODE
41   01  PAY-RATE-TABLE-RECORD          PIC X(36).    116          DISPLAY "Please enter the Status code "
42                                                    117              WITH NO ADVANCING
43   WORKING-STORAGE SECTION.                         118          ACCEPT WA-STATUS-CODE
44                                                    119          SET RT-STATUS-INDEX TO 1
45   01  WORK-FIELDS.                                 120          SEARCH RT-STATUS-ENTRY
46       05  WA-CLASS-CODE              PIC X(2).     121            AT END
47       05  WA-STATUS-CODE             PIC X(2).     122              SET S1-PAY-RATE-NOT-FOUND TO TRUE
48       05  WA-SHIFT-CODE              PIC X.        123              DISPLAY "Invalid Status code"
49       05  WA-DUMMY-RESPONSE-FIELD    PIC X.        124            WHEN RT-STATUS-CODE (RT-CLASS-INDEX,
50                                                    125                            RT-STATUS-INDEX)
51   01  DISPLAY-FIELDS.                              126                    = WA-STATUS-CODE
52       05  DI-PAY-RATE                PIC $$Z.99.   127              DISPLAY "Please enter the Shift code "
53                                                    128                  WITH NO ADVANCING
54   01  PROGRAM-SWITCHES.                            129              ACCEPT WA-SHIFT-CODE
55       05  S1-PAY-RATE-FOUND-SWITCH   PIC X.        130              SET RT-SHIFT-INDEX TO 1
56           88  S1-PAY-RATE-FOUND      VALUE "F".    131              SEARCH RT-SHIFT-ENTRY
57           88  S1-PAY-RATE-NOT-FOUND  VALUE "N".    132                AT END
58       05  S2-REPEAT-TEST-SWITCH      PIC X.        133                  SET S1-PAY-RATE-NOT-FOUND TO TRUE
59           88  S2-REPEAT-TEST         VALUE "Y"     134                  DISPLAY "Invalid Shift code"
60                                            "y".    135                WHEN RT-SHIFT-CODE (RT-CLASS-INDEX,
61           88  S2-DO-NOT-REPEAT-TEST  VALUE "N".    136                                RT-STATUS-INDEX,
62                                                    137                                RT-SHIFT-INDEX)
63   * Copy the table-load data-items.                138                        = WA-SHIFT-CODE
64       COPY PAYTBLE8.DTA.                           139
65                                                    140                  SET S1-PAY-RATE-FOUND TO TRUE
66                                                    141                  MOVE RT-PAY-RATE (RT-CLASS-INDEX,
67   PROCEDURE DIVISION.                              142                                RT-STATUS-INDEX,
68                                                    143                                RT-SHIFT-INDEX)
69   000-TABLE-TEST-PROGRAM.                          144                        TO DI-PAY-RATE
70                                                    145              END-SEARCH
71   ************Initialization Sequence************  146          END-SEARCH
72       DISPLAY "Look up a table entry"              147      END-SEARCH
73             WITH BLANK SCREEN                      148      .
74       DISPLAY " "
75       PERFORM 110-LOAD-PAY-RATE-TABLE
```

General Format of
the COPY Statement

The modules stored in the source libraries can be made available to programmers as dictated by needs of the individual application. To accommodate this, the COPY statement allows you to designate the name of the library in which the required source module is stored; the following limited general form shows this:

$$\underline{\text{COPY}} \text{ text-name } \left[\left\{ \begin{matrix} \underline{\text{OF}} \\ \underline{\text{IN}} \end{matrix} \right\} \text{ library-name} \right]$$

The implication to the personal computer MS-DOS user is that source modules can be stored in a different subdirectory than the program that uses them. For instance, assume that Interplanetary Transport's payroll application is stored on disk as follows:

Programs   In the PAY-PROG subdirectory
                        (identified as \PAY-PROG).

Source library   In the SRCE-LIB subdirectory of PAY-PROG
                        (identified as \PAY-PROG\SRCE-LIB).

Then the COPY statements take the following form:

```
COPY PAYTBLE8.DTA OF \PAY-PROG\SRCE-LIB
COPY PAYTBLE8.PRO OF \PAY-PROG\SRCE-LIB
```

Replacing Elements of
the Copied Source Code

Generally, the programmer who plans to use code from the source code library must write his or her program as if the code were physically included in the program. This means that data-names used in the copying program must conform to those of the copied source module. However, a certain amount of latitude is possible because the COPY statement does allow changes to be made during the copying operation. For instance, assume that you wrote the PAYTBLE8 program and that your table references were

```
RT-JOB-CLASSIF-ENTRY instead of RT-JOB-CLASS-ENTRY
RT-JOB-CLASSIF instead of RT-JOB-CLASS
RT-CLASSIF-INDEX instead of RT-CLASS-INDEX
```

So, for example, lines 111–115 of your program are as shown in Figure 16-6. Without correction, the compiler will issue appropriate error messages regarding undefined fields. The obvious way to handle this is to make appropriate changes so that the main program names correspond to those of the table definition in the source code. However, that is clumsy and error-prone. To accommodate this,

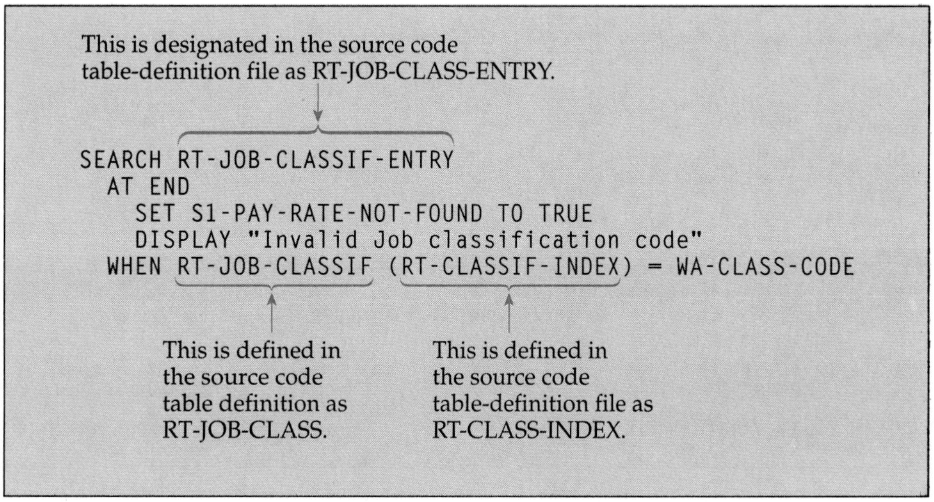

Figure 16-6
Program code that differs
from source code to be
copied.

COBOL provides the REPLACING clause, which identifies changes to be made to the source code when it is copied into the main program. Its use is demonstrated in Figure 16-7(a), where three REPLACING clauses identify the data-item names to be replaced and their replacement values. Figure 16-7(b) shows the original source code and Figure 16-7(c) shows the modified code as it is inserted into the program. Be aware that the original source code file remains unchanged.

After making this change to the copied DATA DIVISION source code, you must make the corresponding change of the copied PROCEDURE DIVISION code because it also refers to the original field names. So, the second of the two COPY statements becomes

```
COPY PAYTBLE8.PRO
    REPLACING RT-JOB-CLASS-ENTRY WITH RT-JOB-CLASSIF-ENTRY
    REPLACING RT-CLASS-INDEX     WITH RT-CLASSIF-INDEX
    REPLACING RT-JOB-CLASS       WITH RT-JOB-CLASSIF
```

Any entry of the copied source code can be changed, including reserved words (except another COPY statement). The full general form of the COPY is

$$\underline{COPY}\ \text{text-name}\ \left[\left\{\genfrac{}{}{0pt}{}{\underline{OF}}{\underline{IN}}\right\}\ \text{library-name}\right]$$

$$\left[\underline{REPLACING}\ \left\{\left(\begin{array}{l}==\text{pseudo-text-1}==\\ \text{identifier-1}\\ \text{literal-1}\\ \text{word-1}\end{array}\right)\ \underline{BY}\ \left\{\begin{array}{l}==\text{pseudo-text-2}==\\ \text{identifier-2}\\ \text{literal-2}\\ \text{word-2}\end{array}\right\}\right\}\ ...\right]$$

Here, *word* is any reserved word except COPY, *literal* is any alphanumeric or numeric literal, and *identifier* is any programmer-defined name. *Pseudo-text* is defined as any sequence of text words, comment lines, or the separator space in a source program.

Figure 16-7 Using the REPLACING clause with the COPY statement.

(a) The COPY/REPLACING statement.

(b) Code in the source file.   (c) Code when copied into program.

Calling a Separate Program from Another Program

Data Definition Considerations with Multiple Modules

To include in a source library commonly used code that can be copied into programs as needed saves coding and debugging time—and promotes standardization. One potential problem in using this technique for procedures relates to the use and definition of data-items.

As you have learned, one of structured programming's objectives is modularization: the organization of a program's components into relatively independent modules that can be coded and tested independent of one another. For large projects on which two or more programming teams might be working, division of the overall task into independent components is critical. Although we speak of the components as independent of one another, the output of one commonly serves as input for another. Obviously, this requires coordination among programmers or programming teams.

To illustrate, let's consider the pay-benefits table-lookup program as two independent components: (1) a program to load the table and (2) a program to process the table. Each includes (1) input, (2) processing within the program, and (3) output, as Figure 16-8 illustrates. As you can see, the output of the table-load program serves as the input to the pay-rate inquiry program.

To implement this technique, COBOL allows you to link separate, independent programs together at execution time. For example, referring to Figure 16-8, the table-load program would be a separately compiled program that is executed from the pay-rate inquiry program. In this respect, the table-load program is subordinate to the pay-rate inquiry program—as such, it is often referred to as a **subprogram**. The execution scenario will be as follows:

1. Entering the appropriate run command causes the pay-rate inquiry program to be loaded from disk into memory, as Figure 16-9(a) illustrates. Execution of the program begins.
2. The pay-rate inquiry program "calls" the table-load program, causing it to be loaded into memory, as Figure 16-9(b) illustrates. As you can see, both programs now reside in memory.
3. Control of the computer is passed to the table-load program (the **called program**), which then loads the table.
4. Upon completion of the table load, execution returns to the **calling program** (the pay-rate inquiry program) and processing continues.

Actually, the action is somewhat like a "super-perform" in that control is transferred to another segment of the overall program and then returned when complete. However, unlike the PERFORM statement, the module to which control

Figure 16-8
Input to and output from independent programs.

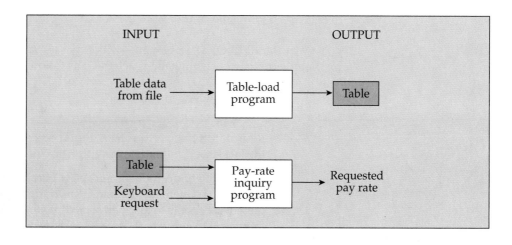

Figure 16-9
Using subprograms.

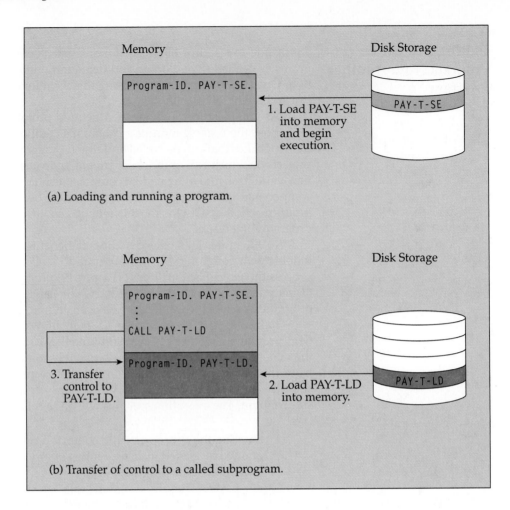

(a) Loading and running a program.

(b) Transfer of control to a called subprogram.

is passed is an entirely separate program—a subprogram. Most programming languages, including machine-languages, include special capabilities for linking programs and subprograms. This requires the following three entities, commonly called **subprogram linkage**:

- The name (or location) of the subprogram.

- The ability to return to the calling program from the subprogram when its execution is complete.

- Communication between the two components of the input to the subprogram and output from it.

With the PERFORM statement—which passes control to a paragraph within a single program—the linkage is achieved as follows:

- The PERFORM includes the paragraph-name of the paragraph to be executed.

- Return from the performed paragraph occurs automatically after the last statement in the paragraph is executed.

- Because the performed paragraph is part of the same program as the PERFORM statement, all data-items defined in the program are completely accessible to any performed paragraph. Any data-item that is accessible to every part of a program is said to be **global**. Later in this chapter, you will see data that is not global.

Calling and Called Programs

All that the table-load and pay-rate inquiry programs have in common is the pay table—including the switch indicating whether or not the table was loaded. So, the subprogram must somehow be able to "transmit" the table to the calling program; remember, these are separately compiled programs. In *both* programs, it is necessary to define and identify the common data-items. To do this, COBOL includes special LINKAGE features, which Figure 16-10 illustrates. (In the COBOL standards, these fall under the **inter-program communication** category.) Let's first look at the called program in Figure 16-10 (b). Special requirements for this application—in which the pay-rate inquiry program is calling the table-load program—are as follows:

1. In the DATA DIVISION, a LINKAGE-SECTION is required. It defines the common data-items under an 01 entry.
2. A USING clause in the PROCEDURE DIVISION header identifies the name of the record (in the LINKAGE SECTION) containing the common data-items. The item listed in the USING is called a **parameter**.

These entries alert the compiler that this program will be called by another, thereby allowing the compiler to incorporate special inter-program communication components into the program.

In the calling program, a slight rearrangement of entries in the WORKING-STORAGE SECTION is required.

1. The data-items to receive values from the called program (components of the parameter) are grouped under a single record in exactly the same form as that of the LINKAGE SECTION in the called program. The data-items must correspond in number, type, and size. The particular choice of the record-name—TABLE-LINKAGE-ITEMS—is not a reserved word; it is a programmer-selected name chosen for its documentation value.

Figure 16-10   Inter-program communication linkage elements.

```
IDENTIFICATION DIVISION.                                    IDENTIFICATION DIVISION.
PROGRAM-ID. PAY-T-SE.                                       PROGRAM-ID. PAY-T-LD.
       :                                                           :
       :                                                           :
WORKING-STORAGE SECTION.                                    LINKAGE SECTION.

01  TABLE-LINKAGE-ITEMS.                                    01  LINKAGE-DATA-ITEMS.
    05  S3-TABLE-LOADED-SWITCH        PIC X.                    05  TABLE-LOADED-SWITCH.
        88  S3-TABLE-LOAD-ERROR       VALUE "E".                    10  S2-TABLE-LOADED-RESULT       PIC X.
                                                                        88  S2-TABLE-LOAD-COMPLETE       VALUE "C".
    05  RT-RATE-TABLE.                                                  88  S2-TABLE-LOAD-ERROR          VALUE "E".
        10  RT-JOB-CLASS-ENTRY   OCCURS 7 TIMES                        88  S2-TABLE-LOAD-NOT-COMPLETE   VALUE "N".
                                 INDEXED BY RT-CLASS-INDEX.
                                                               05  PT-PAY-TABLE.
            15  RT-JOB-CLASS      PIC X(2).                        10  PT-JOB-CLASSIF-ENTRY OCCURS 7 TIMES
            15  RT-STATUS-ENTRY   OCCURS 2 TIMES                                            INDEXED BY PT-CLASSIF-INDEX.
                                  INDEXED BY RT-STATUS-INDEX.
                                                                       15  PT-JOB-CLASSIF       PIC X(2).
                20  RT-STATUS-CODE   PIC X(2).                          15  PT-JOB-STATUS-ENTRY  OCCURS 2 TIMES
                20  RT-SHIFT-ENTRY   OCCURS 3 TIMES                                          INDEXED BY PT-STATUS-INDEX.
                                     INDEXED BY RT-SHIFT-INDEX.
                                                                           20  PT-STATUS         PIC X(2).
                    25  RT-SHIFT-CODE  PIC X(1).                            20  PT-SHIFT-ENTRY    OCCURS 3 TIMES
                    25  RT-PAY-RATE    PIC 99V99.                                            INDEXED BY PT-SHIFT-INDEX.
       :                                                                       25  PT-SHIFT-CODE    PIC X(1).
       :                                                                       25  PT-RATE          PIC 99V99.
PROCEDURE DIVISION.                                                :
       :                                                           :
       :                                                    PROCEDURE DIVISION USING LINKAGE-DATA-ITEMS.
    CALL "PAY-T-LD" USING TABLE-LINKAGE-ITEMS
```

(a) From the pay-rate inquiry (calling) program.   (b) From the table-load (called) program.

2. The subprogram is "performed" by the CALL statement, which includes the called program name and a USING statement. The USING statement refers to the record-name under which the common data-items are defined.

Perhaps you noticed that most of the data-item names of the table-load program were changed so that they are slightly different from their counterparts in the pay-rate inquiry program. This was done to illustrate the point that the names do not need to be the same. Data-items of the called program are associated with corresponding names of the calling program strictly by their relative positions.

Figure 16-11 lists the complete pay-rate inquiry program, PAY-T-SE (PAY Table SEarch). You can see the CALL described in the preceding section at line 75. Also, notice that the program does not include an ENVIRONMENT DIVISION; it does not need one because it has no file to process.

Figure 16-12 lists the complete pay-rate table-load program, PAY-T-LD (PAY Table LoaD). You can see that the LINKAGE SECTION was included following the WORKING-STORAGE SECTION. One other inter-program communication element is necessary to implement this application: the EXIT PROGRAM statement. When execution of the called program is complete, this statement is required in order that control be returned to the calling program. This is the exact form of the statement; both reserved words are required.

The pay-rate table of PAY-T-LD differs slightly from that of Figure 16-10 in that it does not designate index items for PT-JOB-STATUS-ENTRY and PT-SHIFT-ENTRY. They are not needed because the program operates only on the PT-JOB-CLASSIF-ENTRY index. Actually, in this program, the table entry could be defined as follows:

```
05  PT-JOB-CLASSIF-ENTRY PIC X(36)
                 OCCURS 7 TIMES
                 INDEXED BY PT-CLASSIF-INDEX.
```

The disadvantage of this form is the potential for having a mismatch between the length of the field PT-JOB-CLASSIF-ENTRY and the actual table. (It is easy to calculate the length incorrectly.) Also, it is not compatible with another feature of the USE statement REFERENCE phrase, which is described later.

Other Inter-Program Communication Features

Techniques used in this example illustrate some of the features of inter-program communication; other notable points are as follows:

- Coding a LINKAGE SECTION in a program follows most of the same rules as coding a WORKING-STORAGE SECTION. However, the VALUE clause is not allowed, except to define conditional names (88-level items).

- In this example, the CALL statement lists only one parameter: TABLE-LINKAGE-ITEMS. Generally, COBOL places no limit on the number of parameters that can be listed in the CALL, but they must be either 01-level or elementary items. They can be defined in either the FILE SECTION or the WORKING-STORAGE SECTION.

- The PROCEDURE DIVISION header of the called subprogram must contain a USING clause that corresponds to the CALL statement USING clause of the calling program. If two or more parameters are listed following the USING, then the correspondence between parameters is based on position. That is, the first listed parameter in the calling program corresponds to the first listed parameter of the called program, and so on.

Figure 16-11   The pay-rate table search program—PAY-T-SE.

```
1     IDENTIFICATION DIVISION.
2     PROGRAM-ID. PAY-T-SE.
3
4   * Interplanetary Transport, Inc.
5   * Pay Table Lookup Test Program
6   * Written by W. Price    3/28/95
7
8   * Table:   Loaded from a file with a subprogram.
9   * Input:   Keyboard entry of
10  *              Job classification code
11  *              Job status code
12  *              Shift code
13  * Output:  Pay rate accessed from Pay rate table
14  * Comment: Pay rate table is three level
15  *              including arguments as follows
16  *              (all three levels indexed):
17  *              Job classification
18  *              Job status
19  *              Shift code
20  *          Nested SEARCH statements are used
21  *          for first level (classification),
22  *          second level (status), and
23  *          third level (shift) access.
24
25
26    DATA DIVISION.
27
28    WORKING-STORAGE SECTION.
29
30    01  WORK-FIELDS.
31        05  WA-CLASS-CODE            PIC X(2).
32        05  WA-STATUS-CODE           PIC X(2).
33        05  WA-SHIFT-CODE            PIC X.
34        05  WA-DUMMY-RESPONSE-FIELD  PIC X.
35        05  WA-TABLE-ENTRY-COUNT     PIC 9.
36            88  CORRECT-TABLE-COUNT      VALUE 7.
37
38    01  DISPLAY-FIELDS.
39        05  DI-PAY-RATE              PIC $$Z.99.
40
41    01  PROGRAM-SWITCHES.
42        05  S1-PAY-RATE-FOUND-SWITCH  PIC X.
43            88  S1-PAY-RATE-FOUND        VALUE "F".
44            88  S1-PAY-RATE-NOT-FOUND    VALUE "N".
45        05  S2-REPEAT-TEST-SWITCH    PIC X.
46            88  S2-REPEAT-TEST           VALUE "Y"
47                                               "y".
48            88  S2-DO-NOT-REPEAT-TEST    VALUE "N".
49
50    01  TABLE-LINKAGE-ITEMS.
51        05  S3-TABLE-LOADED-SWITCH   PIC X.
52            88  S3-TABLE-LOAD-ERROR      VALUE "E".
53
54        05  RT-RATE-TABLE.
55            10  RT-JOB-CLASS-ENTRY    OCCURS 7 TIMES
56                                      INDEXED BY RT-CLASS-INDEX.
57                15  RT-JOB-CLASS      PIC X(2).
58                15  RT-STATUS-ENTRY   OCCURS 2 TIMES
59                                      INDEXED BY RT-STATUS-INDEX.
60                    20  RT-STATUS-CODE  PIC X(2).
61                    20  RT-SHIFT-ENTRY  OCCURS 3 TIMES
62                                        INDEXED BY RT-SHIFT-INDEX.
63                        25  RT-SHIFT-CODE  PIC X(1).
64                        25  RT-PAY-RATE    PIC 99V99.
65
66
67    PROCEDURE DIVISION.
68
69    000-TABLE-TEST-PROGRAM.
70
71    ************Initialization Sequence************
72        DISPLAY "Look up a table entry"
73               WITH BLANK SCREEN
74        DISPLAY " "
75        CALL "PAY-T-LD" USING TABLE-LINKAGE-ITEMS
76
77    *************Processing Sequence**************
78        IF S3-TABLE-LOAD-ERROR
79           DISPLAY "TABLE LOAD ERROR - RUN ABORTED"
80           DISPLAY "Press ENTER to exit"
81           ACCEPT WA-DUMMY-RESPONSE-FIELD
82           SET S2-DO-NOT-REPEAT-TEST TO TRUE
83        ELSE
84           SET S2-REPEAT-TEST TO TRUE
85        END-IF
86
87        PERFORM UNTIL S2-DO-NOT-REPEAT-TEST
88          PERFORM 200-LOOKUP-PAY-RATE
89          IF S1-PAY-RATE-FOUND
90            DISPLAY "Pay rate: ", DI-PAY-RATE
91          END-IF
92          DISPLAY " "
93          DISPLAY "Do you want to make another test <Y/N>? "
94                 WITH NO ADVANCING
95          ACCEPT S2-REPEAT-TEST-SWITCH
96        END-PERFORM
97
98    **************Termination Sequence*************
99        STOP RUN
100       .
101   ***************************************************
102   200-LOOKUP-PAY-RATE.
103       DISPLAY " "
104       DISPLAY "Please enter the job classification "
105              WITH NO ADVANCING
106       ACCEPT WA-CLASS-CODE
107       SET RT-CLASS-INDEX TO 1
108       SEARCH RT-JOB-CLASS-ENTRY
109         AT END
110             SET S1-PAY-RATE-NOT-FOUND TO TRUE
111             DISPLAY "Invalid Job classification code"
112         WHEN RT-JOB-CLASS (RT-CLASS-INDEX) = WA-CLASS-CODE
113             DISPLAY "Please enter the Status code "
114                    WITH NO ADVANCING
115             ACCEPT WA-STATUS-CODE
116             SET RT-STATUS-INDEX TO 1
117             SEARCH RT-STATUS-ENTRY
118               AT END
119                   SET S1-PAY-RATE-NOT-FOUND TO TRUE
120                   DISPLAY "Invalid Status code"
121               WHEN RT-STATUS-CODE (RT-CLASS-INDEX,
122                                    RT-STATUS-INDEX)
123                       = WA-STATUS-CODE
124                   DISPLAY "Please enter the Shift code "
125                          WITH NO ADVANCING
126                   ACCEPT WA-SHIFT-CODE
127                   SET RT-SHIFT-INDEX TO 1
128                   SEARCH RT-SHIFT-ENTRY
129                     AT END
130                         SET S1-PAY-RATE-NOT-FOUND TO TRUE
131                         DISPLAY "Invalid Shift code"
132                     WHEN RT-SHIFT-CODE (RT-CLASS-INDEX,
133                                         RT-STATUS-INDEX,
134                                         RT-SHIFT-INDEX)
135                             = WA-SHIFT-CODE
136
137                         SET S1-PAY-RATE-FOUND TO TRUE
138                         MOVE RT-PAY-RATE (RT-CLASS-INDEX,
139                                           RT-STATUS-INDEX,
140                                           RT-SHIFT-INDEX)
141                             TO DI-PAY-RATE
142                   END-SEARCH
143               END-SEARCH
144       END-SEARCH
145       .
```

■ The data-items that compose the LINKAGE SECTION of the called sub-program can be operated on in the called subprogram, just as any other data-items. However, a change in any of them changes the value of the corresponding data-item of the calling program (unless the REFERENCE phrase is included).

Figure 16-12 The pay-rate table load subprogram—PAY-T-LD.

```
1     IDENTIFICATION DIVISION.                              52
2     PROGRAM-ID. PAY-T-LD.                                 53
3                                                           54    PROCEDURE DIVISION USING LINKAGE-DATA-ITEMS.
4    * Interplanetary Transport, Inc.                       55
5    * Pay Table Load Program                               56    000-TABLE-LOAD-PROGRAM.
6    * Written by W. Price   3/28/95                        57        OPEN INPUT PAY-RATE-TABLE-FILE
7                                                           58        PERFORM 100-INITIALIZE-VARIABLE-FIELDS
8     ENVIRONMENT DIVISION.                                 59        PERFORM 200-LOAD-PAY-RATE-TABLE-ENTRY
9                                                           60            VARYING PT-CLASSIF-INDEX
10    INPUT-OUTPUT SECTION.                                 61                FROM 1 BY 1
11                                                          62                UNTIL S2-TABLE-LOAD-COMPLETE
12    FILE-CONTROL.                                         63                OR S2-TABLE-LOAD-ERROR
13        SELECT PAY-RATE-TABLE-FILE                        64        CLOSE PAY-RATE-TABLE-FILE
14            ASSIGN TO (system dependent).                 65        EXIT PROGRAM
15                                                          66        .
16                                                          67    100-INITIALIZE-VARIABLE-FIELDS.
17    DATA DIVISION.                                        68        SET S1-NOT-END-OF-TABLE-FILE TO TRUE
18                                                          69        SET S2-TABLE-LOAD-NOT-COMPLETE TO TRUE
19    FILE SECTION.                                         70        INITIALIZE WA-TABLE-ENTRY-COUNT
20                                                          71        .
21    FD  PAY-RATE-TABLE-FILE.                              72    200-LOAD-PAY-RATE-TABLE-ENTRY.
22    01  PAY-RATE-TABLE-RECORD        PIC X(36).           73        READ PAY-RATE-TABLE-FILE
23                                                          74            AT END SET S1-END-OF-TABLE-FILE TO TRUE
24    WORKING-STORAGE SECTION.                              75        END-READ
25                                                          76        EVALUATE
26    01  PROGRAM-SWITCH.                                   77            S1-END-OF-TABLE-FILE also WA-VALID-TABLE-COUNT
27        05  S1-TABLE-FILE-SWITCH        PIC X.            78    *       --------------------      --------------------
28            88  S1-END-OF-TABLE-FILE      VALUE "E".      79
29            88  S1-NOT-END-OF-TABLE-FILE  VALUE "N".      80    *       Valid table entry so store it
30    01  WA-WORK-AREA.                                     81            WHEN     FALSE       also        FALSE
31        05  WA-TABLE-ENTRY-COUNT       PIC 9.             82    *       --------------------      --------------------
32            88  WA-VALID-TABLE-COUNT      VALUE 7.        83                MOVE PAY-RATE-TABLE-RECORD
33                                                          84                    TO PT-JOB-CLASSIF-ENTRY (PT-CLASSIF-INDEX)
34    LINKAGE SECTION.                                      85                ADD 1 TO WA-TABLE-ENTRY-COUNT
35                                                          86
36    01  LINKAGE-DATA-ITEMS.                               87    *       Table file contains too many entries
37        05  TABLE-LOADED-SWITCH.                          88            WHEN     FALSE       also        TRUE
38            10  S2-TABLE-LOADED-RESULT   PIC X.           89    *       --------------------      --------------------
39                88  S2-TABLE-LOAD-COMPLETE     VALUE "C". 90                SET S2-TABLE-LOAD-ERROR TO TRUE
40                88  S2-TABLE-LOAD-ERROR        VALUE "E". 91
41                88  S2-TABLE-LOAD-NOT-COMPLETE VALUE "N". 92    *       Table file contains insufficient entries
42                                                          93            WHEN     TRUE        also        FALSE
43        05  PT-PAY-TABLE.                                 94    *       --------------------      --------------------
44            10  PT-JOB-CLASSIF-ENTRY OCCURS 7 TIMES       95                SET S2-TABLE-LOAD-ERROR TO TRUE
45                    INDEXED BY PT-CLASSIF-INDEX.          96
46                15  PT-JOB-CLASSIF     PIC X(2).          97    *       Table file is properly loaded
47                15  PT-JOB-STATUS-ENTRY  OCCURS 2 TIMES.  98            WHEN     TRUE        also        TRUE
48                    20  PT-STATUS      PIC X(2).          99    *       --------------------      --------------------
49                    20  PT-SHIFT-ENTRY   OCCURS 3 TIMES. 100                SET S2-TABLE-LOAD-COMPLETE TO TRUE
50                        25  PT-SHIFT-CODE  PIC X(1).     101
51                        25  PT-RATE        PIC 99V99.    102        END-EVALUATE
                                                          103        .
```

BY REFERENCE and BY CONTENT Phrases

Consider another subprogram application: one in which a routine is required that will compute the mean and standard deviation of an array's data elements.* The subprogram will have input and output, as Figure 16-13 illustrates. The significance of this example is that the input data array to the subprogram will be used in calculations by the subprogram, *but it must not be changed*. The sole function of the subprogram is mean and standard deviation calculation. What if, due to an undetected error in the subprogram, some of the array elements were changed? In many applications, small changes could go undetected—thereby corrupting all calculations associated with the data array.

COBOL-85 provides for this with the BY REFERENCE and BY CONTENT phrases. The default for the USING is the BY REFERENCE phrase; it provides for changing values of data in the calling program. Specifically, execution of the called program proceeds as if the called program data-items occupy the same computer storage areas as those of the calling program.

The easiest way to understand the BY CONTENT phrase is to think of it as functioning in the following manner:

---

*The 1989 Intrinsic Function Module includes functions for computing the mean and standard deviation of an array. We will ignore those functions for this discussion and consider a subprogram to do the calculations.

Figure 16-13
Communication between a
program and a subprogram.

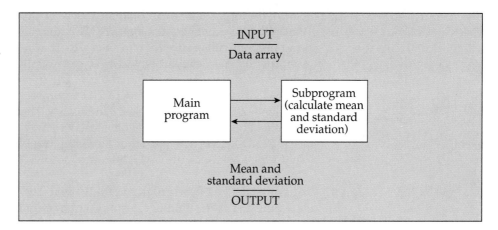

1. All BY CONTENT parameter values of the calling program are copied into the corresponding LINKAGE SECTION area of the called program.
2. The called program operates on its copy of the parameter items, changing them if necessary for calculations within the called program.
3. At the conclusion of the called program, the parameter values used by the called program are *not* copied back to the calling program.

This provides a valuable **data isolation** feature; data is available to a called program, but is protected from change.

Figure 16-14's code skeleton illustrates how these phrases would be employed in the array processing example. The BY CONTENT identification of SA-STUDENT-SCORES-ARRAY means that its elements will be available to the called program for processing, but not for change. However, the *copy* of those elements transmitted to IA-INPUT-DATA-ARRAY can be changed if necessary. In contrast, the BY REFERENCE identification of SR-STUDENT-SCORE-RESULTS means that these entries can be changed by the called program. Notice that in the source code of the called program, you cannot distinguish between BY CONTENT and BY REFERENCE parameters.

The two parameters have another distinction concerning their implementation. That is, the data description of each parameter in the BY CONTENT phrase of the CALL statement must be the same as the data description of the corresponding parameter in the USING phrase of the PROCEDURE DIVISION header. In contrast, with the BY REFERENCE, the data-item description in the called program only needs to correspond in length to the corresponding data-item in the calling program.

Figure 16-14   Illustrating BY CONTENT and BY REFERENCE.

```
01  SA-STUDENT-SCORES-ARRAY.                          LINKAGE SECTION.
    05  SA-STUDENT-SCORE      OCCURS 500 TIMES
                              PIC 999.                 01  IA-INPUT-DATA-ARRAY.
01  SR-STUDENT-SCORE-RESULTS.                              05  IA-ARRAY-ELEMENTS   OCCURS 500 TIMES
    05  SR-STUDENT-MEAN       PIC 999.                                             PIC 999.
    05  SR-STUDENT-STD-DEV    PIC 999.                 01  SR-STAT-RESULTS.
                                                           05  SR-MEAN             PIC 999.
      .                                                    05  SR-STD-DEV          PIC 999.
      .
      .                                                      .
    CALL "STD-DEV" USING BY CONTENT SA-STUDENT-SCORES-ARRAY   .
                         BY REFERENCE SR-STUDENT-SCORE-RESULTS .

                                                       PROCEDURE DIVISION USING IA-INPUT-DATA-ARRAY
                                                                                SR-STAT-RESULTS

  (a) Calling program.                                 (b) Called program.
```

Error Handling

One of the topics stressed in Chapter 15 was error recovery; for example, you need the ability to recover from a disk WRITE failure. Regarding subprograms, what if your program calls a subprogram and (1) there is insufficient memory for it or (2) the subprogram was deleted from disk? The answer: Your program crashes unless you have made provisions for error handling. The solution to this dilemma is to use the ON EXCEPTION/NOT ON EXCEPTION phrases of the CALL statement—in conjunction with the END-CALL scope terminator. These have exactly the same form as the other equivalent forms you have used; for instance, READ/AT END/NOT AT END/END-READ. The format of the CALL is included at the end of this chapter. For COBOL-74 users, the CALL includes the ON OVERFLOW for error handling.

The CANCEL Statement

Although the PAY-T-SE program calls the PAY-T-LD program to load the table only one time, in many situations, a subprogram might be called numerous times. For instance, an employee benefits program might call—for processing of each employee—a separate subprogram for tax-sheltered annuity calculations.

In this respect, after a subprogram is called (loaded and executed) and control returns to the calling program, the called subprogram remains in memory undisturbed. If the subprogram is called a second time, the program state remains unchanged from when control was previously returned to the calling program. For instance, any changes that were made to the values of data-items will remain, files that were opened and not closed will stay open, and so on. In many cases, this is desirable—but in some, it is not. In two circumstances, you might not want the subprogram to remain unchanged in memory.

First, the program needs might be such that with each execution of the subprogram, it must be in its initial state (that is, all data-items at their initial values).

Second, if you have a large application with numerous subprograms, they might exceed the computer's memory capacity. In most programs that call many subprograms, some of them are used only one time and are no longer needed. Furthermore, it is rare that all of the subprograms need to be in memory at the same time.

The solution to both of these situations is to direct the system to remove one or more subprograms from memory. This is done with the CANCEL statement. For example, inserting the following statement immediately after the CALL (line 75 of PAY-T-SE—Figure 16-11, page 579) causes the subprogram to be removed from memory following its execution:

```
CANCEL "PAY-T-LD"
```

The memory occupied by this program will then be made available for other use. If the needs of PAY-T-SE were such that it was needed again later in the program, another CALL reloads it into memory and runs it from its initial state.

Called Subprograms Calling Other Subprograms

A called program may call another program, and so on.* For instance, assume that special actions are required by PAY-T-LD after opening the table file, but before beginning the table-load process. If desired, these actions could be coded as a separate subprogram—for example, FILE-CHK—called by PAY-T-LD. So, you now have:

PAY-T-SE would call PAY-T-LD

PAY-T-LD would call FILE-CHK

The only restriction is that a CALL statement cannot reference any called program to which control was transferred and that has not yet completed execution. In other words, a program cannot be re-entered until an EXIT occurs.

---

*The Educational version of RM/COBOL-85 does not allow a called subprogram to call another subprogram.

Nested Programs

Characteristics of Nested Programs

This chapter's third major topic is nested programs. Basically, a **nested program** is a complete program that is contained within another program. On the surface, the nested program may appear to be similar to using source code from a library with the COPY command (or to the called subprogram), but it is not. Although subprograms allow a program to be divided into separate, independent modules of code, the primary function of subprograms is to make available to the programmer common functions in a preprogrammed, compiled form. On the other hand, program nesting provides COBOL with the basic tools to implement modular programming principles within a program to an extent impossible using the techniques described in this book's previous chapters.

To illustrate how program nesting might be used in a business environment, assume that an employee payroll system was designed for Interplanetary Transport, Inc. The primary processing program was broken into four components, each assigned to a programming team. During the design phase of the program, the input to and output from each component was carefully defined. Each programming team knows exactly the file formats it will be using and the data-items required to interface to the other components. So, each group can write its component independent of the other groups. When all four groups are finished, the four components can be combined to form the desired program.

However, a problem exists regarding data-names. Each group will create numerous data-items for use within their component. So, some convention must be established for selecting names so that names used in one program component are not accidentally selected by another team. You can appreciate this from your knowledge of PAYTBLE8, in which the table-loading function is copied from a source library. The programmer who uses the table-load source code must be careful to avoid using data-names already used in the copied code. Remember, the names selected are global, meaning that they are available throughout the program.

Called subprograms avoid this conflict because they are separately compiled; in fact, special features must be employed to allow the programs to share data. You have *independence of data* between the program and the called subprograms. Data-names defined in the subprogram are said to be **local** data-names because they are meaningful only within the subprogram and not within the program that calls the subprogram.

PAY-T-LD As a Nested Program

The code skeleton of Figure 16-15 shows how the existing PAY-T-LD program would be nested within the PAY-T-SE program. No changes are required to either program. The only additions are the END PROGRAM statements. The END PROGRAM statement does exactly as the English indicates: It tells the compiler that it has reached the end of the named program. Its general form is

Format:

<u>END</u> <u>PROGRAM</u> program-name.

Notice the similarity of this nested program to nested IF statements in which PROGRAM-ID corresponds to IF and END PROGRAM corresponds to END-IF. Technically, PAY-T-SE includes its own code plus the nested program PAY-T-LD—everything up to the corresponding END PROGRAM PAY-T-SE statement. However, the end of the PAY-T-SE PROCEDURE DIVISION code is signaled by the PROGRAM-ID of the nested program. In other words, you will never see code of a program split by a nested program.

Although the illustration of Figure 16-15 shows one program nested within another (one level of nesting), programs can be nested to any desired level. For instance, assume that PAY-T-SE requires two nested programs: PAY-T-LD and ADJ-RATE. Furthermore, PAY-T-LD itself requires the nested programs FILE-CHK and TBLE-MOD. This means two levels of nesting and is illustrated in

Figure 16-15
A nested program.

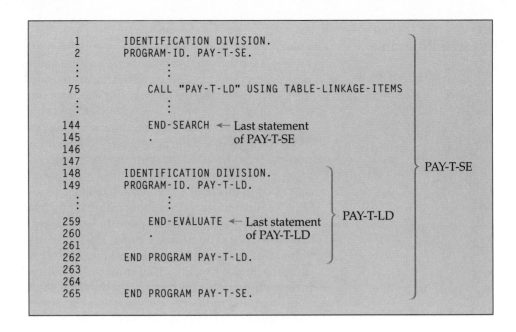

```
        1         IDENTIFICATION DIVISION.
        2         PROGRAM-ID. PAY-T-SE.
        :             :
        :             :
       75            CALL "PAY-T-LD" USING TABLE-LINKAGE-ITEMS
        :             :
        :             :
      144            END-SEARCH ← Last statement
      145            .              of PAY-T-SE
      146
      147
      148            IDENTIFICATION DIVISION.
      149            PROGRAM-ID. PAY-T-LD.
        :             :
        :             :
      259               END-EVALUATE ← Last statement
      260               .              of PAY-T-LD
      261
      262            END PROGRAM PAY-T-LD.
      263
      264
      265         END PROGRAM PAY-T-SE.
```

Figure 16-16. Notice that PAY-T-LD, which itself contains two nested programs, is at the same nesting level (within PAY-T-SE) as is ADJ-RATE.

The IS GLOBAL Clause

The significant feature of the nested program capability is that it provides data independence between program modules of a single program. That is, data-items defined within one of the program modules are local to that module and have nothing to do with data of other modules. This way, they are protected from accidental corruption by the other modules of the program. In the context of Figure 16-15, this means that names defined in PAY-T-LD (including file-names, record-names, data-names, and procedure-names) have no meaning outside of PAY-T-LD (which is nested in PAY-T-SE). Similarly, names used in PAY-T-SE are not available to PAY-T-LD *unless specifically indicated*.

From the subprogram example of Figures 16-11 and 16-12, you know that communicating data between a calling program and a called subprogram is achieved through the LINKAGE SECTION and USING clause. Data isolation and modular independence for nested programs are enhanced by communicating data between a calling program and the called nested program in exactly the same way: through a LINKAGE SECTION and a USING clause.

There is, however, another technique you will often encounter: using global data items. Although global data items compromise data isolation, the technique is implemented in this example to give you an idea of how it works. Any data-item declared as GLOBAL becomes available to any nested program included within the program containing the global declaration. To illustrate, consider two examples in the context of Figure 16-16:

- If the data-item SAVE-TABLE is declared global in PAY-T-SE, then it is available to all nested programs (PAY-T-LD, FILE-CHK, TBLE-MOD, and ADJ-RATE).

- If the data-item HOLD-RATE is declared global in PAY-T-LD, it is available only within PAY-T-LD and its nested programs TBLE-MOD and ADJ-RATE. It is not available in ADJ-RATE or in PAY-T-SE itself.

Note that there is no reason to use a global declaration in FILE-CHK, TBLE-MOD, or ADJ-RATE because they do not contain nested programs.

Figure 16-16
Two-level nesting.

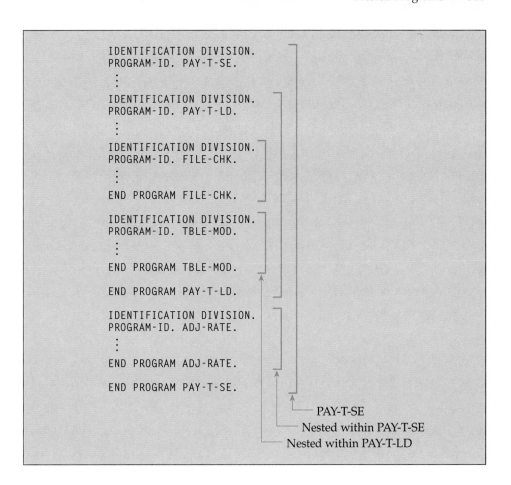

```
        IDENTIFICATION DIVISION.
        PROGRAM-ID. PAY-T-SE.
          :
        IDENTIFICATION DIVISION.
        PROGRAM-ID. PAY-T-LD.
          :
        IDENTIFICATION DIVISION.
        PROGRAM-ID. FILE-CHK.
          :
        END PROGRAM FILE-CHK.

        IDENTIFICATION DIVISION.
        PROGRAM-ID. TBLE-MOD.
          :
        END PROGRAM TBLE-MOD.

        END PROGRAM PAY-T-LD.

        IDENTIFICATION DIVISION.
        PROGRAM-ID. ADJ-RATE.
          :
        END PROGRAM ADJ-RATE.

        END PROGRAM PAY-T-SE.
```

PAY-T-SE
Nested within PAY-T-SE
Nested within PAY-T-LD

You must be aware that the GLOBAL clause can be used only with a data-item defined as a level 01; it *cannot* be used at any lower level. However, all data-items subordinate to the 01 declared as global are themselves global.

The Pay-Rate Program As a Nested Program

The program solution for this example is shown in Figure 16-17. This program should look familiar; most of its points were already covered. As you study this program, notice the following:

1. Data-items defined in the DATA DIVISION of PAY-T-GL (starting line 51) are those needed by PAY-T-LD. They are included under the 01 entry GLOBAL-ITEMS, which is declared as GLOBAL. Remember, all subordinate items to an 01 entry declared as global are themselves global. So, they are available to the nested program PAY-T-LD—as well as to PAY-T-GL.
2. PAY-T-LD contains no corresponding set of data-item definitions (see lines 167–182) since the needed data-items are available from PAY-T-GL.
3. During execution, control is transferred to the nested program PAY-T-LD using the CALL statement (see line 78); this is the same CALL used to transfer control to a subprogram. It does not include a USING phrase because no parameters are being passed.
4. During execution, control is returned from the nested program to the calling program by the EXIT PROGRAM statement (see line 196); this is the same EXIT PROGRAM used to return control from a subprogram.

There is one final note of caution regarding global data-names. That is, if a data-name used for a data-item declared as global in a program is used to define a

Figure 16-17 A nested program—PAY-T-GL.

```
1     IDENTIFICATION DIVISION.
2     PROGRAM-ID. PAY-T-GL.
3
4     * Interplanetary Transport, Inc.
5     * Pay Table Lookup Test Program
6     * Written by W. Price   3/28/95
7
8     * Table:  Loaded from a file with a nested program.
9     * Input:  Keyboard entry of
10    *              Job classification code
11    *              Job status code
12    *              Shift code
13    * Output: Pay rate accessed from Pay rate table
14    * Comment: Pay rate table is three-level
15    *          including arguments as follows
16    *          (all three levels indexed):
17    *              Job classification
18    *              Job status
19    *              Shift code
20    *          Nested SEARCH statements are used
21    *          for first level (classification),
22    *          second level (status), and
23    *          third level (shift) access.
24
25
26    DATA DIVISION.
27
28    WORKING-STORAGE SECTION.
29
30    01  WORK-FIELDS.
31        05  WA-CLASS-CODE           PIC X(2).
32        05  WA-STATUS-CODE          PIC X(2).
33        05  WA-SHIFT-CODE           PIC X.
34        05  WA-DUMMY-RESPONSE-FIELD PIC X.
35        05  WA-TABLE-ENTRY-COUNT    PIC 9.
36            88  CORRECT-TABLE-COUNT     VALUE 7.
37
38    01  DISPLAY-FIELDS.
39        05  DI-PAY-RATE             PIC $$Z.99.
40
41    01  PROGRAM-SWITCHES.
42        05  S1-PAY-RATE-FOUND-SWITCH   PIC X.
43            88  S1-PAY-RATE-FOUND          VALUE "F".
44            88  S1-PAY-RATE-NOT-FOUND      VALUE "N".
45        05  S2-REPEAT-TEST-SWITCH      PIC X.
46            88  S2-REPEAT-TEST             VALUE "Y"
47                                                 "y".
48            88  S2-DO-NOT-REPEAT-TEST      VALUE "N".
49
50    01  GLOBAL-ITEMS IS GLOBAL.
51        05  S3-TABLE-LOADED-SWITCH     PIC X.
52            88  S3-TABLE-LOAD-COMPLETE     VALUE "C".
53            88  S3-TABLE-LOAD-ERROR        VALUE "E".
54            88  S3-TABLE-LOAD-NOT-COMPLETE VALUE "N".
55
56        05  RT-RATE-TABLE.
57            10  RT-JOB-CLASS-ENTRY   OCCURS 7 TIMES
58                                     INDEXED BY RT-CLASS-INDEX.
59                15  RT-JOB-CLASS     PIC X(2).
60                15  RT-STATUS-ENTRY  OCCURS 2 TIMES
61                                     INDEXED BY RT-STATUS-INDEX.
62                    20  RT-STATUS-CODE   PIC X(2).
63                    20  RT-SHIFT-ENTRY   OCCURS 3 TIMES
64                                         INDEXED BY RT-SHIFT-INDEX.
65                        25  RT-SHIFT-CODE  PIC X(1).
66                        25  RT-PAY-RATE    PIC 99V99.
67
68
69    PROCEDURE DIVISION.
70
71
72    000-TABLE-TEST-PROGRAM.
73
74    ************Initialization Sequence************
75        DISPLAY "Look up a table entry"
76               WITH BLANK SCREEN
77        DISPLAY " "
78        CALL "PAY-T-LD"
79
80    *************Processing Sequence*************
81        IF S3-TABLE-LOAD-ERROR
82            DISPLAY "TABLE LOAD ERROR - RUN ABORTED"
83            DISPLAY "Press ENTER to exit"
84            ACCEPT WA-DUMMY-RESPONSE-FIELD
85            SET S2-DO-NOT-REPEAT-TEST TO TRUE
86        ELSE
87            SET S2-REPEAT-TEST TO TRUE
88        END-IF
89
90        PERFORM UNTIL S2-DO-NOT-REPEAT-TEST
91            PERFORM 200-LOOKUP-PAY-RATE
92            IF S1-PAY-RATE-FOUND
93                DISPLAY "Pay rate: ", DI-PAY-RATE
94            END-IF
95            DISPLAY " "
96            DISPLAY "Do you want to make another test <Y/N>? "
97                   WITH NO ADVANCING
98            ACCEPT S2-REPEAT-TEST-SWITCH
99        END-PERFORM
100
101   *************Termination Sequence*************
102       STOP RUN
103       .
104   *********************************************
105   200-LOOKUP-PAY-RATE.
106       DISPLAY " "
107       DISPLAY "Please enter the job classification "
108              WITH NO ADVANCING
109       ACCEPT WA-CLASS-CODE
110       SET RT-CLASS-INDEX TO 1
111       SEARCH RT-JOB-CLASS-ENTRY
112           AT END
113               SET S1-PAY-RATE-NOT-FOUND TO TRUE
114               DISPLAY "Invalid Job classification code"
115           WHEN RT-JOB-CLASS (RT-CLASS-INDEX) = WA-CLASS-CODE
116               DISPLAY "Please enter the Status code "
117                      WITH NO ADVANCING
118               ACCEPT WA-STATUS-CODE
119               SET RT-STATUS-INDEX TO 1
120               SEARCH RT-STATUS-ENTRY
121                   AT END
122                       SET S1-PAY-RATE-NOT-FOUND TO TRUE
123                       DISPLAY "Invalid Status code"
124                   WHEN RT-STATUS-CODE (RT-CLASS-INDEX,
125                                        RT-STATUS-INDEX)
126                       = WA-STATUS-CODE
127                       DISPLAY "Please enter the Shift code "
128                              WITH NO ADVANCING
129                       ACCEPT WA-SHIFT-CODE
130                       SET RT-SHIFT-INDEX TO 1
131                       SEARCH RT-SHIFT-ENTRY
132                           AT END
133                               SET S1-PAY-RATE-NOT-FOUND TO TRUE
134                               DISPLAY "Invalid Shift code"
135                           WHEN RT-SHIFT-CODE (RT-CLASS-INDEX,
136                                               RT-STATUS-INDEX,
137                                               RT-SHIFT-INDEX)
138                               = WA-SHIFT-CODE
139
140                               SET S1-PAY-RATE-FOUND TO TRUE
141                               MOVE RT-PAY-RATE (RT-CLASS-INDEX,
142                                                 RT-STATUS-INDEX,
143                                                 RT-SHIFT-INDEX)
144                                 TO DI-PAY-RATE
145                       END-SEARCH
146               END-SEARCH
147       END-SEARCH
148       .
```

data-item in a nested program, then the data-name of the nested program becomes local to the nested program. For instance, consider a modification to the previous nesting example shown in Figure 16-18. In PAY-T-SE, the data-item ERROR-FLAG is global because it is defined under GLOBAL-DATA, which is declared global. That two-position numeric item is available to all nested programs *except* FILE-CHK because the name is defined within FILE-CHK. The one-position alphanumeric version of ERROR-FLAG is local to FILE-CHK and therefore available only to FILE-CHK.

Figure 16-17   (continued)

```
149
150
151    ******TABLE LOAD PROGRAM******
152    IDENTIFICATION DIVISION.
153    PROGRAM-ID. PAY-T-LD.
154
155  * Interplanetary Transport, Inc.
156  * Pay Table Load Program
157  * Written by W. Price    3/28/95
158
159    ENVIRONMENT DIVISION.
160
161    INPUT-OUTPUT SECTION.
162
163    FILE-CONTROL.
164        SELECT PAY-RATE-TABLE-FILE
165            ASSIGN TO (system dependent).
166
167    DATA DIVISION.
168
169    FILE SECTION.
170
171    FD  PAY-RATE-TABLE-FILE.
172    01  PAY-RATE-TABLE-RECORD        PIC X(36).
173
174    WORKING-STORAGE SECTION.
175
176    01  PROGRAM-SWITCH.
177        05  S1-TABLE-FILE-SWITCH        PIC X.
178            88  S1-END-OF-TABLE-FILE        VALUE "E".
179            88  S1-NOT-END-OF-TABLE-FILE    VALUE "N".
180    01  WA-WORK-AREA.
181        05  WA-TABLE-ENTRY-COUNT        PIC 9.
182            88  WA-VALID-TABLE-COUNT        VALUE 7.
183
184
185    PROCEDURE DIVISION.
186
187    000-TABLE-LOAD-PROGRAM.
188        OPEN INPUT PAY-RATE-TABLE-FILE
189        PERFORM 100-INITIALIZE-VARIABLE-FIELDS
190        PERFORM 200-LOAD-PAY-RATE-TABLE-ENTRY
191            VARYING RT-CLASS-INDEX
192                FROM 1 BY 1
193                UNTIL S3-TABLE-LOAD-COMPLETE
194                    OR S3-TABLE-LOAD-ERROR
195        CLOSE PAY-RATE-TABLE-FILE
196        EXIT PROGRAM
197        .
198    100-INITIALIZE-VARIABLE-FIELDS.
199        SET S1-NOT-END-OF-TABLE-FILE TO TRUE
200        SET S3-TABLE-LOAD-NOT-COMPLETE TO TRUE
201        INITIALIZE WA-TABLE-ENTRY-COUNT
202        .
203    200-LOAD-PAY-RATE-TABLE-ENTRY.
204        READ PAY-RATE-TABLE-FILE
205            AT END SET S1-END-OF-TABLE-FILE TO TRUE
206        END-READ
207        EVALUATE
208            S1-END-OF-TABLE-FILE also WA-VALID-TABLE-COUNT
209  *      -------------------    -------------------
210
211  *      Valid table entry so store it
212        WHEN      FALSE      also      FALSE
213  *      -------------------    -------------------
214        MOVE PAY-RATE-TABLE-RECORD
215            TO RT-JOB-CLASS-ENTRY (RT-CLASS-INDEX)
216        ADD 1 TO WA-TABLE-ENTRY-COUNT
217
218  *      Table file contains too many entries
219        WHEN      FALSE      also      TRUE
220  *      -------------------    -------------------
221        SET S3-TABLE-LOAD-ERROR TO TRUE
222
223  *      Table file contains insufficient entries
224        WHEN      TRUE      also      FALSE
225  *      -------------------    -------------------
226        SET S3-TABLE-LOAD-ERROR TO TRUE
227
228  *      Table file is properly loaded
229        WHEN      TRUE      also      TRUE
230  *      -------------------    -------------------
231        SET S3-TABLE-LOAD-COMPLETE TO TRUE
232
233        END-EVALUATE
234        .
235
236    END PROGRAM PAY-T-LD.
237
238    END PROGRAM PAY-T-GL.
```

Chapter Summary

From this chapter, you have learned the following three techniques for managing programs:

- The COPY statement, which allows source code to be standardized and stored in source statement libraries. When needed in a program, the COPY causes a designated source code module to be inserted into the program during the compiling operation. Code can be inserted into any division of the program.

- Subprograms that allow you to program common operations, compile them, and store them as separate code in an object library. A subprogram is incorporated into a program with the CALL statement.

- Data is passed between a program and a called subprogram through the LINKAGE SECTION of the subprogram and the USING clause of the CALL statement.

- One or more programs can be fully contained within another program. This is called program nesting. Nesting provides the means to isolate program functions and data in separate programs.

Figure 16-18
A local definition over-riding a global declaration.

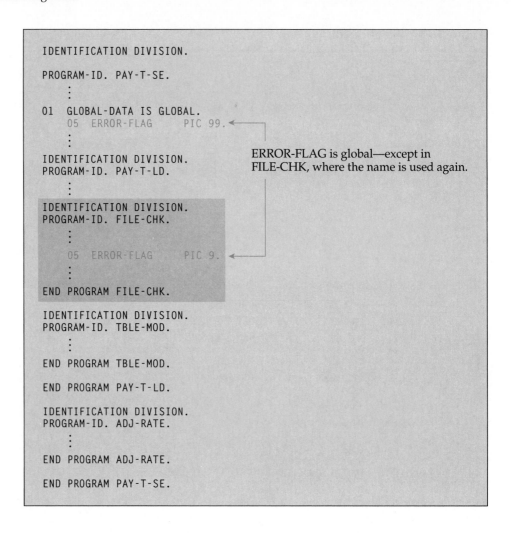

```
IDENTIFICATION DIVISION.

PROGRAM-ID. PAY-T-SE.
      :
01  GLOBAL-DATA IS GLOBAL.
    05  ERROR-FLAG    PIC 99.
      :
IDENTIFICATION DIVISION.
PROGRAM-ID. PAY-T-LD.
      :
IDENTIFICATION DIVISION.
PROGRAM-ID. FILE-CHK.
      :
    05  ERROR-FLAG    PIC 9.
      :
END PROGRAM FILE-CHK.

IDENTIFICATION DIVISION.
PROGRAM-ID. TBLE-MOD.
      :
END PROGRAM TBLE-MOD.

END PROGRAM PAY-T-LD.

IDENTIFICATION DIVISION.
PROGRAM-ID. ADJ-RATE.
      :
END PROGRAM ADJ-RATE.

END PROGRAM PAY-T-SE.
```

ERROR-FLAG is global—except in FILE-CHK, where the name is used again.

COBOL Language Elements

The COBOL statements you have studied in this chapter are as follows:

CALL The CALL statement causes control to be transferred from one object program to another. Its general format (to the extent used in this book) is

$$\underline{CALL} \quad \begin{Bmatrix} \text{identifier-1} \\ \text{literal-1} \end{Bmatrix} \left[\text{USING} \begin{Bmatrix} \text{[BY \underline{REFERENCE}] \{identifier-2\}..} \\ \text{BY \underline{CONTENT} \{identifier-2\}...} \end{Bmatrix} ... \right]$$

[ON <u>EXCEPTION</u> imperative-statement-1]
[<u>NOT</u> ON <u>EXCEPTION</u> imperative-statement-2]
[<u>END-CALL</u>]

CANCEL The CANCEL statement ensures that the next time the referenced program is called, it will be in its initial state.

$$\underline{CANCEL} \quad \begin{Bmatrix} \text{identifier-1} \\ \text{literal-1} \end{Bmatrix} ...$$

COPY The COPY statement provides the means to copy text from a source statement library into a source program.

$$\underline{\text{COPY}} \text{ text-name} \left[\begin{Bmatrix} \underline{\text{OF}} \\ \underline{\text{IN}} \end{Bmatrix} \text{ library-name} \right]$$

$$\left[\underline{\text{REPLACING}} \left\{ \begin{Bmatrix} \text{==pseudo-text-1==} \\ \text{identifier-1} \\ \text{literal-1} \\ \text{word-1} \end{Bmatrix} \underline{\text{BY}} \begin{Bmatrix} \text{==pseudo-text-2==} \\ \text{identifier-2} \\ \text{literal-2} \\ \text{word-2} \end{Bmatrix} \right\} \cdots \right]$$

EXIT PROGRAM The EXIT PROGRAM statement marks the logical end of a called program.

> <u>EXIT</u> <u>PROGRAM</u>

Other language elements you have studied in this chapter are as follows:

END PROGRAM The END PROGRAM header indicates the end of the named source program to the compiler.

> <u>END</u> <u>PROGRAM</u> program-name.

LINKAGE SECTION The LINKAGE SECTION provides the means for communication between a program and a called subprogram. Its structure is identical to that of the WORKING-STORAGE SECTION. Its general format (to the extent used in this book) is

> <u>LINKAGE</u> <u>SECTION</u>.
> record-description-entry

GLOBAL clause The GLOBAL clause specifies that a data-name (level 01 only) or a file-name is available to every program within the program that declares it.

> IS <u>GLOBAL</u>

PROCEDURE DIVISION header The PROCEDURE DIVISION header for a program called by another program must include a USING phrase if parameters are passed.

> <u>PROCEDURE</u> <u>DIVISION</u> [<u>USING</u> {data-name-1}...].

Programming Conventions

Standardize record descriptions and save them in a source statement library. Any program using a particular file should include a COPY statement to copy the record description into the programming. This promotes standardization and reduces the possibility of errors.

Often-used routines and procedures should be set up as independent subprograms, compiled and stored in an object library. This reduces redundant effort.

Whenever possible in preparing a subprogram, group the linkage data-items into a single record. Then the USING can designate that record-name.

For a very large program, break the program down into major independent components and program them as nested components of a controlling program. This provides data independence otherwise not available in COBOL.

Error Prevention/ Detection

When using the COPY statement, always check data definitions of the copied code carefully before writing your program in order to avoid duplicating names of the copied code.

If a subprogram does not appear to be returning data to the calling program correctly, check to ensure that the formats of the LINKAGE SECTION and the data definition in the calling program are identical. For instance, accidentally switching two fields might not cause a compiler error, but it will give incorrect results.

If a result is not returned to a global data-item in a called program from a nested program, check to ensure that the linkage data-item used in the nested program was not accidentally defined in the nested program.

Exercises

Terms for Definition

called program
calling program
data isolation
global
inter-program communication
local
nested program

object code
parameter
source code
source code libraries
subprogram
subprogram linkage

Questions About the Example Programs

1. A programmer inserts the COPY PAYTBLE8.DTA statement immediately following the DATA DIVISION header at line 36 of the PAYTBLE8 program (Figure 16-5). Does this make any difference during either compiling or execution? Explain your answer.

2. A programmer inserts the COPY PAYTBLE8.PRO statement following the last statement of PAYTBLE8 (Figure 16-5). Does this make any difference during either compiling or execution? Explain your answer.

3. In the nested PAY-T-GL program of Figure 16-17, a programmer uses the data-name S3-TABLE-LOADED-SWITCH at line 177 (instead of S1-TABLE-FILE-SWITCH). Describe the problem this causes.

Programming Project

Each of the programming assignments of preceding chapters dealt with a single element of some programming application. This project is much more comprehensive: It involves several elements of an order-processing system for UNISOFT, Incorporated—a mail-order vendor of computer software. The basic component of the project consists of three parts: order entry, invoice preparation, and a controlling menu system. Additional components provide for payment processing and customer billing.

For your first insight to the application, let's consider what happens when an order is placed. Assume that the customer Karen Richardson (customer number 12555) is placing an order for two copies of QBase 7000 and one copy of Orchestra II.

1. The salesperson enters customer number 12555, Richardson's customer number. The program must access her record from the customer file and display needed data.
2. The salesperson enters the product number for QBase 7000.
3. The program must access and display product information for that item from the inventory file.
4. The salesperson enters 2 for a Quantity of 2. The program must calculate the Charge-amount as the Unit-price times the Quantity.

5. The program must subtract the Quantity 2 from the Quantity-on-hand field of the inventory record and write that record back to disk.
6. The process must be repeated for the next item—Orchestra II.
7. When the order-entry process is complete, information about this order is written to an order file.

A typical order-entry screen into which the salesperson makes the entries appears as shown in Figure 16-19.

From the preceding descriptions, it is apparent that an order-entry system will include at least three data files: a customer file, an inventory file, and an order file. The order file contains information such as the customer number of the person placing the order, the date of the order, the amount due from the order, and a list of items ordered. In this project, the order file is actually two separate files: an invoice file and an invoice line-item file.

About the Invoice Files   In this application, each order is identified by an invoice number. Figure 16-20 illustrates the relationship between records of the invoice file and the invoice line-item file. The link between the two is established by the invoice number field: the key field for the invoice file.

Figure 16-19   Typical order-entry screen.

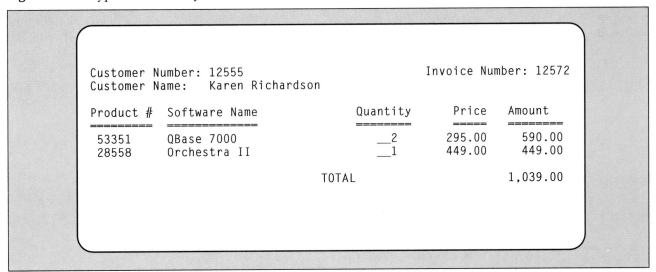

```
Customer Number: 12555                              Invoice Number: 12572
Customer Name:    Karen Richardson

Product #   Software Name         Quantity      Price     Amount
=========   =============         ========      =====     ========
  53351     QBase 7000                  _2      295.00      590.00
  28558     Orchestra II                _1      449.00      449.00

                                 TOTAL                    1,039.00
```

Figure 16-20
Interrelating records of the invoice file and the invoice line-item file.

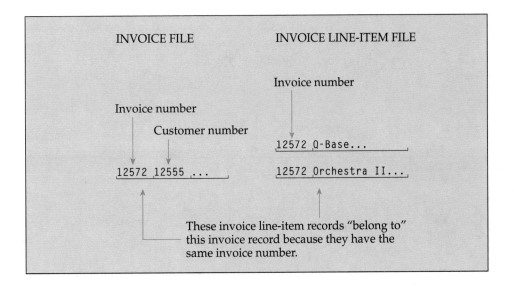

However, the invoice line-item file presents a special problem in that it can contain more than one record for a single invoice record. Yet it must include the invoice number in its key to establish the "linkage" between the invoice master and line-item files. This is done, and the uniqueness of the key field preserved, by adding a line number suffix to the invoice number. That is, the first two fields of the invoice line-item file are the invoice number and a two-digit line-item number. The combination of these two fields, which is unique, serves as the key field for the file. The invoice-number part of it provides the desired random access for processing line-item records together with their corresponding invoice record.

As each order is taken and a new invoice created, it must be given an invoice number that is one greater than the preceding invoice number. To do that, the first record of the invoice file is a header record containing the next available invoice number. Creation of a new invoice record includes the following steps:

1. Access the header record (from the invoice master file).
2. Increment the Last-invoice-number value from the header record as the invoice number for the new invoice record.
3. Build and write the new invoice master record.
4. Rewrite the header record.

System Files

This application requires four indexed files: SOFTWARE.DAI, CUST-MAS.DAI, INVOICE.DAI, and LINEITEM.DAI. The first two can be generated by compiling and running the program ORD-CRE8.CBL, which creates the empty files and loads them with data from the sequential files SOFTWARE.DAT and CUST-MAS.DAT. Compiling and running the program INV-CRE8 creates the needed empty indexed files INVOICE.DAI and LINEITEM.DAI. If you are using a compiler other than Micro Focus or Ryan-McFarland, you may need to change FILE-CONTROL entries.

Inventory file (SOFTWARE.DAI)

Contains one record for each inventory item.

Organization is indexed

Key field: Stock number

Positions	Field	Format
1–5	Stock number	
6–35	Software name	
36–55	Vendor name	
56–58	Quantity on hand	S999
59–61	Reorder level	999
62–66	Price	999V99

Customer master file (CUST-MAS.DAI)

Contains one record for each customer.

Organization is indexed

Key field: Customer number

Positions	Field	Format
1–5	Customer number (key field)	
6–35	Name	
36–65	Street address	
66–85	City	
86–87	State	
88–96	Zip code	
97–104	Balance owed on account	S999999V99

Invoice file (INVOICE.DAI)

Contains one record for each invoice. First record is a header record. Invoice numbers are assigned beginning with the number 00001.

Organization is indexed

Key field: Invoice number

Alternate key: Customer number (with duplicates)

Positions	Field	Format
Header record		
1–5	Invoice number: value 00001	
6–10	Not used	
11–15	Last used invoice number	
16–30	Not used	
Subsequent records		
1–5	Invoice number—key field	
6–10	Customer number for this sale	
11–16	Date of invoice	*yymmdd*
17–23	Total billed amount of invoice	99999V99
24–30	Amount paid on this invoice	99999V99

Invoice line-item file (LINEITEM.DAI)

Contains one record for each item ordered of each invoice. The key field is composed of the key code plus the invoice number plus a two-digit number, which is the line number of that entry on the invoice.

Organization is indexed

Key field: Key code + Invoice number + line number

Alternate key: Invoice number (with duplicates)

Positions	Field	Format
1	Key code	Value "K"
2–6	Invoice number	
7–8	Line number of this invoice entry	
9–13	Customer number	
14–18	Stock number of item purchased	
19–48	Description of item purchased	
49–51	Quantity purchased of this item	
52–56	Item price	999V99
57–63	Amount (quantity purchased times price)	99999V99

Order Entry

An order-processing system is required for UNISOFT that will allow salespeople to enter orders interactively. As each order is entered, customer data will be accessed from a customer master file and product information for each item will be accessed from the inventory file. The customer file and inventory file will be updated to reflect activity of the order. Order information will be written to invoice files for later preparation of invoices.

Required files:

>Inventory file
>Customer master
>Invoice file
>Invoice line-item

Program operations—Order entry:

1. Accept the customer number of the customer placing the order.

2. Access the customer record from the customer file.

3. Repeat the following for each ordered item:
    a. Accept the product number of the item ordered.
    b. Access the product record from the inventory file.
    c. Accept the quantity for the entered product.
    d. If the quantity on hand is insufficient for this order, display an error message and do not accept this line entry.
    e. If the quantity on hand is sufficient for this order:
       ■ Calculate:
         Charge-amount = Quantity times Price
       ■ Subtract the Quantity ordered from the inventory record Quantity-on-hand field and rewrite the record.
       ■ Accumulate the Charge-amount for the ordered item.

4. Add the accumulated amount to the Customer-balance field of the customer record and rewrite the record.

5. Write an invoice record to the invoice file for this order.

6. Update the invoice file header record to contain the invoice number of the last invoice in the file.

7. Write one record to the invoice transaction (line-item) file for each line-item of the order.

Invoice Preparation

Another element of the order-processing system is printing invoices for mailing to the customer (or including with the order when it is shipped).

Required files:

>Customer master
>Invoice file
>Invoice line-item

Printed output:

Figure 16-21 shows a typical invoice.

Figure 16-21   A typical customer invoice.

```
                        UNISOFT, INCORPORATED
                        *********************

                              INVOICE

    Invoice number: 12572                    Date: 11/11/95


        Karen Richardson          12555
        315 San Benito Avenue
        San Jose     CA  95130




    Product                              Unit
    Number    Description        Quantity Price      Amount
    -------------------------------------------------------------
    53351     QBase 7000               2  295.00      590.00
    28558     Orchestra II             1  449.00      449.00











    -------------------------------------------------------------
                                     Invoice Total    1,039.00

              Thank you for your patronage
```

Program operations—Invoice preparation:

1. If this program is entered immediately after order entry, then print invoices for those orders entered during that session.

2. Otherwise, ask the user to designate the beginning and ending invoice numbers of the invoices to be printed. Check to ensure that the requested beginning invoice number is not less than 00002 and the ending invoice number is not larger than the number of the last invoice in the file.

3. For each invoice record in the requested invoice number range:
   a. Read the invoice record.
   b. Using the Customer-number value from the invoice master, read the customer record corresponding to this invoice record.
   c. Print the upper portion of the invoice.
   d. Read each invoice line-item record corresponding to this invoice master and print a detail line.
   e. After the last invoice transaction record for this invoice is processed, print the invoice total line.

4. Print appropriate descriptions needed to identify fields of the invoice—see the sample invoice, Figure 16-21.

Menu Control

Access to order entry and invoice preparation is through a controlling menu program. This menu program must also provide access to additional options, as described next.

Program operations—Menu-controlling program:

1. Access to the order-processing system must be through a "front-end" menu that lists the available options.

2. The order-entry and invoice-processing programs must be compiled as separate subprograms that are called by the menu program.

Payment Processing

One of the essential activities of UNISOFT is collecting money due from customers. As each payment is received from a customer, a record is created in the payment file, the amount is deducted from the balance field in the customer file, and the amount paid is applied to one or more invoice master records. Regarding updating the invoice file, consider a typical example in which the file contains the following four records:

Invoice number	Invoice amount	Amount paid	Balance owed
00037	245.95	245.95	0.00
00049	182.50		182.50
00063	212.00		212.00
00089	722.49		722.49

If this customer submits a 300.00 payment, 182.50 is applied to invoice 00049 and the balance, 117.50, is applied to invoice 00063—with the following result:

Invoice number	Invoice amount	Amount paid	Balance owed
00037	245.95	245.95	0.00
00049	182.50	182.50	0.00
00063	212.00	117.50	94.50
00089	722.49		722.49

Required files:

Invoice file
Payment file (PAYMENT.DAI)

Contains a header record and one record for each payment received. You must create this file and insert the header record—your program will be similar to INV-CRE8.

Organization is indexed

Key field: Payment number

Alternate key: Customer number

Positions	Field	Format
Header record (record 1)		
1–5	00001	
6–10	Unused	
11–15	Last used payment number	
16–30	Unused	
Subsequent records		
1–5	Payment number—key field	
6–10	Customer number for this payment	
11–16	Date entered	*yymmdd*
17–23	Total amount of payment	99999V99

Program operations—Payment processing:

For each payment-received record, the program must:

1. Accept the payment data from the keyboard.

2. Insert a record into the payment file. To do so, access the header record to obtain the last payment number used (required to generate the key field value). Update the header record.

3. Get the first invoice record for this customer.

4. If in this invoice record, the Amount-paid field is equal to the Invoice-amount field, get subsequent records for this customer until one is encountered in which the Amount-paid field is less than the Invoice-amount field.

5. If the payment amount is greater than the remaining amount on the invoice, set the Amount-paid field equal to the Invoice-amount field; decrease the remaining payment amount accordingly.

6. If a payment amount remains, repeat the process for subsequent invoice records for this customer.

7. If after processing the last invoice record for this customer, a payment amount still remains, ignore it because it will be handled by the customer-billing program.

Customer Billing

At the end of each month, UNISOFT prepares customer bills listing all transactions for that month. This program requires that data from the customer, invoice, and payment files be merged. If a customer has no transactions and no balance due, then no bill will be created.

Required files:

> Customer file
> Invoice file
> Payment file

Printed output:

One bill must be printed for each customer with activity during the month or with an outstanding balance. The bill will be output on a preprinted customer statement form, as Figure 16-22 shows.

Figure 16-22 Sample customer bill.

```
                        UNISOFT, INCORPORATED
                        *********************

                          CUSTOMER STATEMENT

     CUSTOMER NUMBER  12555                Statement date: 12/01/95

     Karen Richardson
     315 San Benito Avenue
     San Jose      CA  95130



     Please return this portion
     with your payment           AMOUNT ENCLOSED _____


     ------------------------------------------------------------

               INVOICE
      DATE     NUMBER   DESCRIPTION              AMOUNT   BALANCE
      -------------------------------------------------------------
                        Opening balance                   863.25

      11/07/95          Payment received         700.00
      11/19/95          Payment received         160.00

      11/11/95  01012                          1,039.00
      11/16/95  01033                             68.95
      11/27/95  01315                            212.49




                        BALANCE DUE                     1,323.69
```

Program operations—Customer billing:

1. Prepare a bill for each customer having (1) a Customer-balance field not equal to zero or (2) one or more payments or purchases during the processing period.

2. The processing cycle is monthly (based on the calendar month).

3. Print the customer number, statement date, and customer name and address on the upper portion of the form.

4. For each payment received during the current month:
   a. Print one line on the customer statement.
   b. Subtract the amount from the Customer-balance field (in the customer record).

5. For each invoice processed during the current month:
   a. Print one line on the customer statement.
   b. Add the amount to the Customer-balance field (in the customer record).

6. For the summary line, print:
   a. "Balance due" and the amount if the Customer-balance field is positive.
   b. "Account is current" if the Customer-balance field is zero.
   c. "Customer credit" and the amount followed by the letters CR if the Customer-balance field is negative.

THE COBOL REPORT WRITER FEATURE

COBOL's Report Writer feature provides program-mers with the ability to write report programs that have a reduced amount of COBOL coding. PROCE-DURE DIVISION coding is reduced because much of the report logic is handled through the specification of programming requirements in the REPORT SECTION of the DATA DIVISION. Coding requirements for the DATA DIVISION are sometimes also lessened because the need to define report control, accumulator, and FILLER fields is decreased. The Report Writer feature is not available on all COBOL compilers, however.

Although not documented in the Personal COBOL manual, Personal COBOL includes the Report Writer feature. The three example programs in this appendix were tested with Personal COBOL.

APPENDIX OUTLINE

Creating a Report with a Report Total

Chapter 7 gave you your first insight into the intricacies of report design. Recall that a report page is commonly vertically divided into different report page areas, as Figure AA-1 illustrates. Through appropriate program coding—sometimes very complex—you have controlled printing from page to page, as illustrated by this figure. That is, your programs have included detailed instructions of *how* to produce the desired report. In contrast, with Report Writer, you only need to designate *what* you require for a report—Report Writer handles the required logic automatically.

Report Requirements

To illustrate, let's consider a minor variation of PATLIST3 (Figure 7-12, page 213). For this example, the output must be as illustrated by the print chart of Figure AA-2. From this print chart, you see the following requirements:

1. The first four lines of the report page are to be blank—these compose the top margin.
2. The heading lines printed on each page begin at line 5 and occupy five lines (including line 9, which is blank).
3. The first detail lines must be printed on line 10.
4. The report summary consists of two lines (the first is blank).

Two items are not illustrated by this print chart: the number of lines in the body of the report and the length of the form to be used.

Since the patron file includes a limited number of records, only 15 detail lines are printed per page. Then the complete output requirements are as illustrated in the sample printout of Figure AA-3.

As a minimum, we will need to describe for Report Writer the following characteristics of this report:

Figure AA-1
Sample page layout.

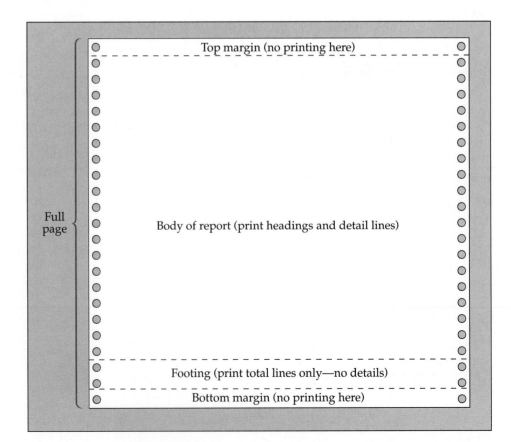

Figure AA-2   Print chart for Report Writer example.

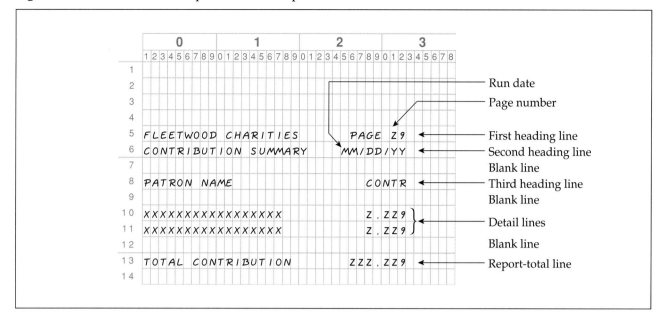

1. The line location of each heading line and its contents.
2. The first and last positions on which detail lines may be printed.
3. The data-items to be printed on detail lines.
4. What will be printed on the report-total line and its location relative to the last detail line.

Figure AA-3   Sample patron file report.

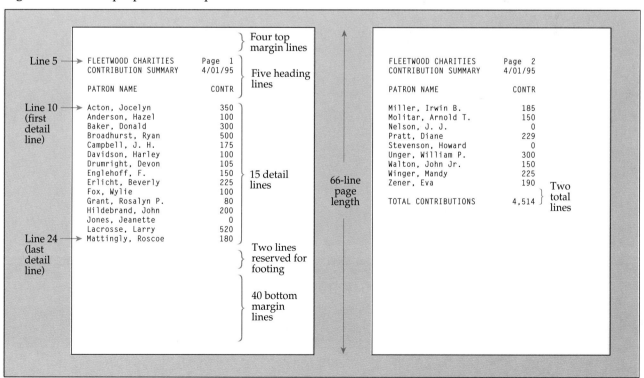

With this information, Report Writer automatically provides for page control (including a page counter), accumulates the field to be totaled (the contributions field), and prints all of the output lines.

The RPATLIST Program   Figure AA-4 shows a program using the COBOL Report Writer feature to produce this report. Notice that in this program, named RPATLIST (the R indicating Report Writer PATLIST program), the PROCEDURE DIVISION is much shorter than those of PATLIST2 and PATLIST3 in Chapter 7. Key Report Writer features are highlighted in this program listing.

Figure AA-4   The RPATLIST program.

```
1        IDENTIFICATION DIVISION.
2        PROGRAM-ID.    RPATLIST.
3
4    *      Price/Welburn  4/1/95
5    *      Report total program using Report Writer
6
7        ENVIRONMENT DIVISION.
8
9        INPUT-OUTPUT SECTION.
10
11       FILE-CONTROL.
12           SELECT PATRON-FILE
13           ASSIGN TO (system dependent).
14
15           SELECT PATRON-LIST
16           ASSIGN TO (system dependent).
17
18
19       DATA DIVISION.
20
21       FILE SECTION.
22
23       FD  PATRON-FILE.
24       01  PATRON-RECORD          PIC X(68).
25
26       FD  PATRON-LIST
27           REPORT IS CONTRIBUTION-SUMMARY.  ◄——— Report clause
28
29       WORKING-STORAGE SECTION.
30
31       01  PROGRAM-SWITCHES.
32           05  S1-END-OF-FILE-SWITCH PIC X(1).
33               88  S1-END-OF-FILE        VALUE "Y".
34               88  S1-NOT-END-OF-FILE    VALUE "N".
35
36       01  WA-WORK-AREAS.
37           05  WA-CURRENT-DATE.
38               10  WA-CURRENT-YEAR   PIC 9(2).
39               10  WA-CURRENT-MONTH  PIC 9(2).
40               10  WA-CURRENT-DAY    PIC 9(2).
41
42       01  PR-PATRON-RECORD.
43           05  PR-NAME               PIC X(18).
44           05                        PIC X(46).
45           05  PR-ACTUAL-CONTR       PIC 9(4).
46
```

```
47       REPORT SECTION.                                       REPORT SECTION
48
49       RD  CONTRIBUTION-SUMMARY
50           CONTROL IS FINAL
51           PAGE LIMIT IS 66
52           FIRST DETAIL  10
53           LAST DETAIL   24.
54
55       01  TYPE IS PAGE HEADING.                             Heading lines
56           03  LINE NUMBER 5.
57               05  COLUMN  1 PIC X(19)   VALUE "FLEETWOOD CHARITIES".
58               05  COLUMN 26 PIC X(4)    VALUE "Page".
59               05  COLUMN 31 PIC Z(2)    SOURCE PAGE-COUNTER.
60
61           03  LINE NUMBER 6.
62               05  COLUMN  1 PIC X(20)   VALUE "CONTRIBUTION SUMMARY".
63               05  COLUMN 25 PIC Z9      SOURCE WA-CURRENT-MONTH.
64               05  COLUMN 27 PIC X(1)    VALUE "/".
65               05  COLUMN 28 PIC 9(2)    SOURCE WA-CURRENT-DAY.
66               05  COLUMN 30 PIC X(1)    VALUE "/".
67               05  COLUMN 31 PIC 9(2)    SOURCE WA-CURRENT-YEAR.
68
69           03  LINE NUMBER 8.
70               05  COLUMN  1 PIC X(11)   VALUE "PATRON NAME".
71               05  COLUMN 28 PIC X(5)    VALUE "CONTR".
72
73       01  DL-DETAIL-LINE                                    Detail line
74           TYPE IS DETAIL.
75           03  LINE PLUS 1.
76               05  COLUMN  1 PIC X(18)   SOURCE PR-NAME.
77               05  COLUMN 28 PIC Z,ZZ9   SOURCE PR-ACTUAL-CONTR.
78
79       01  TYPE IS CONTROL FOOTING FINAL.                    Summary lines
80           03  LINE PLUS 2.
81               05  COLUMN  2 PIC X(19)   VALUE "TOTAL CONTRIBUTIONS".
82               05  COLUMN 26 PIC ZZZ,ZZ9 SUM PR-ACTUAL-CONTR.
83
84
85       PROCEDURE DIVISION.
86
87       000-PRINT-PATRON-LIST.
88
89       ************Initialization Sequence************
90           OPEN INPUT PATRON-FILE
91                OUTPUT PATRON-LIST
92           INITIATE CONTRIBUTION-SUMMARY  ◄——————— Begins the report
93           PERFORM 100-INITIALIZE-VARIABLE-FIELDS
94
95       ************Processing Sequence*************
96           PERFORM UNTIL S1-END-OF-FILE
97               READ PATRON-FILE INTO PR-PATRON-RECORD
98                   AT END
99                       SET S1-END-OF-FILE TO TRUE
100                  NOT AT END
101                      PERFORM 200-PROCESS-PATRON-RECORD
102              END-READ
103          END-PERFORM
104
105      ************Termination Sequence*************
106          TERMINATE CONTRIBUTION-SUMMARY  ◄——————— Ends the report
107          CLOSE PATRON-FILE
108                PATRON-LIST
109          STOP RUN
110          .
111      *************************************************
112      100-INITIALIZE-VARIABLE-FIELDS.
113          SET S1-NOT-END-OF-FILE TO TRUE
114          ACCEPT WA-CURRENT-DATE FROM DATE
115          .
116      200-PROCESS-PATRON-RECORD.
117          GENERATE DL-DETAIL-LINE  ◄——————— Prints report lines
118          .
```

DATA DIVISION— The FILE SECTION

As you know, every file used in a program (including report files) requires an FD. So RPATLIST includes two FDs: one for the input file and the other for the report file. This pertains to output files generated by Report Writer as well. The only difference between an FD for a regular printer file and that for a Report Writer output file is that the 01 entry is replaced by the REPORT IS clause. This clause specifies the name of the report, CONTRIBUTION-SUMMARY in RPATLIST.

In addition to the REPORT IS clause, the FD may include BLOCK CONTAINS, RECORD CONTAINS, and LABEL RECORDS clauses, the same as a conventional FD.

When the REPORT clause is coded in the FD, no 01-level record-description entries are coded for that file in the FILE SECTION. Instead, the 01-level report-line records are described in the REPORT SECTION; let's consider it next.

DATA DIVISION— The REPORT SECTION's RD

The first entry you see in the REPORT SECTION of Figure AA-4 is the report-description (RD) entry. One of these is required for each report to be prepared by the program. (Each example program in this appendix includes only one report definition.)

The RD-entry format is shown in Figure AA-5—together with the entry from RPATLIST. Because most programs prepare a single report, just one RD entry is typically coded in a Report Writer program. The RD name—CONTRIBUTION-SUMMARY, in this case—must match the report-name specified in the FD entry. The RD entry contains two clauses: CONTROL IS and PAGE LIMIT.

Figure AA-5
The RD-entry format.

Format:

RD report-name

$$\left[\left\{ \begin{array}{l} \underline{\text{CONTROL}} \text{ IS} \\ \underline{\text{CONTROLS}} \text{ ARE} \end{array} \right\} \left\{ \begin{array}{l} \text{data-name-1 [data-name-2]}\ldots \\ \underline{\text{FINAL}} \text{ [data-name-1 [data-name-2]}\ldots\text{]} \end{array} \right\}\right]$$

$$\left[\underline{\text{PAGE}} \left[\begin{array}{l} \underline{\text{LIMIT}} \text{ IS} \\ \underline{\text{LIMITS}} \text{ ARE} \end{array} \right] \text{integer-1} \left[\begin{array}{l} \text{LINE} \\ \text{LINES} \end{array} \right] \right.$$

$$\begin{array}{l} \text{[}\underline{\text{HEADING}} \text{ integer-2]} \\ \text{[}\underline{\text{FIRST}} \ \underline{\text{DETAIL}} \text{ integer-3]} \\ \text{[}\underline{\text{LAST}} \ \underline{\text{DETAIL}} \text{ integer-4]} \\ \text{[}\underline{\text{FOOTING}} \text{ integer-5]} \end{array} \Bigg] .$$

Example from RPATLIST:

```
49    RD   CONTRIBUTION-SUMMARY  ←──── This name must be the
50         CONTROL IS FINAL              name designated in
51         PAGE LIMIT IS 66              the FD for the report.
52         FIRST DETAIL   10
53         LAST DETAIL    24.
```

The CONTROL IS Clause

The CONTROL IS clause specifies control-break hierarchies within the report. Because the RPATLIST is a read-and-print program with only end-of-report totals (no control totals), CONTROL IS FINAL is specified. The reserved word FINAL provides for the printing of final totals at the end of the report. (Actually, CONTROL IS FINAL is the default; if a report contains only final totals and no control totals, it is not necessary to explicitly code the CONTROL IS FINAL clause.)

The PAGE LIMIT Clause

The PAGE LIMIT clause identifies the vertical line-span parameters to be used for the report. In Figure AA-5's general format, you can see that phrases are included that allow you to designate the page size, the start of the heading area, the detail-line span, and the footing area. However, the needs of RPATLIST are satisfied by designating:

1. PAGE LIMIT IS 66 is coded to designate the physical size of the printer paper (an 11-inch form with printing at 6 lines per inch).
2. FIRST DETAIL 10 designates line 10 as the first line on which a detail line may be printed.
3. LAST DETAIL 24 designates line 24 as the last line on which a detail line may be printed. Note that these two entries provide for 15 detail lines, as required by Figure AA-3.

In this program, it is not necessary to designate values for the HEADING and FOOTING phrases because they are controlled by subsequent REPORT SECTION entries.

DATA DIVISION—01-Level Report Lines in the REPORT SECTION

Following the RD entry is one 01-level report line for each type of line that will be printed. The 01 includes:

- Optionally, a record-name.

- A designation of the type of line being defined. Report Writer provides for seven broad types of lines. RPATLIST uses three of them: heading, detail, and final total.

- An indication of where the line will be printed, designated by a line number or relative to another line.

- The format of the line, including the column designations, PICTURE symbols, and literals or data to be printed.

Let's begin with the PAGE HEADING record, which is reproduced here in Figure AA-6(a) from the RPATLIST program.

TYPE IS PAGE HEADING

PAGE HEADING lines are printed at the top of each page. Only one 01-level TYPE IS PAGE HEADING entry is permitted within an RD entry. Notice that no record-name was affixed to the 01-level TYPE IS PAGE HEADING entry. A record-name is not required if the report-line record is not called out in the PROCEDURE DIVISION. Because PAGE HEADING lines are seldom referenced this way, record-names are usually omitted from the 01-level record-description entry. Figure AA-6(b) shows the identical record definition in which the name PAGE-HEADING-RECORD is included. In RPATLIST, the name would serve no useful function. Even its documentation value is minimized by the presence of the TYPE phrase.

Figure AA-6   The PAGE HEADING record.

```
01  TYPE IS PAGE HEADING.                              01  PAGE-HEADING-RECORD
    03  LINE NUMBER 5.                                     TYPE IS PAGE HEADING.
        05  COLUMN   1 PIC X(19)   VALUE "FLEETWOOD CHARITIES".   03  H1-HEADING-LINE
        05  COLUMN 265 PIC X(4)    VALUE "Page".                      LINE NUMBER 5.
        05  COLUMN  31 PIC Z(2)    SOURCE PAGE-COUNTER.                  05  COLUMN   1 PIC X(19)   VALUE "FLEETWOOD CHARITIES".
                                                                        05  COLUMN  26 PIC X(4)    VALUE "Page".
                                                                        05  COLUMN  31 PIC Z(2)    SOURCE PAGE-COUNTER.

    03  LINE NUMBER 6.                                     03  H2-HEADING-LINE
        05  COLUMN  1 PIC X(20)   VALUE "CONTRIBUTION SUMMARY".           LINE NUMBER 6.
        05  COLUMN 25 PIC Z9      SOURCE WA-CURRENT-MONTH.                  05  COLUMN  1 PIC X(20)   VALUE "CONTRIBUTION SUMMARY".
        05  COLUMN 27 PIC X(1)    VALUE "/".                                05  COLUMN 25 PIC Z9      SOURCE WA-CURRENT-MONTH.
        05  COLUMN 28 PIC 9(2)    SOURCE WA-CURRENT-DAY.                    05  COLUMN 27 PIC X(1)    VALUE "/".
        05  COLUMN 30 PIC X(1)    VALUE "/".                               05  COLUMN 28 PIC 9(2)    SOURCE WA-CURRENT-DAY.
        05  COLUMN 31 PIC 9(2)    SOURCE WA-CURRENT-YEAR.                   05  COLUMN 30 PIC X(1)    VALUE "/".
                                                                           05  COLUMN 31 PIC 9(2)    SOURCE WA-CURRENT-YEAR.

    03  LINE NUMBER 8.                                     03  H3-HEADING-LINE
        05  COLUMN  1 PIC X(11)   VALUE "PATRON NAME".                     LINE NUMBER 8.
        05  COLUMN 28 PIC X(5)    VALUE "CONTR".                            05  COLUMN  1 PIC X(11)   VALUE "PATRON NAME".
                                                                           05  COLUMN 28 PIC X(5)    VALUE "CONTR".
```

(a) From RPATLIST.   (b) With optional record/field names.

The LINE Clause

Each line of output is defined by an entry subordinate to the 01. In Figure AA-6, you see three 03-level entries. As with the 01-level entry, no data-name is required because these items are not referenced directly from the PROCEDURE DIVISION. (Names are assigned to them in Figure AA-6(b) solely to illustrate naming.) The LINE clause is an essential element of these entries. It functions exactly as the English suggests; for instance, the first heading line must be printed on line number 5 of the report. When preparing the program code, you can pick these numbers right off the print chart (see Figure AA-2). Notice that the line number clause is part of the 03 entry, as the period following it indicates.

Although the first entry under the 01 (03, in this example) can be an elementary item, it is more commonly broken down into components, as done here with the succession of 05 elementary entries.

Breakdown into Elementary Items

Each elementary entry (coded at the 05 level, in this example) includes three components. The first is the beginning position on the print line where the item is to be printed—the COLUMN phrase. Inspecting, for example, the first heading line definition, you can see that the beginning column numbers (1, 26, and 31) correspond to the beginning print positions for the three components of the first heading line in Figure AA-2's print chart.

The second element of the 05 entries is the PIC, which has exactly the same form you used for a print line defined in the WORKING-STORAGE SECTION.

The third element of the 05 entries designates the literal value or the data to be printed. The VALUE clause is utilized in exactly the same way you used it in the past. However, each data-item whose value will be printed must be identified by preceding its name with the reserved word SOURCE. In the three heading line definitions of Figure AA-6, you see four fields designated following the word SOURCE. Three of them—in the second heading line—define the run date as required by the print chart.

The other, PAGE-COUNTER, is a special element that illustrates one of the many features of Report Writer. It is a specific field provided by Report Writer that contains the current page number. It is both defined and tallied automatically by Report Writer.

TYPE IS DETAIL

Definition of the detail line in RPATLIST—repeated in Figure AA-7—is similar to those of the heading lines. Because the detail line must be referenced in the PROCEDURE DIVISION, a record-name—DL-DETAIL-LINE, in this case—is always required for a TYPE IS DETAIL line.

Instead of the absolute line numbers that normally apply to heading lines, relative line numbers are typically used for DETAIL lines to indicate line spacing (that is, single-, double-, and so on). Relative line numbers are coded with the reserved word PLUS. So, because the patron list detail lines must be single-spaced, LINE PLUS 1 is coded as the line number for the DETAIL line. This causes advancing of one line before each detail line is printed. Positioning of the first and last detail lines on each page is controlled by the RD entries (see lines 52 and 53 of RPATLIST in Figure AA-4).

Similar to the coding for the heading lines, each field to be printed on the detail line is coded with a level-number, a COLUMN number, a PICTURE clause, and either a SOURCE or a VALUE clause.

Although only one detail line is included in RPATLIST, there is no limit to the number of different TYPE IS DETAIL entries that may be coded under an RD.

TYPE IS CONTROL FOOTING FINAL

The last entry in RPATLIST's RD, the CONTROL FOOTING, is shown in Figure AA-8. A TYPE IS CONTROL FOOTING FINAL line is used for an end-of-report total line and is printed at the termination of the report, after all other lines are printed. Like the PAGE HEADING entry, only one TYPE IS CONTROL FOOTING FINAL entry is permitted within an RD entry. Also, like the TYPE IS PAGE HEADING entry, the FINAL total line is not usually referenced in the PROCEDURE DIVISION, so a record-name is not usually coded in the 01-level record-description entry.

Because the report-total line will be double-spaced from the last detail line, the LINE clause is coded as LINE PLUS 2.

The SUM Clause

In the detail line, you designate data-item values to be printed with the SOURCE clause. In contrast, the report summary line requires that the sum of PR-ACTUAL-CONTR for all records be printed (the report total). The SUM clause provides for this. During compilation, Report Writer creates a special data-item—called a sum counter—for each field designated by a SUM clause. At the beginning of execution, each sum counter is initialized to zero; as each input record is processed, the sum counter is automatically increased by the value in the designated field.

You can also perform a counting function using the SUM clause. For instance, assume that a count of the number of contributors was to be printed as the first of two report summary lines in RPATLIST. This is easily accomplished by inserting the code of Figure AA-9 into RPATLIST. As you can see, WA-CONSTANT-ONE is the name of a field in WORKING-STORAGE that contains a VALUE of 1.

Figure AA-7
The TYPE IS DETAIL line.

```
73        01  DL-DETAIL-LINE
74                TYPE IS DETAIL.
75            03  LINE PLUS 1.
76                05  COLUMN  1 PIC X(18)   SOURCE PR-NAME.
77                05  COLUMN 28 PIC Z,ZZ9   SOURCE PR-ACTUAL-CONTR.
```

Figure AA-8
The TYPE IS CONTROL FOOTING line.

```
79        01  TYPE IS CONTROL FOOTING FINAL.
80            03  LINE PLUS 2.
81                05  COLUMN  2 PIC X(19)   VALUE "TOTAL CONTRIBUTIONS".
82                05  COLUMN 26 PIC ZZZ,ZZ9 SUM PR-ACTUAL-CONTR.
```

Figure AA-9   Adding a counter to RPATLIST.

```
        05  WA-CONSTANT-ONE     VALUE 1.          Add this to the
                                                  WORKING-STORAGE SECTION
                                                  (following line 40) of RPATLIST.

    01  TYPE IS CONTROL FOOTING FINAL.
        03  LINE PLUS 2.
            05  COLUMN  2 PIC X(19)    VALUE "CONTRIBUTOR COUNT".
            05  COLUMN 26 PIC ZZ9      SUM WA-CONSTANT-ONE.
        03  LINE PLUS 2.
            05  COLUMN  2 PIC X(19)    VALUE "TOTAL CONTRIBUTIONS".
            05  COLUMN 26 PIC ZZZ,ZZ9 SUM PR-ACTUAL-CONTR.
                                                  Insert this entry
                                                  into the CONTROL
                                                  FOOTING definition.
```

This means that each time a detail line is printed for an employee, the sum counter for the total number of contributors is incremented by 1. When the first total line is printed, the total number of employees accumulated in this sum counter is printed.

In general, the object of the SUM clause (the identifier coded after it) must be either (1) a numeric field specified as the object of a SOURCE clause, (2) the name of a REPORT SECTION field specified with the SUM clause (that is, another sum counter), or (3) a numeric field in the FILE SECTION or the WORKING-STORAGE SECTION.

Be aware that the SUM clause can be specified only in a TYPE IS CONTROL FOOTING line. Also, a data-item that contains a SUM clause must have a numeric or a numeric-edited PICTURE.

Format for Record Definitions

The output record definitions for the RD entry includes two general formats: one for the 01-level entry and the other for data-item description entries. You should recognize most of the entries in Figure AA-10's format for the 01-level entry from the 01-level entry of RPATLIST. Most of the entries not illustrated in RPATLIST are used in remaining example programs or code segments.

The other data-item entries—levels 02–48—must conform to the format shown in Figure AA-11. As with the 01-level entry, you are already familiar with most of these elements. The UPON and RESET clauses are described in a later example.

The PROCEDURE DIVISION

Actually, there is not very much to investigate in the PROCEDURE DIVISION. Report Writer adds only five new statements. The three most commonly used are highlighted in RPATLIST's PROCEDURE DIVISION, repeated in Figure AA-12.

The INITIATE Statement

The INITIATE statement begins Report Writer processing. The INITIATE statement sets all SUM accumulators to zero and sets the variable PAGE COUNTER to 1. It also initializes to zero the variable LINE-COUNTER, a Report Writer–defined data-item in which Report Writer maintains the current-page line number.

Notice that the report file is opened just like any other file (line 91). This output file, named in the FD entry, must be opened *before* the INITIATE statement is executed.

Figure AA-10
Report Writer 01-level
report-line format.

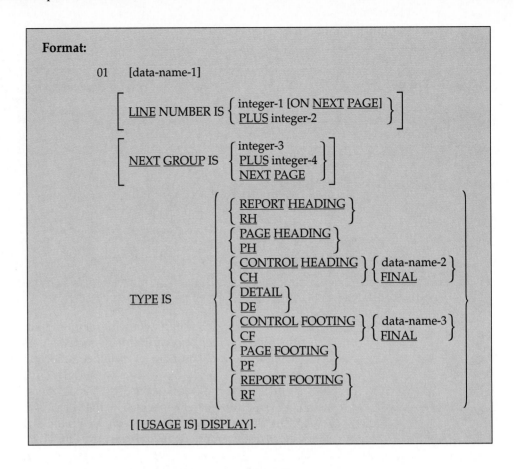

Format:

01   [data-name-1]

$$\left[\underline{LINE} \text{ NUMBER IS} \left\{ \begin{array}{l} \text{integer-1 [ON } \underline{NEXT} \underline{PAGE}] \\ \underline{PLUS} \text{ integer-2} \end{array} \right\} \right]$$

$$\left[\underline{NEXT} \underline{GROUP} \text{ IS} \left\{ \begin{array}{l} \text{integer-3} \\ \underline{PLUS} \text{ integer-4} \\ \underline{NEXT} \underline{PAGE} \end{array} \right\} \right]$$

$$\underline{TYPE} \text{ IS} \left\{ \begin{array}{l} \left\{ \begin{array}{l} \underline{REPORT} \underline{HEADING} \\ \underline{RH} \end{array} \right\} \\ \left\{ \begin{array}{l} \underline{PAGE} \underline{HEADING} \\ \underline{PH} \end{array} \right\} \\ \left\{ \begin{array}{l} \underline{CONTROL} \underline{HEADING} \\ \underline{CH} \end{array} \right\} \left\{ \begin{array}{l} \text{data-name-2} \\ \underline{FINAL} \end{array} \right\} \\ \left\{ \begin{array}{l} \underline{DETAIL} \\ \underline{DE} \end{array} \right\} \\ \left\{ \begin{array}{l} \underline{CONTROL} \underline{FOOTING} \\ \underline{CF} \end{array} \right\} \left\{ \begin{array}{l} \text{data-name-3} \\ \underline{FINAL} \end{array} \right\} \\ \left\{ \begin{array}{l} \underline{PAGE} \underline{FOOTING} \\ \underline{PF} \end{array} \right\} \\ \left\{ \begin{array}{l} \underline{REPORT} \underline{FOOTING} \\ \underline{RF} \end{array} \right\} \end{array} \right\}$$

[[<u>USAGE</u> IS] <u>DISPLAY</u>].

**The GENERATE
Statement**

The GENERATE statement causes a detail line to be written to the report. The name of the TYPE IS DETAIL line is typically coded as the object of the GENERATE verb (refer to line 117 of Figure AA-12).

When the GENERATE statement is executed, the Report Writer logic checks to see if a PAGE HEADING is required. If so, the report page is advanced and the heading lines are printed before the detail line is processed. Think back to the report programs of Chapter 7 and the detailed logic you needed. It is all controlled automatically by Report Writer.

Figure AA-11
Report Writer data-item
description format.

Format:

level-number [data-name-1]

$$\left[\underline{LINE} \text{ NUMBER IS} \left\{ \begin{array}{l} \text{integer-1 [ON } \underline{NEXT} \underline{PAGE}] \\ \underline{PLUS} \text{ integer-2} \end{array} \right\} \right]$$

$$\left[\underline{COLUMN} \text{ NUMBER IS integer-3} \right]$$

$$\left\{ \begin{array}{l} \underline{PICTURE} \\ \underline{PIC} \end{array} \right\} \text{ IS character-string}$$

$$\left\{ \begin{array}{l} \underline{SOURCE} \text{ IS identifier-1} \\ \underline{VALUE} \text{ IS literal} \\ \left\{ \underline{SUM} \text{ identifier-2 [, identifier-3]...} \right. \\ \qquad \left[\underline{UPON} \text{ data-name-2 [, data-name-3]...} \right] \right\}... \\ \qquad \left[\underline{RESET} \text{ ON} \left\{ \begin{array}{l} \text{data-name-4} \\ \underline{FINAL} \end{array} \right\} \right] \end{array} \right\}$$

Figure AA-12
The PROCEDURE
DIVISION for RPATLIST.

```
85      PROCEDURE DIVISION.
86
87      000-PRINT-PATRON-LIST.
88
89      ************Initialization Sequence************
90          OPEN INPUT PATRON-FILE
91               OUTPUT PATRON-LIST
92          INITIATE CONTRIBUTION-SUMMARY        ←
93          PERFORM 100-INITIALIZE-VARIABLE-FIELDS
94
95      **************Processing Sequence**************
96          PERFORM UNTIL S1-END-OF-FILE
97              READ PATRON-FILE INTO PR-PATRON-RECORD
98                  AT END
99                      SET S1-END-OF-FILE TO TRUE
100                 NOT AT END
101                     PERFORM 200-PROCESS-PATRON-RECORD
102             END-READ
103         END-PERFORM
104
105     **************Termination Sequence*************
106         TERMINATE CONTRIBUTION-SUMMARY       ←
107         CLOSE PATRON-FILE
108               PATRON-LIST
109         STOP RUN
110         .
111     ***********************************************
112     100-INITIALIZE-VARIABLE-FIELDS.
113         SET S1-NOT-END-OF-FILE TO TRUE
114         ACCEPT WA-CURRENT-DATE FROM DATE
115         .
116     200-PROCESS-PATRON-RECORD.
117         GENERATE DL-DETAIL-LINE              ←
118         .
```

Designates the report
file named in the
REPORT clause of
the FD.

Designates the name
of the detail line
to be printed.

In RPATLIST, the GENERATE statement is included in a separate module.
This is not necessary and was done here only to show generality. In fact, it would
be logical in this case to replace the PERFORM at line 101 with the GENERATE of
line 117, thereby eliminating the 200 module.

**The TERMINATE
Statement**

The TERMINATE statement ends Report Writer processing. Before the report file is
closed, the report must be named in a TERMINATE statement. When the TERMI-
NATE statement is executed, a FINAL control break is triggered, which causes all
TYPE CONTROL FOOTING lines to be printed (RPATLIST has only one report-
total line). After the TERMINATE statement is coded for the report, the CLOSE
statement for the report file typically follows. As a result, the mainline module for
a Report Writer program typically appears as the following:

```
OPEN files.
INITIATE report.
PERFORM initialize-variable fields.
PERFORM UNTIL end-of-file
  AT END
    SET END-OF-FILE to true
  NOT AT END
    PERFORM Process-record module.
TERMINATE report.
CLOSE files.
STOP RUN.
```

**A Single-Level
Control-Break Report**

**The RSCTLBRK
Program**

In Chapter 9, you learned how to write control-break programs—a task that was
somewhat formidable. Control-break programs using Report Writer involve relatively simple extensions of principles you already learned from RPATLIST. Almost
all of the coding revolves around defining the various record types in the DATA
DIVISION. As you will see, all control-break logic is handled automatically by
Report Writer.

The single-level control-break print chart of Chapter 9 is repeated in Figure AA-13. Recall that in the SCTLBRK program, the Sales-revenue for each input record is calculated as the product of the Unit-price and Quantity-sold.

Figure AA-14 shows the RSCTLBRK program, which uses Report Writer to produce the report. First, notice that the PROCEDURE DIVISION differs from that of RPATLIST only in the need to calculate the Sales-revenue for each sales representative (lines 167–168).

In addition to the Report Writer features used in RPATLIST for a report with end-of-report totals, this single-level control-footings report illustrates four other coding considerations:

- An additional entry in the CONTROL IS clause of the RD.

- Determination of the LAST DETAIL value (of the RD) considering footing requirements.

- Designating a control field in the TYPE IS CONTROL FOOTING clause of the 01-report-line entry.

- The NEXT GROUP clause in the 01-report-line entry.

The CONTROL IS Clause

In the RPATLIST program with end-of-report totals (Figure AA-4, page 602), CONTROL IS FINAL was specified in the RD entry. For this single-level control-break report, two control totals are required: one for each group of sales representatives and the other for the entire report. You designate this in the CONTROL IS clause by including both the reserved word FINAL and the name of the control field that triggers the break. In Figure AA-14's RSCTLBRK program, that control field is SR-SALES-REP, and so it is specified after the reserved word FINAL (see lines 71 and 72).

When a data-name is specified in the CONTROL IS clause, that field must be defined in either the FILE SECTION or in the WORKING-STORAGE SECTION. When more than one entry appears in the CONTROL IS clause, the entries must be listed in order of descending significance—that is, in major to minor sequence. So, FINAL is listed first, followed by the control field SR-SALES-REP.

Figure AA-13 Single-level sales-report print chart.

Figure AA-14   A single-level control-break program—RSCTLBRK.

```
1        IDENTIFICATION DIVISION.
2        PROGRAM-ID.  RSCTLBRK.
3
4      * Written by T. Welburn 3-27-86.
5      * Revised 3/1/95 by W. Price.
6      * PYRAMID SALES COMPANY.
7
8      * This program uses the COBOL Report Writer feature
9      * to read sales records, compute the sales
10     * revenue for each sales record, and print a sales
11     * detail line for each sales record.
12
13     * When the Sales Rep number changes, a Sales-Rep
14     * total line is printed.
15
16     * After all records are processed, a report-total line
17     * is printed.
18
19
20       ENVIRONMENT DIVISION.
21
22       INPUT-OUTPUT SECTION.
23
24       FILE-CONTROL.
25           SELECT SALES-FILE
26               ASSIGN TO (system dependent).
27
28           SELECT SALES-REPORT-FILE
29               ASSIGN TO (system dependent).
30
31
32       DATA DIVISION.
33
34       FILE SECTION.
35
36       FD  SALES-FILE.
37       01  SALES-RECORD.
38           05  PIC X(48).
39
40       FD  SALES-REPORT-FILE
41           REPORT IS SALES-REPORT.
42
43       WORKING-STORAGE SECTION.
44
45       01  PROGRAM-SWITCHES.
46           05  S1-END-OF-FILE-SWITCH     PIC X(1).
47               88  S1-END-OF-FILE            VALUE "E".
48               88  S1-NOT-END-OF-FILE        VALUE "N".
49
50       01  WA-WORK-AREAS.
51           05  WA-RUN-DATE.
52               10  WA-RUN-YEAR       PIC 9(2).
53               10  WA-RUN-MONTH      PIC 9(2).
54               10  WA-RUN-DAY        PIC 9(2).
55           05  WA-SALES-REVENUE      PIC S9(5)V99.
56
57       01  SR-SALES-RECORD.
58           05  SR-RECORD-CODE        PIC X(2).
59           05  SR-STATE              PIC X(2).
60           05  SR-BRANCH             PIC X(3).
61           05  SR-SALES-REP          PIC X(5).
62           05  SR-DATE-OF-SALE       PIC X(6).
63           05  SR-PRODUCT-CODE       PIC X(7).
64           05  SR-PRODUCT-DESCRIPTION PIC X(16).
65           05  SR-QUANTITY-SOLD      PIC S9(3).
66           05  SR-UNIT-PRICE         PIC 9(2)V99.
67
68       REPORT SECTION.
69
70       RD  SALES-REPORT
71           CONTROL IS FINAL
72                     SR-SALES-REP
73           PAGE LIMIT IS 66 LINES
74           FIRST DETAIL 10
75           LAST DETAIL   57.
76
77       01  TYPE IS PAGE HEADING.
78           03  LINE 4.
79               05  COLUMN  1 PIC X(21) VALUE "PYRAMID SALES COMPANY".
80               05  COLUMN 71 PIC X(4)  VALUE "PAGE".
81               05  COLUMN 76 PIC ZZZ9  SOURCE PAGE-COUNTER.
82
83           03  LINE 5.
84               05  COLUMN  1 PIC X(37)
85                       VALUE "SALES REPORT - SEQUENCED BY SALES REP".
86               05  COLUMN 72 PIC Z9   SOURCE WA-RUN-MONTH.
87               05  COLUMN 74 PIC X(1) VALUE "/".
88               05  COLUMN 75 PIC 9(2) SOURCE WA-RUN-DAY.
89               05  COLUMN 77 PIC X(1) VALUE "/".
90               05  COLUMN 78 PIC 9(2) SOURCE WA-RUN-YEAR.
91
92           03  LINE 7.
93               05  COLUMN  1 PIC X(5)  VALUE "SALES".
94               05  COLUMN 23 PIC X(25)
95                       VALUE "DATE    PRODUCT     PRODUCT".
96               05  COLUMN 59 PIC X(20) VALUE "UNIT QTY.      SALES".
97
98           03  LINE 8.
99               05  COLUMN  1 PIC X(35)
100                      VALUE "REP. STATE BRANCH  OF SALE   CODE".
101              05  COLUMN 40 PIC X(40)
102                      VALUE "DESCRIPTION      PRICE   SOLD    REVENUE".
103
104      01  DL-DETAIL-LINE
105          TYPE IS DETAIL.
106          LINE IS PLUS 1.
107          05  COLUMN  1 PIC X(5)      SOURCE SR-SALES-REP.
108          05  COLUMN  9 PIC X(2)      SOURCE SR-STATE.
109          05  COLUMN 15 PIC X(3)      SOURCE SR-BRANCH.
110          05  COLUMN 21 PIC XX/XX/XX  SOURCE SR-DATE-OF-SALE.
111          05  COLUMN 31 PIC X(7)      SOURCE SR-PRODUCT-CODE.
112          05  COLUMN 40 PIC X(16)     SOURCE SR-PRODUCT-DESCRIPTION.
113          05  COLUMN 58 PIC ZZ.99     SOURCE SR-UNIT-PRICE.
114          05  COLUMN 65 PIC ZZ9-      SOURCE SR-QUANTITY-SOLD.
115          05  COLUMN 71 PIC ZZ.ZZZ.99- SOURCE WA-SALES-REVENUE.
116
117      01  ST-SALES-REP-TOTAL-LINE
118          TYPE IS CONTROL FOOTING SR-SALES-REP.
119          LINE IS PLUS 2.
120          NEXT GROUP IS PLUS 2.
121          05  COLUMN  1 PIC X(5)         SOURCE SR-SALES-REP.
122          05  COLUMN 34 PIC X(16)        VALUE "SALES REP. TOTAL".
123          05  COLUMN 70 PIC ZZZ,ZZZ.99- SUM WA-SALES-REVENUE.
124          05  COLUMN 81 PIC X(1)         VALUE "*".
125
126      01  RT-REPORT-TOTAL-LINE
127          TYPE IS CONTROL FOOTING FINAL.
128          LINE IS PLUS 3.
129          05  COLUMN 51 PIC X(12)        VALUE "REPORT TOTAL".
130          05  COLUMN 68 PIC Z,ZZZ,ZZZ.99- SUM WA-SALES-REVENUE.
131          05  COLUMN 81 PIC X(2)         VALUE "**".
132
133
134      PROCEDURE DIVISION.
135
136      000-PRINT-SALES REPORT.
137
138      ************Initialization Sequence************
139          OPEN INPUT SALES-FILE
140               OUTPUT SALES-REPORT-FILE
141          INITIATE SALES REPORT
142          PERFORM 100-INITIALIZE-VARIABLE-FIELDS
143
144      *************Processing Sequence*************
145          PERFORM UNTIL S1-END-OF-FILE
146              READ SALES-FILE INTO SR-SALES-RECORD
147                  AT END
148                      SET S1-END-OF-FILE TO TRUE
149                  NOT AT END
150                      PERFORM 200-PROCESS-DETAIL-RECORD
151              END-READ
152          END-PERFORM
153
154      **************Termination Sequence************
155          TERMINATE SALES-REPORT
156          CLOSE SALES-FILE
157                SALES-REPORT-FILE
158          STOP RUN
159          .
160      ************************************************
161
162      100-INITIALIZE-VARIABLE-FIELDS.
163          SET S1-NOT-END-OF-FILE TO TRUE
164          ACCEPT WA-RUN-DATE FROM DATE
165          .
166      200-PROCESS-DETAIL-RECORD.
167          MULTIPLY SR-UNIT-PRICE BY SR-QUANTITY-SOLD
168              GIVING WA-SALES-REVENUE
169          GENERATE DL-DETAIL-LINE
170          .
```

The LAST DETAIL Clause

The line number you designate for the last detail line of the page determines the beginning of the footing area. So, you need to do some simple arithmetic to determine its position. Referring to Figure AA-13, this report has the following bottom-of-page needs:

Sales rep total	2 (including 1 blank)
Report total	3 (including 2 blanks)
Bottom margin	4 (an arbitrary choice)
Total	9
Last detail line is	$66 - 9 = 57$

As you see, the size of the footing area and the bottom margin are determined implicitly by the designation of the last detail line number and the number of summary lines printed. The value 57 provides sufficient space to ensure that summary lines are never printed at the top of a new page if the last detail line on a page is also the last line for a control group. So, for each page of the report, the last printed line is on line 57 unless it contains the last line of a control group—in which case, the sales-representative control total will be on line 59 and (if the last page) the report total will be on line 62.

The TYPE IS CONTROL FOOTING Data-Name Option

Corresponding to each entry in the CONTROL clause of the RD, one TYPE IS CONTROL FOOTING record must be defined. RSCTLBRK includes one 01 record for the report total (lines 126–131) and one for the sales-rep breaks (lines 117–124). Here you see that each of these records is given a record-name (lines 117 and 126). Recall from your study of RPATLIST that these control footing records are not referenced in the PROCEDURE DIVISION, so they do not need to be named. Names are included here—and in the next example—merely for documentation value. Otherwise, the FINAL footing record is identical in form to that of RPATLIST.

The sales representative total line differs in two respects: the inclusion of the control field and the NEXT GROUP clause.

The field of the input record that triggers the control break must be specified as the data-name. In the RSCTLBRK report, the SR-SALES-REP field is the control field. So, in line 118, TYPE IS CONTROL FOOTING SR-SALES-REP is specified for the ST-SALES-REP-TOTAL-LINE. (The data-name must match a field specified in the CONTROL IS clause of the RD entry.)

The NEXT GROUP Clause

Refer to the print chart of Figure AA-13 and you will see that the sales-rep group total line is followed by two blank lines before the next detail line is printed.

This spacing is achieved with the NEXT GROUP clause, which is specified on the 01-level control-total footing line (program line 120 of RSCTLBRK). A value of PLUS 2 is specified in the RSCTLBRK program. This causes double-spacing after the control-total footing line is printed, resulting in one blank line. Then printing the next detail line (which includes LINE IS PLUS 1) causes a second blank line to be inserted before the detail is printed.

Detailed Actions of Report Writer

Recall from Chapter 9 that you must program the following actions to process a record when writing a single-level control-break program:

1. Compare the value of the control field to the control-field value from the preceding record.
2. If the control-field values are the same:
   a. Check to determine if the page is full. If it is, progress to a new page and print report headings.
   b. Format and print the detail line.
   c. Add the fields to be totaled to their corresponding accumulators.

3. If the control-field values are different:
    a. Print the control-total line.
    b. Initialize appropriate control-total fields.

All of these actions are carried out automatically by Report Writer when the GENERATE statement is executed. No PROCEDURE DIVISION coding is required to produce the control breaks. This is indeed a powerful feature.

A Multiple-Level Control-Break Report

The second program from Chapter 9, the multiple-level MCTLBRK, produces a report grouped by sales representative, within branch, within state. The sales report format is repeated in Figure AA-15. Interestingly, the Report Writer program to produce this report is a relatively simple extension of RSCTLBRK. In fact, the changes are confined to the RD, as Figure AA-16 shows. (This RD is taken from the program RMCTLBRK, stored on the diskette that accompanies this book.)

In addition to the Report Writer features just covered for a single-level control-break report, a multiple-level control-break report has three other significant coding considerations: (1) the sequence of data-names in the CONTROL IS clause, (2) the arrangement of 01-level lines in the REPORT SECTION, and (3) the rolling of totals.

The RD Entry

Because RMCTLBRK is a three-level control-break program with end-of-report totals, the reserved word FINAL plus the three control fields—SR-STATE, SR-BRANCH, and SR-SALES-REP—are specified in the CONTROL IS clause (lines 71–74). Remember that the control fields must be listed in order of decreasing significance—that is, in major to minor field sequence. So, FINAL is specified first and the minor field—SR-SALES-REP—is coded last.

Figure AA-15 Multiple-level sales-report print chart.

Figure AA-16 The RD entry from the multiple-level control-break program RMCTLBRK.

```
68    REPORT SECTION.                                    114   01  DL-DETAIL-LINE
69                                                       115           TYPE IS DETAIL
70    RD  SALES-REPORT                                   116           LINE IS PLUS 1.
71        CONTROL IS FINAL                               117           05  COLUMN   2  PIC X(2)     SOURCE SR-STATE.
72                    SR-STATE                           118           05  COLUMN   8  PIC X(3)     SOURCE SR-BRANCH.
73                    SR-BRANCH                          119           05  COLUMN  14  PIC X(5)     SOURCE SR-SALES-REP.
74                    SR-SALES-REP                       120           05  COLUMN  21  PIC XX/XX/XX SOURCE SR-DATE-OF-SALE.
75        PAGE LIMIT IS 66 LINES                         121           05  COLUMN  31  PIC X(7)     SOURCE SR-PRODUCT-CODE.
76            FIRST DETAIL 10                            122           05  COLUMN  40  PIC X(16)    SOURCE SR-PRODUCT-DESCRIPTION.
77            LAST DETAIL  54.                           123           05  COLUMN  58  PIC ZZ.99    SOURCE SR-UNIT-PRICE.
78                                                       124           05  COLUMN  65  PIC ZZ9-     SOURCE SR-QUANTITY-SOLD.
79    01  TYPE IS PAGE HEADING.                          125           05  COLUMN  71  PIC ZZ,ZZZ.99- SOURCE WA-SALES-REVENUE.
80        03  LINE 4.                                    126
81            05  COLUMN  1  PIC X(21) VALUE "PYRAMID SALES COMPANY".   127   01  ST-SALES-REP-TOTAL-LINE
82            05  COLUMN 71  PIC X(4)  VALUE "PAGE".     128           TYPE IS CONTROL FOOTING SR-SALES-REP
83            05  COLUMN 76  PIC ZZZ9  SOURCE PAGE COUNTER.   129           LINE IS PLUS 2
84                                                       130           NEXT GROUP IS PLUS 2.
85        03  LINE 5.                                    131           05  COLUMN   2   PIC X(2)      SOURCE SR-STATE.
86            05  COLUMN  1  PIC X(37)                   132           05  COLUMN   8   PIC X(3)      SOURCE SR-BRANCH.
87                    VALUE "SALES REPORT - SEQUENCED BY SALES REP".   133           05  COLUMN  14   PIC X(5)      SOURCE SR-SALES-REP.
88            05  COLUMN 72  PIC Z9    SOURCE WA-RUN-MONTH.   134           05  COLUMN  34   PIC X(16)     VALUE "SALES REP. TOTAL".
89            05  COLUMN 74  PIC X(1)  VALUE "/".        135           05  COLUMN  70   PIC ZZZ,ZZZ.99- SUM WA-SALES-REVENUE.
90            05  COLUMN 75  PIC 9(2)  SOURCE WA-RUN-DAY.   136           05  COLUMN  81   PIC X(1)      VALUE "*".
91            05  COLUMN 77  PIC X(1)  VALUE "/".        137
92            05  COLUMN 78  PIC 9(2)  SOURCE WA-RUN-YEAR.   138   01  BT-BRANCH-TOTAL-LINE
93                                                       139           TYPE IS CONTROL FOOTING SR-BRANCH
94        03  LINE 7.                                    140           LINE IS PLUS 2
95            05  COLUMN 14  PIC X(5)  VALUE "SALES".    141           NEXT GROUP IS PLUS 2.
96            05  COLUMN 23  PIC X(4)  VALUE "DATE".     142           05  COLUMN   2   PIC X(2)      SOURCE SR-STATE.
97            05  COLUMN 31  PIC X(7)  VALUE "PRODUCT".  143           05  COLUMN   8   PIC X(3)      SOURCE SR-BRANCH.
98            05  COLUMN 42  PIC X(7)  VALUE "PRODUCT".  144           05  COLUMN  38   PIC X(12)     VALUE "BRANCH TOTAL".
99            05  COLUMN 59  PIC X(4)  VALUE "UNIT".     145           05  ST-SALES-REP-TOTAL
100           05  COLUMN 65  PIC X(3)  VALUE "QTY".      146               COLUMN  70   PIC ZZZ,ZZZ.99- SUM WA-SALES-REVENUE.
101           05  COLUMN 74  PIC X(5)  VALUE "SALES".    147           05  COLUMN  81   PIC X(2)      VALUE "**".
102                                                      148
103       03  LINE 8.                                    149   01  TT-STATE-TOTAL-LINE
104           05  COLUMN  1  PIC X(5)  VALUE "STATE".    150           TYPE IS CONTROL FOOTING SR-STATE
105           05  COLUMN  7  PIC X(6)  VALUE "BRANCH".   151           LINE IS PLUS 2
106           05  COLUMN 15  PIC X(3)  VALUE "REP".      152           NEXT GROUP IS PLUS 2.
107           05  COLUMN 22  PIC X(7)  VALUE "OF SALE".  153           05  COLUMN   2   PIC X(2)      SOURCE SR-STATE.
108           05  COLUMN 33  PIC X(4)  VALUE "CODE".     154           05  COLUMN  39   PIC X(11)     VALUE "STATE TOTAL".
109           05  COLUMN 40  PIC X(11) VALUE "DESCRIPTION".   155           05  TT-STATE-TOTAL
110           05  COLUMN 58  PIC X(5)  VALUE "PRICE".    156               COLUMN  70   PIC ZZZ,ZZZ.99- SUM ST-SALES-REP-TOTAL.
111           05  COLUMN 65  PIC X(4)  VALUE "SOLD".     157           05  COLUMN  81   PIC X(3)      VALUE "***".
112           05  COLUMN 73  PIC X(7)  VALUE "REVENUE".  158
113                                                      159   01  RT-REPORT-TOTAL-LINE
                                                         160           TYPE IS CONTROL FOOTING FINAL
                                                         161           LINE IS PLUS 3.
                                                         162           05  COLUMN 51  PIC X(12)      VALUE "REPORT TOTAL".
                                                         163           05  COLUMN 68  PIC Z,ZZZ,ZZZ.99- SUM TT-STATE-TOTAL.
                                                         164           05  COLUMN 81  PIC X(4)       VALUE "****".
```

The allowance for a footing area is like that of RSCTLBRK, except that the footing must provide for the possibility of eight footing lines (refer to Figure AA-15). This requirement exists if the last detail line of the report falls on the last allowable detail line of the form. It requires the entry LAST DETAIL 54 to maintain a minimum four-line bottom margin.

Generation of Control Footing Lines

When the GENERATE statement is executed for a detail line, Report Writer first checks the control fields—as listed in the CONTROL IS clause—in major to minor sequence. When a control break is detected, the control footing lines are generated before the detail line is printed. The control footing lines are printed in minor to major sequence up to the level at which the control break occurred. That is, when a branch control break happens, the sales-rep control footing line is printed, then the branch control footing line is printed. After that, the detail line for the record that triggered the control break—the first detail line for the next control group— is printed.

As you can see in Figure AA-16, the control-total 01-level records are included in minor to major order (sales-rep total record first and the report-total record last). As in Chapter 9, their physical order has no bearing on the actual processing sequence; the CONTROL IS clause of the RD entry determines the printing order of the total lines.

Rolling the Totals

For simplicity in the single-level RSCTLBRK program, the WA-SALES-REVENUE field was used to increment both the sales-rep-total and the report-total sales-revenue fields—refer to lines 123 and 130 of RSCTLBRK (Figure AA-14, page 611). A more common practice is to add the contents of a given level accumulator to the next control-level accumulator when a control break occurs. For instance, in the MCTLBRK program (Figure 9-17, page 305), the following occurs:

1. With each record, the calculated field WA-SALES-REVENUE is added to the Sales-rep accumulator TA-TOTAL-SALES-REP-ACCUM (line 201 of MCTLBRK).
2. When a Sales-rep break occurs, TA-TOTAL-SALES-REP-ACCUM is added to the branch accumulator TA-TOTAL-BRANCH-ACCUM (line 258 of MCTLBRK).
3. A similar action occurs for the Branch break (line 274) and the State break (line 290).

This technique, called rolling the totals, is employed in RMCTLBRK. To provide for it, a data-name must be assigned to each sum counter. For instance, consider the following code (lines 145–146 of Figure AA-16):

```
05  ST-SALES-REP-TOTAL
        COLUMN  70    PIC ZZZ,ZZZ.99-   SUM WA-SALES-REVENUE.
```

This entry defines the accumulator field ST-SALES-REP-TOTAL; it will serve as the accumulator for the WA-SALES-REVENUE values as each data record is processed. Then that accumulator is used as the sum field for the next higher-level accumulator—the branch (lines 155–156 of Figure AA-16):

```
05  TT-STATE-TOTAL
        COLUMN  70    PIC ZZZ,ZZZ.99-   SUM ST-SALES-REP-TOTAL.
```

In other words, each higher-level sum counter references the field with the SUM clause at its immediately lower level. So, after each line is printed, the total field is added to the next higher level and the printed total is zeroed. You may want to review MCTLBRK in Chapter 9 (Figure 9-17); the accumulator names here are identical to those used in MCTLBRK.

Regarding the assignment of names to data-items in the REPORT SECTION, you should recognize that a data-name can be assigned to any of the group or elementary items (refer to the formats of Figures AA-10 and AA-11, page 608). Few entries require names, however.

Other Report Writer Facilities

The HEADING and FOOTING Phrases of the PAGE Clause

Referring to the general form of the RD (Figure AA-5, page 603), you see two phrases not used in the example programs of this chapter: HEADING and FOOT-ING. The HEADING phrase designates the first line on which headings can be printed. If, for instance, you included a heading phrase in RMCTLBRK, you would code:

```
HEADING 4
```

However, in all three example programs, inclusion of this phrase would be redundant because the line number for the first heading line is explicitly indicated in each record definition. For example, refer to program line 80 of Figure AA-16, where you see the entry LINE 4.

The FOOTING phrase designates the last line on which a footing line is allowed to be printed. In, for instance, RMCTLBRK, you might include FOOTING 62, which tells Report Writer that no footing line is allowed beyond line 62. However, this limit is implicit from the establishment of line 54 as the last detail line and the inclusion of up to eight summary lines. Although not evident from the examples in this appendix, the FOOTING phrase is useful in certain instances. However, in this appendix's programs, the phrase is of little value.

The RESET ON Clause

Sum counters are normally zeroed after they are printed. Sometimes, however, cumulative (running) totals are required. Figure AA-17 shows an example of the single-level sales report with cumulative sales-revenue totals printed on each control footing line.

To override the automatic zeroing of sum counters, the RESET ON clause is specified after the SUM clause. Its format is shown in Figure AA-18. The identifier field must be a field (or the reserved word FINAL) named in a CONTROL IS clause. The identifier field must be a higher level of control to—that is, major to—the group in which the RESET ON clause is coded.

The GROUP INDICATE Clause

Group indication is used to enhance the readability of a report by eliminating repeated fields from adjacent report lines. When group indication is applied to a field, that field is printed only on the first detail line after a control break and on the first detail line of a new page. Figure AA-19 provides an example of the single-level sales report with group indication of the sales representative number.

Figure AA-17   Example of single-level sales report with cumulative totals.

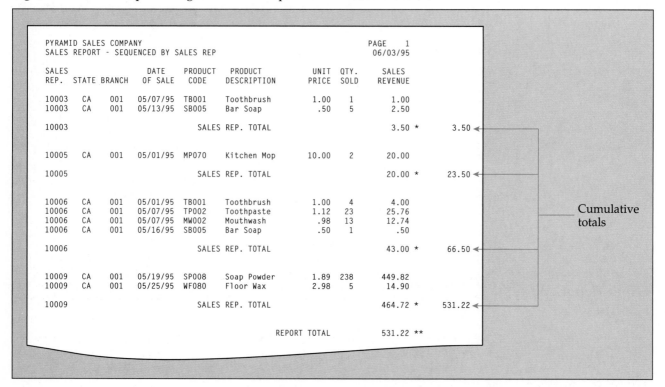

Figure AA-18
RESET ON clause format.

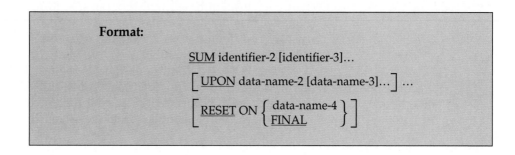

Figure AA-19   Single-level report group indication.

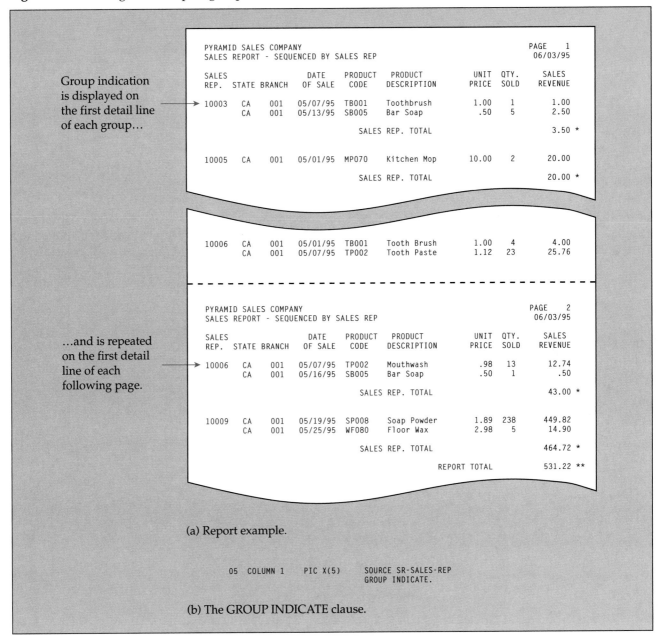

(a) Report example.

```
05  COLUMN 1    PIC X(5)    SOURCE SR-SALES-REP
                            GROUP INDICATE.
```

(b) The GROUP INDICATE clause.

The Report Writer GROUP INDICATE clause provides this group indication. It can be specified only with elementary fields within a TYPE IS DETAIL line.

A Report with TYPE IS CONTROL HEADING Lines

Control heading lines are sometimes also used to enhance the readability of control-break reports. Figure AA-20 shows an example of a control heading line for each sales rep in the single-level sales report. Control headings are sometimes used when it is necessary to conserve horizontal space on a report line; the control fields can thus be omitted from the detail line. The extra heading lines increase vertical line-space requirements, however.

The code necessary to produce these control heading lines is shown in Figure AA-20(b). Like a control footing line, the identifier specified as the SOURCE (SR-SALES-REP, in this case) must be either a field named in the CONTROL IS clause or the reserved word FINAL.

Figure AA-20   Using control headings.

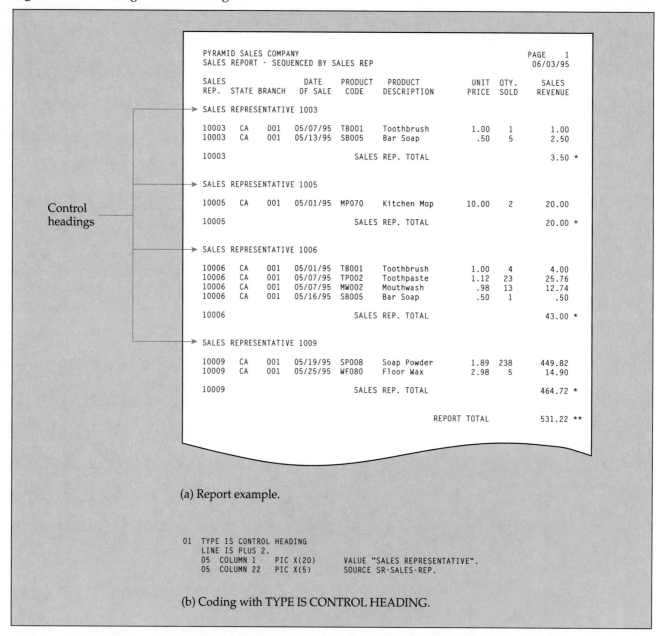

Control
headings

```
        PYRAMID SALES COMPANY                                          PAGE   1
        SALES REPORT - SEQUENCED BY SALES REP                          06/03/95

        SALES                  DATE    PRODUCT   PRODUCT           UNIT  QTY.    SALES
        REP.   STATE BRANCH   OF SALE  CODE      DESCRIPTION       PRICE SOLD   REVENUE

        SALES REPRESENTATIVE 1003

        10003   CA    001    05/07/95  TB001     Toothbrush        1.00   1      1.00
        10003   CA    001    05/13/95  SB005     Bar Soap           .50   5      2.50

        10003                                    SALES REP. TOTAL                3.50 *


        SALES REPRESENTATIVE 1005

        10005   CA    001    05/01/95  MP070     Kitchen Mop      10.00   2     20.00

        10005                                    SALES REP. TOTAL               20.00 *


        SALES REPRESENTATIVE 1006

        10006   CA    001    05/01/95  TB001     Toothbrush        1.00   4      4.00
        10006   CA    001    05/07/95  TP002     Toothpaste        1.12  23     25.76
        10006   CA    001    05/07/95  MW002     Mouthwash          .98  13     12.74
        10006   CA    001    05/16/95  SB005     Bar Soap           .50   1       .50

        10006                                    SALES REP. TOTAL               43.00 *


        SALES REPRESENTATIVE 1009

        10009   CA    001    05/19/95  SP008     Soap Powder       1.89 238    449.82
        10009   CA    001    05/25/95  WF080     Floor Wax         2.98   5     14.90

        10009                                    SALES REP. TOTAL              464.72 *


                                                 REPORT TOTAL                  531.22 **
```

(a) Report example.

```
01  TYPE IS CONTROL HEADING
    LINE IS PLUS 2.
    05  COLUMN 1     PIC X(20)      VALUE "SALES REPRESENTATIVE".
    05  COLUMN 22    PIC X(5)       SOURCE SR-SALES-REP.
```

(b) Coding with TYPE IS CONTROL HEADING.

The printing of control heading lines is triggered by the execution of the GENERATE statement. When a control break occurs, the control heading lines are printed—in major to minor order—after the control footing lines for the previous group and before the detail line for the current record. Control heading lines are also printed before the first detail line of the report is generated.

A Report with TYPE IS REPORT HEADING Lines

Often a report heading describing the report is printed at the beginning of the report, usually on a separate page preceding the detail output. This is accomplished with the TYPE IS REPORT HEADING clause, as illustrated by Figure AA-21's example for RMCTLBRK. Here you can see that the various printed lines are defined in the same way as heading lines by using the LINE and COLUMN phrases to designate their positions. The printed output for this specification appears as shown in Figure AA-21(b). Including the NEXT GROUP IS NEXT PAGE clause in the 01 causes printing of the report itself to begin on the next page. So this report heading is printed by itself on the first page of the report.

Other Types of Report Writer Lines

Recall from Figure AA-10's general format for the 01-level Report Writer entry (page 608) that the TYPE IS clause allows for seven options. You have seen five of them in this appendix: REPORT HEADING, PAGE HEADING, CONTROL HEADING, DETAIL, and CONTROL FOOTING. Report Writer also provides for two additional—less frequently used—types of report lines:

- TYPE IS PAGE FOOTING
- TYPE IS REPORT FOOTING

TYPE IS PAGE FOOTING allows you to print at the end of each page. It is sometimes used for footing descriptions, page numbers, and page totals. However, if you intend to print page totals, remember that the SUM clause (for accumulating) can only be used with TYPE IS CONTROL FOOTING; it cannot be used with TYPE IS PAGE FOOTING. So, to print page totals, you must define appropriate accumulators in the WORKING-STORAGE SECTION and include necessary program logic in the PROCEDURE DIVISION.

A TYPE IS REPORT FOOTING line is printed at the end of a report, after all other lines. REPORT FOOTING lines are used for legends and other report-ending material. Report Writer allows a report footing to be printed in the bottom margin of the report (as indicated by the line number values in the RD for the FOOTING and PAGE phrases).

A Report with Summary Group-Printed Lines

A summary, or group-printed, line represents an accumulation of detail records. Summary lines are used to shorten the length of reports when the individual detail-entry information is not required.

A control footing line is, in effect, a summary line. Figure AA-22(a) shows the single-level sales report printed without detail lines as an example of a summary report.

Figure AA-21
The TYPE IS REPORT HEADING.

```
01  TYPE IS REPORT HEADING
    NEXT GROUP IS NEXT PAGE.
    03  LINE 15  COLUMN 30
                 PIC X(21) VALUE "PYRAMID SALES COMPANY".
    03  LINE PLUS 1 COLUMN 30
                 PIC X(21) VALUE "*********************".
    03  LINE PLUS 2 COLUMN 33
                 PIC X(16) VALUE "SALES REPORT--A5".
    03  LINE PLUS 3 COLUMN 30
                 PIC X(21) VALUE "SUBTOTALS PRINTED FOR".
    03  LINE PLUS 1 COLUMN 29
                 PIC X(24) VALUE "SALES REP, BRANCH, STATE".
    03  LINE PLUS 2
        05  COLUMN 30  PIC X(12)  VALUE "REPORT DATE:".
        05  COLUMN 44  PIC Z9     SOURCE WA-RUN-MONTH.
        05  COLUMN 46  PIC X(1)   VALUE "/".
        05  COLUMN 47  PIC 9(2)   SOURCE WA-RUN-DAY.
        05  COLUMN 49  PIC X(1)   VALUE "/".
        05  COLUMN 50  PIC 9(2)   SOURCE WA-RUN-YEAR.
```

(a) Report Writer coding.

```
              PYRAMID SALES COMPANY
              *********************

                SALES REPORT--A5

              SUBTOTALS PRINTED FOR
              SALES REP, BRANCH, STATE

              REPORT DATE:  06/03/95
```

(b) Report example.

Figure AA-22
Printing a summary report.

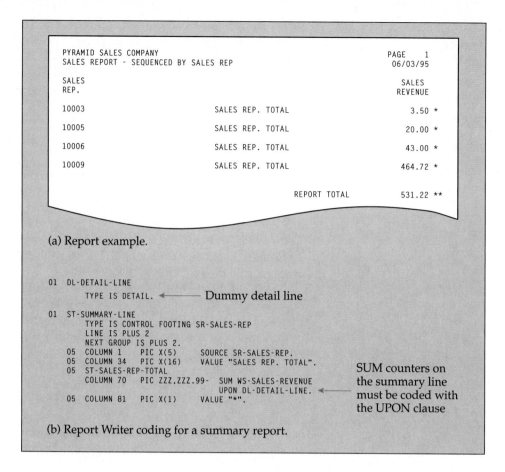

(a) Report example.

```
01  DL-DETAIL-LINE
        TYPE IS DETAIL.  ◄——— Dummy detail line

01  ST-SUMMARY-LINE
        TYPE IS CONTROL FOOTING SR-SALES-REP
        LINE IS PLUS 2
        NEXT GROUP IS PLUS 2.
    05  COLUMN 1    PIC X(5)     SOURCE SR-SALES-REP.
    05  COLUMN 34   PIC X(16)    VALUE "SALES REP. TOTAL".
    05  ST-SALES-REP-TOTAL
        COLUMN 70   PIC ZZZ,ZZZ.99-   SUM WS-SALES-REVENUE
                                      UPON DL-DETAIL-LINE.  ◄———
    05  COLUMN 81   PIC X(1)     VALUE "*".
```

SUM counters on the summary line must be coded with the UPON clause

(b) Report Writer coding for a summary report.

In order to accomplish the printing of summary lines without detail lines, a dummy, or null, TYPE IS DETAIL line must be coded. The dummy entry is required because incrementing the SUM counter is triggered by detail-line generation.

Figure AA-22(b) shows the coding that produces a summary report. A dummy TYPE IS DETAIL line contains only the record-name—DL-DETAIL-LINE—and the TYPE IS DETAIL entry. No printing action occurs because no LINE clause, no fields, and no COLUMN clauses are coded.

Sum counters to be incremented for each detail item must be coded with the UPON clause as shown.

The USE BEFORE REPORTING Statement

Sometimes, it is necessary to execute a routine before a certain report line is printed. Examples of such situations are (1) a table lookup before a control heading line is printed, (2) arithmetic calculations other than summation that must be performed on a line, and (3) the need to count the number of control groups.

Suppose you want to count the number of sales representatives printed on the single-level sales report and to print the total on the end-of-report total line. The easiest way to do this is to count the number of control breaks that occur. This is done with the USE BEFORE REPORTING statement, as Figure AA-23 illustrates.

As you can see, the USE BEFORE REPORTING statement is coded in the DECLARATIVES area of the PROCEDURE DIVISION. (As described in Chapter 15, the DECLARATIVES must physically precede the rest of the PROCEDURE DIVISION.) After the reserved words USE BEFORE REPORTING, the name of the total line that will be accessed is coded.

Actually, the statement does exactly as the English suggests. That is, you can read it as: "USE this procedure BEFORE REPORTING (printing) the group-total line ST-SALES-REP-TOTAL-LINE." So, during execution, whenever a sales-rep control break occurs and before the total line is printed, the procedure is executed. Because the number of sales representatives is the same as the number of control groups, the desired result is achieved.

In the program logic, the field WA-NBR-SALES-REPS, defined in WORKING-STORAGE, is incremented. Then, in the FINAL total line, the WA-NBR-SALES-REPS fields is coded as the object of a SOURCE clause.

Be aware that a TYPE IS DETAIL line cannot be referenced in the USE BEFORE REPORTING statement. However, this restriction causes no problems. Detail-processing routines are handled in the regular PROCEDURE DIVISION coding between the READ statement and its following GENERATE statement.

Figure AA-23   The USE BEFORE REPORTING statement.

```
                              DATA DIVISION.
                                 :
                                 :

                              WORKING-STORAGE SECTION
                                 :
                                 :

                                05  WA-NBR-SALES-REPS   PIC S9(4)     VALUE ZERO.
                                 :
                                 :

                              REPORT SECTION.
                                 :
                                 :

                              01  ST-SALES-REP-TOTAL-LINE
                                      TYPE IS CONTROL FOOTING SR-SALES-REP
                                      LINE IS PLUS 2
                                      NEXT GROUP IS PLUS 2
                                    05  COLUMN 1   PIC X(5)     SOURCE SR-SALES-REP.
                                    05  COLUMN 34  PIC X(16)    VALUE "SALES REP. TOTAL".
                                    05  ST-SALES-REP-TOTAL
                                        COLUMN 70  PIC ZZZ,ZZZ.99- SUM WA-SALES-REVENUE.
                                    05  COLUMN 81  PIC X(1)     VALUE "*".

                              01  RT-REPORT-TOTAL-LINE.
                                      TYPE IS CONTROL FOOTING FINAL
                                      LINE IS PLUS 3.
                                    05  COLUMN 13  PIC ZZZ9     SOURCE WA-NBR-SALES-REPS.
                                    05  COLUMN 23  PIC X(10)    VALUE "SALES REPS".
                                    05  COLUMN 51  PIC X(12)    VALUE "REPORT TOTAL".
                                    05  COLUMN 63  PIC Z,ZZZ,ZZZ.99- SUM WS-SALES-REVENUE.
                                    05  COLUMN 81  PIC X(2)     VALUE "**".

                              PROCEDURE DIVISION.

                              DECLARATIVES.

                              TALLY-SALES-REPS SECTION.
                                  USE BEFORE REPORTING ST-SALES-REP-TOTAL-LINE.
                                 :
                                 :

                              D010-COUNT-EACH-SALES-REP.
                                  ADD 1 TO WA-NBR-SALES-REPS
                                 .

                              END DECLARATIVES.

                              000-PRINT-SALES-REPORT.
                                 :
                                 :
```

Add these two entries for the sales-rep count in the total line.

This 01 data-name is designated in the USE BEFORE REPORTING statement.

DECLARATIVES must be at the beginning of the PROCEDURE DIVISION.

Modules must be formed as SECTIONs within DECLARATIVES.

END DECLARATIVES must terminate DECLARATIVES.

Appendix Summary

**DATA DIVISION—
FILE SECTION**

The REPORT IS clause is coded in the FD entry to name the report file.

**DATA DIVISION—
REPORT SECTION**

An RD (report-description) entry is coded in the REPORT SECTION for each report file named in an FD entry. The RD-name must match the report-name specified in the FD. The RD entry contains two clauses: CONTROL IS and PAGE LIMIT.

The CONTROL IS clause specifies control-break hierarchies within the report. Control fields (including the reserved word FINAL) must be listed in major to minor sequence.

The PAGE LIMIT clause identifies line-span parameters. It is recommended that the value entered after the reserved words PAGE LIMIT corresponds to the physical length of the printed form. The HEADING entry specifies the line number at which the report headings will begin; in this appendix's examples, it is redundant because of line numbers associated with the first heading line. The FIRST DETAIL entry specifies the first line number at which the first detail line is printed. The LAST DETAIL entry specifies the last line number at which a detail line is printed on each page. The FOOTING entry specifies the last line number at which a CONTROL FOOTING line is printed. It is not needed in this appendix's examples.

One 01-level report entry must be coded for each required report line.

The LINE clause specifies the vertical line-spacing requirements. It can be included at either the group level or the elementary level. The LINE clause can be coded with either (1) an absolute line number or (2) a relative line number through specification of the reserved words LINE IS PLUS.

The COLUMN clause specifies the horizontal line positioning for each field to be printed.

The VALUE clause stores constant data into a REPORT SECTION field. To place variable data into a REPORT SECTION field, either a SOURCE or a SUM clause is specified.

The SOURCE clause requires specification of either (1) the name of a field or (2) the reserved word PAGE-COUNTER, which is a special Report Writer field that keeps track of the page number.

The SUM clause causes Report Writer to establish a sum counter. The SUM clause can be specified only in a TYPE IS CONTROL FOOTING line. The identifier coded after the reserved word SUM must be either (1) a numeric field specified as the object of a SOURCE clause, (2) the name of a REPORT SECTION field specified with the SUM clause (that is, another sum counter), or (3) a numeric field in the FILE SECTION or the WORKING-STORAGE SECTION.

Sum counters are automatically incremented when the GENERATE statement is executed. They are automatically zeroed after they are printed. To provide for the rolling of totals, a lower-level (more minor) sum counter is named in the SUM clause.

To override automatic zeroing of sum counters, the RESET ON clause is coded. The GROUP INDICATE clause can be specified on TYPE IS DETAIL fields to provide for group indication.

For summary (group-printed) reports, a dummy (null) TYPE IS DETAIL LINE must be coded. A dummy TYPE IS DETAIL line contains only the record-name and the TYPE IS DETAIL entry. No detail-line printing action occurs because no LINE clause, no fields, and no COLUMN clauses are coded.

**PROCEDURE
DIVISION**

The INITIATE statement begins Report Writer processing. The file named in the FD entry must be opened before the report named in the INITIATE statement can be initiated. The INITIATE statement handles the following processing:

- All SUM counters are set to 0.

- The LINE-COUNTER is set to 0.

- The PAGE-COUNTER is set to 1.

The GENERATE statement causes a detail line to be written to the report. The name of the TYPE IS DETAIL line is typically coded as the object of the GENERATE verb. The first time the GENERATE statement is executed, the following processing occurs:

- The REPORT HEADING group (if specified) is printed.

- The PAGE HEADING group is printed.

- CONTROL HEADING lines (if specified) are printed in major to minor order.

- The first DETAIL line is printed.

For each GENERATE statement executed after the first GENERATE, the following processing occurs:

- Tests are made to see if a PAGE FOOTING group should be printed. If a PAGE FOOTING group is required during GENERATE processing, it is printed.

- Tests are made to see if a PAGE HEADING group should be printed. If a PAGE HEADING group is required during GENERATE processing, it is printed.

- A test is made to see if one or more CONTROL FOOTING lines should be printed. If so, they are printed in minor to major order up to the most major level at which the control break occurred.

- A test is made to see if one or more CONTROL HEADING lines should be printed. If so, they are printed in major to minor order from the most major level at which the control break occurred.

- The DETAIL line is printed.

The TERMINATE statement ends Report Writer processing. Before the report file is closed, the report named in the TERMINATE STATEMENT must be terminated. When the TERMINATE statement is executed, the following processing occurs:

- Tests are made to see if a PAGE FOOTING group should be printed. If a PAGE FOOTING group is required during TERMINATE processing, it is printed.

- Tests are made to see if a PAGE HEADING group should be printed. If a PAGE HEADING group is required during TERMINATE processing, it is printed.

- All CONTROL FOOTING lines are printed, in major to minor order.

- The REPORT FOOTING group (if specified) is printed.

The USE BEFORE REPORTING statement can be coded in the DECLARATIVES area of the PROCEDURE DIVISION to enable the execution of a routine before a certain report line is printed. After the reserved words USE BEFORE REPORTING, the name of the report line that will be accessed is coded. A TYPE IS DETAIL line cannot be referenced in the USE BEFORE REPORTING statement.

INTRINSIC FUNCTIONS

The publication ANSI X3.23a-1989, entitled *Intrinsic Functions Module for COBOL,* describes the addition of 42 functions to the 1985 COBOL Standard. A function is a preprogrammed procedure that performs a particular task. A simple example is a square root function. You designate a value and the function calculates and returns the square root. To illustrate, assume that WA-INPUT-AREA contains a number of which you want the square root; you could obtain it with the following statement:

```
COMPUTE WA-INPUT-AREA-SQ-ROOT = FUNCTION SQRT (WA-INPUT-AREA)
```

Similarly, if WA-DESCRIPTION is an alphanumeric field whose contents consist of both upper- and lowercase letters, and you want all uppercase, you could use the following:

```
MOVE UPPER-CASE (WA-DESCRIPTION) TO WA-DESCRIPTION
```

Both cases deal with two entities: the input to and output from the function. The input to the function is called the argument (some functions may have multiple arguments); this is the data-item enclosed within parentheses in the preceding examples. The output is called the function—note that this results in a somewhat ambiguous use of the word *function.*

As you can see, some functions operate on alphanumeric data and others, on numeric data. With some functions (none illustrated here), the argument and the value returned by the function are of different data types.

Functions that return alphanumeric (or alphabetic) results can be used in any statement in which you would normally use an alphanumeric data-item—for instance, a MOVE or an IF condition in which the field to which the function value is being compared is alphanumeric. However, functions that return numeric results can be used only in arithmetic expressions. All such examples in this appendix use the COMPUTE statement to illustrate use of the numeric functions.

Date Functions

FUNCTION CURRENT-DATE

Type	Alphanumeric
Argument	None
Example	MOVE FUNCTION CURRENT-DATE TO WA-HOLD-DATE

Action	Places the current date and time in the programmer-defined 21-character alphanumeric field WA-HOLD-DATE, according to the following format:

1–4	Year (for example, 1995)
5–6	Month of year (01–12)
7–8	Day of month (01–31)
9–10	Time—number of hours past midnight
11–12	Minutes past the hour (00–59)
13–14	Seconds past the hour (00–59)
15–21	Other data

FUNCTION WHEN-COMPILED

Type	Alphanumeric
Argument	None
Example	`MOVE FUNCTION WHEN-COMPILED TO WA-COMPILED-DATE`
Action	Places the date and time that the program was compiled in the programmer-defined 21-character alphanumeric field WA-COMPILED-DATE. The format is identical to that for CURRENT-DATE.

The next two functions are used in performing operations with dates common to business programming. For instance, you can use them to determine the number of elapsed days between July 21, 1995, and September 19, 1995, or the calendar date of the day 60 days from today. They use, as their basis, a starting date of December 31, 1600.

FUNCTION INTEGER-OF-DATE

Type	Integer
Argument	Must be numeric of form *yyyymmdd* (and a valid date)
Example	`COMPUTE WA-DAY-COUNT = FUNCTION INTEGER-OF-DATE (WA-DATE)`
Action	Calculates the number of days elapsed since December 31, 1600, until the date in the date field WA-DATE and places the result in WA-DAY-COUNT.

FUNCTION DATE-OF-INTEGER

Type	Integer (of form *yyyymmdd*)
Argument	Integer (the number of days since December 31, 1600)
Example	`COMPUTE WA-DATE = FUNCTION DATE-OF-INTEGER (WA-DAY-COUNT)`
Action	Determines the calendar date that is WA-DAY-COUNT days after December 31, 1600, and places the result (in *yyyymmdd* form) in WA-DATE.

The following two examples illustrate common use of the date functions:

1. Determine the number of days between two dates—stored in WA-DATE-FIRST and WA-DATE-LAST:

```
COMPUTE WA-ELAPSED-DAYS = FUNCTION INTEGER-OF-DATE (WA-DATE-FIRST)
                        - FUNCTION INTEGER-OF-DATE (WA-DATE-LAST)
```

2. Determine the calendar date of the day 120 days from today:

```
05  WA-CURRENT-DATE-X    PIC X(21).
05  WA-CURRENT-DATE REDEFINES WA-CURRENT-DATE-X
                            PIC 9(8).

MOVE FUNCTION CURRENT-DATE TO WA-CURRENT-DATE-X
COMPUTE WA-DAY-COUNT = FUNCTION INTEGER-OF-DATE (WA-CURRENT-DATE)
                    + 120
COMPUTE WA-FUTURE-DATE = FUNCTION DATE-OF-INTEGER (WA-DAY-COUNT)
```

Mathematical Functions

FUNCTION RANDOM

Type	Numeric
Argument	Optional—if used, must be zero or positive integer. The absence of an argument always produces the same sequence of random numbers.
Example	`COMPUTE WA-RANDOM = FUNCTION RANDOM (WA-SEED-VALUE)`
Action	Returns a value in WA-RANDOM that is equal to or greater than zero and less than one.

FUNCTION SQRT

Type	Numeric
Argument	Numeric (zero or positive)
Example	`COMPUTE WA-ROOT= FUNCTION ROOT (WA-NUMBER)`
Action	Computes the square root of the number WA-NUMBER and places it in WA-ROOT.

Mathematical Functions— Array Processing

The following functions operate on two or more data-items. These functions are most commonly used with arrays (tables). Each of the examples operates on the data-item WA-DATA-ARRAY—which, you can assume, is defined with an OCCURS clause. In the examples, the array name appears with the argument ALL; that is, WA-DATA-ARRAY(ALL). ALL is a reserved word signifying all of the array elements. If the table is defined with the OCCURS DEPENDING ON clause, the range of values is determined by the clause object.

FUNCTION MEAN

Type	Numeric
Argument	Numeric
Example	`COMPUTE WA-MEAN = FUNCTION MEAN (WA-DATA-ARRAY(ALL))`
Action	Calculates the arithmetic average of the elements of WA-DATA-ARRAY and stores it in WA-MEAN.

FUNCTION MEDIAN

Type	Numeric
Argument	Numeric
Example	`COMPUTE WA-MEDIAN= FUNCTION MEDIAN (WA-DATA-ARRAY(ALL))`
Action	Determines the middle value of the elements of WA-DATA-ARRAY by arranging its elements in sorted order and stores it in WA-MEDIAN.

FUNCTION RANGE

Type	Numeric
Argument	Numeric
Example	`COMPUTE WA-RANGE= FUNCTION RANGE (WA-DATA-ARRAY(ALL))`
Action	Determines the difference between the largest and the smallest values of the array WA-DATA-ARRAY and stores it in WA-RANGE.

FUNCTION STANDARD-DEVIATION

Type	Numeric
Argument	Numeric
Example	`COMPUTE WA-STD-DEV=` `        FUNCTION STANDARD-DEVIATION (WA-DATA-ARRAY(ALL))`
Action	Computes the standard deviation of the elements of WA-DATA-ARRAY and stores it in WA-STD-DEV.

FUNCTION SUM

Type	Numeric
Argument	Numeric
Example	`COMPUTE WA-SUM = FUNCTION SUM (WA-DATA-ARRAY(ALL))`
Action	Computes the sum of the elements of WA-DATA-ARRAY and stores it in WA-SUM.

FUNCTION MAX

Type	Numeric Alphanumeric
Argument	Numeric Alphanumeric
Example	Numeric—WA-DATA-ARRAY is defined with 9 PICTURE symbols. `COMPUTE WA-MAX = FUNCTION MAX (WA-DATA-ARRAY(ALL))`
Action	Determines the largest value in WA-DATA-ARRAY and stores it in WA-MAX.

Example	Alphanumeric—WA-DATA-ARRAY is defined with X (or A) PICTURE symbols.

```
MOVE FUNCTION MAX (WA-DATA-ARRAY(ALL)) TO WA-MAX-X
```

Action	Determines the largest value in WA-DATA-ARRAY and stores it in WA-MAX-X (defined with X PICTURE symbols).

FUNCTION MIN

Type	Numeric Alphanumeric
Argument	Numeric Alphanumeric
Example	Numeric—WA-DATA-ARRAY is defined with 9 PICTURE symbols.

```
COMPUTE WA-MIN = FUNCTION MIN (WA-DATA-ARRAY(ALL))
```

Action	Determines the smallest value in WA-DATA-ARRAY and stores it in WA-MIN.
Example	Alphanumeric—WA-DATA-ARRAY is defined with X (or A) PICTURE symbols.

```
MOVE FUNCTION MIN (WA-DATA-ARRAY(ALL)) TO WA-MIN-X
```

Action	Determines the smallest value in WA-DATA-ARRAY and stores it in WA-MIN-X (defined with X PICTURE symbols).

The preceding examples illustrate multiple arguments with the single-dimensioned array WA-DATA-ARRAY. However, you can include a list of entries or a multi-dimensioned array, as the following examples using SUM illustrate:

Example	`COMPUTE WA-SUM = FUNCTION SUM (WA-DATA-ARRAY(1, ALL))`
Action	Computes the sum of the elements of the first row of the two-dimensional table WA-DATA-ARRAY and stores it in WA-SUM.
Example	`COMPUTE WA-SUM = FUNCTION SUM (WA-DATA-ARRAY(WA-ROW, ALL))`
Action	Computes the sum of the elements of the row designated by the contents of WA-ROW of the two-dimensional table WA-DATA-ARRAY and stores it in WA-SUM.
Example	`COMPUTE WA-SUM = FUNCTION SUM (WA-F1, WA-F2, SC-AMNT)`
Action	Computes the sum of the three listed data-items and stores it in WA-SUM.

String Functions

FUNCTION LOWER-CASE

Type	Alphanumeric
Argument	Alphanumeric or alphabetic
Example	`MOVE FUNCTION LOWER-CASE (WA-ALPHA) TO WA-ALPH-LOWER`
Action	Converts the letters contained in WA-ALPHA to lowercase and places the result in WA-ALPH-LOWER. The contents of WA-ALPHA are unchanged.

FUNCTION UPPER-CASE

Type	Alphanumeric
Argument	Alphanumeric or alphabetic
Example	`MOVE FUNCTION LOWER-CASE (WA-ALPHA) TO WA-ALPHA`
Action	Converts the letters contained in WA-ALPHA to uppercase.

PRINTER CONTROL FROM COBOL

The "standard" printer output is 10 characters per inch. This means that when using 8½-inch wide paper, the output line can be a maximum of 85 characters wide (for most printers, the width is 80). However, almost all printers have the capability to print smaller-sized characters—17 characters per inch is common—thereby effectively increasing the line width for an 8½-inch form. Some printers allow the print mode to be set from printer switches or buttons. Others require that the computer send an appropriate binary code or sequence of codes.

So, by creating the appropriate code sequence in a COBOL program and then writing it to the printer (as part of your initialization sequence), you can set your computer to print condensed type.

The technique used here for defining the needed binary codes revolves around defining data-items usage as binary. In personal computer COBOL, this ordinarily results in a two-byte field. The technique is as follows:

- In the WORKING-STORAGE SECTION, define appropriate binary codes to produce the desired printer control.

- In the PROCEDURE DIVISION initialization sequence, move these codes to the output line and print them.

The IBM Graphics/Epson Printer

The ASCII code to change the IBM Graphics/Epson printer to condensed printing mode is 15; the code to return it to standard printing is 18. Figure AC-1 is a simple listing program that (1) sets an IBM Graphics/Epson printer to condensed mode, (2) prints records from the patron file, and (3) resets the printer to standard mode. (Note: The FILE CONTROL is that for Micro Focus and Ryan-McFarland.) Lines 35–39 define the binary code for compressed printing; lines 41–45 define the code for standard printing. The appropriate code is moved to the output line and printed (lines 80–82 and 86–88).

By defining USAGE BINARY, a two-byte field results. The right byte contains the binary equivalent of 15 (or 18); the left byte contains binary zeroes. (Warning: Do not use a PIC 9(1) and expect to get a one-byte field. Any field width of 1 through 4 gives a two-byte binary field.)

The printer control techniques in this appendix were implemented and tested by a highly respected friend and colleague, Jack Olson.

Figure AC-1   Setting and resetting the print mode for IBM Graphics/Epson printers.

```
1        IDENTIFICATION DIVISION.                  46
2        PROGRAM-ID.    PRNCTL.                     47
3                                                   48        PROCEDURE DIVISION.
4     *     J. Olson   1/05/95                      49
5     *     Printer control                         50        000-PRINT-PATRON-LIST.
6                                                   51
7        ENVIRONMENT DIVISION.                      52     ************Initialization Sequence************
8                                                   53        OPEN INPUT PATRON-FILE
9        INPUT-OUTPUT SECTION.                      54             OUTPUT PATRON-LIST
10                                                  55             PERFORM 860-SET-PRINTER
11       FILE-CONTROL.                              56        MOVE "NO" TO PS-END-OF-PATRON-FILE
12          SELECT PATRON-FILE                      57
13             ASSIGN TO DISK "PATRON.DAT"          58     **************Processing Sequence**************
14             ORGANIZATION IS LINE SEQUENTIAL.     59        PERFORM UNTIL
15          SELECT PATRON-LIST                      60          PS-END-OF-PATRON-FILE IS EQUAL TO "YES"
16             ASSIGN TO PRINTER "PRN-FILE".        61          READ PATRON-FILE
17                                                  62             AT END
18                                                  63                MOVE "YES" TO PS-END-OF-PATRON-FILE
19       DATA DIVISION.                             64             NOT AT END
20                                                  65                MOVE PATRON-RECORD TO PATRON-LINE-RECORD
21       FILE SECTION.                              66                WRITE PATRON-LINE-RECORD
22                                                  67          END-READ
23       FD  PATRON-FILE.                           68        END-PERFORM
24       01  PATRON-RECORD          PIC X(68).      69
25                                                  70     **************Termination Sequence*************
26       FD  PATRON-LIST.                           71        PERFORM 870-RESET-PRINTER
27       01  PATRON-LINE-RECORD     PIC X(68).      72        CLOSE PATRON-FILE
28                                                  73              PATRON-LIST
29       WORKING-STORAGE SECTION.                   74        STOP RUN
30                                                  75        .
31       01  PROGRAM-SWITCHES.                      76     **************************************************
32          05  PS-END-OF-PATRON-FILE  PIC X(3).    77
33                                                  78        860-SET-PRINTER.
34       01  PC-PRINTER-CONTROL-CODES.              79     *     Set printer to compressed mode
35          05  PC-IBM-COMPRESSED     PIC 9(2)      80        MOVE PC-COMPRESSED TO PATRON-LINE-RECORD
36                            VALUE 15  USAGE BINARY.81        WRITE PATRON-LINE-RECORD
37          05  FILLER REDEFINES PC-IBM-COMPRESSED. 82           AFTER ADVANCING 0 LINES
38             10                    PIC X.         83
39             10  PC-COMPRESSED     PIC X.         84     *     Set printer to standard mode
40                                                  85        870-RESET-PRINTER.
41          05  PC-IBM-STANDARD      PIC 9(2)       86        MOVE PC-STANDARD TO PATRON-LINE-RECORD
42                            VALUE 18  USAGE BINARY.87        WRITE PATRON-LINE-RECORD
43          05  FILLER REDEFINES PC-IBM-STANDARD.   88           AFTER ADVANCING 0 LINES
44             10                    PIC X.         89        .
45             10  PC-STANDARD       PIC X.
```

HP LaserJet Printers

The principle for setting the print mode for LaserJet printers is the same as the preceding, except many more codes are required. The sample program of Figure AC-2 illustrates the technique. A 30-character string is required to set the compressed mode and a 26-character string is required for the standard mode. The positions E1 through E6 require the Escape character (code 27). It is defined at lines 36–40 and moved into the appropriate positions at line 103.

This example illustrates one other item: form feeding. When printing reports from COBOL with a laser printer, the last page usually remains in the printer buffer. To remove it, you must perform a form-feed operation with the printer console buttons. This is done as part of the program (see lines 42–46 and 110–112).

Figure AC-2   Setting and resetting the print mode for HP LaserJet printers.

```
1        IDENTIFICATION DIVISION.                          59        05  PC-LASER-STANDARD.
2        PROGRAM-ID.    PRNCTL-L.                          60            10  E4  PIC X.
3                                                          61            10      PIC X(4)      VALUE "&l00".
4    *      J. Olson 1/5/95                                62            10  E5  PIC X.
5    *      Printer control--HP LaserJet                   63            10      PIC X         VALUE "(".
6                                                          64            10      PIC X         VALUE "8".
7        ENVIRONMENT DIVISION.                             65            10      PIC X         VALUE "U".
8                                                          66            10  E6  PIC X.
9        INPUT-OUTPUT SECTION.                             67            10      PIC X(2)      VALUE "(s".
10                                                         68            10      PIC X(14)     VALUE "0p10h12v0s0b3T".
11       FILE-CONTROL.                                     69
12           SELECT PATRON-FILE                            70
13               ASSIGN TO DISK "PATRON.DAT"               71    PROCEDURE DIVISION.
14               ORGANIZATION IS LINE SEQUENTIAL.          72
15           SELECT PATRON-LIST                            73    000-PRINT-PATRON-LIST.
16               ASSIGN TO PRINTER "PRN-FILE".             74
17                                                         75    ***********Initialization Sequence***********
18                                                         76        OPEN INPUT PATRON-FILE
19       DATA DIVISION.                                    77             OUTPUT PATRON-LIST
20                                                         78        PERFORM 860-SET-PRINTER
21       FILE SECTION.                                     79        MOVE "NO" TO PS-END-OF-PATRON-FILE
22                                                         80
23       FD  PATRON-FILE.                                  81    *************Processing Sequence*************
24       01  PATRON-RECORD          PIC X(68).             82        PERFORM UNTIL
25                                                         83            PS-END-OF-PATRON-FILE IS EQUAL TO "YES"
26       FD  PATRON-LIST.                                  84            READ PATRON-FILE
27       01  PATRON-LINE-RECORD     PIC X(68).             85            AT END
28                                                         86                MOVE "YES" TO PS-END-OF-PATRON-FILE
29       WORKING-STORAGE SECTION.                          87            NOT AT END
30                                                         88                MOVE PATRON-RECORD TO PATRON-LINE-RECORD
31       01  PROGRAM-SWITCHES.                             89                WRITE PATRON-LINE-RECORD
32           05  PS-END-OF-PATRON-FILE  PIC X(3).          90            END-READ
33                                                         91        END-PERFORM
34       01  PC-PRINTER-CONTROL-CODES.                     92
35                                                         93    *************Termination Sequence*************
36           05  PC-ESC-CHARA          PIC 9(2)            94        PERFORM 870-RESET-PRINTER
37                                     VALUE 27  USAGE BINARY.  95        CLOSE PATRON-FILE
38           05  FILLER REDEFINES PC-ESC-CHARA.            96              PATRON-LIST
39               20                    PIC X.              97        STOP RUN
40               20  PC-ESC            PIC X.              98        .
41                                                         99    ***************************************************
42           05  PC-FORM-FEED-CHARA    PIC 9(2)            100       .
43                                     VALUE 12  USAGE BINARY.  101   860-SET-PRINTER.
44           05  FILLER REDEFINES PC-FORM-FEED-CHARA.      102   *    Set printer to compressed mode
45               20                    PIC X.              103       MOVE PC-ESC TO E1, E2, E3, E4, E5, E6
46               20  PC-FORMFEED       PIC X.              104       MOVE PC-LASER-COMPRESSED TO PATRON-LINE-RECORD
47                                                         105       WRITE PATRON-LINE-RECORD
48           05  PC-LASER-COMPRESSED.                      106           AFTER ADVANCING 0 LINES
49               10  E1  PIC X.                            107       .
50               10      PIC X(4)      VALUE "&l00".       108   870-RESET-PRINTER.
51               10  E2  PIC X.                            109   *    Clear last page from printer
52               10      PIC X         VALUE "(".          110       MOVE PC-FORMFEED TO PATRON-LINE-RECORD
53               10      PIC X         VALUE "8".          111       WRITE PATRON-LINE-RECORD
54               10      PIC X         VALUE "U".          112           AFTER ADVANCING 0 LINES
55               10  E3  PIC X.                            113   *    Set printer to standard mode
56               10      PIC X(2)      VALUE "(s".         114       MOVE PC-LASER-STANDARD TO PATRON-LINE-RECORD
57               10      PIC X(18)     VALUE "0p16.66h8.5v0s0b0T".  115   WRITE PATRON-LINE-RECORD
58                                                         116           AFTER ADVANCING 0 LINES
                                                           117       .
```

Other Printers and Other Print Modes

Other printers can be set in exactly the same way as the two previous examples. For instance, assume that you have a printer that allows printing at 12 characters per inch and that the printer manual indicates a three-character code sequence of Escape, ?, and D is needed to set it. Your code sequence would be defined as follows:

```
05  PC-12-CPI.
    10  PC-ESC-1  PIC X.
    10            PIC X(2) VALUE "?D"
```

After moving the Escape character into PC-ESC-1 from its definition (see lines 36–40 of Figure AC-2), you could move PC-12-CPI to the output line and print it.

COMPLETE COBOL-85 LANGUAGE FORMATS

This appendix contains the composite language formats skeleton of the American National Standard COBOL (1985). It displays selected COBOL-85 language formats.

General Format for IDENTIFICATION DIVISION

```
IDENTIFICATION DIVISION.

PROGRAM-ID. program-name  [ IS  { COMMON  }  PROGRAM ] .
                                 { INITIAL }

[AUTHOR. [comment-entry] ...]

[INSTALLATION. [comment-entry] ...]

[DATE-WRITTEN. [comment-entry] ...]

[DATE-COMPILED. [comment-entry] ...]

[SECURITY. [comment-entry] ...]
```

General Format for ENVIRONMENT DIVISION

```
[ENVIRONMENT DIVISION.

[CONFIGURATION SECTION.

[SOURCE-COMPUTER. [computer-name [WITH DEBUGGING MODE.]]

[OBJECT-COMPUTER. [computer-name

  [                    { WORDS      }  ]
  [ MEMORY SIZE integer-1 { CHARACTERS } ]
  [                    { MODULES    }  ]

  [PROGRAM COLLATING SEQUENCE IS alphabet-name-1].]]
```

(continues)

[SPECIAL-NAMES. [[implementor-name-1

$$
\begin{Bmatrix}
\text{IS mnemonic-name-1 [\underline{ON} STATUS IS condition-name-1 [\underline{OFF} STATUS IS condition-name-2]]} \\
\text{IS mnemonic-name-2 [\underline{OFF} STATUS IS condition-name-2 [\underline{ON} STATUS IS condition-name-1]]} \\
\underline{ON} \text{ STATUS IS condition-name-1 [\underline{OFF} STATUS IS condition-name-2]} \\
\underline{OFF} \text{ STATUS IS condition-name-2 [\underline{ON} STATUS IS condition-name-1]}
\end{Bmatrix}
$$
...

[ALPHABET alphabet-name-1 IS

$$
\begin{Bmatrix}
\underline{STANDARD-1} \\
\underline{STANDARD-2} \\
\underline{NATIVE} \\
\text{implementor-name-2} \\
\left\{ \text{literal-1} \left[\begin{Bmatrix} \underline{THROUGH} \\ \underline{THRU} \end{Bmatrix} \text{literal-2} \\ \{ \underline{ALSO} \text{ literal-3} \} ... \right] \right\} ...
\end{Bmatrix}
$$ ...

$$
\left[\underline{SYMBOLIC} \text{ CHARACTERS} \left\{ \left\{ \{\text{symbolic-character-1}\} ... \begin{Bmatrix} \underline{IS} \\ \underline{ARE} \end{Bmatrix} \{\text{integer-1}\} ... \right\} ... \right. \right.
$$

$$
\left. \left. [\underline{IN} \text{ alphabet-name-2}] \right\} \right] ...
$$

$$
\left[\underline{CLASS} \text{ class-name IS} \left\{ \text{literal-4} \left[\begin{Bmatrix} \underline{THROUGH} \\ \underline{THRU} \end{Bmatrix} \text{literal-5} \right] \right\} ... \right] ...
$$

[CURRENCY SIGN IS literal-6]

[DECIMAL-POINT IS COMMA].]]]

[INPUT-OUTPUT SECTION.

 FILE-CONTROL.

   {file-control-entry} ...

General Format for File-Control-Entry

Sequential File:

SELECT [OPTIONAL] file-name-1

   ASSIGN TO $\begin{Bmatrix} \text{implementor-name-1} \\ \text{literal-1} \end{Bmatrix}$ ...

   $\left[\underline{RESERVE} \text{ integer-1} \begin{bmatrix} \text{AREA} \\ \text{AREAS} \end{bmatrix} \right]$

   [[ORGANIZATION IS] SEQUENTIAL]

   $\left[\underline{PADDING} \text{ CHARACTER IS} \begin{Bmatrix} \text{data-name-1} \\ \text{literal-2} \end{Bmatrix} \right]$

   $\left[\underline{RECORD} \underline{DELIMITER} \text{ IS} \begin{Bmatrix} \underline{STANDARD-1} \\ \text{implementor-name-2} \end{Bmatrix} \right]$

   [ACCESS MODE IS SEQUENTIAL]

   [FILE STATUS IS data-name-2].

Relative File:

```
SELECT [OPTIONAL] file-name-1

    ASSIGN TO { implementor-name-1 } ...
              { literal-1          }

    [ RESERVE integer-1 [ AREA  ] ]
                        [ AREAS ]

    [ORGANIZATION IS] RELATIVE

    [                { SEQUENTIAL [RELATIVE KEY IS data-name-1]  } ]
    [ ACCESS MODE IS { { RANDOM  }                               } ]
    [                { { DYNAMIC } RELATIVE KEY IS data-name-1   } ]

    [FILE STATUS IS data-name-2].
```

Indexed File:

```
SELECT [OPTIONAL] file-name-1

    ASSIGN TO { implementor-name-1 } ...
              { literal-1          }

    [ RESERVE integer-1 [ AREA  ] ]
                        [ AREAS ]

    [ORGANIZATION IS] INDEXED

    [                { SEQUENTIAL } ]
    [ ACCESS MODE IS { RANDOM     } ]
    [                { DYNAMIC    } ]

    RECORD KEY IS data-name-1

    [ALTERNATE RECORD KEY IS data-name-2 [WITH DUPLICATES]] ...

    [FILE STATUS IS data-name-3].
```

Sort or Merge File:

```
SELECT file-name-1 ASSIGN TO { implementor-name-1 } ... .
                             { literal-1          }
```

Report File:

```
SELECT [OPTIONAL] file-name-1

    ASSIGN TO { implementor-name-1 } ...
              { literal-1          }

    [ RESERVE integer-1 [ AREA  ] ]
                        [ AREAS ]

    [[ORGANIZATION IS] SEQUENTIAL]

    [ PADDING CHARACTER IS { data-name-1 } ]
                           { literal-2   }

    [ RECORD DELIMITER IS { STANDARD-1          } ]
                          { implementor-name-2  }

    [ACCESS MODE IS SEQUENTIAL]

    [FILE STATUS IS data-name-2].
```

**General Format for
DATA DIVISION**

```
[DATA DIVISION.

[FILE SECTION.

⎡ file-description-entry {record-description-entry} ...            ⎤
⎢ sort-merge-file-description-entry {record-description-entry} ... ⎥ ...
⎣ report-file-description-entry                                    ⎦

[WORKING-STORAGE SECTION.

⎡ 77-level-description-entry ⎤ ...
⎣ record-description-entry    ⎦

[LINKAGE SECTION.

⎡ 77-level-description-entry ⎤ ...
⎣ record-description-entry    ⎦

[COMMUNICATION SECTION.

[communication-description-entry [record-description-entry] ... ] ... ]

[REPORT SECTION.

[report-description-entry {report-group-description-entry} ... ] ... ]]
```

**General Format for
File-Description-Entry**

Sequential File:

```
FD file-name-1

    [IS EXTERNAL]

    [IS GLOBAL]

    ⎡ BLOCK CONTAINS [integer-1 TO] integer-2 { RECORDS    } ⎤
    ⎣                                          { CHARACTERS } ⎦

    ⎡         ⎧ CONTAINS integer-3 CHARACTERS                                       ⎫ ⎤
    ⎢ RECORD  ⎨ IS VARYING IN SIZE [[FROM integer-4] [TO integer-5] CHARACTERS]     ⎬ ⎥
    ⎢         ⎪    [DEPENDING ON data-name-1]                                        ⎪ ⎥
    ⎣         ⎩ CONTAINS integer-6 TO integer-7 CHARACTERS                          ⎭ ⎦

    ⎡ LABEL { RECORD IS   } { STANDARD } ⎤
    ⎣       { RECORDS ARE  } { OMITTED  } ⎦

    ⎡ VALUE OF { implementor-name-1 IS { data-name-2 } } ⎤ ...
    ⎣                                  { literal-1   }   ⎦

    ⎡ DATA { RECORD IS   } {data-name-3} ... ⎤
    ⎣      { RECORDS ARE  }                  ⎦

    ⎡ LINAGE IS { data-name-4 } LINES ⎡ WITH FOOTING AT { data-name-5 } ⎤ ⎤
    ⎢           { integer-8   }       ⎣                  { integer-9   } ⎦ ⎥
    ⎢                                                                     ⎥
    ⎢ ⎡ LINES AT TOP { data-name-6 } ⎤ ⎡ LINES AT BOTTOM { data-name-7  } ⎤ ⎥
    ⎣ ⎣              { integer-10  } ⎦ ⎣                  { integer-11 } ⎦ ⎦

    [CODE-SET IS alphabet-name-1].
```

Relative File:

```
FD file-name-1

   [IS EXTERNAL]

   [IS GLOBAL]

   ┌                                        ┌ RECORDS    ┐ ┐
   │ BLOCK CONTAINS [integer-1 TO] integer-2 │ CHARACTERS │ │
   └                                        └            ┘ ┘

   ┌         ┌                                                            ┐ ┐
   │         │ CONTAINS integer-3 CHARACTERS                              │ │
   │ RECORD  │ IS VARYING IN SIZE [[FROM integer-4] [TO integer-5] CHARACTERS │ │
   │         │       [DEPENDING ON data-name-1]                          │ │
   │         │ CONTAINS integer-6 TO integer-7 CHARACTERS                │ │
   └         └                                                            ┘ ┘

   ┌       ┌ RECORD IS   ┐ ┌ STANDARD ┐ ┐
   │ LABEL │ RECORDS ARE │ │ OMITTED  │ │
   └       └             ┘ └          ┘ ┘

   ┌                                    ┌ data-name-2 ┐ ┐        ┐
   │ VALUE OF │ implementor-name-1 IS   │ literal-1   │ │  ...   │
   └                                    └             ┘ ┘        ┘

   ┌      ┌ RECORD IS   ┐                   ┐
   │ DATA │ RECORDS ARE │ {data-name-3}...  │  .
   └      └             ┘                   ┘
```

Indexed File:

```
FD file-name-1

   [IS EXTERNAL]

   [IS GLOBAL]

   ┌                                        ┌ RECORDS    ┐ ┐
   │ BLOCK CONTAINS [integer-1 TO] integer-2 │ CHARACTERS │ │
   └                                        └            ┘ ┘

   ┌         ┌                                                             ┐ ┐
   │         │ CONTAINS integer-3 CHARACTERS                               │ │
   │ RECORD  │ IS VARYING IN SIZE [[FROM integer-4] [TO integer-5] CHARACTERS] │ │
   │         │       [DEPENDING ON data-name-1]                           │ │
   │         │ CONTAINS integer-6 TO integer-7 CHARACTERS                 │ │
   └         └                                                             ┘ ┘

   ┌       ┌ RECORD IS   ┐ ┌ STANDARD ┐ ┐
   │ LABEL │ RECORDS ARE │ │ OMITTED  │ │
   └       └             ┘ └          ┘ ┘

   ┌                                    ┌ data-name-2 ┐ ┐        ┐
   │ VALUE OF │ implementor-name-1 IS   │ literal-1   │ │  ...   │
   └                                    └             ┘ ┘        ┘

   ┌      ┌ RECORD IS   ┐                    ┐
   │ DATA │ RECORDS ARE │  {data-name-3} ... │  .
   └      └             ┘                    ┘
```

Sort-Merge File:

```
SD file-name-1

   ┌         ┌                                                             ┐ ┐
   │         │ CONTAINS integer-1 CHARACTERS                               │ │
   │ RECORD  │ IS VARYING IN SIZE [[FROM integer-2] [TO integer-3] CHARACTERS] │ │
   │         │       [DEPENDING ON data-name-1]                           │ │
   │         │ CONTAINS integer-4 TO integer-5 CHARACTERS                 │ │
   └         └                                                             ┘ ┘

   ┌      ┌ RECORD IS   ┐                    ┐
   │ DATA │ RECORDS ARE │ {data-name-2} ...  │  .
   └      └             ┘                    ┘
```

Report File:

<u>FD</u> file-name-1

    [IS <u>EXTERNAL</u>]

    [IS <u>GLOBAL</u>]

$$\left[\ \underline{\text{BLOCK}}\ \text{CONTAINS}\ [\text{integer-1}\ \underline{\text{TO}}]\ \text{integer-2}\ \left\{\begin{array}{l}\underline{\text{RECORDS}}\\ \text{CHARACTERS}\end{array}\right\}\ \right]$$

$$\left[\ \underline{\text{RECORD}}\ \left\{\begin{array}{l}\text{CONTAINS integer-3 CHARACTERS}\\ \text{CONTAINS integer-4}\ \underline{\text{TO}}\ \text{integer-5 CHARACTERS}\end{array}\right\}\ \right]$$

$$\left[\ \underline{\text{LABEL}}\ \left\{\begin{array}{l}\underline{\text{RECORD}}\ \text{IS}\\ \underline{\text{RECORDS}}\ \text{ARE}\end{array}\right\}\ \left\{\begin{array}{l}\underline{\text{STANDARD}}\\ \underline{\text{OMITTED}}\end{array}\right\}\ \right]$$

$$\left[\ \underline{\text{VALUE}}\ \underline{\text{OF}}\ \left\{\ \text{implementor-name-1 IS}\ \left\{\begin{array}{l}\text{data-name-1}\\ \text{literal-1}\end{array}\right\}\ \right\}\ \ldots\ \right]$$

    [<u>CODE-SET</u> IS alphabet-name-1]

$$\left\{\begin{array}{l}\underline{\text{REPORT}}\ \text{IS}\\ \underline{\text{REPORTS}}\ \text{ARE}\end{array}\right\}\ \{\text{report-name-1}\}\ \ldots\ .$$

General Format for Data Description Entry

Format 1:

$$\text{level-number}\ \left[\begin{array}{l}\text{data-name-1}\\ \text{FILLER}\end{array}\right]$$

    [<u>REDEFINES</u> data-name-2]

    [IS <u>EXTERNAL</u>]

    [IS <u>GLOBAL</u>]

$$\left[\ \left\{\begin{array}{l}\underline{\text{PICTURE}}\\ \underline{\text{PIC}}\end{array}\right\}\ \text{IS character-string}\ \right]$$

$$\left[\ [\underline{\text{USAGE}}\ \text{IS}]\ \left\{\begin{array}{l}\text{BINARY}\\ \underline{\text{COMPUTATIONAL}}\\ \underline{\text{COMP}}\\ \underline{\text{DISPLAY}}\\ \underline{\text{INDEX}}\\ \underline{\text{PACKED-DECIMAL}}\end{array}\right\}\ \right]$$

$$\left[\ [\underline{\text{SIGN}}\ \text{IS}]\ \left\{\begin{array}{l}\underline{\text{LEADING}}\\ \underline{\text{TRAILING}}\end{array}\right\}\ [\underline{\text{SEPARATE}}\ \text{CHARACTER}]\ \right]$$

$$\left[\begin{array}{l}\underline{\text{OCCURS}}\ \text{integer-2 TIMES}\\ \quad \left[\ \left\{\begin{array}{l}\underline{\text{ASCENDING}}\\ \underline{\text{DESCENDING}}\end{array}\right\}\ \text{KEY IS}\ \{\text{data-name-3}\}\ \ldots\ \right]\ \ldots\\ \quad\quad [\underline{\text{INDEXED}}\ \text{BY}\ \{\text{index-name-1}\}\ \ldots\ ]\\ \underline{\text{OCCURS}}\ \text{integer-1}\ \underline{\text{TO}}\ \text{integer-2 TIMES}\ \underline{\text{DEPENDING}}\ \text{ON data-name-4}\\ \quad \left[\ \left\{\begin{array}{l}\underline{\text{ASCENDING}}\\ \underline{\text{DESCENDING}}\end{array}\right\}\ \text{KEY IS}\ \{\text{data-name-3}\}\ \ldots\ \right]\ \ldots\\ \quad\quad [\underline{\text{INDEXED}}\ \text{BY}\ \{\text{index-name-1}\}\ \ldots\ ]\end{array}\right]$$

$$\left[\ \left\{\begin{array}{l}\underline{\text{SYNCHRONIZED}}\\ \underline{\text{SYNC}}\end{array}\right\}\ \left[\begin{array}{l}\underline{\text{LEFT}}\\ \underline{\text{RIGHT}}\end{array}\right]\ \right]$$

$$\left[\ \left\{\begin{array}{l}\underline{\text{JUSTIFIED}}\\ \underline{\text{JUST}}\end{array}\right\}\ \text{RIGHT}\ \right]$$

[<u>BLANK</u> WHEN <u>ZERO</u>]

[<u>VALUE</u> IS literal-1].

Format 2:

66 data-name-1 <u>RENAMES</u> data-name-2 $\left[\left\{ \begin{array}{c} \underline{THROUGH} \\ \underline{THRU} \end{array} \right\} \text{data-name-3} \right]$.

Format 3:

88 condition-name-1 $\left\{ \begin{array}{c} \underline{VALUE} \text{ IS} \\ \underline{VALUES} \text{ ARE} \end{array} \right\}$ $\left\{ \text{literal-1} \left[\left\{ \begin{array}{c} \underline{THROUGH} \\ \underline{THRU} \end{array} \right\} \text{literal-2} \right] \right\}$ ... .

General Format for Report Description Entry

<u>RD</u> report-name-1

[IS <u>GLOBAL</u>]

[<u>CODE</u> literal-1]

$\left[\left\{ \begin{array}{c} \underline{CONTROL} \text{ IS} \\ \underline{CONTROLS} \text{ ARE} \end{array} \right\} \left\{ \begin{array}{c} \text{\{data-name-1\}} \text{ ...} \\ \underline{FINAL} \text{ [data-name-1] ...} \end{array} \right\} \right]$

$\left[\underline{PAGE} \left[\begin{array}{c} \underline{LIMIT} \text{ IS} \\ \underline{LIMITS} \text{ ARE} \end{array} \right] \text{integer-1} \left[\begin{array}{c} \underline{LINE} \\ \underline{LINES} \end{array} \right] \text{[\underline{HEADING} integer-2]} \right.$

$\quad$ [<u>FIRST</u> <u>DETAIL</u> integer-3] [<u>LAST</u> <u>DETAIL</u> integer-4]

$\quad \left. \text{[\underline{FOOTING} integer-5]} \right]$.

Format 1:

01 [data-name-1]

$\left[\underline{LINE} \text{ NUMBER IS} \left\{ \begin{array}{c} \text{integer-1 ON } \underline{NEXT} \underline{PAGE}] \\ \underline{PLUS} \text{ integer-2} \end{array} \right\} \right]$

$\left[\underline{NEXT} \underline{GROUP} \text{ IS} \left\{ \begin{array}{c} \text{integer-3} \\ \underline{PLUS} \text{ integer-4} \\ \underline{NEXT} \underline{PAGE} \end{array} \right\} \right]$

<u>TYPE</u> IS $\left\{ \begin{array}{l} \left\{ \begin{array}{c} \underline{REPORT} \underline{HEADING} \\ \underline{RH} \end{array} \right\} \\ \left\{ \begin{array}{c} \underline{PAGE} \underline{HEADING} \\ \underline{PH} \end{array} \right\} \\ \left\{ \begin{array}{c} \underline{CONTROL} \underline{HEADING} \\ \underline{CH} \end{array} \right\} \left\{ \begin{array}{c} \text{data-name-2} \\ \underline{FINAL} \end{array} \right\} \\ \left\{ \begin{array}{c} \underline{DETAIL} \\ \underline{DE} \end{array} \right\} \\ \left\{ \begin{array}{c} \underline{CONTROL} \underline{FOOTING} \\ \underline{CF} \end{array} \right\} \left\{ \begin{array}{c} \text{data-name-3} \\ \underline{FINAL} \end{array} \right\} \\ \left\{ \begin{array}{c} \underline{PAGE} \underline{FOOTING} \\ \underline{PF} \end{array} \right\} \\ \left\{ \begin{array}{c} \underline{REPORT} \underline{FOOTING} \\ \underline{RF} \end{array} \right\} \end{array} \right\}$

[[<u>USAGE</u> IS] <u>DISPLAY</u>].

Format 2:

```
level-number [data-name-1]

    [ LINE NUMBER IS { integer-1 [ON NEXT PAGE] } ]
    [                { PLUS integer-2            } ]

    [[USAGE IS] DISPLAY].
```

Format 3:

```
level-number [data-name-1]

    { PICTURE }
    { PIC     } IS character-string

    [[USAGE IS] DISPLAY]

    [ [SIGN IS] { LEADING  } SEPARATE CHARACTER ]
    [           { TRAILING }                    ]

    [ { JUSTIFIED } RIGHT ]
    [ { JUST      }       ]

    [BLANK WHEN ZERO]

    [ LINE NUMBER IS { integer-1 [ON NEXT PAGE] } ]
    [                { PLUS integer-2            } ]

    [COLUMN NUMBER IS integer-3]

    { SOURCE IS identifier-1                              }
    { VALUE IS literal-1                                  }
    { {SUM {identifier-2} ... [UPON {data-name-2}... ]} ... }
    {     [ RESET ON { data-name-3 } ]                    }
    {     [          { FINAL       } ]                    }

    [GROUP INDICATE].
```

General Format for PROCEDURE DIVISION

Format 1:

```
[PROCEDURE DIVISION [USING {data-name-1} ... ].

[DECLARATIVES.

{section-name SECTION [segment-number].

    USE statement.

[paragraph-name.

    [sentence] ... ] ... } ...

END DECLARATIVES.]

{section-name SECTION [segment-number].

[paragraph-name.

    [sentence] ... ] ... }... ]
```

Format 2:

```
[PROCEDURE DIVISION [USING {data-name-1} ... ].

{paragraph-name.

    [sentence] ... }... ]
```

General Format for COBOL Verbs

The general formats of input/output verbs differ from those of other verbs in that their format depends upon the type of file being processed. For instance, CLOSE for a sequential file has a different general format than CLOSE for an indexed file. To indicate these differences, the following letters are included to the left of the verb.

I   Indexed   **R**   Relative   **S**   Sequential   **W**   Report Writer

```
ACCEPT identifier-1 [FROM mnemonic-name-1]

ACCEPT identifier-2 FROM  ┌ DATE        ┐
                          │ DAY         │
                          │ DAY-OF-WEEK │
                          └ TIME        ┘

ADD  { identifier-1 } ... TO {identifier-2 [ROUNDED]} ...
     { literal-1    }

     [ON SIZE ERROR imperative-statement-1]

     [NOT ON SIZE ERROR imperative-statement-2]

     [END-ADD]

ADD  { identifier-1 } ... TO { identifier-2 }
     { literal-1    }        { literal-2    }

     GIVING {identifier-3 [ROUNDED]} ...

     [ON SIZE ERROR imperative-statement-1]

     [NOT ON SIZE ERROR imperative-statement-2]

     [END-ADD]

ADD  { CORRESPONDING } identifier-1  TO identifier-2 [ROUNDED]
     { CORR          }

     [ON SIZE ERROR imperative-statement-1]

     [NOT ON SIZE ERROR imperative-statement-2]

     [END-ADD]

ALTER {procedure-name-1 TO {PROCEED TO} procedure-name-2} ...

CALL { identifier-1 } [ USING { [BY REFERENCE] {identifier-2} ... } ... ]
     { literal-1    }         { BY CONTENT {identifier-2} ...      }

     [ON OVERFLOW imperative-statement-1]

     [END-CALL]

CALL { identifier-1 } [ USING { [BY REFERENCE] {identifier-2} ... } ... ]
     { literal-1    }         { BY CONTENT {identifier-2} ...      }

     [ON EXCEPTION imperative-statement-1]

     [NOT ON EXCEPTION imperative-statement-2]

     [END-CALL]

CANCEL { identifier-1 } ...
       { literal-1    }

SW  CLOSE  { file-name-1 [ { REEL } [FOR REMOVAL]         ] } ...
           {             [ { UNIT }                       ] }
           {             [ WITH { NO REWIND }             ] }
           {             [      { LOCK      }             ] }
```

RI   <u>CLOSE</u> {file-name-1 {WITH <u>LOCK</u>]} ...

<u>COMPUTE</u> {identifier-1 [<u>ROUNDED</u>} ... = arithmetic-expression-1

    [ON <u>SIZE</u> <u>ERROR</u> imperative-statement-1]

    [<u>NOT</u> ON <u>SIZE</u> <u>ERROR</u> imperative-statement-2]

    [<u>END-COMPUTE</u>]

<u>CONTINUE</u>

<u>DELETE</u> file-name-1 RECORD

    [<u>INVALID</u> KEY imperative-statement-1]

    [<u>NOT</u> <u>INVALID</u> KEY imperative-statement-2]

    [<u>END-DELETE</u>]

<u>DISABLE</u> $\left\{ \begin{array}{l} \underline{INPUT}\ [\underline{TERMINAL}] \\ \underline{I-O}\ \underline{TERMINAL} \\ \underline{OUTPUT} \end{array} \right\}$ cd-name-1 $\left[\ WITH\ \underline{KEY}\ \left\{ \begin{array}{l} identifier-1 \\ literal-1 \end{array} \right\} \right]$

<u>DISPLAY</u> $\left\{ \begin{array}{l} identifier-1 \\ literal-1 \end{array} \right\}$ ... [<u>UPON</u> mnemonic-name-1 [WITH <u>NO</u> <u>ADVANCING</u>]

<u>DIVIDE</u> $\left\{ \begin{array}{l} identifier-1 \\ literal-1 \end{array} \right\}$ <u>INTO</u> {identifier-2 [<u>ROUNDED</u>]} ...

    [ON <u>SIZE</u> <u>ERROR</u> imperative-statement-1]

    [<u>NOT</u> ON <u>SIZE</u> <u>ERROR</u> imperative-statement-2]

    [<u>END-DIVIDE</u>]

<u>DIVIDE</u> $\left\{ \begin{array}{l} identifier-1 \\ literal-1 \end{array} \right\}$ <u>INTO</u> $\left\{ \begin{array}{l} identifier-2 \\ literal-2 \end{array} \right\}$

  <u>GIVING</u> {identifier-3 [<u>ROUNDED</u>]} ...

    [ON <u>SIZE</u> <u>ERROR</u> imperative-statement-1]

    [<u>NOT</u> ON <u>SIZE</u> <u>ERROR</u> imperative-statement-2]

    [<u>END-DIVIDE</u>]

<u>DIVIDE</u> $\left\{ \begin{array}{l} identifier-1 \\ literal-1 \end{array} \right\}$ <u>BY</u> $\left\{ \begin{array}{l} identifier-2 \\ literal-2 \end{array} \right\}$

  <u>GIVING</u> {identifier-3 [<u>ROUNDED</u>]} ...

    [ON <u>SIZE</u> <u>ERROR</u> imperative-statement-1]

    [<u>NOT</u> ON <u>SIZE</u> <u>ERROR</u> imperative-statement-2]

    [<u>END-DIVIDE</u>]

<u>DIVIDE</u> $\left\{ \begin{array}{l} identifier-1 \\ literal-1 \end{array} \right\}$ <u>INTO</u> $\left\{ \begin{array}{l} identifier-2 \\ literal-2 \end{array} \right\}$ <u>GIVING</u> identifier-3 [<u>ROUNDED</u>]

  <u>REMAINDER</u> identifier-4

    [ON <u>SIZE</u> <u>ERROR</u> imperative-statement-1]

    [<u>NOT</u> ON <u>SIZE</u> <u>ERROR</u> imperative-statement-2]

    [<u>END-DIVIDE</u>]

```
DIVIDE { identifier-1 } BY { identifier-2 } GIVING identifier-3 [ROUNDED]
       { literal-1    }    { literal-2    }

    REMAINDER identifier-4

    [ON SIZE ERROR imperative-statement-1]

    [NOT ON SIZE ERROR imperative-statement-2]

    [END-DIVIDE]

           ┌ identifier-1 ┐  ┌      ┌ identifier-2 ┐ ┐
           │ literal-1    │  │      │ literal-2    │ │
EVALUATE   { expression-1 }  │ ALSO { expression-2 } │  ...
           │ TRUE         │  │      │ TRUE         │ │
           └ FALSE        ┘  └      └ FALSE        ┘ ┘

    {{WHEN

       ┌ ANY                                                                                    ┐
       │ condition-1                                                                            │
       │ TRUE                                                                                   │
       │ FALSE                                                                                  │
       │        ┌ identifier-3            ┐ ┌ ┌ THROUGH ┐ ┌ identifier-4            ┐ ┐         │
       │ [NOT]  { literal-3               }  │ { THRU    } { literal-4               } │         │
       └        └ arithmetic-expression-1 ┘ └           └ arithmetic-expression-2 ┘ ┘         ┘

    [ALSO

       ┌ ANY                                                                                    ┐
       │ condition-2                                                                            │
       │ TRUE                                                                                   │
       │ FALSE                                                                                  │
       │        ┌ identifier-5            ┐ ┌ ┌ THROUGH ┐ ┌ identifier-6            ┐ ┐         │  ... } ...
       │ [NOT]  { literal-5               }  │ { THRU    } { literal-6               } │         │
       └        └ arithmetic-expression-3 ┘ └           └ arithmetic-expression-4 ┘ ┘         ┘

    imperative-statement-1} ...

    [WHEN OTHER imperative-statement-2]

    [END-EVALUATE]

EXIT

EXIT PROGRAM

GENERATE { data-name-1   }
         { report-name-1 }

GO TO [procedure-name-1]

GO TO [procedure-name-1] ... DEPENDING ON identifier-1

                              ┌ {statement-1}    ┐ ┌ ELSE {statement-2} ... [END-IF] ┐
IF condition-1 THEN { NEXT SENTENCE ... }         │ ELSE NEXT SENTENCE               │
                                                  └ END-IF                           ┘

INITIALIZE {identifier-1} ...

    ┌            ┌ ┌ ALPHABETIC         ┐          ┌ identifier-2 ┐ ┐   ┐
    │ REPLACING  │ │ ALPHANUMERIC       │ DATA BY  { literal-1    } │   │  ...
    │            │ { NUMERIC            }          └              ┘ │   │
    │            │ │ ALPHANUMERIC-EDITED │                          │   │
    └            └ └ NUMERIC-EDITED      ┘                          ┘   ┘

INITIATE {report-name-1} ...
```

```
INSPECT identifier-1 TALLYING
```

$$
\left\{ \text{identifier-2 } \underline{\text{FOR}} \left\{ \begin{array}{l} \underline{\text{CHARACTERS}} \left[\left\{ \begin{array}{l} \underline{\text{BEFORE}} \\ \underline{\text{AFTER}} \end{array} \right\} \text{ INITIAL } \left\{ \begin{array}{l} \text{identifier-4} \\ \text{literal-2} \end{array} \right\} \right] \cdots \\ \left\{ \begin{array}{l} \underline{\text{ALL}} \\ \underline{\text{LEADING}} \end{array} \right\} \left\{ \left\{ \begin{array}{l} \text{identifier-3} \\ \text{literal-1} \end{array} \right\} \left[\left\{ \begin{array}{l} \underline{\text{BEFORE}} \\ \underline{\text{AFTER}} \end{array} \right\} \text{INITIAL} \left\{ \begin{array}{l} \text{identifier-4} \\ \text{literal-2} \end{array} \right\} \right] \cdots \right\} \cdots \end{array} \right\} \cdots \right\} \cdots
$$

```
INSPECT identifier-1 REPLACING
```

$$
\left\{ \begin{array}{l} \underline{\text{CHARACTERS}} \ \underline{\text{BY}} \left\{ \begin{array}{l} \text{identifier-5} \\ \text{literal-3} \end{array} \right\} \left[\left\{ \begin{array}{l} \underline{\text{BEFORE}} \\ \underline{\text{AFTER}} \end{array} \right\} \text{ INITIAL } \left\{ \begin{array}{l} \text{identifier-4} \\ \text{literal-2} \end{array} \right\} \right] \cdots \\ \left\{ \begin{array}{l} \underline{\text{ALL}} \\ \underline{\text{LEADING}} \\ \underline{\text{FIRST}} \end{array} \right\} \left\{ \left\{ \begin{array}{l} \text{identifier-3} \\ \text{literal-1} \end{array} \right\} \underline{\text{BY}} \left\{ \begin{array}{l} \text{identifier-5} \\ \text{literal-3} \end{array} \right\} \left[\left\{ \begin{array}{l} \underline{\text{BEFORE}} \\ \underline{\text{AFTER}} \end{array} \right\} \text{INITIAL} \left\{ \begin{array}{l} \text{identifier-4} \\ \text{literal-2} \end{array} \right\} \right] \cdots \right\} \cdots \end{array} \right\} \cdots
$$

```
INSPECT identifier-1 TALLYING
```

$$
\left\{ \text{identifier-2 } \underline{\text{FOR}} \left\{ \begin{array}{l} \underline{\text{CHARACTERS}} \left[\left\{ \begin{array}{l} \underline{\text{BEFORE}} \\ \underline{\text{AFTER}} \end{array} \right\} \text{ INITIAL } \left\{ \begin{array}{l} \text{identifier-4} \\ \text{literal-2} \end{array} \right\} \right] \cdots \\ \left\{ \begin{array}{l} \underline{\text{ALL}} \\ \underline{\text{LEADING}} \end{array} \right\} \left\{ \left\{ \begin{array}{l} \text{identifier-3} \\ \text{literal-1} \end{array} \right\} \left[\left\{ \begin{array}{l} \underline{\text{BEFORE}} \\ \underline{\text{AFTER}} \end{array} \right\} \text{INITIAL} \left\{ \begin{array}{l} \text{identifier-4} \\ \text{literal-2} \end{array} \right\} \right] \cdots \right\} \cdots \end{array} \right\} \cdots \right\} \cdots
$$

```
      REPLACING
```

$$
\left\{ \begin{array}{l} \underline{\text{CHARACTERS}} \ \underline{\text{BY}} \left\{ \begin{array}{l} \text{identifier-5} \\ \text{literal-3} \end{array} \right\} \left[\left\{ \begin{array}{l} \underline{\text{BEFORE}} \\ \underline{\text{AFTER}} \end{array} \right\} \text{ INITIAL } \left\{ \begin{array}{l} \text{identifier-4} \\ \text{literal-2} \end{array} \right\} \right] \cdots \\ \left\{ \begin{array}{l} \underline{\text{ALL}} \\ \underline{\text{LEADING}} \\ \underline{\text{FIRST}} \end{array} \right\} \left\{ \left\{ \begin{array}{l} \text{identifier-3} \\ \text{literal-1} \end{array} \right\} \underline{\text{BY}} \left\{ \begin{array}{l} \text{identifier-5} \\ \text{literal-3} \end{array} \right\} \left[\left\{ \begin{array}{l} \underline{\text{BEFORE}} \\ \underline{\text{AFTER}} \end{array} \right\} \text{INITIAL} \left\{ \begin{array}{l} \text{identifier-4} \\ \text{literal-1} \end{array} \right\} \right] \cdots \right\} \cdots \end{array} \right\} \cdots
$$

```
INSPECT identifier-1 CONVERTING { identifier-6 } TO { identifier-7 }
                                 { literal-4    }    { literal-5    }
```

$$
\left[\left\{ \begin{array}{l} \underline{\text{BEFORE}} \\ \underline{\text{AFTER}} \end{array} \right\} \text{ INITIAL } \left\{ \begin{array}{l} \text{identifier-4} \\ \text{literal-2} \end{array} \right\} \right] \cdots
$$

```
MERGE file-name-1 { ON { ASCENDING  } KEY {data-name-1} ... } ...
                  {      DESCENDING }

      [COLLATING SEQUENCE IS alphabet-name-1]

      USING file-name-2 {file-name-3} ...

      { OUTPUT PROCEDURE IS procedure-name-1 [ { THROUGH } procedure-name-2 ] }
      {                                        { THRU    }                   }
      { GIVING {file-name-4} ...                                             }

MOVE { identifier-1 } TO {identifier-2} ...
     { literal-1    }

MOVE { CORRESPONDING } identifier-1 TO identifier-2
     { CORR          }

MULTIPLY { identifier-1 } BY {identifier-2 [ROUNDED]} ...
         { literal-1    }

      [ON SIZE ERROR imperative-statement-1]

      [NOT ON SIZE ERROR imperative-statement-2]

      [END-MULTIPLY]
```

```
MULTIPLY  { identifier-1 }  BY  { identifier-2 }
          { literal-1    }      { literal-2    }

     GIVING  {identifier-3 [ROUNDED]} ...

     [ON SIZE ERROR imperative-statement-1]

     [NOT ON SIZE ERROR imperative-statement-2]

     [END-MULTIPLY]
```

```
       ⎧ INPUT  { file-name-1 [ REVERSED        ] } ...  ⎫
       ⎪                      [ WITH NO REWIND   ]        ⎪
S  OPEN⎨                                                 ⎬ ...
       ⎪ OUTPUT {file-name-2  [WITH NO REWIND]}...        ⎪
       ⎪ I-O {file-name-3} ...                            ⎪
       ⎩ EXTEND {file-name-4} ...                         ⎭
```

```
        ⎧ INPUT  {file-name-1} ...  ⎫
        ⎪ OUTPUT {file-name-2} ...  ⎪
RI OPEN ⎨ I-O {file-name-3} ...     ⎬ ...
        ⎪ EXTEND {file-name-4} ...  ⎪
        ⎩                           ⎭
```

```
        ⎧ OUTPUT {file-name-1 [WITH NO REWIND]} ... ⎫
W  OPEN ⎨ EXTEND {file-name-2} ...                  ⎬ ...
        ⎩                                           ⎭
```

```
PERFORM [ procedure-name-1 [ { THROUGH } procedure-name-2 ] ]
                           [ { THRU    }                   ]

     [imperative-statement-1  END-PERFORM]
```

```
PERFORM [ procedure-name-1 [ { THROUGH } procedure-name-2 ] ]
                           [ { THRU    }                   ]

     { identifier-1 } TIMES [imperative-statement-1 END-PERFORM]
     { integer-1    }
```

```
PERFORM [ procedure-name-1 [ { THROUGH } procedure-name-2 ] ]
                           [ { THRU    }                   ]

     [ WITH TEST { BEFORE } ] UNTIL condition-1
     [           { AFTER  } ]

     [imperative-statement-1 END-PERFORM]
```

```
PERFORM [ procedure-name-1 [ { THROUGH } procedure-name-2 ] ]
                           [ { THRU    }                   ]

     [ WITH TEST { BEFORE } ]
     [           { AFTER  } ]

     VARYING { identifier-2  } FROM { identifier-3 }
             { index-name-1  }      { index-name-2 }
                                    { literal-1    }

          BY { identifier-4 } UNTIL condition-1
             { literal-2    }

     [ AFTER { identifier-5 } FROM { identifier-6 }
             { literal-3    }      { index-name-4 }
                                   { literal-3    }

          BY { identifier-7 } UNTIL condition-2 ] ...
             { literal-4    }

     [imperative-statement-1 END-PERFORM]
```

```
SRI READ file-name-1 [NEXT] RECORD [INTO identifier-1]

     [AT END imperative-statement-1]

     [NOT AT END imperative-statement-2]

     [END-READ]
```

R <u>READ</u> file-name-1 RECORD [<u>INTO</u> identifier-1]

    [<u>INVALID</u> KEY imperative-statement-3]

    [<u>NOT</u> <u>INVALID</u> KEY imperative-statement-4]

    [<u>END-READ</u>]

I <u>READ</u> file-name-1 RECORD [<u>INTO</u> identifier-1]

    [<u>KEY</u> IS data-name-1]

    [<u>INVALID</u> KEY imperative-statement-3]

    [<u>NOT</u> <u>INVALID</u> KEY imperative-statement-4]

    [<u>END-READ</u>]

<u>RELEASE</u> record-name-1 [<u>FROM</u> identifier-1]

<u>RETURN</u> file-name-1 RECORD [<u>INTO</u> identifier-1]

    AT <u>END</u> imperative-statement-1

    [<u>NOT</u> AT <u>END</u> imperative-statement-2]

    [<u>END-RETURN</u>]

S <u>REWRITE</u> record-name-1 [<u>FROM</u> identifier-1]

RI <u>REWRITE</u> record-name-1 [<u>FROM</u> identifier-1]

    [<u>INVALID</u> KEY imperative-statement-1]

    [<u>NOT</u> <u>INVALID</u> KEY imperative-statement-2]

    [<u>END-REWRITE</u>]

$$\underline{SEARCH}\ identifier\text{-}1\ \left[\ \underline{VARYING}\ \begin{Bmatrix} identifier\text{-}2 \\ index\text{-}name\text{-}1 \end{Bmatrix} \right]$$

    [AT <u>END</u> imperative-statement-1]

$$\left\{ \underline{WHEN}\ condition\text{-}1\ \begin{Bmatrix} imperative\text{-}statement\text{-}2 \\ \underline{NEXT}\ \underline{SENTENCE} \end{Bmatrix} \right\} \ \ldots$$

    [<u>END-SEARCH</u>]

<u>SEARCH</u> <u>ALL</u> identifier-1 [AT <u>END</u> imperative-statement-1]

$$\underline{WHEN}\ \begin{Bmatrix} data\text{-}name\text{-}1 \begin{Bmatrix} IS\ \underline{EQUAL}\ TO \\ IS\ \underline{=} \end{Bmatrix} \begin{Bmatrix} identifier\text{-}3 \\ literal\text{-}1 \\ arithmetic\text{-}expression\text{-}1 \end{Bmatrix} \\ condition\text{-}name\text{-}1 \end{Bmatrix}$$

$$\left[\underline{AND}\ \begin{Bmatrix} data\text{-}name\text{-}2 \begin{Bmatrix} IS\ \underline{EQUAL}\ TO \\ IS\ \underline{=} \end{Bmatrix} \begin{Bmatrix} identifier\text{-}4 \\ literal\text{-}2 \\ arithmetic\text{-}expression\text{-}2 \end{Bmatrix} \\ condition\text{-}name\text{-}2 \end{Bmatrix} \right] \ \ldots$$

$$\begin{Bmatrix} imperative\text{-}statement\text{-}2 \\ \underline{NEXT}\ \underline{SENTENCE} \end{Bmatrix}$$

    [<u>END-SEARCH</u>]

<u>SEND</u> cd-name-1 <u>FROM</u> identifier-1

$$\underline{SET}\ \begin{Bmatrix} index\text{-}name\text{-}1 \\ identifier\text{-}1 \end{Bmatrix} \ \ldots\ \underline{TO}\ \begin{Bmatrix} index\text{-}name\text{-}2 \\ identifier\text{-}2 \\ integer\text{-}1 \end{Bmatrix}$$

$$\underline{SET}\ \{index\text{-}name\text{-}3\} \ \ldots\ \begin{Bmatrix} \underline{UP}\ \underline{BY} \\ \underline{DOWN}\ \underline{BY} \end{Bmatrix} \begin{Bmatrix} identifier\text{-}3 \\ integer\text{-}2 \end{Bmatrix}$$

```
SET  { {mnemonic-name-1} ... TO { ON  } } ...
                                { OFF }

SET {condition-name-1} ... TO TRUE

SORT file-name-1 { ON { ASCENDING  } KEY {data-name-1} ... } ...
                      { DESCENDING }
```

[WITH DUPLICATES IN ORDER]

[COLLATING SEQUENCE IS alphabet-name-1]

```
{ INPUT PROCEDURE IS procedure-name-1 [ { THROUGH } procedure-name-2 ] }
{                                     [ { THRU    }                   ] }
{ USING {file-name-2} ...                                              }

{ OUTPUT PROCEDURE IS procedure-name-3 [ { THROUGH } procedure-name-4 ] }
{                                      [ { THRU    }                   ] }
{ GIVING {file-name-3} ...                                             }
```

```
                        [      { IS EQUAL TO             }        ]
                        [      { IS =                    }        ]
                        [      { IS GREATER THAN         }        ]
                        [      { IS >                    }        ]
START file-name-1  [ KEY { IS NOT LESS THAN        } data-name-1 ]
                        [      { IS NOT <                }        ]
                        [      { IS GREATER THAN OR EQUAL TO }    ]
                        [      { IS >=                   }        ]
```

[INVALID KEY imperative-statement-1]

[NOT INVALID KEY imperative-statement-2]

[END-START]

```
STOP { RUN       }
     { literal-1 }
```

```
STRING { { identifier-1 } ... DELIMITED BY { identifier-2 } } ...
       { { literal-1    }                  { literal-2    } }
       {                                   { SIZE         } }
```

INTO identifier-3

[WITH POINTER identifier-4]

[ON OVERFLOW imperative-statement-1]

[NOT ON OVERFLOW imperative-statement-2]

[END-STRING]

```
SUBTRACT { identifier-1 } ... FROM {identifier-3 [ROUNDED]} ...
         { literal-1    }
```

[ON SIZE ERROR imperative-statement-1]

[NOT ON SIZE ERROR imperative-statement-2]

[END-SUBTRACT]

```
SUBTRACT { identifier-1 } ... FROM { identifier-2 }
         { literal-1    }          { literal-2    }
```

GIVING {identifier-3 [ROUNDED]} ...

[ON SIZE ERROR imperative-statement-1]

[NOT ON SIZE ERROR imperative-statement-2]

[END-SUBTRACT]

```
SUBTRACT { CORRESPONDING } identifier-1 FROM identifier-2 [ROUNDED]
         { CORR          }

    [ON SIZE ERROR imperative-statement-1]

    [NOT ON SIZE ERROR imperative-statement-2]

    [END-SUBTRACT]

SUPPRESS PRINTING

TERMINATE {report-name-1} ...

UNSTRING identifier-1

    [ DELIMITED BY [ALL] { identifier-2 } [ OR [ALL] { identifier-3 } ] ] ...
    [                    { literal-1    } [        { literal-2    } ] ]

    INTO [identifier-4 [DELIMITER IN identifier-5] [COUNT IN identifier-6]} ...

    [WITH POINTER identifier-7]

    [TALLYING IN identifier-8]

    [ON OVERFLOW imperative-statement-1]

    [NOT ON OVERFLOW imperative-statement-2]

    [END-UNSTRING]
```

```
SRI  USE [GLOBAL] AFTER STANDARD { EXCEPTION } PROCEDURE ON { {file-name-1} ... }
                                 { ERROR     }              { INPUT           }
                                                            { OUTPUT          }
                                                            { I-O             }
                                                            { EXTEND          }
```

```
 W   USE AFTER STANDARD { EXCEPTION } PROCEDURE ON { {file-name-1} ... }
                        { ERROR     }              { OUTPUT           }
                                                   { EXTEND           }

     USE [GLOBAL] BEFORE REPORTING identifier-1

                            { cd-name-1                        }
     USE FOR DEBUGGING ON   { [ALL REFERENCES OF] identifier-1 } ...
                            { file-name-1                       }
                            { procedure-name-1                  }
                            { ALL PROCEDURES                    }
```

```
 S   WRITE record-name-1 [FROM identifier-1]

     [                              { { identifier-2 } [ LINE  ] } ]
     [ { BEFORE } ADVANCING         { { integer-1    } [ LINES ] } ]
     [ { AFTER  }                   {                            } ]
     [                              { { mnemonic-name-1 }        } ]
     [                              { { PAGE            }        } ]

     [ AT { END-OF-PAGE } imperative-statement-1 ]
     [    { EOP         }                        ]

     [ NOT AT { END-OF-PAGE } imperative-statement-2 ]
     [        { EOP         }                        ]

     [END-WRITE]
```

```
 RI  WRITE record-name-1 [FROM identifier-1]

     [INVALID KEY imperative-statement-1]

     [NOT INVALID KEY imperative-statement-2]

     [END-WRITE]
```

General Format for COPY and REPLACE Statements

```
COPY text-name-1 [ { OF } library-name-1 ]
                   { IN }

    [ REPLACING { { ==pseudo-text-1== }    { ==pseudo-text-2== } } ... ]
                { { identifier-1        } BY { identifier-2      } }
                { { literal-1          }    { literal-2         } }
                { { word-1             }    { word-2            } }

REPLACE {==pseudo-text-1== BY ==pseudo-text-2==} ...

REPLACE OFF
```

General Format for Conditions

Relation Condition:

```
{ identifier-1             }   { IS [NOT] GREATER THAN          }   { identifier-2             }
{ literal-1                }   { IS [NOT] >                     }   { literal-2                }
{ arithmetic-expression-1 }   { IS [NOT] LESS THAN             }   { arithmetic-expression-2 }
{ index-name-1            }   { IS [NOT] <                     }   { index-name-2            }
                              { IS [NOT] EQUAL TO              }
                              { IS [NOT] =                     }
                              { IS GREATER THAN OR EQUAL TO    }
                              { IS >=                          }
                              { IS LESS THAN OR EQUAL TO       }
                              { IS <=                          }
```

Class Condition:

```
                        { NUMERIC          }
                        { ALPHABETIC       }
identifier-1 IS [NOT]   { ALPHABETIC-LOWER }
                        { ALPHABETIC-UPPER }
                        { class-name-1     }
```

Condition-Name Condition:

```
condition-name-1
```

Switch-Status Condition:

```
condition-name-1
```

Sign Condition:

```
                                    { POSITIVE }
arithmetic-expression-1 IS [NOT]    { NEGATIVE }
                                    { ZERO     }
```

Negated Condition:

```
NOT condition-1
```

Combined Condition:

```
condition-1 { { AND } condition-2 } ...
            { { OR  }             }
```

Abbreviated Combined Relation Condition:

```
relation-condition { { AND } [NOT] [relational-operator] object } ...
                   { { OR  }                                    }
```

Qualification

Format 1:

$$
\begin{Bmatrix} \text{data-name-1} \\ \text{condition-name-1} \end{Bmatrix}
\begin{Bmatrix}
\left\{ \begin{Bmatrix} \underline{IN} \\ \underline{OF} \end{Bmatrix} \text{data-name-2} \right\} \dots \left[\begin{Bmatrix} \underline{IN} \\ \underline{OF} \end{Bmatrix} \begin{Bmatrix} \text{file-name-1} \\ \text{cd-name-1} \end{Bmatrix} \right] \\
\begin{Bmatrix} \underline{IN} \\ \underline{OF} \end{Bmatrix} \begin{Bmatrix} \text{file-name-1} \\ \text{cd-name-1} \end{Bmatrix}
\end{Bmatrix}
$$

Format 2:

$$
\text{paragraph-name-1} \begin{Bmatrix} \underline{IN} \\ \underline{OF} \end{Bmatrix} \text{section-name-1}
$$

Format 3:

$$
\text{text-name-1} \begin{Bmatrix} \underline{IN} \\ \underline{OF} \end{Bmatrix} \text{library-name-1}
$$

Format 4:

$$
\underline{\text{LINAGE-COUNTER}} \begin{Bmatrix} \underline{IN} \\ \underline{OF} \end{Bmatrix} \text{file-name-2}
$$

Format 5:

$$
\begin{Bmatrix} \underline{\text{PAGE-COUNTER}} \\ \underline{\text{LINE-COUNTER}} \end{Bmatrix} \begin{Bmatrix} \underline{IN} \\ \underline{OF} \end{Bmatrix} \text{report-name-1}
$$

Format 6:

$$
\text{data-name-3}
\begin{Bmatrix}
\begin{Bmatrix} \underline{IN} \\ \underline{OF} \end{Bmatrix} \text{data-name-4} \left[\begin{Bmatrix} \underline{IN} \\ \underline{OF} \end{Bmatrix} \text{report-name-2} \right] \\
\begin{Bmatrix} \underline{IN} \\ \underline{OF} \end{Bmatrix} \text{report-name-2}
\end{Bmatrix}
$$

Miscellaneous Formats

Subscripting:

$$
\begin{Bmatrix} \text{condition-name-1} \\ \text{data-name-1} \end{Bmatrix}
\left(
\begin{Bmatrix}
\text{integer-1} \\
\text{data-name-2} \left[\begin{Bmatrix} + \\ - \end{Bmatrix} \text{integer-2} \right] \\
\text{index-name-1} \left[\begin{Bmatrix} + \\ - \end{Bmatrix} \text{integer-3} \right]
\end{Bmatrix} \dots
\right)
$$

Reference Modification:

data-name-1 (leftmost-character-position: [length])

Identifier:

$$
\text{data-name-1} \left[\begin{Bmatrix} \underline{IN} \\ \underline{OF} \end{Bmatrix} \text{data-name-2} \right] \dots \left[\begin{Bmatrix} \underline{IN} \\ \underline{OF} \end{Bmatrix} \begin{Bmatrix} \text{cd-name-1} \\ \text{file-name-1} \\ \text{report-name-1} \end{Bmatrix} \right]
$$

[({subscript} ...)] [(leftmost-character-position: [length])]

COBOL
Reserved Words

Each COBOL Standard includes a set of reserved words. In addition, every implementation includes additional words, not part of the Standard but unique to that implementation. In the list that follows, Micro Focus enhancements are preceded by the letter m and Ryan-McFarland enhancements by the letter r (mr denotes both Micro-Focus and Ryan-McFarland). Those with no preceding letter code are COBOL-85 Standard. COBOL-85 reserved words not included in COBOL-74 are followed by (n74), meaning not in 1974 COBOL.

ACCEPT	m BACKGROUND-COLOR	COMMA	COPY
ACCESS		m COMMIT	CORR
ADD	m BACKWARD	COMMON (n74)	CORRESPONDING
m ADDRESS	mr BEEP	COMMUNICATION	COUNT
ADVANCING	BEFORE	COMP	m CRT
AFTER	m BELL	m COMP-0	m CRT-UNDER
ALL	BINARY (n74)	mr COMP-1	CURRENCY
ALPHABET (n74)	BLANK	m COMP-2	mr CURSOR
ALPHABETIC	mr BLINK	mr COMP-3	m CYCLE
ALPHABETIC-LOWER (n74)	BLOCK	m COMP-4	
ALPHABETIC-UPPER (n74)	BOTTOM	m COMP-5	DATA
	BY	r COMP-6	DATE
ALPHANUMERIC (n74)		m COMP-X	DATE-COMPILED
ALPHANUMERIC-EDITED (n74)	CALL	COMPUTATIONAL	DATE-WRITTEN
ALSO	CANCEL	m COMPUTATIONAL-0	DAY
ALTER	CD	mr COMPUTATIONAL-1	DAY-OF-WEEK (n74)
ALTERNATE	CF	m COMPUTATIONAL-2	DE
AND	CH	mr COMPUTATIONAL-3	DEBUG-CONTENTS
ANY (n74)	m CHAIN	m COMPUTATIONAL-4	DEBUG-ITEM
ARE	m CHAINING	m COMPUTATIONAL-5	DEBUG-LINE
AREA	m CHANGED	r COMPUTATIONAL-6	DEBUG-NAME
AREAS	CHARACTER	m COMPUTATIONAL-X	DEBUG-SUB-1
ASCENDING	CHARACTERS	COMPUTE	DEBUG-SUB-2
ASSIGN	CLASS (n74)	CONFIGURATION	DEBUG-SUB-3
AT	CLOCK-UNITS	m CONSOLE	DEBUGGING
AUTHOR	CLOSE	CONTAINS	DECIMAL-POINT
m AUTO	COBOL	CONTENT (n74)	DECLARATIVES
m AUTO-SKIP	CODE	CONTINUE (n74)	DELETE
m AUTOMATIC	CODE-SET	CONTROL	DELIMITED
	mr COL	CONTROLS	DELIMITER
	COLLATING	r CONVERT	DEPENDING
	COLUMN	CONVERTING (n74)	DESCENDING

653

	DESTINATION	mr	ERASE		IF	m	MANUAL
	DETAIL		ERROR	m	IGNORE		MEMORY
	DISABLE	m	ESCAPE		IN		MERGE
m	DISK		ESI		INDEX		MESSAGE
	DISPLAY		EVALUATE (n74)		INDEXED		MODE
m	DISPLAY-1		EVERY		INDICATE		MODULES
	DIVIDE		EXCEEDS		INITIAL		MOVE
	DIVISION		EXCEPTION		INITIALIZE (n74)		MULTIPLE
	DOWN	m	EXCESS-3		INITIATE		MULTIPLY
	DUPLICATES	m	EXCLUSIVE		INPUT		
	DYNAMIC	m	EXEC		INPUT-OUTPUT	m	NAME
		m	EXECUTE		INSPECT	m	NAMED
r	ECHO	n	EXHIBIT		INSTALLATION	m	NATIONAL
	EGI		EXIT		INTO	m	NATIONAL-EDITED
m	EJECT		EXTEND		INVALID		NATIVE
	ELSE		EXTERNAL (n74)		IS	m	NCHAR
	EMI						NEGATIVE
m	EMPTY-CHECK		FALSE (n74)	m	JAPANESE		NEXT
	ENABLE		FD		JUST		NO
	END		FILE		JUSTIFIED	m	NO-ECHO
mr	END-ACCEPT		FILE-CONTROL				NOT
	END-ADD (n74)	m	FILE-ID	m	KEPT	m	NULL
	END-CALL (n74)		FILLER		KEY	m	NULLS
m	END-CHAIN		FINAL	m	KEYBOARD		NUMBER
	END-COMPUTE (n74)		FIRST				NUMERIC
	END-DELETE (n74)	m	FIXED		LABEL		NUMERIC-EDITED
mr	END-DISPLAY		FOOTING		LAST		
	END-DIVIDE (n74)		FOR		LEADING		OBJECT-COMPUTER
	END-EVALUATE (n74)	m	FOREGROUND-		LEFT		OCCURS
	END-IF (n74)		COLOR	m	LEFT-JUSTIFY		OF
	END-MULTIPLY (n74)		FROM	m	LEFTLINE		OFF
	END-OF-PAGE	m	FULL		LENGTH		OMITTED
	END-PERFORM (n74)		FUNCTION (n74)	m	LENGTH-CHECK		ON
	END-READ (n74)				LESS		OPEN
	END-RECEIVE (n74)		GENERATE		LIMIT		OPTIONAL
	END-RETURN (n74)		GIVING		LIMITS		OR
	END-REWRITE (n74)		GLOBAL (n74)	m	LIN		ORDER (n74)
	END-SEARCH (n74)		GO		LINAGE		ORGANIZATION
	END-START (n74)	mr	GOBACK		LINAGE-COUNTER		OTHER (n74)
	END-STRING (n74)		GREATER		LINE		OUTPUT
	END-SUBTRACT (n74)	m	GRID		LINES		OVERFLOW
	END-UNSTRING (n74)		GROUP		LINE-COUNTER	m	OVERLINE
	END-WRITE (n74)				LINKAGE		
	ENTER		HEADING	m	LOCAL-STORAGE		PACKED-DECIMAL
m	ENTRY	r	HIGH		LOCK		(n74)
	ENVIRONMENT		HIGH-VALUE	m	LOCKING		PADDING (n74)
r	EOF		HIGH-VALUES	r	LOW		PAGE
mr	EOL	m	HIGHLIGHT		LOW-VALUE		PAGE-COUNTER
	EOP				LOW-VALUES	m	PARAGRAPH
mr	EOS		I-O	m	LOWER		PERFORM
	EQUAL		I-O-CONTROL	m	LOWLIGHT		PF
m	EQUALS	mr	ID				PH
			IDENTIFICATION				PIC

	PICTURE		RESERVE		STATUS		VALUE
	PLUS	m	RESET		STOP		VALUES
	POINTER		RETURN		STRING	m	VARIABLE
r	POS	m	RETURN-CODE		SUBTRACT		VARYING
	POSITION	m	RETURNING		SUB-QUEUE-1		
	POSITIVE	r	REVERSE		SUB-QUEUE-2	m	WAIT
m	PREVIOUS	m	REVERSE-VIDEO		SUB-QUEUE-3		WHEN
r	PRINT		REVERSED		SUM	m	WHEN-COMPILED
mr	PRINTER		REWIND		SUPPRESS		WITH
m	PRINTER-1		REWRITE		SYMBOLIC		WORDS
	PRINTING		RF		SYNC		WORKING-STORAGE
	PROCEDURE		RH		SYNCHRONIZED		WRITE
m	PROCEDURE- POINTER		RIGHT				
		m	RIGHT-JUSTIFY	r	TAB		ZERO
	PROCEDURES	m	ROLLBACK		TABLE	m	ZERO-FILL
	PROCEED		ROUNDED		TALLYING		ZEROES
	PROGRAM		RUN		TAPE		ZEROS
	PROGRAM-ID				TERMINAL		
mr	PROMPT		SAME		TERMINATE		+
m	PROTECTED	m	SCREEN		TEST (n74)		-
	PURGE (n74)		SD		TEXT		*
			SEARCH		THAN		/
	QUEUE		SECTION		THEN (n74)		**
	QUOTE	m	SECURE		THROUGH		=
	QUOTES		SECURITY		THRU		>
			SEGMENT		TIME		<
	RANDOM		SEGMENT-LIMIT	m	TIME-OUT		>= (n74)
m	RANGE	m	SELECT	m	TIMEOUT		<= (n74)
	RD		SEND		TIMES		
	READ		SENTENCE	m	TITLE		
m	READY		SEPARATE		TO		
	RECEIVE		SEQUENCE		TOP		
	RECORD		SEQUENTIAL	m	TRACE		
m	RECORDING		SET		TRAILING		
	RECORDS		SIGN	m	TRAILING-SIGN		
	REDEFINES		SIZE		TRUE (n74)		
	REEL	m	SKIP1		TYPE		
	REFERENCE (n74)	m	SKIP2				
	REFERENCES	m	SKIP3	m	UNDERLINE		
	RELATIVE		SORT	m	UNEQUAL		
	RELEASE		SORT-MERGE		UNIT		
	REMAINDER	m	SORT-RETURN	mr	UNLOCK		
r	REMARKS		SOURCE		UNSTRING		
	REMOVAL		SOURCE-COMPUTER		UNTIL		
	RENAMES		SPACE		UP		
	REPLACE (n74)	m	SPACE-FILL	mr	UPDATE		
	REPLACING		SPACES		UPON		
	REPORT		SPECIAL-NAMES	m	UPPER		
	REPORTING		STANDARD		USAGE		
	REPORTS		STANDARD-1		USE		
m	REQUIRED		STANDARD-2 (n74)	m	USER		
	RERUN		START		USING		

INDEX